HUMAN LEARNING

FOURTH EDITION

Jeanne Ellis Ormrod
University of Northern Colorado (Emerita)
University of New Hampshire

PEARSON

Merrill
Prentice Hall

Upper Saddle River, New Jersey
Columbus, Ohio

Library of Congress Cataloging-in-Publication Data

Ormrod, Jeanne Ellis.
    Human learning / Jeanne Ellis Ormrod.--4th ed.
      p. cm.
    Includes bibliographical references and indexes.
    ISBN 0-13-094199-9
    1. Learning, Psychology of. 2. Behaviorism (Psychology) I. Title.

BF318.O76 2004
153.1'5--dc21
                                           2003056141

Vice President and Executive Publisher: Jeffery W. Johnston
Publisher: Kevin M. Davis
Editorial Assistant: Autumn Crisp
Production Editor: Mary Harlan
Production Coordinator: Holly Henjum, Carlisle Publishers Services
Design Coordinator: Diane C. Lorenzo
Text Design and Illustrations: Carlisle Communications
Cover Design: Ali Mohrman
Cover image: SuperStock. Paul Klee, "Kopf (Head)," 1915, 5
© 2003 Artists Rights Society (ARS), New York/VG Bild-Kunst, Bonn
Production Manager: Laura Messerly
Director of Marketing: Ann Castel Davis
Marketing Manager: Amy June
Marketing Coordinator: Tyra Poole

This book was set in Berkeley Book by Carlisle Communications, Ltd. It was printed and bound by R.R. Donnelley & Sons Company. The cover was printed by The Lehigh Press, Inc.

Pearson Education Ltd.
Pearson Education Singapore Pte. Ltd.
Pearson Education Canada, Ltd.
Pearson Education—Japan

Pearson Education Australia Pty. Limited
Pearson Education North Asia Ltd.
Pearson Educación de Mexico, S.A. de C.V.
Pearson Education Malaysia Pte. Ltd.

10 9 8 7 6 5 4 3 2 1
ISBN: 0-13-094199-9

Preface

Human learning is a fascinating process, and psychologists discover more about it every year. Yet I am saddened and frustrated by how little nonpsychologists seem to know about how they themselves learn and about how they can best help others learn in instructional settings. Research is clear on this point: How something is taught, studied, and thought about definitely *does* make a difference in what people learn, how well they understand it, how long they remember it, and how readily they apply it to new situations and problems.

I have written this textbook with particular students in mind: students who would like to learn about learning but often do not have much background in psychology. Such students may benefit from studying the historical roots of learning theories but prefer to focus their energies on studying contemporary perspectives and ideas. These students might find learning theories fascinating but lose patience when they cannot see the relevance of those theories to everyday practice. These students are capable of reading a dry, terse textbook but probably learn more effectively from a book that shows how different concepts relate to one another, provides numerous examples, and, especially, emphasizes meaningful learning—true *understanding*—of the material it presents.

In This Edition

This fourth edition of *Human Learning* is different in many ways from the third edition of 1998. A new Chapter 2 introduces readers to the anatomy and physiology of the brain, speculates about the physiological bases of learning and memory, and dispels common myths about brain functioning and development. Behaviorist views of learning have been condensed from four chapters into three, with closer attention to how early behaviorists built on one another's ideas. The contents of the "old" Chapter 13 (expository instruction, teaching concepts, mnemonics, etc.) have been integrated into other chapters, where various instructional strategies can be more closely tied to the principles and theories on which they are based. And the virtual explosion of research on human motivation in recent years has made it necessary to expand my discussion of motivation to three chapters.

In addition to the discussion of the brain in chapter 2, many new topics appear throughout the book. Examples include measures of learning (Chapter 1); noncontingent reinforcement as a means of reducing undesirable behaviors (Chapter 4); effects of high-stakes testing (Chapter 5); functional analysis (Chapter 5); collective self-efficacy (Chapter 7); phonological loop and visuospatial sketchpad (Chapter 9); the generation effect (Chapter 10); acquisition of procedural knowledge (Chapter 10); confirmation bias (Chapter 11); false memories (Chapter 12); theory of mind, intentional learning, and epistemic doubt (Chapter 13); near versus far transfer (Chapter 14); visual imagery in problem solving (Chapter 14); the social nature of learning (Chapter 15); technology-based discussions (Chapter 15); arousal and relatedness as basic human needs (Chapter 16); performance-approach, performance-avoidance, work-avoidance, social, and career goals (Chapter 17); dispositions (Chapter 17); interrelationships among motivation, affect, and self-regulation (Chapter 17) process versus product goals (Chapter 17); entity versus incremental views of intelligence (Chapter 18); intrapersonal versus interpersonal attributions, and cultural differences in attributions (Chapter 18). And, more generally, I have rewritten every chapter to reflect the latest developments in learning theory and research.

Acknowledgments

Although I am listed as the sole author, I have certainly not written this book alone. Many people have helped me along the way:

- Frank Di Vesta, my adviser and mentor at Penn State, who taught me a great deal about learning and who absolutely refused to let me graduate until I also learned a great deal about writing.
- Kevin Davis, my editor at Merrill Education, who continues to guide, support, and inspire me in my efforts to shed light on the many ways in which psychology can inform practice in educational and therapeutic settings.
- The editorial staff at Carlisle Publishers Services—especially Holly Henjum, who skillfully transformed my rough manuscript into a polished publication, and Katherine Evancie, who carefully scrutinized every line for grammatical errors, awkward prose, and missing references.
- My colleagues across the nation who read early drafts or editions most thoroughly and conscientiously and whose suggestions have greatly improved the final product: Livingston Alexander, Western Kentucky University; Martha B. Bronson, Boston College; Margaret W. Cohen, University of Missouri at St. Louis; Ralph F. Darr, Jr., The University of Akron; Jean C. Faieta, Edinboro University of Pennsylvania; Sarah Huyvaert, Eastern Michigan University; Jaina Jolley, Clarion University of Pennsylvania; Joseph Kersting, Western Illinois Universtiy; Mary Lou Koran, University of Florida; Gerald Larson, Kent State University; Mark Lewis; University of Texas at Tyler; Michael S. Meloth, University of Colorado; John Newel, University of Florida at Gainesville; Jim O'Connor, California State University at Bakersfield; Sarah Peterson, Northern Illinois University; Steven Pulos, University of Northern Colorado; and Karen Zabrucky, Georgia State University.
- Colleagues who recently reviewed the third edition and offered many helpful suggestions for adding to and in other ways enhancing my discussions in the fourth edition: P. Karen Murphy, The Pennsylvania State University; Jonathan A. Plucker, In-

diana University; Daniel H. Robinson, University of Texas at Austin; and Jack Snowman, Southern Illinois University.

- My husband, Richard, and my children, Christina, Alex, and Jeffrey, who have been eternally supportive of my writing endeavors and who have provided me with numerous examples of human learning in action.
- My parents, James and Nancy Ellis, who long ago taught me the value of higher education.
- My students, who urged me to write the book in the first place and continue to give me feedback about how I can make it better.

Jeanne Ellis Ormrod

Educator Learning Center:
An Invaluable Online Resource

Merrill Education and the Association for Supervision and Curriculum Development (ASCD) invite you to take advantage of a new online resource, one that provides access to the top research and proven strategies associated with ASCD and Merrill—the Educator Learning Center. At **www.EducatorLearningCenter.com** you will find resources that will enhance your students' understanding of course topics and of current educational issues, in addition to being invaluable for further research.

How the Educator Learning Center will help your students become better teachers

With the combined resources of Merrill Education and ASCD, you and your students will find a wealth of tools and materials to better prepare them for the classroom.

Research

- More than 600 articles from the ASCD journal *Educational Leadership* discuss everyday issues faced by practicing teachers.
- A direct link on the site to Research Navigator™ gives students access to many of the leading education journals, as well as extensive content detailing the research process.
- Excerpts from Merrill Education texts give your students insights on important topics of instructional methods, diverse populations, assessment, classroom management, technology, and refining classroom practice.

Classroom Practice

- Hundreds of lesson plans and teaching strategies are categorized by content area and age range.
- Case studies and classroom video footage provide virtual field experience for student reflection.
- Computer simulations and other electronic tools keep your students abreast of today's classrooms and current technologies.

Look into the value of Educator Learning Center yourself

Preview the value of this educational environment by visiting **www.EducatorLearningCenter.com** and clicking on "Demo." For a free 4-month subscription to the Educator Learning Center in conjunction with this text, simply contact your Merrill/Prentice Hall sales representative.

Brief Contents

Contents

Part One

Introduction to Human Learning

CHAPTER 1

Definitions and Perspectives of Learning

When my son Alex was in kindergarten, his teacher asked me *please* to do something about his shoes. I had been sending Alex off to school every morning with his shoelaces carefully and lovingly tied, yet by the time he arrived at his classroom door, the laces were untied and flopping every which way—a state to which they invariably returned within 10 minutes of his teacher's retying them. Alex and I tried a series of shoe-tying lessons but with little success. As an alternative, I proposed that we double-knot the laces when we tied them each morning, but Alex rejected my suggestion as being too babyish. I purchased a couple of pairs of shoes that had Velcro straps instead of laces, but Alex gave the shoes such a workout that the Velcro quickly separated itself from the leather. By March, the teacher, justifiably irritated that she had to retie my son's shoes so many times each day, insisted that Alex learn to tie them himself. So I sat down with him and demonstrated, for the umpteenth time, how to put two laces together to make a presentable bow. This time, however, I accompanied my explanation with a magical statement: "Alex, when you learn to tie your shoes, I will give you a quarter." Alex had shoe-tying perfected in five minutes, and after that we didn't have a single complaint from school—well, not about his shoes anyway.

When my daughter Tina was in fourth grade, she experienced considerable difficulty with a series of homework assignments in subtraction. She had never learned the basic subtraction facts, despite my continually nagging her to practice them, the result being that she could not solve many two- and three-digit subtraction problems successfully. One night, after her typical half-hour tantrum about "these stupid problems," my husband explained to Tina that subtraction was nothing more than reversed addition and that her knowledge of addition facts could help her with subtraction. Something must have clicked in Tina's head, because we weren't subjected to any more tantrums about subtraction. Multiplication, yes, but not subtraction.

Human learning takes many forms. Some instances of learning are readily observable, such as when a child learns to tie shoes. Other instances of learning are fairly subtle, such as when a child gains a better understanding of mathematical principles. And people learn for many different reasons. Some learn for the external rewards their achievements bring—for example, for good grades, recognition, or money (consider my mercenary son). But others learn for less obvious, more internal reasons—perhaps to gain a sense of accomplishment, or perhaps simply to make life easier.

In this book, I describe human learning from the various perspectives that have evolved in psychological theory throughout the twentieth century and are continuing to evolve in the twenty-first century. As you will soon discover, learning is a complicated process, and psychologists disagree even about such basic issues as what learning is, how it occurs, and which factors are necessary for it to occur at all.

IMPORTANCE OF LEARNING

Many species have things easy compared to humans, or at least so it would seem. Birds, for example, are born with a wealth of knowledge that we humans must learn. Birds instinctively know how to build their houses; we either have to be taught something about framing, roofing, and drywalling or else have to hire someone to do these things for us. Birds know, without being taught, exactly when to fly south and how to get there; we have to look at our calendars and road maps. Birds instinctively know how to care for their young; meanwhile, we attend prenatal classes, read child-care books, and watch others demonstrate how to change diapers.

However, it is the humans, not the birds, who are getting ahead in this world. Human beings have learned to make increasingly stronger and more comfortable homes for themselves, while birds are still making the same flimsy, drafty nests they have been living in for thousands of years. Humans have developed fast, dependable modes of transportation for themselves and their possessions, while birds are still winging it. And humans are learning how better to feed and care for themselves and their young, so that each generation grows taller, stronger, and healthier than the previous one. Birds, meanwhile, are still eating worms.

The learning process allows the human race a greater degree of flexibility and adaptability than is true for any other species on the planet. Because so little of our behavior is instinctive and so much of it is learned, we are able to benefit from our experiences. We know which actions are likely to lead to successful outcomes and which are not, and we modify our behavior accordingly. And as adults pass on to children the wisdom gleaned from their ancestors and from their own experiences, each generation is just that much more capable of behaving intelligently. Let's face it: We can get from New York to Miami in three hours, but how long does it take the birds?

DEFINING LEARNING

My son Alex's learning to tie his shoes and my daughter Tina's learning how subtraction relates to addition are both examples of learning. Consider these instances of learning as well:

- The mother of a 10-year-old boy insists that her son assume some household chores, for which he earns a small weekly allowance. The allowance, when saved for two or three weeks, enables the boy to purchase small toys of his own choosing. As a result, he develops an appreciation for the value of money.

- A college student from a small town is, for the first time, exposed to political viewpoints different from her own. After engaging in heated political debates with classmates, she evaluates and modifies her own political philosophy.
- A toddler is overly affectionate with a neighborhood dog, and the dog responds by biting the toddler's hand. After that, the child cries and runs quickly to his mother every time he sees a dog.

As you can see, learning is the means through which we acquire not only skills and knowledge, but values, attitudes, and emotional reactions as well.

Just what do we mean by the term **learning**? Different psychologists conceptualize and define learning differently. Here are two definitions that reflect two common, yet quite different, conceptions of what learning is:

1. Learning is a relatively permanent change in behavior as a result of experience.
2. Learning is a relatively permanent change in mental representations or associations as a result of experience.

What do these definitions have in common? Both describe learning as involving a relatively permanent *change*—a change that will last for some time, although not necessarily forever. And both definitions attribute this change to *experience*; in other words, learning takes place as a result of one or more events in the learner's life. Other changes, such as those caused by maturational changes in the body, organic damage, or temporary body states (e.g., fatigue, drugs), are not attributable to experience and so do not reflect learning.

The two definitions I have presented differ primarily in terms of *what* changes when learning occurs. The first definition refers to a change in *behavior*—an external change that we can observe—and reflects the perspective of a group of theories collectively known as **behaviorism**. Behaviorist theories focus on the learning of tangible, observable behaviors or *responses*, such as tying shoes, solving a subtraction problem correctly, or complaining about a stomachache in order to stay home from school.

In contrast, the second definition focuses on a change in *mental representations or associations*—an internal change that we can*not* see—reflecting the perspective of a group of theories collectively known as **cognitivism**. Cognitive theories focus not on behavioral outcomes but on the *thought processes* (sometimes called *mental events*) involved in human learning. Examples of such processes include finding relationships between addition and subtraction facts, using memory gimmicks to remember French vocabulary words, or constructing idiosyncratic and highly personalized interpretations of classic works of literature.

In this book, I will describe both the behaviorist and cognitive views of learning; I will also describe perspectives that lie somewhere between the two extremes. Most psychologists tend to align themselves with one perspective or the other, and I, whose graduate training and research program have been rooted in cognitive traditions, am no exception. Yet I firmly believe that both the behaviorist and cognitive perspectives have something important to say about human learning and that both provide useful suggestions for helping people learn more effectively.

DETERMINING WHEN LEARNING HAS OCCURRED

Regardless of whether we take a behaviorist or cognitive perspective, we *know* that learning has occurred only when we actually see it reflected in a person's behavior. For example, we might see a learner:

- Performing a completely new behavior—perhaps tying shoes correctly for the first time.
- Changing the frequency of an existing behavior—perhaps more regularly cooperating with (rather than being aggressive toward or in some other way alienating) classmates.
- Changing the speed of an existing behavior—perhaps recalling various subtraction facts more quickly than before.
- Changing the intensity of an existing behavior—perhaps throwing increasingly outrageous temper tantrums as a way of obtaining desired objects.
- Changing the complexity of an existing behavior—perhaps discussing a particular topic in greater depth and detail after receiving instruction about the topic.
- Responding differently to a particular stimulus—perhaps crying and withdrawing at the sight of a dog after having previously been eager to interact with dogs.

Throughout the book, we will continue to see these and other approaches to assessing learning. How we *interpret* such changes, however, will depend on the particular theoretical perspective we are considering at the time.

NATURE OF PRINCIPLES AND THEORIES

The systematic study of behavior, including human and animal learning processes, has emerged only within the past 100 years or so, making psychology a relative newcomer to scientific inquiry. But in a century's time, thousands of experiments have investigated how people and animals learn, and consistent patterns in research findings have led psychologists to generalize about the learning process through the formulation of both principles and theories of learning.

Principles of learning identify specific factors that consistently influence learning and describe the specific effects that these factors have. For example, consider this learning principle:

A behavior that is followed by a satisfying state of affairs (a reward) is more likely to increase in frequency than a behavior not followed by such a reward.

In this principle, a particular factor (a reward that follows a behavior) is identified as having a particular effect (an increase in the behavior's frequency). The principle can be observed in many different situations, including the following:

- A pigeon is given a small pellet of food every time it turns its body in a complete circle. It begins turning more and more frequently.
- Dolphins who are given fish for "speaking" in dolphinese quickly become quite chatty.
- A boy who completes a perfect spelling paper and is praised for it by a favorite teacher works diligently for future success in spelling assignments.
- A high school girl who receives compliments on her new hairstyle continues to style her hair in the same way.

Principles are most useful when they can be applied to a wide variety of situations. The "reward" principle is an example of such broad applicability: It applies to both animals and humans and holds true for different types of learning and for different rewards. When a principle such as this one is observed over and over again—when it stands the test of time—it is sometimes called a **law**.

Theories of learning provide explanations about the underlying mechanisms involved in the learning process. Whereas principles tell us *what* factors are important for learning, theories tell us *why* these factors are important. For example, consider one aspect of social cognitive theory (described in Chapter 7):

> *People learn what they pay attention to. A reward increases learning when it makes people pay attention to the information to be learned.*

Here we have one possible explanation of why a reward affects learning: It increases attention, which in turn brings about learning.

Advantages of Theories

Principles of learning tend to be fairly stable over time: Researchers observe many of the same factors affecting learning time and time again. In contrast, theories of learning continue to evolve, to the point where I must revise this book in significant ways every four or five years. Certainly, the changeable nature of theories can be frustrating, in that we can never be confident that we have the "real scoop" on learning. Yet it is precisely the dynamic nature of learning theories that enables us to gain an increasingly accurate understanding of what is, in fact, a very complex, multifaceted process.

Theories have several advantages over principles. First, they allow us to summarize the results of many research studies and integrate numerous principles of learning. In that sense, theories are often quite concise (psychologists use the term **parsimonious**).

Second, theories provide starting points for conducting new research; they suggest research questions worthy of study. For example, the theory that attention is more important than reward leads to the following prediction:

> *When a particular situation or task draws an individual's attention to the information to be learned, learning occurs even in the absence of a reward.*

In fact, this prediction has frequently been supported by research (e.g., Cermak & Craik, 1979; Faust & Anderson, 1967; Hyde & Jenkins, 1969).

Third, theories help us make sense of research findings. Research conducted outside the context of a particular theoretical perspective can yield results that are trivial and nongeneralizable. Interpreted from a theoretical perspective, however, those same results become significant. For example, consider an experiment by Seligman and Maier (1967). In this classic study, dogs were placed in individual cages and given a number of painful and unpredictable shocks. Some dogs were able to escape the shocks by pressing a panel in the cage, whereas others were unable to escape. The following day, the dogs were placed in different cages, and again shocks were administered. This time, however, each shock was preceded by a signal (a tone) that the shock was coming, and the dogs could avoid the shocks by jumping over a barrier as soon as they heard the tone. The dogs that had been able to escape the shocks on the preceding day learned to avoid the shocks altogether in this new situation, but the dogs that had been unable to escape previously did *not* learn to avoid the shocks. On the surface, this experiment, although interesting, might not seem especially relevant to human learning. Yet Seligman and his colleagues used this and other experiments to develop their theory of *learned helplessness*: People who learn that they have no control over unpleasant or painful events in one situation are unlikely, in later situations, to try to escape or avoid those aversive events even when it is possible for them to do so. In Chapter 5, we will look at learned helplessness more closely, and in Chapter 18, we will incorporate it into a more general theoretical framework known as *attribution theory.*

Theories have a fourth advantage as well: By giving us ideas about the mechanisms that underlie human learning and performance, they can ultimately help us design learning environments that facilitate human learning to the greatest possible degree. For example, consider the teacher who is familiar with the theory that attention is an essential ingredient in the learning process. That teacher may identify and use a variety of approaches—perhaps providing interesting reading materials, presenting intriguing problems, and praising good performance—that are likely to increase students' attention to academic subject matter. In contrast, consider the teacher who is familiar only with the principle that rewarded behaviors are learned. That teacher may use certain rewards—perhaps small toys or trinkets—that are counterproductive because they distract students' attention away from the academic tasks at hand.

Disadvantages of Theories

Despite their advantages, theories also have at least two disadvantages. First, no single theory explains everything that researchers have discovered about learning. Current theories of learning tend to focus on specific aspects of learning. Behaviorist theories, for example, limit themselves to situations in which learning involves specific, overt responses. Cognitive theories tend to focus instead on how people organize, interpret, and remember information. Observed phenomena that do not fit comfortably within a particular theoretical perspective are usually excluded from that perspective.

Second, theories affect what new information is published, therefore biasing the knowledge that we have about learning. For example, imagine that several researchers propose a particular theory of learning and conduct a research study to support their idea. They obtain results that are opposite to what they expected and so cast doubt on their theory. If these researchers are fully committed to demonstrating that their theory is correct, they are unlikely to publish results that will indicate otherwise! In this way, theories may sometimes impede progress toward a truly accurate understanding of the learning process.

A Perspective on Theories and Principles

You should ultimately think of the learning theories I describe in this book as dynamic, changing models of the learning process. Each theory is based on several decades of research results, and each has some validity. However, as research continues in the decades ahead, theories of learning will inevitably be revised to account for the new evidence that emerges. In this sense, no single theory can be considered "fact."

At the same time, you might think of learning principles as relatively enduring conclusions about cause–effect relationships in the learning process. The "reward" principle was introduced by Edward Thorndike in 1898 and has remained with us in one form or another ever since. Thorndike's original theory of *why* reward affects learning, however, has been largely replaced by other explanations.

Both principles and theories help us predict the conditions under which learning is likely to occur. To the extent that they are useful in this way, we are better off with them—imperfect and tentative as they may sometimes be—than without them.

APPLYING PRINCIPLES AND THEORIES TO INSTRUCTIONAL PRACTICE

A great deal of learning takes place in a classroom context, and most of it is beneficial. For example, it is in the classroom that most students learn how to read and how to subtract one number from another. Unfortunately, students may also learn things at school that are *not* in their best interest over the long run. For example, although students may learn to read, they may also learn that the "best" way to remember what they read is to memorize it, word for word, without necessarily trying to understand it. And although students may learn their subtraction facts, they may also learn that mathematics is a boring and sometimes frustrating endeavor.

The learning that takes place in our schools cannot be left to chance. The better we understand the factors that influence learning (principles) and the processes that underlie it (theories), the more effectively we can promote the kinds of learning that will facilitate students' long-term success rather than the kinds of learning that might actually impede their progress.

The theories I have included in the chapters ahead portray human learning from different perspectives; sometimes they even contradict one another. Yet I hope you will take an eclectic perspective as you read the book, resisting the temptation to choose one theory over others as being the "right" one. Different theories are applicable in different situations, depending on the environmental factors under consideration, the specific subject matter being learned, and the objectives of instruction. Furthermore, each theory provides unique insights into how and why human beings learn and how instruction might be designed to enhance student learning (e.g., see Catania, 1985; Epstein, 1991; Reynolds, Sinatra, & Jetton, 1996). It is probably more helpful to think of theories in terms of their *usefulness* than in terms of their correctness.

As theories of learning continue to be revised and refined in the years to come, so, too, will instructional practices be revised and refined. In the meantime, we can use current theories to help people of all ages learn in increasingly effective and efficient ways.

OVERVIEW OF THE BOOK

In Chapter 2, we will continue our introduction to learning by examining the physiological underpinnings of thinking and learning. There we will look at the nature of the human nervous system and consider where and how learning probably occurs in the brain. We will also consider what brain research tells us—as well as what it does *not* tell us—about thinking, learning, and instruction in classroom settings.

In Part II of the book, we will explore principles and theories of learning from the behaviorist perspective, focusing on relationships between environmental events (stimuli) and the behaviors (responses) that people acquire as a result of those events. We will begin by examining the general assumptions of behaviorist theories (Chapter 3) and then explore in depth the two most commonly used models of learning within the behaviorist perspective: classical conditioning (Chapter 3) and operant conditioning (Chapters 4 and 5). We will also consider the role of unpleasant events, such as punishment, in the learning process (Chapter 6).

In Part III (Chapter 7), we will make the transition from behaviorism to cognitivism as we examine social cognitive theory, a theory that has evolved over the years from its behaviorist roots into a blend of behaviorist and cognitive ideas regarding how and what people learn by observing those around them.

In Part IV, we will turn to theories of learning that are almost entirely cognitive in nature. We will first look at a variety of cognitive perspectives, both old and new, that have contributed to our understanding of how people think and learn (Chapter 8). We will then examine in depth the internal mental processes involved in learning and memory (Chapters 9, 10, and 12) and the nature of the "knowledge" that such processes yield (Chapter 11).

As we proceed to Part V, we will continue our exploration of cognitive theories by examining more complex aspects of human learning and cognition. Specifically, we will look at how well people understand and regulate their own thinking processes—a phenomenon known as *metacognition*—and how effectively they can apply what they've learned in one situation to new tasks and problems (Chapters 13 and 14). We will then consider how learning and cognition are sometimes a very social enterprise: People can often make better sense of situations and respond in more adaptive ways when they work together than any one of them might be able to do individually (Chapter 15).

Finally, in Part VI, we will consider the role that motivation plays in learning. We will look at motivation's effects on learning and behavior, examine several theoretical perspectives regarding the nature of motivation, and consider how emotion (*affect*) is closely intertwined with both motivation and learning (Chapter 16). We will also identify the many cognitive factors that enter into and shape motivational processes (Chapters 17 and 18).

Throughout the book, we will frequently identify educational implications of the principles and theories we are studying. I hope that once you have finished the final chapter, you will be convinced, as I am, that psychology has a great deal to offer about how we can enhance teaching and learning both inside and outside of the classroom.

SUMMARY

Learning allows human beings a greater degree of flexibility and adaptability than is true for any other species. Currently, two major theoretical perspectives help us understand how people learn. The *behaviorist* perspective emphasizes relationships among observable stimuli and responses. The *cognitive* perspective emphasizes the role of internal mental processes in learning. Regardless of which perspective we take, however, we know that learning has occurred only when we can actually see a behavior change of some kind—perhaps the appearance of a new response, or perhaps an increase in the frequency of an existing one. *Principles* (descriptions of what factors affect learning) and *theories* (explanations of why those factors have the effects they do) from both behaviorism and cognitivism can help educators optimize instructional practices and maximize students' learning and achievement.

CHAPTER 2

Learning and the Brain

Someone in my family has a broken brain; to protect his privacy, I will simply call him Loved One. As a child, Loved One was in most respects quite normal: He did well in school, spent after-school hours playing typical "boy" games with his friends, and often traveled to places near and far with his parents and siblings. People who knew him described him as smart, sweet, and sensitive. But even then, there were, perhaps, little cracks in his brain. For one thing, he had trouble delaying gratification: He always wanted things now, now, now. And he made many poor choices in his daily decision making—for example, leaving a pet turtle unattended on his bed (the turtle fell off the bed, broke its shell in two, and died the following day) and smashing unwanted toys on the back patio using a hammer that left huge "smash" marks on the patio itself.

When Loved One was 17, something went seriously wrong. Despite curfews and significant consequences for ignoring them, he would stay out until the wee hours of the morning; sometimes he didn't return home until the middle of the next day. He became increasingly hostile and defiant, and his parents found it impossible to reason with him. He often refused to get out of bed to go to school. His grades plummeted, and by December of his senior year, it was clear that he wouldn't have enough credits to graduate with his high school class. In January, his out-of-control behavior landed him in a juvenile detention center. While awaiting trial, he became increasingly lethargic until eventually he could barely move: He wouldn't eat and didn't seem able to walk or talk. When, on the day of his trial, he was brought into the courtroom in a wheelchair—awake but unresponsive—the judge remanded him to the state mental hospital.

Loved One has been officially diagnosed as having *bipolar disorder*, a condition characterized by periods of elation and intense activity (mania) followed by periods of deep sadness and lethargy (depression). Particularly during the manic periods, Loved One has **psychosis:** His thinking is impaired to the point where he cannot function normally. He seems unable to reason, make appropriate decisions, or control his impulses. Furthermore, he often has auditory hallucinations, hearing voices that aren't there. Given such symptoms, some family members and therapists suspect that he has *schizophrenia* as well as bipolar disorder (the combination is known as *schizoaffective disorder*).

Medication does wonders for Loved One: It calms him down, clears his thoughts, gives him back his impulse control, and helps him appropriately interpret and respond to events in his daily life. Medication has enabled him to acquire his graduate equivalency diploma (G.E.D.) and earn a B in a math class at a local community college. But like many people with mental illness, Loved One doesn't always stay on his medication. When he doesn't, his brain goes haywire and his behaviors land him in jail and, if he is lucky, back in the hospital. Loved One typically remembers very little of what he does or what happens to him when he is psychotic. That is probably just as well.

The human brain is an incredibly complex mechanism, and researchers have a long way to go in understanding how it works and why it doesn't always work as well as it should. Yet they had made considerable progress in the past two decades, and their knowledge about brain anatomy and physiology grows by leaps and bounds every year.

In this chapter we will look at the biological underpinnings of thinking and learning. We will begin by putting the basic building blocks of the human nervous system under the microscope. We will then examine structures within the brain and the various functions each appears to have. Later, we will trace the brain's development over time (at that point we will speculate about why Loved One's brain broke down when it did) and look at theorists' beliefs about the physiological basis of learning. Finally, we will consider what educational implications we can draw—as well as what implications we *cannot* draw—from current knowledge and research about the brain. As we address these topics, we will discredit some common myths about the brain that currently run rampant in educational literature.

BASIC BUILDING BLOCKS OF THE HUMAN NERVOUS SYSTEM

The human nervous system has two main components. The **central nervous system,** comprising the brain and spinal cord, is the coordination center: It connects what we sense (e.g., what we see, hear, smell, taste, and feel) with what we do (e.g., how we move our arms and legs). The **peripheral nervous system** is the messenger system: It carries information from *receptor cells*—cells specialized to detect particular kinds of stimulation from the environment (e.g., light, sound, chemicals, heat, pressure)—to the central nervous system, and it carries directions back to various body parts (muscles, organs, etc.) about how to respond to that stimulation.

Nerve cells, or **neurons,** provide the means through which the nervous system transmits and coordinates information. Curiously, however, neurons don't directly touch one another; they send chemical messages to their neighbors across tiny gaps known as **synapses.** And neurons rely on other cells, known as **glial cells,** to give them structure and support. Let's briefly look at the nature of each of these key elements of the nervous system.

Neurons

Each neuron in the human body plays one of three roles. **Sensory neurons** carry incoming information from receptor cells. They convey this information to **interneurons,** which integrate and interpret input from multiple locations. The resulting "decisions" are transmitted to **motor neurons,** which send messages about how to behave and respond to appropriate parts of the body.[1] As you might guess, sensory neurons and motors neurons are located in the peripheral nervous system. The vast majority of interneurons are found in the central nervous system, especially in the brain.

Although neurons vary somewhat in size and shape, all of them have several features in common (see Figure 2–1). First, like all cells, they have a cell body, or **soma,** that contains the cell's nucleus and is responsible for the cell's health and well-being. In addition, they have a number of branchlike structures, known as **dendrites,** that receive messages from other neurons. They also have an **axon,** a long, armlike structure that transmits information on to additional neurons (occasionally, a neuron has more than one axon). The end of the axon may branch out numerous times, and the ends of its tiny branches have **terminal buttons** that contain certain chemical substances (more about these substances shortly). For some (but not all) neurons, much of the axon is covered with a white, fatty substance known as a **myelin sheath.**

When a neuron's dendrites are stimulated by other cells (either receptor cells or other neurons), the dendrites become electrically charged. In some instances, the charges are so small that the neuron "ignores" them. But when the charges reach a certain level (known as the **threshold of excitation**), the neuron "fires," sending an electrical impulse along its axon to the terminal buttons. If the axon has a myelin sheath, the impulse travels quite rapidly, as the message leaps from gap to gap, almost as if it were playing leap frog. If the axon does not have a myelin sheath, the message travels more slowly.

Synapses

The branching ends of a neuron's axon reach out to, but do not quite touch, the dendrites (in some cases, the somas) of other neurons. Whereas transmission of information within a neuron is electrical, transmission of information from one neuron to another is chemical. When an electrical impulse moves down a neuron's axon, it signals the terminal buttons to release chemicals known as **neurotransmitters.** These chemicals travel across the synapses and stimulate the dendrites or somas of neighboring neurons.

Different neurons specialize in different kinds of neurotransmitters. Perhaps in your readings about health, fitness, or related topics, you have seen references to dopamine, epinephrine, norepinephrine, serotonon, amino acids, or peptides. All of these are neurotransmitters, and each of them may play a unique role in the nervous system. For instance, dopamine is a key

---

[1]You may sometimes see the terms *receptor neurons, adjuster neurons,* and *effector neurons* used for sensory neurons, interneurons, and motor neurons, respectively.

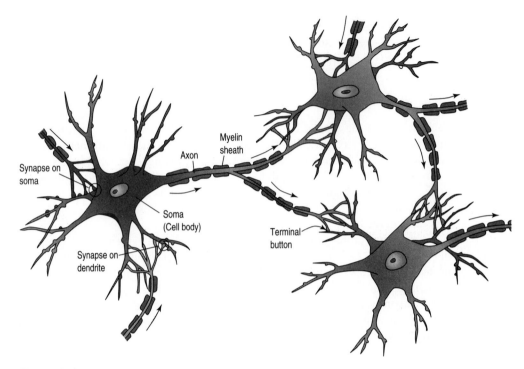

Figure 2–1
The nature of neurons and their interconnections.

neurotransmitter in the frontal cortex, which, as you will discover shortly, is actively involved in consciousness, planning, and the inhibition of irrelevant behaviors and ideas (Goldman-Rakic, 1992). Some theorists suspect that schizophrenia may sometimes be the result of abnormal levels of dopamine (Conklin & Iacono, 2002; Walker, 2002). (Recall Loved One's difficulties with decision making and impulse control.)

Any single neuron may have synaptic connections with hundreds of other neurons (Goodman & Tessier-Lavigne, 1997; R. F. Thompson, 1985). Some neurotransmitters increase the level of electrical activity in the neurons they stimulate, whereas others inhibit (i.e., decrease) the level of electrical activity. Whether a particular neuron fires, then, is the result of how much it is "encouraged" and "discouraged" by its many neighbors.

Glial Cells

Only about 10% of the cells in the nervous system are neurons. The other 90% are glial cells (also known as *neuroglia*). Glial cells do not carry messages themselves; rather, they serve in several supportive roles that enable neurons to do their work. For instance, glial cells provide a stable structure that helps to keep neurons in place and insulated from one another. They provide the chemicals that neurons need to function properly. They form the myelin sheaths that surround the axons of many neurons. And they serve as the clean-up crew, removing dead neurons and excess neurotransmitter substances.

In the human brain, these basic building blocks—neurons, synapses, and glial cells—make it possible for us to survive (e.g., by breathing and sleeping), to identify the stimuli we encounter (e.g., recognizing a friend or the family pet), to feel emotion (e.g., becoming afraid when we encounter danger), and to engage in the many conscious thought processes (e.g., planning, reading, solving mathematical problems) that are distinctly human.

BRAIN STRUCTURES AND FUNCTIONS

In some instances, sensory neurons connect directly with motor neurons in the spinal cord. For instance, if you touch something very hot, the sensory neurons traveling from your fingertips up your arm and into your spinal cord tell the motor neurons traveling back to your arm and hand muscles to quickly pull your fingers away. You make this automatic response, or **reflex**, without any thought whatsoever. Although your brain certainly perceives the heat you have encountered, your spinal cord enables you to remove yourself from danger before your brain deliberates on the situation at all.

For the most part, however, information from the outside world travels to the brain, which then decides whether and how to respond. The human brain is an incredibly complicated mechanism that involves somewhere in the neighborhood of *one hundred billion* neurons (Goodman & Tessier-Lavigne, 1997). These neurons are, of course, microscopic, and they are interconnected in a myriad of ways. Thus, researchers have had quite a challenge in figuring out how the brain works and what parts serve what functions, but they have made considerable progress nevertheless.

In this section, we will look at the methods that researchers use to study the nature and functions of various parts of the brain. We will then examine researchers' findings, identifying particular functions that different structures appear to serve and learning how the two hemispheres of the brain may play somewhat different roles in thinking and learning. Later, as we consider the interconnected nature of the brain, we will find that thinking—and in fact even a single "piece" of knowledge—is rarely, if ever, located in a single spot.

Methods in Brain Research

In their work, researchers have had several methodologies at their disposal:

- *Studies with animals.* Some researchers take liberties with animals (e.g., laboratory rats) that they would never take with human beings. For instance, they may remove a certain part of an animal's brain, insert a tiny needle into a certain location and electrically stimulate it, increase the levels of certain hormones, or inject chemicals that block certain neurotransmitters. They then observe changes in the animal's behavior and assume that these changes reflect the functions that particular brain structures, hormones, or neurotransmitters serve.
- *Case studies of people with brain injuries and other pathological conditions.* Researchers take detailed notes about what people with brain injuries or certain pathologies (e.g., schizophrenia, dyslexia) can and cannot do. After death, they examine the individuals' brains to identify areas of abnormality (e.g., specific sites of an injury, abnormal brain structures). If the absence of certain abilities is consistently associated with certain brain abnormalities, then researchers reasonably conclude that the affected brain areas play a key role in those missing abilities.

- *Electrical recording.* Researchers place electrodes at strategic locations on a person's scalp and record patterns of electrical activity in the brain. The resulting record, known as an *electroencephalograph* (EEG), tends to show different patterns of brain waves for different activities (e.g., for sleep versus wakefulness). Often, researchers will collect EEG data as people perform specific tasks, yielding *event-related potentials* (ERPs) that provide some indication of the nature of the brain activity occurring during those tasks. In one recent study (Farwell & Smith, 2001), researchers using an EEG-based procedure called *memory and encoding related multifaceted electroencephalographic responses* (MERMER) could determine, with an accuracy rate of 90% or higher, which individuals had and had not experienced certain events.
- *Neuroimaging.* Using a variety of recent technological advances, researchers take pictures of blood flow or metabolism rates in various parts of the brain as people perform a particular task. Common techniques are positron emission tomography (PET), single-photo emission computerized tomography (SPECT), computerized axial tomography (CAT), magnetic resonance imaging (MRI), and functional magnetic resonance imaging (fMRI). Presumably, areas of greater blood flow or metabolic rate reflect areas of the brain that contribute in significant ways to the task in question.

None of these methods is perfect. For instance, brain injuries may simultaneously affect multiple regions of the brain, laboratory rats do not have many of the cognitive abilities that humans do, EEGs don't tell us precisely where particular thought processes are occurring, and neuroimaging involves expensive diagnostic equipment with only limited availability for basic research (Byrnes, 2001). Nevertheless, taken together, research using these techniques is helping scientists identify and begin to put together some of the pieces of the puzzle about how the human brain works.

Parts of the Brain

The human brain has three major components (see Figure 2–2), which have emerged at different points along our evolutionary journey. The **hindbrain,** located in the lower part of the brain where the spinal cord enters the skull, appeared first in evolution and appears first in prenatal development. Made up of several smaller structures (e.g., the medulla, pons, and cerebellum), the hindbrain is involved in many basic physiological processes that keep us alive (breathing, swallowing, sleeping, heart rate, etc.). The cerebellum, at the lower rear of the brain, is actively involved in balance and complex motor behaviors (e.g., walking, riding a bicycle, playing racquetball).

Next in both evolutionary and prenatal development is the **midbrain,** which plays supporting roles in vision and hearing (e.g., helping to control and coordinate eye movements). Probably the most essential part of the midbrain is the **reticular formation** (also called the *reticular activating system,* or RAS), which extends into the hindbrain as well. The reticular formation is a key player in attention and consciousness; for example, it alerts us to potentially important stimuli that the body's receptors are encountering.

Last to come along is the **forebrain,** located in the front and upper portions of the brain. The forebrain is where most of the "action" is in primates, especially human beings. Resting on top, like a thick, poorly constructed toupee, is the **cerebral cortex**—often simply called the **cortex**—which is divided into two halves (**hemispheres**) that, on the surface, appear to be mirror images of each other. Neurologists conceptualize the hemispheres of the cortex as having four major parts, or *lobes,* named after the parts of the skull that cover them (see Figure 2–3):

Figure 2–2
Key parts of the brain. The figure shows the middle of the brain; hence, the right and left sides of the cortex are missing.

- *Frontal Lobes.* Located at the front and top of the cortex, the frontal lobes are where much of our conscious thinking seems to occur. The frontal lobes are largely responsible for a wide variety of very "human" activities, including language, attention, reasoning, planning, goal setting, self-monitoring, decision making, judgment, learning strategies, controlled movements, and interpretation of others' behaviors. In addition, the frontal lobes are instrumental in inhibiting irrelevant and inappropriate thoughts and actions. (I suspect that much of Loved One's illness involves malfunctioning of his frontal lobes.)
- *Parietal Lobes.* Located in the upper back portion of the cortex, the parietal lobes receive and interpret somatosensory information—that is, information about temperature, pressure, texture, and pain. These lobes are also actively involved in paying attention, processing word sounds, and thinking about the spatial characteristics of objects and events.
- *Occipital Lobes.* Located at the very back of the brain, the occipital lobes have major responsibility for interpreting and remembering visual information.
- *Temporal Lobes.* At the sides, behind the ears, are the temporal lobes, which interpret and remember complex auditory information (e.g., speech, music). The temporal lobes also appear to be important in memory for information over the long run (something we will later call *long-term memory*), especially for meanings and general world knowledge.

In some cases, researchers have pinned down fairly specific regions of the cortex in which certain kinds of processing seem to occur. But many areas of the cortex are not so neatly specialized. These areas, known as *association areas*, appear to integrate information from various parts of the cortex, as well as from other parts of the brain, and so are essential for complex thinking and behavior.

Inside and below the cortex are several other parts of the forebrain. Following are some especially noteworthy ones:

Frontal lobe

Parietal lobe

Temporal lobe

Occipital lobe

Figure 2–3
Side view of the cortex.

- *Limbic System.* Closely connected with the temporal lobes is a cluster of structures essential to learning, memory, emotion, and motivation. A small, seahorse-shaped structure known as the *hippocampus* (Greek for "seahorse") is intimately involved in attention and learning, especially for things that we consciously (rather than unconsciously) learn. Another structure, the *amygdala*, figures prominently in emotions (especially "negative" ones such as fear, stress, anger, and depression) and in automatic emotional reactions (e.g., aggression). Furthermore, the amygdala enables us to associate particular emotions with particular stimuli or memories (Adolphs & Damasion, 2001; Byrnes, 2001; Cahill et al., 1996).
- *Thalamus.* The thalamus, located in the very middle of the brain, serves as a "switchboard operator" that receives incoming information from various sensory neurons and sends it on to appropriate areas of the cortex. It also plays a role in arousal, attention, and fear.
- *Hypothalamus.* Located beneath the thalamus, the hypothalamus regulates many activities related to survival, such as breathing, body temperature, hunger and thirst, mating, fighting, and fleeing from harm.

The Left and Right Hemispheres

To some degree, the left and right hemispheres have different specialties. Curiously, the left hemisphere is largely responsible for controlling the right side of the body, and vice versa. For most people, the left hemisphere seems to be in charge of language, with particular areas of the left frontal lobe, known as Broca's area and Wernicke's area, being involved in speech and language comprehension, respectively. Reading and mathematical calculation skills also seem to be heavily dependent on the left hemisphere (Byrnes, 2001; Roberts & Kraft, 1987). In contrast, the right hemisphere is more dominant in visual and spatial processing, such as locating objects in space, perceiving shapes, comparing quantities, drawing and painting, mentally manipulating visual images, recognizing faces and facial expressions, and interpreting gestures (Byrnes, 2001; Ornstein, 1997). In general, the left side is more apt to handle details, whereas the right side is better suited for looking at and synthesizing an overall whole (Ornstein, 1997).

Yet contrary to a popular myth, people rarely if ever think exclusively in one hemisphere; there is no such thing as "left-brain" or "right-brain" thinking. The two hemispheres are joined together by a collection of neurons (the *corpus callosum*) that enables constant communication back and forth, and so the hemispheres typically collaborate in day-to-day tasks. Let's take language comprehension as an example. The left hemisphere handles such basics as syntax and word meanings, but it seems to interpret what it hears and reads quite literally. The right hemisphere is better able to consider multiple meanings and take context into account; hence, it is more likely to detect sarcasm, irony, metaphors, and puns (Beeman & Chiarello, 1998; Ornstein, 1997). Without your right hemisphere, you would find no humor in the following joke:

> A woman went to a butcher to buy rabbit for a stew but the hares hanging at the butcher's are quite large. So, she says to the butcher, "I'd like to make some rabbit stew but these things are too big. Could you cut one in two for me?". . . "Sorry ma' am [the butcher replies], we don't split hares here." (Ornstein, 1997, p. 109)

About 80% of human beings have left and right hemispheres that are specialized in the ways I've just described. For instance, the left hemisphere is the primary language hemisphere for more than 90% of right-handed individuals but for only about 60% of left-handed folks. People differ, too, in how "lopsided" their thinking is: Whereas some often rely predominantly on one hemisphere or the other (depending on the circumstances), others regularly think in a fairly balanced, two-sided manner (Ornstein, 1997).

As you can see, then, functions of some areas of the brain (especially in the cortex) are hardly set in stone. Occasionally, one area may take over a function that another area typically serves. For example, if, before age 1, children sustain damage to the left hemisphere or have part of their left hemisphere surgically removed (perhaps to address severe epileptic seizures), the right hemisphere steps in and enables the children to acquire normal language capabilities (Beeman & Chiarello, 1998; Stiles & Thal, 1993). To some extent, which parts of the cortex handle which kinds of information depends on which messages from various sensory neurons end up at which locations; if surgical interventions rearrange where the messages go, the cortex accommodates the change (Byrnes, 2001). Furthermore, different areas of the cortex may take on different roles as a result of what specific stimuli and tasks present themselves while a particular part of the cortex is actively changing and maturing (Ornstein, 1997).

Interconnectedness of Brain Structures

As you may have noticed in our earlier discussion of various brain structures, many aspects of our daily functioning—for instance, attention, learning, memory, and motor skills—are handled in multiple places. And as you just discovered, the two hemispheres usually work together to understand and respond to the world. Remember, too, that any single neuron is apt to have hundreds of synapses with other neurons. As information travels through the brain, messages go every which way—not only from "lower down" in the processing system (i.e., at points where sensory information first reaches the brain) to "higher up" (i.e., at points where information is synthesized and interpreted or where behaviors are chosen and controlled), but also in the opposite direction and across areas that handle very different sensory modalities and motor functions. In essence, learning or thinking about virtually anything tends to be *distributed* across many parts of the brain (Bressler, 2002; Thelen & Smith, 1998). A task as seemingly simple as identifying a particular word while reading a book or listening to speech will activate multiple areas of the cortex (Byrnes, 2001; Rayner, Foorman, Perfetti, Pesetsky, & Seidenberg, 2001).

In fact, probably even a single piece of information—for example, remembering your address, telephone number, or birthday—is probably stashed away in your head in a distributed manner. In the 1920s, Karl Lashley (1929) worked extensively with rats in his efforts to determine where particular memories might be located. Lashley gave his rats a chance to learn their way around a particular maze and then removed certain sections of their brains to see whether they still remembered the maze. Regardless of which sections Lashley removed, the rats did not totally forget the maze; instead, they gradually remembered less and less as more and more of their brains were removed. It appeared that the rats remembered the maze in multiple places simultaneously, with each place contributing to the overall memory.

How does such a complex, interconnected mechanism—the human brain—come into being? Mother Nature's handiwork is quite a marvel. We look now at how the brain emerges and changes over the course of development.

DEVELOPMENT OF THE BRAIN

A second widespread myth about the brain is that it does all of its "maturing" within the first few years of life and that its development can best be nurtured by bombarding it with as much stimulation as possible—reading instruction, violin lessons, art classes, and so on—before its owner ever reaches kindergarten. Nothing could be further from the truth. Although much of the brain's development occurs before birth and the first few years after birth, the brain continues to develop throughout childhood and adolescence, and probably into adulthood as well. The early years are important, to be sure, but the kinds of experiences that nurture the brain's early development are fairly normal ones. In this section, we will trace brain development during the prenatal months and postnatal years and look at factors that influence its development. We will then address two questions with which theorists have wrestled: To what extent are there critical periods in brain development? and To what extent is the brain "prewired" to know or learn certain things? As you will discover, theorists have tentatively answered the first question but are still wrestling with the second.

Prenatal Development

About 25 days after conception, the brain first emerges as a tiny tube. The tube grows longer and begins to fold inward to make pockets (Rayport, 1992). Three chambers appear, and these eventually become the forebrain, midbrain, and hindbrain. Neurons quickly form and reproduce in the inner part of the tube; between the fifth and twentieth weeks of prenatal development, they do so at the astonishing rate of 50,000 to 100,000 new cells per second (Diamond & Hopson, 1998). The vast majority (but apparently not all) of the neurons a person will ever have are formed at this time (Bruer, 1999; R. A. Thompson & Nelson, 2001).

In the second trimester of prenatal development, the neurons migrate to various locations, drawn by a variety of chemicals and supported by glial cells. On their arrival, they send out dendrites and axons in an effort to connect with one another. Those that make contact survive and begin to take on particular functions, whereas those that do not (about half of them) tend to die off (Diamond & Hopson, 1998; Goldman-Rakic, 1986; Huttenlocher, 1993). Such deaths are not to be mourned, however. Programming human beings to overproduce neurons was apparently Mother Nature's way of ensuring that the brain would have a sufficient number with which to work. The excess ones are unnecessary and can quite reasonably be cast aside.

Development in Infancy and Early Childhood

At birth, the human brain is about one-fourth the size it will be in adulthood, but by age 3 it has reached three-fourths of its adult size (Johnson & de Haan, 2001; Kolb & Whishaw, 1990). The cerebral cortex is the least mature part of the brain at birth, and cortical changes that occur in infancy and early childhood probably account for many of the advancements we see in children's thinking and reasoning (e.g., Quartz & Sejnowski, 1997; Siegler, 1998).

Three significant processes characterize brain development in the early years: synaptogenesis, synaptic pruning, and myelination.

Synaptogenesis

Neurons begin to form synapses well before birth. But shortly after birth, the rate of synapse formation increases dramatically. Neurons sprout new dendrites going every which way, and so they come into contact with a great many of their neighbors. Thanks to this process of **synaptogenesis**, young children have many more synapses than adults do (Bruer, 1999; Byrnes, 2001). Eventually, the rapid proliferation of synapses comes to a halt. Exactly when it does varies for different parts of the brain; for instance, synapses reach their peak in the auditory cortex (temporal lobes) at about 3 months, in the visual cortex (occipital lobes) at about 12 months, and in the frontal lobes at age 2 or 3 (Bruer, 1999; Huttenlocher, 1979, 1990).

Synaptic Pruning

As children encounter a wide variety of stimuli and experiences in their daily lives, some synapses come in quite handy and are used repeatedly. Other synapses are largely irrelevant and useless, and these gradually fade away. In fact, the system seems to be set up to *guarantee* that this cutting back, or **synaptic pruning,** occurs. Neurons require chemical substances known as *trophic factors* for their survival and well-being, and by transmitting messages to other neurons, they cause the recipients to secrete such chemicals. If neurons regularly receive trophic factors from the same sources, they form stable synapses with those sources. If they receive trophic factors from some neurons but not others, they pull their axons away from the "unsupportive" ones. And if they are so "unstimulating" that they rarely excite any of their neighbors, they wither and die (Byrnes, 2001). In some areas of the brain, the period of intensive synaptic pruning occurs fairly early (e.g., in the preschool or early elementary years); in other areas, it begins later and continues until well into adolescence (Bruer, 1999; Huttenlocher & Dabholkar, 1997; Johnson & de Haan, 2001).

Why do our brains create a great many synapses, only to eliminate a sizeable proportion of them later on? In the case of synapses, more is not necessarily better (Byrnes, 2001). Theorists speculate that by generating more synapses than we will ever need, we have the potential to adapt to a wide variety of conditions and circumstances. As we encounter certain regularities in our environment, we find that some synaptic connections make no sense, because they aren't consistent with what we typically encounter in the world or with how we typically need to respond to it. In fact, effective learning and behaving require not only that we think and do certain things but also that we *not* think or do *other* things—in other words, that we inhibit certain thoughts and actions (Dempster, 1992; Haier, 2001). Synaptic pruning, then, may be Mother Nature's way of making our brains more efficient.

Myelination

As noted earlier, a neuron's axon is in some cases covered with a myelin sheath, which greatly speeds up the rate with which an electrical charge travels along the axon. When neurons first develop, they have no myelin; this substance arrives a bit later, courtesy of glial cells. The process of coating neural axons, known as **myelination**, occurs gradually over time. Some myelination begins near the end of the prenatal period (e.g., this is true in certain areas necessary for basic survival), but much of it occurs in the first few years after birth, with different areas becoming myelinated in a predictable sequence (Diamond & Hopson, 1998). Myelination accounts for a sizeable proportion of the brain's postnatal increase in size (Byrnes, 2001). Without doubt, it also enhances the brain's capacity to respond to the world quickly and efficiently.

Development in Middle Childhood, Adolescence, and Beyond

Especially in the cortex, synaptic pruning continues into the middle childhood and adolescent years, and myelination continues into the twenties (Johnson & de Haan, 2001; Merzenich, 2001; Paus et al., 1999). Several parts of the brain—notably the frontal and temporal lobes, hippocampus, amygdala, and corpus callosum, all of which play key roles in thinking and learning—increase significantly in size from middle childhood until late adolescence or adulthood (Giedd et al., 1999a; Sowell & Jernigan, 1998; Walker, 2002). The frontal lobes show evidence of considerable maturation during late adolescence and early adulthood, possibly enabling increasing facility in such areas as attention, planning, and impulse control (Pribram, 1997; Sowell, Thompson, Holmes, Jernigan, & Toga, 1999).

With puberty come changes in young people's hormone levels (e.g., estrogen, testosterone), and these hormones affect the continuing maturation of brain structures, and possibly the production and effectiveness of neurotransmitters as well (Achenbach, 1974; Eisenberg, Martin, & Fabes, 1996; Walker, 2002). In any case, it appears that the levels of some neurotransmitters change at puberty; for instance, serotonin decreases, and dopamine increases in some areas of the cortex (Walker, 2002). If a particular hormone or neurotransmitter is abnormally high or low at this point, something can go seriously awry in brain functioning.

Recall how Loved One's symptoms, minor in the early years, intensified in high school. In most cases, bipolar disorder and schizophrenia don't appear until adolescence or early adulthood. Such disorders seem to be caused, at least in part, by abnormal structures or neurotransmitter levels—abnormalities that don't emerge, or least don't have much effect, until after puberty (Carlson, 1999; Giedd et al., 1999b; Jacobsen et al., 1997a, 1997b).

Factors Influencing Brain Development

Heredity certainly plays a role in brain development. For instance, genetic instructions guide such processes as cell migration, synaptogenesis, and myelination (Bruer, 1999). For the most part, heredity ensures that things go right as the brain continues to grow and restructure itself. Occasionally, however, flawed instructions can cause things to go wrong. For instance, identical twins (twins who began as a single fertilized egg, then split in two, and so have the same DNA) have a higher-than-average probability of sharing disabilities such as schizophrenia and dyslexia (Byrnes, 2001; Conklin & Iacono, 2002). Children with Down syndrome, who have an extra 21st chromosome, have fewer cortical neurons, less myelin, and fewer synapses (Byrnes, 2001).

Environmental factors have effects as well. Severe malnutrition is most problematic during prenatal development, when it results in reduced production of neurons and glial cells (Byrnes, 2001). After birth, malnutrition hampers cell growth, myelination, and performance on psychological measures of cognitive development (e.g., intelligence tests), but the effects of short-term impoverishment can often be reversed by better diets later on (Byrnes 2001; Sigman & Whaley, 1998). Good nutrition only goes so far, however: Providing vitamins, minerals, and other food supplements has little effect if children otherwise have reasonably adequate diets (Zigler & Hodapp, 1986).[2]

Environmental toxins, too, make a difference. When future mothers consume significant amounts of alcohol during pregnancy, their children often have *fetal alcohol syndrome*, a condition characterized by distinctive facial features, poor motor coordination, delayed language, and mental retardation (e.g., Dorris, 1989). Ingestion of excessive amounts of lead (perhaps by eating paint chips found in old apartment buildings) can result in deficits in cognitive abilities (Byrnes, 2001; McLoyd, 1998). Exposure to radiation during the period of rapid neuron production in the first few months of prenatal development leads to mental retardation but has little effect after this point (Goldman-Rakic, 1986).

Opportunities to learn also influence brain growth. When rats learn how to navigate a complex maze or difficult obstacle course, researchers later find more and stronger synapses in relevant parts of their cortexes (Black, Isaacs, Anderson, Alcantara, & Greenough, 1990; Greenough, Juraska, & Volkmar, 1979; Kleim et al., 1998). People who have learned to read and write have, in their corpus callosums, a thicker band of fibers connecting their parietal lobes (Castro-Caldas et al., 1999). People who learn to play a musical instrument show detectably different organizational patterns in the brain than nonmusicians (Elbert, Pantev, & Taub, 1995). Intensive interventions for congenital or acquired disabilities (e.g., dyslexia, brain damage from strokes, removal of certain parts of the brain) lead to reorganizations of brain structure or changes in patterns of brain activation (Bach-y-Rita, 1981; Crill & Raichle, 1982; Small, Flores, & Noll, 1998). To the extent that the brain adapts itself in such ways to different circumstances and experiences, we say that it has **plasticity.**

To What Extent Are There Critical Periods in Brain Development?

Let's reconsider a point I made just a moment ago: Radiation has a substantial impact on brain development *only* in the early months of the prenatal period. And consider this intriguing finding: When accomplished musicians play their musical instruments, those who began their musical training before age 10 show greater activation in a certain part of their brains than those who began their training at an older age (Elbert et al., 1995). One group doesn't necessarily play better than the other, but the pattern of activation is different for the two groups.

Such findings raise an important question: To what degree does the *timing* of instruction or intervention make a difference in brain development? More specifically, to what degree are there

---

[2]For a review of research on the possible effects of food supplements on learning and memory in adults, see McDaniel, Maier, and Einstein (2002).

critical periods[3] —certain age ranges in which particular kinds of environmental stimulation have their greatest, and perhaps only, impact—in brain development?

Researchers have consistently found evidence for critical periods in the development of visual perception. If kittens have one eye sewn shut for the first three months of life, they remain functionally blind in that eye throughout life: The eye itself begins to work once the stitches are removed (e.g., receptors in the retina respond to light), but the part of the cortex that receives signals from the previously nonseeing eye isn't able to interpret the information it gets (Hubel & Wiesel, 1970). A similar thing happens when monkeys have one eye sewn shut for the first six months of life, yet monkeys suffer no permanent loss of vision if the eye is sewn shut for six months during adulthood rather than infancy (Bruer, 1999; Hubel, Wiesel, & Levay, 1977; Levay, Wiesel, & Hubel, 1980). And when human beings are born with cataracts that prevent normal vision, early surgery is essential. If the cataracts are removed before age 2, children develop relatively normal vision, but if surgery is postponed until age 5 or older, children remain functionally blind in whichever eye was affected (Bruer, 1999). Curiously, it seems to be the *pattern* of light deprivation, rather than light deprivation per se, that affects development in visual areas of the cortex; when monkeys have *both* eyes sewn shut for the first six months, they develop normal vision (Bruer, 1999; Hubel et al., 1977; Levay et al., 1980). It appears that if, in the early months, one eye is stimulated more than the other, the cortex restructures itself to take advantage of the information it gets from the seeing eye and compensate for what it's not getting from the other eye.

In human beings, we find convincing evidence that there are critical periods in learning language as well. Children who have little or no exposure to language in the early years often have trouble acquiring language later on, even with adequate or enriched language experiences (e.g., Curtiss, 1977; Newport, 1990). Furthermore, in the first few days and weeks of life, infants can discriminate among speech sounds used in a wide variety of languages, but by the time they are 6 months old, they "hear" only those differences important in their own language (Kuhl, Williams, & Lacerda, 1992). As an example, the English language treats "L" and "R" as two separate sounds, whereas Japanese clumps them together into a single sound; thus, children in English-speaking countries continue to hear the difference between them, whereas Japanese children quickly lose the ability to tell them apart. I think back with fondness to Kikuko, one of my apartment mates in graduate school. As a native Japanese speaker who didn't learn English until grade school, Kikuko talked about taking her *umblella* with her on rainy days, and she thought that people counted *raps* to keep track of how many times they had run around the track at the gym.

Additional evidence for critical periods in language development comes from people who learn a second language. Typically, people learn how to pronounce a second language flawlessly only if they study it before midadolescence or, even better, in the preschool or early elementary years (Bialystok, 1994a; Collier, 1989; Flege, Munro, & MacKay, 1995). Children may also have an easier time mastering a language's various verb tenses and complex aspects of syntax when they are immersed in the language within the first 5 to 10 years of life (Bialystok, 1994a, 1994b; Johnson & Newport, 1989). The effects of age on language learning are especially noticeable when the second language is phonetically and syntactically very different from the first (Bialystok, 1994a; Strozer, 1994).

---

[3]Many developmentalists prefer the term *sensitive period,* which connotes a more open-ended, flexible window of opportunity. However, I have seen the term *critical period* more frequently in recent literature about brain development, hence my use of this term here.

Although we see evidence for critical periods in visual perception and language, most theorists doubt very much that there are critical periods for *all* skills and knowledge domains. Oftentimes people become quite proficient in topics or skills that they don't begin to tackle until they are teenagers or adults. For example, I didn't learn to drive until I was 16, didn't begin to study psychology until I reached college, and didn't begin to play racquetball until I was in graduate school, but with time and practice, I have acquired considerable mastery in those domains.

Experience-Expectant Versus Experience-Dependent Plasticity

So when is early experience important, and when is it *not* important? Greenough, Black, and Wallace (1987) have made a distinction that can help us make sense of what appear to be conflicting data. Mother Nature, it seems, has helped our brains to evolve in such a way that we can adapt to the specific physical and cultural environments in which we find ourselves, but she assumes that we will have *some* stimulation early on to shape brain development. For skills that human beings have possessed for many millenia—visual perception, language, and so on—the brain is **experience-expectant:** It uses the experiences that human beings encounter in virtually any environment to fine-tune its powers. For instance, although the brain is initially capable of interpreting visual signals from both eyes, it will restructure itself to compensate for a nonseeing one. And although it comes equipped with what it needs to discriminate among many different speech sounds, it quickly learns to ignore subtle differences that are irrelevant for making sense of its native language, paving the way for more efficient discriminations among sounds that *are* important for language comprehension. Quite possibly, the phenomena of synaptogenesis and synaptic pruning provide the mechanisms by which the brain initially sets itself up to accommodate a wide variety of environments and then begins to zero in on the particular environment in which it actually finds itself (Bruer, 1999).

Many other content domains and skill areas—for instance, reading, music, driving a car, psychology, racquetball—are such recent additions to human culture (and none of these appears in *all* cultures) that Mother Nature hasn't had the time (and for skills such as racquetball, probably hasn't had the inclination) to make them part of our evolutionary heritage (Bruer, 1997, 1999; Byrnes, 2001). Domains and skills that are unique to particular cultures and social groups are **experience-dependent:** They emerge only when environmental conditions nurture them, and they can presumably emerge at any age. In fact, by strengthening weak synapses and forming new ones, human beings and other animals retain considerable experience-dependent plasticity throughout the lifespan (Bruer, 1999; Greenough et al., 1987; Merzenich, 2001; Merzenich, Allard, & Jenkins, 1990). For example, at age 85, my mother-in-law moved from Arizona to be near us in our present home in New Hampshire. She easily learned what she needed to survive and thrive in her new community: how to get to the bank, hardware store, hairdresser, and grocery store (the nearest supermarket is almost 10 miles away); which neighbors have talents and interests similar to her own; what political issues are simmering in town and across the state; and so on.

So let's return to our initial question: To what extent are there critical periods in brain development? It appears that critical periods exist for certain basic abilities such as visual perception and language. Even in these domains, however, the windows of opportunity remain open for different periods of time for different aspects of those abilities; for instance, there are different time frames for the development of color vision, motion perception, and depth perception, and different time frames for sound discrimination, pronunciation, and acquisition of syntactic structures (Bruer, 1999; Locke, 1993). Furthermore, the windows don't necessarily slam shut at particular ages; rather, they close gradually over a prolonged period and in some cases stay open at least a crack for a very long time, particularly if the right kinds of experiences are provided. And for complex, culture-specific acquisitions—including most of the topics and skills that we teach in schools and universities—the windows remain wide open throughout childhood and adulthood (Bruer, 1999; R. A. Thompson & Nelson, 2001).

To What Extent Is the Brain "Prewired" to Know or Learn Things?

Let's look once again at language. Speaking and understanding language is a miraculous accomplishment indeed; children must master not only the subtle motor movements involved in producing various consonants and vowels but also tens of thousands of word meanings plus syntactical structures so numerous and multifaceted that even linguists have been hard pressed to identify and catalog them all. How children master language as quickly as they do remains one of the big mysteries in child development. Many theorists believe that, although children are obviously not born knowing a particular language, they *are* born with some predispositions that assist them in acquiring whichever language they hear spoken around them (e.g., Cairns, 1996; Gopnik, 1997; Hirsh-Pasek & Golinkoff, 1996; Lenneberg, 1967; Lightfoot, 1999). This perspective of language learning, known as **nativism,** is supported by three widely observed phenomena. First, everyday speech seems to be inadequate to enable children to acquire the complex, adultlike language that they eventually *do* acquire. In typical day-to-day conversations, adults often use incomplete sentences, are lax in their adherence to grammatical rules and, when talking to very young children, may use artificially short and simple language. In other words, there is a *poverty of the stimulus* in the language that children hear (Cook & Newson, 1996; Harris, 1992; Lightfoot, 1999). Second, to communicate effectively, children must derive a myriad of unspoken, underlying rules that govern how words are put together and then use these rules to generate sentences they have never heard before (Chomsky, 1959, 1972; Littlewood, 1984; Pinker, 1993). Third, all children in a particular language community learn essentially the *same* language despite widely differing early childhood experiences and a general lack of systematic instruction in appropriate language use (Cromer, 1993; Lightfoot, 1999; Littlewood,1984).

Some theorists have suggested that human beings may be prewired with respect to other domains as well. Consider these findings from research with infants:

* By 24 hours of age, infants have some ability to discriminate between objects that are close to them versus objects that are farther away (Slater, Mattock, & Brown, 1990). It's as if they can judge distance long before they have much opportunity to *learn* about distance.
* Infants as young as 1 or 2 days old may imitate an adult's facial expressions—perhaps pursing their lips, opening their mouths, or sticking out their tongues (Field, Woodson, Greenberg, & Cohen, 1982; Meltzoff & Moore, 1977; Reissland, 1988). It's as if they already connect certain things they see others do with certain things that they themselves can do.
* By 3 or 4 months, infants show signs of surprise when one solid object passes directly through another one, when an object seems to be suspended in midair, or when an object appears to move immediately from one place to another without traveling across the intervening space to get there (Baillargeon, 1994; Spelke, 1994; Spelke, Breinlinger, Macomber, & Jacobson, 1992). It appears, then, that young infants know that objects are substantive

entities with definite boundaries, that they will fall unless something holds them up, and that their movements across space are continuous.

Such findings suggest to some theorists (e.g., Flavell, Miller, & Miller, 1993; Spelke, 2000) that infants have some biologically built-in **core knowledge** about the physical world. Knowledge of this kind would have an evolutionary advantage, of course—it would give infants a head start in learning about their environment—and evidence for it has been observed in other species as well (Spelke, 2000).

Nevertheless, the extent to which the human brain is hardwired with certain knowledge, or perhaps with predispositions to acquire that knowledge, is, at present, an unresolved issue, and it will likely remain so for quite some time. Unless researchers can assess infants' knowledge at the very moment of birth, they cannot rule out the possibility that experience and practice, rather than built-in knowledge, account for infants' early capabilities. Just imagine a couple of scientists in lab coats appearing in the hospital delivery room to ask if they can whisk the new baby away for a "research project." I doubt that they'd find many new parents willing to sign the necessary permission forms.

THE PHYSIOLOGICAL BASIS OF LEARNING

So how and where, from a physiological standpoint, does learning occur? As I suggested in the earlier discussion of brain plasticity, many theorists believe that the basis for learning lies in changes in interconnections among neurons—in particular, in the strengthening of existing synapses and the formation of new ones, perhaps through increases in the number and complexity of dendrites at the "receiving" ends of neurons (Byrnes & Fox, 1998; Greenough et al., 1987; Merzenich, 2001; Rosenzweig, 1986). But another phenomenon may be involved as well. Until recently, it was common "knowledge" that all the neurons a person would ever have are produced in the first few weeks of the prenatal period. Some researchers are finding, however, that **neurogenesis**—the formation of new neurons—continues throughout the lifespan in a particular part of the hippocampus, and possibly also in certain regions of the frontal and parietal lobes (Gould, Beylin, Tanapat, Reeves, & Shors, 1999; Sapolsky, 1999; R. A. Thompson & Nelson, 2001). Neurogenesis appears to be stimulated, in part, by new learning experiences (Gould et al., 1999), but exactly how it enters into the learning process remains an unanswered question.

As for *where* learning occurs, the answer is: many places. The frontal lobes are active when we must pay attention and think about new information and events, and all of the lobes of the cortex may be active to a greater or lesser extent in interpreting new input in light of previously acquired knowledge (Byrnes, 2001). The small, seahorse-shaped hippocampus seems to be a central figure in the learning process, binding together the information it simultaneously receives from various parts of the brain (Bauer, 2002; Squire & Alvarez, 1998). And its neighbor in the limbic system, the amygdala, is probably instrumental in the early, preverbal, emotional memories that young children form (LeDoux, 1998).

Even as researchers pin down how and where learning occurs, we must remember that knowledge of brain anatomy and physiology doesn't begin to tell us everything we need to know about learning, let alone about how we can best foster and enhance it in educational settings. Let's look now at what research about the brain does and does not tell us about appropriate and effective educational practice.

EDUCATIONAL IMPLICATIONS OF BRAIN RESEARCH

Extolling recent advances in brain research, some well-meaning but ill-informed individuals have drawn unsubstantiated inferences about its educational implications. For instance, you might hear people speaking of "building better brains," designing a "brain-based curriculum," or "teaching to the right brain." Such statements often reflect misconceptions about how the brain works. Brain research is only in its infancy, and much of what researchers have learned about brain functioning is still somewhat tentative and controversial (Byrnes, 2001). Following are several conclusions we can draw with some confidence:

- *Some loss of synapses is both inevitable and desirable.* Apparently in an effort to preserve as many of those early synapses as possible, some writers have suggested that infants and young children be immersed in stimulation-rich environments that get them off to a strong start in academics, athletics, and the arts. But as we have seen, synaptic pruning is inevitable, because synapses must compete for a limited supply of the trophic factors that ensure their survival. Furthermore, pruning is beneficial, not detrimental, because it eliminates useless synapses and thereby enhances the brain's efficiency. The sequence of synaptogenesis and synaptic pruning is a primary means by which Mother Nature ensures plasticity and adaptability in human functioning (Bruer, 1999; Byrnes & Fox, 1998). In fact, much learning and many advances in cognitive abilities (e.g., abstract reasoning) occur after most synaptic pruning has already taken place (Bruer, 1999).

- *Many environments nurture normal neurological development.* In domains where development depends on particular kinds of stimulation at particular ages (i.e., in domains characterized by critical periods), the necessary stimulation is found in experiences that children encounter in virtually any culture. For instance, to acquire normal binocular vision, children need regular and balanced visual input to both eyes. To acquire normal facility with language, children need ongoing exposure to a language, either spoken or manually signed (e.g., Newport, 1990). Such experiences can be found not only in "enriching" daycare and preschool environments but also in lower-income, inner-city neighborhoods and even in remote tribal groups in developing countries. To date, we do not know to what extent, or even *if*, intensive, structured educational experiences promote greater brain growth than might otherwise be expected (Bruer, 1999; R. A. Thompson & Nelson, 2001).

One important caveat must be mentioned here, however: A *very* critical period is the prenatal period, especially the first few months after conception, when adequate nutrition and protection from radiation and other environmental hazards are essential if the brain is to get off to a good start. The adverse effects of poor nutrition and environmental insults during this time period appear to be irreversible.

- *The early years are important for learning, but so are the later years.* Although complex environments appear not to be essential for *neurological* development, children often make greater *cognitive* gains—for instance, they have more knowledge and skills, and they earn higher scores on intelligence tests—in enriching preschool programs than they make without such programs (Bronfenbrenner, 1999; Ramey, 1992; Seitz, Rosenbaum, & Apfel, 1985; Zigler & Finn-Stevenson, 1987). Yet the gains made in the early years tend to diminish over time, and may disappear altogether, unless children continue to have stimulating experiences during the school years (Bronfenbrenner, 1999; Campbell & Ramey, 1995; Gustafsson & Undheim, 1996). Educators and policy makers should not put all of their eggs in one age-specific basket; nurturance of learning and cognitive growth must be a long-term enterprise (Brown & Bjorklund, 1998).

- *There is no such thing as teaching to the "left brain" or to the "right brain."* Some writers have suggested that many adults and children specialize in one hemisphere or the other, to the point of being largely "left-brain" or "right-brain" thinkers and learners, and so they urge educators to accommodate the hemispheric preferences of every student. This *dichotomania* is "pseudoscience" that is sometimes used to justify letting students avoid disciplined, rational thinking (Ornstein, 1997; Stanovich, 1998). As we have seen, both hemispheres work in close collaboration in virtually all thinking and learning tasks. In the absence of performing surgical lobotomies (which I obviously don't recommend), attempts to train one side exclusively will be in vain.

- *In developmental domains characterized by critical periods, the windows of opportunity often remain at least a crack open.* The concept of *critical period* tells us the best time for a particular ability to be nurtured, but it doesn't necessarily tell us the *only* time. Sometimes, for a variety of reasons, children have little or no exposure to appropriate stimulation during the optimal time frame; for instance, children may not get needed cataract surgery until their families can afford it, and children who are congenitally deaf may not encounter a language they can actually perceive (e.g., American Sign Language) until they reach school age. Rather than fret over what should have happened but didn't, researchers and educators can better serve young people who have missed critical experiences by devising and testing interventions that enable those individuals to make up some of the lost ground (Bruer, 1999).

- *Brain research can help us refine our theories of learning and cognition, but it can tell us little if anything about what to teach or how best to teach it.* As researchers continue to learn more about the architecture and functioning of the brain, they may find evidence that either supports or refutes various psychological explanations of how people learn and think (Bruer, 1997; Byrnes, 2001). And as psychologists refine their theories of learning and cognition, they can gradually get a better handle on the kinds of instructional methods and therapeutic interventions that are most likely to foster effective learning and behavior.

Nevertheless, we can probably never boil down specific psychological phenomena—thoughts, knowledge, interpretations, and so on—into strictly physiological entities. For instance, brain research is unlikely to tell us much about what information and skills are most important for people to have; such things are often culture specific, and decisions about how to prioritize them are value-laden (Bloom & Tinker, 2001; Chalmers, 1996; Gardner, 2000). Nor does brain research give us many clues about how we can best help learners acquire important information and skills (Byrnes, 2001; Mayer, 1998). Fortunately, as you will discover in the chapters that follow, psychological theories of learning—theories derived from studies of human behavior rather than from brain anatomy and physiology—have a great deal to offer as we work to identify effective instructional and therapeutic techniques.

SUMMARY

Messages travel through the human nervous system (including the brain and spinal cord) via both (1) electrical transmissions that run through individual neurons and (2) chemical transmissions that traverse the synapses between neurons. Synapses in the spinal cord are responsible for a few basic reflexes, but by and large, the brain is the coordination and decision-making center for the body.

Using a growing arsenal of research methods (animal research, case studies with human beings, electrical recordings on the scalp, and neuroimaging technology), scientists have learned a great deal about how the brain works. In human beings, the largest and most recently evolved part of the brain—the *forebrain*—predominates in consciousness, thinking, learning, and the many distinctly "human" activities in which people engage. Even small, seemingly simple tasks (e.g., recognizing and understanding a particular word, remembering a specific bit of information) typically involve many parts of the brain (including both the left and right hemispheres) working in concert.

The beginnings of the brain emerge late in the first month of prenatal development; by the second trimester, the vast majority of neurons a person will ever possess have formed and are migrating to their final locations. Synapses among neurons begin to form before birth; shortly after birth, the rate of synapse formation increases dramatically, to the point where children have many more synapses than adults do. Over the course of childhood and adolescence, the brain cuts back (i.e., *prunes*) little-used synapses, apparently as a means of adapting to its environment and increasing its efficiency. Although most brain development occurs during the prenatal period and early childhood years, some changes in brain structures and neurotransmitters continue into adolescence and early adulthood. Genetic instructions are largely responsible for the course of neurological development, but nutrition, environmental toxins, and learning experiences have effects as well.

Researchers have found evidence for *critical periods* in the development of some basic, long-standing human abilities (e.g., visual perception and language). But many recent human achievements (e.g., literacy, mathematics) can probably be acquired at any age, and certainly the ability to form new synapses (i.e., to *learn*) remains throughout life. Some theorists hypothesize that certain knowledge and skills essential for the human species' survival (e.g., language, basic knowledge about the physical world), or at least a predisposition to acquire these things quickly and easily, may be biologically built in.

Some educators have drawn unwarranted implications from brain research. The early years are important, but providing intensive, structured programs for infants and preschoolers is unlikely to prevent synaptic pruning, and any other potential benefits of such programs for neurological development have yet to be demonstrated. Furthermore, attempts to teach to the "left brain" or "right brain" are fruitless because the two hemispheres collaborate in virtually every task and activity. Educators and other practitioners must remember that learning and mastery of complex tasks can continue throughout the lifespan, and in fact many cognitive advancements (e.g., abstract thinking) don't emerge until late childhood, adolescence, or adulthood.

Part Two

Behaviorist Views of Learning

CHAPTER 3

Behaviorism and Classical Conditioning

I have a "thing" about bees. Whenever a bee flies near me, I scream, wave my arms frantically, and run around like a wild woman. Yes, yes, I know, I will be better off if I remain perfectly still, but somehow I just can't control myself. My overreaction to bees is probably a result of several painful bee stings I received as a small child.

One way to explain how people develop involuntary responses to particular stimuli, such as my fearful reaction to bees, is a theory of learning known as *classical conditioning*. Classical conditioning is an example of *behaviorism*, a perspective I introduced in Chapter 1. The first major theoretical perspective of learning to emerge in the twentieth century, behaviorism is the topic of Chapters 3 through 6. In this chapter, we will identify basic assumptions of the behaviorist approach. We will then examine the nature of classical conditioning, looking at Ivan Pavlov's classic research with dogs and extending his ideas to human learning. Later, we will consider how several other early learning theorists built on Pavlov's work. Finally, we will derive several educational implications of behaviorist theories. In the following three chapters, we will continue our discussion of behaviorism by examining principles and applications of *operant conditioning* (Chapters 4 and 5) and looking at the effects of aversive stimuli on learning and behavior (Chapter 6).

BASIC ASSUMPTIONS OF BEHAVIORISM

Prior to the twentieth century, the two dominant perspectives in psychology were *structuralism* (e.g., Wilhelm Wundt's work) and *functionalism* (e.g., John Dewey's writings). Although these two perspectives differed considerably in their underlying assumptions and topics of study, they shared a common weakness: They lacked a precise, carefully defined research methodology. The primary means of investigating learning and other psychological phenomena, especially for the structuralists, was a method called **introspection:** People were asked to "look" inside their minds and describe what they were thinking. But in the early 1900s, some psychologists began to criticize the introspective approach for its subjectivity and lack of scientific rigor. They worried that, without more objective research methods, psychology as a discipline would never be seen as true "science."

Beginning with the efforts of the Russian physiologist Ivan Pavlov (to be described shortly) and the work of American psychologist Edward Thorndike (to be described in Chapter 4), a more objective approach to the study of learning—one that focused on observable phenomena rather than on nonobservable mental events—emerged. These researchers looked primarily at *behavior*—something that they could easily see and objectively describe—and so the behaviorist movement was born.

Behaviorists have not always agreed on the specific processes that account for learning. Yet many of them have historically shared certain basic assumptions:

• *Principles of learning should apply equally to different behaviors and to different species of animals.* Behaviorists typically assume that human beings and other animals learn in similar ways—an assumption known as **equipotentiality.** (Behaviorists often use the term **organism** to refer generically to a member of any species, human and nonhuman alike.) As a result of this assumption, behaviorists often apply to human learning situations the principles that they have derived primarily from research with such animals as rats and pigeons.

• *Learning processes can be studied most objectively when the focus of study is on stimuli and responses.* Behaviorists believe that psychologists must study learning through objective scientific inquiry, in much the same way that chemists and physicists study phenomena in the physical world. By focusing on two things that they can observe and measure—more specifically, by focusing on **stimuli** in the environment and **responses** that organisms make to those stimuli—psychologists can maintain such objectivity. Behaviorist principles of learning often describe a relationship between a stimulus (**S**) and a response (**R**); hence, behaviorism is sometimes called **S–R psychology.**

• *Internal processes are largely excluded from scientific study.* Many behaviorists believe that because we cannot directly observe and measure internal processes (e.g., thoughts, motives, emotions), we should exclude these processes from research investigations, as well as from explanations of how learning occurs (e.g., Kimble, 2000; Watson, 1925). These behaviorists describe an organism as a "black box," with stimuli impinging on the box and responses emerging from it, but with the things going on inside of it remaining a mystery.[1]

Not all behaviorists take a strict black-box perspective, however. Some insist that internal factors—those within the organism (O)—are also important in understanding learning and behavior. These **neobehaviorist** theorists are sometimes called S–O–R (stimulus–organism–response) theorists rather than S–R theorists. One early neobehaviorist was Clark Hull, who suggested that factors such as motivation and the strength of stimulus–response associations have significant

---

[1]This idea that the study of human behavior and learning should focus exclusively on stimuli and responses is sometimes called *radical behaviorism.*

influences on behavior (we'll look at Hull's work near the end of the chapter). More recently, some behaviorists have asserted that they can effectively understand both human and animal behavior only when they consider cognitive processes as well as environmental events (Church, 1993; DeGrandpre, 2000; Hulse, 1993; Rachlin, 1991; Rescorla, 1988; Schwartz & Reisberg, 1991; Wasserman, 1993). We'll get a flavor of some of these cognitive processes when we examine contemporary perspectives on classical conditioning and operant conditioning later in this chapter and in Chapter 4, respectively.

• *Learning involves a behavior change.* Behaviorists have traditionally defined learning as a change in behavior. After all, as we noted in Chapter 1, we can determine that learning has occurred *only* when we see it reflected in someone's actions. In fact, some behaviorists propose that if no behavior change occurs, then learning cannot possibly be taking place at all.

As some behaviorists have begun to bring cognitive factors into the picture, they have also backed off from this behavior-based definition of learning; rather they treat learning and behavior as separate, albeit related, entities. A number of psychologists (e.g., Brown & Herrnstein, 1975; Estes, 1969a; Herrnstein, 1977; Schwartz & Reisberg, 1991) have suggested that many behaviorist laws are more appropriately applied to an understanding of what influences the *performance* of learned behaviors rather than what influences learning itself.

• *Organisms are born as blank slates.* Aside from certain species-specific instincts (such as the nest-building and migratory behaviors that many birds exhibit) and biologically based disabilities (e.g., mental retardation and mental illness in human beings), organisms are not born with predispositions to behave in particular ways. Instead, organisms enter the world as "blank slates" (an idea often referred to by the Latin equivalent, *tabula rasa*) on which environmental experiences gradually "write." Because each organism has a unique set of environmental experiences, so, too, will it acquire its own unique set of behaviors.

• *Learning is largely the result of environmental events.* Rather than use the term *learning*, behaviorists often speak of **conditioning:** An organism *is conditioned* by environmental events. The passive form of this verb connotes many behaviorists' belief that because learning is the result of one's experiences, learning happens *to* an organism in a way that is often beyond the organism's control.

• *The most useful theories tend to be parsimonious ones.* According to behaviorists, we should explain the learning of all behaviors, from the most simple to the most complex, by as few learning principles as possible; this assumption reflects a preference for **parsimony** (conciseness) in explaining learning and behavior. We will see an example of such parsimony in the first behaviorist theory we explore: classical conditioning.

CLASSICAL CONDITIONING

In the early 1900s, Ivan Pavlov, a Russian physiologist whose work on digestion earned him a Nobel Prize in 1904, was conducting a series of experiments related to salivation in dogs. To study a dog's salivation responses, he would make a surgical incision in the dog's mouth, thus enabling him to collect and measure its saliva. After strapping the dog into an immobile position, he would give it some powdered meat and observe its resulting salivation. Pavlov noticed that after a few of these experiences, the dog began to salivate before it saw or smelled the meat—in fact, it salivated as soon as the lab assistant entered the room with the meat. Apparently, the dog had learned that the lab assistant meant food was on the way and responded accordingly. Pavlov devoted a good part of his later years to a systematic study of this learning process on which he had so inadvertently stumbled, and he eventually summarized his research in his book *Conditioned Reflexes* (Pavlov, 1927).

Pavlov's early studies of classical conditioning went something like this:

1. He first observed whether the dog salivated in response to a particular stimulus—perhaps to a flash of light, the sound of a tuning fork, or the ringing of a bell. For simplicity's sake, we'll continue with our discussion using a bell as the stimulus in question. As you might imagine, the dog did not find the ringing of a bell especially appetizing and so did not salivate.
2. Pavlov then rang the bell again, and this time followed it immediately with the presentation of some powdered meat. The dog, of course, salivated. Pavlov rang the bell several more times, always presenting meat immediately afterward. The dog salivated on each occasion.
3. Pavlov then rang the bell again *without* presenting any meat. Nevertheless, the dog salivated. The bell, to which the dog had previously been unresponsive (in step 1), now led to a salivation response. There had been *a change in behavior as a result of experience*; from the behaviorist perspective, then, *learning* had taken place.

Let's analyze the three steps in Pavlov's experiment in much the same way that Pavlov did:

1. A **neutral stimulus** (**NS**) is a stimulus to which the organism does not respond. In the case of Pavlov's dog, the bell was originally a neutral stimulus that did not elicit a salivation response.
2. The neutral stimulus is presented just before another stimulus, one that *does* lead to a response. This second stimulus is called an **unconditioned stimulus** (**UCS**), and the response to it is called an **unconditioned response** (**UCR**), because the organism responds to the stimulus unconditionally, without having had to learn to do so.[2] For Pavlov's dog, meat powder was an unconditioned stimulus to which it responded with the unconditioned response of salivation.
3. After being paired with an unconditioned stimulus, the previously neutral stimulus now elicits a response, so it is no longer "neutral." The NS has become a **conditioned stimulus** (**CS**) to which the organism has learned a **conditioned response** (**CR**). In Pavlov's experiment, the bell, after being paired with the meat (the unconditioned stimulus) became a conditioned stimulus that led to the conditioned response of salivation. The diagram in Figure 3–1 shows graphically what happened from a classical conditioning perspective.

Pavlov's studies of classical conditioning continued long after these initial experiments, and many of his findings have been replicated with other responses and in other species, including

---

[2]Pavlov's original terms were actually uncondition*al* stimulus and uncondition*al* response, but the mistranslation to uncondition*ed* remains in most classical conditioning literature.

Figure 3–1
A classical conditioning analysis
of Pavlov's dog.

humans. Let's take a closer look at the process of classical conditioning and at some examples of how it might occur in human learning.

The Classical Conditioning Model

Classical conditioning has been demonstrated in many species—not only in dogs and laboratory rats but also in newborn human infants (Lipsitt & Kaye, 1964; Reese & Lipsitt, 1970), human fetuses still in the womb (Macfarlane, 1978), and even organisms as simple as flatworms (Thompson & McConnell, 1955). The applicability of classical conditioning clearly extends widely across the animal kingdom.

As Pavlov's experiments illustrated, classical conditioning occurs when two stimuli are presented at approximately the same time. One of these stimuli is an unconditioned stimulus: It has previously been shown to elicit an unconditioned response. The second stimulus, through its association with the unconditioned stimulus, begins to elicit a response as well: It becomes a conditioned stimulus that brings about a conditioned response. In many cases, conditioning occurs relatively quickly; it is not unusual for an organism to show a conditioned response after the two stimuli have been presented together only five or six times, and sometimes after only one pairing (Rescorla, 1988).

Classical conditioning is most likely to occur when the conditioned stimulus is presented just *before* (perhaps by half a second) the unconditioned stimulus. For this reason, some psychologists describe classical conditioning as a form of **signal learning.** By being presented first, the conditioned stimulus serves as a signal that the unconditioned stimulus is coming, much as Pavlov's dog might have learned that the sound of a bell indicated that yummy meat powder was on its way.

Classical conditioning usually involves the learning of *involuntary* responses—responses over which the learner has no control. When we say that a stimulus **elicits** a response, we mean that the stimulus brings about a response automatically, without the individual having much control over the occurrence of that response. In most cases, the conditioned response is similar to the unconditioned response, with the two responses differing primarily in terms of which stimulus elicits the response and sometimes in terms of the strength of the response. Occasionally, however, the CR is quite different, perhaps even opposite to, the UCR (I'll give you an example a bit later). But in one way or another, the conditioned response allows the organism to anticipate and prepare for the unconditioned stimulus that will soon follow (Rachlin, 1991; Schwartz & Reisberg, 1991).

The conditioned stimulus may serve as a signal that the unconditioned stimulus is coming.

Classical Conditioning in Human Learning

We can use classical conditioning theory to help us understand how people learn a variety of involuntary responses, especially responses associated with physiological functioning or emotion. For example, people can develop aversions to particular foods as a result of associating those foods with an upset stomach (Garb & Stunkard, 1974; Logue, 1979). To illustrate, after associating the taste of creamy cucumber salad dressing (CS) with the nausea I experienced during pregnancy (UCS), I developed an aversion (CR) to cucumber dressing that lasted for several years.

For many people, darkness is a conditioned stimulus for going to sleep, perhaps in part because it has frequently been associated with fatigue. I once became uncomfortably aware of how conditioned I was when I attended my daughter Tina's "astronomy night" at school. We parents were ushered into a classroom and asked to sit down. Then the lights were turned off, and we watched a half-hour filmstrip describing a NASA space museum. Although I am usually quite alert during the early evening hours, I found myself growing increasingly drowsy, and probably only my upright position in an uncomfortable metal chair kept me from losing consciousness altogether. In that situation, the darkness elicited a go-to-sleep response, and there were no stimuli (certainly not the filmstrip) to elicit a stay-awake response.

Attitudes, too, may be partly the result of classical conditioning. In one recent study (Olson & Fazio, 2001), college students sat at a computer while various cartoon characters (Pokemon characters with which they were unfamiliar) were presented on the screen. One character was consistently presented in conjunction with words and images that evoked positive feelings (e.g., "excellent," "awesome," pictures of puppies, and a hot fudge sundae). A second character was consistently presented along with words and images that evoked negative feelings (e.g., "terrible," "awful," pictures of a cockroach, and a man with a knife). Other characters were paired with more neutral words and images. Afterward, when the students were asked to rate some of the cartoon characters and other images they had seen on a scale of −4 (unpleasant) to +4 (pleasant), they rated the character associated with pleasant stimuli far more favorably than the character associated with unpleasant stimuli. Curiously, a positive attitude toward an initially neutral stimulus doesn't necessarily emerge only when people experience it in the company of other pleasant things. Simply experiencing it repeatedly in the *absence* of *un*pleasant things may be enough to engender a preference for it (Zajonc, 2001).

Classical conditioning is also a useful model for explaining some of the fears and phobias that people develop. For example, my bee phobia can probably be explained by the fact that bees (CS) were previously associated with a painful sting (UCS), such that I became increasingly fearful (CR) of the nasty insects. In a similar way, people who are bitten by a particular breed of dog sometimes become afraid of that breed, or even of all dogs.

Probably the best-known example of a classically conditioned fear of an animal is the case of "Little Albert," an infant who learned to fear white rats through procedures used by John Watson and Rosalie Rayner (1920). Albert was an even-tempered, 11-month-old child who rarely cried or displayed fearful reactions. One day, Albert was shown a white rat. As he reached out and touched the rat, a large steel bar behind him was struck, producing a loud, unpleasant noise. Albert jumped, obviously very upset by the startling noise. Nevertheless, he reached forward to touch the rat with his other hand, and the steel bar was struck once again. After five more pairings of the rat (CS) and the loud noise (UCS), Albert was truly rat-phobic: Whenever he saw the rat he cried hysterically and crawled away as quickly as his hands and knees would allow. Watson and Rayner reported that Albert responded in a similarly fearful manner to a rabbit, a dog, a seal-skin coat, cotton wool, and a Santa Claus mask with a fuzzy beard, although none of these had ever been paired with the startling noise. (Watson and Rayner never "undid" their conditioning of poor Albert. Fortunately, the ethical standards of the American Psychological Association now prohibit such negligence.)

When I was growing up, my mother had an effective means of keeping my behavior within reasonable limits. Whenever I began to step out of bounds, she simply gave me The Look, a scowl accompanied by a wrinkled brow and sinister, piercing eyes. I suspect that this facial expression must have been paired with physical punishment sometime in my early childhood years, because The Look alone was eventually sufficient to send me to my bedroom in quick retreat. A threat of punishment such as The Look can arouse sufficient anxiety to control a child's behavior without one's actually having to resort to the punishment threatened. From a classical conditioning perspective, however, a threat can become a conditioned stimulus only if it has in fact been associated with punishment at one time or another, with that punishment following the threat in close proximity (Klein, 1987).[3]

Fear of failure is still another example of a response that may be classically conditioned. In some cases, people who are unusually afraid of failing may have previously associated failure with unpleasant circumstances; perhaps they've associated failure with painful punishment from an angry parent or ridicule by insensitive classmates. Yet occasional failure is a natural consequence of attempting new tasks, whether in school, at home, or elsewhere. Teachers and parents must be

---

[3]The use of punishment is controversial because any stimulus that is frequently associated with it—perhaps the home or school environment, or perhaps a child's parent or teacher—can become a conditioned stimulus that also elicits fear and anxiety responses. When we examine punishment in more detail in Chapter 6, I'll offer suggestions that should minimize such negative side effects.

careful that failure does not become such a strong conditioned stimulus for children that they resist new activities and challenging but potentially risky problems.

These examples of classical conditioning at work will, I hope, help you recognize a classically conditioned response when you see one. We now turn to several general phenomena associated with classical conditioning.

Basic Concepts in Classical Conditioning

Pavlov and other behaviorists have described a number of phenomena related to classical conditioning. Here we examine several of them: extinction, spontaneous recovery, stimulus generalization, stimulus discrimination, higher-order conditioning, and sensory preconditioning.

Extinction

Let's return for a moment to Pavlov's dog. Remember that the dog learned to salivate at the sound of a bell alone after that bell had rung in conjunction with meat powder on several occasions. But what would happen if the bell continued to ring over and over without the meat powder's ever again being presented along with it? Pavlov discovered that repeated presentations of the conditioned stimulus alone led to successively weaker and weaker conditioned responses. Eventually, the dog no longer salivated at the sound of the bell; in other words, the conditioned response disappeared.

The disappearance of a conditioned response when a conditioned stimulus is repeatedly presented *without* the unconditioned stimulus is a phenomenon Pavlov called **extinction.** For example, The Look from my mother no longer has the effect it used to. Whatever punishment was once associated with it has long since disappeared (and besides, now I'm bigger than she is).

Sometimes conditioned responses will extinguish, and sometimes they will not. The unpredictability of extinction is a source of frustration to anyone working with people who have acquired inappropriate, yet involuntary, conditioned responses. Later in the chapter, we will identify some reasons why extinction doesn't always occur.

Spontaneous Recovery

Even though Pavlov quickly extinguished his dog's conditioned salivation response by repeatedly presenting the bell in the absence of meat powder, when he entered his laboratory the following day he discovered that the bell once again elicited salivation in the dog, almost as if extinction had never taken place. This reappearance of the salivation response after it had previously been extinguished is something Pavlov called **spontaneous recovery.**

In more general terms, spontaneous recovery is a recurrence of a conditioned response when a period of extinction is followed by a rest period. For example, if I am near lots of bees for a period of time, I eventually settle down and regain my composure. However, my first response on a later encounter with a bee is to fly off the handle once again.

Pavlov found that when a conditioned response appears in spontaneous recovery, it is typically weaker than the original conditioned response and extinguishes more quickly. In situations in which a CR spontaneously recovers several times, each time after a period of rest has elapsed, the response appears in a weaker form than it had previously and disappears more rapidly.

Stimulus Generalization

You may recall that Little Albert, after being conditioned to fear a white rat, also became afraid of a rabbit, a dog, a white fur coat, cotton wool, and a fuzzy-bearded Santa Claus mask. When individuals respond to other stimuli in the same way that they respond to conditioned stimuli, **stimulus generalization** is occurring. The more similar a stimulus is to the conditioned stimulus, the greater the probability of generalization. Albert exhibited fear of all objects that were white and fuzzy like the rat, but he was not afraid of his nonwhite, nonfuzzy toy blocks. In a similar way, a child who fears an abusive father may generalize that fear to other men, but not to women.

Generalization of conditioned responses to new stimuli is a common phenomenon (Bouton, 1994). In some cases, generalization of conditioned fear responses may actually increase over time; that is, as time goes on, an individual may become fearful of an increasing number of objects (McAllister & McAllister, 1965). Thus, dysfunctional conditioned responses that do not quickly extinguish may actually become more troublesome as the years go by.

Stimulus Discrimination

Pavlov observed that when he conditioned a dog to salivate in response to a high-pitched tone, the dog would generalize that conditioned response to a low-pitched tone. To teach the dog the difference between the two tones, Pavlov repeatedly presented the high tone in conjunction with meat powder and presented the low tone without meat. After several such presentations of the two tones, the dog eventually learned to salivate only at the high tone. In Pavlov's terminology, *differentiation* between the two tones had taken place. Psychologists today more frequently use the term **stimulus discrimination** for this phenomenon.

Stimulus discrimination occurs when one stimulus (the CS+) is presented in conjunction with an unconditioned stimulus, and another stimulus (the CS−) is presented in the absence of the UCS. The individual learns a conditioned response to the CS+ but does not generalize the response to the CS−. For example, if a child who is abused by her father simultaneously has positive interactions with other adult men, she is not as likely to generalize her fear of her father to those other individuals.

Higher-Order Conditioning

Pavlov also described a phenomenon known as **second-order conditioning,** or more generally as **higher-order conditioning.** When a dog had been conditioned to salivate at the sound of a bell, and the bell was later presented in conjunction with a neutral stimulus such as a flash of light, that neutral stimulus would also begin to elicit a salivation response, even though it had never been directly associated with meat. In other words, the light flash became a conditioned stimulus through its pairing, not with the unconditioned stimulus, but with another conditioned stimulus.

Higher-order conditioning works like this: First, a neutral stimulus (NS_1) becomes a conditioned stimulus (CS_1) by being paired with an unconditioned stimulus (UCS), so that it soon elicits a conditioned response (CR). Next, a second neutral stimulus (NS_2) is paired with CS_1, and it, too, begins to elicit a conditioned response; that second stimulus has also become a conditioned stimulus (CS_2).

A diagram of higher-order conditioning appears in Figure 3–2. Steps 1 and 2 depict the original conditioning; steps 3 and 4 depict higher-order conditioning, in which a second neutral stimulus becomes a CS_2 by virtue of its being paired with the CS_1.

Higher-order conditioning is a possible explanation for some of the fears that students exhibit in the classroom (e.g., Klein, 1987). Let's say, first of all, that failure has previously been associated

Figure 3–2
An example of higher-order conditioning.

Step 1:   **NS$_1$**
           (bell)

                        UCR
                        (salivate)

           UCS
           (meat)

Step 2:   **CS$_1$**   ⟶   **CR**
           (bell)   (salivate)

Step 3:   **NS$_2$**
           (light)

                        CR
                        (salivate)

           CS$_1$
           (bell)

Step 4:   **CS$_2$**   ⟶   **CR**
           (light)   (salivate)

with painful physical punishment. Then another situation—perhaps a test, an oral presentation in front of classmates, or even school itself—becomes associated with failure. The painful punishment is the UCS. Failure, originally a neutral stimulus (NS$_1$), becomes a CS$_1$ after its association with the UCS. Some other aspect of school (e.g., a test), while first a neutral stimulus (NS$_2$), becomes an additional conditioned stimulus (CS$_2$) through its association with CS$_1$. In this way, a student may develop test anxiety, fear of public speaking, or even school phobia—fear of school itself.

Higher-order conditioning probably also explains the attitudes that college students developed in the Pokemon study (Olson & Fazio, 2001) described earlier. People aren't born with particular feelings about the words *awesome* or *awful*, nor do they necessarily have built-in reactions to pictures of hot fudge sundaes or cockroaches. Rather, people probably acquire particular feelings about the words and images through their experiences over time, to the point where these stimuli can provide a starting point for further classical conditioning.

Sensory Preconditioning

Higher-order conditioning is one way an individual can develop a conditioned response to a stimulus that has never been directly paired with an unconditioned stimulus. **Sensory preconditioning** is very similar to higher-order conditioning, except that the steps occur in a different order. Let me first illustrate the process by once again conditioning Pavlov's poor, overworked dog. Suppose that we first present the sound of a bell and a flash of light simultaneously. Then we pair the bell with meat powder. Not only does the dog salivate in response to the sound of a bell, we discover that it also salivates in response to the flash of light!

In more general terms, sensory preconditioning occurs like this: First, two neutral stimuli (NS$_1$ and NS$_2$) are presented simultaneously. Then one of these neutral stimuli (NS$_1$) is associated with an unconditioned stimulus (UCS), thus becoming a conditioned stimulus (CS$_1$) and eliciting a conditioned response (CR). In cases of sensory preconditioning, the second neutral stimulus (NS$_2$) *also* elicits the conditioned response (i.e., NS$_2$ has become CS$_2$) by virtue of its prior association with CS$_1$.

Figure 3–3
An example of sensory preconditioning.

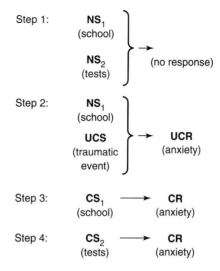

Step 1: NS_1 (school)

NS_2 (tests)   (no response)

Step 2: NS_1 (school)

UCS (traumatic event)   →   UCR (anxiety)

Step 3: CS_1 (school)   ⟶   CR (anxiety)

Step 4: CS_2 (tests)   ⟶   CR (anxiety)

Klein (1987) has suggested that sensory preconditioning may be an alternative explanation for some cases of test anxiety. School (NS_1) is first associated with tests (NS_2). If school is later associated with some traumatic event (UCS), then not only will school become a conditioned stimulus (CS_1) eliciting anxiety (CR) but tests may become a conditioned stimulus (CS_2) as well. A diagram of how test anxiety might develop through sensory preconditioning is presented in Figure 3–3.

Contemporary Perspectives on Classical Conditioning

Numerous psychologists have followed up on Pavlov's original studies of the classical conditioning phenomenon. Their research has led to several recent developments in our understanding of when and how classical conditioning occurs:

• *Contingency between the conditioned and unconditioned stimuli is probably more important than their contiguity.* Pavlov proposed that classical conditioning occurs when the unconditioned stimulus and the would-be conditioned stimulus are presented at approximately the same time; in other words, there must be **contiguity** between the two stimuli. In fact, as we noted earlier, classical conditioning is most likely to occur when the conditioned stimulus is presented just before the unconditioned stimulus. Conditioning is less likely to occur when the CS and UCS are presented at *exactly* the same time, and it rarely occurs when the CS is presented *after* the UCS (e.g., Miller & Barnet, 1993). In some cases, people develop an aversion to certain foods (recall my aversion to creamy cucumber dressing) when the delay between the conditioned stimulus (food) and the unconditioned stimulus (nausea) is as much as 24 hours (Logue, 1979). As you can see, contiguity between the two stimuli is an overly simplistic explanation of how a conditioned response is acquired.

More recent theorists (e.g., Gallistel & Gibbon, 2001; Granger & Schlimmer, 1986; Rachlin, 1991; Rescorla, 1967, 1988) have proposed that *contingency* is the essential condition: The potential conditioned stimulus must occur *only* when the unconditioned stimulus is going to follow—in other words, when the CS serves as a signal that the UCS is coming (recall my earlier reference to classical conditioning as "signal learning"). When two stimuli that are usually presented separately occur together a few times by coincidence, classical conditioning is unlikely to occur.

•   *Characteristics of the would-be conditioned stimulus affect the degree to which conditioning occurs.* The more noticeable (*salient*) a neutral stimulus—in other words, the extent to which it is bright, loud, or otherwise intense—the more likely it is to become a conditioned stimulus when presented in conjunction with an unconditioned stimulus (Rachlin, 1991; Schwartz & Reisberg, 1991). Furthermore, some stimuli are especially likely to become associated with certain unconditioned stimuli; for example, food is more likely to become a conditioned stimulus associated with nausea (a UCS) than, say, a light or the sound of a tuning fork. In other words, associations between certain stimuli are more likely to be made than are associations between others—a phenomenon known as **associative bias** (Garcia & Koelling, 1966; Hollis, 1997; Schwartz & Reisberg, 1991). Quite possibly, evolution has been at work here: Our ancestors could better adapt to their environments when they were predisposed to make associations that reflected true cause–effect relationships, such as associating nausea with the new food that instigated it (Timberlake & Lucas, 1989).

•   *Classical conditioning may involve cognition as well as responding.* Some theorists now believe that classical conditioning often involves the formation of associations not between two stimuli but between internal *mental representations* of those stimuli (Bouton, 1994; Forsyth & Eifert, 1998; Furedy & Riley, 1987; Miller & Barnet, 1993; Rachlin, 1991; Rescorla, 1988; Schwartz & Reisberg, 1991; Wagner, 1981). Furthermore, the conditioned stimulus may enable an organism to *predict* (in a decidedly mental fashion) that the unconditioned stimulus is coming (Hollis, 1997; Martin & Levey, 1987; Rescorla, 1967, 1988; Rescorla & Wagner, 1972; Schwartz & Reisberg, 1991; Wagner & Rescorla, 1972). As you can see, then, some behaviorists are now beginning to talk about the thinking processes that they so deliberately steered clear of in earlier years.

Classical conditioning does not *necessarily* involve cognition, however (Papka, Ivry, & Woodruff-Pak, 1997; Schwartz & Reisberg, 1991). In some cases, a classically conditioned response may be one of which the organism is not consciously aware. For instance, when organisms receive certain drugs (e.g., morphine or insulin), the drugs, as unconditioned stimuli, naturally lead to certain physiological responses (e.g., reduced pain sensitivity or hypoglycemia). Curiously, stimuli presented prior to these drugs—perhaps a light, a tone, or the environmental context more generally—begin to elicit an *opposite* response (e.g., increased pain sensitivity or hyperglycemia), presumably to prepare for—in this case, to counteract—the pharmaceutical stimuli that will soon follow (e.g., Flaherty et al., 1980 Siegel, 1975, 1979). Such effects, which are almost certainly not consciously controlled by the recipients of the drugs, are one probable reason why habitual drug users often develop increasing tolerance to their drug of choice and need increasing quantities to gain the same "high" or other sought-after physiological state (Siegel, Hinson, Krank, & McCully, 1982; Tiffany & Baker, 1981).

Changing Inappropriate Conditioned Responses

Conditioned responses are often difficult to eliminate because they are involuntary; people have little or no control over them. Yet some classically conditioned responses (e.g., some irrational fears) may be detrimental to an individual's functioning. How can we get rid of counterproductive conditioned responses? Extinction and counterconditioning are two possible methods.

Extinguishing Undesirable Responses

One obvious way to eliminate a conditioned response is through the process of extinction. If the conditioned stimulus is presented in the absence of the unconditioned stimulus frequently enough, the conditioned response should disappear. Often this is exactly what happens.

Unfortunately, however, extinction is notoriously undependable as a means of eliminating conditioned responses: It simply doesn't always work. There are at least three reasons why:

1. The speed at which extinction occurs is unpredictable. If, during the conditioning process, the conditioned stimulus was sometimes presented in conjunction with the unconditioned stimulus but sometimes alone (i.e., the stimulus pairings were inconsistent), extinction is likely to be especially slow (Humphreys, 1939).

2. People tend to avoid a stimulus they have learned to fear, thus reducing the chances that they might eventually encounter the conditioned stimulus in the absence of the unconditioned stimulus. For example, a student who has learned to fear mathematics after a history of failing at mathematical tasks typically avoids math as much as possible, thus minimizing any chance of experiencing math *without* failure.

3. Even when a response has been extinguished, it may reappear through spontaneous recovery. We can never be totally sure when a response will spontaneously recover and when it will not. Spontaneous recovery is especially likely to occur if extinction has occurred in only one context; the conditioned response is apt to reappear in contexts in which extinction has not taken place (Bouton, 1994).

Counterconditioning More Desirable Responses

In an alternative procedure to extinction, called **counterconditioning,** one conditioned response is replaced with a new, more productive conditioned response. Counterconditioning tends to be more effective than extinction in eliminating undesirable conditioned responses; it also decreases the chances that those responses will recur through spontaneous recovery.

Mary Cover Jones's (1924) classic work with "Little Peter" provides an excellent example of counterconditioning. Peter was a 2-year-old boy who had somehow acquired a fear of rabbits. To rid Peter of his fear, Jones placed him in a high chair and gave him some candy. As he ate, she brought a rabbit into the far side of the same room. Under different circumstances the rabbit might have elicited anxiety; however, the pleasure Peter felt as he ate the candy was a stronger response and essentially overpowered any anxiety he might have felt about the rabbit's presence. Jones repeated the same procedure every day over a two-month period, each time sitting Peter in a high chair with candy and bringing the rabbit slightly closer than she had the time before, and Peter's anxiety about rabbits eventually disappeared.

In general, counterconditioning involves the following components:

1. A new response that is **incompatible** with the existing conditioned response is chosen. Two responses are incompatible with each other when they cannot be performed at the same time. Because classically conditioned responses are often emotional in nature, an incompatible response is often some sort of opposite emotional reaction. For example, in the case of Little Peter, happiness was used as an incompatible response for fear. Because fear and anxiety create bodily tension, any response involving relaxation would be incompatible.

2. A stimulus that elicits the incompatible response must be identified; for example, candy elicited a "happy" response for Peter. If we want to help someone develop a happy response to

a stimulus that has previously elicited displeasure, we need to find a stimulus that already elicits pleasure—perhaps a friend, a party, or a favorite food. If we want someone instead to acquire a relaxation response, we might ask that person to imagine lying in a cool, fragrant meadow or on a lawn chair by a swimming pool.

3. The stimulus that elicits the new response is presented to the individual, and the conditioned stimulus eliciting the undesirable conditioned response is *gradually* introduced into the situation. In treating Peter's fear of rabbits, Jones first gave Peter some candy; she then presented the rabbit at some distance from Peter, only gradually bringing it closer and closer in successive sessions. The trick in counterconditioning is to ensure that the stimulus eliciting the desirable response is always *stronger* than the stimulus eliciting the undesirable response; otherwise, the latter response might prevail.

Counterconditioning provides a means for decreasing or eliminating many conditioned anxiety responses. For example, in **systematic desensitization,** people who become excessively anxious in the presence of certain stimuli are asked to relax while imagining themselves in increasingly stressful situations involving those stimuli; in doing so, they gradually replace anxiety with a relaxation response (Wolpe, 1958, 1969; Wolpe & Plaud, 1997). Systematic desensitization has been widely used as a means of treating such difficulties as test anxiety and fear of public speaking (Hughes, 1988; Morris, Kratochwill, & Aldridge, 1988; Silverman & Kearney, 1991). I should point out, however, that treating test anxiety alone, without remediating possible academic sources of a student's poor test performance as well, may reduce test anxiety without any concurrent improvement in test scores (Covington, 1992; Naveh-Benjamin, 1991; Tryon, 1980).

A technique I recommend to many graduate students who dread their required statistics courses because of mathematics anxiety is to find a math textbook that begins well below their own skill level—at the level of basic number facts, if necessary—so that the problems are not anxiety arousing. As they work through the text, the students begin to associate mathematics with success rather than failure. Programmed instruction (described in Chapter 5) is another technique that can be useful in reducing anxiety about a given subject matter, because it allows a student to progress through potentially difficult material in small, easy steps.

BUILDING ON PAVLOV'S IDEAS: THE WORK OF WATSON, GUTHRIE, AND HULL

Pavlov was hardly the only early learning theorist to espouse behaviorist ideas. In this section we look at three additional theorists—John Watson, Edwin Guthrie, and Clark Hull—who built directly on Pavlov's work. In the following chapter, we consider two more early behaviorists—Edward Thorndike and B. F. Skinner—who took a somewhat different tack, examining the effects that stimuli that *follow* responses (i.e., consequences and, in particular, *rewards*) have on learning and behavior.

John Watson

It was actually John Watson (1913) who introduced the term *behaviorism* and served as the most vocal advocate for the behaviorist perspective in the early part of the twentieth century. In his major writings, Watson (1914, 1916, 1919, 1925) adamantly called for the introduction of scientific objectivity and experimentation into the study of psychological phenomena. He emphasized the need for focusing scientific inquiry on observable behaviors rather than on such nonobservable phenomena as "thinking." Not only did Watson oppose the study of internal mental events but he also denied any existence of the mind at all! Thought, he proposed, was nothing more than tiny movements of the tongue and larynx and thus was a behavior just like any other.

Greatly influenced by the work of both Pavlov and another Russian, Vladimir Bechterev (1913), Watson adopted the classically conditioned S–R **habit** as the basic unit of learning and extended it to human learning (e.g., recall Watson and Rayner's study with Little Albert, described earlier).[4] Watson proposed two laws that described how such habits develop. First, his *law of frequency* stressed the importance of repetition:

> *The more frequently a stimulus and response occur in association with each other, the stronger that S–R habit will become.*

Second, Watson's *law of recency* stressed the importance of timing:

> *The response that has most recently occurred after a particular stimulus is the response most likely to be associated with that stimulus.*

In other words, the last response that an organism has made to a stimulus is the one that is most likely to occur the next time the stimulus is presented.

Watson believed that past experience accounts for virtually all behavior. His extreme environmentalism, which denied that hereditary factors had any effect on behavior whatsoever, was reflected in the following infamous quote:

> Give me a dozen healthy infants, well-formed, and my own specified world to bring them up in and I'll guarantee to take any one at random and train him to become any type of specialist I might select—doctor, lawyer, artist, merchant-chief, and yes, even beggar-man and thief, regardless of his talents, penchants, tendencies, abilities, vocations and race of his ancestors. (Watson, 1925, p. 82)

Watson's influence continued to be felt long after he retired from academia in 1920. His strong advocacy of psychology as an objective and precise science and his insistence that environment plays a key role in human behavior led to a behaviorist tradition that dominated psychological research and theory in the western hemisphere until the 1960s.

Edwin Guthrie

Edwin Guthrie's **contiguity theory** (Guthrie, 1935, 1942) was similar to John Watson's perspective in that it placed S–R connections at the center of the learning process. Guthrie's basic principle of learning was as follows:

---

[4]The use of the term *habit* can be tracked back to the writings of an early cognitive psychologist, William James (1890). James did not conceptualize a habit as an "unthinking" stimulus–response relationship, but rather as a behavior that requires relatively little conscious control: "A strictly voluntary act has to be guided by idea, perception, and volition, throughout its whole course. In an habitual action, mere sensation is a sufficient guide, and the upper regions of brain and mind are set comparatively free" (James, 1890, pp.115–116). Watson and several other early behaviorists adopted James's term but rejected James's proposal that other actions are more "thoughtful" in nature.

A stimulus that is followed by a particular response will, upon its recurrence, tend to be followed by the same response again. This S–R connection gains its full strength on one trial.

In other words, if an organism responds to a particular stimulus in a particular way on one occasion, the organism will make the same response the next time it encounters the same stimulus; in this manner, a habit is formed. Guthrie contended that the critical factor in learning is the *contiguity*—the more or less simultaneous occurrence—of a stimulus and a response. Guthrie also shared Watson's belief that *recency* is critical in learning: An organism will respond to a stimulus in the way that it has most recently responded to that stimulus.

Guthrie's notion of **one-trial learning**—that an S–R connection is fully formed on one pairing—was a radical one in its time. Most other early behaviorists believed that S–R connections were acquired only gradually, primarily through practice. Guthrie explained the seemingly gradual learning of complex behaviors by proposing that such behaviors are actually composed of many tiny S–R connections; with each practice trial, more and more appropriate S–R connections are formed, thus leading to slow, incremental changes observed in overall performance.

The parsimony of Guthrie's theory—his proposal that the contiguity of stimuli and responses is the basis of all learning—is certainly appealing. Guthrie conducted little research to support his views, however, and later research has cast doubt on the notion that learning is as simple as Guthrie described it (Bower & Hilgard, 1981). Nevertheless, three techniques for breaking S–R habits that Guthrie derived from his theory continue to be used in educational and therapeutic practice. We will look at these techniques shortly.

Clark Hull

It was primarily the work of Clark Hull (1943, 1951, 1952) that introduced *organismic* characteristics—characteristics unique to different individuals—into behaviorist learning theory. Like some of his predecessors, Hull maintained that learned S–R habits form the basis of behavior. He also agreed with Edward Thorndike and B. F. Skinner—two theorists we'll examine in Chapter 4—that rewards are important in the learning process. However, he believed that the presence of a particular stimulus and one's past experiences with that stimulus are not the only determinants of whether a particular response will occur or how strongly it will be made. Hull proposed that a number of other factors (**intervening variables**) unique to each organism and each occasion must be considered in order to predict the likelihood and strength of a response's occurrence. Thus, Hull's ideas comprised an S–O–R theory, rather than an S–R theory, of learning.

According to Hull, one intervening variable influencing the occurrence of a response is **habit strength,** the degree to which a particular stimulus and a response are associated. The more often a response has previously been rewarded in the presence of the stimulus, the greater is the habit strength and the more likely the response is to occur.

A second intervening variable critical for a response to occur is the organism's **drive,** an internal state of arousal that motivates its behavior. Hull suggested that some drives (e.g., hunger and thirst) are directly related to an organism's survival. Other drives (called *acquired drives*) serve no apparent biological purpose; they develop over time when initially "unexciting" stimuli are associated with such drive-reducing stimuli as food or drink. To illustrate, one might become "driven" by a need for approval if approval has previously been associated with a candy bar. From

Hull's perspective, rewards increase the strength of an S–R habit by reducing the organism's drive; for example, food reduces hunger.

Hull proposed that intervening variables such as habit strength, drive, stimulus intensity (with an intense stimulus bringing about a stronger response than a weak stimulus), and incentive (based on the amount and immediacy of reward) all work together to increase the likelihood and relative strength of a particular response. At the same time, **inhibitory factors** (e.g., fatigue) decrease the likelihood and strength of the response.

According to Hull, an organism might learn several different responses to the same stimulus, each with a different degree of habit strength. The combination of the various S–R habits for a given stimulus, with their respective habit strengths, is known as a **habit-family hierarchy.** When a stimulus is presented, an organism will, if possible, make the response for which the habit strength is the strongest. If the organism is somehow prevented from making that response, it will try to make the second response, or, if again foiled, the third response, and so on down the hierarchy.

As an illustration of this concept of habit-family hierarchy, consider George, who faces a homework assignment involving the multiplication of fractions. George may first try to complete the assignment using the technique his teacher taught him for multiplying fractions. If he finds that he cannot remember the technique, he may instead ask his friend Angela if he may copy her answers. If Angela refuses his request, he may resort to a third response in his hierarchy: telling his teacher that the family dog ate his homework.

Hull developed a series of mathematical formulas through which the occurrence and strength of responses might be predicted once the various intervening variables were measured and their values entered. The precision of Hull's formulas permitted a careful testing of his theory through research, and many specifics of the theory were found to be inaccurate (Bower & Hilgard, 1981; Klein, 1987). For example, learning apparently can take place in the absence of drive; as you will discover in Chapters 7 and 9, attention to new information may ultimately be more important than motivation to learn the information. In addition, Hull proposed that a reward is a stimulus that reduces drive, yet, as you will discover when you read Chapter 16, some rewards actually appear to *increase* drive (e.g., Olds & Milner, 1954).

Hull's theory was a predominant force in behaviorism throughout the 1940s and 1950s. Although many details of the theory did not hold up under empirical scrutiny, Hull's emphasis on intervening variables made such notions as *motivation* and *incentive* prominent concepts in learning research. And his many productive students—among them Kenneth Spence, Neil Miller, John Dollard, and O. H. Mowrer—continued to advance and modify Hullian ideas for many years.

EDUCATIONAL IMPLICATIONS OF BEHAVIORIST PRINCIPLES AND CLASSICAL CONDITIONING

From what we have learned about behaviorist ideas so far, we can derive several implications for instructional practice:

• *Practice is important.* From a behaviorist perspective, people are more likely to learn when they have a chance to *behave*—for instance, when they can talk, write, experiment, or demonstrate (e.g., see Drevno et al., 1994). Ideally, then, students should be active respondents throughout the learning process, rather than simply passive recipients of whatever information is being taught.

Many behaviorists have stressed the idea that repetition of stimulus–response habits strengthens those habits. If people need to learn responses to particular stimuli thoroughly, then practice is essential. For example, students will learn basic addition and subtraction facts better and recall them more quickly if they repeat those facts numerous times (perhaps through the use of flash cards, or perhaps by applying those facts frequently in mathematical problem-solving tasks). In a similar way, many reading teachers believe that the best way for students to improve their reading level is simply to read, read, read.

• *Students should encounter academic subject matter in a positive climate and associate it with positive emotions.* The durability and generalizability of some classically conditioned responses point to the need for a positive classroom climate for students beginning on day one. Students should experience academic tasks in contexts that elicit pleasant emotions—feelings of enjoyment, enthusiasm, or excitement, for instance—rather than in contexts that elicit anxiety, disappointment, or anger. When students associate academic subject matter with positive feelings, they are more likely to pursue it of their own accord. For example, when children's early experiences with books are enjoyable ones, they are more likely to read frequently and widely in later years (Baker, Scher, & Mackler, 1997).

When schoolwork, a teacher, or even the school environment itself is associated with punishment, humiliation, failure, or frustration, school and its curriculum can become sources of excessive anxiety. Some classroom activities—for example, tests, oral presentations, and difficult subject matter—are especially likely to be associated with unpleasant circumstances such as failure or embarrassment, and many students may soon become anxious when involved in them. Teachers should, therefore, take special precautions when asking students to engage in any such "risky" activities. For example, I suspect that many students have early unpleasant experiences in public speaking because they receive little, if any, instruction about how to prepare and deliver an effective oral presentation. If students are asked to speak in front of a group, they should be given specific suggestions regarding what material to present and how to present it in such a way that classmates will react favorably rather than with boredom or ridicule.

Mathematics is a difficult and anxiety-arousing subject for many students, and students often dislike it because they find it so frustrating (Stodolsky, Salk, & Glaessner, 1991). I firmly believe that mathematics anxiety is so prevalent because most schools teach too much, too fast, and too soon, so that students quickly begin to associate mathematics with frustration and failure. Part of the problem may lie in the tendency to teach mathematical concepts before children are cognitively ready to deal with them. For instance, many developmental researchers have found that the ability to understand the concept of *proportion*, which underlies fractions and decimals, tends not to appear until age 11 or 12 at the earliest (Schliemann & Carraher, 1993; Tourniaire & Pulos, 1985; also see the discussion of Piaget's theory in Chapter 8). Yet schools typically introduce fractions and decimals sometime around fourth grade, when students are only 9 or 10 years old.

Educators have often argued that school should be a place where a student encounters more success than failure, and classical conditioning provides a justification for their argument. This is not to say, however, that students should never experience failure; as we will discover in Chapter 8, challenging activities are more apt to promote cognitive growth than easy ones, and errors are inevitable when students must wrestle with difficult problems and tasks. But when students experience failure *too* frequently, either in their schoolwork or in their social relationships, school may quickly become a conditioned stimulus that leads to such counterproductive conditioned responses as fear and anxiety. These responses, once conditioned, may be very resistant to extinction and may interfere with a student's ability to learn effectively for years to come.

• *To break a habit, a person must replace one S–R connection with another one.* Guthrie's notion of recency—the idea that an organism will respond to a stimulus in the same way that it responded in the most recent previous encounter with that stimulus—implies that habits, once formed, are difficult to break. The trick in breaking a habit, from the perspective of the recency principle, is to lead an individual, in one way or another, to make a new response to the same stimulus.

As an example, Guthrie (1935) described a girl who, on returning home from school each day, had the nasty habit of throwing her hat and coat on the floor rather than hanging up her garments. Despite her mother's repeated entreaties to change the sloppy behavior, the habit persisted. One day, rather than admonishing the girl, Mother insisted that she put her hat and coat back on, go outside, reenter the house, and hang up her clothes. The hanging-up response, being the one most recently exhibited, now became a new habit for the girl, and the throwing-on-the-floor response disappeared.

Guthrie proposed three ingenious techniques specifically designed to break habits; the second and third reflect the *counterconditioning* approach we discussed earlier:

- *Exhaustion method:* One way to break a stimulus–response habit is to continue to present the stimulus until the individual is too tired to respond in the habitual way. At that point, a new response will occur and a new S–R habit will form. For example, when breaking a bucking bronco, the persistent rider (the stimulus) stays on the horse's back until the horse is too exhausted to continue bucking; a new response (behavior reflecting acceptance of the rider, such as standing still) then becomes associated with the "rider" stimulus. Similarly, a teacher might eliminate a child's spitball-throwing behavior by having that child stay after school to make and throw spitballs until the child is too tired to continue.

- *Threshold method:* Another way of breaking a habit is to begin by presenting the stimulus so faintly that the individual does not respond to it in the habitual manner. The intensity of the stimulus is then increased so gradually that the individual continues *not* to respond to it. For example, when a student has test anxiety (in other words, when a test stimulus leads to an anxiety response), a teacher might eliminate that child's anxiety by first presenting tasks that are enjoyable to the child and that only remotely resemble a test. Over time, the teacher can present a series of tasks that increasingly (but gradually) begin to take on testlike qualities.

- *Incompatibility method:* A third method for breaking an S–R connection is to present the stimulus when the habitual response cannot occur and when an opposite, or *incompatible*, response will occur. For example, Guthrie recommended tying a dead chicken around a dog's neck to teach the dog not to catch and eat chickens. The dog will struggle to get rid of the annoying chicken, thereby making a response that is incompatible with catching and eating the chicken. Similarly, imagine a classroom of highly achievement motivated students who are overly competitive with one another. To reduce such a competitive spirit, the teacher might divide the class into small groups and assign each group an academic task that requires cooperation rather than competition (e.g., developing an argument for one side of an issue in a class debate). Assigning grades on the basis of group performance rather than individual performance should further increase the likelihood that students will cooperate rather than compete. Under such conditions, cooperative behavior should replace competitive behavior.

- Assessing learning involves looking for behavior changes. Regardless of how effective teachers think a certain activity, lecture, or set of curriculum materials might be, they should never assume that students are learning anything unless they actually observe students' behaviors changing as a result of instruction. Only behavior changes—for example, higher test scores, improved athletic performance, more appropriate social interaction skills, or better study habits—can ultimately confirm that learning has taken place.

SUMMARY

Behaviorism encompasses a group of theories that share several common assumptions, including the generalizability of learning principles across species, the importance of focusing on observable events, and the "blank slate" nature of organisms. Early behaviorists insisted that psychology could be a true science only if it defined learning as a behavior change, and they focused solely on stimulus–response relationships. Today, however, some behaviorists make a distinction between learning and behavior, and some believe that relationships between stimuli and responses can be better understood when cognitive factors are also considered.

One groundbreaking researcher in the behaviorist tradition was Ivan Pavlov, who proposed that many involuntary responses are acquired through a process of *classical conditioning*. Such conditioning occurs when two stimuli are presented at approximately the same time. One is an *unconditioned stimulus* that already elicits an *unconditioned response*. The second stimulus, through its association with the unconditioned stimulus, begins to elicit a response as well: It becomes a *conditioned stimulus* that brings about a *conditioned response*. But if the conditioned stimulus is later presented numerous times in the absence of the unconditioned stimulus, the conditioned response decreases and may eventually disappear *(extinction)*; nevertheless, it may reappear after a period of rest *(spontaneous recovery)*.

Once an organism has learned to make a conditioned response in the presence of one conditioned stimulus, it may respond in the same way to a similar stimulus *(stimulus generalization)* unless the latter stimulus has repeatedly been experienced in the absence of the unconditioned stimulus *(stimulus discrimination)*. Classically conditioned associations can build on one another through the processes of *higher-order conditioning* and *sensory preconditioning*; in both cases, a neutral stimulus may become a conditioned stimulus (eliciting a conditioned response), not directly by its association with the unconditioned stimulus, but indirectly by its association with a stimulus that either has been or will be experienced in conjunction with that UCS.

Classical conditioning provides one possible explanation of how human beings acquire physiological responses (e.g., nausea), emotional responses (e.g., anxiety, phobic reactions), and attitudes (e.g., like or dislike) toward particular stimuli. It also offers two strategies for eliminating such responses: extinction and *counterconditioning* (i.e., replacing unproductive S–R relationships with more productive ones).

Several other early behaviorists built on Pavlov's work. John Watson and Edwin Guthrie suggested that practice enhances learning, perhaps because it increases the strength of a particular S–R habit (Watson) or perhaps because it increases the number of appropriate S–R habits required to perform a complex behavior (Guthrie). Clark Hull argued that S–R relationships can be better understood, and behavior can be more accurately predicted, when *intervening variables*, such as habit strength, drive, incentives, and inhibitory factors, are considered. All of these early theorists have made us aware of the fact that past and present events have a strong influence on the behaviors we exhibit.

Our discussion of behaviorism thus far has yielded several educational implications. First, active responding and practice are important for increasing habit strength. Second, the classical conditioning paradigm underscores the importance of helping students experience academic subject matter in contexts that elicit pleasant rather than unpleasant emotions. Third, eliminating undesirable behaviors (i.e., breaking a "bad habit") must in one way or another involve replacing existing S–R connections with more productive ones. And fourth, teachers can ultimately determine that learning has occurred *only* when they observe changes in students' behaviors.

CHAPTER 4

Operant Conditioning

Different individuals work for different rewards. As a child, when my son Alex needed money to buy something he desperately wanted, he engaged in behaviors he never did otherwise—for example, mowing the lawn or scrubbing the bathtub. In contrast, financial incentives rarely enticed my son Jeff into doing household chores, yet he would readily clean up the disaster area he called his bedroom if doing so enabled him to have a friend spend the night.

    The idea that rewards affect behavior has influenced psychologists' thinking for more than 100 years, and it has been especially prominent in behaviorist learning theories. In this chapter we will examine the work of two early behaviorists—Edward Thorndike and B. F. Skinner—who emphasized the importance of rewards (Skinner called them *reinforcers*) in learning. Our major focus will be on Skinner's model of learning, which he called *operant conditioning*. In our discussion of Skinner's work, we will first look at the basic operant conditioning model and see how it differs from the classical conditioning model that we studied in Chapter 3. We will then examine concepts central to our understanding of operant conditioning, including extinction, shaping, positive versus negative reinforcement, and continuous versus intermittent reinforcement. As we consider the topic of stimulus control, we will find that, although reinforcers are stimuli that follow responses, stimuli that *precede* responses can influence behavior as well. Toward the end of the chapter, we will discuss several ways in which contemporary views of operant conditioning differ somewhat from Skinner's original ideas. At numerous points in the chapter we will derive strategies for classroom practice, but we will save more systematic applications of operant conditioning principles (e.g., applied behavior analysis) for Chapter 5, where we can give them our full attention.

THORNDIKE'S EARLY RESEARCH

In 1898, Edward Thorndike introduced a theory of learning that emphasized the role of experience in the strengthening and weakening of stimulus–response connections; this perspective is sometimes referred to as **connectionism**[1] (Thorndike, 1898, 1911, 1913). In his classic first experiment (his doctoral dissertation), Thorndike placed a cat in a "puzzle box" with a door that opened when some device (e.g., a wire loop) was appropriately manipulated. Thorndike observed the cat initiating numerous, apparently random movements in its attempts to get out of the box; eventually, by chance, the cat triggered the mechanism that opened the door and allowed escape. When returned to the box a second time, the cat again engaged in trial-and-error movements but managed to escape in less time than it had previously. With successive trials in the box, the cat, although continuing to demonstrate trial-and-error behavior, managed to escape within shorter and shorter time periods.

From his observations of cats in the puzzle box, Thorndike concluded that the learning of a behavior is affected by the consequence of that behavior (e.g., escape from a confining situation). We can sum up Thorndike's *law of effect* as follows:

> Responses to a situation that are followed by satisfaction are strengthened;
> responses that are followed by discomfort are weakened.

According to Thorndike, learning consists of trial-and-error behavior and a gradual "stamping in" of some behaviors (those leading to satisfaction) and "stamping out" of other behaviors (those leading to discomfort). In other words, rewarded responses increase, and punished responses diminish and disappear.

Thorndike proposed that practice influences S–R connections as well. His *law of exercise* can be paraphrased as follows:

> Stimulus–response connections that are repeated are strengthened;
> stimulus–response connections that are not used are weakened.

[1]Thorndike's connectionism should not be confused with a more contemporary form of connectionism (also known as parallel distributed processing), which we will discuss in Chapter 11.

In other words, practice facilitates the learning of responses. Responses that are not practiced gradually disappear.

Thorndike eventually revised his law of effect and discarded his law of exercise (Thorndike, 1935). The original law of effect implied that reward and punishment have opposite but equal effects on behavior: One strengthens and the other weakens. But Thorndike's later research (1932a, 1932b) indicated that punishment may not be effective in weakening responses. For example, in one experiment (Thorndike, 1932a), college students completed a multiple-choice Spanish vocabulary test in which they were to choose the English translation for each of a long list of Spanish words. Every time a student chose the correct English word out of five alternatives, the experimenter said "Right!" (presumably rewarding the response); every time a student chose an incorrect alternative, the experimenter said "Wrong!" (presumably punishing the response). In responding to the same multiple-choice questions over a series of trials, the students increased the responses for which they had been rewarded but did not necessarily decrease those for which they had been punished. In his *revised law of effect*, Thorndike continued to maintain that rewards strengthen the behaviors they follow, but he deemphasized the role of punishment. Instead, he proposed that punishment has an *indirect* effect on learning: As a result of experiencing an annoying state of affairs, an organism may engage in certain other behaviors (e.g., crying or running away) that interfere with performance of the punished response.

Thorndike also conducted research (described by Trowbridge & Cason, 1932) that casts doubt on the effect of practice alone on learning. For example, in one experiment, people were blindfolded and asked to draw a series of four-inch lines. They could not see the results of their efforts, and they received no information from the experimenter about the correctness of their drawings. Without feedback, they did not improve in accuracy despite their practice, a result that led Thorndike to repudiate his law of exercise.

Although not all of Thorndike's original ideas have stood the test of time, his belief that satisfying consequences bring about changes in behavior—in other words, that rewards promote learning—continues to be a key component of behaviorist perspectives today. Thorndike's influence has been especially noticeable in Skinner's model of operant conditioning.

SKINNER'S OPERANT CONDITIONING

B. F. Skinner (1938, 1953, 1958, 1966b, 1971, 1989; Skinner & Epstein, 1982) is unquestionably the best-known learning theorist in the behaviorist tradition. Originally a fiction writer, Skinner was lured into psychology by the ideas of Pavlov and Watson (Skinner, 1967). Like Thorndike, Skinner proposed that we acquire those behaviors that are followed by certain consequences. Unlike Thorndike, however, Skinner spoke only about the strengthening of responses, not the strengthening of S–R connections.

To study the effects of consequences using precise measurement of responses in a carefully controlled environment, Skinner developed a piece of equipment, now known as the Skinner box, that has gained widespread popularity in animal learning research. As shown in Figure 4–1, the Skinner box used in studying rat behavior includes a metal bar that, when pushed down, causes a food tray to swing into reach long enough for the rat to grab a food pellet. In the pigeon version of the box, instead of a metal bar, a lighted plastic disk (a "key") is located on one wall; when the pigeon pecks the key, the food tray swings into reach for a short time.

Figure 4–1
A prototypical Skinner box: The
food tray swings into reach to
provide reinforcement.

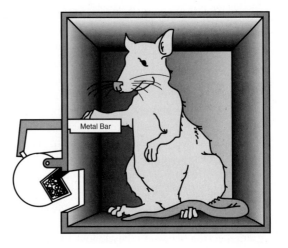

Metal Bar

By observing rats and pigeons in their respective Skinner boxes under various conditions, Skinner developed a set of principles that is better described as a *description* of learning than an explanation of it; hence, some psychologists view Skinner's perspective more as a "nontheory" than as a theory of learning. Skinner's principles of operant conditioning, first proposed in 1938, underwent little change in the five decades prior to his death in 1990. Operant conditioning principles have served as the basis for thousands of research studies and have been applied extensively in both educational and therapeutic settings.

Skinner's Basic Law of Conditioning

We can paraphrase Skinner's (1938) basic principle of **operant conditioning** as follows:

> A response that is followed by a reinforcer is strengthened and is therefore more likely to occur again.

In other words, responses that are reinforced tend to increase in frequency. Because a response increase is a change in behavior, then, from a behaviorist viewpoint, reinforcement brings about learning. For example, Skinner found that rats will learn to press metal bars, and pigeons will learn to peck at round plastic disks, to get pellets of food. Likewise, my son Jeff would increase his house-keeping behavior if it allowed him to see a friend, and my son Alex would do just about anything if the price was right.

Skinner intentionally used the term *reinforcer* instead of *reward* to describe a consequence that increases the frequency of a behavior. The word *reward* implies that the stimulus following a behavior is somehow both pleasant and desirable, an implication that Skinner tried to avoid for two reasons. First, some individuals will work for what others believe to be unpleasant consequences; for example, as a child, my daughter Tina occasionally did something she knew would irritate me because she enjoyed watching me blow my stack. Second, "pleasantness" and "desirability" are subjective judgments, and behaviorists such as Skinner prefer that psychological principles be restricted to the domain of objectively observable events. A reinforcer is defined not by allusion to its pleasantness or desirability but instead by its effect on behavior:

A **reinforcer** is a stimulus or event that increases the frequency of a response it follows. (The act of following a response with a reinforcer is called **reinforcement**.)

Notice how I have just defined a reinforcer totally in terms of observable phenomena, without reliance on any subjective judgment.

Now that I have given you definitions of both operant conditioning and a reinforcer, I need to point out a major problem with my definitions: Taken together, they constitute circular reasoning. I have said that operant conditioning is an increase in a behavior when it is followed by a reinforcer, but I cannot seem to define a reinforcer in any other way except to say that it increases behavior. I am therefore using reinforcement to explain a behavior increase, and a behavior increase to explain reinforcement! Fortunately, a paper by Meehl (1950) has enabled learning theorists to get out of this circular mess by pointing out the **transituational generality** of a reinforcer: The same reinforcer will increase many different behaviors in many different situations.

Important Conditions for Operant Conditioning

Three important conditions are necessary for operant conditioning to occur:

• *The reinforcer must follow the response.* "Reinforcers" that precede a response rarely have an effect on that response. For example, many years ago, a couple of instructors at my university were concerned that grades, because they were "threatening," interfered with student learning; therefore, they announced on the first day of class that everyone would receive an A for the course. Many students never attended class after that first day, so there was little learning with which any grade could interfere. Reinforcers must always, always *follow* the desired behavior.

• *The reinforcer must follow immediately.* A reinforcer tends to reinforce the response that immediately preceded it. Thus, reinforcement is less effective when its presentation is delayed. In the meantime, an organism may make one or more responses that are reinforced instead. Once, when I was teaching a pigeon named Ethel to peck a lighted plastic disk, I made a serious mistake: I waited too long after she had pecked the disk before reinforcing her, and in the meantime she had begun to turn around. After eating her food pellet, Ethel began to spin frantically in counterclockwise circles, and it was several minutes before I could get her back to the pecking response I had in mind for her.

Our schools are notorious for delayed reinforcement.How many times have you completed an exam or turned in a written assignment only to receive your grade days or even weeks later? Immediate reinforcers are typically more effective than delayed reinforcers in classroom situations (Kulik & Kulik, 1988). Immediate reinforcement is especially important for young children and animals (e.g., Critchfield &Kollins, 2001; Green, Fry, & Myerson, 1994).

• *The reinforcer must be contingent on the response.* Ideally, the reinforcer should be presented *only* when the desired response has occurred—that is, when the reinforcer is *contingent* on the response.[2] For example, teachers often specify certain conditions that children must meet before

---

[2]Conditioning can occur (albeit more slowly) without one-to-one contingency—that is, when some responses go unreinforced (more about this point in the section on schedule of reinforcement) and when reinforcement is occasionally presented in the absence of the desired response. What is essential is *conditional probability*: Reinforcement must be *more likely* to occur when the response is made than when it is not (Vollmer & Hackenberg, 2001).

going on a field trip: They must bring their permission slips, they must complete previous assignments, and so on. When these teachers feel badly for children who have not met the stated conditions and allow them to go on the field trip anyway, the reinforcement is not contingent on the response, and the children are not learning acceptable behavior. If anything, they are learning that rules can be broken!

What Behaviors Can Be Reinforced?

Virtually any behavior—academic, social, psychomotor—can be learned or modified through operant conditioning. As a teacher, I keep reminding myself of what student behaviors I want to increase and try to follow those behaviors with positive consequences. For example, when typically quiet students raise their hands to answer a question or make a comment, I call on them and give them whatever positive feedback I can. I also try to make my classes lively, interesting, and humorous, as well as informative, so that students are reinforced for coming to class in the first place.

Unfortunately, undesirable behaviors can be reinforced just as easily as desirable ones. Aggression and criminal activity often lead to successful outcomes: Crime usually *does* pay. In school settings, disruptive behaviors may often get teachers' and classmates' attention when more productive behaviors do not (e.g., Craft, Alberg, & Heward, 1998; Flood, Wilder, Flood, & Masuda, 2002; Taylor & Romanczyk, 1994). Getting "sick" allows the school-phobic child to stay home from school. Students occasionally come to me at the end of the semester pleading for a higher grade than their class performance has warranted or else for the opportunity to complete an extra-credit project. I almost invariably turn them down, for a simple reason: I want good grades to be contingent on good study habits and high achievement throughout the semester, not on begging behavior at my office door. Teachers must be extremely careful about what they reinforce and what they do not.

CONTRASTING OPERANT CONDITIONING AND CLASSICAL CONDITIONING

Skinner suggested that there are really two different kinds of learning: classical conditioning (he used the term *respondent conditioning*) and operant conditioning. The two forms of conditioning are different in several major respects; these differences are summarized in Figure 4–2.

Classical conditioning results from the pairing of two stimuli, the UCS and the CS. The learned response is a direct and immediate reaction to the stimulus that precedes it; that is, the conditioned stimulus brings about, or *elicits*, the conditioned response. The conditioned response is automatic and involuntary, such that the organism has virtually no control over what it is doing. Skinner's term *respondent* reflects the fact that the organism's behavior is an involuntary response to a stimulus.

In contrast, operant conditioning results when a response is followed by a reinforcing stimulus. The response is a voluntary one *emitted* by the organism, with the organism having complete control over whether the response occurs. Skinner's term **operant** reflects the fact that the organism voluntarily *operates* on, and thereby has some effect on, the environment. Because operant conditioning reflects an R—>S_{Rf} model, where S_{Rf} symbolizes a reinforcing stimulus, Skinner was not really an S–R psychologist at all—he was actually an R–S psychologist.

	Classical Conditioning	**Operant Conditioning**
Occurs when	Two stimuli (UCS and CS) are paired	A response (R) is followed by a reinforcing stimulus (S_{Rf})
Nature of response	Involuntary: elicited by a stimulus	Voluntary: emitted by the organism
Association required	CS ⟶ CR	R ⟶ S_{Rf}

Figure 4–2
Differences between classical and operant conditioning.

Some theorists have suggested that both classical and operant conditioning are based on the same underlying learning processes (e.g., see Bower & Hilgard, 1981). In most situations, however, the classical and operant conditioning models are differentially useful in explaining different learning phenomena, so many psychologists continue to treat them as two distinct forms of learning.

BASIC CONCEPTS IN OPERANT CONDITIONING

Several concepts are central to our understanding of operant conditioning, including free operant level, terminal behavior, extinction, superstitious behavior, shaping, and chaining. Let's look briefly at each of them.

Free Operant Level (Baseline)

As we noted earlier, an *operant* behavior is a voluntary response that has a particular effect on the environment. The **free operant level** is the frequency of an operant behavior in the absence of reinforcement; in other words, it is the prereinforcement, or **baseline**, frequency of that response. People vary in their free operant levels for different responses. For example, for some students, getting-out-of-seat behavior is quite frequent, whereas for others it is rare. Similarly, some students read frequently without being asked to do so, whereas others seldom read on their own initiative.

Terminal Behavior

The **terminal behavior** is the form and frequency of a desired response at the end of a planned reinforcement program. Let's say, for example, that a second-grade boy rarely stays in his seat for more than five minutes at a time, and when he does sit down, he slouches so low in the chair that his head is barely level with the desk. A teacher who plans to alter this child's classroom behavior through reinforcement might specify the terminal behavior as "sitting up straight for a 10-minute period."

When we use reinforcement to change behavior, it is essential that we describe the terminal behavior in concrete terms ahead of time. Specifying the exact form of the desired behavior (e.g., sitting up straight) and the frequency or duration of the behavior (e.g., for a 10-minute period) enables us to determine objectively whether our reinforcement program has been effective.

Extinction

In classical conditioning, when the CS is repeatedly presented in the absence of the UCS, the CR decreases and eventually disappears—that is, the response is extinguished. In operant conditioning, **extinction** occurs when a response is no longer followed by a reinforcer. A nonreinforced response decreases and eventually returns to its baseline rate. For example, class clowns who find that no one laughs at their jokes anymore are likely to decrease their joke telling. Students who are never called on when they raise their hands may stop trying to participate in class discussions. Students who continue to fail exams despite hours of studying may eventually stop studying.

We should note here that in the initial stages of the extinction process, we may sometimes see a brief *increase* in the behavior being extinguished—a phenomenon known as an **extinction burst** (Lerman & Iwata, 1995; Lerman, Iwata, & Wallace, 1999; McGill, 1999). We may also see increased variability in the kinds of responses that are exhibited (Rachlin, 1991). For example, students who find themselves doing poorly on exams may try studying more or studying differently; if such efforts continue to meet with failure, however, their studying behavior will eventually decrease and perhaps disappear altogether.

Although we want to extinguish undesirable behaviors, such as disruptive joke telling, we need to take precautions that *desirable* behaviors are reinforced frequently enough that they *don't* extinguish. For example, if we see students failing classroom exams time after time despite their best efforts, we should look for the root of the problem. If only one student is failing, perhaps that student needs help in developing more appropriate study techniques, more individualized instruction, or placement in a situation better matched to his or her current knowledge and skills. If many other students find the same exams too difficult to pass, something may be wrong with those exams or with classroom instruction.

Superstitious Behavior

What happens when reinforcement is random and not contingent on any particular behavior? Skinner once left eight pigeons in their cages overnight with the food tray mechanism adjusted to present reinforcement at regular intervals, regardless of what responses the pigeons were making at the time. By morning, six of the pigeons were acting bizarrely. For example, one repeatedly thrust its head into an upper corner of the cage, and two others were swinging their heads and bodies in rhythmic pendulum movements (Skinner, 1948).

Randomly administered reinforcement tends to reinforce whatever response has occurred immediately beforehand, and an organism will increase that response, thus displaying what Skinner called **superstitious behavior.** A nonbehaviorist way of describing the learning of a superstitious behavior is that the organism thinks that the response and reinforcement are related, when in fact they are not. For example, a student may have a "lucky sweater" to wear on exam days, or a football player may, before every game, perform a ritual totally unrelated to successful football.

Superstitious behavior in the classroom can occur either when reinforcement is not contingent on behavior or when students do not know which of their many responses are responsible for bringing about reinforcement. It behooves teachers to ensure that classroom reinforcers such as praise, attention, and grades *are* contingent on desired behaviors and that response–reinforcement contingencies are clearly specified.

Shaping

Before we can reinforce someone for exhibiting a particular response, the person must first *make* the response. But sometimes an individual's free operant level of a response is so low that it rarely, if ever, occurs. To handle such a situation, Skinner introduced a method called **shaping,** a technique also known as **successive approximations.** Shaping is a means of teaching a behavior when the free operant level for that behavior is very low or when the desired terminal behavior is different in form from any responses that the organism exhibits.

To shape a particular behavior, we begin by reinforcing the first response that in any way approximates the desired behavior and then continue to reinforce it until the organism is emitting it fairly frequently. At that point, we reinforce only those responses that more closely resemble the desired behavior, then those that resemble it more closely still, until eventually only the desired behavior itself is being reinforced. In other words, shaping is a process of reinforcing successively closer and closer approximations to the terminal behavior until the terminal behavior is exhibited.

To illustrate, when I taught my pigeon Ethel to peck a lighted disk in her Skinner box, I began by reinforcing her every time she faced the wall on which the disk was located. Once this response was occurring frequently, I began to reinforce her only when she moved her beak near the wall, then only when she touched the wall with her beak, then only when she pecked within a two-inch radius of the disk, and so on. Within an hour, I had Ethel happily pecking the disk and eating the food pellets that followed each correct peck.

Legend has it that a group of students once shaped a professor of mine a few days after he had given a lecture on shaping. Every time the professor stood on the side of the classroom near the door, the students all appeared interested in what he was saying, sitting forward in their seats and taking notes feverishly. Every time he walked away from the door, they acted bored, slouching back in their seats and looking anxiously at their watches. As the class went on, they reinforced the professor only as he moved closer and closer to the door until, by the end of class, he was lecturing from the hallway.

In much the same way, teachers gradually shape a variety of academic skills and classroom behaviors as children move through the grade levels. For example, kindergarten children are taught to print their letters on wide-lined paper; they are praised for well-formed letters and for letters whose bottoms rest on one line and whose tops touch the line above. As children progress through the primary grades, the spaces between the lines become smaller, and teachers are more particular about how well the letters are written. Eventually, many children begin to write consistently sized and carefully shaped letters with the benefit of only a lower line, and eventually with no line at all. Teachers also shape the sedentary behavior of their students: As students grow older, teachers expect them to sit quietly in their seats for longer and longer periods. To some degree, we can think of mathematics as a shaped set of skills as well: Teachers introduce complex problem solving only after students have mastered more basic skills, such as counting, number recognition, and addition.

In a similar manner, teachers may inadvertently shape undesirable behavior. For example, let's say that Molly frequently exhibits such disruptive responses as talking out of turn and physically annoying other students. Molly's teacher, Mr. Smith, realizes that, because he has been reprimanding her for these responses, he has actually been giving her the attention that he knows she craves and so in essence has been reinforcing her for her disruptiveness. Mr. Smith decides to eliminate Molly's disruptive behavior by ignoring it—in other words, by using extinction. Unfortunately, although Mr. Smith can easily ignore minor infractions, he finds himself unable to ignore more extreme disruptions and so reprimands Molly for them. Rather than extinguishing Molly's disruptive behavior, then, Mr. Smith is actually shaping it: He is insisting that Molly be *very* disruptive, rather than just a little disruptive, in order to get reinforcement.

Chaining

Organisms can also learn a sequence, or *chain,* of responses through shaping. For example, when visiting a tourist trap in South Dakota many years ago, I watched a chicken play a solitary version of "baseball": As soon as the chicken heard the appropriate signal (triggered by the quarter

I deposited in the side of its cage), it hit a ball with a horizontal bar (a bat of sorts) that it could swivel at home plate, then ran counterclockwise around a three-foot-square baseball diamond back to home plate again (at which point it found some food in its feeding tray). The chicken's trainer had probably taught the chicken this complex chain of responses by first reinforcing only the last response in the sequence (running to home plate), then reinforcing the last two responses (running to third base and then to home plate), then reinforcing the last three (running to second base, third base, and home plate), and so on, eventually reinforcing only the entire sequence.

This process of teaching a chain of responses by first reinforcing just one response, then reinforcing two responses in a row, then reinforcing a sequence of three, and so on is known as **chaining**.[3] Just as a chicken can learn to play baseball, so, too, can people learn lengthy, fairly complex behaviors through chaining. For example, students in a tennis class might learn to hold their rackets a certain way, then stand with their feet apart facing the net as they watch for the ball, then move toward an approaching ball and adjust their position appropriately, and then swing their rackets to meet the ball. Similarly, students in a first-grade classroom might learn to put their work materials away, sit quietly at their desks, and then line up single file at the classroom door before going to lunch. Such complex actions are often acquired more easily one step at a time—in other words, through chaining.

THE NATURE OF REINFORCERS

We have talked at length about how reinforcers can be used to change behavior. It is time now to talk more about reinforcers themselves. We'll first distinguish between primary and secondary reinforcers and between positive and negative reinforcement (which we will also contrast with punishment). We'll then consider the different kinds of reinforcers that teachers can use to change student behavior.

Primary and Secondary Reinforcers

A **primary reinforcer** is one that satisfies a built-in, perhaps biological, need or desire. Some primary reinforcers, such as food, water, oxygen, and warmth, are essential for physiological well being. Others, such as a chocolate bar or a glass of wine, aren't essential, but they can enhance a *sense* of well being. Still other primary reinforcers, such as physical affection, cuddling, and a smile, are more social in nature, and human beings have probably evolved to appreciate them as a way of enhancing social cohesiveness and so, indirectly, enhancing their chances of survival (Harlow & Zimmerman, 1959; Vollmer & Hackenberg, 2001). There may be individual differences regarding the consequences that serve as primary reinforcers; for example, sex is reinforcing to some individuals but not to others, and a particular drug may be a primary reinforcer for a drug addict but not necessarily for a nonaddicted individual (e.g., Lejuez, Schaal, & O'Donnell, 1998).

---

[3]When teaching the chicken to play basketball, the trainer probably used *backward chaining*, starting with the final response in the sequence and then adding, one by one, the response that needed to precede it. In other situations, trainers or teachers might use *forward chaining*, reinforcing the first response in the sequence and then adding subsequent responses to the sequence that is reinforced. Research yields mixed results regarding the relative effectiveness of these two approaches with human beings (Zirpoli & Melloy, 2001).

Primary versus secondary reinforcers.

A **secondary reinforcer,** also known as a **conditioned reinforcer,** is a previously neutral stimulus that has become reinforcing to an organism through repeated association with another reinforcer (e.g., Wolfe, 1936). Examples of secondary reinforcers, which do not satisfy any built-in biological or social needs, are praise, good grades, money, and feelings of success.[4]

How do secondary reinforcers become reinforcing? An early explanation was that some stimuli become secondary reinforcers through the process of classical conditioning. A neutral stimulus is paired with an existing reinforcer (UCS) that elicits some form of biological satisfaction (UCR). That neutral stimulus becomes a CS (i.e., it becomes a secondary reinforcer) that elicits the same satisfaction (CR). For example, my daughter Tina learned very early that she could use money (CS) to buy candy (UCS) to satisfy her sweet tooth. The more often a secondary reinforcer has been associated with another reinforcer, and the stronger that other reinforcer is, the more powerful the secondary reinforcer will be (Bersh, 1951; D'Amato, 1955).

More recently, some theorists have proposed that secondary reinforcers are effective to the extent that they give an organism information that a primary reinforcer is coming (Bower, McLean, & Meachem, 1966; Green & Rachlin, 1977; Mazur, 1993; Perone & Baron, 1980). This explanation has a decidedly cognitive flavor to it: An organism is *seeking information* about the environment rather than simply responding to that environment in a "thoughtless" manner.

The relative influences of primary and secondary reinforcers in our lives probably depend a great deal on economic circumstances. When such biological necessities as food and warmth are scarce, these primary reinforcers, as well as the secondary reinforcers closely associated with them (e.g., money), may be major factors in reinforcing behavior. But in times of economic well being, when cupboards are full and houses are warm, such secondary reinforcers as praise, grades, and feelings of success, are more likely to play a major role in the learning process.

Positive Reinforcement and Negative Reinforcement

In addition to distinguishing between primary and secondary reinforcers, we can also distinguish between positive and negative reinforcement. Let's examine these two forms of reinforcement and look at how they differ from punishment.

---

[4]One could argue that praise enhances social relationships and so might be a primary reinforcer. However, praise involves language—a learned behavior—and not all individuals find it reinforcing, hence its categorization as a secondary reinforcer (e.g., see Vollmer & Hackenberg, 2001).

Positive Reinforcement

Up to this point, the reinforcers I have mentioned have all been positive reinforcers. **Positive reinforcement** involves the *presentation* of a stimulus after the response. Food, a smile, praise, and success are all positive reinforcers.

Negative Reinforcement

In contrast to positive reinforcement, **negative reinforcement** increases a response through the *removal* of a stimulus, usually an aversive or unpleasant one.[5] For example, when rats learn to press a bar to terminate an electric shock, removal of the aversive shock is negative reinforcement that increases bar pressing. Many cars sound a loud buzzer if the keys are still in the ignition when the driver's door is opened; removal of the keys from the ignition is negatively reinforced (so will presumably increase in frequency) because the buzzer stops. Children will sometimes complain of stomachaches or behave disruptively as a way of wiggling out of academic activities they find difficult and frustrating; when engaging in such behaviors allows them to escape the troublesome tasks, the behaviors are likely to continue.

The removal of guilt or anxiety can be an extremely powerful negative reinforcer. A child may confess to a crime committed days or even weeks earlier because she has been feeling guilty about the transgression all that time and needs to get it off her chest. Anxiety may drive one student to complete a term paper early, thereby removing an item from his things-to-do list. Another student confronted with the same term paper might procrastinate until the last minute, thereby removing anxiety—although only temporarily—about the more difficult aspects of researching for and writing that paper.

We must keep in mind that negative reinforcement can affect the behavior of teachers as well as the behavior of students. Teachers may often behave in ways that get rid of aversive stimuli; for example, they may use classroom discipline strategies (responses such as yelling at students or promising less homework) that eliminate unpleasant stimuli (disorderly conduct in the classroom) over the short run but are ineffective over the long run. As an illustration, if Ms. Jones yells at Marvin for talking too much, Marvin may temporarily stop talking, which negatively reinforces Ms. Jones's yelling behavior.[6] But if Marvin likes getting Ms. Jones's attention (a positive reinforcer for him), he will be chattering again before very long.

Contrasting Positive and Negative Reinforcement With Punishment

Both positive reinforcement and negative reinforcement increase the responses that they follow. **Punishment,** however, is likely to *decrease* those responses. We will consider the effects of punishment in more detail in Chapter 6, but let's briefly define punishment here so you understand how it differs from negative reinforcement.

Punishment takes one of two forms, frequently referred to as Punishment I and Punishment II. **Punishment I** involves the *presentation* of a stimulus, usually an aversive one. Scolding and spanking are examples of this form of punishment. **Punishment II** involves the *removal* of a stimulus, usually a pleasant one. Examples include fines for misbehaviors (because money is being taken away)

---

[5]Don't let the word "negative" *in negative reinforcement* lead you astray here. It is not a value judgement; it simply refers to the fact that something is being *taken away* from the situation.

[6]Note that, although behaving in a disruptive fashion is a response that Marvin makes, in this situation it serves as a *stimulus* that Ms. Jones wants to eliminate.

Nature of Stimulus

Stimulus is	Pleasant	Aversive
Presented after the response	Positive reinforcement (response increases)	Punishment I (response decreases)
Removed after the response	Punishment II (response decreases)	Negative Reinforcement (response increases)

Figure 4–3
Positive reinforcement, negative reinforcement, and punishment.

and loss of privileges. Figure 4–3 illustrates the differences among positive reinforcement, negative reinforcement, Punishment I, and Punishment II.

Many people mistakenly use the term *negative reinforcement* when they are really talking about punishment. Although both phenomena may involve aversive stimuli, they differ in two critical respects. First, as we just noted, they have opposite effects: Negative reinforcement *increases* the frequency of a response, whereas punishment often *decreases* the frequency of a response. A second crucial difference concerns the order of events. With negative reinforcement, the aversive stimulus *stops* when the response is emitted. With Punishment I, however, the aversive stimulus *begins* when the response is emitted. Figure 4–4 illustrates this difference graphically. The termination of an aversive stimulus negatively reinforces a response; the initiation of an aversive stimulus punishes a response.

The Variety of Consequences That Human Beings Find Reinforcing

When using reinforcement in the classroom, teachers often unnecessarily limit themselves to only a handful of reinforcers. In fact, a wide variety of events can be reinforcing to students and other human beings. Let's look at several possibilities.

Material Reinforcers

A **material reinforcer,** or tangible reinforcer, is an actual object; food and toys are examples. For many people, the word *reinforcer* brings to mind such tangible consequences for good behavior. But in school situations at least, most psychologists recommend that we use material reinforcers only as a last resort, when absolutely no other reinforcer works. Food, toys, trinkets, and similar

Figure 4–4
Negative reinforcement and punishment differ in terms of which occurs first—the aversive stimulus or the response.

items have a tendency to distract students' attention from the things they should be doing in class and so may be counterproductive in the long run.

Social Reinforcers

A **social reinforcer** is a gesture or sign from one person to another that communicates positive regard. Praise, a smile, a pat on the back, and a hug are all social reinforcers. Social reinforcement is a common occurrence in the classroom and can be quite effective. Teacher attention, approval, praise, and appreciation are powerful classroom reinforcers (Becker, Madsen, Arnold, & Thomas, 1967; Craft et al., 1998; Drabman, 1976; Madsen, Becker, & Thomas, 1968).[7] The attention and approval of peers can be effective as well (Bowers, Woods, Carlyon, & Friman, 2000; Evans & Oswalt, 1968; Flood et al., 2002).

Activity Reinforcers

Speaking nonbehavioristically, an **activity reinforcer** is an opportunity to engage in a favorite activity. (A quick quiz: Which word is the nonbehaviorist part of my definition, and why?) David Premack (1959, 1963) discovered that people will often perform one activity if doing so enables them to perform another. His **Premack principle** for activity reinforcers is as follows:

> A normally high-frequency response, when it follows a normally low-frequency response, will increase the frequency of the low-frequency response.

A high-frequency response is, in essence, a response that an organism enjoys doing, whereas a low-frequency response is one that the organism does not enjoy. Another way of stating the Premack principle, then, is that organisms will perform less-preferred tasks so that they can subsequently engage in more-preferred tasks.

To illustrate, my own free operant level for housework is extremely low. I have found that I am more likely to do household chores if I make a higher-frequency behavior, such as reading a mystery novel or having a party, contingent on doing the housework. In a similar way, appropriate classroom behavior can be improved through the Premack principle. For instance, young children can quickly be taught to sit quietly and pay attention if they are allowed to engage in high-frequency, high-activity behaviors (e.g., interacting with classmates) only after they have been quiet and attentive for a certain period of time (Homme, deBaca, Devine, Steinhorst, & Rickert, 1963).

Although psychologists agree that the Premack principle works, they disagree as to *why* it works. If you are interested in exploring the theoretical underpinnings of the Premack principle, see the discussions by Bower and Hilgard (1981) and Timberlake and Allison (1974).

Positive Feedback

In some instances, material and social reinforcers may improve classroom behavior and lead to better learning of academic skills because they provide **feedback** to students about which responses are desirable and which are not (Butler, 1987; Gagné & Driscoll, 1988). Positive

---

[7]We should note here that praise has a potential downside, depending on the specific message that it contains and the context in which it is given. We will consider the possible negative side effects of praise in Chapter 18.

feedback is clearly effective in bringing about desired behavior changes (Kladopoulos & McComas, 2001; Lhyle & Kulhavy, 1987; Smith & Smoll, 1997).

I once spent a half hour each day for several weeks working with Michael, a nine-year-old boy with a learning disability who was having difficulty learning his cursive letters. Over the first three weeks, neither Michael nor I could see any improvement, and we were both becoming increasingly frustrated. To give ourselves more concrete feedback on the results of our sessions together, I decided to start graphing Michael's daily performance. I explained to Michael how we would chart his progress on a sheet of graph paper by marking off the number of cursive letters he could remember each day. I also told him that as soon as he had reached a dotted line near the top of the page (a line indicating that he had written all 26 letters correctly) for three days in a row, he could have a special treat (his choice was a purple felt-tip pen).

At the beginning of each subsequent work session, I tested Michael on his cursive letters, and together we counted the number that he had correctly remembered. We entered his performance on the chart in the form of a bar of the appropriate height, and then Michael practiced the letters he had missed. Michael's daily performance began to improve dramatically. Not only was he making noticeable progress, but he also looked forward to charting his performance and seeing a higher bar each day. Within two weeks, Michael had successfully met the criterion for his felt-tip pen: He had written all 26 cursive letters for three days in succession. As it turns out, the pen was probably not the key ingredient in our success: Michael didn't seem bothered by the fact that he lost it within 24 hours of earning it. Instead, I suspect that the concrete positive feedback about his own improvement was the true reinforcer that helped Michael to learn.

Feedback is especially likely to be effective when it communicates what students have and have not learned and when it gives them guidance about how they might improve their performance (Butler & Winne, 1995; Lhyle & Kulhavy, 1987). Under such circumstances, even *negative* feedback can lead to enhanced performance (e.g., Barbetta, Heward, Bradley, & Miller, 1994). It is difficult to interpret such findings within a strictly behaviorist framework, however; it appears that students must be *thinking* about the specific meaning of the feedback they receive and using it to adjust their future behavior.

Intrinsic Reinforcers

In many situations, individuals engage in certain responses not because of any external reinforcers but because of the internal good feelings—the **intrinsic reinforcers**—that such responses bring. Feeling successful after solving a difficult puzzle, feeling proud after returning a valuable item to its rightful owner, and feeling relieved after completing a difficult assignment are all examples of intrinsic reinforcers. People who continue to engage in responses for a long time without any obvious external reinforcers for their efforts are probably working for intrinsic sources of satisfaction.

For many students, the true reinforcers for learning are probably the internal reinforcers—the feelings of success, competence, mastery, and pride—that their accomplishments bring. For such students, other reinforcers are more helpful if they provide feedback that academic tasks have been performed well. Grades may be reinforcing for the same reason: Good grades reflect high achievement—a reason to feel proud.

From a teacher's perspective, positive feedback and the intrinsic reinforcement that such feedback brings are probably the most desirable forms of classroom reinforcement. Keep in mind, however, that consistent positive feedback and resulting feelings of success and mastery can occur only when instruction has been carefully tailored to individual skill levels and abilities, and only when students have learned to value academic achievement. When, for whatever reasons, children are not motivated to achieve academic success, then other reinforcers, such as social and activity reinforcers, can be helpful.

Always remember that what is reinforcing for one individual may not be reinforcing for another. Reinforcement, like beauty, is in the eyes of the beholder. And even for the same individual, a reinforcer on one occasion may not be a reinforcer on another. Several other factors influence the effectiveness of reinforcers, as we shall see now.

FACTORS INFLUENCING THE EFFECTIVENESS OF REINFORCEMENT

Several factors influence the effectiveness of reinforcement in operant conditioning, including timing, magnitude and appeal, and consistency.

Timing

Earlier in the chapter, I stressed the importance of *immediate* reinforcement for operant conditioning. In most cases, greater delays in reinforcement lead to slower acquisition of responses (e.g., Hockman & Lipsitt, 1961; Lett, 1973, 1975; Terrell & Ware, 1961). Fortunately, in situations when immediate reinforcement is impossible, environmental cues indicating that reinforcement will come later can be helpful (Fowler & Baer, 1981; Perin, 1943). For example, a teacher who wants to reinforce her students' persistence through a difficult lesson might say, "Because we have all worked so hard this morning, after lunch we will practice the class play that you all have been enjoying so much." Furthermore, children also become better able to work for delayed reinforcers (that is, to delay *gratification*) when the waiting period is increased gradually and when they learn strategies for coping with the wait—for instance, by engaging in an activity or telling themselves "If I wait a little longer, I will get a bigger cookie" (Binder, Dixon, & Ghezzi, 2000; Dixon & Cummings, 2001; Freeland & Noell, 1999).

Magnitude and Appeal

The larger and more appealing the reinforcer, the faster a response will be learned and the more frequently it will be exhibited (e.g., Atkinson, 1958; Siegel & Andrews, 1962). For example, in a study by Siegel and Andrews (1962), 3- to 5-year-old boys learned more quickly when they were reinforced with such treats as candy, coins, balloons, and small toys than when the reinforcers were unexciting buttons. In fact, for older children and adults, large, delayed reinforcers are often more effective than small, immediate ones, provided that the individuals know the reinforcers will eventually appear (e.g., Green et al., 1994).

Interestingly enough, it is not always the absolute magnitude of reinforcement that affects behavior as much as it is the *relative* magnitude compared with prior experience. For example, in a classic study by Crespi (1942), rats ran a runway to reach a food reinforcer at the far end. When rats accustomed to a small quantity of food were suddenly reinforced with a greater amount, they ran faster than rats who had always received that same large amount. Similarly, rats accustomed to a large amount of reinforcement who then began receiving less food ran more slowly than rats who had always had that smaller amount. Crespi's results have been replicated in other rat stud-ies (e.g., McHale, Brooks, & Wolach, 1982), although the results of analogous studies with infants have been inconsistent (e.g., Fagen & Rovee, 1976; Lipsitt & Kaye, 1965).

The changes in behavior observed when quantities of reinforcement increase or decrease are commonly known as **contrast effects.** One contrast effect—the **elation effect**—occurs when the amount of reinforcement is increased: The response rate becomes *faster* than it would be if the reinforcement had always been at that higher level. The opposite contrast effect—the **depression effect**—occurs when the amount of reinforcement is decreased: The result is that the response rate becomes *slower* than it would be if reinforcement had always been that low. The depression effect may be at least partly due to negative emotions associated with a reduction in reinforcement (Flaherty, 1985).

Consistency

One of the most critical factors affecting both the rate at which responses are learned and the rate at which they can be extinguished is the consistency of reinforcement (e.g., Staddon & Higa, 1991). To illustrate how consistency plays a role, consider this fantasy I have for the handful of students in my classes each semester who don't read their textbook:

> The student is locked in a small room. The assigned textbook lies on a nearby table. Every time the student opens the book to one of the assigned pages and looks at the page, a small piece of delicious junk food falls from a hole in the ceiling.

Essentially, I would like to put unmotivated students into my own version of a Skinner box—the Ormrod box!

Now imagine 20 students in 20 Ormrod boxes. Ten of these students, randomly selected, are in Group A: They receive a piece of junk food every time they open the textbook and look at it. The other 10 are in Group B: They get junk food for some of their book-reading responses (perhaps one response out of every four) but receive nothing for their efforts the rest of the time. Group A is receiving **continuous reinforcement:** Every response is reinforced. Group B is receiv-ing **intermittent reinforcement:** Some of the responses are reinforced and some are not. Which group is going to increase its textbook-reading behavior faster? The answer, of course, is Group A, the group with continuous reinforcement. Continuously reinforced responses are acquired faster than intermittently reinforced responses.

Now suppose that, after a few hours in their respective Ormrod boxes, all 20 students have begun to show a high frequency of textbook-reading responses, so I turn off the junk-food-dropping mechanisms. Which students are first going to notice that they are no longer being reinforced? The answer again is Group A. Students who have been reinforced for every single response will notice rather quickly that reinforcement has stopped, and their textbook reading should extinguish rapidly (unless, of course, they find such behavior intrinsically reinforcing). In contrast, Group B students have been receiving reinforcement for only 25% of their responses, so they are accustomed to non-reinforcement; these students will probably continue to read their textbooks for some time before they realize that reinforcement has ceased. Intermittently reinforced responses are extinguished more slowly than continuously reinforced responses.

Behaviorists usually recommend reinforcing a response continuously until the terminal behavior is reached and then maintaining the response through intermittent reinforcement so that it does not extinguish. Intermittent reinforcement can follow a variety of **reinforcement schedules,** each of which has different effects on resistance to extinction and on the frequency and pattern of the response being reinforced. We now look at several different schedules and the behavior patterns that result from each one.

SCHEDULES OF REINFORCEMENT

In this section I will describe three different groups of intermittent reinforcement schedules: ratio schedules (those in which reinforcement occurs after a certain number of responses), interval schedules (those in which reinforcement occurs for the first response after a certain time interval has elapsed), and differential schedules (those in which reinforcement is contingent on a certain rate of responding).

Ratio Schedules: Reinforcing a Certain Number of Responses

A **ratio schedule** is one in which reinforcement occurs after a certain number of responses have been emitted. That particular number can either be constant (a fixed-ratio schedule) or vary from one reinforcement to the next (a variable-ratio schedule).

Fixed Ratio (FR)

In a **fixed-ratio** reinforcement schedule, a reinforcer is presented after a certain constant number of responses have occurred. For example, reinforcement might occur after every third response (a 1:3 ratio schedule) or after every fiftieth response (a 1:50 schedule). Such a reinforcement schedule can lead to a high and consistent response rate over an indefinite period of time; for example, pigeons whose pecking is maintained on a high ratio schedule will peck as often as 10 times per second (Ferster & Skinner, 1957).

Whitlock (1966) has described the use of a series of ratio schedules with a 6-year-old boy who had been unable to acquire basic reading skills. At first, the boy was asked to read words presented to him on flash cards. Every time he read a word correctly, he received a plastic poker chip as a reinforcer, reflecting a continuous reinforcement schedule. He could trade jars of 36 poker chips for a variety of activities; for example, with two jars he could play a game, and with seven jars he could watch a cartoon. Once the boy was able to read from beginning reader storybooks, he was reinforced on a 1:2 fixed-ratio schedule; that is, he received one chip for every two words he read correctly. Eventually he was reinforced for every four words (a 1:4 schedule), then for every page (one reinforcer for every 10 to 25 words), then for every story (one reinforcer for every 50 to 70 words), and finally for every four stories. After 15 sessions of such individualized instruction, reinforcement was phased out altogether, and the boy was placed in his classroom's regular reading program; three months later, he was still reading at grade level. (One thing has always struck me about this study: Because so many poker chips were required to make a "purchase," the boy must have actually bought very few activities. I suspect that his increasing success in reading was the true reinforcer in this case.)

Ratio schedules even as high as 1:1000, when introduced through a series of successively higher ratios (as was done in the Whitlock study), have been found to maintain a response (Ferster & Skinner, 1957). In fact, high ratios typically lead to higher rates of responding than low ratios (Collier, Hirsh, & Hamlin, 1972; Stephens, Pear, Wray, & Jackson, 1975), although organisms operating under high-ratio schedules tend to exhibit a **postreinforcement pause** (a temporary decrease in responding) after each reinforced response (Ferster & Skinner, 1957).

Variable Ratio (VR)

A **variable-ratio** reinforcement schedule is one in which reinforcement is presented after a particular, yet *changing,* number of responses have been emitted. This kind of schedule is described by the average number of responses needed to obtain reinforcement. For example, in a 1:5 VR schedule, reinforcement might first take place after four responses, then after seven more, then after three, and so on. As you can see, the occurrence of reinforcement in a VR schedule is somewhat unpredictable.

Playing a Las Vegas slot machine is an example of a response that is reinforced on a variable-ratio schedule. The more times you insert a quarter into the machine, the more times you will be reinforced by having quarters come back out again, but those quarters do not come out after any predictable number of quarters have been inserted. In a similar way, telephone solicitation is reinforced on a VR schedule. The greater the number of calls made, the greater the number of sales, but the soliciting caller never knows just which call will lead to reinforcement.

Margaret, a friend of my daughter Tina during their elementary school years, was always very persistent when she wanted something; she seldom took no for an answer. A possible source of her persistence became clear to me one evening when Tina and I had dinner at a restaurant with

Telephone solicitation is reinforced on a variable-ratio schedule.

Margaret and her mother. The girls gobbled their food quickly and went off to explore the restaurant while we ladies nursed our coffee. Margaret quickly returned to the table to make a request of her mother:

> "Mom, can I have a quarter for a video game?"
> "No."
> "Please, mom?"
> "I said no, Margaret."
> "But Tina has one." (I look absentmindedly into space.)
> "No."
> "I'll pay you back as soon as we get home."
> "*No,* Margaret."
> "*Pretty please?*!" (Margaret puts on a desperate face.)
> "Oh, all right, here's a quarter."

Margaret's asking behaviors were probably on a variable-ratio reinforcement schedule: She had learned that persistence eventually paid off.

Variable-ratio schedules result in higher response rates than fixed-ratio schedules. Furthermore, responses reinforced on a VR schedule are highly resistant to extinction. In fact, pigeons working on very high VR schedules may expend more energy responding than they gain in food reinforcement, thus eventually working themselves to death (Swenson, 1980).

Interval Schedules: Reinforcing the First Response After a Time Period

An **interval schedule** is one in which reinforcement is contingent on the first response emitted after a certain time interval has elapsed. The time interval can either be constant (a fixed-interval schedule) or vary from one reinforcement to the next (a variable-interval schedule).

Fixed Interval (FI)

With a **fixed-interval** reinforcement schedule, reinforcement is contingent on the first response emitted after a certain fixed time interval has elapsed. For example, the organism may be reinforced for the first response emitted after five minutes have elapsed, regardless of how many responses may or may not have been made during those five minutes. Following reinforcement, another five-minute interval must elapse before a response is again reinforced.

A fixed-interval schedule produces a unique response pattern: Following reinforcement, the response rate tapers way off in a postreinforcement pause until the end of the time interval approaches, at which point responding picks up again (e.g., Ferster & Skinner, 1957; Shimoff, Catania, & Matthews, 1981). To illustrate, when my daughter Tina was in fifth grade, she had a spelling test every Friday. She got the week's list of spelling words each Monday and so had four evenings in which to study the list. Occasionally she began on Wednesday, but she more often waited until Thursday night to study her spelling. If we were to graph Tina's studying behavior, it might look something like the graph in Figure 4–5. This "scallop" pattern is typical of behaviors reinforced on a fixed-interval schedule. We do not see the high rate of responding with a FI schedule that is observed for fixed- and variable-ratio schedules, nor do we see as much resistance to extinction.

Figure 4–5
Responses reinforced on a fixed-interval schedule show a "scallop" pattern.

Variable Interval (VI)

In a **variable-interval** reinforcement schedule, reinforcement is contingent on the first response emitted after a certain time interval has elapsed, but the length of that interval keeps changing from one occasion to the next. For example, the organism may be reinforced for the first response after five minutes, then the first response after eight minutes, then the first response after two minutes, and so on, with the VI schedule being identified by the average time interval.

As an illustration, you may have a friend who really enjoys talking on the telephone, so that when you try to call this individual, you often hear a busy signal. If you have an urgent need to get in touch with your friend, you may continue to dial the phone number once every few minutes until eventually your call goes through. In a similar way, students who have been told that there is always the possibility of an unannounced ("pop") quiz in class are likely to study a little bit every night. They never know on exactly which day their studying will pay off. Your pattern of dialing your gabby friend and students' patterns of studying for pop quizzes are typical of the response pattern observed for variable-interval schedules: a slow, steady rate of responding. The longer the average time interval until reinforcement, the slower the response rate will be (e.g., Catania & Reynolds, 1968). (Please note that for other reasons, pop quizzes are generally not recommended. They may increase students' anxiety levels in the classroom, and, as you will discover in Chapter 16, high levels of anxiety interfere with learning. Furthermore, pop quizzes don't allow for the fact that students' extracurricular activities and family obligations sometimes prevent completion of schoolwork the same day it is assigned.)

For both ratio and interval schedules, then, variable schedules lead to steadier response rates than fixed schedules do, probably because of the unpredictability of reinforcement after a correct response. With a variable schedule, there is always the possibility that the next correct response will pay off. Variable schedules also appear to lead to greater resistance to extinction, again possibly because of their unpredictable nature.

When using ratio or interval schedules of reinforcement to prevent the extinction of a previously acquired response, the best schedule to use depends on the rate of response desired. In most cases, a variable ratio is recommended for a high rate of responding, with a variable-interval schedule being better for a slow yet steady rate. Ideally, when continuous reinforcement is first replaced by intermittent reinforcement, the ratio should be small (e.g., 1:2 or 1:3) or the time interval short. The ratio or interval can then gradually be increased until the responses continue with very little reinforcement at all.

Differential Schedules: Reinforcing Rates of Responding

When a particular *rate* of responding is required, a **differential schedule of reinforcement** is appropriate: A specific number of responses occurring within a specific length of time leads to reinforcement. Researchers have investigated the effects of several such schedules, including these:

- Reinforcement of a differential rate of high responding
- Reinforcement of a differential rate of low responding
- Reinforcement of the *non*occurrence of the response (differential reinforcement of other behaviors)

Differential Rate of High Responding (DRH)

A **DRH schedule** provides reinforcement only when a specific, *large* number of responses (or even more responses than that) have occurred within a particular period of time. For example, consider Tina's friend Margaret, the girl who persistently asked her mother for money to play a video game. Margaret may actually have been on a DRH schedule rather than a variable-ratio schedule, in that she had to ask for a quarter several times *all at once* to get reinforcement. With a ratio schedule, the time it takes to emit the necessary number of responses is irrelevant, but with a DRH schedule, this time period is critical. Because a DRH schedule requires many responses in a short amount of time, a high response rate is typical.

Theoretically, studying for regularly scheduled exams is really on a DRH schedule: The more studying that occurs, the greater the probability of reinforcement at exam time. However, as Klein (1987) has pointed out, too many students instead treat exams as fixed-interval schedules, thus showing the "goof off now, cram later" study pattern.

Differential Rate of Low Responding (DRL)

A **DRL schedule** reinforces the first response after a certain time interval has elapsed in which the organism has *not* made the response at all. This might sound like a fixed-interval schedule, but remember that in an FI schedule, responses during the time interval, although not reinforced, are otherwise acceptable. One example of a response on a DRL schedule is trying to start a car with a flooded engine. Repeated attempts at starting it will fail; you must wait for a few minutes, then try again, before you are likely to succeed.

Students' requests for their teacher's assistance are an example of responses that might be most appropriately reinforced on a DRL schedule. Reinforcing students continuously when they ask for the teacher's help might lead to a high rate of such requests and a resulting overdependence on the teacher. However, reinforcing students who ask for help only after they have been working independently for a period of time will teach them that independence with occasional questions is more acceptable.

We should note here that learning the appropriate response pattern for a DRL schedule often takes time, because it requires one *not* to perform a behavior that has previously been reinforced (Reynolds, 1975).

Differential Reinforcement of Other Behaviors (DRO)

In a **DRO schedule**, the organism is reinforced for doing anything *except* for making a certain response during a certain time period; in this situation, the organism must never make that particular response at all. As an example, consider the teacher who says, "I am going to write on the chalkboard the name of every student who speaks out of turn today. If your name is not on the board by three o'clock, you may have a half hour of free time." That teacher is using a DRO schedule, because she is reinforcing children for *not* talking without permission.

Continuous reinforcement is clearly the most effective way of teaching a new response. Once the terminal behavior has been reached, however, the various intermittent reinforcement schedules—ratio, interval, and differential—can be beneficial both in preventing extinction (the DRO schedule excepted) and in controlling the frequency and pattern of that response.

STIMULUS CONTROL

Earlier in the chapter, I described Skinner's operant conditioning as an $R \longrightarrow S_{Rf}$ model (where S_{Rf} is reinforcement) rather than the $S \longrightarrow R$ model more typical of other early behaviorists. Actually, a stimulus that precedes a response *can* influence the likelihood that the response will occur again, although the role of this **antecedent stimulus** in operant conditioning is different from the role it plays in other behaviorist models such as classical conditioning.

To illustrate, here is a typical scenario in a high school class: The teacher begins to describe the evening's homework assignment to a class of quiet and attentive students but is interrupted by a bell marking the end of the class period. Immediately the students, no longer interested in hearing their assignment, slam their notebooks shut and begin to push and shove their way toward the classroom door. These students are under **stimulus control:** They have learned that a particular response (leaving class) is acceptable under certain stimulus conditions (e.g., when the bell rings). A wise teacher would stand in front of the door while giving the homework assignment and not let the students leave their seats—bell or no bell. In that way, students would learn that leaving class is permissible only after a different stimulus—the teacher's movement away from the door—has occurred.

In operant conditioning, the antecedent stimulus does not directly elicit the response as it does in classical conditioning. Instead, the stimulus *sets the occasion* for a response to be reinforced. When an antecedent stimulus increases the likelihood that a response will occur, we call that stimulus a **discriminative stimulus,** often symbolized as **S+,**[8] and say that the response is under stimulus control. Responses to stimuli in operant conditioning often show stimulus generalization and stimulus discrimination—phenomena similar to the generalization and discrimination observed in classical conditioning.

Stimulus Generalization

When an organism has learned to respond in a certain way in the presence of one stimulus (the S+), it is likely to respond in the same way in the presence of similar stimuli; this operant conditioning phenomenon is known as **stimulus generalization.** Just as is true in classical conditioning, stimulus generalization is more likely to occur when stimuli are similar to the discriminative stimulus. For example, students in a kindergarten classroom (the classroom being the S+) may learn such appropriate classroom behaviors as raising their hands and waiting to be called on

---

[8]If you read any of Skinner's writings on this topic, keep in mind that he used the symbol S^D instead of S+.

before speaking. Such behaviors are more likely to generalize to a similar situation (such as first grade) than to a dissimilar situation (such as the family dinner table). This tendency of organisms to generalize more readily as stimuli become more similar to the discriminative stimulus is known as a **generalization gradient.**

Stimulus Discrimination

In classical conditioning, stimulus discrimination occurs when one stimulus (the CS+) is presented in conjunction with an unconditioned stimulus, and another stimulus (the CS–) is presented in the absence of the UCS. A similar phenomenon happens in operant conditioning: A response may be reinforced in the presence of one stimulus (S+) but not in the presence of another stimulus, symbolized as **S–:**[9]

$$(S+) \ R \longrightarrow S_{Rf}$$

$$(S-) \ R \longrightarrow (nothing)$$

Learning under what circumstances a response will and will not be reinforced is operant conditioning's form of **stimulus discrimination.** Stimulus discrimination is essentially a process of learning that a conditioned response made in the presence of S+ should not be generalized to S–.

Consider the preschooler who has learned to say "bee" whenever she sees this symbol:

b

She then sees a similar stimulus:

d

and responds "bee" once again—that is, she generalizes. (Anyone who has worked with young children who are learning their alphabet letters has probably observed that, consistent with the generalization gradient, children are much more likely to generalize the "bee" response to the letter *d* than to less similar letters, such as *s* or *y*.) If the teacher does not reinforce the child for the "bee" response to the symbol *d,* the student should eventually learn to discriminate between the letters *b* and *d*.

Stimulus Control in the Classroom

At school, as in most other situations, different responses are desirable at different times. For example, it is perfectly appropriate, and in fact quite desirable, to talk with classmates at certain times (e.g., during a classroom discussion) but not at others (e.g., during the weekly spelling test). Likewise, running may be appropriate in the gymnasium but can be dangerous in the school corridors. How can teachers encourage their students to exhibit different behaviors on different occasions? Psychologists have suggested two strategies: cueing and setting events.

Cueing

In the classroom, the discriminative stimuli that set the occasion for certain desired behaviors are not always obvious ones; for example, the only naturally occurring stimulus that sets the occasion for cleaning up work materials and getting ready to go to lunch might be a clock on the wall

[9]Skinner used the symbol S^Δ instead of S-.

that says 11:55. Under such circumstances, teachers can provide additional discriminative stimuli that let students know how to behave—a strategy often called **cueing** or **prompting** (e.g., Krumboltz & Krumboltz, 1972; Shabani et al., 2002; Taylor & Levin, 1998).

In some situations, teachers can provide nonverbal cues to indicate desired responses. For example, during a cooperative learning activity, they might quickly flash the overhead light on and off a few times to remind students to talk quietly rather than loudly. In other situations, teachers can give verbal cues to encourage appropriate behavior. For example, an elementary teacher whose students are preparing to go to the lunchroom might cue students by saying, "Walk quietly and in single file." The teacher can then reinforce the desired behavior by allowing students to proceed only when they behave as they have been instructed. A teacher who wants to give students a subtle reminder about the necessity for accomplishing a reading assignment quickly might say, "After you have all finished reading about recycling on pages 69 and 70 of your geography book, I will tell you about tomorrow's field trip to a recycling plant."[10]

Setting Events

Thus far, we have focused our discussion of stimulus control on specific stimuli (e.g., the letter *b* or a teacher's cue to "walk quietly") that encourage students to behave in particular ways. Some psychologists talk not about specific stimuli but instead about complex environmental conditions—**setting events**—under which certain behaviors are most likely to occur (Brown, Bryson-Brockmann, & Fox, 1986; Hoch, McComas, Johnson, Faranda, & Guenther, 2002; Kantor, 1959; Morris, 1982; Wahler & Fox, 1981). For example, preschoolers are more likely to interact with their classmates during free play time if they have a relatively small area in which to play and if the toys available to them (balls, puppets, toy housekeeping materials) encourage group activity (Brown, Fox, & Brady, 1987; Martin, Brady, & Williams, 1991). Similarly, the nature of the games that children are asked to play influences the behaviors they exhibit: Cooperative games promote increases in cooperative behavior, whereas competitive games promote increases in aggressive behavior (Bay-Hinitz, Peterson, & Quilitch, 1994). Teachers are well advised, then, to create the kinds of environments that are likely to encourage the very behaviors they want their students to exhibit.

CONTEMPORARY PERSPECTIVES ON OPERANT CONDITIONING

As we noted earlier in the chapter, B. F. Skinner's ideas about operant conditioning underwent little change from 1938 until his death in 1990. The views of other behaviorists have evolved considerably over time, however. Following are some examples of how contemporary perspectives of operant conditioning differ from Skinner's original notions:

- *Behavior is better understood by looking at a larger context and longer time frame than has traditionally been the case.* Early behaviorists tended to think in terms of specific S–R relationships within a relatively short time period; for example, a researcher might look at the immediate

---

[10]Simple cues are often effective in nonclassroom settings as well. For instance, when grocery store workers or restaurant hosts say good-bye to departing customers and add a reminder to "buckle up," customers are more likely to fasten their seatbelts when they get into their cars (Austin, Alvero, & Olson, 1998; Engerman, Austin, & Bailey, 1997).

consequence of a particular response. In contrast, many behaviorists are now looking at larger and longer environment–behavior relationships (e.g., see Herrnstein, 1990; Rachlin, 1990, 1991). The *setting events* that we just discussed illustrate this trend in that they are relatively complex environmental conditions rather than specific stimuli. Some psychologists look at the choices that organisms make in situations in which several different behaviors—each leading to a different reinforcer—are possible (de Villiers, 1977; Rachlin, 1991). Others examine the conditions under which certain behaviors are likely to persist despite *changes* in environmental stimuli—a phenomenon sometimes known as **behavioral momentum** (Belfiore, Lee, Vargas, & Skinner, 1997; Mace et al., 1988; Nevin, Mandell, & Atak, 1983).

A study by Belfiore and colleagues (1997) illustrates behavioral momentum nicely. Two girls (Allison, who was 14, and Roberta, who was 15) had a history of refusing to do the academic tasks that their teachers assigned. The researchers found that they could encourage the two students to work on difficult three-digit multiplication problems if they first gave the girls some simple one-digit problems. More generally, teachers can promote behavioral momentum by assigning easy or enjoyable tasks that lead naturally to more complex and potentially frustrating ones.

• *Operant conditioning involves cognition as well as behavior.* Many theorists now propose that operant conditioning can best be understood when we consider nonobservable mental processes as well as observable stimuli and responses (Colwill, 1993; Rachlin, 1991; Schwartz & Reisberg, 1991; Vaughan, 1988; Wasserman, 1993). For example, they talk about an organism forming *expectations* as to what reinforcer is likely to follow a particular response (Colwill, 1993; Rachlin, 1991; Schwartz & Reisberg, 1991). They find that humans and nonhumans alike develop *categories* of stimuli to which they respond; to illustrate, pigeons can be trained to discriminate (by making different responses) between members of different categories, including cats versus flowers, cars versus trucks, pictures of Charlie Brown versus those of other Peanuts characters, and even different lengths of time (Killeen, 1991; Rachlin, 1991; Vaughan, 1988; Wasserman, 1993). And behaviorists are beginning to use such phrases as *paying attention* to discriminative stimuli, mentally *encoding* and finding *meaning* in response–reinforcement relationships, and *seeking information* about the environment—phrases with definite cognitive overtones (Colwill, 1993; Colwill & Rescorla, 1986; DeGrandpre, 2000; Rachlin, 1991; Rescorla, 1987; Schwartz & Reisberg, 1991).

• *Operant and classical conditioning, taken together, do not completely determine the behaviors that an organism will exhibit on any given occasion.* B. F. Skinner was a **determinist:** He proposed that if we were to have complete knowledge of an organism's past reinforcement history and present environmental circumstances, as well as knowledge of any genetic predispositions that the organism might have to behave in certain ways, we would be able to predict the organism's next response with total accuracy. The views of some contemporary behaviorists are not so deterministic in nature: They propose that any organism's behavior reflects a certain degree of variability that S–R relationships cannot explain (Epstein, 1991; Rachlin, 1991). For example, if you think about it, shaping behavior— refining it through successively "fussier" reinforcement contingencies—would not be possible unless an organism varied its responses somewhat from one occasion to another. Ultimately, it is only by making changes in responses (however small those changes might be) and experiencing their consequences that new and perhaps more adaptive behaviors can emerge over time (Epstein, 1991).

• *Just as reinforcement increases the frequency of a response, punishment can be an effective means of decreasing a response.* Early research by Thorndike (1932a, 1932b) and Skinner (1938) indicated that punishment was unlikely to reduce the behavior that it followed. But later research studies have shown that punishment *can* be effective in many situations. As a result, some theorists have revived the "punishment" part of Thorndike's original law of effect, asserting that responses followed by discomfort are in fact weakened (e.g., Aronfreed, 1968; Aronfreed & Reber, 1965; Lentz, 1988; Parke, 1972, 1977; Rachlin, 1991). We should note that when behaviorists describe the effects of both reinforcement and punishment in learning and behavior, they typically use the term **instrumental conditioning** rather than Skinner's *operant conditioning*.

We will discuss punishment, including its effects and guidelines for its use, in Chapter 6. For now, we will look at reinforcement-based methods for eliminating undesirable behavior.

ELIMINATING UNDESIRABLE BEHAVIORS

We have talked at length about how new responses are learned, modified, and maintained through operant conditioning. But sometimes we may instead want to get rid of a behavior that has previously been acquired through reinforcement. Four possible methods of reducing and eliminating misbehavior are extinction, noncontingent consequences, differential reinforcement of other behaviors, and reinforcement of incompatible behaviors.

Extinguishing Responses

A psychologist was once consulted about Jimmy, a child who had been hospitalized for an extended period. Nurses in the children's ward were very concerned because Jimmy kept banging his head on the side of his crib; whenever they heard him doing so, they would rush to his room and stop the behavior, thereby inadvertently reinforcing and maintaining the head-banging behavior. The psychologist successfully eliminated Jimmy's head banging through a process of extinction: A protective helmet was strapped on Jimmy's head to prevent injury, and the nurses were instructed to ignore Jimmy during his head-banging episodes. At the same time, because Jimmy clearly craved attention, the nurses *did* attend to him on other occasions.

Extinction—making sure that a particular response no longer leads to reinforcement—is sometimes an effective means of eliminating inappropriate behavior. Students who engage in disruptive behavior in class may stop if such behavior no longer results in the teacher attention they seek (i.e., if the teacher ignores them). Cheating on classroom assignments may soon disappear if students never receive credit for the scores they obtain on those assignments. We don't necessarily want to eliminate the particular reinforcers (e.g., attention, class credit) that have been operating in such circumstances; we simply need to make sure that those reinforcers are *not* contingent on the responses we are trying to eliminate (e.g., Fischer, Iwata, & Mazaleski, 1997).

Unfortunately, extinction is often not the most dependable method of eliminating unwanted behavior, for several reasons. First, it is not always possible to identify the specific consequence that is actually reinforcing a response; for example, children who, like Jimmy, engage in head-banging behavior do so for different reasons—perhaps to gain adult attention, escape from academic tasks (a form of negative reinforcement), or provide self-stimulation (Iwata, Pace, Cowdery, & Miltenberger, 1994). Second, there may often be several reinforcers involved in maintaining a response, including some that are difficult to remove; for example, although a teacher may be able to ignore the comments of a class clown, other students in the class may continue to reinforce those comments. Third, even if all sources of reinforcement can be removed, the behavior may show an extinction burst, increasing in frequency before it begins to decline (Lerman et al., 1999; McGill, 1999). Fourth, extinguished behaviors sometimes show spontaneous recovery: A response that has been extinguished one day may pop up again at a later date, perhaps in a different context (Alberto & Troutman, 2003; Skinner, 1953). Finally, some responses may be particularly resistant to extinction because they have previously been reinforced on an intermittent schedule. When responses cannot be extinguished for any of these reasons, other methods may be more useful.

Presenting Desired Consequences Noncontingently

As we have seen, children sometimes behave inappropriately to achieve certain desired results, perhaps to gain teacher attention or to escape frustrating tasks. In recent years, some researchers have found that presenting desired consequences noncontingently—for instance, giving attention at unpredictable times or providing regular breaks from difficult tasks—can lead to a decrease in inappropriate behavior (Coleman & Holmes, 1998; Hagopian, Crockett, van Stone, DeLeon, & Bowman, 2000; Ringdahl, Vollmer, Borrero, & Connell, 2001).[11] In this way, children gain the consequences they seek *without* having to act out to do so. The primary disadvantage of this approach, of course, is that children don't necessarily learn more appropriate behaviors to replace the counterproductive ones.

Reinforcing Other Behaviors

As we noted earlier, the differential reinforcement of other behaviors—a DRO reinforcement schedule—is a procedure whereby an organism is reinforced for *not* exhibiting a particular behavior during a specified time interval. For example, when a teacher praises a student who manages to get through an entire recess without fighting with any of his classmates, that teacher is using a DRO schedule. The differential reinforcement of other behaviors tends to be a more effective and long-lasting technique than extinction (Uhl, 1973; Uhl & Garcia, 1969; Zeiler, 1971) and has been shown to be effective in reducing a variety of inappropriate classroom behaviors (Parrish, Cataldo, Kolko, Neef, & Egel, 1986; Pinkston, Reese, LeBlanc, & Baer, 1973; Repp, Barton, & Brulle, 1983; Repp & Deitz, 1974). Its major drawback is that we are not fussy about *which* other behaviors an individual exhibits, and some of them may be inappropriate. The next strategy—reinforcing of incompatible behaviors—gets around this problem.

Reinforcing Incompatible Behaviors

We have previously encountered the use of incompatible responses in the discussions of counterconditioning and breaking habits in Chapter 3. Within the operant conditioning model, the notion of incompatibility is equally useful. The first step is to identify a response that is incompatible with the undesirable response—a response that cannot be performed at the same time as the undesirable response. That incompatible behavior is then reinforced. For example, a child's

[11]Theorists have used various terms for this approach, including *time-based schedule, noncontingent reinforcement,* and *noncontingent escape.*

inappropriate out-of-seat behavior may be reduced by reinforcing the child whenever he is sitting down. An aggressive student can be reinforced whenever she is interacting in a prosocial manner with her classmates. A tennis player who displays inappropriate emotional outbursts every time he misses a shot can be reinforced for keeping his frustration under control by standing still, taking several deep breaths, and then continuing to play (Allen, 1998). Krumboltz and Krumboltz (1972) have described how reinforcing an incompatible behavior was effective in handling the chronic litterbug at a junior high school: The student was put in charge of his school's antilitter campaign and given considerable recognition and praise for his efforts.

The reinforcement of incompatible behaviors sounds similar to the DRO schedule, but an important difference exists between the two methods. The DRO schedule involves reinforcing an individual simply for *not* making a particular response. Reinforcing incompatible behaviors involves reinforcing a *specific, opposite* response. Like a DRO schedule, it is typically more effective than extinction in eliminating undesirable behaviors (Allen, 1998; Lentz, 1988; Woods & Miltenberger, 1995; Zirpoli & Melloy, 2001).[12]

WHEN REINFORCEMENT DOESN'T WORK

The basic principle of operant conditioning—that a response increases in frequency when it is followed by reinforcement—has been used successfully in many different situations to change a wide variety of behaviors. When reinforcement doesn't work, the source of difficulty can often be traced to one of four circumstances:

- *The "reinforcer" isn't reinforcing.* A first-grade teacher once consulted me about one of her students, a boy so disruptive that he was only able to spend a half day in the classroom. In an effort to modify the disruptive behavior, the teacher had attached to the boy's desk a large sheet of heavy cardboard that was cut and painted to look like a clown, with a small red lightbulb for a nose. When the boy exhibited appropriate classroom behaviors, such as sitting quietly or attending to an assigned task, the teacher would push a button on a remote control that lit up the red nose. "I don't understand why his behavior isn't changing," she told me. "Maybe this clown isn't reinforcing to the boy," I suggested. "Nonsense!" exclaimed the teacher. "The clown has always worked with *other* children!"

One of the most common mistakes that teachers make in using operant conditioning techniques is to assume that certain consequences will be reinforcing for all students. Not everyone will work for the same reinforcers; a consequence that increases desired behaviors for one child may not increase such behaviors for another. For example, although most students find their teacher's praise reinforcing, some students do not (e.g., Pfiffner, Rosén, & O'Leary, 1985). Some students may be afraid of being labeled "teacher's pet," especially if they value the friendship of

---

[12]Reinforcing an incompatible behavior is sometimes referred to as a *differential reinforcement of incompatible behavior* (DRI) schedule (e.g., Allen, 1998). You may also see behaviorists refer to a *differential reinforcement of alternative behavior* (DRA) schedule (e.g., Lerman, Kelley, Vorndran, Kuhn, & LaRue, 2002; Vollmer, Roane, Ringdahl, & Marcus, 1999). The DRA approach, which can be quite effective, involves reinforcing one or more *specific* other behaviors (rather that *any* other behavior, as is true of the DRO schedule). However, the alternative behaviors are not necessarily incompatible with the behavior to be eliminated.

The "reinforcer" must be reinforcing.

peers who shun high achievers. Many Native American students, although they appreciate praise for group achievements, may feel uncomfortable when their own individual efforts are singled out as being noteworthy (Fuller, 2001).

How can teachers determine what events will be reinforcing for different students? One way is to ask the students' parents, or even the students themselves. Children don't always have a good sense of what consequences they are truly likely to work for, however (Northup, 2000), so perhaps a better approach is to observe them over a period of time to see what kinds of consequences seem to affect their behavior. The one thing *not* to do is guess.

We should note here that any single reinforcer won't necessarily maintain its reinforcing value indefinitely, especially if it is presented quite frequently (Bowman, Piazza, Fisher, Hagopian, & Kogan, 1997; Viken & McFall, 1994). For example, as much as you probably enjoy good food, you can only eat so much, and as much as you enjoy the praise of people you respect, constant praise gets tiresome after a while. It's certainly possible to get too much of a good thing. A strategy we'll discuss in Chapter 5—a token economy—offers one simple way to provide variety in the reinforcers offered.

• *Reinforcement isn't consistent.* Sometimes it is inconvenient to reinforce a behavior every time it occurs. But remember, continuous reinforcement brings about more rapid behavior change than intermittent reinforcement. If a student's behavior has been particularly disruptive and time consuming, a little extra time devoted *now* to the continuous reinforcement of appropriate behaviors, inconvenient as that may occasionally be, will probably save time in the long run.

• *An individual either loses too much or gains too little by changing a behavior.* Consider the teenager who shies away from teacher praise because his peer group doesn't approve of academic achievement. It may be that teacher praise *is* a reinforcer to this student, but he risks losing his status in the group if he is praised too frequently or profusely. Praise given privately, out of the earshot of peers, will probably be much more reinforcing than public praise in this case.

Sometimes the desired behavior simply requires too much effort to be worth the payoff (e.g., Friman & Poling, 1995). For example, people often recycle paper and aluminum cans when recycling containers are placed close at hand; they are much less likely to do so when they have to walk across the room or down the hall (Brothers, Krantz, & McClannahan, 1994; Ludwig, Gray, & Rowell, 1998). And consider the college student who estimates that she will have to study at least 20 hours a week to get an A in a history class. Although the A may be an effective reinforcer, it may not be worth the amount of time she will have to spend to earn it.

Consciously or otherwise, people may sometimes engage in a cost–benefit analysis when looking at the consequences of different behaviors (Eccles & Wigfield, 1985; Feather, 1982; Perry & Fisher, 2001). Although they may have learned that a certain response will be reinforced, they will nevertheless not respond in that way if they have too much to lose, or too little to gain, by doing so. For people to respond positively to reinforcement, it must be worth their while.

• *Shaping proceeds too quickly.* In many situations, encouraging a desirable behavior requires a process of *shaping* that behavior. Remember that shaping involves the reinforcement of a series of responses that more and more closely approximate the terminal behavior. Each response should be well learned before reinforcement proceeds to a closer approximation. If an attempt at shaping moves too quickly, such that each response is not well established before a more sophisticated one is expected, the reinforcement program will be ineffective in bringing about behavior change.

To illustrate, let's say that Ms. Garcia, a third-grade teacher, wants to reinforce Jack, an especially hyperactive student, for sitting quietly in his seat; her goal (the terminal behavior) is for him to sit quietly for 20 minutes. On the first morning of the intervention program, Jack sits quietly for one minute, and so Ms. Garcia reinforces him. She probably does *not* want to move on to a two-minute criterion after he has met the one-minute criterion only once. Instead, she should continue reinforcing Jack for one-minute "sits" until it is clear, from the frequency of his sitting behavior, that she can begin to expect that behavior for a longer period of time.

SKINNER ON EDUCATION

B. F. Skinner wrote prolifically on the weaknesses of schools from an operant conditioning perspective (e.g., Skinner, 1953, 1954, 1958, 1968, 1973). He contended that reinforcement in the classroom usually occurs inconsistently and too long after a desired response has occurred. Although "natural" reinforcers (e.g., the opportunity to control one's environment or the intrinsically rewarding value of the subject matter) can sometimes reinforce (and therefore increase) appropriate academic behaviors, in fact most classroom reinforcers are artificially imposed. A problem inherent in our educational system is that teachers must teach behaviors that will be useful to students in the *future* rather than in the present, so these behaviors are not likely to lead to the naturally positive consequences now that they might later on (e.g., although a student might find algebra useful when she becomes a mechanical engineer, she does not find it particularly useful in her current life). As a result, teachers resort to artificial reinforcers such as teacher approval, grades, stickers, or free time to foster academic achievement. These reinforcers are often ineffective, however, in part because their relationships to the responses that students make are often unclear.

In desperation, teachers often find themselves punishing *mis*behaviors, through such aversive consequences as displeasure, ridicule, and failing grades, rather than reinforcing appropriate responses; as Skinner puts it, teachers "induce students to learn by threatening them for not learning" (Skinner, 1968, p. 57). Not only is such aversive control of behavior ineffective, it may also encourage students to engage in behaviors that allow them to escape school tasks or avoid them altogether.

Skinner urged educators to focus on reinforcing student successes rather than on punishing student failures. He proposed a "technology of teaching" whereby instruction is individualized, complex verbal behaviors are gradually shaped, reinforcement for appropriate responses is consistent and immediate, and learned behaviors are maintained through intermittent reinforcement schedules. Skinner's suggestions for how operant conditioning might be successfully applied to classroom situations, and the suggestions of other psychologists and educators as well, are the subject of the next chapter.

SUMMARY

While observing cats in a puzzle box as part of his doctoral research, Edward Thorndike concluded that consequences producing satisfaction (rewards) increase the strength of responses and that consequences producing discomfort (punishment) weaken responses. In later years, Thorndike revised this *law of effect*, suggesting that a reward strengthens a response but that punishment does not necessarily weaken it.

Building on Thorndike's work, Skinner offered his basic principle of *operant conditioning*: Responses that are followed by reinforcement increase in frequency. For operant conditioning to occur, a reinforcer must follow immediately after a response and be contingent on that response. Operant conditioning is different from classical conditioning in at least three ways: (1) it occurs as a result of a response being followed by a reinforcing stimulus rather than as a result of two stimuli being paired, (2) it involves voluntary rather than involuntary responses, and (3) it is better described as an R→S relationship than as an S→R relationship.

The *free operant level*, or baseline, of a response is its frequency in the absence of reinforcement; the *terminal behavior* is the form and frequency of the desired response at the end of a reinforcement program. Even when a response–reinforcer sequence occurs by coincidence rather than by design, an increase in the frequency of that response may be observed (*superstitious behavior*). A response that has previously been reinforced but is no longer being reinforced tends to decrease in frequency to its baseline rate (*extinction*). Complex behaviors can be taught by reinforcing successive approximations to the desired terminal behavior (*shaping*) or by reinforcing an increasingly longer sequence of responses (*chaining*).

Reinforcement takes a variety of forms. A *primary reinforcer* is one that satisfies a built-in need, perhaps providing something essential for survival; a *secondary reinforcer* is one that becomes reinforcing through repeated association with another reinforcer. Whereas *positive reinforcement* involves the presentation of a (presumably pleasant) stimulus, *negative reinforcement* involves the removal of a (presumably aversive) stimulus; because negative reinforcement increases behavior just as positive reinforcement does, it is *not* a form of punishment. A reinforcer is not always a material object; for instance, it can also be a social event, a favorite activity, positive feedback, or an intrinsic feeling of satisfaction.

Timing, magnitude, appeal, and consistency of reinforcement affect the rate at which new behaviors are learned. Different schedules of reinforcement influence the frequency with which responses occur, as well as the rates at which those responses are acquired and extinguished.

Antecedent stimuli also affect the occurrence of a response. For example, when an organism has learned to respond in a certain way in the presence of one stimulus, it is likely to respond in the same way in the presence of other, similar stimuli *(stimulus generalization)*. However, if a particular response has been reinforced in the presence of one stimulus but not in the presence of another, the organism will exhibit the response only when the former stimulus is presented *(stimulus discrimination)*. Teachers can use a variety of antecedent stimuli, perhaps taking the form of *cues* or *setting events*, that encourage appropriate classroom behaviors.

Contemporary perspectives of operant conditioning differ somewhat from Skinner's original notions. For example, some theorists propose that behavior is better understood by looking beyond specific S–R relationships to a larger context and longer time frame. In addition, some current explanations of why operant conditioning takes place include a discussion of the cognitive factors that underlie conditioning. And many theorists now believe that

behavior may never be totally predictable—that human and nonhuman behavior is somewhat variable even when reinforcement histories and stimulus conditions remain constant.

In addition to punishment (which, according to many contemporary behaviorists, *does* lead to a response decrease), several reinforcement-based techniques—extinction, presenting desired consequences noncontingently, differentially reinforcing other behaviors, and reinforcing incompatible behaviors—serve as viable means of eliminating undesirable behaviors. Yet reinforcement is unlikely to be effective if the consequence isn't truly reinforcing or is presented infrequently, if the learner loses too much or gains too little by changing behavior, or if shaping proceeds too quickly. B. F. Skinner contended that, in classroom situations, appropriate behaviors are usually reinforced inconsistently and undesirable behaviors are often unintentionally reinforced.

CHAPTER 5

Applications of Operant Conditioning

Over the past 40 years, operant conditioning has had a significant influence on educational and therapeutic practices. Several educational innovations can be attributed either directly or indirectly to operant conditioning and its principles, including instructional objectives, programmed instruction, computer-assisted instruction, mastery learning, and applied behavior analysis. In this chapter, we will look at the basic components of these techniques and consider empirical evidence concerning their effectiveness. We will then address frequently expressed concerns regarding the use of reinforcement in the classroom.

INSTRUCTIONAL OBJECTIVES

In its 1947 report, the President's Commission on Higher Education described the primary goal of the U.S. educational system as "the full, rounded, and continuing development of the person" (cited in Dyer, 1967, p. 14). At first glance, this might seem to be a worthwhile and appropriate goal for education, but on closer inspection, the statement provides very little *specific* information regarding what an educated person should be like. The President's Commission report is a good example of "word magic": It sounds nice, but we eventually realize that we don't have a clue as to what the words really mean (Dyer, 1967). When we don't know exactly what our educational objectives are, we don't know what or how to teach, nor do we know whether instruction is effectively accomplishing its goals.

As we noted in the preceding chapter, a standard practice in using operant conditioning is to specify the terminal behavior in precise, observable terms before conditioning begins, thereby helping us develop appropriate methods of shaping the desired behavior and of determining when that behavior has been acquired. This principle of a priori specification of the terminal behavior in observable, measurable terms has been applied to classroom instruction in the form of instructional objectives. Initially, such objectives were often quite behavioral in nature.

Behavioral Objectives

Ideally, a **behavioral objective** has three components (Mager, 1962, 1984; Schloss & Smith, 1994). First, the outcome is stated in terms of an observable and measurable behavior. Consider this objective:

> The student will be aware of current events.

A student's "awareness" is not easily observable. The same objective can be stated in terms of one or more specific behaviors that a student should exhibit; consider this one as an example:

> The student will describe the major points of dissension between the Israelis and the Palestinians.

Some verbs (e.g., *understand*, *appreciate*, *know*, *be aware of*, *remember*) tell us little, if anything, about what students should actually be able to do, but others (e.g., *write*, *compute*, *list*, *describe*, *select*) clearly communicate observable responses. We can probably conceptualize almost any objective in behavioral terms if we think about the specific things people would have to do to convince someone that they had met the objective (Mager, 1972).

Second, a behavioral objective specifies the conditions under which the behavior should be exhibited. Sometimes we expect desired behaviors to occur in specific situations (stimulus conditions). For example, one of my objectives for my graduate course in educational assessment is as follows:

> The student will correctly compute test-retest reliability.

I do not expect students to memorize the formula for calculating test-retest reliability, however. Hence, there is a condition under which I expect the behavior to occur:

> Given the formula for a correlation coefficient, the student will correctly compute test-retest reliability.

Finally, the objective includes a criterion for judging the acceptable performance of the behavior. Many behaviors are not strictly right or wrong; instead, they vary on a continuum of relative "rightness" and "wrongness." In cases where right and wrong behaviors are not obvious, a behavioral objective should specify the criterion for acceptable performance, perhaps in terms of a certain percentage of correct answers, a certain time limit, or the degree of acceptable deviation from the correct response (Mager, 1962, 1984). Following are some examples to illustrate this point:

On weekly written spelling tests, the student will correctly spell at least 85% of the year's 500 spelling words.

Given a sheet of 100 addition problems involving the addition of two single-digit numbers, including all possible combinations of the digits 0 through 9, the student will correctly write the answers to these problems within five minutes.

Given the formula for a correlation coefficient, the student will correctly compute test-retest reliability, with differences from a computer-calculated coefficient being attributable to rounding-off errors.

The Current Perspective on Instructional Objectives

Behavioral objectives have frequently been criticized for focusing on concrete, picayune details rather than on more central, but probably more abstract, educational goals. Many lists of behavioral objectives emphasize behaviors that depend on the rote memorization of facts rather than on behaviors that reflect more complex and sophisticated learning (Trachtenberg, 1974); in other words, they focus on **lower-level skills** rather than **higher-level skills.** Such lower-level objectives may be prevalent simply because they are the easiest ones to conceptualize and write.

School personnel have many goals in mind for each classroom in any given year, and these goals typically encompass both lower-level and higher-level skills. Writing behavioral objectives that cover each and every goal can sometimes become a burdensome, if not impossible, task. As a result, many educators have proposed that a smaller number of general, nonbehavioral objectives provide a reasonable alternative (e.g., Dressel, 1977; Gronlund, 2000; Popham, 1995; Posner & Rudnitsky, 1986). But in such situations, it is helpful to list examples of behaviors that reflect each abstract objective. To illustrate, imagine that we want high school students to understand, evaluate, and critique the things that they read—an objective that certainly involves higher-level thinking skills. We might list behavioral manifestations of critical reading such as the following:

1. Distinguishes between main ideas and supporting details
2. Distinguishes between facts and opinions
3. Distinguishes between facts and inferences
4. Identifies cause–effect relations
5. Identifies errors in reasoning
6. Distinguishes between valid and invalid conclusions
7. Identifies assumptions underlying conclusions (Gronlund, 2000, p. 52; format adapted)

This is hardly an exhaustive list of what critical reading entails, but it does give us an idea of the terminal behaviors we want to see.

Formulating Different Levels of Objectives

Sometimes objectives that reflect basic knowledge and skills are appropriate. But in many circumstances, objectives reflecting relatively sophisticated levels of learning are desired, especially as students get older (e.g., see Cole, 1990). In such situations, **taxonomies** of objectives—the various behaviors we might want to see students demonstrate, often listed in order of increasing complexity—are helpful (e.g., see Bloom, Englehart, Furst, Hill, & Krathwohl, 1956; Harrow,

1. **Knowledge:** rote memorizing of information in a basically word-for-word fashion; for example, reciting definitions of terms or remembering lists of items.
2. **Comprehension:** translating information into one's own words; for example, rewording a definition or paraphrasing a rule.
3. **Application:** using information in a new situation; for example, applying mathematical principles to the solution of word problems or applying psychological theories of learning to educational practice.
4. **Analysis:** breaking information down into its constituent parts; for example, discovering the assumptions underlying a philosophical essay or identifying fallacies in a logical argument.
5. **Synthesis:** constructing something new by integrating several pieces of information; for example, developing a theory or presenting a logical defense for a particular point of view.
6. **Evaluation:** placing a value judgement on data; for example, critiquing a theory or determining the appropriateness of conclusions drawn from a research study.

Figure 5–1
Bloom's taxonomy of educational objectives.
(Bloom, Englehart, Furst, Hill, & Krathwohl, 1956)

1972; Krathwohl, Bloom, & Masia, 1964; Stiggins, 2001). One early and widely used example, Bloom's Taxonomy of Educational Objectives (Bloom et al., 1956), describes six general levels of knowing and using information—that is, six possible objectives in the **cognitive domain.** These six levels are summarized in Figure 5–1.

Bloom and his colleagues originally presented the six levels as a hierarchy, with each one depending on those preceding it in the list. Although the hierarchical nature of Bloom's cognitive domain is in doubt (L. W. Anderson et al., 2001; Furst, 1981; Krathwohl, 1994; Seddon, 1978), the taxonomy nevertheless provides a useful reminder that instructional objectives should often encompass higher-level cognitive skills as well as the knowledge of simple, discrete facts (Gronlund, 2000; Hastings, 1977; Popham, 1988). In Chapter 12, we'll look at a recent revision of Bloom's taxonomy that incorporates contemporary theoretical perspectives of learning and cognition.

Usefulness and Effectiveness of Objectives

Although educators have largely drifted away from identifying specific behavioral objectives, more general instructional objectives—perhaps labeled as *outcomes, standards, proficiencies, targets,* or *benchmarks*—continue to play a key role in curriculum design and assessment practices. From a teacher's perspective, instructional objectives serve several useful functions (Gronlund, 2000; Mager, 1962, 1984; Stiggins, 2001). First, specification of a lesson's objectives in precise terms helps a teacher choose the most effective method of teaching that lesson. For example, when teaching a unit on basic addition, a teacher might use flash cards if the objective is *knowledge* of number facts but should probably use word problems or real-life problem-solving activities if the objective is the *application* of those number facts. A second advantage is that objectives, especially when described in behavioral terms, are easily communicated from one teacher to another. For example, although teachers may differ in their perception of what "application of addition principles" means, they will be likely to interpret "correct solution of addition word problems" similarly. Finally, objectives facilitate the evaluation of both students and instructional programs: Student accomplishment and program effectiveness can be evaluated on the basis of whether manifestations of the desired behaviors are observed. From a student's perspective, instructional objectives have additional advantages: Students who are told what they should be able to do at the conclusion of instructional unit know what they must focus on, have tangible goals to strive for, and are better able to judge how successfully they have learned (Gronlund, 2000; McAshan, 1979; Stiggins, 2001).

Despite such potential benefits, research studies investigating the effectiveness of objectives for improving academic performance have yielded mixed results (Melton, 1978). Objectives tend to focus teachers' and students' attention toward certain information and skills (those things that are included in the objectives) and away from other subject matter (e.g., Slavin, 1990b). If the stated objectives encompass *everything* that students should learn, the use of objectives in the classroom will enhance learning. But if the objectives include only a portion of what the teacher deems to be important, while excluding other, equally important material, some critical information and skills are not as likely to be learned as completely as they might otherwise be. Basing major decisions on whether students achieve predetermined objectives (i.e., making decisions about promotion, graduation, teacher salaries, school funding, etc., based on students' scores on a single **high-stakes test**) exacerbates this problem. When teachers are held accountable for their students' performance on a particular test, many of them will understandably devote many class hours to the knowledge and skills that the test assesses, and students may focus their studying efforts on that same material (Darling-Hammond, 1991; Linn, 2000; Resnick & Resnick, 1996). The result is often that students perform at higher levels on the test *without* improving their achievement and abilities more generally (Amrein & Berliner, 2002).[1]

PROGRAMMED INSTRUCTION AND COMPUTER-ASSISTED INSTRUCTION

From the perspective of operant conditioning, reinforcement must occur immediately after a response to have a significant impact on that behavior. Yet many reinforcers of classroom learning are delayed by hours, days, or, in the case of a high school diploma or college degree, even years. To provide a means by which responses can be reinforced immediately, Skinner (1954) developed a technique most frequently known as **programmed instruction,** or **PI.** Initially, programmed instruction involved a "teaching machine," a box enclosing a long roll of printed material that a student could advance past a display window, exposing small portions of information successively and systematically. In the 1960s and 1970s, PI increasingly took the form of programmed textbooks and, eventually, computer-assisted instruction.

Regardless of its medium, programmed instruction consists of several standard features. First, the material to be learned is presented through a series of discrete segments, or **frames.** The first frame presents a new piece of information and poses a question about it. The student responds to the question and then turns to the next frame; that frame provides the correct answer

---

[1]In the United States, the No Child Left Behind Act of 2001 promises to increase the emphasis on high-stakes testing. As I write this fourth edition, we do not yet know how this legislation will affect students' overall academic achievement. The intent behind the legislation (i.e., to boost children's academic achievement, especially that of children from minority groups and low-income backgrounds) is certainly laudable. However, many experts fear that its focus on increasing test scores and accountability, rather than on supporting and rewarding effective instructional practice, will render it ineffective, possibly even detrimental. Time (and research) will tell.

to the question posed in the previous frame, presents more information, and asks another question. The student continues through the frames, encountering new information, responding to questions, and checking answers.

Intrinsic to programmed instruction are several concepts and principles based on operant conditioning, including the following:

1. *Active responding.* The student is required to make a response in each frame.
2. *Shaping.* Instruction begins with information that the student already knows. New information to be learned is broken into tiny pieces, and instruction proceeds through a gradual presentation of increasingly more difficult pieces. As the successive pieces are presented and questions of increasing difficulty are answered, the terminal behavior is gradually shaped.
3. *Immediate reinforcement.* Shaping proceeds so slowly that students virtually always make a correct response; in this way, they practice appropriate responses, not inappropriate ones, and so the probability of reinforcement is quite high.[2] Each correct answer is reinforced immediately in the form of feedback that it is correct.
4. *Individual differences in learning rate.* Programmed instruction is self-paced, allowing students to progress through an instructional unit at their own rate of speed.

Early programmed instruction involved a **linear program:** All students proceeded through exactly the same sequence of frames in exactly the same order. In 1961, Crowder and Martin introduced the **branching program,** which typically progresses in larger steps than a linear program (each frame presents more information), so that error rates in responding are somewhat higher. A student who responds incorrectly is directed to one or more "remedial" frames for further practice on that part of the lesson before being allowed to continue with new material.

The major advantage of a branching program is that it provides remedial instructional frames only for students who have difficulty with a particular concept; other students can move on to new information without having to spend time on practice they don't need. Unfortunately, however, a branching program can be cumbersome, at least in its textbook form. Students are referred to different frames, and often to different pages, for different responses, so progression through the program is rarely smooth. Fortunately, this drawback of the branching program was virtually eliminated by the advent of computer-assisted instruction.

Computer-assisted instruction, or **CAI,** is programmed instruction presented by means of a computer. It has several advantages not characteristic of paper-and-pencil forms of programmed instruction. First, branching programs can be used without having to instruct students to proceed to one frame or another; the computer automatically presents the appropriate frame for any response the student gives. Second, because of the graphics capabilities of computers (e.g., complex moving visual displays can be included in lessons), CAI can present information in a way that traditional programmed instruction cannot. Third, the computer can record and maintain ongoing data for each student, including information such as how far a student has progressed in the program, how often he or she is right and wrong, how quickly he or she responds, and so on.

---

[2]Skinner believed that making errors interferes with learning, in large part because students practice incorrect responses. In contrast, many cognitive theorists believe that errors can sometimes be helpful in that they encourage students to examine and reevaluate their reasoning and problem-solving strategies (e.g., see the discussion of conceptual change in Chapter 13).

With such data, a teacher can monitor each student's progress through the program and identify students who are having unusual difficulty with the material. And, finally, a computer can be used to provide instruction when flesh-and-blood teachers are not available; for example, CAI has been used to deliver college instruction in rural areas far removed from university settings.

Effectiveness of PI and CAI

Most research indicates that traditional (i.e., noncomputer-based) programmed instruction provides little if any advantage over traditional instructional methods (Kulik, Cohen, & Ebeling, 1980; Kulik, Schwalb, & Kulik, 1982). In contrast, CAI can sometimes lead to greater academic achievement and improved student attitudes toward schoolwork, at least in comparison with traditional instructional methods (Blok, Oostdam, Otter, & Overmaat, 2002; Christmann, Badgett, & Lucking, 1997; Fletcher-Flinn & Gravatt, 1995; Hativa & Shorer, 1989; Kulik, Kulik, and Cohen, 1980; Lepper & Gurtner, 1989; Liao, 1992). However, the differences in achievement for CAI versus traditional methods are typically small or moderate, rather than large.

A cautionary note regarding the use of PI and CAI is in order. Some programmed instruction packages may be poorly conceived (Bell-Gredler, 1986; O'Leary & O'Leary, 1972); for example, they may not always adequately incorporate such principles as active responding, immediate reinforcement of responses, or gradual shaping of the terminal behavior. Generally speaking, PI and CAI are less likely to be effective when such principles of operant conditioning are violated (e.g., Kritch & Bostrow, 1998; Tudor, 1995), but exceptions have been noted. In one study of programmed instruction at the college level, occasional 10-second delays in feedback actually *enhanced* students' learning, apparently because the delays gave students more time to study the material in front of them (Crosbie & Kelly, 1994).

As cognitivism increasingly dominates theories of human learning, computer instruction is no longer restricted to the traditional, behaviorism-based CAI approach; hence, you may sometimes see reference to such terms as *computer-based instruction (CBI)* or *computer-assisted learning (CAL)* rather than CAI. Today's computer-based instruction encompasses a wide variety of innovations, including simulations that engage students in realistic activities (e.g., dissecting an animal, flying an airplane), "intelligent tutors" that diagnose and address specific problem areas, computer tools (e.g., word processing programs, spreadsheets, graphing programs, music composition software), and challenging problems and games. Later in the book, we will consider how computer technology has been used to promote complex problem-solving skills (Chapter 14) and to enhance group learning and meaning-making (Chapter 15).

MASTERY LEARNING

Inherent in the behaviorist perspective, and especially in the operant conditioning model, is the belief that, given appropriate environmental conditions (e.g., consistent reinforcement of desirable behaviors and gradual shaping of responses over time), people are capable of acquiring many complex behaviors. As an example of such optimism, you may remember John Watson's famous quote presented in Chapter 3: "Give me a dozen healthy infants, well-formed, and my own specified world to bring them up in and I'll guarantee to take any one at random and train him to become any type of specialist I might select. . . ."

The optimism of behaviorism is reflected in **mastery learning**—an approach to instruction in which students must learn one lesson well (they must *master* the content) before proceeding to the next lesson. Underlying this approach is the assumption that most students *can* learn school subject matter if they are given sufficient time and instruction to do so.

Mastery learning is based, in part, on the operant conditioning concept of *shaping*: At first, a relatively simple response is reinforced until it is emitted frequently (i.e., until it is mastered), then a slightly more difficult response is reinforced, and so on until eventually the desired terminal behavior is acquired. Consistent with shaping, mastery learning usually includes the following components:

1. *Small, discrete units.* Course content is broken up into a number of separate units or lessons, with each unit covering a small amount of material.
2. *A logical sequence.* Units are sequenced such that basic concepts and procedures— those that provide the foundation for later units—are learned first. More complex concepts and procedures, including those that build on basic units, are learned later. For example, a unit in which students learn what a fraction *is* would obviously come before a unit in which they learn how to add two fractions together. The process through which the component parts of course content are identified and sequenced, going from simpler to more complex, is called **task analysis.**
3. *Demonstration of mastery at the completion of each unit.* Before "graduating" from one unit to the next, students must show that they have mastered the current unit—for example, by taking a test on the content of that unit.
4. *A concrete, observable criterion for mastery of each unit.* Mastery of a topic is defined in specific, concrete terms. For example, to pass a unit on adding fractions with the same denominator, students might have to answer at least 90% of test items correctly.
5. *Additional remedial activities for students needing extra help or practice.* Students do not always demonstrate mastery on the first try. Additional support and resources—perhaps alternative approaches to instruction, different materials, workbooks, study groups, and individual tutoring—are provided for students who need them (e.g., Guskey, 1985).

Mastery learning gained prominence during the 1960s, and many educators still advocate it in one form or another (Block, 1980; Bloom, 1968, 1974, 1976, 1981, 1984; Boschee & Baron, 1993; Carroll, 1963, 1989; Guskey, 1985, 1994; Hunter, 1982; Keller, 1968; Lee & Pruitt, 1984). A particular form of mastery learning—Fred Keller's personalized system of instruction—has been used extensively at the college level. Let's take a closer look at what this approach entails.

Keller's Personalized System of Instruction (PSI)

As Michael (1974) has pointed out, traditional college instruction has definite weaknesses when viewed from the perspective of operant conditioning principles. For example, students may not learn what grades they've earned for their work until days or weeks after they've submitted the work; hence, achievement is not immediately reinforced. Furthermore, students must frequently proceed to advanced material before they have mastered the more basic information necessary to understand it.

To remedy such weaknesses, Keller (1968, 1974) developed the **personalized system of instruction** (also known as **PSI** or the **Keller Plan**) as an alternative approach to teaching college students. In addition to the discrete modules, logical sequence, and frequent measures of mastery characteristic of other mastery learning approaches, PSI encompasses the following features:

1. *Emphasis on individual study.* Most learning occurs through students' independent study of such written materials as textbooks and study guides. One-on-one tutoring provides additional assistance when necessary.
2. *Unit exams.* An examination on each module assesses students' mastery of the material. Students receive immediate feedback about how well they have performed on unit exams.
3. *Self-pacing.* Students report to class to take exams when they are ready to do so; in this sense, learning is self-paced. Some students proceed through the course very quickly, others more slowly. (Self-pacing is sometimes, but not always, a component of other mastery approaches as well.)
4. *Supplementary instructional techniques.* Traditional group instructional methods (e.g., lectures, demonstrations, and discussions) are occasionally provided to supplement the material that appears in the textbook or other assigned readings. These group classes are optional but serve to motivate and stimulate students.
5. *Use of proctors.* Proctors, usually more advanced students, administer and score exams and tutor students on topics with which they are having difficulty.

The teacher of a PSI course plays a different role from that of someone using a more conventional approach to instruction. The PSI teacher is less of a lecturer and more of a curriculum developer, exam writer, proctor coordinator, and record keeper. Rather than leading students through course content, the PSI teacher instead provides an elaborate system whereby students, with the assistance of study guides and tutors, find their own way through the content.

Effectiveness of Mastery Learning and PSI

Several reviews of research findings (Arlin, 1984; Block & Burns, 1976; Kulik, Kulik, & Bangert-Drowns, 1990; Kulik, Kulik, & Cohen, 1979; Shuell, 1996) indicate that mastery learning (including PSI) facilitates student learning and often leads to higher achievement than more traditional approaches (although note that Slavin [1987, 1990b] found no substantial differences). Furthermore, students in mastery learning programs often retain the things they have learned for longer periods of time (DuNann & Weber, 1976; Kulik et al., 1979); to illustrate, in one study, college students in mastery-based psychology classes remembered 75 to 85% of the material after 4 months and 70 to 80% after 11 months (Semb, Ellis, & Araujo, 1993). And PSI, at least, facilitates better study habits: Although PSI students don't appear to study more than other students, they study regularly rather than procrastinating and cramming the way students in traditional courses often do (Born & Davis, 1974; Kulik et al., 1979). Low-achieving students in particular seem to benefit from a mastery learning approach (DuNann & Weber, 1976; Kulik et al., 1990).

Mastery learning and PSI are not without their problems, however. In many cases, students who learn quickly receive less instruction than their classmates, raising a concern about possibly inequitable treatment of these students (Arlin, 1984). Furthermore, for logistical reasons, fast-learning students must sometimes wait until their slower classmates have also mastered the material before they can proceed to the next unit; as a result, they learn less than they might otherwise (Arlin, 1984). Yet when all students are allowed to work at their own pace, teachers must assist and keep track of perhaps 25 or 30 students working on different tasks and succeeding at different rates; hence, they may do more "managing" (e.g., distributing materials, grading tests) than actual teaching (Berliner, 1989; Prawat, 1992).

Additional weaknesses have been noted for PSI in particular. One difficulty lies in the required mastery of material; some students are unable to meet the criterion for passing exams, despite repeated assessments (Sussman, 1981). A second weakness is the lack of interaction among students—interaction that many students see as beneficial to their learning (Gasper, 1980). A third problem is related to the self-paced nature of a PSI course, which is sometimes compromised if university policy requires that students complete a course within one quarter or semester (Sussman, 1981). Poorly motivated students are likely to procrastinate until finally they must withdraw from the course (Sussman, 1981; Swenson, 1980). Although, in general, withdrawal rates for PSI courses are not appreciably higher than those for traditional courses, they can be quite high if students take the course entirely on-line, without ever seeing a classroom or fellow classmates (Kulik et al., 1979, 1990; Pear & Crone-Todd, 1999). Several techniques have been shown to reduce procrastination and withdrawal from PSI, among them setting target dates for the completion of different modules (Reiser & Sullivan, 1977), giving bonus points for early completion of modules (Bufford, 1976), and eliminating the necessity for completing the course within a single college term (Sussman, 1981).

Mastery learning is probably most appropriately used when a teacher's main objective is for students to learn specific skills or a specific body of information prerequisite to later topics. In such situations, the immediate feedback and emphasis on mastery of course material may well be reasons why mastery learning increases student achievement, especially for low-achieving students. When the objective is something other than acquiring information or skills, however—for example, when the objective is for students to gain a better understanding of controversial issues or to work cooperatively with classmates to solve complex problems—a mastery approach may not be the method of choice.

APPLIED BEHAVIOR ANALYSIS

Applied behavior analysis (ABA), sometimes called *behavior modification*, *behavior therapy*, or *contingency management*, is probably the most straightforward application of operant conditioning principles. Based on the assumption that behavior problems are the result of past and present environmental circumstances, applied behavior analysis encompasses a number of procedures whereby an individual's present environment is modified to promote the reinforcement of acceptable behaviors and the nonreinforcement of inappropriate ones. Central to ABA techniques are such operant conditioning concepts as reinforcement, extinction, shaping, stimulus control, and the reinforcement of incompatible behaviors. The concepts of punishment and modeling, though not components of Skinner's model of operant conditioning, are also frequently used in ABA interventions; these two aspects of ABA will be addressed in Chapters 6 and 7, respectively.

Components of Applied Behavior Analysis

Although ABA encompasses a number of different techniques, several strategies are common to many of them:

Antecedent		Peer teased him			None observed	Peer hit him	
Target behavior (hitting)	no	yes	no	no	yes	yes	no
Consequence		scolded			scolded	none	
	9:00	9:02	9:04	9:06	9:08	9:10	9:15

(Times indicate start of each 2-minute interval)

Figure 5–2
A time sample of target behaviors in conjunction with antecedent and consequent events.

- *Both the present behaviors and the desired behaviors are specified in observable, measurable terms.* Consistent with behaviorist tradition, teachers and therapists who use ABA focus their attention on specific, concrete responses. The actual behaviors to be increased or decreased are often called **target behaviors**. For example, in a program designed to decrease a child's aggressiveness, such target behaviors as screaming, hitting other people, and throwing objects might be identified (Morris, 1985).

- *Behavior is measured both before and during the intervention.* Only through objective measurement of the target behavior during both baseline and intervention can we determine whether a particular ABA procedure is effectively changing a target behavior. One way of measuring the target behavior is simply to count the overall *frequency* of a given response; for example, if we have designed a program to modify Johnny's hitting-others behavior, we would count each instance of hitting. A second method of behavior measurement is to examine the *rate* of responding by counting the number of responses occurring within a specified time interval; for example, we might count the number of times Johnny hits in each hour of the day. Still a third method, called **time-sampling,** involves dividing the time period during which the individual is being observed into equal intervals and then checking whether the target behavior occurred in each interval. For example, we might measure Johnny's hitting behavior by dividing his school day into five-minute intervals and then counting the intervals in which hitting was observed.

Behaviorists urge that target behaviors be observed and recorded as objectively as possible. Ideally, they recommend that one person (e.g., a teacher or therapist) administer the ABA intervention and at least two other individuals trained in observation techniques observe and record occurrences of the target behavior. If the method of behavior measurement is such that the behavior is being objectively and accurately recorded, the agreement between the recordings of the two observers (the **interrater reliability**) should be very high.

- *Environmental conditions that may be encouraging problem behaviors are identified.* It is often helpful to collect information not only about target behaviors but also about events that immediately precede and follow the behaviors. A teacher or therapist typically takes an *ABC* approach, observing the individual in his or her daily environment and collecting ongoing information about the following:

Figure 5–3
Frequency of Jeb's ear-covering responses under various antecedent and consequent conditions.
Reprinted with permission from "Functional Analysis of Stereotypical Ear Covering in a Child with Autism" by J.-C. Tang, C. H. Kennedy, A. Koppekin, & Mary Caruso, 2002, *Journal of Applied Behavior Analysis, 35*, p. 96. Copyright 2002 by the Society for the Experimental Analysis of Behavior, Inc.

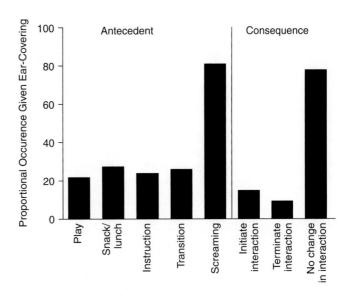

- **A**ntecedents: stimuli and events that the individual encounters
- **B**ehaviors: responses that the individual subsequently makes
- **C**onsequences: stimuli and events that immediately follow the behaviors

Figure 5–2 illustrates a short time sample of Johnny's hitting responses, with events antecedent and consequent to those responses also recorded.

Once such information is collected, the teacher or therapist looks for patterns in the data and identifies specific events that may be triggering or reinforcing a target behavior—an approach known as **functional analysis.**[3] As an example, consider Jeb, a 5-year-old boy with autism. Jeb's teachers reported that he spent a great deal of each school day covering his ears. Researchers Tang, Kennedy, Koppekin, and Caruso (2002) set out to determine why ear-covering behavior was so frequent. At 30-second intervals, they recorded (1) each occurrence of ear covering, (2) specific events occurring at the time (i.e., whether the response occurred during playtime, snack or lunch, instruction, and transition between activities, and whether another child was screaming), and (3) teacher behavior following each response (i.e., whether a teacher began, stopped, or continued interacting with Jeb). Figure 5–3 shows the frequency with which the ear-covering behavior occurred under various antecedent and consequent conditions. As you can see, the teachers did not change their behavior toward Jeb when he covered his ears, and so they were apparently not reinforcing the target behavior. A look at the antecedent stimuli is more enlightening: Eighty percent of the ear-covering incidents occurred immediately after a classmate screamed. Quite possibly, Jeb had heightened sensitivity to loud noises, a characteristic seen in many children with autism (Sullivan, 1994; Williams, 1996).

---

[3]In some functional analyses, the teacher or therapist systematically *manipulates* the environment as a way of testing various hypotheses about influential antecedent stimuli and consequences (Iwata, Dorsey, Slifer, Bauman, & Richman, 1982/1994; Van Camp et al., 2000). For examples of this approach, see Jones, Drew, and Weber (2000); Ellington et al. (2000); Magee and Ellis (2000); K. Meyer (1999); Mueller, Sterling-Turner, & Scattone (2001); and Piazza et al. (1999).

• *A specific intervention or treatment plan is developed.* Developing a treatment plan involves determining the method by which the target behavior is to be modified. Sometimes a behavior's frequency can be increased simply by reinforcing the behavior every time it occurs. When the free operant level (baseline) of a desired response is very low, however, the response may have to be shaped through the reinforcement of successively closer and closer approximations. An undesirable behavior can be eliminated through such methods as extinction, the differential reinforcement of other behaviors (a DRO schedule), the reinforcement of incompatible behaviors, or stimulus control (i.e., limiting the situations in which the behavior is allowed).

As we noted in the preceding chapter, we should never assume that particular consequences will be reinforcing to particular learners. Instead, we can identify one or more reinforcers that are likely to change learners' behaviors by observing what they will work for (e.g., through a functional analysis) or perhaps by asking them outright. When an ABA program is instituted in a school setting, social reinforcers (such as praise) or activity reinforcers (such as special privileges or the opportunity to spend time with a favorite classmate) are often effective (Bates, 1979; Brophy, 1981; Northup et al., 1995; Piersel, 1987). In some cases, immediate feedback that a student has done something correctly is all the reinforcement a student needs, especially when it is not otherwise clear that the student has been successful (Bangert-Drowns, Kulik, Kulik, & Morgan, 1991; Harris & Rosenthal, 1985; Kulik & Kulik, 1988). If material reinforcers are called for (primarily because other reinforcers don't work), having parents provide those reinforcers at home for behaviors exhibited at school often works quite well (Barth, 1979; Kelley & Carper, 1988; Miller & Kelley, 1994; Wielkiewicz, 1986).

In many cases, explicit instruction is part of the intervention as well (e.g., Craft et al., 1998; Heck, Collins, & Peterson, 2001). For example, imagine that a few students have been engaging in off-task behaviors as a way of gaining their teacher's attention. These students might be taught strategies for getting attention for *on*-task behavior instead, perhaps by (1) raising their hands or approaching the teacher's desk; (2) waiting quietly until the teacher acknowledges them; and (3) requesting feedback through such questions and comments as "How am I doing?" "I don't understand this," and "Look, I'm all finished!" (Craft et al., 1998, p. 402).

• *When appropriate, the individual is involved in treatment planning.* In some instances, a teacher and student develop a **contingency contract**, an agreement that specifies certain expectations for the student (the terminal behavior) and the consequences of the student's meeting those expectations (the reinforcer). For example, a student and teacher may agree that the student should turn in all homework assignments, on time and with at least 80% accuracy, every day for a week. If the student accomplishes this task, the contract might specify that the student will have some time to engage in a favorite activity, or that the teacher and student will spend time after school studying a topic of particular interest to the student. Although a contingency contract can be as simple as a verbal agreement, more often it is an actual written contract. The student and teacher negotiate the conditions of the contract in one or more meetings, and then both of them sign and date the contract. Ideally, initial contracts require small tasks that a student can accomplish within a short period of time, and both the desired behavior and the reinforcer are specified in precise, concrete terms (Homme, Csanyi, Gonzales, & Rechs, 1970; Walker & Shea, 1995).

A contingency contract can be used to encourage academic achievement; it can also be used to modify classroom behavior. For example, when a teacher and student develop a contract specifying that certain behaviors will lead to desired consequences, the contract might help the student to spend more class time attending to assigned work or to engage in more prosocial behaviors on the playground. Contingency contracting has been shown to be effective for addressing such diverse problems as poor study habits (Brooke & Ruthren, 1984; Miller & Kelley, 1994), juvenile delinquency (Rueger & Liberman, 1984; Welch, 1985), and drug addiction (Anker & Crowley, 1982; Crowley, 1984; Rueger & Liberman, 1984).[4]

• *The treatment is monitored for effectiveness as it progresses, and it is modified if necessary.* When a desired behavior increases or an unwanted behavior decreases during the intervention program (compared with the baseline rate), the logical conclusion is that the ABA program is effective. When little change is observed from baseline to treatment, however, a modification of the program is warranted. Perhaps the teacher or therapist is trying to shape behavior too quickly. Perhaps the "reinforcer" is not really reinforcing, and a different reinforcer should be substituted. Perhaps an undesired behavior that the teacher or therapist is attempting to eliminate through extinction is being maintained by reinforcers beyond his or her control. An unsuccessful intervention program should be carefully examined for these and other possible explanations for its ineffectiveness and then modified accordingly.

• *Measures are taken to promote generalization of newly acquired behaviors.* Although people often generalize the responses they learn in one situation to other situations (e.g., R.V. Hall, Cristler, Cranston, & Tucker, 1970; Walker, Mattsen, & Buckley, 1971), there is no guarantee that they will do so. In fact, many ABA programs have limited success precisely because responses that are learned under some stimulus conditions do not generalize to others (Alberto & Troutman, 2003; Hughes, 1988; Schloss & Smith, 1994). Psychologists have suggested several strategies for promoting generalization during an ABA program:

  • Teach the desired behavior in a wide variety of contexts, including many realistic ones; if possible, teach the behavior in the actual situations in which it is ultimately desired (Anderson-Inman, Walker, & Purcell, 1984; Emshoff, Redd, & Davidson, 1976; R. V. Hall et al., 1970; Haring & Liberty, 1990; Stokes & Baer, 1977).
  • Teach many different versions of the behavior; for example, when teaching interpersonal skills, teach a variety of ways to interact appropriately with others (Stokes & Baer, 1977).
  • Teach the relationship of the desired behavior to reinforcers that occur naturally in the environment; for example, point out that better personal hygiene leads to positive attention from others (Bourbeau, Sowers, & Close, 1986; Stokes & Baer, 1977).
  • Reinforce the behavior when it spontaneously occurs in new situations; in other words, specifically reinforce generalization (Stokes & Baer, 1977).

• *Treatment is phased out after the desired behavior is acquired.* Once the terminal behavior has been reached, the ABA program is gradually phased out. In many instances, the newly learned behaviors begin to have their own rewards; for example, the aggressive student who learns more acceptable social behaviors begins to acquire new friends, and the student who has finally learned to read begins to feel successful and enjoy reading. In other situations, maintaining the target behavior may require intermittent reinforcement, such as a series of successively higher variable-ratio reinforcement schedules.

---

[4]Because a contingency contract enables learners to have a say in their treatment plans, it should enhance their *sense of self-determination* and so increase the likelihood that they will change their behaviors. We will examine the nature and effects of self-determination in Chapter 17.

Using Applied Behavior Analysis With Large Groups

Our emphasis until now has been on the use of applied behavior analysis with individuals. But ABA techniques can also be used to change the behavior of *groups* of people—for example, the behavior of an entire class of students. Two methods are particularly effective in working with groups: a group contingency and a token economy.

Group Contingency

In a **group contingency,** the entire group must perform a desired behavior in order for reinforcement to occur. For example, in one study (Lovitt, Guppy, & Blattner, 1969) the performance of a class of 32 fourth graders on their weekly spelling tests improved with a group contingency. In phase 1 of the study, baseline data indicated that about 12 students (38%) had perfect spelling tests in any given week. In phase 2, spelling tests were administered each of four days during the week; any student who obtained a perfect test score one day was given free time on any successive days that the same test was repeated. During this individually based contingency period, the average number of perfect spelling tests a week more than doubled to 25.5 (80%). In phase 3, the individual contingencies of phase 2 continued to apply; in addition, when the entire class achieved perfect spelling tests by Friday, the class was permitted to listen to the radio for 15 minutes. The group contingency of phase 3 led to 30 perfect spelling tests (94% of the class) a week!

The "good behavior game" is an example of how a group contingency can reduce classroom misbehaviors. In research conducted by Barrish, Saunders, and Wolf (1969), a class of particularly unruly fourth graders (seven of the students had repeatedly been referred to the principal for problem behaviors) was divided into two teams whose behaviors were carefully observed during reading and mathematics lessons. Every time a team member engaged in out-of-seat or talking-out behavior, that team received a mark on its designated part of the chalkboard. The team that had fewer marks during the lesson received special privileges (e.g., first in the lunch line or free time at the end of the day); if both teams had five marks or fewer, both won privileges.

Figure 5–4 shows the results of Barrish and colleagues' study. Notice how baseline data were first collected for both math and reading periods. The good behavior game was instituted in the mathematics period on day 23; out-of-seat and talking-out behaviors decreased sharply during math instruction while continuing at a high frequency during reading. On day 45, the game was initiated during reading instruction and stopped during math instruction; notice how the frequencies of misbehaviors changed accordingly. On day 51, the game was reinstated in the math period, and again the misbehavior decreased to a low level in that class. By the way, collecting data from two different situations (**multiple baseline** data) and switching from reinforcement to nonreinforcement and then back again (a technique called **reversal**) are common techniques in ABA research for ruling out coincidence as the reason for observed behavior changes.

Numerous other studies support the effectiveness of group contingencies, particularly when they are used within the context of cooperative learning activities (Barbetta, 1990; Johnson & Johnson, 1987; Pigott, Fantuzzo, & Clement, 1986; Slavin, 1983a, 1983b). Peer pressure and social reinforcement are clearly among the reasons that group contingencies are effective (O'Leary & O'Leary, 1972; Swenson, 1980). Misbehaving students are encouraged by other students to change their behaviors and are frequently praised when those changes occur (Johnson & Johnson, 1987; Slavin, 1983b). In addition, when increased academic achievement is the desired behavior, high-achieving students often assist their lower-achieving classmates by tutoring and providing extra practice in the subject matter (Bronfenbrenner, 1970; Johnson & Johnson, 1987; Pigott et al., 1986).

Figure 5–4

Percentage of one-minute intervals in which talking-out and out-of-seat behaviors occurred during math and reading periods. From "Good Behavior Game: Effects of Individual Contingencies for Group Consequences on Disruptive Behavior in a Classroom" by H. H. Barrish, M. Saunders, & M. M. Wolf, 1969, *Journal of Applied Behavior Analysis, 2,* p. 122. Copyright 1969 by *Journal of Applied Behavior Analysis.* Reprinted by permission.

Token Economy

A **token economy**, undoubtedly the most prevalent ABA technique in group settings, involves a situation in which individuals who behave appropriately are reinforced with **tokens**—items that can later be traded in for **backup reinforcers,** which are objects or privileges of each individual's choice. For example, a teacher using a token economy in the classroom might reinforce students with one poker chip for each completed assignment. Just before lunch, students can use their poker chips to "buy" small treats, free time in the reading center, or a prime position in the lunch line. A token economy typically includes the following components:

1. *A set of rules* describing the responses that will be reinforced. The rules should be relatively few in number so that they can be remembered easily.
2. *Token reinforcers* that can be awarded immediately when appropriate behaviors are exhibited. Such items as poker chips, checkmarks on a grid sheet, play money, or points can be used. Even class grades have been successfully used as tokens (McKenzie, Clark, Wolf, Kothera, & Benson, 1968).
3. *A variety of backup reinforcers* (objects, activities, and privileges) for which tokens can be exchanged. Examples of backup reinforcers that have been shown to be effective in classroom token economies include free time (Osborne, 1969), participation in special events (Bushell, Wrobel, & Michaelis, 1968), and parent-awarded allowances (McKenzie et al., 1968).
4. *A "store" at which the backup reinforcers can be "purchased."* Young children should be allowed at least one purchase opportunity a day; for older children, one or two opportunities a week may be sufficient.

Token reinforcers are advantageous because teachers can use them to reward individual behaviors immediately and conveniently within a group setting. The fact that students can trade tokens for many different backup reinforcers is another advantage; every individual can probably find at least one desirable item. In fact, children and adults alike seem to prefer having some choice in the reinforcers for which they work (Bowman et al., 1997; Fisher & Mazur, 1997; Geckeler, Libby, Graff, & Ahearn, 2000). The tokens themselves often become effective reinforcers as well (Hundert, 1976). Perhaps they become secondary reinforcers through repeated association with other reinforcing objects and events, or perhaps they are effective simply because they provide feedback that students are doing something right.

Adding a Cognitive Component to ABA

In recent years, many practitioners have added a cognitive element to ABA techniques, using such terms as *cognitive behavior modification*, *cognitive behavior therapy*, or *cognitive-behavioral intervention* to describe their approaches (Elliott & Busse, 1991; Hughes, 1988; Robinson, Smith, Miller, & Brownell, 1999; Yell, Robinson, & Drasgow, 2001). In such approaches, the teacher or therapist frequently models the desired behavior, the assumption being that such modeling helps the student understand the particular behavior that is desired and thereby facilitates the learning process. Another common strategy is **coaching,** whereby the teacher or therapist verbally instructs and guides the student as the latter practices appropriate behaviors. Cognitive approaches also focus on problem solving; for example, the teacher or therapist might ask the student to think carefully about the effects that various behaviors may have in problem situations and to choose those behaviors that are likely to bring about desired consequences.

Effectiveness of ABA

Applied behavior analysis has often been shown to bring about behavior change, and it frequently works where other techniques fail (e.g., O'Leary & O'Leary, 1972). Numerous studies point to its effectiveness in improving academic performance and study habits (Braukmann, Ramp, & Wolf, 1981; Glover & Gary, 1976; Harris & Sherman, 1973; Iwata, 1987; Lovitt et al., 1969; McLaughlin

& Malaby, 1972; McLaughlin & Williams, 1988; McNamara, 1987; Piersel, 1987; Rapport & Bostow, 1976). It can also promote improvements in classroom attentiveness, social skills, and personal hygiene (Braukmann et al., 1981; Iwata, 1987; McLaughlin & Williams, 1988; Packard, 1970; Schloss & Smith, 1994; Taylor & Kratochwill, 1978). Furthermore, it can effectively reduce such undesirable behaviors as hyperactivity, impulsivity, aggression, and violence (Ayllon, Layman, & Kandel, 1975; Braukmann et al., 1981; Frankel & Simmons, 1985; Mayer & Butterworth, 1979; Northup et al., 1995; Plummer, Baer, & LeBlanc, 1977; Robinson, Smith, Miller & Brownell, 1999; Shafto & Sulzbacher, 1977; Wulbert & Dries, 1977).

Applied behavior analysis is particularly beneficial for students who must be continually motivated to engage in appropriate academic and social behaviors. It is therefore used frequently in the education and therapy of students with special needs, especially those with either learning difficulties or behavioral problems (Braukmann et al., 1981; Haring, Roger, Lee, Breen, & Gaylord-Ross, 1986; Hobbs & Holt, 1976; McLaughlin & Williams, 1988; Northup et al., 1995; O'Leary & Becker, 1967; Pfiffner & Barkley, 1998; Plummer et al., 1977; Witt, Elliott, & Gresham, 1988; Wolf, Braukmann, & Ramp, 1987).

Although we know that ABA techniques work, we don't always know just *why* they work. One likely factor underlying their effectiveness is the use of clearly specified response–reinforcement contingencies. Because desired behaviors are described in specific, concrete terms, learners know exactly what is expected of them. And the immediate feedback that learners receive through reinforcement provides them with clear guidance as to when their behaviors are on target and when they are not.

CRITICISMS OF USING REINFORCEMENT IN THE CLASSROOM

Although instructional techniques based on operant conditioning principles are clearly effective, these techniques are not without their critics. Some criticisms are probably ill founded, whereas others should be considered more seriously. We will first examine some of the common "bogus" complaints and then turn to more genuine concerns.

Bogus Complaints

Many criticisms directed toward the use of reinforcement in the classroom reflect either a misunderstanding of operant conditioning principles or an ignorance of empirical findings. Following are some typical examples of such criticisms:

• *Reinforcement is bribery.* The bribery argument is probably the most frequent complaint leveled against the use of reinforcement in the classroom. However, the word *bribery* implies that the behavior being reinforced is somehow illegal or unethical. On the contrary, the appropriate use of reinforcement in the classroom can facilitate the attainment of educational objectives, all of which involve academically and socially desirable behaviors.

• *Reinforcement develops dependence on concrete, external rewards for appropriate behavior.* Some critics propose that students should engage in learning simply for learning's sake; by

Reinforcement as bribery.

Pssst, kid! Want to learn to read?

reinforcing learning, they argue, teachers foster the expectation that students will always receive rewards for their accomplishments. This argument can be countered in two ways. First, ABA techniques do not necessarily involve material reinforcers. Social reinforcers, activities, feedback, and intrinsic reinforcers (e.g., feelings of success or accomplishment) are also effective in changing behavior, and the sensible teacher will use them instead of material reinforcers whenever possible.

Second, even when a teacher must use material reinforcers to change behavior, these reinforcers bring about desired changes that apparently *will not occur any other way*. Reinforcement is often used when more traditional methods of changing behavior have failed to increase important academic and social skills or to decrease counterproductive behaviors. If the choice comes down to teaching Mary to read by reinforcing her for reading or not teaching her to read at all, obviously Mary must learn to read using whatever means possible. We must remember, too, that when material reinforcers are used, social events (e.g., praise) that are paired with them should eventually become secondary reinforcers and so can be used instead.

• *Reinforcing one student for being good teaches other students to be bad.* "Hmmm," Leslie thinks. "Linda has been such a loudmouth the past few weeks that the teacher is now giving her raisins so she'll keep quiet. Maybe if I start shooting my mouth off, I'll start getting some raisins, too." If students are thinking along these lines, then something is clearly wrong with the way reinforcement is being administered in the classroom. All students should be reinforced for their appropriate behaviors. Praise and positive feedback should not be limited to a handful of chronic misbehavers but should be awarded consistently to all students. If the behavior of a particular student can be modified *only* with material reinforcers such as raisins, such reinforcement should be administered discretely and in private.

• *Changing a problem behavior does not change the underlying cause of that behavior, and so other behavioral manifestations of that underlying cause may appear.* Reflected in this criticism is Sigmund Freud's notion of *symptom substitution*: Problem behaviors are a function of deep-rooted psychological conflicts, so that when a behavior is eliminated without treatment of its underlying cause, another problem behavior will emerge in its place. The best rebuttal to the symptom substitution criticism is an empirical one: When problem behaviors are treated through applied behavior analysis, symptom substitution rarely occurs (e.g., Rimm & Masters, 1974).

One likely reason for this finding is that changing an individual's behavior may indirectly address its underlying causes as well. For example, consider the girl who is inappropriately aggressive on the playground. This girl might truly want to interact with her peers, but aggression is the only way she knows of initiating that interaction. Reinforcing the girl for more appropriate methods of social interaction not only helps her develop friendships but also addresses the underlying cause of her aggression—her desire for companionship.

Genuine Concerns

The bogus complaints just listed can be easily rebutted. Three major criticisms of operant conditioning techniques should be taken more seriously, however:

- *Attempts at changing behaviors ignore cognitive factors that may be interfering with learning.* When students are capable of learning a new skill but are not motivated to do so, the use of reinforcement may be all that is needed to bring about the desired behavior change. But when cognitive deficiencies (e.g., specific learning disabilities) exist that interfere with the acquisition of a new skill, reinforcement alone may be insufficient. In the latter situation, teachers may need to employ teaching techniques based more on cognitive learning theories—theories that we will explore in later chapters.

- *Reinforcement of some behaviors may interfere with maximal learning and performance over the long run.* Reinforcement for accomplishing a certain task focuses students' attention and effort more on getting that task done quickly, perhaps at a minimally acceptable level, than on *learning* from that task (Brophy, 1986; Clifford, 1990; Lepper & Hodell, 1989; McCaslin & Good, 1996). When teachers want their students to engage in complex, higher-level thinking—for example, to think flexibly and creatively about the subject matter—then extrinsic reinforcement simply for task accomplishment may sometimes be counterproductive (Brophy, 1986; Deci & Ryan, 1985; Hennessey & Amabile, 1987; Lepper & Hodell, 1989).

- *Extrinsic reinforcement of a behavior already motivated by intrinsic reinforcement may undermine the intrinsically reinforcing value of that behavior.* Individuals often engage in activities because of the intrinsic rewards—for example, pleasure or feelings of success—that those activities bring. A number of research studies indicate that enjoyable activities can be increased by extrinsic reinforcers but will then *decrease* to a below-baseline frequency once the extrinsic reinforcers are removed. For example, in one early study, preschool children who were promised a fancy "good player award" for drawing pictures were, later on, *less* likely to draw pictures in a free-play situation than either (a) children who were given a similar award but not told about it in advance or (b) children who were not reinforced for drawing pictures (Lepper, Greene, & Nisbett, 1973). Similar results have been obtained in a study with college students: Students who received a dollar for each correct solution of a series of block puzzles were less likely to continue to work at such puzzles in the absence of reinforcement than students who had not been paid for their correct solutions (Deci, 1971). Particularly when initial interest in an activity is high, when newly offered reinforcers are tangible (e.g., toys or money), when people know in advance that such reinforcers will be coming, and when simply doing the activity (rather than doing it *well*) is reinforced, intrinsic motivation to perform the activity is likely to be undermined (Cameron, 2001; Deci, Koestner, & Ryan, 2001). We will consider a possible explanation for such findings in our discussion of self-determination in Chapter 17.

WHEN OPERANT CONDITIONING TECHNIQUES ARE MOST APPROPRIATE

Instructional methods based on principles of operant conditioning are probably more appropriate for certain groups of students than for others. Among the students who appear to benefit the most from the structure and clearly specified response–reinforcement contingencies of operant conditioning techniques are students with a history of academic failure, poorly motivated students, anxious students, and students for whom nothing else works.

Frequent success experiences and reinforcements, such as those provided by mastery learning or programmed instruction, are particularly beneficial to students who have previously had little success in their academic careers (e.g., Gustafsson & Undheim, 1996; Snow, 1989). Children officially identified as having a "developmental delay" or "learning disability" fall into this category, as do many students with chronic behavior problems. A regular pattern of academic success is exactly what such students need to bolster the low self-confidence resulting from a long string of academic failures.

Students with little motivation to engage in academic tasks can also benefit from operant conditioning techniques. Although some students thrive on the feelings that academic success can bring, others do not value academic achievement. The introduction of extrinsic reinforcers (material, social, or activity reinforcers) contingent on academic accomplishments may be helpful in motivating seemingly "uninterested" students to master essential skills (Cameron, 2001; Covington, 1992; Lepper, 1981).

Highly anxious students appear to need structure in the classroom to perform well on academic tasks (Corno et al., 2002; Dowaliby & Schumer, 1973; Grimes & Allinsmith, 1961; Helmke, 1989). Such students need a classroom environment that specifies expectations for behavior and clearly lays out response–reinforcement contingencies. They also seem to require frequent success experiences and positive feedback. Many of the methods derived from operant conditioning principles address the needs of anxious children especially well: Instructional objectives spell out desired behaviors in concrete terms, programmed instruction and mastery learning provide success and positive feedback, and applied behavior analysis techniques clearly communicate which behaviors will yield the reinforcers the students seek.

Finally, there are some students for whom nothing else works. Techniques based on operant conditioning principles have been shown to be effective methods of changing even the most resilient of problem behaviors (Greer, 1983; Rimm & Masters, 1974). Such stubborn conditions as childhood autism and serious behavior disorders have been dealt with more successfully by applied behavior analysis than by any other method currently available.

Yet methods based on operant conditioning are probably not well suited for everyone. Bright students may find the gradual, inch-by-inch approach of programmed instruction slow and tedious. A token economy in a classroom of highly motivated college-bound students may undermine the intrinsic desire of these students to achieve at a high level. Other learning theories, notably cognitive theories, are probably more useful for helping these students learn.

SUMMARY

Instructional objectives, and especially behavioral objectives (which describe educational goals in terms of precise, observable responses), are a direct outgrowth of the concept of terminal behavior. Objectives facilitate communication among students and teachers; they also help in the selection of appropriate instructional strategies and evaluation techniques. Objectives tend to focus teachers' and students' attention on the information and skills they identify (an advantage) and away from other information and skills (a decided disadvantage if *all* important objectives have not been identified or are not being assessed).

Programmed instruction, *computer-assisted instruction*, and *mastery learning* incorporate such operant conditioning principles as active responding, shaping, and immediate reinforcement. In general, noncomputer-based programmed instruction appears to be no more effective than traditional instructional methods, whereas traditional computer-assisted instruction can have small to mo derate positive effects. Mastery learning is often superior to traditional instruction, especially for low-achieving students, and is most appropriate for teaching basic information and skills that are prerequisites for more advanced topics.

Applied behavior analysis (ABA) involves the planned, systematic use of behaviorist principles to encourage more productive behaviors. Typically, it involves precise measurement of target behaviors, manipulation of antecedent events and consequences (e.g., reinforcement, punishment) to change the frequency of various responses, ongoing monitoring of an intervention to ensure its effectiveness, and specific plans for generalization and phase out. Such mechanisms as contingency contracts and group contingencies allow teachers and therapists to use reinforcement effectively even in large-group settings. ABA techniques have been shown to improve a wide variety of academic and social behaviors, often in situations where other approaches have been unsuccessful.

Use of reinforcement in the classroom has drawn a number of criticisms; some reflect a misunderstanding of common behaviorist practices, but others are legitimate. Operant conditioning techniques are probably best used with certain kinds of students (e.g., those with high anxiety, poor motivation, or a history of academic failure) rather than as a matter of course with all students.

CHAPTER 6

Effects of Aversive Stimuli

I n our discussion of operant conditioning in Chapters 4 and 5, we focused on the role that desirable consequences (reinforcers) play in learning and behavior. In this chapter, we will consider the impact of *aversive* events on learning and behavior, with particular attention to three different situations. We will first examine how people and animals learn to escape and avoid unpleasant situations. We will then look at the effects of punishing consequences on learning and behavior. Finally, we will examine a phenomenon that occurs when people and animals are exposed to aversive stimuli that they can neither avoid nor escape—a phenomenon known as learned helplessness.

ESCAPE AND AVOIDANCE LEARNING

My former university in Colorado, like most other colleges and universities, had many faculty committees. When I first joined the faculty as an assistant professor, I eagerly agreed to serve on committees whenever I could, perceiving them to be a means of meeting other faculty members and having input into university decision making. Before long, however, I discovered that most faculty committees spent years chewing on the same old issues without ever arriving at consensus or otherwise accomplishing very much. Frustrated by the amount of time I was wasting, I soon found myself inventing excuses to leave committee meetings early ("I'm *so* sorry, but I have to take my son to the dentist."). Eventually, I stopped volunteering to join committees in the first place, thus avoiding them altogether.

    Committee meetings had become aversive events for me. My learning to make excuses so I could leave meetings early and then learning not to serve on committees at all is typical of what happens when an aversive stimulus is presented: Organisms learn to *escape* and eventually to *avoid* that stimulus if they possibly can.

Escape Learning

Escape learning is the process of acquiring a response that terminates an aversive stimulus. For example, in Neal Miller's (1948) classic study of escape learning, rats were placed in one compartment of a two-compartment cage and then given a series of electric shocks. The rats quickly learned to turn a wheel that enabled them to run to the other compartment, thereby escaping the aversive shocks. In an analogous study with humans (Hiroto, 1974), people readily learned to move a knob to turn off an unpleasantly loud noise.

Just as in the laboratory, students learn various ways of escaping unpleasant tasks or situations in the classroom and elsewhere. Making excuses ("My dog ate my homework!") and engaging in inappropriate classroom behaviors provide means of escaping tedious or frustrating academic assignments (e.g., Magee & Ellis, 2000; Taylor & Romanczyk, 1994). Lying about one's own behaviors ("I didn't do it—*he* did!") is potentially a way of escaping the playground supervisor's evil eye. Hypochondria, chronic truancy, and dropping out of school are ways of escaping the school environment altogether. Some escape responses are productive ones, of course; for instance, many teenagers acquire tactful ways of rebuffing unwanted sexual advances or leaving a party where alcohol or drugs are in abundance.

Because escape from an aversive stimulus terminates that stimulus, the escape response is *negatively reinforced*. When rats make a response that stops an electric shock, when children make a response that terminates the evil eye,[1] and when I make an excuse to leave a committee meeting, we are all reinforced by virtue of the fact that an unpleasant event is removed.

The more aversive a stimulus is, the more likely people are to learn to escape it (e.g., Piliavin, Dovidio, Gaertner, & Clark, 1981; Piliavin, Piliavin, & Rodin, 1975). For example, children who have particular difficulty with assignments are more likely to have dogs who allegedly eat their homework. And students who drop out before earning their high school diplomas are often those who have encountered repeated academic and social failure at school (e.g., Garnier, Stein, & Jacobs, 1997; Rumberger, 1995).

Avoidance Learning

Avoidance learning is the process of learning to stay away from an aversive stimulus altogether. For avoidance learning to occur, an organism must have some sort of **pre-aversive stimulus**, a cue signaling the advent of the aversive stimulus. For example, rats who hear a buzzer and are then given an electric shock (making the buzzer a pre-aversive stimulus) easily learn to jump a hurdle as soon as the buzzer sounds, thereby avoiding the painful shock (Mowrer, 1938, 1939). Similarly, children quickly learn to pull a brass handle as soon as a light flashes so that they can avoid an unpleasantly loud noise (Robinson & Robinson, 1961).

---

[1]The evil eye may remind you of The Look, described in Chapter 3's discussion of classical conditioning. Although some stimuli (e.g., those that cause physical pain) are naturally aversive, others (e.g., certain facial expressions) may become aversive over time through their association with other unpleasant stimuli—in other words, through classical conditioning.

Common escape and avoidance responses.

Avoidance learning appears in two forms: active avoidance learning and passive avoidance learning. In **active avoidance learning,** the organism must actively make a particular response to avoid an aversive event. To illustrate, studying behavior is, in many cases, an instance of active avoidance learning. Ideally, studying should be an enjoyable activity in its own right (thereby providing intrinsic reinforcement), but unfortunately many people do not enjoy it in the least (I, for example, would much rather read a mystery novel or watch a television game show). Yet by studying fairly frequently, most students are able to avoid an aversive stimulus—a failing grade. Consider how rarely studying behavior occurs when there is no signal of possible impending doom (i.e., no pre-aversive stimulus), such as an assigned research report or an upcoming exam.

In other situations, organisms learn that *not* making a particular response allows them to avoid an aversive event (e.g., Lewis & Maher, 1965; Seligman & Campbell, 1965); this form of learning is called **passive avoidance learning.** For example, people who feel awkward and uncomfortable in social situations tend not to go to parties or other social events. Likewise, students who have difficulty with mathematics rarely sign up for advanced math classes if they can help it.

What learning processes underlie avoidance learning? An early and widely cited theory of avoidance learning is Mowrer's two-factor theory (Mowrer, 1956; Mowrer & Lamoreaux, 1942). According to Mowrer's theory, avoidance learning is a two-step process that involves both classical conditioning and operant conditioning. In the first step, because the pre-aversive stimulus and the aversive stimulus are presented close together in time, the organism learns to fear the pre-aversive stimulus through a process of classical conditioning, as illustrated in Figure 6–1. In the second step, an avoidance response results in negative reinforcement because it leads to escape from the fear-inducing pre-aversive stimulus.

Figure 6–1
Learning to fear a pre-aversive stimulus through classical conditioning.

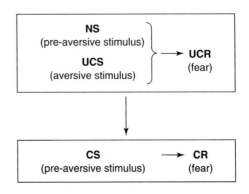

Logical as Mowrer's proposal may appear, research does not completely support it. For example, rats can learn to avoid an aversive stimulus even when they are unable to escape the pre-aversive stimulus (Kamin, 1956); this finding refutes Mowrer's notion that escape from the pre-aversive stimulus negatively reinforces the avoidance response. Furthermore, once an avoidance response has been well learned, organisms may exhibit little if any fear of the pre-aversive stimulus; thus, the avoidance response can no longer be negatively reinforced by a reduction of that fear (e.g., Kamin, Brimer, & Black, 1963).

Since Mowrer's time, several other theories of avoidance learning have been advanced (Bolles, 1975; D'Amato, 1970; Herrnstein, 1969; Seligman & Johnston, 1973). For example, some theorists postulate that the actual reinforcer of an avoidance response is a feeling of relief (D'Amato, 1970; Denny & Weisman, 1964). However, because avoidance behavior can occur in the absence of fear, other theorists (Bolles, 1975; Seligman & Johnston, 1973) have abandoned behaviorism for a cognitive explanation of avoidance learning: Organisms form *expectations* about what situations are aversive and what behaviors enable them to avoid those situations.

Extinguishing Avoidance Responses

Although there is disagreement about the best theoretical explanation of avoidance learning, there is general agreement about one thing: Avoidance responses are difficult to extinguish. When a previously aversive situation loses all sources of unpleasantness, organisms nevertheless continue to avoid it. For example, dogs will continue to escape from a box that has been previously associated with shock long after the shock has been eliminated (Solomon & Wynne, 1954).

One likely reason for the high resistance of avoidance responses to extinction is that when an organism avoids a formerly aversive situation, it has no opportunity to learn that the situation is no longer aversive. Let's consider students' avoidance of mathematics as an example. As I suggested in Chapter 3, mathematics anxiety may be a conditioned response acquired at a time when children are not cognitively ready to master abstract mathematical concepts. Students with math anxiety may avoid math classes indefinitely, even though they may eventually develop the cognitive maturity necessary for comprehending previously troublesome concepts. If students never again enroll in another math class, they will never learn that they have nothing to fear!

Many psychologists believe that the best way to get rid of an avoidance response is to extinguish the fear that leads to the avoidance behavior in the first place. One way of doing this is through *systematic desensitization,* a technique I mentioned in Chapter 3: Having someone relax while imagining a series of increasingly anxiety-arousing scenarios can reduce fear of certain situations, such as tests or public speaking engagements. Another approach is to prevent a person from making the avoidance response. By doing so, we create an occasion in which the person experiences the conditioned stimulus *without* the fear-eliciting unconditioned stimulus; thus, we encourage the extinction of a classically conditioned fear response. For example, a math-anxious student whom we know possesses adequate cognitive skills to succeed in mathematics might be required to enroll in a math class; once in class, the student can discover that mathematics is a rewarding experience rather than a frustrating one. In some circumstances, it is probably true that students don't always know what is best for them.

Undoubtedly, the best way to deal with both escape and avoidance behaviors in the classroom is to *prevent* such behaviors from being learned in the first place—something we can accomplish only by minimizing aversive classroom stimuli. For example, educators should have students' existing knowledge, skills, and cognitive maturity in mind when they develop instructional objectives, and they should then provide the resources and assistance that students need to accomplish those objectives successfully. When students achieve success at classroom tasks (a positive reinforcer), rather than experiencing frustration and failure at every turn, they are more likely to seek out those tasks than to avoid them.

In escape learning and avoidance learning, an organism makes a response that allows it to either terminate or avoid an aversive stimulus—a stimulus that, especially in the case of escape learning, is already present in the environment. But when an aversive stimulus occurs only *after* the organism makes a response, we have an instance of punishment instead. We turn to an examination of this phenomenon now.

PUNISHMENT

Punishment can take either of two forms. **Punishment I** is the more commonly recognized form; it involves the *presentation* of a stimulus, which decreases the strength of the response it follows. Typically, Punishment I involves the presentation of an aversive stimulus—for example, a spanking or a failing grade. **Punishment II** decreases the strength of a response by virtue of the *removal* of a stimulus, usually a pleasant one. Losing a privilege and being fined (in which case money is lost) are examples of Punishment II.[2] Punishment is a common occurrence in our daily lives; some theorists believe that even the *absence of reinforcement* can be punishing (we'll explore this idea in Chapter 7).

Views on the effectiveness of punishment have changed considerably over the past 60 years. Early research indicated that punishment was a very *ineffective* means of changing behavior. For example, Thorndike (1932b) found that, although positive feedback facilitated students' learning of correct responses, negative feedback did not reduce *incorrect* responses. Similarly, Skinner (1938) found that when rats were punished for a response that had previously been reinforced, the response was temporarily suppressed but soon returned to its prepunishment frequency. As a result, many early behaviorists discouraged the use of punishment.

Probably because of the negative views of punishment held by prominent learning theorists during the early decades of the twentieth century, punishment as a means of behavior control was largely ignored until the 1960s. Until that time, concern centered more on disadvantages than on any possible advantages of punishment. More recently, however, research evidence has emerged to indicate that punishment *can* be effective in certain situations.

In the following pages, we will explore the multifaceted topic of punishment. We will begin by examining punishment's numerous disadvantages. We will then look at evidence supporting the use of punishment as an effective means of behavior change and consider various theoretical explanations for its effects on behavior. Finally, we will discuss some guidelines for using punishment appropriately in classroom contexts.

---

[2]You may also see Punishment I referred to as *positive punishment* (because something is being added to the situation) or *presentation punishment*. You may also see Punishment II referred to as *negative punishment* (because something is being taken away from the situation) or *removal punishment*.

Disadvantages of Punishment

Over the years, psychologists have cited a number of disadvantages associated with the use of punishment:

- *A punished behavior is not eliminated; it is only suppressed.* Punishment *suppresses* a response: It makes the response less likely to occur. However, this suppression effect is often only temporary: The punished behavior may eventually reappear, perhaps when the punishment stops or when the punisher is absent (Appel & Peterson, 1965; Azrin, 1960; Griffore, 1981; Holz & Azrin, 1962; Skinner, 1938).

- *Punishment sometimes leads to an increase in the punished behavior.* In some cases, this effect may be due to the fact that the "punishment" is actually reinforcing. For example, a teacher's reprimands may be reinforcing to the girl who craves her teacher's attention or to the boy who wants to look "cool" in front of his classmates. Yet even in situations in which the punishment is truly punishing, it may nevertheless lead to an increase in the response that it follows. More specifically, when a behavior is punished in one situation, it may decrease in that situation but *increase* in a situation in which it has *not* been punished—a phenomenon known as **behavioral contrast** (e.g., Reynolds, 1975; Swenson, 1980). For example, some children who behave badly at school may be described by their parents as being little angels at home. Such children are possibly being held to strict behavioral rules on the home front, with severe punishment following any infractions; if so, they may engage in the forbidden behaviors at school, where they can do so with milder consequences.

- *The response–punishment contingency may not be recognized.* Punishment, particularly physical punishment, can distract an individual's attention away from the behavior that was punished. People are often less aware of the response that was punished than they are of the punishment itself (Maurer, 1974). Punishment is clearly ineffective if people do not know what they are being punished for.

- *Punishment often elicits undesirable emotional responses and may lead to escape and avoidance behaviors.* When punishment involves an especially aversive stimulus, the association of that stimulus with other stimuli (e.g., with the punisher or with the situation in which punishment occurred) can, through classical conditioning, lead to undesirable emotional responses to those other stimuli (Skinner, 1938). For example, when a teacher punishes a student at school, that punishment (the UCS) may be associated with the teacher, the task, or the classroom, any of which may then become conditioned stimuli (CSs) that elicit conditioned responses (CRs) such as fear and anxiety. In a similar manner, when an athletic coach continually yells at children for their poor performance during a game, negative attitudes toward the sport may result (Feltz, Chaase, Moritz, & Sullivan, 1999; Smith & Smoll, 1997).

    Furthermore, a stimulus that has become fear inducing because of its association with punishment may lead to escape or avoidance behavior (e.g., Redd, Morris, & Martin, 1975). Escape and avoidance responses at school take many forms, including inattention, cheating, lying, refusal to participate in classroom activities, and truancy (e.g., Becker, 1971; Magee & Ellis, 2000; Skinner, 1938; Taylor & Romanczyk, 1994).

- *Punishment may lead to aggression.* When punishment produces pain, it evokes emotional arousal in an individual—arousal that may result in anger and aggression, especially in people

Physical punishment models aggression.

already predisposed to making aggressive responses (Azrin, 1967; Berkowitz & LePage, 1967; Walters & Grusec, 1977). Aggressive behavior appears to reduce this emotional arousal and, more generally, to "feel good," the result being that aggression is reinforced (Bramel, Taub, & Blum, 1968; Hokanson & Burgess, 1962).

Furthermore, some forms of punishment provide a model of aggression, thus communicating the message that aggression is acceptable. I am reminded of the many hypocritical interactions I have witnessed in the grocery store. A mother yells, "How many times have I told you not to hit your sister?!" and then gives her child a solid whack. Children who observe others being aggressive are more likely to be aggressive themselves; we'll consider research on aggression and modeling in Chapter 7.

• *Punishment does not illustrate the correct behavior.* As Skinner (1938) pointed out, punishment tells an individual what *not* to do but not what should be done instead. Consider the boy who is consistently aggressive on the playground; perhaps aggression is the only way he knows of interacting with other children. Punishing this child for aggressive behavior without simultaneously teaching him more appropriate social skills does little to help him develop friendly relationships with classmates.

• *Severe punishment may cause physical or psychological harm.* Obviously, severe physical punishment can lead to bodily injury. Severe psychological punishment, such as extreme embarrassment or deflation of one's self-esteem, can be equally harmful. The mother of a college friend of mine constantly degraded my friend with such remarks as "How can you be so *stupid*!" and "Can't you ever do *anything* right?" Throughout our four years in college, my friend fought numerous bouts with depression and was in and out of mental institutions. The line between punishment and abuse is a thin and fuzzy one indeed.

Despite these many potential disadvantages, punishment *can* be an effective method of bringing about desired behavior change. In the next few pages, we'll look at some instances in which punishment *does* work. A bit later in the chapter, I'll offer some guidelines for using punishment that can help avert the disadvantages I have just listed.

Effectiveness of Punishment

Although early research cast doubt on the idea that punishment decreases the responses it follows, some researchers have found that punishment *can* successfully reduce or eliminate undesirable behaviors (Azrin & Holz, 1966; Dinsmoor, 1954, 1955; Rachlin, 1991; Tanner & Zeiler, 1975; Walters & Grusec, 1977). Punishment is often used when methods such as extinction, the differential reinforcement of other behaviors (DRO schedule), or the reinforcement of an incompatible response are ineffective or impractical; furthermore, it appears that punishment may sometimes be more effective than any of these other techniques (Boe & Church, 1967; Corte, Wolf, & Locke, 1971; Frankel & Simmons, 1985; Pfiffner & O'Leary, 1987; Walters & Grusec, 1977). Punishment is especially advised when a behavior might harm either oneself or others; in such cases, using punishment to eliminate such behavior rapidly may actually be the most humane course of action.

In a series of studies, R. Vance Hall and his colleagues (1971) demonstrated the speed with which punishment can bring about behavior change. For example, in one study, consistent punishment virtually eliminated the aggressive behavior of a seven-year-old deaf girl named Andrea. Initially, this girl pinched and bit both herself and anybody else with whom she came in contact; the frequency of such responses (an average of 72 per school day) was so high that normal academic instruction was impossible. Following a baseline period, punishment for each aggressive act began: Whenever Andrea pinched or bit, her teacher pointed at her sternly and shouted "No!" Figure 6–2 shows the changes in Andrea's behavior (the brief *reversal* to nonreinforcement for a few days was used to rule out coincidence as an explanation for the behavior changes). Even though Andrea was deaf, the shouting and pointing virtually eliminated her aggressiveness.

In a second study, Hall and his colleagues (1971) modified the whining and complaining behaviors of a boy named Billy. Billy frequently cried, whined, and complained of stomachaches whenever he was given a reading or arithmetic assignment, while apparently being quite happy and healthy the rest of the day. The treatment program consisted of giving Billy five slips of

Figure 6–2

Number of bites and pinches by Andrea during the school day. Reprinted with permission from "The Effective Use of Punishment to Modify Behavior in the Classroom" by R. V. Hall, S. Axelrod, M. Foundopoulos, J. Shellman, R. A. Campbell, & S. S. Cranston, 1972, in K. D. O'Leary & S. O'Leary (Eds.), *Classroom Management: The Successful Use of Behavior Modification*, p. 175. Copyright 1972 by Pergamon Press, Ltd.

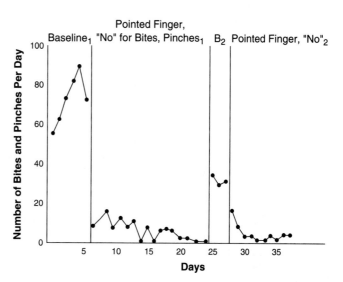

Figure 6–3

Frequency of Billy's cries (C), whines (W), and complaints (C_1) during reading and arithmetic periods.
Reprinted with permission from "The Effective Use of Punishment to Modify Behavior in the Classroom" by R. V. Hall, S. Axelrod, M. Foundopoulos, J. Shellman, R. A. Campbell, & S. S. Cranston, 1972, in K. D. O'Leary & S. O'Leary (Eds.), *Classroom Management: The Successful Use of Behavior Modification,* p. 177. Copyright 1972 by Pergamon Press, Ltd.

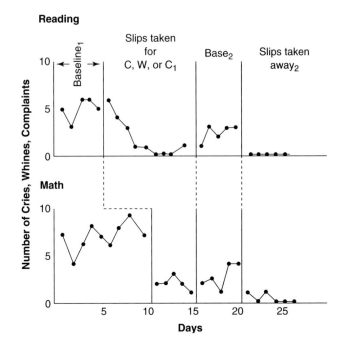

colored paper bearing his name at the beginning of reading and arithmetic periods every day and then removing one slip of paper (Punishment II) each time Billy cried, whined, or complained. Treatment was instituted on day 6 for Billy's reading period and on day 11 for his math period (this *multiple baseline* approach was used to rule out the coincidence factor). Figure 6–3 shows the effectiveness of such obviously mild punishment (note the temporary reversal to non-punished baseline similar to that shown in Figure 6–2).

In yet another study by Hall and his colleagues (1971), 3 tenth-grade students enrolled in a French class earned higher grades when after-school tutoring was the "punishment" for low grades. These students—Dave, Roy, and Debbie—had been consistently earning Ds and Fs on daily quizzes. Their teacher informed them that because they were obviously having difficulty with their French, they would have to come in for a half hour of tutoring after school whenever they received a grade lower than C. Quiz grades during baseline and during the time when poor quiz performance would be punished are shown in Figure 6–4 (note the multiple baseline approach once again). As you can see, none of the students ever needed to report for after-school tutoring. Apparently, the threat of punishment alone was sufficient to bring about desired study behaviors. Perhaps temporary removal of the threat—by studying for each quiz—was sufficient negative reinforcement to increase regular study habits.

What is unique about the studies by Hall and his colleagues is that none of the punishments could be construed as being either physically or psychologically harmful. Yet all of them—pointing and yelling "No," taking away colored slips of paper, and requiring after-school tutoring—were clearly effective in bringing about dramatic behavior changes in different students. But just why does punishment work? Let's explore some possible explanations.

Figure 6–4

Quiz grades for three high school French
class students.
Reprinted with permission from "The Effective
Use of Punishment to Modify Behavior in
the Classroom" by R. V. Hall, S. Axelrod,
M. Foundopoulos, J. Shellman, R. A. Campbell, &
S. S. Cranston, 1972, in K. D. O'Leary &
S. O'Leary (Eds.), *Classroom Management: The
Successful Use of Behavior Modification*, p. 180.
Copyright 1972 by Pergamon Press, Ltd.

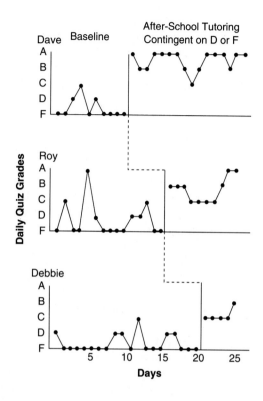

Theoretical Perspectives on Punishment

Several theories have been advanced to explain why punishment decreases the behavior that precedes it. Guthrie (1935) and Skinner (1953) offered two early theories based on the notion of
incompatibility: Punishment reduces a response only when it leads to a behavior (such as escape
from the situation) that is incompatible with the punished response. Thus, Guthrie and Skinner
argued that punishment affects the punished behavior indirectly (by bringing about a new
response) rather than directly. An alternative theory (Estes, 1969b; Walters & Grusec, 1977) is
also based on the notion of incompatibility, albeit the incompatibility of motives rather than
behaviors. According to this explanation, punishment leads to motives (e.g., fear) incompatible
with the motives that originally led to the behavior being punished. For example, when a rat that
has learned to press a bar to obtain food is then punished for pressing the bar, the fear induced
by the punishment may essentially lower the rat's appetite.

Mowrer (1960) proposed a two-stage theory of punishment similar to his theory of avoidance learning. First, when an organism is punished for a particular behavior, fear of the environment in which punishment occurred is established through a process of classical conditioning.
Second, escape from that environment is reinforced because such escape reduces that fear (negative reinforcement). Punishment is effective to the extent that the escape response is incompatible with the punished response. In contrast, Aronfreed (1968; Aronfreed & Reber, 1965)
proposed that anxiety is associated not with stimuli in the environment but with the initiation of
the punished response and perhaps also with the thoughts that precede the response; suppressing the response—*not* emitting it—is negatively reinforced by anxiety reduction.

Still other theorists (e.g., Azrin & Holz, 1966; Fantino, 1973; Rachlin, 1991; Rachlin & Herrnstein, 1969) have reverted to Thorndike's original law of effect and view punishment in the same way they view reinforcement—as a consequence that alters the frequency of future behaviors. Many of these researchers advocate an atheoretical approach to punishment; they focus more on the factors influencing the effectiveness of punishment than on the reasons underlying its effectiveness (Walters & Grusec, 1977).

Using Punishment in Classroom Settings

The use of punishment as a means of behavior control is widespread in both child-rearing and educational practice (Sears, Maccoby, & Levin, 1957; Straus, 2000a, 2000b; Wielkiewicz, 1986). One likely reason for the prevalence of punishment as a disciplinary measure is that, because it tends to decrease or eliminate an undesirable behavior fairly quickly, the punisher is *negatively reinforced:* By using punishment, he or she gets rid of an unwanted state of affairs.

Two particular forms of punishment—time-out and response cost—are frequently used in classroom situations. Both involve the withdrawal of reinforcers and so are examples of Punishment II. Three other types of punishment—verbal reprimands, restitution, and overcorrection—are also useful in some instances; these involve imposing unpleasant consequences and so are examples of Punishment I. Let's examine the evidence for each of these.

Time-Out

Time-out involves placing the misbehaving individual in an environment with no reinforcers—in other words, in a dull, boring situation. Often, this time-out environment is a separate room, furnished sparsely or not at all, in which the individual cannot interact with others. At other times, it may be a corner of the classroom screened from the rest of the room by partitions or tall furniture. In any event, the time-out environment should be neither reinforcing, as the hall or the principal's office is likely to be, nor frightening, as a dark closet might be (Walker & Shea, 1995; Wielkiewicz, 1986). Foxx and Shapiro (1978) have developed a procedure that easily incorporates time-out into a classroom context without requiring any special facilities. Students wear ribbons that make them eligible to participate in rewarding classroom activities. Students who misbehave remain in the classroom, but their ribbons are removed, making them ineligible to receive the reinforcers available to their classmates.

Time-out effectively reduces a variety of disruptive, aggressive, and dangerous behaviors (Frankel & Simmons, 1985; Lentz, 1988; Mace, Page, Ivancic, & O'Brien, 1986; MacPherson, Candee, & Hohman, 1974; Mathews, Friman, Barone, Ross, & Christophersen, 1987; Pfiffner & Barkley, 1998; Rortvedt & Miltenberger, 1994). Short time-outs that do not allow students to escape classroom tasks and so do not interfere with students' academic learning are often quite effective (Skiba & Raison, 1990); many psychologists argue that durations of 10 minutes (even as few as two minutes for preschool children) are sufficient. A key to using time-out effectively is that the inappropriate behavior must *stop* before the child is released from the time-out situation; release from time-out (a negative reinforcer) is therefore contingent on appropriate behavior.

Response Cost

Response cost involves the withdrawal of a previously earned reinforcer; a ticket for speeding (resulting in the payment of a fine) and the loss of previously earned privileges are examples. Response cost has been shown to reduce such misbehaviors as aggression, inappropriate speech, disruptiveness, hyperactivity, and tardiness (Iwata & Bailey, 1974; Kazdin, 1972; McLaughlin & Malaby, 1972; Rapport, Murphy, & Bailey, 1982) and appears to be particularly effective when combined with reinforcement of appropriate behavior (Phillips, Phillips, Fixsen, & Wolf, 1971).

Verbal Reprimand

Although some students find teacher attention of any kind to be reinforcing, most students regard a **verbal reprimand**—a scolding or admonishment—as punishment (O'Leary, Kaufman, Kass, & Drabman, 1970; Van Houten, Nau, MacKenzie-Keating, Sameoto, & Colavecchia, 1982). In addition to suppressing undesirable behavior, occasional reprimands also appear to enhance the positive reinforcement value of praise (Pfiffner & O'Leary, 1987).

Reprimands are often more effective when they are immediate, brief, and accompanied by eye contact (e.g., The Look) or a firm grip (Pfiffner & O'Leary, 1993; Van Houten et al., 1982). They may also be more effective when spoken quietly and in close proximity to the child being punished (O'Leary et al., 1970; Van Houten et al., 1982); such unobtrusive reprimands are less likely to attract the (potentially reinforcing) attention of other individuals in the room. Ideally, too, a reprimand should communicate that a student is capable of better performance (Parsons, Kaczala, & Meece, 1982; Pintrich & Schunk, 2002).

Restitution and Overcorrection

Restitution and overcorrection involve requiring people to take actions that correct the results of their misdeeds. In **restitution**, a misbehaving individual must return the environment to the same state of affairs that it was in prior to the misbehavior. As examples, a child who breaks a window must pay for a new one, and a child who makes a mess must clean it up. Restitution is a good example of a *logical consequence*, whereby the punishment fits the crime.

In the case of **restitutional overcorrection**, the punished individual must make things *better* than they were prior to the inappropriate behavior (Foxx & Azrin, 1973; Foxx & Bechtel, 1983; Rusch & Close, 1976). For example, a student who throws food in the lunchroom might be asked to mop the entire lunchroom floor, or the student who offends a classmate might be asked to apologize to the entire class.

Positive-practice overcorrection involves having an individual repeat an action, but this time doing it correctly, perhaps in an exaggerated fashion. For example, a student who runs dangerously down the school corridor might be asked to back up and then *walk* (perhaps at a normal pace, or perhaps very slowly) down the hall. Similarly, a student in a drivers' education class who neglects to stop at a stop sign might be asked to drive around the block, return to the same intersection, and come to a complete stop (perhaps counting aloud to five) before proceeding.

Practitioners have mixed views regarding the value of restitutional overcorrection and positive-practice overcorrection as methods of bringing about behavior improvement in school settings; in some cases, these techniques may be overly time consuming and draw unnecessary attention to the punished behavior (Schloss & Smith, 1994; Zirpoli & Melloy, 2001). When such approaches *are* used, however, teachers should portray them more as means for helping students acquire appropriate behavior than as punishment per se (Alberto & Troutman, 2003; Carey & Bucher, 1986; Zirpoli & Melloy, 2001).

The punishments I've just described appear to have fewer negative side effects than either physical punishment, such as spanking, or psychological punishment, such as withdrawal of love (Walters & Grusec, 1977). Yet teachers who use recommended forms of punishment to reduce inappropriate behavior must nevertheless monitor their effects on the behaviors being punished. For example, some individuals find time-out to be reinforcing rather than punishing (Alberto & Troutman, 2003; Solnick, Rincover, & Peterson, 1977), and so their "punished" behaviors will increase rather than diminish.

In Chapter 4, I discussed the importance of reinforcement as a means of providing feedback about what constitutes appropriate behavior. In much the same way, punishment is probably effective to the extent that it gives feedback about inappropriate behavior. Sometimes students are truly unaware of how frequently they misbehave (e.g., Krumboltz & Krumboltz, 1972), and the occasional punishment of inappropriate responses can provide reminders that keep these students on task. But how do we avoid such side effects as aggression, escape responses, and negative emotional reactions? Let's turn to some guidelines for using punishment in the classroom.

Guidelines for Using Punishment Effectively

Psychologists and educators have offered numerous suggestions on how to use punishment effectively, many of which decrease the chances of negative side effects. The guidelines that follow are among those most commonly cited:

• *The "punishment" must be punishing.* Punishment, like reinforcement, is defined by its effect on behavior: True punishment decreases the response it follows. If a given consequence does not decrease the response it is meant to punish, that consequence may not be aversive to the individual being "punished"; in fact, it may even be reinforcing.

Teachers and parents often make assumptions about what consequences will be punishing for children. For example, when my children were growing up, a common "punishment" around our house was to be sent to one's room. For my two sons, such a consequence was truly aversive because they would much rather socialize with the family in the kitchen or living room than be isolated in their rooms for any length of time. But when my daughter Tina was banished to her bedroom, she was probably being reinforced: She rearranged her furniture, listened to her radio, or settled under the covers with a good book. And the behaviors for which she was most often punished in this way—behaviors related in one way or another to annoying and teasing her brothers—seemed to increase rather than decrease.

Tina is "punished."

- *The punishment must be strong enough to be effective but not overly severe.* Punishment that is too short or mild is not effective (e.g., Parke & Walters, 1967). For example, fines for such behaviors as speeding and drunken driving are obviously insufficient deterrents for some individuals. Similarly, grades in many college classrooms may be too lenient to discourage a student from academically unproductive behaviors. A college teacher may believe that by giving some students Cs, she is in some way punishing those students for their lack of class attendance and poor exam performance. Yet a C average is quite acceptable at most institutions, so the students may not be sufficiently "punished" to reduce their frequency of party-going and Frisbee-throwing at times when they should be attending classes or reading their textbooks.

At the same time, punishment must not be overly severe, or it might lead to such undesirable side effects as resentment, hostility, aggression, or escape behavior. Furthermore, although severe punishment may quickly suppress a response, that response may reappear at its original level once the punisher has left the scene (Appel & Peterson, 1965; Azrin, 1960). The ultimate purpose of administering punishment is to communicate that the limits of acceptable behavior have been exceeded; it should not be so excessive that it undermines the personal relationship between the punisher and the person being punished (Spaulding, 1992).

- *Punishment should be threatened once before it is administered.* (My use of the term *threaten* here means only that people should be warned ahead of time, not that they should be intimidated.) Punishment is most likely to deter behavior when an individual *knows* that the behavior will lead to punishment (e.g., Aronfreed, 1968; also see Chapter 7). Therefore, people should know ahead of time that a particular behavior will be punished and what the punishment will be. I remember an incident, when I was about four years old, in which I was punished without warning. Sitting at lunch one day, apparently considering the old adage "Waste not, want not," I proceeded to lick a large quantity of peanut butter off my butter knife. An adult scolded me sternly for my behavior, and I was devastated. Being the Miss Goody Two-Shoes that I was at the time, I would never have engaged in knife-licking behavior if I had known it was an unacceptable response.

One common mistake many teachers and parents make is to continue to threaten punishment without ever following through. One threat is advisable, but repeated threats are not. The mother who continually says to her son, "If you hit your sister again, Tommy, I'll send you to your room for the rest of the week," but never sends Tommy to his room, is giving her son the message that no response–punishment contingency really exists.

One of the reasons that teachers and parents often fail to follow through with threatened punishment is that they too often *bluff*, proposing punishment that is impractical or unrealistically extreme. Tommy's mother does not punish her son because forcing Tommy to spend "the rest of the week" in his room would be a major inconvenience for both of them. A teacher who threatens that certain behaviors will result in students not going on a promised field trip should do so only if he or she knows that leaving some students behind at school is logistically possible.

- *The behavior to be punished should be described in clear, concrete terms.* Students should understand exactly which responses are unacceptable. A student who is told, "If you disrupt the class again this morning, you will lose your free time," may not understand exactly what the teacher means by "disrupt" and so may continue to engage in inappropriate classroom behavior. The teacher should instead take the student aside and say something like this: "Sharon, there are two behaviors that are unacceptable in this classroom. When you talk without permission and when you get out of your seat during quiet reading time, you keep other children from getting their work done. This morning I expect you to talk and get out of your seat only when I give you permission to do so. Otherwise, you will have to sit quietly at your desk this afternoon when the other children have their free time."

- *Punishment should be consistent.* Just as is true for reinforcement, punishment is much more effective when it is a consistent consequence of a particular response (Leff, 1969; Parke & Deur, 1972; Rachlin, 1991). When a response is punished only occasionally, with other occurrences of that response being either reinforced or ignored, the response disappears slowly, if at all. Consistent with this principle is the fact that many adolescents who exhibit serious behavior problems (e.g., getting in trouble with the law) come from home environments in which parental discipline has been administered inconsistently (Glueck & Glueck, 1950; McCord, McCord, & Zola, 1959).

Unfortunately, people can be punished only when they are caught in the act. Thieves are rarely apprehended, and speeders are ticketed only when they drive on roadways that are patrolled. Many undesirable classroom behaviors, such as talking out, getting out of one's seat, being aggressive, and cheating, may be reinforced as frequently as they are punished. To deal with the difficulty of detecting some undesirable student behaviors, the next two guidelines—changing the situation so the misbehavior is less likely to occur and providing a positively reinforceable alternative behavior—are especially critical.

- *Whenever possible, the environment should be modified so that the misbehavior is less likely to occur.* The temptation to engage in a misbehavior should be reduced or, if possible, eliminated. People on diets should not stock their kitchens with junk food. Troublemaking friends should be placed on opposite sides of the classroom or in different classes. Cheating on an exam can be reduced by having students sit apart from one another or by administering two different forms of the exam (perhaps the same test items in two different orders).

- *Desirable alternative behaviors should be taught and reinforced.* Punishment of misbehavior is typically more effective when it is combined with support for, as well as reinforcement of, appropriate behavior (Carey & Bucher, 1986; Rimm & Masters, 1974; Ruef, Higgins, Glaeser, & Patnode, 1998; Walters & Grusec, 1977). A misbehavior is more likely to be suppressed permanently when alternative behaviors are reinforced, especially when those behaviors are incompatible with the punished behavior. For example, when punishing aggression on the playground, teachers should remember also to reinforce appropriate social behavior. Teachers can punish a student for cheating, but they should also reinforce that student for demonstrating good study habits and for working well independently.

- *Whenever possible, punishment should immediately follow the inappropriate behavior.* As is true for reinforcement, the effectiveness of punishment decreases dramatically when it is delayed (Trenholme & Baron, 1975; Walters, 1964; Walters & Grusec, 1977). The more closely punishment follows a misbehavior, the more effective it will be. Punishment is particularly effective when it is administered as soon as the misbehavior *begins* (Aronfreed, 1968; Aronfreed & Reber, 1965). When, for whatever reason, punishment cannot be administered immediately, delayed punishment may be effective provided that the punished behavior is clearly described (Aronfreed & Reber, 1965).

- *An explanation of why the behavior is unacceptable should be given.* Although behaviorists tend to focus attention on responses and their consequences, a significant body of research indicates that punishment is more effective when *reasons* why certain behaviors cannot be tolerated are given (Baumrind, 1983; Hess & McDevitt, 1984; Hoffman, 1975; Parke, 1977;

Perry & Perry, 1983). For example, in an example presented earlier, Sharon's teacher incorporated reasoning into her description of Sharon's inappropriate behaviors: "When you talk without permission and when you get out of your seat during quiet reading time, *you keep other children from getting their work done.*"

Providing reasons as to why behaviors are unacceptable has at least four advantages (Cheyne & Walters, 1970; Walters & Grusec, 1977):

1. When punishment is accompanied by reasoning, it appears to make the immediacy of punishment a less critical factor in its effectiveness.

2. Reasoning increases the likelihood that when one behavior is punished, similar misbehaviors are also suppressed; that is, the effect of the punishment generalizes to other misbehaviors.

3. If reasons are given, misbehaviors are likely to be suppressed even when the punisher is absent.

4. Older children apparently *expect* to be told why they cannot engage in certain behaviors and are likely to be defiant when reasons are not provided.

• *Some punishments are ineffective and should be avoided.* Among the punishments generally *not* recommended are physical punishment, psychological punishment, extra classwork, and suspension from school.

Physical punishment may be the only means of keeping very young children from engaging in potentially harmful behaviors. For example, the toddler who takes delight in sticking metal objects into electrical outlets must be quickly informed in no uncertain terms that such behavior cannot continue. However, the use of physical punishment with older children may provide a model of aggression for those children: Consider as evidence the finding that the great majority of abusive parents have been themselves abused as children (Steele & Pollack, 1968; Steinmetz, 1977; Straus, Gelles, & Steinmetz, 1980). Occasional *mild* physical punishment (e.g., a mild spanking) does not appear to be correlated with behavior problems later on, although in some cases it can intensify into physical abuse (Baumrind, Larzelere, & Cowan, 2002; Gunnoe & Mariner, 1997).

Psychological punishment, such as embarrassing or insulting a child, also is not recommended (Davis & Thomas, 1989; Walker & Shea, 1995). Children who are consistently made to feel inferior or inadequate are likely to develop low self-esteem, which will interfere with their ability to engage in appropriate and constructive behaviors on future occasions.

Extra classwork is appropriate when it is a logical consequence of the misbehavior (e.g., when students are failing at academic tasks because of their inattentiveness in class), but in other situations it transmits the message that schoolwork is not fun. When Marcus is punished for his disruptive classroom behaviors by being assigned an additional 100 math problems, he is unlikely to perceive mathematics in a positive light.

Finally, suspension from school is typically an ineffective remedy for misbehavior (Doyle, 1990; Moles, 1990; Nichols, Ludwin, & Iadicola, 1999). Many chronically misbehaving students are those who have difficulty with their academic work; many high school troublemakers, for example, are students with poor reading skills. Suspending such students from school puts these students at an even greater disadvantage and decreases still further the likelihood of academic success. Additionally, when students find school to be an aversive situation, removal from that

Suspension is not an effective punishment.

environment is negatively reinforcing rather than punishing. (It is also negatively reinforcing to the school administrators who have gotten rid of their troublemakers!)

An alternative, potentially more effective punishment for chronic misbehavers is **in-house suspension.** In-house suspension is similar to a time-out in that punished students are placed in a quiet, boring room within the school building. In-house suspension typically lasts one or more days rather than only a few minutes, however, and students suspended in this manner are continually monitored by a member of the school staff. Students bring their schoolwork with them and must keep up with their classroom assignments. In-house suspension tends to be effective because it does not allow students to escape the school environment yet prevents the social interactions with peers that most students find reinforcing. Although in-school suspension programs have not been systematically investigated through controlled research studies, practitioners report that these programs are often effective in reducing chronic misbehaviors, particularly when part of the suspension session is devoted to teaching appropriate behaviors and tutoring academic skills and when the supervising teacher acts as a supportive resource rather than as a punisher (Gootman, 1998; Huff, 1988; Nichols et al., 1999; Pfiffner & Barkley, 1998; Sullivan, 1989).

• *Punishment should be used sparingly.* The studies by Hall and his colleagues (1971) that I depicted earlier in Figures 6–2, 6–3, and 6–4 provide several illustrations of how quickly punishment can reduce inappropriate behavior. An effective punishment is one that does not need to be administered very often to be effective. Only when punishment is a frequent occurrence (in which case it is obviously not effective anyway) are the numerous disadvantages of punishment likely to appear.

When used properly, punishment is the quickest way of reducing or eliminating unacceptable behaviors. Remember, behaviorists define punishment as a consequence that decreases the response it follows. A "punishment" that clearly is not suppressing an undesirable behavior very quickly should be replaced by a different consequence.

LEARNED HELPLESSNESS

Imagine that you are a student who is continually failing assignments and exams. You try all kinds of strategies to improve your grades—studying longer, memorizing your textbooks word for word, having a friend drill you on key points, and even sleeping with your books open over your head (hoping that the information will sink in)—and still you get F after F after F. Eventually, you would probably just stop trying to achieve academic success and accept the "fact" that you have no control over the grades you receive.

When aversive stimuli are presented repeatedly, and when an organism cannot avoid, escape from, or otherwise terminate them, the organism will eventually give up and passively accept those stimuli. This passive acceptance of uncontrollable aversive events is known as **learned helplessness.**

Let me illustrate the phenomenon by describing research conducted by Seligman and Maier (1967). In the first phase of this classic experiment, dogs received numerous painful and unpredictable shocks. Some dogs were able to escape the shocks by pushing a panel in the cage, whereas other dogs could not escape the shocks regardless of what they did. The following day, each dog was placed in a box that was divided into two compartments by a barrier. While in this box, the dog was presented with a series of tone-shock combinations, with a tone always preceding a shock; the dog could avoid the shock by jumping over the barrier into the other compartment as soon as it heard the tone. Dogs that had been able to escape the shocks on the previous day quickly learned to avoid the shocks on the second day. In contrast, dogs that previously had been unable to escape displayed learned helplessness: They made few attempts to escape, instead simply sitting still and whining as the shocks were presented.

People, too, begin to exhibit symptoms of learned helplessness when they cannot control the occurrence of aversive events (Hiroto, 1974; Hiroto & Seligman, 1975; Peterson, Maier, & Seligman, 1993). According to Maier and Seligman (1976), learned helplessness is manifested in three ways. First, there is a *motivational* effect: The individual is slow to exhibit responses that will yield reinforcement or enable escape from punishment. Second is a *cognitive* effect: The individual has difficulty learning in future situations in which control of consequences is possible. Even when the individual's responses do lead to reinforcement or escape from an aversive stimulus, the individual tends not to learn from those experiences. The third effect is an *emotional* one: The individual tends to be passive, withdrawn, fearful, and depressed.

Learned helplessness has been offered as an explanation of clinical depression (Seligman, 1975, 1991): Depressed people typically perceive that they have less control over their lives than nondepressed people. It may also be characteristic of some schoolchildren, particular those who experience consistent difficulty completing academic tasks (Dweck, 1986; Holliday, 1985; Jacobsen, Lowery, & DuCette, 1986; Stipek & Kowalski, 1989). As an example, consider the child with a learning disability. Often remaining unidentified as a student with special educational needs, the child may encounter repeated failure in academic work, despite reasonable efforts to succeed, and so may eventually stop trying. I have also seen the learned helplessness phenomenon in presumably nondisabled students when I talk with them about certain subject areas. Many students, for example, attribute their mathematics anxiety to the fact that, as elementary school students, they could not comprehend how to solve certain problems no matter what they did or how hard they tried. Others show learned helplessness in the area of spelling: Even when they know they have spelled a word incorrectly, they do not try to correct the spelling, excusing their behavior by such statements as "I'm just a bad speller" or "I never could spell very well" (Ormrod & Wagner, 1987).

Learned helplessness is clearly a situation in which aversive consequences occur unpredictably rather than being contingent on certain behaviors. Ultimately, individuals experiencing such seemingly random consequences may begin to believe, perhaps justifiably, that they have little or no control over the things that happen to them. We will look in more detail at the effects of perceived control (or lack thereof) as we discuss the cognitive side of learned helplessness in Chapter 18.

In this and the previous two chapters, we have seen how response–reinforcement contingencies increase certain responses and how response–punishment contingencies decrease others. To succeed in the school environment, students must be aware of those contingencies and be able to exhibit the responses that lead to positive outcomes. When students are unable to learn despite clearly specified contingencies and a slow, carefully designed curricular sequence, they may have cognitive problems that teachers cannot address from a strictly behaviorist perspective. In such situations, cognitive learning theories, which I will describe in Part IV of the book, may provide a more useful framework.

In Part III (Chapter 7), we will make a gradual transition to the study of cognition. There we will look at social cognitive theory, a theory that originated within the behaviorist perspective (especially operant conditioning) but has more recently begun to use cognitive ideas in its explanation of human behavior.

SUMMARY

Escape learning is the process of learning to terminate an aversive stimulus. *Avoidance learning* is the process of learning to avoid an aversive stimulus altogether. Unfortunately, when organisms (including human beings) avoid a particular situation, they never have the opportunity to discover when the situation is no longer aversive; hence, avoidance responses, once learned, are difficult to extinguish.

Views on *punishment* have changed considerably over the past 60 years: Early researchers found that punishment did little to reduce behaviors and cited numerous disadvantages of its use; for instance, its effects are often temporary rather than permanent, and it may lead to undesirable emotional reactions, aggressive behavior, or physical or psychological harm. More recently, however, some forms of punishment (e.g., time-outs, response cost, repri-

mands) have been found to be effective in decreasing a variety of inappropriate behaviors. A number of strategies enhance punishment's effectiveness; for instance, punishment is more effective when it immediately follows the inappropriate behavior and when it is accompanied by reasons why the behavior is unacceptable.

When aversive stimuli are repeatedly presented regardless of how a person behaves, he or she may develop a sense of *learned helplessness*—a sense of having little control over the environment—with motivational, cognitive, and emotional side effects. Students with a history of academic failure (e.g., students with learning disabilities) sometimes display learned helplessness in classroom settings, exerting little effort even at tasks that they should easily be able to master.

Part Three

Social Cognitive Theory

CHAPTER 7

Social Cognitive Theory

One summer, my sons Alex and Jeff spent quite a bit of time with their Uncle Pete, a large man who could pick them both up at the same time and carry them around on his shoulders. Uncle Pete's feats of strength were quite a contrast to Mom's and Dad's difficulties in lifting either boy alone, or even in opening pickle jars. For several years after that summer, Alex and Jeff spoke often of wanting to be like Uncle Pete, and I found that I could talk them into eating many foods they had previously shunned simply by saying, "This is what helps Uncle Pete get big and strong." The ploy never did work for broccoli, however.

When my daughter Tina was in junior high school, some of her friends got in the habit of calling her every morning to find out what she would be wearing to school that day. Tina was apparently somewhat of a fashion trendsetter at school, and several other girls were mimicking her attire. Given the apparel in which Tina left for school most mornings, I shudder at the thought of what her cronies must have looked like.

My daughter the trendsetter.

Almost daily, we see instances of people watching others and learning from them. Little boys often emulate hero figures such as Superman, Batman, and Uncle Pete. Through watching and copying one another, preadolescent girls often begin to behave in similar ways: dressing alike, wearing their hair in faddish styles, and lusting after the same boys. Children imitate their parents by developing similar hobbies and interests, by expressing similar political and religious beliefs, and by eventually raising their own children using the same disciplinary techniques with which they were raised. Students in the classroom learn many academic skills, including reading, writing, adding, and subtracting, at least partly through watching and imitating what their teachers and classmates do.

Such learning by observation and modeling is the focus of **social cognitive theory** (e.g., Bandura, 1977b, 1986; Rosenthal & Zimmerman, 1978; Schunk, 1989c). Initially known as *social learning theory*, it evolved from behaviorism but now includes many of the ideas that cognitivists also hold, hence the gradual shift in label to social *cognitive* theory. In this chapter, we will consider social cognitive theory's perspective on how both environmental and cognitive factors interact to influence human learning and behavior. We will explore the phenomenon of *modeling*, examining the mental processes involved, the effects of modeling on behavior, and the characteristics of effective models. We will find that people's beliefs about their own ability to execute various behaviors successfully (their *self-efficacy*) play a role in the responses they choose to make and the effort they exert in making those responses. And we will discover how, through the process of *self-regulation*, people become less and less influenced by environmental conditions as time goes on. At the end of the chapter, we will examine a number of implications of social cognitive theory for educational practice.

THE SOCIAL COGNITIVE APPROACH

Social cognitive theory focuses on what and how people learn from one another, encompassing such concepts as observational learning, imitation, and modeling. Although many species of animals can learn by imitation (Hayes & Hayes, 1952; Herbert & Harsh, 1944; Kaiser, Zentall, & Galef, 1997; Zentall, Sutton, & Sherburne, 1996), social cognitive theory deals primarily with human learning, and so we will be putting research involving rats and pigeons aside at this point.

The study of learning through imitation was launched by two of Clark Hull's students, Neal Miller and John Dollard (1941). It was not until the early 1960s, however, that a theory of imitation and modeling separate from its behaviorist roots began to take shape. Development of this theory, originally called *observational learning,* was due in large part to the research and writings of Albert Bandura of Stanford University (e.g., Bandura, 1969, 1973, 1977b, 1986, 1989; Bandura & Walters, 1963). Bandura's perspective has evolved considerably over the years and continues to be a driving force in studies of imitation and modeling. You will find numerous references to Bandura and others who build on his ideas (e.g., Dale Schunk, Barry Zimmerman) throughout the chapter.

General Principles of Social Cognitive Theory

Several general principles underlie social cognitive theory, including the following:

• *People can learn by observing the behaviors of others, as well as by observing the outcomes of those behaviors.* Many early behaviorists viewed learning largely as a matter of trial and error: People learn by making a variety of responses and then modifying their behavior based on the consequences (e.g., the reinforcement) that their responses bring. In contrast, social cognitive theorists propose that most learning takes place not through trial and error but instead through watching the behavior of other individuals **(models).**

• *Learning can occur without a change in behavior.* As we noted in Chapters 1 and 3, behaviorists define learning as a change in behavior; thus, no learning can occur unless behavior *does* change. In contrast, social cognitive theorists argue that because people can learn through observation alone, their learning will not necessarily be reflected in their actions. Something learned at one time may be reflected in behavior exhibited at the same time, at a later time, or never.

• *The consequences of behavior play a role in learning.* The role of consequences in social cognitive theory has evolved as the theory itself has evolved. In Miller and Dollard's (1941) early theoretical analysis of learning new behaviors through imitation, reinforcement of those behaviors was a critical factor. Operant conditioning continued to be a major component of Albert Bandura's early work as well (e.g., Bandura & Walters, 1963). More recently, however, the role of consequences has been reconceptualized (Bandura, 1977b, 1986; Rosenthal & Zimmerman, 1978). Contemporary social cognitive theorists propose that both reinforcement and punishment have less critical, *indirect* effects on learning—effects that we will examine shortly.

• *Cognition plays a role in learning.* Over the past 30 years, social cognitive theory has become increasingly "cognitive" in its analysis of human learning. For example, contemporary social cognitive theorists maintain that an individual's *awareness* of response–reinforcement and response–punishment contingencies is an essential component of the learning process. They also assert that *expectations* of future reinforcements and punishments can have a major impact on the behaviors that people exhibit. Finally, as you will soon see, social cognitive theorists incorporate such cognitive processes as *attention* and *retention* (memory) into their explanations of how learning occurs.

We turn now to the ways in which environmental factors—reinforcement and punishment in particular—play a role in learning by observation. We will then look at how cognition is also involved.

ENVIRONMENTAL FACTORS IN SOCIAL LEARNING: REINFORCEMENT AND PUNISHMENT

If we were to explain imitation from an operant conditioning perspective, we might propose that people imitate others because they are reinforced for doing so. In fact, this explanation is exactly what Miller and Dollard proposed back in 1941. According to these theorists, an individual uses another person's behavior as a discriminative stimulus for an imitative response. The observer is then reinforced in some way for displaying imitation. For example, let's say that a French teacher carefully enunciates:

Comment allez vous?   (Discriminative stimulus)

Students repeat the phrase in more or less the same way:

Comma tally voo?   (Response)

The teacher then praises them for their efforts:

Trés bien! Very good!   (Reinforcement)

From an operant conditioning perspective, imitation of other people's behavior is maintained by an intermittent reinforcement schedule: Individuals are not *always* reinforced for mimicking the responses of others, but they are reinforced often enough that they continue to copy those around them. Eventually imitation itself becomes a habit, a phenomenon Miller and Dollard called **generalized imitation.**

How the Environment Reinforces and Punishes Modeling

People are often reinforced for modeling the behaviors of others. Bandura has suggested that the environment reinforces modeling, and also may occasionally punish modeling, in several possible ways:

• *The observer is reinforced by the model.* In the French lesson I described earlier, the model—the teacher—reinforced students for imitative behavior. People often reinforce others who copy what they themselves do. For example, a group of teenage girls is more likely to welcome another girl into the group if she dresses as they do. A gang of antisocial boys will probably accept a new member only if he acts "tough."

Adults, such as parents and teachers, most often reinforce children for copying those behaviors that their culture deems to be appropriate. For example, when my children were young, I would occasionally hear one of them use polite, "adult" language on the telephone, perhaps along this line: "I'm sorry, but my mother is busy right now. If you will give me your name and number, I'll have her call you back in a few minutes." Such a statement was similar to what I myself would tell callers, and I was likely to praise the child profusely. However, a statement such as,

"Ma! Telephone! Hurry up and get off the potty!" was definitely *not* learned through observation of the adults in the house, and I certainly never reinforced it.

• *The observer is reinforced by a third person.* On some occasions an individual is reinforced by a third person rather than by the model. For example, children are often reinforced by parents and teachers when they imitate other children. Something I used to tell my youngest child, Jeff, was this: "Oh, you're such a big boy now! You're getting dressed all by yourself, just like Alex does!"

During the Beatlemania of the 1960s, many teenage boys began sporting "moppet" haircuts like those of the Beatles. Such haircuts were "in," at least in my high school, and none of us girls would have ever been caught dead with a boy who had hair shorter than John Lennon's. My friends and I were, in essence, reinforcing boys who modeled themselves after the Beatles. In earlier days, we would have reinforced anyone who could play the guitar and bat his eyelashes in a come-hither fashion, just as Ricky Nelson used to do in the television show *Ozzie and Harriet.*

• *The imitated behavior itself leads to reinforcing consequences.* Many behaviors that we learn through observing others produce satisfying (reinforcing) results. For example, a French student who pronounces his *Comment allez vous?* correctly will have greater success communicating with a Parisian. An individual who can closely model a tennis instructor's body positions and arm movements is more likely to get the ball over the net.

• *Consequences of the model's behavior affect the observer's behavior vicariously.* When people observe a model making a particular response, they may also observe the consequence of that response. If a model is reinforced for a response, then the *observer* may show an increase in that response; this phenomenon is known as **vicarious reinforcement.** For example, if Andy sees Adam gain popularity among the girls because he can play the guitar and bat his eyelashes in a come-hither fashion, Andy may very well buy a guitar and take a few guitar lessons; he may also stand in front of the mirror practicing eyelash batting.

Reinforcement of the model affects the observer's behavior as well.

The power of vicarious reinforcement (and of **vicarious punishment** as well) was dramatically illustrated in an early study by Bandura (1965b). Children watched a film of a model hitting and kicking an inflated punching doll. One group of children saw the model reinforced for such aggressive behavior, a second group saw the model punished, and a third group saw the model receive no consequences for the aggression. When the children were then placed in a room with the doll, those who had seen the model being reinforced for aggression displayed the most aggressive behavior toward the doll: They had been vicariously reinforced for aggression. Conversely, those children who had seen the model punished for aggression were the least aggressive of the three groups: They had been vicariously punished for such behavior.

Vicarious punishment indicates to the observer that a particular behavior will not be tolerated; vicarious reinforcement indicates that a behavior is acceptable. Apparently, a *lack of punishment* to the model may also be a form of vicarious reinforcement in that it conveys the message that a behavior will be tolerated (Bandura, 1973, 1977b, 1986; Walters & Parke, 1964; Walters, Parke, & Cane, 1965). For example, in a study by Walters and Parke (1964), children in three different experimental groups watched a film in which a boy (the model) was told by a female experimenter not to play with a number of toys that lay on the table in front of him but instead to read a book that she had given him. Yet as soon as the woman left the room, the boy began to play with the toys. At this point, the film was different for the three experimental groups, as follows:

1. *Reward.* The woman returned, handed the boy some toys, and played with him affectionately.
2. *Punishment.* The woman returned, snatched away the toys the boy was playing with, shook him vigorously, and sat him back down with the book.
3. *No consequence.* The woman did not return to the room.

Children in these three groups, and children in a control group who did not view a film, were then taken to a room full of toys, told not to touch them, given a book to read, and left alone for 15 minutes. Children in the no-consequence group played with the toys (thus disobeying the experimenter's instructions) just as much as the reward group did. Children in the punishment group were more obedient, but the most obedient children were those in a fourth (control) group, who had not watched the disobedient model at all.

When people see others misbehave without negative consequences, they are more likely to misbehave themselves. For example, when my daughter was in elementary school, she came home almost daily with complaints about who had gotten away with what on the playground that day. When playground supervisors ignore transgressions day after day, their inaction not only perpetuates those misbehaviors but may even cause them to increase. In the same way, I often wonder whether individuals who see others quite literally get away with murder aren't more likely to engage in criminal activities themselves.

Problems With a Strict Operant Conditioning Analysis of Social Learning

Although early social learning theorists tried to explain imitative behavior from the perspective of operant conditioning, they encountered several problems in doing so. For one thing, operant conditioning does not address the effects of punishment, yet, as we saw in Bandura's (1965b) study of children watching a boy playing with prohibited toys, punishment *can* influence behavior.

A second problem is that completely new behaviors can be learned simply by watching others perform them (Bandura, 1977b, 1986; Rosenthal, Alford, & Rasp, 1972). As you should recall, operant conditioning must start with an emitted response, a response that can then be modified through shaping. The acquisition of entirely novel responses—responses that an individual has seen but never previously emitted in any form—is difficult to explain from a strictly Skinnerian perspective.

A third difficulty in explaining modeling as an instance of operant conditioning is the phenomenon of **delayed imitation:** Some behaviors that are learned through observing others do not appear until a later time. The operant conditioning paradigm, if we consider the role of the antecedent stimulus, looks like this:

$$(S +) R \rightarrow S_{Rf}$$

These three parts of the model—discriminative stimulus (S+), response (R), and reinforcement (S_{Rf})—follow one right after the other, with the response occurring in the presence of the discriminative stimulus. Yet as Bandura (1977b) has pointed out, the response and resulting reinforcement do not always appear immediately after the discriminative stimulus but may instead occur days or even weeks later. For such delayed imitation to be exhibited, learning must actually take place when the discriminative stimulus is presented, despite the absence of reinforcement at that time.

Still a fourth problem lies in the powerful effect of vicarious reinforcement: Individuals sometimes exhibit behaviors for which they themselves are *never* reinforced.

A Contemporary Social Cognitive Perspective of Reinforcement and Punishment

More recently, social cognitive theorists (e.g., Bandura, 1977b, 1986; Rosenthal & Zimmerman, 1978) have suggested that direct consequences of behavior are not necessary for learning to occur. Instead, consequences have the following effects on learning and behavior:

• *Reinforcement and punishment influence the extent to which an individual exhibits a behavior that has been learned.* Social cognitive theorists believe that, although people may learn new behaviors, they will not demonstrate those behaviors unless there is a reason (i.e., reinforcement) for doing so. For example, I learned many years ago that the capital of Alaska is Juneau. Yet I have never had a reason to demonstrate that knowledge because I have never been tested on the capital of Alaska, nor have I ever been in Alaska desperately seeking the state capital. Now, of course, I do have a reason: I want to impress you with the fact that I know the capital of at least one of the 50 states.

Bandura (1977b, 1986) has proposed that a person forms *hypotheses* about what responses are most appropriate in different situations. These hypotheses are formed and modified with the feedback that reinforcement and punishment, either of one's own actions or those of others, provide. Although an individual may learn both appropriate and inappropriate behaviors equally well, the appropriate behaviors—those that will lead to reinforcement—are the ones more likely to occur.

• *The expectation of reinforcement influences cognitive processes that promote learning.* As an example of a cognitive process involved in learning, social cognitive theorists (e.g., Bandura,

1977b, 1986) maintain that *attention* plays a critical role in learning. And attention is influenced by the expectation of reinforcement: People are more likely to pay attention to someone else's behavior when they think they will be reinforced for modeling that behavior.

I have learned the hard way that when I tell my students they will not be held responsible for certain information, I am making a BIG MISTAKE. All I have to do is say something like, "Now I want you to listen carefully to what I have to say for the next five minutes, but *it won't be on the next test*," and students put their pens down and settle back in their seats; if I'm teaching an early morning class, a few in the back row may start to nod off. People are less likely to pay attention to information when they do not anticipate a payoff for learning it.

As you can see, social cognitive theorists stress the role of environmental factors in learning, but they acknowledge the importance of cognitive factors as well. Let's now turn our own attention to those cognitive factors.

COGNITIVE FACTORS IN SOCIAL LEARNING

The cognitive side of social cognitive theory is evident in many aspects of the theory; examples include learning without performance, cognitive processing during learning, expectations, and the awareness of response–consequence contingencies.

Learning Without Performance

Bandura makes a distinction between learning through observation (something he calls **vicarious acquisition**) and the actual imitation of what has been learned. As we noted earlier, people can learn by watching others without necessarily imitating the behaviors they have seen (Bandura, 1977b, 1986; Rosenthal & Zimmerman, 1978). At least two sources of evidence indicate that this is true. For one thing, people can verbally describe a behavior they have observed without actually performing it (Bandura, 1965a). Second, people who observe a model perform a behavior may not demonstrate that behavior until some later time when they have a reason for doing so. For example, I previously described a study by Bandura (1965b) in which children watched a film of a model acting aggressively toward an inflated punching doll. As you may recall, the consequences of the aggression to the model (reinforcement, punishment, or no consequence) influenced the extent to which children themselves engaged in aggressive acts toward the doll. Later in the study, however, all of the children were promised rewards (stickers and fruit juices) if they could imitate the model's behavior. At that point, differences among the three groups of children disappeared! Clearly they had all *learned* the model's behavior equally well; the consequences to the model apparently affected their earlier performance but not their learning.

Cognitive Processing During Learning

Social cognitive theorists describe the cognitive processes (i.e., thinking) that occur when people are learning. For example, they contend that *attention* is a critical factor in learning. Furthermore, they propose that people are more likely to remember information when they mentally repeat (*rehearse*) it and when they develop verbal and visual mental representations (*memory codes*) of this information. I will illustrate each of these concepts when, later in the chapter, I describe the four processes that Bandura suggests are necessary for modeling to occur.

Expectations

Social cognitive theorists believe that, in part as a result of being reinforced for some behaviors and punished for others, people form **outcome expectations,** beliefs about the consequences that future behaviors are likely to bring (Bandura, 1977b, 1986, 1989, 1997; Rosenthal & Zimmerman, 1978). People often have expectations of what is likely to happen in different situations; they expect certain behaviors to lead to reinforcement and others to lead to punishment. The concept of **incentive**—anticipating that a particular reinforcement will occur if a particular behavior is performed—reflects this idea of expectation. Obviously, when people expect to be rewarded for imitating a behavior, they will be more likely to pay attention to that behavior and try to remember how it is performed. Furthermore, they will be motivated to demonstrate the behavior they have learned. You should notice a critical difference here between the role of reinforcement in operant conditioning and in social learning. In operant conditioning, reinforcement influences learning of the behavior it *follows*. In social learning, however, an *expectation* of reinforcement influences the learning of a behavior it *precedes* (Bandura, 1977b, 1986).

As we discovered earlier, the nonoccurrence of expected punishment can be reinforcing. Conversely, the nonoccurrence of expected reinforcement is often a form of punishment (Bandura, 1977b, 1986). Both of these principles involve situations in which outcome expectations are not being met. For example, imagine yourself as a student in a class in which the teacher has clearly described the criteria necessary to earn an A. You work hard, and your performance meets the specified criteria, so you are naturally expecting an A. But at the last minute, your teacher adds an additional requirement: To earn an A, students must write a 20-page term paper. You are probably angry and frustrated (in a sense, you feel punished), because you had expected reinforcement based on the work you had already completed, and that reinforcement is now being withheld.

Not only do people form expectations about the likely outcomes of various behaviors, they also form **efficacy expectations,** beliefs about their own *ability* to perform the behaviors successfully (Bandura, 1997). Imagine once again that you are in a class in which the instructor has described the criteria for an A. But imagine, too, that you don't believe that you have the knowledge and skills to meet those criteria. In this case, even though you know what it takes for a high grade, you don't *have* what it takes (not in your own eyes, at least), and so you cannot achieve an A no matter what you do. We will examine the nature and effects of efficacy expectations, commonly known as *self-efficacy*, later in the chapter.

Awareness of Response–Consequence Contingencies

According to social cognitive theorists, reinforcement and punishment have little effect on learning and behavior unless people are *aware* of the response–reinforcement and response–punishment contingencies (Bandura, 1977b, 1986; Spielberger & DeNike, 1966). Reinforcement increases a response only when an individual realizes which particular response has led to the reinforcement. Similarly, an individual must recognize what particular behavior is being punished before that behavior is likely to decrease. For example, consider a situation in which a student receives an F on a writing assignment, with comments such as "Poorly written" and "Disorganized" noted in the margins. For many students, such feedback is insufficient to bring about an improvement in writing because, among other things, it does not identify the specific parts of the assignment that are poorly written and disorganized.

It should be clear by now that social cognitive theory incorporates elements of both behaviorism and cognitivism. We have examined some of the environmental and cognitive factors that, from a social cognitive perspective, are involved in the learning process. We must also consider how environment and cognition *interact* with one another. Let's turn next to that topic—in particular, to Bandura's concept of reciprocal causation.

RECIPROCAL CAUSATION

We have already seen how the environment influences behavior and how mental processes occurring within the learner (e.g., attention, expectations) influence behavior. Bandura (1989) has proposed that, in a reciprocal fashion, behavior can also influence both the environment and the person. In fact, each of these three variables—environment, person, and behavior—influences the other two, a phenomenon Bandura calls **reciprocal causation**.[1] The interaction of environment (E), person (P), and behavior (B) can be depicted like this:

Certainly the environment influences a person's behavior. For example, the occurrence of a desirable or undesirable consequence as a result of a particular response influences the probability that an individual will make that response again. But an individual's *perception* of the environment (a "person" variable) can be equally influential on behavior. For example, I mentioned earlier that awareness of response–reinforcement contingencies influences the extent to which those contingencies affect behavior. Consider an experiment by Kaufman, Baron, and Kopp (1966) as a case in point. Participants in the experiment were all placed on a variable-interval reinforcement schedule, with the average interval before reinforcement being one minute, and told one of three different things about the schedule they were on. People in Group 1 were told that they were on a one-minute variable-interval schedule (i.e., they were told the truth). People in Group 2 were told that they were on a one-minute *fixed*-interval schedule. People in Group 3 were told that they were on a variable-ratio (1:150) schedule. People's response patterns corresponded to the reinforcement schedules they *believed* they were on: Group 3 showed the fastest response rate, and Group 2 showed the slowest response rate, consistent with the response

[1]Prior to 1989, Bandura used the term *reciprocal determinism*.

patterns that are actually observed for these different reinforcement schedules. Baron, Kaufman, and Stauber (1969) reported similar results.

Yet behavior affects both the environment that individuals encounter and the personal characteristics that they develop. The responses people make (e.g., the academic courses they choose, the extracurricular activities they pursue, and the company they keep) determine the situations they find themselves in and the consequences they experience (environmental variables). For example, individuals typically behave in ways that increase reinforcement and decrease punishment, and their actions may put them in situations that present new response–reinforcement contingencies.[2] Furthermore, the pattern of one's responses over time affects one's self-confidence and expectations for future success (person variables). For example, a boy who stumbles and falls frequently may begin to think that he is a klutz. By consistently performing well on mathematics assignments, a girl may begin to believe that she is a mathematics whiz.

Finally, person variables and environmental variables affect each other. For example, by directing attention (a person variable) to one stimulus and not to another, certain aspects of the environment will be experienced and others will not. And we have already seen how the consequences of past behaviors (an environmental variable) affect the expectations that people have (a person variable) regarding the outcomes of future behaviors.

One prime example of the interplay among environment, person, and behavior variables is modeling. Let's now look more closely at the modeling process.

MODELING

Children begin to imitate others soon after birth. When infants are 1 or 2 days old, they change their faces noticeably (e.g., moving muscles near their mouths, eyes, and brows) when an adult shows a happy, sad, or surprised expression, and an observer who doesn't know which expression the babies are observing can guess it with greater-than-chance accuracy (Field et al., 1982). By 6 to 9 months, infants can learn new ways of manipulating objects (e.g., pushing a button on a box, shaking an egg-shaped rattle) by watching a model display those behaviors, and the infants will often remember the behaviors a day later (Collie & Hayne, 1999; Meltzoff, 1988a, 1988b). By 18 months, they may remember and imitate an action they have seen as much as a month earlier (Collie & Hayne, 1999).

According to Bandura (1977b, 1986), many of the behaviors people exhibit have been acquired through observing and modeling what others do. In this section, we will explore several topics related to modeling. We will first consider the different types of models we may see and the kinds of behaviors that can be modeled. We will then look at four processes essential for learning to occur through modeling and at the various ways in which models can affect behavior. Finally, we will identify several characteristics of effective models. Before we proceed, however, I should point out that social cognitive theorists sometimes use the term *modeling* to describe what

---

[2]In recent years, I have seen a similar idea in behaviorist literature. Rosales-Ruiz and Baer (1997) define the term *behavioral cusp* as "any behavior change that brings the organism's behavior into contact with new contingencies that have even more far-reaching consequences" (p. 533). For example, when infants begin to crawl, they gain greater access to toys, other family members, and potentially hazardous objects. When students begin to read fluently, they open up many new opportunities for learning and instruction.

a model does (i.e., demonstrate a behavior) and at other times to describe what the observer does (i.e., copy that behavior). I have tried to write this section in such a way that the term's meaning is always readily discernible from the context in which it is used.

Types of Models

Bandura identifies three different types of models. When we think of modeling, we most frequently think of a **live model**—an actual person demonstrating a particular behavior. But we can also learn by observing a **symbolic model**—a person or character portrayed in a film, television show, book, or other medium. For example, many children model their behavior after football players; rock singers; or such fictional characters as Superman, Harry Potter, or Pippi Longstocking. And finally, we can learn from **verbal instructions**—descriptions of how to behave—without another human being, either live or symbolic, being present at all.

Behaviors That Can Be Learned Through Modeling

Many behaviors are learned, at least in part, through modeling. For example, students

- Are better readers when their parents read frequently at home (Hess & McDevitt, 1989).
- Master new athletic skills more effectively when shown specific techniques for improving their performance (Kitsantas, Zimmerman, & Cleary, 2000; Zimmerman & Kitsantas, 1997).
- Are more likely to resist the enticements of a stranger when a peer has modeled techniques for resisting such enticements (Poche, Yoder, & Miltenberger, 1988).
- Begin to deal with a fear-inducing situation with little or no fear after seeing a model behave fearlessly in that situation (Bandura, Grusec, & Menlove, 1967; Bandura & Menlove, 1968; Silverman & Kearney, 1991).
- Are more likely to show intolerance of racist statements when people around them refuse to tolerate such statements (Blanchard, Lilly, & Vaughn, 1991).
- Are more likely to violate traditional gender stereotypes—that is, to behave without regard to what is "appropriate" behavior for males and females—when they see others behaving in a nonstereotypical manner (Carlson, 1984; Hoffman, 1984; Ruble & Ruble, 1982; Selkow, 1984; Weinraub et al., 1984).

Considerable research has been conducted concerning the impact of modeling on three kinds of behavior in particular: academic skills, aggression, and morality.

Academic Skills

Students learn many academic skills by seeing others demonstrate those skills. For instance, they may learn how to solve long-division problems or write a cohesive paragraph or story partly by observing how their teachers and peers do these things (Braaksma, Rijlaarsdam, & van den Bergh, 2002; Sawyer, Graham, & Harris, 1992; Schunk, 1981; Schunk & Hanson, 1985; Schunk & Swartz, 1993). In small groups with classmates, they may also adopt one another's strategies for conducting discussions about literature, for instance soliciting one another's opinions ("What do you think, Jalisha?"), voicing agreement or disagreement ("I agree with Kordell because . . . ," "I disagree with Janelle . . . "), and justifying their points of view ("I think it shouldn't be allowed, because if he got to be king, who knows what he would do to the kingdom.") (R. Anderson et al., 2001, pp. 14, 16–17, 25).

Often, students learn academic skills more effectively when models demonstrate not only how to do something but also how to *think about* something—in other words, when models engage in **cognitive modeling** (Sawyer et al., 1992; Schunk, 1981, 1998; Schunk & Swartz, 1993). As an example, consider how a teacher might model the thinking processes involved in long division:

> First I have to decide what number to divide 4 into. I take 276, start on the left and move toward the right until I have a number the same as or larger than 4. Is 2 larger than 4? No. Is 27 larger than 4? Yes. So my first division will be 4 into 27. Now I need to multiply 4 by a number that will give an answer the same as or slightly smaller than 27. How about 5? $5 \times 4 = 20$. No, too small. Let's try 6. $6 \times 4 = 24$. Maybe. Let's try 7. $7 \times 4 = 28$. No, too large. So 6 is correct." (Schunk, 1998, p. 146)

Aggression

Numerous research studies indicate that children become more aggressive when they observe aggressive or violent models (Bandura, 1965b; Bandura, Ross, & Ross, 1961, 1963; Goldstein, Arnold, Rosenberg, Stowe, & Ortiz, 2001; Mischel & Grusec, 1966; Steuer, Applefield, & Smith, 1971; Walters & Thomas, 1963; Walters, Thomas, & Acker, 1962). In the classic study in this area (Bandura et al., 1961), preschoolers were taken one at a time to a playroom containing a variety of toys and were seated at a table where they could draw pictures. Some of these children then observed an adult (an aggressive model) enter the room and engage in numerous aggressive behaviors toward an inflatable punching doll, including kicking the doll in the air, straddling it and hitting it over the head with a wooden mallet, and making statements like "Pow!" "Kick him," and "Punch him in the nose." Other children instead observed an adult (a nonaggressive model) come in and play in a constructive way with building blocks. Still other children saw no model while they were in the playroom. The children were then led to another room where they were mildly frustrated: Just as they began to play with some very attractive, entertaining toys, the toys were taken away from them. Finally, the children were taken to a third room in which both nonaggressive and aggressive toys (including the inflatable punching doll and wooden mallet) were present; their behaviors were recorded and coded for aggressive content by observers on the other side of a one-way mirror. Children who had seen the aggressive model were clearly the most aggressive of the three groups, and, in fact, they mimicked many of the same behaviors that they had seen the aggressive model display (e.g., straddling the doll and hitting it with the mallet). Children who had seen a nonaggressive model were even less aggressive than the no-model group. With regard to aggression, then, models can have an impact either way: Aggressive models will lead to increased aggression in children, and nonaggressive models will lead to decreased aggression.

Children can also learn aggression from observing it in films, on television, or in video games (Anderson & Bushman, 2001; Rushton, 1980). In another study by Bandura and his colleagues (Bandura et al., 1963), preschool children who had seen a film of either an adult or a cartoon character being aggressive exhibited just as much aggression toward an inflatable doll as did children who had seen a live adult model; all of these children were significantly more aggressive than children who had not observed a model at all. But modeled aggression is hardly limited to dolls and other toys: In a study by Steuer, Applefield, and Smith (1971), children who watched cartoons depicting aggressive and violent behavior were significantly more aggressive toward their peers than children who had not seen the cartoons.

The fact that children model aggressive behavior depicted in the media has obvious implications for television and movie violence. Children not only model aggression but also tend to model the same *forms* of aggression that they observe (Bandura et al., 1963; Mischel & Grusec, 1966). Even cartoons that display violent behaviors, including such classics as *Tom and Jerry* and *Roadrunner*, may not be as harmless as they appear.

Morality

Many aspects of moral thinking and moral behavior are apparently influenced by observation and modeling. Research has demonstrated the importance of modeling for such behaviors as generosity (Elliott & Vasta, 1970; Radke-Yarrow, Zahn-Waxler, & Chapman, 1983; Rushton, 1975, 1982), self-control (Harter, 1983; Stevenson & Fantuzzo, 1986), and resistance to temptation (Wolf & Cheyne, 1972). Consider a study by Rushton (1975) as an example: Children first observed a model playing a bowling game and reinforcing himself with tokens for high performance. Some children saw the model donate half of the earned tokens to a poor boy named Bobby pictured on a poster in the room; other children observed the model keep all of his winnings for himself despite the presence of the poster. The children then had the opportunity to play the game and to reward themselves with tokens. The more tokens they earned, the better prize they could purchase (therefore, donating to Bobby meant that they would have to purchase a lesser prize for themselves). Children who had watched generous models were more likely to donate some of their own tokens to Bobby than were children who had watched selfish models. This difference was true not only in the initial experimental session but also in a follow-up session two months later.

Moral judgments regarding right and wrong may also develop, at least in part, through modeling (Bandura & McDonald, 1963; Prentice, 1972; Schliefer & Douglas, 1973). For example, in a study by Bandura and McDonald (1963), experimenters presented children with pairs of stories such as these:

1. John was in his room when his mother called him to dinner. John goes down, and opens the door to the dining room. But behind the door was a chair, and on the chair was a tray with fifteen cups on it. John did not know the cups were behind the door. He opens the door, the door hits the tray, bang go the fifteen cups, and they all get broken.

2. One day when Henry's mother was out, Henry tried to get some cookies out of the cupboard. He climbed up on a chair, but the cookie jar was still too high, and he couldn't reach it. But while he was trying to get the cookie jar, he knocked over a cup. The cup fell and broke. (Bandura & McDonald, 1963, p. 276)

In each pair, stories portrayed one well-intended child (such as John) who caused major damage and another child with less appropriate intentions (such as Henry) who did minor damage. For each pair of stories, the children were asked which child was naughtier. Some children consistently picked the child with the bad intentions as being naughtier; these children were then exposed to a model who used amount of damage as the criterion for naughtiness. Other children had a pattern of judging the well-meaning but more destructive child as being naughtier; they were exposed to a model who used bad intentions as the criterion for naughtiness. Observing the model had a profound effect on the children's later moral judgments: Children began to make moral decisions similar to those the model had made and opposite to their own previous judgments.

We have already seen that when models on film depict aggressive behavior, that behavior is often imitated. But visual media can model appropriate social responses as well, often quite effectively (Huston, Watkins, & Kunkel, 1989; Rushton, 1980). For example, in a study by Friedrich and Stein (1973), a group of preschool children watched *Mister Rogers' Neighborhood*— a television show that stresses such prosocial behaviors as cooperation, sympathy, and sharing— for 30 minutes each day over a four-week period. These children displayed more socially appropriate behavior and less aggression than children who instead watched shows with aggressive content (e.g., *Batman* and *Superman*) during the same time period.

What about situations in which a model preaches one set of moral values and practices another? A review of research by Bryan (1975) leads to a clear conclusion: When children hear a model say one thing and do something else, they are more likely to imitate what the model *does* than what the model *says*. In other words, to be effective, models must practice what they preach.

Processes Necessary for Effective Modeling to Occur

According to Bandura (1969, 1973, 1977b, 1986), four processes are necessary before an individual can successfully model the behavior of someone else: attention, retention, motor reproduction, and motivation.

Attention

To imitate a behavior accurately, a person must first pay attention to the model and especially to the significant aspects of the modeled behavior. For example, if Martha wishes to learn how to swing a golf club, she should watch how the golf pro stands, how her legs are placed, how she holds the club, and so on. Paying attention to the irrelevant parts of the model or her behavior— how the pro clears her throat or how her socks don't quite match—will, of course, not be helpful.

I still remember my first French teacher, a woman who came to my fifth-grade class for an hour one day each week. This woman always wore the same dark green wool dress, which, unfortunately, turned to a turquoise color in places where she perspired. I remember focusing on those turquoise spots, fascinated that a wool dress could actually change color so dramatically just because of a little human sweat. Yes, I was paying attention to my model, but, no, I did not learn much French, because I did not pay attention to the important aspect of the model's behavior—her voice.

Retention

The second step in learning from a model is to remember the behavior that has been observed. One simple way to remember what one has seen is **rehearsal**—repeating whatever needs to be remembered over and over again. For example, in a study by Weiss and Klint (1987), elementary school students were asked to remember a sequence of actions (do a crabwalk, pick up a beanbag, gallop, do a log roll, and skip) that they needed to perform on mats on the gymnasium floor. Students remembered the sequence more successfully if they were instructed to repeat, or *rehearse*, it to themselves while they executed it.

According to Bandura, people store both verbal representations (such as step-by-step instructions or labels that describe the actions to be performed) and visual images of the behaviors they have seen. These verbal and visual **memory codes** serve as guides when people perform the observed behavior, whether they perform it immediately after the model has

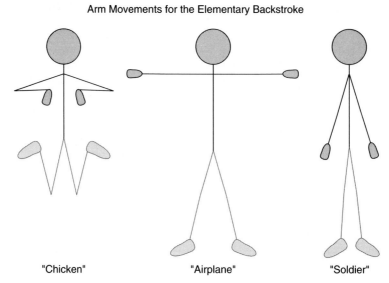

Arm Movements for the Elementary Backstroke

"Chicken"   "Airplane"   "Soldier"

Figure 7–1
Students often remember a model's behaviors more easily when those behaviors have verbal labels.

demonstrated it or at some time in the future. To illustrate such memory codes, my son Jeff's swimming teacher used the words *chicken*, *airplane*, and *soldier* to describe the three arm movements of the elementary backstroke (see Figure 7–1). The words provided Jeff with verbal codes for these actions; the teacher's demonstration of them facilitated the formation of visual images.

Considerable evidence indicates that learning from a model is easier if learners have assistance in forming memory codes for the behaviors they observe (Alford & Rosenthal, 1973; Bandura & Jeffery, 1973; Bandura, Jeffery, & Bachicha, 1974; Coates & Hartup, 1969; Cohen, 1989; Gerst, 1971; Rosenthal et al., 1972). For example, in a study by Gerst (1971), college students studied a number of words (hand signals) in sign language for the deaf. Students who were instructed either to describe the signals verbally or to form mental images of them remembered the signals more successfully than an uninstructed control group; students who were instructed to develop verbal labels descriptive of the hand movements remembered the signals most accurately. Teachers, too, can provide memory codes for learners. For example, in a study by Rosenthal, Alford, and Rasp (1972), second graders more effectively remembered the actions that an adult model demonstrated when she simultaneously described what she was doing.

The storage of information in memory and the different forms that such stored information can take are topics that have been studied more extensively by cognitive theorists than by social cognitive theorists. So we will return to this topic of memory storage again, and in much greater detail, in Chapters 10 and 11.

Modeling cannot occur without the physical capability.

Motor Reproduction

The third process involved in modeling is replicating the behavior that the model has demonstrated. When an individual cannot reproduce an observed behavior, perhaps because of physical immaturity, lack of strength, or disability, this third process obviously does not occur. For example, a child with articulation difficulties may never be able to pronounce *sassafras* correctly, no matter how many times she hears the word spoken. And a toddler who watches his teenage brother throw a football does not possess the muscular coordination to mimic that throw.

In my never-ending battle with the bulge, I used to turn on Jane Fonda's physical workout videocassette tape religiously every night (well, at least twice a month). Jane performed exercises in various pretzel-like contortions that I, even in my wildest dreams, would never be able to do. My body wasn't built to be folded in that many ways. Motor reproduction of everything I watched Model Jane do was simply not possible.

Reproduction of an observed behavior at the same time it is observed facilitates learning for at least two reasons. For one thing, it enables learners to encode that behavior not only in verbal and visual forms but perhaps in a *motoric* form as well—that is, in terms of the specific actions it encompasses (Cohen, 1989). Furthermore, by modeling a behavior in the presence of the model, learners can get feedback about how to improve their performance (Bandura, 1977b; Schunk, 1981).[3] For instance, when children who have historically struggled with math are learning division, instruction that includes an opportunity for practice and immediate feedback about the quality of performance is clearly superior to instruction that provides no opportunity for such practice and feedback (Schunk, 1981).

---

[3]We should note, however, that some children may prefer to practice newly learned behaviors in private before showing an adult what they have learned. For example, this may be the case for many Native American children (Fuller, 2001; Suina & Smolkin, 1994).

Motivation

The final necessary ingredient for modeling is motivation: Learners must want to demonstrate what they have learned. For example, many people who have grown up in our society have seen models on television point a gun in someone's ribs and say "Reach for the sky" (or something to that effect). Fortunately, very few people are motivated to model that behavior, at least with a real gun.

Although parents and teachers are often models for children, children do not model *all* of the behaviors they observe their parents and teachers performing. For example, although my children model my ways of speaking to people on the telephone and my cookie-baking techniques, for some reason they don't seem to copy my broccoli-cooking or floor-scrubbing behaviors. Children model behaviors only when they are motivated to do so.

To review, Bandura's four processes essential for modeling to occur are attention, retention, motor reproduction, and motivation. Because these processes vary among individuals, different people will model the same behavior differently. For example, Martha and Mary might pay attention to different aspects of their tennis instructor's tennis swing: Martha may focus on how the instructor is standing, whereas Mary may attend more to the way the instructor grips her racket. Or the two girls might store different visual images of the swing, Martha remembering that the instructor was facing the net and Mary remembering her standing with the left shoulder toward the net. Martha may be stronger, but Mary may be more motivated to play tennis well. The end result is that Martha and Mary will model the same tennis swing differently. Not only will the four essential processes for modeling lead to individual differences in modeled behaviors, but the absence of any one of them will make modeling unlikely to occur at all.

Effects of Modeling on Behavior

In what ways do models influence behavior? Social cognitive theorists (e.g., Bandura, 1969, 1973, 1977b, 1986; Bandura & Walters, 1963; Rosenthal & Zimmerman, 1978) have proposed that modeling has several effects:

• *Modeling teaches new behaviors.* People can learn entirely new behaviors by observing others perform those behaviors. For example, by listening to and imitating the sounds made by others, a person learns to speak new words. And by watching how a parent swings a baseball bat and following the parent's verbal instructions ("Keep your eye on the ball!"), a child learns to hit a baseball.

• *Modeling influences the frequency of previously learned behaviors.* As we noted earlier, people are more likely to exhibit behaviors they have previously learned when they see others being reinforced for such behaviors; in other words, vicarious reinforcement has a **facilitation** effect. By the same token, people are less likely to perform behaviors for which they have seen others being punished; in other words, vicarious punishment has an **inhibition** effect.

• *Modeling may encourage previously forbidden behaviors.* In some situations, when people observe a model engaging in behavior that has previously been described as forbidden or "wrong," and especially when the model is reinforced for engaging in that behavior, they themselves are more likely to display the behavior. On these occasions, vicarious reinforcement has a *disinhibition* effect (because previously inhibited behavior is now reoccurring). For example, in studies by Walters and his colleagues (Walters & Thomas, 1963; Walters, Thomas, & Acker, 1962), adults viewed either a film depicting aggression and violence (*Rebel without a Cause*) or a neutral film (*Picture Making by Teenagers*), then were asked to administer "shocks" to other individuals. (These other individuals were confederates of the experimenter who did not really receive any shocks but behaved as if they did.) People who had watched the violent, aggressive film administered more frequent and more intense "shocks" to the confederates. The film had apparently disinhibited previously learned aggressive behavior.

• *Modeling increases the frequency of similar behaviors.* When a person observes a model performing a particular behavior, that person may display similar rather than identical behavior. For example, a boy who sees his older brother excel at basketball, but who lacks his brother's height advantage, may instead try to become a successful soccer player. As a high school student, I would have given my eye teeth to become a "cool" cheerleader but did not have the gymnastic skills necessary for cheerleading. Instead, I became a majorette in the marching band, a position that was almost as cool.

Characteristics of Effective Models

People who are most likely to serve as live or symbolic models for others tend to have one or more characteristics:

• *The model is competent.* People demonstrating a particular behavior are more likely to be imitated by others if they are viewed as being competent, capable individuals (Bandura, 1986; Schunk, 1987). For example, a person trying to learn tennis is more likely to model the techniques of a successful tennis player than those of a friend who seldom gets the ball over the net. And a student trying to learn how to write a good term paper is more likely to look at the work of someone who has consistently received high grades on term papers than at the work of a student who tends to do poorly on such assignments. Even 3-year-olds have some ability to discriminate between the effective and ineffective behaviors they see modeled, and they are more likely to imitate those that produce desired outcomes (Want & Harris, 2001).

• *The model has prestige and power.* Individuals who have high status, respect, and power, either within a small group or within society as a whole, are more likely to serve as models for others (Bandura, 1986). A child is more likely to imitate the behaviors of a student leader or a famous rock star than the behaviors of a class dunce or a rock-and-roll "has-been." To illustrate, Sasso and Rude (1987) taught a number of nondisabled children (some of whom were popular with their peers and some of whom were not) methods of initiating appropriate social interactions with children who had physical disabilities. Other children who saw their popular classmates interacting with disabled children were likely to do so as well, but children who saw unpopular students modeling the same behavior were unlikely to follow suit.

• *The model behaves in stereotypical "gender-appropriate" ways.* Males are more likely to model behavior that is consistent with male stereotypes; similarly, females are more likely to model behaviors that follow traditional female patterns (Schunk, 1987). For example, in studies in which children watched adult models of both genders being aggressive (Bandura et al. 1961, 1963), boys were more likely than girls to imitate the aggressive behaviors, presumably because aggression is a trait more frequently associated with males than with females.

• *The model's behavior is relevant to the observer's situation.* Individuals are more likely to model behaviors that have functional value in their own circumstances (Rosenthal & Bandura, 1978; Schunk, 1987). For example, my daughter models many of my behaviors, but she definitely does not model the way I dress. She has told me, in so many words, that she would be laughed out of town if she dressed the way I do.

Models are often competent, prestigious, and powerful.

Parents and teachers are among the people whom children most often model, particularly when those parents and teachers are seen as competent, respected, and powerful. Children also frequently model their behavior after famous personalities and fictional heroes. And children's peer groups—other children of the same gender and age—can be a source of powerful and influential models as well.

Yet characteristics of the model are not the only variables determining whether modeling takes place. Another important variable is the observer's self-efficacy, a topic to which we turn now.

SELF-EFFICACY

People are more likely to engage in certain behaviors when they believe they are capable of executing those behaviors successfully—that is, when they have high **self-efficacy** (Bandura, 1977a, 1982, 1986, 1989; Schunk, 1989b). For example, I hope you believe that you are capable of understanding and remembering the ideas I present in this book; in other words, I hope you have high self-efficacy for learning about learning. You may or may not believe that with instruction and practice you will eventually be able to perform a passable swan dive; in other words, you may have high or low self-efficacy about learning to dive. You are probably quite skeptical that you could ever walk barefoot over hot coals, so my guess is that you have low self-efficacy regarding this activity.

Self-efficacy is a concept similar to *self-concept* but with an important distinction. Self-concept, though conceptualized somewhat differently by different theorists, is typically depicted as pervading a wide variety of activities; thus, people are described as having generally high or low self-concepts. Self-efficacy is more specific to particular domains, tasks, or situations. For instance, students may have higher self-efficacy about learning in social studies than in mathematics (Stodolsky et al., 1991). They may have high self-efficacy about learning to perform a swan dive but low self-efficacy about swimming the entire length of a swimming pool underwater. In recent years, self-efficacy has been more prevalent than self-concept in theoretical explanations of research results, in part because researchers have defined it more narrowly and consistently (Bong & Clark, 1999).

How Self-Efficacy Affects Behavior

According to social cognitive theorists (e.g., Bandura, 1977a, 1982, 1997, 2000; Phillips & Zimmerman, 1990; Schunk, 1989c; Zimmerman, 1998; Zimmerman, Bandura, & Martinez-Pons, 1992), people's feelings of self-efficacy affect several aspects of their behavior, including their choice of activities, their goals, their effort and persistence, and ultimately their learning and achievement.

Choice of Activities People tend to choose tasks and activities at which they believe they can succeed; they also tend to avoid those at which they think they will fail. For example, students who believe they can succeed at mathematics are more likely to take math courses than students who believe they are mathematically incompetent (Eccles, Wigfield, & Schiefele, 1998). Those who believe they can win a role in the school play are more likely to try out for the play than students with little faith in their acting or singing abilities.

Goals People set higher goals for themselves when they have high self-efficacy in a particular domain. For instance, adolescents' choices of careers and occupational levels reflect subject areas in which they have high rather than low self-efficacy (Bandura, Barbaranelli, Caprara, & Pastorelli, 2001). Their choices are often consistent with traditional gender stereotypes: Boys are more likely to have high self-efficacy for, and so aspire to careers in science and technology, whereas girls are more likely to feel efficacious about, and so choose careers in education, health, and social services (Bandura et al., 2001).

Effort and Persistence People with a high sense of self-efficacy are more likely to exert effort in attempting to accomplish a task; they are also more likely to persist when they encounter obstacles. Students with low self-efficacy about a task put less effort into it and give up more quickly in the face of difficulty.

Learning and Achievement Students with high self-efficacy tend to learn and achieve more than students with low self-efficacy, even when actual ability levels are the same (Assor & Connell, 1992; Bandura, 1986; Pajares, 1996; Schunk, 1989a; Zimmerman et al., 1992). In other words, when several students have equal ability, those students who believe they can do a task are more likely to accomplish it successfully than those who do not believe they are capable of success.

Factors in the Development of Self-Efficacy

Students usually hold fairly accurate opinions about their own self-efficacy: They typically have a good sense of what they can and cannot do (Bandura, 1986). Ideally, it is probably best for students to slightly overestimate their competence; by doing so, they are more likely to try those activities that can help them develop new skills and abilities (Assor & Connell, 1992; Bandura, 1997). Unfortunately, students sometimes seriously underestimate their chances of success, perhaps because of a few bad experiences (Phillips & Zimmerman, 1990). For example, a girl who gets a C in science from a teacher with exceptionally strict grading criteria may erroneously believe that she is "no good" in science. A new boy at school whose attempts at being friendly are rejected by two or three thoughtless classmates may erroneously believe that no one likes him.

According to social cognitive theorists (e.g., Bandura, 1986, 1997; Schunk, 1989a; Schunk, Hanson, & Cox, 1987), several factors affect the development of self-efficacy, including one's own previous successes and failures, the messages that others communicate, the successes and failures of others, and the successes and failures of the group as a whole.

Previous Successes and Failures

Students feel more confident that they can succeed at a task—that is, they have greater self-efficacy—when they have succeeded at that task or at similar ones in the past (Bandura, 1986; Klein, 1990; Nicholls, 1984). For example, a student is more likely to believe he can learn to divide fractions if he has successfully mastered the process of multiplying fractions. Similarly, a student will be more confident about her ability to play field hockey or rugby if she has already developed skills in soccer. In some cases, students' judgments of success are based on the progress they make over time; in other instances, their judgments are based on how well they perform in comparison with their peers (Butler, 1998a; Pintrich & Schunk, 2002; Schunk & Zimmerman, 1997).

Once students have developed a high sense of self-efficacy, an occasional failure is unlikely to dampen their optimism very much. In fact, when historically successful people encounter small setbacks on the way to achieving success, they learn that sustained effort and perseverance are key ingredients for that success; in other words, they develop **resilient self-efficacy** (Bandura, 1989). When students meet with *consistent* failure in performing a particular task, however, they tend to have little confidence in their ability to succeed at that task in the future. Each new failure confirms what they already "know" about the task—they can't do it.

It is not surprising, then, that students with a history of academic success have higher self-efficacy for academic tasks than students with lower school performance. For example, students with learning disabilities—students who typically have encountered failure after failure in classroom activities—often have low self-efficacy with regard to the things they study in school (Schunk, 1989c).

Messages From Others

To some extent, students' self-efficacy beliefs are enhanced when others praise good performance or provide assurances that success is possible. Statements such as "You can do this problem if you work at it" or "I'll bet Judy will play with you if you just ask her" do give students a slight boost in self-confidence. This boost is short-lived, however, unless students' efforts at a task ultimately meet with success (Schunk, 1989a).

We should note, too, that the messages students receive are sometimes implied rather than directly stated, yet they can influence self-efficacy nonetheless. For example, by giving constructive criticism about how to improve a poorly written research paper—criticism that indirectly communicates the message that "I know you can do better, and here are some suggestions how"—a teacher may boost students' self-efficacy for writing such research papers (Pintrich & Schunk, 2002). In some cases, actions speak louder than words. For example, the teacher who provides a great deal of assistance to a struggling student—more assistance than the student really needs—is communicating the message that "I don't think you can do this on your own" (Schunk, 1989b).

Successes and Failures of Others

People often acquire information about their own self-efficacy by observing the successes and failures of other individuals, especially those who appear to be similar to themselves (Schunk, 1983b, 1989c). As an example, students often consider the successes and failures of other students, especially those of similar ability, when appraising their own chances of success on academic tasks. Thus, seeing a classmate model a behavior successfully is often more effective than seeing a teacher do it. In one research study (Schunk & Hanson, 1985), elementary school children having difficulty with subtraction were given 25 subtraction problems to complete. Those who had seen another student successfully complete the problems got an average of 19 correct, whereas those who saw a teacher complete the problems got only 13 correct, and those who saw no model at all solved only 8!

Curiously, it is sometimes better to watch a peer model who struggles with a task at first and then gradually masters it, rather than one who executes it perfectly at first shot (Kitsantas et al., 2000; Schunk et al., 1987). Presumably observing such a **coping model** shows students that success does not necessarily come easily—that they must work and practice to achieve success—and allows them to observe the strategies that the model employs to gain proficiency.

Successes and Failures of the Group as a Whole

Students may have greater self-efficacy when they work in a group than when they work alone, and especially when they achieve success as a group. Such **collective self-efficacy** is a function not only of students' perceptions of their own and others' capabilities but also of their perceptions of how effectively they can work together and coordinate their roles and responsibilities (Bandura, 1997, 2000).

The concept of collective self-efficacy is a fairly new one, and research to date has focused primarily on adults (Bandura, 1997; Goddard, 2001; Tschannen-Moran, Woolfolk Hoy, & Hoy, 1998). We can reasonably assume that children, too, are likely to have higher self-efficacy when they work in groups, provided that those groups are functioning smoothly and effectively. We will consider strategies for fostering effective group work in Chapter 15.

Yet students must ultimately also learn skills for independent learning and performance. Social cognitive theorists believe that people can and should ultimately regulate their own behavior. We therefore turn to a topic gaining increasing prominence in psychological and educational literature—the topic of *self-regulation*.

SELF-REGULATION

As social cognitive theory has evolved over the years, it has increasingly emphasized the role of **self-regulation** of behavior (Bandura, 1977b, 1982, 1986; Zimmerman, 1989). Through both direct and vicarious reinforcement and punishment, growing children gradually learn which behaviors are and are not acceptable to the people around them. Eventually, they develop their *own* ideas about appropriate and inappropriate behavior, and they choose their actions accordingly.

Social cognitive theorists are hardly the only ones who have considered the nature of self-regulation; behaviorists have addressed it (e.g., see Belfiore & Hornyak, 1998), as have many cognitive theorists (e.g., see the discussion of Vygotsky's theory in Chapter 8). Yet social cognitive theorists have, to a considerable degree, been responsible for laying the groundwork on which other theorists have built. In this chapter, we will, in a typically social cognitive manner, blend elements of behaviorism and cognitivism to explore the nature of self-regulated behavior.

Elements of Self-Regulation

From the perspective of social cognitive theorists, self-regulation entails at least four processes: setting standards and goals, self-observation, self-judgment, and self-reaction (Bandura, 1986; Schunk, 1989c, 1998; Schunk & Zimmerman, 1996).[4]

Setting Standards and Goals

As mature human beings, we tend to set standards for our own behavior; in other words, we establish criteria regarding what constitutes acceptable performance. We also establish certain goals that we value and toward which we direct many of our behaviors.

The kinds of performance standards that people establish for their own behavior depend to some degree on the standards they see other people adopt (Bandura, 1977b, 1986). In a study by Bandura and Kupers (1964), for example, children watched adult or child models reward themselves with candy and self-praise for their performance in a bowling game. Some of the children watched the models reward themselves only after achieving 20 points or more (reflecting very high performance); these models admonished themselves for lower performance. Other children observed models reward themselves after achieving as few as 10 points. All of the children then had the opportunity to play the game themselves and to help themselves to candy whenever they chose. Bandura and Kupers found that the children tended to reinforce themselves using performance standards very similar to those they had seen the models use.

People are most apt to adopt the kinds of standards that models similar to themselves in ability adopt (Bandura, 1977b). They are unlikely to adopt the standards of models who are much more competent or who apply performance standards inconsistently (Bandura, 1977b; Bandura & Whalen, 1966).

Self-Observation

An important part of self-regulation is to observe oneself in action. To make progress toward important goals, people must be aware of how well they are doing at present; in other words, they must know what parts of their performance are working well and what parts need improvement.

---

[4]When social cognitive theorists identify elements of self-regulation, they typically list only the last three: self-observation, self-judgment, and self-reaction. However, they invariably refer to the importance of setting standards and goals, hence my decision to add this process as the first item on the list.

Self-Judgment

People's behaviors are frequently judged by others—for example, by relatives, teachers, classmates, friends, and the general public. Eventually, people begin to judge and evaluate their *own* behaviors based on the standards they hold for themselves.

Self-Reaction

As people become increasingly self-regulating, they begin to reinforce themselves—perhaps by feeling proud or telling themselves that they did a good job—when they accomplish their goals. They also begin to punish themselves—perhaps by feeling sorry, guilty, or ashamed—when they do something that does not meet their own performance standards. Such self-praise and self-criticism can be as influential in altering behavior as the reinforcements and punishments that others administer (Bandura, 1977b, 1986).

To illustrate, consider Jason, a student who perceives himself to have average intelligence. Jason is likely to form standards for his own academic achievement that match the achievement of other "average" students; he is, therefore, likely to pat himself on the back for "B" work and to maintain a similar level of effort on future tasks. In contrast, consider Joanna, a student whose close friends are the high achievers of the class. If Joanna believes that her ability is similar to that of her friends, she is likely to adopt high standards for herself and to admonish herself for the same B-level achievement of which Jason is so proud. Provided that the B does not appreciably undermine her self-efficacy, Joanna is likely to try harder on the same task the next time around (Bandura, 1989).

Promoting Self-Regulated Behavior

Writing a textbook is a major undertaking. As I sit here in my office tapping at the keys of my word processor day after day, I sometimes wonder why in the world I ever committed myself to such a project when I could instead be in my warm, comfortable living room reading mystery novels or watching television game shows. Yet each day I drag myself to my office to produce a few more pages. How do I do it? I do it by reinforcing myself every time I finish a small section of the book. For example, as soon as I finished the section on self-efficacy that you just read, I gave myself permission to go watch my favorite game show. Before I can watch another one, though, I need to finish this section on self-regulation.

The author engages in self-regulation.

Let's see what's behind door number 1...

Theorists have offered several techniques for promoting self-regulated behavior. These techniques (sometimes called *self-control*[5] or *self-management*) include self-instructions, self-monitoring, self-reinforcement, and self-imposed stimulus control.

Self-Instructions

One effective strategy is to teach learners to give themselves instructions that guide their behavior (Mace, Belfiore, & Shea, 1989; Meichenbaum, 1985; Schunk, 1989c; Shaffer, 1988). As one simple illustration, beginning tennis students improve the accuracy of their returns when they give themselves these four verbal cues:

- "Ball" (to remind them to keep their eyes on the ball)
- "Bounce" (to continue tracking the path of the ball)
- "Hit" (to focus on contacting the ball with the racket)
- "Ready" (to get into position for the next ball) (Ziegler, 1987)

Other studies show self-instructions to be effective in helping students acquire more effective approaches to academic tasks, develop better social skills, and keep their impulsive and aggressive behavior in check (Alberto & Troutman, 2003; Guevremont, Osnes, & Stokes, 1988; Hughes, 1988; Leon & Pepe, 1983; Meichenbaum, 1977).

Meichenbaum (1977) has successfully used five steps in teaching children how to give themselves instructions to guide their behavior.

1. *Cognitive modeling:* An adult model performs the desired task while verbalizing instructions that guide performance.
2. *Overt, external guidance:* The child performs the task while listening to the adult verbalize the instructions.
3. *Overt self-guidance:* The child repeats the instructions aloud while performing the task.
4. *Faded, overt self-guidance:* The child whispers the instructions while performing the task.
5. *Covert self-instruction:* The child silently thinks about the instructions while performing the task.

As you can see, then, the adult initially serves as a model not only for the behavior itself but also for self-instructions. Responsibility for performing the task *and* for guiding that performance is gradually turned over to the child.

Self-Monitoring

Another method that can help people control their own behavior is simply to have them observe and measure their own responses, just as someone else might measure those responses in traditionally applied behavior analysis. The mere recording of responses is often enough to alter the

---

[5]Some theorists make a distinction between the terms *self-control* and *self-regulation*. For instance, Díaz, Neal, and Amaya-Williams (1990) define self-control as complying with someone else's standards for appropriate behavior even when the latter individual is absent, whereas self-regulation involves setting one's *own* standards for appropriate behavior. Schunk and Zimmerman (1997; Kitsantas et al., 2000; Zimmerman & Kitsantas, 1999) suggest that self-control is heavily dependent on comparing one's own performance with internal standards that have been acquired from a model's performance, whereas true self-regulation is more automatic and flexible, allowing adaptation to changing circumstances.

frequency of a behavior. For example, my family was once part of a research project in which randomly selected households recorded their television-watching habits over a period of several weeks. We were instructed to mark down every instance of television viewing—including the date, time of day, length of time, and programs watched—on a specially designed record sheet. Each time I thought about turning on the television set, I remembered all of the work I would have to go through to record my viewing, and, as often as not, I found something else to do instead. Thus, the simple process of having to record my television-watching behavior altered that behavior.

Self-monitoring can be instituted in a classroom setting as well. For example, in one study (Harris, 1986), students having difficulty keeping their minds on their spelling assignments were given tape recorders that emitted a small beep at random intervals about 45 seconds apart. Whenever students heard a beep, they asked themselves, "Was I paying attention?" This simple technique doubled their time on task and tripled their productivity on spelling assignments. Other studies have obtained similar results in terms of increased on-task behavior and assignment completion (Belfiore & Hornyak, 1998; Hallahan, Marshall, & Lloyd, 1981; Harris, 1986; Heins, Lloyd, & Hallahan, 1986; Mace et al., 1989; Mace & Kratochwill, 1988; Webber, Scheuermann, McCall, & Coleman, 1993).

Just as desirable behaviors can be increased, undesirable behaviors can be *decreased* through self-monitoring. For example, self-recording of a target behavior has been found to reduce such disruptive classroom behaviors as talking out of turn, leaving one's seat without permission, and hitting classmates (Bolstad & Johnson, 1972; Mace et al., 1989; Moletzsky, 1974; Webber et al., 1993).

Self-Reinforcement

People are often able to change their behavior by reinforcing themselves when they behave in a desired fashion and withholding reinforcement when they do not (Mace et al., 1989; Mahoney & Thoresen, 1974; O'Leary & O'Leary, 1972; Rimm & Masters, 1974). For example, I am able to maintain my book-writing behavior by applying the Premack principle: I let myself engage in enjoyable activities only after I have completed less enjoyable ones. (To refresh your memory on the Premack principle, see the section "Activity Reinforcers" in Chapter 4.)

When students learn to reinforce themselves for their accomplishments—perhaps by giving themselves some free time, helping themselves to a small treat, or simply praising themselves—their study habits and academic performance improve (Beneke & Harris, 1972; Greiner & Karoly, 1976; Hayes et al., 1985; Stevenson & Fantuzzo, 1986). In one research study (Stevenson & Fantuzzo, 1986), students who had been performing poorly in arithmetic were taught to give themselves points when they did well on their assignments; they could later use these points to "buy" a variety of items and privileges. Within a few weeks, these students were doing as well as their classmates on both in-class assignments and homework. In another study (Bandura & Perloff, 1967), self-reinforcement was just as effective in modifying student behaviors as reinforcement administered by a teacher.

Self-Imposed Stimulus Control

As you should recall from our discussion of operant conditioning in Chapter 4, a response is under stimulus control when it is emitted in the presence of some stimuli but not in the presence of others. This idea can be translated into an effective means of promoting self-regulation (Mahoney & Thoresen, 1974); I call it self-imposed stimulus control. To increase a particular desired behavior, an individual might be instructed to seek out an environment in which that behavior is most likely to occur. For example, a student who wishes to increase the time actually spent studying each day should sit down at a table in the library rather than on a bed at home. Conversely, to decrease an undesired behavior, an individual should engage in that behavior only in certain situations. For example, I once knew a professor who, in an effort to stop smoking, gradually reduced the number of locations in which he allowed himself to smoke. Eventually, he was able to smoke in only one place, facing a back corner of his office; at that point, he successfully stopped smoking.

We should note here that techniques designed to promote self-regulation work only when learners are motivated to change their own behavior. Under such circumstances, such techniques can help learners discover that they have some control, not only over their behavior but over their environment as well. Three precautions must be taken, however. First, people being trained in self-regulation strategies must have the capability for performing the desired behaviors; for example, students who want to modify their study habits will achieve higher grades only if they possess adequate academic skills to ensure success. Second, people must *believe* that they can make the necessary behavior changes; in other words, they must have high self-efficacy (Schunk, 1998). And third, people must be cautioned not to expect too much of themselves too quickly. Many individuals would prefer overnight success, but shaping, either of oneself or of another, is usually a slow, gradual process. Just as the dieter will not lose 40 pounds in one week, it is equally unlikely that a habitually poor student will achieve honor roll status immediately. For self-regulation techniques to be effective, one's expectations for oneself must be practical and realistic.

The Cognitive Side of Self-Regulation

We have seen numerous indications that self-regulation involves cognitive processes as well as behavior. As a concrete example, in Meichenbaum's final step for teaching self-instructions, the learner does not verbalize, but merely *thinks* about the instructions that a model has provided. More generally, such elements of self-regulation as setting standards for performance, self-judgment, and self-reaction (e.g., feeling proud or ashamed) are probably more cognitive than behavioral in nature.

In recent years, psychologists have applied the concept of self-regulation more explicitly to the control of one's mental processes; in particular, they now talk about *self-regulated learning* as well as self-regulated behavior. For example, self-regulated learners set goals for a learning activity, choose study strategies that are likely to help them accomplish the goals, monitor their progress toward the goals, and change their study strategies if necessary (Winne, 1995a). We will talk more about self-regulated learning when we discuss metacognition and study strategies in Chapter 13, where we will draw from the work of both cognitive and social cognitive theorists.

EDUCATIONAL IMPLICATIONS OF SOCIAL COGNITIVE THEORY

Social cognitive theory has numerous implications for classroom practice. Let's look at some of the most important ones:

- *Students often learn a great deal simply by observing others.* According to many behaviorists (e.g., B. F. Skinner), people must make active responses for learning to occur. But in this chapter, I have presented examples of how learning can also occur through observations of what other people do. For instance, we have seen that children can acquire new skills, make moral judgments, and develop standards for their own behavior in large part by observing those around them.

Furthermore, people may learn what behaviors are and are not acceptable through their vicarious experiences—more specifically, by seeing others receive reinforcement or punishment for various responses. Therefore, teachers and other school personnel must be consistent in the rewards and punishments they administer—not only from time to time but also from student to student.

• *Describing the consequences of behaviors can effectively increase appropriate behaviors and decrease inappropriate ones.* As you should recall, social cognitive theorists propose that reinforcement and punishment affect behavior only when people are consciously aware of response–consequence contingencies. Thus, promises of rewards for good behaviors and warnings of unpleasant consequences for misdeeds can be effective means of improving student behavior. But administering reinforcement or punishment when students do not recognize the relationship between a particular response they have made and its consequence is unlikely to bring about behavior change.

• *Modeling provides an alternative to shaping for teaching new behaviors.* Operant conditioning provides one means—shaping—for teaching a new response. But to shape a particular behavior, one must begin by reinforcing an existing behavior and then gradually modifying that behavior through differential reinforcement; for complex behaviors, this process can be quite time consuming. Social cognitive theory offers a faster, more efficient means for teaching new behavior: the modeling process.

To promote effective modeling, a teacher must make sure that four essential conditions exist: attention, retention, motor reproduction, and motivation. First of all, the teacher must make sure that students pay attention to the model and particularly to the relevant aspects of the model's behavior. Second, the teacher can facilitate students' retention of what they observe by helping them form appropriate memory codes (perhaps verbal labels or visual images) for their observations. Third, giving students opportunities to practice the behaviors they see and providing corrective feedback about their efforts will aid their motor reproduction of the responses they are modeling. Finally, the teacher must remember that students will display behaviors they have learned only if they have the motivation to do so. Many children are intrinsically motivated to perform, but others may require external incentives and reinforcers. (We will consider numerous motivational strategies, with a particular focus on those that foster intrinsic motivation, in Chapters 16 through 18.)

• *Teachers, parents, and other adults must model appropriate behaviors and take care that they don't model inappropriate ones.* Adults often possess characteristics (e.g., competence, prestige, power) that make them influential models for children. Accordingly, they must be careful that they model appropriate behaviors for the children with whom they interact. I am delighted when I see teachers and other adults show characteristics such as open-mindedness, empathy, and concern for physical fitness; I cringe when I see them express disdain for particular points of view, disregard the needs and concerns of other human beings, or smoke cigarettes.

A child I know once tried out for a role in a school Christmas pageant. Lisa went off to school on the morning of pageant tryouts, aware that students could each try out for one part only and thinking that she had a good chance of winning the role of Mrs. Claus. Lisa was convinced that the teacher would award the leading role of Santa Claus to a girl named Ann; however, because Ann was late that morning and the teacher had announced that latecomers would not be allowed to try out, Lisa instead tried out for Santa himself. When Ann arrived 10 minutes late, the teacher disregarded her rule about latecomers being ineligible, allowed Ann to try out for Santa Claus, and ultimately awarded the role to Ann. In doing so, this teacher, one of the school's most visible role models, modeled hypocrisy and favoritism.

As an educational psychologist who helps future teachers learn how to teach, my job is a particularly challenging one because I must practice what I preach. If I tell my students that immediate feedback, organization of information, vivid examples, hands-on experiences, and assessment practices that match instructional objectives are all important components of effective teaching, my students' learning will obviously be enhanced when I model all of those things as well. To say one thing but do another would be not only hypocritical but also counterproductive.

• *Teachers should expose students to a variety of other models.* Adult models need not be limited to children's teachers and parents. Other adults can be invited to visit classrooms on occasion; for example, police officers, prominent city officials, businesspeople, and nurses might demonstrate appropriate behaviors and attitudes related to safety, good citizenship, responsibility, and health. Symbolic models can also be effective; for example, studying the lives of such individuals as Helen Keller, Martin Luther King, Jr., and Eleanor Roosevelt is a viable method of illustrating many desirable behaviors.

Models don't simply demonstrate appropriate behaviors. Carefully chosen ones can also help break down traditional stereotypes regarding what different groups of people can and cannot do. For example, teachers might introduce students to male nurses, female engineers, African American physicians, Hispanic business executives, or athletes who are wheelchair bound. By exposing students to successful individuals of both genders, from many cultural and socioeconomic backgrounds, and with a variety of physical disabilities, teachers can help students realize that they themselves may also have the potential to accomplish great things.

• *Students must believe that they are capable of accomplishing school tasks.* As we have seen, students' self-efficacy affects their learning and academic achievement. Yet students are likely to differ widely in their confidence about performing tasks successfully. For example, at the adolescent level, boys are likely to have higher self-efficacy than girls with regard to mathematics and sports; meanwhile, girls are likely to have higher self-efficacy than boys for assignments in an English class (Wigfield, Eccles, & Pintrich, 1996).

To enhance students' self-efficacy related to school activities, teachers can make use of the factors that appear to promote self-efficacy. For instance, they can tell students that individuals similar to themselves have mastered the things they are learning. They might also have students actually observe their peers successfully accomplishing tasks; it may be especially beneficial for students to see a peer struggling with a task or problem at first—something they themselves are likely to do—and then eventually mastering it. In addition, teachers can plan group activities in which students collaborate on challenging assignments. But most importantly, teachers can foster high self-efficacy by helping students achieve classroom success themselves—for example, by helping them master essential basic skills and providing guidance and support for tackling more advanced, difficult ones.

• *Teachers should help students set realistic expectations for their academic accomplishments.* As growing children become increasingly self-regulating, they begin to adopt standards for their own behavior. Such standards are often based on those that people around them have adopted, and so they may in some cases be either overly optimistic or overly pessimistic (Paris & Cunningham, 1996; Phillips & Zimmerman, 1990). When a student's standards for performance are unrealistically high, as might be true for a perfectionist, continual disappointment and frustration are likely to result. Yet when a student's standards are too low, underachievement will be the outcome. Teachers can facilitate students' academic and social progress by helping them form self-expectations commensurate with their current skills and ability levels.

> • *Self-regulation techniques provide effective methods for improving student behavior.* Earlier in the chapter, I described four techniques for promoting self-regulation: self-instructions, self-monitoring, self-reinforcement, and self-imposed stimulus control. When students are intrinsically motivated to change their own behaviors, such techniques can provide a viable alternative to behaviorist approaches.

As social cognitive theorists have so clearly shown, we cannot ignore the social context of the classroom. Students can and do learn from the models—the parents, teachers, and peers—that they see every day. Social cognitive theorists have also made it clear that we must consider cognitive as well as environmental factors when trying to explain how human beings learn and behave. As we move into cognitivism in the next chapter, we will begin to focus on such cognitive factors more closely.

SUMMARY

Social cognitive theory focuses on the ways in which individuals learn from observing one another. This perspective reflects a blending of behaviorist concepts (e.g., reinforcement and punishment) and cognitive notions (e.g., awareness and expectations). Environmental and cognitive variables continually interact with one another and with behavior, such that each influences the others in a reciprocal fashion.

Many behaviors, beliefs, and attitudes are acquired through *modeling*; academic skills, aggression, and morality are three examples. Four processes are necessary for modeling to occur: attention, retention, motor reproduction, and motivation. Effective models are likely to be competent, prestigious, and powerful, and to exhibit behaviors that are "gender-appropriate" and relevant to the observer's own situation.

Individuals with high *self-efficacy*—those who believe they can successfully accomplish a particular task—are more likely to choose challenging activities, exert effort and persist at those activities, and exhibit high levels of achievement over the long run. Self-efficacy can be enhanced through encouraging messages, successes of others, group accomplishments, and, perhaps most importantly, one's own individual successes.

Social cognitive theorists propose that, although the environment influences behavior, over time people begin to regulate their own behavior; they do so by developing their own standards for performance, observing and judging themselves on the basis of those standards, and reinforcing or punishing themselves (even if only mentally and emotionally) for what they have or have not done. Teachers can help their students become more self-regulating by teaching such techniques as self-instructions, self-monitoring, self-reinforcement, and self-imposed stimulus control.

Social cognitive theory offers numerous implications for educational practice. For example, describing response–reinforcement and response–punishment contingencies makes students aware of what those contingencies are; hence, such descriptions are likely to affect behavior before any consequences are ever imposed. When instruction involves teaching new skills, modeling provides an effective, and often more efficient, alternative to operant conditioning techniques. Modeling is not restricted to planned instruction, however: Teachers and other adults model a variety of behaviors, attitudes, and values in their daily interactions with students, and so they must be careful that their behaviors reflect fairness, acceptance of diverse viewpoints, a healthy lifestyle, and high ethical standards. When teaching potentially challenging subject matter, teachers must give students reason to believe that they are truly capable of mastering that subject matter.

Part Four

Cognitive Views of Learning

CHAPTER 8

Antecedents and Assumptions of Cognitivism

Since the 1960s, cognitivism (also known as *cognitive psychology*) has been the predominant perspective within which learning research has been conducted and theories of learning have evolved. As we begin to explore this perspective, you will undoubtedly notice a change in emphasis. In earlier chapters, we focused largely on the roles of environmental conditions (stimuli) and observable behaviors (responses) in learning, although social cognitive theory also provided a window into such mental phenomena as attention, expectations, and self-efficacy. At this point, we will begin to look more directly at **cognitive processes,** considering how people perceive, interpret, remember, and otherwise think about the environmental events they experience.

As you should recall, early behaviorists chose not to incorporate mental events into their learning theories, arguing that such events were impossible to observe and measure and so could not be studied objectively. During the 1950s and 1960s, however, many psychologists became increasingly dissatisfied with such a "thoughtless" approach to human learning. Major works with a distinctly cognitive flavor began to emerge; publications by Noam Chomsky (1957) in psycholinguistics and by Bruner, Goodnow, and Austin (1956) in concept learning are examples. Ulric Neisser's *Cognitive Psychology*, published in 1967, was a landmark book that helped to legitimize cognitive theory as a major alternative to behaviorism (Calfee, 1981). Increasingly, cognitivism began appearing in educational psychology literature as well, with Jerome Bruner (1961a, 1961b, 1966) and David Ausubel (1963, 1968; Ausubel & Robinson, 1969) being two well-known early proponents. By the 1970s, the great majority of learning theorists had joined the cognitive bandwagon (Robins, Gosling, & Craik, 1999).

Yet the roots of cognitive psychology preceded the mass discontentment with strict S–R psychology by several decades. Some cognitive learning theories appeared in the early decades of the twentieth century, notably those of the American psychologist Edward Tolman, the Gestalt psychologists of Germany, the Swiss developmentalist Jean Piaget, and the Russian developmentalist Lev Vygotsky. These early theories have had considerable influence on contemporary cognitivism, and Piaget's and Vygotsky's theories in particular continue to provide dominant perspectives for developmental research.

Equally important to the cognitive movement was research conducted in the early and middle decades of the twentieth century in an area known as *verbal learning*. Verbal learning theorists originally attempted to apply a stimulus–response analysis to human language and verbal behavior, but they soon discovered that the complexities of human language-based learning were sometimes difficult to explain from the behaviorist perspective. Increasingly, verbal learning theorists began to incorporate cognitive processes into their explanations of research results.

In this chapter, we will consider some of the contributions of Tolman, the Gestaltists, Piaget, Vygotsky, and the verbal learning theorists. We will then look at the basic assumptions of contemporary cognitivism and at several specific theoretical perspectives that cognitivists offer. Finally, we will identify some general educational implications of the cognitive perspective.

EDWARD TOLMAN'S PURPOSIVE BEHAVIORISM

Edward Chace Tolman (1932, 1938, 1942, 1959) was a prominent learning theorist during the heyday of behaviorism, yet his work had a distinctly cognitive flair. Like his behaviorist contemporaries, Tolman valued the importance of objectivity in conducting research and used nonhuman species (especially rats) as the subjects of his research. Unlike his contemporaries, however, Tolman included internal mental phenomena in his explanations of how learning occurs and adopted a more holistic view of learning than was true of S–R theorists.

Tolman developed his mentalistic view of learning by using some rather ingenious adaptations of traditional behaviorist research methods. We will see examples of his approach as we consider the central ideas of his theory:

- *Behavior should be studied at a molar level.* Early theorists in the behaviorist tradition, such as Pavlov, Watson, and Thorndike, attempted to reduce behavior to simple stimulus–response connections. In contrast, Tolman was adamant in his position that more global (molar) behaviors are the appropriate objects of study. Tolman argued that breaking behavior down into isolated S–R reflexes, rather than looking at it in its totality, obscures the meaning and purpose of that behavior.

- *Learning can occur without reinforcement.* Tolman opposed the behaviorist idea that reinforcement is necessary for learning to occur, and he conducted several experiments to support his contention. As an example, let's look at a study by Tolman and Honzik (1930) in which three groups of rats ran a difficult maze under different reinforcement conditions. Group 1 rats were reinforced with food each time they successfully completed the maze. Group 2 rats received no reinforcement for successful performance. Group 3 rats were not reinforced during the first 10 days in the maze but began receiving reinforcement on the eleventh day.

Before we examine the results of this experiment, let's predict what should have happened in this situation if reinforcement were an essential condition for learning to occur. Because Group 1 rats were continuously reinforced, we would expect their performance to improve over time. Because Group 2 rats were *not* reinforced, we would expect their performance to stay at a constant

Figure 8–1
Maze performance of rats receiving food, no food, or food at day 11.
Adapted from "Introduction and Removal of Reward, and Maze Performance in Rats" by E. C. Tolman and C. H. Honzik, 1930, *University of California Publications in Psychology, 4*, p. 267. Copyright 1930 by University of California Press. Adapted with permission.

low level. And we would expect the rats in Group 3 to show no improvement in performance until after day 11, at which point they should show a pattern of behavior similar to the Group 1 rats' first few days of performance.

The actual results of the Tolman and Honzik experiment appear in Figure 8–1; the data points indicate the average number of wrong turns (errors) each group made while traveling the maze each day. Notice that the performance of Groups 2 and 3 improved somewhat even when they were not receiving reinforcement. Notice also that once the rats in Group 3 began receiving reinforcement, their performance in the maze equaled (in fact, it surpassed!) Group 1's performance. Apparently, Group 3 rats had learned as much as Group 1 rats despite their lack of reinforcement during the first 10 days. Such results cast doubt on Thorndike's law of effect: Perhaps reinforcement is not as critical a factor in learning as behaviorists have suggested.

• *Learning can occur without a change in behavior.* Although early behaviorists equated learning with behavior changes, Tolman argued that learning can occur *without* being reflected in a change in behavior, using the term **latent learning** for such unobservable learning. The Tolman and Honzik study just described provides an example of latent learning: Group 3 rats must have been learning just as much as Group 1 rats during the first 10 days, even though their behavior did not reflect such learning. (Presumably, Group 2 rats were also learning more than they let on.) Tolman proposed that reinforcement influences *performance* rather than learning, in that it increases the likelihood that a learned behavior will be exhibited. (As we noted in the preceding chapter, social cognitive theorists have come to conclusions similar to those of Tolman, proposing that learning can occur without a change in behavior and that reinforcement increases the likelihood that people will demonstrate what they have learned.)

- *Intervening variables must be considered.* As you may recall from Chapter 3, Clark Hull incorporated **intervening variables** into his theory of learning, arguing that variables such as drive, habit strength, and incentive play critical roles. The concept of intervening variables did not originate with Hull, however; as early as 1932, Tolman proposed that variables within the organism (e.g., cognitions and physiological states) affect the behaviors observed. Thus, with Tolman's work, we have an early concern for *individual differences* in the learning process, a concern that continues in contemporary cognitivism.

- *Behavior is purposive.* Tolman believed that learning should be viewed not as the formation of S–R connections but as a process of learning that certain events lead to other events (e.g., that following a particular path through a maze leads to reinforcement). He proposed that once an organism has learned that a behavior leads to a certain end result, the organism behaves in order to achieve that end. In other words, behavior has a *purpose*, that of goal attainment. Because Tolman stressed the goal-directed nature of behavior, his theory of learning is sometimes referred to as **purposive behaviorism.**

- *Expectations affect behavior.* According to Tolman, once an organism learns that certain behaviors produce certain kinds of results, it begins to form expectations about the outcomes of its behaviors. Rather than reinforcement affecting the response that it follows, the organism's *expectation* of reinforcement affects the response that it *precedes*. (Once again, we see a similarity with social cognitive theory.)

When an organism's expectations are not met, its behavior may be adversely affected. For example, in an experiment by Elliott (cited in Tolman, 1932), rats received one of two different reinforcers for running a maze: An experimental group received a favorite rat delicacy—bran mash—whereas a control group received relatively unenticing sunflower seeds. The experimental group ran the maze faster than the control group, apparently because they were expecting a yummier treat at the end of the maze. On the tenth day, the experimental group rats were switched to the sunflower seed reinforcement that the control group rats had been getting all along. After discovering the change in reinforcement, these rats began to move through the maze more slowly than they had previously, and even more slowly than the control rats. Because both groups were being reinforced identically at this point (i.e., with boring sunflower seeds), the inferior performance of the rats in the experimental group was apparently due to the change in reinforcement, resulting in a *depression effect* similar to what I described in Chapter 4. As Tolman might put it, the rats' expectation of reinforcement was no longer being confirmed. As you or I might say, the rats were very disappointed with the treat awaiting them.

- *Learning results in an organized body of information.* Through a series of studies, Tolman demonstrated that rats who run a maze learn more than just a set of independent responses. It appears that they also learn how the maze is arranged—the lay of the land, so to speak. For example, in a classic study by Tolman, Ritchie, and Kalish (1946), rats ran numerous times through a maze that looked like maze 1 of Figure 8–2. They were then put in a situation similar to maze 2 of Figure 8–2. Because the alley that had previously led to food was now blocked, the rats had to choose among 18 other alleys. Using S–R theory's notion of stimulus generalization, we would expect the rats to make their running response to a stimulus very similar to the blocked alley. We would therefore predict that the rats would choose alleys near the blocked one—particularly alley 9 or alley 10. However, few of the rats chose either of these routes. By far, the most common choice was alley 6, the one that presumably would provide a shortcut to the location in which the rats had come to expect food.

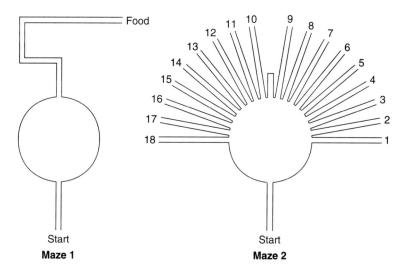

Figure 8–2
Mazes used by Tolman, Ritchie, and Kalish (1946).

Based on such research, Tolman proposed that rats (and presumably many other species as well) develop **cognitive maps** of their environments: They learn where different parts of the environment are situated in relation to one another. Knowing how things are organized in space enables an organism to get from one place to another quickly and easily, often by the shortest possible route. The concept of a cognitive map (sometimes called a *mental map*) has continued to be a topic of research for contemporary researchers, psychologists and geographers alike (e.g., Downs & Stea, 1977).

Tolman's notion of a cognitive map reflects his belief that learning is *organized*: Rats integrate their experiences into an organized body of information from which they can then draw inferences (e.g., about shortest routes). In developing his views about the organized nature of what organisms learn, Tolman was influenced by the ideas of the Gestalt psychologists of Germany. It is to Gestalt psychology that we turn now.

GESTALT PSYCHOLOGY

During the early decades of the twentieth century, a perspective emerged in German psychology that was largely independent of behaviorism-dominated American psychology. This perspective, known as **Gestalt psychology,** was advanced by such theorists as Max Wertheimer (1912, 1945, 1959), Wolfgang Köhler (1925, 1929, 1938, 1940, 1947, 1959, 1969), and Kurt Koffka (1935). Gestalt psychologists emphasized the importance of organizational processes in perception, learning, and problem solving and believed that individuals were predisposed to organize information in particular ways. Following are several basic ideas of Gestalt psychology:

• *Perception is often different from reality.* The origin of Gestalt psychology is usually attributed to Wertheimer's (1912) description and analysis of an optical illusion known as the *phi*

phenomenon. Wertheimer observed that when two lights blink on and off sequentially at a particular rate, they often appear to be only one light moving quickly back and forth. (This effect can be observed in the blinking lights of many roadside signs.) The fact that an individual "sees" motion when observing stationary objects led Wertheimer to conclude that perception of an experience is sometimes different from the experience itself.

- *The whole is more than the sum of its parts.* Gestaltists believed that human experience cannot be successfully understood when various aspects of experience are studied in isolation from one another. For example, we perceive the illusion of movement in the *phi* phenomenon only when two or more lights are present; no motion is perceived in a single light. Similarly, we recognize a particular sequence of musical notes as being the melody of "Jingle Bells," but we hear the same song even when the key changes and so the specific notes that are played are different (Rachlin, 1995). A combination of stimuli may show a pattern not evident in any of the stimuli alone; to use a Gestaltist expression, the whole is more than the sum of its parts.

The importance of the interrelationships among elements in a situation can be seen in Köhler's (1929) **transposition** experiments with chickens. Hens were shown two sheets of gray paper, one a darker shade of gray than the other. Grain was placed on both sheets, but the hens were allowed to feed only from the darker one. On a subsequent occasion, the hens were shown a sheet of paper the same shade as that on which they had previously been fed, along with a sheet of an even darker shade. In this second situation, the hens tended to go to the darker of the two sheets—in other words, to one on which they had *not* previously been reinforced. The hens had apparently learned something about the relationship between the two sheets of paper; in a sense, they learned that darker is better.

- *The organism structures and organizes experience.* The German word *Gestalt*, roughly translated, means "structured whole." Structure is not necessarily inherent in a situation; instead, the organism imposes structure and organization on that situation. For example, the *phi* phenomenon represents a person's synthesis of two flashing lights into the perception of a single moving light.

Figure 8–3 provides another example of how experiences are organized. As you look at this figure, you probably perceive four pairs of lines with individual lines at each end. Yet turn your attention to Figure 8–4, in which the same lines appear within a particular context. You probably now see the lines differently—as five pairs forming the sides of five rectangles. The lines themselves are identical in both cases, but the way in which you organize them (i.e., how you group the lines together) is different. The "structure" of the lines is something that you yourself impose on the figure.

Figure 8–3

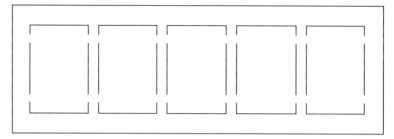

Figure 8–4

• *The organism is predisposed to organize experience in particular ways.* Gestaltists believed that organisms (especially human beings) are predisposed to structure their experiences in similar, and therefore predictable, ways. They proposed several principles to describe how people organize their experiences. One of the dominant principles affecting how people organize information is the **law of proximity:** People tend to perceive as a unit those things that are close together in space. For example, look at the following dots:

● ● ●   ● ● ●   ● ● ●

Not only do you see nine dots, but you probably also perceive an arrangement of three groups of three dots each; that is, you see those dots that are in closer proximity to one another as somehow belonging together. In the same way, when you looked at Figure 8–3, you perceived lines that were close together as forming pairs. And notice how you read this phrase:

One very high way

and this one:

On every highway

In both phrases, the same letters appear in exactly the same sequence:

Oneveryhighway

Yet because of the different ways the letters are grouped together, you read the phrases differently.

Another organizational principle from Gestalt psychology is the **law of similarity:** People tend to perceive as a unit those things that are similar to one another. For example, look at the dots in Figure 8–5. Can you see the letter Y among them? Perhaps not. But now look at the dots in Figure 8–6. This time a letter Y is obvious. The arrangement of the dots in both cases is the same, but in the second case the dots forming the Y are all black, and you tend to perceive those similar black dots as a unit. Yet you probably haven't noticed other letters, such as the letter E,

Figure 8–5   ○ ○ ● ○ ○   **Figure 8–6**   ● ○ ○ ○ ●
                   ○ ● ○ ○ ○   ○ ● ○ ● ○
                   ○ ○ ○ ○ ●   ○ ○ ● ○ ○
                   ● ○ ● ○ ○   ○ ○ ● ○ ○
                   ○ ○ ● ○ ●   ○ ○ ● ○ ○

that are also formed by some of the dots. As early as 6 or 7 months of age, children show evidence that they perceive the world in accordance with the law of similarity (Quinn, Bhatt, Brush, Grimes, & Sharpnack, 2002).

Still another Gestaltist principle is the **law of closure:** People tend to fill in missing pieces to form a complete picture. For example, when you looked at Figure 8–4, you filled in missing segments of what appeared to be continuous straight lines to perceive five rectangles. Similarly, when you look at Figure 8–7, you are probably able to read "Singing in the rain," even though 50% of the print is missing. You simply fill in what isn't there.

Gestaltists further proposed that individuals always organize their experience as simply, concisely, symmetrically, and completely as possible, a principle known as the **law of Prägnanz** (i.e., "terseness" or "preciseness") (Koffka, 1935). For example, you are likely to see rectangles in Figure 8–4 because rectangles are simple, symmetric figures. It is unlikely that you would mentally fill in the missing pieces of that figure in a wild and crazy fashion such as that shown in Figure 8–8. People are very simple folks after all!

• *Learning follows the law of Prägnanz.* According to Gestalt psychologists, learning involves the formation of **memory traces.** These memory traces are subject to the law of Prägnanz, so that over time they tend to become simpler, more concise, and more complete than the actual input. For example, after seeing the somewhat irregular objects in Figure 8–9, people are likely to remember them later as being a "circle" and a "square." As another example, consider a study by Tversky (1981), in which people studied maps and then drew them from memory. Distortions in people's reproductions often followed the law of Prägnanz: Curvy, irregular lines were straightened, slanted lines were represented as north–south or east–west lines, and map features were placed in better alignment with one another than they had been in the original maps.

• *Problem solving involves restructuring and insight.* As we noted in Chapter 4, Thorndike (1898) described problem solving (such as that exhibited by cats in puzzle boxes) as a process of trial and error. Gestaltists proposed a very different view of how organisms solve problems. Köhler (1925), for instance, suggested that problem solving involves mentally combining and recombining various elements of a problem until a structure that solves the problem is achieved. He described numerous observations of chimpanzees solving problems through what he perceived to be the mental manipulation of the problem situation. In one situation, a chimpanzee named Sultan was faced with a dilemma: Some fruit was placed far enough

Figure 8–7   Singing in the rain

Figure 8–8

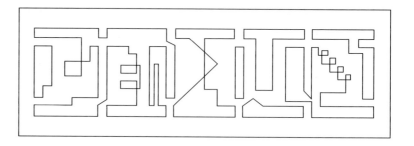

outside his cage that he could not reach it. Sultan had had earlier experiences in which he had successfully used sticks to rake in fruit; however, the only stick inside the cage was too short. A longer stick was outside the cage, but, like the fruit, was beyond Sultan's reach. The following scenario ensued:

> Sultan tries to reach the fruit with the smaller of the two sticks. Not succeeding, he tears at a piece of wire that projects from the netting of his cage, but that, too, in vain. Then he gazes about him (there are always in the course of these tests some long pauses during which the animals scrutinize the whole visible area). He suddenly picks up the little stick, once more goes up to the bars, directly opposite to the long stick, scratches it towards him with the [short stick], seizes it, and goes with it to the point opposite the [fruit], which he secures. From the moment that his eyes fall upon the long stick, his procedure forms one consecutive whole, without hiatus. . . . (Köhler, 1925, p. 180)

In another situation, Sultan, again confronted with fruit placed outside the cage beyond his reach, had two hollow bamboo rods, one somewhat thinner than the other, and both too short to reach the fruit. After numerous "fruitless" attempts, he seemingly gave up and resorted to playing indifferently with the sticks. At one serendipitous point, Sultan found himself holding the two sticks end to end in such a way that they appeared to form a long, straight line. He immediately pushed the end of the thinner stick into the end of the thicker one (thus making a single long stick), ran over to the edge of the cage, and successfully obtained the elusive bananas.

In neither of the situations I have just described did Sultan engage in the random trial-and-error learning that Thorndike had observed for cats. Instead, it appeared to Köhler as if Sultan thought about possible solutions to the problem, arranging the problem elements in various ways, until he arrived at a sudden **insight** as to a problem solution.

Gestalt psychology continues to influence how cognitive psychologists conceptualize learning and cognition (e.g., Henle, 1985; Quinn et al., 2002; Vecera, Vogel, & Woodman, 2002). For example,

Figure 8–9
Irregularly shaped
objects may later be
remembered as
"circles" or "squares."

we will examine another basic organizing principle—figure-ground—when we look at the nature of attention in Chapter 9. We will see *closure* at work when we examine constructive processes in perception and memory in Chapters 10 and 12. We will revisit the Gestaltist idea of *insight* in our exploration of problem solving in Chapter 14. And the general idea that people organize the things that they learn will come up repeatedly in our discussion of learning and cognition in the chapters to come.

JEAN PIAGET'S DEVELOPMENTAL THEORY

Independent of Tolman's work in the United States and of the Gestalt movement in Germany, the Swiss biologist Jean Piaget began a research program during the 1920s that has probably had a greater impact on contemporary theories of cognitive development than that of any other single researcher. Piaget had interests in philosophy as well as biology and was particularly curious about the origins of knowledge, a branch of philosophy known as *epistemology*. To discover where knowledge comes from and the forms that it takes as it develops, Piaget and his colleagues undertook a series of studies that provided some unique insights into how children think and learn about the world around them (e.g., Inhelder & Piaget, 1958; Piaget, 1928, 1952, 1959, 1970, 1971, 1972, 1980; Piaget & Inhelder, 1969).

Although Piaget's theory dates from the 1920s, its impact on psychological thought in the Western Hemisphere was not widely felt until the 1960s, probably for several reasons. One likely reason is that Piaget, being Swiss, wrote in French, making his early work less accessible to English-speaking psychologists. Although his writings were eventually translated into English, Piaget's ideas gained widespread prominence and visibility largely through a summary of his early work written by the American psychologist John Flavell (1963).

A second reason that the Geneva research program was largely overlooked for more than three decades was Piaget's unconventional research methodology. Piaget employed what he called the **clinical method:** He gave children a variety of tasks and problems, asking a series of questions about each one. He tailored his interviews to the particular responses that the children gave, with follow-up questions varying from one child to the next. Such a procedure was radically different from the standardized, tightly controlled conditions typical of behaviorist animal research and was, therefore, unacceptable to many of Piaget's contemporaries in North America.

But perhaps the most critical reason that Piaget's theory did not immediately become part of the mainstream of psychological thought was its philosophical incompatibility with the behaviorist perspective that dominated the study of learning until the 1960s. Piaget focused on mental events—for example, on logical reasoning processes and the structure of knowledge—at a time when such mentalism was still being rejected by many learning theorists. The cognitivism that began to emerge in the 1960s was more receptive to Piagetian ideas.

Piaget's work is probably so popular today because it is the single most global theory of intellectual development; it incorporates such diverse topics as language; logical reasoning; moral judgments; and conceptions of time, space, and number. In addition, Piaget's unique studies with children, often involving cleverly designed problem situations, reveal a great deal about the nature of children's thought. In the next few pages, we will look at Piagetian ideas that are especially relevant to our understanding of human learning and cognition:

- *People are active processors of information.* Whereas behaviorists portrayed organisms, including humans, as passive respondents to environmental conditions, Piaget portrayed human beings as being *actively involved* in interpreting and learning from the events around them. Rather than simply responding to the stimuli they encounter, people manipulate those stimuli and observe the effects of their actions. For example, consider Piaget's observation of his son Laurent at 16 months of age:

> Laurent is seated before a table and I place a bread crust in front of him, out of reach. Also, to the right of the child I place a stick about 25 cm. long. At first Laurent tries to grasp the bread without paying attention to the instrument, and then he gives up. I then put the stick between him and the bread. . . . Laurent again looks at the bread, without moving, looks very briefly at the stick, then suddenly grasps it and directs it toward the bread. But he grasped it toward the middle and not at one of its ends so that it is too short to attain the objective. Laurent then puts it down and resumes stretching out his hand toward the bread. Then, without spending much time on this movement, he takes up the stick again, this time at one of its ends . . . and draws the bread to him.
>
> An hour later I place a toy in front of Laurent (out of his reach) and a new stick next to him. He does not even try to catch the objective with his hand; he immediately grasps the stick and draws the toy to him. (Piaget, 1952, p. 335)

In this situation, Laurent is acting on his environment; he is obviously experimenting with the elements of the situation to see what outcomes he can achieve. (You may have noticed a similarity between Laurent's behavior and that of the chimpanzee Sultan described earlier. Sultan, too, was an active problem solver rather than a passive respondent to environmental events.)

- *Knowledge can be described in terms of structures that change with development.* Piaget proposed the concept of **scheme** as being the basic structure through which an individual's knowledge is mentally represented. Although Piaget's notion of scheme is somewhat abstract, it can be defined roughly as a mental unit that represents a class of similar actions or thoughts. For example, an infant might have a scheme for grasping and use it for grabbing everything from bottles to rubber ducks. A teenager may have certain schemes related to logical thinking that might be applied to reasoning about a variety of social, political, or moral issues. As children develop, new schemes emerge, and existing schemes are repeatedly practiced, occasionally modified, and sometimes integrated with one another into **cognitive structures.** A good deal of Piaget's theory focused on the development of the cognitive structures that govern logical reasoning—structures that Piaget called **operations.**

- *Cognitive development results from the interactions that children have with their physical and social environments.* By interacting with the environment, growing children develop and modify their schemes. For example, in the anecdote involving Laurent that I presented earlier, we see a toddler actively manipulating parts of his physical environment—more specifically, manipulating the stick and bread—and presumably learning that some objects can be used as tools to obtain other objects. Equally essential to children's development is their interaction with other people. For example, Piaget described young children as being **egocentric**—as having difficulty understanding that others don't share their perspective of the world. Through social interactions, both positive (e.g., conversations) and negative (e.g., conflicts over such issues as sharing and fair play), children begin to discover that they hold a perspective of the world uniquely their own.

- *The processes through which people interact with the environment remain constant.* According to Piaget, people interact with their environment through two unchanging processes (he called them *functions*) known as assimilation and accommodation. In **assimilation,** an individual interacts with an object or event in a way that is consistent with an existing scheme. For example, the infant who sees Mama's flashy, dangling earrings may assimilate those earrings to his grasping scheme, clutching and pulling at them in much the same way that he grasps bottles. A second grader who has developed a scheme for adding two apples and three apples to make five apples may apply this scheme to a situation involving the addition of two dollars and three dollars. In **accommodation,** an individual either modifies an existing scheme or forms a new one to account for a new event. For example, an infant who has learned to crawl must adjust her style of crawling somewhat when she meets a flight of stairs. A boy who calls a spider an "insect" must revise his thinking when he learns that insects have six legs but spiders have eight.

Assimilation and accommodation are complementary processes: Assimilation involves modifying one's perception of the environment to fit a scheme, and accommodation involves modifying a scheme to fit the environment. According to Piaget, these two processes typically go hand in hand, with individuals interpreting new events within the context of their existing knowledge (assimilation) but also modifying their knowledge as a result of those events (accommodation).

Learning results from the conjoint processes of assimilation and accommodation. Learning is especially reflected in the process of accommodation, because it is through accommodation that major cognitive changes occur. An environmental event cannot lead to accommodation of schemes, however, unless that event can be related (assimilated) to those schemes in the first place. For example, consider this sentence:

D. O. Hebb proposed that learning is a process of developing cell assemblies and phase sequences.

Unless you know who D. O. Hebb was, and unless you are familiar with the concepts of *cell assembly* and *phase sequence*, you can learn very little from the sentence. Assimilation is almost always a necessary condition for accommodation to occur: You must be able to relate a new experience to what you already know before you can learn from it. This necessity for overlap between prior knowledge and the material to be learned is an important principle not only in Piagetian theory but in contemporary cognitive views of learning as well.

• *People are intrinsically motivated to try to make sense of the world around them.* According to Piaget, people are sometimes in a state of **equilibrium;** they can comfortably explain new events in terms of their existing schemes. But this equilibrium doesn't continue indefinitely, because people sometimes encounter new events that they cannot adequately explain in terms of their current understanding of the world. Such inexplicable events create **disequilibrium,** a "mental discomfort" of sorts. Only through replacing, reorganizing, or better integrating their schemes (in other words, through accommodation) do people become able to understand and explain previously puzzling phenomena. The movement from equilibrium to disequilibrium and back to equilibrium again is known as **equilibration**—a process that promotes increasingly complex levels of thought and knowledge.

• *Cognitive development occurs in distinct stages, with thought processes at each stage being qualitatively different from those at other stages.* A major feature of Piaget's theory is the identification of four distinct stages of cognitive development, each with its own unique patterns of thought. The schemes of each stage are modified and incorporated into the schemes of the following stage, thereby providing a foundation for that next stage. As a result, children progress through the four stages in the same, invariant sequence. The characteristics of Piaget's four stages are more completely described in other secondary sources (e.g., see Flavell, 1963; Flavell et al., 1993; Siegler, 1998; Wadsworth, 1996), but I will discuss them briefly here.

The first stage, the **sensorimotor stage,** is evident from birth until about 2 years of age (the exact ages of each stage vary from child to child). Much of the sensorimotor stage is characterized by behavior- and perception-based schemes, rather than by internal, mental schemes that we might think of as being "thought." According to Piaget, infants do not yet possess schemes that enable them to think about objects other than those directly in front of them; in other words, the expression "out of sight, out of mind" definitely applies. Near the end of the sensorimotor stage, however, **symbolic thinking**—the ability to represent external objects and events in terms of internal, mental symbols—emerges, marking the beginning of true thought as Piaget defined it.

The second stage, which Piaget called the **preoperational stage,** emerges when children are about 2 years old and continues until they are about 6 or 7. Language skills virtually explode during this stage; the words in children's rapidly increasing vocabularies reflect the many new mental schemes that they are developing. However, the preoperational stage is characterized by thinking that is often illogical by adult standards. For example, young children tend to confuse psychological phenomena (e.g., thoughts and emotions) with physical reality, a confusion manifested by such actions as attributing feelings to inanimate objects and insisting that monsters and bogeymen are lurking under the bed.

A commonly cited example of the illogical thinking of preoperational children is their reaction to a **conservation of liquid** problem. Imagine three glasses: Glasses A and B are tall, thin, and filled to equal heights with water, while Glass C is short, fat, and empty, as is shown in the "before" part of Figure 8–10. Clearly Glasses A and B contain the same amount of water. But now the contents of Glass B are poured into Glass C, thereby creating the situation shown in the "after" part of Figure 8–10. Do Glass A and Glass C contain the same amount of water, or does one contain more?

Being a logical adult, you would probably conclude that the two glasses hold identical amounts of water (excluding a few drops that might have been lost in the process of pouring). The preoperational child, however, is likely to say that the glasses hold different amounts of water: Most will say that Glass A has more because it is taller, although a few will say that Glass C has more because it is fatter. The child's thinking depends more on perception than logic during the

Figure 8–10
The water in Glass B ("before") is poured into Glass C ("after"). Does Glass C have the same amount of water that Glass B did?

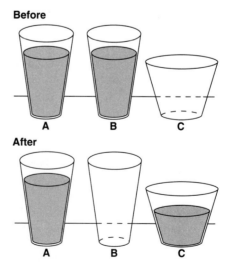

preoperational stage and so is susceptible to outward appearances: The glasses *look* different and so must *be* different.

According to Piaget, the third stage of cognitive development, **concrete operations,** appears when children are about 6 or 7 years old and continues until they are about 11 or 12. Children at this stage begin to think logically about conservation problems and other situations as well. Concrete operational children are limited in one very important respect, however: They can apply their logical operations only to concrete, observable objects and events. They have difficulty dealing with abstract information and with hypothetical ideas contrary to their own reality. For example, the concrete operational child should readily agree with the logic that

If all first graders are children,

And if all children are people,

Then all first graders are people.

yet will have trouble recognizing the logical validity of a similar problem that includes a contrary-to-fact premise:

If all first graders are children,

And if all children are hippopotamuses,

Then all first graders are hippopotamuses.

Concrete operational children, although generally very logical, cannot readily distinguish between logic and reality, and, after all, first graders are *not* hippopotamuses.

The fourth and final stage, **formal operations,** appears when children are about 11 or 12 years of age and continues to evolve for at least several years after that. During formal operations, the child develops the ability to reason with abstract, hypothetical, and contrary-to-fact information. Other abilities essential to mathematical and scientific reasoning emerge as well. For example, proportional thinking develops, through which the child truly begins to understand the concept of *proportion*, as reflected in such mathematical entities as fractions and decimals. The child also begins to separate and control variables: In testing a hypothesis about which factor among many may bring about a particular result, the child tests one variable at a time while holding all others constant. In addition, with the onset of formal operations children are able to examine their own thought processes and evaluate the quality and logic of those thoughts; for example, a child may notice a logical fallacy in something that he or she has said.

It is important to note here that recent research, though sometimes confirming Piaget's assertions regarding characteristics of the different stages (Flavell, 1996), does not support Piaget's proposed stage characteristics in their entirety. For example, it appears that infants and young children are cognitively more sophisticated than Piaget's descriptions of the sensorimotor and preoperational stages would indicate (Baillargeon, 1994; Carey, 1985a; Donaldson, 1978; Flavell et al., 1993; Metz, 1995; Siegler, 1998). At the same time, Piaget may have overestimated the capabilities of adolescents and even adults; for instance, many adults (including many college students) show behavior more characteristic of concrete operations than of formal operational thought (Kuhn, Garcia-Mila, Zohar, & Andersen, 1995; Pascarella & Terenzini, 1991; Siegler, 1998; Ward & Overton, 1990).

A second problem with Piaget's notion of stage-related logical thinking skills is that children often use a given logical thinking skill in one situation while being unable to use what is presumably the same skill in another situation (Case, 1985; Ceci & Roazzi, 1994; Flavell et al., 1993; Girotto & Light, 1993; Siegler & Ellis, 1996). Children's knowledge about the specific topics under consideration appears to be influential here (Carey, 1985a; Metz, 1995; Pulos & Linn, 1981). For example, in one study (Pulos & Linn, 1981), many seventh graders living in a rural school district demonstrated the formal operational ability to separate and control variables on a problem related to fishing but not on Piaget's traditional laboratory methods for assessing the same ability.

• *The rate of cognitive development is controlled to some extent by maturation.* One unique aspect of Piaget's theory is his assertion that children's progression through the four stages is limited by maturation—that is, by genetically controlled physiological changes. Piaget contended that a necessary prerequisite for the transition to each successive stage is the occurrence of certain neurological changes that allow more sophisticated cognitive structures to develop. Because of physiological limitations, it would be virtually impossible for a 2-year-old child to think logically like a concrete operations child or for a 7-year-old to deal successfully with abstract ideas.

As we discovered in Chapter 2, the brain continues to develop throughout childhood and adolescence, and even in the early adult years. Quite possibly, this continuing neurological development, and especially the development of the frontal cortex, may allow growing human beings to think in increasingly sophisticated ways. Although some researchers have found evidence that significant neurological changes do occur at the typical transition ages for progression from one of Piaget's cognitive stages to the next (Epstein, 1978; Hudspeth, 1985), whether such changes are specifically *related to* the cognitive changes that Piaget described is still very much an open question. Furthermore, researchers sometimes find that, with proper training, children become capable of thinking in ways that Piaget suggested were possible only for older individuals; such findings cast some doubt on maturation as a limiting factor in cognitive development (Case, 1985; Field, 1987; Mayer, 1992; Murray, 1978; Siegler, 1978).

Many of Piaget's ideas are evident in contemporary cognitivism. The current notion that knowledge is structured and organized can be seen in Piaget's work as well as in that of Tolman and the Gestaltists. Also important in contemporary theories of learning is Piaget's proposal that for learning to occur, an individual must be able to assimilate new information into existing cognitive structures; in other words, a new experience and prior knowledge must overlap. Many motivation theorists believe that conflicting perceptions or ideas do, in fact, create mental discomfort (disequilibrium) and motivate learners to seek out additional information to resolve the discrepancy (see Chapter 16). Finally, although many psychologists now question the idea that cognitive development can be characterized as a series of distinct stages (Flavell et al., 1993; Kuhn, 2001b; Rosser, 1994; Siegler & Ellis, 1996), Piaget's analyses of how children think about a variety of tasks and problems have provided the impetus for many studies of the development of cognition. Thus, although not all of Piaget's ideas have been validated by research, his theory continues to be an influential force in both the thinking and research methodologies of cognitive psychology.

While Piaget was conducting his early, groundbreaking research, another psychologist had ideas of his own about the factors that facilitate cognitive development. We turn to Lev Vygotsky's ideas now.

LEV VYGOTSKY'S DEVELOPMENTAL THEORY

The Russian psychologist Lev Vygotsky conducted numerous studies of children's thinking from the 1920s until his premature death from tuberculosis in 1934. Many Western psychologists did not fully appreciate the value and usefulness of his work until several decades later, when his major writings were translated into English (Vygotsky, 1962, 1978, 1987, 1997). Although Vygotsky never had the chance to develop his theory fully, his views are clearly evident in our views of learning and instruction today.

As you should recall, Piaget proposed that through assimilation and accommodation, children develop increasingly advanced and integrated schemes over time. In Piaget's view, learning is largely an individual enterprise; growing children do most of the work themselves. In contrast, Vygotsky believed that the adults in a society foster children's learning and development in an intentional and somewhat systematic manner: They continually engage children in meaningful and challenging activities and help them perform those activities successfully. Because Vygotsky emphasized the importance of society and culture for promoting cognitive growth, his theory is sometimes referred to as the **sociocultural perspective.** We can summarize this perspective in terms of several major assumptions:

- *Complex mental processes begin as social activities; as children develop, they gradually internalize these processes and can use them independently of the people around them.* Vygotsky proposed that many thinking processes have their roots in the social interactions (conversations, arguments, etc.) that children have with other people. As children discuss objects and events with adults and other knowledgeable individuals, they gradually incorporate into their own thinking the ways that people around them talk about and interpret the world, and they begin to use the words, concepts, symbols, and other representations—in essence, the *cognitive tools*—that are typical for their culture. The process through which social activities evolve into internal mental activities is called **internalization.**

Not all mental processes emerge through children's interactions with adults; some also develop as children interact with their peers. As an example, children frequently argue with one another about a variety of matters—how best to carry out an activity, what games to play, who did what to whom, and so on. According to Vygotsky, childhood arguments help children discover that there are often several points of view about the same situation. Eventually, children can, in essence, internalize the "arguing" process, developing the ability to look at a situation from several different angles on their own.

- *Thought and language become increasingly interdependent in the first few years of life.* For us as adults, thought and language are closely interconnected. For one thing, we often think in terms of the specific words that our language provides; for example, when we think about household pets, words such as *dog* and *cat* are likely to pop up repeatedly in our heads. In addition, we usually express our thoughts when we converse with others; as we often like to put it, we "speak our minds."

Vygotsky proposed that, in contrast to the state of affairs for adults, thought and language are distinctly separate functions for infants and young toddlers. In these early years of life, thinking occurs independently of language, and when language appears, it is first used primarily as a means of communication rather than as a mechanism of thought. But sometime around two years of age, thought and language become intertwined: Children begin to express their thoughts when they speak, and they begin to think in terms of words.

When thought and language merge, we begin to see **self-talk** (also known as *private speech*), whereby children talk to themselves out loud. Self-talk eventually evolves into **inner speech:** Children "talk" to themselves mentally rather than aloud. According to Vygotsky, both self-talk and inner speech have a similar purpose: By talking to themselves, children learn to guide and direct their own behaviors through difficult tasks and complex maneuvers in much the same way that adults have previously guided them. Self-talk and inner speech, then, are examples of the internalization process: Children gradually internalize the directions that they have initially received from those around them, so that they are eventually giving *themselves* directions.

Recent research has supported Vygotsky's views regarding the progression and role of self-talk and inner speech. The frequency of children's audible self-talk decreases during the preschool years, but this decrease is accompanied by an increase in whispered mumbling and silent lip movements, presumably reflecting a transition to inner speech (Bivens & Berk, 1990; Owens, 1996). Furthermore, self-talk increases when children are performing more challenging tasks—tasks at which they must work harder to complete successfully (Berk, 1994; Schimmoeller, 1998).

• *Through both informal conversations and formal schooling, adults convey to children the ways in which their culture interprets and responds to the world.* In their interactions with children, adults share the *meanings* that they attach to objects, events, and, more generally, human experience. In the process, they transform, or *mediate*, the situations that children encounter. Meanings are conveyed through a variety of mechanisms, including language (spoken words, writing, etc.), symbols, mathematics, art, music, literature, and so on.

Informal conversations are one common method through which adults pass along culturally appropriate ways of interpreting situations. No less important in Vygotsky's eyes is formal education, where teachers systematically impart the ideas, concepts, and terminology used in various academic disciplines (Vygotsky, 1962). Although Vygotsky, like Piaget, saw value in allowing children to make some discoveries themselves, he also saw value in having adults describe the discoveries of previous generations (Karpov & Haywood, 1998).

To the extent that specific cultures pass along unique concepts, ideas, and beliefs, children of different cultural backgrounds will develop somewhat different knowledge, skills, and ways of thinking. Thus, Vygotsky's theory leads us to expect greater diversity among children, at least in terms of cognitive development, than Piaget's theory does. For example, some cultures use a wide variety of maps (road maps, maps of subway systems, shopping mall layouts) and expose children to them early and frequently, whereas other cultures rarely if ever use maps (Trawick-Smith, 2000; Whiting & Edwards, 1988).

• *Children can accomplish more difficult tasks when they have the assistance of people more advanced and competent than themselves.* Vygotsky distinguished between two kinds of abilities that children are likely to have at any particular point in their development. A child's **actual developmental level** is the upper limit of tasks that he or she can perform independently, without help from anyone else. A child's **level of potential development** is the upper limit of tasks that he or she can perform with the assistance of a more competent individual. To get a true sense of children's cognitive development, Vygotsky suggested, we should assess their capabilities both when performing alone *and* when performing with assistance.

Children can typically do more difficult things in collaboration with adults than they can do on their own. For example, children just learning how to use a baseball bat can hit a baseball more successfully when adults are present to guide their swings. Children can play more difficult piano pieces when adults help them locate some of the notes on the keyboard. Students can solve more difficult mathematics problems when their teacher helps them identify critical problem components and potentially fruitful problem-solving strategies. And students can often read more complex prose within a reading group at school than they are likely to read independently at home (e.g., Burron & Claybaugh, 1992).

*   *Challenging tasks promote maximum cognitive growth.* The range of tasks that children cannot yet perform independently but *can* perform with the help and guidance of others is, in Vygotsky's terminology, the **zone of proximal development (ZPD).** A child's zone of proximal development includes learning and problem-solving abilities that are just beginning to develop within the child—abilities that are in an immature, "embryonic" form. Naturally, any child's ZPD will change over time; as some tasks are mastered, more complex ones will appear to present new challenges.

Vygotsky proposed that children learn very little from performing tasks they can already do independently. Instead, they develop primarily by attempting tasks they can accomplish only in collaboration with a more competent individual—that is, when they attempt tasks within their zone of proximal development. In a nutshell, it is the challenges in life, rather than the easy successes, that promote cognitive development.

Vygotsky focused more on the processes through which children develop than on the characteristics that children of particular ages are likely to exhibit. Furthermore, his descriptions of such processes were often imprecise and lacking in detail (Gauvain, 2001; Haenan, 1996; Hunt, 1997; Wertsch, 1984). For these reasons, Vygotsky's theory has been more difficult for researchers to test and either verify or disprove than has the case for Piaget's theory.

Nevertheless, contemporary theorists and practitioners have made considerable use of Vygotsky's ideas. For example, as we saw in the preceding chapter on social cognitive theory, self-instructions (in other words, self-talk) are a recommended strategy for helping children regulate their own behavior. If you look back at Meichenbaum's five steps for teaching self-instructions (described in Chapter 7), you should notice how each step promotes increasing internalization of what is initially a social interaction between the teacher and student.

In addition, we are seeing an increasing interest in teaching methods that involve social interaction. Some methods, such as classroom discussions and cooperative learning, involve frequent interaction among students themselves. Others, such as reciprocal teaching and apprenticeships, involve ongoing interactions between students and their teachers. I will describe each of these approaches in more detail in Chapter 15.

Finally, theorists and educators have given considerable thought to the kinds of assistance that can help students complete challenging assignments. The term **scaffolding** is often used here: Adults and other more competent individuals provide some form of structure or guidance that enables students to engage in activities and perform tasks that are in their zone of proximal development. For example, a teacher might

*   Work with students to develop a plan for dealing with a new task.
*   Demonstrate the proper performance of the task in a way that students can easily imitate.
*   Divide a complex task into several smaller, simpler tasks.
*   Provide structure or guidelines regarding how the task should be accomplished.
*   Provide a calculator, computer software (word processing programs, spreadsheets, etc.), or other technology that makes some aspects of the task easier.
*   Ask questions that get students thinking in appropriate ways about the task.
*   Keep students' attention focused on the relevant aspects of the task.

- Keep students motivated to complete the task.
- Remind students what their goal is in performing the task (e.g., what a problem solution should look like).
- Give frequent feedback about how students are progressing.
  (Gallimore & Tharp, 1990; Good, McCaslin, & Reys, 1992; Lajoie & Derry, 1993; Merrill et al., 1996; Rogoff, 1990; Rosenshine & Meister, 1992; Wood, Bruner, & Ross, 1976)

As students become more adept at performing tasks, scaffolding is gradually phased out, and the students eventually perform those tasks on their own.

The perspectives that we've examined so far—those of Tolman, Gestalt psychologists, Piaget, and Vygotsky—had a cognitivist flavor from their inception. At about the same time, certain other theorists began with the best of behaviorist intentions, but over time found it increasingly difficult to explain their research results using stimulus–response principles alone. We turn now to the work of these verbal learning theorists—psychologists who helped pave the way for a wider acceptance of cognitive views of learning.

VERBAL LEARNING RESEARCH

One outgrowth of the behaviorist movement was an extension of behaviorist principles to a uniquely human behavior—language. In the early and middle decades of the twentieth century (and especially from the 1930s through the 1960s), many researchers attempted to study verbal behavior and the learning of verbal material by applying an S–R approach to these phenomena. The results of this research program are collectively known as **verbal learning** research.

Central to verbal learning research were two learning tasks, serial learning and paired associate learning, that could easily be analyzed in terms of an S–R perspective. **Serial learning** involves learning a sequence of items in a particular order; the alphabet, the days of the week, and the nine planets of our solar system are examples. Verbal learning theorists explained serial learning in this way: The first item in the list is a stimulus to which the second item is learned as a response, the second item then serves as a stimulus to which the third item is the learned response, and so on.

Paired associate learning involves learning pairs of items. Learning foreign language vocabulary words and their English equivalents (e.g., *le papier* is French for "paper") and learning state capitals (e.g., Juneau is the capital of Alaska) are two examples. Verbal learning theorists described paired associates as being distinct stimulus–response associations: The first item in each pair is the stimulus, and the second item is the response.

Increasingly, verbal learning studies yielded results that could not be easily explained in terms of S–R connections, and theorists began to introduce a variety of mental phenomena into their discussions of learning processes. In this section, I will describe some general learning principles that emerged from verbal learning research. Some of the findings are relatively easy to explain from a behaviorist perspective, but others are more troublesome.

- *Serial learning is characterized by a particular pattern.* In a serial learning task, a **serial learning curve** is usually observed: People learn the first few items and last few items more quickly and easily than they learn the middle items (Hall, 1971; McCrary & Hunter, 1953; Roediger & Crowder, 1976). If we were to graph the speed with which the various items in a

Figure 8–11
A typical serial learning curve.

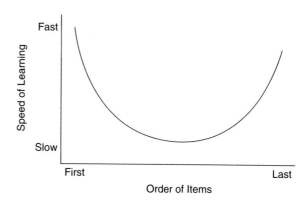

serial list are learned, we might obtain results similar to what you see in Figure 8–11. An example of the serial learning curve is the way in which most children learn the alphabet: They learn the first letters (*A, B, C, D*) and the last letters (*X, Y, Z*) before they learn the middle letters (e.g., *J, K, L, M*).

The tendency for the first items in a serial learning curve to be learned quickly is called the **primacy effect.** The tendency for the last items to be learned quickly is called the **recency effect.** Verbal learning theorists explained both effects by proposing that the end points of the list (i.e., the first and last items) served as *anchors* to which the other items would then be attached in a stimulus–response fashion.

• *Overlearned material is more easily recalled at a later time.* What happens when you learn information perfectly and then continue to study it? This process of **overlearning,** in which you learn material to mastery and then practice the material for additional study trials, enables you to remember the information much more accurately at a later time (Krueger, 1929; Underwood, 1954). For example, Krueger (1929) found that overlearning of a list of words enhanced recall for up to a month after the learning session. As you may recall from Chapter 3, many early behaviorists emphasized the importance of practice for learning, presumably because it strengthens stimulus–response connections.

• *Distributed practice is usually more effective than massed practice.* Imagine that you have to study for a test. You estimate that you need six hours to master the test material. Would you do better on the test if you studied for six hours all at once or if you broke your study time into smaller chunks of time—say, 6 one-hour sessions? Research has indicated that **distributed practice,** spreading study time out over several occasions, usually leads to better learning than **massed practice,** in which study time occurs all at once (Glenberg, 1976; Underwood, 1961; Underwood, Kapelak, & Malmi, 1976). Thus, studying for a test over several short sessions is more likely to be effective than one long cram session. Furthermore, the further apart the study sessions are, the better one's recall for the learned information is likely to be over the long run (Bahrick, Bahrick, Bahrick, & Bahrick, 1993). From a behaviorist perspective, massed practice might eventually lead to fatigue, which would cause the learner to begin practicing inappropriate responses.

• *Learning in one situation often affects learning and recall in another situation.* Imagine yourself having to learn two sets of paired associates. The first set looks like this:

Set 1

house – dragon
plant – sled
lamp – music
onion – pillow

The second one looks like this:

Set 2

house – paper
plant – clock
lamp – turkey
onion – chair

After you have first learned Set 1 and then learned Set 2, you are asked to remember the responses to each of the stimulus words in Set 1. Will you have difficulty? You probably will, because you learned different responses to those same words when you learned Set 2. You would have an easier time remembering the correct responses you learned in Set 1 if you had *not* had to learn the Set 2 responses as well.

Verbal learning theorists observed that when people learn two sets of paired associates in succession, their learning of the second set often diminishes their ability to recall the first set (Hall, 1971), a phenomenon known as **retroactive inhibition.** They further observed that individuals in this situation often have difficulty remembering the second set as well as the first (Hall, 1971), a phenomenon known as **proactive inhibition.** The tendency for a set of paired associates learned at one time to interfere with the recall of a set learned either earlier or later is especially likely to occur when the two sets have the same or similar stimulus words but different response words (Osgood, 1949).

Under different circumstances, learning one set of information may actually improve the recall of information learned at another time, a phenomenon that verbal learning theorists called either **retroactive facilitation** or **proactive facilitation,** depending on the order in which the two sets of information were learned (Hall, 1971). Facilitation is most likely to occur when two situations have similar or identical stimuli and when they have similar responses as well (Osgood, 1949). As an example, after learning the stimulus–response pair "house — dragon," you would probably learn "house — monster" fairly easily.

Verbal learning theorists (e.g., McGeoch, 1942; Melton & Irwin, 1940; Underwood, 1948) proposed that retroactive and proactive inhibition were major factors in *forgetting* verbal information; therefore, they were among the first to discuss theoretical ideas related to *memory.* Many contemporary cognitive psychologists also suggest that inhibition plays a significant role in memory and forgetting, although they are less likely to focus on specific S–R associations that may be involved.

• *Characteristics of the material affect the speed with which people can learn it.* Verbal learning researchers discovered a number of characteristics that affect the ease of learning verbal material:

Some items are more
meaningful than others.

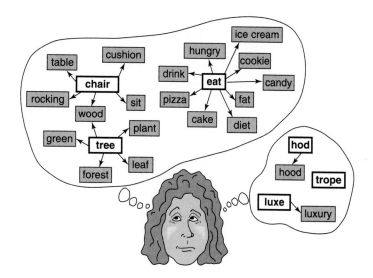

1. Items are more quickly learned when they are *meaningful*—that is, when they can be easily associated with other ideas (Cofer, 1971; Paivio, 1971). This principle was discovered very early by the German psychologist Hermann Ebbinghaus (1913). Ebbinghaus, who served as his own subject of study for a number of experiments in serial learning, observed that the associations he could make with words helped him learn those words. He attempted to eliminate the influence of associations by using presumably meaningless **nonsense syllables** ("words" such as JAD, MON, and ZIV). Yet even many nonsense syllables often have meaningfulness and evoke associations, thus making them relatively easy to learn (Hall, 1971). For example, the nonsense syllable JAD might make you think of "jade," and the syllable MON might remind you of "money."

2. Items are easier to learn when they are *pronounceable* (Di Vesta & Ingersoll, 1969; Underwood & Schulz, 1960). For example, the nonsense syllable DNK should be learned faster than BPX because most people can pronounce DNK more easily.

3. *Concrete* items are easier to learn than abstract items (Gorman, 1961; Paivio, 1963); for example, items such as

    turtle, hammer, sandwich

    are learned faster than items such as

    truth, joy, experience

4. One probable reason that the concreteness of items makes them easier to learn is that concrete items can be *mentally visualized*. The extent to which we form visual images of items appears to influence the ease with which we learn those items (Clark & Paivio, 1991; Paivio, 1971; Sadoski, Goetz, & Fritz, 1993). For example, it is easier to form a mental image of a turtle than it is to form an image of truth. Notice how, in discussing visual imagery, verbal learning theorists were beginning to talk about mental events. This phenomenon of visual imagery is quite difficult to explain from an S–R perspective.

- *People often impose meaning when learning new information.* The effect of meaningfulness on learning can be explained from an S–R perspective: When a stimulus word has many other words associated with it, one of those associations may in turn be associated with the response to be learned. What is more troublesome for an S–R approach is the fact that people will go out of their way to *make* information meaningful when they are trying to learn it. For example, when Bugelski (1962) asked adults to learn paired associates involving nonsense syllables, they invariably reported that they imposed meanings to help them learn the pairs. To illustrate, when given this pair

DUP — TEZ

one person used the word *deputize* to help form the connection. Cognitive theories have emerged that probably better explain this tendency for human beings to search for meaning.

- *People organize what they learn.* When people are allowed to recall items of a serial learning task in any order (a task known as **free recall**), they typically do *not* recall those items in the original presentation order. Instead, the order in which people recall items often reflects an organizational scheme of some kind (Bousfield, 1953; Buschke, 1977; Jenkins & Russell, 1952). In a classic experiment by Bousfield (1953), college students were given a list of 60 words, 15 from each of four categories: animals, names, vegetables, and professions. Although the words were presented in a random order, the students tended to recall them in category clusters. For example, a typical recall order might have been something like this:

camel, giraffe, zebra, donkey, Jason, Adam, Howard, pumpkin,
cabbage, carrot, lettuce, radish, milkman, baker, dentist

People even try to organize seemingly unorganized material (Tulving, 1962). This tendency people have to insist on organizing the information they learn is difficult to explain from behaviorist principles. As you will see in later chapters, however, it lends itself quite easily to an explanation based on cognitive learning theories.

- *People often use encoding strategies to help them learn.* As the earlier example of remembering - *DUP-TEZ* as "deputize" illustrates, people often change, or *encode*, information in some way to make it easier to learn (Bugelski, 1962; Dallett, 1964; Underwood & Erlebacher, 1965). Furthermore, when experimenters specifically tell people to use a certain encoding strategy to help them learn information, learning improves (Bugelski, Kidd, & Segmen, 1968; Hall, 1971). For instance, when people are instructed in techniques for forming mental visual images, they are able to remember a list of words more accurately than individuals who have not been given such instructions (Bugelski et al., 1968).

- *People are more likely to learn general ideas than to learn words verbatim.* In fact, when people focus on learning ideas rather than on learning information word for word, their learning is faster and their recall more accurate (Briggs & Reed, 1943; English, Welborn, & Killian, 1934; Jones & English, 1926). Verbal learning research focused on the learning of verbatim information. In doing so, it may very well have ignored the way in which human beings actually learn most verbal material.

Clearly, verbal learning research provided us with a number of useful learning principles. It also provided us with two learning tasks, serial and paired associate learning, that continue to be used in learning research. At the same time, in trying to stretch S–R models of learning to explain human verbal behavior, it began to demonstrate some weaknesses of the behaviorist perspective.

In more recent decades, the focus of verbal learning research has been on how people learn meaningful verbal material (e.g., prose passages) rather than artificially constructed serial lists or paired associates. In fact, the term *verbal learning* was largely abandoned (e.g., the *Journal of Verbal Learning and Verbal Behavior* became the *Journal of Memory and Language* in 1985) as verbal learning researchers began to embrace cognitivist ideas.

INTRODUCTION TO CONTEMPORARY COGNITIVISM

We have just seen how, even during the heyday of behaviorism, the work of Tolman, Gestalt psychologists, Piaget, Vygotsky, and verbal learning researchers was laying a foundation for cognitive learning theories. During the 1960s, discontent with the inadequacies of behaviorism became more widespread. The behaviorist perspective could not easily explain why people attempt to organize and make sense of the information they learn or sometimes even alter the form of that information (e.g., by remembering general meanings rather than verbatim input). Among learning psychologists grew the realization that mental events—cognition—could no longer be ignored (e.g., see Kendler, 1985).

In this section of the chapter, we will examine some of the major assumptions that underlie most cognitive explanations of learning. We will also look at three different approaches to understanding learning—information processing theory, constructivism, and contextual views—that fall within the larger theoretical perspective we call cognitivism.

General Assumptions of Cognitive Theories

The assumptions underlying contemporary cognitive theories of learning are radically different from those underlying behaviorism. What follow are some of the most central ones:

* *Some learning processes may be unique to human beings.* Because people possess abilities unique to the species (complex language is an example), the processes involved in learning may be different for human beings than they are for other animals. Accordingly, almost all research within the cognitivist perspective is conducted with human beings, and theories formulated from this research are typically not generalized to other species.

* *Cognitive processes are the focus of study.* Mental events are centrally involved in human learning and must be incorporated into theories of learning processes. To the extent that individuals think about the same situation differently, they will learn different things from that situation.

* *Objective, systematic observations of people's behavior should be the focus of scientific inquiry; however, inferences about unobservable mental processes can often be drawn from behavior.* Cognitive psychologists share with behaviorists the beliefs that the study of learning must be objective and that learning theories should be based on the results of empirical research. Cognitivists differ from behaviorists in one critical respect, however: By observing the responses that individuals make to different stimulus conditions, they believe they can draw reasonable inferences about the nature of the internal mental events that lead to those responses. In fact, researchers have become increasingly more ingenious in designing research studies that enable them to draw conclusions about specific cognitive processes.

A classic study by Bransford and Franks (1971) provides an example of inference drawing in cognitive research. In this experiment, undergraduate students listened to 24 sentences and answered simple questions about each one. The sentences were variations on four general ideas:

a rock rolling down a hill, a man reading a newspaper, a breeze blowing, and ants eating jelly. To illustrate, the six sentences about the ants eating jelly were as follows:

The ants ate the sweet jelly which was on the table.

The ants in the kitchen ate the jelly which was on the table.

The ants in the kitchen ate the jelly.

The ants ate the sweet jelly.

The ants were in the kitchen.

The jelly was on the table.

The students then listened to a second set of 28 sentences (variations on the same themes as before) and were asked to indicate whether or not each had been in the first set. Most of the sentences (24 out of 28) were *new* sentences; here are some examples:

The ants in the kitchen ate the sweet jelly which was on the table.

The ants in the kitchen ate the sweet jelly.

The ants ate the jelly which was on the table.

The jelly was sweet.

The students erroneously "recognized" most of these new sentences as being "old" ones. Sentences that contained a lot of information were especially likely to be recognized as having been heard before; for instance, "The ants in the kitchen ate the sweet jelly which was on the table" was more likely to be recognized than "The jelly was sweet." From such results, Bransford and Franks concluded that people abstract ideas from the verbal information they receive (rather than learning it verbatim) and organize similar ideas together in their memories. Sentences in the experiment that included most or all of the information related to a single theme may have more closely resembled the students' organized memories and so seemed more familiar to them.

Obviously, Bransford and Franks did not directly observe the cognitive processes that they described. Yet such processes seem to be reasonable explanations of the behaviors they *did* see.

• *Individuals are actively involved in the learning process.* Rather than being passive victims of environmental conditions, people are active participants in the learning process and in fact *control* their own learning. Individuals themselves determine how they mentally process the information they receive, and these cognitive processes in turn determine what, if anything, will be learned in a given situation.

• *Learning involves the formation of mental representations or associations that are not necessarily reflected in overt behavior changes.* Like Tolman, who advanced the concept of *latent learning*, contemporary cognitive psychologists believe that learning involves an internal, mental change rather than the external behavior change that many behaviorists describe. Learning can, therefore, occur without being reflected in an individual's observed performance. (Of course, as we noted in Chapter 1, other people have no way of knowing that learning has taken place until there *is* a behavior change of some sort.)

- *Knowledge is organized.* An individual's knowledge, beliefs, attitudes, and emotions are not isolated from one another but are instead all associated and interconnected. This emphasis on organization is one that we saw in several early cognitive theories, notably those of Tolman, the Gestaltists, and Piaget.

- *Learning is a process of relating new information to previously learned information.* Similar to Piaget's assertion that accommodation almost always involves assimilation, contemporary cognitive theorists believe that learning is most likely to occur when individuals can relate a new experience to the information they have acquired from earlier experiences.

Despite sharing certain common assumptions, cognitivists take somewhat different approaches in their attempts to portray how learning occurs. The predominant approach to the study of human learning, as reflected in ongoing research and journal space, is a group of theories known collectively as *information processing theory*. In recent years, however, two other perspectives—*constructivism* and *contextual views*—have also gained popularity, especially among psychologists who concern themselves with instructional practice and other educational issues. Let's look briefly at each of these three perspectives.

Information Processing Theory

Many cognitive theories focus on how people think about (i.e., *process*) the information they receive from the environment—how they perceive the stimuli around them, how they "put" what they've perceived into their memories, how they "find" what they've learned when they need to use it, and so on. Such theories are collectively known as **information processing theory.**

Many early information processing theories (e.g., those that emerged in the 1960s) portrayed human learning as being similar to how computers process information. To illustrate, theorists talked about "storing" information in and "retrieving" it from memory, borrowing the terms *storage* and *retrieval* so often used in reference to computer memory. It soon became clear, however, that the computer analogy was overly simplistic—that people often think about and interpret information in ways that are difficult to explain in the rigid, algorithmic ways that computers process information (e.g., see Bereiter, 1997; Bransford & Franks, 1971; Mayer, 1996a; Reisberg, 1997). At this point, the general perspective known as information processing theory includes a variety of specific theories about how people mentally think about the information they receive; some of these theories are computerlike in nature, but many others are not.

Information processing theory has been quite helpful for identifying the many processes that human cognition involves. It has yet to put those processes all back into an integrated whole that explains how human beings think and behave, however. Furthermore, it has told us more about *how* people learn than about *what* specific mental entities they acquire in the learning process (Alexander, White, & Daugherty, 1997).

Constructivism

Within the past three decades, it has become increasingly apparent that learners don't just absorb information as they encounter it. Instead, people do a great deal with the information they acquire, actively trying to organize and make sense of it, often in unique, idiosyncratic ways. Most cognitive theorists now portray learning more as *constructing* knowledge from the information one receives rather than directly receiving that information from the outside world (e.g., see Marshall, 1992; Mayer, 1996a; Prawat, 1993; Spivey, 1997). In some (although not all) cases, such theorists refer to their perspective as **constructivism** rather than information processing theory.

In this chapter, we have already seen several theoretical perspectives that are distinctly constructivist in flavor. For example, Tolman's concept of *cognitive map*, the Gestaltist concept of *closure*, and Piaget's concept of *cognitive structure* all involve constructing knowledge for oneself rather than absorbing it exactly as it has been presented. In these situations, we see the process of construction occurring separately within each learner, reflecting a perspective known as **individual constructivism.**

In other situations, people work together to make sense of their world. For example, several students may form a study group when they have a difficult and confusing textbook; helping one another, they may be able to interpret and understand the book in ways that they may not have been able to do on their own. As another example, astronomers have, over the course of several centuries, made increasingly better sense of the phenomena they've observed through their telescopes; the discipline of astronomy provides a view of the universe that innumerable scientists have pieced together over many centuries. Theories of learning that focus on how people work together, either at a single sitting or over the course of many years, reflect a perspective known as **social constructivism.**

Constructivist perspectives have directed psychologists' attention back to *what* is learned; the *schemas*, *scripts*, and *personal theories* that will be described in Chapter 11 are examples of the forms that learner-constructed knowledge might take. These perspectives also place the reins for directing learning squarely in the hands of the learner. Teachers cannot "pour" knowledge into the heads of students as they might pour lemonade into a glass; rather, students must make their own lemonade. Yet critics argue that some constructivists have taken this idea too far, suggesting that teachers have little control over how students interpret subject matter and learn from classroom activities (e.g., see critiques by Hirsch, 1996; Marton & Booth, 1997). In fact, a voluminous body of research (not to mention the countless personal experiences of students in elementary, secondary, and college classrooms) tells us that a wide variety of teaching methods, from teacher-directed lectures to more student-directed group discussions, very definitely *do* affect what students learn and how effectively they learn it. To use the "reins" metaphor once again, although learners are in the driver's seat in the learning process, teachers can provide a road map and offer suggestions about how to move the horse and wagon forward. To revert to the lemonade metaphor, teachers can supply the lemons, sugar, and water, as well as some directions about the relative proportions of each that will yield a flavorful drink.

Contextual Views

Within the past few years, several cognitive theories have emerged that place considerable emphasis on the importance of the immediate environment—the *context*—in learning and behavior. As an example of this perspective, we noted earlier in the chapter that, contrary to Piaget's belief that different forms of logic are associated with different developmental stages, children of a particular age actually show considerable variability in their logical thinking skills, depending on the specific subject matter with which they're dealing. As another example, people can often think more "intelligently" when they have calculators, computers, diagrams, equations, or paper and pencil to help them (Greeno, Collins, & Resnick, 1996; Pea, 1993; Perkins, 1995; Sternberg & Wagner, 1994). As a third example, consider Vygotsky's concepts of *actual developmental level* (the extent to which a person can perform a task independently) and *level of potential development* (the extent to which that person can perform a task with someone else's help). As Vygotsky pointed out, one's level of potential development will always be higher than one's actual developmental level; in other words, people can always accomplish more difficult tasks when they have the assistance of those around them. Furthermore, they can advance cognitively *only* when they work on tasks that they cannot do alone—tasks that are in their zone of proximal development.

Contextual perspectives of learning have a variety of labels attached to them. Terms such as *situated learning, situated cognition, distributed learning,* and *distributed intelligence* all refer to situations in which learning and thinking are influenced by the physical and social contexts in which people are immersed; for example, the term *distributed intelligence* refers, in part, to the notion that we often think more "intelligently" when we think about and discuss ideas with others than when we think alone. (Social constructivist theories, because they involve cognition within a social context, can often be classified as contextual views as well.)

Contextual views remind us that learning is to some degree connected to the context in which it occurs. They also help us understand why people don't always apply what they've learned in one situation to a different situation; in other words, people don't necessarily *transfer* their learning. Yet people sometimes *do* transfer what they learn at one time to a very different context; for instance, they may use the arithmetic they learned in elementary school to develop household budgets and balance their checkbooks, and they can read materials very different from the storybooks and textbooks they studied in the classroom (Anderson, Reder, & Simon, 1996, 1997; Bereiter, 1997; Perkins, 1992). In Chapter 14, we'll look more closely at the nature of transfer and at the conditions that tend to facilitate and discourage it.

Integrating Cognitive Perspectives

It is important to note that complete consensus does not exist, even among cognitivists, about how different cognitive theories can best be categorized (for various possibilities, see Bredo, 1997; Case, 1996; Derry, 1996; Greeno et al., 1996; Mayer, 1996a, 1996b; Reynolds et al., 1996). As one simple example, some theorists portray contemporary information processing theory as being decidedly constructivist in nature (Derry, 1996; Mayer, 1996a, 1996b; Phye, 1997; Prawat, 1996; Pressley, Whaston-McDonald, et al., 1997).

Despite the fuzziness of the boundaries between various cognitive perspectives, some psychologists and educators have insisted on drawing sharp distinctions among them. This tendency to dichotomize theoretical perspectives—to portray one as black and another as white, to suggest that one points strictly to "teacher-centered" instructional methods whereas another supports more "learner-centered" methods, and in some cases to imply that one is a "good guy" and another is a "bad guy"—drives me nuts. In recent years, a few of my colleagues in the field have expressed similar frustration (Bereiter & Scardamalia, 1996; Clancey, 1997; Harris & Alexander, 1998; Hynd, 1998; Salomon, 1993; Sfard, 1998).

In my own mind, ideas from information processing theory, constructivism, and contextual views, as well as the theories we've already considered (e.g., social cognitive theory, Piaget's and Vygotsky's theories) all make significant contributions to our understanding of how human beings think and learn, and taken together, they can give us a more complete understanding of human cognition than any single approach offers alone.[1] Accordingly, we will be pulling from a variety of cognitive perspectives, in a somewhat eclectic manner, as we explore how people think and learn in the next few chapters.

GENERAL EDUCATIONAL IMPLICATIONS OF COGNITIVE THEORIES

Theories of human cognition give us many ideas about how we can best help others learn. We will derive some very specific educational applications in later chapters. At this point, let's identify some of the more general educational implications of the cognitive perspective, including those of early cognitive theories.

• *Cognitive processes influence learning.* If learning is a function of how information is mentally processed, then students' cognitive processes should be a major concern to educators. Students' learning difficulties often indicate ineffective or inappropriate cognitive processes; for example, children with learning disabilities tend to process information less effectively than nondisabled children (e.g., Swanson, 1987). Teachers must be aware not only of *what* students are trying to learn but also of *how* they are trying to learn it.

• *As children grow, they become capable of increasingly more sophisticated thought.* Both Piaget and Vygotsky have pointed out that children acquire more complex reasoning processes over time. Piaget described such development in terms of four qualitatively different stages, whereas Vygotsky spoke more in terms of a continually advancing zone of proximal development. Regardless of whose perspective we take, we come to the same conclusion: Teachers must consider their students' current levels of cognitive functioning when planning topics and methods of instruction. For example, children in the elementary school grades are likely to have difficulty with abstract ideas that don't relate to their own experiences (using Piaget's terms, they are in either the preoperational or concrete operational stage rather than in the formal operational stage) and so will learn more effectively if information is presented through concrete, hands-on activities. Even high school and college students, if they have not completely acquired formal operational ways of thinking and reasoning, may benefit from having concrete experiences before studying abstract material. In fact, verbal learning research tells us that students of *all* ages and developmental levels should benefit from concrete learning materials.

• *People organize the things they learn.* Teachers can facilitate students' learning by presenting information in an organized fashion and by helping students see how one thing relates to another. We will identify some strategies for promoting such organization in Chapter 10.

• *New information is most easily acquired when people can associate it with things they have already learned.* Therefore, teachers can help students learn by showing them how new ideas relate to old ones (once again, we will identify more specific strategies in Chapter 10). When students are unable to relate new information to anything with which they are familiar, learning is apt to be slow, frustrating, and ineffective.

• *People control their own learning.* The behaviorist B. F. Skinner (1954, 1968) argued that students must make active responses in the classroom if they are to learn anything. Cognitivists

---

[1]For various perspectives on how two or more theories might be combined, I refer you to Anderson, Greeno, Reder, and Simon (2000); Gauvain (2001); P. A. Ornstein and Haden (2001); Packer and Goicoechea (2000); and Zimmerman (1981).

share Skinner's view; however, they emphasize *mental* activity rather than physical activity. Students who are not mentally active in the classroom—those who do not attend to, think about, and in other ways cognitively process the subject matter at hand—will learn very little. For those who *do* become mentally engaged with the subject matter, the nature of their cognitive processes will determine what they learn and how effectively they learn it.

OVERVIEW OF UPCOMING CHAPTERS

In the next seven chapters, we will explore cognitivist views of learning in greater detail. In the remaining chapters of Part IV, we will examine the nature of human memory, looking at the basic components of memory (Chapter 9), the various ways in which people store information in memory (Chapter 10), the nature of the knowledge they create (Chapter 11), and the factors that promote long-term retention of the things they've learned (Chapter 12). At various points throughout these chapters, we will identify specific implications of memory theory for classroom instruction.

We will continue our discussion of cognitivist ideas in Part V, where we will focus on more complex aspects of learning and cognition. In Chapters 13 and 14, we will look at how people think about their own thinking (a phenomenon known as *metacognition*) and at how they apply what they've learned to new situations (phenomena known as *transfer* and *problem solving*). In Chapter 15, we will consider how learners often work together to construct complex interpretations and understandings of the topics they study.

SUMMARY

Cognitivism is currently the predominant perspective within which human learning is described and explained. The roots of cognitive theory can be found in research and theories dating back to the 1920s and 1930s. For example, Edward Tolman, while conducting animal laboratory studies similar to those of behaviorists, included mental phenomena in his perspective of how learning occurs and adopted a more holistic view of learning than was true of S–R theorists. Gestalt psychologists emphasized the importance of organizational processes in perception, learning, and problem solving, proposing that people are predisposed to organize information in particular ways. Jean Piaget portrayed children as active and motivated learners who, through numerous interactions with their physical and social environments, construct an increasingly complex understanding of the world around them.

Lev Vygotsky proposed that social activities are precursors to, and form the basis for, complex mental processes; he also suggested that adults promote children's cognitive development by passing along the meanings that their culture assigns to objects and events and by assisting children with challenging tasks. In the middle decades of the twentieth century, verbal learning theorists, who initially attempted to apply an S–R analysis to the study of human language-based learning, further stoked the fire of cognitivism by increasingly incorporating mental events into explanations of their research results.

Contemporary cognitivism emphasizes mental processes and proposes that many aspects of learning are probably unique to the human species. Cognitivists share behaviorists' belief that the study of learning must be objective and that learning theories should be based on empirical research; however, they suggest that by observing the responses people make to different stimulus conditions, they can draw inferences about the cognitive processes that have led to those responses. Cognitivism encompasses several perspectives—information processing theory, constructivism, and contextual views—that all contribute to our understanding of how human beings think and learn. Teachers must consider students' cognitive processes when considering how best to help students succeed in the classroom.

CHAPTER 9

Basic Components of Memory

Imagine yourself studying for an upcoming exam that will cover a lengthy and somewhat confusing reading assignment. You understand most of the material you have read and are confident that you will remember it. But you have trouble with one section of the assignment, mainly because it doesn't make much sense to you. In desperation, you try to memorize this section word for word, but your learning becomes slow, arduous, and not much fun.

Now imagine yourself taking the exam. It was not as difficult as you had thought it would be, but you can't remember the answer to a particularly trivial question: "What was Edward C. Tolman's middle name?" You know you studied the relevant section in the book, but you simply cannot remember the information called for. After considering all of the names you can think of that begin with *C*, you finally give up and turn in your exam paper with the question unanswered.

Immediately afterward, you congregate with your classmates in the hall and rehash the questions. "What was Tolman's middle name?" you ask. Your friend Harry responds smugly, "It was Chace. I can remember that easily because my sister married a guy named Marvin Chace." And then your friend Carol adds, "I learned the name by imagining Tolman *chacing* his rats down their mazes." You grit your teeth, thinking it ridiculous that Harry and Carol would do better than you on a question because of a coincidental brother-in-law or a silly visual image. But let's face it, your classmates remembered and you did not.

Learning a piece of information at one point in time does not guarantee that you will remember it later on. Many variables determine what information gets into memory in the first place and what information stays there long enough for you to recall it when you need it. In this chapter, we will begin our examination of how human memory seems to work and how various factors influence its effectiveness. After defining basic terminology that psychologists use when they talk about memory, we will spend much of the chapter looking at the various components that memory may include, using the *dual-store* model that underlies many contemporary memory theories. Later in the chapter, we will turn to two alternative views of human memory: *levels-of-processing* theory and *activation* theory. Finally, we will identify several generalizations that seem to hold true regardless of which theoretical perspective we take.

BASIC TERMINOLOGY IN MEMORY THEORY

Memory theorists make a distinction between *learning* and *memory*. They also refer frequently to the processes of *storage*, *encoding*, and *retrieval*.

Learning Versus Memory Up to this point, we have not really separated learning and memory, but memory theorists do draw a distinction between the two terms. *Learning* is viewed, quite simply, as the acquisition of new information or skills; as we defined it in Chapter 1, learning involves a relatively permanent change in mental representations or associations as a result of experience. In contrast, **memory** is related to the ability to recall information that has previously been learned. In some instances, the word *memory* is used to refer to the process of retaining information for a period of time. In other instances, it is used to refer to a particular "location" where learned information is kept; for example, we will be talking about *working memory* and *long-term memory*. The distinction between learning and memory is an important one; for a number of reasons that you will discover in subsequent chapters, not everything that is learned is necessarily remembered over the long run.

Storage The process of "putting" new information in memory is known as **storage.** For example, if you can put this fact in your head:

Jeanne Ormrod's birthday is August 22nd.

then you are *storing* the information. We will talk a little bit about storage processes in this chapter, and we will examine them in more depth in Chapter 10.

Encoding As people store information in memory, they usually modify it in some way; this process of **encoding**[1] often helps them store the information more easily. Sometimes encoding involves *changing the form* of the information. For example, I once had a combination lock for which the

---

[1]In our discussion of modeling in Chapter 7, we noted that people can often remember a model's behavior more accurately when they form verbal or visual *memory codes* to help them remember the specific actions that the model has demonstrated. Such memory codes are examples of encoding in action.

combination was 22–8–14. I quickly learned the first two numbers by encoding them as "the day and month of my birthday." In this case, I changed numerical information into a verbal form. Encoding may also involve *adding to* new information using one's existing knowledge of the world. For example, consider this information:

> Jeanne Ormrod was born in Providence, Rhode Island.

On reading this, you might conclude that I am a native New Englander or that I am a U.S. citizen—inferences that you might store along with the information I actually gave you. Yet another encoding process is one of *simplifying* information that has been presented—for example, by remembering the overall meaning or gist of a situation rather than the specific details of what happened. For example, you might remember that the author of one of your textbooks talked about her birthday without remembering the actual date.

Retrieval The process by which people "find" information they have previously stored so that they can use it again is called **retrieval**. For example, I am hoping that, come mid-August, you will retrieve the date of my birthday and send me a tasteful card. Because I get cards from few of my readers (and primarily from students in my own classes), we can conclude that retrieval is quite easy in some cases but more difficult in others. (An alternative hypothesis, of course, is that information retrieval is occurring but is not resulting in a behavior change.)

A DUAL-STORE MODEL OF MEMORY

Late in the nineteenth century, Harvard psychologist William James (1890) proposed that human memory has three components: an after-image, a primary memory, and a secondary memory. James's model was largely ignored during the behaviorism-dominated early decades of the twentieth century, but the advent of cognitivism in the 1960s brought a renewed interest in human memory, and in 1968 Richard Atkinson and Richard Shiffrin (1968, 1971) proposed a model of memory similar to that of James. This model laid the groundwork for what has become the most prevalent view of human memory today—a **dual-store model** of memory, depicted in simplified form in Figure 9–1.

    Like William James, Atkinson and Shiffrin proposed that memory has three components, using the terms *sensory register* (SR), *short-term memory* (STM), and *long-term memory* (LTM). (The model is called *dual*-store in reference to the distinction between short-term memory and long-term memory.) Information from the environment—input—first enters the sensory register, where it is held for a very short time (a few seconds at the most). If the information is

Figure 9–1
A simplified dual-store
model of memory.

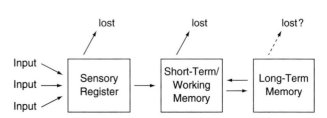

processed in a particular way, it moves on to short-term memory. Information is held in short-term memory for less than a minute, however, and must be processed further if it is to move on to long-term memory. Processing of information in short-term memory frequently involves the use of information from long-term memory as well (hence the two-way arrows between short-term and long-term memory in Figure 9–1). If a piece of information reaches the sensory register or short-term memory but is not then processed sufficiently for its transference to the next component of the memory system, that information is assumed to be lost from the memory system—in other words, it is forgotten. Whether information can be lost from long-term memory as well (note the dotted arrow and question mark in Figure 9–1) is still an open question, one that we will address in Chapter 12.

A dual-store model of human memory can be likened to an information selection and storage system similar to one you might use to store important documents at home. You undoubtedly acquire numerous pieces of paper in your home over the course of a few months; among this mass of paper may be such items as newspapers, personal letters, bills, a driver's license, university transcripts, junk mail, and grocery store receipts. You probably discard some items (such as junk mail and grocery receipts) almost as soon as you get them; these things get no further than the "sensory register" of your storage system. You need to deal with others (such as bills) briefly (e.g., you need to pay them) and then you can more or less forget them; they are processed for a short time in your system's "short-term storage." Still others (such as a driver's license and transcripts) may be important enough that you want to put them in a safe, organized place where you can find them later; thus, they end up in a "long-term storage" compartment such as a wallet, file cabinet, or safe-deposit box.

Over the years, learning theorists have continued to build on and modify Atkinson and Shiffrin's dual-store model. For example, they have theorized about the forms in which information is stored and the processes through which it is moved from short-term memory to long-term memory. But perhaps the most noticeable change is an increasing reference to short-term memory as a "working" memory that processes information in addition to storing it (hence, the term *working* in the second box of Figure 9–1). To be consistent with contemporary memory theorists, we will primarily use the term *working memory* from this point on.

In the pages that follow, we will examine the three components of the dual-store model; we will also look at the various **control processes** that affect the retention of information and its movement from one component to another. As we proceed, remember that the language we will use in our discussion of human memory is largely metaphorical in nature (Roediger, 1980; Rosenfield, 1988). For example, the three components of memory are not necessarily three separate "places" in the brain. Furthermore, when we talk about memory processes, we are not necessarily saying anything about neurological events. As you discovered in Chapter 2, psychologists still have much to learn about how memory processes occur physiologically and how brain structure relates to psychological models of human memory. At a couple of points in the chapter, I will suggest where in the brain certain structures and functions may be located. I will do so in footnotes, however, because our emphasis here will be on what psychologists have learned about memory by studying human behavior and performance (e.g., what kinds of things people seem to be able to remember, and under what circumstances they remember most effectively), not by studying the anatomy and physiology of the brain.

SENSORY REGISTER

The first component of the dual-store model, the **sensory register**[2], holds incoming information long enough for it to undergo preliminary cognitive processing. All of the environmental information that we are capable of sensing probably stays with us in the sensory register for a very brief time. For example, if you have ever waved a flashlight or sparkler in the air on a dark night, you've undoubtedly noticed that the light leaves a trail behind it. This trail does not exist in the air itself; it is the result of your sensory register holding the light you have seen for a short time after you saw it. As another example, when you sit in a classroom for an hour or more, your attention will almost inevitably wander away from the instructor at some point. You may have noticed that when you tune back in to what the instructor is saying, you can often recall two or three words that the instructor has said *before* you tuned in. Virtually everything the instructor has uttered has probably been recorded in your sensory register despite your mental absence from class, but, alas, only those last two or three words are still there when you decide to be mentally "present" again.

Characteristics of the Sensory Register

Let's look specifically at three characteristics of the sensory register: capacity, form of storage, and duration.

Capacity
The capacity of the sensory register is, as far as psychologists can tell, unlimited. All of the environmental information that human beings are capable of sensing is probably stored briefly in the sensory register.

Form of Storage
Information appears to be stored in the sensory register in basically the same form in which it has been sensed: visual input is stored in a visual form, auditory input in an auditory form, and so on (Coltheart, Lea, & Thompson, 1974; Cowan, 1995; Howard, 1983; Turvey & Kravetz, 1970). At this point, information has not yet been understood or interpreted by the learner. In other words, the sensory register holds information *before* it is processed.[3]

Duration
Information remains in the sensory register for only a very brief time, but measuring its exact duration is difficult. One problem in studying the characteristics of information in the sensory register is that when we ask people to report or in some other way process something that they've stored there, the information automatically moves on to working memory and so is no longer in the place where we want to study it!

---

[2]You may also see labels such as *sensory memory, brief sensory store, iconic memory,* and *echoic memory.*

[3]As we discovered in Chapter 2, different parts of the brain seem to be responsible for processing different kinds of sensory input. We can reasonably guess, then, that the sensory register is not a single structure located in a particular spot in the brain. Rather, different areas may act as sensory registers for different sensory modalities.

The classic experiment designed to assess the duration of the sensory register was conducted by George Sperling (1960). Recruiting adults to participate in his experiment, Sperling presented displays of three rows of four letters and digits each; following is a typical display:

7	1	V	F
X	L	5	3
B	4	W	7

Each display was presented for a fraction of a second, then participants were asked to recall either one particular row of symbols or all 12 symbols. When asked to recall a single row, people were able to do so with 76% accuracy; because they were not told *which* row they would need to recall until after the display had disappeared, they apparently remembered approximately 76% of the symbols they had seen. Yet when asked to recall all 12 symbols, they could do so with only 36% accuracy. Sperling's explanation of this result was that most of the symbols were stored initially but faded from memory before the participants had a chance to report them all. In a follow-up experiment, Sperling (1960) varied the amount of time that elapsed between the display and the signal indicating which row was to be remembered. People could recall little of a display after a delay of more than a quarter of a second.

From the results of research studies such as Sperling's, it appears that the duration of visual information in the sensory register is probably less than a second (Loftus & Loftus, 1976; Wingfield & Byrnes, 1981). Auditory information probably lasts longer, with a duration of two to four seconds (Conrad & Hull, 1964; Darwin, Turvey, & Crowder, 1972; Moray, Bates, & Barnett, 1965).

Why does auditory input last longer than visual input? One possible explanation (e.g., Wingfield & Byrnes, 1981) is that a major source of auditory input—human speech—can be understood only within its sequential context. For example, consider this sentence:

I scream for ice cream.

You can interpret the first two words as either *I scream* or *ice cream*. Only when you hear the third word—*for*—can you begin to interpret the first two words accurately. The task of understanding speech, which is frequently filled with temporarily ambiguous sounds, is often easier if we can hold those sounds in memory in an uninterpreted form until we receive additional, clarifying information. As we human beings have acquired a greater capacity for language, then, evolution must also have given us a greater capacity to retain uninterpreted sequential auditory input.

Two factors probably account for the rapid disappearance of information from the sensory register. First, *interference* may be a factor: New information coming in effectively replaces (and thereby erases) the information already there (e.g., Breitmeyer & Ganz, 1976). Many psychologists also believe that, even without new input, existing information in the sensory register simply fades away, or *decays*, over time (e.g., Loftus & Loftus, 1976; Wingfield & Byrnes, 1981). Regardless of the reasons for the sensory register's short duration, in most instances people don't need to store information there for very long. Important information is probably going to be processed so that it enters working memory. Unimportant information, like junk mail, is probably best dealt with by throwing it away.

MOVING INFORMATION ON TO WORKING MEMORY: THE ROLE OF ATTENTION

If we want to move information from the sensory register into working memory, it appears that, at least in most cases, we must *pay attention* to it (Atkinson & Shiffrin, 1968; Cowan, 1995; Kulhavy, Peterson, & Schwartz, 1986). For example, as you read this book, you are probably attending to only a small part of the visual input that your eyes sense right now (I hope you are attending to the words on this page!). In the same way, you do not worry about all of the sounds you hear at any particular time; you select only certain sounds to pay attention to. In essence, information that an individual pays attention to moves on to working memory, whereas information that is not attended to may be lost from the memory system.

One reason that people don't remember something they've seen or heard, then, is that they never really paid attention to it. If you are sitting in class with your mind a thousand miles away from the professor's lecture, you might say that you forgot what the instructor said, or you might say that you never heard it in the first place. The reality of the situation is somewhere in between: The lecture reached your sensory register but was not sufficiently processed to move on to your working memory.

Factors Influencing Attention

What kinds of stimuli are likely to capture one's attention? Certain kinds of stimuli tend to draw attention, whereas other kinds do not (e.g., Cowan, 1995; Horstmann, 2002; Sergeant, 1996). Following are some important factors affecting what people pay attention to and, therefore, what they store in working memory.

Size Which of the following letters first draw your eye?

A B c d E f g

You probably noticed the B and E before the other letters because of their larger size. Attention tends to be drawn to large objects, a fact that newspaper publishers employ when they typeset front-page headlines in large letters and that advertisers use when they put potentially unenticing information in fine print.

Intensity More intense stimuli—bright colors and loud noises, for instance—attract attention. Teachers frequently speak more loudly than usual—"**Be quiet!**"—when they want to get their students' attention. Similarly, toy manufacturers emphasize bright colors in the toys they produce, knowing that young children browsing store shelves will be more attracted to vivid reds and yellows than to subtle pinks and beiges.

Novelty Stimuli that are novel or unusual in some way tend to draw people's attention. For example, look at the women in Figure 9–2. You probably find yourself attending more to the woman on the right than to the other three. A woman with two heads and three legs is not someone you see every day.

Incongruity Objects that are incongruous—those that don't make sense within their context—tend to capture people's attention. For example, read this sentence:

I took a walk to the rabbit this morning.

Figure 9–2
Novelty draws attention.

Did you spend more time looking at the word *rabbit* than at the other words? If so, it may have been because *rabbit* doesn't make much sense within the context of the sentence.

Emotion Stimuli with strong emotional associations attract attention. A nude body flashing through a crowded room usually draws the attention (and astonished expressions) of just about everyone present. Words such as *blood* and *murder* also are attention getters because of their emotional overtones.

Personal Significance The other factors I've listed—size, intensity, novelty, incongruity, and emotion—tend to capture attention but don't necessarily hold it for very long. In contrast, personal significance—the meaning and relevance people find in an object or event—can both capture and *maintain* attention (Cohen, 1972; Gibson & Rader, 1979; Voss & Schauble, 1992; Vurpillot & Ball, 1979). When a student sits in front of a television set with an open textbook, the stimulus that the student attends to—the television or the book—depends in large part on which stimulus is more closely related to the student's motives at that particular moment. If the textbook is interesting or if an important examination is scheduled for the next day, the student will attend to the book. But if a popular situation comedy or a cliff-hanging soap opera is on, or if the textbook is dry and unenticing, the student may very well forget that the text is even in the same room.

Think, for a moment, about curriculum materials, including textbooks, that you have seen recently. Do they possess characteristics that are likely to catch a student's eye? Do important words and concepts stand out, perhaps because they are larger or **more intense** or *unusual*? Are certain topics likely to grab a student's interest because they are interesting and relevant to the age group? If your answer to these questions is no, then students may very well have difficulty attending to and learning from those materials.

Nominal Versus Effective Stimuli

Even when several people are all paying attention to the same stimulus, they may all be attending to different *aspects* of that stimulus. For example, suppose that a first-grade teacher shows his students a picture of a girl and asks them to shout out the first letter of the word that the picture represents. Most students will probably shout out "G" for *girl*. But if Louise is focusing on the girl's dress rather than on the entire picture, she may instead shout "D."

The stimulus that appears to us, as outsiders, to be presented (sometimes called the **nominal stimulus**) is not necessarily the stimulus to which people are actually attending (the **effective stimulus**).

Once, when I was teaching introductory psychology to first-year college students, a student who had failed my first two examinations came to my office and expressed frustration about her lack of success in my class. When I asked her to describe how she went about completing the assigned readings in the textbook, she told me, "Well, I start looking through the chapter, and when I get to a page that looks important, I read it." With further probing, I discovered that this young woman had been reading approximately one out of every three pages assigned! In this case, the effective stimulus was only one-third of the nominal stimulus.

As another example of how differences in attention can lead to differences in learning, let's look at an experiment by Faust and Anderson (1967) in which students studied Russian vocabulary words under one of two conditions. Some students read single statements presenting an English word and its Russian equivalent and then were required to write the Russian word. Following is an example of the materials that these students received:

> *A table is a stohl.*

> *A table is a _____.*

Other students were shown short paragraphs, each containing several Russian words and their English equivalents, following which was a fill-in-the-blank item in which they wrote one of the Russian words. An example follows:

> *A rag is a tryapka. A bridge is a*
> *mohst. A table is a stohl. A college*
> *is a vooz. An onion is a look.*

> *A table is a _____.*

Faust and Anderson found that students who were given the paragraphs learned the English meanings of more Russian words than students who were given the single sentences; they reasoned that differences in attention explained the differences in achievement. To understand how attention might differ in the two situations, pretend for a moment that you are a student who wants to complete the Russian vocabulary task with a minimum of time and effort. Now look at the first set of stimulus materials. You don't have to read (attend to) the English word to answer correctly with *stohl*. If you know that the Russian word consistently appears as the last word of the sentence, then you only need to attend to that last word and copy it on the blank line. As a result, you may learn the Russian word but not connect it to its English meaning.

Now look at the second set of stimulus materials. Because several Russian words appear in the paragraph, you must determine which of them is the correct answer. At the very least, you must look at the English word *table* in the incomplete statement at the bottom and then locate that word in the preceding paragraph. You find "A table is a stohl" and so write *stohl* in the blank. You may or may not have paid attention to other sentences in the paragraph, but at least you have attended to both the English word in question and its Russian equivalent. Hence you are more likely to learn that *stohl* means "table." Clearly, then, characteristics of the task at hand influence what you must pay attention to in order to perform that task successfully and, therefore, what you ultimately learn from completing the task.

Nature of Attention

What cognitive processes underlie people's ability to attend to certain aspects of the environment and to ignore others? On the surface, the answer might appear simple: People just focus their eyes directly on what they want to pay attention to. Yet you can probably think of many times when you have directed your eyes toward a specific object yet not paid attention to it at all: Perhaps you were listening intently to a piece of music or were deep in thought about something that wasn't anywhere in sight.

Furthermore, people are able to focus the attention of senses other than vision without having to physically orient themselves in a particular direction. Consider the case of auditory attention: You can go to a party at which numerous conversations are going on simultaneously and successfully attend to just one of them, regardless of where your ears are "aimed." You may be listening to the person standing directly in front of you, or, if that person has been rambling on for more than an hour about the difficulty he has had cultivating rhubarb in his garden, you may instead tune in to a more interesting conversation a few feet to your right or left. Even though you may be looking directly at the rhubarb grower and nodding in mock agreement, your attention is somewhere else altogether.

The ability to attend to one spoken message while ignoring others—aptly called the **cocktail party phenomenon**—has been studied using a technique called **shadowing:** A person participating in a research study is asked to listen through earphones to two simultaneously spoken messages and to repeat the message presented by one of the speakers. By assessing the accuracy of the person's repetition, researchers have been able to speculate about cognitive processes underlying attention.

In pioneering research by Cherry (1953), people who listened simultaneously to two speeches (each consisting of numerous clichés strung together) spoken by the same individual were unable to attend to just one of the speeches: Although these people were able to repeat entire clichés accurately, they pulled these clichés equally from the two speeches. However, when they heard two messages on different topics by different speakers with different voices coming from different directions, repetition of one of the messages was much more accurate.

People who shadow one of two messages notice very little of the other message. They can seldom report any of the words included in the unattended message and typically do not even notice whether the language spoken is their native tongue. Superficial characteristics, such as a change from a man's voice to a woman's voice, are noticed, but the content of the message is not (Cherry, 1953). Because of Cherry's findings, an early theory of attention (Broadbent, 1958) likened auditory attention to a filter that enabled the listener to select one message on the basis of physical characteristics and screen out others, much as a television tuner zeroes in on one frequency and shuts out the rest.

Yet research subsequent to this proposed filter theory has indicated that people do not totally filter out information from a supposedly unattended message. People who participate in shadowing experiments notice particularly meaningful words (such as their own names) in the unattended message (Treisman, 1964). They also hear words from that message if those words fit meaningfully into the attended message (Gray & Wedderburn, 1960; Treisman, 1964). For example, suppose you hear these two sentences simultaneously and are asked to shadow only the first one:

Speaker 1:   I bought candy at the plate today.
Speaker 2:   Put the rhubarb on my store, please.

You might very well "hear" the first speaker say, "I bought candy at the store today" (borrowing the word *store* from the second speaker) because such a sentence makes more sense than what the speaker really did say.

Although most psychologists now reject the idea that attention is like a filter, they continue to have difficulty pinning down its precise nature. It almost certainly involves both automatic responses (e.g., immediately turning to look in the direction of a loud, unexpected noise) and conscious control (e.g., deciding which conversation to listen to at a cocktail party).[4] Generally speaking, you might think of attention as being *focused cognitive processing of particular aspects of the environment* (Barkley, 1996a; Cowan, 1995; Johnston, McCann, & Remington, 1995). As we have seen, however, such processing does not necessarily exclude other stimuli in the environment. At a cocktail party, people might select the sounds that resemble a particular person's voice and that seem to fit into a meaningfully constructed sentence. If a word from another speaker also fits the meaning, however, it might very well be incorporated into what is heard.

Attention as a Limited Capacity

Perhaps life would be simpler if people didn't have to choose certain stimuli to pay attention to, but could instead attend to *everything* that they record in their sensory registers. Unfortunately, it turns out that people are incapable of attending to everything at once. For example, look at Figure 9–3. At first glance, you probably see a white goblet. But if you look at the black spaces on either side of the goblet, you should also be able to see two silhouettes ("Peter" and "Paul") staring at each other.

Now try this little exercise: See if you can focus on both the goblet and the two silhouettes at *exactly* the same time, so that you can clearly see the details of both. Can you do it? Most people are unable to attend to the goblet and the faces at exactly the same time, although they may be able to shift their focus from the goblet to the faces and back again very quickly.

The Peter-Paul goblet illustrates a phenomenon that early Gestalt psychologists called **figure-ground:** An individual can attend to one object (the **figure**) and notice the details of that object. Whatever the individual is not paying attention to (i.e., the background, or **ground**) is not carefully inspected: The individual may notice a few salient characteristics, such as color, but is likely to overlook more specific information about unattended objects.[5]

Gestalt psychologists proposed that people can pay attention to only one thing at a time— hence the difficulty most folks have in attending to both the goblet and the faces simultaneously. Since their time, other theorists (e.g., Broadbent, 1958; Cherry, 1953; Shapiro, 1994; Treisman, 1964; Welford, 1977) have proposed something similar: People can only attend to one *complex* source of information at a time. In situations in which more than one stimulus requires attention, one's attention must be switched quickly back and forth from one to another.

But now consider a situation in which you are driving your car while also carrying on a conversation with a friend. Are you not attending to two things, the road and the conversation, at once? To account for such a situation, some theorists (e.g., J. R. Anderson, 1990; Cowan, 1995; Kahneman, 1973; Norman & Bobrow, 1975; Pashler, 1992) have described attention as involving

---

[4]The hindbrain, midbrain, and forebrain all have some involvement in attention. The reticular formation, hippocampus, and frontal and parietal lobes of the cortex are especially important (see Chapter 2).

[5]For contemporary analyses of the figure-ground phenomenon, see Peterson (1994); Peterson and Gibson (1994); and Vecera, Vogel, and Woodman (2002).

Figure 9–3
The Peter-Paul goblet.

a **limited processing capacity,** with the number of stimuli being attended to depending on how much cognitive processing is required for each one. If you are engaging in a difficult task, such as learning to drive a car with a standard transmission, you may very well need to devote your full attention to that task and so not hear a thing that your friend is telling you. However, if you are doing something more habitual or automatic, such as driving a standard transmission after years of driving experience, you can easily devote some attention to what your friend is saying. Many tasks, such as driving, become increasingly automatic over time, therefore requiring less and less of our attention (I'll say more about this phenomenon, known as *automaticity*, in Chapter 10). Even so, when people carry on a conversation (say, on a cellular phone) while driving, they have slower reaction times and are less likely to notice traffic signals (Strayer & Johnston, 2001). Occasionally, people do become adept at splitting their attention among two complex tasks, but only when they have considerable practice in performing both of those tasks at the same time (Hirst, Spelke, Reaves, Caharack, & Neisser, 1980; Reisberg, 1997; Spelke, Hirst, & Neisser, 1976).

Regardless of how we view attention, one thing is clear: People's ability to attend to the stimuli around them is limited, such that they usually cannot attend to or otherwise learn from two complex situations at the same time. Thus, people must be quite selective about the information they choose to process and must ignore (and so lose) a lot of the information they receive. Frustrating as it may sometimes seem, people simply cannot attend to, learn, and remember everything they encounter.

Attention is closely connected with working memory, although theorists continue to debate *how* closely the two are linked (e.g., Downing, 2000; Woodman, Vogel, & Luck, 2001). As you will see now, working memory controls attention to some extent, and it, like attention, has a limited capacity.

WORKING MEMORY

Atkinson and Shiffrin (1968) used the term **short-term memory** to refer to a storage mechanism that holds information for a brief time after it is attended to so that it can be mentally processed. But as I mentioned earlier, most theorists now believe that this component of memory is also where cognitive processing itself takes place, hence their more frequent use of the term **working memory** (e.g., Baddeley, 1986; Cowan, 1995; Daneman & Carpenter, 1980).

As an example of the storage and processing functions of working memory, try solving the following long-division problem in your head, without referring back to the page until you have solved it:

$$37\overline{)4281}$$

Almost impossible, isn't it? You may have found that while you were dividing 37 into 42, you forgot what the last two digits of the dividend were. Although you probably had no trouble holding six numbers in your working memory, you may not have been able to hold all six while also doing something with them.

Working memory is the component of memory in which the active processing of information takes place. It identifies information in the sensory register that warrants attention, saves the information for a longer period of time, and processes it further. It may also hold and think about information that it retrieves from long-term memory—information that will help in interpreting newly received environmental input.

Many theorists portray working memory as playing the role of **central executive,** controlling and monitoring a person's overall thinking and memory processes (Baddeley, 1986, 2001; Barkley, 1996b; Cowan, 1995; Demetriou, Christou, Spanoudis, & Platsidou, 2002; Haberlandt, 1997). In essence, working memory is the component in which "thinking" occurs; therefore, you might think of it as the "awareness" or "consciousness" of the memory system (e.g., Bellezza, 1986).[6]

Characteristics of Working Memory

As we examine the nature of working memory, we'll address the same three characteristics we considered for the sensory register: capacity, form of storage, and duration.

Capacity

Unlike the sensory register, working memory appears to have a very limited capacity for storing information. After reviewing a number of early studies, George Miller (1956) proposed that its capacity can be characterized as the *magical number seven, plus or minus two:* People can hold from five to nine units of information in working memory at one time, with the average number of memorable units being about seven.

Miller further proposed that although the *number* of information units in working memory cannot be increased beyond 7 ± 2, the *amount* of information in each unit can be increased. For example, consider this nine-digit string:

6 3 1 9 8 0 2 5 7

People are more successful in learning long strings of digits if they group the digits into larger numbers, perhaps storing them something like this:

6−3−1   9−8−0   2−5−7

[6]To a considerable degree, processes associated with the central executive appear to be located in the frontal lobes of the cortex; for instance, individuals with damage to their frontal lobes may have trouble controlling attention, planning a course of action, and inhibiting inappropriate responses (Baddeley, 2001; Byrnes, 2001; Kimberg, D'Esposito, & Farah, 1997).

This process of combining pieces of information, called **chunking,** increases the amount of information that the limited space of working memory can hold. To use Miller's analogy, if you can hold only seven coins, you are far richer holding seven quarters, or even seven gold pieces, than seven pennies.

Current theorists believe that Miller's original assessment of 7 ± 2 is overly simplistic (e.g., J. R. Anderson, 1990; Baddeley, 2001; Schneider & Detweiler, 1987). The number of items that can be stored depends on how much information each item includes. For example, Simon (1974) found that, although he himself could remember a list of 7 one- or two-syllable words, he could remember only 6 three-syllable words, 4 two-word phrases, and even fewer phrases of more than two words. In other words, the larger the chunks, the fewer of them working memory can hold at a time. Therefore, as Anderson (1990) has pointed out, it may be difficult to identify the true capacity of working memory, at least in terms of a specific number of discrete items that can be stored there. Furthermore, there may be a trade-off between how much processing is necessary and how much information can be held in working memory: Cognitive processing may take up some of its capacity, leaving less room for information storage.

Form of Storage

Regardless of the form in which information is received, it appears that much of the information stored in working memory is stored in an *auditory* form, especially when the information is language based (Alegria, 1998; Baddeley, 1986; Baddeley & Logie, 1992; Conrad, 1962, 1964). For example, in a study by Conrad (1964), adults were shown six-letter sequences, with letters being presented visually, one at a time, at intervals of three-fourths of a second. As soon as the last letter of a sequence had been presented, participants in the study wrote down all six of the letters they had seen, guessing at any letters that they could not easily recall. When people recalled letters incorrectly, the letters they said they had seen were more likely to resemble the actual stimuli in terms of how they *sounded* than how they looked. For example, the letter *F* was "remembered" as the auditorially similar letter *S* 131 times but as the visually similar letter *P* only 14 times. Similarly, the letter *V* was remembered as *B* 56 times but as *X* only 5 times.

Yet working memory probably includes a means of storing and manipulating information in a visual or spatial form as well (Baddeley, 1986, 2001; Baddeley & Hitch, 1974; Conrad, 1972; E. E. Smith, 2000). An example can be found in an ingenious experiment by Shepard and Metzler (1971) involving pictures of three-dimensional block configurations similar to those shown in Figure 9–4. In this experiment, adults compared pairs of these pictures and determined whether they represented the same three-dimensional configuration. For example, *a* and *b* in Figure 9–4 constitute a "match": if *b* were rotated 90 degrees clockwise, it would be identical to

Figure 9–4
Figures similar to those used by Shepard and Metzler (1971).

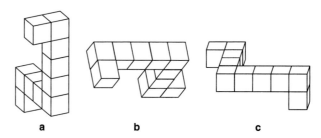

a   b   c

a. However, *a* and *c* are not a match: if *c* were rotated 90 degrees counterclockwise, it would become apparent that its top branch points in a different direction from that of *a.* Shepard and Metzler measured people's reaction time to each pair of figures, assuming that more extensive cognitive processing would be reflected in longer reaction times. Results were quite dramatic: Reaction times were almost entirely a function of how much a figure would have to be rotated for it to be lined up with another figure. In other words, the participants were responding as if they were mentally "rotating" mental images, with more rotation resulting in a longer reaction time. Similar results were obtained when people compared rotated letters (Cooper & Shepard, 1973).

Many theorists believe that working memory actually involves two or more separate storage systems that specialize in different sensory modalities (Baddeley, 1986, 2001; Schacter, 1999; Shah & Miyake, 1996; E. E. Smith, 2000). Neurological evidence supports this idea: Tasks involving the processing of verbal, auditory information activate different parts of the brain than do tasks involving the processing of visual and spatial information (Awh et al., 1996; Goldman-Rakic, 1992; MacAndrew, Klatzky, Fiez, McClelland, & Becker, 2002). Even different aspects of a single task—for instance, *holding* auditory information versus mentally *repeating* it— may occur in different parts of the brain (Schacter, 1999).

As an example of these separate storage systems, Alan Baddeley (e.g., 1986, 2001) has suggested that a mechanism he calls a **phonological loop**[7] can keep a small amount of auditory information fresh through constant repetition (more about such repetition shortly). Meanwhile, a **visuospatial sketchpad** allows manipulation and short-term retention of visual material. Presumably, working memory also includes a "place" where information from multiple modalities can be integrated into an overall understanding of a particular situation (or episode); Baddeley (2001) calls this component the **episodic buffer.**

Having modality-specific storage mechanisms seems to help us "stretch" our working memory capacity somewhat. We have an easier time performing two tasks at the same time when one task involves primarily auditory information and the other task is more visual in nature—for instance, when we are asked simultaneously to judge whether a series of sentences are true or false (an auditory, verbal task) and to perform tasks similar to that in Figure 9–4 (Baddeley, 1999; Just et al., 2001; Mayer & Moreno, 1998). Even so, people in such situations do not devote the amount of mental "energy" to either of the tasks that they would use if they were doing only one of them (Just et al., 2001).

Duration

Working memory is just what its alternative name, *short-term memory,* implies: short. An experiment by Peterson and Peterson (1959) gives us some idea of how long information in working memory lasts. In this experiment, adults were told three consonant letters (e.g., *D X P*) and then immediately asked to count backward by threes from a three-digit number, which was different in each trial. At a signal that occurred anywhere from 3 to 18 seconds after the three consonants had been presented, the participants were asked to recall the consonants. When recall was delayed only 3 seconds, people were able to remember the letters with 80% accuracy; after an 18-second interval, however, their accuracy was only about 10%.

---

[7]In his early writings, Baddeley called this an *articulatory loop.* However, he changed the term to reflect the fact that it involves the *sounds* (phonemes) of speech but does not necessarily involve actual speaking (articulation).

Considering research results such as those of Peterson and Peterson, psychologists believe that the duration of working memory is probably somewhere between 5 and 20 seconds. As is true for the sensory register, both decay and interference have been offered as explanations for the short time span of working memory. Some information stored in working memory may simply fade away (i.e., decay) if it is not processed further (Peterson & Peterson, 1959; Reitman, 1974; Shiffrin & Cook, 1978). Other information may be replaced ("bumped out," as one of my professors used to put it) by new input (Cowan, Wood, Nugent, & Treisman, 1997; Keppel & Underwood, 1962; Melton, 1963; Reitman, 1974). For example, as a woman who for many years had a husband, three children, a dog, and two cats all living in the house, I found myself frequently being interrupted in the middle of tasks. If I had a batch of cookies in the oven, and Jeff asked me to make him a snack and Tina asked me to help her find something she'd misplaced, my cookies were very likely to be pushed from my working memory until I was confronted with new environmental input: The smell of something burning. My husband called me absentminded, but I knew better. My mind was definitely present, but the working component of it had a limited capacity, and new input interfered with the information already stored there. (We're now down to just me, my husband, two pets, and occasionally a kid or two; I find that the more of them who are in the house at once, the less I can concentrate on a single task, such as writing this book.)

Control Processes in Working Memory

Working memory, and especially its central executive component, appears to be the home of many processes important for learning, thinking, and behavior—for example, directing attention, coordinating information from different sensory systems, making sense of situations, drawing inferences, reasoning, planning, making decisions, solving problems, and inhibiting irrelevant thoughts and actions (Baddeley, 2001; Carlson & Moses, 2001; Demetriou et al., 2002; Engle, 2002). For now we'll look at three control processes that primarily affect the functioning of working memory: organization, retrieval, and maintenance rehearsal. In Chapter 10, we'll look at several working memory processes that help information move *beyond* working memory into long-term memory.

Organization

Earlier, I described Miller's (1956) proposal that the process of chunking helps increase the amount of information that can be stored in working memory. As they develop, children show an increasing tendency to chunk information, thereby enhancing the capacity of their working memories (Farnham-Diggory, 1972).

Chunking is an organizational process, in that two or more pieces of information are combined. Information can be organized in a variety of ways. For example, consider again the nine-digit string I presented earlier:

6 3 1 9 8 0 2 5 7

I have already described one way of chunking this string: grouping it into three groups of three digits each. Another frequently observed organizational strategy is to impose a rhythm, or even a melody, on the numbers (Bower & Springston, 1970). Still another way of organizing the digits is to attach some meaning to them—a process that involves retrieving information that has previously been stored in long-term memory. For example, I can store the numbers just listed as three meaningful pieces of information: My son Alex's birthday (the 6th month and 3rd day of *1980*), a quarter (25 cents), and a week (7 days). (Note here that by attaching meaning to the numbers, we also facilitate their storage in long-term memory; in Chapter 10, we will look at such *meaningful learning* more closely.)

Retrieval

Retrieval of information from working memory depends largely on how much information is stored there, a point illustrated in a study by Sternberg (1966). In this experiment, college students were given a set of one to six numbers, which the students presumably stored in working memory. An additional number was then presented, and the students were asked whether that number had been among the original set. The time it took for students to answer the question depended almost entirely on the size of number set already stored in working memory, with each successively larger set yielding a reaction time of about 40 milliseconds longer. Apparently, retrieval of information from working memory is simply a process of scanning all of the contents of working memory, successively and exhaustively, until the desired information is found.

Maintenance Rehearsal

You look up a friend's telephone number and store that number in your working memory; its seven digits are about the limit of what your working memory can hold. But then you find that someone else is using the telephone, and so you must wait to place your call. How do you keep your friend's number in working memory? If you are like most people, you probably repeat it to yourself over and over again.

Repeating information to keep it alive in working memory is a process known as **maintenance rehearsal,** which often takes the form of subvocal speech (Landauer, 1962; Sperling, 1967). Maintenance rehearsal provides a means for saving information from the forgetting processes of decay and interference; when such rehearsal isn't possible, information in working memory disappears quickly. As an example, recall Peterson and Peterson's (1959) examination of the duration of working memory that I described earlier. After participants in the experiment were given the three consonants that they needed to remember, they were asked to count backward by threes until the signal for recall. Such backward counting kept them from rehearsing the three letters; otherwise, they might have kept them in working memory indefinitely simply by repeating them over and over as long as necessary.

There is apparently an upper limit to the amount of information people can keep in working memory simply through repetition, and this upper limit reflects how much can be repeated before some of it starts to fade (Baddeley, 1999). As an illustration, try remembering the following two lists of words. After reading the words in List 1 once or twice, cover the page and rehearse the words until you've written them all down on a piece of scrap paper:

List 1:

beg, far, hum, late, kick, wheel

Now try the same thing with the following words:

List 2:

caterpillar, university, ostentatious, alimony, calamity, interrogation

Each list has six items, but you probably found the first list easier to remember than the second because the words were shorter and so you could repeat them all fairly quickly. In contrast, you may have found that the words in the second list each took so long to pronounce that by the time you got to the end of the list, one or two of the earlier words were starting to fade away. This phenomenon—being able to remember a greater number of short items than longer items—is known as the *word length effect* (e.g., Baddeley, 2001). Here's where Baddeley's concept of *phonological loop* comes into play. Baddeley likens the phenomenon to the circus performer who tries to spin a number of plates at the same time: Just as the performer must periodically return to each plate to keep it spinning, so, too, must a learner frequently return to and repeat each word to keep it fresh in memory. In both cases, there's an upper limit to the number of items that can simultaneously be kept active.

Maintenance rehearsal is observed more frequently in older children and adults than in younger children (Bjorklund & Coyle, 1995; Gathercole & Hitch, 1993; Rosser, 1994), so it is probably to some degree a learned skill. I myself used rehearsal frequently in high school and college whenever I had difficulty remembering something I would be tested on—perhaps when I needed to know a complicated formula, a verbatim definition, or a lengthy list of items. I would continue to repeat the information to myself as test papers were distributed, then immediately write it in the margin so it would be there for me if and when I needed it.

Although maintenance rehearsal can indeed be a useful strategy for keeping information in working memory, teachers must remember that information in working memory will disappear once rehearsal stops. If students are using maintenance rehearsal frequently, their teachers might suspect that they are having trouble storing that information in their long-term memories. Yet long-term memory is where important information *should* be stored. We turn now to this final component of the dual-store model.

LONG-TERM MEMORY

Long-term memory is perhaps the most complex component of the human memory system. As such, it has been studied more extensively than either the sensory register or working memory, and psychologists have offered numerous theories about its nature. I will give you an overview of it here and then describe its characteristics and relevant control processes in more depth in the following three chapters.

Characteristics of Long-Term Memory

As we did for both the sensory register and working memory, we will look at the capacity, form of storage, and duration of long-term memory. We will then look briefly at control processes.

Capacity
As far as theorists can determine, the capacity of long-term memory is unlimited. In fact, as you will discover in Chapter 10, the more information that is already stored in long-term memory, the easier it is to store additional information there.

Form of Storage

Information is probably stored in long-term memory in a variety of ways. For example, language provides one basis of storing information, and visual imagery may provide another. However, most psychologists agree that the bulk of information in long-term memory is probably stored in terms of meanings—that is, *semantically*. In any case, information is rarely remembered exactly as it was received from the environment. Individuals tend to remember the gist of what they see and hear, rather than word-for-word sentences or precise mental images.

Another noteworthy characteristic of long-term memory is its *interconnectedness*: Related pieces of information tend to be associated together. Ultimately, every piece of information is probably directly or indirectly connected with every other piece.[8]

Theorists have made several distinctions among the kinds of information that long-term memory includes. Some especially critical ones are the distinctions among episodic, semantic, procedural, and conceptual knowledge, and the distinction between explicit and implicit knowledge.

Episodic, Semantic, Procedural, and Conceptual Knowledge Tulving (1983, 1991, 1993) has made a distinction between **episodic memory**—one's memory of personal life experiences[9]—and **semantic memory**—one's general knowledge of the world independent of those experiences. The two forms of memory are different in numerous ways. For instance, we *remember* events we have experienced (episodic) but *know* things about the world (semantic). We can often recall when a particular event happened to us (episodic) but usually can*not* recall when we acquired specific facts about the world (semantic). We are most likely to remember certain episodes in our lives when we are in the same context in which we first experienced them, yet we can usually recall general information about the world regardless of the specific context in which we find ourselves. And our semantic memories typically stay with us longer than our episodic memories; for example, we are far more likely to recall the typical menu items at a particular fast-food restaurant than to remember what we actually ordered at that restaurant a year ago last Tuesday.

Both episodic memory and semantic memory relate to the nature of "how things were or are"—something that many theorists refer to as **declarative knowledge.** But we also have something called **procedural knowledge:** We know "how to do things" (J.R. Anderson, 1983a, 1995).[10] For example, you probably know how to ride a bicycle, wrap a gift, and add the numbers 57 and 94. To do such things successfully, we must adapt our actions to changing conditions; for example, when riding a bicycle, we must be able to turn left or right when we find an object directly in our path, and we must be able to come to a complete stop when we reach our destination. Accordingly, as you will learn in our discussion of *productions* in Chapter 11, our procedural knowledge must include information about how to respond under different circumstances; that is, it includes *conditional knowledge.*

---

[8]As you should recall from Chapter 2, most neurons in the brain have synaptic connections with hundreds of other neurons. Presumably many of these synapses account for the organized nature of long-term memory.

[9]Some theorists have developed the idea of episodic memory further, often using the term *autobiographic memory*; for example, see Conway and Rubin (1993), Eacott (1999), and Nelson (1993a, 1993b).

[10]When theorists talk about *skill learning*, in most cases they are talking about the acquisition of procedural knowledge.

As you might guess, episodic, semantic, and procedural forms of knowledge are interconnected in long-term memory. For instance, when I think about what *dogs* are like (semantic knowledge), I may be reminded of how our dog Anna once ate the leftover chocolate cake we brought home after Tina's birthday party at McDonald's (episodic knowledge), and I might be reminded, too, of how I need to put our current dog Tobey's boots on his feet so that they stay on in deep snow (procedural knowledge). How did Anna get the chocolate cake? Why does Tobey need boots to walk in the snow? And why does putting the boots on one way work better than putting them on another? Perhaps there is yet another kind of knowledge—**conceptual knowledge**—that reflects our understanding of *why* certain events happened, why certain things are the way they are, and why certain procedures are effective but others are not (J. R. Anderson, 1995; Byrnes, 2001). Whether such knowledge is distinctively different from the other forms we've identified, or whether it simply reflects relationships among those other forms, is as yet unclear (Byrnes, 2001).

Explicit Versus Implicit Knowledge How do you grow flowers from a packet of flower seeds? You can probably describe the process fairly accurately, explaining that you need to plant the seeds in soil, make sure they have plenty of sunlight, water them regularly, and so on. But how do you keep your balance when you ride a bicycle? How do you move your legs when you skip? What things do you do to form a grammatically correct sentence when you speak? Such questions are more difficult to answer: Even though such activities are probably second nature to you, you really can't put your finger on exactly what you do when you perform them.

Many theorists make a distinction between **explicit knowledge**—knowledge that we can easily recall and explain—and **implicit knowledge**—knowledge that we cannot consciously recall or explain but that nevertheless affects our behavior (e.g., Graf & Masson, 1993; Newcombe & Fox, 1994; Roediger, 1990; Schacter, 1993; Siegler, 2000). Sometimes people have no conscious awareness that they have learned something, yet what they have learned clearly shows up in their actions. This is the case, for example, for people who have suffered certain types of brain damage (Bachevalier, Malkova, & Beauregard, 1996; Cermak, 1993; Gabrieli, Keane, Zarella, & Poldrack, 1997; Kolers, 1975; Schacter, 1993). There is also evidence that we acquire some implicit knowledge when we learn either a first or second language: We can produce grammatically correct sentences even though we cannot explain how we do it (Ellis, 1994; Reber, 1993).

Sometimes memories are sufficiently "dim" that they affect us only in subtle ways. For example, when 9-year-olds look at pictures of classmates from their preschool days, they may have no conscious recollection of some of them, but their physiological responses suggest that they *do* recognize these children at some level (Newcombe & Fox, 1994). As another example, when college students are asked to specify which direction well-known cultural images face (e.g., when students in England are asked which way Queen Elizabeth faces on a 10-pence coin, and when students in Japan are asked which side the cartoon character Hello Kitty wears her bow on), they can rarely tell you. However, when forced to choose between the correct orientation and its mirror image, they guess correctly about 65 to 80% of the time—hardly stellar performance, but certainly better than chance (Kelly, Burton, Kato, & Akamatsu, 2001).

Duration

As you will learn in Chapter 12, theorists disagree regarding the duration of long-term memory. Some theorists believe that information, once stored in long-term memory, remains there permanently. Others, however, believe that information can disappear from long-term memory through a variety of forgetting processes. In fact, although some information may remain in long-term memory for long periods, there is probably no way to show conclusively that *all* information stored there remains permanently. The question about the duration of long-term memory is still an open one, and the best we can say is that long-term memory's duration is indefinitely *long*.

Control Processes in Long-Term Memory

In Chapters 10 and 12, we will examine long-term memory storage and retrieval processes in depth. But at this point, let's get a general idea of what these processes entail.

Storage

Storage processes in the first two components of memory are fairly straightforward: Anything sensed is stored in the sensory register, and anything attended to is stored in working memory. However, as we shall see in the next chapter, storage of information in long-term memory is not so simple. Although some information may be stored easily (visual images are an example), most information must be consciously and actively processed before it is stored. People store information in long-term memory most successfully when they understand it, organize it, and integrate it with information they already have.

Recall that the processing necessary for storing information in long-term memory is accomplished in working memory. Recall, too, that working memory has a limited capacity and can handle only so much information at one time. The result is that long-term memory storage occurs slowly, and a great deal is lost from working memory along the way. In essence, working memory is the bottleneck in the memory system: It prevents most information from ever getting into long-term memory.[11]

Retrieval

Retrieval of information from either the sensory register or working memory is simple and easy: If the information is still there, it will probably be found. Retrieval of information from long-term memory is more difficult: Long-term memory has much more information than an individual can realistically search through at one time, so the success of retrieval depends largely on whether the individual searches in the right "location." Furthermore, retrieval from long-term memory is closely tied to storage processes: The more completely information has been understood, the better it has been organized, and the more closely it has been integrated with previously stored concepts, the more easily that information can be remembered.

Speaking of retrieval from long-term memory, what was Edward C. Tolman's middle name? Did you perhaps remember your friend Harry's brother-in-law, Marvin *Chace*? Or did you think of Tolman *chacing* his rats down their mazes? The more ways that people store a piece of information in long-term memory, the better their chances of retrieving the information when they need it.

---

[11]Some advocates for *speed-reading* programs claim that speed-reading greatly increases the amount of information that a person can learn and remember within a certain time period. Contemporary views of memory indicate that such results are highly unlikely. In fact, research tells us that people's comprehension of text is significantly lower when they speed-read than when they read at a normal rate (Carver, 1990; Crowder & Wagner, 1992). Speed-reading is probably effective only when readers already know much of the information they are reading (Carver, 1971, 1990; Crowder & Wagner, 1992).

ARE WORKING MEMORY AND LONG-TERM MEMORY REALLY DIFFERENT?

Up to this point, we have been talking about working memory and long-term memory as two distinctly different components of memory. Some theorists have proposed, however, that working and long-term memory are really a single entity. Let's look at the evidence both in favor of and against the working memory/long-term memory distinction.

Evidence Supporting the Distinction

Several research findings have been cited as evidence for the distinction between working and long-term memory. For one thing, the major form of storage in the two memories appears to be different, working memory placing a heavy emphasis on acoustic encoding and long-term memory being largely semantic in nature.

As another source of evidence, let's reconsider the serial learning curve described in Chapter 8 (to refresh your memory, refer back to Figure 8–11). Given a list of items to remember, individuals more often remember the first few items in the list (the *primacy effect*) and the last few items (the *recency effect*) than they remember the middle items. Some theorists have explained the serial learning curve in terms of a dual-store model of memory (Glanzer & Cunitz, 1966; Norman, 1969). From this perspective, people can process the first few items in a list sufficiently to store them in long-term memory, and they continue to hold the last few items in working memory after the entire list has been presented. They lose many of the middle items, however, because they don't have enough time to process them adequately for long-term memory storage and lose them from working memory as later items are presented. In support of the view that early items in a serial learning list are stored in long-term memory is the finding that when the presentation rate is slowed down (thus allowing for more processing), the primacy effect is increased (Glanzer & Cunitz, 1966). Conversely, when processing of list items is prevented, the primacy effect disappears; that is, items early in the list are remembered no better than items in the middle of the list (Peterson & Peterson, 1962). In contrast, the recency effect seems to be more affected by the recall interval: The longer that recall of the list is delayed, the less people are able to remember items at the end of the list, a finding consistent with the notion that these items are stored in the short-lived working memory (Glanzer & Cunitz, 1966; Postman & Phillips, 1965).

Third, studies of people who have undergone certain brain injuries or neurosurgical procedures sometimes show an impairment of one kind of memory without a corresponding loss of function in the other (Atkinson & Shiffrin, 1968; Eysenck & Keane, 1990; Scoville & Milner, 1957). For example, some individuals can recall events experienced before the brain trauma but are unable to retain new experiences, indicating a possible problem with working memory while long-term memory remains intact. Other individuals can recall new experiences long enough to talk briefly about them but cannot remember them a few minutes later; these are cases in which working memory is functioning, but new information seemingly cannot be transferred into long-term memory. Consistent with such findings, some evidence indicates that working memory and long-term memory processes may occur in different parts of the brain (Zola-Morgan & Squire, 1990).

Evidence Against the Distinction

Other research findings indicate that working memory and long-term memory may not be as distinctly different as I have portrayed them. For example, although information is frequently stored acoustically in working memory and semantically in long-term memory, there is also evidence for *semantic* storage in working memory (Shulman, 1971, 1972) and for *acoustic* storage in long-term memory (Nelson & Rothbart, 1972).

Furthermore, some research studies have cast doubt on the idea that the recency effect in serial learning necessarily reflects the use of a working memory separate from long-term memory (Crowder, 1993; Greene, 1986; Reisberg, 1997; Wickelgren, 1973). For example, in a study by Thapar and Greene (1993), college students viewed a list of words presented two words at a time on a computer screen; they also performed a 20-second "distractor" task (mentally adding a series of digits) after each pair of words. The students remembered the last few words in the list much better than the middle words, even though, thanks to the distractor task, *none* of the words could possibly have still been in working memory. Considering results such as these, theorists have suggested that the serial learning curve can be explained as easily by a single-store model as by a dual-store model. One possible explanation is simply that forgetting occurs rapidly at first and then slowly tapers off—a pattern that holds true for many different species and many different tasks (Wickelgren, 1973; Wixted & Ebbesen, 1991). From this perspective, the recency effect may simply be a result of the fact that the last items of a list have not yet undergone that rapid decay. Another possibility is that items in a list are easier to remember if they are distinctive in some way; items near the end of the list have more memorable positions (e.g., a word may be "the last one" or "the next-to-last one") and so may be more memorable as result (Greene, 1986; Reisberg, 1997).

Alternative explanations also exist for the impairments in memory observed in individuals who have undergone brain traumas (Eysenck & Keane, 1990; Glass, Holyoak, & Santa, 1979; Zechmeister & Nyberg, 1982). These impairments may reflect specific difficulties in storage or retrieval processes rather than in working memory or long-term memory per se.

The debate regarding dual-store and single-store models is by no means resolved; more complete discussions of the issue are presented elsewhere (e.g., Cowan, 1994, 1995; Crowder, 1993; Eysenck & Keane, 1990). In the meantime, many theorists are more concerned about how information is processed than about how many separate components human memory might have. In the next section, I present two examples.

ALTERNATIVE VIEWS OF HUMAN MEMORY

At least two alternatives to the dual-store model of memory have been proposed: a levels-of-processing model and an activation model. These theories emphasize the cognitive processes involved in human memory rather than the possible structures that may comprise it.

Levels of Processing

The **levels-of-processing** model of human memory (Cermak & Craik, 1979; Craik & Lockhart, 1972) was the first major theoretical alternative to the dual-store model. According to this view, incoming information is processed by a **central processor** (similar to the *central executive* aspect of working memory I spoke of earlier) at any one of a number of different levels of complexity. This central processor has a limited capacity, in that it can hold only so much at one time; the information temporarily held there is what we are aware of at any given point in time.

How long and how well information is remembered depends on how thoroughly the central processor deals with it. Information that isn't processed at all leaves only a very brief impression (much as it does in the sensory register of the dual-store model). Information that is processed superficially, such that only surface characteristics (e.g., appearance, brightness) are attended to, may last a few seconds (much as it does in the dual-store model's working memory). Only when information undergoes "deep" processing—that is, when it is interpreted, understood, and related to previously learned information—do we remember it for any length of time.

An experiment by Turnure, Buium, and Thurlow (1976) illustrates how different levels of processing lead to different degrees of information recall. Children 4 and 5 years old were asked to remember pairs of common objects (e.g., remembering that *soap* and *jacket* go together). Children processed the information in one of five different ways, as follows:

1. *Labels.* They repeated the names of the objects.
2. *Sentence generation.* They made up sentences that included both objects in a pair.
3. *Sentence repetition.* They repeated experimenter-generated sentences that stated a relationship between the two objects (e.g., "The soap is hiding in the jacket.").
4. *"What" question.* They answered a question about a relationship between the objects (e.g., "What is the soap doing in the jacket?").
5. *"Why" question.* They answered a question concerning why a particular relationship existed between the objects (e.g., "Why is the soap hiding in the jacket?").

In this experiment, children learned most effectively when they were forced to think about (i.e., process) a relationship between the objects: The question-answering conditions (conditions 4 and 5) led to the greatest recall of the word pairs. Repeating a sentence that expressed such a relationship (condition 3) led to some recall; presumably repetition promoted some processing of the association between each pair. Least effective for learning were the first two conditions. In the labeling condition (condition 1), no relationship between objects was processed, and children in the sentence-generation condition (condition 2) often constructed sentences that did not effectively connect the two objects (e.g., "I have some soap and a jacket.").

One element that frequently arises as an important factor in learning is **intention to learn:** People who intend to learn something are more likely to learn and remember it than people who do not specifically try to learn that information. Proponents of the levels-of-processing model have argued that people process information more thoroughly when they are intending to learn it but that the depth of processing, rather than intention to learn per se, affects the success of learning. In fact, research supports this point: When individuals process material deeply, they often learn it successfully even when they are not specifically *trying* to learn it (Postman, 1964). In other words, nonintentional learning (often called **incidental learning**) is just as effective as intentional learning if the degree of processing is equal in the two situations.

A study by Hyde and Jenkins (1969) provides an example of successful incidental learning as a result of deep processing. College students were shown a list of 24 words presented at a rate of one word every two seconds. Some students (a control group) were merely told to learn the words; thus, they would be intentionally learning the words. Different experimental groups received different instructions, as follows:

1. *Pleasantness rating.* Students were told to rate each word for its degree of pleasantness; for example, a word such as *love* might be rated as relatively pleasant, whereas *hate* might be rated as less pleasant.

2. *Counting letters.* Students were told to count the number of letters in each word.

3. *Counting letter* Es. Students were told to count the number of letter *Es* in each word.

At the same time, some of the students receiving each of the different instructions were told to learn the words as they went along; these students were presumably engaged in intentional learning of the words. Other students were not told to learn the words; for these students, any recall of the words would presumably be the result of incidental learning.

The different tasks that Hyde and Jenkins assigned should lead to different levels of processing. In counting all of the letters or the number of *Es* in a word, the learner would need to look only at the superficial characteristics of the word and would not have to interpret the word's meaning; thus, a counting task should lead to relatively shallow processing. In rating a word's pleasantness, the learner must examine the word's meaning; hence, deeper, semantic processing should result. Consistent with levels-of-processing theory, students who rated words for their pleasantness remembered more words than students who counted letters. More interesting, however, is the fact that incidental learning students who rated the words for their pleasantness generally remembered as many words as any of the intentional learning groups (in fact, they did *better* than the intentional counting groups). Here was a case where learning was facilitated simply by virtue of the fact that students had to focus on the underlying meaning of the material to be learned. Depth of processing, not intention to learn, was the critical factor affecting the degree of learning.

The levels-of-processing model has certainly had its impact on psychologists' conceptualizations of learning and memory; for instance, I often see learning theorists talking about processing information "deeply" or in a more "shallow" manner. Nevertheless, weaknesses of this approach have surfaced. For one thing, the idea of *depth* of processing is a vague notion that is difficult to define or measure in precise terms (Baddeley, 1978). Furthermore, some research indicates that degree of learning is not always a function of the degree of processing in the way that the model predicts. For example, the more frequently information is repeated, the better it can be remembered *regardless* of the depth of processing it has undergone (Nelson, 1977). Even more damaging, however, is the finding that, in some cases, superficial processing actually leads to *better* recall than deeper processing. In an experiment by Morris, Bransford, and Franks (1977), college students were given a series of words and asked (1) whether each word fit appropriately into a sentence (a task involving "deep" semantic processing) or (2) whether the word rhymed with another word (a task involving "superficial" phonetic processing). Students recalled more words on an unexpected recall test when they had processed them semantically; however, they were more successful at identifying rhymes of the original words when they had processed them phonetically. Stein (1978) has reported similar results.

Other thinking related to the levels-of-processing approach is that information processing is most effective not necessarily when it is semantic but rather when it is *elaborative*—that is, when the learner adds information to the material to be learned in such a way that the new material is encoded more precisely, more meaningfully, and more completely (Craik & Tulving, 1975; Ellis & Hunt, 1983). We will examine the process of elaboration in more detail in the next chapter.

Activation

Some theorists (e.g., J. R. Anderson, 1983b, 1984, 1995; Collins & Loftus, 1975; Cowan, 1995; Kimberg, D'Esposito, & Farah, 1997) have proposed that working and long-term memory are not necessarily separate entities but may instead simply reflect different **activation** states of a single memory. According to this view, all information stored in memory is in either an active or an inactive state. Information that is currently active, which may include both incoming information and information previously stored in memory, is the information that individuals are paying attention to and processing—information I have previously described as being in working memory. As attention shifts, other pieces of information in memory become activated, and the previously activated information gradually becomes inactive. The bulk of the information stored in memory is in an inactive state, so that we are not consciously aware of it—I have previously described this information as being in long-term memory.

A key principle in activation theory is that activation almost invariably spreads from one piece of information to associated pieces. As evidence for this idea, theorists point to a phenomenon called **priming.** For example, let's consider a study by Ratcliff and McKoon (1981). College students first studied a series of sentences (e.g., *The doctor hated the book.*). After the students knew the sentences well, they were shown a number of nouns, one at a time, and asked to identify those that had been included in the sentences they learned earlier. Sometimes the nouns were immediately preceded by another noun from the same sentence (e.g., they might see *book* right after seeing *doctor*); when such was the case, the students correctly indicated having seen the second noun significantly faster than they would have otherwise. It's as if presentation of the first noun activated memories associated with that noun and so made those other memories more readily available. That is, activation of one noun stimulated, or *primed*, activation of the second.

Activation theory doesn't help us understand why, as noted earlier, different kinds of stimuli (e.g., auditory versus visual, verbal versus spatial) seem to be processed in somewhat different areas of the brain (Baddeley, 2001). Nevertheless, this approach is particularly useful in understanding how people retrieve information from long-term memory. Accordingly, we will encounter it again in Chapter 12.

The author activates part of her memory.

GENERALIZATIONS ABOUT MEMORY
AND THEIR EDUCATIONAL IMPLICATIONS

Clearly, theorists don't entirely agree about how memory is structured or how it functions. But regardless of how we conceptualize the human memory system, there are several things we can conclude about how memory operates. At this point, let's make a few generalizations and consider their implications for educational practice:

- *Attention is essential for learning.* Regardless of which model of memory we use, we know that attention is critical for long-term retention of information. People will *not* learn the things that they don't process in some way, and paying attention is the first step that they must take.

There is an old saying, "You can lead a horse to water, but you can't make him drink." Ormrod's corollary is "The horse can't possibly drink if you don't at least lead him to the water." Helping students to focus their attention on important information is the first step in helping them learn it: It gets them to the water trough.

Yet classrooms are usually lively environments with many stimuli competing for students' attention. For example, think of yourself in one of your college classes. Sometimes you pay attention to what the teacher is saying, but at other times your attention drifts to such things as the shape of the instructor's nose, the style of another student's clothes, the doodles in your notebook, or the plans you've made for the upcoming weekend. If adults cannot pay attention during every minute of a class session, how can we reasonably expect younger learners to do so?

Actually, the things that teachers do in the classroom make a big difference in the extent to which students pay attention to the tasks at hand. Here are several effective strategies for capturing and holding students' attention:

- *Include variety in topics and presentation styles.* Repetition of the same topics and the same procedures day after day can lead to boredom and reduced attention (Zirin, 1974). Variety and novelty in the subject matter and mode of presentation will help keep students' attention focused on a lesson (Berlyne, 1960; Good & Brophy, 1994; Keele, 1973; Keller, 1987).
- *Provide frequent breaks, especially when working with young children.* After prolonged periods of sitting quietly and attentively, even adults are apt to become restless and distracted. Frequent breaks are especially important for students in the early and middle elementary grades. For example, children are often more attentive after recess than before, even if recess has involved playing quietly in the classroom rather than running around the schoolyard (Pellegrini & Bjorklund, 1997; Pellegrini, Huberty, & Jones, 1995).
- *Ask questions.* Questions are an excellent way of maintaining students' attention when it might otherwise wander away from the topic at hand (Grabe, 1986; Piontkowski & Calfee, 1979; Samuels & Turnure, 1974). By asking questions periodically, and perhaps by occasionally addressing questions to particular students, teachers can help students keep their attention where it should be. (We will consider additional benefits of teacher questions in Chapter 12.)
- *Minimize distractions when independent work is assigned.* Most students are better able to concentrate on challenging independent assignments when their work environment is relatively quiet and subdued.
- *Seat students near the teacher if they have difficulty paying attention.* Students are more apt to pay attention when they are placed at the front of the room and near the teacher (Doyle, 1986a; Schwebel & Cherlin, 1972). Front row seats may be especially appropriate for students with a history of being easily distracted.

• *Monitor students' behaviors.* Behaviors often provide a clue to whether students are paying attention. For example, students should be directing their eyes at the teacher, textbook, or other appropriate stimulus and should be clearly working on the task at hand (Grabe, 1986; Piontkowski & Calfee, 1979; Samuels & Turnure, 1974).

• *Different people may attend differently to the same stimulus.* As we discovered in our discussion of nominal versus effective stimuli, even when teachers successfully draw students' attention to instructional events or materials, they cannot always control *how* students attend to them. The Faust and Anderson (1967) study described earlier in the chapter (the one in which students studied Russian vocabulary words by reading either single sentences or several-sentence paragraphs) points to one important strategy for helping students attend effectively: Teachers should design classroom tasks in such a way that students can perform the tasks successfully *only* by paying attention to the things that are most important for them to learn.

• *People can process only a limited amount of information at a time.* We have characterized both attention and the "working" aspect of memory as having a limited capacity; in other words, people can pay attention to and think about only a small amount of information at any one time. Accordingly, getting information into long-term memory will be a slow process. Educators must remember this point in pacing their lectures and choosing their instructional materials. When too much information is presented too fast, students will simply not be able to remember it all.

• *Memory is selective.* Because learners usually receive much more information than they can possibly process and remember, they must continually make choices about what things to focus on and what things to ignore. Unfortunately, teachers and textbooks often load students up with more details than any normal person can possibly remember (Calfee, 1981; E. Gagné, 1985). In such situations, students must inevitably select some information to the exclusion of other information, but they aren't always the best judges of what material is most important for them to learn.

Details are often important means of illustrating, clarifying, and elaborating on the main points of a lecture or textbook. In this sense, they are indispensable. At the same time, teachers must help their students sort through essential and nonessential information so that the students don't lose sight of the forest because of the trees.

• *The limited capacity of working memory is not necessarily a bad thing.* The working memory bottleneck forces learners to condense, organize, and synthesize the information they receive (e.g., Gagné & Driscoll, 1988). These processes may be in learners' best interest over the long run, as you will discover in our discussion of long-term memory storage in the following chapter.

SUMMARY

Memory theorists often distinguish between *learning* (acquisition of new information) and *memory* (saving information for a period of time); occasionally, they also use *memory* in reference to a particular "spot" (metaphorically speaking) where information is saved. Some of their terminology is borrowed from computer lingo: *Storage* means "putting" information in memory, *encoding* involves changing information to store it more

effectively, and *retrieval* is the process of "finding" information that was stored at an earlier time.

Currently the most prevalent view of human memory—a *dual-store model*—maintains that memory has three distinct components. The first component, the *sensory register*, holds virtually all of the information that has been sensed for a very short period of time (a fraction of a second for visual information, two to four seconds for auditory information). If the information held in the sensory register is not processed in some fashion—at a minimum, by being paid attention to—it appears to disappear from memory.

Attention involves the selection of certain stimuli in the environment for further processing. Attention is influenced by several stimulus characteristics (size, intensity, novelty, incongruity, emotion, and personal significance), and what people actually pay attention to (the effective stimulus) is not always what outside observers *think* they are paying attention to (the nominal stimulus). Attentional capacity is limited: People usually cannot pay attention to more than one demanding task at any given time.

Information that is attended to moves on to *working memory* (also called short-term memory), where it is actively processed; in essence, working memory is the "thinking" center of the memory system. Working memory has a limited capacity; for example, most people can hold no more than five to nine digits there at a single time. Furthermore, information stored in working memory lasts only about 5 to 20 seconds unless it is processed further.

Information that undergoes further processing (e.g., integration with previously stored information) moves on to the third component—*long-term memory.* Long-term memory appears to have the capacity to hold a great deal of information for a relatively long period of time.

Theorists disagree about whether working memory and long-term memory are distinctly different entities, and research investigating this issue has yielded mixed results. At least two alternatives to the dual-store model have been proposed: a *levels-of-processing* model, in which information processed in depth is retained longer than is information processed only superficially, and an *activation* model, in which the information stored in memory is either in an "active," conscious state or in an "inactive," unconscious state.

Despite differing perspectives regarding the exact nature of the human memory system, we can make several generalizations about how memory operates. For one thing, attention is essential for effective learning. Also, people can process only a limited amount of information at any one time, so they must be selective about the things they study. Finally, the processing bottleneck of the memory system is not necessarily a bad thing; it forces people to condense and integrate information in ways that are often beneficial over the long run.

Long-Term Memory I: Storage

Over the years, I've had a number of students appear at my office door after receiving a low score on one of my exams. "But I studied so *hard*!" a student might whine, displaying a look of frustrated desperation. "I studied twice as long as my roommate did, yet my roommate got an A while I got a C-!"

Storing information in long-term memory and retrieving it later can be a tricky business. If the two roommates are equally motivated to achieve in my class, the difference between them may be the result of their storage and retrieval processes. After almost 30 years of talking with students about how they typically study, I have come to the conclusion that many are sadly uninformed about how best to learn and remember information.

Even when students effectively store information in their long-term memories, they don't always learn what their teachers *think* they are learning. For example, when my daughter Tina was in fourth grade, she came home one day complaining about a song she was learning in the school choir. "It has bad words in it, Mom," she told me. I was quite surprised to learn that she was talking about "America the Beautiful," but then she recited the guilty line from the second verse:

    All the bastard cities gleam.

After shuddering about the richness of my daughter's vocabulary, I patiently explained to her that the line in question was actually "Alabaster cities gleam." Two weeks later the rest of the family went to hear Tina's choir performing in concert. As the children began to sing "America the Beautiful," 6-year-old Alex turned to me and whispered, "Why are they singing about *spaceship* skies?"

Long-term memory provides a mechanism for saving information over a relatively long period of time. It also provides a knowledge base from which to interpret new information. As we shall see, people frequently store incoming information in long-term memory by relating it to things they already know—in other words, to things already existing in long-term memory. Different people are likely to store the same information differently, then, because they have previously stored different kinds of information in their respective long-term memories. Alex had never heard the word *spacious* before, but *spaceship* was a frequent word in his world of science fiction cartoons. Similarly, Tina was unfamiliar with *alabaster*, but . . . well, let's not go there.

In this chapter, we will explore the multifaceted nature of long-term memory storage. We will first consider how storage is often constructive in nature and look at examples of construction in action. We will then examine cognitive processes that may be involved in long-term memory storage, as well as activities and characteristics that either facilitate or interfere with storage. Finally, we will identify strategies for promoting effective long-term memory storage in instructional settings. In the following two chapters, we will look at the nature of the knowledge that people acquire and at the processes involved in retrieving that knowledge from long-term memory.

CONSTRUCTION IN STORAGE

Imagine, for a minute, that your mind worked like a videocassette recorder, such that you recorded everything you saw and heard. Your memory of an event would involve a simple process of finding and replaying the appropriate cassette, and you would be able to remember the event as completely and accurately as if you were reliving it. Studying for an exam would be easy, you might think—no need for reading the textbook more than once or for mindless repetition of meaningless facts.

Unfortunately, our minds are not accurate recorders of life events. As we discovered in the preceding chapter, we can process only a small amount of information in working memory at any one time, and so we quickly lose most of what we've stored in our sensory registers. In a manner of speaking, most of the information we receive from the environment goes in one ear (or eye) and out the other. In part because we retain such a small percentage of the information we receive, many learning theorists believe that long-term memory storage often involves a process of *construction*, whereby we use the bits and pieces of information we do retain to build a reasonable understanding of the world around us.

Examples of Construction in Action

At any given point in time, our interpretation of the environment (**perception**) is usually both less and more than the information we actually receive from the environment (**sensation**). Perception is *less* than sensation because people cannot possibly interpret all of the information that bombards their sensory receptors at any given moment. Right now, as you are looking at this book, light waves are bouncing off of the page and hitting the light-sensitive cells in the retinas of your eyes. At the same time, you may also be receiving light waves from the table at which you are working, the carpet on the floor, and the pictures on the walls. Your ears are probably receiving numerous sound waves, perhaps from a radio, a nearby conversation, an air conditioner, or traffic outside your window. Perhaps a certain smell is drifting through the air, or a certain taste from your last meal lingers in your mouth. It is neither necessary nor possible for you to interpret *all* of these sensations, so you will attend to some of them and ignore the others.

But perception is also much *more* than sensation, because sensation alone provides insufficient information for an adequate interpretation of ongoing events. It appears that people use the data they receive from their sensory receptors to put together, or construct, an overall perception of any given situation (Neisser, 1967; Ornstein, 1972). As an example, consider the fact that our eyes do not provide a continual report of visual stimulation; rather, they jump from one focal point to another, taking periodic "snapshots" of the visual field. These jumps in focus, or **saccades**, occur four or five times a second, with visual sensation occurring primarily during the rest periods between them (Abrams, 1994; Irwin, 1996). If we receive only four or five snapshots of visual information each second, our visual world should appear jerky and erratic, much as an old-time movie does. The fact that we instead see smooth-flowing motion is due, in large part, to the mental "filling in" that occurs as our minds interpret visual sensations. (This principle should remind you of the Gestalt concept of *closure*.)

Even if human eyes functioned 100% of the time, they would typically provide an incomplete picture of the environment, and we would have to fill in mentally the information that we did not sense. For example, imagine walking into a bookstore and seeing the store clerk behind the counter. You probably sense only the clerk's head and upper torso, yet you perceive an entire person. You assume that the clerk has a lower torso and two legs, and in fact you would be quite surprised if the clerk's lower body looked any other way!

As another example of construction in perception, look at the three pictures in Figure 10–1. Most people perceive the picture on the left as being that of a woman, even though many of her features are missing. Enough features are visible—an eye and parts of the nose, mouth, chin, and hair—that you can construct a meaningful perception from them. Do the other two figures provide enough information for you to construct two more faces? Construction of a face from the figure on the right may take you a while, but it can be done.

Consider, too, how much is missing from the spoken language that we hear. For example, let's say that you are in a noisy room and hear someone say:

I -an't -ear a thing in this -lace!

People often make assumptions about what they don't see and may be quite surprised when such assumptions are inaccurate.

Figure 10–1
Can you construct a person from each of these pictures?
Reprinted from "Age in the Development of Closure Ability in Children" by C. M. Mooney,
1957, *Canadian Journal of Psychology*, *11*, p. 220. Copyright 1957 by Canadian
Psychological Association. Reprinted with permission.

Although you haven't heard everything the person said, you may have enough information to
perceive the sentence:

I can't hear a thing in this place!

Even when you do hear everything the speaker says, what you *really* hear is a continu-
ousstreamofsoundwaves rather than . . . separate . . . words . . . spoken . . . like . . . this. Only
when you are familiar with the particular language you are listening to can you mentally divide
the one long sound you actually sense into separate words. For instance, you can easily understand the following sentence when you hear it:

I read a book.

even though the identical sentence in Mandarin Chinese would give you trouble:

Wǒkànshū.

To an individual fluent in Mandarin Chinese but not in English, the situation would be reversed;
that person would "hear" this:

Ireadabook.

and this:

Wǒ kàn shū.

Curiously, once you have constructed meaning from what you have seen or heard, that
meaning then seems so obvious to you. Furthermore, you tend to perceive the same pattern of
sensory information in the same way at a future time; a particular construction of sensory input

Figure 10–2
Reprinted from "The Role of Frequency in Developing Perceptual Sets" by B. R. Bugelski & D. A. Alampay, 1961, *Canadian Journal of Psychology, 15*, p. 206. Copyright 1961 by Canadian Psychological Association. Reprinted with permission.

tends to stick. For example, if you were to close this book now and not pick it up again for a week or more, you would see the three faces in Figure 10–1 almost immediately, even if you had had difficulty perceiving them originally.

Different people may construct different interpretations of any given event. For instance, consider Tina's and Alex's rather unconventional interpretations of "America the Beautiful." As another example, take a close look at the picture in Figure 10–2. Describe to yourself what you see. Notice the shape of the head, the eye, the nose, the mouth, the jaw line. But just what is it that you *do* see? Is this a picture of a man? Or is it, perhaps, a picture of a rat or a mouse?

The man-rat picture in Figure 10–2 is an example of an **ambiguous stimulus,** something that readily lends itself to more than one possible construction. Some people perceive the figure as a bald man with an overbite, a strangely shaped ear, and a backward tilt to his head. Others instead perceive a rat or mouse with a very short front leg and a long tail curling beneath its body (Bugelski & Alampay, 1961).

As you can see, then, people often perceive the world in their own unique ways, and all may arrive at different conclusions about what they have seen and heard. As a result, several people witnessing the same event often store very different things in their long-term memories. Let's now look more closely at the processes involved in long-term memory storage.

LONG-TERM MEMORY STORAGE PROCESSES

Before we begin our discussion of long-term memory storage processes, try this exercise. Here is a short story entitled "The War of the Ghosts." Read it silently *one time only,* then cover the page and write down as much of the story as you can remember.

The War of the Ghosts

One night two young men from Egulac went down to the river to hunt seals, and while they were there it became foggy and calm. Then they heard war-cries, and they thought, "Maybe this is a war-party." They escaped to the shore, and hid behind a log. Now canoes came up, and they heard the noise of paddles, and saw one canoe coming up to them. There were five men in the canoe, and they said:

"What do you think? We wish to take you along. We are going up the river to make war on the people."

One of the young men said: "I have no arrows."

"Arrows are in the canoe," they said.

"I will not go along. I might be killed. My relatives do not know where I have gone. But you," he said, turning to the other, "may go with them."

So one of the young men went, but the other returned home.

And the warriors went on up the river to a town on the other side of Kalama. The people came down to the water, and they began to fight, and many were killed. But presently the young man heard one of the warriors say, "Quick, let us go home: that Indian has been hit." Now he thought: "Oh, they are ghosts." He did not feel sick, but they said he had been shot.

So the canoes went back to Egulac, and the young man went ashore to his house, and made a fire. And he told everybody and said, "Behold I accompanied the ghosts, and we went to fight. Many of our fellows were killed, and many of those who attacked us were killed. They said I was hit, and I did not feel sick."

He told it all, and then he became quiet. When the sun rose he fell down. Something black came out of his mouth. His face became contorted. The people jumped up and cried.

He was dead. (Bartlett, 1932, p. 65)

Now cover the story and write down everything you can remember of it.

Once you have finished, compare your reproduction with the original. What differences do you notice? Your reproduction is probably shorter than the original. Some details are almost certainly omitted. Perhaps you even added some things. But you probably maintained the gist of the story: You included its main ideas and events, mostly in their proper sequence.

Using this Native American ghost story, Frederic Bartlett (1932) conducted one of the earliest studies of the long-term memory of meaningful verbal information. Bartlett asked his students at Cambridge University to read the story two times, then to recall it at various times later on. Students' recalled stories differed from the actual story in a number of ways:

1. *The words themselves were changed.* In other words, recall was not verbatim.
2. *The gist of the story, including the major sequence of events, was usually retained.* Some details, especially those that were essential to the story and those that were particularly striking, were retained. Unimportant details and meaningless information, however, were omitted. For example, such details as "something black came out of his mouth" and "he was dead" were likely to be remembered; such details as "the young man . . . made a fire" and "a town on the other side of Kalama" were frequently forgotten.
3. *Parts of the story were distorted and additional information was inserted to make the story more logical and consistent with English culture.* For example, people rarely go "to the river to hunt seals," because seals are saltwater animals. Students might, therefore, say that the men went to the river to *fish.* Similarly, the supernatural element did not fit comfortably with the religious beliefs of most Cambridge students and was often altered. In the following recollection, written by a student six months after he had read the original story, several additions and distortions are evident:

   Four men came down to the water. They were told to get into a boat and to take arms with them. They inquired, "What arms?" and were answered "Arms for battle." When they came to the battle-field they heard a great noise and shouting, and a voice said: "The black man is dead." And he was brought to the place where they were, and laid on the ground. And he foamed at the mouth. (Bartlett, 1932, pp. 71–72)

The main idea of the story—a battle—is retained. But after six months, the story has been so distorted that it is barely recognizable.

4. *There was a tendency to explain the story's events as well as describe them.* For example, one student insisted on explaining events in parentheses:

> The young man did not feel sick (i.e., wounded), but nevertheless they proceeded home (evidently the opposing forces were quite willing to stop fighting). (Bartlett, 1932, p. 86)

Bartlett's findings illustrate several general principles of long-term memory storage. First, individuals select some pieces of information to store and exclude others. Second, they are more likely to store underlying meanings than verbatim input. Third, they use their existing knowledge about the world (i.e., things they have already stored in long-term memory) to help them make sense of and understand new information. And fourth, some of that existing knowledge may be *added* to the new information, such that what is learned is more than, and perhaps qualitatively different from, the information actually presented.

In this section of the chapter, we will look at six cognitive processes that affect long-term memory storage—selection, rehearsal, meaningful learning, internal organization, elaboration, and visual imagery—with a particular focus on the acquisition of *declarative knowledge*. We will then look at how some of these processes may also promote the acquisition of *procedural knowledge*.

Selection

In some cases, once information has been attended to, it is automatically stored in long-term memory, even if it is not specifically selected for further processing (Hasher & Zacks, 1984; Zacks, Hasher, & Hock, 1986). For example, consider this question:

Which word occurs more frequently in English—bacon or pastrami?

You probably had no difficulty answering correctly that *bacon* is the more frequently occurring word. Hasher and Zacks (1984) found that people could easily answer such questions about the frequency of events even though they had never been concerned about counting them. Similarly, they could answer questions about where various events occurred without having intentionally processed such information. Such automatic storage of frequency information and locations begins quite early in life and may help to establish a basic knowledge base on which future learning can build (Siegler, 1998).

However, more meaningful information apparently must be encoded as well as attended to if it is to be stored effectively in long-term memory. Such encoding takes time and requires the active involvement of working memory, which, as we discovered in Chapter 9, has a very limited capacity. One theorist (Simon, 1974) has estimated that each new piece of information takes about 10 seconds to encode. Using this estimate and the additional estimate that 30 new pieces of information may be presented in a minute of a typical classroom lecture, another theorist (E. Gagné, 1985) has estimated that students can process only six pieces of information per minute—*one-fifth* of the lecture content! Obviously, learners must be extremely selective about the information they choose to process and so must have a means of determining what is important and what is not.

Although the selection process itself is largely directed by working memory (presumably by the central executive component mentioned in Chapter 9), long-term memory also plays a critical role. People's knowledge about the world, their priorities, and their predictions about what environmental input is likely to be useful affect what they pay attention to and think about

(Schwartz & Reisberg, 1991; Voss & Schauble, 1992). A student who has learned that a teacher's lecture content will probably reappear on an upcoming exam is likely to listen closely to what the teacher is saying. A student who has learned that a teacher's exam questions are based entirely on outside reading assignments or has decided that an active social life is more important than classroom achievement may instead attend to something more relevant or interesting—perhaps the flattering sweater worn by the student on her right.

Given the capacity and time constraints of human memory, how can teachers help students select important information? An obvious way is simply to tell students what information is important and what is not; when students are told *not* to remember certain information, that information is less likely to go beyond working memory (Bjork, 1972). Another way is to build redundancy into lectures and instructional materials by repeating important points several times. For example, when I am presenting an important idea to my students, I typically present it several different times. I state the idea once and then state it again using different words. I then illustrate it with at least two examples (often as many as five), and I present the idea itself once again. Notice the redundancy in the last four sentences—it should have been very difficult not to process my meaning at least once! (We'll identify additional strategies in our discussion of *signals* later in the chapter.)

Rehearsal

You should recall from the preceding chapter that rehearsal provides a means of maintaining information in working memory indefinitely. In their early dual-store model of memory, Atkinson and Shiffrin (1971) proposed that rehearsal is also a method of storing information in long-term memory, and there is some evidence that they were right. Several studies have shown that people remember frequently rehearsed items better than less frequently rehearsed ones (Nelson, 1977; Rundus, 1971; Rundus & Atkinson, 1971).

Yet a number of theorists have argued that rehearsal leads to storage in long-term memory only if, in the process, the learner associates the new information with existing knowledge—in other words, if rehearsal also involves *meaningful learning* (Craik & Watkins, 1973; Klatzky, 1975; Watkins & Watkins, 1974). From their perspective, mere repetition of information—maintenance rehearsal—is sufficient to keep the information in working memory but *in*sufficient to move it into long-term memory. Rehearsal that in some way helps learners make associations between the new information and things they already know—sometimes known as **elaborative rehearsal**—does facilitate storage in long-term memory. As an example, in a study by Craik and Watkins (1973), college students were asked to perform two tasks simultaneously: They had to keep one word in their working memories (by rehearsing it) while at the same time examining additional words to see if they met certain criteria. In this situation, the amount of rehearsal did *not* influence the extent to which the students were able to recall the words they had rehearsed; apparently the second task kept them busy enough that they were unable to make associations with the rehearsed words. When the additional words were presented at a slower rate, however, recall of the rehearsed words improved, presumably because the students could devote more working memory capacity to forming associations with those words.

Learning information primarily through repetition is sometimes called **rote learning** (Ausubel, Novak, & Hanesian, 1978; Hiebert & Lefevre, 1986; Mayer, 1996b). In rote learning, there is little or no attempt to make the information meaningful or to understand it in terms of things one already knows. If such information is stored in long-term memory at all, it is stored in relative isolation from other information. As you will discover when you read Chapter 12, information stored in this unconnected fashion becomes difficult to retrieve.

So many times I have seen students engage in simple repetition as a means of trying to learn new information. This process, often referred to as "memorizing," emphasizes the learning of verbatim information rather than the learning of underlying meanings. Although young children (e.g., elementary school students) are especially likely to use this strategy when trying to learn new information (Cuvo, 1975; Gathercole & Hitch, 1993; Rosser, 1994), I have observed high school and college students using it as well. Teachers must help students understand that mere repetition is an inefficient means of storing information for the long run, if it even works at all. The four processes we turn to now—meaningful learning, internal organization, elaboration, and visual imagery—are clearly more effective methods of long-term memory storage.

Meaningful Learning

Look at this string of 15 letters:

MAIGUWRSENNFLOD

And now look at this string:

MEANINGFULWORDS

Both strings are the same length, and both contain exactly the same letters. Which string is easier to learn? No doubt you will agree that the second is easier because you can relate it to words you already know. In the same way, my daughter Tina related a phrase from "America the Beautiful" to her existing knowledge about the world (which unfortunately included *bastard* but not *alabaster*), as did my son Alex, who heard *spaceship skies* instead of *spacious skies*. By relating new information to knowledge already stored in their long-term memories, people find *meaning* in that information. Hence, this process is frequently known as **meaningful learning**; it is also what we are referring to when we talk about understanding or comprehension.

We learn information meaningfully by storing it in long-term memory in association with similar, related pieces of information. Meaningful learning appears to facilitate both storage and retrieval: The information is stored more quickly and remembered more easily (J. R. Anderson, 1995; Ausubel et al., 1978; Mayer, 1996b). To illustrate, consider the following passage from an experiment by Bransford and Johnson (1972):

> The procedure is actually quite simple. First you arrange things into different groups. Of course, one pile may be sufficient depending on how much there is to do. If you have to go somewhere else due to lack of facilities that is the next step, otherwise you are pretty well set. It is important not to overdo things. That is, it is better to do too few things at once than too many. In the short run this may not seem important, but complications can easily arise. A mistake can be expensive as well. At first the whole procedure will seem complicated. Soon, however, it will become just another facet of life. It is difficult to foresee any end to the necessity for this task in the immediate future, but then one never can tell. After the procedure is completed one arranges the materials into different groups again. Then they can be put into their appropriate places. Eventually they will be used once more and the whole cycle will then have to be repeated. However, that is part of life. (p. 722)

Figure 10–3
Droodles from Bower, Karlin, and Dueck
(1975).
From "Comprehension and Memory for
Pictures" by G. H. Bower, M. B. Karlin, and
A. Dueck, 1975, *Memory and Cognition, 3*,
p. 217. Reprinted by permission of
Psychonomic Society, Inc.

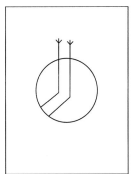

All of the words in this passage were undoubtedly familiar to you, yet you may have had some difficulty understanding what you were reading. If you didn't know what the passage was about, you would have had trouble relating it to things in your long-term memory. But now try reading the passage again, this time thinking of it as a description of washing clothes. Bransford and Johnson found that college students who knew the topic of the passage remembered twice as much as those who had no topic with which to connect things.

People can also store nonverbal material more easily when it has meaning for them. For example, in a study by Bower, Karlin, and Dueck (1975), students were asked to remember somewhat meaningless line drawings; examples of these "droodles" appear in Figure 10–3. Students who were given meaningful labels for such pictures, such as "a midget playing a trombone in a telephone booth" or "an early bird who caught a very strong worm" were more likely to remember them correctly a week later than students who weren't given such labels.

Relating new information to *oneself* can have a particularly dramatic effect on learning. This point was clearly illustrated in a study by Rogers, Kuiper, and Kirker (1977). College students were given a list of 40 adjectives (some words were presented in large type and some in small type) and asked to respond to one of four questions about each word. They were then unexpectedly asked to remember as many of the 40 adjectives as they could. Following are the four questions asked about different adjectives and the amount of incidental learning that resulted from answering each of them:

Question	Percentage Recalled
1. Does it have big letters?	3%
2. Does it rhyme with _____?	7%
3. Does it mean the same as _____?	13%
4. Does it describe you?	30%

When the students were required to relate the word to something they already knew (question 3), they remembered more than when they were asked to consider superficial characteristics of the word (questions 1 and 2). But when they were asked to relate the word to themselves (question 4), incidental learning was more than *twice* what it was for meaningful but not self-related processing.

Because meaningful learning allows new information to be organized with previously learned information, it is sometimes referred to as **external organization** (e.g., E. Gagné, 1985). Another equally important process is the organization of a new body of information within itself—a process known as **internal organization.**

Internal Organization

A body of new information to be learned is stored more effectively and remembered more completely when it is organized—in other words, when the various pieces are interconnected in some way. In fact, people seem to have a natural tendency to organize and integrate the information they receive. For example, in our discussion of verbal learning research in Chapter 8, we noted that people who are asked to remember a list of words often put those words into categories as they learn them (e.g., remembering all of the animals together, all of the vegetables together, and so on). You may also recall the Bransford and Franks (1971) study described in Chapter 8, in which students learned that "The ants in the kitchen ate the sweet jelly which was on the table" by integrating the content of several shorter sentences.

You have undoubtedly had teachers whose lectures were unorganized, with one point following another in an unpredictable sequence. As you might expect, material presented in such an unorganized fashion is more difficult to learn than clearly organized material. An experiment by Bower, Clark, Lesgold, and Winzenz (1969) demonstrates just how significant internal organization can be. College students were given four study trials in which to learn 112 words that fell into four categories (e.g., minerals, plants, etc.). Some students had words arranged randomly, whereas other students had words arranged in four conceptual hierarchies (the minerals hierarchy in Figure 10–4 is an example). After one study trial, students who had studied the organized words could remember more than three times as many words as those who had studied the randomized words. After four study trials, the students in the organized group remembered all 112, whereas those in the random group remembered only 70.

Many good students organize information spontaneously as they learn it, and such student-generated organization can be quite effective (Britton, Stimson, Stennett, & Gülgöz, 1998; Buschke, 1977; McDaniel & Einstein, 1989; Tulving, 1962). Furthermore, providing students with specific organizational schemes can often help students learn more effectively (Atkinson et al.,

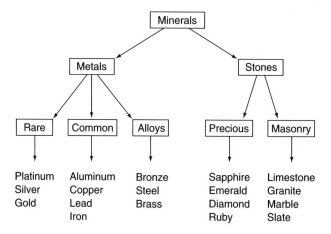

Figure 10–4
Example of a conceptual hierarchy from Bower et al. (1969).
From "Hierarchical Retrieval Schemes in Recall of Categorized Word Lists" by G. H. Bower, M. C. Clark,
A. M. Lesgold, and D. Winzenz, 1969, *Journal of Verbal Learning and Verbal Behavior, 8*, p. 324. Copyright
1969 by Academic Press. Reprinted by permission.

1999; DuBois, Kiewra, & Fraley, 1988; DuBois, Staley, Guzy, & DiNardo, 1995; Kiewra et al., 1988). We will explore ways of facilitating students' organizational processes when we examine metacognition and study strategies in Chapter 13.

Elaboration

Suffering from cold symptoms? Consider this:

> Aren't you tired of sniffles and runny noses all winter? Tired of always feeling less than your best? Get through a whole winter without colds. Take Eradicold Pills as directed. (Harris, 1977, p. 605)

Do Eradicold Pills prevent colds? If you believe that they do, then you have been the unwitting victim of **elaboration**: You added your own information to the passage you read and "learned" that information along with what you had actually read. In a study by Harris (1977), people who read the preceding passage asserted that Eradicold Pills prevented colds almost as frequently as those who read an explicit statement to that effect.

When people receive new information, they often impose their own interpretations on it—perhaps making assumptions, drawing inferences, and so on—and learn those interpretations right along with the information they've actually received. Elaboration, then, is a process of learning *more* than the material actually presented; I like to think of it as *learning between the lines*.[1] As an example, my son Jeff tells me that when he first heard the expression "losing one's voice" when he was in first or second grade, he concluded that people eventually lose their voices permanently. From this, he deduced that people are born with a finite amount of "voice" that they eventually use up. So as not to waste his own supply, he would mouth the words, rather than actually sing them, during his weekly choir sessions at school.

Numerous studies lead to the same conclusion: People frequently elaborate on the information they receive and later have difficulty distinguishing between the actual "truth" and their elaborations of it (Bower, Black, & Turner, 1979; Graesser & Bower, 1990; Harris, 1977; Johnson, Bransford, & Solomon, 1973; Owens, Bower, & Black, 1979; Reder, 1982; Reder & Ross, 1983). To illustrate, the following is a passage from an experiment by Owens et al. (1979). Read it *one time only*:

> Nancy woke up feeling sick again and she wondered if she really were pregnant. How would she tell the professor she had been seeing? And the money was another problem.
>
> Nancy went to the doctor. She arrived at the office and checked in with the receptionist. She went to see the nurse, who went through the usual procedures. Then Nancy stepped on the scale and the nurse recorded her weight. The doctor entered the room and examined the results. He smiled at Nancy and said, "Well, it seems my expectations have been confirmed." When the examination was finished, Nancy left the office. (Owens et al., 1979, pp. 185–186)

Did the doctor tell Nancy she was pregnant? The fact is, he did not. Yet in the study conducted by Owens and his colleagues, when students read the passage and then were asked a day later to

---

[1]*Meaningful learning* and *elaboration* might strike you as very similar processes, and theorists sometimes use the terms interchangeably. In my mind, it is helpful to distinguish between the two. Whereas meaningful learning involves *connecting* new information to existing knowledge, elaboration also involves *embellishing on* new information.

recall information about it, they "remembered" considerably more than they had actually read. Many of their recalled elaborations were directly related to Nancy's suspected condition. Other students in the experiment read only the second paragraph of the passage and so were unaware that Nancy thought she was pregnant; these students added far fewer elaborations.

As was the case for my son Jeff when he heard the expression "losing one's voice," and as may also have been the case for you when you read about Eradicold Pills, elaboration sometimes leads to distortions and errors in what is learned. But most of the time, elaboration is a highly effective means of long-term memory storage: Elaborated information is typically learned and remembered far more easily than nonelaborated information (J.R. Anderson, 1990, 1995; Bobrow & Bower, 1969; Craik & Tulving, 1975; Greeno et al., 1996; McDaniel & Einstein, 1989; Myers & Duffy, 1990; Pressley, 1982; Stein & Bransford, 1979; van der Broek, 1990). As Anderson (1990) has pointed out, most elaborations reflect correct assumptions and interpretations of an event, not incorrect ones.

Elaboration appears to be especially effective when it helps to tie new information together—that is, when it also helps to organize it. For example, in studies by Stein, Bransford, and their colleagues (Stein & Bransford, 1979; Stein et al., 1982), fifth graders and college students were instructed to learn a series of sentences. Each sentence involved a particular kind of man and a particular activity; here are some examples:

The fat man read the sign.

The hungry man got into the car.

The sentences were elaborated with phrases added on to them—elaborations generated either by the experimenters or by the students themselves. Some of the elaborative phrases (*precise* elaborations) provided a connection between a man's characteristic and his activity, for example:

The fat man read the sign warning about the thin ice.

The hungry man got into the car to go to the restaurant.

Other elaborative phrases (*imprecise* elaborations) did not tie the characteristic and activity together; here are some examples:

The fat man read the sign that was two feet high.

The hungry man got into the car and drove away.

Precise elaborations were much more effective than imprecise ones in helping the students learn the sentences.

In some cases, learners elaborate on and integrate new information to the point where they construct an entirely new idea, concept, procedure, or line of reasoning. Oftentimes, learning something by constructing it *on one's own* makes it more memorable than having someone else present it in a prepackaged format; this phenomenon is known as the **generation effect.** Self-constructed knowledge (provided that it is accurate, of course) appears to be beneficial primarily in situations where learners engage in greater elaboration of new material than they might otherwise (McDaniel, Waddill, & Einstein, 1988; McNamara & Healy, 1995; Wiley & Voss, 1999).

Elaboration probably facilitates long-term memory for several reasons. First, elaborated information is less likely to be confused with other, similar information stored in long-term memory (Ellis & Hunt, 1983). Second, elaboration provides additional means through which the information can later be retrieved (J. R. Anderson, 1990, 1995); in a sense, it provides more places to "look" for the information. And third, elaboration may help with inferences about what the information was *likely* to have been when the information itself cannot be accurately recalled (J. R. Anderson, 1990).

Unfortunately, many students try to learn information strictly at face value, without trying to understand it, organize it, or elaborate on it (Linn, Songer, & Eylon, 1996; Snow, Corno, & Jackson, 1996). (As we shall discover in Chapter 12, teachers' frequent overreliance on assessment techniques that require verbatim knowledge may encourage such an ineffective approach to learning.) To learn classroom subject matter effectively, students should instead develop study strategies that involve meaningful learning, internal organization, and elaboration processes. For instance, they can be encouraged to state ideas in their own words, generate their own examples of ideas, make connections between new concepts and their own past experiences, and draw logical inferences from the data they receive. We will identify several ways to help them acquire such strategies in Chapter 13.

Visual Imagery

Without looking back at Figure 10–3, can you remember what the "midget playing a trombone in a telephone booth" looked like? Can you remember the "early bird who caught a very strong worm"? If so, then you may have stored these things not only as the verbal labels that I gave them but also in terms of **visual imagery**—that is, as mental "pictures" that captured how the figures actually looked.

As we will discover in the next chapter, theorists disagree about the exact nature of visual imagery. Nevertheless, research consistently indicates that forming visual images can be a powerful means of storing information in long-term memory. People of all ages have a remarkably accurate memory for visual information (Bower, 1972; Brown & Campione, 1972; Bruck, Cavanagh, & Ceci, 1991; Levin & Mayer, 1993; Standing, 1973). For example, in an experiment by Shepard (1967), college students looked at more than 600 pictures (color photos and illustrations from magazines), with an average inspection time of less than six seconds per picture. The students were then given pairs of dissimilar pictures and asked to identify which picture in each pair they had seen; they were able to do so with 98% accuracy. (Their accuracy on a similar task using words was only 88%.) Furthermore, images may be relatively enduring. For instance, in a study by Mandler and Ritchey (1977), people's memory for meaningfully organized pictures showed little decline over a four-month period.

We should note, however, that visual imagery does not always provide a complete, accurate representation of the information that has been received. Images tend to be fuzzy and less detailed than the original environmental input (J. R. Anderson, 1990; Loftus & Bell, 1975). They can also be distorted by the learner's general knowledge, as an early study by Carmichael, Hogan, and Walters (1932) illustrates. The experimenter asked adults to remember simple pictures like the ones shown on the left side of Figure 10–5. Two different groups were given two different sets of labels for these pictures, and the participants tended to remember the pictures in ways that more closely fit the specific labels they were given. For instance, as you can see in Figure 10–5, the first picture was reproduced differently depending on whether it had been labeled as eyeglasses or dumbbells. Similarly, recall of the second picture was influenced by its identity as a kidney bean or a canoe.

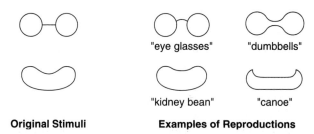

Figure 10–5
Experimental stimuli and examples of participants' reproductions, from Carmichael, Hogan, & Walters (1932). Adapted from "An Experimental Study of the Effect of Language on the Reproduction of Visually Perceived Form" by L. Carmichael, H. P. Hogan, and A. A. Walters, 1932, *Journal of Experimental Psychology, 15*, p. 80.

Because images tend to be incomplete and inaccurate, they may not be helpful when precise, detailed information must be stored. For example, many educators have advocated the use of visual imagery in learning to spell (e.g., Harris, 1985; Radebaugh, 1985), and some research has provided support for this practice (Kernaghan & Woloshyn, 1994; Roberts & Ehri, 1983). Although imagery may help spelling, we should remember that one's visual image of a word will not necessarily include *all* of its letters (Ormrod & Jenkins, 1988). To illustrate, my mental image of the word *silhouette*, until I looked it up in the dictionary just now, was something along these lines:

<h1 style="text-align:center">sil🔲🔲ette</h1>

I had an image of the word that was sufficient to recognize it when I read it but not sufficiently detailed for spelling it correctly.

Despite this drawback of visual imagery, its increased use in the classroom has been widely recommended. Visual images can be stored quickly and retained over long periods of time. Thus, students tend to learn more material and remember it longer when whatever they are studying is concrete and easily visualizable (Clark & Paivio, 1991; Edens & McCormick, 2000; Rice, Hauerwas, Ruggiero, & Carlisle, 1996; Sadoski et al., 1993; Sadoski & Paivio, 2001; Thrailkill & Ormrod, 1994). Students also benefit when pictures and diagrams are provided to support and supplement ideas presented verbally (Carney & Levin, 2002; Clark & Paivio, 1991; Kulhavy, Lee, & Caterino, 1985; Mayer, 1989a; Small, Lovett, & Scher, 1993; Waddill, McDaniel, & Einstein, 1988).

Encouraging students to form their *own* mental images of information can also be an effective instructional technique (Clark & Paivio, 1991; Gambrell & Bales, 1986; Sadoski & Quast, 1990). For example, when students form visual images while reading stories or listening to explanations of school subject matter, they more effectively understand and remember what they have read or heard (Cothern, Konopak, & Willis, 1990; Dewhurst & Conway, 1994; Sadoski & Paivio, 2001). Imagery can even help students form simple associations. For example, when students are instructed to form visual images connecting pairs of objects, memory for those pairs is enhanced (Bower, 1972). Accordingly, imagery provides the foundation for a number of memory strategies called *mnemonics*—strategies that we will consider in Chapter 13.

It is important to note that people differ in their ability to use visual imagery: Some form images quickly and easily, whereas others form them only slowly and with difficulty (Behrmann, 2000; Clark & Paivio, 1991; Kosslyn, 1985; Riding & Calvey, 1981). Visual supplements and encouragements to visualize are most apt to help learners who can easily create images as they study new material (e.g., Carney & Levin, 2002).

Of the six long-term memory storage processes we've just examined, the last three—internal organization, elaboration, and visual imagery—are clearly constructive in nature. Each of these processes involves combining new information with things that we already know. When we organize information, we often use a familiar framework (perhaps a hierarchy of well-known categories) to give new material a meaningful structure. When we elaborate, we use both new information and our existing knowledge to construct a reasonable interpretation of an event. When we use visual imagery, we often create those images for ourselves based on what we know about how objects typically appear.

How Procedural Knowledge Is Acquired

Some of the procedures that people learn—for example, driving a stick shift, planting flowers, serving a volleyball—consist primarily of overt behaviors. Many others—for instance, writing an essay, solving for *x* in an algebraic equation, surfing the Internet—have a significant mental component as well. Most procedures probably involve a combination of physical behaviors and mental activities.

Procedural knowledge ranges from relatively simple actions (e.g., holding a pencil correctly or using scissors) to far more complex ones. Complex procedures are usually not learned in one fell swoop. Instead, they are acquired slowly over a period of time, often only with a great deal of practice (J. R. Anderson, 1983a; Ericsson & Chalmers, 1994; Proctor & Dutta, 1995).

Researchers are just beginning to identify the storage processes involved in acquiring procedural knowledge. To some degree, of course, learners store procedures in terms of actual behaviors (e.g., Willingham, 1999; Willingham & Goedert-Eschmann, 1999). Yet some procedures, complex ones especially, may also be learned as declarative knowledge—in other words, as *information* about how to do something rather than as the actual *process* of doing it. Learners may initially use such information to guide them as they execute a procedure (recall our discussions of self-instructions in Chapter 7 and self-talk in Chapter 8). To the extent that they must do so, however, their performance is apt to be slow and laborious and require considerable concentration (i.e., it consumes considerable working memory capacity). As they continue to practice the procedure, their performance gradually becomes faster, easier, and more efficient. People who show exceptional talent in a particular skill—say, in figure skating or playing the piano—typically practice a great deal, usually a minimum of three to four hours a day over a period of 10 years or more (Ericsson, 1996).

Exactly how the informational and behavioral aspects of procedural knowledge are interrelated in the learning process is not yet clear. One theorist (J. R. Anderson, 1983a, 1987) has suggested that declarative knowledge is acquired first and, with practice, gradually *evolves* into procedural knowledge. More recently, other theorists (Willingham & Goedert-Eschmann, 1999) have proposed that people simultaneously learn both information and behaviors in the process of acquiring a new procedure. However, people learn the information—that is, they learn explicit declarative knowledge—fairly quickly, whereas they learn the appropriate behaviors in a more gradual, *implicit* fashion. When the behaviors are still imperfect and unreliable, people use their declarative information to help them remember what they need to do, presumably by engaging in overt or subvocal self-talk. Such verbal self-support becomes less necessary as they increasingly fine-tune and master the behavioral aspects of the procedure.

Nevertheless, some of the storage processes we've already discussed play a role in acquiring procedural knowledge as well as declarative knowledge. For instance, verbally rehearsing a sequence of steps in a motor skill enhances people's ability to perform that skill (Weiss & Klint, 1987). Illustrations or live demonstrations of a procedure, which presumably foster visual imagery, are also quite helpful (R. Gagné, 1985; Kitsantas et al., 2000; Zimmerman & Kitsantas, 1999). In fact, imagining *yourself* performing an action (e.g., executing a gymnastics skill or a basketball shot) can enhance acquisition of a procedure, although such imagined behaviors are obviously not as effective as actual practice (Feltz, Landers, & Becker, 1988; Kosslyn, 1985).

FACTORS AFFECTING LONG-TERM MEMORY STORAGE

A number of factors affect how learners store information in long-term memory. In this section, we will consider cognitive factors—working memory, prior knowledge, prior misconceptions, and expectations—and behavioral factors—verbalization, enactment, repetition, and review— that appear to be especially influential.

Working Memory

As we have seen, long-term memory storage is most likely to be effective when new material is connected with existing knowledge. For learners to make a connection between a new piece of information and a piece of information that they already have, they must be *aware* of the relationship between the two; in other words, both pieces must be in working memory at the same time (Daneman, 1987; Kintsch & van Dijk, 1978; Mayer, Moreno, Boire, & Vagge, 1999; Nuthall, 2000).

An experiment by Hayes-Roth and Thorndyke (1979) illustrates this idea. In this experiment, students read one of two passages describing a fictional country. The same pieces of information appeared in both passages but in a different order: In one passage, related pieces of information appeared in sequential sentences, whereas in the other, they appeared in separate paragraphs. Students more frequently made the connection between the two related pieces of information (and thus could draw an inference from them) when those pieces of information were presented one right after the other, presumably because both pieces were more likely to be in working memory at the same time.

People don't necessarily have to experience two things in sequence to make connections between them, however. In many cases, new information reminds learners of something they already know, leading them to retrieve that knowledge to working memory. In other cases, a wise teacher might point out the relationships between the new information and previously learned material, thus encouraging retrieval of relevant prior knowledge.

Prior Knowledge

People can connect new information to prior knowledge only when they actually *have* knowledge that relates to what they are learning. One of the most important factors affecting long-term memory storage, then, is what a person *already knows* (Ausubel et al., 1978; Novak, 1998). Learners who have a

large body of information already stored in long-term memory have more ideas to which they can relate their new experiences and so can more easily engage in such processes as meaningful learning
and elaboration. Learners who lack relevant knowledge must resort to inefficient rote-learning strategies. In other words, the rich (in knowledge) get richer, and the poor stay relatively poor.

Our prior knowledge about the world often affects our ability to encode even the most
basic kinds of information. For example, when you see someone walking away from you, that
person does not appear to shrink, even though the image on your retinas is in fact getting
smaller. You have learned from past experience that people do not shrink just because they
move away from you, and so you make certain mental adjustments regarding people's sizes.
What would happen if you had no such prior experience with perceiving people and other
things at varying distances? The anthropologist Colin Turnbull (1961) observed exactly this
situation while studying the Ba Mbuti pygmies, a tribe living in the thick jungle of the African
Congo rain forest. With no open spaces in their environment, the Ba Mbuti never had the opportunity to see objects more than a few feet away from them. Turnbull described an incident
in which a member of the tribe, a man named Kenge, traveled for the first time to an area of
open grasslands. When Kenge spied a herd of buffalo grazing in the far distance, he asked,
"What insects are those?" and dismissed as folly Turnbull's reply that they were actually buffalo that were very far away. A short time later, as the men approached the buffalo by car,
Kenge grew increasingly frightened as he watched the buffalo "grow" in size, fearful that a
magic trick was being played on him.

Numerous studies have illustrated the importance of previous knowledge for encoding and
storing new information (Alexander, Kulikowich, & Schulze, 1994; Chiesi, Spilich, & Voss, 1979;
Dole, Duffy, Roehler, & Pearson, 1991; Gauntt, 1991; Hall, 1989; Machiels-Bongaerts, Schmidt,
& Boshuizen, 1991; Novak & Musonda, 1991; Rouet, Favart, Britt, & Perfetti, 1997; Schneider,
1993). As an example, some of my colleagues and I once conducted a study of how well people from
different disciplines learn and remember maps (Ormrod, Ormrod, Wagner, & McCallin, 1988). We
asked faculty members and students in three disciplines—geography, sociology, and education—to
study two maps and then reproduce them from memory. The first of these maps, shown in Figure
10–6, depicts a city arranged in accordance with usual citylike patterns; that is, its arrangement is
logical. Notice how the downtown business district is located at a point where it can be easily reached
from different directions (this is typical), and the mills, lumberyard, and low-income housing are
situated near the railroad tracks (also typical). The second map, shown in Figure 10–7, is on a larger
scale and depicts several political regions (countries, perhaps). Several things about this map make
no sense; that is, its arrangement is *illogical*. Notice how a river originates in the plains and runs *up*
into the mountains, transportation networks do not interconnect, and towns are not located at transportation junctions. My colleagues and I predicted that geographers would remember more of the
logical city map than either sociologists or educators because they could use their knowledge of typical urban patterns to learn the map meaningfully. We also predicted that the geographers would
have no advantage over the other disciplines on the illogical "countries" map because geographic
principles were largely inapplicable in making sense out of the map. Our predictions were confirmed: Geographers showed better recall than the other two groups for the logical city map but not
for the illogical countries map. Because we had asked the participants to "think aloud" as they
studied the maps, we were also able to examine the strategies they employed; as we expected, the
geographers learned the maps more meaningfully than the other groups, and all three groups learned
the city map more meaningfully than the countries map. Our nongeographers used primarily rote-
learning strategies, mostly in the form of simple repetition.

Figure 10–6
The logical city map from Ormrod et al. (1988).
Reprinted from "Reconceptualizing Map Learning" by J. E. Ormrod, R. K. Ormrod, E. D. Wagner, &
R. C. McCallin, 1988, *American Journal of Psychology, 101*, p. 428. Reprinted with permission of
the University of Illinois Press.

Other studies have yielded similar results. For example, children who know a lot about spiders remember more from reading a passage about spiders than do children who initially know very little (Pearson, Hansen, & Gordon, 1979). People who know a lot about baseball or basketball can remember more new facts about those sports and more about what happened in a particular game than can people who are relatively uninformed about the two sports (Hall & Edmondson, 1992; Kuhara-Kojima & Hatano, 1991; Spilich, Vesonder, Chiesi, & Voss, 1979). Experts at the game of chess can remember the locations of chess pieces on a chessboard more accurately than chess novices, but only when the placement of pieces is logical within the framework of an actual game (Chase & Simon, 1973; deGroot, 1965). Second graders in Brazil who have experience as street vendors learn basic arithmetic more easily than students without street-vending experience (Saxe, 1988). Eighth graders who know a lot about American history engage in more elaborative processing when they read a history textbook (e.g., they are more likely to summarize the material, make inferences, and identify unanswered questions) than classmates who have less history knowledge (Hamman et al., 1995).

Although older children and adults usually learn most things more easily than younger children, we sometimes find the reverse to be true if younger children have more knowledge

Figure 10–7
The illogical country map from Ormrod et al. (1988).
Reprinted from "Reconceptualizing Map Learning" by J. E. Ormrod, R. K. Ormrod, E. D. Wagner, &
R. C. McCallin, 1988, *American Journal of Psychology*, *101*, p. 429. Reprinted with permission of the
University of Illinois Press.

about the subject matter (Chi, 1978; Lindberg, 1991; Schneider, Körkel, & Weinert, 1990). For example, children who are expert chess players can better remember where chess pieces are on a chessboard than adults who are relative novices at chess (Chi, 1978). Similarly, 8-year-olds who know a lot about soccer remember more from a passage they read about soccer than 12-year-olds who know very little about the game (Schneider et al., 1990).

Because everyone has somewhat different knowledge about the world, people are likely to elaborate on the same information in different ways and, as a result, to learn different things. For example, how would you interpret this newspaper headline (from Leinhardt, 1992)?

VIKINGS CREAM DOLPHINS

Your interpretation might depend on whether you are more attuned to American football or to possible early Scandinavian cuisine (Leinhardt, 1992). And consider the following passage from a study conducted by Anderson, Reynolds, Schallert, and Goetz (1977):

Rocky slowly got up from the mat, planning his escape. He hesitated a moment and thought. Things were not going well. What bothered him most was being held, especially since the charge against him had been weak. He considered his present situation. The lock that held him was strong but he thought he could break it. He knew, however, that his timing would have to be perfect. Rocky was aware that it was because of his early roughness that he had been penalized so severely—much too severely from his point of view. The situation was becoming frustrating; the pressure had been grinding on him for too long. He was being ridden unmercifully. Rocky was getting angry now. He felt he was ready to make his move. He knew that his success or failure would depend on what he did in the next few seconds. (Anderson et al., 1977, p. 372)

Is this story about a wrestling match? Or is it about a prison escape? Read the passage again, and you should notice that it could be about either one. Anderson and his colleagues found that students' interpretations of the story depended on their background: Physical education majors more frequently viewed it as a wrestling match, whereas music education majors (most of whom had little or no knowledge of wrestling) were more likely to interpret it as a prison escape. Obviously, people elaborate on the same information in different ways, depending on their depth of knowledge about particular topics.

It is entirely possible, however, to have existing knowledge about a topic and yet *not* relate new information about it to what is already stored in long-term memory. As noted earlier, a learner will make connections between the "new" and the "old" only if both are simultaneously in working memory. To switch from a dual-store model of memory to an activation model for a moment, we might say that both the new and the old must be *activated* at the same time. As we consider instructional strategies later in the chapter, we'll identify a variety of ways in which teachers might promote meaningful learning and elaboration by activating students' prior knowledge.

Prior Misconceptions

When people engage in elaboration, they use what they already know about a topic to expand on, and presumably make better sense of, new information. But what happens when people use inaccurate "knowledge"—**misconceptions**[2]—to elaborate? If people think that new information is clearly "wrong" within the context of what they currently believe about the world, they may sometimes ignore the information altogether. In other situations, they may distort the information to be consistent with their "knowledge"; as a result, they learn something quite different from what they actually saw, heard, or read (Alexander & Judy, 1988; Bishop & Anderson, 1990; Dole et al., 1991; Lipson, 1982, 1983; Roth & Anderson, 1988; Sneider & Pulos, 1983). In some instances, having *mis*information is more detrimental than having *no* information about a topic (e.g., Lipson, 1982).

We saw one instance of such *mis*learning in Bartlett's (1932) study involving "The War of the Ghosts": Many students distorted the story to make it consistent with English culture. A study by Eaton, Anderson, and Smith (1984) provides another example. Fifth graders spent several weeks studying a unit on light in their science curriculum. A pretest had shown that many students had a particular misconception about light: They believed that people see things only because the light shines on them and makes them brighter. During the unit, the correct explanation of human sight was presented: Light reflects off objects and continues to travel *to the eye*, which then detects the

---

[2]Some theorists prefer terms such as *naive beliefs* or *naive conceptions* to reflect the fact that such inaccuracies, though not a good match with contemporary scientific understandings, may be reasonable conclusions from a child's early knowledge and experiences.

light and so makes vision possible. Despite reading and hearing this information, most students retained their misconceptions about vision in a test given at the end of the unit. Only 24 to 30% of them correctly indicated in their answers that light must travel not only from the light source to the object but also from the object to the eye.

We see effects of prior misconceptions even at the college level (Bishop & Anderson, 1990; Clement, 1982; Holt-Reynolds, 1992; Winer, Cottrell, Gregg, Fournier, & Bica, 2002). For example, undergraduates who study the nature of vision in a psychology course—including the idea that light must travel from the object to the eye—often leave the course thinking that vision occurs because something travels in the *opposite* direction—that is, from the eye to the object (Winer et al., 2002). Similarly, students in teacher education programs may disregard a professor's definition of a concept, instead using their previous understanding of the concept, and they are likely to ignore any recommendations for teaching practice that are inconsistent with their own beliefs about what "good teaching" is (Holt-Reynolds, 1992). I have seen such phenomena in some of my own undergraduate teacher education students. For instance, they may stick to their existing definitions of such terms as *egocentrism*, *maturation*, and *elaboration*, even though I point out quite emphatically that a psychologist defines these words differently than a layperson does. And, despite the evidence I present regarding the effectiveness of meaningful learning, a few of them continue to insist that rote learning is a better approach.

Teachers often present information to students with the assumption that the information will correct students' erroneous beliefs. Unfortunately, what often happens instead is that students stubbornly hold onto their preconceived notions about the world and distort the new information to fit those notions. Changing students' misconceptions can therefore be a difficult, although not impossible, task. As we examine the nature of *personal theories* in Chapter 11, we'll look in greater depth at the kinds of misbeliefs children and adults are likely to have. And as we consider *conceptual change* later in that chapter, we'll identify strategies for promoting more accurate understandings.

Expectations

Read this sentence:

> I pledge allegiance to the flag of the United Stetes of American, and to the Repulbic for which it stends, one nation, under God, indivsible, with liberty and justice for all.

You may have noticed one or two typographical errors in the passage. But did you catch them all? Altogether there were *five* mistakes, italicized below:

> I pledge allegiance to the flag of the United St*e*tes of Americ*a*n, and to the Repul*b*ic for which it st*e*nds, one nation, under God, indiv*s*ible, with liberty and justice for all.

If you didn't notice all of the errors—and many people don't—then your expectation of what words *should* have been there influenced your interpretation of the sentence. If you have seen and heard the U.S. Pledge of Allegiance as many times as I have, you know that the phrase "I pledge allegiance . . . " is usually followed by a certain sequence of words, and so you may have seen what you expected to see.

We often form expectations about the things we will see and hear—expectations based on our knowledge, and perhaps also on our misconceptions, about how the world typically operates. Such expectations can influence the ways in which we encode and store new information in long-term memory (Kaiser, McCloskey, & Proffitt, 1986; Schacter, 1999). In many cases we perceive and learn something more quickly when we have a good idea ahead of time about the information we are going to receive, perhaps because relevant portions of long-term memory have already been activated (e.g., recall the discussion of *priming* in Chapter 9). The process of reading is a case in point. Beginning readers pay close attention to the letters on the page as they read and, as a result, often read slowly and comprehend little. More mature readers tend not to look as carefully at the printed page. Instead, they rely on such things as context, sentence syntax, prior knowledge about a topic, and expectations about what the author is trying to communicate in order to draw hasty, although usually accurate, conclusions about what is on the page. It is precisely because mature readers *do* jump to such conclusions that they read as quickly and efficiently as they do (Dole et al., 1991; Owens, 1996; Smith, 1988).

Yet such an efficient approach to reading has a potential drawback as well: Readers risk jumping to the *wrong* conclusions and misperceiving or misinterpreting what is on the page. They may have difficulty proofreading accurately, "seeing" correctly spelled words that are actually misspelled. And they may have trouble learning how to spell the many new vocabulary words (e.g., *psychology*, *environment*, *reinforcement*) that they encounter in their reading (Frith, 1978, 1980; Ormrod, 1985, 1986a, 1986b, 1986c). For example, people frequently misread my name—Jeanne Ormrod—as "Jeanne Orm*ond*," an error that I find quite annoying. But let's face it: Ormrod is an unusual name, whereas Ormond is more common. One can almost not blame readers who see *Orm . . .* and just assume that the rest of the word is . . . *ond*. Using the first few letters of a word to identify that word is a common strategy in reading (Lima, 1993).

Earlier in the chapter, I introduced the concept of *ambiguous stimulus*, a stimulus that can be interpreted in more than one way. Ambiguous stimuli are especially likely to be encoded in accordance with people's expectations (Eysenck & Keane, 1990; Sherman & Bessenoff, 1999). For instance, when I show the man-mouse picture (Figure 10–2) to students in my classes, I consistently find that the great majority of students who have been led to expect a mouse—by previously viewing a picture that is clearly a rodent—*do* in fact see a mouse or rat. Students who have similarly been led to expect a man see the bald-headed man. And notice how your expectations concerning how people typically behave influence your initial interpretation of the first statement in this verbal exchange (from Gleitman, 1985, p. 432):

> "We're going to have my grandmother for Thanksgiving dinner."
> "You are? Well, we're going to have turkey."

The behaviors that we see other people exhibit are often subject to numerous interpretations and so are prime examples of ambiguous stimuli. For example, if you see me smile at you (my behavior), you might draw any number of possible conclusions: I'm happy to see you, I'm *not* happy to see you but am being polite, I detest you but need a favor, I think the outfit you're wearing is pretty ridiculous, and so on. People tend to interpret the behaviors of others in accordance with their own expectations (Juvonen, 1991; Nisbett & Bellows, 1977; Ritts, Patterson, & Tubbs, 1992; Snyder & Swann, 1978). People expect positive behaviors from a person they like or admire and so are likely to perceive that person's behaviors in a positive light—a phenomenon known as the **halo effect.** In much the same way, they expect inappropriate behaviors from a person they dislike, and their perceptions of that person's behaviors are biased accordingly—we could call this the **horns effect.** For example, imagine that Mr. Brighteyes, a fifth-grade teacher, has one student, Mary, who consistently performs well in classwork, and another, Susan, who typically turns in sloppy and incomplete work.

Let's say that both girls turn in an assignment of marginal quality. Mr. Brighteyes is likely to *over*rate Mary's performance and *under*rate Susan's.

Many factors affect people's expectations, and hence their interpretations, of another's behaviors. For instance, people often expect higher-quality performance from people who are clean and well groomed than from people who are dirty and disheveled—hence the adage "Dress for success." Teachers expect well-behaved students to be more academically successful than poorly behaved students; thus, their judgments of a specific student's academic performance are likely to be influenced by the way the student behaves in the classroom (Bennett, Gottesman, Rock, & Cerullo, 1993). Stereotypes about people of different genders, races, ethnic backgrounds, and socioeconomic groups also have an effect (Darley & Gross, 1983; C. Reyna, 2000; Sherman & Bessenoff, 1999; Stephan & Stephan, 2000). An experiment by Darley and Gross (1983) provides an example. Undergraduate students were told that they were participating in a study on teacher evaluation methods and were asked to view a videotape of a fourth-grade girl named Hannah. Two versions of the videotape were designed to give two different impressions about Hannah's socioeconomic status; Hannah's clothing, the kind of playground on which she played, and information about her parents' occupations indirectly conveyed to some students that she was from a low socioeconomic background and to others that she was from a high socioeconomic background. All students then watched Hannah taking an oral achievement test (on which she performed at grade level) and were asked to rate Hannah on a number of characteristics. Students who had been led to believe that Hannah came from wealthy surroundings rated her ability well above grade level, whereas students who believed she lived in an impoverished environment evaluated her as being below grade level. The two groups of students also rated Hannah differently in terms of her work habits, motivation, social skills, and general maturity.

Individuals' expectations and perceptions may even be influenced by other people's names. In an experiment by Harari and McDavid (1973), elementary school teachers were asked to grade essays written by 10-year-old children. Teachers who read an essay supposedly written by "Lisa" gave it a better grade than teachers who read the same essay but thought it was written by "Bertha." In the same way, "David" received better grades than "Hubert." Perhaps we should think of student essays as being ambiguous stimuli, because the criteria for perceiving (grading) them are often somewhat subjective. Grading of such ambiguous stimuli may be especially influenced by teachers' past experiences with—and therefore their expectations for—their students.

Verbalization

An activity that clearly facilitates long-term memory storage is **verbalization**—talking or writing about an experience that either has happened or is happening. Children often talk with their parents or teachers about past and current events, and their memory for those events is enhanced as a result (Haden, Ornstein, Eckerman, & Didow, 2001; Hemphill & Snow, 1996; Nelson, 1993b; Tessler & Nelson, 1994). As an example, consider the following dialogue, in which 6-year-old Kerry and her mother talk about a recent whale-watching expedition:

Mother:	And we went with, who'd we go with?
Kerry:	David.
Mother:	David. Who else?
Kerry:	And Nana and Papa.
Mother:	And who else? Daddy went too, didn't he?
Kerry:	Yeah.

Mother:	Yeah. Who else?
Kerry:	That's all.
Mother:	Oh, and Auntie Karen and Uncle Pete, right?
Kerry:	Yeah.
Mother:	And David's two brothers.
Kerry:	Mmhm.
Mother:	We went whale watching and um I think it turned out to be a disaster because it was rough out there and we got kind of seasick. We did see whales, but not as good as we wanted to.
Kerry:	I saw one.
Mother:	Yeah, we saw them. They're big, huh?
Kerry:	[Nods.]
Mother:	How many were there?
Kerry:	About thirteen.
Mother:	About thirteen! There were only two or three!
Kerry:	No, there wasn't, because they were runnin' back and forth like fifty times! (Hemphill & Snow, 1996, p. 182)

Such discussions, sometimes called **co-constructed narratives,** can help the participants make better sense of an event and perhaps apply labels to it (e.g., *whale watching, seasick*). By doing these things, they encode and remember the event more effectively.

For older children and adults, verbalization sometimes takes the form of **self-explanation,** a form of self-talk in which learners engage while attempting to understand difficult subject matter. For example, when reading a challenging textbook chapter, students might paraphrase the parts they understand, identify parts they're having difficulty with (e.g., "This is confusing"), draw inferences from the ideas presented, and summarize what they've read. When students are encouraged to engage in overt self-explanation as they study, they better understand the content (Atkinson, Derry, Renkl, & Wortham, 2000; deLeeuw & Chi, 2003).

Writing provides yet another form of verbalization that can facilitate long-term memory storage. For instance, when students write about what they are reading in their textbooks—answering study questions, relating the material to things they already know, analyzing various points of view, and so on—they are more likely to engage in such storage processes as meaningful learning, organization, and elaboration (Benton, 1997; Burnett & Kastman, 1997; Durst & Newell, 1989; Greene & Ackerman, 1995; Konopak, Martin, & Martin, 1990; Marshall, 1987).

Enactment

By **enactment,** I mean engaging in an overt behavior—actually *doing* something—that in some way reflects what is being learned. The importance of enactment has popped up in previous chapters under different guises: In our discussion of behaviorism (Chapters 3 through 5), we noted the importance of *active responding* in learning, and in our discussion of social cognitive theory (Chapter 7), we noted the importance of *motor reproduction* in modeling.

A wide variety of physical actions seem to promote long-term memory storage. Young children more easily remember geometric shapes when they can actually draw those shapes (Heindel & Kose, 1990). Children in the upper elementary grades better understand what they learn in science when they create illustrations of scientific concepts; for instance, they might show

how the nervous system works by drawing a diagram of a neuron, or they might illustrate gravity, friction, and kinetic energy by drawing a picture of a roller coaster (Edens & Potter, 2001; Van Meter, 2001). Seventh graders better understand concepts related to map interpretation (e.g., latitude, longitude, scale, map symbols) when they use such concepts to construct their *own* maps rather than simply answering questions about existing maps (Gregg & Leinhardt, 1994a). Undergraduate students studying physics can better apply the things they learn about how pulley systems work when they can experiment with actual pulleys rather than simply looking at diagrams of various pulley systems (Ferguson & Hegarty, 1995).

Physical enactment is, of course, especially helpful when people are learning complex motor skills—that is, when they are acquiring procedural knowledge. In such instances, people typically learn most effectively when they get regular *feedback* about how they are doing (R. Gagné, 1985; Proctor & Dutta, 1995). Sometimes such feedback follows directly from their performance; for instance, a new tennis player can see where he hits each ball, and a new driver knows that she needs more practice with a standard transmission if she keeps stalling the engine every time she tries to move forward. In other cases, however, people learn more effectively when a more advanced individual (e.g., a coach) commends them for proper form or gives them constructive suggestions on what they might do differently (Kladopoulos & McComas, 2001; Kluger & DeNisi, 1998; Schunk & Zimmerman, 1997).

As we discovered in Chapter 4, behaviorists think of feedback as a form of *positive reinforcement*. And as we noted in Chapter 7, social cognitive theorists propose that feedback affects learners' *self-efficacy*. Here we see a third role that feedback can play: a source of *information* that can help learners improve their performance.

Repetition and Review

As we've already seen, rehearsal—repeating information over and over within the course of a few seconds or minutes—can maintain the information in working memory indefinitely (recall the discussion of maintenance rehearsal in Chapter 9) but is probably a relatively *ineffective* way to promote long-term memory storage. In contrast to such short-lived rehearsal, reviewing and practicing information and procedures at periodic intervals over the course of a few weeks, months, or years clearly enhances retention and performance. This principle seems to hold true for people of all ages, even young infants (Anderson & Schooler, 1991; Belfiore, Skinner, & Ferkis, 1995; Dempster, 1991; Linton, 1986; Proctor & Dutta, 1995; Rovee-Collier, 1993; West & Stanovich, 1991).

In essence, recent researchers have supported early verbal learning theorists' finding that *overlearning* facilitates memory. A second verbal learning principle is also relevant here: Additional learning and practice sessions are typically more effective when they are spaced out over a period of time—that is, when they reflect *distributed practice* rather than *massed practice* (J. R. Anderson, 1990; Bahrick et al., 1993; Dempster, 1991). In the lingo of contemporary cognitive psychology, this phenomenon is known as the **spacing effect.** It is important to note that initial learning is sometimes a bit *slower* when it is spread out over time; its benefits are most clearly seen when we look at *long-term retention* rather than speed of initial learning (e.g., Bahrick et al., 1993).

By reviewing and practicing what we have learned over a period of time, we probably accomplish several things. First, we engage in additional processing—processing that may allow us to elaborate on learned information in new ways and so understand it more thoroughly (Dempster, 1991; McDaniel & Masson, 1985). Second, by reviewing the same information repeatedly, especially in different contexts, we form more and stronger associations with other things in memory; as a result, we will more readily recall it when we need it at a future time

(J. R. Anderson, 1990, 1995; Calfee, 1981). Continued practice seems to have a third benefit as well: it promotes automaticity, as we shall see now.

Development of Automaticity

Schneider and Shiffrin (1977; Shiffrin & Schneider, 1977) have distinguished between two types of information processing: controlled and automatic. **Controlled processing** requires much of a learner's attention and is likely to use most or all of the learner's working memory capacity. In other words, controlled processing requires conscious thought and effort. An example is the cognitive processing necessary for learning to drive a car. I still remember the summer evening many years ago when my father tried to teach me to drive a standard shift in our 1951 Ford convertible (no, I'm not *that* old; the car was almost an antique at the time). Trying to steer the car in the right direction while simultaneously monitoring the speed and negotiating the stick shift and clutch consumed all of my attention and working memory capacity. In fact, my working memory must have been overflowing, because I kept forgetting to step on the clutch, thus jerking the car forward and almost catapulting my father into outer space. (Dad enrolled me in a drivers' education class the following morning.)

In contrast, **automatic processing,** more frequently known as **automaticity,** occurs with little or no conscious attention or effort and requires little working memory capacity; it is, in a sense, "thoughtless." Controlled processes become increasingly automatic through repetition and practice (J. Anderson, 1983a; Cheng, 1985; Schneider & Shiffrin, 1977; Shiffrin & Schneider, 1977). As I continued to drive that 1951 Ford, I gradually became more proficient, and I was able to devote less and less mental effort to the task of driving. With several months of persistent practice, I was cruising Main Street with my friends, tapping my fingers to early Beatles music on the radio, munching McDonald's french fries (12 cents a bag in those days), and watching the sidewalk for male classmates of particular interest. Even though my car had a standard transmission, driving had essentially become an automatic activity for me.

As you should recall from Chapter 9, people can usually attend to only one demanding task—one task that requires conscious, controlled processing—at a time. However, people can probably attend to several tasks simultaneously when each of them involves only automatic processing. How many mental activities they can conduct at the same time, then, depends on how automatically they can perform each activity. Remember, working memory has a limited capacity; people can perform only as many activities simultaneously as that capacity will allow.

Many academic tasks require performing a number of "subtasks" at more or less the same time. For successful performance of these tasks, some of the subtasks should probably be automatic (Lesgold, 1983; Mayer & Wittrock, 1996; Perfetti, 1983; Resnick, 1989; Resnick & Johnson, 1988). Consider the case of reading. Comprehending what one reads is often a difficult task involving controlled, conscious effort. If students are to understand what they read, basic reading processes such as letter and word identification must occur automatically. In fact, research is clear on this point: The more effort a student must devote to identifying the words on the page, the lower the student's comprehension of a passage is apt to be (Greene & Royer, 1994; LaBerge & Samuels, 1974; Perfetti & Hogaboam, 1975; Perfetti & Lesgold, 1979).

Writing, too, is a multifaceted process that can easily exceed the limits of working memory unless some processes are automatic (Berninger, Fuller, & Whitaker, 1996; Flower & Hayes, 1981; McCutchen, 1996). Good writers devote most of their attention to the communicative aspect of writing—that is, to expressing their thoughts in a clear, logical, and organized fashion (Birnbaum, 1982; Pianko, 1979). Apparently, these individuals have already learned the mechanics of writing (e.g., spelling, grammar, punctuation) thoroughly enough to apply them automatically. In contrast, poor writers devote a considerable amount of attention to writing mechanics and so can give little thought to communicating their ideas clearly (Birnbaum, 1982; Pianko, 1979). Becoming a good writer, then, is at least partly a matter of automatizing basic skills. People can devote themselves to the task of clear self-expression only if they are not bogged down with concerns about subject–verb agreement or the correct spelling of *psychology*.

Similarly, some aspects of mathematics—especially basic math facts—need to become second nature (e.g., R. Gagné, 1983). For example, in my course on educational assessment, students must be able to solve problems such as the following before they can learn to interpret intelligence test (IQ) scores:

$$\frac{70 - 100}{15} = ?$$

To solve such a problem easily, my students must have certain arithmetic facts at their fingertips; in this case, they must be able to subtract 100 from 70 quickly and must automatically recognize that -30 divided by 15 equals -2. I have frequently observed that when my students must consciously and effortfully calculate a simple arithmetic problem, they lose sight of the overall task they are trying to accomplish.

Earlier in the chapter, I emphasized the importance of meaningful learning. Meaningful learning is certainly important for basic knowledge and skills. To the extent possible, students must be able to make sense of simple facts and procedures, relating them to other things already known about the world. At the same time, meaningful learning is not enough for things that must be recalled quickly and automatically. These things should be repeated and practiced often enough that they become second nature.

Yet automaticity has its downsides as well. For one thing, people may perform habitual actions without even thinking about them, to the point where they can't remember whether they've done them or not (Reason & Mycielska, 1982). For example, sometimes I know that I've fed the dog only by checking his dish to see if it's still damp, and sometimes I know that I've let the cat in for the night only by looking all around the house until I find her or, alternatively, by calling for her outside and waiting to see if she comes running. A more serious disadvantage of automaticity is that it increases the likelihood that an individual will quickly recall certain ideas or perform certain procedures when other, less automatic ideas or procedures are more useful (Langer, 2000; LeFevre, Bisanz, & Mrkonjic, 1988). People are far more flexible, and so far more likely to identify unique approaches to situations or creative solutions to problems, when they aren't automatically "locked in" to a particular response (Killeen, 2001; Langer, 2000). We'll revisit this issue in our discussion of *mental set* in problem solving in Chapter 14.

PROMOTING EFFECTIVE STORAGE PROCESSES

I often hear educators and educational psychologists making the distinction between teacher-centered and student-centered approaches to instruction. By *teacher-centered instruction*, they mean methods in which the instructor directly presents the material to be learned—for instance, through lectures, explanations, textbooks, and educational videos. Because teacher-centered methods often present information in essentially the same form that students are expected to learn it, they are sometimes called *expository instruction*. In contrast, *student-centered instruction* encourages students to construct their *own* knowledge and understandings, although usually within the context of planned activities and some degree of teacher guidance. Discovery learning, whole-class and small-group discussions, cooperative learning, and group problem-solving activities are all examples of student-centered instruction.

In my opinion, the terms *teacher-centered* and *student-centered* are misnomers. Presumably students are at the center of *any* form of instruction, in that teachers design their lessons with students' learning, rather than their own learning, in mind. The key difference is not one of focus but rather one of *control*: Students direct the course of learning to a greater degree in student-centered approaches than in teacher-centered approaches. Hence, I suggest that we use slightly different terminology. In **teacher-directed instruction,** the teacher calls most of the shots, choosing what topics will be addressed, directing the course of the lesson, and so on. In **student-directed instruction,** students have considerable say in the issues they address and how to address them.

Historically, most instruction has been the teacher-directed variety. Yet some psychologists have criticized such instruction—especially the lecture method—as being a relatively ineffective pedagogical technique. For example, B. F. Skinner (e.g., 1968; Skinner & Epstein, 1982) proposed that learning occurs most effectively when students make active responses; because the typical classroom lecture does not allow much active responding, it is unlikely to promote learning. Jerome Bruner (e.g., 1961a, 1961b) has been similarly critical of lectures, suggesting that students can better understand ideas when they have concrete, firsthand experiences with those ideas, perhaps through hands-on discovery sessions.

In recent years, many educators and educational psychologists have called for an increasing use of student-directed approaches, and a growing body of research indicates that these approaches can be highly effective. Because they are especially valuable for encouraging complex cognitive skills, we'll examine them in Chapter 15, after we've had a chance to discuss metacognition and problem solving.

In the meantime, we should note that teacher-directed instruction has many advocates among contemporary cognitive theorists (e.g., Ausubel et al., 1978; Pressley, with McCormick, 1995; Rosenshine & Stevens, 1986; Tarver, 1992; Weinert & Helmke, 1995). These theorists suggest that students listening to a teacher's explanation or lecture are not necessarily the passive nonresponders that Skinner portrayed. Instead, students, although perhaps not overtly active, are nevertheless *cognitively* active: They busily attend to and meaningfully interpret the information they hear. Furthermore, although some students (those whom Piaget would describe as concrete operational) may require the concrete experiences that discovery learning provides, other students (those whom Piaget would describe as formal operational) are quite capable of understanding concepts presented at an abstract, verbal level. For the latter group of students, a concise, organized, teacher-directed lesson may be the most rapid and efficient means of presenting classroom subject matter.

Ultimately, what matters most about any instructional method is not whether it is teacher- or student-directed, but *how well it promotes effective storage processes.* Unfortunately, some educators seem to forget this basic principle. All too often, classroom instruction and assessment methods emphasize the learning of classroom material at a verbatim level, with little or no regard for its underlying meaning (Dansereau, 1978; Doyle, 1983, 1986b; Fennema, Carpenter, & Peterson, 1989; Schoenfeld, 1985b). Many school textbooks are equally guilty, presenting lists of facts with few interrelationships between them and without regard for what students know beforehand (Alleman & Brophy, 1992; Beck and McKeown, 1988, 1994; Berti, 1994; Calfee & Chambliss, 1988; Chambliss, Calfee, & Wong, 1990; McKeown & Beck, 1990). To get a sense of what students may encounter in their textbooks, read the following textbook passage:

> *The Langurian and Pitok War.* In 1367 Marain and the settlements ended a 7-year war with the Langurian and Pitoks. As a result of this war Languria was driven out of East Bacol. Marain would now rule Laman and other lands that had belonged to Languria. This brought peace to the Bacolian settlements. The settlers no longer had to fear attacks from Laman. The Bacolians were happy to be a part of Marain in 1367. Yet a dozen years later, these same people would be fighting the Marish for independence, or freedom from United Marain's rule. This war was called the Freedom War or the Bacolian Revolution. A revolution changes one type of government or way of thinking and replaces it with another. (Beck & McKeown, 1994, p. 239)

Are you confused? I certainly am. The passage is from an actual American history textbook, albeit with a few modifications:

- *1763* has been changed to *1367*
- *Britain* has been changed to *Marain*
- *Colonies* has been changed to *settlements*
- *French* has been changed to *Langurian*
- *Indians* has been changed to *Pitoks*
- *North America* has been changed to *East Bacol*
- *Canada* has been changed to *Laman*
- *War for Independence* has been changed to *Freedom War*
- *American* has been changed to *Bacolian*

If I were to show you the original passage, you would understand it easily *if* you grew up in the United States or for some other reason already know about the French and Indian War and the American Revolution. But for many American fifth graders, the original passage is almost as confusing as the modified one I just presented, because they have little prior knowledge about the countries and events described (Beck & McKeown, 1994).

Perhaps as a result of instruction, textbooks, assignments, and evaluation methods that downplay the importance of learning classroom subject matter in a meaningful fashion, students often engage in rote learning (Novak & Musonda, 1991; Perkins & Simmons, 1988; Prawat, 1989). Yet even the most teacher-directed lesson can promote meaningful learning and other effective storage processes. Following are a number of principles that can guide instructional practice regardless of whether it is teacher-directed or student-directed:

  • *Meaningful learning can occur only when students have prior knowledge to which they can relate new ideas.* Students have considerable difficulty learning and remembering material that does not overlap with their existing knowledge. When students are observed processing material in a rote manner (e.g., rehearsing it), they probably either lack the appropriate background knowledge for learning that material effectively or are unaware of the relevant knowledge that they *do* have. For example, American history textbooks frequently refer to the colonists' distress over Britain's "taxation without representation" policy, yet they don't always provide an adequate explanation of why this policy was so upsetting to the colonists (Beck & McKeown, 1994). Many adults can easily relate the idea of taxation without representation to their own frustrations with high taxes. Most fifth graders, however, have little if any experience on which to draw in understanding the colonists' situation.

Whenever they introduce a new topic, teachers must consider what knowledge students already have about the topic and begin instruction at that point. As an example, early mathematics instruction might build on informal counting procedures children have developed on their own (Fennema et al., 1989). Teachers can incorporate students' own backgrounds, both personal and cultural, into topics being introduced (Garcia, 1992). Teachers can also use new material within the context of everyday activities and problems—for example, by using mapping skills to map the school or neighborhood or by studying metric units as part of a cooking class (Brophy & Alleman, 1991; Reesink, 1984).

When students seem to have very little knowledge about a particular topic, teachers might provide actual experiences to which the students can then relate new concepts. For example, a teacher might introduce the idea of *taxation without representation* by conducting an activity in which students are told to give valued objects to fellow students (only temporarily) without regard for their own wishes in the matter. I frequently use this create-an-experience strategy myself, not only in my classes but also in my books; asking you to read the passage about the Langurian and Pitok War a moment ago was an example of the kinds of things I do. I then follow up by relating new concepts and principles to the experience that my students or readers have just had.

Analogies that relate classroom subject matter to familiar concepts and situations can also be quite effective (Bulgren, Deshler, Schumaker, & Lenz, 2000; Donnelly & McDaniel, 1993; English, 1997b; Simons, 1984; Stepich & Newby, 1988; Zook, 1991). Figure 10–8 presents examples of effective analogies for a variety of classroom topics. Analogies help students learn information more meaningfully and retrieve it more easily, particularly when the topic is a new one for students or when the material is relatively abstract. At the same time, teachers must be careful to point out ways in which the two things being compared are *different*; otherwise, students may take an analogy too far and draw incorrect conclusions (Duit, 1990; Glynn, 1991; Sfard, 1997; Zook & Di Vesta, 1991).

Even when students do have existing knowledge to which they can relate new material, they frequently do not recognize the connections they might make (Paris & Lindauer, 1976; Spires & Donley, 1998; Spires, Donley, & Penrose, 1990; Stodolsky et al., 1991). Hence, theorists recommend that instruction include **prior knowledge activation**—some means of encouraging students to retrieve relevant knowledge from long-term memory to working memory. For example, teachers and students might discuss a topic in class before they begin a reading assignment about that topic (Hansen & Pearson, 1983; Wilson & Anderson, 1986). And when content learned earlier in the year (or perhaps in previous years) is important for understanding something new, teachers might provide a quick review of that content—a "refresher," if you will.

• Students are more apt to engage in meaningful learning when they are explicitly encouraged to do so. Students must approach new information with the attitude that they can understand and make sense of it; in other words, they must approach it with a meaningful learning set (Ausubel et al., 1978). Students are more likely to have this attitude when teachers emphasize understanding rather than verbatim recitation—for instance, when students know that they will be expected to explain it in their own words rather than having to reproduce textbook definitions (Ausubel et al., 1978). A meaningful learning set is also more likely to occur when students are confident that they can understand new material. Students who have learned

- If we think of the earth's history as a *24-hour day*, then humans have been in existence only for the last minute of that day (Hartmann, Miller, & Lee, 1984).
- The growth of a glacier is like *pancake batter being poured into a frying pan*. As more and more substance is added to the middle, the edges spread farther and farther out (courtesy of R. K. Ormrod).
- The Ural Mountains in Russia are like *the Appalachian Mountains in the United States*. They are old, worn-down mountains that served as temporary barriers to migration (Andrews, 1987).
- The human circulatory system is similar to a *parcel delivery system*. "Red blood cells work like trucks, carrying needed materials from a central distribution point for delivery throughout the body. Arteries and veins are like roads, acting as access routes through which the various points of delivery are reached. The heart is like the warehouse or the central point in which vehicles are loaded and dispatched, and to which empty vehicles are returned to be reloaded" (Stepich & Newby, 1988, p. 136).
- Peristalsis, a process that moves food through the digestive system, is ". . . like *squeezing ketchup out of a single-serving packet*. You squeeze the packet near one corner and run your fingers along the length of the packet toward an opening at the other corner. When you do this, you push the ketchup through the packet, in one direction, ahead of your fingers, until it comes out of the opening" (Newby, Ertmer, & Stepich, 1994, p. 4, emphasis added).

- Any horizontal surface, such as a table, exerts force on an object that rests on it. You might think of the table as a *spring* that is compressed when something is put on top of it. The spring pushes up against the object (D.E. Brown, 1992).
- The process of heat flow is similar to *falling dominos.* In both cases, one thing affects the thing next to it, which in turn affects the thing next to *it,* and so on (Royer & Cable, 1976).
- Electricity going through a wire is like *people going through a tunnel*. Everything that enters at one end comes out at the other (Gentner & Gentner, 1983).
- Tying a bowline knot is like *a rabbit guarding the territory around its home*. You hold the rope vertically and make a loop near the middle. The loop is the rabbit hole, the upper end of the rope is the tree, and the lower end is the rabbit. The rabbit goes up and out of the hole, around the tree, and back down the hole (Hayes & Henk, 1986).
- A dual-store model of memory is like *the information selection and storage system you use at home*. Some things (e.g., junk mail) are discarded as soon as they arrive, others (e.g., bills) are dealt with only briefly, and still others (e.g., driver's license) are used regularly and saved for a long period of time (see Chapter 9 of this book).
- Retrieval from long-term memory is like *looking for something in a large, dark room with only a small flashlight*. You can look at only one small spot at a time, and it is virtually impossible to look everywhere (Lindsay & Norman, 1977).

Figure 10–8
Examples of analogies that promote connections between new ideas and things students already know.

through past experience that a certain subject is confusing are more likely to resort to a rote-learning approach (Ausubel & Robinson, 1969).

- *Students learn more effectively when a lesson begins with an advance organizer.* Earlier in the chapter, I distinguished between *internal organization*—how various ideas within a body of new information are interrelated—and *external organization*—how that information is related to what students already know. One means of facilitating both forms of organization is the use of **advance organizers** (Ausubel et al., 1978). An advance organizer is a general introduction to new material that is typically designed to accomplish either or both of two purposes. An **expository organizer** provides a rough overview or outline of the material, describing the general topics that will be presented and their relationship to one another; thus, it provides the beginnings of an internal organizational scheme. A **comparative organizer** shows how the new material relates to students' previous experiences, to information they have previously learned in school, or possibly to their own purposes for studying the material; it also points out the similarities between the new information and the old. In this way, the organizer facilitates external organization (i.e., meaningful learning). An additional advantage of a comparative organizer is that it establishes a meaningful learning set: Students anticipate being able to understand the new material at a meaningful level and thus are more likely to approach the learning task with meaningful learning in mind.

Research consistently demonstrates the effectiveness of advance organizers in facilitating student learning, especially when material is not clearly organized and students have trouble organizing it on their own (Ausubel et al., 1978; Corkill, 1992; Mayer, 1979a, 1979b). Advance organizers also appear to promote more meaningful learning and greater transfer of classroom material to new situations (Mayer, 1987).

Advance organizers are usually more effective when they are fairly concrete (Corkill, 1992; Corkill, Glover, & Bruning, 1988; Mayer & Bromage, 1980; Zook, 1991). A variety of formats of advance organizers—overviews, outlines, analogies, examples, and thought-provoking questions—all appear to be effective (Alexander, Frankiewicz, & Williams, 1979; Corkill, 1992; Frase, 1975; Glynn & Di Vesta, 1977; Mayer, 1984; Zook, 1991). For example, here is how a teacher might introduce a lesson on radar by means of an analogy—a comparative advance organizer:

> Radar means the detection and location of remote objects by reflection of radio waves. The phenomenon of acoustic echoes is familiar. Sound waves reflected from a building or cliff are received back at the observer after a lapse of a short interval. The effect is similar to you shouting in a canyon and, seconds later, hearing a nearly exact replication of your voice. Radar uses exactly the same principle except that the waves involved are radio waves, not sound waves. These travel very much faster than sound waves, 186,000 miles per second, and can cover much longer distances. Thus, radar involves simply measuring the time between transmission of the waves and their subsequent return or echo, and then converting that to a distance measure. (Mayer, 1984, p. 30)

In some situations, an advance organizer might even take a graphic rather than strictly verbal form. For example, when introducing a unit on minerals, a hierarchical diagram similar to the one in Figure 10–4 might provide a helpful visual overview—an expository advance organizer.

• *Students often need guidance in determining what things are most important to learn.* When instruction provides a great deal of information, students may have trouble deciding which things are important and which things are not (Alexander & Jetton, 1996; Dole et al., 1991; Garner, Alexander, Gillingham, Kulikowich, & Brown, 1991; Reynolds & Shirey, 1988). For example, students may focus their attention on interesting, relatively trivial details at the expense of less interesting but more important ideas (Alexander & Jetton, 1996; Garner et al., 1991; Ward, 1991). Or they may look at the equations they see in a scientific proof while disregarding any verbal explanation of those equations (Dee-Lucas & Larkin, 1991).

A variety of **signals** as to what information is most important can facilitate students' learning from expository forms of instruction (Armbruster, 1984; Lorch, Lorch, & Inman, 1993; Reynolds & Shirey, 1988). For example, writing key points on the chalkboard is a means of emphasizing those points. Underlining or italicizing important phrases and sentences in a textbook passage makes them more prominent (Hartley, Bartlett, & Branthwaite, 1980; McAndrew, 1983). Specific instructional objectives for a lesson let students know what they should focus on (see Chapter 5). Questions interspersed throughout a lecture or textbook passage draw students' attention to particular ideas (Anderson & Biddle, 1975; Andre, 1979; McDaniel & Einstein, 1989). Even simply telling students what's important probably facilitates learning (Reynolds & Shirey, 1988).

• *In as many ways as possible, students should interconnect the new ideas they are learning.* Expository instruction tends to be more effective when it presents new information in the basic organizational format in which students should store it in memory (Dansereau, 1995; Tennyson & Cocchiarella, 1986; Tennyson, Tennyson, & Rothen, 1980; Wade, 1992). For example, teachers facilitate students' learning when they present ideas in a logical sequence, identify any hierarchical relationships that exist among concepts, and make cause–effect relationships clear. Showing how material should be organized and interrelated may be especially important for students who have little relevant background knowledge and for students who have a history of learning difficulties (Buckland, 1968; deLeeuw & Chi, 2003; Krajcik, 1991; Mayer, 1989a).

One strategy for showing how the concepts and ideas of a lesson interrelate is a **concept map** or **knowledge map**—a diagram of the concepts or main ideas of a unit (often identified by circles) and the interrelationships among them (often designated by lines and by words or phrases that link two concepts or ideas together). As an illustration, Figure 10–9 presents a concept map that a teacher might use to organize some of the key concepts in a lesson on ancient Egyptian art. Such organizational maps can frequently help students learn, organize, and remember the things that they hear in a lecture or read in a textbook (Krajcik, 1991; Linn et al., 1996; Novak, 1998; O'Donnell, Dansereau, & Hall, 2002).

• *Generally speaking, students learn and remember new material more effectively when they elaborate on it.* Students are more likely to remember classroom material over the long run if they expand on that material based on the things they already know. As examples, they might draw an inference that has not been explicitly stated, speculate on the motives of historical figures, or think about how they might apply a scientific principle at home.

Many classroom activities can potentially promote student elaboration of classroom subject matter. For example, asking students to talk about a topic, perhaps within the context of a class discussion or cooperative learning activity, almost forces them to do *something* (mentally) with that material (Brown & Campione, 1986; Hiebert & Raphael, 1996; Prawat, 1989; Reiter, 1994; Yager, Johnson, & Johnson, 1985). Asking students to write about what they are learning—perhaps in a research paper or on an essay question—enables them to pull their thoughts together and perhaps to identify and resolve gaps and inconsistencies in their understanding (Prawat, 1989). And when students tutor their classmates on subject matter they presumably know quite well, they learn it at an even higher level of understanding (Brown & Palincsar, 1987; Inglis & Biemiller, 1997; Semb et al., 1993).

Teachers must remember, however, that elaboration can sometimes lead students to acquire erroneous ideas, especially if they already have misconceptions about the topic at hand. Teachers must continually monitor students' understanding of classroom material—perhaps by asking questions, assigning regular homework, or giving occasional quizzes—and then take steps to correct any misinterpretations that students' responses reveal. Some of their misconceptions may be

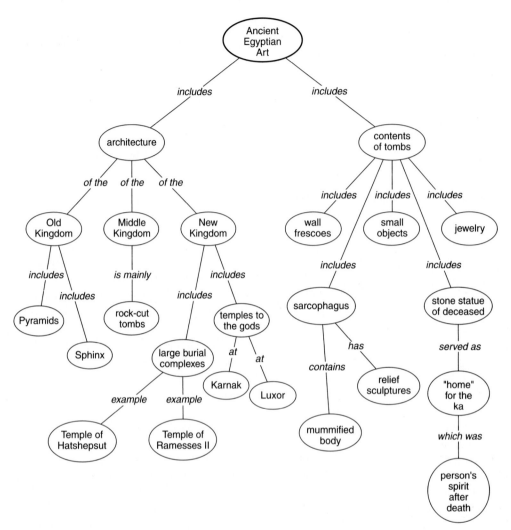

Figure 10–9
A possible concept map for a lesson on ancient Egyptian art.

"stubborn" ones that are not easily corrected; we will identify strategies for changing such misconceptions in our discussion of *conceptual change* in Chapter 11.

• *Visual aids facilitate visual imagery.* As we have seen, visual imagery can be a highly effective way of encoding information. It may be particularly valuable when used in conjunction with other storage processes such as meaningful learning or elaboration. Thus, presenting information in visual form—through physical objects, pictures, maps, diagrams, graphs, live models, and so on—is often a helpful supplement to verbal material (Carney & Levin, 2002; Clark & Paivio, 1991; Prawat, 1989; Small et al., 1993; Verdi & Kulhavy, 2002; Verdi, Kulhavy, Stock, Rittschof, & Johnson, 1996; Waddill et al., 1988; Winn, 1991).

In most situations, visual aids should be simple, concise, and clear, presenting major ideas without overwhelming students with detail (Mayer, 1989b; Shah & Hoeffner, 2002; Vekiri, 2002). In addition to promoting visual imagery, many visual aids can also show students how major ideas relate to and affect one another; thus they provide one more way of helping students organize information (Levin & Mayer, 1993; Mayer, 1989a; Winn, 1991). It is important, however, that pictures and other visual aids be relevant to the material students are studying; for example, irrelevant visual material in a reader or textbook, although possibly increasing the book's attractiveness, is unlikely to facilitate learning and can sometimes distract the learner's attention away from the more important part of the book—the text (Carney & Levin, 2002; Levin, Anglin, & Carney, 1987; Samuels, 1967, 1970).

• *A variety of instructional strategies promote acquisition of procedures.* Theorists have suggested several teaching strategies that seem to help students learn and remember procedures more effectively. For instance, teachers can demonstrate a procedure or show pictures of the specific behaviors it involves (R. Gagné, 1985). They can verbalize their own thoughts—thereby demonstrating *mental* procedures—as they engage in a complex task (recall our discussion of *cognitive modeling* in Chapter 7). They can encourage students to use verbal rehearsal while learning a new skill—in other words, to repeat the required steps over and over to themselves (Weiss & Klint, 1987). And, of course, students will be more likely to remember a procedure when teachers give them a chance to carry it out themselves and provide feedback about their performance (Cohen, 1989; Heindel & Kose, 1990; Proctor & Dutta, 1995). When procedures are fairly complicated, teachers may want to break them down into smaller tasks and have students practice each one separately at first (J.R. Anderson et al., 1996). Chapters 13 and 14 describe additional strategies for facilitating the acquisition of procedural knowledge related to metacognition and problem solving.

• *Students learn new material more effectively when they have sufficient time to process it effectively.* Effective long-term memory storage processes—meaningful learning, internal organization, elaboration, visual imagery—take *time*. In student-directed learning sessions, students have considerable control over how they spend their time; therefore, they can stop when they need to in order to think things through. But in teacher-directed learning sessions, the teacher is largely in control of the pacing and must be sure to give students the processing time they need. For example, when giving a lecture, teachers might lecture for 8 or 10 minutes and then give students a 2-minute interval in which to compare notes and clarify subject matter with one another (Rowe, 1987).

• *End-of-lesson summaries promote learning and retention.* As we noted earlier in our discussion of advance organizers, students tend to learn more effectively when they receive advance notice of the things they will be learning. Students also tend to benefit from summaries presented at the end of a verbal lecture or written passage: They learn more effectively when they hear or read a synopsis of the information they have just studied (Hartley & Trueman, 1982; Lorch et al., 1993).

Summaries probably serve multiple functions for students. Among other things, they may help students to review material, determine which of the many ideas they have studied are most important, and pull key ideas into a more cohesive organizational structure.

• *Periodic review and practice enhances learning.* As we have seen, rehearsal of information within a short period of time (e.g., less than a minute) is a relatively ineffective way to store information in long-term memory. But occasional repetition of learned information over a longer period of time (e.g., over the course of a few days, weeks, or months) *does* enhance storage and retention. Teachers might find it helpful, then, to have students review and practice important material throughout the school year, perhaps by integrating that material into the context of new lessons. Repetition is particularly important for facts and skills that students need every day—for example, for basic number facts, words frequently encountered in reading, and rules of punctuation. (Computer software can sometimes make such drill and practice more palatable; e.g., see Lesgold [1983], Perfetti [1983], and Resnick & Johnson [1988].) Basic information and skills should certainly be learned as meaningfully as possible, but they should also be practiced until students can retrieve them quickly and automatically.

- *Learning quickly does not always mean learning better.* Earlier in the chapter, we noted that distributed practice sometimes leads to slower learning than massed practice but that it tends to promote greater retention of material over the long run. More generally, how *quickly* students learn something is not necessarily a good indication of how *well* they learn it (Bahrick et al., 1993; Phye, 2001; Salomon, 1979/1994; Schmidt & Bjork, 1992). To truly master a topic, students must relate it to things they already know, form many interconnections among its various parts, draw inferences about and in other ways elaborate on it, and perhaps learn certain aspects of it to automaticity. Such things take time—in some cases a great deal of time—but for important topics and skills, it will be time well spent.

Furthermore, although a certain amount of feedback is essential for learning to take place, occasional rather than continual feedback about one's performance may sometimes promote performance over the long run, even though it may result in slower improvement initially (Schmidt & Bjork, 1992). It may be that learners need practice not only in performing certain tasks but also in retrieving relevant knowledge about each task and giving *themselves* feedback about their performance (Schmidt & Bjork, 1992).

SOME FINAL REMARKS ABOUT LONG-TERM MEMORY STORAGE

Before we leave our discussion of long-term memory storage, we should note a few final points about storage processes:

- *Long-term memory storage is idiosyncratic.* Any two people store different information from the same situation, for several reasons. First, they attend to different aspects of the situation, and so different information is placed in their working memories. Second, they encode that information differently; for example, some people use visual imagery more than others. And third, they bring their own unique background experiences to the situation so that the interpretations of what they observe are truly their own.

- *Storage of new information sometimes affects previously learned information as well.* Consistent with the process of elaboration, learners sometimes distort new material to fit their existing beliefs. Yet in other situations, a new piece of information may help learners recognize that something they stored earlier is inaccurate or that two previously learned pieces of information are related in a way they had not previously recognized.

- *The ways in which people store new information affect both the nature of the knowledge they possess and the ease with which they can retrieve that knowledge later on.* In the next two chapters, we will consider two other topics related to long-term memory: the nature of knowledge (Chapter 11) and retrieval (Chapter 12). As we address these topics, we will continually find that long-term memory storage processes are inextricably related both to what we know and how easily we can remember it.

SUMMARY

Many theorists believe that long-term memory storage processes are often constructive in nature. We typically store *less* than what we have sensed because our working memories cannot hold all of the input that our sensory registers temporarily record. At the same time, we also store *more* than what we have sensed, using the often incomplete data we receive to construct a logical understanding of the events around us.

Long-term memory storage involves a variety of cognitive processes. *Selection* is the process of determining what information we should process further and what information is irrelevant to our needs. *Rehearsal* is repeating something over and over again in a relatively meaningless (rote) fashion; its effectiveness in promoting long-term memory storage is questionable at best. *Meaningful learning* is connecting new material with similar ideas already stored in memory; in other words, it is a process of making sense out of the material. *Internal organization* is the integration of various pieces of new information into a cohesive, interrelated whole. *Elaboration* involves imposing one's own previously acquired knowledge and beliefs on new information. And *visual imagery* is encoding information in a mental "picture" that maintains its physical appearance to some extent.

Most research investigating the effectiveness of such processes has involved declarative knowledge (e.g., facts, concepts, principles). But these processes may play a role in the acquisition of procedural knowledge (e.g., motor skills, problem-solving strategies) as well, perhaps because declarative knowledge can either evolve into procedural knowledge or support learners' efforts in the early stages of acquiring a new skill.

Several cognitive factors affect long-term memory storage. People are likely to relate new material to their existing knowledge only when both things are in working memory at the same time. A greater amount of existing knowledge about a topic, provided that it is *accurate*, usually facilitates long-term memory storage. Expectations about what will be seen or heard often yield more rapid and efficient learning. However, misconceptions and inaccurate predictions about the topic under consideration may often lead to distortions in what is learned and remembered.

Overt behaviors can affect long-term memory storage as well. It is often helpful to talk about, write about, or physically enact aspects of the things that are being learned. Furthermore, although repetition of information within a period of a few seconds or minutes (rehearsal) is not an effective way of storing information in the first place, occasional repetition of information stretched out over time makes that information easier to remember over the long run. Knowledge and skills needed on a regular basis should, in many cases, be practiced over and over until they are learned to a level of *automaticity*—that is, until they can be retrieved quickly and effortlessly.

Contemporary psychologists have made a distinction between teacher-centered and student-centered instruction; the two approaches might better be described as *teacher-directed* versus *student-directed* instruction. Although some theorists have argued that one approach is better than the other, in fact the effectiveness of either approach depends on the cognitive processes it encourages students to engage in. Regardless of the instructional methods used, teachers can foster effective long-term memory storage processes in a wide variety of ways—for instance, by activating students' prior knowledge about a topic, helping students organize and integrate new material, giving signals about what is most important to learn and remember, encouraging students to draw inferences and in other ways elaborate on ideas, and providing numerous opportunities for practice and review.

Long-Term Memory II: The Nature of Knowledge

T ake a few minutes to answer the following questions:

1. What did you do yesterday?
2. In what kind of house or apartment did you live when you were 10 years old?
3. What is a *noun*?
4. How are rote learning and meaningful learning different?
5. How do you ride a bicycle?
6. When buying things at the grocery store, how do you decide which checkout line to go to?
7. What are some reasons why people own horses?
8. Why do many people prefer grass to gravel in their front yards?

These questions asked you about eight very different topics, but I suspect that you could easily answer most of them. Even if you always lose at Trivial Pursuit and would never dream of becoming a contestant on the television game show *Jeopardy*, you nevertheless have a great deal of information stored in your long-term memory. Some of what you know relates to your own personal life experiences (i.e., it reflects *episodic memory*), but much more of it is general knowledge about the world (i.e., *semantic memory*). You've acquired some of your knowledge from teachers or textbooks, but you've probably picked up a vast amount on your own over the years. Furthermore, you don't only know things about your own past history and about the world around you (all of which comprises your *declarative knowledge*), you also know how to do a great many things (i.e., you have considerable *procedural knowledge*). And you've pulled some of the things you know about and the things you know how to do to help you understand why the world is the way it is (this is your *conceptual knowledge*). Some of the things you know come readily to mind when you're asked to think about or describe them (this is *explicit knowledge*), but other things, such as how to ride a bicycle, may be more difficult to put a finger on (this is *implicit knowledge*).

Do these terms sound familiar? They should, because you read about all of them in the section on long-term memory in Chapter 9. I'm asking you now to keep them in mind as you learn more about the nature of knowledge in this chapter. Consistent with one of my recommendations near the end of Chapter 10, I'm encouraging you to *activate your prior knowledge*.

As you will discover, theorists have gone in many different directions in describing the possible nature of human knowledge, and it will be virtually impossible for us to roll all of their ideas into a tight little package. We will begin by exploring various perspectives regarding possible forms of encoding and possible organizational schemes. We will then examine several structures that knowledge might take, with a focus on *concepts*, *schemas* and *scripts*, and *personal theories*. Later, we will consider the overall quality of knowledge that people acquire and look at how expertise related to a particular field or discipline develops over the years. Finally, we will derive a few generalizations about the nature of knowledge.

HOW INFORMATION IS ENCODED IN LONG-TERM MEMORY

Take a minute and think about a rose. What things come to mind? Perhaps words such as *flower*, *red*, *beautiful*, *long-stemmed*, or *expensive* pop into your head. Perhaps you can picture what a rose looks like or recall how it smells. Perhaps you can even feel a thorn prick your finger as you imagine yourself reaching out to clip a rose from its bush.

Information is probably encoded in long-term memory in a number of ways. For one thing, it may be encoded *symbolically*, represented in memory by words (e.g., "Roses are red, violets are blue"), mathematical expressions, or other symbolic systems. Sometimes environmental input is stored as an *image* that retains some of its physical characteristics; for example, a rose has a certain look and a particular smell. Input may also be represented as one or more *propositions*, such that its underlying abstract meaning is stored; for example, the fact that "a rose is a flower" may be stored as an abstract idea. Still another way in which information can be stored in long-term memory is *productions*—the procedures involved in performing a particular task; for example, one learns the procedure necessary for clipping a rose from a rose bush. These four ways of encoding information—symbols, imagery, propositions, and productions—appear frequently in theories of long-term memory, and so we will look at each of them more closely.

Encoding in Terms of Symbols: Words, Numbers, Etc.

A **symbol** is something that represents an object or event, often without bearing much direct resemblance to that object or event. As human beings, we probably represent much of our experience as symbols—as words, numbers, maps, graphs, and so on (DeLoache, 1995; Flavell et al., 1993; Salomon, 1979/1994).

There is no question that some information is stored in terms of actual words—in other words, as **verbal codes** (Bower, 1972; Clark & Paivio, 1991; Paivio, 1986; Salomon, 1979/1994).[1] Support for this idea comes both from everyday human experiences and from several theoretical perspectives. First, people have verbal labels for most of the objects and events in their lives; for instance, you think of this thing you are reading as a *book*. Second, people sometimes learn information in a verbatim fashion; Hamlet's soliloquy ("To be or not to be . . . ") and the lyrics of "Jingle Bells" are examples of things that people typically learn word for word. Third, people use language to help them associate things in memory. For example, the French word for "dog" is *chien*; I remember this word by thinking "dog chain." Many of the principles that emerged from verbal learning research (e.g., the serial learning curve) probably apply primarily to information stored in a verbal code. And finally, as we have seen, people often talk to themselves as a way of guiding themselves through new tasks and procedures (recall our discussions of *self-instructions* in Chapter 7 and *self-talk* in Chapter 8).

Encoding in Terms of Appearance: Imagery

Can you imagine your mother's face? The melody of a favorite song? The smell of a rose? If so, then you are probably using mental imagery. Many psychologists believe that individuals store images in several modalities, including visual, auditory, and olfactory (smelling).[2] However, research and theory have emphasized visual imagery, so that is what we will focus on here.

Although at least one theorist has argued against the existence of visual imagery (Pylyshyn, 1973, 1979, 1981, 1984), most psychologists believe that it is a distinct form of information storage (e.g., Bower, 1972; Clark & Paivio, 1991; Farah, Hammond, Levine, & Calvanio, 1988; Kosslyn, 1994; Paivio, 1986; Sadoski & Paivio, 2001). People often say that they "see pictures" in their minds. Yet as you may recall from Chapter 3, early behaviorists pointed out that asking people to "look at" and describe their own thought processes—that is, to engage in *introspection*—lacks the objective rigor that many psychologists believe to be essential for scientific inquiry. Furthermore, some researchers have discovered that people cannot always describe their own cognitive processes accurately (Nisbett & Wilson, 1977; Zuriff, 1985).

Researchers have found other convincing evidence for the existence of mental imagery as a distinct form of encoding in long-term memory, however.[3] For one thing, people's memory for

---

[1] We previously encountered this idea in our discussion of social cognitive theory in Chapter 7. At the time, we used Bandura's terminology, talking about words as one form of a *memory code*.

[2] For more on auditory imagery, see Intons-Peterson (1992), Intons-Peterson, Russell, and Dressel (1992), and Reisberg (1992).

[3] The idea that people store information in two different ways—verbally and visually—is the essence of Allan Paivio's *dual coding theory* (e.g., Clark & Paivio, 1991; Paivio, 1971, 1986; Sadoski & Paivio, 2001). Do not confuse dual coding theory with the *dual-store model* of memory described in Chapter 9. Dual coding theory distinguishes between two different forms of encoding in long-term memory, whereas the dual-store model distinguishes between working memory and long-term memory.

visual material is often better than it is for strictly verbal material (Clark & Paivio, 1991; Dewhurst & Conway, 1994; Edens & McCormick, 2000; Shepard, 1967). In fact, people tend to remember information better when it is presented in *both* verbal and visual forms, rather than in only one form or the other (Kulhavy et al., 1985; Paivio, 1975, 1986; Sadoski & Paivio, 2001). And specifically instructing people to form visual images of what they are studying helps them to learn the material more quickly and remember it more effectively (Jones, Levin, Levin, & Beitzel, 2000; Pressley, Johnson, Symons, McGoldrick, & Kurita, 1989).

The exact nature of visual imagery is still an open question, but one thing is clear: A visual image is probably *not* a mental snapshot. Visual imagery probably involves some of the same cognitive processes as visual perception (Behrmann, 2000; Kosslyn, 1994; Peterson, Kihlstrom, Rose, & Glisky, 1992). In some instances, it may involve motion (e.g., mentally "seeing" a galloping horse or "scanning" different parts of a picture) rather than a static image (Sadoski & Paivio, 2001). Yet visual images tend to be imprecise representations of external objects, with many details omitted, blurry, or altered (Chambers & Reisberg, 1985; Reed, 1974; Sadoski & Paivio, 2001). Furthermore, individuals can construct mental images of things they have never seen; for example, you can probably visualize a rhinoceros with a pumpkin stuck on its horn even though you have never seen a rhino in that predicament.

I've often suspected that people's *gestures*—especially the ways they move their hands as they speak—reflect their attempts to communicate their visual images to others. For instance, my husband talks with his hands as much as with his mouth, and he consistently uses certain motions when he talks about certain kinds of things. Whenever he talks about something wavy in shape (e.g., a snake in the grass or a windy mountain road), he will move his hand forward in a snakelike manner. Whenever he talks about the size or shape of an object, he will use his hands to show its contour. (I once asked him to describe the dimensions of something while he was driving in the mountains of Colorado. Big mistake. He took both hands off the steering wheel to gesture while he described the object, and it was a miracle we didn't end up in a ditch.) Researchers have only begun to examine the reasons why we gesture, but they are finding that our gestures do seem to represent aspects of thought—perhaps including visual images or other spatial information— that are not necessarily reflected in what we say (Alibali, Bassok, Solomon, Syc, & Goldin-Meadow, 1999; Bassok, 1997; Goldin-Meadow, 1997, 2001; Koschmann & LeBaron, 2002; Krauss, 1998; Roth, 2001).

Encoding in Terms of Meanings: Propositions

People are more apt to remember the general meaning of what they see or hear than precise, word-for-word detail. For example, think about the section you just read on imagery. What do you remember about it? You probably do not remember the specific words you read, but you should be able to recall the general ideas of the section. (If you cannot, go back and read the section again!)

Many learning theorists (J. R. Anderson, 1995; Ellis & Hunt, 1983; E. D. Gagné, 1985; van Dijk & Kintsch, 1983; Weaver & Kintsch, 1991) believe that meanings are stored as **propositions**—that is, as small units of knowledge concerning relationships among objects or events. To paraphrase John Anderson's (1990) definition, a proposition is the smallest unit of knowledge that (1) can stand as a separate statement or assertion and (2) can be judged as being either true or false. To illustrate, consider the following sentence:

Mary's uncle, whom she adores, owns a red Ferrari.

We can break up this complex sentence into four smaller assertions, each containing part of its meaning:

1. Mary has an uncle.

2. Mary adores the uncle.

3. The uncle owns a Ferrari.

4. The Ferrari is red.

Each assertion is either true or false; if any one of them is false, then the entire sentence is false. The four assertions are rough verbal analogs of the abstract propositions that may be stored in memory when the sentence itself is encountered.

Any proposition has two components. First, it includes one or more **arguments**—objects or events that are the topics of the proposition. Second, it involves a single **relation**—a description of an argument or a relationship among two or more arguments. For example, the assertion "Mary has an uncle" contains two arguments ("Mary" and "uncle") and one relation ("has"). Arguments are usually reflected by nouns and pronouns in a sentence, whereas relations are more typically reflected by verbs, adjectives, and adverbs.

Propositions provide a theoretical model of how meanings may be stored. It is becoming increasingly clear that a great deal of the information individuals receive is stored primarily in terms of underlying meanings. For example, participants in research studies can often remember information verbatim if asked to do so immediately after that information has been presented. When recall is delayed, their ability to remember the exact input declines rapidly, yet they continue to remember its *meaning* fairly accurately (J. R. Anderson, 1990; Brainerd & Reyna, 1992; Crowder & Wagner, 1992; Kintsch, 1977; Reder, 1982; Reyna, 1995).

Nonverbal visual information also appears to be stored at least partly in terms of meanings (Mandler & Johnson, 1976; Mandler & Parker, 1976; Mandler & Ritchey, 1977). An experiment by Mandler and Johnson (1976) illustrates this point well. In the experiment, college students looked at line drawings that included a number of different objects; for instance, one picture was a classroom scene that included a teacher, student, desk, bookshelf, flag, clock, globe, and large map. The students were then shown another set of pictures and asked whether each of the pictures was identical to a previous picture or had been changed in some way. Students were far more likely to notice changes in the pictures that reflected a change in the general meaning (e.g., a teacher was talking about a child's drawing instead of a world map) than in those that reflected a nonmeaningful change (e.g., the teacher's skirt and hairstyle were different).

Encoding in Terms of Actions: Productions

As already noted, some of our knowledge is *procedural*; that is, we know how to perform various actions and activities. Some theorists have suggested that procedural knowledge is encoded in the form of **productions** (J. R. Anderson, 1983a, 1987, 1990, 1995; E. D. Gagné, 1985). Productions can best be described as a set of IF–THEN rules. For example, productions for riding a bicycle would include rules such as these:

1. IF I want to speed up, THEN I pedal at a faster rate.
2. IF I want to slow down, THEN I pedal at a slower rate.

3. IF my route turns to the right, THEN I turn the handlebars in a clockwise direction.
4. IF my route turns to the left, THEN I turn the handlebars in a counterclockwise direction.
5. IF an object is directly in front of me, THEN I must turn either right or left.
6. IF I want to stop, THEN I squeeze the brakes on the handlebars.

Similarly, productions for adding 2 two-digit numbers would include these rules:

1. IF the sum of the digits in the "ones" column equals 9 or less, THEN I write that sum in the "ones" column of the answer space.
2. IF the sum of the digits in the "ones" column equals 10 or more, THEN I write the digit that appears in the "ones" column of that sum in the "ones" column of the answer space and carry the "1" to the "tens" column of the problem.
3. IF the sum of the digits in the "tens" column equals 9 or less, THEN I write that sum in the "tens" column of the answer space.
4. IF the sum of the digits in the "tens" column equals 10 or more, THEN I write the digit that appears in the "ones" column of that sum in the "tens" column of the answer space and write the "1" in the "hundreds" column of the answer space.

As you can see, the "IF" part of a production specifies the condition under which a particular behavior will occur, and the "THEN" part specifies what that behavior will be. Productions, then, provide a means through which individuals can be responsive to different environmental conditions. Although some psychologists have described such **conditional knowledge** as a form of knowledge distinct from the other forms I have already described, from this *production* perspective, it is an integral part of procedural knowledge (Byrnes, 2001).

We may store information using any one of the four methods of encoding I have just described—symbols, images, propositions, or productions—or perhaps in some other way that theorists have not yet identified. Furthermore, we may sometimes encode the same information simultaneously in two or more different ways. In support of this idea, college students in an experiment by Pezdek (1977) confused information they had seen in pictures with information they had read in sentences. For example, some students first saw a picture of a car parked by a tree, then read the sentence, "The car by the tree had ski racks on it." These students tended to recognize a picture of a car with ski racks as being one they had seen before, even though the original picture had not included a rack; hence, they were probably storing the same information in both visual and verbal forms. Similarly, in the study by Carmichael, Hogan, and Walters (1932) that I described in the preceding chapter (the study in which people looked at figures given one of two labels; see Figure 10–5 as a reminder), people probably stored the stimulus figures both as images (e.g., two balls connected by a line) and as words (e.g., *eyeglasses* or *dumbbells*). As we discovered in our earlier discussion of visual imagery, people are more likely to remember information when they store it in multiple ways.

When the same information is encoded in two or more different ways, those different codes are probably associated together in long-term memory (Heil, Rösler, & Hennighausen, 1994; Reisberg, 1997; Sadoski & Paivio, 2001; Sporer, 1991). It also appears that different but related pieces of information are frequently stored in connection with one another (e.g., Brown & Schopflocher, 1998). We shall now look more closely at such interconnections—in other words, at the general organization of long-term memory.

THE ORGANIZATION OF LONG-TERM MEMORY

Contemporary theories of long-term memory are **associationistic:** They propose that pieces of information stored in long-term memory are associated, or connected, with one another. To show you what I mean, get a piece of paper and try this exercise. In just a minute, you will read a common, everyday word. As soon as you read it, write down the first word that comes into your head. Then write down the first word that *that* word reminds you of. Continue writing down the first word that each successive word brings to mind until you have a list of 10 words.

Ready? Here is the word to get your mind rolling:

beach

Once you have completed your list of 10 words, examine it carefully. It should give you an idea of what ideas are associated with what other ideas in your long-term memory.

Here is the list that I constructed using the same procedure and my own long-term memory:

sand
castle
king
queen
Elizabeth
England
London
theater
Hair
nude

Some of my associations might be similar to yours. For example, beach–sand and king–queen are common associates. Others might be unique to me. For instance, the last five items on my list reflect my trip to London in my college days when I attended a different theater production every night. The most memorable of the productions I saw was the musical *Hair*, in which several actors briefly appeared nude (quite shocking in 1969!).

Psychologists believe that virtually all pieces of information stored in long-term memory are directly or indirectly related to one another. Different individuals relate and organize their long-term memories somewhat idiosyncratically because their past experiences have been different. Nevertheless, the organizational schemes that people use may share some common features. At least three models of long-term memory organization have been proposed: the hierarchy, the propositional network, and parallel distributed processing.

Long-Term Memory as a Hierarchy

An early view of long-term memory organization was that information was stored in a hierarchical arrangement, with more general, superordinate information at the top of the hierarchy and more specific, subordinate information below it (Ausubel, 1963, 1968; Ausubel & Robinson, 1969; Collins & Quillian, 1969, 1972). An example of such a hierarchy is my own knowledge of the animal kingdom, part of which is depicted in Figure 11–1. Notice how the most general category—animals—is at the top of the hierarchy. Next are two major categories of animals—vertebrates and invertebrates—followed by more and more subordinate categories, until finally

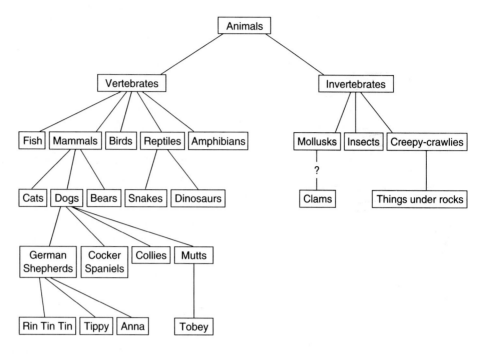

Figure 11–1
The author's hierarchical knowledge of the animal kingdom.

specific instances of a category (e.g., Rin Tin Tin, Tippy, and Anna are all German shepherds) are reached. As you can see, part of my hierarchy would resemble that of a biologist (my classes of vertebrates, for instance), but other parts are uniquely my own.

In a classic study, Collins and Quillian (1969) demonstrated how long-term memory might be organized hierarchically. Adults were given a number of statements (e.g., "A canary can sing") and asked to indicate whether they were true or false; people's reaction times to confirm or reject the statements were recorded. Following are some examples of true statements and approximate reaction times to them:

Statements About Category Membership	Reaction Times (msec)
A canary is a canary.	1000
A canary is a bird.	1160
A canary is an animal.	1240

Statements About Characteristics	Reaction Times (msec)
A canary can sing.	1300
A canary can fly.	1380
A canary has skin.	1470

Notice how the reaction times increased for the three sentences regarding category membership: Participants most quickly verified that a canary is a canary and least quickly verified that a canary is an animal. Now notice the different reaction times for the three statements concerning a canary's characteristics: Participants found the statement about singing easiest and that about having skin most difficult. Collins and Quillian argued that the two sets of sentences are actually parallel, because most people associate singing directly with canaries, whereas they associate flying with birds and having skin with animals.

Collins and Quillian suggested that an individual's knowledge about categories and category characteristics is arranged in a hierarchical fashion similar to that depicted in Figure 11–2. To verify the statements, subjects had to locate the two components of the statement (e.g., "canary" and "skin") within their long-term memories and determine whether they were associated, either directly or indirectly. The farther apart the two components were in the hierarchy, the longer it would take to verify a statement (hence, the longer the reaction times).

Strictly hierarchical models of long-term memory have been the object of considerable criticism (Bourne, Dominowski, Loftus, & Healy, 1986; Loftus & Loftus, 1976; Wingfield & Byrnes, 1981). First, information is not always hierarchical in nature. Second, predictions consistent with hierarchically arranged information are not always confirmed. For example, just as people more quickly verify that a canary is a bird than they verify that a canary is an animal, we should expect that people would agree with the statement "A collie is a mammal" faster than the statement "A collie is an animal," because *collie* is closer to *mammal* than it is to *animal* in a logical hierarchy of animals. Yet the opposite holds true: People more quickly agree that a collie is an animal than that it is a mammal (Rips, Shoben, & Smith, 1973).

At this point, it appears that some information in long-term memory may be arranged hierarchically but that most information is probably organized less systematically. An alternative view of long-term memory, the propositional network, may provide a more useful and flexible theoretical model.

Long-Term Memory as a Propositional Network

A **network** model portrays memory as consisting of many pieces of information interconnected through a variety of associations. To illustrate, let's return again to my own previous list of

Figure 11–2
A simplified version of the Collins and Quillian (1969) knowledge hierarchy.
Based on "Retrieval Time from Semantic Memory" by A. M. Collins & M. R. Quillian, 1969, *Journal of Verbal Learning and Verbal Behavior, 8*, pp. 240–247.

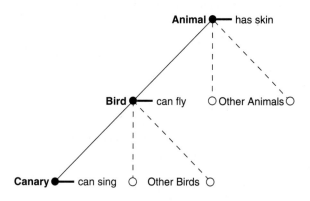

successive associations resulting from the word *beach*: sand, castle, king, queen, Elizabeth, England, London, theater, *Hair*, nude. Such a list might have been generated from a long-term memory network such as the one in Figure 11–3. Different individuals should have networks with somewhat different associations and so should generate different lists. Some individuals, depending on their past experiences at the beach, might even associate *beach* and *nude* directly with each other!

One widely used model of long-term memory organization is the **propositional network** (J.R. Anderson, 1976, 1983a, 1983b, 1990; Anderson & Bower, 1973; E.D. Gagné, 1985; Lindsay & Norman, 1977; Norman & Rumelhart, 1975). A propositional network is one in which propositions and their interrelationships are stored in a networklike fashion. As an illustration, let's return to a sentence we considered earlier in the chapter:

Mary's uncle, whom she adores, owns a red Ferrari.

and to the four assertions it contains:

1. Mary has an uncle.

2. Mary adores the uncle.

3. The uncle owns a Ferrari.

4. The Ferrari is red.

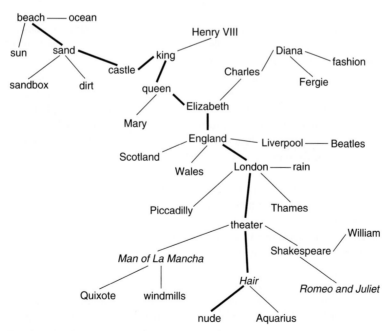

Figure 11–3
A hypothetical network of information in long-term memory.

Figure 11–4

Diagrams of separate propositions.

1. Mary has an uncle.

2. Mary adores the uncle.

3. The uncle owns a Ferrari.

4. The Ferrari is red.

The four assertions can be diagrammed as propositions, as shown in Figure 11–4. These diagrams, using Anderson's (1990) symbols, each show a proposition (symbolized by an oval) that encompasses one relation and one or more arguments.

As you should notice, the four diagrams in Figure 11–4 share several objects, or arguments; in particular, *Mary*, *uncle*, and *Ferrari* each appear in two or more propositions. Such commonalities allow the propositions to be linked in a network; an example is shown in Figure 11–5. A propositional network model of long-term memory is obviously more flexible than a hierarchical model. A hierarchy includes only superordinate–subordinate relationships; in contrast, a network can easily include a wide variety of relationships (e.g., possession, location, opposition).

Network models are often conceptualized as including not only propositions (meanings) but other memory codes (such as imagery and productions) as well (E. D. Gagné, 1985; Glass et al., 1979; Paivio, 1986; Sadoski & Paivio, 2001). For example, you might have a visual image of a Ferrari stored in association with the information about Mary's uncle and his red sports car. Perhaps not too far away in the same network are productions related to how you drive a car.

In the preceding chapter, I described the process of *meaningful learning*—storing new information by relating it to knowledge already in long-term memory. Both hierarchical and propositional network models of memory give us an idea of how such meaningful learning might occur. For example, using a hierarchical model of long-term memory organization, Ausubel described meaningful learning as involving **subsumption**, whereby people place new

Figure 11–5
A propositional network.

Mary's uncle, whom she adores, owns a red Ferrari.

information under an appropriate superordinate category in their knowledge hierarchy (Ausubel, 1963, 1968; Ausubel et al., 1978; Ausubel & Robinson, 1969). To illustrate, students are more likely to learn meaningful information about an animal called a skink if they are told that it is "a kind of lizard that looks like a snake" than if they are told that it is "brightly colored" or "a shy, seldom-seen creature." In the former case, they can store the concept *skink* under the more general concept *lizard*; in the latter two situations, they aren't really sure just *where* to put it.

Using a propositional network model of long-term memory, we can characterize meaningful learning as a process of storing new propositions with related propositions in the network. For example, let's assume that you have already stored some propositions concerning Mary's uncle and his red Ferrari in a form similar to what I depicted in Figure 11–5. You then read the following sentence:

The uncle is named Charles.

You might connect this proposition to your existing propositions about the uncle and perhaps to propositions concerning another Charles that you know of, as illustrated in Figure 11–6.

A propositional network model of memory gives us greater flexibility in the nature of interrelationships than a strictly hierarchical model offers. The black-and-white nature of propositions—each one must be definitely true or false—is troublesome, however. Many aspects of human experience that are stored in long-term memory, such as an interpretation of a Shakespearian play or an emotional reaction to a work of art, cannot be easily classified as right or wrong (Eisner, 1994).

Parallel Distributed Processing

Until now, we have been speaking as if various bits of information are each stored in a single "location" in long-term memory. But let's return to a couple of research findings we encountered in our discussion of the brain in Chapter 2. First, even when people think about something fairly simple—perhaps a single word—numerous areas of the cortex are activated. Second, recall

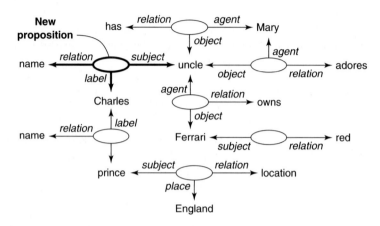

Figure 11–6
Meaningful learning in a propositional network.

Lashley's (1929) work with maze-running rats. As Lashley gradually removed more and more of their brains, the rats gradually remembered less and less about mazes they had mastered; no single surgery marked a dramatic change from "knowing" to "not knowing" a maze. In both people and rats, and presumably in many other species as well, knowledge about a particular thing seems to be distributed across many parts of the brain.

With such findings in mind, some theorists have proposed that each piece of information is stored in the form of an integrated collection of entities, called **nodes,** that are located throughout long-term memory. Any single node may be associated with many different pieces of information. Each separate idea that you have stored in your long-term memory is represented, then, not as a single node but rather as a *unique network of interconnected nodes.* As one idea (network) is activated, other ideas that share some of its nodes may also be activated.

Such a view of long-term memory is often called **parallel distributed processing** (PDP): Pieces of information are stored in a *distributed* fashion throughout long-term memory, with numerous nodes being processed simultaneously—that is, in *parallel* (Ackley, Hinton, & Sejnowski, 1985; Ballard, 1986; Hinton & Anderson, 1981; Hinton, McClelland, & Rumelhart, 1986; McClelland & Rumelhart, 1986; Plunkett, 1996; Rumelhart & McClelland, 1986). Parallel distributed processing is also known as **connectionism,** but it should not be confused with Edward Thorndike's connectionism described in Chapter 4.

The parallel distributed processing model is useful for understanding the multidimensional nature of even the simplest of ideas (e.g., Rayner et al., 2001; Siegler, 1998). For example, when we read the word

beach

in a textbook, we may simultaneously retrieve not only what it means but also how it sounds, how it is pronounced, and what a typical beach looks like. The model also helps us understand how we can often fill in missing information when a stimulus is incomplete: Enough nodes of an idea are activated that the entire network becomes activated.

The PDP model is still in the early stages of development, and it is far from perfect (Fodor & Pylyshyn, 1988; Holyoak, 1987; Lachter & Bever, 1988; McClelland, 2001; Pinker & Prince, 1988; Sternberg, 1996). It tends to portray learning as a gradual process of strengthening and weakening associations and so does not explain how we can sometimes learn something very rapidly or, alternatively, quickly revise our beliefs about something in the face of contradictory information (Ratcliff, 1990; Schacter, 1989). And although it was presumably developed to be consistent with research findings about brain functioning, its relationship to brain anatomy is a loose one at best (McClelland, 2001; Siegler, 1998).

Regardless of how long-term memory is organized, it clearly *is* organized. To some extent, people organize all of the information they store in their long-term memories. To an even greater extent, they organize their knowledge regarding very specific objects, events, and topics. At this point, let's turn to several specific examples of how people might organize their experiences, as we look at *concepts*, *schemas*, *scripts*, and *personal theories*.

CONCEPTS

One night in late May many years ago, my son Jeff and I had a discussion about the seasons. It went something like this:

Jeff:	When are spring and summer coming?
Mom:	Spring is already here. Haven't you noticed how warm it is, and how the leaves are back on the trees, and how the birds are singing again?
Jeff:	Oh. Then when is summer coming?
Mom:	Well, you have only one more week of school, and then a couple of weeks after that, summer will be here.
Jeff:	Summer is when we go swimming, right?
Mom:	[I pause and think about how to answer.] Right.

As a 4-year-old, Jeff had not yet precisely defined the concepts of *spring* and *summer*. When I was a child, summer was a season of heat, humidity, and no school. As an adult, I now define it more formally as the three-month period between the summer solstice and the autumn equinox. To Jeff, however, summer was simply the time when he could swim.

Children begin to categorize aspects of their world as early as 3 months of age (Behl-Chadha, 1996; Eimas & Quinn, 1994; Quinn, 2002, 2003), and their categories undoubtedly form the basis for their first concepts. Generally speaking, you might think of a **concept** as a class of objects or events that share one or more similarities (Flavell et al., 1993; Klausmeier, 1990; Schwartz & Reisberg, 1991). Some concepts are defined by readily observable characteristics and are fairly easy to learn. For example, the word *milk* refers to a white liquid with a particular taste. Similarly, the word *red* refers to a certain range of light wavelengths (although people disagree about exactly where "red" ends and "orange" begins). Other concepts are defined by less salient attributes, so are more slowly learned and more easily misconstrued. For instance, the four seasons of the year are "officially" designated by the occurrences of solstices

One cannot learn abstract (defined) concepts such as *cousin* through physical examination alone.

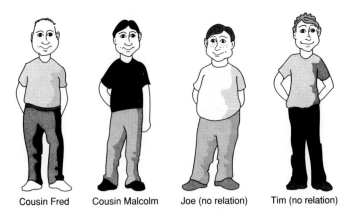

Cousin Fred   Cousin Malcolm   Joe (no relation)   Tim (no relation)

and equinoxes that most people are unaware of, so many people erroneously define them in terms of different weather conditions. Still other concepts may be even harder to grasp because they are based on abstract, relativistic, and sometimes elusive criteria. For example, psychologists have wrestled with the concept of *intelligence* for many years and still cannot agree on what the term means.

Some theorists have found it useful to distinguish between two general kinds of concepts (Cohen, 1983; R. M. Gagné, 1985; Newby & Stepich, 1987; Wasserman, DeVolder, & Coppage, 1992). **Concrete concepts** are easily identified by their physical appearance; *cow*, *red*, and *round* are examples. From a behaviorist perspective, concrete concepts may develop, at least in part, as a result of stimulus generalization: Once an organism has learned to respond in a certain way to one stimulus, it tends to respond in the same way to similar stimuli. In contrast, **abstract concepts** are difficult to conceptualize in terms of specific, observable characteristics; examples include *intelligence*, *charisma*, and *work*. Abstract concepts are probably best described in terms of a formal definition (R. M. Gagné, 1985). Consider the concept *cousin* as an example. There is no way to learn what a cousin is simply by looking at examples of cousins and noncousins; all will have one head, two arms, two legs, and so on. Instead, a person probably learns a rule (definition) for identifying cousins: A *cousin* is an offspring of a parent's sibling. Because stimulus generalization is unlikely to occur when objects or events don't *look* similar, abstract concepts are most likely to develop as a result of specific training or instruction (Hull, 1943; Wasserman et al., 1992).

In many cases, people first learn a concept in a concrete form, then later acquire a more abstract definition of it (e.g., R. M. Gagné, 1985; Liu, Golinkoff, & Sak, 2001). When I was a child, *summer* was a concrete concept for me: Heat, humidity, and no school were easily observable characteristics. I later acquired an abstract concept of summer as I learned how the seasons are determined by the tilt of the Earth in relation to the sun. In a similar way, children first learn about a *circle* as a concrete concept (i.e., a "roundish" thing); later, perhaps in a high school geometry class, they may develop an abstract concept of a circle (i.e., all points on a plane equidistant from another single point). And they will initially conceptualize various family members (cousins, uncles, etc.) in terms of things they can actually see, rather than in terms of the nature of the relationship (Keil, 1989). The following two conversations, each between an experimenter (E) and a child (C), illustrate:

[E:]	This man your daddy's age loves you and your parents and loves to visit and bring presents, but he's not related to your parents at all. He's not your mommy or daddy's brother or sister or anything like that. Could that be an uncle?
C:	Yes.
E:	What is an uncle?
C:	An uncle is that he brings you presents at Christmas.
E:	What else?
C:	An uncle is that he lets you come over to his house.
E:	Could I be your uncle?
C:	No . . . because I don't know you.
E:	If I got to know you and brought you presents, could I be your uncle?
C:	Yes. (Keil, 1989, pp. 71, 76)
[E:]	Suppose your mommy has all sorts of brothers, some very old and some very, very young. One of your mommy's brothers is so young he's only 2 years old. Could that be an uncle?
C:	No . . . because he's little and two years old.
E:	How old does an uncle have to be?
C:	About 24 or 25.
E:	If he's 2 years old, can he be an uncle?
C:	No . . . he can be a cousin. (Keil, 1989, pp. 71, 74, 76)

Most concepts are identified by a label—a word that symbolizes the concept and represents it in both thought and communication. For example, you have probably formed a concept that encompasses the many things you have seen with the following characteristics:

- Shorter and wider than most adult humans
- Covered with a short, bristly substance
- Appended at one end by an object similar in appearance to a paintbrush
- Appended at the other end by a lumpy thing with four pointy objects sticking upward (two soft and floppy, two hard and curved around)
- Held up from the ground by four spindly sticks, two at each end
- Usually observed in pastures or barns
- Almost always eating grass

You have no doubt attached a particular label to these similar-looking things: *cow*.

We haven't truly acquired a concept until we can correctly identify all positive and negative instances of it. A **positive instance** is a particular example of a concept. To illustrate, you and I are positive instances of the concept *person*, and this thing you are reading is a positive instance of the concept *book*. A **negative instance** is a nonexample of the concept. You and I are negative instances of the concept *cow*, and this book is a negative instance of the concept *pencil*.

People often have "sort-of" understandings of concepts, in that they cannot always accurately distinguish positive instances from negative instances. A child who vehemently denies that a Chihuahua is a dog has not completely learned the concept of *dog*; neither has the child who calls the neighbor's cow "doggie." Denying that a Chihuahua is a dog—**undergeneralization**—

reflects an inability to recognize all positive instances. Identifying a cow as a dog—**overgenera-lization**—reflects an inability to reject all negative instances. The various theories of concept learning that we will consider now can help us to understand how such "sort-of" knowledge might exist.

Theories of Concept Learning

Several terms will be useful to us as we examine the various theories of concept learning that psychologists have proposed. In particular, I need to explain what I mean when I talk about different kinds of *features* and *rules*.

Features (some theorists instead use the term **attributes**) are the characteristics of a concept's positive instances. For instance, my dog Tobey has numerous features worthy of note, including these:

- Hairy
- At one time physiologically equipped to impregnate female dogs
- Wearing a red collar
- Likely to bark loudly at any negative instance of an Ormrod
- Presently located on my office floor

Some features are important for identifying positive instances of a concept, whereas others are not. **Defining features** are characteristics that must be present in all positive instances. For example, to be a dog, Tobey should have hair and, as a male member of the species, should have (or once have had) the capability of impregnating a female, who would then eventually give birth to live young. **Correlational features** are frequently found in positive instances but are not essential for concept membership. For example, most dogs bark and many dogs wear collars, but neither of these features is a characteristic of *all* dogs. **Irrelevant features** are characteristics that are unrelated to membership in the concept. Tobey's location on my office floor is totally irrelevant to his dogness.

Let's pause here for a brief exercise. Figure 11–7 presents eight positive instances and eight negative instances of the concept *gudge*. Can you identify one or more defining features of a gudge?

As you may have surmised, the two defining features of a gudge are that it be gray and square. A large black dot is a correlational feature: Black dots are found on six of the eight gudges but on only one nongudge. White dots and topside "whiskers" are irrelevant features, because they are found equally often on gudges and nongudges.

From some theoretical perspectives, concept learning is a process of learning what features are important for identifying positive instances of that concept. In essence, one must learn that certain features are essential components of the concept and that other features are frequently present but unessential. Learning to differentiate between a concept's defining and correlational features takes time and experience, often many years' worth (Keil, 1989; Mervis, 1987). For example, consider this question that Saltz (1971) posed to children:

> A father goes to work. On the way home from work in the evening he stops at a bar to have a drink. His friends there are drunkards and he becomes a drunkard too. Is he still a father? (Saltz, 1971, p. 28)

Saltz found that, even at the age of 8, most children denied that a drunkard could still be a father. Apparently, many young children believe that "goodness" defines fatherhood rather than

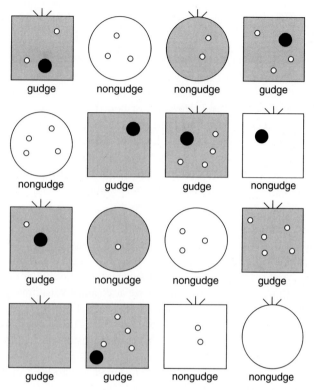

Figure 11–7
Positive and negative instances of a *gudge*.

correlating with it, a belief that they are likely to abandon only when they encounter enough "bad" positive instances of a father.

Some concepts have a single defining feature; others are apt to have two or more features that may or may not all need to be present at the same time. For instance, the concept *red* has one defining feature: a particular range of wavelengths. In contrast, the concept *gudge* has two that must both be present: square and gray. An *out* in baseball is an example of a concept for which no single defining feature is always present; for example, it can be three strikes while a player is at bat, the tagging of a player who is running from base to base, or a fly ball caught before it touches the ground. Concept **rules** specify how defining features are combined to define the concepts. Theorists (Bourne, 1967; Bruner et al., 1956; Dodd & White, 1980; Klein, 1987; Saltz, 1971) have identified a number of different concept rules. Four rules are most commonly described:

1. *Simple:* Only one particular feature must be present; for example, *red* is a specific range of wavelengths.
2. *Conjunctive:* Two or more features must all be present; for example, a *circle* must be two-dimensional and must have all points equidistant from a center point.
3. *Disjunctive:* Two or more defining features are not all present at the same time; for example, an *out* in baseball occurs in any one of several different situations.

4. *Relational:* The relationship between two or more features determines the concept; for example, the concept *between* requires three objects, two located on opposite sides of a third.

When early researchers examined the effects of various concept rules on learning, they discovered that simple rules (in which only one feature determines concept membership) are easiest to learn, conjunctive and disjunctive rules are moderately difficult, and relational rules are most difficult (Bourne, 1967; Haygood & Bourne, 1965; Neisser & Weene, 1962). Consistent with this finding, young children often have trouble understanding such common relational concepts as *under, over, more,* and *less;* for example, children as old as 7 years often do not fully understand what the concept *less* means (Owens, 1996; Palermo, 1973).

With these "concepts about concepts" in mind, let's look at four views of concept learning that psychologists have proposed: hypothesis testing, prototypes, feature lists, and exemplars.[4]

Hypothesis Testing

Take a few minutes to learn the concept *studge* using Figure 11–8. Your first step is to get two index cards or similar-sized pieces of paper. Use one card to cover the right side of the figure. Now take the second card and cover the left side, exposing only the top section above the first horizontal line. In this top section, you will see a rectangle with three gray circles inside; take a wild guess and decide whether the rectangle is a studge. Once you have made your guess, move the left card down to the next horizontal line, revealing the correct answer. In this section you will also see a second rectangle, one with a gray square inside; decide whether you think it is a studge. Keep moving the card down the page, one section at a time, on each occasion getting your feedback and then deciding whether the next rectangle is a studge. Continue the process with the rectangles on the right side of the figure.

Now that you have finished, you have, I hope, learned that the concept *studge* is "two or three circles." Shape and number are defining features for the concept; color is irrelevant to studgeness. In learning about studges, perhaps you found yourself forming different hypotheses about what is and is not a studge. For instance, the first example was a studge. You may have used that positive instance to generate one or more hypotheses, such as the following:

- A studge is anything gray.
- A studge is round.
- A studge is three of something.
- A studge is three gray circles.

The second example in Figure 11–8 was a nonstudge, so, had you held the hypothesis that a studge is gray, you would have eliminated that particular hypothesis at that point. A hypothesis such as "three of something," however, would have been confirmed with the second example but disconfirmed with the third. Eventually you may have ended up with the correct hypothesis: A studge is a set of two or three circles.

---

[4]For early behaviorist and neobehaviorist views of concept learning, I refer you to the first two editions of this book (published in 1990 and 1995, respectively) or to my original sources (R. M. Gagné, 1985; Hull, 1920; Kendler & Kendler, 1959, 1961, 1962).

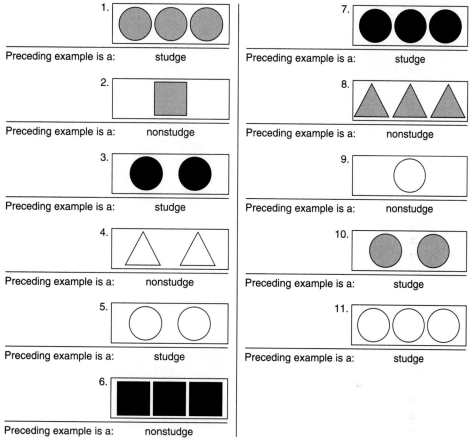

Figure 11–8
Positive and negative instances of a *studge*.

In an early theory of concept learning, Bruner, Goodnow, and Austin (1956) proposed that concept learning is a process of forming various hypotheses about the features and rules that define a concept and then using positive and negative instances to confirm or reject those hypotheses. To support their theory, they used stimuli similar to my positive and negative instances of studges to study concept learning in adults. They gave participants in their experiment one positive instance of the concept and then asked them to try to select other positive instances from among an array of stimuli varying on four dimensions (shape, color, number of objects, and number of borders around the objects). By noting the selections that were made, Bruner and his colleagues observed several different approaches that the participants used in formulating and testing their hypotheses. Some people appeared to test one hypothesis at a time, choosing stimuli that varied on only one feature from a previous positive instance. If they received feedback that confirmed their hypothesis, they continued to test it; if they received contradictory feedback, they would form a different hypothesis and begin to test that one. Other people appeared to hold several hypotheses in mind at the same time and test them simultaneously as they chose various stimuli. This latter strategy would, of course, be faster, but it would also place greater demands on memory, hence leading to more errors. This tendency to test several hypotheses simultaneously was also observed by Levine (1966).

Although some hypothesis testing may very well occur when people learn concepts, it is probably not the only process involved in concept learning. Experiments in which hypothesis testing has been observed, such as those of Bruner and colleagues (1956) and Levine (1966), have been criticized as being artificial and not resembling real-world concept learning conditions (Glass et al., 1979; Rosch, 1973a). People rarely encounter a situation in which they can pick possible examples of a concept in a systematic manner; more typically, they find a positive instance here, a negative instance there, and so on, in a somewhat haphazard fashion over a period of time. Furthermore, in several experiments (Brooks, 1978; Reber & Allen, 1978; Reber, Kassin, Lewis, & Cantor, 1980), people who were instructed to identify the rules underlying certain classification schemes (i.e., to form hypotheses) actually performed more poorly than people who were not so instructed. In these cases, the more successful learners were the less analytic ones: They simply remembered early positive instances and compared new examples with them. A different theory of concept learning—one involving the formation of prototypes—better explains such findings.

Prototypes

Eleanor Rosch (1973a, 1973b, 1977a; Rosch, Mervis, Gray, Johnson, & Boyes-Braem, 1976) and other theorists (Eysenck & Keane, 1990; Kemler Nelson, 1990; Smith, 1988; Wittgenstein, 1958) have argued that many real-world concepts are difficult to delineate in terms of defining features and precise rules. Objects can lack important features yet still be identified as positive instances of a particular concept. For example, a salient feature of human beings is that they have two legs, but you can still recognize a person who has no legs as being a human. Similarly, although dogs typically have hair, a few breeds with little or no hair have recently emerged. Thus, people must often use correlational features rather than defining features to identify positive instances of a concept.

Furthermore, concepts may have fuzzy boundaries, so that in certain borderline cases correct identification of positive and negative instances is difficult (Labov, 1973; Oden, 1987; Rosch, 1973a, 1978; Zazdeh, Fu, Tanak, & Shimura, 1975). For example, is a stroke a *disease*? In a study by McCloskey and Glucksberg (1978), some people believed that it was and others did not. Is turquoise a shade of *blue* or a shade of *green*? My husband insists that turquoise is green, but I know better: It's blue.

Rosch (1973a, 1973b, 1977a, 1977b, 1978; Rosch & Mervis, 1975; Rosch, Mervis, et al., 1976) and others (Attneave, 1957; Tennyson & Cocchiarella, 1986; Walton & Bower, 1993) have proposed that people form concepts by developing a **prototype**, or representative example, of a typical member of that category. As an illustration, form an image in your mind of a *bird*. What probably comes to mind is a small creature, perhaps about the shape and size of a robin or sparrow. It is unlikely that you would instead imagine a penguin or an ostrich because these animals, although they are birds, are not as typically birdlike in appearance as robins and sparrows. Similarly, imagine a *vehicle*. Your image probably resembles a car or a truck rather than a canoe or hot-air balloon, because cars and trucks are more commonly observed instances of vehicles. Now imagine *red*. You probably picture a color similar to that red crayon you had when you were five rather than pink or maroon.

A prototype is likely to incorporate features of the most typical, commonly observed positive instances of the concept. For instance, your prototype of a human being probably has two arms and two legs, stands upright, and is slightly less than two meters tall. Your prototype of a table is likely to be a rectangular flat surface held up by four legs, one of them at each of the four corners. You identify new objects as positive instances of a particular concept when you compare them with the concept prototype and find them to be sufficiently similar. A positive identification does not require that all features be present, however. Thus, you can still recognize a legless man as a human being, and you can still recognize a three-legged object as a table.

At least two sources of evidence support the idea that many concepts may be represented in memory in the form of prototypes. First, people easily identify positive instances of a concept that closely resemble the prototype but have difficulty identifying positive instances that are less similar (Glass, Holyoak, & O'Dell, 1974; Posner & Keele, 1968, 1970; Rips et al., 1973; Rosch, 1973b, 1978; Rosch & Mervis, 1975; Rosch, Simpson, & Miller, 1976; Wilkins, 1971). In one experiment by Rosch (1973b), elementary school and undergraduate students identified as birds those creatures that looked particularly birdlike (e.g., robins and sparrows) more quickly than they identified creatures less similar to the prototype (e.g., chickens and ducks).

A second source of evidence for prototypes is the finding that people usually recognize positive instances they have never encountered before when those instances closely resemble the prototype. In fact, people recognize them more easily than positive instances they *have* encountered that do *not* closely match the prototype (Franks & Bransford, 1971; Posner, Goldsmith, & Welton, 1967; Posner & Keele, 1968). For example, in an experiment by Franks and Bransford (1971), college students viewed a series of geometric patterns that involved one or more variations from a particular "base" pattern; the base pattern itself was not presented. The students were then shown another series of patterns (including the base pattern) and asked to identify which ones they had previously seen; they had actually seen *none* of these patterns earlier. Students were especially likely to "recognize" patterns that closely resembled the base pattern; they were most confident that they had seen the base pattern itself. Presumably, the base pattern represented the single best example of the various stimuli that the students had originally seen and thus most closely approximated the pattern prototype that they had formed. Similar results have been observed with a sample of three- and four-year-old children (Bomba & Siqueland, 1983).

Rosch, Mervis, and their colleagues (1976) have suggested that conceptual prototypes may be organized in a three-level hierarchy—a hierarchical organizational scheme similar to what I described earlier in the chapter. **Basic-level concepts** are the ones we use most frequently—for instance, the ones we use when we name objects (this is a *chair*, this is a *hat*, this is a *car*, and so on). **Superordinate concepts** are more general categories that encompass a number of basic-level concepts (e.g., chairs and tables are both *furniture*, hats and shoes are two kinds of *clothing*, and cars and trucks are *vehicles*). **Subordinate concepts** are more specific subdivisions of basic-level concepts (e.g., *rocking chairs* and *lawn chairs* are types of chairs, *berets* and *bowlers* are types of hats, and *Volkswagen Beetles* and *Ford Mustangs* are types of cars). You can think of the three levels as reflecting varying degrees of abstraction: The superordinate concepts are most abstract, and the subordinate concepts are most concrete.

We probably cannot explain all human concept learning strictly in terms of the development of prototypes, however. For one thing, how we categorize an object depends on the context in which we find it. For instance, if a cuplike object contains flowers, we might identify it as a *vase* rather than a *cup*; if it contains mashed potatoes, we might instead identify it as a *bowl* (Labov, 1973; Schwartz & Reisberg, 1991). Furthermore, not all concepts lend themselves readily to a single prototypical representation (Eysenck & Keane, 1990; Hampton, 1981). For instance, I have a difficult time identifying a typical example of *music*: Classical, rock, jazz, and country-western are all quite different.

Feature Lists

Feature list theory (Bourne, 1982; Bourne et al., 1986; Neumann, 1974, 1977; Rips et al., 1973; Smith, Shoben, & Rips, 1974; Ward, Vela, & Haas, 1990) is in some ways similar to prototype theory but focuses more on a concept's defining and correlational features. From this perspective, learning a concept involves developing a **feature list** that includes the following:

- Relevant features, both defining and correlational, of the concept
- The probability that each of these features is likely to be present in any specific instance—that is, the frequency with which each feature occurs
- The relationships among the features—that is, the rules for their combination

Recognizing an object as a positive instance of a concept, then, is a matter of determining whether the object possesses enough relevant features. Prototypes are recognized more quickly than other positive instances only because they encompass most or all of the concept's relevant features.

A prediction from feature list theory is that negative instances will be erroneously identified as positive instances if a sufficient number of relevant features are present. Bourne (1982) confirmed this prediction in an experiment involving an *exclusive disjunctive* concept. Earlier in the chapter, I described a disjunctive concept as being one with two or more defining features that do not all need to be present at once (the example I gave you was an *out* in baseball). An exclusive disjunctive concept is a subcategory of this kind of concept: An item possessing any of the defining features is a positive instance, but an item possessing all of them is not. (For example, a *pludge* is anything that is red or square, but things that are both red and square are nonpludges.) In an experiment involving college students, Bourne presented numerous positive and negative instances of an exclusive disjunctive concept that had two relevant features; an item that had one, but not both, of the features was a positive instance. Despite their training, when the students were later asked to identify examples of the concept, they were more likely to "recognize" those stimuli possessing both relevant features than those possessing only one of the two features.

As we discovered in Chapter 10, we human beings have a natural tendency to pick up on the relative frequencies of various objects and events in our lives (recall how you knew that the word *bacon* occurs more frequently in the English language than *pastrami*). We also seem to acquire some knowledge about the statistical odds with which various features are likely to be present in positive instances of a concept (Ariely, 2001). Yet feature list theory is probably not the perfect explanation of concept learning, either: As we noted earlier, we cannot always identify the specific features on which concepts are based. To the extent that we can identify defining and correlational features, however, our awareness of them undoubtedly comprises part of our knowledge about concepts.

Exemplars

In some cases, our knowledge of a concept may be based more on a variety of examples—that is, on **exemplars**—than on a single prototype (Carmichael & Hayes, 2001; Reisberg, 1997; Ross & Spalding, 1994; Sadoski & Paivio, 2001). Exemplars can give us an idea of the variability we are likely to see in any category of objects or events. As an illustration, consider the concept *fruit*. Many different things are likely to come to mind here: Apples, bananas, grapes, mangos, and kiwifruit are all possibilities. If you encounter a new instance of fruit—a blackberry, let's say—you could compare it with the variety of exemplars you have already stored and find one (a raspberry, perhaps) that is relatively similar.

It is possible that prototypes or exemplars are used to identify positive instances in clear-cut situations, whereas formal definitions (which include defining features) are used in other, more ambiguous ones (Andre, 1986; Glass et al., 1979; Glass & Holyoak, 1975). To illustrate, abstract concepts such as *rule*, *belief*, and *instinct* are difficult to conceptualize in terms of a typical example. In some cases, it may also be true that children rely on prototypes or exemplars initially and then acquire a more general, abstract understanding (perhaps including a formal definition) later on (e.g., Liu et al., 2001). For example, as a preschooler, my son Jeff adamantly denied that the concept *animal* includes people, fish, and insects. The belief that these groups are nonanimals is a common phenomenon among young children, who often restrict their conception of animals to four-legged mammals (Carey, 1985b; Kyle & Shymansky, 1989; Saltz, 1971). I suspect that Jeff's animal prototype might have resembled the family dog or perhaps the cows he often saw in the surrounding countryside. When he began studying the animal kingdom in school, he learned a biology-based definition of an animal that incorporates some of its major features: a form of life that derives its food from other organisms, responds immediately to its environment, and can move its body. At that point Jeff acknowledged that people, fish, and creepy-crawlies are legitimate animals. (If he takes college biology at a later date, however, he may learn that biologists do not really agree on a definition of *animal* and that true defining features of the concept are difficult to identify.)

I suspect that each of the theories of concept learning we have just examined has an element of truth. As human beings, perhaps we represent any single concept in long-term memory as a prototype, a set of defining and correlational features, *and* a number of exemplars (e.g., Armstrong, Gleitman, & Gleitman, 1983). Perhaps we also form and test hypotheses about the nature of particular concepts. We do not necessarily need to choose just one theory of concept learning as being the "right" one, to the exclusion of the other three.

In our discussion of concepts, two factors have emerged as essential components of the concept learning process. First, people must learn the characteristics that determine concept membership (and discover which of those characteristics, if any, are truly definitive). Second, they must develop awareness of the degree of acceptable variation from best examples of the concept. For example, an ostrich is a bird even though it is much larger than the prototypical bird; however, a certain other creature that is the same size and also walks on two legs—a human being—falls outside of the bird category. In other words, to learn a concept completely, one must eventually learn the boundaries of that concept.

Researchers have identified a number of factors that affect the ease with which people learn new concepts. As we look at these factors in the following section, we'll also identity strategies for facilitating concept learning in instructional settings.

Facilitating Concept Learning

The following principles capture important factors affecting concept learning and yield strategies for helping learners of all ages acquire new concepts:

• *Concepts are easier to learn when defining features are salient and irrelevant features are not.* The more obvious a concept's defining features are—the more they stand out in positive instances—the easier the concept is to master. For example, as a young child my son Jeff easily learned the correct meanings of *milk, hot,* and *television,* presumably because the features that define these concepts are readily observable. However, he struggled with words such as *spring, summer, work,* and *university*—concepts whose defining features are not so apparent.

Meanwhile, irrelevant features that consistently appear in positive instances hinder the course of concept learning, especially if they are prominent (Good & Brophy, 1986). For instance, the concept *animal* is difficult for many children, because many of the salient features of positive instances—body covering, nature and number of limbs, facial features, shape, and size—are somewhat irrelevant. So, too, might a true understanding of the concept *art* be a tough one to acquire. Things that stand out about a particular work of art are characteristics such as shape, color, medium (e.g., paint or clay), and subject matter (e.g., people or objects), yet these characteristics are only tangentially related to what art *is.*

Because young children typically pay more attention to obvious features, their early understandings of concepts are apt to be based on such features. For example, in a study by DeVries (1969), children ranging in age from 3 to 6 played for a short time with a good-natured cat named Maynard. Then, as they watched, the experimenter placed a ferocious-looking dog mask on Maynard and asked them, "What is this animal now?" Many of the 3-year-olds asserted that Maynard was now a dog and refused to pet him. The 6-year-olds, however, could overlook the dog mask, recognizing that it did not change Maynard's catness. As children grow older, they begin to attend less to perceptually salient features and focus more on abstract qualities (Anglin, 1977; Ausubel et al., 1978; Keil, 1989).

One logical strategy for enhancing concept learning, then, is to highlight a concept's defining features while downplaying its irrelevant ones. For instance, a science teacher who creates a line drawing to illustrate the concept of *insect* might make an insect's essential characteristics (e.g., six legs, three body parts) more noticeable by outlining them with dark, thick lines. Similarly, a music teacher who wants to help students learn about *three-quarter time* might have them tap out the rhythm with drumsticks or their fingers as they listen to waltzes and other songs that have three beats to a measure.

• *Concepts are easier to learn when defining and correlational features are numerous and redundant.* As defining and correlational features become increasingly numerous and redundant, positive instances become easier to pick out (Good & Brophy, 1986). For example, the concept *bird* is relatively easy to learn, because many characteristics—feathers, wings, beak, small size, and scrawny legs and feet—are either defining or correlational features. The concept *weed* is more difficult because it has only two defining features, and one of them is fairly abstract: It is a plant, and it is in the wrong place at the wrong time.

Although correlational features often make positive instances easier to identify, students who are overly dependent on them will sometimes make errors. More specifically, they may either overgeneralize (i.e., identify something as an example of a concept when in fact it is not) or undergeneralize (i.e., overlook a true example of a concept). Clearly, then, teachers must make clear to students which features are truly essential for concept membership and which features are present only some of the time.

• *Definitions facilitate concept learning* (Fukkink & de Glopper, 1998; R. M. Gagné, 1985; Tennyson & Cocchiarella, 1986). A good definition includes defining features plus any rules related to them (e.g., "all defining features must be present"). Furthermore, it describes the concept in terms of other concepts with which students are already familiar (R. M. Gagné, 1985). Definitions and other explicit descriptions may be especially helpful when concepts involve a number of defining features or reflect certain relationships among features—in other words, when they involve conjunctive, disjunctive, or relational rules.

• *Numerous and varied positive instances help to illustrate a concept* (Clark, 1971; R. M. Gagné, 1985; Merrill & Tennyson, 1977, 1978; Tennyson & Cocchiarella, 1986). Through encountering many instances of concepts, people can form prototypes of those concepts. In some situations, in fact, providing a "best example" is more helpful than offering a definition. To illustrate, Park (1984) used two instructional methods to teach basic psychology concepts (e.g., positive and negative reinforcement) to high school students. For some students, instruction focused on the defining features of the concepts; for others, it focused on illustrative examples of the concepts. Students for whom defining features were emphasized were better able to classify new examples during instruction. However, students who had been given examples of the concepts remembered more of what they had learned after instruction was completed. Ideally, of course, definitions and examples should be presented hand in hand, and, in fact, this combination of methods leads to more effective concept learning than either method alone (Dunn, 1983; Tennyson, Youngers, & Suebsonthi, 1983).

Concepts are better learned with many examples than with only one or two (Kinnick, 1990; Tennyson & Park, 1980; Tennyson & Tennyson, 1975). First examples should be simple and straightforward, with as few irrelevant features as possible (Clark, 1971; Merrill & Tennyson, 1977, 1978). Later examples should be more difficult, with more irrelevant features present (Clark, 1971; Kinnick, 1990; Merrill & Tennyson, 1977). Ultimately, examples should illustrate the full range of the concept so that students do not undergeneralize (Merrill & Tennyson, 1978; Tennyson & Cocchiarella, 1986); for example, the concept *mammal* should be illustrated by whales and platypuses as well as by cats and dogs.

• *Negative instances are useful in demonstrating what a concept is **not*** (Clark, 1971; Freiburgs & Tulving, 1961; R. M. Gagné, 1985; Merrill & Tennyson, 1977; Tennyson & Cocchiarella, 1986; Winston, 1973). Although negative instances were viewed as relatively unimportant by early theorists (Hovland & Weiss, 1953; Smoke, 1932), their importance has more recently been recognized. Negative instances, especially when they are *near misses* to the concept, are helpful in defining the concept's limits and in preventing overgeneralization (Merrill & Tennyson, 1977; Winston, 1973). For example, in learning about dogs, students can be shown that such similar-looking animals as cats, goats, and cows are nondogs in order to learn just where to draw the line on dogness.

• *Positive and negative instances are more effective when presented simultaneously.* In their everyday lives, people typically learn concepts through **sequential presentation:** They encounter a series of positive and negative instances one at a time over a period of weeks, months, or years and in the process they may gain information about what is and is not an example of the concept. A faster way to learn concepts is **simultaneous presentation,** in which

Concepts are best learned through a simultaneous presentation of both positive and negative instances.

Each of these is a dog.

None of these is a dog.

people can see a number of positive and negative instances all at once (Bourne, Ekstrand, & Dominowski, 1971; Ellis & Hunt, 1983; R. M. Gagné, 1985). One likely reason for the difference in effectiveness of the two presentation methods is that in sequential presentation, the learner must store in memory what is learned from each instance, and that information can be forgotten from one instance to the next. In simultaneous presentation, however, the information to be gleaned from positive and negative instances is available all at once, so demands on memory are not as great.

• *Classroom assessment tasks can enhance as well as monitor concept learning.* Do students truly understand what a concept is, or have they simply memorized a definition in a rote, meaningless fashion? To find out, teachers can ask students to select positive instances of the concept from among numerous possibilities (Kinnick, 1990; Merrill & Tennyson, 1977; Tennyson & Cocchiarella, 1986). One theorist has called this strategy an *eg hunt*, a tongue-in-cheek variation of "e.g." (Thiagarajan, 1989). Students who have not completely mastered a concept will be unable to identify all positive and negative instances accurately, particularly in borderline cases. For instance, in one study (P. Wilson, 1988), sixth and eighth graders were asked to define the concept *rectangle*: Many of them defined a rectangle in such a way that squares were (appropriately) included. Yet, when shown a variety of shapes and asked to identify the rectangles, the great majority of students who had correctly defined the concept of rectangle nevertheless did *not* identify any squares as being positive instances.

In addition, teachers might ask students to generate their *own* examples and applications of a concept; by doing so, they encourage students to check and refine their current understandings (Ellis & Hunt, 1983; Watts & Anderson, 1971). The benefits of self-generated examples and applications are illustrated in an experiment in which high school students received instruction in basic psychological concepts (Watts & Anderson, 1971). Students who were asked to apply those concepts to new situations remembered more of the material than students who were asked merely to recall certain facts.

Concepts are among the simplest ways in which we organize the world around us. Oftentimes we organize concepts into larger, more comprehensive understandings. Our next topics of discussion, *schemas* and *scripts*, are examples of how we might pull several concepts together.

SCHEMAS AND SCRIPTS

As you should recall from Chapter 8, Jean Piaget used the term *scheme* to refer to a mental unit representing a class of similar actions or thoughts. More recently, psychologists have been using a similar term but in a somewhat different sense. In contemporary cognitive theory, the term **schema** usually refers to a closely connected set of ideas (including concepts) related to a specific object or event (Anderson & Pearson, 1984; Bartlett, 1932; Dansereau, 1995; Derry, 1996; Rumelhart & Ortony, 1977). For example, you probably have a schema for what a faculty member's *office* is typically like: It is usually a small room that contains a desk, one or more chairs, bookshelves with books, and other items useful in performing academic duties. You undoubtedly also have a schema about the nature of physical *substances*—a schema that includes ideas such as the following:

- A substance has a location: It is somewhere in particular.
- A substance is stable: It doesn't simply appear or disappear without cause.
- A substance is sensitive to gravity: It will fall toward the Earth if nothing holds it up.
- A substance can move: For instance, it can be pushed. (Reiner, Slotta, Chi, & Resnick, 2000)

Our schemas often influence how we perceive and remember new situations. For instance, your schema of a faculty office might distort your later memory of what a particular office was actually like. In a study by Brewer and Treyens (1981), 30 college students were brought, one at a time, to a room they believed to be the experimenter's university office. After waiting in the office for less than a minute, they were taken to another room and asked to write down everything they could remember about the room. Most students correctly remembered things that one would expect to find in an office (e.g., a desk, a chair, and shelves). Relatively few of them remembered items not likely to be part of an office schema (e.g., a skull, a clown-shaped light switch, and a tennis racket). And 9 of the 30 "remembered" books that weren't there at all!

People often form schemas about events as well as objects; such event schemas are sometimes called **scripts** (Bower et al., 1979; Dansereau, 1995; Schank, 1975; Schank & Abelson, 1977). As an illustration, consider the following situation:

> John was feeling bad today so he decided to go see the family doctor. He checked in with the doctor's receptionist, and then looked through several medical magazines that were on the table by his chair. Finally the nurse came and asked him to take off his clothes. The doctor was very nice to him. He eventually prescribed some pills for John. Then John left the doctor's office and headed home. (Bower et al., 1979, p. 190)

You probably had no trouble understanding the passage because you have been to a doctor's office yourself and have a script for how those visits usually go. You can therefore fill in a number of details that the passage doesn't ever tell you. You probably inferred that John must have *traveled* to the doctor's office, although the story omits this essential step. Likewise, you probably concluded that John took his clothes off in the examination room, *not* in the waiting room, even though the story never makes it clear where John did his striptease. As you can see, then, a person's mental script for an event will influence what information is "learned" from a given instance of that event. In a study by Bower and colleagues (1979), college students read the same passage you just read. The students in the experiment "remembered" reading about many activities that were likely to be part of a visit to the doctor (e.g., arriving at the doctor's office) but that they had in fact *not* read.

Other research provides further support for the idea that schemas and scripts influence how learners process, store, and remember new information. To illustrate, people have an easier time making sense of poems from various historical periods when they have well-developed schemas for poems written in each of those periods (Peskin, 1998). Many people (especially those with stereotypical schemas about how males and females behave) more accurately remember pictures and films that portray men and women behaving in a gender-stereotypical rather than counter-sterotypical manner (Cordua, McGraw, & Drabman, 1979; Martin & Halverson, 1981; Signorella & Liben, 1984). People also have an easier time remembering events similar to those in their own culture, presumably because such events are consistent with recognizable scripts (Lipson, 1983; Reynolds, Taylor, Steffensen, Shirey, & Anderson, 1982; Steffensen, Joag-Dev, & Anderson, 1979). And consider the following story about two boys playing hooky:

> The two boys ran until they came to the driveway. "See, I told you today was good for skipping school," said Mark. "Mom is never home on Thursday," he added. Tall hedges hid the house from the road so the pair strolled across the finely landscaped yard. "I never knew your place was so big," said Pete. "Yeah, but it's nicer now than it used to be since Dad had the new stone siding put on and added the fireplace."
>
> There were front and back doors and a side door which led to the garage which was empty except for three parked 10-speed bikes. They went in the side door, Mark explaining that it was always open in case his younger sisters got home earlier than their mother.
>
> Pete wanted to see the house so Mark started with the living room. It, like the rest of the downstairs, was newly painted. Mark turned on the stereo, the noise of which worried Pete. "Don't worry, the nearest house is a quarter of a mile away," Mark shouted. Pete felt more comfortable observing that no houses could be seen in any direction beyond the huge yard.
>
> The dining room, with all the china, silver, and cut glass, was no place to play so the boys moved into the kitchen where they made sandwiches. Mark said they wouldn't go to the basement because it had been damp and musty ever since the new plumbing had been installed. (Pichert & Anderson, 1977, p. 310)

You will probably remember different details from the story, depending on whether you read it from the perspective of a potential home buyer or a potential burglar (Anderson & Pichert, 1978). Different schemas and scripts come into play for buying versus burgling a home.

As we noted in Chapter 9, the human memory system typically encounters more information than it can possibly handle. Schemas and scripts provide a means for reducing this information overload: They help people to focus their attention on things that are likely to be important and to ignore what is probably unimportant (Goetz, Schallert, Reynolds, & Radin, 1983; Martin & Halverson, 1981; Wilson & Anderson, 1986). For example, when going to see the doctor, it is more important to check in with the receptionist than to remember the pictures on the waiting room wall. Schemas also enable people to make sense of incomplete information (R. C. Anderson, 1984; Dansereau, 1995; Martin & Halverson, 1981; Rumelhart & Ortony, 1977; Wilson & Anderson, 1986). As a result, individuals may "remember" things that they never specifically encountered but instead filled in using their existing schemas and scripts (Bower et al., 1979; Farrar & Goodman, 1992; Flavell et al., 1993; Kardash, Royer, & Greene, 1988).

Schema theory has intuitive appeal as a way of helping us understand how we organize our past experiences and use what we've learned to predict and interpret future experiences. It has been criticized for being somewhat vague, however; for example, theorists have not been very precise regarding what schemas and scripts actually *are* (Dansereau, 1995; Reynolds et al., 1996). Furthermore, although we can reasonably assume that people form and modify schemas and scripts based on the specific objects and events they encounter in their lives (Flavell et al., 1993; Pressley, with McCormick, 1995; Rumelhart, 1980), the cognitive processes that occur during this learning are not at all clear.

Schemas and scripts usually relate to relatively specific objects and events. Another concept—that of *personal theories*—may help us understand how people may organize their knowledge and beliefs on a much grander scale.

PERSONAL THEORIES

Numerous psychologists have speculated that people form general **personal theories**[5]—coherent belief systems that encompass cause–effect relationships—about many aspects of the world around them, including physical phenomena, biological phenomena, social relationships, political entities, and mental events (e.g., diSessa, 1996; Flavell, 2000; Hatano & Inagaki, 1996; Keil & Silberstein, 1996; Kuhn, 2001b; Torney-Purta, 1994; Wellman & Gelman, 1992). This perspective of how people organize knowledge is sometimes known as **theory theory.** No, you're not seeing double here: We're discussing a theoretical perspective about people's everyday theories.

As an illustration of this approach, take a minute to read the two scenarios in Figure 11–9 (which appears on the following page) and answer the questions that each one poses.

Chances are, you concluded that the coffeepot had been transformed into a bird feeder but that the raccoon was still a raccoon despite its radical surgery; even fourth graders come to these conclusions (Keil, 1986, 1989). Now how is it possible that the coffeepot could be made into something entirely different, whereas the raccoon could not?

The concepts that people form are influenced in part by the theories they have about how the world operates (Keil, 1986, 1989, 1994; Medin, 1989; Neisser, 1987; Reisberg, 1997). For instance, even young children seem to make a basic distinction between man-made objects (e.g., coffeepots and bird feeders) and biological entities (e.g., raccoons and skunks) (Hatano & Inagaki, 1996; Massey & Gelman, 1988). Furthermore, children seem to conceptualize the two categories in fundamentally different ways: Man-made objects are defined largely by the *functions* they serve (e.g., keeping coffee warm or feeding birds), whereas biological entities are defined primarily by their origins (e.g., the parents who brought them into being or their DNA). Thus, when a coffeepot begins to hold birdseed rather than coffee, it becomes a bird feeder by virtue of the fact that its function has changed. But when a raccoon is surgically altered to look like a skunk, it still has raccoon parents and raccoon DNA and so cannot possibly *be* a skunk (Keil, 1987, 1989). Thinking along similar lines, even preschoolers will tell you that you cannot change a yellow finch into a bluebird by giving it a coat of blue paint or dressing it in a "bluebird" costume (Keil, 1989).

---

[5]Theorists typically refer simply to *theories* (occasionally, they use the term *folk theories*) rather than to personal theories. I use the term *personal theories* here to distinguish these mental entities from the psychological theories we've been discussing throughout the book.

1.   Doctors took a coffeepot that looked like this:

They sawed off the handle, sealed the top, took off the top knob, and sawed off and sealed the spout. They also sawed off the base and attached a flat piece of metal. They attached a little stick, cut a window in it, and filled the metal container with bird food. When they were done, it looked like this:

After the operation, was this a coffeepot or a bird feeder?

2.   Doctors took this raccoon:

and shaved away some of its fur. They dyed what was left all black. Then they bleached a single stripe all white down the center of its back. Then, with surgery, they put in its body a sac of super-smelly odor, just like a skunk has. When they were all done, the animal looked like this:

After the operation, was this a skunk or a raccoon?

Figure 11–9
What the doctors did.
Both scenarios based on Keil, 1989, p. 184.

People's personal theories about the world seem to guide them as they identify potential defining features of concepts they are learning (Keil, 1987, 1989; McCauley, 1987; Mervis, 1987). For example, if you were trying to learn what a *horse* is, the fact that you know it's an animal would lead you to conclude that its location (in a stable, a pasture, a shopping mall, or wherever) is an irrelevant feature. In contrast, if you were trying to learn what the *equator* is, knowing it's something on a map of the world should lead you to suspect that location is of the utmost importance.

More generally, personal theories help people organize and make sense of personal experiences, classroom subject matter, and other new information (Reiner et al., 2000; Wellman & Gelman, 1998). Although theory theory has been criticized for offering only vague descriptions of the nature and structure of a personal theory (Siegler, 1998), it is nevertheless quite useful in helping us understand why people sometimes misconstrue the world around them, as we shall see now.

Personal Theories Versus Reality

A few theorists have argued that we can never completely know what is "real" or "true" about the world because knowledge and reasoning processes are constructed, and therefore man-made, entities (e.g., Lakoff & Núñez, 1997; von Glasersfeld, 1995).[6] Be that as it may, some ways of understanding the world are certainly more *useful* than others: They align themselves fairly closely with our day-to-day observations, and they enable us to make predictions about future events with considerable accuracy (Chinn, 1998; Tobin & Tippins, 1993).

Theories about the world begin to emerge in the early months of life, long before children encounter formal scientific theories at school. In our discussion of *core knowledge* in Chapter 2, we saw evidence that 3- to 4-month-old infants have already begun to form a theory about the physical world: They are surprised when solid objects seem to be suspended in midair or appear to pass directly through other objects. Apparently, then, their early theories of physics include rudimentary understandings of gravity and of the principle that only one object can occupy a particular place at a particular time (Baillargeon, 1994; Spelke, 1994; Wynn & Chiang, 1998). Young infants also seem to know that people are fundamentally different from inanimate objects: People, but not objects, are active, self-propelling, and responsive to others (Poulin-Dubois, 1999). As children grow older and encounter many new experiences and a great deal of new information, they continually expand on and revise their theories about the physical world, the biological world, and the social and mental aspects of human beings (e.g., Keil & Silberstein, 1996; Wellman & Gelman, 1992).

The personal theories that children form are not always consistent with the theories that experts in a particular field have developed, however (e.g., diSessa, 1996; Duit, 1991; Halldén, 1994; C. L. Smith, Maclin, Grosslight, & Davis, 1997). For example, what is *rain*? Here is one seven-year-old's explanation:

> Clouds think it's too hot, and one day they start sweating. I guess they start sweating and then the sweat falls on us. (Stepans, 1991, p. 95)

And what shape is the earth that the rain falls on? Some fifth graders might tell you that it's "round, like a thick pancake" (Vosniadou, 1994). Many Japanese children believe that plants and inanimate objects have "minds" similar to those of humans; although this idea isn't consistent with contemporary scientific thinking, it *is* consistent with certain aspects of Japanese culture (Hatano & Inagaki, 1996).

Even adults don't always have their facts straight. For example, my husband, who teaches geography at the college level, tells me that some of his students believe that rivers always run from north to south (after all, water can only run "downhill") and that the Great Lakes contain saltwater. I find misconceptions in my own college classes as well, such as the belief that negative reinforcement involves the presentation of an aversive stimulus (see Chapter 4 for the correct explanation) and the belief that rote learning is more effective than meaningful learning (Lennon, Ormrod, Burger, & Warren, 1990). And many adults, especially before they take a course in physics, think that in order to keep an object moving through space, one must continually apply force to the object; this notion is inconsistent with physicists' principle of *inertia* (diSessa, 1996).

Figure 11–10 lists some of the misconceptions that researchers have observed in children, and in some cases, in adults as well. People's erroneous notions about the world probably have a variety of sources. Sometimes misconceptions result from how things *appear* to be (Byrnes,

---

[6]This perspective is sometimes called *radical constructivism.*

In biology

- A living thing is something that moves and/or grows. The sun, wind, clouds, and fire are living things (Kyle & Shymansky, 1989).
- Plants "eat" soil, fertilizer, and water, just as people eat more "humanly" food (Roth & Anderson, 1988). (From the perspective of biology, plants produce their own food through the process of photosynthesis.)
- Vision involves something moving outward from the eye toward the object being seen (Winer & Cottrell, 1996; Winer et al., 2002). (In reality, the opposite is true: Light rays bounce off the object to the eye.)

In astronomy

- The Earth is bigger than the sun and stars (Vosniadou, 1991).
- The sun revolves around the Earth. It "rises" in the morning and "sets" in the evening, at which point it "goes" to the other side of the Earth (Vosniadou, 1991; Vosniadou & Brewer, 1987).
- The Earth is shaped like a round, flat disk (Nussbaum, 1985; Sneider & Pulos, 1983; Vosniadou, 1994; Vosniadou & Brewer, 1987).
- Space has an absolute "up" and "down"; people standing at the South Pole will fall off the Earth (Sneider & Pulos, 1983).

In physics

- Objects exist for a purpose. For example, some rocks are pointy so that animals that live nearby can scratch themselves when they have an itch (Kelemen, 1999).

- Any moving object has a force acting on it. For example, a ball thrown in the air continues to be pushed upward by the force of the throw until it begins its descent (Carey, 1986; diSessa, 1996; Kyle & Shymansky, 1989). (In reality, force is needed only to change the direction or speed of an object; otherwise, *inertia* is at work.)
- Gravity is the "glue" that holds people to the Earth. There is no gravity without air (Kyle & Shymansky, 1989).
- When an electric current lights up a lightbulb, it is "used up" (consumed) by the lightbulb and disappears (Kyle & Shymansky, 1989). (In reality, the current flows back to the power source from which it originated.)

In geography, history, and social studies

- The lines separating countries or states are marked on the Earth (Gardner, Torff, & Hatch, 1996).
- Islands float on top of the ocean (Gardner et al., 1996).
- Christopher Columbus was the first person to believe that the world is round rather than flat (Hynd, 2003).
- People are poor only because they don't have enough money to buy a job. Giving a poor person a small amount of money will make that person rich (Delval, 1994).
- People can move from one social class to another by making superficial changes, perhaps by changing from rags to nice clothing, furs, and jewelry (Delval, 1994).

Figure 11–10
Examples of common misconceptions.

1996; diSessa, 1996; Duit, 1991); for example, from our perspective living here on the Earth's surface, the sun looks as if it moves around the Earth, rather than vice versa. Sometimes misconceptions are fostered by common expressions in language; for instance, we often talk about the sun "rising" and "setting" (Duit, 1991; Mintzes, Trowbridge, Arnaudin, & Wandersee, 1991; Roth & Anderson, 1988; Stepans, 1991). Sometimes people infer incorrect cause–effect relationships between two events simply because those events often occur at the same time

(Byrnes, 1996; Keil, 1991). Perhaps even fairy tales and television cartoon shows play a role in promoting misconceptions (Glynn, Yeany, & Britton, 1991); as an example, after cartoon "bad guys" run off the edge of a cliff, they usually remain suspended in air until they realize that there's nothing solid holding them up. And unfortunately, it is sometimes the case that we acquire erroneous ideas because we have seen or heard them from others; in some instances, teachers or textbooks even give us such misinformation (Begg, Anas, & Farinacci, 1992; Duit, 1991).

The Challenge of Conceptual Change

In some cases, replacing an erroneous belief with a more accurate one is fairly straightforward. For instance, if you think that my birthday is January 1, I can simply tell you that, no, January 1 is *my brother's* birthday—*mine* is August 22—and you may very well make the mental adjustment. But when a naïve belief or misconception is part of a larger theory about the world, a major overhaul may be in order. The process of replacing one personal theory or belief system with another, presumably better one is known as **conceptual change**.[7]

Research in classrooms indicates that students of all ages often hold quite stubbornly to their misconceptions about the world, even after considerable instruction that explicitly contradicts those misconceptions (Anderson, Sheldon, & Dubay, 1990; Borko & Putnam, 1996; Carey, 1986; Chambliss, 1994; Champagne, Klopfer, & Gunstone, 1982; Chinn & Brewer, 1993; Holt-Reynolds, 1992; Roth, 1990; Shuell, 1996; Winer et al., 2002). Why are people's misconceptions often so resistant to change? Theorists have offered several possible explanations:

- *People's existing beliefs affect their interpretations of new information.* Thanks to the processes of meaningful learning and elaboration—processes that usually facilitate learning—learners are more likely to interpret new information in ways that are consistent with what they already "know" about the world, to the point where they continue to believe what they have always believed. Generally speaking, maintaining existing perspectives, rather than considering alternative and possibly conflicting ones, is the "default" mode in human cognition (De Lisi & Golbeck, 1999).

- *Most people have a confirmation bias.* Learners of all ages (college students included) tend to look for information that confirms their existing beliefs and to ignore or discredit any contradictory evidence—a phenomenon known as **confirmation bias** (Chinn & Brewer, 1993; Duit, 1991; Kuhn, Amsel, & O'Loughlin, 1988; Minstrell & Stimpson, 1996; Schauble, 1990). For example, when students in a high school science lab observe results that contradict what they expected to happen, they might complain that "Our equipment isn't working right" or "I can never do science anyway" (Minstrell & Stimpson, 1996).

- *People's existing beliefs are often consistent with their everyday experiences.* Truly accurate explanations of physical phenomena (e.g., commonly accepted principles or theories in physics) are often fairly abstract and difficult to relate to everyday reality (Alexander, 1997; Driver, Asoko, Leach, Mortimer, & Scott, 1994; Linn et al., 1996; Mintzes et al., 1991). For example, although the

---

[7]Some theorists use the term *conceptual change* in reference to *any* situation in which one belief or set of beliefs is replaced by another, even a situation as simple as revising a belief about a person's birthday. They may refer to more extensive changes (the "overhaul" variety) as *radical conceptual change, restructuring,* or *reconstruction.*

law of inertia tells us that force is needed to *start* an object in motion but not to *keep* it in motion, we know from experience that if we want to move a heavy object across the floor, we must keep on pushing it until we get it where we want it (Driver et al., 1994). Consider, too, Newton's second law: Force is a product of mass and acceleration ($F = ma$). This law tells us that acceleration must *always* accompany force—an idea that many people have difficulty relating to their own observations. A young woman taking an introductory college physics course expressed her confusion this way:

> I want it to be true, but there's just no way it is, you know . . . I don't know why I just started doubting myself because that stupid force formula. . . . I mean I want what seems logical to me to make sense with what I've learned and what you can, like, you know, like when we were talking about the formulas. I mean you learn these formulas and you apply them to all these problems. But when something that you know is true—I mean to me it makes so much sense that it's crazy to even debate it, that if you're pushing this with a constant force, and you see it moving, that it's not accelerating. (diSessa, Elby, & Hammer, 2003, pp. 275–276, emphasis removed)

• *Some erroneous beliefs are integrated into a cohesive whole, with many interrelationships existing among various ideas.* In such instances, changing misconceptions involves changing an entire organized body of knowledge—an entire theory—rather than a single belief (Chambliss, 1994; Derry, 1996; Duit, 1991). For example, the belief that the sun revolves around the Earth may be part of a more general "Earth-centered" view of things, perhaps one that includes the moon, stars, and various other heavenly bodies revolving around the Earth as well. In reality, of course, the moon revolves around the Earth, the Earth revolves around the sun, and the other stars are not directly involved with the Earth one way or the other. Yet the Earth-centered view is a much easier one to understand and accept (on the surface, at least), and everything fits so nicely together.

• *People may fail to see an inconsistency between new information and their prior beliefs.* In many situations, people learn new information without letting go of their prior beliefs, so that two inconsistent ideas remain in long-term memory simultaneously (Chambliss, 1994; Keil & Silberstein, 1996; Mintzes et al., 1991; Winer & Cottrell, 1996). Sometimes this happens because people learn the new information at a rote level, without relating it to the things they already know and believe (Chambliss, 1994; Strike & Posner, 1992). In other cases, it may occur because existing misconceptions take the form of *implicit knowledge*—knowledge that cannot consciously be accessed (Keil & Silberstein, 1996; Strike & Posner, 1992). In either situation, people do not realize that the new things they have learned contradict what they already believe, and they may continue to apply their misconceptions when interpreting new situations (Champagne et al., 1982; Hynd, 2003; Luque, 2003).

• *People may have a personal or emotional investment in their existing beliefs.* For one reason or another, people may be especially committed to certain beliefs, perhaps insisting that "This theory is what I believe in! Nobody can make me change it!" (Mason, 2003, p. 228). In some instances, their beliefs may be an integral part of their religion or culture (Hatano & Inagaki, 1996; Southerland & Sinatra, 2003). In other cases, people may interpret challenges to their belief systems as threats to their overall self-esteem (Linnenbrink & Pintrich, 2003; Luque, 2003; Minstrell & Stimpson, 1996; Sherman & Cohen, 2002).

• *Sometimes people's existing beliefs are supported by their social environment.* To the extent that others in a learner's support network (e.g., one's family, peer group, or political party) hold a particular set of beliefs, the learner will have less reason to abandon those beliefs (Hatano & Inagaki,

2003). We see the effect of social context even in highly educated academic communities. For instance, the dominance of behaviorism in North American psychology in the first few decades of the twentieth century encouraged most budding psychologists to take an S-R approach to learning and to reject quite adamantly any suggestion that they look at the decidedly nonobservable phenomenon called *thinking*.

When students have few prior misunderstandings about a particular phenomenon, helping them acquire more sophisticated theories about that phenomenon is relatively easy. When they have many naïve beliefs and misconceptions about the topic, however, helping them acquire scientifically acceptable understandings is more difficult. In the latter situation, teachers face a twofold challenge: They must not only help students learn new things but also help them *unlearn*, or at least *inhibit*, existing misconceptions (Hynd, 2003). We look now at strategies for (1) fostering theory development when students are "starting from scratch" in the subject matter and (2) promoting conceptual change when students already have well-ingrained but counterproductive ideas about a topic.

Fostering Theory Development

Because personal theories (like all theories) are integrated bodies of knowledge, long-term memory storage processes that enhance such integration—for instance, meaningful learning, internal organization, and elaboration—are, of course, likely to enrich those theories. Psychologists and educators have offered additional suggestions for educators as well:

- *Physical models can help learners tie ideas together.* In some cases, learners' personal theories include **mental models**—representations of how particular concepts and principles interrelate or how a specific system works—that reflect the structure of external reality (English, 1997a; Greeno, 1991; Halford, 1993; Perfetti, Britt, Rouet, Georgi, & Mason, 1994). Instructors can facilitate the formation of accurate models by presenting physical versions of them, for example in the form of a flowchart that shows how a computer program works, a diagram that shows why pulleys can help someone lift heavy objects more easily, or a three-dimensional double helix that depicts the structure of DNA (Carney & Levin, 2002; Mayer, 1989a; Reiner et al., 2000).

- *Group interaction can enhance learners' theoretical understandings.* Often, learners acquire more sophisticated understandings when they discuss a phenomenon they have observed, exchange perspectives about it, and build on one another's ideas (e.g., Lamon, Chan, Scardamalia, Burtis, & Brett, 1993; O'Donnell & King, 1999). We will look at the nature and benefits of group interactions more closely in Chapter 15.

- *Some personal theories and mental models can be helpful even when they aren't entirely accurate.* Sometimes theories and models can help learners understand and predict phenomenon even though they don't precisely reflect what experts believe to be the "true" state of affairs. For instance, in Chapter 9, I presented the dual-store model of memory, and I have continued to refer to working memory and long-term memory as distinctive entities. Not all research findings support the dual-store model (see the section "Are Working Memory and Long-Term Memory Really Different?" in Chapter 9), and my gut instincts tell me that it is almost certainly an oversimplification of how human cognition and memory operate. Nevertheless, the working memory–long-term memory distinction is a very *useful* one that can often help us predict how students are likely to learn and perform in the classroom. Similarly, a *flow* model of how a warm substance heats a colder one (heat travels from one to the other) does not accurately capture the molecular nature of heat (molecules move more quickly in a warm substance than in a cold one). Yet the "flow" notion can often help students make reasonably accurate predictions about temperature and is especially useful when learners have only a limited ability to think abstractly about the nature of heat (Linn & Muilenburg, 1996; Reiner et al., 2000).

We mustn't take this idea too far, however. When learners' theories and models are substantially different from experts' views, they may wreak havoc with new learning. In such situations, conceptual change is clearly in order.

Promoting Conceptual Change

Theorists and researchers have offered several suggestions for getting students on the road to conceptual change:

- *Before instruction begins, teachers should determine what misconceptions about a topic exist.* Teachers can more easily address students' misconceptions when they know what those misconceptions *are* (Kyle & Shymansky, 1989; Roth & Anderson, 1988; Stepans, 1991; Vosniadou & Brewer, 1987). Thus, a lesson might begin with informal questioning or a formal pretest to probe students' current views of the subject at hand. Teachers may need to ask a series of questions to get a clear understanding of what their students really believe. The following dialogue illustrates the kinds of questions that may be in order:

Adult:	What is rain?
Child:	It's water that falls out of a cloud when the clouds evaporate.
Adult:	What do you mean, "clouds evaporate"?
Child:	That means water goes up in the air and then it makes clouds and then, when it gets too heavy up there, then the water comes and they call it rain.
Adult:	Does the water stay in the sky?
Child:	Yes, and then it comes down when it rains. It gets too heavy.
Adult:	Why does it get too heavy?
Child:	'Cause there's too much water up there.
Adult:	Why does it rain?
Child:	'Cause the water gets too heavy and then it comes down.
Adult:	Why doesn't the whole thing come down?
Child:	Well, 'cause it comes down at little times like a salt shaker when you turn it upside down. It doesn't all come down at once 'cause there's little holes and it just comes out.
Adult:	What are the little holes in the sky?
Child:	Umm, holes in the clouds, letting the water out. (dialogue from Stepans, 1991, p. 94)

This conception of a cloud as a "salt shaker" of sorts is hardly consistent with the scientifically accepted view of how and why rain comes about. As teachers gain more experience teaching a particular topic over the years, they can begin to anticipate what students' prior beliefs and misbeliefs about that topic are likely to be (e.g., Hollon, Roth, & Anderson, 1991).

• *Students should learn correct information in a meaningful rather than rote fashion.* Students will notice inconsistencies between new information and prior beliefs only when they try to make connections between the new and the old. To use levels-of-processing terminology for a moment, students are most likely to modify their misconceptions in light of new data if they process those data *in depth*—in other words, if they become actively engaged in learning and truly try to understand the information being presented (D. E. Brown, 1992; Chinn & Brewer, 1993; Howe, Tolmie, Greer, & Mackenzie, 1995; Lee & Anderson, 1993; Pintrich, Marx, & Boyle, 1993; Slusher & Anderson, 1996). Instruction is most likely to encourage meaningful learning, and therefore to promote conceptual change, when it focuses on a few key ideas rather than covering many topics superficially (diSessa, 1996; Kyle & Shymansky, 1989; Roth & Anderson, 1988).

• *Students are more apt to revise their current way of thinking when they believe revision is in order.* Many theorists suggest that conceptual change is most likely to occur when people encounter evidence that clearly contradicts what they currently believe—in other words, when they experience what Piaget called *disequilibrium.* For example, one first-grade teacher wanted to challenge her students' belief that rocks always sink in water. She showed her class two stones, a small piece of granite and a considerably larger piece of pumice. Pumice, of course, results when molten lava cools; because it has many pockets of air, it is relatively light and so can float. Before the teacher dropped the stones into a container of water, she asked the class to make a prediction, and a girl named Brianna predicted that both stones would sink. The small piece of granite did sink, but the piece of pumice floated. Brianna was noticeably agitated: *"No! No! that's not right! That doesn't go with my mind (student grabs her head) it just doesn't go with my mind"* (Hennessey, 2003, p. 121).

Theorists have offered several suggestions for how teachers might create disequilibrium and then encourage students to address it:

• Ask questions that challenge students' current beliefs.
• Present phenomena that students cannot adequately explain within their existing perspectives.
• Ask students to make predictions about what will happen in various circumstances—predictions that, given their present beliefs, are apt to be wrong.
• Encourage students to conduct experiments to test various hypotheses.
• Ask students to provide possible explanations for puzzling phenomena they have observed.
• Engage students in discussions of the pros and cons of various explanations.
• Show how one explanation of an event or phenomenon is more plausible (i.e., makes more sense) than others.
  (Andre & Windschitl, 2003; Chinn & Brewer, 1993; Chinn & Malhotra, 2002; Guzzetti, Snyder, Glass, & Gamas, 1993; Hatano & Inagaki, 2003; Howe et al., 1995; Pine & Messer, 2000; Posner, Strike, Hewson, & Gertzog, 1982; Prawat, 1989; Roth, 1990; C. L. Smith et al., 1997; Vosniadou & Brewer, 1987)

Such strategies must encompass a wide variety of instructional methods, including demonstrations, hands-on experiments, teacher explanations, and student discussions. There is certainly no single "best" instructional method for promoting conceptual change (Hynd, 1998).

• *Students must explicitly compare their existing beliefs with alternative explanations.* Students are more likely to replace a misconception with a more accurate understanding, rather than to accept the accurate understanding while also *retaining* the misconception, if they are thinking about both ideas at the same time. In other words, the erroneous and accurate beliefs should both be in working memory simultaneously. Unfortunately, many textbook authors seem to be oblivious to this point: When they present new ideas in science or history, they neglect to point out that these ideas may be inconsistent with what students currently believe. The result is that students often do *not* shed their misconceptions in the face of contradictory information (deLeeuw & Chi, 2003; McKeown & Beck, 1990; Otero, 1998; Southerland & Sinatra, 2003).

One strategy for encouraging students to compare various beliefs and explanations is to engage them in discussions about the pros and cons of each one (Prawat, 1989; C. Smith et al., 1997). Yet textbooks can present the pros and cons of various perspectives as well. One effective approach is **refutational text,** in which possible objections to a particular explanation are presented but then discredited. In this way, students are persuaded to "buy into" the preferred explanation and also "inoculated" against accepting counterarguments that they might encounter at a future time (Hynd, 2003).

• *Students must **want** to learn the correct explanation.* Students are most likely to engage in deep processing and meaningful learning when they are motivated to do so (Hatano & Inagaki, 1993; Lee & Anderson, 1993; Pintrich et al., 1993). At a minimum, they must be interested in the subject matter, believe it will help them achieve their personal goals, set their sights on mastering it, and have sufficient self-efficacy to believe that they *can* master it (Andre & Windschitl, 2003; Hynd, 2003; Pintrich et al., 1993). Furthermore, students must not see the new, contradictory information as in some way threatening their self-esteem (Minstrell & Stimpson, 1996; Sherman & Cohen, 2002). And ideally, the classroom should be socially and emotionally supportive of conceptual change (Hatano & Inagaki, 2003). For instance, students must feel confident that their teacher and classmates will not ridicule them for expressing logical but incorrect ideas, and they must believe that the ultimate goal of a lesson is understanding the subject matter rather than simply performing well on a quiz or assignment. As we consider motivation in Chapters 16 through 18, we'll identify strategies for accomplishing such things.

Some theorists have suggested that it may sometimes be easier to help students *understand* new explanations than to make students *believe* and *accept* them, especially when the subject matter involves controversial issues such as evolution, capital punishment, or abortion (Eagly, Kulesa, Chen, & Chaiken, 2001; Kuhn, Shaw, & Felton, 1997; Sinatra, Southerland, McConaughy, & Demastes, in press; Southerland & Sinatra, 2003). Probably the most defensible approach when dealing with controversial issues is to help students understand the reasoning behind various perspectives, as well as the evidence for and against each one, but to acknowledge that students must ultimately come to conclusions consistent with their own moral and religious convictions (Sinatra et al., in press; Southerland & Sinatra, 2003).

• *Throughout a lesson, students' understanding should be monitored for particularly tenacious misconceptions.* Because of human beings' natural tendency to reinterpret new information in light of what they already "know," some misconceptions may persist in spite of a teacher's best efforts. These misconceptions are sometimes blatantly incorrect; at other times, they may be sort-of-but-not-quite correct. To illustrate the latter situation, let's consider an example offered by Roth and Anderson (1988), once again dealing with students' understanding of vision. Students sometimes define *transparent* as "something you can see through." Although such a definition is consistent with how we generally speak about transparency, it may nevertheless reflect the erroneous belief that sight originates with the eye and goes outward to and through the transparent object. *Transparent* is more accurately defined as "something light passes through." In the following class discussion, the teacher probes students' reasoning about transparency, uncovers a potential misconception, and encourages students to offer a scientifically more accurate explanation:

Ms. Ramsey:	(Puts up transparency) Why can't the girl see around the wall?
Annie:	The girl can't see around the wall because the wall is opaque.
Ms. Ramsey:	What do you mean when you say the wall is opaque?
Annie:	*You can't see through it. It is solid.*
Brian:	(calling out) The rays are what can't go through the wall.
Ms. Ramsey:	I like that answer better. Why is it better?
Brian:	The rays of light bounce off the car and go to the wall. They can't go through the wall.
Ms. Ramsey:	Where are the light rays coming from originally?
Students:	The sun.
Annie:	*The girl can't see the car because she is not far enough out.*
Ms. Ramsey:	So you think her position is what is keeping her from seeing it. (She flips down the overlay with the answer.) Who was better?
Students:	Brian.
Ms. Ramsey:	(to Annie) Would she be able to see if she moved out beyond the wall?
Annie:	Yes.
Ms. Ramsey:	Why?
Annie:	*The wall is blocking her view.*
Ms. Ramsey:	Is it blocking her view? What is it blocking?
Student:	Light rays.
Ms. Ramsey:	Light rays that are doing what?
Annie:	If the girl moves out beyond the wall, then the light rays that bounce off the car are not being blocked. (Roth and Anderson, 1988, pp. 129–130)

Notice how Ms. Ramsey is not satisfied with Annie's original answer that the wall is opaque. With further questioning, it becomes clear that Annie's understanding of opaqueness is off target: She talks about the girl being unable to "see through" the wall rather than light's inability to pass through the wall. With Ms. Ramsey's continuing insistence on precise language, Annie eventually begins to bring light rays into her explanation (Roth & Anderson, 1988).

Assessment of students' comprehension is important *after* a lesson as well. Teachers are more likely to detect misconceptions when they ask students to *use* and *apply* the things they have learned (as Ms. Ramsey does in the conversation just presented) rather than simply to spit back facts, definitions, and formulas memorized at a rote level (Roth, 1990; Roth & Anderson, 1988).

As you have seen, teachers can do a variety of things to nudge learners toward conceptual change. But ultimately, learners themselves are in control of the cognitive processes (meaningful learning, internal organization, elaboration, etc.) that will enable them to make sense of new ideas and thereby acquire more accurate understandings. Their proficiency in directing their own learning efforts and their understanding of what it actually *means* to learn something are key elements in their ability to revise their thinking about classroom subject matter. Accordingly, we will revisit the topic of conceptual change after we have discussed metacognition in Chapter 13.

How readily conceptual change comes about may also be partly a function of how much knowledge learners have about a topic and how well they have already organized and integrated what they currently know and believe. We look now at how people's knowledge about a topic may change over time—that is, at the development of expertise.

DEVELOPMENT OF EXPERTISE

Obviously, people acquire an increasing amount of information in their long-term memories over time. Many people eventually acquire a great deal of information about a particular topic or subject matter, to the point where we can say they are *experts* in their field. It appears, however, that experts don't just know more than their peers; their knowledge is also *qualitatively* different from that of others. In particular, their knowledge tends to be tightly organized, with many interrelationships among the things that they know and with many abstract generalizations unifying more concrete details (Alexander & Judy, 1988; Bédard & Chi, 1992; Proctor & Dutta, 1995; Zeitz, 1994). Such qualities enable experts to retrieve the things they need more easily, to find parallels between seemingly diverse situations, and to solve problems more effectively (Chi, Glaser, & Rees, 1982; De Corte, Greer, & Verschaffel, 1996; Rabinowitz & Glaser, 1985; Voss, Greene, Post, & Penner, 1983).

Patricia Alexander (1997, 1998) has suggested that there may be three somewhat distinct stages in the development of knowledge related to a particular subject matter. At the first stage, which she calls *acclimation*, learners familiarize themselves with a new content domain, much as someone might do by taking an introductory course in biology, economics, or art history. At this point, they pick up a lot of facts that they tend to store in relative isolation from one another. As a result of such "fragmented" learning, they are likely to hold on to many misconceptions that they may have acquired before they started studying the subject systematically.

At the second stage, which Alexander calls *competence*, learners acquire considerably more information about the subject matter, and they also acquire some general principles that help tie the information together. Because learners at the competence stage make numerous interconnections among the things they learn, they are likely to correct many of the specific misconceptions they have previously developed. Those misconceptions that remain, however, are apt to pervade much of their thinking about the subject. At the competence stage, learners' entire approach to the subject matter begins to resemble that of experts; for example, they may start to "think like a historian" or to engage in some of their own scientific research. Competence is something that people acquire only after studying a particular subject in depth, perhaps through an undergraduate major, a master's degree, or several years of professional experience.

At the final stage—*expertise*—we can say that learners have truly mastered their field. They know a great deal about the subject matter, and they have pulled much of their knowledge together into a tightly integrated whole. At this point, they are helping to lead the way in terms of conducting research, proposing new ways of looking at things, solving problems, and, in general, making new knowledge. Expertise comes only after many years of studying and experience in a particular field; as a result, few learners ever reach this stage.

Because knowledge at the competence and expertise stages is fairly well integrated, any misconceptions at either of these stages may be especially resistant to change (Alexander, 1998).

As an example, let's return to our discussion of verbal learning research in Chapter 8. Initially, verbal learning researchers (most of them certainly experts in psychology) tried to explain human language–based learning within the context of behaviorism, the predominant theoretical perspective of the time. It was only after several *decades*, as evidence that behaviorist principles could *not* explain continued to mount up, that these researchers abandoned their S–R explanations for more cognitive ones.[8]

Alexander points out that the development of expertise depends not only on the acquisition of knowledge but also on effective learning strategies and a strong interest in the subject matter. We will identify many effective learning strategies in Chapter 13, and we will examine the specific benefits of interest in Chapter 17.

GENERALIZATIONS ABOUT THE NATURE OF KNOWLEDGE

In this chapter we have considered a variety of perspectives about how knowledge in long-term memory might be encoded and organized. At this point, let's make some final generalizations about the nature of knowledge:

• *There can be considerable redundancy in how information is stored.* Earlier in the chapter, I mentioned a finding by Rips et al. (1973) that people can verify that "A collie is an animal" more quickly than they can verify that "A collie is a mammal." It is probably a more economical use of long-term memory "space" to remember that a collie is a mammal and that a mammal is an animal; people can then easily infer that a collie must be an animal. Yet it appears from these researchers' results that people store the fact that a collie is an animal as well—a fact that is redundant with other knowledge in long-term memory. Such redundancy may simply be a matter of convenience: If we have plenty of "room" in long-term memory, why not store the same information in the variety of ways in which we might need it later on?

As we've noted, too, the same information may be encoded in two or more different forms, for instance as both words and a visual image (recall the car with ski racks by the tree). Different forms of encoding facilitate different ways of thinking about a topic (Eisner, 1994; Salomon, 1979/1994). A picture may sometimes be worth a thousand words, depicting spatial relationships that are difficult to capture in any other way. Yet words and meanings may more easily allow us to interrelate similar ideas (perhaps through the propositions they have in common) in ways that spatial representations would not allow.

• *Most of our knowledge is a summary of our experiences rather than information about specific events.* The bulk of our knowledge appears to be semantic rather than episodic in nature: As we go through life, we continually combine the specific experiences we have into a general knowledge of the world that is somewhat independent of those experiences.

Concepts are a good example of how we summarize the objects and events that we encounter. As summaries of the things we have learned, concepts have several advantages:

---

[8]More generally, such *paradigm shifts* in scientific communities occur only after considerable evidence and a great deal of discussion and debate. For a classic discussion of paradigm shifts, see T. Kuhn's (1970) *The Structure of Scientific Revolutions*.

1. *They reduce the world's complexity* (Bruner, 1957; Sokal, 1977). Classifying similar objects and events makes life simpler and easier to understand. For example, when you drive along a country road, it is easier to think to yourself "There are some cows" than to think "There is a brown object, covered with bristly stuff, appended by a paintbrush and a lumpy thing, and held up by four sticks. Ah, yes, and I also see a black-and-white spotted object, covered with bristly stuff, appended by a paintbrush and a lumpy thing, and held up by four sticks. And over there is a brown-and-white spotted object. . . ."

2. *They facilitate inferences and generalization to new situations* (Johnson-Laird & Wason, 1977; Rosser, 1994; Sloutsky, Lo, & Fisher, 2001; Welder & Graham, 2001). When we learn a concept, we associate certain characteristics with it. Then, when we encounter a new instance of the concept, we can draw on our knowledge of associated characteristics to make assumptions and inferences about the new instance. For example, if you see a herd of cattle as you drive through the countryside, you can assume that you are passing through either dairy or beef country, depending on whether you see large udders hanging down between two of the spindly sticks. If you purchase a potted flower, you know that you must water it regularly because of something you have learned about the concept *flower*: It needs water to live. Thanks to concepts, we don't have to learn from scratch in each new situation.

3. *They allow abstraction of the environment* (Bruner, 1966). An object covered with bristly stuff, appended by a paintbrush and a lumpy thing, and held up by four sticks is a very concrete thing. The concept *cow*, however, can be more abstract: It incorporates such characteristics as "female," "supplier of milk," and, to the dairy farmer, "economic asset." Concepts and their labels allow individuals to think about their experiences without necessarily having to consider all of their concrete, perceptual aspects.

4. *They enhance the power of thought* (Bruner, 1966). When you are thinking about an object covered with bristly stuff, appended by a paintbrush and a lumpy thing, held up by four sticks, and so on, you can think of little else; to express this point in terms of contemporary memory theory, your working memory capacity is filled to the brim. But when you simply think *cow*, you can also think about *horse*, *dog*, *goat*, and *pig* at the same time.

5. *They make it easier for us to make connections among the things we know* (Bruner, 1957; Bruner et al., 1956). Once we have condensed and abstracted information into concepts, we can more easily make associations among those concepts in long-term memory. For instance, we can relate the concept *cow* to the concepts *bull* and *calf* in a familial sort of way and to *mammal*, *animal*, and *living thing* in a hierarchical fashion.

We must remember, however, that our summaries of the world will sometimes cause us to make mistakes. For example, when we identify a new stimulus as being a positive instance of a particular concept, we are likely to react to that stimulus as we would to any other instance of the concept. In the process, we may lose sight of the unique qualities of that particular stimulus. Furthermore, if we have identified a stimulus incorrectly, our response to it may be inappropriate. I remember as a young child trying to make a wagon using square pieces of wood for wheels. Calling those pieces of wood *wheels* was an inaccurate identification, and, as you can imagine, my wagon didn't move very far. Finally, in some situations we may *over*classify our experiences. For example, when we form **stereotypes** of certain groups of people (perhaps people of specific genders, races, or cultural backgrounds), we are apt to draw many incorrect inferences about how particular members of that group are apt to behave (Murray & Jackson, 1982/1983; Nelson & Miller, 1995; Oskamp, 2000).

• *In most situations, integrated knowledge is more useful than fragmented knowledge.* When we integrate the things we know, we are more likely to draw inferences that go beyond the specific things we have learned. Furthermore, as we will discover in the next chapter, organized information is easier to remember—in other words, to retrieve—than unorganized information.

Many theorists now stress the importance of teaching an integrated body of knowledge— knowledge that includes general principles, cause–effect relationships, and so on—rather than simply teaching isolated facts (e.g., Gregg & Leinhardt, 1994b; Linn et al., 1996; White & Rumsey, 1994). In the case of mathematics, for example, teachers should help students make associations between general concepts and principles of mathematics, on the one hand, and specific procedures for solving mathematical problems, on the other (Hiebert et al., 1997; Hiebert & Lefevre, 1986). When students learn specific mathematical procedures (e.g., how to do long division, or how to add two fractions by finding a common denominator) in association with the overall "logic" of mathematics, they are more likely to apply problem-solving procedures appropriately and to recognize occasions when they have obtained illogical and therefore incorrect problem solutions.

• *The in-depth study of a few topics is often more beneficial than the superficial study of many topics.* Historically, many people have seen the role of schools as being one of promoting **cultural literacy**—that is, of helping children learn the many facts that a seemingly "educated" person should know (e.g., see Hirsch, 1996). For example, we are often chagrined when we hear how many children don't know the capital of France, can't list the nine planets of the solar system, or have no idea who wrote *Romeo and Juliet.*

Certainly, schooling should, in part, be about helping children acquire a basic knowledge of the world and culture in which they live so that they can participate more fully and effectively in their society (Hirsch, 1996). Yet if schools focus exclusively on imparting isolated facts, an integrated body of knowledge about the world is unlikely to develop. Many theorists now suggest that teachers focus more on teaching a few topics in depth than on covering many topics at a superficial level (Berliner & Biddle, 1995; Brophy & Alleman, 1992; Gardner, 2000; Onosko & Newmann, 1994; Sizer, 1992). They advocate the idea that **less is more:** When students study *less* material so that they can study it more thoroughly, they learn it *more* completely and with greater understanding, and they are more likely to undergo conceptual change when such change is warranted.

SUMMARY

People probably encode information in a variety of forms, including symbols (e.g., verbal codes), imagery (e.g., visual images), meanings (e.g., propositions), and actions (e.g., productions), and information encoded in these different ways is interconnected. Some information may be organized in a hierarchical format that reflects superordinate and subordinate categories, but much more is probably organized as a network (perhaps consisting of interrelated propositions) that encompasses many different kinds of relationships. Building loosely on neurological research, some theorists have proposed that any single piece of information is represented in long-term memory in a distributed fashion, that is, as a network of scattered but interconnected nodes that activate simultaneously.

Concepts are classes of objects or events that share one or more common properties. Some concepts are concrete, in that they are easily identified by their physical appearance, whereas others are more abstract and difficult to pin down in terms of observable characteristics. Learning a concept often involves learning the features that determine which objects and events are members of that concept (i.e., positive instances) and which are nonmembers (i.e., negative instances). Drawing from several theories of concept learning, we can speculate that learning a concept may involve testing hypotheses about the nature of a particular concept, forming a prototype of a typical positive instance, developing a feature list for the concept, and storing exemplars that represent the variability of positive instances. Teachers can help students master concepts in the classroom when they capitalize on factors that facilitate concept learning—for instance, when they provide definitions, highlight defining features, simultaneously present both positive and negative instances, and ask students to generate their own examples.

A *schema* is a closely connected set of ideas related to a specific object or event. Schemas that summarize how common events typically transpire (e.g., what a visit to the doctor's office is usually like) are sometimes called *scripts*. Schemas and scripts often influence how we process, store, and remember new situations; for example, they allow us to fill in any missing information with our own knowledge about how the world typically operates.

Some of the knowledge stored in long-term memory takes the form of *personal theories*, coherent belief systems that encompass cause–effect relationships about physical, biological, social, political, or mental phenomena. Personal theories influence concept learning by giving learners some idea about the features that are likely to be important. Such theories are not always accurate reflections of the world,

however; they may include incomplete or inaccurate understandings. When students are starting from scratch about a new topic (i.e., when they have minimal information and few if any misconceptions about the topic), then helping them acquire theoretical knowledge may be relatively straightforward. For instance, teachers can present physical models that depict structures or cause–effect relationships, and they can encourage students to build on one another's ideas in small-group or whole-class discussions. But when students must replace existing misconceptions with more accurate explanations—that is, when they must undergo *conceptual change*—the teacher's task is more difficult, in part because students are likely to distort new information to be consistent with what they already believe and in part because students may have a personal, emotional, or social stake in keeping their existing conceptions. Theorists have offered numerous suggestions for promoting conceptual change; for instance, teachers should encourage meaningful learning of a few key ideas rather than rote learning of many isolated facts, and they must show students how new explanations are more plausible and useful than existing ones.

The development of *expertise* in a particular subject area involves acquiring an increasing amount of knowledge, making numerous interconnections within that knowledge base, and eventually integrating what has been learned into a cohesive whole. People typically become experts in their field only after many years of intensive study and practice.

Most of our knowledge probably represents a summary of our life experiences. For example, concepts summarize what we have learned about particular objects or events; as such, they reduce the complexity of the environment and facilitate generalization to new situations. By and large, integrated knowledge about a topic is more useful than knowledge of separate facts.

CHAPTER 12

Long-Term Memory III: Retrieval and Forgetting

H ere are definitions of five words in the English language. Can you identify the specific words to which they refer?

- The fluid part of blood
- A picture form of writing used in ancient Egypt
- A game whose object is to snap small plastic disks into a container
- A zigzag trim used to decorate clothing
- A small, hard-shelled, ocean-dwelling animal that attaches itself to rocks and ships

You probably identified some of these words almost without thinking. But there is a good chance that you could not retrieve all five instantaneously. For one or more of them, you may have found yourself looking around in your long-term memory, perhaps for a lengthy period of time, in "places" where a word might be located. (In case you could not retrieve all five words, they are *plasma, hieroglyphics, tiddlywinks, rickrack,* and *barnacle.*)

Retrieving information from long-term memory is sometimes easy and automatic, at other times slow and strenuous, and at still other times virtually impossible. We tend to remember frequently used information without conscious effort. For instance, we can quickly retrieve the locations of our homes and the names of our close friends. It is more difficult to retrieve information that we seldom use. For example, we often have trouble remembering words that we rarely encounter in our everyday lives (words such as *hieroglyphics* and *barnacle*); in some cases, we may feel that such words are on the "tips of our tongues," yet we still cannot recall them (A. Brown, 1991; Brown & McNeill, 1966). Similarly, we may experience difficulty in identifying people whom we have not seen recently or frequently (Yarmey, 1973).

In this chapter, we will look at how memory theorists believe long-term memory retrieval works and at how retrieval, like storage, is often constructive in nature. Later, we will explore several explanations of why we are sometimes unable to retrieve the things we think we have learned—in other words, why we forget. Finally, we will make use of our knowledge about retrieval to identify additional implications of memory theory for instructional practice.

HOW RETRIEVAL WORKS

How easily we retrieve something from long-term memory depends in large part on how well we stored it in the first place. Unlike working memory, which is functionally quite small, long-term memory is so large that an exhaustive exploration of it all is probably impossible. A search of long-term memory must therefore be selective and explore only certain "sections" (e.g., Hopkins & Atkinson, 1968). If the sought-after information is not stored in one of those sections, we will not retrieve it.

Our success in retrieving information from long-term memory depends to some extent on whether we initially stored the information in a well-organized fashion. To understand the role that organization plays in retrieval, let's first look at an analogous situation—your great-grandmother's attic. (I am going back three generations, because young families typically have homes without much attic space, and many grandparents seem to live in condominiums these days.) Granny probably kept many things in her attic, including furniture, books, old clothes, seldom-used cooking utensils, and holiday decorations. Granny may have been a very organized woman, one who stored all of the books in one place, all of the clothes in another, and all of the holiday decorations somewhere else. Alternatively, she may have been more haphazard, throwing things up there any old place, so that some cooking utensils were with books, others were with clothes, and still others were stuffed in an old dresser or on the top shelf of a dilapidated armoire. How Granny stored items in her attic undoubtedly affected her ability to find them later on. If she stored things systematically (e.g., books with books and cooking utensils with cooking utensils), she would have been able to find them easily when she needed them. But if she stored them in a helter-skelter fashion, she may have had to purchase new canning jars every summer because she couldn't locate her jars from any of the previous 13 years.

So it is with long-term memory. Retrieval is easier when related pieces of information are stored in close association with one another, because we then have a good idea about where to find a certain piece of information. To illustrate, try answering this question about a concept I presented in an earlier chapter:

What is a discriminative stimulus?

You may be able to answer the question quickly and easily, or you may have to search your long-term memory for a while. Your ability to retrieve the answer depends partly on how well you have

An organized long-term memory makes things easier to retrieve.

organized the information you acquired from previous chapters. The word *stimulus* should, of course, lead you to look among the many pieces of information you have stored about behaviorist learning theories. The word *discriminative* might suggest to you that you look more specifically in your information about discrimination. If your knowledge about discrimination is stored with what you know about stimulus control (and it should be, because the two concepts are related), then you should find the answer to the question. A discriminative stimulus lets you know that a particular response is likely to be reinforced; it *sets the occasion* for a particular response-reinforcement contingency.

Lindsay and Norman (1977) have characterized long-term memory retrieval as being similar to looking for something in a large, dark room with only a small flashlight. Imagine that the electricity goes off in Granny's house on a dark, moonless night. Because Granny can no longer use either her electric can opener or her electric lights, she takes a flashlight up to the attic to find the manual can opener she put there last October. She switches on her flashlight and begins her search. Unfortunately, the flashlight cannot illuminate the whole attic at once. Instead, she must aim the light first at one spot, then at another, until eventually she finds the can opener. The necessity to search the attic one spot at a time will not be a problem if Granny knows the exact location of the can opener (e.g., in a drawer with other small cooking utensils), but she may search all night without success if she has no idea where she might have put the thing. In much the same way, retrieval from long-term memory may be a process of looking in various small "locations" in memory, one location at a time. Information that has been stored in a logical place (i.e., associated with similar ideas) will probably be found quickly. Information that has been stored haphazardly, in a rote-learning fashion, will turn up only after a great deal of searching, or possibly not at all.

An experiment by Bower and Holyoak (1973) illustrates the dependence of retrieval on earlier storage. In this study, college students listened to a set of tape-recorded sounds and identified something that each sound might be (e.g., chirping crickets or soldiers clumping down stairs). Two weeks later, they listened to a second set of sounds, including some sounds they had heard previously and some new sounds as well. Once again they were asked to identify what each sound might be and to indicate whether they had heard that exact sound during the first session. When students labeled a sound in the same way in the second session as they had in the first session, they were likely to recognize it as being one they had heard before. When they labeled it in a different way in the two sessions (e.g., once as a bouncing ball and once as a heartbeat), they were less likely to recognize it as being a familiar one. Other students, who had labels provided for them by the experimenter, showed similar results. By using a label they had used before, the students apparently were more likely to search the part of long-term memory where the previous sound was stored.

Let's return to the activation model of memory described in Chapter 9. According to this model, all information stored in memory is in either an active or inactive state. Information in an active state is what we might think of as being in working memory, whereas inactive information is in long-term memory. The activation model lends itself particularly well to an understanding of how long-term memory retrieval might work. From this perspective, our starting point in long-term memory might be an idea triggered by something in the environment. Retrieval is then a process of **spreading activation,** with the activation flowing through connections within the network of stored information (e.g., J. R. Anderson, 1990; Collins & Loftus, 1975; E. D. Gagné, 1985). Only a small part of the network can be activated at once, thus accounting for the limited-capacity, "flashlight" quality of retrieval. If the activation eventually spreads to that part of the network in which the information is located—something that is more likely to happen if similar ideas are closely associated in the network—we will retrieve the desired information.

Generally speaking, retrieval is easier for things that we know *well*—things that we have practiced a lot and use frequently—and especially for things that we have learned to automaticity. It's as we go to those "places" often enough that we don't even have to think about where to go in order to find them.

In addition, retrieval is usually easier when we are relaxed rather than anxious about retrieving information, particularly if we are looking for *non*automatized information. To illustrate, think about what happens when you are looking for your car keys and are desperate to find them quickly because you are already late for an important appointment. As you begin to panic, your search strategies become less and less efficient. You look in the same places over and over again; you don't think creatively about the wide variety of places in which the keys might be lurking. So, too, does anxiety adversely affect retrieval: We don't search long-term memory in an "open-minded" manner, reducing our chances of finding the desired information.

Retrieval Cues

Retrieval is obviously easier when we have a good idea where to "look" in long-term memory—that is, when we know which part of long-term memory to activate. Accordingly, hints about where to find information—**retrieval cues**—are often helpful. Essentially, retrieval cues are likely to activate the part of long-term memory where a desired piece of information can be found (recall our discussion of *priming* in Chapter 9).

In Chapter 10, you read a story called "The War of the Ghosts." Can you fill in the blank in this sentence from the story?

And the warriors went on up the river to a town on the other side of _____.

See if you can remember the name of the town before you continue reading.

Any luck? If not, then perhaps you will recognize the town from among these four choices: (1) Bisantri, (2) Dormro, (3) Muckaruck, (4) Kalama. Is it any easier to fill in the blank now? It should be. Perhaps you have now correctly identified Kalama as the answer. In this question, I gave you a type of retrieval cue known as an **identity cue** (Bourne et al., 1986), because it was identical to the information you were trying to retrieve. Recognition tasks, such as multiple-choice tests, are often easier than recall tasks (e.g., Semb et al., 1993), presumably because of the identity cues that recognition tasks provide.

Now try this exercise. Read the following list of 24 words *one time only*. I will ask you to recall them as soon as you have finished.

tulip	pencil	spoon	bed	baker	ruby
hat	mountain	doctor	paper	daisy	shirt
chair	fork	diamond	canyon	knife	table
hill	soldier	rose	pen	shoe	emerald

Now that you have read all 24 words, cover the page and write as many of them as you can remember. *Do not peek back at the list just yet.*

If you cannot remember all 24, see if these words and phrases help you:

clothing	professions
eating utensils	writing supplies
gemstones	furniture
flowers	land forms

These category names should help you remember more of the words, because all of the 24 words fall into one of those categories. Such **associate cues** are related to the words you were searching for; as such, they should direct your search toward relevant parts of your long-term memory.

Still a third kind of retrieval cue is an organizational structure, or **frame,** that systematically guides the search of long-term memory (e.g., Calfee, 1981). For example, in Chapter 10, I described an experiment by Bower and his colleagues (1969) in which presenting words in an organized format (e.g., the "minerals" hierarchy shown in Figure 10–4), rather than in a random order, facilitated learning. An overall organizational structure provides numerous cues that should facilitate retrieval (e.g., "Hmmm, now that I've remembered the rare and common metals, I need to remember the alloys").

Consider this sentence that biology students often tell me they use to remember the biological classification system:

King Philip comes over for good spaghetti.

The students use the first letter of each word in the sentence to help them remember these terms in their correct order: *kingdom, phylum, class, order, family, genus,* and *species.* Each word in the sentence provides a retrieval cue—it limits the search of long-term memory to words that begin with a particular letter. The sentence is a good example of a *superimposed meaningful structure*—a type of mnemonic that we'll discuss in Chapter 13.

Oftentimes when we learn new information, we store it in association with the other things we are encountering at the same time—a phenomenon known as **encoding specificity** (Tulving, 1983). Those other things can later help us retrieve the information; in other words, they provide **contextual cues.** Accordingly, we are more apt to retrieve the information when we are in the same context in which we learned it, rather than in a different one. For instance, as we will see in our discussion of *situated learning* in Chapter 14, students may associate things they learn in a particular class (e.g., social studies or physics) primarily with that content domain and so may fail to retrieve it in other classes where it may be quite relevant to the topic at hand.

In some instances, even the physical environment in which something has been learned can serve as a retrieval cue (Godden & Baddeley, 1975; Smith, Glenberg, & Bjork, 1978). In an unusual demonstration of this principle, Godden and Baddeley (1975) had scuba divers learn 36 unrelated words in either of two environments: on shore or 20 feet below the water's surface. They were then asked to remember the words in either the same or a different environment. On a free recall task, the divers were able to recall more words when they were in the same environment in which they had learned the words than when they were in the other environment. Yet even when the environment itself is not the specific one in which we originally learned something, exposure to some of the characteristics of that environment—perhaps the same smells or the same background music—can help us remember (Balch, Bowman, & Mohler, 1992; Cann & Ross, 1989; Schab, 1990).

Retrieval cues definitely aid recall of information.[1] They are likely to be most effective when we have associated them frequently with the specific information we are trying to remember (Tulving, 1968, 1975; Tulving & Thomson, 1971; Underwood, 1983). For example, when retrieving the list of 24 words I gave you earlier, once you remembered *table*, you should have had little trouble remembering *chair* as well (or vice versa), because the two words often occur together in conversation.

Although retrieval cues usually facilitate our recall of information, they can hinder it when they direct our search to a part of long-term memory *other* than that which holds the information. For instance, in a study by Brown (1968), an experimental group of college students was given a list of 25 U.S. states to read, while a control group had no such list. Both groups were then asked to recall as many of the 50 states as they could. Compared with the control group, the experimental group remembered more of the states they had previously read but *fewer* of the states they had *not* read. Thus, retrieval cues are helpful only to the extent that they direct us to that part of long-term memory containing the desired information.

CONSTRUCTION IN RETRIEVAL

Read the following passage *one time only*:

Carol Harris' Need for Professional Help

Carol Harris was a problem child from birth. She was wild, stubborn, and violent. By the time Carol turned eight, she was still unmanageable. Her parents were very concerned about her mental

---

[1]Retrieval cues may even affect the extent to which organisms exhibit classically conditioned responses; see Bouton (1994) for an explanation.

health. There was no good institution for her problem in her state. Her parents finally decided to take some action. They hired a private teacher for Carol. (Sulin & Dooling, 1974)

Now cover the passage and answer this question: Did you read the statement "She was deaf, dumb, and blind" anywhere in the passage?

You probably answered "no" to my question. But do you think you might have been fooled if you had read the same passage with the name Helen Keller substituted for Carol Harris? Sulin and Dooling (1974) compared what happened when people read a Carol Harris version of the story versus when they read a Helen Keller version: Immediately after reading the passage, 20% of the "Helen Keller" group stated that the passage had included a statement about the woman being "deaf, dumb, and blind," yet no one in the "Carol Harris" group made that mistake. One week later, the number asserting they had read such a statement rose to 50% for the "Helen Keller" group but only to 5% for the "Carol Harris" group. In a follow-up study using the same passage, Dooling and Christiaansen (1977) found that people who read about Carol Harris, but who were told at recall a week later that the passage was really about Helen Keller, were also likely to "remember" the statement about her being "deaf, dumb, and blind." At retrieval time, the participants in the two studies were apparently using their prior knowledge about Helen Keller as well as their actual memory of what they had read. The longer the time interval between storage and retrieval, the greater the impact their prior knowledge had.

Such results indicate that long-term memory retrieval, like long-term memory storage, may involve constructive processes. Individuals often retrieve only a portion of the information that has previously been presented to them; on such occasions, they may fill in holes in what they remember based on what is logical or consistent with their existing knowledge and beliefs about the world (R. C. Anderson, 1984; Halpern, 1985; Heit, 1993; Kolodner, 1985; Loftus, 1991; Neisser, 1981; Spiro, 1980a, 1980b; Wilson & Anderson, 1986).

Construction can occur in retrieval of nonverbal as well as verbal material. For example, in Chapter 10, I described research by Carmichael and colleagues (1932), in which people's reproductions of line drawings reflected the labels (e.g., eyeglasses or dumbbells) assigned to them. The participants probably remembered only parts of those drawings and filled in the rest based on what they knew about the objects that the labels identified. Another example of constructive retrieval of nonverbal material can be found in the recall of a crime one has witnessed. Eyewitness testimony is sometimes an inaccurate representation of what actually happened (Buckhout, 1974; Lindsay, 1993; Loftus, 1991, 1992). People's descriptions of the crime may vary considerably, depending on prior knowledge about the individuals involved, expectations about what typically happens in such a situation, and additional information presented at a later time (more on the last point shortly).

Even especially vivid memories can be partly reconstructed and, therefore, have the potential to be inaccurate. As an example, think about where you were and what you were doing when, on September 11, 2001, you first heard about the attack on the World Trade Center. You can probably recall where you were and what you were doing in considerable detail. But how *accurate* is your recollection? Unless you have a videotape of yourself when you first heard the news, there is no way to be sure.

Neisser and Harsch (1992) studied college students' memory for another disaster, the crash of the space shuttle *Challenger* on January 28, 1986. (To refresh your memory, the *Challenger* plummeted into the ocean soon after liftoff, and seven astronauts perished, including Christa McAuliffe, the first teacher to travel into space.) Neisser and Harsch asked the students to describe the circumstances in which they heard the news both the morning after the incident and then again two and a half years later. Even after more than two years, many students were quite confident about their recollections. Despite their confidence, however, some of them were way off base. For example, one student gave this account the morning after hearing about the disaster:

> I was in my religion class and some people walked in and started talking about [it]. I didn't know any details except that it had exploded and the schoolteacher's students had all been watching which I thought was so sad. Then after class I went to my room and watched the TV program talking about it and I got all the details from that. (Neisser & Harsch, 1992, p. 9)

The same student had this recollection two and a half years later:

> When I first heard about the explosion I was sitting in my freshman dorm room with my roommate and we were watching TV. It came on a news flash and we were both totally shocked. I was really upset and I went upstairs to talk to a friend of mine and then I called my parents. (Neisser & Harsch, 1992, p. 9)

Our memories of hearing about significant and emotion-laden events are often quite vivid, detailed ones with a seemingly "snapshot" quality to them; hence, psychologists call them **flashbulb memories** (Bohannon & Symons, 1992; Brewer, 1992; Brown & Kulik, 1977). Yet we shouldn't let such vividness lead us astray; although many flashbulb memories are quite accurate, many others are not (Brewer, 1992; Rubin, 1992; Schmolck, Buffalo, & Squire, 2000).

Although constructive processes may be responsible for many errors in what we remember, construction usually facilitates long-term memory retrieval. When our memory of an event is incomplete, we can fill in details based on what makes sense (Halpern, 1985; Kintsch, Mandel, & Kozminsky, 1977; Kolodner, 1985; Reder, 1982). For example, a student may not immediately remember which general surrendered at Appomattox at the end of the American Civil War; however, the student might reasonably assume that, because the South lost the war and General Robert E. Lee commanded the Southern troops, it was probably General Lee who surrendered at Appomattox. Similarly, a student trying to remember how to spell the word *ascertain* may surmise that, because the word is related in meaning to the word *certain*, it should be spelled similarly.

The Power of Suggestion: Effects of Subsequently Presented Information

Sometimes people's recollections are influenced not only by their prior knowledge but also by information presented to them sometime *after* they learned whatever they are retrieving. Generally speaking, this is a good thing: People *should* continually update their knowledge and understanding as new information comes in. In some cases, however—for instance, in eyewitness testimony—further information in the form of incorrect statements or misleading questions can be detrimental.

As an illustration of how constructive processes can lead people astray in eyewitness testimony, consider an experiment by Loftus and Palmer (1974). Five different groups of adults watched a film depicting a car accident, and then people in each group were asked one of five questions about how fast the car was going. The participants' estimates of the speed varied significantly, depending on how the question was worded (italics highlight the variations in wording):

Question Asked	Estimated Speed (mph)
About how fast were the cars going when they *contacted* each other?	31.8
About how fast were the cars going when they *hit* each other?	34.0
About how fast were the cars going when they *bumped* into each other?	38.1
About how fast were the cars going when they *collided* into each other?	39.3
About how fast were the cars going when they *smashed* into each other?	40.8

As you can see, the participants' reconstructions of the accident were influenced to some extent by the severity of the crash implied by the questions they were asked.

As another example, let's consider what has become a classic study of eyewitness testimony in young children (Leichtman & Ceci, 1995). A man identified as "Sam Stone" briefly visits a preschool classroom; he comments on the story the teacher is reading to the children, strolls around the perimeter of the room, waves goodbye, and leaves. Later, an adult asks, "When Sam Stone got that bear dirty, did he do it on purpose or as an accident?" and "Was Sam Stone happy or sad that he got the bear dirty?" When asked such questions, children may recall that Sam soiled a teddy bear, even though he never touched a stuffed animal during his visit (Leichtman & Ceci, 1995, p. 571). Susceptibility to leading questions is more common in 3- and 4-year-olds than in 5- and 6-year-olds; older children are less likely to be swayed by suggestive remarks (Leichtman & Ceci, 1995).

Such results illustrate the **misinformation effect:** People's memory for an event may become distorted when they subsequently receive inaccurate information about the event (Bruck & Ceci, 1997; Lindsay, 1993; Loftus, 1991, 1992; Thelen, 1989; Titcomb & Reyna, 1995; Toglia, 1996; Zaragoza & Mitchell, 1996). Apparently, people integrate the misinformation with their original knowledge of the event and may use the two in combination to reconstruct what "must" have happened.

Constructing Entirely New "Memories"

In some cases, retrieval is almost entirely constructive, in that an individual is asked to provide information that has never actually been stored. For example, consider this arithmetic problem:

$$\frac{1}{2} \times 0 = ?$$

You may never have been given the answer to this specific problem, yet you no doubt learned long ago that anything times zero equals zero. Hence you are able to construct the correct answer:

$$\frac{1}{2} \times 0 = 0$$

Constructive retrieval enables individuals to produce information beyond what they have specifically stored. Such construction takes time, however (J. R. Anderson, 1985). In a study by Stazyk, Ashcraft, and Hamann (1982), students easily retrieved multiplication facts they had practiced many times over and so quickly answered such problems as 2×3 and 4×6. However, they were slower to answer "zero" problems such as 2 × 0 and 0 × 6. Many students probably store a general rule for such problems (i.e., anything times zero equals zero) rather than specific answers to each problem, and they must therefore construct their answer from the rule each time such a problem is presented. When fast reaction times are essential (e.g., when numerous basic math facts are needed to solve complex problems), it is probably to a student's advantage to learn the specific information required rather than a more general rule from which the information can be derived.

Occasionally, entirely new "memories" have little or no basis in fact. In particular, they are **false memories** for events that never happened (Loftus, 1997; Pezdek, Finger, & Hodge, 1997; Seamon, Luo, & Gallo, 1998). False memories are especially likely for things that might reasonably or logically have occurred. For example, in word-list learning tasks, people may "remember" seeing words that they never actually saw but that are close associates of words they *did* see, presumably because the unseen words were activated during the learning session (Brainerd & Reyna, 1998; Brainerd, Reyna, & Brandse, 1995; Roediger & McDermott, 2000; Seamon et al., 1998). Consider, too, a study by Pezdek and colleagues (1997) in which high school students were asked whether certain events happened when they were eight years old. Some of the events actually did happen, but the experimenters fabricated two others, one involving a common religious ritual for Catholic children and another involving a common ritual for Jewish children. As you might guess, Catholic students were more likely to "remember" the Catholic event, whereas Jewish students were more apt to "remember" the Jewish one, and their scripts for such events allowed them to "recall" a fair number of details about what had transpired.

Remembering Earlier Recollections

In their study of memory about the *Challenger* disaster, Neisser and Harsch (1992) interviewed many students a third time, three years after the disaster itself and so six months after the second recall session. On this third occasion, most students essentially repeated their stories from six months earlier. When those who inaccurately remembered the occasion were given hints as to the truth about where they had been and what they had been doing, they stuck with their prior misrecollections; furthermore, they were quite surprised when they were shown their original, morning-after descriptions. It appeared that these students were remembering not what had actually had happened but what they had previously *said* had happened.

As the Neisser and Harsch study illustrates, recalling an event that has happened to us often affects our later memory for the event, especially when we verbally describe the event. Such **narratives** can definitely be constructive in nature (Bohannon & Symons, 1992; Rubin, 1992; Schank & Abelson, 1995). Author Marion Winik has described the process this way:

> Sometimes I think childhood memories are fabricated like pearls around a grain of sand. You know how it works: take one old photograph and the quick current of memory it sparks; add what you heard happened, what could have happened, what probably happened; then tell the story over and over until you get the details down. It doesn't take a degree in psychology to reverse-engineer your childhood based on the adult it produced.
>
> Even if I've made it all up, it doesn't matter. I'm stuck with the past I believe in, even if it's wrong. (Winik, 1994, p. 40)

In some instances, people "recall" things that never happened simply because at an earlier time, someone else insisted that they think or talk about it. For instance, asking people to picture an imaginary event transpiring increases the likelihood that, later on, they will remember that it *actually* happened; young children have an especially difficult time distinguishing fact from fantasy (Foley, Harris, & Herman, 1994; Garry & Polaschek, 2000; Parker, 1995). And confirming people's responses to questions they don't know the answers to—perhaps telling them that they're correct when they identify someone in a lineup of unfamiliar faces or when they provide details that they never actually observed——increases the chances that they will "remember" something they never witnessed (Wells & Bradfield, 1999; Zaragoza, Payment, Ackil, Drivdahl, & Beck, 2001).

Although people occasionally "remember" something that they never learned, it is more often the case that they can't retrieve something they *did* learn. We turn our attention now to explanations of why attempts at retrieval sometimes prove fruitless—in other words, to explanations of forgetting.

FORGETTING

Over time, people recall less and less about the events they have experienced and the information they have acquired (J. R. Anderson, 1995; Wixted & Ebbesen, 1991). Theorists have offered a number of explanations about why we forget much of what we learn. Here we look at seven possibilities: decay, obliterative subsumption, interference, failure to retrieve, repression, construction error, and failure to store. We then consider possible reasons why our earliest experiences are especially difficult to recall.

Decay

In the early decades of cognitive psychology, many theorists thought that once information is stored in long-term memory, it remains there permanently in some form (Loftus & Loftus, 1980). Increasingly, however, psychologists have come to believe that information can fade away, or **decay**, and eventually disappear from memory altogether, especially when the information is not being used (Altmann & Gray, 2002; Byrnes, 2001; Loftus & Loftus, 1980; Schacter, 1999).

The observations of neurosurgeon Wilder Penfield (1958, 1959; Penfield & Roberts, 1959) have been cited as evidence for the permanence of long-term memory. Penfield sometimes operated on locally anesthetized but otherwise conscious patients. In doing so, he discovered that stimulating portions of the brain with a weak electric current could promote vivid sensations in his patients. Patients would describe hearing a song, delivering a baby, or going to a circus as if the experience were actually happening to them at that very moment. They acted almost as if they were reliving previous events in their lives. Unfortunately, however, Penfield never determined whether the events his patients "remembered" had actually occurred.

Some evidence indicates that information may indeed remain in long-term memory for a long time (Bahrick, 1984; Semb & Ellis, 1994). For example, in a study by Bahrick (1984), individuals remembered a considerable amount of the Spanish they had learned in high school or college as many as 50 years before, even if they had not spoken Spanish since that time. Other evidence is found in experiments in which people *re*learn information they have previously learned but can no longer recall or recognize: These individuals learn the information more quickly than people who have not previously learned the same material (Nelson, 1971, 1978).

Unfortunately, no conclusive evidence confirms the permanence of long-term memory: Research findings do not (and quite possibly *cannot*) demonstrate that *all* information stored in long-term memory remains there for the life of the individual (Eysenck & Keane, 1990). Yet it is probably equally impossible to determine whether information can entirely disappear from long-term memory; perhaps a person who seemingly forgets is simply not "looking" in the right place. It does appear, however, that unused memories weaken and become less accessible over time.

Obliterative Subsumption

A variation of the decay theory is Ausubel's notion of **obliterative subsumption** (Ausubel, 1963, 1968; Ausubel et al., 1978; Ausubel & Robinson, 1969). According to Ausubel, meaningful learning is a process of subsuming new pieces of information into long-term memory under more general, superordinate pieces of information. Over time, these specific pieces of information may be absorbed by their superordinates; in other words, they are *obliteratively subsumed*. For example, a teacher may present a general concept and then illustrate that concept with a number of examples; the student probably subsumes the examples under the concept. Over time, however, some of the examples may lose their distinctiveness from the concept itself and eventually blend in with the subsuming concept. At that point, the concept continues to be remembered, but the examples are forgotten.

As evidence for his theory, Ausubel has pointed out that general ideas are more likely to be remembered than specific details. Furthermore, details that are distinctive in some way are remembered, whereas less distinctive ones are forgotten or become a general blur (Eysenck, 1979; Reisberg, 1997). To illustrate, when I think back to my early lessons in U.S. history, I remember the general idea behind the American Revolution: The colonists were fighting for independence from British rule. I also remember certain distinctive details; for example, the Battle of Bunker Hill is commemorated by a monument I visited frequently as a child, and the Boston Tea Party was a unique and colorful illustration of American dissatisfaction with British taxation policies. However, I have forgotten the details of many other events, because, to my young mind, they consisted of nondistinctive people and places.

The notion of obliterative subsumption is certainly consistent with what we commonly observe to be true regarding the kinds of information we remember versus the kinds we forget. However, as is true regarding decay theory, little evidence to date either supports or refutes its validity as a major, distinct factor in forgetting.

Interference

In Chapter 8, I described the phenomena of proactive and retroactive inhibition: In both situations, learning one set of verbal material interferes with the ability to recall another set. Verbal learning theorists (McGeoch, 1942; Melton & Irwin, 1940; Postman & Underwood, 1973; Underwood, 1948) proposed that such inhibition is a major cause of forgetting verbal information. Some contemporary memory theorists agree, although they often use the term **interference** rather than inhibition (Altmann & Gray, 2002; Dempster & Corkill, 1999; Schacter, 1999). In support of this explanation of forgetting, recall of word lists can be as high as 85% when sources of interference are removed from a serial learning task (Underwood, 1957).

Imagine that you need to learn a list of 20 words. You are then asked to learn another list of 20 more words. Now try to remember the first list. Learning the second list has probably made it more difficult to recall the first list; to some extent, you have forgotten which words are in which list. The interference theory of forgetting might best be described as a theory of confusion: An individual has learned numerous responses and gets them mixed up. Using more conventional behaviorist terminology, verbal learning theorists called this phenomenon **response competition** (e.g., Melton & Irwin, 1940).

An experiment by John Anderson (1974) helps us place interference within a contemporary cognitive framework. College students learned a long list of single-proposition sentences, each of which involved a person and a place; here are some examples:

A hippie is in the park.
A hippie is in the church.
A policeman is in the park.
A sailor is in the park.

The people and places appeared in varying numbers of sentences; some items (e.g., the policeman) appeared in only one sentence, whereas others (e.g., the park) appeared several times. The students studied the sentences until they knew them very well—more specifically, until they could respond to a long list of questions (e.g., "Who is in the park?" "Where are the hippies?") with 100% accuracy. At that point, they were given a new set of sentences and asked to indicate whether or not these had been among the previous set. The more frequently the person and the place had appeared in the previous set of sentences, the longer it took the students to determine whether the person and place had appeared *together* in that first set. Anderson (1974, 1976, 1983a, 1990) has explained these results as being a function of the numerous associations the students developed to the frequently appearing people and places. For example, the more frequently that certain places had been associated with *hippie* in the original set of sentences, the longer students would take to search among their associations with *hippie* to determine whether a new sentence about a hippie had been among the previous set. Thus, multiple associations with a concept can slow down retrieval time for information connected with that concept, a phenomenon that Anderson calls the **fan effect.**

Interference is probably more relevant in the forgetting of rote-learned information than in meaningfully learned information (Good & Brophy, 1986). In other words, response competition and confusion are more likely to be a problem when associations between pieces of information are arbitrary rather than logical.

Failure to Retrieve

You can probably think of occasions when you couldn't remember something at first, yet recalled it later on. Clearly, then, the information was still in your long-term memory; you just couldn't retrieve it the first time around.

Using our "flashlight" analogy again, we might say failure to retrieve occurs when people neglect to "look" in that part of long-term memory that holds the desired information. Perhaps the information was stored with very few connections to other ideas; as a result, even a broad search of memory doesn't focus the flashlight on (i.e., activate) it (J. R. Anderson, 1995). Given appropriate retrieval cues, however, people may eventually find what they are looking for (Tulving, 1975; Tulving & Psotka, 1971; Underwood, 1983).

Some instances of failure to retrieve involve forgetting to do something that needs to be done. As an example, when I was considerably younger, I often forgot to turn off my car lights after driving to work on a foggy morning. I occasionally forgot important meetings. Sometimes I forgot to bring crucial handouts or transparencies to class. Yes, yes, I know what you're thinking: I was suffering from the absentminded professor syndrome.

It's not that I would lose information from my long-term memory. When I went to the parking lot at the end of the day and discovered that my car battery was dead, I would readily remember that I had turned on my car lights that morning. When I was reminded of an important meeting I'd missed or got to the point in a class session where I needed the handout I'd forgotten to bring, I would think, "Oh, yes, of course!" My problem was that I *forgot to retrieve* important information at the appropriate time. Fortunately, as I've learned more about memory, I've also developed a strategy to overcome my absentmindedness. I'll share it with you near the end of the chapter.

Repression

Earlier in the chapter, we discovered that emotionally laden news sometimes results in a flash-bulb memory—a particularly vivid recollection of where we were and what we were doing when we heard the news. But in some situations we may have an experience that is so painful or emotionally distressing that we tend either not to remember it at all or else to remember only isolated fragments of it (Arrigo & Pezdek, 1997; Loftus & Kaufman, 1992; Nadel & Jacobs, 1998). This phenomenon, often known as **repression**,[2] was first described by Sigmund Freud (1915/1957, 1922); more recently, several theorists have explained it within a contemporary cognitivist framework (Erdelyi, 1985; Erdelyi & Goldberg, 1979; Jones, 1993; Wegman, 1985). To describe repression in contemporary memory terminology, painful information begins to produce anxiety whenever the relevant part of long-term memory is approached. Because anxiety itself is unpleasant, the memory search will tend to steer clear of the anxiety-arousing part of long-term memory. Thus, the painful memory, as well as any other information stored in close association with it, remains out of reach and so is essentially "forgotten."

Repression is reportedly quite common in clinical settings (Erdelyi, 1985; Erdelyi & Goldberg, 1979; Pezdek & Banks, 1996). Over a series of therapy sessions, perhaps with the help of hypnosis (which induces relaxation), a client gradually recalls bits and pieces of a traumatic incident; eventually, the client may remember the entire event. Recalling the incident often relieves the symptoms for which the client has sought the therapist's assistance (Erdelyi & Goldberg, 1979). Unfortunately, however, many presumably repressed "memories" are never checked for accuracy; thus, they may or may not be based on something that actually occurred (Holmes, 1990; Loftus, 1993). For instance, although a hypnotic state may increase people's confidence and willingness to talk about past events, it doesn't necessarily improve their memory for what transpired (Lynn, Lock, Myers, & Payne, 1997; Reisberg, 1997).

A few laboratory research studies support the existence of repression (Davis, 1987; Davis & Schwartz, 1987; Eriksen & Kuethe, 1956; Zeller, 1950), but overall the evidence is more spotty than that found in therapeutic settings. Repression is apparently difficult to create in the

---

[2]Arrigo and Pezdek (1997) prefer the term *psychogenic amnesia*, which describes the nature of the phenomenon without offering the "repression" explanation of why it occurs.

laboratory, leading at least one theorist to question its existence (Holmes, 1974, 1990). It may be, however, that events sufficiently traumatic to bring about repression cannot easily or ethically be created in a laboratory setting; it may also be that many adults simply do not repress painful information as a matter of course (Erdelyi, 1985; Jones, 1993). Until these various possibilities are systematically investigated, theorists will undoubtedly have difficulty reaching consensus about the extent to which repression plays a role in human forgetting.

Construction Error

We have already seen how construction can lead to errors in recall. Construction may occur either at storage (i.e., learner-invented information is stored) or at retrieval (i.e., the learner "remembers" information that was never encountered). Construction at retrieval time is particularly likely to occur when there are holes in the information retrieved—holes possibly due to decay, interference, or unsuccessful retrieval. So, as you might expect, erroneous reconstruction of an event or a body of learned information is increasingly likely to occur as time goes on (Anderson & Pichert, 1978; Dooling & Christiaansen, 1977; Spiro, 1977).

Failure to Store

A final explanation of "forgetting" is the fact that some information may never have been learned in the first place (Bourne et al., 1986; Ellis & Hunt, 1983). Perhaps we didn't pay attention to the information, so it never entered working memory. Or perhaps we didn't process it sufficiently to get it into long-term memory. As you well know, mere exposure to information does not guarantee long-term memory storage.

The Case of Infantile Amnesia

You probably remember very little of your infancy and early childhood years. I remember a couple of snippets—for instance, I recall waiting patiently in my crib one morning until my parents woke up, and I recall being held lovingly by my Nana one day in her flower garden—but for all I know, these "memories" never really happened. I certainly don't remember the first birthday party my parents gave me, even though all the photos of it suggest that it must have been a very festive occasion. Generally speaking, people remember little or nothing about specific events in their lives that occurred before age three (Newcombe, Drummey, Fox, Lie, & Ottinger-Albergs, 2000; Pillemer & White, 1989).

Children have *some* capacity to remember information from a very early age, however. In fact, a study by DeCasper and Spence (1986) suggests that memory begins even before birth. In this study, pregnant women read aloud a passage from a children's book (e.g., Dr. Seuss's *The Cat and the Hat*) twice a day for the final six weeks of their pregnancies. Later, their newborn babies were given pacifiers, and the babies' sucking rates (either fast or slow) determined whether they heard a recording of their mother reading the prebirth story or a different one. Even though the infants were only 2 or 3 days old, they began to adjust their sucking rate so that they could hear the familiar story—the one they had previously heard only while still in the womb!

We see evidence that young infants remember things they encounter after birth as well. For instance, when a ribbon connected to a mobile is tied to a baby's foot, even a 2-month-old easily learns that kicking makes the mobile move and remembers the connection over a period of several days—longer if the child has an occasional reminder (Rovee-Collier, 1999). Infants age 3 to 6 months show evidence that they remember the order in which they've seen a sequence of three mobiles (Gulya, Rovee-Collier, Galluccio, & Wilk, 1998). At age 6 months, they can recall and imitate actions they have seen 24 hours earlier, and their memory for observed actions increases in duration in the months that follow (Bauer, 1995; Collie & Hayne, 1999). By the time children are 2 years old, they are highly accurate in identifying pictures they have seen previously (Brown & Scott, 1971; Perlmutter & Lange, 1978).

Much of what infants learn and remember appears to be in the form of *implicit knowledge*—knowledge that affects their behavior even though they cannot consciously recall it (Nelson, 1995; Newcombe et al., 2000). Theorists have offered two plausible explanations for why we consciously recall so little of our early years. First, brain structures that are actively involved in explicit memories, such as the hippocampus and frontal cortex, are not fully developed at birth, and the frontal cortex in particular continues to mature in significant ways for several years thereafter (LeDoux, 1998; Nell, 2002; Newcombe et al., 2000). Second, as we have seen, talking about experiences enhances memory for them (recall our discussions of **verbalization** in Chapter 10 and of **narratives** earlier in this chapter), but infants and toddlers don't have the language skills to talk about events. As they gain proficiency in language, and particularly when people around them engage them in conversations about what they are experiencing, their memories improve dramatically (Eacott, 1999; Haden et al., 2001; Nelson, 1996; Simcock & Hayne, 2002; Tessler & Nelson, 1994). Presumably, talking about events enables them to encode the events in a verbal (language-based) form, making the events more easily retrievable at a later time.

Perhaps all of the explanations I've just presented are partially responsible for the universal human problem of forgetting. Yet forgetting isn't necessarily a bad thing. Many of the things we learn on any particular occasion have little use to us later (especially *much* later), and we rarely need to remember things *exactly* as we originally experienced them (Anderson & Schooler, 1991; Reisberg, 1997; Schacter, 1999). As Byrnes (2001) has put it, "our minds seem to be naturally equipped to retain only those events that repeat on a regular basis" (p. 59).

In classroom settings, however, students sometimes forget things related to important instructional objectives. In the final section of the chapter, we will pull together what we have learned about retrieval and forgetting, as well as about memory more generally, into several general principles that have implications for classroom practice.

GENERAL PRINCIPLES OF RETRIEVAL FOR INSTRUCTIONAL SETTINGS

In the preceding three chapters, we've identified numerous principles about memory and knowledge that have implications for classroom practice. Following are several additional ones that have particular relevance for retrieval of academic subject matter:

- *The internal organization of a body of information facilitates its retrieval.* When material is presented in an organized fashion—for instance, when hierarchical structures, cause–effect relationships, and so on are clearly specified—students are more likely to store it in a similar organizational network. And when information in long-term memory is organized, it can more easily be retrieved.

Some of my own students have found the following analogy useful in helping them understand the importance of organization for retrieval:

> Imagine 10,000 buttons scattered on a hardwood floor. Randomly choose two buttons and connect them with a thread. Now put this pair down and randomly choose two more buttons, pick them up, and connect them with a thread. As you continue to do this, at first you will almost certainly pick up buttons that you have not picked up before. After a while, however, you are more likely to pick at random a pair of buttons and find that you have already chosen one of the pair. So when you tie a thread between the two newly chosen buttons, you will find three buttons tied together. In short, as you continue to choose random pairs of buttons to connect with a thread, after a while the buttons start becoming interconnected into larger clusters. . . . (Kauffman, 1995, p. 56)

Eventually, you will form a single giant cluster of buttons. At this point, you can pick up almost any button in the pile and have most of the others follow. Now think of the buttons as being individual pieces of information related to a particular topic, and think of the threads as being your associations among those pieces. Eventually, you make enough associations that when you retrieve one idea about the topic, you can also retrieve, either directly or indirectly, most of the other things you know about that topic.[3]

• *How something is retrieved at one time affects how it is apt to be retrieved later on.* As we've seen, retrieval can be quite constructive. We've seen, too, that people tend to remember things in the same way time after time. Once they remember something incorrectly once, they're apt to remember it in the same incorrect way on a future occasion.

When students don't know the appropriate interconnections to make among the ideas they are studying, they may pull the ideas together in a way that seems logical but isn't necessarily accurate (recall our discussion of *theory theory* in Chapter 11). As an illustration, when a researcher asks fourth graders from Michigan why the Americas were once called the New World, a girl named Rita has this to say:

> Because they used to live in England, the British, and they didn't know about . . . they wanted to get to China 'cause China had some things they wanted. They had some cups or whatever—no, they had furs. They had fur and stuff like that and they wanted to have a shorter way to get to China so they took it and they landed in Michigan, but it wasn't called Michigan. I think it was the British that landed in Michigan and they were there first and so they tried to claim that land, but it didn't work out for some reason so they took some furs and brought them back to Britain and they sold them, but they mostly wanted it for the furs. So then the English landed there and they claimed the land and they wanted to make it a state, and so they got it signed by the government or whoever, the big boss, then they were just starting to make it a state so the British just went up to the Upper Peninsula and they thought they could stay there for a little while. Then they had to fight a war, then the farmers, they were just volunteers, so the farmers went right back and tried to get their family put together back again. (VanSledright & Brophy, 1992, p. 849)

---

[3]I am indebted to one of my former students, Jason Cole, for originally making the analogy between Kauffman's scenario and the organization of memory.

Rita has taken bits and pieces of information she has learned in school and pulled them into a scenario that makes sense to her. In the process, she has made some creative connections indeed. For instance, she associates China with both cups (after all, many cups *are* made of china) and furs (which early traders actually obtained in western North America). Notice, too, how Rita maintains that the British found a shorter way to get to China—one that apparently went right through Michigan. At the same time, Rita doesn't make at least one essential connection that would help her understand early American history—the fact that the "British" and the "English" were the same group of people.

Although Rita's description of American history has a few elements of truth, these elements have been combined to form an overall "knowledge" of history that could give any historian heart failure. If teachers want students to connect and remember classroom subject matter in a particular way, then, they should make the appropriate connections clear *right from the start.*

• *Information that must be retrieved within a particular context should be stored within that context.* People are most likely to retrieve information relevant to a situation when they have stored it in close association with other aspects of that situation. If they have stored it elsewhere, they are much less likely to stumble on it at times when it will be useful. Thus, information should be stored with retrieval in mind.

In light of this principle, teachers should give students numerous opportunities to relate classroom material to the various situations that are later likely to require its retrieval. For example, a student is more likely to retrieve mathematical ideas relevant to accounting, surveying, or engineering if the mathematics teacher incorporates problems involving accounting, surveying, and engineering into instruction. Similarly, a student studying for a psychology test stressing application becomes better prepared by using study time to consider numerous situations in which psychological principles can be applied. Furthermore, students should have opportunities to use the things they learn in real-world contexts; we will consider such *authentic activities* in Chapter 14.

• *External retrieval cues minimize failure to retrieve.* Earlier I mentioned the common problem of *forgetting to retrieve*—in particular, forgetting to do something you need to do. The best way to address this problem, I've found, is to provide an **external retrieval cue**—a physical reminder outside of (external to) the memory system. The classic example is a string around the finger: The string is tied in a spot impossible to overlook and serves as a reminder that something needs to be remembered.[4]

Finger strings are terribly unfashionable, but other external retrieval cues can be equally effective. Over the years, I've developed several that have made me one of the *least* absentminded professors on the planet. I keep a weekly calendar open by the telephone on my desk, and I write in it not only the meetings and appointments I need to go to but also the things I do regularly every week—teaching class Monday afternoons, playing racquetball Wednesday evenings, and so on. I write notes to myself about things I need to do on a particular day or accomplish by the end of the week, and I put them in plain sight on my desk. And if I need to be sure to bring something

---

[4] An *external retrieval cue* should remind you of the concept *cueing* (or *prompting*) described in Chapter 4. Behaviorists think of cues as evoking desired responses, whereas cognitivists think of them as facilitating retrieval. The effect is the same—a desired behavior is more likely to occur—but the explanation of why the cue has an effect is different.

with me to class or an appointment, I put it on the floor between my desk and my office door, so that I will definitely see it as I leave. Essentially, what I'm doing is guaranteeing retrieval of the things I need to remember.

As we'll discover in Chapter 13, students are typically quite naïve about how their memories work (and don't work), and teachers are in an excellent position to help them learn to use their memories most effectively. Teachers can, of course, provide occasional verbal reminders (e.g., "Don't forget to bring your permission slips back tomorrow!"). But ultimately, students should also be shown how to develop their *own* retrieval cues—appointment books, to-do lists, self-reminder sticky notes, and so on—so that they can eventually become responsible for their own retrieval.

• *Questions about previously learned material can promote both review and further elaboration.* In our discussion of instructional objectives in Chapter 5, we made a distinction between lower-level skills and higher-level skills. This was essentially a distinction between simply *knowing* something versus *doing* something (mentally) with that knowledge—for example, applying, analyzing, synthesizing, or evaluating it. We can make a similar distinction between **lower-level questions** and **higher-level questions:** The former ask students to retrieve something pretty much as they have stored it in memory, whereas the latter ask students to elaborate on that retrieved information.

Teacher questioning is a widely used teaching technique (e.g., Mehan, 1979), probably because it has several benefits. We noted one such benefit in Chapter 9: Questions help to focus students' attention on classroom activities. Questions also provide a feedback mechanism through which teachers and students alike can discover how much students have learned from a current lesson or can remember from previous lessons (Airasian, 1994; Connolly & Eisenberg, 1990; Fox & LeCount, 1991). When questions focus students' attention on previously studied material, they encourage review of that material—review that should promote greater recall later on (Wixson, 1984). And higher-level questions have the additional advantage of encouraging students to go beyond the information itself and construct more sophisticated understandings (Aulls, 1998; Meece, 1994; Minstrell & Stimpson, 1996). As examples, consider these questions from a lesson on the telegraph:

> Was the need for a rapid communications system [in North America] greater during the first part of the nineteenth century than it had been during the latter part of the eighteenth century? Why do you think so? (Torrance & Myers, 1970, p. 214)

To answer these questions, students must recall what they know about the eighteenth and nineteenth centuries (including the increasing movement of settlers to distant western territories) and pull that knowledge together in a way they have perhaps never done before.

All too often, however, teachers and instructional materials pose lower-level, fact-based questions, with few if any higher-level questions to facilitate student elaboration (Armbruster & Ostertag, 1993; Aulls, 1998; Raudenbush, Rowan, & Cheong, 1993; Tobin, 1987). Such a state of affairs is unfortunate. Fact-based questions are certainly quite useful for helping students acquire and review basic knowledge and skills. Yet research indicates quite clearly that teachers and instructional materials (e.g., textbooks) promote greater student achievement when they ask higher-level questions in addition to lower-level ones—for example, when they call for inferences, applications, justifications, and solutions to problems as well as asking for knowledge (Armbruster & Ostertag, 1993; Brophy, 1992b; Frederiksen, 1984b; Liu, 1990; Redfield & Rousseau, 1981).

The revised taxonomy includes six *cognitive processes,* each of which is potentially relevant to four different *types of knowledge.*

Cognitive Processes

1. **Remember:** recognizing or recalling information learned at an earlier time and stored in long-term memory
2. **Understand:** constructing meaning from instructional materials and messages (e.g., drawing inferences, identifying new examples, summarizing)
3. **Apply:** using knowledge in a familiar or new situation
4. **Analyze:** breaking information into its constituent parts, and perhaps identifying interrelationships among those parts
5. **Evaluate:** making judgments about information using certain criteria or standards
6. **Create:** putting knowledge and/or procedures together to form a coherent, structured, and possibly original whole

Types of Knowledge

A. **Factual knowledge:** knowing specific pieces of information (e.g., facts, terminology)
B. **Conceptual knowledge:** knowing more general structures and interrelationships among pieces of information (e.g., general principles, schemas, models, theories)
C. **Procedural knowledge:** knowing how to do something (e.g., using algorithms, employing scientific research methods), and possibly applying certain criteria in choosing the procedure to use
D. **Metacognitive knowledge:** knowing about the nature of thinking and about effective learning strategies, and being aware of one's own cognitive processes

Figure 12–1
A two-dimensional revision of Bloom's taxonomy (L. W. Anderson et al., 2001).

- *Taxonomies of objectives can be useful reminders of the various ways in which students might be asked to think about and apply what they have learned.* In our discussion of instructional objectives in Chapter 5, we looked at Bloom's Taxonomy of Educational Objectives, which suggests six, increasingly complex levels of behavior that teachers might encourage and assess. Recently, a collaborative group of educational psychologists (L. W. Anderson et al., 2001) has revised the taxonomy, in part to reflect theoretical advances in learning and cognition. The revision is a two-dimensional taxonomy that includes six *cognitive processes,* each of which is potentially relevant to four different *types of knowledge* (see Figure 12–1). The six cognitive processes are similar to the six levels in Bloom's original taxonomy (see Figure 5–1 on page 85). However, the cognitive processes are described by verbs rather than nouns, and the last two, *evaluate* and *create,* reflect a reversal of Bloom's *synthesis* and *evaluation* levels. The four types of knowledge include two forms of declarative knowledge, *factual knowledge* and *conceptual knowledge,* as well as *procedural knowledge* and *metacognitive knowledge* (we will look at the nature of the last one more closely in Chapter 13).

The two dimensions of the revised taxonomy are intended to represent two continuums that progress from very simple cognitive processes and types of knowledge to more complex ones. The continuums are not intended to be hard and fast, however; for example, some forms of conceptual knowledge can be fairly complex and abstract, whereas some forms of procedural knowledge are quite simple and concrete (L. W. Anderson et al., 2001). Rather than nitpick about the extent to which certain cognitive processes or types of knowledge are truly more complex than others, a more useful perspective of the revised taxonomy is to regard it as a helpful reminder of the various kinds of knowledge that students might have and the various ways in which they might use and apply it in new tasks and situations.

  • *Retrieval can take time.* Sometimes retrieval happens quickly and easily, especially for material that has been used repeatedly and perhaps been learned to automaticity. But in other instances, searching long-term memory for information relevant to a particular question or task can take a considerable amount of time. People need even more time if they must pull together what they can recall to draw new inferences, make new comparisons, generate new applications, and so on.

In the classroom, then, it is unreasonable to expect students to formulate insightful, creative responses to higher-level questions in a split second. Yet when teachers ask students a question, they typically wait one second or less for a response; if students don't respond in that short time interval, teachers tend to speak again, perhaps by asking different students the same question, rephrasing the question, or even answering the question themselves (Rowe, 1974, 1987). Teachers are equally reluctant to let much time elapse after students answer questions or make comments in class; once again, they typically allow one second or less of silence before responding to a statement or asking another question (Rowe, 1987).

The amount of time teachers allow to pass after their own and students' questions and comments is known as **wait time.** In many instances, one second is probably *not* sufficient time for students to think about (process) the questions teachers ask and the comments students make in class. After all, they must retrieve the things they know and, in the case of higher-level questions, must construct a response they have not previously stored.

Research indicates that students benefit tremendously simply from being given a little time to think. For example, when teachers increase their wait time by allowing at least three seconds to elapse (instead of only one) after both their own questions and students' remarks, we see changes in student behavior such as the following (Mohatt & Erickson, 1981; Rowe, 1974, 1987; Tharp, 1989; Tobin, 1987):[5]

Increased Student Participation:

- Students talk more and are more likely to answer questions correctly.
- More students participate in class; previously quiet students (including many minority students) become more active contributors.
- Students are more likely to contribute spontaneously to a class discussion—for example, by asking questions and presenting their own perspectives.
- Students are more likely to talk *to one another* (as well as to their teacher) within the context of a classroom discussion.

Better Quality of Student Responses:

- Students' responses are longer and more sophisticated.
- Students are more likely to support their responses with evidence or logic.
- Students are more likely to give a variety of responses to the same question.
- Students are more likely to speculate when they don't know an answer.

---

[5]Note, however, that waiting *too* long may be detrimental because students' attention begins to drift elsewhere, so that important information is no longer in working memory (Duell, 1994).

Better Classroom Performance:

- Students are less likely to feel confused by course content; they are more likely to feel confident that they can master the material.
- Students' motivation to learn class material increases.
- Students show higher achievement, especially for complex material.
- Discipline problems decrease (as one fifth-grade boy put it, "It's the first time in all my years in school that anybody cared what I really thought—not just what I am supposed to say" [Rowe, 1987, p. 40]).

We also see changes in teacher behavior when we increase wait time to at least three seconds. More specifically, we see changes such as the following (Rowe, 1974, 1987; Tobin, 1987):

Different Kinds of Questions:

- Teachers ask fewer "simple" questions (e.g., questions requiring the recall of facts).
- Teachers ask more complex questions (e.g., questions requiring students to elaborate or develop alternative explanations).

Increased Flexibility in Instruction:

- Teachers modify the direction of discussion to accommodate students' comments and questions.
- Teachers allow their classes to pursue a topic in greater depth than they originally anticipated.

Changes in Expectations:

- Teachers' expectations for many students, especially previously low-achieving students, begin to improve.

Increasing wait time during class discussions and question–answer sessions benefits student learning in two ways (Tobin, 1987). First, it allows students more time to process information. Second, it appears to change the very nature of teacher–student discussions; for example, teachers are more likely to ask challenging, thought-provoking questions. In fact, the nature of the questions that teachers ask is probably as important as—and perhaps even more important than—the amount of wait time per se (Giaconia, 1988).

When the objective is recall of facts—when students need to retrieve information very quickly, to "know it cold"—then wait time during a question–answer session should be short. There is a definite advantage to rapid-fire drill and practice for skills that teachers want students to learn to a level of automaticity (Tobin, 1987). But when objectives include more complex processing of ideas and issues, longer wait time provides both teachers and students the time they need to retrieve relevant ideas and think them through.

- *Classroom assessments promote retrieval and review; they also influence storage processes.* As a college professor, I give regular quizzes—usually every two or three weeks in undergraduate classes and at least once a month in masters' level classes. I also give frequent out-of-class assignments in which students must apply what they are learning to their personal and professional lives. My assessments encourage review, of course, but they also encourage students to reflect on classroom material in new ways. Even my multiple-choice questions require students to elaborate on what they have learned, often by asking them to recognize new examples of concepts or to evaluate various classroom strategies using principles of effective learning and memory.

My assessment practices don't just affect what students do at retrieval time, however. They also affect how students study classroom subject matter to begin with; in other words, they affect students' storage processes. Because my students know from day one that I am going to assess their *understanding* and *application* of what they learn in my class, most of them focus on meaningful learning and elaboration when they listen, speak, read, and study. A few of them, alas, do what they've always done in other classes—they rote-memorize—and these students typically struggle on my quizzes and assignments until they either seek my assistance or else stumble on more effective approaches themselves.

Research tells us that classroom assessments, *when designed appropriately*, can enhance students' learning and memory in at least four ways:

1. *By promoting effective storage processes.* Students tend to read and study differently depending on how they expect their learning to be assessed (Frederiksen, 1984b; Frederiksen & Collins, 1989; Lundeberg & Fox, 1991). For example, students are likely to focus on memorizing isolated facts at a rote level if they believe a test will require verbatim recall. They are more likely to try to make sense of what they are studying—that is, to engage in meaningful learning—when they know they will have to put things in their own words. And they are more likely to elaborate on class material if such elaboration will be required at assessment time—for example, if they know they will have to apply, analyze, or synthesize the material.

2. *By encouraging review before the assessment.* As we discovered in Chapter 10, students have a better chance of remembering things over the long run if they review those things periodically. Preparing for assessments is one way of reviewing classroom material. For instance, most students study class material more and learn it better when they are told they will be tested on it than when they are simply told to learn it (Frederiksen, 1984b; Halpin & Halpin, 1982). We should note, however, that students typically spend more time studying the information they think will be on an assessment than the things they think an assessment won't cover (Corbett & Wilson, 1988; Frederiksen, 1984b; Frederiksen & Collins, 1989).

3. *By requiring review during the assessment itself.* Taking a test or completing an assignment is, in and of itself, an occasion for retrieving and reviewing learned information. Generally speaking, the very process of completing an assessment on classroom material helps students learn that material better (Dempster, 1991; Foos & Fisher, 1988; Frederiksen, 1984b; Nungester & Duchastel, 1982). But once again, the nature of the assessment probably makes a difference here: Tasks that require students to go beyond the material itself (e.g., to draw inferences) are more likely to be effective than those that ask only for recall of previously learned facts (Foos & Fisher, 1988). And tasks that require a broad search of long-term memory promote more comprehensive review than do relatively specific test questions (Frederiksen & Ward, 1978; Murnane & Raizen, 1988).

4. *By providing feedback.* Assessments provide a concrete mechanism for letting students know what things they have learned correctly and what things they have learned either *incorrectly* or not at all. For example, when students get constructive comments on their essays—comments that point out the strengths and weaknesses of each response, indicate where answers are ambiguous or imprecise, suggest how an essay might be more complete or better organized, and so on—their understanding of class material and their writing skills are both likely to improve (Baron, 1987; Krampen, 1987).

When we look at typical classroom tests, we are more apt to see test items that focus on lower-level skills (e.g., knowledge of simple facts), perhaps because such items are the easiest ones to write (Frederiksen & Collins, 1989; Nickerson, 1989; Poole, 1994; Silver & Kenney, 1995). If teachers want students to do *more* than memorize facts, they must develop assessments that encourage students to process information in certain ways—perhaps to rephrase ideas in their own words, generate their own examples of concepts, relate principles and procedures to real-world situations, use class material to solve problems, or examine ideas with a critical eye. Sometimes, of course, well-constructed test items can encourage such processes. In many cases, however, teachers may want to use other kinds of assessment tasks—perhaps writing stories, keeping journals, constructing maps, collecting and synthesizing data, comparing contradictory historical accounts, critiquing government policies, creating portfolios—that more readily allow students to apply classroom subject matter to new problems and situations, including those in their own lives (Gregg & Leinhardt, 1994a; Lester, Lambdin, & Preston, 1997; Mehrens, 1992; Paris & Paris, 2001; Shepard, 2000).

• *Long-term memory can probably never be a totally reliable record of information.* Long-term memory storage and retrieval are both constructive processes and so will always be fallible. Students' memories will never be perfect. At the same time, students can certainly learn how to capitalize on the strengths of the human memory system and how to compensate for its weaknesses. In our discussion of metacognition and self-regulated learning in the next chapter, we'll identify numerous strategies that students can use, as well as numerous ways that teachers can help them acquire such strategies.

SUMMARY

Retrieval from long-term memory appears to be a process of searching, in one "location" at a time, until the desired information is found. Retrieval is easier when information has previously been stored in a meaningful, organized fashion and when *retrieval cues* are present; presumably interconnections among ideas and appropriate retrieval cues increase the probability that looked-for information will be activated.

Retrieval is often a constructive process: Some pieces of information are directly retrieved and other, nonretrieved details are filled in to create a logical, coherent (albeit sometimes incorrect) recollection. Recall of information and events can also be affected by information or misinformation (e.g., misleading suggestions) presented at a later time. People sometimes "remember" things they have never specifically learned, perhaps because they draw correct inferences from what they *have* learned

or perhaps because related ideas in their long-term memories were activated during a learning experience. Describing a previous event in a particular way increases the likelihood that the learner will remember it in the same way on future occasions; in a sense, people remember their previous *recollections* of an event as much as (or even more than) they remember the event itself.

Theorists have offered numerous explanations for why people "forget" things they have presumably learned, including *decay, obliterative subsumption, interference, failure to retrieve, repression, construction error,* and *failure to store* information in the first place. *Infantile amnesia*—remembering little or nothing about what happens during the first few years of life—may be the result of both immature brain structures and an inability to talk about (and thereby verbally encode) experiences. Forgetting is not necessarily a bad thing, however: We typically have little use for the trivial details of everyday life, and we rarely need to remember important information word for word.

Numerous instructional practices facilitate students' ability to retrieve the things they've learned. When students learn a new body of information in an organized manner, and when they also associate that information with contexts in which it is apt to be useful, they are more likely to retrieve

ideas when potentially applicable or helpful. Yet retrieval is never guaranteed, and so *external retrieval cues* (e.g., "notes to self") can ensure that important things are remembered. Teacher questions and assessment practices can encourage retrieval and review. Lower-level questions and tasks may promote automaticity, but higher-level ones (those that ask students to infer, apply, justify, problem solve, etc.) are more likely to encourage further elaboration.

CHAPTER 13

Metacognition, Self-Regulated Learning, and Study Strategies

When I look back on my days as a high school student, I think about how I used to learn, or at least *tried* to learn, and I shudder. Although I was a reasonably good student, my ideas about how I could best study for my classes were incredibly naïve. For example, I remember sitting on my bed "reading" my history textbook at night: My eyes dutifully went down each page, focusing briefly on every line, but my mind was a thousand miles away. After completing the reading assignment, I couldn't remember a thing I had read, yet I had the crazy notion that my supposed "knowledge" of history would miraculously come to mind at test time (it didn't). I remember, too, studying vocabulary words for my class in Mandarin Chinese: I truly believed that simply repeating those words over and over again would get them through my thick skull. In retrospect, the only subject I learned well was mathematics, because the various mathematical concepts and principles I studied seemed quite logical based on what I already knew.

When I went to college, I continued to bumble along, spending too much time in mindless "reading" and taking notes in class that I can now make very little sense of (I have to wonder how much they helped me even then). It was only after a great deal of studying experience and considerable trial and error that I began to realize how important it was that I pay attention to course material with my mind as well as my eyes and that I try to understand the things I was studying.

How, as a metacognitively naïve high school student, the author read her history textbook.

A critical turning point of World War II was. . . hmmm, wonder what I should wear to school tomorrow. . . December 7, 1941. . . I'm really angry at what Marjorie said to me in P.E. today. . . next time I'll say something nasty back to her. . . I bet I can come up with something clever. . . let's see. . . goodness, I've finished the first part of the chapter already.

HISTORY

As you have been reading this book, I hope you have been learning a great deal about how *you* learn and remember; perhaps you have also been modifying your approach to your own learning tasks. For example, you may now be trying to pay closer attention to what you read in textbooks and what you hear in class. You may also be focusing more on understanding, organizing, and elaborating on your course material. In any case, I hope you are not reading this book the way I used to read my history text.

People's knowledge of their own learning and cognitive processes, as well as their regulation of those processes to enhance learning and memory, are collectively known as **metacognition**.[1] The more metacognitively sophisticated students are, the higher their school learning and achievement are likely to be. Unfortunately, many students of all ages (even many adults) appear to know little about effective ways to learn and remember (Dryden & Jefferson, 1994; Mayer, 1996b; Pintrich & De Groot, 1990; Schofield & Kirby, 1994; Thomas, 1993).

Metacognition is closely related to that *central executive* I spoke of in Chapter 9. You might think of it as the "manager" or "coach" of a person's learning (Schoenfeld, 1985b): It guides information processing and monitors the effectiveness of the various strategies the learner is applying to a particular learning task. But just as the coach of a basketball team might be either quite knowledgeable about playing basketball or instead harbor some very counterproductive misconceptions about how best to play the game, so, too, can a learner's metacognitive knowledge be either a help or a hindrance in the learning process.

In this chapter, we will look at the many things that people's metacognitive knowledge and skills may include. We will revisit social learning theorists' notion of self-regulation, this time applying it to an understanding of how learners regulate their learning and cognitive processes in the pursuit

---

[1]You may occasionally see the terms *metamemory* and *hypercognition*.

of specific learning tasks. We will examine numerous learning and study strategies that appear to promote effective learning and retention of classroom material and consider how students' *epistemological beliefs*—their beliefs about the nature of knowledge and learning—influence how they study and learn. We will discover that students' learning strategies improve with age but that students don't always use effective strategies even when they may be capable of doing so. Finally, we will identify instructional practices that can help students become metacognitively more sophisticated, and thus better able to learn and achieve in the classroom, over the long run.

METACOGNITIVE KNOWLEDGE AND SKILLS

Metacognition includes knowledge and skills such as the following:

- *Being aware of what one's own learning and memory capabilities are and of what learning tasks can realistically be accomplished* (e.g., recognizing that it is probably not possible to learn everything in a 200-page reading assignment in a single evening)
- *Knowing which learning strategies are effective and which are not* (e.g., realizing that meaningful learning is more effective than rote learning for long-term retention)
- *Planning an approach to a learning task that is likely to be successful* (e.g., finding a place to study where there will be few distractions)
- *Using effective learning strategies* (e.g., taking detailed notes when lecture material is likely to be difficult to remember otherwise)
- *Monitoring one's present knowledge state* (e.g., recognizing when information has been successfully learned and when it has not)
- *Knowing effective strategies for retrieval of previously stored information* (e.g., thinking about the context in which a certain piece of information was probably learned)

In essence, metacognition is *thinking about thinking*. As you can see, it involves some fairly complex (and often abstract) ideas and processes. Many of these ideas and processes are not specifically taught in the classroom. Thus, it should not surprise you to learn that students typically acquire metacognitive knowledge and skills slowly and only after many challenging learning experiences, nor should it be surprising that some students develop few if any effective study strategies at all.

As an example of metacognition, let's consider what happens when students study their school textbooks. Their reading in this situation is not just a process of identifying the words on the page, nor is it just making sense of the sentences and paragraphs in which those words appear. The students are also trying to store the information they read in long-term memory so that they can retrieve it later on. In other words, they are *reading for learning*.

What specifically do students do when they read for learning? Good readers—those who understand and effectively remember what they read—do many of the following:

- Clarify their purpose for reading something
- Read differently depending on whether they want to ascertain the general gist of a passage, learn the passage's content thoroughly and in great detail, or simply read for pleasure
- Determine what is most important to learn and remember, and focus their attention and efforts on that material

- Try to make sense of and elaborate on (e.g., draw inferences from and identify logical relationships within) what they read
- Bring their prior knowledge into play in understanding and elaborating on what they read
- Envision possible examples and applications of the ideas presented
- Make predictions about what they are likely to read next in a passage
- Ask themselves questions that they try to answer as they read
- Periodically check themselves to make sure they understand and remember what they have read
- Attempt to clarify any ambiguous points they encounter.
- Persist in their efforts to understand when they have initial difficulty comprehending what they are reading
- Read for possible conceptual change—in other words, read with the understanding that the ideas they encounter may be inconsistent with things they currently believe
- Critically evaluate what they read
- Summarize what they have read
  (Baker, 1989; Barnett, 1999; Brown & Palincsar, 1987; Brown, Palincsar, & Armbruster, 1984; Chan, Burtis, & Bereiter, 1997; Dole et al., 1991; Hacker, 1998b; Myers & Duffy, 1990; Palincsar & Brown, 1989; Roth & Anderson, 1988; Schraw & Bruning, 1995; van der Broek, 1990)

In contrast, poor readers—those who have trouble learning and remembering the things they read—use few of the strategies I've just listed. For example, they have little focus and sense of purpose as they read a passage (Brown & Palincsar, 1987). They have difficulty drawing

How the author *should* have read her history textbook.

A critical turning point of World War II was the Japanese attack on Pearl Harbor on December 7, 1941. . . why would the attack on Pearl Harbor have been so important for the outcome of the war?. . . probably because it forced the United States to enter the war, greatly increasing the number of ships, guns, and troops available to the Allies.

inferences from the ideas they encounter (Oakhill, 1993). They rarely ask themselves questions about the material, predict what's coming next, clarify ambiguous statements, or summarize what they have read (Palincsar & Brown, 1984). They overlook inconsistencies among ideas within the text, as well as inconsistencies between those ideas and their prior beliefs about the world (Brown & Palincsar, 1987; Roth & Anderson, 1988). And, in general, poor readers seem to have little metacognitive awareness of the things they should do mentally as they read (Baker, 1989). As examples, consider three high school students' descriptions of how they studied:

- I stare real hard at the page, blink my eyes and then open them—and cross my fingers that it will be right here (points at head).
- It's easy. If [the teacher] says study, I read it twice. If she says read, it's just once through.
- I just read the first line in each paragraph—it's usually all there. (Brown & Palincsar, 1987, p. 83)

As you might guess, these students did *not* learn very effectively from the things they were reading (Brown & Palincsar, 1987).

Not all students are so metacognitively naive. For example, as 9-year-old Eamon describes what he does when he encounters new ideas in science, he seems to have a fairly good understanding of meaningful learning and the dynamic nature of knowledge:

I try to look for a fit. Like if it doesn't fit with any . . . of the ideas that I have in my head I just leave it and wait for other ideas to come in so that I can try to fit them together with my ideas. Maybe they will go with my ideas and then another idea will come in and I can fit it together with that idea and my understanding just keeps on enlarging. An idea usually does fit. (M. G. Hennessey, 2003, p. 123)

It appears, then, that Eamon has some explicit knowledge of his own thought processes: He can actively think about and describe them. Yet a good deal of metacognition may be *implicit*: People often regulate their learning processes without conscious awareness that they are doing so.[2]

The process of metacognition is consistent with social learning theorists' notion of *self-regulation*: It provides the mechanism through which people begin to regulate one aspect of their lives—their own learning. Let's look more closely at what self-regulated learning involves.

SELF-REGULATED LEARNING

In our discussion of self-regulation in Chapter 7, we discovered that as children grow older, most of them begin to set standards and goals for their own performance. They then choose behaviors that they think will help them meet such standards and goals, and they evaluate the effects of their actions.

Social learning theorists and cognitivists alike have begun to portray effective learning in a similar manner—as a process of setting goals, choosing learning strategies that are likely to help one achieve those goals, and then evaluating the results of one's efforts (Paris & Cunningham, 1996; Schunk & Zimmerman, 1994; Winne, 1995a; Zimmerman, 1998). Yet increasingly,

---

[2]Some theorists propose that metacognition includes both explicit and implicit knowledge, but others suggest that we should use the term only to refer to knowledge and processes of which people are consciously aware (e.g., Brown, Bransford, Ferrara, & Campione, 1983; diSessa et al., 2003; Hacker, 1998a; Siegler, 1998). I will use the term in its broader sense, which encompasses both explicit and implicit knowledge.

theorists have begun to realize that effective learning includes control of one's motivation and emotions as well. Thus, **self-regulated learning** typically includes most or all of the following:

- *Goal setting:* Identifying a desired end result for the learning activity. Self-regulated learners know what they want to accomplish when they read or study; for instance, they may want to learn specific facts, get an overall understanding of the ideas being presented, or simply acquire sufficient knowledge to do well on a classroom exam (Mayer, 1996b; Nolen, 1996; Winne & Hadwin, 1998; Wolters, 1998; Zimmerman & Bandura, 1994). Typically, they tie their goals for a particular learning activity to their longer-term goals and aspirations (Zimmerman, 1998). And especially as they reach college, they may set deadlines for themselves as a way of making sure they don't leave important learning tasks until the last minute (Ariely & Wertenbroch, 2002).

- *Planning:* Determining how best to use the time available for the learning task. Self-regulated learners plan ahead with regard to a learning task and use their time effectively to accomplish their goals (Zimmerman, 1998; Zimmerman & Risemberg, 1997).

- *Self-motivation:* Maintaining intrinsic motivation to complete a learning task. Self-regulated learners are apt to have high self-efficacy regarding their ability to accomplish the learning task successfully (Schunk & Zimmerman, 1997; Zimmerman & Risemberg, 1997). In addition, they use a variety of strategies to keep themselves on task—perhaps embellishing on the task to make it more fun, reminding themselves of the importance of doing well, visualizing their eventual success, or promising themselves a reward when they are finished (Corno, 1993; Wolters, 2000; Wolters & Rosenthal, 2000).

- *Attention control:* Maximizing attention on the learning task. Self-regulated learners try to focus their attention on the subject matter at hand and to clear their minds of potentially distracting thoughts and emotions (Harnishfeger, 1995; Kuhl, 1985; Winne, 1995a).

- *Application of learning strategies:* Selecting and using appropriate ways of processing the material to be learned. Self-regulated learners choose different learning strategies depending on the specific goal they wish to accomplish; for example, they read a magazine article differently, depending on whether they are reading it for entertainment or studying for an exam (Linderholm, Gustafson, van den Broek, & Lorch, 1997; Schunk & Zimmerman, 1997; Winne, 1995a).

- *Self-monitoring:* Checking periodically to see whether progress is being made toward the goal. Self-regulated learners continually monitor their progress during a learning activity, and they change their learning strategies or modify their goals if necessary (Butler & Winne, 1995; Carver & Scheier, 1990; Zimmerman, 1998).

- *Self-evaluation:* Assessing the final outcome of one's efforts. Self-regulated learners determine whether what they have learned is sufficient for the goals they have set for themselves (Butler & Winne, 1995; Schraw & Moshman, 1995; Zimmerman & Risemberg, 1997).

- *Self-reflection:* Determining the extent to which one's learning strategies have been successful and efficient, and possibly identifying alternatives that may be more effective in future learning situations (Kuhn, 2001b; Winne & Stockley, 1998; Zimmerman, 1998).

When students are self-regulated learners, they set higher academic goals for themselves, learn more effectively, and achieve at higher levels in the classroom (Bronson, 2000; Butler & Winne, 1995; Winne, 1995a; Zimmerman & Bandura, 1994; Zimmerman & Risemberg, 1997). Unfortunately, few students acquire a high level of self-regulation, perhaps in part because traditional instructional practices do little to promote it (Paris & Ayres, 1994; Zimmerman & Bandura, 1994).

To some extent, self-regulated learning probably develops from opportunities to engage in independent, self-directed learning activities appropriate for the age group (Paris & Paris, 2001; Vye et al., 1998; Zimmerman, 1998). But if we take Vygotsky's perspective for a moment, we might reasonably suspect that self-regulated learning also has roots in socially regulated learning (Stright, Neitzel, Sears, & Hoke-Sinex, 2001; Vygotsky, 1962). At first, other people (e.g., parents or teachers) might help children learn by setting goals for a learning activity, keeping children's attention focused on the learning task, suggesting effective learning strategies, monitoring learning progress, and so on. Over time, children assume increasing responsibility for these processes; that is, they begin to set their *own* learning goals, stay on task with little prodding from others, identify potentially effective strategies, and evaluate their own learning.

Developmentally speaking, a reasonable bridge between other-regulated learning and self-regulated learning is **co-regulated learning,** in which an adult and one or more children share responsibility for directing the various aspects of the learning process (McCaslin & Good, 1996). For instance, the adult and children might mutually agree on the specific goals of a learning endeavor, or the adult might describe the criteria that indicate successful learning and then have children evaluate their own performance in light of those criteria. Initially, the adult might provide considerable structure, or scaffolding, for the children's learning efforts; in a true Vygotskian fashion, such scaffolding is gradually removed as children become more effectively self-regulating.

Later in the chapter, we will consider several strategies that teachers can use to facilitate the development of self-regulation in students at a variety of age levels. Before we can do so, however, we must find out more about what metacognitive processes entail. At this point, let's consider what research has to say about effective learning and study strategies.

EFFECTIVE LEARNING AND STUDY STRATEGIES

In our discussion of cognitive theories in the previous few chapters, we have often mentioned people's strategies for learning, studying, solving problems, and so on. Perhaps we should stop for a moment to consider what we actually mean by the term *strategy*. Sometimes people engage in effective storage processes with little conscious awareness of what they are doing (Kintsch, 1998; Stanovich, 1999). For instance, as you read an enjoyable novel, you may automatically relate events in the story to similar events in your own life. But generally speaking, when psychologists use the terms **learning strategy** and **study strategy,** they are talking about the *intentional* use of one or more cognitive processes to accomplish a particular learning task (Alexander, Graham, & Harris, 1998; Siegler, 1998; Snowman, 1986).[3]

People do a lot of things "in their heads" when they want to learn and remember new material, but some strategies are clearly more effective than others. In the next few pages, we will consider research findings regarding several effective learning and study strategies. The first three—meaningful learning, elaboration, and organization—are long-term memory storage processes that we initially encountered in Chapter 10. The others—note taking, identifying important information, summarizing, comprehension monitoring, and mnemonics—are additional strategies that researchers have consistently found to be valuable techniques in academic learning tasks.

---

[3]Snowman (1986) has suggested that we distinguish between more general *learning strategies* (overall plans for accomplishing a learning task) and *learning tactics* (more specific techniques executed during the learning task itself). For the most part, the strategies I describe in this chapter are of the more specific, tactical type.

Meaningful Learning and Elaboration

In Chapter 10, I described *meaningful learning* as a process of relating new material to knowledge already stored in long-term memory and *elaboration* as a process of using prior knowledge to interpret and expand on that new material. Both processes involve making connections between new information and the things we already know, and both processes clearly facilitate our learning as we study (Dole et al., 1991; Pressley, 1982; Waters, 1982; Weinstein, 1978; Wittrock & Alesandrini, 1990).

A study by Van Rossum and Schenk (1984) illustrates this point well. College students studied and took notes on a historical passage, then took a test on the contents of the passage and answered questions about how they had studied. Approximately half of the students described rote-learning approaches to studying; they interpreted the objective of the assignment as one of memorizing facts (as one student described it, "learning everything by heart"). The other half described meaningful and elaborative approaches to the study process: They attempted to understand, interpret, abstract meaning, and apply what they read. One student's self-report illustrates the latter approach:

> First I read the text roughly through and try to form a picture of the content. The second time I read more accurately and try through the structure of the text to make the small connections in and between the paragraphs. The third or fourth time I try to repeat to myself, without looking at the text, the main lines of the argument, emphasizing reasonings. This is my usual way to study texts. (Van Rossum & Schenk, 1984, p. 77)

There were no differences between the two groups of students in their performance on multiple-choice questions that tested their knowledge of facts in the passage. However, students who used meaningful learning strategies performed better on multiple-choice questions that required drawing inferences and produced better-integrated and qualitatively superior responses on an essay test on the same material.

In Chapter 10, I introduced the concept of *prior knowledge activation*, reminding students of what they already know about a topic. In fact, students can be taught to think about relevant prior knowledge on their own as they study a new topic. When they use this strategy, they can more easily engage in meaningful learning and elaboration, and they can more effectively apply what they learn to new situations (Spires & Donley, 1998).

Students appear to interpret information differently depending on whether they are trying to remember facts or generate applications—in other words, depending on whether they are trying to elaborate on what they learn. In a study conducted by one of my doctoral students, Rose McCallin (McCallin, Ormrod, & Cochran, 1997), undergraduate education majors enrolled in two educational psychology classes completed a questionnaire that assessed their approach to learning the course material. Some students described themselves as wanting to learn specific teaching techniques; in other words, they wanted to be told exactly what they should do in the classroom. Other students described themselves as preferring to understand psychological principles of human learning and behavior so that they could develop their *own* classroom procedures. Following the course's unit on educational assessment and measurement, McCallin gave the students a list of basic concepts in educational testing and asked them to draw a diagram (concept map) that showed how the concepts were related to one another. Students with a tell-me-what-to-do attitude tended to depict relationships among concepts that were simplistically factual or procedural (e.g., "*Raw scores* are used to compute a *mean*"). In contrast, students with a let-me-apply-it-myself attitude described conceptual interrelationships that reflected more sophisticated processing, including hierarchical structures, cause–effect relationships, and deductive reasoning (e.g., "*Reliability* affects the *standard error of measurement*"). Although McCallin did not study how well the students remembered course material after the semester was over, we could reasonably predict that the latter kind of students—those who developed a well integrated and elaborated understanding of the topic in question so that they could apply it themselves—would be able to retrieve and reconstruct the course material more effectively. And, for reasons that you will discover in our discussion of transfer and problem solving in the next chapter, such students should also be able to apply principles of educational psychology more readily to new situations and problems.

Organization

In Chapter 10, we examined evidence for the importance of *internal organization*—finding connections and interrelationships within a body of new information—for long-term memory storage. Making oneself aware of the inherent organizational structure of new material facilitates learning; so, too, does imposing an organizational structure on material when that structure doesn't initially exist (Britton et al., 1998; Gauntt, 1991; Kail, 1990; Wade, 1992).

Nevertheless, students often fail to construct appropriate organizational structures for information presented in lectures and written materials. Rather than recognizing and taking advantage of the interrelationships inherent in a body of information, students frequently "organize" various ideas simply as a list of unrelated facts (Meyer, Brandt, & Bluth, 1980). Furthermore, students are less likely to organize learning material as it becomes more difficult for them (Kletzien, 1988).

Students can use several techniques to help them organize classroom material effectively. One frequently used approach involves creating an outline of the major topics and ideas. When students learn how to outline the things they hear in lectures and read in textbooks, their classroom learning often improves (McDaniel & Einstein, 1989; Wade, 1992). Curiously, however, good students are *less* likely to outline the things they read than their more "average" classmates (Baker, 1989). It may be that better students organize material easily enough in their heads that paper-and-pencil outlines aren't necessary.

A second approach involves creating a graphic representation of the information to be learned—perhaps a map, flow chart, pie chart, or matrix (Dansereau, 1995; B. F. Jones, Pierce, & Hunter, 1988/1989; Scevak, Moore, & Kirby, 1993; Van Patten, Chao, & Reigeluth, 1986). For example, high school students can remember historical events more effectively when they put information about important events on a map depicting where each event took place (Scevak et al., 1993). As another example, consider how students might better remember the sequence in which various historical events took place. A few years ago, my son Alex (then a high school senior) and I took an undergraduate art history course at my university. The first unit of the course covered a 40,000-year span, including prehistoric art (e.g., cave paintings), Mesopotamian art (e.g., the Gates of Ishtar), and ancient Egyptian art (e.g., the pyramids at Giza). As we studied for our first test, Alex and I had a hard time keeping the time periods of all of the cultures and artistic styles straight. We finally constructed a time line, depicted in Figure 13–1, which organized what was happening when and kept us from going into severe numbers shock. The time line didn't necessarily help us make better sense of events, but it did help us keep track of them. It also provided a way for us to encode the information visually as well as verbally (B. F. Jones et al., 1988/1989).

Still another technique for organizing information is concept mapping (Krajcik, 1991; Mintzes, Wandersee, & Novak, 1997; Novak & Gowin, 1984). In Chapter 10, I described

Figure 13–1
The Ormrod time line for prehistoric, Mesopotamian, and ancient Egyptian art.

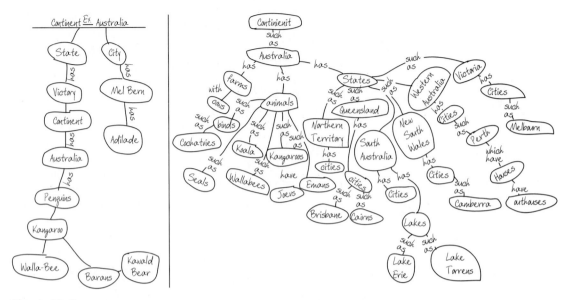

Figure 13-2
Concept maps constructed by two fifth-grade students after watching a slide lecture on Australia.
From *Learning How to Learn* (pp. 100–101) by J. D. Novak & D. B. Gowin, 1984, Cambridge, England: Cambridge University Press. Copyright 1984 by Cambridge University Press. Reprinted with the permission of Cambridge University Press.

concept maps as a way that teachers can depict the overall organizational structure of a lesson or unit (refer back to Figure 10–9 as an example). Yet students can also create their *own* concept maps for a lesson. Figure 13–2 shows concept maps constructed by two fifth-grade students after they watched a slide-show lecture on Australia. Notice how very different the knowledge of the two children appears to be, even though both children received the same information.

Concept maps, constructed either by a teacher or by students themselves, often facilitate students' classroom performance (Alvermann, 1981; Hawk, 1986; Holley & Dansereau, 1984). Students benefit in numerous ways from constructing their own concept maps for classroom material (Mintzes et al., 1997; Novak, 1998; Novak & Gowin, 1984). By focusing on how concepts relate to one another, students organize material better. They are also more likely to notice how new concepts are related to things they already know; thus, they are more likely to learn the material meaningfully. And, like such graphic techniques as maps and time lines, concept maps can help students encode information in long-term memory visually as well as verbally. Concept maps are especially helpful to low-achieving students, perhaps because they provide a means of helping these students process information in ways that high-achieving students do more regularly (Dansereau, 1995; Lambiotte, Dansereau, Cross, & Reynolds, 1989; Mintzes et al., 1997; Stensvold & Wilson, 1990).

Student-constructed concept maps can provide information to teachers as well as to students; in particular, such maps may indicate possible misconceptions and "holes" in students' understanding (Novak, 1998; Novak & Gowin, 1984; Novak & Musonda, 1991). If you look carefully at the concept map on the left side of Figure 13–2, you should detect several misconceptions that the student has about Australia. For example, Adelaide is *not* part of Melbourne, it is a different city altogether! If geographic knowledge about Australia is an instructional objective, then this student clearly needs further instruction to correct such misinformation.

Note Taking

In general, taking notes on information presented in lectures and textbooks is positively correlated with student learning (Benton, Kiewra, Whitfill, & Dennison, 1993; Cohn, Hult, & Engle, 1990; Hale, 1983; Kiewra, 1989; Shrager & Mayer, 1989). Note taking probably serves two functions for students (Di Vesta & Gray, 1972; Kiewra, 1989). For one thing, it facilitates *encoding* of material: By writing information down and looking at it on paper, students are likely to encode it both verbally and visually. As evidence for the encoding function of note taking, students remember more when they take notes even if they have no opportunity to review those notes (Howe, 1970; Weinstein & Mayer, 1986). In addition, notes serve as a form of concrete *external storage* for information presented in class: Given the notorious fallibility of long-term memory (see Chapter 12), pen and paper often provide a dependable alternative (Benton et al., 1993). Once lecture content is recorded on paper, it can be reviewed at regular intervals later on.

In my own classes, I have often observed how very different the notes of different students can be, even though all of the students sit through the same class sessions. Some students write extensively; others write very little. Some students try to capture all of the main ideas of a lecture or explanation, whereas others only copy the specific words I write on the board—mostly terms and their definitions. Some students include details and examples in their notes; others do not.

Not surprisingly, the effectiveness of note taking depends on the type of notes taken. Notes are more useful to students when they are relatively complete representations of the presented material (Benton et al., 1993; Cohn et al., 1990; Kiewra, 1989). They are more likely to promote learning when they represent an encoding of the information that is consistent with the objectives of the instructional unit; hence, those objectives should be clear to students (Barnett, Di Vesta, & Rogozinski, 1981; Snowman, 1986). Notes are also more likely to be effective when they summarize main ideas and include details that support those ideas (Brown, Campione, & Day, 1981; Doctorow, Wittrock, & Marks, 1978; Kiewra, 1985; Taylor, 1982). And notes that go beyond the material—those that include students' own elaborations of it—may be especially beneficial (Barnett et al., 1981; Kiewra, 1989; King, 1992).

The effectiveness of note taking depends on the type of notes taken.

Another effective technique is reorganizing and elaborating on notes that have previously been taken during a lecture or reading assignment (DuBois et al., 1988; Kiewra, 1985; Kiewra et al., 1988; Shimmerlick & Nolan, 1976). Especially in a lecture situation, students have no control over how fast information is presented and may not have time to process everything meaningfully. In such a case, students may need to focus merely on writing information during class and then organizing and encoding it appropriately afterward.

Unfortunately, many students (especially those at the junior high and high school, rather than college, levels) have difficulty understanding their own notes when they use them to review class material at a later time (Yokoi, 1997). Teachers can do some very simple things to improve the quality and completeness of the notes that students take. Writing important ideas on the chalkboard may be helpful: Students are far more likely to write down those things that their teacher writes. Emphasizing important ideas (e.g., by repeating them) also increases the likelihood that students will record those ideas on paper. Furthermore, providing some kind of general organizational framework—a skeletal outline, a compare-and-contrast matrix, or the like—facilitates students' ability to organize information in the ways that the teacher envisions (Benton et al., 1993; Kiewra, 1989; Pressley, Yokoi, Van Meter, Van Etten, & Freebern, 1997; Van Meter, Yokoi, & Pressley, 1994; Yokoi, 1997).

Identifying Important Information

Students frequently encounter more information than they can possibly store in their long-term memories within a reasonable time period. As a result, they must determine which things are most important for them to learn and study—for instance, they must separate main ideas from trivial details (Dole et al., 1991; Reynolds & Shirey, 1988). The task is often a challenging one, in part because the relative "importance" of different ideas is ultimately determined by the teacher, who may have a different perspective on the material than students do (Alexander & Jetton, 1996; Broekkamp, Van Hout-Wolters, Rijlaarsdam, & van den Bergh, 2002; Schellings, Van Hout-Wolters, & Vermunt, 1996).

The various *signals* that are present in a lecture or textbook (e.g., specified objectives of a lesson, boldfaced or italicized words, ideas written on the chalkboard) can help students discriminate between important and unimportant information (recall our discussion of signals near the end of Chapter 10). In some instances, however, students may overlook or misinterpret such signals; in other instances, existing signals may be few and far between. In the absence of useful signals, students often have trouble identifying the main points of a lecture or reading assignment; this is particularly true when they have little background knowledge about the subject matter they are studying (Byrnes, 1996; Dole et al., 1991; Garner et al., 1991). Many students use relatively inadequate methods of selecting information—for example, focusing on first sentences of paragraphs or on distinctive pieces of information (such as definitions and formulas)—and often miss critical ideas as a result (Mayer, 1984; Pallock & Surber, 1997; Surber, 2001).

Once students become proficient at identifying important information, underlining or highlighting the information, at least in purchased textbooks and students' class notes, is apt to be beneficial. I encourage my own students to underline or highlight the important points that their textbooks present; doing so is less time consuming than taking notes on a book's content, and it keeps specific information within its larger context. But underlining and highlighting are probably only effective when used sparingly to emphasize main ideas and essential details (Snowman, 1986). Highlighting an entire page, as if with a paint roller, can hardly be of much value.

Summarizing

Students are sometimes encouraged to summarize the material they read and hear—for instance, by condensing and integrating it, deriving abstract representations of it, or identifying suitable headings to label it. Doing so seems to facilitate learning and retention of that material (Dole et al., 1991; Jonassen, Hartley, & Trueman, 1986; King, 1992; Rinehart, Stahl, & Erickson, 1986; Wittrock & Alesandrini, 1990).

Unfortunately, many students have difficulty adequately summarizing the things they read and hear (Anderson & Hidi, 1988/1989; Brown & Palincsar, 1987; Byrnes, 1996; Jonassen et al., 1986). If we think about it, we realize that developing a good summary is not an easy task at all: Students must discriminate between important and unimportant information, identify main ideas that may or may not be explicitly stated, and organize critical elements into a cohesive whole (Anderson & Hidi, 1988/1989; Greene & Ackerman, 1995; Spivey, 1997). In classroom situations, students must also have some sense of how they are going to be evaluated and tailor their summaries to the evaluation criteria (Snowman, 1986).

Theorists have offered several suggestions for helping students create good summaries of classroom subject matter:

- Have students first practice developing summaries for short, easy, and well-organized passages (perhaps those only a few paragraphs in length), then gradually introduce longer and more difficult texts for them to summarize.
- When students are writing a summary, suggest that they:
  - Identify or invent a topic sentence for each paragraph or section.
  - Identify superordinate concepts or ideas that subsume several more specific points.
  - Find supporting information for each main idea.
  - Delete trivial and redundant information.
- Have students compare and discuss their summaries, considering what ideas they thought were important and why.
  (Anderson & Hidi, 1988/1989; Brown & Day, 1983; Rinehart et al., 1986; Rosenshine & Meister, 1992)

Such strategies do seem to help students write better summaries and, ultimately, to learn and remember classroom material more effectively (Bean & Steenwyk, 1984; Pressley, with McCormick, 1995; Rinehart et al., 1986).

Comprehension Monitoring

Students who learn most effectively check themselves periodically to be sure they are understanding and remembering what they hear in class or read in a textbook. They also take steps to remediate any comprehension difficulties they have—for example, by asking questions or rereading a passage. In other words, good students engage in **comprehension monitoring**[4] (Baker, 1989; Dole et al., 1991; Hacker, Dunlosky, & Graesser, 1998; Haller, Child, & Walberg, 1988; Otero & Kintsch, 1992).

Unfortunately, many students of all ages *don't* carefully monitor their comprehension as they sit in class or read a textbook (Baker & Brown, 1984; Flavell, 1979; Hacker, Bol, Horgan,

---

[4]Theorists are talking about a similar idea when they use the terms *metacomprehension, self-regulated comprehension, calibration, judgment of learning,* and *metamnemonic evaluation.*

Students are not always accurate judges of what they know and what they do not.

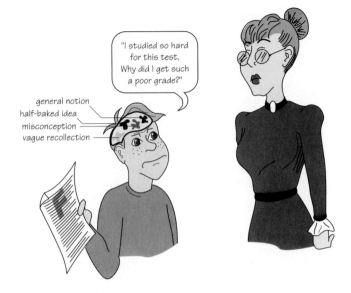

"I studied so hard for this test. Why did I get such a poor grade?"

general notion
half-baked idea
misconception
vague recollection

& Rakow, 2000; Otero, 1998). As a result, they are often ignorant about what they know and what they don't know, and they may think they understand something they actually *misunderstand*. In other words, they have an **illusion of knowing**[5] (Baker, 1989; Brown, 1978; Butler & Winne, 1995; Hacker, 1998b; Voss & Schauble, 1992). Students are especially likely to have an illusion of knowing something when they have little prior knowledge about the subject matter or when the material is especially difficult for them (Hacker, 1998a; Maki, 1998; Stone, 2000; Winne & Jamieson-Noel, 2001). Illusions of knowing are also more common when students have overly simplistic ideas of what it means to "know" something (more on this idea in the upcoming section on epistemological beliefs).

When students think they know classroom material, they are likely to stop studying it. Thus, students who have only the *illusion* of knowing it will stop studying prematurely (Horgan, 1990; Voss & Schauble, 1992). And they are apt to be quite puzzled when, as a result, they perform poorly on an exam or assignment (Hacker et al., 2000; Horgan, 1990). For example, students occasionally approach me to express their confusion about why they did so poorly on an exam when they "knew" the information so well. When I ask these students specific questions about the material, I usually find that they don't really have a good grasp of it at all.

One strategy for facilitating students' comprehension monitoring is to have them draw pictures or diagrams of the material they are studying (Van Meter, 2001); such a strategy may be especially useful for topics that involve spatial arrangements or cause–effect relationships. Another approach is to have students formulate questions before a lesson or reading assignment that they then answer as they go along (Bragstad & Stumpf, 1982; Robinson, 1961; Rosenshine, Meister, & Chapman, 1996; Thomas & Robinson, 1972). For instance, before reading a textbook, a student might turn each heading and subheading into a question to be answered and then read sec-

[5]You may also see the term *secondary ignorance*.

tions of text with the intention of finding answers to those questions (Robinson, 1961). Such **self-questioning** is probably even more effective when students do it *throughout* a lesson or reading assignment (Brozo, Stahl, & Gordon, 1985; Dole et al., 1991; Haller et al., 1988; Wong, 1985). For example, undergraduate students who ask themselves questions as they take notes during a class lecture take better notes, understand the material better, and remember it longer (King, 1992; Spires, 1990).

By asking themselves questions periodically, students are more likely to know when they know something and when they do not. After reviewing research on the effectiveness of self-questioning, however, Snowman (1986) concluded that positive effects are limited to the acquisition of facts, without any noticeable impact on more sophisticated behaviors such as application or evaluation of those facts. This may be because most students ask themselves primarily fact-based questions (e.g., "When did Columbus reach the New World?") rather than higher-level questions (e.g., "Why did Columbus risk his life to find a new route to India?"), perhaps because they have learned to expect mostly fact-based questions on their classroom examinations (Jackson, Ormrod, & Salih, 1996, 1999). To promote meaningful learning, elaboration, and, in general, higher-level processing of information, teachers might encourage students to continually ask themselves questions such as the following:

- Explain why (how) . . . .
- What is the main idea of . . . ?
- How would you use . . . to . . . ?
- What is a new example of . . . ?
- What do you think would happen if . . . ?
- What is the difference between . . . and . . . ?
- How are . . . and . . . similar?
- What conclusions can you draw about . . . ?
- How does . . . affect . . . ?
- What are the strengths and weaknesses of . . . ?
- What is the best . . . and why?
- How is . . . related to . . . that we studied earlier?
  (King, 1992, p. 309)

Ideally, students should assess their understanding of class material at some later time as well. People are often inaccurate and overly optimistic judges of how much they will remember about something they have just read (Nelson & Dunlosky, 1991; Pressley, Borkowski, & Schneider, 1987; Weaver & Kelemen, 1997). In a simple illustration of this principle (Nelson & Dunlosky, 1991), undergraduate students studied a series of 60 paired associates (e.g., *ocean–tree*) for eight seconds apiece. Students were asked how confident they were that in 10 minutes' time they would be able to remember the second word in each pair when cued with the first; this question was sometimes asked immediately after a word pair had been presented (the immediate condition) and sometimes asked after several minutes had elapsed (the delayed condition). After studying all 60 pairs, students were tested for their actual ability to recall the second word in every pair. Their estimates of how much they would remember were far more accurate for word pairs in the delayed condition than for pairs in the immediate condition; in the latter condition, students believed they would remember many more pairs than they actually did. The problem with judging one's knowledge of something immediately after studying it, Nelson and Dunlosky reasoned, is that the information is still in working memory and therefore can easily be retrieved. Ideally, students need to judge the likelihood that they can retrieve information from long-term memory as well—something they can do only when they monitor their comprehension after several minutes, hours, or days have elapsed.

Mnemonics

Most of the strategies we've discussed so far are based on the assumption that the material makes sense and can be logically organized. But if you reflect back on your own educational experiences, you can probably recall many situations in which you had trouble learning important information because it didn't "hang together" in any logical way. Perhaps the troublesome material consisted of long lists of items, unfamiliar vocabulary words in a foreign language, or particular rules of grammar, spelling, or mathematics. **Mnemonics**—memory "tricks"—are devices that facilitate the learning and recall of many forms of hard-to-remember material. Here we will look at three general types of mnemonics: verbal mediation, visual imagery, and superimposed meaningful structures.

Verbal Mediation

Imagine that you are trying to learn that the German word *Handschuh* means *glove*. Playing off how the word sounds phonetically, you might remember this word by thinking of a glove as a "shoe for the hand." Such a mnemonic is an example of the use of **verbal mediation,** in which two words or ideas are associated by a word or phrase (the verbal mediator) that connects them. Here are some examples of verbal mediators for other German vocabulary words:

German Word	English Meaning	Mediator
der Hund	dog	hound
das Schwein	pig	swine
die Gans	goose	gander
der Stier	bull	steer

Notice that in every case, the verbal mediator bridges the gap between the German word and its English equivalent. By storing the mediator, you can make a connection between the two words.

Verbal mediators clearly facilitate learning (e.g., Bugelski, 1962), and their use is not necessarily restricted to the learning of foreign vocabulary words. For example, here is a mnemonic sometimes seen in spelling instruction:

The principal is my pal.

Retrieving this sentence will enable a student to remember that the correct spelling for a school administrator is "princi*pal*" rather than "princi*ple*." As a high school student, my daughter remembered the chemical symbol for gold—Au—by thinking "*Ay, you* stole my *gold* watch!"

Visual Imagery

As we discovered in Chapter 10, a visual image is a powerful storage mechanism that can be formed quickly and retained for a relatively long period of time. Accordingly, visual imagery forms the basis for a number of effective mnemonic devices. Here we will focus on three of them: the method of loci, the pegword method, and the keyword method.

Method of Loci In the days of the Greek and Roman empires, orators used a particular technique to help them remember the major ideas they wished to include in their hours-long harangues at the local forum (lecture notes were apparently not acceptable in those days). These orators would think about a familiar route that they walked frequently—the route from home to the forum, for example—and about the significant landmarks along the way—perhaps a bridge, a large tree, and a brothel, in that order. Then, when planning a speech, they would translate each key point into some sort of concrete, observable object and form a visual image of each successive key point located at each landmark along the familiar route. For example, let's say that the first three points in an orator's speech were the frequent traffic jams near the forum, the importance of a mass transit system in downtown Rome, and the consequent necessity for a tax increase. He might store images such as these: (1) numerous horses and pedestrians entangled in a traffic jam on the bridge (first landmark), (2) a gigantic, 30-person chariot perched among the branches of the large tree (second landmark), and (3) several toga-clad prostitutes pitching coins at a tax collector from the upstairs window of the brothel (third landmark). Later, when pontificating at the forum, the orator would take a mental walk along his familiar route; as he passed each landmark, he would readily retrieve the image of that landmark and the object symbolizing the next major point of his speech. In this manner, he could easily remember all of the main ideas of the oration and their correct order.

This **method of loci** (*loci* is the Latin word for *places*) is clearly an effective mnemonic technique (Christen & Bjork, 1976; Groninger, 1971; Snowman, 1986) and lends itself readily to the storage and retention of lists of items. For example, in a study by Groninger (1971), some participants learned a list of 25 words using the method of loci while others learned the words simply by grouping them. People using the method of loci learned the words faster and remembered more of them on a free recall task five weeks later. Both groups performed equally well, however, when asked to recognize (rather than recall) the words; thus, it appears that the benefit of the method of loci may lie in the imagery-based retrieval cues it provides.

Pegword Method The **pegword method** is another technique for effectively learning a list of items and their relative positions (Bower, 1972; Bugelski et al., 1968; Higbee, 1976; Mastropieri & Scruggs, 1989, 1992). This method consists of using a well-known or easily learned list of items that then serves as a series of "pegs" on which another list is "hung" through visual imagery. To illustrate, the following poem is sometimes used as a pegboard:

> One is a bun.
> Two is a shoe.
> Three is a tree.
> Four is a door.
> Five is a hive.
> Six is sticks.
> Seven is heaven.
> Eight is a gate.
> Nine is a line; and
> Ten is a hen.
> (Miller, Galanter, & Pribram, 1960, p. 135)

This poem should be an easy one to remember because its lines are composed of the numbers 1 through 10 in conjunction with rhyming nouns. Now suppose you need to remember a list of items in a certain order. You take the first item on the list and form a visual image of it interacting with the noun that rhymes with *one* (in this case, *bun*), then take the second list item and

Using a keyword to remember that a horse
is a *Pferd*.

imagine it interacting with the noun that rhymes with *two* (*shoe*), and so on. Images can be formed quickly and typically need not be practiced to be remembered.

Consider this food chain as an example of a list to be learned using the "One is a bun" poem:

Algae in a lake are eaten by
Water fleas, which are eaten by
Minnows, which are eaten by
Larger fish, which are eaten by
Eagles.

Using the pegword method, you form an image of algae and a bun together—perhaps a hamburger bun covered with green algae. Similarly, you visualize water fleas in conjunction with a shoe—perhaps you see a shoe filled with water and several water fleas doing the backstroke across the surface. For the last three items of the food chain, you might form images of a tree with minnows hanging down like fruit, a door with a large fish stuffed through the keyhole, and an eagle wearing a beehive for a hat. Remembering the food chain, then, is simply a matter of thinking "One is a bun," conjuring up the image of the bun with algae, then thinking "Two is a shoe," retrieving the shoe image, and so on.[6]

Keyword Method I have already described the use of verbal mediation in learning foreign language words. But as you may have noticed, the German words I chose for my illustrations of verbal mediation closely resembled English words. More often, however, words in a foreign language are not so obviously related to their English meanings. In such situations, the **keyword method** provides an effective alternative. This technique, which is actually a combination of verbal mediation and visual imagery, involves two steps: (1) identifying an English word or phrase (the keyword) that sounds similar to the foreign word and then (2) forming a visual image of the English sound-alike word with the English meaning. For example, consider how we might remember these German words:

German Word	English Meaning	Keyword(s)	Visual Image
das Pferd	horse	Ford	A *horse* driving a *Ford*
das Kaninchen	rabbit	can on chin	A *rabbit* with a *can* on its *chin*
der Waschbär	raccoon	wash, bar	A *raccoon wash*ing with a *bar* of soap
das Stachelschwein	porcupine	stash, swine	A *porcupine stash*ing nuts under a pig (*swine*)

[6]My cousin Natalie Powell, who worked at Gallaudet College for many years, has given me a version of "One is a bun" that students who are deaf can use: *One is you, two is vegetable, three is rooster, four is football, five is paper, six is water, seven is smoking, eight is pumpkin, nine is Indian, ten is nut.* Each number is matched with a word that is very similar to it in American Sign Language.

The keyword method has been shown to be an effective instructional device in teaching both English and foreign language vocabulary words. It is also useful in teaching such paired associates as states and their capitals, cities and their products, painters and their master-pieces, and names and faces (Atkinson, 1975; Carney & Levin, 2000; Carney, Levin, & Stack-house, 1997; M. S. Jones et al. 2000; Levin, 1981; Levin, McCormick, Miller, Berry, & Pressley, 1982; Pressley, Levin, & Delaney, 1982). Furthermore, older students (such as eighth graders) often spontaneously apply this mnemonic to new learning tasks once they have been trained in its use (Carney & Levin, 2000; B. F. Jones & Hall, 1982; M. S. Jones et al., 2000; Mastropieri & Scruggs, 1989). Although only concrete objects can actually be visualized, the technique can be used with more abstract words as well, provided that they can be adequately represented by a concrete object. For example, consider the Spanish word for love, *el amor*: This word might be learned by picturing a heart (symbolizing *love*) wearing a suit of armor (the keyword).

Identifying keywords when numbers are involved can be a bit trickier; for example, you might have trouble identifying sound-alike words for numbers such as 239 or 1861. To address this prob-lem, Lorayne and Lucas (1974) suggested that learners use specific consonant sounds as substitutes for different digits and then create words using those sounds. For example, imagine that you want to remember that the painting on the left side of Figure 13–3 was painted by Jean-Louis-Ernest Meissonier in 1861. To remember the artist's name, use the keyword *messenger*. To remember the date, you can create a word using the number-letter equivalents on the right side of Figure 13–3. To keep things simple, we'll assume that you already know that Meissonier lived in the 1800s and so address only the last two digits of the year. If we use *J* to represent the 6 and *T* to represent the 1, we can form a second keyword, *jet*. Now, form a visual image of the man as a *messenger* who has just walked down the steps from his *jet* in the background (Carney & Levin, 1994). Although this approach may seem complicated, in fact college students learn it fairly easily, and using it helps them remember the artists and dates of paintings more easily than they would otherwise (Carney & Levin, 1994).

When encouraging students to use mnemonics based on visual imagery, teachers must keep three things in mind. First, many young children cannot generate effective images on their own and so probably need to have pictures provided for them (Mayer, 1987). Second, for imagery to be an effective means of remembering a connection between two items (e.g., between a bridge and mass transit, or between love and *amor*), the two items must be incor-porated into the same image in an *interacting* fashion (Bower, 1972; Dempster & Rohwer, 1974). Thus, while an image of a heart wearing armor is an effective way of remembering the Spanish word for *love*, an image of a heart standing beside a suit of armor probably is not. Third, as noted in Chapter 10, imagery does not preserve details very effectively; therefore, it may not help one remember such specific information as the exact shape of a heart or the number of dents on a suit of armor.

Superimposed Meaningful Structure

One of my most vivid memories from my years as an undergraduate psychology major is being required to learn the 12 cranial nerves: olfactory, optic, oculomotor, trochlear, trigeminal, abducens, facial, auditory, glossopharyngeal, vagus, spinal accessory, and hypoglossal. It is not the nerves themselves that I remember but rather how painfully difficult it was to learn them all in

Number-Letter Equivalents

1 = T or D

2 = N

3 = M

4 = R

5 = L

6 = J, soft G, SH, or CH

7 = K, hard C, or hard G

8 = F or V

9 = P or B

10 = S, Z, or soft C

To remember that this masterpiece was painted by Jean-Louis-Ernest *Meissonier* in 18*61*, form a visual image of the man as a *messenger* who has just walked down the steps from his *jet* (*J* for 6 and *T* for 1) in the background (Carney & Levin, 1994). (Number-letter equivalents are from Lorayne & Lucas, 1974.)

Figure 13–3
Using the keyword method to remember the artist and year of a masterpiece.
A Cavalier: Time of Louis XIII, 1861, Jean-Louise-Ernest Meissonier. By kind permission of the Trustees of the Wallace Collection, London.

their correct order. I had little luck drilling the list into my thick skull (I was using the tried-and-not-so-true method of rehearsal) until a friend passed along this mnemonic:

On old Olympus' towering top, a Finn and German viewed some hops.

Notice that the first letters of the words in the sentence correspond with the first letters of the 12 cranial nerves: Just like in the list of nerves, the first three words in the sentence begin with *O*, the next two begin with *T*, and so on. And the sentence, though a bit strange, is fairly easy to remember because of the structure provided by its rhythm and rhyme.

"On old Olympus" illustrates a mnemonic I call a **superimposed meaningful structure.**[7] The technique is simple: The learner imposes a familiar structure on the body of information to be learned. That structure can be a sentence, story, rhythm, acronym, or anything else already familiar to the learner. For instance, during a recent trip to visit my brother-in-law in England, I stumbled on the following mnemonic for remembering the kings and queens of England, beginning with King William I and ending with Queen Elizabeth II:

> Willie, Willie, Harry, Steve,
> Harry, Dick, John, Harry Three.
> Edward One, Two, Three, Dick Two,
> Henry Four, Five, Dick the Bad,
> Harrys twain and Ned, the lad.
> Mary, Lizzie, James, the Vain,
> Charlie, Charlie, James again.
> William and Mary, Anne o' Gloria,
> Four Georgies, William, and Victoria.
> Edward Seven, Georgie Five,
> Edward, George, and Liz (alive).

Figure 13–4 lists additional examples of mnemonics, some for declarative information and others for procedures.

Superimposed meaningful structures clearly facilitate memory for lists of items (Bower & Clark, 1969; Bulgren, Schumaker, & Deshler, 1994). As an example, let's look at an experiment by Bower and Clark (1969). Two groups of college students learned 12 lists of 10 nouns: Group 1 learned each list by using repetition, whereas group 2 composed narrative stories that included all 10 words of each list. Here is an example of such a group 2 story (the nouns to be remembered are in capital letters):

> A LUMBERJACK DARTed out of a forest, SKATEd around a HEDGE past a COLONY of DUCKS. He tripped on some FURNITURE, tearing his STOCKING while hastening toward the PILLOW where his MISTRESS lay. (Bower & Clark, 1969, p. 182)

After the students had learned each of the 12 lists perfectly, they were then asked to recall all 120 words (the first word of each list was given as a retrieval cue). Students in group 1 (repetition) recalled only 13% of the words; in contrast, students in group 2 (stories) recalled 93%!

It should be clear by now that mnemonics can be extremely helpful learning aids. As you may have noticed, their effectiveness lies in their conformity with a few critical principles of storage and retrieval. First, they often impose a structure or organization on the material to be learned. Second, they help the learner relate the new material to information already stored in long-term memory (e.g., to the number system or a familiar poetic meter). And third, they provide retrieval cues (such as the *associate cues* and *frames* described in Chapter 12) that help learners find the information at a later time.

---

[7]I have also seen the terms *semantic elaboration* and *acrostic* used in reference to this technique.

The Mnemonic	What It Represents
	For Declarative Information
ROY G. BIV	The spectrum: red, orange, yellow, green, blue, indigo, violet
HOMES	The five Great Lakes: Huron, Ontario, Michigan, Erie, Superior
Every good boy does fine.	The lines on the treble clef: E G B D F
Campbell's ordinary soup does make Peter pale.	The geologic time periods of the Paleozoic era: Cambrian, Ordovician, Silurian, Devonian, Mississippian, Pennsylvanian, Permian
When the "mites" go up, the "tites" go down.	The distinction between stalagmites and stalactites
A "boot"	The shape of Italy
A "bearskin rug"	The shape of France
George Ellen's old grandmother rode a pig home yesterday.	The correct spelling of *geography*
I before E, except after C.	The correct spelling of words such as receive
Thirty days has September	The number of days in each month
	For Procedural Information
Righty, tighty; lefty, loosy.	Turning a screw (clockwise to tighten it, counterclockwise to loosen it)
BEEF	Good form for a free throw in basketball: *b*alance the ball, *e*lbows in, *e*levate the arms, *f*ollow through
FOIL	Multiplying a mathematical expression of the form *(ax + b) (cx + d)*: Multiply the *f*irst terms in each set of parentheses, then the *o*uter terms, the *i*nner terms, and finally the *l*ast terms

Figure 13–4
Examples of superimposed meaningful structures.

Yet people rarely use mnemonics (Morris, 1977), perhaps because they are unaware of their existence or their benefits. Teachers can obviously help students learn difficult information if they identify or create mnemonics for that information. Furthermore, they can help students become more independent learners by showing them how to develop effective mnemonics on their own.

In the past few pages, we have identified a number of effective learning and study strategies. Some of these, such as outlining, taking notes, and writing summaries, are **overt strategies**; in other words, they are behaviors that we can actually see. Others—such as elaborating, identifying important information, and monitoring comprehension—are **covert strategies**; they are internal mental processes that we often can*not* see. Ultimately, it is probably the ways in which students process the information they receive—the covert strategies—that determine how effectively they learn and remember that information (Kardash & Amlund, 1991).

What kinds of learning and study strategies are we likely to see in students of different ages? Let's look at trends in the development of metacognitive knowledge and skills.

DEVELOPMENT OF METACOGNITIVE KNOWLEDGE AND SKILLS

Developmental psychologists have observed several trends in the development of metacognition:

- *Children become increasingly aware of the nature of thinking.* In Chapter 11, we examined *theory theory*, a perspective that focuses on the personal theories that children develop about various aspects of their world. "Theory theorists" propose that children develop personal theories not only about their physical and social worlds but also about their internal, psychological world. More specifically, children develop a **theory of mind,** which includes increasingly complex understandings of their own and others' mental states—thoughts, beliefs, perspectives, feelings, motives, and so on (e.g., Flavell, 2000; Lillard, 1998; Wellman, 1990).

Young children have only a limited ability to look inward at their own thinking and knowledge (Flavell, Green, & Flavell, 2000). Although many preschoolers have the words *know, remember,* and *forget* in their vocabularies, they don't fully grasp the nature of these mental phenomena. For instance, 3-year-olds use the term *forget* simply to mean "not knowing" something, regardless of whether they knew the information at an earlier time (Lyon & Flavell, 1994). When 4- and 5-year-old children are taught a new piece of information, they may say that they've known it for quite some time (Taylor, Esbensen, & Bennett, 1994).

During the elementary and secondary school years, children and adolescents become better able to reflect on their own thought processes and so are increasingly aware of the nature of thinking and learning (Flavell, Miller, & Miller, 1993; Wellman & Hickling, 1994). To some extent, adults may foster such development by talking about the mind's activities—for instance, by referring to "thinking a lot" or describing someone's mind as "wandering" (Wellman & Hickling, 1994).

- *Children become increasingly realistic about their memory capabilities and limitations.* Young children tend to be overly optimistic about how much they can remember. As they grow older and encounter a wide variety of learning tasks, they discover that some things are more difficult to learn than others (Bjorklund & Green, 1992; Flavell et al., 1993). They also begin to realize that their memories are not perfect—that they cannot possibly remember everything they see or hear. For example, in a study by Flavell, Friedrichs, and Hoyt (1970), four age groups of children (ranging from nursery school to fourth grade) were shown strips of paper picturing from 1 to 10 objects and asked to predict how many objects they thought they could remember at a time (a working memory task). The children were then tested to determine how many objects they actually could remember. All four groups of children tended to overestimate their working memory capacities, but the estimates of the older children were more realistic. For example, kindergarten children predicted that they could remember an average of 8.0 objects but in fact remembered only 3.6. In contrast, the fourth graders estimated that they could remember 6.1 objects and actually recalled 5.5 (a much closer prediction).

- *Children increasingly become aware of and use effective learning and memory strategies.* Young children have little metacognitive awareness of effective strategies. Older children are more likely to have a variety of strategies, to apply them broadly and flexibly, and to know when to use each one (Alexander et al., 1998; A. L. Brown et al., 1983; Flavell et al., 1993; Siegler, 1998). Consider these research findings as illustrations:

  - When asked to study and remember 36 common objects (e.g., a bell, a flag, a wagon) over a series of learning trials, and when given the opportunity to review half of the items after each trial, first graders choose their study items randomly, without consideration of past memory failures. In contrast, third graders choose to study those items they were unable to recall on the previous trial (Masur, McIntyre, & Flavell, 1973).

- When young children use rehearsal to learn a list of items, they typically repeat each item a few times by itself. When they reach 9 or 10 years of age, they begin to use *cumulative rehearsal*, reciting the entire list at once and continuing to add any new items (Gathercole & Hitch, 1993). Furthermore, children in the early elementary grades are not terribly discriminating about the things they rehearse; older children are more likely to emphasize important material in the process (Kail, 1990).

- Children increasingly organize the things they need to remember, perhaps by putting items into categories (Hacker, 1998a; Moely, 1977; Siegler, 1998). They also become more flexible in their organizational strategies, especially as they reach adolescence (Plumert, 1994).

- The use of elaboration continues to increase throughout the school years (Flavell et al., 1993; Kail, 1990; Schneider & Pressley, 1989). For example, tenth graders are more likely than eighth graders to use elaboration when trying to remember paired associates (e.g., *doctor–machine, acorn–bathtub*) (Waters, 1982). Sixth graders often draw inferences from the things they read, whereas first graders rarely do (Chan, Burtis, Scardamalia, & Bereiter, 1992).

Even when young children can verbally describe which learning and memory strategies are effective and which are not, if left to their own devices they tend to use relatively ineffective strategies (Strage et al., 1988).

- *Children engage in more comprehension monitoring as they get older.* Children's ability to monitor their own comprehension improves throughout the school years, and so children and adolescents become increasingly aware of when they actually know something (Hacker, 1998a; van Kraayenoord & Paris, 1997). Young children (e.g., those in the early elementary grades) often think they know or understand something before they actually do. As a result, they don't study things they need to learn as much as they should, and they often don't ask questions when they receive incomplete or confusing information (Dufresne & Kobasigawa, 1989; Flavell et al., 1970; Markman, 1977; McDevitt, Spivey, Sheehan, Lennon, & Story, 1990). Yet even college students sometimes have difficulty assessing their own knowledge accurately; for instance, they often overestimate how well they will perform on an exam (Hacker et al., 2000).

- *Some learning processes may be used unconsciously and automatically at first but become more conscious and deliberate with development.* It is not unusual to see learners organizing or elaborating on the things they are learning without being consciously aware that they are doing so (Bjorklund, 1987; Flavell et al., 1993; Howe & O'Sullivan, 1990). For example, young children may automatically group things into categories as a way of learning them more effectively; only later do they *try* to categorize the things they need to learn (Bjorklund, 1987). Thus, children's learning processes become more intentional—and therefore more *strategic*—with age.

The specific learning strategies that students use depend, to some extent, on their beliefs about the nature of the knowledge they are trying to acquire, as well as about the nature of learning itself. Such *epistemological beliefs* are our next topic.

EPISTEMOLOGICAL BELIEFS

Earlier in the chapter, I described how, as a high school student, I believed that I was "reading" my history textbook even when I was thinking about something else and that I could effectively "study" my Chinese vocabulary words by repeating them aloud to myself a few times. It is clear that I had a very naïve notion of what learning involves: I thought that it was a relatively mindless process that would magically happen regardless of how much effort I invested.

I also had some pretty shaky beliefs about what "knowledge" is. I thought that the academic disciplines I was studying—history, science, literature—were pretty much set in stone, with definite "right" and "wrong" ways of looking at things. Experts didn't know everything just yet (e.g., they still hadn't figured out how to cure the common cold), but that knowledge was "out there" somewhere and they would eventually find it. In the meantime, it was my job as a student to acquire as many facts as I could; I wasn't quite sure what I would do with them all, but I knew, deep down, that they would somehow make me a better person.

As people who learn new things every day, we all have ideas about what "knowledge" and "learning" are—ideas that are collectively known as **epistemological beliefs.**[8] In many cases, such beliefs are pulled together into cohesive, although not necessarily accurate, personal theories about human learning and cognition (Hofer & Pintrich, 1997; Kuhn, 2000; Lampert, Rittenhouse, & Crumbaugh, 1996). Included in these theories are beliefs about such things as the following:

- *The certainty of knowledge:* Whether knowledge is a fixed, unchanging, absolute "truth" *or* a tentative, dynamic entity that will continue to evolve over time[9]
- *The simplicity and structure of knowledge:* Whether knowledge is a collection of discrete and isolated facts *or* a set of complex and interrelated ideas
- *The source of knowledge:* Whether knowledge comes from outside of the learner (i.e., from a teacher or an "authority" of some kind) *or* is derived and constructed by learners themselves
- *The criteria for determining truth:* Whether an idea is accepted as true when it is communicated by an expert *or* when it is logically evaluated based on available evidence
- *The speed of learning:* Whether knowledge is acquired quickly if at all (in which case people either know something or they don't, in an all-or-none fashion) *or* is acquired gradually over a period of time (in which case people can partially know something)
- *The nature of learning ability:* Whether people's ability to learn is fixed at birth (i.e., inherited) *or* can improve over time with practice and use of better strategies
(Elder, 2002; Hammer, 1994; Hofer & Pintrich, 1997; King & Kitchener, 2002; Linn et al., 1996; Schommer, 1994a; Wood & Kardash, 2002)

Keep in mind that epistemological beliefs are not as "either–or" as I have just described them. Some theorists have suggested that the elements I've listed probably reflect *continuums* rather than strict dichotomies (Baxter Magolda, 2002; King & Kitchener, 2002; Kuhn & Weinstock, 2002; Marton & Booth, 1997).

---

[8]You may also see such terms as *personal epistemology, intuitive epistemology, epistemic cognition, ways of knowing,* or *meta-knowing* (diSessa et al., 2003; Hofer, 2002; Kuhn, 1999).

[9]The belief that there is an ultimate "truth" that experts will eventually determine is sometimes called *logical positivism.* This view contrasts sharply with *radical constructivism,* a perspective maintaining that there is no "reality" separate from people's constructed understandings and beliefs.

Whether and in what ways people's various beliefs about knowledge and learning hang together as an integrated belief system is a matter of considerable debate (Buehl & Alexander, 2001; diSessa et al., 2003; Hofer & Pintrich, 1997, 2002; Qian & Alvermann, 1995; Schommer-Aikins, 2002). Concerns about research methodologies fuel this debate. Researchers obtain information about learners' beliefs primarily from interviews and questionnaires, yet some theorists suspect that learners' true beliefs may be implicit rather than explicit and so are far removed from conscious awareness (diSessa et al., 2003; Hammer & Elby, 2002; Schraw & Moshman, 1995). In addition, the particular measures and statistical methods used seems to influence the kinds of beliefs and interrelationships among them that researchers identify (Schraw, Bendixen, & Dunkle, 2002).

Increasingly, theorists are beginning to realize that people's epistemological beliefs are somewhat context- and situation-specific (Andre & Windschitl, 2003; Bell & Linn, 2002; diSessa et al., 2003; Hammer & Elby, 2002; Schommer-Aikins, 2002; Schraw, 2000). For example, even though you and I may believe that scientific views of the world will probably continue to evolve over time (thus believing that knowledge is not certain), we know that other things are fairly black and white. Two plus two is four, the capital of France is Paris, and William Shakespeare wrote *Romeo and Juliet*; these facts are unlikely to change any time in the foreseeable future. Furthermore, learners' epistemological beliefs may be specific to particular content domains. Following are some examples:

- Many students believe that knowledge in some disciplines is more certain than knowledge in others. For example, they may believe that knowledge in mathematics and the natural sciences is more of a "sure thing" than knowledge in the social sciences (De Corte, Op't Eynde, & Verschaffel, 2002; Hofer, 2000; Schommer, 1994b).
- Many students think that learning mathematics and physics means memorizing procedures and formulas. Furthermore, there is usually only one "correct" way to solve a problem and one "correct" answer to it (De Corte et al., 2002; Hammer, 1994).
- Many students think that when they work on mathematics problems, they will either solve the problems in a couple of minutes or else not solve them at all. Many also think that when an answer to a math problem isn't a whole number, it is probably wrong (Schoenfeld, 1988).

People's epistemological beliefs often change over time. For example, young children typically believe in the certainty of knowledge; they think that there is an absolute truth about any topic out there somewhere (Astington & Pelletier, 1996; Kuhn & Weinstock, 2002). As they reach the high school and college years, some (but by no means all) of them begin to realize that knowledge is a subjective entity and that different perspectives on a topic may be equally valid (Belenky, Clinchy, Goldberger, & Tarule, 1986/1997; Kuhn & Weinstock, 2002; Perry, 1968; Schommer, 1997). Other changes may also occur at the high school level; for example, students in twelfth grade are more likely than ninth graders to believe that knowledge consists of complex interrelationships (rather than discrete facts), that learning happens slowly (rather than quickly), and that learning ability can improve with practice (rather than being fixed at birth) (Schommer, 1997).[10] Cultural differences in epistemological beliefs may exist as well; for instance, college students in Ireland are more likely to view learning as a complex and constructive process that results in somewhat tentative understandings of a topic, whereas their counterparts in the United States are more likely to view learning as a process of attending carefully to presented information and memorizing it as a set of isolated facts (McDevitt, Sheehan, Cooney, Smith, & Walker, 1994).

---

[10]Epistemological beliefs may continue to evolve in the adult years; for example, see Baxter Magolda (2002).

Effects of Epistemological Beliefs

Students' epistemological beliefs clearly influence how they study and learn. Following are some of the specific effects that different beliefs are likely to have:

- *Beliefs regarding the certainty of knowledge.* When students believe that knowledge related to a topic is a fixed, certain entity, they are apt to jump to quick and potentially inaccurate conclusions based on the information they receive. In contrast, when students view knowledge as something that continues to evolve and doesn't necessarily include definitive right and wrong answers, they are more apt to enjoy cognitively challenging tasks, engage in meaningful learning, read course material critically, undergo conceptual change when it is warranted, and recognize that some issues are controversial and not easily resolved (Kardash & Howell, 2000; Kardash & Scholes, 1996; Mason, 2003; Schommer, 1994a).

- *Beliefs regarding the simplicity and structure of knowledge.* Students who believe that knowledge is a collection of discrete facts are more likely to use rote-learning processes when they study and more likely to hold on to their misconceptions about a topic. They also tend to believe that they "know" the material they are studying if they can recall basic facts and definitions. In contrast, students who believe that knowledge is a complex set of interrelated ideas are more likely to engage in meaningful learning, organization, and elaboration when they study and more likely to evaluate the success of their learning efforts in terms of how well they understand and can apply what they have learned (Hammer, 1994; Hofer & Pintrich, 1997; Mason, 2003; Purdie, Hattie, & Douglas, 1996; Schommer-Aikins, 2002).

- *Beliefs regarding the source of knowledge.* Students who believe that knowledge originates outside of the learner and is passed along directly by authority figures are apt to be fairly passive learners, perhaps listening quietly to explanations without trying to clarify confusing ideas, or perhaps exerting little effort when lessons consist of discovery activities and class discussions rather than lectures. In contrast, students who believe that knowledge is something that one constructs for oneself are apt to be cognitively engaged in learning activities, make interconnections among ideas, read and listen critically, work to make sense of seemingly contradictory pieces of information, undergo conceptual change, and get emotionally involved with the things they are studying (Chan et al., 1997; Haseman, 1999; Hogan, 1997; McDevitt et al., 1990; Schommer, 1994b; Schraw & Bruning, 1995).

- *Beliefs regarding the criteria for determining truth.* When students believe that something is probably true if it comes from an "expert" of some sort, they are apt to accept information from authority figures without question. But when they believe that ideas should be judged on their logical and scientific merit (rather than on their source), they are apt to critically evaluate new information on the basis of available evidence (King & Kitchener, 2002). The following interview with a student, concerning the belief that the Egyptians (rather than, say, an earlier civilization or extraterrestrials) built the pyramids, illustrates the latter perspective:

> Interviewer: Can you ever say you know for sure about this issue?
>
> Student: It . . . is very far along the continuum of what is probable.
>
> Interviewer: Can you say that one point of view is right and one is wrong?
>
> Student: Right and wrong are not comfortable categories to assign to this kind of item. It's more or less likely or reasonable, more or less in keeping with what the facts seem to be. (dialogue from King & Kitchener, 1994, p. 72)

As students grow older, and especially as they move into higher levels of education (e.g., gradu-ate school), they become increasingly adept at distinguishing between weak and strong evidence for a particular idea or point of view (Kuhn, 2001a).

  • *Beliefs regarding the speed of learning.* When students believe that learning happens quickly in an all-or-none fashion, they are apt to believe that they have learned something before they really have, perhaps after only a single reading of their textbooks; they are also apt to give up quickly in the face of failure and to express discouragement or dislike regarding the topic they are studying. In contrast, when students believe that learning is a gradual process that often takes time and effort, they are likely to use a wide variety of learning strategies as they study and to persist until they have made sense of the ideas presented (Butler & Winne, 1995; Kardash & Howell, 2000; Schommer, 1990, 1994b).

  • *Beliefs regarding the nature of learning ability.* As you might guess, students' beliefs about the nature of learning ability are correlated with their persistence in learning. If they think that learn-ing ability is a fixed commodity, they will quickly give up on challenging tasks. In contrast, if they think that their ability to learn something is under their control, they will pursue a variety of sup-portive learning activities and try, try again until they have mastered the subject matter (Hartley & Bendixen, 2001; Schommer, 1994a, 1994b).

Not surprisingly, students with more sophisticated epistemological beliefs—for example, those who believe that knowledge is complex and uncertain and that learning is often a slow, gradual process—achieve at higher levels in the classroom (Schommer, 1994a). Furthermore, more advanced levels of academic achievement may bring about more advanced views about knowledge and learning (Schommer, 1994b; Strike & Posner, 1992). The more students can get beyond the "basics" and explore the far reaches of a discipline—whether it be science, mathematics, history, literature, or some other domain—the more they will discover that learning involves acquiring an integrated and cohesive set of ideas, that even experts don't know everything about a topic, and that truly complete and accurate "knowledge" of how the world operates may ultimately be an unat-tainable goal.

It is important to note here that students are not the only ones who can have relatively naïve beliefs about the nature of knowledge and learning; some *teachers* appear to have such beliefs as well. Some teachers seem to believe that knowledge about a particular subject matter is a fixed and well-defined entity, that students need to "absorb" this knowledge in isolated bits and pieces, and that learning is a process of mindless memorization and rehearsal (L. M. Anderson, 1997; Berliner, 1997; Hofer & Pintrich, 1997; Schommer, 1994b). Such beliefs are likely to influence the ways that teachers teach and assess their students; for example, teachers holding these beliefs will be more likely to focus on lower-level skills in their instructional objectives, classroom activities, assignments, and tests (Grossman, 1990; Hofer & Pintrich, 1997).

THE INTENTIONAL LEARNER

Earlier I described learning and study strategies as involving the *intentional* use of certain cogni-tive processes to learn. Truly effective learning, it appears, involves **intentional learning,** in which a learner is actively and consciously engaged in cognitive and metacognitive activities directed specifically at thinking about and learning something (Bereiter, 1997; Bereiter &

Scardamalia, 1989; Langer, 1997, 2000; Sinatra & Pintrich, 2003a).[11] Intentional learners have particular goals they want to accomplish as they learn, and they make use of the many self-regulatory strategies they have at their disposal to achieve those goals. Long gone is that reactive responder to environmental stimuli that we encountered in the early days of behaviorism. Instead, we now have the learner squarely in the driver's seat with an itinerary, a road map, and considerable knowledge about how to drive the car.

Without a doubt, intentional learning involves both automatic and controlled processes. Many of the basic components of learning—retrieving word meanings, connecting new ideas to very similar information already in long-term memory, and so on—have been practiced to a level of automaticity, and so the learner carries them out with little thought or effort. But overseeing the process is a very conscious, goal-directed individual who brings into play a variety of strategies—deciding what to focus on, trying to make sense of ambiguous text passages, drawing inferences for one's own life circumstances, and the like—as necessary (diSessa et al., 2003; Kintsch, 1998; Sinatra & Pintrich, 2003b).

Intentional learning may be especially important when learners need to overhaul their current understandings of a topic or issue—in other words, when they must undergo *conceptual change* (Gunstone, 1994; Sinatra & Pintrich, 2003a). Intentional learning evokes several processes that are critical for revising one's understandings in any significant fashion (Luque, 2003; Mason, 2003). First, intentional learners actively attend to and think about the new information, and so they are more likely to notice discrepancies with what they currently believe. Second, they are eager to acquire mastery of the subject matter, and so they exert considerable effort to make sense of it. Third, they bring to the table a variety of learning and self-regulatory strategies—elaboration, self-motivation, self-monitoring, and so on—that maximize their chances for revising their beliefs in line with what they are hearing or reading. But in addition to such processes, intentional learners must have epistemological beliefs consistent with the notion of conceptual change. More specifically, they must believe that knowledge about a topic continues to evolve and improve over time and that learning something *well* can take time, effort, and perseverance (Southerland & Sinatra, 2003).

Intentional learning is the ideal situation. Unfortunately, what is more typical is that students don't regularly, consistently, or actively use effective learning and self-regulatory strategies. We now look at reasons why.

WHY STUDENTS DON'T ALWAYS USE EFFECTIVE STRATEGIES

As we have seen, many students continue to use ineffective learning and study strategies (e.g., rote memorization) throughout their academic careers. Given what you have learned about metacognition up to this point, can you generate some hypotheses about why this might be so? In this section, I will suggest several possible reasons why effective learning strategies emerge slowly, if at all. You will, I hope, find some of your own ideas in my list.

- *Students are uninformed or misinformed about effective strategies.* Many students, even those at the high school and college levels, are metacognitively naïve about how they can best learn

---

[11]The concepts *mindful learning* and *mindfulness* (Langer, 1997, 2000) reflect a similar idea.

(Alexander & Judy, 1988; Barnett, 2001; Palmer & Goetz, 1988; Thomas, 1993; Wood, Motz, & Willoughby, 1997). For example, some students believe that all they need to do to learn information better is to exert more effort—that is, to *try harder*—with little regard for how they should mentally process that information (O'Sullivan & Joy, 1990; Pressley, Borkowski, & Schneider, 1987). When I present a unit on cognitive psychology to my junior-level educational psychology class, my description of such basic strategies as organizing information and relating it to familiar concepts and experiences appears to be a major revelation to about half of my students; sadly, too many of these students have viewed learning as being best approached through rote memorization throughout their many years in school.[12] Furthermore, many students believe (incorrectly) that trying to learn information meaningfully—that is, trying to understand and make sense of the things they study—interferes with their ability to do well on classroom tests that emphasize rote memorization and knowledge of isolated facts (Crooks, 1988).

• *Students have epistemological beliefs that lead them to underestimate or misrepresent a learning task.* Students are unlikely to use effective strategies if they believe that the learning task before them is an easy one or that their success in learning is unrelated to the effort they put forth (Butler & Winne, 1995; Winne, 1995a). And as we have already seen, they will certainly not engage in such processes as meaningful learning, organization, and elaboration if they think that "knowledge" is nothing more than a collection of unrelated facts.

• *Students mistakenly believe that they are already using effective strategies.* Perhaps because they are not monitoring their comprehension or perhaps because they have defined learning in an overly simplistic manner, many low-achieving students erroneously believe that their current approach to learning and studying is a good one (Loranger, 1994; Starr & Lovett, 2000). In some cases, feedback that students are *not* mastering the material will spur them to adopt more effective strategies, at least in the short run (Starr & Lovett, 2000). In other instances, however, students may attribute their poor performance to factors outside of themselves—perhaps to poor instruction or a "picky" test (we'll discuss the nature and effects of such *attributions* in Chapter 18).

• *Students have little relevant prior knowledge on which they can draw.* Students who use ineffective learning and study strategies tend to know less about the subject matter they are studying, and less about the world in general, than students who use effective strategies (Alexander & Judy, 1988; Chi, 1981; Schneider, 1993). For example, students may know too little about a topic to determine what is important and what is not (Alexander & Jetton, 1996; Carpenter & Just, 1986; McDaniel & Einstein, 1989). They may have few concepts or experiences to which they can relate new material in a meaningful fashion; thus, they have greater difficulty comprehending the things they read (Dole et al., 1991; Hall, 1989; Wilson & Anderson, 1986; Woloshyn, Pressley, & Schneider, 1992). And they are likely to have fewer organizational frameworks and schemas that they can impose on what might otherwise appear to be an unrelated set of ideas (Carpenter & Just, 1986).

---

[12]A belief in the value of rehearsal and drill-and-practice is especially prevalent among students from China and Japan (Ho, 1994; Purdie & Hattie, 1996). Many of these students do not depend *solely* on rehearsal, however. Rather, they supplement it with meaningful learning and elaboration (Marton & Booth, 1997; Tweed & Lehman, 2002). At the same time, cultures of the Far East may foster more simplistic epistemological beliefs—for instance, that knowledge is fact based and cut-and-dried, and that it can often be gained from authority figures (Qian & Pan, 2002).

- *Assigned learning tasks do not lend themselves to sophisticated strategies.* In some situations, teachers may assign tasks for which effective strategies are either counterproductive or impossible. For example, when teachers assign simple tasks that involve lower-level skills (e.g., when they insist that facts and definitions be learned verbatim), students are unlikely to engage in such processes as meaningful learning and elaboration (Thomas, 1993; Turner, 1995; Van Meter et al., 1994). When teachers expect a great deal of material to be mastered for each test, students may have to devote the limited time that they have to getting a general "impression" of everything rather than to developing an in-depth understanding and integration of the subject matter (Thomas, 1993). When teachers tell students exactly what questions will be asked on a particular classroom test or assignment, students are likely to focus only on material related to those questions, without regard for the larger context in which the material appears (Thomas, 1993).

- *Students have goals that are inconsistent with effective learning.* Students are not always interested in learning for understanding; instead, they may be more interested in remembering information only long enough to get a passing grade, or they may want to complete an assigned task in as little time and with as little effort as possible. Effective learning strategies may be largely irrelevant to such motives (Mayer, 1996b; Nolen, 1996).

- *Students think that sophisticated learning strategies require too much effort to make them worthwhile.* If students believe that certain strategies involve too much time and effort, they are unlikely to use them, no matter how effective those strategies might be (Guttentag, 1984; Palmer & Goetz, 1988; Pressley et al., 1990). In many cases, students seem to be unaware of how much a few simple strategies can help them learn and remember classroom material (Pressley, Levin, & Ghatala, 1984; Zimmerman, 1994). In other instances, they may have little experience with a particular strategy; thus, they have learned few (if any) of the strategy's components to automaticity, and so using it effectively *does* require a great deal of effort (Alexander et al., 1998; Siegler, 1998).

- *Students have low self-efficacy about their ability to learn in an academic setting.* Some students, especially those with a history of academic failure, develop the belief that they are incapable of learning regardless of what they do. Such students may believe (erroneously) that *no* strategy is likely to make any appreciable difference in their school achievement (Alexander et al., 1998; Palmer & Goetz, 1988; Pressley, Borkowski, & Schneider, 1987).

Teachers often assume that students will use the same relatively sophisticated study strategies that they themselves use—an assumption that is clearly unwarranted in many cases. But can metacognitive knowledge and skills be taught? Most psychologists believe that they can, and furthermore, that they *should*, be taught. Let's look at some approaches to teaching metacognitive knowledge and skills.

PROMOTING EFFECTIVE LEARNING AND STUDY STRATEGIES

As students move through the grade levels—from elementary school to middle or junior high school, then to high school, and perhaps eventually on to college—their learning tasks become increasingly more complex and challenging (e.g., Eccles & Midgley, 1989; J. E. Wilson, 1988). For example, students must remember more information, do more with it (in terms of application, problem solving, critical analysis, etc.), and understand it at a more abstract level. Thus, there is a greater need for sophisticated learning and study strategies as the years go by (Baker, 1989).

Unfortunately, when teaching complex subject matter, teachers rarely teach effective strategies for learning it (Hamman, Berthelot, Saia, & Crowley, 2000; Pressley et al., 1990; J. E. Wilson, 1988; Wood et al., 1997). Yet when left to their own devices, students typically acquire effective strategies slowly if at all, and some students develop counterproductive misconceptions about how best to learn.

Many learning theorists suggest that schools should provide explicit instruction in how to study and learn. This instruction may be especially valuable for at-risk students—those with a history of academic difficulties and a high probability of dropping out of school prematurely (Alderman, 1990; Brown & Palincsar, 1987; Weinstein, Hagen, & Meyer, 1991). In this final section of the chapter, we will examine research regarding the effectiveness of study skills training; we will also consider some specific classroom strategies for promoting and enhancing students' metacognitive knowledge and skills.

Effectiveness of Study Skills Training Programs

Initially, most programs designed to enhance metacognitive knowledge and skills were at the college level (J. E. Wilson, 1988). But in recent years we have also seen these programs at the high school, junior high, and even upper-elementary levels, and short, strategy-specific training sessions have been offered for children as young as four or five. The collective results of research studies indicate that learners at all levels *can* be taught more effective learning and study strategies, with consequent improvements in their memory, classroom performance, and academic achievement; such training appears to be especially beneficial for low-achieving students (Baker, 1989; Carr & Schneider, 1991; DuBois et al., 1995; Fletcher & Bray, 1996; Haller et al., 1988; Hansen & Pearson, 1983; Hattie, Biggs, & Purdie, 1996; Holley & Dansereau, 1984; Kulik, Kulik, & Shwalb, 1983; Lange & Pierce, 1992; Mastropieri & Scruggs, 1989; Pressley, 1982; Pressley, Borkowski, & Schneider, 1987; Shrager & Mayer, 1989; Wade, 1983; Weinstein, Goetz, & Alexander, 1988; J. E. Wilson, 1988).

Effective study skills programs tend to be multifaceted, teaching a wide variety of learning and study strategies. For example, successful reading-for-learning instruction is likely to teach students to (1) determine their purpose in reading a particular passage and modify their reading behavior accordingly, (2) activate background information and experiences relevant to the topic, (3) identify and attend to main ideas, (4) draw inferences from the things they read, and (5) monitor their reading comprehension as they go along. And general learning and study strategies programs typically include instruction about meaningful learning, organizational strategies, elaboration, mnemonics, note taking, and summarizing. Aside from such commonalities, training programs often differ markedly from one another; I invite you to explore some of the possibilities by consulting the references listed in the preceding paragraph.

Guidelines for Promoting Effective Strategies

Theorists and researchers have identified a number of practices that appear to promote the development of more sophisticated metacognitive knowledge and skills. Following are some guidelines to keep in mind:

- *Students learn strategies more effectively when those strategies are taught within the context of specific subject domains and actual academic learning tasks* (Hattie et al., 1996; Paris & Paris, 2001; Pressley, El-Dinary, Marks, Brown, & Stein, 1992; Pressley, Harris, & Marks, 1992). As students encounter specific academic content, they should simultaneously learn ways to study that content. For example, when presenting new information in class, a teacher might (1) suggest how students can organize their notes, (2) describe mnemonics for things that are difficult to remember, and (3) ask various students to summarize the ideas presented. When assigning textbook pages to be read at home, a teacher might (4) suggest that students consider what they know about a topic *before* they begin reading about it, (5) ask students to use headings and subheadings to make predictions about upcoming content, and (6) provide questions for students to ask themselves as they read.

- *Students can use sophisticated learning strategies only when they have a knowledge base to which they can relate new material* (Brown et al., 1981; Greene, 1994; Weinstein & Mayer, 1986). The knowledge and skills that students bring to the classroom affect their ability to learn new information meaningfully, identify main ideas, and engage in such elaborative activities as drawing inferences and clarifying ambiguities. Teachers must be careful not to present difficult material until students have mastered the prerequisite knowledge and skills essential for a genuine understanding of that material.

- *Students should learn a wide variety of strategies, as well as the situations in which each one is appropriate* (Mayer & Wittrock, 1996; Nist, Simpson, Olejnik, & Mealey, 1991; Paris, 1988; Pressley, El-Dinary, et al., 1992; Pressley, Harris, & Marks, 1992). Different strategies are useful in different situations; for example, meaningful learning may be more effective for learning general principles within a discipline, whereas mnemonics may be more effective for learning hard-to-remember pairs and lists. Organizing ideas in a hierarchical fashion may be appropriate for one unit (e.g., see Figure 10–4); organizing them in a two-by-two matrix may be appropriate for another (e.g., see Figure 4–2).

- *Effective strategies should be practiced with a variety of tasks and on an ongoing basis* (Brown & Palincsar, 1987; Collins, Brown, & Newman, 1989; Pressley, El-Dinary, et al., 1992; Pressley, Harris, & Marks, 1992). When students learn a strategy only within the context of one particular task, they are unlikely to use that strategy in other contexts (Pressley et al., 1990). But when they learn to apply the same strategy to many different tasks over a long period of time, they are likely to recognize the strategy's value and to generalize its use to new situations. Effective strategy instruction is clearly not a one-shot deal.

- *Strategy instruction should include covert as well as overt strategies* (Kardash & Amlund, 1991). Certainly students stand to benefit from guidance about how to take notes from a lecture, underline the material they read in their textbooks, and write summaries of the material they study. But the sophisticated cognitive processes that underlie these behaviors—learning meaningfully, organizing, elaborating, comprehension monitoring, and so on—are ultimately the most important strategies for students to acquire.

- *Teachers can model effective strategies by thinking aloud about new material* (Brown & Palincsar, 1987; Pressley, El-Dinary, et al., 1992; Pressley, Harris, & Marks, 1992). When teachers think aloud about the content their classes are studying (e.g., "I remember that *Au* is the symbol for gold by remembering, '*Ay, you* stole my gold watch!' " or "Hmm . . . it seems to me that Napoleon's military tactics were quite similar to those of the ancient Assyrians"), they give their students specific, concrete examples of how to process information effectively.

- *Teachers should scaffold students' initial attempts at using new strategies, gradually phasing out the scaffolding as students become more proficient.* In Chapter 8, I introduced the concept of *scaffolding*, whereby a competent individual (e.g., a teacher) guides and supports a student's early attempts at a difficult task; as the student becomes more skilled at performing the task independently, such support is gradually removed. Many of the metacognitive activities we have considered in this chapter (e.g., note taking, comprehension monitoring, summarizing) are challenging tasks indeed, and some teacher scaffolding to facilitate them is clearly in order (Dole et al., 1991; Katayama & Robinson, 2000; Pontecorvo, 1993; Pressley, Harris, & Marks, 1992; Rogoff, 1990).

Earlier in the chapter, we saw several illustrations of how teachers can scaffold students' learning and study strategies. For instance, teachers can provide a general organizational framework that students can follow while taking notes. They can provide examples of questions that students can use to monitor their comprehension as they read (e.g., "Explain how . . . " or "What is a new example of . . . ?"). They can provide guidance about how to develop a good summary (e.g., "Identify or invent a topic sentence" or "Find supporting information for each main idea"). Such scaffolding is most likely to be helpful when students are studying subject matter they find difficult to comprehend yet *can* comprehend if they apply appropriate metacognitive strategies (Pressley, El-Dinary, et al., 1992). As students become more proficient in the use of these strategies, instruction can gradually proceed through increasingly more challenging material (Rosenshine & Meister, 1992).

- *Students can often learn effective strategies by working cooperatively with their classmates.* A rapidly growing body of research indicates that group learning activities, especially when structured in particular ways, can promote more sophisticated cognitive processing. One effective approach is to teach students to ask one another, and then answer, higher-level questions about the material they are studying—for instance, "Why is it that such-and-such is true?" (Kahl & Woloshyn, 1994; King, 1994, 1999; Martin & Pressley, 1991; Palincsar & Brown, 1984; Rosenshine et al., 1996; Woloshyn et al., 1992). Depending on the size of the student group, this approach may make take the form of either *guided peer questioning* (also known as *elaborative interrogation*) or *reciprocal teaching*. We'll look at both of these techniques in Chapter 15.

- *Students must understand why the study skills they are being taught are helpful.* Research indicates that strategy instruction is more successful when students not only learn effective strategies but also learn *how* and *why* these strategies are effective (Hattie et al., 1996; Paris & Paris, 2001; Pressley, Borkowski, & Schneider, 1987; Pressley, Harris, & Marks, 1992). In my own classes, I sometimes do little "experiments," presenting information that is difficult to learn and remember, then giving some students a mnemonic for learning the information but giving other students no guidance at all. We find out how much students in each group can recall by writing students' "test" scores on the board, and then we compare the two sets of numbers. The performance of the two groups is usually so dramatically different that my students readily acknowledge the usefulness of the mnemonic I've taught them.

Earlier I mentioned that students often don't realize just how ineffective their current strategies are. In several studies, Pressley and his colleagues trained students at a variety of age levels (ranging from 10 years to adulthood) to use keyword mnemonics to learn lists of vocabulary words (Pressley, Levin, & Ghatala, 1984, 1988; Pressley, Ross, Levin, & Ghatala, 1984). Although the students mastered the technique, many of them chose *not* to use it for a similar learning task later on. Students who were explicitly asked to consider just how much the keyword method had helped them learn the earlier words were far more likely to use it again in the new learning task. In a similar manner, teachers might occasionally need to show their students in a very concrete fashion (perhaps by using an ungraded quiz) just how little they are actually learning and remembering using their current, ineffective strategies and how much more they can learn using a different approach.

• *Students should have epistemological beliefs that are consistent with effective strategies.* As we have seen, students' epistemological beliefs influence the learning strategies that they use, and study strategies training, in and of itself, will not necessarily change those beliefs (Schraw & Moshman, 1995). Because students' beliefs about the nature of knowledge and learning may be in the form of implicit rather than explicit knowledge, they may be especially resistant to change (Schraw & Moshman, 1995).

Not only do epistemological beliefs affect students' ability to undergo conceptual change, but in fact revising epistemological beliefs involves conceptual change in and of itself. To nudge students toward increasingly sophisticated epistemological understandings, then, teachers should ideally create situations in which students find reason to doubt, and so feel dissatisfied with, their current beliefs (Hofer, 2002). Piaget called such dissatisfaction *disequilibrium*; more recently, it has been called **epistemic doubt** (Bendixen, 2002).

One possible way to change students' epistemological beliefs is to talk specifically about the nature of knowledge and learning—for instance, to describe learning as an active, ongoing process of finding interconnections among ideas and eventually constructing one's own understanding of the world (Schommer, 1994b). Possibly an even more effective approach is to provide classroom experiences that lead students to discover that knowledge must necessarily be a dynamic, rather than static, entity and to realize that successful learning sometimes occurs only through effort and persistence. For example, teachers can have students address complex issues and problems that have no clear-cut right or wrong answers (Kardash & Scholes, 1996; King & Kitchener, 2002; Schommer, 1994b). They can teach strategies for gathering data and testing competing hypotheses (Andre & Windschitl, 2003; King & Kitchener, 2002; C. L. Smith, Maclin, Houghton, & Hennessey, 2000). They can ask students to compare several explanations of a particular phenomenon or event and consider the validity and strength of evidence supporting each one (Andre & Windschitl, 2003; King & Kitchener, 2002; Linn et al., 1996). And they can show students, perhaps by presenting puzzling phenomena, that their own current understandings, and in some cases even those of experts in the field, do not yet adequately explain all of human experience (Chan et al., 1997; Vosniadou, 1991).

Teachers must be careful how far they take such strategies, however. When students are firmly rooted in their *learning-involves-facts-that-I-can-get-only-from-an-expert* beliefs, they may find little of value in—and so may gain little from—lessons that emphasize diverse perspectives and offer few solid answers (Andre & Windschitl, 2003).

• *Students should develop mechanisms for monitoring and evaluating their own learning.* As we noted earlier, self-regulated learners monitor their progress throughout a learning task and then evaluate their ultimate success in mastering the material they have been studying. In addition to teaching students self-questioning (a technique that facilitates comprehension monitoring), theorists have offered several recommendations for promoting self-monitoring and self-evaluation in students:

• Have students set specific goals and objectives for each study session, and then describe achievements in relation to them (Eilam, 2001; Morgan, 1985).
• Ask students to keep ongoing records of their performance, and to reflect on their learning in writing assignments, journals, or portfolios (Belfiore & Hornyak, 1998; Paris & Paris, 2001; Perry, 1998).
• Provide specific criteria that students can use to judge their performance (Paris & Ayres, 1994; Winne, 1995b).

- On some occasions, delay teacher feedback so that students first have the opportunity to evaluate their own performance (Butler & Winne, 1995; Schroth, 1992).
- Encourage students to evaluate their performance realistically, and then reinforce them (e.g., with praise or extra-credit points) when their evaluations match the teacher's (McCaslin & Good, 1996; Schraw, Potenza, & Nebelsick-Gullet, 1993; Zuckerman, 1994).

Even kindergartners and first graders can be encouraged to reflect on their performance and progress, perhaps through questions such as "What were we doing that we're proud of?" and "What can we do that we didn't do before?" (Perry, VandeKamp, Mercer, & Nordby, 2002, p. 10). By engaging regularly in self-monitoring and self-evaluation of classroom assignments, students should eventually develop appropriate standards for their performance and apply those standards regularly to the things they accomplish—true hallmarks of a self-regulated learner.

- *Students must believe that, with sufficient effort and appropriate strategies, they **can** learn and understand challenging material.* Strategy instruction must give students a sense of self-efficacy about their ability to learn classroom material (McCombs, 1988; Palmer & Goetz, 1988; Paris, 1988; Shapley, 1994). And it must show them that their success in learning is, in fact, related to the specific strategies they use (Butler & Winne, 1995; Pressley, Borkowski, & Schneider, 1987; Pressley, El-Dinary, et al., 1992).

Once students believe that they can learn academic subject matter successfully, they are more likely to *want* to learn it. Self-efficacy is one key ingredient in students' motivation to achieve in the classroom, for reasons we'll identify in Chapter 17.

By teaching students the metacognitive knowledge and skills they need to learn challenging classroom material, teachers not only help students learn that specific material more successfully but also help them become more effective learners over the long run. And it is the long run for which teachers must ultimately prepare their students.

Yet even with effective learning and self-regulatory skills, and even with high self-efficacy, students will not necessarily become intentional, "thoughtful" learners who gain maximum benefit from their classroom experiences. Ultimately, *motivating* students to learn is as important as *helping them learn how to learn.* Thus, the motivational strategies we identify in Chapters 16 to 18 will be an important complement to the instructional strategies we've identified here.

SUMMARY

People's knowledge of effective learning and cognitive processes and their use of such processes to enhance learning are collectively known as *metacognition*. Students' metacognitive knowledge and skills are significantly related to their classroom performance and academic achievement. The most successful students are *self-regulated learners*: They set goals for their own performance, plan how best to use their learning time, keep themselves motivated as they study, focus their attention on learning tasks, use effective learning strategies, monitor their progress,

evaluate the final outcome of their efforts, and reflect on the overall effectiveness of their approach in order to improve future learning efforts.

Effective learning and study strategies include meaningful learning, elaboration, organizing, note taking, identifying important information, summarizing, comprehension monitoring, and, when necessary, using mnemonics for hard-to-remember facts and lists. Most important are the internal mental processes (covert strategies) that students use; any observable study behaviors (overt strategies) are likely to be effective only when the covert strategies that underlie them are productive ones. Children show increasing metacognitive sophistication as they grow older and gain more experience with academic learning tasks; nevertheless, many students at the high school and college levels are surprisingly uninformed about how best to learn.

People's *epistemological beliefs* are the things they believe about the nature of knowledge (e.g., whether it is static or continually evolving, whether it involves isolated facts or a cohesive body of interrelated ideas, whether it comes from an outside authority or is constructed within) and the nature of learning (e.g., whether it occurs in an all-or-none fashion or slowly over a period of time, and whether it is determined more by inherited ability or more by effort and strategies). Students' epistemological beliefs influence the approaches they take to learning tasks and the criteria they use to decide when they have learned something successfully.

Ideally, students should be *intentional* learners. That is, they should be actively and consciously engaged in the learning process, should identify particular goals to accomplish as they study, and should bring a wide variety of learning and self-regulatory strategies to any study session. Intentional learning is especially important when students must undergo considerable conceptual change to truly understand the subject matter.

There are numerous reasons why students don't use effective strategies to learn classroom subject matter. For example, students may be uninformed about effective strategies or have overly simplistic beliefs about what "knowing" something means. They may have insufficient prior knowledge about a topic to enable meaningful learning and elaboration, or assigned classroom tasks may not lend themselves to such strategies. Students may be uninterested in mastering classroom subject matter or else believe that they cannot master it regardless of what they do.

Research indicates that training in effective learning and study strategies can significantly enhance students' classroom achievement. Theorists and researchers have offered a number of suggestions for promoting more sophisticated metacognitive knowledge and skills. For example, instruction regarding effective learning strategies is more successful when presented within the context of specific academic content rather than as a topic separate from academic subject areas. Strategy instruction is also more successful when students have numerous opportunities to practice specific strategies and when teachers and classmates scaffold early efforts. Students must develop epistemological beliefs consistent with effective learning strategies, and they must acquire mechanisms for monitoring and evaluating their learning efforts. Ultimately, students must discover that, with sufficient effort and appropriate strategies, they *can* learn and understand challenging classroom material.

Transfer and Problem Solving

Most semesters, I teach an undergraduate course in educational psychology for students who are preparing to become elementary or secondary teachers. In various class sessions, I introduce such topics as contemporary memory theory, operant conditioning, cognitive development, motivation, classroom management, and educational assessment. Many of my students seem to learn the material well: They carry on informed discussions in class and demonstrate comprehension and application on assignments and exams. But I always wonder about what happens to these students when they finish my course. Do the things they have learned in my class make a difference in the way they eventually teach their own students? Do they really apply the concepts I have taught them? Do principles and theories of educational psychology help them solve classroom problems?

When something you learn in one situation affects how you learn or perform in another situation, **transfer** has occurred. Sometimes you transfer knowledge and skills you have previously learned to solve a problem; hence, **problem solving** is a form of transfer.

Ideally, transfer and problem solving should be two of our educational system's top priorities. Schools at all levels, from preschools to doctoral programs, teach knowledge and skills with the assumption that students will somehow apply what they have learned to the "real world." Yet the things people learn in school do not always seem to transfer to new situations and new problems. Many adults cannot use basic addition and subtraction procedures to balance their checkbooks. Many teachers reinforce inappropriate behaviors in their classrooms, ignoring the basic operant conditioning principles they learned in their undergraduate psychology classes. People of all ages may be able to describe the difference between "right" and "wrong" without relating the distinction to their own behavior.

In this chapter, we will examine concepts, principles, theories, and research related to both transfer and problem solving. We will also consider a variety of factors that either facilitate or interfere with the successful application of acquired knowledge and skills to new situations and problems. At the end of the chapter, we will look at implications for educational practice.

TRANSFER

Transfer is a part of everyday life: People continually encounter new situations and draw on previously acquired knowledge and skills to deal with them. In fact, transfer is an essential component of human functioning. Without it, people would have to learn from scratch about how to behave in every new circumstance and would spend much of their time in trial-and-error learning.

If you think back to our discussions of classical and operant conditioning in Chapters 3 and 4, you might realize that we have already talked about transfer to some extent. In those chapters we considered the phenomenon of *generalization*: After an organism learns a response to one stimulus, it often makes the same response to similar stimuli. Generalization is clearly an instance of transfer because learning in one stimulus situation influences behavior in a slightly different situation. But here we will hardly be limiting ourselves to the behaviorist perspective; as you will discover, most contemporary explanations of transfer are decidedly cognitivist in nature.

In this first section of the chapter, we will explore various aspects of transfer. After considering different types of transfer, we will examine several theoretical perspectives of how transfer occurs, looking at both early theories and more contemporary views. We will also identify factors that influence the likelihood that transfer will take place.

Types of Transfer

Theorists have made several distinctions among types of transfer: positive versus negative transfer, vertical versus lateral transfer, near versus far transfer, and specific versus general transfer.

Positive Versus Negative Transfer

When learning in one situation facilitates learning or performance in another situation, we say that **positive transfer** has occurred. Learning basic mathematics procedures should facilitate a person's ability to balance a checkbook. Learning principles of reinforcement should improve a teacher's ability to modify student behavior. Knowing the difference between right and wrong should have a positive impact on moral and ethical behavior.

In a sense, the processes of meaningful learning and elaboration are instances of positive transfer, because previously learned information is used in understanding and remembering new ideas (Ausubel et al., 1978; Brooks & Dansereau, 1987; Voss, 1987). "Old" information can help meaningful and elaborative learning in a variety of ways; for instance, it can serve as a conceptual framework to which new material is attached, help the learner fill in the holes when new ideas are ambiguous or incomplete, or provide an analogy that helps make those ideas understandable.

In contrast, when something learned in one situation hinders a person's ability to learn or perform in a second situation, then **negative transfer** has occurred. For example, when I play tennis after having played racquetball the day before, I find myself missing the ball a lot: I keep positioning myself too close to the ball because I am accustomed to a short racquetball racquet rather than to the much longer tennis racket. People accustomed to driving a standard transmission who then find themselves behind the wheel of a car with an automatic transmission often step on a clutch that isn't there. People who learn a second language typically apply patterns of speech production characteristic of their native tongue, thus giving them a foreign accent; they may also mistakenly apply spelling patterns from their native language (Fashola, Drum, Mayer, & Kang, 1996; Schmidt & Young, 1987). Students accustomed to memorizing facts in other college courses often don't perform well on my own application-oriented exams.

An example of a situation in which negative transfer frequently rears its ugly head is in work with decimals: Students often erroneously apply mathematical rules they have learned for whole numbers. For example, when asked to compare two decimals such as these:

2.34 versus 2.8

students sometimes apply the rule that "more digits mean a larger number," thus concluding that 2.34 is the larger of the two decimal numbers (Behr & Harel, 1988). Another rule inappropriately transferred to decimals is this whole-number rule: "When a number is divided, the result is a smaller number." Even college students show negative transfer of this rule; for instance, many assert that the answer to this problem:

$$5 \div 0.65$$

is a number smaller than 5 (Tirosh & Graeber, 1990). The answer is actually about 7.69, a *larger* number.

As you can see, transfer may or may not be beneficial for performance. At the end of the chapter, we will look at ways to maximize positive transfer while minimizing negative transfer.

Vertical Versus Lateral Transfer

In some subject areas, topics build on one another in a hierarchical fashion, so that an individual must almost certainly know one topic before moving to the next. For example, a student should probably master principles of addition before moving on to multiplication, because multiplication is an extension of addition. Similarly, a medical student must have expertise in human anatomy before studying surgical techniques: It's difficult to perform an appendectomy if you can't find the appendix. **Vertical transfer** refers to such situations—an individual acquires new knowledge or skills by building on more basic information and procedures.

In other situations, knowledge of one topic may affect learning a second topic even though the first is not a prerequisite to the second. Knowledge of French is not essential for learning Spanish, yet knowing French should facilitate one's learning of Spanish because many words are similar in the two languages. When knowledge of the first topic is not essential to learning the second one but is helpful in learning it just the same, we say that **lateral transfer** has occurred.

Near Versus Far Transfer

Near transfer involves situations or problems that are similar in both superficial characteristics and underlying relationships. For example, consider the following problem:

An automotive engineer has designed a car that can reach a speed of 50 miles per hour within 5 seconds. What is the car's rate of acceleration?

Let's assume that you have learned how to solve this problem by applying the formula $v = a \times t$ (velocity = acceleration × time elapsed). You then encounter this problem:

A car salesperson tells a customer that a particular model of car can reach a speed of 40 miles per hour within 8 seconds. What is the car's rate of acceleration?

The two problems have similar surface characteristics (they both involve cars) and similar underlying structures (they both involve the relationship among velocity, acceleration, and time). But now imagine that after solving the first problem, you instead encounter this problem:

> A biologist reports that a cheetah she has been observing can attain a speed of 60 kilometers per hour within a 10-second period. How quickly can the cheetah increase its speed?

Although the general structure is the same as before (once again, the $v = a \times t$ formula applies), we have now switched topics (from cars to cheetahs) and units of measurement (from miles per hour to kilometers per second). **Far transfer** involves two situations that are similar in their underlying relationships but *different* in their surface features.

Specific Versus General Transfer

Both near and far transfer are instances of **specific transfer.** In specific transfer, the original learning task and the transfer task overlap in some way. For example, having knowledge about the anatomy of a human should help a veterinary student learn the anatomy of a dog because the two species have many parallel anatomical features. A student who knows Spanish should easily learn Portuguese because the two languages have similar vocabulary and syntax.

In **general transfer,** the original task and the transfer task are different in both content and structure. For example, if knowledge of Latin helps a student learn physics, or if the study habits a student develops in a physics course facilitate the learning of sociology, then general transfer is occurring.

Research clearly shows that near transfer is more common than far transfer and that specific transfer is more common than general transfer (Bassok, 1997; Di Vesta & Peverly, 1984; Gray & Orasanu, 1987; Perkins & Salomon, 1989). In fact, the question of whether general transfer can occur at all has been the subject of much debate over the years. We turn now to both early and contemporary theories of transfer, which vary considerably in their perspectives of what things transfer and when.

Theories of Transfer

How does transfer occur? Let's look first at an early view of transfer—one that predates twentieth-century learning theories—and then see what both behaviorists and cognitivists have had to say about how and when transfer takes place.

A Historical Perspective: Formal Discipline

In days of yore, serious scholars often studied rigorous and difficult topics—for instance, Latin, Greek, and formal logic—that are not as frequently studied today. Although these subject areas may have had no specific applicability to one's day-to-day functioning, scholars believed that learning such subjects would nevertheless improve their learning and performance in many other aspects of their lives. As recently as the middle of the twentieth century, students were given frequent practice in memorizing things (poems, for example), apparently as a method of improving their general learning capabilities. Such practices reflect the notion of **formal discipline:** Just as you exercise muscles to develop strength, you exercise your mind to learn more quickly and deal with new situations more effectively.

The theory of formal discipline, a predominant view in educational circles in the nineteenth century and early decades of the twentieth century, emphasized the importance and likelihood of general transfer, the idea being that learning in one situation improves learning and performance in another situation regardless of how different the two situations might be. As human learning began to be studied empirically, however, this notion of "mind as muscle" was soon discarded. For example, William James[1] (1890) memorized a new poem each day over the course of several weeks, assuming that he would begin to learn poems more quickly with practice. Yet he found that his poem learning did not improve; if anything, he learned his later poems more *slowly* than his early ones. More recently, researchers have found that learning computer programming—a skill requiring precise, detailed thinking about a logical sequence of events—does *not* facilitate people's logical thinking in areas unrelated to computer use (Mayer & Wittrock, 1996; Perkins & Salomon, 1989). The consensus of contemporary learning theorists is that general transfer, in the extreme sense portrayed by the formal discipline perspective, probably does not occur.

An Early Behaviorist Theory: Thorndike's Identical Elements

Edward Thorndike (1903, 1924) proposed a theory of transfer that emphasized specific transfer: Transfer occurs only to the extent that the original and transfer tasks have *identical elements*. In an early study supporting Thorndike's theory (Thorndike & Woodworth, 1901), people received extensive training in estimating the areas of rectangles. This training improved their subsequent ability to estimate the areas of rectangles and other two-dimensional forms (e.g., triangles and circles). However, training had less of an impact on the judgment of nonrectangular shapes, presumably because nonrectangles had elements both similar and dissimilar to the elements of rectangles. In a later study, Thorndike (1924) examined the interrelationships of high school students' academic achievement in various curricular areas. Achievement in one subject area appeared to facilitate students' achievement in another only when the two subjects were similar. For example, arithmetic achievement was related to performance in a bookkeeping course, but Latin proficiency was not. Thorndike concluded that the value of studying specific topics was due not to the benefits of mental exercise but to "the special information, habits, interests, attitudes, and ideals which they demonstrably produce" (Thorndike, 1924, p. 98).

A Later Behaviorist Perspective: Similarity of Stimuli and Responses

Since Thorndike's work, behaviorist views of transfer have focused on how transfer is affected by stimulus and response characteristics in both the original and transfer situations. As an illustration, consider these four lists of paired associates:

List 1	List 2	List 3	List 4
lamp–shoe	lamp–sock	rain–shoe	lamp–goat
boat–fork	boat–spoon	bear–fork	boat–shop
wall–lawn	wall–yard	sofa–lawn	wall–rice
corn–road	corn–lane	book–road	corn–fish

---

[1]As you may recall, William James was the Harvard psychologist who, back in 1890, suggested that human memory has three components. Atkinson and Shiffrin's dual-store model (see Chapter 9) was based in part on James's ideas.

Imagine that you first learn List 1 and then are asked to learn List 2. Will your knowledge of the pairs in List 1 help you learn the pairs in List 2? Based on the results of verbal learning studies (Hall, 1966, 1971), the answer is yes: The stimulus words are identical in the two situations and the responses are similar, so positive transfer from one list to the other is likely to occur.

Now, however, imagine that you have to learn List 1 and then List 3. Will prior learning of List 1 help with List 3? The answer again is yes (Hall, 1966, 1971). Even though the stimulus words are very different, the responses in List 3 are identical to those of List 1—hence they have already been learned—and merely need to be attached to the new stimuli.

But now let's now suppose that, after learning List 1, you need to learn List 4. Here is a case in which very different responses from those of List 1 must be learned to the very same stimuli. Learning List 1 is likely to make learning List 4 more difficult because you will sometimes remember the List 1 response instead of the List 4 response (Hall, 1966, 1971), and negative transfer will result.

In general, principles of transfer that have emerged from behaviorist literature (Osgood, 1949; Thyne, 1963) include the following:

1. When stimuli and responses are similar in the two situations, maximal positive transfer will occur.
2. When stimuli are different and responses are similar, some positive transfer will occur.
3. When stimuli are similar and responses are different, negative transfer will occur.

As an example of this last point, I remember one year as a high school student when my class schedule included second-period Latin and third-period French. The word for "and" (*et*) is spelled the same in both languages but pronounced very differently ("et" in Latin and "ay" in French), hence meeting the conditions for negative transfer (similar stimuli, different responses). On several occasions I blurted out an "et" in my French class—a response that inevitably evoked a disgusted scowl from my French teacher.

As learning theorists have moved away from behaviorist perspectives to more cognitive explanations of how human beings learn, they have spoken less and less of specific stimulus–response connections. Nevertheless, we see hints of behaviorist notions even in today's conceptions of transfer. For example, similarity between something already learned and the demands of a new situation clearly *is* an important factor affecting the extent to which transfer occurs. And John Anderson (1987) has proposed that transfer occurs to the extent that procedures (productions) used in one situation apply to a second situation—a cognitive variation on Thorndike's theory of identical elements.

An Information Processing Perspective: Importance of Retrieval

From a cognitive perspective, we can probably best understand transfer as involving a process of retrieval: People are apt to transfer previously learned information and skills to a new situation only when they retrieve the information and skills at the appropriate time (Cormier, 1987; Prawat, 1989). To make a connection between their current situation and any prior knowledge that might be relevant to the situation, people must have both things in working memory at the same time. Given the low probability that any particular piece of information will be retrieved, as well as the limited capacity of working memory, many potentially relevant pieces of information may very well *not* be transferred in situations in which they would be helpful.

The presence or absence of retrieval cues in the transfer situation determines what relevant knowledge, if any, is retrieved to working memory. A new event is more likely to call to mind previously learned information when aspects of the event are closely associated with the relevant information in long-term memory. This will happen, for instance, if the learner anticipated the situation when storing the new information, so that the situation and information relevant to it were stored in a connected fashion.

A Contextual Perspective: Situated Learning

In recent years, some cognitivists have proposed that most learning is context specific—that it is "situated" in the environment in which it takes place.[2] Such **situated learning** is unlikely to result in transfer to new contexts, especially when they are very different from the ones in which learning originally occurred (Brown, Collins, & Duguid, 1989; Greeno et al., 1996; Greeno, Moore, & Smith, 1993; Lave & Wenger, 1991; Light & Butterworth, 1993; Singley & Anderson, 1989).

Research indicates that some skills may indeed be context bound (Butterworth, 1993; Hirschfeld & Gelman, 1994; Snow, 1994). For example, children who sell candy, gum, and other items on the street may readily use basic mathematical procedures when they calculate prices for various quantities of items or when they determine the amount of change they should give a customer yet not transfer such procedures to classroom math lessons (Carraher, Carraher, & Schliemann, 1985; Schliemann & Carraher, 1993). Carpenters may learn mathematical concepts such as *parallel* and *perpendicular* within the context of carpentry yet not realize that their knowledge is applicable in other situations requiring the same concepts (Millroy, 1991). Furthermore, as we discovered in our discussion of Piaget's theory in Chapter 8, children can often apply logical thinking skills (e.g., proportional reasoning, or separation and control of variables) to situations with which they have had previous experience yet *not* be able to use them in less familiar contexts.

Even in a school context, skills don't necessarily transfer from one classroom to another (Bassok & Holyoak, 1990, 1993). A study by Saljo and Wyndham (1992) provides an illustration. High school students were asked to figure out how much postage they should put on an envelope that weighed a particular amount, and they were given a table of postage rates that would enable them to determine the correct amount. When students were given the task in a social studies class, most of them used the postage table to find the answer. But when students were given the task in a math class, most of them ignored the postage table and tried to *calculate* the postage in some manner, sometimes figuring it to several decimal places. Thus, the students in the social studies class were more likely to solve the problem correctly; as a former social studies teacher myself, I suspect that, in that context, they were well accustomed to looking for information in tables and charts. In contrast, many of the students in the math class drew on strategies they associated with that class (using formulas and performing calculations) and so overlooked the more efficient and accurate approach.

It is important to note here that not all cognitivists believe that learning is as situated as some of their colleagues claim (e.g., see J. Anderson, Reder, & Simon, 1996, 1997; Bereiter, 1997; Perkins, 1992). Critics argue that in its present form, situated learning theory is too vague to allow us to predict exactly when transfer will and will not take place (J. R. Anderson et al., 1997; Renkl, Mandl, & Gruber, 1996). They also point out that people often *do* use the things they have learned in school in real-world situations; for example, most individuals in our society engage in reading and simple mathematics—two skills they've probably learned at school—in nonschool contexts

[2]This idea is similar to Tulving's notion of *encoding specificity*, which I described in Chapter 12.

almost every day (J. R. Anderson et al., 1996). A key factor here appears to be the extent to which students *perceive* a content domain to be applicable to a wide variety of circumstances. For example, college students often transfer skills they learn in algebra to a physics class, but they rarely transfer skills in the other direction, from physics to algebra (Bassok, 1997). Typically, algebra is taught as a subject area that has relevance for many different situations and problems, whereas physics is more apt to be portrayed as a self-contained discipline (Bassok, 1997).

Despite such concerns, situated learning theory has numerous supporters, many of whom argue that classroom learning activities should be as similar to real-world tasks as possible. We will consider such *authentic activities* later in the chapter.

A Current View on General Transfer: Learning to Learn

We have already seen two extreme perspectives regarding general transfer. Advocates of formal discipline argued that learning rigorous and demanding subject matter facilitates later learning tasks because it strengthens and "disciplines" the mind. Thorndike, however, argued that learning in one situation will transfer to another situation only to the extent that the two situations have identical elements. Current views concerning general transfer are somewhere in between: General transfer is not as common as specific transfer, but learning occurring at one time *can* facilitate learning at another time if, in the process, the individual *learns how to learn*.

In several early studies of learning to learn, Harry Harlow (1949, 1950, 1959) found that monkeys and young children became progressively faster at discrimination-learning tasks. More recently, a number of studies have examined the transfer value of metacognitive knowledge and skills; as we noted in Chapter 13, effective study methods and habits often do generalize from one subject matter to another (see also Brooks & Dansereau, 1987; A. L. Brown, 1978; Pressley, Snyder, & Cariglia-Bull, 1987).

As long as two tasks have something in common, the possibility of transfer from one situation to the other exists (Gray & Orasanu, 1987). But commonalities among tasks do not guarantee transfer. In fact, regardless of theoretical orientation, most theorists agree that transfer does not occur nearly as often as it could or should. Much school learning seems to yield **inert knowledge** that students never use outside of the classroom (Mayer, 1996b; Perkins & Salomon, 1989; Renkl et al., 1996; Whitehead, 1929).

Factors Affecting Transfer

A number of factors influence the probability that information or skills learned in one situation will transfer to another situation. Following are several principles that can help us predict when transfer is most likely to occur:

• *Meaningful learning promotes better transfer than rote learning.* We have previously seen that meaningfully learned information is more easily stored and retrieved than information learned at a rote level. Now we see an additional advantage of meaningful learning: It promotes positive transfer (Ausubel et al., 1978; Brooks & Dansereau, 1987; Mayer & Wittrock, 1996; Prawat, 1989). For example, in a study by Brownell and Moser (1949, cited in Mayer, 1977), third-grade students were taught the idea of borrowing in subtraction in a presumably meaningful manner: Two-digit numbers were represented by individual sticks and groups of 10 sticks bundled together, with borrowing represented by the untying of one group of 10. These students solved a variety of subtraction problems more successfully than students taught the same information simply through verbally presented rules. Along a similar vein, in an experiment by Mayer and Greeno (1972), two groups of college students received one of two methods of instruction on a formula related to basic probability theory. Group 1 received instruction that focused on the formula itself, whereas group 2 received instruction that emphasized the relationship of the formula to students' general knowledge. Group 1 students were better able to apply the formula to problems similar to those they had studied during instruction, but group 2 students were better able to use the formula in ways that had not specifically been covered in instruction—that is, they could transfer the formula to a wider variety of situations. Apparently, group 2 students had made more connections between the new material and existing information in their long-term memories, and those connections enabled them to transfer probability theory in ways that group 1 students could not.

• *The more thoroughly something is learned, the more likely it is to be transferred to a new situation.* Research is clear on this point: The probability of transfer increases when students know something *well* (Brophy, 1992b; Cormier & Hagman, 1987; Gick & Holyoak, 1987; Voss, 1987).

Acquiring knowledge and skills thoroughly takes time. In fact, some conditions that make initial learning slower and more difficult may actually be beneficial both for retention (see Chapter 10) and for transfer over the long run. For example, increasing the variability of the tasks learners are asked to practice during instruction—having them perform several different tasks or several variations on the same task within a single instructional unit—lowers their performance initially but enhances their ability to transfer what they have learned to new situations later on (Chen, 1999; Schmidt & Bjork, 1992).

Clearly, then, there is a trade-off between expediency and transfer. Teachers who teach a few things in depth are more likely to promote transfer than those who teach many things quickly—the *less is more* principle I introduced in Chapter 11. Students should demonstrate thorough mastery of material if they will be expected to apply that material in future situations.

• *The more similar two situations are, the more likely it is that what is learned in one situation will be applied to the other situation.* Behaviorists have argued that similarity of either stimuli or responses is necessary for transfer to occur. Cognitivists have proposed instead that because transfer depends on retrieval of relevant information at the appropriate time, the *perceived* similarity rather than actual similarity of the two situations is important (Bassok & Holyoak, 1993; Di Vesta & Peverly, 1984; Gick & Holyoak, 1987; Voss, 1987). Either way, one thing is clear: Similarity between two situations makes a difference.

• *Principles are more easily transferred than discrete facts.* General principles and rules are more applicable than specific facts and information (Cheng, Holyoak, Nisbett, & Oliver, 1986; Fong, Krantz, & Nisbett, 1986; Gick & Holyoak, 1987; Judd, 1932; Perkins & Salomon, 1987; Perry, 1991; Singley & Anderson, 1989). For example, if you have read Chapter 4's discussion of operant conditioning, then you probably remember the general principle of reinforcement: A reinforcer is a stimulus that increases the later frequency of a response it follows. This principle is easily transferable to a wide variety of situations, whereas specific facts that I mentioned in the same chapter (e.g., who did what research study and when) are not. Similarly, when students are trying to understand such current events as revolutions and international wars, general principles from history—for example, the principle that two groups of people will engage in battle when other attempts at reaching a mutually satisfying state of affairs have failed—are probably more applicable than precise knowledge of World War II battles. And when students study geography, general map interpretation skills—for instance, determining why various features are located where they are—are probably more useful than the names and locations of specific rivers, mountain ranges, and state capitals (Bochenhauer, 1990). General and perhaps somewhat abstract principles are especially helpful when a new situation does not, on the surface, appear to be similar to previous experiences but when it shares underlying structural or conceptual similarities with those experiences—in other words, when the new situation requires *far transfer* (J. R. Anderson et al., 1996; Perkins, 1995; Perkins & Salomon, 1989).[3]

• *Numerous and varied examples and opportunities for practice increase the extent to which information and skills will be applied in new situations.* As situated learning theorists have suggested, knowledge is often stored in association with the context in which it has been encountered. People who store a particular skill or piece of information in connection with one situation are likely to retrieve that knowledge—and thus may use it—when they encounter the same situation once again; they are *less* likely to retrieve it when they are in a somewhat different situation (Di Vesta & Peverly, 1984; Stein, 1989; Sternberg & Frensch, 1993). For example, many elementary students don't recognize that the things they learn in science are useful in solving real-world problems (Rakow, 1984). And, in general, students don't see the connections between the things they learn in school and the situations they encounter in the outside world (Alexander & Judy, 1988; diSessa, 1982; Gick & Holyoak, 1987; Mayer & Wittrock, 1996; Perkins & Simmons, 1988; Schoenfeld, 1985a; Sternberg & Frensch, 1993).

People are most likely to transfer something they have learned when they have encountered it in a wide variety of examples and practice situations (J. R. Anderson et al., 1996; Cormier, 1987; Cox, 1997; Gick & Holyoak, 1987; Kotovsky & Fallside, 1989; Perkins, 1995; Schmidt & Bjork, 1992; see Bassok & Holyoak, 1993, for an exception). Learners instructed in this fashion store the material they are studying in association with multiple contexts; therefore, they are more likely to retrieve the information when they again find themselves in one of those contexts. As an illustration, when students are learning basic arithmetic principles, they might be asked to apply those principles in determining best buys at a grocery store, dividing items equitably among friends, running a lemonade stand, and so on. Arithmetic will then be associated in long-term memory with all of these situations, and when the need arises to determine which of two grocery products yields the most for the money, relevant arithmetic procedures should be readily retrieved.

• *The probability of transfer decreases as the time interval between the original task and the transfer task increases.* Most research on transfer has focused on very short delays between the original task and the transfer task (Gick & Holyoak, 1987). Yet transfer decreases as the time interval between the original and transfer situations increases (Gick & Holyoak, 1987). Here is another principle that is probably a result of retrieval: Information that has been learned recently is more likely, and more able, to be retrieved than information acquired further back in time (recall our discussion of *decay* in Chapter 12).

How and when do people transfer information they have learned to find solutions to problems? It is to this topic—problem solving—that we turn next.

---

[3]Perkins and Salomon (1989) have made a distinction between low-road transfer and high-road transfer. *Low-road transfer* occurs when a new situation is superficially quite similar to prior experiences, such that relevant knowledge and skills are readily retrieved. But in *high-road transfer*, people must make a conscious and deliberate connection between a new situation and their previous experiences; such a connection is often made on the basis of an underlying, abstract principle. In other words, low-road transfer is most likely to occur in situations involving near transfer, whereas high-road transfer is required in situations involving far transfer.

PROBLEM SOLVING

Can you solve these three problems?

1. What number is obtained when 3354 is divided by 43?
2. How can a middle-aged educational psychologist be helped to control her junk food habit?
3. How can two groups of people of differing political persuasions and a mutual lack of trust be convinced to curtail their proliferation of military weapons and instead work toward cooperation and peaceful coexistence?

The world presents us with many different kinds of problems. Some, such as problem 1, are straightforward: All of the information necessary for a solution is presented, and the solution is definitely right or wrong. Others, such as problem 2, may necessitate seeking out additional information (e.g., does the educational psychologist keep physically active, or does she sit around the house all day reading mystery novels and watching television game shows?), and there may be two or more solutions to the problem (e.g., self-reinforcement for altered eating habits, six months on a tropical island with no grocery stores). Still others, such as problem 3, may be so complicated that, even after considerable research and creative thought, no easy solution emerges (as I write this, events in the Middle East come to mind). Different kinds of problems require different procedures and different solutions; this multifaceted nature of problem solving has made the theoretical study of problem solving a very challenging endeavor indeed.

In the following pages, we will explore a number of topics related to the complex activity of human problem solving. We will first define some basic concepts that appear in problem-solving literature and then examine both behaviorist and cognitive theories of problem solving. Because cognitive theories predominate at the present time, we will also look in depth at aspects of memory and cognitive strategies that are often involved when people solve problems successfully.

Basic Concepts in Problem Solving

Several basic concepts will be helpful to us as we explore the nature of problem solving: problem components, algorithms, heuristics, and well-defined problems versus ill-defined problems.

Components of a Problem

Any problem has at least three components (Glass et al., 1979; Wickelgren, 1974):

- *Givens:* Pieces of information that are provided when the problem is presented
- *Goal:* The desired end state—what a problem solution will hopefully accomplish
- *Operations:* Actions that can be performed to approach or reach the goal

Operations are frequently described in terms of *productions*, the "if–then" conditional actions described in Chapter 11 (e.g., see J. R. Anderson, 1983a, 1987). When one or more operations can be applied to reach the goal state, the problem is successfully solved.

Algorithms and Heuristics

Some problems can be approached using a set of specified operations that always lead to a correct solution. For example, the problem of dividing 3354 by 43 can be solved using either of two procedures: (1) applying prescribed methods of long division or (2) pushing the appropriate series of buttons on a calculator. Either approach leads to the correct answer: 78. Similarly, a pumpkin pie recipe, if followed to the letter in terms of ingredients, measurements, and oven temperatures, provides a series of steps that guarantees a delicious dessert. Such specific, step-by-step procedures for solving problems are called **algorithms.**

Unfortunately, not all problems can be solved with algorithms. No specific algorithms exist for eliminating a junk food addiction or establishing world peace. In such situations, people use other approaches to problem solving—approaches that may or may not work. These approaches, known collectively as **heuristics,** include general problem-solving strategies, rules of thumb, and "best guesses" based on past experience with similar problems. For example, in helping an educational psychologist reduce her junk food intake, one heuristic is to think of as many different solutions as possible (a technique known as **brainstorming**), in hopes that one of them will be acceptable. The problem of disarmament of two warring factions can perhaps be solved by analogy: If two co-workers can resolve their differences when they sit down and talk about them, maybe the same strategy will be effective with political groups (hence the frequent summit conferences among world leaders).

Heuristics are also used when algorithms are impractical or time consuming. For example, I once coordinated a chili supper for the parent–teacher association (PTA) of my children's elementary school and needed numerous volunteers to assist me. The PTA board suggested an algorithm for me to use: Contact the more than 200 individuals who had indicated on a questionnaire several months earlier that they would help at PTA functions. Being pressed for time, I instead chose a heuristic: I contacted people I knew personally, aware that I could arm-twist many of them into helping out. Similarly, although an algorithm exists for determining the best move in a game of checkers, people tend not to use it because of its impracticality. This algorithm is as follows: Consider every possible move, then consider every possible next move that the opponent could make in response to each of those moves, then consider every follow-up move that could be made in response to each of *those* moves, and so on until the winner is projected for every conceivable series of moves (Samuel, 1963). Such an algorithm would take either a sophisticated computer programmer or a lifetime of complete dedication to a single game of checkers.

Well-Defined Versus Ill-Defined Problems

Problems vary greatly in terms of how well they are structured or defined. Many theorists have found it helpful to distinguish between well-defined and ill-defined problems (Eysenck & Keane, 1990; Frederiksen, 1984a; Reitman, 1964, 1965; Simon, 1973, 1978), a distinction that actually reflects a continuum of problem structure rather than a rigid dichotomy (Frederiksen, 1984a). At one extreme is the **well-defined problem,** one for which goals and givens are clearly stated, all of the necessary information for solving the problem is presented, and an algorithm exists that will lead to a correct solution. At the other extreme is the **ill-defined problem,** one in which the desired goal is ambiguous, some information necessary for the solution is lacking, and no relevant algorithm for the problem exists. Well-defined problems often have only one right solution, whereas ill-defined problems often have several possible solutions that vary in terms of their relative "rightness" or acceptability. The problem of dividing 3354 by 43 is well defined, while that of military disarmament is ill defined (e.g., the goal of "cooperation and peaceful coexistence" is ambiguous).[4]

---

[4]For a detailed discussion of ill-defined problems in international relations, see Voss, Wolfe, Lawrence, and Engle (1991).

As you might guess, ill-defined problems are typically more difficult to solve and require more complex problem-solving strategies than well-defined problems.

Unfortunately, researchers have focused more on well-defined problems (often somewhat artificial ones) than on the ill-defined problems that life so often presents (Eysenck & Keane, 1990; Ohlsson, 1983; Rosenshine et al., 1996). You will undoubtedly notice this bias as we proceed with our discussion of problem solving. Nevertheless, most of the theories and principles I will present presumably apply to both kinds of problems. And in fact, later in the chapter we will find that one strategy for solving ill-defined problems is to define them more specifically and concretely—in other words, to make them well defined.

Theories of Problem Solving

Since Edward Thorndike's early work with the cat in the puzzle box, several theories of problem solving have emerged from both the behaviorist and cognitive perspectives. We will first look at two behaviorist views: trial-and-error and response hierarchy. We will then examine three more cognitive approaches: Gestalt psychology, stages of problem solving, and information processing theory.

Trial-and-Error Learning

In Chapter 4, you read about Thorndike's (1898) classic work with a cat in a puzzle box. The cat needed to solve a problem: how to get out of a confining situation. It explored the box, manipulating its various parts, and eventually triggered the mechanism that opened the door. Once again the cat was put back into the box, and once again it tried different behaviors until it triggered the release mechanism. In each succeeding trial, escape from the box took less time than in the previous trial. The cat's approach to the problem situation appeared to be one of trial and error, with the correct solution being followed by a positive consequence (escape from the box).

A trial-and-error approach is often observed in the problem-solving behavior of children. For example, consider the way many young children assemble jigsaw puzzles: They try to fit different pieces into the same spot, often without considering each piece's shape and appearance, until eventually they find a piece that fits. Such an approach to problem solving is a workable one if there are only a limited number of possibilities that one can try; otherwise, it can be extremely time consuming, with no guarantee of finding a successful solution (Chi & Glaser, 1985). One advantage of children's early play experiences is that play provides opportunities to discover the properties of a wide variety of objects, and such discoveries may enable children to more readily solve problems with those objects at a later time (Christie & Johnsen, 1983).

Response Hierarchy

A concept you encountered in Chapter 3 was Clark Hull's notion of a habit-family hierarchy, now more generally known as a **response hierarchy:** An organism learns several different responses to the same stimulus, each of which is associated with that stimulus with a certain degree of habit strength. When a stimulus is presented, an organism will, if possible, make the response for which the habit strength is the strongest. If that response fails or is prevented from occurring, the organism will make the second response, and so on down the hierarchy (Hull, 1934, 1937, 1938).

A response hierarchy can be graphically depicted like this:

In this case, three responses have been learned to the same stimulus, with stronger stimulus–response associations being indicated by thicker arrows. The organism first emits the response with the strongest association to the stimulus (R_1). If that response fails to achieve its goal, the response with the second strongest association (R_2) is emitted, then the third strongest response (R_3), and so on until eventually the goal is attained.

A number of behaviorists (e.g., Davis, 1966; Mayzner & Tresselt, 1958, 1966; Skinner, 1966a) have applied the notion of response hierarchy to a problem-solving situation. Stimuli in the problem situation may evoke several different responses, and those responses will be produced, one at a time and in order of their strength, until either the problem is solved or the organism exhausts its repertoire of responses. To illustrate, as my daughter Tina was growing up, she was often confronted with the same problem: getting permission from her parents to do something we didn't want her to do. Given this problem, she typically tried three different responses, usually in the same order. First she would smile sweetly and describe how much she wanted to engage in the forbidden activity (such a response, apparently, was associated most strongly with this particular problem situation). If that tactic was unproductive, she would speak indignantly about how her parents never let her do anything. As a last resort, she would run off to her room, slamming her door and shouting that her parents hated her. Unfortunately, Tina never did learn that some problems, such as gaining permission to engage in forbidden activities, would be solved over her parents' dead bodies.

In their emphasis on trial-and-error learning and habit strength, behaviorists have obviously focused on the role that stimulus–response connections play in problem solving. Although such an approach can often be used to explain problem-solving behavior, contemporary theorists have largely abandoned it to focus more on the mental processes involved in problem solving. Consistent with this trend, we, too, will abandon behaviorism at this point and embrace a more cognitively oriented perspective for the rest of our discussion.

Gestalt Psychology

In Chapter 8, I described Wolfgang Köhler's (1925) observations of chimpanzee behavior in problem-solving situations. Köhler observed little trial-and-error behavior of the form that Thorndike had described. Rather, it appeared to him that the chimpanzees carefully examined the components of a problem situation (sizing things up, so to speak) and mentally combined and recombined those components until they eventually found a winning combination. At this point of **insight,** the chimps would immediately move into action, performing the required responses in a deliberate manner until the problem was solved. From such observations, Köhler (1925, 1929) concluded that problem solving was a process of mentally **restructuring** a problem situation until insight into the problem's solution was reached. Similar instances of insight have been observed in young children (Smith & Dutton, 1979; Sylva, Bruner, & Genova, 1976).

Stages of Problem Solving

Another early cognitive approach to problem solving was to identify the mental stages through which problem solving proceeded. For example, Wallas (1926) identified four steps in problem solving:

1. *Preparation:* Defining the problem and gathering information relevant to its solution
2. *Incubation:* Thinking about the problem at a subconscious level while engaging in other activities
3. *Inspiration:* Having a sudden insight into the solution of the problem
4. *Verification:* Checking to be certain that the solution is correct

Similarly, Polya (1957) listed these four steps:

1. *Understanding the problem:* Identifying the problem's knowns (givens) and unknowns and, if appropriate, using suitable notation, such as mathematical symbols, to represent the problem
2. *Devising a plan:* Determining appropriate actions to take to solve the problem
3. *Carrying out the plan:* Executing the actions that have been determined to solve the problem and checking their effectiveness
4. *Looking backward:* Evaluating the overall effectiveness of the approach to the problem, with the intention of learning something about how similar problems may be solved on future occasions

Unfortunately, Wallas and Polya derived their conceptualizations of problem solving more from introspection and informal observation than from controlled experimentation, and they were somewhat vague about how each of their four steps could be accomplished (Lester, 1985; Mayer, 1992; Schoenfeld, 1992). For example, Wallas's notion of incubation revealed little about how to behave to facilitate the occurrence of inspiration. Similarly, Polya recommended devising a plan with little consideration of just how one would go about doing that. For such reasons, early stage theories of problem solving were of limited usefulness in helping psychologists determine what specific cognitive processes are involved in solving problems successfully.

Information Processing Theory

Most contemporary theories focus less on the steps people follow in solving problems and more on the specific mental processes they use to reach problem solutions. These information processing theories emphasize the role of such factors as working memory capacity, meaningful learning, organization of long-term memory, retrieval of relevant information, and specific cognitive strategies. The bulk of current research in problem solving reflects inquiry into the nature of these cognitive processes. In the following pages, we will look at them in detail.

Cognitive Factors in Problem Solving

The ability to solve problems successfully depends on a number of factors related to the human information processing system. Here we will focus on several factors: working memory capacity, encoding and storage in long-term memory, long-term memory retrieval, the knowledge base relevant to the problem, and metacognition. As we go along, we will identify several differences between problem-solving experts and novices within a particular content domain, discovering reasons why some people solve problems quickly, easily, and effectively, while others solve them either with great difficulty or not at all.

Working Memory Capacity

As you should recall, working memory is the component of memory in which the active, conscious processing of information occurs. Yet this component has a limited capacity: It can hold and process only a small amount of information at a time. If the information and processes necessary to solve a problem exceed working memory capacity, the problem cannot be solved (J. R. Anderson, 1987; Johnstone & El-Banna, 1986; Pulos, 1980; Salthouse, 1991; Tourniaire & Pulos, 1985). For example, you may remember from Chapter 9 how difficult it can be to solve long-division problems in your head.

The working memory limitation can be overcome in problem-solving situations in a couple of ways. First, some of the information necessary to solve the problem can be stored externally (e.g., by writing it down on paper) or perhaps even processed externally (e.g., by using a calculator). Second, as I suggested in Chapter 10, some skills involved in problem solving should be learned well enough that they become automatic, thus requiring only minimal working memory capacity.

Encoding and Storage of the Problem

Consider this classic children's riddle:

> As I was going to St. Ives,
> I met a man with seven wives.
> Every wife had seven sacks.
> Every sack had seven cats.
> Every cat had seven kits.
> Kits, cats, sacks, wives.
> How many were going to St. Ives?

Many people take this logical approach to the problem: 1 traveler plus 1 man plus 7 wives plus 7^2 sacks (49) plus 7^3 cats (343) plus 7^4 kits (2401) equal a total of 2802 going to St. Ives. People who solve the problem in this manner have encoded the problem incorrectly. In particular, they have overlooked the first line of the riddle: "As *I* was going to St. Ives." The problem statement doesn't tell us where the polygamist was taking his harem and menagerie—perhaps to St. Ives, perhaps not.

Here is a passage containing some information you will need to solve a mathematical problem. Read the information; then, after you have finished, turn the page to read the problem:

I went to the store and made the following purchases:

- A roasting chicken for $4
- A dozen eggs for $1 per dozen
- Three avocados for 50¢ each
- Two cans of tomato sauce for 25¢ each
- Five apples for 20¢ each

Now for the problem:

How many items did I buy?

Did you find that you stored the wrong information? You may have been expecting the problem "How much did I spend?" If so, then you probably determined the total amount spent in each line of the problem and added the amounts together for a grand total. Using this approach, however, you would not have stored the information actually necessary for solving the problem: the number of items mentioned in each line.

One critical factor in problem solving is *what* specific information is stored in memory (Chi, Glaser, & Farr, 1988; Glaser, 1987; Sternberg, 1985; Sternberg & Davidson, 1982, 1983). A difficulty you may have had with the grocery shopping problem is that some irrelevant information was presented (i.e., the prices of items), and you may have stored that information instead of more essential data. Irrelevant information can be distracting, thus interfering with successful problem solving. For example, when my daughter Tina was in elementary and middle school, she often had trouble with math problems that included superfluous facts. She behaved almost as if she had learned that she needed to use *all* of the information she was given. This attitude may have been the result of her prior school experiences: Most of the problems she had previously encountered (especially word problems in mathematics) presented only the information needed to solve the problem—no more, no less.

A second critical factor related to long-term storage is *how* a problem is encoded in memory (Mayer, 1986; Ormrod, 1979; Prawat, 1989; Resnick, 1989; Schwartz, 1971; Sternberg & Davidson, 1982). For example, consider these two ways of presenting the same situation:

- There are 5 birds and 3 worms. How many more birds are there than worms?
- There are 5 birds and 3 worms. How many birds won't get a worm?

First graders often struggle with the first problem, yet they solve the second one quite easily (Hudson, 1983). The first problem requires students to store *relational* information—how one thing compares to another. Relational information seems to be difficult to encode, even for adults. For instance, Mayer (1982) examined undergraduate students' ability to remember problems such as this one:

A truck leaves Los Angeles en route to San Francisco at 1 P.M. A second truck leaves San Francisco at 2 P.M. en route to Los Angeles going along the same route. Assume the two cities are 465 miles apart and that the trucks meet at 6 P.M. If the second truck travels at 15 mph faster than the first truck, how fast does each truck go? (Mayer, 1982, p. 202)

The students in Mayer's study had considerable difficulty remembering relational information (e.g., one truck traveling *15 mph faster* than another): They made three times as many errors in recalling relational aspects of problems as they did in recalling basic assertions (e.g., two cities being 465 miles apart).

Wertheimer (1945) has provided another example of the importance of encoding in problem solving: calculating the area of a parallelogram. As you probably know, the area of a rectangle is determined by multiplying its height by its width. But how is the area of a parallelogram determined? The problem solution is easier once you realize that the extra "triangle" at one end of the parallelogram is identical to the missing triangle at the other end, as illustrated in Figure 14–1.

Figure 14–1
Finding the area of a parallelogram.

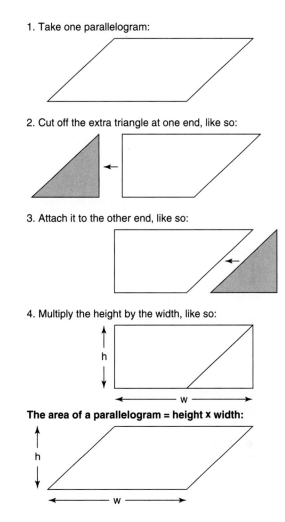

1. Take one parallelogram:

2. Cut off the extra triangle at one end, like so:

3. Attach it to the other end, like so:

4. Multiply the height by the width, like so:

h

w

The area of a parallelogram = height x width:

h

w

How people encode a problem—and therefore how they solve it—is partly a function of how they classify the problem to begin with (Hinsley, Hayes, & Simon, 1977; Resnick, 1989; Sternberg & Davidson, 1982, 1983). For example, consider this situation:

> The students in Alice's ninth-grade social studies class have been working in pairs on an assigned project; their teacher has said that he will give a prize for the best project that a pair completes. Alice is now complaining to her younger sister Louisa that her partner, Meg, no longer wants to work with her; Meg thinks Alice is too bossy. Louisa suggests that the best course of action is simply for Alice and Meg to buckle down and finish the project so that they can win the prize. Alice, however, is thinking that she should instead talk with Meg and promise that she will be less bossy. (based on Berg & Calderone, 1994)

Louisa and Alice are classifying the problem in different ways here, and so they arrive at different solutions. In Louisa's eyes, the problem is one of completing the project. Alice sees the problem quite differently—as one of resolving an interpersonal conflict (Berg & Calderone, 1994).

As another example of problem classification, consider this problem:

> Ana went shopping. She spent $3.50 and then counted her money when she got home. She had $2.35 left. How much did Ana have when she started out? (Resnick, 1989, p. 165)

If you recognize this as an addition problem, you will probably get the correct answer of $5.85. However, if the word *left* in the problem leads you to classify the problem as one requiring subtraction (because many subtraction problems ask questions such as "How many are *left*?"), you may very well get the incorrect answer of $1.15 (Resnick, 1989).

Expert and novice problem solvers within a particular content domain seem to classify problems differently (Anzai, 1991; Chi et al., 1988; De Corte et al., 1996; Di Vesta & Peverly, 1984; Larkin, 1983; Novick, 1988; Schoenfeld & Herrmann, 1982). Experts generally classify a problem on the basis of abstract concepts and underlying principles and patterns. They seem to have a well-developed set of **problem schemas** that they use to represent different kinds of problems. Novices, however, tend to focus on specific, concrete aspects of a problem and so are apt to retrieve information related only to those aspects. As an illustration, Schoenfeld and Herrmann (1982) compared the ways that mathematics professors and students categorized a variety of mathematical problems. Professors classified them on the basis of abstract principles related to problem solution; for example, those solved by analogy were grouped together, as were those solved by contradiction, and so on. In contrast, students classified the problems on the basis of more superficial characteristics, such as whether they contained polynomial expressions or whether they included figures from plane geometry. After a course in mathematics, the students were asked to repeat the classification task; at this point, they began to classify the problems as their professors did.

Experts may also spend more time defining ill-defined problems before attempting to solve them (Mitchell, 1989; Swanson, O'Connor, & Cooney, 1990; Voss, Tyler, & Yengo, 1983; Voss, Wolfe, Lawrence, & Engle, 1991). Consider this problem as an example:

> Imagine that the year is 1983 and that you are the Minister of Agriculture in the Soviet Union. Crop productivity has been low for the past several years, and people are beginning to go hungry. What would you do to increase crop production? (based on Voss, Greene, Post, & Penner, 1983; Voss, Tyler, & Yengo, 1983)

Take a few minutes to jot down some of your ideas.

How much time did you spend defining the problem? Chances are, you didn't spend much time at all; you probably went right to work thinking about possible problem solutions. If you were a political scientist specializing in the Soviet Union, however, you might have spent considerable time identifying various aspects of the problem—perhaps considering Soviet political policies, the amount of land available for farming, and so on—before thinking about how you might solve it (Mitchell, 1989; Voss, Greene, et al., 1983; Voss, Tyler, & Yengo, 1983).

Mental Sets in Encoding People are often predisposed to approach and encode problems in particular ways—a phenomenon known as **mental set**.[5] Here is a problem for which people are often the victims of mental set:

> How can you throw a tennis ball so that it goes a short distance, comes to a complete stop, then reverses its direction? You may not bounce the ball against a surface, nor may you attach any other object (such as a string) to it. (Based on Gardner, 1978)

---

[5]Gestalt psychologists introduced this idea, using the term *Einstellung*.

I once gave this problem to a masters-level learning theories class, and only a handful of my 35 students were able to solve it. Most of them worked on the assumption that the ball had to be thrown horizontally (some even said that they encoded the problem as a visual image of a pitcher). Once you break this mental set, the answer is quite simple: You throw the ball *up*.

As another example of mental set, consider this "candle" problem adapted from a similar one used by Duncker (1945):

> You are in a room with a bulletin board firmly affixed to the wall. Your task is to stand a candle upright beside the bulletin board about 4 feet above the floor. You do not want the candle touching the bulletin board, because the candle's flame must not singe the bulletin board. Instead, you need to place the candle about a centimeter away. How can you accomplish the task, given the following materials:
>
> • A small candle (birthday cake size)
> • A match
> • A box of thumbtacks
> • A 12-inch wooden ruler
> • A metal knitting needle

Develop a solution for the problem before you continue reading.

When I bring these materials to my graduate classes, students typically identify three different solutions. One solution is to stab the knitting needle through the candle and into the bulletin board; this action inevitably splits the candle and gouges the bulletin board. A second solution is to form a horizontal surface with the ruler, propping it against the bulletin board with thumbtacks (perhaps also sticking the knitting needle in the bulletin board just below it), and then place the candle on top; however, the precariously placed ruler usually falls to the floor once the candle is added. Only a third solution works: Take the thumbtacks out of the box, use the tacks to attach the box to the bulletin board, then affix the candle to the top side of the box (with either melted wax or a tack). The solution is obvious once you think about it, but many people have difficulty with the problem because they encode the box as a container and fail to consider its other possible functions.

The tendency to think of objects as having only one function, thereby overlooking other possible uses, is a form of mental set known as **functional fixedness** (Birch & Rabinowitz, 1951; Duncker, 1945; Maier & Janzen, 1968). The degree to which individuals experience functional fixedness depends, in part, on situational conditions. People more easily solve the candle problem if the tacks are presented *outside* of the box, presumably because they are less likely to think of the box only as a container for the tacks (Duncker, 1945). The problem is also easier to solve if the box itself is labeled "BOX" (Glucksberg & Weisberg, 1966), possibly because the label draws attention to the box as something that can be used in solving the problem.

Mental set and functional fixedness are partly the result of past experience: If a particular approach to a problem has worked in the past, a person is likely to continue using it and perhaps learn it to a level of automaticity. The person is then likely to apply this approach, often in a relatively "mindless" fashion, even in situations where it is inappropriate or unnecessarily cumbersome. (Recall our discussion of automaticity's downsides in Chapter 10.)

Luchins's experiments with water jar problems (1942; Luchins & Luchins, 1950) illustrate just how strongly one's past experiences can influence problem solving. Imagine, if you will, that you have three jars of three different sizes:

Jar A holds 20 ounces of water.
Jar B holds 59 ounces of water.
Jar C holds 4 ounces of water.

You need exactly 31 ounces of water. Assuming that you have an unlimited amount of water, how can you get the exact amount of water using only the three jars you have? Try to find a solution before you read further.

The solution to the water jar problem is as follows:

1. Fill jar B. This gives you 59 ounces of water.
2. Pour water from jar B into jar A until A is full. This leaves 39 ounces in jar B.
3. Pour water from jar B into jar C until C is full. This leaves 35 ounces in jar B.
4. Pour the water out of jar C.
5. Once again pour water from B into C. At this point you have 31 ounces in jar B, the exact amount you need.

Mathematically speaking, the solution to the problem is

$$B - A - 2C$$

Luchins (1942) gave participants in his study a series of such problems, with the answer always being the same: $B - A - 2C$. He then presented the following three problems:

Jar A holds:	Jar B holds:	Jar C holds:	Obtain this amount:
23	49	3	20
15	39	3	18
28	76	3	25

Almost everyone solved the first two problems using the same formula as before: $B - A - 2C$. They had difficulty solving the third problem because the standard formula did not apply. But notice that all three can be solved quite easily: The solution for the first and third problems is $A - C$, and that for the second problem is $A + C$. The participants in Luchins's study (who were professors and graduate students—hardly mental slouches!) were victims of a problem-solving mental set established through prior experience.

In most situations, one's predisposition to approach similar problems in similar ways facilitates successful problem solving (Maier, 1945). A mental set influences the way in which a problem is encoded in memory, however, and this encoding in turn influences the parts of long-term memory that are searched for potentially relevant information and procedures. If a problem's encoding steers an individual in the wrong "direction" in long-term memory, then it hinders problem-solving performance (Alexander & Judy, 1988; Mayer, 1992; Stein, 1989). Let's now consider retrieval from long-term memory as yet another cognitive factor affecting problem-solving success.

Retrieval From Long-Term Memory
To use previously learned information to solve a problem, people must retrieve that information at the time they are thinking about the problem. Thus, the factors that facilitate long-term memory retrieval—for example, meaningful learning and organized storage—facilitate problem-solving success as well (Ausubel et al., 1978).

When people search long-term memory for information relevant to a problem, they begin by looking in logical "places." They tend to retrieve familiar ideas first, identifying original or unusual problem solutions later or not at all (Bourne et al., 1986). They also tend to retrieve information closely associated with aspects of the problem situation; for example, people more easily solve the candle problem when they have previously learned a paired-associate list that includes the pair *candle–box* (Weisberg, DiCamillo, & Phillips, 1979). Hints that provide important retrieval cues can be helpful, at least if individuals perceive their relevance (Bassok & Holyoak, 1993; Bourne et al., 1986; Gick & Holyoak, 1987). For example, the solution of anagrams such as this one:

Unscramble these letters to form a real word: NEEPLATH

is easier when you know that the solution belongs to a particular category such as *animals* (Safren, 1962). (The solution, by the way, is *elephant*.)

As I mentioned in Chapter 12, anxiety interferes with retrieval by restricting the part of long-term memory that is searched. Anxious individuals are therefore apt to have difficulty solving problems whose solutions are not readily apparent. For example, Glucksberg (1962) asked four groups of people to solve the candle problem presented earlier. For two groups, the tacks were out of the box (the easy version of the problem), and for the other two groups, the tacks were in the box (the difficult version). Two groups were given no reason to be anxious about solving the problem; their success or failure in finding a solution had no consequences. The other two groups had an incentive to make them more eager and anxious about finding a solution: The fastest 25% of the problem solvers would receive $5, and the fastest individual of all would receive $25 (a tidy sum back in 1962). Here are the mean reaction times (in minutes) for the four groups of problem solvers; larger numbers indicate greater difficulty in solving the problem:

	Easy version	Difficult version
Low anxiety	4.99	7.41
High anxiety	3.67	11.08

When the box was empty, its use as a platform for the candle was obvious, and anxiety facilitated problem solving. But when the box was already being used as a container, anxiety made the problem even more difficult to solve than it already was.

The effects of anxiety on problem solving seem to be reduced or eliminated when individuals know where to search in long-term memory. Although high-anxiety individuals typically perform more poorly than low-anxiety individuals on problem-solving tasks, performance of the two groups is similar when memory aids that promote appropriate retrieval are provided (Gross & Mastenbrook, 1980; Leherissey, O'Neil, & Hansen, 1971).

If information relevant to a problem is to be retrieved from long-term memory, it must obviously be *in* long-term memory to begin with. So another factor affecting problem-solving success is an individual's knowledge base in a particular content domain, as we shall see now.

Knowledge Base

Successful (expert) problem solvers have a more complete and better organized knowledge base for the problems they solve (Anzai, 1991; Bédard & Chi, 1992; Chi et al., 1982; Lawson & Chinnappan, 1994). For example, using the concept mapping technique described in Chapters 10 and 13, Cochran (1988) examined the achievement (much of which involved problem solving) of high school physics students studying a unit on electricity. The higher achievers were students who had better organized information about concepts related to electricity in long-term memory; not only did they know better which concepts should be associated with which other concepts, but they also knew the particular relationships that different concepts had with one another. Low achievers were often uncertain about just how the different aspects of electricity fit together and more often misconstrued relationships among concepts. By having more information relative to a specific content domain, as well as more interconnections among various bits of information, expert problem solvers can more quickly and easily retrieve the things they need to solve a problem; they can also make inferences about the problem that may facilitate its solution (J.R. Anderson, 1993; Bédard & Chi, 1992; Chi et al., 1982; Hiebert & Lefevre, 1986; Stein, 1989).

Successful problem solvers also appear to have more knowledge of specific strategies they can use to solve problems within their area of expertise. For instance, once they have categorized a problem as falling into a particular category or being consistent with a certain problem schema, they readily apply certain procedures to solve it (Chi & Glaser, 1985; Gick, 1986; Mayer, 1986; Prawat, 1989; Reed, 1993). And they have often learned basic problem-solving procedures to automaticity (Chi et al., 1988; Glaser, 1987). Novice problem solvers, lacking the rich knowledge base of experts, are more likely to engage in ineffective problem-solving strategies—for example, resorting to trial and error, persevering with unproductive procedures, making unwarranted assumptions, and applying procedures and equations in a rote, meaningless fashion (Perkins & Simmons, 1988).

Metacognition

Metacognition plays a key role in problem solving. In particular, successful problem solvers must

- Believe that they are capable of solving the problem successfully.
- Understand that some problems may take considerable time and effort to accomplish.
- Analyze a problem into its component parts.
- Select appropriate problem-solving strategies.
- Plan a course of action.
- Monitor progress toward a solution, and change strategies if necessary.
  (Cardelle-Elawar, 1992; Davidson & Sternberg, 1998; De Corte et al., 1996; Dominowski, 1998; Geary, 1994; Kilpatrick, 1985; Lesgold & Lajoie, 1991; Lester, 1985; Pfeiffer, Feinberg, & Gelber, 1987; Schoenfeld, 1992; Silver, 1982)

The more metacognitively engaged people are in the problems they are tackling, the more likely they are to be flexible in their choice of strategies, to solve complex problems successfully, and to transfer effective problem-solving strategies to new situations (Delclos & Harrington, 1991; Dominowski, 1998; King, 1991).

As an illustration, consider this train of thought regarding a particular problem:

> I'm sloppy at doing [algorithm]; I'd better go slow. This is complicated. I should go through the steps carefully. This method isn't working. I'll try something else. I need to vocalize what I'm doing to help me keep on track. I need to write these steps out. (Lester, 1985, p. 63)

This individual, while obviously not an expert at solving the problem in question, is bringing several beneficial metacognitive skills to bear on the problem—for example, acknowledging the need to go slowly and carefully, recognizing when a strategy is unproductive, and identifying specific behaviors that may facilitate problem-solving success.

Unfortunately, students sometimes have epistemological beliefs that interfere with effective problem solving. In the case of mathematics, for instance, many students believe that successful problem solving is largely a matter of luck, that a problem can have only one right answer, that there's only one way to solve any particular problem, and that a problem is either solvable within a few minutes' time or else not solvable at all (De Corte et al., 1996; Geary, 1994; Schoenfeld, 1992). When students have naïve beliefs about the nature of a subject area or about knowledge more generally—perhaps thinking that there is a single "right" answer to virtually any issue—they are especially likely to have difficulty addressing ill-defined problems (Schraw, Dunkle, & Bendixen, 1995).

We have spoken of the need to have appropriate strategies for solving particular problems and to regulate (metacognitively) the effectiveness of those strategies in achieving a problem solution. But what specific strategies do people use? We turn to this topic now.

Problem-Solving Strategies

Some types of problems—long-division problems, for instance—have specific algorithms associated with them that always yield a correct solution. Such algorithms are typically domain specific: They are useful with particular problems in a particular content area but are, for the most part, inapplicable to problems in other areas.

As an example, let's consider some of the algorithms that children use when they are given a problem such as this one:

If I have 2 apples and you give me 4 more apples, how many apples do I have altogether?

Young children can often solve such problems even if they have not yet had specific instruction in addition at school. A strategy that emerges early in development is simply to put up two fingers and then four additional fingers and count all the fingers to reach the solution of "6 apples." Somewhat later, children may begin to use a *min* strategy, whereby they start with the larger number (for the apple problem, they would start with 4) and then add on, one by one, the smaller number (e.g., counting "four apples . . . then five, six . . . six apples altogether") (Siegler & Jenkins, 1989). Still later, of course, children learn the basic addition facts (e.g., "2 + 4 = 6") that enable them to answer easier addition problems without having to count at all. As new strategies emerge, children may initially have trouble using them effectively, and so they may often resort to the earlier, less efficient, but more dependable ones. Eventually, they acquire sufficient proficiency with their new strategies that they can comfortably leave the less efficient ones behind (Siegler, 1998).

But what do people do when they haven't learned an algorithm for solving a problem, or perhaps when no algorithm for a problem exists? In such cases, they typically rely on more general heuristic strategies (Gick, 1986; Perkins & Salomon, 1989; Prawat, 1989). Among such strategies are combining algorithms, hill climbing, means–ends analysis, working backward, using visual imagery, drawing analogies, and "shortcut" heuristics.

Combining Algorithms

Sometimes, when a single algorithm is insufficient to solve a problem, several algorithms in combination may lead to a correct solution (R. M. Gagné, 1985). Mathematics problems (e.g., algebraic equations, geometric proofs) are frequently solved through a combination of algorithms.

Combining algorithms is not necessarily as easy as it sounds (e.g., Mayer & Wittrock, 1996). In some cases, individuals may have to learn, through either formal classroom instruction or informal experiences, the process of combining algorithms. A study by Scandura (1974) illustrates this point. Elementary school children were taught trading rules such as these:

$$n \text{ caramels} = n + 1 \text{ toy soldiers}$$
$$n \text{ toy soldiers} = n + 2 \text{ pencils}$$

They were then asked to make trades that involved combining two of these rules (e.g., trading caramels for pencils). Children who were unable to combine rules successfully were identified, and half of them were given specific instruction on how to combine the rules. Subsequently, all of these instructed children effectively combined the trading rules (one of them first required additional instruction), whereas none of the children in an untrained control group were able to do so.

Hill Climbing

Hill climbing (Andre, 1986; Chi & Glaser, 1985; Mayer, 1983; Wickelgren, 1974) is a problem-solving strategy in which individuals make any move that brings them closer to the problem goal. For example, consider this problem:

> You have a pile of 24 coins. Twenty-three of these coins have the same weight, and one is heavier. Your task is to determine which coin is heavier and to do so in the minimum number of weighings. You are given a beam balance (scale), which will compare the weight of any two sets of coins out of the total set of 24 coins. (Wickelgren, 1974, p. 34)

Stop to figure out a solution before you continue.

You probably used hill climbing to solve the problem, weighing different groups of coins against one another and gradually eliminating some of them, until eventually only the single heavier coin remained. How many weighings did you use? In fact, as Wickelgren (1974) has pointed out, the heavy coin can be identified with only *three* weighings, like so:

1. Divide the 24 coins into three groups of 8 coins each. Whichever of the three groups is heavier than the other two must contain the heavy coin. Weigh one group against a second; if one group tips the scale, it must contain the heavy coin. If the two groups balance each other, the third group must contain the heavy coin.
2. Divide the 8-coin group containing the heavy coin into three smaller groups, with two groups of 3 coins and one group of 2 coins. Weigh the two 3-coin groups against each other. As before, the scale will tell you if one group is heavier (in which case it contains the heavy coin). If the two groups balance each other, the group of 2 coins must contain the heavy coin.
3. Using the same reasoning as in the previous two steps, the heavy coin can be identified from the group of 2 or 3 coins with only one additional weighing.

Hill climbing often leads to a correct problem solution. It is ineffective, however, in situations in which the problem solution requires one or more temporary steps *backward*. To illustrate, consider this problem:

> A zookeeper must transport three lions and three giraffes across a river. She has a small barge that can hold only her and two of her animals, so she will have to make several trips

and leave some of the animals unattended some of the time. However, whenever she leaves a group of animals, the giraffes must outnumber the lions; a single giraffe is no match for a lion, and so a one-to-one ratio might give the lions a tasty meal. How can the zookeeper transport all six animals safely across the river?

Try to solve the zookeeper's problem before you read further.

The zookeeper can transport her animals across the river in this manner:

1. She takes two lions to the other side, leaving three giraffes and one lion behind. (The giraffes will be safe because they outnumber the lion.)
2. She comes back alone.
3. She takes one giraffe to the other side, leaving two giraffes and one lion behind.
4. She *brings back* the two lions, leaving one giraffe alone on the other side.
5. She takes the two giraffes to the other side, leaving the three lions behind.
6. She comes back alone, leaving the three giraffes behind.
7. She takes two lions to the other side, leaving one lion behind.
8. She comes back alone, leaving three giraffes and two lions behind.
9. She takes the last lion across the river.

The problem solution, then, requires a step backward: The zookeeper must bring two of the lions back to the first side of the river (step 4). A person using a hill-climbing strategy would not consider such a step and would be unable to solve the problem.

Means–Ends Analysis

Means–ends analysis (J. R. Anderson, 1993; Newell & Simon, 1972; Resnick & Glaser, 1976; Restle & Davis, 1962) is a process whereby an individual breaks a problem into two or more subgoals and then works successively on each of them. To illustrate, consider this situation:

I have just had a brick barbecue built in my backyard. I have had it built with metric dimensions: The grill is 1 meter wide and 1.5 meters long. Rich and Marcy Jones look over from their yard next door and say, "Oooo, nice barbecue . . . almost as big as ours."

"Mine is bigger," I reply.

"Can't be," they say. "Our grill is 3.5 feet by 5 feet."

The question: Have I kept up with the Jones family by buying a bigger barbecue grill? I can solve this problem by breaking it into four subgoals and solving each one in turn:

1. Convert the dimensions of the Joneses' grill into metric units. One foot equals approximately 0.30 meters; multiplying the "feet" dimensions by 0.30 yields dimensions of 1.05 by 1.5 meters.
2. Compute the area of the Joneses' grill. Multiplying 1.05 by 1.5 equals 1.575 square meters.
3. Compute the area of my grill. Multiplying 1 by 1.5 equals 1.5 square meters.
4. Compare the areas of the two grills. Rich and Marcy's grill is still larger than mine. I have not kept up with the Joneses.

Means–ends analysis appears to be a relatively common method of solving problems (Greeno, 1973; Newell & Simon, 1972) and is most likely to be used when the goal is clearly specified (Sweller & Levine, 1982). However, a potential disadvantage of this approach is that, by attending to only one subgoal at a time, a person may lose sight of the problem as a whole (Sweller & Levine, 1982).

Children show some ability to use means–ends analysis as early as their first birthday. For example, imagine that an infant sees an attractive toy beyond her reach. A string is attached to the toy; its other end is attached to a cloth closer at hand. Between the cloth and the infant is a foam rubber barrier. Many 12-month-old infants can put two and two together and realize that to accomplish the goal (getting the toy), they first have to do several other things. Accordingly, they remove the barrier, pull the cloth toward them, grab the string, and reel in the toy (Willatts, 1990).

Working Backward

Consider this game, similar to one described by Wickelgren (1974):

> There are 21 pennies on a table. Two players, Mary and Susan, take turns removing pennies from the table; in any given turn, a player must take one, two, or three pennies. The player who removes the last penny from the table wins the game and keeps all 21 pennies. Mary begins by taking two pennies. What strategy can Susan use to be sure that she wins the game?

See if you can solve the problem before you read further.

The problem is solved by beginning at the *end* of the game, at the point where Susan removes the last penny, and then going backward to the first move. In what situation will Mary be in the position of enabling Susan to win? Remember, each player can remove one, two, or three pennies on a turn. Let's look at the solution as a series of steps:

1. Mary must be forced into a situation in which she has to leave one, two, or three pennies on the table. Susan can then take them all, and victory is hers.
2. If, on the preceding turn, Susan leaves four pennies, then Mary's options are such that she must leave one to three pennies on her turn.
3. For Susan to leave four pennies, Mary must, on the previous turn, leave five, six, or seven pennies.
4. For Mary to leave five to seven pennies, Susan must leave eight pennies for Mary to choose from.

Continuing the steps in this manner, we see a pattern: Susan must always leave a number divisible by four. Therefore, when Mary removes 2 pennies, leaving 19 on the table, Susan should take 3 pennies.

The method I used to help Susan figure out how to win the game every time illustrates the process of **working backward** (Chi & Glaser, 1985; Newell, Shaw, & Simon, 1958; Wickelgren, 1974). This strategy is to begin at the problem goal and then work backward, one step at a time, toward the initial problem state. In each step backward, the individual identifies one or more conditions that would produce the present condition. In a sense, working backward is the opposite approach to that of means–ends analysis.

Working backward is frequently used in solving algebra and geometry proofs. Students are given an initial situation—a formula or a geometric configuration with certain characteristics—and then are asked to prove, through a series of mathematically logical steps, how another formula or another characteristic (the goal) must also be true. Sometimes it is easier to move logically from the goal backward to the initial state; mathematically speaking, this approach is just as valid.

Using Visual Imagery

In Chapter 9, I introduced you to the *visuospatial sketchpad*, a component of working memory that allows short-term storage and manipulation of visual material. In Chapters 10 and 11, we discovered that visual imagery provides a potentially powerful means of storing information in long-term memory. So when problems are easily visualizable or have an obviously spatial structure, people sometimes use visual imagery to solve them (English, 1997a; Hegarty & Kozhevnikov, 1999; Kosslyn, 1985; Wheatley, 1997).

As an example, let's go back in time a few years and look at my doctoral dissertation research (J. O. Ellis, 1975; Ormrod, 1979). I was investigating the nature of people's problem-solving processes when they solved *three-term series problems*, in which three items (terms) are compared, two at a time, with regard to a particular characteristic. The task is to determine the relative ordering of the three terms. For instance, we might compare the elevation of three dining implements:

> The plate is higher than the napkin.
> The cup is lower than the napkin.
> Which is lowest?

or the temperature of three different days:

> Wednesday is hotter than Tuesday.
> Thursday is colder than Tuesday.
> Which is coldest?

At the time I conducted the study, two theorists had offered competing explanations of how people solved such problems, one (H. H. Clark, 1969) suggesting that people encode and solve them verbally and the other (J. Huttenlocher, 1968) suggesting that people encode and solve them spatially (e.g., mentally "putting" a plate higher than a napkin and then "putting" a cup below the napkin). I reasoned that whether people use verbal or visual strategies depends partly on the nature of the problem: Problems that can be easily visualized (e.g., those involving items on a dinner table) should lend themselves more readily to visual imagery than problems that are hard to picture (e.g., those involving temperature and days of the week). I also reasoned that people would be more likely to use visual imagery when they didn't have all of the information in front of them as they solved the problem—in other words, when they had to store it all in working memory at once. My results suggested that I was right on both counts: People's use of visual imagery depended on both the visualizability of the problem and on the demands on working memory during the problem-solving process.

Drawing Analogies

See if you can solve the following problem originally used by Duncker (1945) and adapted by Gick and Holyoak (1980):

> Suppose you are a doctor faced with a patient who has a malignant tumor in his stomach. It is impossible to operate on the patient, but unless the tumor is destroyed the patient will die. There is a kind of ray that can be used to destroy the tumor. If the rays reach the tumor all at once at a

sufficiently high intensity, the tumor will be destroyed. Unfortunately, at this intensity the healthy tissue that the rays pass through on the way to the tumor will also be destroyed. At lower intensities the rays are harmless to healthy tissue, but they will not affect the tumor either. What type of procedure might be used to destroy the tumor with the rays, and at the same time avoid destroying the healthy tissue? (Gick & Holyoak, 1980, pp. 307–308)

If you are having difficulty with the problem, then consider this situation:

A general wishes to capture a fortress located in the center of a country. There are many roads radiating outward from the fortress. All have been mined so that, while small groups of men can pass over the roads safely, any large force will detonate the mines. A full-scale direct attack is therefore impossible. The general's solution is to divide his army into small groups, send each group to the head of a different road, and have the groups converge simultaneously on the fortress. (Gick & Holyoak, 1980, p. 309)

Now go back to the tumor problem. Perhaps the general's strategy in capturing the fortress has given you an idea about how to destroy the tumor. It can be destroyed by shooting a number of low-intensity rays from different directions, such that they all converge on the tumor simultaneously. Gick and Holyoak found that people are more likely to solve the tumor problem when they have first read the solution to the fortress problem because the two problems can be solved in analogous ways.

Drawing an analogy between a problem situation and another situation often provides insights into how a problem can be solved (A.L. Brown, Kane & Echols, 1986; Clement, 1987; English, 1997b; Holyoak, 1985; Mayer & Wittrock, 1996; Schultz & Lochhead, 1991). For example, a student might solve a math problem by finding a similar, "worked out" problem— one that has already been solved correctly using a particular procedure (Atkinson et al., 2000; Mwangi & Sweller, 1998; Reimann & Schult, 1996; Zhu & Simon, 1987). As another example, consider a problem that the Greek scientist Archimedes confronted sometime around 250 B.C.:

King Hiero asked a local goldsmith to make him a gold crown and gave the craftsman the gold he should use. When he received the finished crown, the king suspected that the goldsmith had cheated him by replacing some of the gold with silver, a cheaper metal. The only way to determine the goldsmith's honesty was to compare the crown's weight against its volume. Any metal has a particular volume for any given weight, and that ratio is different for each metal. The crown could be weighed easily enough. But how could its volume be measured?

Archimedes was pondering the problem one day as he stepped into a bathtub. He watched the bath water rise and, through analogy (and perhaps visual imagery as well), immediately identified a solution to the king's problem: The crown's volume could be determined by placing it in a container of water and measuring the amount of water that was displaced.

Using analogies to solve problems has its disadvantages, however. For one thing, people may make an incorrect analogy and solve a problem incorrectly as a result (Novick, 1988). Even when they identify a truly analogous situation, they may draw inappropriate parallels (Mayer & Wittrock, 1996). But the major drawback to using analogies as a problem-solving strategy is that individuals seldom retrieve analogous situations when they face a particular problem situation.

Analogies are
sometimes helpful
in solving problems.

The fact is, people rarely use analogies in solving problems unless a problem and its analogue are quite similar in terms of superficial features (Bassok, 1997; Hayes & Simon, 1974; Holyoak & Koh, 1987; Mayer & Wittrock, 1996; Reed, Ernst, & Banerji, 1974). For instance, in the Gick and Holyoak (1980) study described earlier, although reading about the fortress problem certainly facilitated problem solving, nevertheless only 30% of the students who learned the fortress solution (splitting the troops into small groups) successfully applied it in addressing the tumor problem. In a follow-up study (Holyoak & Koh, 1987), students read an analogy that more closely resembled the tumor situation: A lab assistant repaired the filament of a very expensive lightbulb by shooting low-intensity laser beams simultaneously from different directions. This time, a majority (69%) of the students solved the tumor problem correctly, but even so, a fair number of them did not.

When people *do* use analogies, it may be because someone else (e.g., a teacher or researcher) points out parallels between the two situations or because they serendipitously encounter both the problem and the analogous situation at the same time (A. L. Brown et al., 1986; Crisafi & Brown, 1986; Holyoak & Thagard, 1995). To some extent, using analogies to solve a problem may be a matter of luck—of simply happening to think of (i.e., retrieve) the right idea at the right time.

Shortcut Heuristics: Representativeness and Availability
Some problem-solving strategies can be executed quickly and simply. Two commonly described examples are representativeness and availability (Kahneman & Tversky, 1972, 1973; Klein, 1987; Mayer, 1992; Tversky & Kahneman, 1973, 1974). Unfortunately, such shortcuts sometimes lead to inaccurate problem solutions.

Representativeness involves jumping to conclusions about a solution based on obvious characteristics of the problem. Let me illustrate by adapting a problem used by Kahneman and Tversky (1973). Imagine that I have a stack of 100 personality profiles of 30 engineers and 70 lawyers, all of whom are successful in their careers. I pull this description randomly from the pile:

> Jack is a 45-year-old man. He is married and has four children. He is generally conservative, careful, and ambitious. He shows no interest in political and social issues and spends most of his free time on his many hobbies, which include home carpentry, sailing, and mathematical puzzles. (Kahneman & Tversky, 1973, p. 241)

Now for the problem: What is the probability that this man is one of the 30 engineers?

The probability that the man is an engineer is 30%, because the stack of 100 personality profiles contained profiles of 30 engineers. Yet many people in Kahneman and Tversky's study gave a higher figure; they jumped to a conclusion based on obvious characteristics about Jack that many people associate stereotypically with engineers (e.g., conservative views and enjoyment of mathematical puzzles).

A second shortcut heuristic, **availability,** is a strategy wherein a problem is solved based only on information that comes immediately to mind (i.e., is retrieved) when the problem is encountered. Typically, the problem will be solved using recently acquired information rather than information acquired in the distant past because recent experiences are more likely to be retrieved than those from long ago. For example, imagine that you are trying to decide whether to go to California or Florida for a sunny March vacation at the beach. You learned many years ago that Florida has more rainfall than California. In February, just as you are about to make your choice, you hear on the news that California has just been drenched in a heavy rainstorm. You may easily book a flight to Florida, retrieving the available information about the California rainstorm rather than the overall frequency of rainfall in the two states.

At this point, we have examined a variety of different problem-solving strategies. Because many problems have no right or wrong solutions, no single "best" strategy may exist for solving them. Obviously, different strategies are appropriate in different situations. But sometimes people use strategies at the wrong times, often because they have learned such strategies at a rote, meaningless level. Let's look at what happens when individuals use problem-solving strategies meaninglessly.

Meaningless Versus Meaningful Problem Solving

See if you can solve this problem before you read further:

> The number of quarters a man has is seven times the number of dimes he has. The value of the dimes exceeds the value of the quarters by two dollars and fifty cents. How many has he of each coin? (Paige & Simon, 1966, p. 79)

If you found an answer to the problem—any answer at all—then you overlooked an important point: Quarters are worth more than dimes. If there are more quarters than dimes, the value of the dimes cannot possibly be greater than the value of the quarters. The fact is, the problem makes no sense, and so it cannot be solved.

When people learn algorithms at a rote level, without understanding their underlying logic, they may sometimes apply those algorithms "unthinkingly" and inappropriately (De Corte et al., 1996; Perkins & Simmons, 1988; Prawat, 1989; Resnick, 1989). As a result, they may obtain illogical or physically impossible results. Consider the following instances of meaningless mathematical problem solving as examples:

- A student is asked to figure out how many chickens and how many pigs a farmer has if the farmer has 21 animals with 60 legs in all. The student adds 21 and 60, reasoning that, because the problem says "how many in all," addition is the logical operation (Lester, 1985).
- A student uses subtraction whenever a word problem contains the word *left*—even when a problem actually requiring addition includes the phrase "John left the room to get more apples" (Schoenfeld, 1982).
- Middle school students are asked to calculate how many 40-person buses are needed to transport 540 people to a baseball game. The majority give an answer that includes a fraction, without acknowledging that in the case of buses, only whole numbers are possible (Silver, Shapiro, & Deutsch, 1993).

All too often, when schools teach problem solving, they focus on teaching algorithms for well-defined problems but neglect to help students understand why the algorithms work and how they can be used with real-world problems (Carr & Biddlecomb, 1998; Cooney, 1991; Perkins & Salomon, 1989; Porter, 1989; Silver et al., 1993). For example, perhaps you can remember learning how to solve a long-division problem, but you probably don't remember learning *why* you multiply the divisor by each digit in your answer and write the product in a particular location below the dividend. Or perhaps you were taught a "key word" method for solving word problems: Words such as *altogether* indicate addition, and words such as *left* mean subtraction. This approach is a meaningless one indeed and, as we noted in both the "Ana" and "John" examples presented earlier, often leads to an erroneous solution.

How can teachers help students engage in more meaningful problem solving? And, in general, how can they help students become more expert at problem solving and other forms of transfer? We turn now to the topic of facilitating transfer and problem solving in instructional settings.

FACILITATING TRANSFER AND PROBLEM SOLVING IN THE CLASSROOM

As we noted earlier in the chapter, students often fail to see the relevance of what they have learned in school to new school tasks or to out-of-school problems. Thus, a major objective of our educational system—positive transfer—is not being achieved as well as we would like. At the same time, students sometimes erroneously apply what they have learned to situations in which it is not appropriate—a case of negative transfer.

Learning theorists still have much to learn about the complex processes of transfer and problem solving. Nevertheless, theories and research in both areas provide numerous suggestions for educational practice:

- *Students need to learn information meaningfully and thoroughly.* Theorists agree that a solid knowledge base is a prerequisite for successful transfer and problem solving (Frederiksen, 1984a; Greeno, 1973; Hiebert & Lefevre, 1986; Mayer, 1975; Reif & Heller, 1982; Simon, 1980). In the process of acquiring this knowledge base, students should develop a multitude of interconnections and relationships among the concepts and ideas they learn; they should also discover the potential relevance of such concepts and ideas for the various situations they may encounter later on (Bereiter, 1995; Brophy & Alleman, 1991; Perkins, 1995; Perkins & Salomon, 1987; Prawat, 1989; Sternberg & Frensch, 1993).

Unfortunately, many school curricula include long lists of topics that must be taught, the result being that no single topic is taught very thoroughly (e.g., see Porter, 1989). Breadth of coverage occurs at the expense of depth of coverage—and at the expense of successful transfer and problem solving as well.

• *Students should also learn problem-solving strategies in a meaningful manner.* All too often, students learn problem-solving algorithms as procedures separate from anything they have previously learned about the world. For example, they may learn mathematics—its symbols, principles, and algorithms—in total isolation from the concrete physical world they deal with on a daily basis (Carpenter, 1985; Davis, 1987; Hiebert & Wearne, 1993; Resnick, 1989). When students learn an algorithm in a rote, meaningless fashion, they are likely to use it mechanically, thoughtlessly, and often incorrectly, and they are *unlikely* to recognize many of the situations in which it might legitimately be applied (Greeno, 1991; Hiebert & Wearne, 1993; Kilpatrick, 1985; Perkins & Simmons, 1988).

Rather than simply learning algorithms at a rote level, students should understand *why* they do the things they do in order to solve problems; in other words, they should connect abstract, symbol-based procedures to things they already know about the subject matter and to concrete reality (Carpenter, 1985; Geary, 1994; Prawat, 1989; Resnick, 1989; Rittle-Johnson & Alibali, 1999; Rittle-Johnson, Siegler, & Alibali, 2001).

• *Students must have a mental set for transfer.* We noted earlier that mental sets in problem solving—predispositions to solve problems in particular ways—sometimes interfere with successful problem solving. Yet a *general* mental set to transfer school learning—a predisposition to use and apply the things learned in the classroom—is clearly beneficial (Stein, 1989; Sternberg & Frensch, 1993). To promote such a mental set, teachers can point out how academic content can be applied to a variety of situations both in and out of school (Cox, 1997; Fennema et al., 1989; Perkins & Salomon, 1989; Sternberg & Frensch, 1993; Voss, 1987). And they can encourage their students to be constantly thinking "How might I use this information?" as they listen, read, and study (Perkins, 1992; Stein, 1989; Sternberg & Frensch, 1993).

• *Some prerequisite skills should be practiced until they are learned to the point of automaticity.* Remember that problem solving occurs in working memory—a component of the memory system that has a limited capacity for holding and processing information at any single time. To the extent that students can process the simple and familiar aspects of a problem automatically, thereby using only a minimal amount of working memory capacity, they can devote more "space" to the problem's difficult and novel aspects (Frederiksen, 1984a; Geary, 1994; Mayer, 1985; Perkins & Salomon, 1987; Resnick, 1989).

• *Students more effectively transfer concepts and procedures to new situations and problems when they have many and varied examples and opportunities for practice.* Numerous and diverse examples and practice opportunities promote associations in long-term memory between newly learned information and a variety of relevant situations; hence, the new information is more likely to be retrieved when it is needed later on (Chase & Chi, 1980; Cormier, 1987; Gagné & Driscoll, 1988; Geary, 1994; Perkins & Salomon, 1987). Furthermore, to the extent that students must use a concept or procedure in a slightly different way each time they apply it, they are more likely to develop a general (perhaps abstract) understanding of it—one that doesn't depend on obvious surface features of the situation—and they are less likely to develop mental sets that limit their flexibility in applying it (Carr & Biddlecomb, 1998; Chen, 1999). As an example, try to solve each of the following problems:

- Mary needs to locate her wood stove 6 inches from the wall. She does not have a ruler with her. However, she has three sticks that measure 15, 7, and 2 inches, respectively. Using these, how can she get the right distance (6 inches)?
- John needs exactly 20 cups of fertilizer to spray his backyard. He has a bucket of fertilizer but only three jars that hold 9, 8, and 3 cups, respectively. How can he get 20 cups of fertilizer?
- One day Chef Smith needed to get 7 ounces of flour for his cooking but had only a balance scale and three weights of 9, 5, and 3 ounces available to him. How did he get exactly 7 ounces of flour? (all three problems from Chen, 1999, p. 715)

As you may have realized, all three problems can be solved using the same general strategy that Luchins' water jar problems require, in particular using three known amounts that, when added and subtracted, can yield a needed fourth amount. But notice how each problem has very different surface features, including different forms of measurement (length, volume, weight) and different contexts and goals (positioning a stove, measuring fertilizer for gardening, weighing flour for cooking). Furthermore, each problem requires a different solution ($A - B - C$, $A + B + C$, $A - B + C$). Learning a problem-solving strategy with such varied problems is apt to take longer than learning it with very similar problems (e.g., with a series of water jar problems), but learners will then apply the strategy more broadly and flexibly (Chen, 1999).

Occasionally, teachers should present problems in a somewhat mixed-up order (rather than having students solve a set of problems that all require the same procedure), so students have practice classifying problems before solving them (Geary, 1994; Mayer, 1985; Mayfield & Chase, 2002). Ideally, too, students should have opportunities to apply newly learned strategies to real-life problems as well as more traditional word problems (De Corte et al., 1996; Lave, 1988, 1993). For instance, a teacher might have students predict how much helium they would need to put in a balloon to make it float or calculate the volume of a cylindrical punch bowl to determine whether it's large enough to hold a certain amount of punch for a class party.

- *Students should have experience identifying problems for themselves.* Teachers usually provide the problems they want their students to solve. But beyond the classroom—for example, at home and in the world of employment—people must often identify and define for themselves the problems that stand in their way. Some theorists suggest that students may benefit from getting a head start on such problem finding in the classroom (Brown & Walter, 1990; Eisner, 1994; Hiebert et al., 1996; Porter, 1989; Resnick, Bill, Lesgold, & Leer, 1991). For example, in a math lesson, students might be given data describing the quantities and prices of items in a grocery store and asked to generate a number of questions that could be answered by those data. Or, in a history lesson, students might be given a scenario of an American Civil War battle in progress, instructed to identify the problems facing either the North or the South, and asked to propose possible solutions to those problems.

- *To minimize negative transfer, differences between two ideas should be emphasized.* Insects and spiders are similar stimuli—they are both small arthropods with exoskeletons and a generally creepy-crawly nature—and so students may inappropriately transfer what they know about one group of creepy-crawlies to the other. For similar stimuli, negative transfer can be reduced if differences rather than similarities are emphasized (Sternberg & Frensch, 1993). For instance, insects and spiders are different in a number of ways (e.g., six legs vs. eight legs, three body parts vs. two, antennae vs. no antennae); if emphasized, those differences could reduce negative transfer from one group to the other. Additionally, if negative transfer between two ideas is anticipated, it can be reduced by teaching each in a different environment (Bilodeau & Schlosberg, 1951; Greenspoon & Ranyard, 1957)—for example, by teaching students about insects while sitting in the classroom and teaching them about spiders while on a field trip to the natural history museum.

   • *Problem-solving skills are sometimes better learned through a discovery approach.* Although expository instruction is often the most efficient means of transmitting information to students in an organized fashion, instructional approaches that emphasize guided discovery learning may facilitate better transfer of problem-solving skills to new situations (Hiebert et al., 1997; Kline & Flowers, 1998; Mayer, 1974; McDaniel & Schlager, 1990; Shymansky, Hedges, & Woodworth, 1990). Discovery is probably most appropriate when problems are ill structured and students have a solid knowledge base (Doyle, 1983; Frederiksen, 1984a). However, for well-structured problems that can be solved by a specific algorithm (e.g., long-division problems), and for students relatively unsophisticated about a particular topic, direct instruction of the algorithm may sometimes be preferable (Frederiksen, 1984a; R. M. Gagné, 1985).

   • *Teaching general learning and problem-solving skills (both cognitive and metacognitive) may be helpful.* As I indicated in Chapter 13, training in study skills can be effective and appears to improve classroom learning and achievement. Similarly, many theorists believe that teaching general problem-solving strategies can enhance students' ability to solve problems successfully (Cardelle-Elawar, 1992; E. D. Gagné, 1985; Glaser, 1979; Mayer, 1987; Resnick, 1976; Schoenfeld, 1979, 1992; Simon, 1980). A study by Herrnstein, Nickerson, de Sánchez, and Swets (1986) provides some optimism about the effectiveness of training problem-solving skills: Seventh-grade Venezuelan students who took a year-long course in reasoning, problem-solving, and decision-making skills showed greater improvement in both the specific skills taught and general intellectual ability than did students in an untrained control group. Yet we should note here that, just as study strategies may be better learned when taught within the context of specific academic content areas (see Chapter 13), so, too, may general problem-solving strategies be more effectively learned when connected with content domains to which they are applicable (Mayer, 1992; Resnick, 1987; Schoenfeld & Herrmann, 1982).

   Several problem-solving strategies may be transferable to a wide variety of problem situations. One helpful strategy is talking aloud about the problem and about the problem-solving strategies being applied; doing so can enhance students' ability to identify appropriate approaches and to guide and monitor their own progress (in a metacognitive sense) toward solutions (Berardi-Coletta, Buyer, Dominowski, & Rellinger, 1995; Crowley & Siegler, 1999; deLeeuw & Chi, 2003; Vygotsky, 1962). A second strategy is using paper and pencil to diagram a problem or list its components; this tactic may help students encode a problem more concretely and see the interrelationships among various elements more clearly (Anzai, 1991; Fuson & Willis, 1989; Lindvall, Tamburino, & Robinson, 1982; Mayer, 1992; Prawat, 1989; Schultz & Lochhead, 1991; Wickelgren, 1974). Still a third strategy is brainstorming—thinking of as many hypothetical problem solutions as possible without initially evaluating any of them (Halpern, 1997; Osborn, 1963). The absence of evaluation when brainstorming ideas can potentially facilitate a broader search of long-term memory for unusual and creative possibilities. After generating a long and seemingly exhaustive list of problem solutions, an individual can critically examine the various solutions to identify workable and unworkable ones.

Some theorists (e.g., Davidson & Sternberg, 1998; Ellis & Hunt, 1983; Wallas, 1926) have suggested that *incubating* a problem—letting it remain unsolved in memory for a period of time—can be a helpful strategy, although there are mixed reviews on its effectiveness (J. R. Anderson, 1990; Bourne et al., 1986; Dominowski & Jenrick, 1972). The benefits of an incubation period are more likely to be evident for difficult problems than for easy ones. For one thing, some of the factors that interfere with problem solving, such as fatigue and anxiety, may diminish during the incubation period (Ellis & Hunt, 1983). In addition, the individual may find more appropriate mental sets or more relevant information in long-term memory after leaving the problem alone for a while (J. R. Anderson, 1990; Davidson & Sternberg, 1998; Ellis & Hunt, 1983).

In my own experience as a textbook writer, I have found incubation to be a highly effective strategy. Probably the biggest problem I face when I write is figuring out how best to organize the ever-expanding body of research findings related to learning and motivation. As my field continues to grow and evolve, I find that organizational structures I've used in previous editions of this book are no longer useful in a later edition, and so I begin to experiment with alternative arrangements. Yet my mind seems to be able to handle only so much mini-paradigm-shifting in any single day. Oftentimes, the best thing I can do is to turn my computer off midafternoon, walk the dog, perhaps watch a television game show or two, and essentially let the mental "dust" settle. When I return to my computer the following morning, I often have fresh ideas that did not occur to me the day before.

• *Students should learn strategies for defining ill-defined problems.* Most problems presented in classroom situations are well defined (Frederiksen, 1984a; Sternberg et al., 2000). Students are asked to identify the protagonist and antagonist in a story, use a dictionary to find two different pronunciations of the word *wind*, or calculate how many candy bars six boys can each have if there are 18 bars altogether. In contrast, most real-world problems are ill defined. People need to find viable means of home financing, decide what life insurance policy to purchase (if any), and maintain friendly and productive relationships with obnoxious coworkers.

Ill-defined problems often require an individual to search outside sources to find relevant and potentially helpful information (Simon, 1978). Students should therefore be well versed in techniques for finding information through such resources as libraries, computer databases, and government agencies. Students should also learn techniques for more precisely defining ill-defined problems; for example, one helpful technique is to break a larger problem into a number of subproblems and to define and impose constraints on each of those subproblems (Chi & Glaser, 1985; Reitman, 1965; Simon, 1973). Finally, to the extent that students possess a solid knowledge base, they will be better able to define the problems they encounter (Bédard & Chi, 1992; Frederiksen, 1984a).

• *Students' early attempts to solve difficult problems should be scaffolded.* In Chapter 8, we encountered the concept of scaffolding—providing a structure that supports students in their efforts on difficult tasks. Then, in Chapter 13, we noted the importance of scaffolding students' early attempts to use sophisticated metacognitive strategies. Some theorists suggest that scaffolding may facilitate problem-solving performance as well (Heller & Hungate, 1985;

Wood et al., 1976). Teachers can do several things to help students in their initial attempts at challenging problems: They can simplify early problems, model problem solutions, ask probing questions that encourage students to consider certain features, point out errors along the way, and in general keep students' frustration at a reasonable level. They can also give students questions to ask themselves as they proceed through a problem (King, 1991; Schoenfeld, 1992); here are some examples:

> What (exactly) are you doing? Can you describe it precisely? Why are you doing it? How does it fit into your solution? (Schoenfeld, 1992, p. 356)

As students become more adept at solving problems on their own, such scaffolding can be gradually phased out.

• *The development of effective problem-solving strategies can often be facilitated through cooperative group problem solving.* Numerous theorists have suggested that a cooperative learning environment may be ideal for promoting successful problem solving (e.g., Carr & Biddlecomb, 1998; Hiebert et al., 1997; Palincsar & Herrenkohl, 1999; Qin, Johnson, & Johnson, 1995). By discussing concepts and principles relevant to the problem solution, students may identify more interrelationships among things they know and clarify things about which they are confused (Kilpatrick, 1985; Noddings, 1985). By thinking aloud about how to solve a problem, they may gain a better understanding of what they are mentally doing (Schoenfeld, 1985b; Whimbey & Lochhead, 1986). And, by observing the more effective strategies that their classmates sometimes use, they may begin to adopt those strategies themselves, leaving their own, less efficient strategies behind (Mayer, 1985; Noddings, 1985; Schoenfeld, 1985b). As an illustration of the last point, consider this incident in a cooperative problem-solving setting:

> A youngster suggested that the group should "add, subtract, and multiply these two numbers" and then see which answer "looked" best. Other members of the group were shocked and said, "Donna! We can't do that. We have to figure it out." Donna tried that strategy only once more and then it disappeared from her public repertoire. (Noddings, 1985, pp 350–351)

In Chapter 15, we'll identify many specific strategies for facilitating effective group learning and problem solving.

• *Authentic activities may increase the probability that students will transfer knowledge, skills, and problem-solving strategies to real-world contexts.* **Authentic activities** are tasks that are identical or similar to those that students will eventually encounter in the outside world (De Corte et al., 1996; Greeno et al., 1996; Hiebert & Fisher, 1992; Lave, 1993). Given what we have learned about learning, we can speculate that such activities are likely to have several benefits. For one thing, when students work in a naturalistic context, using the physical and social resources (e.g., tools, colleagues) that such a context offers, students should be able to accomplish more than they might accomplish in relatively artificial and unscaffolded classroom tasks (Greeno et al., 1996). Second, complex authentic tasks can help students make meaningful connections among the various ideas and skills they have learned in the classroom. Finally, because authentic activities resemble real-world tasks and problems, they should help students transfer the things they learn at school to out-of-school situations (Collins et al., 1989).

Authentic activities can be developed for virtually any area of the school curriculum. For example, teachers might have students:

- Give an oral presentation
- Write an editorial
- Write a letter to a business or government agency
- Participate in a debate
- Find information in the library
- Conduct an experiment
- Graph data
- Construct a chart, model, or map
- Design an electrical circuit
- Create a museum display
- Create and distribute a class newsletter

- Converse in a foreign language
- Play in an athletic event
- Conduct fieldwork to study and document local flora and fauna
- Complete an art project
- Perform in a concert
- Design a model city
- Make a video tape
- Perform a workplace routine
- Plan a family budget
- Write a computer program
- Develop a home page for the Internet

It may occasionally be possible to assign authentic activities as homework; for example, teachers might ask students to write an editorial, design an electrical circuit, or plan a family budget while working at home in the evening. But many authentic activities may require considerable classroom dialogue, with students asking questions of one another, sharing their ideas, offering explanations of their thinking, and synthesizing their efforts into an integrated whole (Newmann & Wehlage, 1993; Paris & Turner, 1994). For example, creating a school newspaper, designing a model city, debating controversial social or political issues, and conversing in a foreign language may be activities that students can perform only as a group. Furthermore, because authentic activities are typically more complex and less defined than traditional classroom tasks, they may require considerable teacher scaffolding (Brophy, 1992a; Hickey, 1997). For such reasons, many authentic activities can be accomplished more effectively in class than at home, or perhaps through a combination of group work during class and independent work after school hours.

Researchers consistently find that authentic activities have positive effects. For example, preschoolers acquire and use new problem-solving strategies when they actively participate in realistic problem situations while watching the children's television program *Blue's Clues* (Crawley, Anderson, Wilder, Williams, & Santomero, 1999). Older children gain a more complete understanding of how to use and interpret maps when they construct their own maps than when they engage in workbook exercises involving map interpretation (Gregg & Leinhardt, 1994a). Students are more likely to transfer scientific principles (e.g., nutritional values of different food groups, design of solar-powered airplanes) to real-life situations if, while they are studying, they are asked to plan a trip to the desert rather than if they are simply told they will be tested on the material (Bransford, Franks, Vye, & Sherwood, 1989). Students' writing skills may show greater improvement in both quality and quantity when they practice writing stories, essays, and letters to real people rather than completing short, artificial writing exercises (Hiebert & Fisher, 1992).

We find a technology-based version of authentic problem-solving activities in the *Adventures of Jasper Woodbury* series,[6] in which middle school students encounter a number of

---

[6]For on-line information about the series, visit http://peabody.vanderbilt.edu/ctrs/lsi and then click on Products.

real-life problem situations presented through videodisk technology. In one episode, *Journey to Cedar Creek*, Jasper has just purchased an old boat and is hoping to pilot the boat home the same day. Because the boat has no running lights, he must figure out whether he can get home by sunset, and because he has spent all his cash and used his last check, he must figure out whether he has enough gas to make the trip. Throughout the video, all the information students need to answer these questions is embedded in authentic contexts (e.g., a marine radio announces time of sunset, and mileage markers are posted at various landmarks along the river), but students must sift through a lot of irrelevant information to find it. In another episode, *The Right Angle*, teenager Paige Littlefield is searching for a cave in which her Native American grandfather left her a special gift before he died. The grandfather gave her directions to the cave that require knowledge and use of geometric principles (e.g., "From the easternmost point of Black Hawk Bluff, travel at a bearing of 25° until you are almost surrounded by rock towers. Go to Flat Top Tower. . . . You will know Flat Top Tower because at a distance of 250 feet from the northern side of its base, the angle of elevation of its top is 45°"). Using the grandfather's directions and a topographical map of Paige's ancestral home region, students must locate the cave. There are numerous ways to approach each Jasper problem, and students work in small groups to brainstorm and carry out possible problem solutions. Students of all ability levels find the *Jasper* series highly motivating, and they transfer what they learn from one problem when solving similar problems (Cognition and Technology Group at Vanderbilt, 1990; Learning Technology Center at Vanderbilt, 1996).

Theorists have suggested that an authentic activity is most likely to be effective when it has characteristics such as the following:

- It requires a fair amount of background knowledge about a particular topic; in other words, students must know the subject matter thoroughly and have learned it in a meaningful fashion.
- It promotes higher-level thinking skills; for example, it may involve synthesizing information, forming and testing hypotheses, solving problems, and drawing conclusions.
- It requires students to seek out information in a variety of contexts and perhaps from a variety of academic disciplines.
- It conveys high expectations for students' performance yet also encourages students to take risks and experiment with new strategies.
- Its final outcome is complex and somewhat unpredictable; there is not necessarily a single "right" response or answer.
  (Newmann & Wehlage, 1993; Paris & Turner, 1994)

We should note, however, that it is not necessarily desirable to fill the entire school day with complex, authentic tasks. For one thing, students can often master basic skills more effectively when they practice them in relative isolation from other activities; for example, when learning to play the violin, they need to master their fingering before they join an orchestra, and when learning to play soccer, they need to practice dribbling and passing before they play in a game (J. R. Anderson et al., 1996). Second, some authentic tasks may be too expensive and time consuming to warrant their use on a regular basis in the classroom (Griffin & Griffin, 1994). It is probably most important that classroom tasks encourage students to engage in such cognitive processes as meaningful learning, organization, and elaboration—processes that promote long-term retention and transfer of classroom subject matter—than that tasks always be authentic in nature (J. R. Anderson et al., 1996).

• *Classroom evaluation practices should include measures of transfer and problem solving.* As noted in Chapter 12, traditional classroom tests too often emphasize the learning of specific facts. Certainly basic knowledge and skills are important; among other things, they form the foundation for more sophisticated academic behaviors. But when teachers' instructional objectives also include transfer and problem solving, classroom assessment tasks should ask students to demonstrate the ability to apply classroom subject matter to a variety of situations (Foos & Fisher, 1988; Massialas & Zevin, 1983; Sternberg & Frensch, 1993). This practice can help successful transfer and problem solving become common phenomena rather than rare occurrences.

Teaching for effective transfer and problem solving takes time. Too often, schools seem to rush through a curriculum at the expense of providing sufficient practice at any single point along the way. Educators should probably slow down and give learners time to use and apply the information and skills they learn. Under such conditions, students are likely to accomplish more over the long run.

SUMMARY

Transfer is the process of applying information and skills learned in one situation to learning or performance in another situation. Although most instances of transfer are beneficial, once in a while learning something at one time can negatively impact learning or performance at a later time. Early behaviorists proposed that similarity of stimuli or responses (or both) is essential for transfer to occur. More recently, cognitivists have suggested that transfer depends on retrieval: People are most apt to apply what they've learned if their present context reminds them of potentially useful prior knowledge. Regardless of which theoretical perspective we take, it appears that transfer from one situation to another is most likely to occur when the two situations are similar in some way. Among the factors that facilitate transfer are meaningful learning, thoroughness of learning, acquisition of general principles, and number and variety of examples and opportunities for practice.

Problem solving is a form of transfer, in that previously learned information is applied to resolve a problem situation. Behaviorists and cognitive theorists have offered several theories of problem solving. Cognitive theories—which focus on such factors as working memory, encoding, retrieval, prior knowledge base, and metacognition—predominate at the present time. Some problems can be solved through specific *algorithms*, procedures that guarantee correct solutions. But many others may be solved only through more general *heuristics*, shortcuts without guaranteed outcomes (e.g., conducting a means–ends analysis, using visual imagery, drawing analogies). People typically apply problem-solving procedures more effectively and appropriately when they understand the logic behind the procedures.

Theory and research yield numerous suggestions for promoting transfer and problem solving in classroom settings. For example, a school's prescribed curriculum should make it possible for teachers to teach a few things thoroughly and meaningfully rather than many things superficially and at a rote level (the "less is more" idea). Students should have a *mental set* for transfer; that is, they should approach school subject matter with the idea that they may be able to use it on future occasions. Such techniques as discovery learning, cooperative learning, and authentic activities often facilitate the development and transfer of effective problem-solving skills. Ideally, teachers should not only *teach* for transfer and problem solving but also emphasize it in their assessment practices.

CHAPTER 15

Social Processes in Knowledge Construction

On several occasions in earlier chapters, we have noted the value of involving other people in the learning process. In our exploration of social cognitive theory in Chapter 7, we discovered that observing and imitating what other people do—*modeling*—provides an efficient way for learners to acquire new behaviors. In our discussion of Piaget's theory of cognitive development in Chapter 8, we found that social interactions (whether they be amicable conversations or not-so-amicable conflicts) are essential for helping children understand that others do not necessarily share their perspectives of the world. In the same chapter, we encountered Vygotsky's proposal that complex mental processes begin as social activities—that children gradually internalize ways of thinking that they first experience in a social setting. All three perspectives have led many contemporary theorists to realize that learning can be, and perhaps often *should* be, a very social enterprise.

In this chapter we focus more closely on the social nature of learning, with particular dependence on Vygotskian, social constructivist, and contextual perspectives. We then look at one instructional strategy (apprenticeship) that involves close interaction with an experienced adult and at several additional strategies (class discussion, reciprocal teaching, cooperative learning, peer tutoring, community of learners, and technology-based discussion) that involve significant interaction with peers.

THE SOCIAL NATURE OF LEARNING

Human beings are, by nature, very social creatures, and they can acquire language and other aspects of their rich cultural heritage *only* by interacting with those around them. But interactions with adults and interactions with peers have somewhat different benefits.[1] Let's look at what theory and research suggest about each type of interaction.

Interactions With Adults

As we noted in Chapter 8, Vygotsky proposed that adults help children attach meaning to the objects and events around them, in part by sharing the particular words, concepts, and other cognitive tools that their culture uses to represent and think about the world. In recent years, contemporary theorists have expanded on this idea, pointing out that an adult often helps a child make sense of the world through a joint discussion of a phenomenon or event that the two have mutually experienced (Eacott, 1999; Feuerstein, 1990; Feuerstein, Klein, & Tannenbaum, 1991; John-Steiner & Mahn, 1996). Such an interaction, sometimes called a **mediated learning experience**, encourages the child to think about the phenomenon or event in particular ways—to attach labels to it, recognize principles that underlie it, draw certain inferences from it, and so on.

Vygotsky proposed, too, that children are most likely to benefit from tasks and activities that they can successfully accomplish only with the assistance and support of more competent individuals—that is, tasks within their zone of proximal development. Such assistance and support, which contemporary theorists call scaffolding, can take a variety of forms; for instance, it might involve modeling desired behaviors, offering hints or suggestions, or presenting a simplified version of a task. As an example, consider how a mother scaffolds her 4-year-old daughter Sadie's attempt to construct a toy using Duplo blocks (larger versions of Legos) and a set of illustrated instructions:

MOTHER: Now you need another one like this on the other side. Mmmmmm . . . there you go, just like that.

SADIE: Then I need this one to go like this? Hold on, hold on. Let it go. There. Get that out. Oops!

MOTHER: I'll hold it while you turn it. (*Watches Sadie work on toy.*) Now you make the end.

SADIE: This one?

MOTHER: No, look at the picture. Right here (*points to plan*). That piece.

SADIE: Like this?

MOTHER: Yeah. (Gauvain, 2001, p. 32)

Researchers have consistently found adult scaffolding to be a highly effective way of nurturing the acquisition of children's complex reasoning, metacognitive, and problem-solving skills (e.g., D. M. Hogan & Tudge, 1999; K. Hogan, Nastasi, & Pressley, 2000; Radziszewska & Rogoff, 1991; Rogoff, 1995; also see Chapters 13 and 14).

---

[1]To simplify our discussion, we'll assume that the learners are children or adolescents. If the learners are adults, then think about the section "Interactions With Adults" as referring to subject matter experts and the section "Interactions With Peers" as referring to adults who have knowledge and skills similar to the learners themselves.

Even very teacher-directed instructional strategies (e.g., lectures) typically involve social interaction; for instance, a teacher might periodically ask questions, solicit students' opinions, and give feedback. But the more instruction is a one-way street (from teacher to student), the less information a teacher has about what students do and do not know, how students are interpreting new information (if in fact they are thinking about it at all), and so on. In the best of instructional worlds, adult–student communications continually go both ways rather than just one, with the adult constantly adjusting instruction to a student's current understandings and misunderstandings and offering sufficient scaffolding to foster success.[2]

Interactions With Peers

Both Piaget and Vygotsky argued for the importance of peer interactions in learning and cognitive development, perhaps as a means of creating disequilibrium (Piaget) or facilitating the internalization of interpretations (Vygotsky). In Chapter 8, I introduced you to two additional perspectives that are equally pertinent to our discussion of peer interaction. First is *social constructivism*, which focuses on how learners often work together to make better sense of their world. Second is the *contextual* perspective, which emphasizes the importance of the social context—opportunities for discussion, social support mechanisms, and so on—for facilitating and scaffolding learning. These last two perspectives are by no means mutually exclusive; many contemporary theorists align themselves with both, and often with some of Piaget's or Vygotsky's ideas as well.

Increasingly, theorists and practitioners are recognizing the value of having students work together to construct meaning about classroom subject matter—for instance, to explore, explain, discuss, and debate certain topics either in small groups or as an entire class (e.g., Hatano & Inagaki, 1993, 2003; Hiebert et al., 1997; Lampert, 1990; Sosniak & Stodolsky, 1994). Following is an example of what might happen when learners tackle new subject matter and problems as a group:

> A third-grade class was working on the following problem: Bugs Bunny has 75 carrots. If he eats 5 carrots each day, for how many days does he have food? Most students solved the problem by writing 5s until they reached 75 and then counting the number of 5s. Maria solved the problem by writing $10 \times 5 = 50$, $5 \times 5 = 25$, and $10 + 5 = 15$. After the different methods had been presented, the class discussed the ways in which Maria's method was different from the others. Some students decided it was basically the same because Maria had added fives too, just in groups. The teacher then asked Maria why she chose 10 fives to start and not, say, 7 fives. Maria said she knew the answer to 10×5 so it was easy. This class discussion may look rather innocuous, but it had a significant effect on the way many students thought about division. After the discussion, a number of students began division problems by looking for multiples of the divisor, often choosing multiples or powers of 10. These were important breakthroughs in students' understandings and in the development of better methods. (Hiebert et al., 1997, pp. 44–45)

[2]It's ironic that I might say this, given that I am writing this textbook alone in my office, intending that it be used for instructional purposes and yet knowing that I will never meet most of my readers. As I write, I must compensate for your absence as best as I can, drawing on my previous experiences in the college classroom to anticipate what your prior knowledge, understandings, and misconceptions are likely to be; and presenting the material in ways that I hope will help you encode and store it effectively (e.g., by organizing it logically, pointing out interrelationships among ideas, and occasionally giving you little exercises that let you see certain principles of learning in action).

When learners work together in such a manner, they are, in essence, engaging in **distributed cognition**: They spread the learning task across many minds and can draw on multiple knowledge bases and ideas (Hewitt & Scardamalia, 1998; Kuhn, 2001b; Palincsar & Herrenkohl, 1999; Salomon, 1993).

Theorists and researchers have suggested that peer group interactions facilitate learning in numerous ways. In particular, peer group interactions relative to a particular topic, task, or problem can

- Encourage learners to clarify and organize their ideas sufficiently to explain and justify them to others.
- Provide opportunities for learners to elaborate on what they have learned—for example, by drawing inferences, generating hypotheses, and asking questions.
- Expose learners to new and possibly more sophisticated understandings and cognitive strategies.
- Help learners discover how people from different cultural and ethnic backgrounds may interpret the world in different, yet perhaps equally valid, ways.
- Enable learners to monitor their comprehension and possibly discover flaws and inconsistencies in their thinking.
- Encourage learners to find common ground in diverse perspectives and so perhaps to arrive at a more complex understanding than any single learner could arrive at independently.
- Foster more sophisticated epistemological beliefs—for instance, an increasing recognition that acquiring "knowledge" involves acquiring an integrated set of ideas about a topic and that such knowledge is likely to evolve gradually over a lengthy period of time.
- Introduce learners to processes that experts in a discipline use to advance the frontiers of knowledge—for instance, presenting evidence in support of one's conclusions and examining the strengths and weaknesses of various explanations.
  (L. M. Anderson, 1993; R. C. Anderson et al., 2001; Banks, 1991; Bell & Linn, 2002; Carr & Biddlecomb, 1998; Derry, DuRussel, & O'Donnell, 1998; Fosnot, 1996; Hatano & Inagaki, 1993, 2003; Hiebert & Raphael, 1996; Hogan et al., 2000; King, 1999; Lampert et al., 1996; Paris & Paris, 2001; Patrick & Middleton, 2002; Reiter, 1994; Schwarz, Neuman, & Biezuner, 2000; Stevens & Slavin, 1995; Webb & Palincsar, 1996)

In addition, many learners find interactive learning sessions highly motivating, in part because they can address their social needs at the same time they're studying classroom subject matter (Stevens & Slavin, 1995). (We'll look at the social aspects of motivation in Chapters 16 and 17.)

Choosing Between Adult and Peer Interactions in Instructional Settings

Interactions with adults versus those with peers are apt to be useful in different situations. Working with an adult is especially appropriate when the adult has considerable expertise that students are unlikely to gain through independent trial and error or through collaboration with peers. In contrast, working with peers may be more valuable when students are likely to gain a better understanding of a topic by tossing around diverse ideas, considering the strengths and weaknesses of each one, and revising current knowledge and beliefs in light of new evidence and insights.

Interactions with adults and interactions with peers have their disadvantages as well as their advantages, and these should also be considered when deciding whether to go the "adult" or "peer" route. When working with adults, students may be less likely to explore, experiment with, and in other ways take risks with new material (Hogan et al., 2000). Furthermore, considerable adult assistance may foster dependence, rather than self-regulated learning, and the belief that an authority figure "has all the answers."

Peer group interactions have potential drawbacks as well. Some students groups may have difficulty working together effectively and keeping themselves on task for any length of time (D. M. Hogan & Tudge, 1999; K. Hogan et al., 2000). Some students may be concerned more about making a good impression on peers than about mastering the subject matter (Levy, Kaplan, & Patrick, 2000); we'll examine the nature of such *performance goals* in Chapter 17. Students may have insufficient expertise to tackle a task or problem without adult assistance, and even if they do have the expertise, they may have insufficient teaching and communication skills to help others understand their reasoning (Ellis & Rogoff, 1986; Hogan & Tudge, 1999). Students of high social status may dominate discussions, with other students acquiescing to their opinions and suggestions (Derry, DuRussel, & O'Donnell, 1998; Wittenbaum & Park, 2001). Occasionally, students pass along misconceptions and illogical reasoning processes to their peers (Hogan & Tudge, 1999; Stacey, 1992). And if students believe that authority figures are the source of all knowledge and that "knowing" something means accumulating many facts (recall our discussion of *epistemological beliefs* in Chapter 13), they may see little purpose in discussing controversial issues with classmates (Andre & Windschitl, 2003).

In many situations, students probably learn most effectively with a blend of teacher guidance and peer interaction. As you will see in our later explorations of class discussions, reciprocal teaching, cooperative learning, and other student-directed approaches, some degree of teacher guidance and structure typically enhances learning. First, however, we consider an approach that is at the teacher-directed end of the continuum: an apprenticeship.

APPRENTICESHIPS

In an **apprenticeship,** a learner works intensively with an expert to accomplish complex tasks; in doing so, the learner performs activities that he or she could never do independently. The expert provides considerable structure and guidance throughout the process, gradually removing scaffolding and giving the learner more responsibility as competence increases (Rogoff, 1990, 1991). Many cultures use apprenticeships as a way of gradually introducing children to the practices of the adult community—practices that might include such skills as weaving, tailoring, or midwifery (Lave, 1991; Lave & Wenger, 1991; Rogoff, 1990). We also see apprenticeships frequently in music instruction—for instance, in teaching a student how to play a musical instrument (Elliott, 1995).

Through an apprenticeship, an expert often learns not only how to perform a task but also how to *think about* a task; such a situation is sometimes called a **cognitive apprenticeship** (J. S. Brown et al., 1989; Collins et al., 1989; John-Steiner, 1997; Rogoff, 1990). An example is the relationship between a university professor and a graduate student (Roth & Bowen, 1995). For instance, I used to teach a doctoral seminar called Cognition and Instruction. In the course, I assigned a gigantic collection of outside readings (the required articles and book chapters stacked up to a pile about two feet high), but as a class we spent two or three hours over the course of the semester talking about how to read such a large amount of material productively. I shared such strategies as skimming, reading with particular goals in mind, and relating one theorist's perspectives to another's, and I provided a list of focus questions that students should try to answer as they read. Students were also required to complete a major research project by the end of the semester; I met with each of them periodically to help them narrow down their topic, identify fruitful directions to pursue, organize their thoughts, and consider possible conclusions.

Although apprenticeships can differ widely from one context to another, they typically have some or all of the following features (Collins et al., 1989):

- *Modeling.* The teacher carries out the task, simultaneously thinking aloud about the process, while the student observes and listens.
- *Coaching.* As the student performs the task, the teacher gives frequent suggestions, hints, and feedback.
- *Scaffolding.* The teacher provides various forms of support for the student, perhaps by simplifying the task, breaking it into smaller and more manageable components, or providing less complicated equipment.
- *Articulation.* The student explains what he or she is doing and why, allowing the teacher to examine the student's knowledge, reasoning, and problem-solving strategies.
- *Reflection.* The teacher asks the student to compare his or her performance with that of experts, or perhaps with an ideal model of how the task should be done.
- *Increasing complexity and diversity of tasks.* As the student gains greater proficiency, the teacher presents more complex, challenging, and varied tasks to complete.
- *Exploration.* The teacher encourages the student to frame questions and problems on his or her own, and in doing so, to expand and refine acquired skills.

Apprenticeships are clearly labor intensive; as such, their use in the classroom is not always practical or logistically feasible (De Corte et al., 1996). At the same time, teachers can certainly use elements of an apprenticeship model to help their students develop more complex skills. For example, Scardamalia and Bereiter (1985) have used prompts such as the following to help students think about writing tasks in the same ways that expert writers do:

- "My purpose . . . "
- "My main point . . . "
- "An example of this . . . "
- "The reason I think so . . . "
- "To liven this up I'll . . . "
- "I'm not being very clear about what I just said so . . . "
- "I'm getting off the topic so . . . "
- "This isn't very convincing because . . . "
- "I can tie this together by . . . "

Such prompts provide the same sort of scaffolding that an expert writer might provide, and they help students develop more sophisticated writing strategies (Scardamalia & Bereiter, 1985).

CLASS DISCUSSIONS

As noted earlier, social constructivists propose that people often work together to construct meaningful interpretations of their world. Class discussions in which students feel that they can speak freely, asking questions and presenting their ideas and opinions in either a whole-class or small-group context, obviously provide an important mechanism for promoting such socially constructed understandings (Bruning, Schraw, & Ronning, 1995; De Corte et al., 1996; Fosnot, 1996; Greeno et al., 1996; Hiebert & Fisher, 1992; Marshall, 1992; Webb & Palincsar, 1996; White & Rumsey, 1994).

Class discussions lend themselves readily to a variety of academic disciplines. For example, students may discuss various interpretations of classic works of literature, addressing questions that have no easy or "right" answers; when they do so, they are more likely to relate what they are reading to their personal lives and thereby to understand it better (Eeds & Wells, 1989; Hiebert & Raphael, 1996; McGee, 1992). In history classes, students may study and discuss various documents related to a single historical event and so begin to recognize that history is not necessarily as cut-and-dried as traditional history textbooks portray it (Leinhardt, 1994). In social studies, discussing controversial topics (e.g., capital punishment) can help students understand that diverse viewpoints on an issue may all have some legitimacy (Kuhn et al., 1997). In science classes, discussions of various and conflicting theoretical explanations of observed phenomena may help students come to grips with the idea that science is not "fact" as much as it is a dynamic and continually evolving understanding of the world (Bereiter, 1994). And in mathematics, class discussions that focus on alternative approaches to solving the same problem can promote a more meaningful understanding of mathematical principles and lead to better transfer of those principles to new situations and problems (Cobb et al., 1991; Hiebert & Wearne, 1992, 1996; Lampert, 1990).

Guidelines for Promoting Effective Discussions

Although students typically do most of the talking in classroom discussions, teachers nevertheless play a critical role. Theorists have offered several guidelines for how teachers can promote effective classroom discussions:

• *Class discussions should focus on topics that lend themselves to multiple perspectives, explanations, or approaches* (L. M. Anderson, 1993; Hiebert & Raphael, 1996; Lampert, 1990; Onosko, 1996). Controversial topics appear to have several benefits: Students are more likely to express their views, seek out new information that resolves seemingly contradictory data, reevaluate their own positions on the issues under discussion, and develop a meaningful and well-integrated understanding of the subject matter (Cohen, 1994; Johnson & Johnson, 1985a; Smith, Johnson, & Johnson, 1981).

• *Students should have sufficient prior knowledge about a topic to discuss it intelligently.* Such knowledge may come from either previous class sessions or students' personal experiences (Bruning et al., 1995). In many cases, it is likely to come from studying a particular topic in depth (Onosko, 1996).

• *The classroom atmosphere should be conducive to open debate and the constructive evaluation of ideas.* Students are more likely to share their ideas and opinions if their teacher is supportive of multiple viewpoints and if disagreeing with classmates is socially acceptable. To promote such an atmosphere in the classroom, teachers might

- Communicate the message that understanding a topic at the end of the discussion is more important than having the "correct" answer at the beginning of the discussion.
- Communicate the beliefs that asking questions reflects curiosity, that differing perspectives on a controversial topic are both inevitable and healthy, and that changing one's opinion on a topic can be a sign of thoughtful reflection about the topic under discussion.
- Encourage students to try to understand one another's reasoning and explanations.
- Suggest that students build on one another's ideas whenever possible.
- Encourage students to be open in their agreement or disagreement with their classmates—in other words, to "agree to disagree."
- Depersonalize challenges to a student's line of reasoning by framing questions in a third-person voice—for example, by asking, "What if someone were to respond to your claim by saying . . . ?"
- Occasionally ask students to defend a position that is in direct opposition to what they actually believe.
- Require students to develop compromise solutions that take into account opposing perspectives.
  (Cobb & Yackel, 1996; Hatano & Inagaki, 1993, 2003; Herrenkohl & Guerra, 1998; Hogan et al., 2000; Lampert et al., 1996; Onosko, 1996; Reiter, 1994)

- *Small-group discussions encourage a greater number of students to participate.* Many students may speak more openly when their audience is a handful of classmates rather than the class as a whole; the difference is especially noticeable for females (Théberge, 1994). On some occasions, teachers may want to have students discuss an issue in small groups first, thereby allowing students to voice and gain support for their ideas in a relatively private context, and then bring students together for a whole-class discussion (Onosko, 1996).

- *Class discussions are sometimes more effective when they are structured in some way.* Providing a structure for a class discussion—perhaps setting a particular goal toward which students should work, or assigning different roles to different class members (e.g., some evaluate the quality of evidence presented, others evaluate the validity of conclusions, etc.)—often increases the productivity of a discussion (Calfee, Dunlap, & Wat, 1994; Herrenkohl & Guerra, 1998; Palincsar & Herrenkohl, 1999). Before conducting an experiment, a science teacher might ask students to make predictions about what will happen in the experiment and to explain and defend why they think their predictions are correct; later, after students have observed the outcome of the experiment, the teacher might ask them to explain what happened and why (Hatano & Inagaki, 1991; Herrenkohl & Guerra, 1998). Another strategy, useful when the topic under discussion is an especially controversial one, might be to follow a sequence such as this one:

1. The class is divided into groups of four students apiece. Each group of four subdivides into two pairs.
2. Within a group, each pair of students studies a particular position on the issue and presents its position to the other two students.
3. The group of four has an open discussion of the issue, giving each student an opportunity to argue persuasively for his or her own position.
4. Each pair presents the perspective of the *opposing* side as sincerely and persuasively as possible.

5. The group strives for consensus on a position that incorporates all of the evidence presented (Deutsch, 1993).

• *Students may have more productive discussions when they are given guidance about how to behave.* Teachers must take steps to ensure that students' reactions to one another's ideas are not disparaging or mean spirited (Onosko, 1996). For example, they might provide rules such as the following for acceptable behavior during small-group or whole-class discussions:

- Encourage everyone to participate and listen to everyone's ideas.
- Restate what someone else has said if you don't understand.
- Be critical of ideas rather than people.
- Try to pull ideas from both sides together in a way that makes sense.
- Focus not on winning but on resolving the issue in the best possible way.
- Change your mind if the arguments and evidence presented indicate that you should do so. (based on Deutsch, 1993)

• *Some type of closure should be provided at the end of the discussion.* Although students may sometimes come to consensus about a topic at the end of a class discussion, such agreement is not always possible. Nevertheless, a class discussion should have some form of closure that helps students tie various ideas together. For instance, when I conduct discussions about controversial topics in my own classes, I spend about five minutes at the end of class identifying and summarizing the key issues that students have raised during the class period. Another strategy is to have students explain how a particular discussion has helped them understand the topic in question more fully (Onosko, 1996).

As you have seen, class discussions can help students think about and process classroom subject matter more completely. Such discussions can have an additional advantage as well: They can promote more effective learning strategies during reading and listening activities (A. L. Brown & Reeve, 1987; Cross & Paris, 1988; Palincsar & Brown, 1989; Paris & Winograd, 1990). One particular form of discussion—*reciprocal teaching*—is especially effective in this regard.

RECIPROCAL TEACHING

Annemarie Palincsar and Ann Brown (1984) have identified four key strategies that good readers typically use:

- *Summarizing.* They identify the gist and main ideas of what they read.
- *Questioning.* They ask themselves questions to make sure they understand what they are reading, thereby monitoring their comprehension as they proceed through reading material.
- *Clarifying.* They take steps to clarify confusing or ambiguous parts of the text, perhaps by rereading or imposing their own knowledge on those things.
- *Predicting.* They anticipate what they are likely to read next based on cues in the text (e.g., headings) and ideas that have already been presented.

Palincsar and Brown noted that poor readers—students who learn little from textbooks and other things they read—rarely summarize, question, clarify, or predict. For example, many students cannot adequately summarize a typical fifth-grade textbook until high school or even junior college (A. L. Brown & Palincsar, 1987; Palincsar & Brown, 1984).

Yet summarizing, questioning, clarifying, and predicting are activities that typically occur internally rather than externally; they are cognitive processes rather than observable behaviors. Palincsar and Brown reasoned that students might acquire these strategies more easily if they first practiced them out loud and in cooperation with their classmates. In **reciprocal teaching** (A. L. Brown & Palincsar, 1987; Palincsar & Brown, 1984, 1989; Palincsar & Herrenkohl, 1999), a classroom teacher and several students meet in a group to read a section of text, stopping periodically to discuss that text as they proceed. Initially, the teacher leads the discussion, asking questions about the text to promote summarizing, questioning, clarifying, and predicting. But gradually, he or she turns the role of "teacher" over to different students, who then take charge of the discussion and ask one another the same kinds of questions their teacher has modeled. Eventually, students can read and discuss a text almost independently of the teacher, working together to construct its meaning and checking one another for comprehension and possible misunderstandings.

Reciprocal teaching sessions often begin with students making predictions about what they will read based on the title of a passage and their prior knowledge of a topic. Then, as they proceed through the text, they periodically stop to check their comprehension (e.g., by asking one another fact-based and inferential questions), clarify any potentially ambiguous statements or unfamiliar vocabulary, summarize what they have read, and predict what may be coming next. After finishing the passage, the "teacher" summarizes it, with other students possibly adding to and elaborating on that summary.

As an illustration, let's look at a reciprocal teaching session for a group of six first graders reading a passage about snowshoe rabbits. In this particular case, the classroom teacher reads the text in small segments (at higher grade levels, the students themselves take turns reading). After each segment, the teacher pauses while students discuss and process that segment. As you read the dialogue, look for examples of summarizing, questioning, clarifying, and predicting (there is at least one instance of each):

> The children were reading about the snowshoe rabbit and it was the sixteenth day of dialogue. The teacher had just read a segment of text describing the season in which baby rabbits are born and the ways in which the mother rabbit cares for her babies. A student named Kam is the dialogue leader.

Kam:	When was the babies born?
Teacher:	That's a good question to ask. Call on someone to answer that question.
Kam:	Robby? Milly?
Milly:	Summer.
Teacher:	What would happen if the babies were born in the winter? Let's think.

> Several children make a number of responses including: "The baby would be very cold." "They would need food." "They don't have no fur when they are just born."

Kam:	I have another question. How does she get the babies safe?
Kris:	She hides them.

Kam:	That's right but something else. . . .
Teacher:	There is something very unusual about how she hides them that surprised me. I didn't know this.
Travis:	They are all in a different place.
Teacher:	Why do you think she does this?
Milly:	Probably because I heard another story and when they're babies they usually eat each other or fight with each other.
Teacher:	That could be! And what about when that lynx comes?

Several children comment that that would be the end of all the babies.

Travis:	If I was the mother, I would hide mine, I would keep them all together.
Kris:	If the babies are hidden and the mom wants to go and look at them how can she remember where they are?
Teacher:	Good question. Because she does have to find them again. Why? What does she bring them?
Milly:	She needs to bring food. She probably leaves a twig or something.
Teacher:	Do you think she puts out a twig like we mark a trail?

Several children disagree and suggest that she uses her sense of smell. One child, recalling that the snowshoe rabbit is not all white in the winter, suggests that the mother might be able to tell her babies apart by their coloring.

Teacher:	So we agree that the mother rabbit uses her senses to find her babies after she hides them. Kam, can you summarize for us now?
Kam:	The babies are born in the summer. . . .
Teacher:	The mother. . . .
Kam:	The mother hides the babies in different places.
Teacher:	And she visits them. . . .
Kam:	To bring them food.
Travis:	She keeps them safe.
Teacher:	Any predictions?
Milly:	What she teaches her babies . . . like how to hop.
Kris:	They know how to hop already.
Teacher:	Well, let's read and see.

(dialogue courtesy of A. Palincsar)

Reciprocal teaching provides a mechanism through which both teacher and students can model effective reading and learning strategies. When we consider that we are encouraging effective cognitive processes by first having students practice them aloud in group sessions, we realize that Vygotsky's theory is also at work here: Students should eventually *internalize* the processes that they first use in their discussions with others. Furthermore, the structured nature of a reciprocal teaching session scaffolds students' efforts to make sense of the things they read and hear. For instance, if you look back at the previous dialogue for a moment, you may notice how the teacher models elaborative questions and connections to prior knowledge ("What would happen if the babies were born in the winter?"; "Do you think she puts out a twig like we mark a trail?") and provides general guidance and occasional hints about how students should process the passage about snowshoe rabbits ("Kam, can you summarize for us now?"; "And she visits them . . ."). Also notice in the dialogue how students support one another in their efforts to process what they are reading; consider this exchange as an example:

Kam:	I have another question. How does she get the babies safe?
Kris:	She hides them.
Kam:	That's right but something else. . . .

Effectiveness of Reciprocal Teaching

Studies of reciprocal teaching have yielded significant and often dramatic improvements in students' reading and listening comprehension (Alfassi, 1998; A. L. Brown & Palincsar, 1987; Campione, Shapiro, & Brown, 1995; Hart & Speece, 1998; McGee, Knight, & Boudah, 2001; Palincsar, 1986; Palincsar & Brown, 1984, 1989; Rosenshine & Meister, 1994). Furthermore, students continue to show the benefits of this approach for at least six months after instruction (A. L. Brown & Palincsar, 1987). In an early study of reciprocal teaching (Palincsar & Brown, 1984), 6 seventh-grade students with a history of reading difficulty participated in 20 reciprocal teaching sessions, each lasting about 30 minutes. Despite the relatively short intervention, the students showed changes such as the following:

- They became increasingly able to process reading material in an effective manner—for example, by summarizing and questioning—and to do so independently of their classroom teacher.
- They demonstrated increasingly better comprehension of the passages they were reading. Average scores on daily comprehension tests increased from 30% before instruction to 70 to 80% (a level similar to that for average readers) after instruction.
- Three months after the reciprocal teaching intervention, their scores on a standardized reading comprehension test reflected an improvement in reading comprehension typically observed after 15 months of traditional schooling—more than a year's worth!
- They generalized their new reading strategies to other classes; for instance, they showed improved performance in their science and social studies classes, sometimes even surpassing the levels of their classmates (A. L. Brown & Palincsar, 1987; Palincsar & Brown, 1984).

A reciprocal teaching approach to reading instruction has been used successfully with a wide variety of students, ranging from third graders to college students. Furthermore, it can be used to foster more effective listening comprehension beginning in first grade (the snowshoe rabbit dialogue presented earlier is an example). And it can be employed with an entire classroom of students almost as easily as in a small group. Although teachers are often very skeptical of such a radically different approach to teaching and learning, their enthusiasm grows once they have tried it themselves (A. L. Brown & Palincsar, 1987; Palincsar & Brown, 1989). And as students gain increasing proficiency in this approach, they begin to use it more flexibly and creatively (Palincsar & Herrenkohl, 1999).

COOPERATIVE LEARNING

In **cooperative learning**,[3] students work in small groups to achieve a common goal. Cooperative learning groups vary in duration, depending on the task to be accomplished. On some occasions, groups are formed on a short-term basis to accomplish specific tasks—perhaps to study new material, solve a problem, or complete an assigned project. On other occasions, groups are formed to work toward long-term classroom goals. For instance, **base groups** are cooperative groups that last the entire semester or school year; they provide a means through which students can clarify assignments for one another, help one another with class notes, and provide one another with a general sense of support and belonging in the classroom (Johnson & Johnson, 1991).

We find justification for cooperative learning in a number of theoretical perspectives. From a behaviorist point of view, rewards for group success are consistent with the operant conditioning notion of a group contingency. From the standpoint of social cognitive theory, students are likely to have higher self-efficacy for performing a task when they know that they will have the help of other group members; furthermore, students can model effective learning and problem-solving strategies for one another. And from the perspective of contemporary cognitivist ideas, students who collaborate on a learning task create scaffolding for one another's efforts and may co-construct more sophisticated ideas and strategies than any single group member might be able to construct alone.

Common Features of Cooperative Learning

Cooperative learning is not simply a process of putting students in groups and setting them loose to work on an assignment together. Oftentimes, students will be more accustomed to learning on an individual basis, or perhaps even to competing with classmates, than they are to engaging in cooperative endeavors with other students. For a cooperative learning approach to be successful, teachers must structure classroom activities in such a way that cooperation is not only helpful for academic success but in fact even necessary for it (Johnson & Johnson, 1991). Following are several features that enhance the effectiveness of cooperative groups:

- *Students work in small, teacher-assigned groups.* Groups are typically comprised of two to six members; groups of three to four students can be especially effective (Hatano & Inagaki, 1991; Lou et al., 1996). In most cases, the teacher forms the groups, choosing combinations of students that are likely to be most productive (Johnson & Johnson, 1991). Many advocates of cooperative learning suggest that each group be relatively heterogeneous in makeup—that each group include high achievers and low achievers, boys and girls, and children of various ethnic backgrounds (Johnson & Johnson, 1991; Shachar & Sharan, 1994; Slavin, 1983a; Stevens & Slavin, 1995). Research on this practice yields mixed results, however, as we shall see shortly.

---

[3]Some theorists distinguish between *cooperative* learning and *collaborative* learning, although different theorists draw the line somewhat differently (e.g., see Palincsar & Herrenkohl, 1999; Smith & MacGregor, 1992; Teasley & Roschelle, 1993). Part of their reasoning, I suspect, is that the term *cooperative learning* has historically been associated with particular theorists and particular instructional strategies (e.g., Johnson & Johnson, 1991; Slavin, 1983a, 1990a). Here I am using *cooperative learning* more broadly to refer to any instructional method in which students work together in a somewhat structured format to achieve a shared learning goal.

- *Groups have one or more common goals toward which to work.* At the beginning of a cooperative group activity, the teacher should specify clearly and concretely what each group should accomplish (Johnson & Johnson, 1991).

- *Students are given clear guidelines about how to behave.* Without instruction about appropriate group behaviors, students may act in a decidedly uncooperative manner; for example, they may try to dominate discussions, ridicule one another's ideas, or exert pressure to complete the task in a particular way (Blumenfeld, Marx, Soloway, & Krajcik, 1996; Webb & Palincsar, 1996). Instruction on group skills such as the following seems to increase cooperative and productive group behaviors:
  - Listening to others politely and attentively
  - Making sure everyone has an equal chance to participate and that everyone eventually understands the material
  - Asking clear, precise questions when one doesn't understand
  - Giving encouragement to others, and offering assistance as needed
  - Addressing differences of opinion amicably and constructively (Cohen, 1994; Deutsch, 1993; Gillies & Ashman, 1998; Johnson & Johnson, 1991; Lou et al., 1996; O'Donnell & O'Kelly, 1994; Webb & Farivar, 1994, 1999; Webb & Palincsar, 1996)

- *Group members depend on one another for their success.* Group tasks should be structured so that each student's success depends on the help and participation of other group members; furthermore, each student must believe it is to his or her advantage that other group members do well (Deutsch, 1993; Johnson & Johnson, 1991; Lou et al., 1996; Schofield, 1995; Slavin, 1983a). Tasks that involve creative problem solving and have more than one right answer are especially likely to encourage students to work cooperatively with one another (Blumenfeld et al., 1996). In some situations, each student might have a unique and essential function within the group, perhaps serving as group leader, critic, bookkeeper, summarizer, or the like (A. L. Brown & Palincsar, 1989; Johnson & Johnson, 1991). In other situations, the **jigsaw** technique is useful: New information is divided equally among all group members, and each student must teach his or her portion to the other group members (Aronson, 1997).

- *A structure is provided to encourage productive learning behaviors.* When students are novices at cooperative learning, it is often helpful to give them a set of steps (a "script" to follow) that guides their interaction (Cohen, 1994; Dansereau, 1988; Fantuzzo, King, & Heller, 1992; Meloth & Deering, 1994; Palincsar, Anderson, & David, 1993; Webb & Palincsar, 1996). In one approach, known as **scripted cooperation,** students work together in pairs to read and study expository text (Dansereau, 1988; O'Donnell, 1999). One member of the pair might act as "recaller," summarizing the contents of a textbook passage. The other student acts as "listener," correcting any errors and recalling additional important information. For the next passage, the two students switch roles. Such an approach can help students improve such learning strategies as elaboration, summarizing, and comprehension monitoring (Dansereau, 1988).

The particular structure a teacher provides influences the kind of learning that results—for instance, whether students focus on learning facts, on the one hand, or engage in higher-level thinking skills, on the other. As an example, in **guided peer questioning**[4] (A. King, 1997, 1999;

---

[4]Some theorists use the term *elaborative interrogation* (e.g., Kahl & Woloshyn, 1994; Martin & Pressley, 1991; Woloshyn et al., 1992).

A. King, Staffieri, & Adelgais, 1998), student pairs are given a structure that encourages them to ask one another higher-level questions about the subject matter they are studying. More specifically, they are given "starters" such as these for constructing questions:

- Describe . . . in your own words.
- Explain why . . . .
- What is the difference between . . . and . . . ?
- How could . . . be used to . . . ? (A. King, 1999, p. 93)

Students then use a series of such questions to probe and promote their partner's understanding. The following exchange shows two fifth graders using guided peer questioning as they study material about tide pools and tidal zones:

Janelle:	What do you think would happen if there weren't certain zones for certain animals in the tide pools?
Katie:	They would all be, like, mixed up—and all the predators would kill all the animals that shouldn't be there and then they just wouldn't survive. 'Cause the food chain wouldn't work—'cause the top of the chain would eat all the others and there would be no place for the bottom ones to hide and be protected. And nothing left for them to eat.
Janelle:	O.K. But what about the ones that had camouflage to hide them? (King, 1999, p. 95)

We join the girls again later in the session; at this point, Katie is now asking the questions:

Katie:	How are the upper tide zone and the lower tide zone different?
Janelle:	They have different animals in them. Animals in the upper tide zone and splash zone can handle being exposed—have to be able to use the rain and sand and wind and sun—and they don't need that much water and the lower tide animals do.
Katie:	And they can be softer 'cause they don't have to get hit on the rocks.
Janelle:	Also predators. In the spray zone it's because there's predators like us people and all different kinds of stuff that can kill the animals and they won't survive, but the lower tide zone has not as many predators.
Katie:	But wait! Why do the animals in the splash zone have to survive? (King, 1999, p. 97)

Clearly, Janelle and Katie have become skilled at asking and answering higher-level questions. At the end of the second dialogue, we even see Katie questioning a basic assumption of the discussion—that animals in the splash zone need to survive.

- *The teacher serves primarily as a resource and monitor.* During cooperative learning activities, the teacher monitors each group to be sure that interactions are productive and socially appropriate (Johnson & Johnson, 1991; Meloth & Deering, 1999; Webb & Farivar, 1999). The teacher may also provide assistance in situations in which group members are unable to provide information or insights critical for accomplishing the group's goal. Too much intervention may be counterproductive, however: Students tend to talk less with one another when their teacher joins the group (Cohen, 1994).

- *Students are individually accountable for their achievement.* Each student demonstrates individual mastery or accomplishment of the group's goal—for example, by taking a quiz or answering questions in class. This strategy decreases the likelihood that some students will do most or all of the work while others get a free ride (Johnson & Johnson, 1991; Karau & Williams, 1995; Slavin, 1983b, 1990a; Webb & Palincsar, 1996).

•   *Students are rewarded for group success.* In addition to being accountable for their own learning and achievement, group members are typically rewarded in some way for the success of the group as a whole (Lou et al., 1996; Slavin, 1983b, 1990a). Group rewards often promote higher achievement overall, perhaps because students have a vested interest in helping one another learn and so make a concerted effort to help fellow group members understand the material being studied (Slavin, 1983b; Stevens & Slavin, 1995).

It is important to note, however, that not all researchers have found group rewards to be beneficial. In particular, students may sometimes learn better when they focus on using effective learning strategies than when they focus on obtaining a group reward (Meloth & Deering, 1992, 1994). More generally, the effects of extrinsic reinforcers can be a mixed bag, as you will discover in Chapter 17.

•   *At the completion of an activity, each group evaluates its effectiveness.* Once a cooperative group has accomplished its goal, it looks analytically and critically (often with the assistance of the teacher) at the ways in which it has functioned effectively and the ways in which it needs to improve (Cohen, 1994; Deutsch, 1993; Johnson & Johnson, 1991).

How Heterogeneous Should Cooperative Groups Be?

As I mentioned earlier, cooperative groups are often quite heterogeneous with respect to students' achievement levels, with high and low achievers being asked to work together. In recent years, some theorists have begun to question this practice (Cohen & Lotan, 1995; Fuchs, Fuchs, Hamlett, & Karns, 1998; Good et al., 1992; McCaslin & Good, 1996; O'Donnell & O'Kelly, 1994; S.E. Peterson, 1993; Webb & Palincsar, 1996). One potential problem with heterogeneous grouping is that ability differences among students become more obvious. High-ability students may dominate discussions and work efforts and may discourage low-ability students from fully participating. Low-ability students may be reluctant to ask for help in understanding the material being studied, or they may simply sit back and let other group members do most or all of the work. And if a group fails to achieve its goal, the high performers in the group may resent and blame those who contributed little or nothing to the group's efforts.

Findings regarding the achievement gains of students in heterogeneous ability groupings have been somewhat mixed. Some studies indicate that heterogeneous groups benefit both high-ability students, who can sharpen their understanding of class material by explaining it to classmates, and low-ability students, who benefit from hearing such explanations (Cohen, 1994; L. S. Fuchs et al., 1996; Lou et al., 1996; Stevens & Slavin, 1995; Webb & Palincsar, 1996). Yet other studies indicate that high-ability students do not always gain much from working with their low-ability peers; in fact, these students occasionally even lose ground (Lou et al., 1996; Tudge, 1990; Webb, Nemer, Chizhik, & Sugrue, 1998). And middle-ability students may sometimes do better when grouped with *either* high-ability students (who can help them learn) or low-ability students (whom they can help learn), rather than being placed in the middle of a wide range of student abilities (Lou, Abrami, & d'Apollonia, 2001; Lou et al., 1996; McCaslin & Good, 1996; Webb & Palincsar, 1996).

Two strategies that I mentioned earlier—assigning different roles to different group members and providing scripts for interaction—are possible ways of equalizing the participation of students who have varying abilities. A third approach is to assign projects that require such a wide range of talents and skills that every group member is likely to have something truly unique and useful to contribute to the group's overall success (Cohen, 1994; Cohen & Lotan, 1995; Schofield, 1995).

Effectiveness of Cooperative Learning Activities

Numerous research studies indicate that cooperative learning activities, when designed and structured appropriately, are effective in many ways. Students of all ability levels show higher academic achievement; females, members of minority groups, and students at risk for academic failure are especially likely to show increased achievement (Barron, 2000; Ginsburg-Block & Fantuzzo, 1998; Lou et al., 1996; Mathes, Torgesen, & Allor, 2001; Nichols, 1996b; Qin et al., 1995; Shachar & Sharan, 1994; Slavin, 1983a, 1990a; Stevens & Slavin, 1995). Cooperative learning activities may also promote higher-level thinking skills: Students essentially "think aloud," modeling various learning and problem-solving strategies for one another and developing greater metacognitive awareness as a result (A. L. Brown & Palincsar, 1989; Good et al., 1992; Paris & Winograd, 1990).

The benefits of cooperative learning activities are not limited to gains in learning and achievement. Students have higher self-efficacy about their chances of being successful, express more intrinsic motivation to learn school subject matter, participate more actively in classroom activities, and exhibit more self-regulated learning. They better understand the perspectives of others and more frequently engage in prosocial behavior, making decisions about how to divide a task fairly and equitably, resolving interpersonal conflicts, and encouraging and supporting one another's learning. Furthermore, they are more likely to believe that they are liked and accepted by their classmates, and increased numbers of friendships across racial and ethnic groups as well as between students with and without disabilities are likely to form (Deutsch, 1993; Good et al., 1992; Johnson & Johnson, 1985b, 1987; Lou et al., 1996, 2001; Marsh & Craven, 1997; Nichols, 1996a, 1996b; Slavin, 1983a, 1990a; Stevens & Slavin, 1995; Webb & Palincsar, 1996).

Some potential disadvantages of cooperative learning should be noted, however. Students may sometimes be more interested in achieving a group reward with the least possible effort and so will focus more on getting the "right" answer than on ensuring that all group members understand the subject matter being studied (Good et al., 1992; Hatano & Inagaki, 1991; Linn et al., 1996). The students who do most of the work and most of the talking may learn more than other group members (Blumenfeld, 1992; Gayford, 1992; Webb, 1989). Students may occasionally agree to use an incorrect strategy or method that a particular group member has suggested. And in some cases, students may simply not have the skills to help one another learn (O'Donnell & O'Kelly, 1994). Clearly, then, teachers must keep a close eye on the discussions that cooperative groups have and the products that they create, providing additional structure and guidance when necessary to promote maximal learning and achievement.

One of the reasons that cooperative learning is so often effective is that students may tutor one another in the subject matter they are studying. Such peer tutoring is our next topic of discussion.

PEER TUTORING

Teachers cannot always devote as much time as they would like to one-on-one instruction with their students. In such situations, **peer tutoring**,[5] whereby students who have mastered a topic teach those who have not, can provide an effective alternative for teaching fundamental knowledge and skills (A. L. Brown & Palincsar, 1987; Durkin, 1995; Greenwood, Carta, & Hall, 1988; Pigott et al., 1986).

In some cases, peer tutoring leads to greater academic gains than more traditional forms of instruction (Greenwood et al., 1988). One possible reason for its effectiveness is that it provides a context in which struggling students may be more comfortable asking questions when they don't understand something. In one study (Graesser & Person, 1994), students asked 240 times as many questions during peer tutoring as they did during whole-class instruction!

Peer tutoring typically benefits the tutors as well as those being tutored (Biemiller, Shany, Inglis, & Meichenbaum, 1998; Fuchs, Fuchs, Mathes, & Simmons, 1997; Greenwood et al., 1988; Semb et al., 1993; Webb & Palincsar, 1996). When students study material with the expectation that they will be teaching it to someone else, they are more intrinsically motivated to learn it, find it more interesting, process it in a more meaningful fashion, and remember it longer (Benware & Deci, 1984; Semb et al., 1993). Furthermore, in the process of directing and guiding other students' learning and problem solving, tutors may, in a Vygotskian fashion, internalize these processes and so become better able to direct and guide their *own* learning and problem solving; in other words, peer tutoring may foster greater self-regulation (Biemiller et al., 1998). Peer tutoring has nonacademic benefits as well: Cooperation and other social skills improve, classroom behavior problems diminish, and friendships develop between students of different ethnic groups and between students with and without disabilities (Greenwood et al., 1988).

Guidelines for Facilitating Effective Tutoring

Peer tutoring, like other interactive approaches to instruction, is most effective when teachers follow certain guidelines in its use. Following are several suggestions for using peer tutoring effectively:

• *Teachers should be sure that their tutors have mastered the material being taught and use sound instructional techniques.* Good tutors have a meaningful understanding of the subject matter they are teaching and provide explanations that focus on such understanding; poor tutors are more likely to describe procedures without explaining why the procedures are useful (L. S. Fuchs et al., 1996). Good tutors also use teaching strategies that are likely to promote learning: They ask questions, give hints, scaffold responses when necessary, provide feedback, and so on (Lepper, Aspinwall, Mumme, & Chabey, 1990).

Students don't always have the knowledge and skills that will enable them to become effective tutors, especially at the elementary school level (Greenwood et al., 1988; Kermani & Moallem, 1997; Wood, Wood, Ainsworth, & O'Malley, 1995). It is essential, then, that tutoring sessions be

---

[5]Some theorists use the term *peer tutoring* when referring to structured learning sessions in which students of equal ability ask one another questions about classroom subject matter. I have incorporated the literature about such tutoring in my earlier discussion of cooperative learning. I am restricting my use of the term here to situations in which one learner has greater expertise in the subject matter than the other.

limited to subject matter that the student tutors know well. Training in effective tutoring skills is also helpful; for example, student tutors might be shown how to establish a good relationship with the students they are tutoring, how to break a task into simple steps, how and when to give feedback, and so on (Fueyo & Bushell, 1998; Inglis & Biemiller, 1997; Kermani & Moallem, 1997).

   • *Structured interactions can enhance the effectiveness of peer tutoring.* Studies by Lynn and Douglas Fuchs and their colleagues (D. Fuchs et al., 1997; L. S. Fuchs et al., 1996; Mathes et al., 2001) indicate that providing a structure for tutoring sessions can help elementary students effectively tutor their classmates in reading comprehension skills. In one study (D. Fuchs et al., 1997), 20 second- through sixth-grade classes participated in a project called Peer-Assisted Learning Strategies (PALS). In each class, students were ranked with regard to their reading performance, and the ranked list was divided in half. The first-ranked student in the top half of the list was paired with the first-ranked student in the bottom half of the list, the second student in the top half was paired with the second student in the bottom half, and so on down the list; through this procedure, students who were paired together had moderate but not extreme differences in their reading levels. Each pair read reading material at the level of the weaker reader and engaged in the following activities:

   • *Partner reading with retell.* The stronger reader read aloud for five minutes, and then the weaker reader read the same passage of text. Reading something that had previously been read presumably enabled the weaker reader to read the material easily. After the double reading, the weaker reader described the material that the pair had just read.
   • *Paragraph summary.* The students both read a passage one paragraph at a time. Then, with help from the stronger reader, the weaker reader tried to identify the subject and main idea of the paragraph.
   • *Prediction relay.* Both students read a page of text, and then, with help from the stronger reader, the weaker reader would summarize the text and also make a prediction about what the next page would say. The students would read the following page, and then the weaker reader would confirm or disconfirm the prediction, summarize the new page, make a new prediction, and so on.

Such a procedure enabled students in the PALS program to make significantly greater progress in reading than students who had more traditional reading instruction, even though the amount of class time devoted to reading instruction was similar for both groups. The researchers speculated that the superior performance of the PALS students was probably because they had more frequent opportunities to make verbal responses to the things they were reading, received more frequent feedback about their performance, and, in general, were more frequently encouraged to use effective reading strategies.

   • *Teachers must be careful that their use of higher-ability students to tutor lower-ability students is not excessive or exploitive.* As we have seen, tutors often gain just as much from tutoring sessions as the students they are tutoring. When students teach something to a classmate, they must pull their knowledge together sufficiently to explain it in a way that someone else can understand; in the process, they review, organize, and elaborate on the things they have learned. Nevertheless, teachers must not assume that high-achieving students will always learn from a tutoring session; they should regularly monitor the effects of a peer tutoring program to make sure that all students are reaping its benefits.

   • *Teachers can use peer tutoring to help students with special educational needs.* Peer tutoring has been used effectively to help students with learning disabilities, physical disabilities, and other special educational needs (Cushing & Kennedy, 1997; DuPaul, Ervin, Hook, & McGoey, 1998; D. Fuchs et al., 1997). In one study (Cushing & Kennedy, 1997), low-achieving students were assigned as regular tutors for classmates who had moderate or severe intellectual or physical disabilities. The student tutors clearly benefited from their tutoring assignments: They became more attentive in class, completed classroom tasks more frequently, and participated in class more regularly. I suspect that the opportunity to tutor classmates less capable than themselves may have enhanced their own self-efficacy for learning classroom subject matter, which in turn would encourage them to engage in the kinds of behaviors that would ensure (rather than interfere with) academic success.

- *Tutoring does not necessarily need to be limited to same-age pairs.* In many instances, students at one grade level can effectively tutor students at a lower grade level; for example, fourth or fifth graders can tutor students in kindergarten or first grade (Biemiller et al., 1998; A. L. Brown & Campione, 1994; Kermani & Moallem, 1997). Such a practice is consistent with Vygotsky's belief that older and more competent individuals are invaluable in promoting the cognitive development of younger children. Furthermore, low-ability students who tutor younger children on skills they themselves have mastered have the opportunity to regulate others' learning and, in the process, can internalize those regulation strategies for their own use (Biemiller et al., 1998).

COMMUNITY OF LEARNERS

One important prerequisite for interactive instructional methods is a *sense of community*—a sense that teacher and students have shared goals, respect and support one another' s efforts, and believe that everyone makes an important contribution to classroom learning (Emmer, Evertson, Clements, & Worsham, 1994; Hom & Battistich, 1995; Kim, Solomon, & Roberts, 1995; Lickona, 1991). One way to create this sense of community is to transform the classroom into a **community of learners** in which teacher and students actively and cooperatively work to help one another learn (A. L. Brown & Campione, 1994, 1996; A. L. Brown et al., 1993; Campione et al., 1995; Prawat, 1992; Rogoff, 1994). A classroom that operates as a community of learners is likely to have certain characteristics:

- All students are active participants in classroom activities.
- Discussion and collaboration among two or more students are common occurrences and play a key role in learning.
- Diversity in students' interests and rates of progress is expected and respected.
- Students and teacher coordinate their efforts at helping one another learn; no one has exclusive responsibility for teaching others.
- Everyone is a potential resource for the others; different individuals are likely to serve as resources on different occasions, depending on the topics and tasks at hand.
- The teacher provides some guidance and direction for classroom activities, but students may also contribute to such guidance and direction.
- Constructive questioning and critique of one another's work is commonplace.
- The process of learning is emphasized as much as, and sometimes more than, the finished product.
  (A. L. Brown & Campione, 1994, 1996; Campione et al., 1995; Rogoff, 1994; Rogoff, Matusov, & White, 1996)

Brown and Campione (1994) have described one simple example of how a community of learners might be structured. In this situation, students were divided into five groups to study five different subtopics falling within a general theme; for instance, subtopics for the theme *changing populations* were *extinct, endangered, artificial, assisted,* and *urbanized.* Each group conducted research and prepared teaching materials related to its subtopic; in essence, they became the class experts on that subtopic. The class then reassembled into five new groups that included at least one representative from each of the previous groups; within these groups, the students taught one another the things they had learned.

Communities of learners typically incorporate a variety of interactive instructional strategies, including class discussions, cooperative learning, peer tutoring, and perhaps reciprocal teaching (A. L. Brown & Campione, 1996). The *changing populations* unit just described reflects the *jigsaw* technique described earlier in the section on cooperative learning. In addition, older students or subject matter experts may occasionally sit in on group discussions and gently guide the students as they prepare their teaching materials—for example, asking "Remember that the reader hasn't read about echo location; is this enough to make it clear?" (A. L. Brown & Campione, 1996).

Researchers have not yet systematically compared the academic achievement of communities of learners with the achievement of more traditional classes, but case studies indicate that classes structured as communities of learners have several positive effects. These classes appear to promote higher-level thinking processes, including metacognitive reflections (e.g., "They [other students] can't understand X without Y"), for extended periods of time (A. L. Brown & Campione, 1994, 1996). They are also highly motivating for students; for instance, students often insist on going to school even when they are ill, and they are disappointed when summer vacation begins (Rogoff, 1994). Communities of learners may be especially useful as a way of encouraging students with diverse backgrounds, cultural perspectives, and specialized talents to make unique and valued contributions to the classroom learning environment (e.g., Garcia, 1994).

At the same time, communities of learners have a couple of potential weaknesses (A. L. Brown & Campione, 1994; Hynd, 1998). For one thing, what students learn will inevitably be limited to the knowledge that they themselves acquire and share with one another. Second, students may occasionally pass on their misconceptions to their classmates. Obviously, then, teachers who structure their classrooms as communities of learners must carefully monitor student interactions to make sure that instructional objectives are being achieved and that students ultimately acquire accurate understandings of the subject matter they are studying.

TECHNOLOGY-BASED DISCUSSIONS

Effective student interactions don't necessarily have to be face to face. Through such mechanisms as electronic mail (e-mail), Web-based chat rooms, and electronic bulletin boards, computer technology enables students to communicate with their peers (either in their own classroom or elsewhere), exchange perspectives, and build on one another's ideas (Fabos & Young, 1999; Hewitt & Scardamalia, 1996; J. Schacter, 2000). Technology also allows subject matter experts to be pulled occasionally into the conversation (A. L. Brown & Campione, 1996; Winn, 2002).

Researchers do not yet have a good handle on the particular benefits that cross-school and cross-cultural discussions might have (Fabos & Young, 1999), but at least one form of within-class electronic "discussion" shows considerable promise. Researchers at the University of Toronto have developed computer software[6] that allows students to communicate regularly using a class-wide database and essentially creates a computer-based community of learners[7] (Hewitt & Scardamalia, 1996, 1998; Lamon et al., 1993). Using the database, students share their questions, ideas, notes, writing products, and graphic constructions. Their classmates (and sometimes a subject matter expert as well) respond regularly, perhaps by giving feedback, building on ideas, offering alternative perspectives, or summarizing what has been learned.

Early observations of this approach have been encouraging: Students are concerned about truly understanding classroom subject matter rather than simply "getting things done," actively try to relate new material to what they already know (i.e., they engage in meaningful learning), and show an increased ability to remember and apply classroom subject matter (e.g., Lamon et al., 1993). They also build regularly on one another's ideas. As an example, consider how two students (identifying themselves by the initials AR and AD) respond on-line to another student's (JA's) question, "How does heat affect solids?"; note that the students use the headings "My theory" and "I need to understand" to structure their discussion:

JA: *My theory:* I think that heat makes solids burn or melt. I think that my prediction is right because I've seen solds [sic] melt and burn.

AR: *My theory:* I think that if a solid comes in contact with heat, it becomes hot. I also think it might change colour. Generally if any solid comes in contact with heat then it becomes hot. I think that the solid would become hot faster if it could conduct energy well. If an object didn't conduct energy well then it would heat up, but take a longer time than an object that conducts energy well. It might change colour because we think that if something is very hot it is white or red and sort of hot it is orange or yellow. There might be some truth to this.

AD: *My theory:* I think that it depends on how much heat there is. I also think that it depends on what sort of solid it is. For instance, the heat that might melt rubber might not melt metal. (This last sentece [sic] might be wrong, I'm just using it as an example.)
I need to understand: What makes wood burn instead of melt?
My theory: I think that it might have something to do with wood being organic, because I can't think of anything that is organic, and would melt. (Hewitt & Scardamalia, 1998, p. 85; format adapted)

Such on-line discussions give students the time they may need to reflect on one another's ideas; hence, they allow that *wait time* I spoke of in Chapter 12. And they may be especially valuable for students who are shy or for other reasons feel uncomfortable communicating with classmates in a more public fashion (Hewitt & Scardamalia, 1998).

[6]An early version of this software was called Computer Supported Intentional Learning Environment, or CSILE (pronounced like the name *Cecil*). A more recent version is known as Knowledge Forum. For more information, visit http://csile.oise.utoronto.ca/.

[7]Hewitt and Scardamalia use the term *Knowledge-Building Community.*

Students find their on-line interactions highly enjoyable and motivating (Lamon et al., 1993). And ultimately, students are more likely to process information effectively, and so understand it better, if they are truly motivated to learn it. Up to now, we've talked about motivation only occasionally and in passing, but in fact motivation is *critical* to the learning process. In the final three chapters of the book, we'll look at the nature of motivation more closely; we'll also consider many teaching strategies that can keep students regularly engaged in, and perhaps even excited about, studying classroom subject matter.

SUMMARY

Human beings are a very social species; accordingly, their learning is often a very social enterprise. Interactions with adults (or interactions with subject matter experts, when learners are themselves adults) and interactions with peers have somewhat different benefits, the former offering new cognitive tools (e.g., concepts to facilitate thinking and understanding), and the latter providing a means through which learners can explain, clarify, elaborate on, and perhaps revise their understandings. Interactions with adults versus with peers have both advantages and disadvantages, and often a combination of the two approaches promotes greater learning than either approach alone.

In an *apprenticeship,* a learner works intensively with an expert to accomplish a complex task that the learner could never do on his or her own. In some situations (*cognitive apprenticeships*), the expert shares not only ways to perform the task but also ways of thinking about the task. The expert guides the learner's behavior by using such strategies as modeling, coaching, and scaffolding. As the learner develops greater proficiency, more challenging and varied tasks are introduced.

In a *class discussion,* students must clarify and organize their ideas and opinions sufficiently to express them to others, and they may acquire a more accurate and complete understanding of a topic after hearing what their classmates have to say. Class discussions are often more effective when they address complex or controversial issues about which students have some prior knowledge, when the classroom atmosphere supports open debate and constructive evaluation of ideas, and when sufficient

structure is imposed to encourage all students to participate.

Reciprocal teaching is an approach to instruction whereby students learn to ask one another certain kinds of questions about textual material they are reading. Reciprocal teaching significantly enhances students' reading comprehension skills, in large part by fostering more effective metacognitive skills (e.g., making predictions, summarizing what has been learned).

In *cooperative learning,* students work in small groups to accomplish specific goals. Successful cooperative learning groups have several key features: Students (1) have clear guidelines for appropriate behavior, (2) must coordinate their efforts and support one another's learning in order to be successful, (3) are individually accountable for what they have learned, and (4) are rewarded for the overall success of their group. Research consistently confirms the effectiveness of cooperative learning activities, although it yields conflicting data about how heterogeneous groups should be in order to maximize learning.

Peer tutoring involves two students at either the same grade level or two different grade levels. Tutors and tutees typically both benefit from tutoring sessions; this is especially true when tutors have a good command of the subject matter and use sound instructional techniques or when tutoring sessions are structured to promote effective instruction.

A *community of learners* is a classroom in which teacher and students actively and cooperatively work to help one another learn; it often incorporates other interactive approaches such as class discussions and cooperative learning. Although the teacher provides some guidance and direction for classroom activities, students assume much of the responsibility for acquiring information about a topic and facilitating one another's learning.

Modern computer technology provides a way for student discussion and collaboration to go be-yond classroom walls. It can also enhance interaction within a single classroom, for instance by providing a common database in which students can share their questions, insights, essays, and stories and by enabling students to build regularly on one another's ideas.

CHAPTER 16

Motivation and Affect

Over the years, I have learned how to do a great many things. For example, I have learned how to teach and write about psychology. I have learned how to find my favorite junk food in the supermarket and my favorite television game show in *TV Guide*. I have learned how to control my tongue and temper in a university committee meeting. I have learned how to mow the lawn, file a tax return, cook lima beans, clean the garage, and pick up after slovenly children.

Yet you don't see me doing all of these things on a regular basis. I engage in some activities (e.g., writing about psychology, eating junk food, and watching television game shows) because I like doing them. I engage in others (e.g., behaving myself at committee meetings, filing tax returns, and mowing the lawn) not because I enjoy them but because they bring me things I *do* enjoy, such as productive relationships with university colleagues, IRS refunds, or a well-kept backyard. But there are some things that I rarely do because they aren't fun and they reap me few if any rewards. For example, you won't find me cooking lima beans (abominable little things), cleaning the garage (the cars don't care one way or the other), or picking up children's messy bedrooms (a never-ending battle). And there are additional things that I've never learned at all because I've seen little point in doing so. Batting averages of professional baseball players, locations for the "petite" sizes in ladies' clothing at Sears, and strategies for walking barefoot on hot coals all fall into this category.

Motivation—an internal state that arouses us to action, pushes us in particular directions, and keeps us engaged in certain activities—is the key ingredient here. Even if we are perfectly capable of learning something (and I am, mind you, quite capable of learning where to find virtually any clothing size at Sears), motivation often determines whether and to what extent we actually learn it, especially if the behaviors and cognitive processes necessary for learning are voluntary and so under our control.[1] Furthermore, once we *have* learned how to do something, motivation is in large part responsible for whether we continue to do it.

We have touched on the importance of motivation in previous chapters—for instance, within the context of reinforcement in Chapter 4, modeling in Chapter 7, conceptual change in Chapter 11, and self-regulated learning in Chapter 13. In the final three chapters of the book, we will look more closely at the nature in motivation. In this chapter, we will begin by considering how motivation influences behavior, cognition, and learning, and we'll see that two fundamentally different kinds of motivation, extrinsic and intrinsic, may have somewhat different effects. We will then explore various theories about basic human needs—those that characterize virtually everyone—and theories about individual differences in motivation. After briefly looking at the contemporary cognitive perspective of motivation (which we'll explore in depth in Chapter 17 and 18), we'll turn our attention to the role of *affect* (emotion) in learning and behavior. Finally, we'll identify several educational implications of chapter content.

As we proceed, keep in mind that *learners are almost always motivated in one way or another.* For example, students in a sixth-grade classroom have a variety of motives (Lee & Anderson, 1991). Some will almost certainly want to learn the subject matter being presented in class. Others may be more interested in getting good grades, outperforming their classmates, pleasing their teacher and parents, or simply completing assignments as quickly and painlessly as possible. In general, teachers should never question *whether* their students are motivated. Instead, they should try to determine *in what ways* their students are motivated.

GENERAL EFFECTS OF MOTIVATION

Motivation appears to affect learning and performance in at least four ways:

- *It increases an individual's energy and activity level* (Maehr & Meyer, 1997; Pintrich et al., 1993; Vernon, 1969). It influences the extent to which an individual is likely to engage in a certain activity intensively and vigorously or half-heartedly and lackadaisically.

- *It directs an individual toward certain goals* (Dweck & Elliott, 1983; Eccles & Wigfield, 1985; Maehr & Meyer, 1997). Motivation affects the choices people make and the consequences they find reinforcing. In Chapter 17 we will identify a variety of goals toward which people may strive.

- *It promotes initiation of certain activities and persistence in those activities* (Eccles & Wigfield, 1985; Maehr & Meyer, 1997; Pintrich et al., 1993; Stipek, 1993). Motivation increases the likelihood that people will begin something on their own initiative, persist in the face of difficulty, and resume a task after a temporary interruption.

---

[1]Classical conditioning is an example of learning in which motivation plays little if any role. As you should recall from Chapter 3, classical conditioning involves the acquisition of an involuntary response as a result of encountering two stimuli at approximately the same time. In such a situation, the learner has control neither of the stimulus pairing nor of the response.

Educators have long recognized that **time on task** is an important factor affecting school learning and achievement (Brophy, 1988; Davis & Thomas, 1989). The more time students spend engaged in a particular learning activity, the more academically successful they will be. Although time on task is partly determined by how teachers plan and schedule the classroom curriculum—that is, by how much time they devote to different topics and activities—it is also determined to some extent by students' motivation to study and persist with those topics both in and outside of school.

- *It affects the learning strategies and cognitive processes an individual brings to bear on a task* (Dweck & Elliott, 1983; Eccles & Wigfield, 1985). Time on task is, in and of itself, insufficient for successful learning. As contemporary cognitive theories tell us, certain mental processes—paying attention, learning meaningfully, elaborating, monitoring comprehension, identifying inconsistencies between new information and prior knowledge, and so on—are essential for effective learning and long-term retention of new information and skills. In other words, learners must be *thinking about* what they are seeing, hearing, and doing. Such **cognitive engagement** is one of the benefits of a high level of motivation (Lee & Anderson, 1993; Paris & Paris, 2001; Pintrich et al., 1993; Tobin, 1986).

Yet not all forms of motivation have exactly the same effect on human learning and performance. In fact, extrinsic motivation and intrinsic motivation yield somewhat different results, as we shall see now.

EXTRINSIC VERSUS INTRINSIC MOTIVATION

At the beginning of the chapter, I mentioned that I engage in some activities because they bring about desirable consequences (i.e., they are extrinsically reinforced), whereas I engage in others simply because they are enjoyable. Just as operant conditioning theorists distinguish between extrinsic and intrinsic reinforcement, motivation theorists distinguish between extrinsic and intrinsic motivation.

Extrinsic motivation exists when the source of motivation lies outside of the individual and the task being performed. For example, I file an income tax return every year partly because I usually get a refund when I do so and partly because I will be fined (i.e., punished) if I *don't* file. For many years, I attended university committee meetings because university service was part of my job description and I was quite dependent on my monthly paycheck (in my current position, attending committee meetings is, thank goodness, rarely required). I give my house a thorough cleaning when preparing to host a party, because I would hate for my friends to discover I'm a slob.

In contrast, **intrinsic motivation** exists when the source of motivation lies within the individual and task: The individual finds the task enjoyable or worthwhile in and of itself. For example, I frequently read books and articles about human learning and motivation because they continue to shed new light on topics that are, to me, utterly fascinating. I watch television game shows because I enjoy playing along as a home viewer. I eat junk food because it tastes good (an unfortunate consequence is that I have no need for the petite sizes at Sears).

Extrinsic motivation can certainly promote successful learning and productive behavior, as evidenced by the effectiveness of behavior modification programs (see Chapter 5). Extrinsic reinforcement for engaging in a particular activity increases an individual's time on task, and performance is likely to improve as a result (Emmer & Evertson, 1981). Extrinsic motivation in the classroom has its drawbacks, however: Extrinsically motivated students may exert only the minimal behavioral and cognitive effort they need to execute a task successfully (occasionally this may mean copying someone else's work), and they may stop an activity as soon as reinforcement ceases (Flink, Boggiano, Main, Barrett, & Katz, 1992; Lee, 1991).

Intrinsic motivation has numerous advantages over extrinsic motivation. For any particular task, intrinsically motivated learners are more likely to

- Pursue the task on their own initiative, without having to be prodded or cajoled.
- Be cognitively engaged in the task (e.g., by keeping attention focused on it).
- Undertake more challenging aspects of the task.
- Learn information in a meaningful rather than rote fashion.
- Undergo conceptual change when such change is warranted.
- Show creativity in performance.
- Persist in the face of failure.
- Experience pleasure, sometimes even exhilaration, in what they are doing.
- Regularly evaluate their own progress, often using their own criteria.
- Seek out additional opportunities to pursue the task.
- Achieve at high levels.
  (Brophy, 1986; Csikszentmihalyi, 1990, 1996; Csikszentmihalyi & Nakamura, 1989; Flink et al., 1992; Gottfried, 1990; Harter, 1981a; Hennessey, 1995; Hennessey & Amabile, 1987; Lee & Anderson, 1993; Maehr, 1984; Pintrich et al., 1993; Russ, 1993; Spaulding, 1992; Stipek, 1993)

Csikszentmihalyi (1990, 1996; Csikszentmihalyi & Nakamura, 1989) has used the term **flow** to describe an intense form of intrinsic motivation, characterizing it as a state of complete absorption, focus, and concentration in a challenging activity, to the point that the individual loses track of time and completely ignores other tasks.

Obviously, intrinsic motivation is the optimal state of affairs in the classroom. Unfortunately, although many children first enter school with a high degree of intrinsic motivation to learn classroom subject matter, they gradually lose this motivation as they move through the grade levels (Csikszentmihalyi & Nakamura, 1989; Eccles & Midgley, 1989; Harter, 1992). At the end of the chapter, we will identify several ways in which teachers can help students become more intrinsically motivated to learn classroom material. And in Chapter 17, we will discover the cognitive factors that are likely to influence students' intrinsic motivation to achieve academic success.

At the same time, we should not assume that the presence of extrinsic versus intrinsic motivation must be an either–or situation. On many occasions, learners may be *both* extrinsically and intrinsically motivated (Bronson, 2000; Cognition and Technology Group at Vanderbilt, 1996; Hidi & Harackiewicz, 2000). Furthermore, even a single motive may have both extrinsic and intrinsic aspects; for instance, students may strive for good grades not only for the external rewards that such grades bring but also for verification that they have successfully mastered the subject matter (Hynd, 2003). And as we will discover in our disussion of *internalized motivation* in Chapter 17, some motives are midway along the extrinsic–intrinsic continuum.

BASIC HUMAN NEEDS

Over the years, theorists have offered a variety of perspectives about basic human needs—those needs that are more or less universal across the species. Here we focus on early perspectives (drive theory, need for arousal, and Maslow's hierarchy of needs) and more recent ones (needs for competence, self-worth, and relatedness) that are especially relevant to instructional settings.

Drive Theory

Drive theory (Freud, 1915/1949; Hull, 1943, 1951, 1952; Woodworth, 1918) is based on the notion that people and other animals (*organisms*) try to maintain physiological homeostasis; in other words, they try to keep their bodies at an optimal state of functioning. A **drive** is an internal state of need within an organism: Something necessary for optimal functioning (e.g., food, water, warmth, or rest) is missing. When a drive exists, the organism behaves in ways that reduce the need and bring the body back into balance. For example, a hungry person eats, a thirsty person drinks, a cold person seeks out a source of heat, and a tired person goes to bed. If a response that reduces the need is not immediately possible, the organism shows a general increase in activity—activity that may eventually lead to an encounter with a need-reducing stimulus.

From the perspective of drive theory, a reinforcer is effective to the extent that it reduces a need state, thereby simultaneously reducing drive. For example, a drink of water is reinforcing only if an organism is thirsty, and a source of heat is reinforcing only if an organism is cold. Behaviors that reduce a need state—behaviors that are reinforced—are likely to be repeated when the same need emerges at some later point in time.

Probably the most widely cited version of drive theory is that of Clark Hull (1943, 1951, 1952), a perspective I described briefly in Chapter 3. In 1943, Hull proposed that drive is based on physiological needs such as hunger and thirst. All of these needs contribute to the general drive state of the organism; drive itself is not specific to a particular need. Hull further proposed that the strength (or intensity) of a behavior is a function of both *habit strength* (i.e., the degree to which associations between a particular stimulus and response have been learned) and drive:

$$\textit{Strength of behavior} \; = \; \textit{Habit} \times \textit{Drive}$$

In such a multiplicative relationship, both habit (prior learning) and drive must be present; if either is zero, the strength of the behavior—the likelihood that it will occur—is also zero.

Hull based his notion of *habit times drive* on experiments conducted by two of his students (Perin, 1942; Williams, 1938). In these experiments, rats were placed in Skinner boxes and trained to press a bar for a food reinforcer. Different groups of rats received varying amounts of training, with a greater number of reinforced responses presumably leading to greater habit strength. Later, after going without food for either 3 hours (low drive) or 22 hours (high drive), the rats were once again placed in Skinner boxes, and their frequency of bar pressing was recorded under nonreinforcement (extinction) conditions. The hungrier rats pressed the bar many more times than the less hungry rats; similarly, rats who had received more training pressed the bar more often than those who had undergone little training. Rats with little drive (3 hours of food deprivation) and low habit strength (5 training trials) pressed the bar, on average, only once.

In 1951, Hull revised his thinking in two significant ways. First, he observed that some behaviors serve no apparent biological purpose. He therefore proposed that some drives are

acquired drives: They develop when previously neutral stimuli are associating with drive-reducing stimuli such as food. (To repeat the example I presented in Chapter 3, an individual might become "driven" by a need for approval if approval has previously been associated with candy.) Thus, reinforcement became strictly a function of drive reduction rather than a result of the reduction of specific physiological needs.

In addition, Hull took into account research by Crespi (1942) and others indicating that reinforcers may affect performance rather than learning. (We encountered Crespi's experiment in our discussion of reinforcement in Chapter 4. To refresh your memory, rats running down a runway for food began to run faster when the amount of reinforcement was increased; they began to run more slowly when the amount of reinforcement was decreased.) Accordingly, Hull introduced the concept of *incentive* into his theory, acknowledging that behaviors are influenced by the characteristics of a goal object—for example, by the amount of food at the end of a runway. Incentive became a third essential ingredient for a behavior to occur, as follows:

$$Strength\ of\ behavior\ =\ Habit\ \times\ Drive\ \times\ Incentive$$

When any of these three factors—habit strength, drive, or incentive—is absent, the behavior is not exhibited.

Other theorists expanded on Hull's notion that the characteristics of goal objects (incentives) are motivating forces in behavior (Mowrer, 1960; Overmier & Lawry, 1979; Spence, 1956). From their perspective, **incentive motivation** serves as a mediator (M) between stimuli and responses, affecting which stimuli are responded to and which are not. Symbolically, we could describe the relationship this way:

$$S \rightarrow M_{incentive} \rightarrow R$$

For example, I find a bag of Cheetos quite enticing after several hours of food-free book writing (thus leading to a reach-in-and-grab-a-handful response); however, the same bag provokes no response whatsoever right after a Thanksgiving dinner, when I have stuffed myself with turkey, mashed potatoes, and pumpkin pie.

Incentives undoubtedly play a role in human motivation. Just as Crespi's rats ran faster when they knew that mass quantities of food lay waiting at the end of the runway, so, too, do we humans apparently work harder when incentives are more attractive (Klinger, 1975, 1977). When our progress toward particular goals is temporarily stymied, we often intensify our efforts (Klinger, 1975). And when our progress is permanently blocked, we are likely to respond with immature behavior or aggression (Barker, Dembo, & Lewin, 1941; Dollard, Doob, Miller, Mowrer, & Sears, 1939; Hinton, 1968; Johnson, 1972).

Incentives remain in vogue as a probable source of motivation (see the discussion of social cognitive theory in Chapter 7), and behaviorists acknowledge that different objects and events may be more or less reinforcing depending on whether an organism has been deprived of them for any significant time period (McGill, 1999; Michael, 1993, 2000). But theorists have largely left drive reduction theory by the wayside (Bolles, 1975; Graham & Weiner, 1996). For one thing, learning sometimes occurs in the absence of any apparent drive reduction (Sheffield & Roby, 1950; Sheffield, Roby, & Campbell, 1954; Sheffield, Wulff, & Backer, 1951). For example, male rats will make responses that allow them to mount receptive female rats, even though they are pulled away from the females before they can consummate their affectionate relationship and reduce their sexual drive (Sheffield et al., 1951). Second, a great deal of human behavior seems to be aimed at accomplishing long-term goals rather than satisfying short-term needs (Pintrich &

Schunk, 2002). Third, organisms sometimes behave in ways that actually *increase* their drive states (Olds & Milner, 1954; Rachlin, 1991; Sheffield, 1966a, 1966b). For example, when rats have electrodes implanted in particular areas of their brains (called "pleasure centers"), they eagerly press a bar to obtain electrical stimulation of those areas, and they continue in their bar pressing until they're completely exhausted (Olds & Milner, 1954). In much the same way, we humans voluntarily increase our drive states by going to scary movies, reading suspense novels, and riding roller coasters; some of us are even **sensation seekers**, putting ourselves in risky or dangerous situations on a regular basis for the physiological thrills that such situations yield (Zuckerman, 1994). Perhaps such sensation seeking is an extreme form of a more basic need, a need for arousal.

Arousal

Psychologists use the term **arousal** to refer to the level of internal energy an organism is currently experiencing. Organisms experiencing low levels of arousal are relaxed, perhaps even asleep. Organisms experiencing high levels of arousal are highly energized, perhaps to the point of being excessively anxious. Some research indicates that people have a basic need for stimulation; in other words they have a **need for arousal**.[2]

As an example, let's consider a classic study by Heron (1957). Male college students were given $20 a day (quite an incentive in the 1950s) to stay as long as they were willing to do so in a boring environment—and I mean a *really* boring environment. Aside from occasional brief breaks for eating and other biological necessities, the students spent the time lying on a bed in a small cubicle in which the only sound was the continuous hum of an air conditioner. They wore plastic visors that allowed them to see only diffused, unpatterned light (making them functionally blind) and thick gloves and cardboard sleeves that prevented them from feeling different shapes and textures (minimizing the information they could gain from touching things). Naturally, many students began by catching up on their sleep. Students spent their first few waking hours thinking about college coursework, personal issues, past experiences, and so on. Eventually, they were apt to run out of things to think about and simply let their minds wander aimlessly. As time went on, cognitive functioning deteriorated: The students had trouble concentrating, reported distorted perceptual processes (e.g., the room seemed to move, and objects appeared to change size and shape), and generally seemed quite disoriented. Some began to hallucinate, perhaps seeing a row of cartoon-like men with open mouths or a line of marching squirrels with bags over their shoulders, or perhaps hearing a music box playing or a church choir singing. Some also reported feelings of touch or movement: "One had a feeling of being hit in the arm by pellets fired from a miniature rocket ship he saw" (p. 54). More generally, people seem to have exceptional difficulty functioning under conditions of *sensory deprivation* for any length of time (Solomon et al., 1961).

Some theorists have suggested that not only do people have a basic need for stimulation but they also strive for a certain *optimal level* of arousal (e.g., Berlyne, 1960). Too little stimulation is unpleasant, but so is too much. For example, you may enjoy watching a television game show or listening to music, but you would probably rather not have three television sets, five compact disk

---

[2]Occasionally one of my students assumes that this term refers to sexual activity. On the contrary, *need for arousal* refers to a basic need for stimulation of *any* kind.

players, and a live rock band all blasting in your living room at once. Different people have different optimal levels: Some are sensation seekers whereas others prefer a quieter existence. I, for one, like things a bit on a dull side. Although I certainly enjoy a suspenseful mystery novel on occasion, you'll never catch me riding a roller coaster or bungee jumping.

I've seen very little reference to need for arousal in the motivation literature in recent years, but this simple concept does seem to explain some of the things we see in classrooms. For instance, it explains why students create their own excitement (perhaps passing notes or playing practical jokes on one another) when their teacher drones on at length about a dry topic. (In a sociology class I took as a first-year college student, the girl who sat next to me kept a running tally of how many times the professor cleared his throat. This simple activity kept us both amused, which was fortunate, because the professor certainly did not.) Furthermore, a more cognitive version of the same idea—the *need for cognition*—has recently appeared on the scene (Cacioppo, Petty, Feinstein, & Jarvis, 1996). We'll return to the latter concept in our discussion of *dispositions* in Chapter 17.

Maslow's Hierarchy of Needs

Another early perspective of motivation was that of Abraham Maslow (1959, 1973a, 1973b, 1987). Maslow's theory is a central feature of **humanism**, a movement in psychology that gained prominence in the 1960s and 1970s. Humanism has its roots in counseling psychology and focuses its attention on how individuals acquire emotions, attitudes, values, and interpersonal skills. Humanist perspectives tend to be grounded more in philosophy than in research, but they provide useful insights into human motivation nevertheless.

In an attempt to pull together his informal observations of human behavior, Maslow proposed that people have five different sets of needs:

1. **Physiological needs.** People are motivated to satisfy needs related to their immediate physical survival—needs for food, water, oxygen, warmth, exercise, rest, sex, and so on. For example, if you've been sitting still in class for a long time, you may find yourself getting restless and fidgety, and if you're hungry, you may think more about your growling stomach than about a professor's lecture. Maslow's physiological needs are essentially the same as those of Hull's early drive theory.

2. **Safety needs.** People have a need to feel safe and secure in their environment. Although they may enjoy an occasional surprise, generally speaking they prefer structure and order in their lives. For example, most students like to know what things are expected of them and prefer classroom routines that are somewhat predictable.

3. **Love and belongingness needs.** People seek affectionate relationships with others and like to feel that they "belong" and are accepted as part of a group. For example, a fourth grader may place great importance on having a best friend. And many young adolescents take great pains to fit in with the cool crowd—for example, by wearing a certain hairstyle or buying clothes with a certain brand name conspicuously displayed on them.

4. **Esteem needs.** People need to feel good about themselves (**need for self-esteem**) and to believe that others also feel positively about them (**need for esteem from others**). To develop positive self-esteem, individuals strive for achievement and mastery of their environment. To attain the esteem and respect of others, they behave in ways that gain them

recognition, appreciation, and prestige. For example, a second grader can partially satisfy the need for self-esteem by reading a book "all by myself" or by achieving a special merit badge in Cub Scouts or Campfire Girls. A high school student may try to satisfy the need for esteem from others by running for student council treasurer or becoming a star athlete. When their esteem needs are satisfied, people are self-confident and have a sense of self-worth; when these needs go unmet, people feel weak and inferior.

5. **Need for self-actualization.** People have a need to **self-actualize**—to develop and become all they are capable of becoming (also see Rogers, 1951, 1961). Individuals striving toward self-actualization seek out new activities as a way of expanding their horizons and want to learn simply for the sake of learning. For example, people seeking self-actualization might be driven by their own curiosity to learn everything they can about a particular topic, or they might pursue an active interest in ballet both as a means of developing muscle tone and as an outlet for creative self-expression.

Maslow proposed that the five sets of needs form a hierarchy, as illustrated in Figure 16–1. When two or more of these needs are unmet, people tend to satisfy them in a particular sequence. They begin with the lowest needs in the hierarchy, satisfying physiological needs first, safety needs next, and so on. They attempt to fulfill higher needs only when lower needs have been at least partially met.

To illustrate Maslow's hierarchy, a boy with a need for exercise (a physiological need) may become excessively restless in class even though he is scolded by his teacher for his hyperactivity (thereby *not* satisfying his need for esteem from others). A girl with an unfulfilled need for love and belonging may choose not to enroll in intermediate algebra—a class that would satisfy her desire to learn more math—if the peers whose friendships she most values tell her the class is only for nerds and various other uncool individuals. I once met a boy living in a Philadelphia ghetto who had a strong interest in learning yet often stayed home from school to avoid the violent gangs that hung out on the local street corner. This boy's need for safety took precedence over any higher needs that he might have had.

According to Maslow, the first four needs on the hierarchy—physiological, safety, love and belonging, and esteem needs—result from things that a person *lacks*; hence, Maslow called them **deficiency needs.** Deficiency needs can be met only by external sources—by people or

Figure 16–1

Maslow's hierarchy of needs.

events in one's environment. Furthermore, once these needs are fulfilled, there is no reason to satisfy them further. In contrast, self-actualization is a **growth need:** Rather than addressing a deficiency in a person's life, it serves to enhance the person's growth and development and thus is rarely satisfied completely. Self-actualizing activities tend to be intrinsically motivated: People engage in them because doing so gives them pleasure and satisfies their desire to know and grow.

Needs that are satisfied most of the time have little effect on behavior. For example, many people in our society routinely satisfy their physiological and safety needs. The needs for love and esteem are more likely to go unfulfilled; hence, people may direct much of their effort toward developing self-respect and gaining the acceptance and respect of others. But people are likely to strive for self-actualization—a need that is almost never completely satisfied—only when all four deficiency needs are at least partially met.

According to Maslow, self-actualized individuals have a number of noteworthy characteristics. For example, they are independent, spontaneous, creative, and sympathetic to the plights of others. They perceive themselves, other people, and the world in general in an objective, realistic light, and they are quite comfortable with who they are. They typically have a mission in life—an important problem that they are concerned about solving. Maslow suggested that few people—probably less than 1% of the population—become fully self-actualized, and then only in the later years of life.

Despite its intuitive appeal, Maslow's hierarchy has been criticized on several counts. For one thing, little hard evidence exists to substantiate the hierarchical nature of human motivation. Maslow derived his theory from his informal, subjective observations of presumably "self-actualized" personal friends and from published descriptions of such historical figures as Thomas Jefferson and Abraham Lincoln; it would be almost impossible for other investigators to confirm that these individuals had the characteristics Maslow identified. Furthermore, self-actualization is so rare that the hierarchy may not provide an accurate description of people in general (Petri, 1991). Finally, people's various motives are probably too diverse to be boiled down into such a short list of basic needs (Pintrich & Schunk, 2002). (You'll get a better sense of this diversity of motives in Chapters 17 and 18.)

At the same time, aspects of Maslow's theory clearly have some merit. It makes sense that people will worry about their physiological well-being and personal safety before they try to address more social needs. And Maslow's notions of *esteem needs* and *love and belonging needs* are clearly reflected in contemporary theories about self-worth and relatedness—topics we turn to next.

Competence and Self-Worth

Maslow has hardly been the only one to suggest that people have a need for esteem. In 1959, Robert White proposed that people (and other animals as well) have a basic need for **competence**—a belief that they can deal effectively with their environment. More recently, other theorists have echoed this belief, asserting that the need for competence is a fundamental human need (e.g., Ryan & Deci, 2000).

To achieve a sense of competence, young children spend a great deal of time engaged in exploring and attempting to master the world. As an illustration, let's look once again at an example I presented in Chapter 8, in which Jean Piaget's son Laurent tried to reach a piece of bread that was beyond his reach:

> Laurent is seated before a table and I place a bread crust in front of him, out of reach. Also, to the right of the child I place a stick about 25 cm. long. At first Laurent tries to grasp the bread without paying attention to the instrument, and then he gives up. I then put the stick between him and the bread. . . . Laurent again looks at the bread, without moving, looks very briefly at the stick, then suddenly grasps it and directs it toward the bread. But he grasped it toward the middle and not at one of its ends so that it is too short to attain the objective. Laurent then puts it down and resumes stretching out his hand toward the bread. Then, without spending much time on this movement, he takes up the stick again, this time at one of its ends . . . and draws the bread to him. (Piaget, 1952, p. 335)

Laurent was only 16 months old at the time, yet he clearly had an intrinsic desire to master at least one aspect of his environment. According to White, the need for competence has biological significance and probably evolved with our species: It pushes people to develop ways of dealing more effectively with environmental conditions and thus increases their chances of survival.

More recently, Martin Covington (1992) has proposed that *protecting* one's sense of competence—something he calls **self-worth**—is one of people's highest priorities. Obviously, achieving success on a regular basis is one way of maintaining, perhaps even enhancing, this self-worth. But consistent success isn't always possible, especially when people face challenging tasks. In such situations, an alternative way to maintain self-worth is to *avoid failure*, because failure gives the impression of low ability (Covington, 1992; Covington & Müeller, 2001; Urdan & Midgley, 2001). Failure avoidance manifests itself in a variety of ways; for instance, people may refuse to engage in an activity, devalue its importance for themselves, set very low expectations for themselves, or refuse to relinquish their prior beliefs in the face of considerable contradictory evidence[3] (Covington, 1992; Harter, 1990; Martin, Marsh, & Debus, 2001; Sherman & Cohen, 2002).

In some situations, however, people can't avoid tasks at which they expect to do poorly, and so they use alternative strategies to protect their self-worth. Sometimes they make excuses that seemingly justify their poor performance (Covington, 1992; Urdan & Midgley, 2001). Yet they may also do things that actually *undermine* their chances of success—a phenomenon known as **self-handicapping.** Self-handicapping takes a variety of forms, including these:

- *Setting unattainably high goals.* Working toward goals that even the most able individuals couldn't achieve
- *Taking on too much.* Taking on so many responsibilities that a person could not possibly accomplish them all successfully
- *Procrastinating.* Putting a task off until success is virtually impossible
- *Reducing effort.* Putting forth an obviously insufficient amount of effort to succeed
- *Cheating in class.* Presenting others' work as one's own
- *Using alcohol or drugs.* Taking substances that will inevitably reduce performance (Anderman, Griesinger, & Westerfield, 1998; Covington, 1992; D. Y. Ford, 1996; Jones & Berglas, 1978; Riggs, 1992; Urdan & Midgley, 2001; Urdan, Midgley, & Anderman, 1998)

It might seem paradoxical that people who want to be successful would engage in such behaviors. But if people believe they are unlikely to succeed at a particular task, they increase their chances

---

[3]Hence, the need to protect one's self-worth may be one reason why people don't undergo *conceptual change*.

of *justifying* their lack of success (and therefore they maintain self-worth) by acknowledging that, under the circumstances, success wasn't very likely to begin with (Covington, 1992; Jones & Berglas, 1978; Riggs, 1992). Curiously, some people are more likely to perform at their best, and less likely to display self-handicapping behaviors, when their chances of success are slim; in such situations, failure does not indicate low ability and so does not threaten their sense of self-worth (Covington, 1992).

To date, most research on self-worth theory and self-handicapping has focused on academic tasks and accomplishments. Some theorists suggest, however, that academic achievement isn't always the most important thing affecting people's sense of self-worth; for many people, such factors as social success or physical appearance may be more influential (Eccles et al., 1998). Also troubling is the finding that people sometimes seem more comfortable maintaining *consistent* self-perceptions, even if those self-perceptions are negative ones (Hay, Ashman, van Kraayenoord, & Stewart, 1999; Osborne & Simmons, 2002; Steele, 1997).[4] Yet in most instances, positive self-perceptions do appear to be a high priority; we'll return to this point in Chapter 18.

Relatedness

To some extent, we are all social creatures: We live, work, and play with our fellow human beings. Some theorists have proposed that people of all ages have a fundamental need to feel socially connected and to secure the love and respect of others; in other words, people have a **need for relatedness** (Connell, 1990; Connell & Wellborn, 1991; Ryan & Deci, 2000). As is true for the need for competence, the need for relatedness may be important from an evolutionary standpoint, in that people who live in cohesive, cooperative social groups are more likely to survive than people who go it alone (Wright, 1994).

In the classroom, students' need for relatedness may manifest itself in a wide variety of behaviors. Many children and adolescents place high priority on interacting with friends, often at the expense of getting their schoolwork done (Dowson & McInerney, 2001; Doyle, 1986a; Wigfield, Eccles, Mac Iver, Reuman, & Midgley, 1991). They may also be concerned about projecting a favorable public image—that is, by looking smart, popular, athletic, or "cool" to others (Juvonen, 2000). And some may exhibit their need for relatedness by showing concern for other people's welfare or helping peers who are struggling with classroom assignments (M. E. Ford, 1996; Dowson & McInerney, 2001). The need for relatedness seems to be especially high in the middle school years (Brown, Eicher, & Petrie, 1986; Juvonen, 2000; Ryan & Patrick, 2001). Young adolescents tend to be overly concerned about what others think, prefer to hang out in tight-knit groups, and are especially susceptible to peer influence.

In Chapter 17, the need for relatedness will show up in our discussions of *performance goals* and *social goals*. In Chapter 18, it will pop up again in our discussion of *image management*. Yet although the need for relatedness may, to some extent, be a universal phenomenon, some children and adolescents seem to have a greater need for interpersonal relationships than others (Kupersmidt, Buchele, Voegler, & Sedikides, 1996). In the next section, we look at these and other individual differences in motivation.

---

[4]In different contexts, this phenomenon has been called *self-verification* or *stereotype threat*.

INDIVIDUAL DIFFERENCES IN MOTIVATION

Up to this point, we have been talking about forms of motivation that might characterize all of us at one time or another. But some theorists suggest that motivation takes the form of relatively enduring personality characteristics that people have to a greater or lesser extent. For example, I mentioned earlier that some people tend to be *sensation seekers*, whereas others prefer not to live so much "on the edge."

Theories that propose fairly stable individual differences in motivation are known as **trait theories** of motivation. Historically, researchers have focused considerable attention on individual differences in the needs for affiliation, approval, and achievement. We'll look at these three individual difference variables here. As we pursue the more cognitive aspects of motivation in Chapters 17 and 18, we'll find additional examples of individual differences in motivation, including *personal interests*, *dispositions*, and *learned helplessness*.

Need for Affiliation

The **need for affiliation** is the degree to which a person wants and needs friendly relationships with others (Boyatzis, 1973; Connell & Wellborn, 1991; M. E. Ford & Nichols, 1991; Hill, 1987; McClelland, 1984). For example, as high school students, my oldest two children couldn't stand the thought of being home "alone" (i.e., with their parents) on a Friday or Saturday night and so always found something to do with their friends. When they *were* home on a weeknight, they spent long hours talking to friends on the telephone, to the point where schoolwork sometimes didn't get done. In contrast, my youngest child, Jeff, has always been able to work or play alone quite happily for hours at a time.

People with a high need for affiliation have a number of characteristics in common. For example, they tend to become nervous when other individuals observe their performance (Boyatzis, 1973). They spend considerable time communicating with others, and their attitudes and opinions are easily influenced by those around them (Boyatzis, 1973). They are more interested in interpersonal relationships than in task accomplishment; hence, when choosing a work partner, they are apt to select an incompetent friend over a competent person they don't particularly care for (Boyatzis, 1973; French, 1956; Vernon, 1969). Children with a high need for affiliation tend to have lower grade point averages than their equal-ability peers (Ringness, 1967), and they earn better classroom grades when they have warm, nurturing teachers (McKeachie, 1961; McKeachie, Lin, Milholland, & Isaacson, 1966).

Need for Approval

In addition to having a high need for affiliation, some people have a strong desire to "look good" to others; in other words, they have a high **need for approval** (Boyatzis, 1973; Crowne & Marlowe, 1964; Urdan & Maehr, 1995). For example, one student may continually seek teacher recognition for even the smallest accomplishments in the classroom. Another may do everything possible to appear cool in front of peers.

Many elementary school students have a strong desire to attain the approval of their teacher; at the secondary level, students are more likely to seek the approval of peers (Juvonen & Weiner, 1993; Urdan & Maehr, 1995). Students with a high need for approval are often those with low self-esteem (Crowne & Marlowe, 1964). They may go out of their way to behave in ways they think will please others, sometimes compromising any standards that they themselves may have regarding appropriate behavior (Berndt & Keefe, 1996; Crowne & Marlowe, 1964). But such efforts are often counterproductive: Perhaps because they are trying *too* hard to be liked, students with a high need for approval tend to be relatively unpopular with peers (Boyatzis, 1973; Crowne & Marlowe, 1964).

Need for Achievement

The **need for achievement,** sometimes called **achievement motivation,** is the need for excellence for its own sake, without regard for any external rewards that one's accomplishments might bring (Atkinson, 1957, 1964; Atkinson & Feather, 1966; McClelland, Atkinson, Clark, & Lowell, 1953; Vernon, 1969; Veroff, McClelland, & Ruhland, 1975). For example, a person with a high need for achievement might work diligently to maintain a 4.0 grade point average, practice long hours to become a professional basketball player, or play Monopoly with a vengeance.

People with a high need for achievement are realistic about the tasks they can accomplish, and they persist at tasks that are challenging yet achievable (Vernon, 1969; Veroff et al., 1975). They rarely rest on their laurels; instead, they set increasingly high standards for excellence as their current standards are met (Veroff et al., 1975). And they are willing and able to delay gratification: They put off small, immediate rewards for the larger rewards that their long-term efforts are likely to bring (French, 1955; Vernon, 1969; Veroff et al., 1975).

An early and widely cited theory of achievement motivation is that of John Atkinson and his associates (Atkinson, 1957, 1964; Atkinson & Birch, 1978; Atkinson & Feather, 1966; Atkinson & Raynor, 1978). These theorists proposed that the tendency to strive for achievement is a function of two related needs: the **motive for success,** or M_s (the desire to do well and accomplish goals), and the **motive to avoid failure,** or M_{af} (anxiety about failing to accomplish goals and reluctance to engage in activities that may lead to failure). For many people, one of these needs is stronger than the other, and achievement behavior depends on which need predominates.

Individuals with a stronger motive for success tend to seek and tackle moderately difficult tasks—those that are challenging yet can feasibly be accomplished. Because these individuals have a relatively low motive to avoid failure, they don't worry about the mistakes they may make or the stumbling blocks they may encounter. Furthermore, they recognize that success on difficult tasks is more noteworthy than success on easy tasks.

In contrast, individuals with a stronger motive to avoid failure typically forego such risks in favor of a sure thing. They steer clear of the moderately difficult tasks that their high M_s counterparts select. Instead, they often choose tasks they can almost certainly accomplish. Even though their success on such tasks may be meaningless, they are nevertheless able to avoid the failure they fear. Curiously, though, high M_{af} individuals sometimes choose extremely difficult tasks, those at which they cannot possibly succeed. When they fail at such tasks, they have a built-in explanation— after all, the task was impossible—and so the failure is easily rationalized. This tendency to choose very difficult tasks should remind you of the self-handicapping phenomenon I described earlier.

Atkinson and Litwin (1960) demonstrated the hypothesized effects of M_s and M_{af} in a concrete fashion. Their experiment involved a ring toss game: throwing rings to land around an upright peg. Male undergraduate students, some of whom had been identified as having a higher M_s and others as having a higher M_{af}, were told that they could stand wherever they wished, within a 15-foot range, as they attempted to throw 10 rings, one at a time, around the peg. The great majority of the high M_s students opted to stand about 8 to 12 feet away from the peg (thus taking on a moderate challenge). Of the high M_{af} students, only half stood in the 8- to 12-foot range; the other half stood either

Table 16–1

Characteristics of learners with high versus low needs to approach success and avoid failure (based on Covington & Omelich, 1991).

		Motive for Success (M$_s$)	
		High	Low
Motive to Avoid Failure (M$_{af}$)	High	*Overstrivers* are exceptionally hard working (perhaps too much so), in part to prevent failure. They take failures very hard.	*Failure avoiders* engage in self-handicapping behaviors to minimize the likelihood that failures will reflect low ability.
	Low	*Optimists* are self-confident about their ability to learn. They engage in behaviors and cognitive processes that maximize learning.	*Failure accepters* become increasingly convinced of their low ability as their excuses for failure become decreasingly plausible. They apply minimal effort on learning tasks.

within 7 feet of the peg (thus making the task an easy one) or at least 13 feet away from it (thus making it extremely difficult). Isaacson (1964) found the same pattern in the course selections of college students: Those with a higher M$_s$ tended to choose classes of moderate difficulty, whereas those with a higher M$_{af}$ chose either very easy or very difficult classes.

More recently, Covington and Omelich (1991) have suggested that various combinations of high and low M$_s$ and M$_{af}$ (they actually use the terms *need to approach success* and *need to avoid failure*) result in four different kinds of learners—overstrivers, optimists, failure avoiders, and failure accepters—that are described in Table 16–1. Of the four, the optimists (who are concerned about success but not about failure) are apt to be the most effective learners because they engage in the very behaviors and cognitive processes that make learning possible. The other three groups are more concerned about protecting their sense of self-worth than in mastering new knowledge and skills.

In its earliest conceptualization, the need for achievement was thought to be a general trait that people exhibit consistently in a variety of activities across many domains. More recently, however, many theorists have proposed that this need may instead be somewhat specific to particular tasks and environments (Bong, 2001; Dweck & Elliott, 1983; Eccles & Wigfield, 1985; Paris & Turner, 1994; Stipek, 1996; Wigfield, 1997). Theorists are also beginning to explain people's need for achievement in terms of specific cognitive factors that influence the choices they make, the goals they set for themselves, and the tasks they pursue. In the next section, we will look briefly at what the contemporary cognitive perspective of motivation encompasses.

THE CONTEMPORARY COGNITIVE VIEW OF MOTIVATION

Within the past few decades, theorists have radically changed their approach to the study of human motivation (Dweck, 1986; Graham & Weiner, 1996). Talk of physiological needs and drives has largely gone by the wayside. Concrete, external reinforcers play less of a role in conceptions of human learning (e.g., consider the declining popularity of the operant conditioning perspective in recent years). And interest in global needs that may vary from one individual to another—needs for achievement, affiliation, and the like—is diminishing.

Most contemporary theorists describe human motivation as being a function of human cognition. For example, people set specific *goals* toward which they strive. They form *expectations* regarding the likelihood of success in different activities. They construct *interpretations* (in Chapter 18, we will use the term *attributions*) of why certain consequences come their way, and they make *predictions* about the future consequences of their behavior. As we noted at the beginning of the chapter, motivation affects cognition as well—for example, by increasing attention and cognitive engagement and by promoting effective learning strategies. Ultimately, motivation and cognition are probably inextricably intertwined (Nenniger, 1992; Winne & Marx, 1989).

Some contemporary cognitive theorists also propose that motivation, rather than being a relatively permanent characteristic that people bring with them to various situations, is largely a function of the particular context in which people find themselves; this phenomenon is sometimes called **situated motivation** (Graham & Weiner, 1996; Greeno et al., 1996; Paris & Turner, 1994; Rueda & Moll, 1994). In school classrooms, many factors are likely to influence students' motivation. For instance, the kinds of instructional materials that a teacher uses (whether they are interesting, challenging, relevant to students' needs, and so on), the extent to which students find themselves having to compete with one another, and the ways in which students are evaluated are all likely to play a role (Boykin, 1994; Paris & Turner, 1994; Stipek, 1996).

Cognitive theorists have offered a number of ideas regarding the cognitions involved in motivation and the specific circumstances under which various "motivating" cognitions are most likely to occur; we will explore many of these ideas in Chapters 17 and 18. In the meantime, let's turn to a concept that has implications for our understanding of both motivation and cognition—the concept of *affect*.

THE ROLE OF AFFECT

When we talk about motivation, it is difficult not to talk about **affect**—the feelings, emotions, and general moods that a learner brings to bear on a task—at the same time.[5] For example, earlier in the chapter we noted that intrinsically motivated individuals typically find pleasure in what they are doing. Yet too much motivation—perhaps wanting something too much—may lead to an intense sense of anxiety. Pleasure, anxiety, excitement, pride, depression, anger, guilt—all of these are forms of affect. Affect is interrelated with motivation, learning, and cognition in a variety of ways, as we shall see now.

---

[5]Some theorists use the terms *affect* and *emotion* almost interchangeably. But others suggest that we use *emotion* to refer only to short-term states and *affect* in a broader sense to include both short-term states and longer-term moods and predispositions (Forgas, 2000; Linnenbrink & Pintrich, 2002; Rosenberg, 1998).

How Affect Is Related to Motivation

As people make plans and set goals for themselves, they are more likely to be optimistic about what they can accomplish if they are feeling cheerful rather than depressed (Harter, 1988). But they also consider how they are apt to feel later on—in particular, how good a success will feel (e.g., making them happy or proud) and how bad a failure will feel (e.g., making them sad or ashamed) (Mellers & McGraw, 2001).

Affect comes into play after people complete an activity as well. People of course react emotionally to their successes and failures. They are more apt to feel excited about their successes when they didn't expect to be successful, and they experience more intense negative emotions about their failures when they didn't expect to fail (Bower & Forgas, 2001; Mellers, Schwartz, Ho, & Ritov, 1997). Furthermore, the specific reactions they have depend on how they *interpret* the outcomes of events—in particular, whether they hold themselves, other people, environmental circumstances, or something else responsible for what has happened. For example, if they believe they themselves are responsible for a failure, they may feel ashamed, but if they instead think that someone else was to blame, they are more apt to be angry (Hareli & Weiner, 2002; Neumann, 2000). Here I'm giving you a brief glimpse into the emotional repercussions of people's *attributions*; we'll take up this topic in more detail in Chapter 18.

How Affect Is Related to Learning and Cognition

Affect is clearly intermingled with learning and cognition (Eisner, 1994; Meyer & Turner, 2002; Ochsner & Lieberman, 2001). For example, while learning how to perform a task, we simultaneously learn whether we like doing it (Zajonc, 1980). Problem solving is easier when we enjoy what we are doing, and successful attempts at learning and problem solving often bring on feelings of excitement, pleasure, and pride (Carver & Scheier, 1990; McLeod & Adams, 1989; Snow et al., 1996; Thompson & Thompson, 1989). Our failed attempts at a task are likely to make us feel frustrated or anxious, especially if the task is an easy one, and we are apt to develop a dislike for that task (Carver & Scheier, 1990; Shepperd & McNulty, 2002; Stodolsky et al., 1991).

As we are thinking about, learning, or remembering something, our very thoughts and memories may have emotional overtones—a phenomenon known as **hot cognition** (e.g., Hoffman, 1991; Lazarus, 1991). Often the nature of the material we are trying to learn or remember induces hot cognition and, as a result, affects cognitive processing. When information is emotionally charged, we are more likely to pay attention to it, continue to think about it over a period of time, and repeatedly elaborate on it (Bower, 1994; Edwards & Bryan, 1997; Heuer & Reisberg, 1992; Schacter, 1999). Encountering information that conflicts with what we currently know or believe can cause considerable mental discomfort, which Piaget called *disequilibrium* but many contemporary theorists call **cognitive dissonance.** Such dissonance typically leads learners to try to resolve the inconsistency in some way, perhaps revising existing beliefs (thus undergoing *conceptual change*) or perhaps ignoring the new information (Buehl & Alexander, 2001; Harmon-Jones, 2001; Pintrich et al., 1993).

The emotional nature of what we have stored may influence our ability to retrieve it later on. Although we may occasionally repress extremely painful memories (see Chapter 12), in general we can more easily retrieve information with high emotional content than we can recall relatively nonemotional information (Baddeley, 1982; Bower, 1994; Heuer & Reisberg, 1992; Kleinsmith & Kaplan, 1963; Reisberg, 1997; Russ, 1993; Winograd & Neisser, 1992). As one

People often remember more when
information packs an emotional wallop.

The Serial Killer,
the Relentless
Nymphomaniac,
and Me

example, recall our discussion of *flashbulb memories* in Chapter 12. As another, let's consider an experiment by Heuer and Reisberg (1990). Undergraduate students looked at a series of slides that depicted one of two stories. Both stories involved a boy and his mother visiting the boy's father at his workplace. For some students (the emotional-content group), the father was a surgeon operating on an accident victim; among other things, these students saw slides of surgery in progress (with a person's internal organs in full view) and the badly scarred legs of a child. For other students (the neutral-content group), the father was an auto mechanic repairing a broken-down car; these students saw the internal workings of the car, including a piece that was clearly broken. Two weeks later, all of the students were given an unexpected quiz about the things they had observed. Students who had seen the emotion-laden sequence remembered both the general gist of the story and many of the tiny details depicted in the slides far more accurately than did students who had seen the neutral sequence. In fact, although they did not expect to be tested on what they had seen, people in the emotional-content group remembered more than people who had watched the neutral sequence and specifically been told to remember its plot and details.

General mood states, too, can affect learning and memory. When we are in a good mood (e.g., when we feel happy or excited, rather than sad or depressed), we are more likely to pay attention to information, relate it to things we already know, and so store it effectively (Bower, 1994; Hertel, 1994; Hettena & Ballif, 1981; Isen, Daubman, & Gorgoglione, 1987; Oatley & Nundy, 1996; Snow et al., 1996). A good mood is also likely to help us retrieve things we have previously stored in long-term memory (Oatley & Nundy, 1996). But in addition, we can sometimes retrieve information from long-term memory more successfully when our mood at the time of retrieval is the same as our mood when we initially stored the information—an effect known as **mood-dependent memory** (Bower, 1994; Bower & Forgas, 2001; Eich, 1995).

Some cognitive theorists have suggested that affective responses to objects and events are integral parts of the network of associations that comprises long-term memory (Bower & Forgas, 2001). Affective responses may, in fact, be an important source of *information* that learners have about objects and events (Clore, Gasper, & Garvin, 2001; M. E. Ford, 1996; Smith & Kirby, 2001). For instance, it is quite helpful to know that reading a good book will be a source of pleasure but that spending time with a verbally abusive relative will not. And just as people can easily categorize events on the basis of concepts or schemas, so, too, can they easily categorize events on the basis of affect—what things make them happy, sad, angry, and so on (Bower & Forgas, 2001).

In some circumstances, the affective components of a memory are so intense that they are easily retrieved, perhaps to the point where they are hard to ignore and unlikely to be confused with other memories[6] (Bower & Forgas, 2001; M. E. Ford, 1996; Schacter, 1999). In other cases, affective components may be sufficiently subtle that learners aren't consciously aware of them; that is, they are *implicit* rather than explicit knowledge (Bower & Forgas, 2001; Ito & Cacioppo, 2001). Occasionally, people show physiological responses to a stimulus that they have no conscious recollection of at all; in such situations, previous affective responses to that stimulus are the *only* things that appear to remain in memory (Nadel & Jacobs, 1998; Zajonc, 2000).

Probably the most widely studied form of affect, at least within the context of human learning, is anxiety. For example, in Chapter 3 we discovered that anxiety may be acquired through classical conditioning, becoming a conditioned response to previously neutral stimuli. In Chapter 6, we noted that fear or anxiety may play a prominent role in avoidance learning. In Chapters 12 and 14, we found that anxiety often interferes with both long-term memory retrieval and problem-solving performance. Anxiety has numerous other effects as well; some are beneficial while others are not. We now look more closely at how anxiety influences learning and performance.

Anxiety

Anxiety is a feeling of uneasiness and apprehension about a situation, typically one with an uncertain outcome. Fear and anxiety are related concepts, in that both reflect the high end of the *arousal* continuum. Yet they have one critical difference that sets them apart: Fear is a response to a specific threat, whereas anxiety is vague and relatively unfocused. For example, people are *afraid* of certain things, but they don't always know exactly what they're *anxious* about (Lazarus, 1991).

Anxiety probably has two components: worry and emotionality (Liebert & Morris, 1967; Tryon, 1980; Zeidner, 1998). **Worry** is the cognitive aspect of anxiety, which includes troubling thoughts and beliefs about one's ability to deal with a situation. **Emotionality** is the affective aspect of anxiety, which includes such physiological responses as muscular tension (e.g., stomach "butterflies"), increased heartbeat, and perspiration and such behavioral responses as restlessness and pacing.

Psychologists have found it useful to distinguish between two types of anxiety: state versus trait. **State anxiety** is a temporary condition elicited by a particular stimulus. For example, you might experience state anxiety when working on an especially challenging mathematics problem or when thinking about an upcoming exam in a notoriously difficult class. **Trait anxiety** is a relatively stable state of affairs, such that an individual is chronically anxious in certain situations. For example, you might have general mathematics anxiety or test anxiety, becoming anxious whenever you encounter numbers or think about exams.

---

[6]In other words, emotionally intense memories are less prone to *interference* from other memories (Bower & Forgas, 2001).

Figure 16–2
The inverted U curve, depicting a curvilinear relationship between arousal and performance.

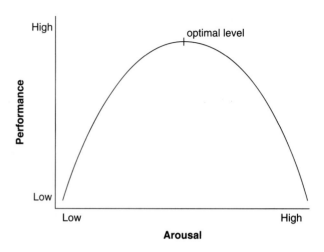

Effects of Anxiety

Early studies focused on the effects of anxiety on learning and performance. More recently, with the advent of cognitivism, studies have investigated the effects that anxiety is likely to have on cognitive processes. Let's consider the evidence in each of these areas.

Effects on Learning and Performance Earlier I mentioned that people may strive to seek an *optimal level* of arousal, a "comfort zone" somewhere between too little and too much. But what is optimal may depend not only on the individual but also on the task at hand. Early researchers found that arousal affects learning and performance in a curvilinear ("inverted U") fashion (Broadhurst, 1959; Fiske & Maddi, 1961; Hebb, 1955; Yerkes & Dodson, 1908). More specifically, a small degree of arousal (e.g., a low level of anxiety) facilitates learning and performance. A high degree of arousal (e.g., high anxiety) may facilitate learning and performance when the task is easy but is likely to interfere when the task is more difficult. For any task, there is probably some optimal level of arousal (reflected by the top point of the inverted U) at which learning and performance are maximized (see Figure 16–2).

A classic experiment with mice by Yerkes and Dodson (1908) provides a concrete illustration of how arousal level and task difficulty interact. Each mouse was placed in a chamber from which it could escape by either of two doors. The wall opposite the doors was slowly moved to make the chamber smaller and smaller, until the mouse was eventually forced to escape through one door or the other. One door led to a safe, comfortable "nest box"; the other led to electric shock. The experimenters provided a clue to help the mouse determine which door was which: The doorway leading to the nest box was consistently lighter in color than the doorway leading to shock.

For different groups of mice, the experimenters varied arousal level by the amount of shock they administered—mild, intense, or somewhere in between—when the "wrong" door was entered. They varied task difficulty by varying the relative similarity or difference between the two doorways: some mice had to choose between white and black (an easy task), others chose between light and dark gray (a moderately difficult task), and still others chose between similar shades of gray (a very difficult, although not impossible, task).

The experimenters established a criterion of 30 correct door choices in a row as an indication that a mouse had successfully learned the discrimination. Figure 16–3 shows the average

Figure 16–3

Arousal level interacts with task difficulty, resulting in different optimal levels for different tasks. From data reported in "The relation of strength of stimulus to rapidity of habit-formation" by R. M. Yerkes and J. D. Dodson, 1908, *Journal of Comparative Neurology and Psychology, 18*, pp. 459–482.

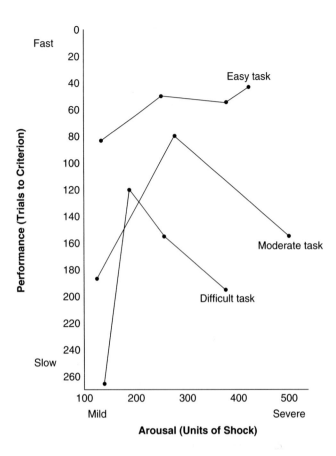

number of learning trials for mice in each condition; because the Y axis reflects quality of performance (speed of learning), groups needing fewer trials to criterion appear higher in the figure than groups with more trials. Notice how the mice with an easy choice performed best under high arousal (intense shock) conditions. Those with a moderately difficult task performed better with moderate arousal (moderate shock). Those with an extremely difficult discrimination performed best when shock and arousal were relatively low.

This principle—that easy tasks are best accomplished with a relatively high level of arousal but more difficult tasks are better accomplished with a low or moderate level—is often known as the **Yerkes–Dodson law.** The principle holds true not only for mice but for human beings as well. A high level of anxiety enhances our performance on easy and automatic tasks, such as running a mile or reciting the alphabet; here we have a case of **facilitating anxiety.** But the same high level interferes with our performance on a difficult task, such as writing a psychology textbook or speaking before a large audience; in this situation, we have **debilitating anxiety.**

We find the Yerkes–Dodson law at work in the classroom as well. For example, students who experience a small amount of muscular tension during mathematical problem solving are more successful problem solvers than students who experience no tension at all (Bloom & Broder, 1950). Highly anxious students sometimes perform better than low-anxiety students on tasks requiring verbatim recall of simple information; however, they perform comparatively poorly on tasks requiring flexible, creative thought (Kirkland, 1971). Low levels of anxiety throughout the course of instruction may facilitate students' learning; a high degree of anxiety at the tail end of the same course (e.g., at final exam time) is apt to be counterproductive (Kirkland, 1971). And the same degree of anxiety about a test may enhance the performance of high-ability students, for whom the test is easy, while lowering the performance of low-ability students, for whom the test is more difficult (Spielberger, 1966).

A useful distinction in this context is the difference between threat and challenge (Combs, Richards, & Richards, 1976). A **threat** is a situation in which learners believe they have little chance of success—they see failure as an almost inevitable outcome. In contrast, a **challenge** is a situation in which learners believe they can probably succeed if they try hard enough. Students are likely to have debilitating anxiety when they perceive a situation to be threatening. They respond to challenges more favorably; for example, they are likely to be highly motivated to do their best, and they express considerable excitement and satisfaction when they succeed (Cobb, Yackel, & Wood, 1989; Natriello & Dornbusch, 1984; Thompson & Thompson, 1989).

For most students, school tasks are (and should be) challenging more often than easy. Accordingly, we should expect students with lower levels of anxiety to perform more effectively in the classroom, which is in fact the case: Students with relatively low trait anxiety achieve greater academic success (e.g., higher grade point averages) than their peers of equal ability who have high trait anxiety (Gaudry & Spielberger, 1971; Stipek, 1993; Tobias, 1980).

Effects on Cognition   Imagine yourself sitting in class taking a test. Here are some possible thoughts running through your mind as you do so:

- Oh, yes, my professor introduced this concept last week. It refers to. . . .
- Here is something we didn't specifically talk about in class. Let me see if I can relate it to something we *did* talk about. . . .
- The best way to solve this problem might be to. . . .
- These questions are getting harder and harder. . . .
- Oh, no, I only have 10 minutes left. I can't possibly finish. . . .
- What if I fail this test? It's required for my program. . . .

The first three thoughts are clearly relevant to the task at hand and should help you do your best on the test. In contrast, the last three are irrelevant to your task: You are spending your time worrying rather than thinking about how to answer the test questions. As you should recall from our discussion of attention and working memory in Chapter 9, we can attend to and process only a small amount of information at any one time. The more time and attention we devote to worrying about a test we are taking, the less capacity we have for dealing with and responding to the test itself.

Anxiety interferes with an individual's attention to a task (Easterbrook, 1959; Eysenck, 1992; Tobias, 1980; Wine, 1980). And because "worrying" thoughts take up a certain amount of working memory capacity, anxiety also interferes with effective storage and retrieval processes (Mueller, 1980; Naveh-Benjamin, 1991; Tobias, 1985; Turner, Thorpe, & Meyer, 1998). Such effects are particularly likely when a learning or memory task is a difficult one and when it involves considerable retrieval of information from long-term memory (Tobias, 1980).

In general, anxiety's debilitative effect is a distractive one: When performing a difficult task, highly anxious people are more likely to think irrelevant thoughts, be diverted by irrelevant stimuli, and exhibit irrelevant responses (Dusek, 1980; Eccles & Wigfield, 1985; Eysenck & Keane, 1990; Wine, 1980).

Common Sources of Anxiety

People become anxious about a variety of things. For example, they may be concerned about their personal appearance (King & Ollendick, 1989). They may worry about how they perform in comparison with their peers and about what their peers might think of them as a result (Hill & Wigfield, 1984; King & Ollendick, 1989). They may feel uncomfortable when they encounter ideas that conflict with what they currently believe; recall our earlier discussion of *cognitive dissonance* (Bendixen, 2002; Harmon-Jones, 2001).[7] They are likely to feel insecure when entering a new, unknown, and perhaps unsettling situation—for instance, when, as young adolescents, they make the transition from elementary school to junior high school (Eccles & Midgley, 1989). Adolescence brings additional sources of anxiety as well, including the high expectations that many secondary school teachers have for students' performance, the increasingly challenging nature of class material, and general concerns about what the future will bring (Eccles & Midgley, 1989; Phelan, Yu, & Davidson, 1994; Snow et al., 1996). And, in general, people are likely to become anxious whenever their sense of self-worth or self-efficacy is threatened—for instance, when they know they are being evaluated or when they receive some form of feedback that portrays them in an unflattering light (Covington, 1992; Eccles et al., 1998).

Two forms of trait anxiety—test anxiety and mathematics anxiety—have been the focus of considerable study. Let's look at what research tells us about each of these.

Test Anxiety Most of us get a little bit anxious about tests, and, as we have already seen, a small amount of anxiety may actually help us do better on them. But some students become extremely anxious in test-taking situations, and these students typically get lower test scores than their less anxious classmates (Cassady & Johnson, 2002; Hembree, 1988; Hill, 1984; S. B. Sarason, 1972). Such students appear to be concerned primarily about the *evaluative* aspect of tests: They are terribly concerned that someone else (such as their teacher) will make negative judgments about them (Harter, Whitesell, & Kowalski, 1992; Phillips, Pitcher, Worsham, & Miller, 1980; Wine, 1980). Test anxiety interferes not only with retrieval at the time of the test, but also with encoding and storage when learners are studying for the test (Cassady & Johnson, 2002). Thus, highly test-anxious students don't just "test" poorly; they also learn poorly.

Test anxiety is rare in the early grades but increases throughout the elementary school years (Kirkland, 1971; S. B. Sarason, 1972). Many secondary and upper elementary students have test anxiety that interferes with their test performance; we are especially likely to see such debilitative test anxiety in students from minority groups, students with special needs, and students with a history of academic failure (Kirkland, 1971; Phillips et al., 1980).

Mathematics Anxiety Of all the subjects taught in schools, none seems to elicit as much anxiety for as many students as mathematics. Mathematics anxiety has both worry and emotionality components. First, math-anxious people firmly believe that they are incapable of succeeding at mathematical tasks. Second, they have negative emotional reactions to math: They fear and dislike it, often intensely (Wigfield & Meece, 1988).

---

[7]Bendixen (2002) suggests that encountering more sophisticated ideas about the nature of knowledge may create a form of cognitive dissonance she calls *epistemic doubt*. This state can be highly anxiety arousing, yet it may spur learners to reflect deeply about their beliefs and eventually construct more sophisticated understandings.

One possible reason why students become anxious about math is that, as we noted in our discussion of classical conditioning (Chapter 3), school curricula sometimes introduce mathematical concepts and procedures before students are cognitively ready to handle them. For example, developmentalists have proposed that the abilities to understand proportions and to deal with abstract ideas don't usually emerge until early adolescence and then continue to develop for several years after that (Schliemann & Carraher, 1993; Tourniaire & Pulos, 1985; also see the discussion of Piaget's theory in Chapter 8). Yet we often expose students to such proportions as fractions and ratios, and to such abstract ideas as negative numbers and *pi* (π), in the upper elementary and early junior high school years. If students are asked to deal with mathematical tasks they can't understand, many of them will undoubtedly encounter frustration and failure. And when students associate frequent failure with math, we can expect them to develop a dislike for the subject and a belief that they are incapable of doing well in it.

As you might expect, students with high math anxiety do more poorly in mathematics classes than students with low math anxiety; furthermore, highly math-anxious students are less likely to enroll in additional mathematics classes of their own volition (Eccles & Jacobs, 1986; McCoy, 1990; Meece, Wigfield, & Eccles, 1990). Such differences between high-math-anxious and low-math-anxious students appear even when the two groups of students have done equally well in previous math classes. In fact, math anxiety may have a greater influence on students' future plans for taking (or not taking) mathematics than do their previous achievement levels and history of success in math (Eccles & Jacobs, 1986). Math anxiety, which is more common in girls than in boys even when achievement levels are the same, may be a key reason why so few girls pursue advanced study or careers in mathematics (Eccles & Jacobs, 1986; Fennema, 1980). And for students of both genders, math anxiety may inhibit the desire to pursue a career in science (Chipman, Krantz, & Silver, 1992).

To perform most effectively in the classroom, students should be motivated to do their best yet not be overly anxious about their performance. In the final section of this chapter, we will consider some general strategies for promoting students' motivation to achieve academic success and for keeping their anxiety at productive levels.

CREATING A MOTIVATING CLASSROOM ENVIRONMENT

All too often, I hear people (including some teachers) complain that students "just aren't motivated" to learn. But one thing should be clear by now: Motivation to learn classroom subject matter is not necessarily something that students bring to school with them—it can also be something that teachers *instill* in students (recall our earlier discussion of *situated motivation*). The school environment definitely does have an impact on students' desire to learn and achieve in the classroom (Osterman, 2000).

The principles and theories we've examined in this chapter offer several ideas about how we can promote motivation in instructional settings:

• *Students learn more effectively and demonstrate more productive classroom behaviors when they are intrinsically motivated to learn and achieve.* Historically, parents, teachers, and society in general have emphasized the extrinsic advantages of classroom success (Harter, 1992; Spaulding, 1992).

For example, parents give their children money and privileges for good report cards. Schools award athletic letters for sports participation. Teachers and guidance counselors point out that students will gain admission to college, find more employment opportunities, and earn higher salaries if they obtain their high school diplomas. Yet as we have seen, *intrinsically* motivated students are more likely to exhibit initiative, independence, ambition, meaningful learning, and enjoyment regarding academic activities than is true for their extrinsically motivated counterparts, and they ultimately achieve at higher levels in the classroom.

Unfortunately, children's intrinsic need to learn and achieve at school tends to decrease as they progress through the school grades, and it may be especially low when they make the often anxiety-arousing transition from elementary school to junior high school (Eccles & Midgley, 1989; Eccles et al., 1998; Gottfried, Fleming, & Gottfried, 2001; Harter, 1981b). And children's very conception of what achievement *is* changes as they develop: As they progress through the elementary school years, they increasingly define success as doing better than their peers rather than as mastering knowledge and skills per se (Feld, Ruhland, & Gold, 1979; Ruble, 1980).

Researchers have identified several strategies that appear to promote intrinsic motivation to learn classroom subject matter. Talking about intrinsic rather than extrinsic motives for pursuing classroom activities is one effective approach (Amabile & Hennessey, 1992; Graham & Weiner, 1996). For example, a teacher might say, "It's always nice to get good grades, but it's more important that you understand what you are studying and enjoy what you are doing," or, "You must be very proud of yourself for passing the district writing test." Adult models who visibly pursue their own interests and express intrinsic enjoyment of something they are doing (e.g., saying "I feel wonderful" after generously doing something for someone else) promote observers' intrinsic motivation for the same activities (Bryan, 1971; Csikszentmihalyi, Rathunde, & Whalen, 1993). And relating classroom topics to students' own lives, experiences, needs, and feelings (e.g., in geography, identifying students with roots in the regions being studied, or, in history, having students imagine how they might have felt leaving home at the age of 12 to work as an apprentice during the Middle Ages) increases the likelihood that students will genuinely want to study those topics (Brophy, 1986; Wlodkowski & Ginsberg, 1995; Zahorik, 1994).

Intrinsic motivation is also more likely to emerge when certain cognitive factors are present—for example, when students believe they are capable of accomplishing tasks successfully and when they feel in control of their lives. As we study such cognitive factors in the following chapter, we will identify additional strategies for helping students genuinely *want* to learn and achieve.

• *Extrinsic motivation can also promote learning.* Although intrinsic motivation is the optimal situation, extrinsic motivation is not necessarily a bad thing, and it is certainly better than *no* motivation to learn. Oftentimes, students are motivated both by an intrinsic desire to master classroom subject matter and by the external rewards that such mastery brings—the good grades, public recognition, access to desirable educational opportunities and careers, and so on (Cameron, 2001; Covington, 2000; Hidi & Harackiewicz, 2000). Only when students place a *priority* on external rewards over intrinsic benefits of learning does extrinsic motivation become problematic; we'll explore this issue in our discussions of self-determination and performance goals in Chapter 17.

It is important to note, too, that students' intrinsic motivation to learn classroom material is not likely to appear overnight but instead will emerge slowly over time, especially if students have previously become accustomed to receiving extrinsic reinforcement for their efforts. In such situations, teachers might want to increase their focus on the intrinsic rewards of learning while only gradually weaning their students from an overdependence on external reinforcers (Covington, 1992; Lepper, 1981; Stipek, 1996).

• *Students are more likely to focus on their schoolwork when their nonacademic needs have been met.* As we examined drive theory, Maslow's hierarchy, self-worth theory, and individual differences, we identified a number of nonacademic needs that students may have. They are likely to have physiological needs on some occasions; for example, they may be hungry, thirsty, tired, or restless. They may feel uncertain or insecure about what will happen to them in class, in the schoolyard, or on the way home from school. Many students will have a strong desire to socialize with others (classmates and teachers alike), gaining the companionship, acceptance, approval, and respect of those around them. And students will want to maintain their own sense of self-worth—to believe that they are competent, capable individuals.

Teachers can do a number of simple things to ensure that students' physiological needs are met. For example, they can help students from low-income families apply for free lunch programs. They can alternate quiet, in-seat tasks with opportunities for physical activity. They can refer students with apparently untreated illnesses to the school nurse. And they should certainly include restroom breaks and trips to the drinking fountain in the daily schedule.

To meet students' need for safety and security in the classroom, and to keep their anxiety about academic tasks and activities at a reasonable, facilitative level, teachers must create an environment that is somewhat orderly and predictable (Brophy, 1987; Dowaliby & Schumer, 1973; Grimes & Allinsmith, 1970; Klein, 1975). For example, teachers might have regular procedures for handing out and sharing materials, meeting with cooperative learning groups, doing homework, and turning in assignments. They should clearly describe expectations for academic performance and classroom behavior. They should deal with misbehaviors in a fair and consistent fashion. And they should provide opportunities for students to voice any questions and concerns that may arise.

Students' needs for love, belonging, affiliation, and approval—and in general, relatedness—can be met in a variety of ways. Teacher–student relationships are, by their very nature, somewhat businesslike; after all, both teachers and students have a job to do. At the same time, teachers can express their interest and affection for students through the many little things they do throughout the day—for example, by acknowledging birthdays and other special occasions, taking students' ideas and opinions seriously, and offering a supportive and nonjudgmental ear when a particular student seems angry or depressed. Teachers should also provide opportunities for students to interact frequently with their classmates—for example, through such group-oriented instructional techniques as discussions, cooperative learning, reciprocal teaching, and role playing. Recall, too, the *sense of community* I described in Chapter 15: Students are more likely to be academically successful—and more likely to stay in school rather than drop out—when they believe that their teachers and peers like and respect them and when they feel that they are valued members of the classroom (Certo, Cauley, & Chafin, 2002; Goodenow, 1993; Hymel, Comfort, Schonert-Reichl, & McDougall, 1996; Ladd, 1990; Osterman, 2000; Ryan & Patrick, 2001).

To help students gain the esteem of others and maintain their own sense of self-worth, teachers can acknowledge students' accomplishments both in and out of class. They can schedule activities in such a way that all students are able to demonstrate their particular strengths at some point during the school day or at special events after school (e.g., Jenlink, 1994). They can "brag" about their students' accomplishments in many subtle ways—for example, by posting students' art projects on the wall, describing noteworthy achievements at parent–teacher conferences, displaying students' best work at open houses, and sending occasional good-news reports home to parents. But most importantly, teachers must do everything they can to help students achieve classroom success.

- *Teachers can capitalize on the role that affect plays in learning.* There is no reason that academic subject matter needs to be dry and emotionless. On the contrary, students will probably remember more if they have feelings about the things they study. For example, a scientific discovery might be exciting. A look at social injustices might make students angry. A poem might convey peace and serenity. One simple way that teachers can promote positive affect is to model their own enthusiasm and excitement about classroom subject matter—perhaps by bringing in newspaper articles and other outside materials they have run across, presenting material in an animated or even impassioned fashion, and sharing the particular questions and issues about which they themselves are concerned (Brophy, 1987, 1999; Perry, 1985; Wlodkowski, 1978).

We must remember, too, that students should associate pleasure and other forms of positive affect with classroom activities. For example, although teachers don't necessarily want to give the impression that schoolwork is all fun and games, they can occasionally incorporate a few gamelike features into classroom tasks and activities (Brophy, 1986)—perhaps by using simple crossword puzzles to introduce new spelling words or by using a television game show format for a class history review (the latter strategy also addresses social needs). And, in general, teachers must make sure that most of students' experiences with any task or subject matter, and especially their *early* experiences, are positive and nonthreatening ones (Wlodkowski, 1978).

- *Assessments of students' performance should be portrayed as means of enhancing future achievement rather than as judgments of ability and worth.* Under the best of circumstances, tests and other forms of classroom assessment *can* serve as effective motivators (albeit extrinsic ones) for student learning. For example, most students study class material more and learn it better when they are told that their learning will be assessed than when they are simply told to learn it (Blumenfeld, Hamilton, Bossert, Wessels, & Meece, 1983; Frederiksen, 1984b; Halpin & Halpin, 1982). Classroom assessments are especially effective as motivators when they challenge students to perform at their very best (Natriello & Dornbusch, 1984). However, we should note several situations in which an assessment will definitely *not* motivate students to do well or—even worse—may motivate them to do *poorly*:

  - When they believe they will be penalized for doing too well on the assessment—for example, when they think they will receive more challenging work (e.g., extra readings or more difficult assignments) if they attain a high score
  - When they think they will lose the esteem of their peers for doing too well—for example, when they are afraid of becoming nerds or "school girls"
  - When they think their teacher's high standards for performance on the assessment are impossible to attain
  - When they consistently perform at lower levels than most of their classmates
  - When they believe an assessment is a poor reflection of what they know
    (Natriello, 1987; Natriello & Dornbusch, 1984; Paris, Lawton, Turner, & Roth, 1991; Paris & Turner, 1994; Sax, 1989)

Thus, a classroom assessment tool is most likely to serve as a motivator for learning when students perceive it to be a valid measure of course objectives, when they believe that successful performance on the assessment is possible, and when they are confident that successful performance will be rewarded rather than punished.

But as we discovered in our discussion of test anxiety, many students are so concerned about performing well on classroom assessments that they become overly anxious when encountering them. There are probably several reasons that high school and upper elementary students experience debilitative anxiety in assessment situations. Perhaps teachers too often imply that an upcoming assessment is an event to be feared or revered. Perhaps teachers too often stress the dire consequences of failing. Perhaps teachers and other school personnel make too many major decisions—about grades, scholarships, admission to special programs, and so on—based on the results of a single test score.

Researchers and theorists offer numerous suggestions for keeping students' anxiety about classroom assessments at a facilitative level. First, teachers should help students master class material and effective study strategies to the point where successful performance on an assessment is highly likely (Covington, 1992; Naveh-Benjamin, 1991). Second, teachers can base students' classroom grades on many sources of data (perhaps including scores on numerous small assessments) instead of on only one or two test scores (Gaudry & Bradshaw, 1971; Gaynor & Millham, 1976; Sax, 1989). Third, teachers can encourage students to do their best without creating unnecessary anxiety about the consequences of doing poorly (I. G. Sarason, 1980; S. B. Sarason, 1972; Sax, 1989; Sinclair, 1971). Fourth, a classroom assessment should be short enough that students can easily complete it within the allotted time; this strategy is especially beneficial for high-anxiety students (Brophy, 1986; Hill, 1984). Fifth, teachers should minimize (and ideally, eliminate) opportunities for students to compare their performance with that of classmates (Hill & Wigfield, 1984). And finally, students should be given whatever support (scaffolding) is appropriate to help them perform successfully on a classroom assessment task. For example, students can be given pretests for practice and feedback, instructed on effective test-taking strategies, and allowed to use notes or other resources when there is no inherent value in committing certain information (e.g., formulas, trivial facts) to memory (Brophy, 1986; Kirkland, 1971; Leherissey et al., 1971; Sax, 1989; Sieber, Kameya, & Paulson, 1970; Stipek, 1993; Wine, 1980).

Above all, teachers and students alike must keep tests and other forms of classroom assessment in the proper context—as means of promoting learning and achievement, especially over the long run, rather than as means of making judgments about students' ability and worth. Evaluation procedures should provide frequent and informative feedback to students about what they have mastered and how they can improve (Brophy, 1986; Spaulding, 1992; Wine, 1980). Such procedures should also allow for the mistakes that are an inevitable part of the learning process. When students know they will have the chance to correct their errors, they are more likely to take on challenging, risky tasks (Brophy, 1986; Wlodkowski, 1978).

Students are more likely to exhibit high motivation to achieve, and therefore to gain the maximum benefits of classroom instruction, when they know they are capable of achieving instructional objectives, when they believe that classroom subject matter is valuable and interesting, and when they are more concerned about learning than about looking "good" for their teacher and classmates. We will consider these points further when we examine cognitive factors in motivation in the next chapter.

SUMMARY

Motivation is an internal state that arouses us to action, pushes us in certain directions, and keeps us engaged in certain activities. Motivation determines the extent to which we exhibit the particular responses we have learned; it also affects whether and in what ways we process the information we receive. *Intrinsic motivation* is ultimately more beneficial than *extrinsic motivation*; for example, intrinsically motivated individuals do things on their own initiative, maintain attention on tasks, and process information in a meaningful fashion. Yet intrinsic and extrinsic motivation are not necessarily mutually exclusive; often learners are simultaneously both intrinsically and extrinsically motivated.

Numerous theorists have speculated about the nature of human beings' basic, universal needs. Early *drive* theorists believed that human beings and other organisms behave in ways that satisfy their physiological needs and thus maintain homeostasis; a bit later, they modified drive theory to include *incentives*, suggesting that characteristics of goal objects mediate a stimulus–response relationship and thereby affect which stimuli are responded to and which are not. In addition to maintaining homeostasis, people may also have a need for stimulation, or *arousal*: People who have little access to environmental stimulation for extended periods have difficulty thinking clearly and may even begin to hallucinate. From the perspective of *Maslow's hierarchy*, people have five different sets of needs (ranging from physiological needs to self-actualization) that they strive to meet in a particular order. More recently, some theorists have suggested that people have a need to believe that they are competent, capable individuals and that they may paradoxically undermine their own success as a way of protecting their sense of *self-worth*. Other contemporary theorists have argued that a need for *relatedness* is equally fundamental—that people have

a basic need to interact with and feel psychologically connected to others.

Trait theorists focus not on needs common to everyone but rather on individual differences that exist in such motives as the *need for affiliation*, the *need for approval*, and the *need for achievement*. Increasingly, however, motivation theorists have emphasized the cognitions that underlie motivation and suggested that motivation may be more a function of the environment than of a learner's personality.

Related to motivation is the concept of *affect*—the feelings, emotions, and moods that an individual brings to bear on a task. Affect influences motivation; for example, people choose their goals in part based on how they think they will feel if they achieve or don't achieve those goals. Affect also influences learning; for example, people can typically store and retrieve information with highly emotional content more easily than they can recall relatively nonemotional information. Of the various forms that affect may take, *anxiety* is the one that researchers have investigated most thoroughly. Anxiety facilitates performance on easy tasks, but high levels interfere with performance on difficult tasks, presumably by interfering with effective cognitive processing and in other ways distracting people from what they are doing.

Theorists and researchers offer numerous suggestions for promoting students' motivation to achieve and succeed in the classroom. For example, teachers should emphasize the intrinsically motivating aspects of school learning yet remember that extrinsic rewards can also be effective motivators in a pinch. Assessment of students' performance should be portrayed as a means of enhancing future achievement rather than as a judgment of ability and worth. And students are more likely to focus on school tasks and activities when their nonacademic needs have been met.

CHAPTER 17

Cognitive Factors in Motivation

Many of the people I meet marvel at how anyone could have the fortitude and persistence to get a doctoral degree. And, to be honest, when I was growing up in the 1950s and 1960s, I expected only to become a housewife and mother, certainly not a college professor with "Ph.D." attached to my name. So how did I get here? It all boils down to motivation.

For one thing, I've always been concerned about children, and in particular about their education. While attending a small liberal arts college during the late 1960s—the era of the Vietnam War, the civil rights movement and sit-ins on the home front, and heightened soul-searching on many campuses across the country—I realized that I wanted my life to have an impact on society far beyond that of my own family and friends. By the end of my senior year, I had identified what I wanted to do when I grew up: I wanted to make education better for my children's generation than it had been for mine.

I began applying to graduate schools and ultimately chose Penn State's educational psychology program, partly because of the reputation of its faculty, partly because of the financial package it offered, and partly because of central Pennsylvania's pastoral charm and serenity. I had been a psychology major as an undergraduate and knew that psychology was something I was "good at." I had also done well in the required statistics courses that led half of my fellow psychology majors to find a different major before their junior year. I worked hard during my years in graduate school, knowing I would certainly be successful if I was conscientious about my studies.

Besides, I found educational psychology absolutely fascinating; the many books and articles I read were hard to put down because they gave me innumerable insights into how human beings learn and many intriguing ideas about how to help people learn more effectively. My doctoral dissertation took longer than I had anticipated (a year and a half from start to finish), but with each passing month I came noticeably closer to completing it, and I *did* complete it in time to graduate in June of 1975.

So why did I initiate and persist in my efforts to earn a doctoral degree? Because, among other things, I valued a better world, had a goal for myself, and discovered an interest in human learning theory. Furthermore, I believed I was capable of graduate work in educational psychology. All of these things—values, goals, interests, and beliefs about myself—are among the cognitive factors that kept me motivated throughout my doctoral program.

In this chapter, we will explore cognitive aspects of human motivation. We will discover how self-perceptions, especially learners' sense of *self-efficacy* and *self-determination*, influence intrinsic motivation. We will see how *expectancies* and *values* affect learners' decisions to pursue particular activities, examine the personal characteristics and situational variables that determine whether learners find *interest* in a particular topic or task, identify various *goals* that learners are apt to strive for, and look at the relatively stable *dispositions* that reflect how learners tend to approach learning tasks and problems. Later, we will consider how learners become increasingly able to *self-regulate* their motivations and emotions, and we will discover that some behaviors that are initially motivated extrinsically may become *internalized* over time, to the point where an individual eventually engages in them freely and willingly. Finally, we will identify strategies for promoting cognitive processes that enhance student motivation.

SELF-PERCEPTIONS AND INTRINSIC MOTIVATION

As you should recall from the preceding chapter, intrinsic motivation has several advantages over extrinsic motivation. For instance, when people are intrinsically motivated, they are more likely to pursue a task on their own initiative, keep their attention focused on it, learn meaningfully, and persist in the face of failure. Edward Deci and Richard Ryan (1985, 1987, 1992; Ryan & Deci, 2000) and other theorists as well (Boggiano & Pittman, 1992; Connell & Wellborn, 1991; Spaulding, 1992) have proposed that intrinsic motivation is most likely to be present when two conditions exist. First, individuals must believe that they are capable of successfully executing the tasks before them; that is, they must have a sense of **competence.** Second, individuals must believe that they can, to some extent, choose and regulate the course of their lives; in other words, they must have a sense of **self-determination.** When both conditions are present, people experience greater pleasure and satisfaction in performing a task.

Let's look more closely at the concepts of competence and self-determination. As we do so, we'll identify a number of variables likely to promote intrinsic motivation.

Competence (Self-Efficacy)

In the preceding chapter, I suggested that people have a need to feel competent and maintain a sense of self-worth; in other words, they need to believe that they can deal effectively with their environment. In our discussion of social cognitive theory in Chapter 7,

I introduced the concept of *self-efficacy*, the belief that one is capable of executing behaviors or performing tasks successfully. On the surface, these two ideas are very similar, but there are, at least in theory, two key differences between the needs for competence and self-worth, on the one hand, and self-efficacy, on the other. First, some motivation theorists have proposed that the need to feel competent (i.e., to have a sense of self-worth) is a basic human need. In contrast, social cognitive theorists have suggested that self-efficacy is certainly a *good* thing, but they do not go so far as to speculate that it is an essential driving force of human nature. Second, competence and self-worth have been conceived as being fairly general, overarching self-perceptions (i.e., what you think about yourself overall), whereas self-efficacy is more task specific.

But now let's muddy the waters a bit. To some degree, how competent you think you are overall is apt to affect the confidence with which you approach a particular task, and how self-efficacious you feel about performing a task is apt to contribute in some way to your overall sense of competence and self-worth. Furthermore, in my own reading of the motivation literature, I find that theorists sometimes use the term *sense of competence* (or something similar) when talking about fairly specific tasks or situations, and they sometimes use the term *self-efficacy* to refer to a fairly general self-perception (e.g., Bandura, 1997).

One point everyone agrees on is that a sense of competence and self-efficacy are important variables influencing motivation, especially *intrinsic motivation.* Conversely, feelings of incompetence lead to decreased interest and motivation (Deci, 1992; Deci & Ryan, 1985, 1987; Harter, 1992; Harter et al., 1992; MacIver, Stipek, & Daniels, 1991).

As we discussed self-efficacy in Chapter 7, we identified several variables that help us believe we can succeed at a task, including encouraging messages, the successes of peers, and, most importantly, one's *own* successes (either individually or as part of a group) at a task or activity. The last of these—actual successes—are, of course, the most powerful. Sometimes learners' successes are obvious; winning a bicycle race and constructing a sturdy bookcase from a set of instructions are examples. But many others are not so clear-cut, and in such instances feedback is often helpful. Curiously, even class grades and other extrinsic reinforcers can promote *intrinsic* motivation to the extent that they signal successful performance and therefore enhance self-efficacy (Cameron, 2001; Covington, 2000; Hynd, 2003; Schunk & Zimmerman, 1997).

Ideally, learners should probably have a reasonably accurate sense of what they can and cannot accomplish, with perhaps just a tad of overoptimism to encourage them to take on new challenges[1]. Learners who underestimate their abilities will set unnecessarily low goals for themselves and give up easily in the face of small obstacles. Those who overestimate their abilities (perhaps because they have been lavished with praise by parents or teachers, or perhaps because school assignments have been consistently easy and nonchallenging) may set themselves up for failure by forming unrealistically high expectations for themselves or by not exerting a sufficient amount of effort to succeed (Bandura, 1997; Paris & Cunningham, 1996; Phillips & Zimmerman, 1990; Stevenson, Chen, & Uttal, 1990). Learners are likely to maximize their overall performance when they have a realistic understanding of their strengths and weaknesses and so know how best to focus their efforts (Försterling & Morgenstern, 2002).

[1]In Vygotskian lingo, a little bit of overoptimism would increase the probability that learners work in their zone of proximal development.

Self-Determination

Numerous motivation theorists have proposed that people are more likely to be intrinsically motivated when they have a sense of self-determination—in other words, when they have some sense of *autonomy* regarding the things they do and the directions their lives take (Boggiano & Pittman, 1992; deCharms, 1972; Deci, 1992; Deci & Ryan, 1992; Spaulding, 1992; Turner, 1995). For example, when we think "I *want* to do this" or "I would *find it valuable* to do that," we have a high sense of self-determination. In contrast, when we think "I *have to*" or "I *should*," we are telling ourselves that someone or something else is making our choices for us.

When circumstances and events confirm our feelings of self-determination, we are likely to engage in tasks for long periods, to think meaningfully and creatively about those tasks, to experience pleasure in our activities, and to achieve at higher levels (Amabile & Hennessey, 1992; deCharms, 1972; Deci, 1992; Deci & Ryan, 1987; Wang & Stiles, 1976). Furthermore, we are likely to undertake the challenges that will maximize our long-term learning and development (Deci & Ryan, 1985).

In contrast, when environmental circumstances and events lead us to conclude that we have little involvement in determining the course of our lives, we may comply with external demands but are unlikely to have much intrinsic motivation (Deci & Ryan, 1987). As an example, I think back to 1989 in the months after the Berlin Wall came down: Many East German workers reportedly showed little initiative or stick-to-itiveness on the job, quite possibly because they had for so long been told exactly what to do and what not to do under the Communist regime. Furthermore, when our reasons for doing something lie outside of ourselves, we are likely to undertake the easy things we know we can do rather than challenges at which we might fail (Stipek, 1993).

Deci and Ryan (1987) have identified several variables that influence people's sense of self-determination one way or the other, including choices, threats and deadlines, controlling statements, extrinsic rewards, and surveillance and evaluation.

Choices

People have a greater sense of self-determination, and are therefore more intrinsically motivated, when they are able to make choices, within reasonable limits, about the things that they do (Deci & Ryan, 1987, 1992; Morgan, 1984; Stipek, 1993). For example, in an early study by Lewin, Lippitt, and White (1939), 10-year-old boys participating in after-school recreational programs were in one of three experimental conditions. In the *autocratic* group, adults made all of the decisions about what the boys would do. In the *laissez-faire* group, the boys did as they pleased, with little if any adult input. In the *democratic* group, the adults and boys engaged in group decision making about daily activities. The boys were most productive in the democratic setting: They showed greater initiative and on-task behavior related to group projects, and they were less likely to be aggressive toward other group members. Other researchers have found similar results in classroom settings: When students have choices (again, within appropriate limits) about the activities in which they engage, they show greater interest and involvement in their classwork, and they display fewer off-task behaviors (Condry, 1977; Dunlap et al., 1994; Foster-Johnson, Ferro, & Dunlap, 1994; Morgan, 1984; Paris & Turner, 1994; Powell & Nelson, 1997; Stipek, 1993, 1996; Vaughn & Horner, 1997).

Threats and Deadlines

Threats (e.g., "Do this or else!") and deadlines (e.g., "This is due by January 15—no exceptions!") are typically experienced as controlling people's behaviors. As a result, they reduce self-determination and intrinsic motivation (Clifford, 1990; Deci & Ryan, 1987).

Controlling Statements

Some of the things that people say to us, even though they aren't threatening in nature, never-theless convey the message that others control our fate and so may undermine our sense of self-determination (Amabile & Hennessey, 1992; Boggiano, Main, & Katz, 1988; Koestner, Ryan, Bernieri, & Holt, 1984). As an example, in an experiment by Koestner and colleagues (1984), first and second graders were asked to paint a picture of a house in which they would like to live. The children were given the materials they needed—a paintbrush, a set of watercolor paints, two sheets of paper, and several paper towels—and then told some rules about how to proceed. For some children (the controlling-limits condition), restrictions described things that they could and could not do, as follows:

> Before you begin, I want to tell you some things that you will have to do. They are rules that we have about painting. You have to keep the paints clean. You can paint only on this small sheet of paper, so don't spill any paint on the big sheet. And you must wash out your brush and wipe it with a paper towel before you switch to a new color of paint, so that you don't get the colors all mixed up. In general, I want you to be a good boy (girl) and don't make a mess with the paints. (Koestner et al., 1984, p. 239)

For other children (the informational-limits condition), restrictions were presented only as infor-mation, like this:

> Before you begin, I want to tell you some things about the way painting is done here. I know that sometimes it's really fun to just slop the paint around, but here the materials and room need to be kept nice for the other children who will use them. The smaller sheet is for you to paint on, the larger sheet is a border to be kept clean. Also, the paints need to be kept clean, so the brush is to be washed and wiped in the paper towel before switching colors. I know that some kids don't like to be neat all the time, but now is a time for being neat. (Koestner et al., 1984, p. 239)

Each child was allowed 10 minutes of painting time. The experimenter then took the child's paint-ing to another room, saying he would return in a few minutes. As he departed, he placed two more sheets of paper on the child's table, saying, "You can paint some more on this piece of paper if you like, or, if you want, you can play with the puzzles over on that table." In the experimenter's absence, the child was surreptitiously observed, and painting time was measured. Children in the informational-limits condition spent more time painting (so were apparently more intrinsically motivated to paint), and their paintings were judged to be more creative, than was true for their counterparts in the controlling-limits condition.

Extrinsic Rewards

In Chapter 5, I expressed the concern that using extrinsic reinforcement may undermine the intrinsic reinforcement that an activity provides. Extrinsic reinforcers are most likely to have this adverse influence when people perceive them as controlling or manipulating their behavior rather than as providing information about their progress.[2] Rewards are unlikely to be beneficial, at least

---

[2]Theorists haven't specifically talked about the informational or controlling messages that *punishment* might communicate, but we can logically deduce that a similar pattern exists here as well. Certainly, punishment can be presented in either of two ways—as a means of control or as a source of information about appro-priate behavior. As we discovered in Chapter 6, punishment is more effective when it is accompanied by rea-sons (information) about why the punished behavior is unacceptable.

over the long run, when people interpret them as bribes or as limits on their freedom (Deci et al., 2001; Hennessey, 1995; Lepper & Hodell, 1989; Ryan, Mims, & Koestner, 1983; Spaulding, 1992). This finding may be, in part, a result of the fact that providing rewards for particular behaviors communicates the message that a task is not worth doing for its own sake (Hennessey, 1995; Stipek, 1993).

Rewards appear to have *no* adverse effects when they're unexpected—for instance, when scientists win the Nobel Prize for groundbreaking research findings—or when they're not contingent on specific behaviors (Cameron, 2001; Deci et al., 2001). Furthermore, as we have noted on previous occasions, extrinsic reinforcement may be useful when desirable behaviors will apparently not occur any other way. People may initially find a new activity boring, difficult, or frustrating and therefore need external encouragement to continue (Cameron, 2001; Deci et al., 2001; Hidi & Harackiewicz, 2000). With continuing practice, however, their competence and skill are likely to improve, and they may eventually begin to find the activity intrinsically rewarding.

Surveillance and Evaluation
People who know they are going to be evaluated on their performance have a lower sense of self-determination and, as a result, are less intrinsically motivated; this is especially likely to be true when the task at hand is a difficult one (Clifford, 1990; Deci & Ryan, 1987, 1992; Harter et al., 1992; Hennessey, 1995; Stipek, 1996). In fact, the mere presence of a potential evaluator is likely to undermine intrinsic motivation (Clifford, 1990; Deci & Ryan, 1987). For example, even though I have a mediocre singing voice, I like to sing and will often do so when no one else is around to hear me (e.g., when I'm mowing the lawn or driving alone on business). But my intrinsic motivation to sing vanishes when anyone else is in earshot.

In Chapter 12, we discovered that formal classroom assessments (e.g., assignments and tests) often promote long-term memory storage. Among other things, they encourage students to review classroom material more regularly and process information more thoroughly. In Chapter 16, we noted a potential downside of tests and other formal assessments: They may elicit debilitating anxiety that interferes with effective cognitive processing and learning. Here we see an additional disadvantage of formal assessments: They may undermine students' intrinsic motivation

Feelings of self-determination and intrinsic motivation are often greater when potential evaluators are absent from the scene.

to learn (Benware & Deci, 1984; Grolnick & Ryan, 1987; Hatano & Inagaki, 2003; Spaulding, 1992; Stipek, 1993). A study by Benware and Deci (1984) illustrates this point well. College students studied an article about brain functioning under either of two conditions: Some studied it with the expectation of being tested on it, while others studied it with the expectation that they would have to teach the material to someone else (a presumably nonevaluative situation). Compared with those in the first group, students in the second group enjoyed their learning experience more, found the material more interesting, and learned it in a more meaningful (rather than rote) fashion. Grolnick and Ryan (1987) have found similar results with fifth graders.

Curiously, people can undermine their own sense of self-determination simply by *imagining* that others may be evaluating their performance (Deci & Ryan, 1992; Ryan, 1982). For example, in a study by Ryan (1982), undergraduate students worked on a series of hidden-figure puzzles, in which they had to find drawings of particular objects embedded within the context of more complex drawings. Some students were told that the task was an indication of "creative intelligence." Even though these students were not specifically told that their performance would be evaluated, they were less likely than students in a control group to continue doing the puzzles in a free-choice situation later on. The mere idea that the task was indicative of intelligence may have led these students to consider how an outside person might evaluate their performance and, accordingly, to have less intrinsic motivation for engaging in the task (Deci & Ryan, 1992; Ryan, 1982).

We should keep in mind that no amount of self-determination is going to make us feel intrinsically motivated to do something if we don't also have a sense of competence. To show you what I mean, let's consider a study by Spaulding (1992, pp. 54–55). Seventh-grade students, including some who believed themselves to be competent writers and some who did not, were asked to write an essay concerning what they had learned in English class that year. Some students were asked to write it for their teacher, someone they believed would evaluate their work; hence, this group experienced low self-determination. Other students were asked to write the essay for the researcher so that she could tell future teachers what students study in English; without the threat of evaluation looming over them, these students presumably experienced relatively high self-determination. As the students wrote their essays, Spaulding measured their task engagement (and, indirectly, their intrinsic motivation) in several different ways. Students who believed themselves to be competent writers showed greater intrinsic motivation in the high self-determination condition—that is, when writing for the researcher. In contrast, students who believed they were poor writers were more engaged in the task when writing for the teacher. Apparently, self-determination in the absence of perceived competence did not promote intrinsic motivation.

Effects of Feedback

In Chapter 4, we talked about positive feedback as a form of reinforcement; from an operant conditioning perspective, feedback has a *direct* effect on behavior. In Chapter 10, we noted that feedback should also promote learning and performance *indirectly* by giving learners information about how they can improve. As we have just seen, motivation theorists suggest that feedback has two additional indirect effects on behavior: It enhances performance to the extent that it affirms an individual's feelings of competence or self-determination (or both). Positive feedback is *unlikely* to be beneficial, at least over the long run, when it either diminishes one's sense of competence or communicates an attempt to control one's behavior (Deci & Ryan, 1992; Ryan et al., 1983; Stipek, 1996). For example, I respond to my children more favorably when they tell me

> Boy, Mom, these brownies you made are really good. *(a competence-enhancing statement)*

than when they say

> It's a good thing you finally baked something around here, Ma. All my friends' mothers do it all the time. *(a controlling statement)*

Compliments about things I do well are always welcome. But statements about what "good" parents are supposed to do make me feel as if I'm not really in charge in my own home. Furthermore, I have no intention of letting my children tell *me* how to behave.

Even *negative* feedback can be effective when it promotes competence and self-determination (Butler, 1987, 1988; Butler & Nisan, 1986; Corno & Rohrkemper, 1985; Stipek, 1996). If it provides information about how to improve in the future, thereby implying that the individual can be successful eventually, it is likely to facilitate intrinsic motivation. If it instead conveys the message that an individual is incompetent or imposes a feeling of outside control, it is apt to undermine any intrinsic motivation to continue engaging in a task.

EXPECTANCIES AND VALUES

Some theorists (e.g., Atkinson, 1964; Dweck & Elliott, 1983; Eccles [Parsons], 1983; Feather, 1982; Wigfield, 1994; Wigfield & Eccles, 1992, 2000) have proposed that motivation for performing a particular task is a function of two variables. First, people must believe they can succeed; in other words, they must have a high **expectancy** about their task performance (a concept that overlaps with social cognitive theorists' concept of self-efficacy). Second, people must believe that there are direct or indirect benefits in performing a task; in other words, they must place **value** on the task itself or on the outcomes that are likely to result.

From this perspective, motivated behavior occurs only when both expectancy and value are present. For example, as a doctoral student in educational psychology, I found value in human learning theory and had a high expectancy that I could master it; thus, I was motivated to learn as much as I could about how human beings learn. I value good music, too, but have a low expectancy for becoming an accomplished musician (I haven't yet learned basic piano-playing skills to automaticity despite five years of lessons), so I don't work very hard or very often at my music. I'm much better at cooking lima beans than I am at singing, but I never cook them because I find no value in eating them. And there are some things that, for me, are associated with both low expectancy and low value; playing violent video games and walking barefoot on hot coals are two activities that spring to mind.

People's expectancies are probably the result of several factors. Prior successes and failures at a particular task, of course, make a difference; for example, people will lower their expectations after experiencing a series of failures (Dweck, Goetz, & Strauss, 1980). Other factors affect expectancy level as well: the perceived difficulty of a task, one's general work habits, environmental resources, the quality of instruction, and the anticipated effort necessary to succeed are all apt to make a difference (Eccles [Parsons], 1983; M. E. Ford, 1996; Wigfield & Eccles, 1992; Zimmerman et al., 1992). From such factors, an individual comes to a conclusion—perhaps correct, perhaps not—about the likelihood of success.

Value is equally subjective in nature. Eccles and Wigfield (1985; Eccles [Parsons], 1983; Wigfield & Eccles, 2000) have suggested several possible reasons why value might be high or low. Some activities are valued because they are associated with desirable personal qualities; for example, a boy who wants to be smart and thinks that smart people do well in school will place a premium on academic success. Other activities have high value because they are seen as means to a desired goal; for example, much as she detests mathematics, my daughter Tina struggled through four years of high school math classes because many colleges require that much math (also see Bong, 2001). Still other activities are valued simply because they bring pleasure and enjoyment; for example, junk food doesn't help me achieve any of my long-range goals (in fact, it interferes with my goal of losing 15 pounds this year), but it sure does taste good.

We can also anticipate the circumstances in which an activity will probably *not* be valued very much (Eccles [Parsons], 1983; Eccles & Wigfield, 1985; Wigfield & Eccles, 2000). Some activities may require so much effort that they are simply not worth it. For example, I could undoubtedly improve my piano-playing skills with lessons and practice, but right now I have more important things to which I need to devote my time and energy. Other activities may be associated with too many bad feelings. For example, I can't imagine hang gliding or bungee jumping because I am deathly afraid of heights. And anything likely to threaten one's self-esteem is a "must" to avoid (Harter, 1990; Wigfield, 1994). For example, you may know individuals who rarely make the first move with people they would like to date for fear that they might be rejected.

As you may have inferred from the preceding discussion, expectancies and values are somewhat interdependent (Eccles et al., 1998). More specifically, people who don't expect to do well in a particular activity may find reasons to devalue it. And people who don't value an activity are less likely to work hard at it and so have lower expectancies about their performance. Even children in the early elementary grades recognize a difference between what they are good at and what is important to them (Eccles et al., 1998). But as they get older, they increasingly find value in the things they are good at and devalue the things they do poorly (Wigfield, 1994).

While examining operant conditioning in Chapter 4, we discovered that people may sometimes not exhibit certain behaviors, despite potential reinforcement, because they have too much to lose or too little to gain by doing so. We can explain such a cost–benefit analysis quite easily within an expectancies/values framework (Eccles [Parsons], 1984; Eccles & Wigfield, 1985; Feather, 1982; Paris & Byrnes, 1989). We will see people engage in a particular activity when they believe that (1) they can perform the activity successfully with a reasonable amount of effort (high expectancy) and (2) the activity or its outcome is worthwhile (high value). We will probably *not* see them engage in that activity if they think they will have to exert an inordinate amount of effort to achieve success (if they achieve it at all), or if they place little value on the activity and its consequence.

INTEREST

When we say that people have **interest** in a particular topic or activity, we mean that they find the topic or activity intriguing and enticing. Interest, then, is one form of intrinsic motivation. Positive affect accompanies interest; for example, people pursuing a task in which they are interested experience such feelings as pleasure, excitement, and liking (Hidi & Anderson, 1992; Schiefele, 1998).

Theorists distinguish between two general types of interest. Some interests reside within the individual; people tend to have personal preferences regarding the topics they pursue and the activities in which they engage. Because such **personal interests**[3] are relatively stable over time, we see a consistent pattern in the choices that people make. For example, my husband has a strong interest in football and so can often be found in front of the television set on Saturdays, Sundays, and Monday nights from September to January. (Fortunately, these are not the times when my favorite television game shows are broadcast.) And each of my children has shown unique personal interests from an early age. When Tina was growing up, she spent many hours either talking to or talking about boys, and as a college student, she lived in a coeducational "fraternity" house with a ratio of three males to every female. For many years, Alex had a thing for critters; he was fascinated with ants as a toddler, and he had an intense interest in various kinds of reptiles (lizards, snakes, dinosaurs) throughout the elementary and middle school years. Jeff has always been a Lego man, in his younger days putting all of his allowance toward Lego sets and spending many long hours in the basement designing architectural wonders. Even now as a college student, he occasionally retreats to the basement during semester breaks to expand on his latest construction.

In contrast to personal interest, **situational interest** is evoked by something in the environment—something that is perhaps new, unusual, or surprising. For instance, as I was driving through the plains of eastern Colorado one day many years ago, I saw what looked like a llama out of the corner of my eye. Well, I knew quite well that the Colorado plains are cattle and horse country, not llama country, so I slowed down to take a closer look, eventually confirming the unlikely llama hypothesis. For the time being, I was more interested in identifying the strange creature I saw than in getting to my destination. In much the same way, you might have your interest temporarily piqued by a traffic accident at the side of the road, a strange-but-true tidbit in the newspaper, or a large, brightly wrapped gift with your name on it.

Effects of Interest

In general, interest promotes more effective information processing. People who are interested in a particular topic devote more attention to it and become more cognitively engaged in it (McDaniel, Waddill, Finstad, & Bourg, 2000; Schiefele & Wild, 1994; Wigfield, 1994). They are also more likely to process information in a meaningful, organized, and elaborative fashion—for instance, by relating it to things they already know, interrelating ideas, drawing inferences, forming visual images, generating their own examples, and identifying potential applications (Hidi & Anderson, 1992; Pintrich & Schrauben, 1992; Schiefele, 1991, 1992; Schraw & Lehman, 2001; Tobias, 1994). And, provided they are not too attached to particular perspectives about a topic, they are more likely to undergo conceptual change if they encounter information that contradicts their existing understandings (Andre & Windschitl, 2003; Linnenbrink & Pintrich, 2003).

As you might guess, then, students who are interested in the things they study are more likely to remember them over the long run and thus are able to build on them in future learning (Garner, Brown, Sanders, & Menke, 1992; Garner et al., 1991; Hidi, 1990; Renninger, 1992; Scholes & Kardash, 1996; Wigfield, 1994). As a result, interested students show higher academic achievement (Hidi & Harackiewicz, 2000; Krapp, Hidi, & Renninger, 1992; Schiefele, Krapp, & Winteler, 1992).

---

[3]You may also see the term *individual interests.*

In this context, personal interest is ultimately more beneficial than situational interest: Whereas the latter may temporarily capture a learner's attention, personal interest is the force that ultimately sustains involvement in an activity over the long run (Alexander et al., 1994).

Factors Promoting Interest

Researchers have identified several sources of situational interest (Renninger, Hidi, & Krapp, 1992; Schank, 1979; Schraw & Lehman, 2001). Some topics—for example, death, destruction, danger, money, romance, and sex—appear to be inherently interesting for human beings. Things that are new, different, or unexpected often generate interest, as do things with a high activity level or intense emotions. Reading material is more interesting when it is concrete and easy to understand and when relationships among ideas are clear. Works of fiction—novels, short stories, movies, and so on—are more engaging when they include themes and characters with which people can personally identify. And, for children at least, challenging tasks are often more interesting than easy ones (Danner & Lonky, 1981; Harter, 1978), a fortunate state of affairs if, as Lev Vygotsky proposed, challenges promote cognitive growth.

Interesting information sometimes appears within the context of larger, less interesting content. Consider this passage as an example:

> Some insects live alone, and some live in large families. Wasps that live alone are called solitary wasps. A Mud Dauber Wasp is a solitary wasp. Click beetles live alone. When a click beetle is on its back, it flips itself into the air and lands right side up while it makes a clicking noise. Ants live in large families. There are many kinds of ants. Some ants live in trees. Black Ants live in the ground. (Garner, Gillingham, & White, 1989, p. 46)

If you are like me, you may have found the sentence about an upside-down beetle making a clicking noise as it rights itself to be the one interesting detail in an otherwise ho-hum passage. Such *seductive details* are apt to draw your attention and get you more cognitively engaged in what you are reading. If they are relevant to the topic you are reading about, they may enhance your understanding (Harp & Mayer, 1998; Sadoski & Paivio, 2001; Schraw, 1998). But if they distract your attention away from more central ideas or activate the wrong schemas in your long-term memory, they are likely to interfere with your overall learning (Garner et al., 1992; Harp & Mayer, 1998; Wade, 1992). For instance, in the preceding paragraph about insects, the description of a click beetle's strategy for turning itself over is definitely irrelevant to the paragraph's main idea (the social versus solitary nature of different insects) and so is unlikely to contribute to your learning (Garner et al., 1989). Seductive details are most apt to be distracting when readers have only limited background knowledge about a topic and therefore have little basis for determining what is and what is not important (Alexander & Jetton, 1996; Garner et al., 1991).

The origins of personal interest have not been investigated to the extent that sources of situational interest have. Many personal interests probably come from people's prior experiences with various topics and activities; for example, objects or events that initially invoke situational interest may provide the seed from which personal interest eventually grows (Alexander, 1997; Hidi & Harackiewicz, 2000). People may also find that acquiring more knowledge and skill in a particular area enhances their sense of self-efficacy, thereby providing intrinsic reinforcement. To some extent, interest and knowledge seem to perpetuate each other: Personal interest in a topic fuels a quest to learn more about the topic, and the increasing knowledge that one gains in turn promotes greater interest (Alexander, 1997; Hidi & McLaren, 1990; Kintsch, 1980; Tobias, 1994).

GOALS

As we discovered in our discussions of social cognitive theory and metacognition in Chapters 7 and 13, setting goals is an important part of self-regulated behavior and learning. People's internal goals and standards for success motivate them to move in particular directions. Self-regulated learners know what they want to accomplish when they read or study, they direct their thoughts and learning strategies accordingly, and they continually monitor their progress toward the goals they have set for themselves (Carver & Scheier, 1990; Schunk & Zimmerman, 1994). Goal attainment results in considerable self-satisfaction; it also leads to greater self-efficacy and higher standards for future performance (Bandura, 1986, 1989). Furthermore, people are more likely to work toward goals, and therefore are more likely to accomplish them, when they have set those goals for themselves rather than when others have imposed goals on them (Schunk, 1985). We must note, however, that goals are beneficial only to the extent that they are accomplishable; if they are unrealistically high, consistent failure to achieve them may result in excessive stress, frustration, or depression (Bandura, 1986).

Goals figure prominently in theories of motivation. In our discussion of motivation's general effects in the preceding chapter, we noted that motivation revolves around the accomplishment of certain goals, with such goals influencing both the choices people make and the consequences they find reinforcing. People's goals also influence their cognitive processing; for instance, goals affect the extent to which learners become cognitively engaged in particular tasks and the cognitive strategies that they use to study and learn (Anderman & Maehr, 1994; Brickman, Miller, & Roedel, 1997; Locke & Latham, 2002; Nolen, 1996; Winne & Marx, 1989).

Researchers have identified a wide variety of goals that people may set for themselves. Following are some of the possibilities:

- Gaining physical comfort and personal well-being
- Achieving and maintaining a sense of competence and self-worth
- Mastering information or skills
- Gaining a better understanding of the world
- Finding novelty and adventure
- Engaging in activities requiring intellectual or artistic challenge and creativity
- Obtaining extrinsic rewards
- Doing well in school (e.g., getting good grades)
- Making a good impression on others
- Gaining the recognition or approval of superiors or peers
- Bringing honor to one's family or social group
- Developing productive interpersonal relationships
- Developing long-term, intimate relationships (e.g., getting married, having children)
- Helping others
- Doing better than others in competitive situations
- Becoming a productive member of society
- Achieving a desired career
- Gaining material wealth
- Gaining social or political power
- Achieving a sense of spiritual understanding or harmony (Cacioppo, Petty, Feinstein, & Jarvis, 1996; Durkin, 1995; M. E. Ford, 1996; Lee & Anderson, 1991; McInerney,

Roche, McInerney, & Marsh, 1997; Schutz, 1994; Urdan & Maehr, 1995; Wentzel, 1989; Wolters, 1998)

Most of us have and work for many of these goals; for example, I achieve some degree of physical comfort by occasionally popping Cheetos into my mouth, I strive to confirm my high sense of self-worth by playing along at home as I watch television game shows, and I try to make a good impression in front of family and friends (or at least try not to look like a complete klutz) as I attempt parallel turns on the ski slope. But many of us have **core goals**—general goals of considerable priority for us at any given point in time—that seem to drive much of what we do (Schutz, 1994). For instance, my number one goal for many years has been to be a productive member of society—to leave the world a better place than I found it—and many of my behaviors (e.g., trying to raise socially responsible children, supporting my friends through difficult times, and writing books that can help teachers and other professionals understand and apply psychological principles) have been in one way or another directed toward that end.

Here we will focus on research findings related to several kinds of goals: achievement goals, work-avoidance goals, social goals, and career goals. We will then look at strategies people use for coordinating their efforts toward multiple goals. Near the end of the chapter, I will offer strategies for capitalizing on students' goals to enhance their motivation to learn and achieve in instructional settings.

Achievement Goals

As I mentioned in the preceding chapter, the need for achievement (also known as achievement motivation) was originally conceptualized as a general characteristic that people exhibit consistently across a variety of tasks and in many domains. But some contemporary theorists have proposed that achievement motivation takes one of several forms, depending on the specific goal an individual has in mind (Ames & Archer, 1988; Dweck & Elliott, 1983; Stipek, 1993). To illustrate, let's consider what three different girls might be thinking during the first day of a basketball unit in a physical education class:

Jane: This is my chance to show all the girls what a great basketball player I am. If I stay near the basket, Joan and June will keep passing to me, and I'll score a lot of points. I can really impress Coach and my friends.

Joan: Boy, I hope I don't screw this up. If I shoot at the basket and miss, I'll look like a real jerk. Maybe I should just stay outside the three-point line and keep passing to Jane and June.

June: I'd really like to become a better basketball player. I can't figure out why I don't get more of my shots into the basket. I'll ask Coach to give me feedback about how I can improve my game. Maybe some of my friends will have suggestions, too.

All three girls want to play basketball well but for different reasons. Jane is concerned mostly about her performance—that is, about looking good in front of her coach and classmates—so she wants to maximize opportunities to demonstrate her skill on the court. Joan is also concerned about the impression she will make, but she just wants to make sure she *doesn't* look *bad*. Unlike Jane and Joan, June isn't even thinking about how her performance will appear to others. Instead, she is interested mainly in developing her skill—in mastering the game of basketball—and doesn't expect herself to be an expert on the first day. For June, making mistakes is an inevitable part of learning a new skill, not a source of embarrassment or humiliation.

June's approach to basketball illustrates a **mastery goal**[4]—a desire to achieve competence by acquiring additional knowledge or mastering new skills. In contrast, Jane and Joan are each setting a **performance goal**[5]—a desire to present oneself as competent in the eyes of others. More specifically, Jane has a **performance-approach goal:** She wants to look good and receive favorable judgments from others. Meanwhile, Joan has a **performance-avoidance goal:** She wants *not* to look bad and receive unfavorable judgments. In some cases, performance goals have an element of social comparison: People are concerned about how their accomplishments compare to those of their peers (Elliot & McGregor, 2000; Elliot & Thrash, 2001; Midgley et al., 1998). In essence, a mastery goal focuses on the *task*, whereas a performance goal focuses on the *self* (Maehr & Kaplan, 2000; Nicholls, 1992).[6]

Mastery goals, performance-approach goals, and performance-avoidance goals are not necessarily mutually exclusive; people may simultaneously have two kinds, or even all three (Anderman & Maehr, 1994; Covington & Müeller, 2001; Hidi & Harackiewicz, 2000; Meece & Holt, 1993). For example, returning to our basketball example, we could imagine another girl, Jeanne, who wants to improve her basketball skills *and* look good in front of peers *and* not come across as a klutz.

Before they reach school age, children seem to focus primarily on mastery goals. For instance, even infants seek out experiences that are likely to increase their competence and mastery of the environment, and they derive genuine pleasure from new accomplishments (Dweck & Elliott, 1983). But when children enter school at five or six years of age, two things happen that orient them more toward performance goals (Dweck & Elliott, 1983). First, they suddenly have many peers around them to whom they can compare their own behavior; as a result, they may begin to define success more in terms of doing better than their classmates than in terms of task mastery. Second, whereas they have previously dealt primarily with physical tasks (e.g., learning to walk, fasten buttons, and ride a tricycle), they are now being asked to deal with tasks of an intellectual and somewhat abstract nature (e.g., learning to read, write, and add). The value of these school tasks may not be readily apparent to them, and their efforts in accomplishing them might therefore seem unnecessarily laborious. Furthermore, they may have greater difficulty assessing their progress on such tasks, to the point where they must rely on others (e.g., their teachers) to make judgments about their competence. As learners approach adolescence, yet another factor kicks in: They are much more likely to worry about what others think of them than they were in their early years (Elkind, 1981; Hartup, 1983; Juvonen, 2000; Midgley, 1993).

---

[4]In previous editions of the book, I have used the term *learning goal*, but the term *mastery goal* seems to be gaining favor among motivation theorists. Other theorists are referring to a similar idea when they talk about *task goals*, *task involvement*, or *task orientation*. Theorists sometimes like to stick to certain terminology to indicate the particular theoretical traditions on which they are building (Murphy & Alexander, 2000). (My earlier discussion of competence versus self-efficacy is another example of this phenomenon). However, the inconsistency in terms can be frustrating for newcomers to the field, because it interferes with their ability to synthesize what they are seeing in the research literature. As I present research findings in this section, I will be drawing on multiple programs of research and basically ignoring any subtle distinctions that theorists assign to the terms they use.

[5]You may also see the terms *ability goal*, *ego involvement*, or *ego orientation*.

[6]Some theorists have speculated that mastery goals may, like performance goals, be either approach oriented or avoidance oriented in nature (Elliot, 1999; Linnenbrink & Pintrich, 2002). However, research has not focused on this distinction, and so we will not consider it here.

Effects of Achievement Goals

A considerable body of research indicates that mastery goals are the optimal situation. As Table 17–1 illustrates, students with mastery goals tend to engage in the very activities that will help them learn: They pay attention in class, process information in ways that promote effective long-term memory storage, and learn from their mistakes. Furthermore, students with mastery goals have a healthy perspective about learning, effort, and failure: They realize that learning is a process of trying hard and continuing to persevere even in the face of temporary setbacks. Consequently, it is usually these students who learn the most from their classroom experiences (Gabriele & Montecinos, 2001; Wentzel & Wigfield, 1998).

In contrast, students with performance goals—especially those with performance-*avoidance* goals—may stay away from some of the very tasks that, because of their challenging nature, would do the most to promote mastery of new skills. Furthermore, these students often experience debilitating anxiety about tests and other classroom tasks. Performance-*approach* goals are a mixed bag: They sometimes have very positive effects, spurring students on to achieve at high levels, especially in the secondary grades and especially in combination with mastery goals (Hidi & Harackiewicz, 2000; McNeil & Alibali, 2000; Pintrich, 2000; Rawsthorne & Elliot, 1999; Urdan, 1997). Yet by themselves, performance-approach goals may be less beneficial than mastery goals: To achieve them, students may use relatively superficial learning strategies (e.g., rote memorization), exert only the minimal effort necessary to achieve desired outcomes, engage in self-handicapping behaviors, and perhaps even cheat (Anderman et al.,1998; Brophy, 1987; Midgley, Kaplan, & Middleton, 2001). Performance-approach goals appear to be most detrimental when students are younger (e.g., in the elementary grades), have relatively low ability in the subject matter, and have low self-efficacy for classroom tasks (Hidi & Harackiewicz, 2000; Kaplan, 1998; Kaplan & Midgley, 1997; Midgley et al., 2001).[7]

Some people seem to choose mastery goals over performance goals fairly consistently. These people can be thought of as having a strong **motivation to learn**—a tendency to find learning activities meaningful and worthwhile and therefore to attempt to get the maximum benefit from them (Brophy, 1986, 1987; McCombs, 1988). The motivation to learn puts a new twist on the concept of achievement motivation: People want to engage in the cognitive processes that lead to successful learning as well as the behaviors that lead to observable achievements.

Origins of Achievement Goals

In some cases, mastery goals come from within. People are more likely to have mastery goals when they have high interest in, and high self-efficacy for, learning something (Bandura, 1997; Murphy & Alexander, 2000; Schiefele, 1992). For example, for a year or so, my son Alex's interest in lizards led him to subscribe to a herpetologists' magazine and to read every issue from cover to cover. Similarly, people interested in antique automobiles might tinker with an old Model T engine until they know the engine inside and out. And people interested in gymnastics might spend a good portion of their free time at the gym practicing, practicing, practicing.

---

[7]Early studies contrasting the effects of mastery goals versus performance goals did not distinguish between performance-approach and performance-avoidance goals. Although theorists have begun to make the distinction in their research within the past few years, they have not yet reached consensus about the benefits and liabilities of performance-approach goals, probably in part because they have defined and measured such goals differently and in part because they have studied different populations of learners (Harackiewicz, Barron, Pintrich, Elliot, & Thrash, 2002; Kaplan, 1998).

Table 17–1
Characteristics of people with learning versus performance goals.

People With Mastery Goals	People With Performance Goals (Especially Those With Performance-Avoidance Goals)
Are more likely to be interested in and intrinsically motivated to learn school subject matter	Are more likely to be extrinsically motivated (i.e., motivated by expectations of external reinforcement and punishment) and more likely to cheat to obtain good grades
Believe that competence develops over time through practice and effort	Believe that competence is a stable characteristic (people either have talent or they don't); think that competent people shouldn't have to try very hard
Exhibit more self-regulated learning and behavior	Exhibit less self-regulation
Use learning strategies that promote true comprehension of course material (e.g., meaningful learning, elaboration, comprehension monitoring)	Use learning strategies that promote only rote learning (e.g., repetition, copying, word-for-word memorization); may procrastinate in their studying
Choose tasks that maximize opportunities for learning; seek out challenges	Choose tasks that maximize opportunities for demonstrating competence; avoid tasks and actions (e.g., asking for help) that might make them look incompetent
Are more likely to undergo conceptual change when confronted with convincing evidence that contradicts current beliefs	Are less likely to undergo conceptual change, in part because they are less likely to notice the discrepancy between new information and existing beliefs
React to easy tasks with feelings of boredom or disappointment	React to success on easy tasks with feelings of pride or relief
Seek feedback that accurately describes their ability and helps them improve	Seek feedback that flatters them
Willingly collaborate with peers when doing so is apt to enhance learning	Willing to collaborate with peers primarily when collaboration offers opportunities to look competent or enhance social status
Evaluate their own performance in terms of the progress they make	Evaluate their own performance in terms of how they compare with others
Interpret failure as a sign that they need to exert more effort	Interpret failure as a sign of low ability and therefore predictive of continuing failure in the future
View errors as a normal and useful part of the learning process; use errors to improve performance	View errors as a sign of failure and incompetence; engage in self-handicapping to provide apparent justification for errors and failures
Persist in efforts to learn, even in the face of failure	Give up easily when they fail and avoid tasks that have previously led to failure
Are satisfied with their performance if they try hard and make progress, even if their efforts result in failure	Are satisfied with their performance only if they succeed
View a teacher as a resource and guide to help them learn	View a teacher as a judge and as a rewarder or punisher

Continued

Table 17–1
Continued

People With Mastery Goals	People With Performance Goals (Especially Those With Performance-Avoidance Goals)
Remain relatively calm during tests and classroom assignments	Are often quite anxious about tests and other assessments
As students, are more likely to be enthusiastic about, and become actively involved in, school activities	As students, are more likely to distance themselves from the school environment

Sources: Ablard & Lipschultz, 1998; C. Ames & Archer, 1988; R. Ames, 1983; Anderman et al., 1998; Anderman & Maehr, 1994; Dweck, 1986; Dweck & Elliott, 1983; Entwisle & Ramsden, 1983; L. S. Fuchs et al., 1997; Gabriele & Boody, 2001; Graham & Weiner, 1996; Jagacinski & Nicholls, 1984, 1987; Kaplan, 1998; Kaplan & Midgley, 1999; Levy et al., 2000; Linnenbrink & Pintrich, 2002, 2003; McCombs, 1988; McGregor & Elliot, 2002; Meece, 1994; Middleton & Midgley, 1997; Murphy, 2000; Murphy & Alexander, 2000; Newman & Schwager, 1995; Nolen, 1996; Powell, 1990; Rawsthorne & Elliot, 1999; A. M. Ryan, Pintrich, & Midgley, 2001; Schiefele, 1991, 1992; Shernoff & Hoogstra, 2001; Skaalvik, 1997; Southerland & Sinatra, 2003; Stipek, 1993; Turner, Thorpe, & Meyer, 1998; Urdan & Midgley, 2001; Urdan et al., 1998.

Yet the instructional environment can encourage mastery goals as well (Church, Elliot, & Gable, 2001; Newman, 1998; Wentzel, 1999). For instance, teachers might describe the intrinsic benefits of learning a skill, focus students' attention on the progress being made, or communicate their own goal of having students understand rather than rote-memorize classroom subject matter. In fact, *insisting* that students understand—a **press for understanding**—may be especially helpful (Middleton & Midgley, 2002; J. C. Turner, Meyer, et al., 1998). For example, teachers might continually ask students to explain and justify their reasoning, and they might refuse to accept substandard work that reflects little thought or effort (Middleton & Midgley, 2002).

Unfortunately, however, performance goals seem to be far more prevalent than mastery goals among today's students, at least those in the secondary grades (Blumenfeld, 1992; Doyle, 1986b; Elliot & McGregor, 2000; Harter, 1992). Most students, if they are motivated to succeed in their schoolwork, are primarily concerned about getting good grades, and they prefer short, easy tasks to lengthier, more challenging ones. Performance goals are also common in team sports, where the focus is often more on winning and gaining public recognition than on developing new skills and improving over time (Roberts, Treasure, & Kavussanu, 1997).

In some instances, students adopt performance goals as a means of avoiding failure, protecting their sense of self-worth, or—especially if their need for relatedness is high—enhancing relationships with peers (Anderman & Anderman, 1999; Covington, 1992; Elliot & McGregor, 2000; Urdan, 2000). In other cases, they may adopt performance goals because they believe that ability is something that they either have or don't have (rather than something they can improve with hard work)[8] and so try to assess their "natural" ability by continually comparing their own

---

[8]In other words, they have an *entity view*, rather than an *incremental view*, of intelligence. We'll look at this distinction more closely in Chapter 18.

performance with that of others (Dweck, 1999). In still other cases, students realize that performing at high levels—in particular, getting good grades—is critical for their future educational and professional opportunities (Covington & Müeller, 2001). Yet many common teaching and coaching practices also contribute to the development of performance goals (Anderman & Anderman, 1999; Church et al., 2001; Newman, 1998; Roberts et al., 1997; Wentzel & Wigfield, 1998). Scoring tests on a curve, reminding students that they need to get good grades if they want to go to college, displaying grades for everyone to see, and focusing on surpassing other schools and teams—all of these strategies, though undoubtedly well intended, encourage learners to focus their attention more on "looking good" than on learning.

Work-Avoidance Goals

As we have just seen, students sometimes want to avoid looking bad as they perform classroom tasks. On other occasions, they may want to avoid having to do classroom tasks *at all*, or at least they will try to put as little effort as possible into those tasks. In other words, they may have a **work-avoidance goal** (Dowson & McInerney, 2001; Gallini, 2000; Nicholls, Cobb, Yackel, Wood, & Wheatley, 1990).

To date, research on work-avoidance goals has focused on the middle school grades, where such goals seem to be fairly common (Dowson & McInerney, 2001; Gallini, 2000). Students with work-avoidance goals use a variety of strategies to minimize their workload; for instance, they may engage in off-task behavior, solicit help on easy tasks and problems, pretend that they don't understand something even when they *do*, complain loudly about challenging assignments, and select the least taxing alternatives whenever choices are given (Dowson & McInerney, 2001). They rarely use effective learning strategies or pull their weight in small-group activities (Dowson & McInerney, 2001; Gallini, 2000).

Given the paucity of research findings on work-avoidance goals at present, we can only speculate about how these goals originate. In some instances, peers may encourage and model work-avoidance behaviors (Nolen, 1996). But we can reasonably guess that students are also likely to adopt such goals when they find little value in academic subject matter, have low self-efficacy for learning it, and see no long-term payoffs for mastering it (e.g., Garner, 1998). In other words, students are most likely to have work-avoidance goals when they have neither intrinsic nor extrinsic motivation to achieve instructional objectives. Students with work-avoidance goals may thus be teachers' biggest challenges, and teachers will have to use a wide variety of motivational strategies—probably including extrinsic reinforcers—to get them truly engaged in, and eventually committed to mastering, academic subject matter.

Social Goals

In Chapter 16, we noted that most students make social relationships a high priority, and in fact all students probably have some need for relatedness. Students are apt to have a variety of social goals, perhaps including the following:

- Forming and maintaining friendly or intimate relationships with others
- Becoming part of a cohesive, mutually supportive group
- Gaining other people's approval
- Achieving status and prestige among peers

- Meeting social obligations and keeping interpersonal commitments
- Assisting and supporting others, and ensuring their welfare (Dowson & McInerney, 2001; M. E. Ford, 1996; Hicks, 1997; Hinkley, McInerney, & Marsh, 2001; Schutz, 1994)

The nature of students' social goals will undoubtedly affect their classroom behavior and academic performance. If students want to gain their teacher's attention and approval, they are apt to strive for good grades and in other ways shoot for performance goals (Hinkley et al., 2001). If they want to gain the approval of low-achieving peers, they may exert little effort in their studies and possibly even adopt work-avoidance goals (B. Brown, 1990; M. E. Ford & Nichols, 1991). If they are seeking friendly relationships with classmates or are concerned about others' welfare, they may eagerly and actively engage in such activities as cooperative learning and peer tutoring; concern for others' welfare may also foster mastery goals (Anderman & Anderman, 1999; Dowson & McInerney, 2001).

Career Goals

Many students include career goals among their long-term goals. Young children set such goals with little thought and change them frequently; for instance, a 6-year-old may want to be a firefighter one week and a professional basketball player the next. By late adolescence, some (though by no means all) have reached some tentative and relatively stable decisions about the career paths they want to pursue (Marcia, 1980).

In general, boys set higher aspirations for themselves than girls do, especially in domains that are stereotypically masculine (Deaux, 1984; Durkin, 1995; Lueptow, 1984). Many girls, especially those raised in fairly traditional cultures, tend to limit themselves to stereotypically "female" occupations (Durkin, 1995; Olneck, 1995; Taylor, 1994). And many girls, but few boys, further limit themselves to careers that they believe will be compatible with their future roles as spouses and parents (Eccles [Parsons], 1984). Gender stereotypes and future family roles are not the only things affecting students' career goals; self-efficacy, expectancies for success, and values are almost certainly involved as well.

Coordinating Multiple Goals

At any one time, individuals are apt to be striving for several goals, perhaps including a desire to learn and understand classroom subject matter, a need to earn the good grades so important for gaining admission to college, and a longing to maintain and enhance social relationships with peers. Achieving multiple goals simultaneously can be a challenging task indeed. People use a variety of strategies to juggle their diverse goals (Dodge, Asher, & Parkhurst, 1989; McCaslin & Good, 1996). They may find activities that allow them to achieve several goals simultaneously; for instance, they may satisfy both achievement goals and social goals by participating in cooperative learning activities (Dodge et al., 1989; Phelan et al., 1994; Urdan & Maehr, 1995). They may pursue some goals while putting others on the "back burner." For example, they might complete assignments that will yield good grades while ignoring more interesting topics they would like to pursue further (Covington, 2000). Likewise, as I pursue the goal of completing this book, I leave dirty dishes in the sink, thereby ignoring my lower-priority goal of having a clean house. People may also modify their ideas of what it means to achieve a particular goal. For example, as I have become increasingly busy with my professional writing in recent years (thereby, I hope, satisfying my desire to make the world a better place), my definition of a clean house has deteriorated rapidly from being a spotless home that would make Martha Stewart green with envy to one in which family members can successfully find a pathway through the clutter on the family room floor.

In some situations, accomplishing one goal may be incompatible with accomplishing another; for example, achieving at a high level in the classroom may interfere with one's ability to maintain a friendship with a peer who doesn't value academic achievement (Berndt & Perry, 1990; Dodge et al., 1989; Phelan et al., 1994). On such occasions, people may have little choice but to abandon one goal in favor of another (McCaslin & Good, 1996). Quite possibly, the species' evolutionary heritage comes into play here, leading people to forsake the "luxuries" of one's culture (e.g., learning to read) for more basic needs (e.g., maintaining social connectedness with others) (Geary, 1998).

DISPOSITIONS

A **disposition**[9] is a general inclination to approach learning and problem-solving situations in a particular way. Dispositions are intentional rather than accidental, and they encompass cognition, motivation, and personality characteristics (Kardash & Scholes, 1996; Kuhn, 2001a; Stanovich, 1999). Following are examples of productive dispositions that theorists have identified:

- *Stimulation seeking.* Eagerly interacting with one's physical and social environment
- *Need for cognition.* Regularly seeking and engaging in challenging cognitive tasks
- *Learned industriousness.* Persisting and persevering even when considerable effort is required
- *Open-mindedness.* Being willing to consider alternative perspectives and multiple sources of evidence, and to suspend judgment rather than leaping to immediate conclusions
- *Critical thinking.* Consistently evaluating information or arguments in terms of their accuracy, logic, and credibility rather than accepting them at face value
- *Consensus seeking.* Seeking a synthesis of diverse perspectives, rather than assuming that perspectives must necessarily be mutually exclusive
- *Future time perspective.* Predicting and considering the long-term consequences of various courses of action (Cacioppo et al., 1996; Eccles et al., 1998; Eisenberger, 1992; Halpern, 1997; Husman & Freeman, 1999; Kardash & Scholes, 1996; Onosko & Newmann, 1994; Raine, Reynolds, & Venables, 2002; Southerland & Sinatra, 2003; Stanovich, 1999; Toplak & Stanovich, 2002)

Research on the nature and effects of dispositions is still in its infancy, but it is becoming increasingly clear that dispositions can be important factors affecting learning, motivation, and achievement. For instance, children who, at age 3, are eager to seek out physical and social stimulation are, at age 11, better readers and earn higher grades at school (Raine et al., 2002). People who have a strong future time perspective are more motivated to engage

---

[9]Theorists are addressing a similar idea when they talk about *habits of mind.*

in activities that will help them achieve their future goals (Husman & Freeman, 1999; Raynor, 1981). People with a high need for cognition learn more from what they read and are more likely to base conclusions on sound evidence and logical reasoning (Cacioppo et al., 1996; Dai, 2002). People who critically evaluate new evidence and are receptive to and open-minded about diverse perspectives show more advanced reasoning capabilities; they are also more likely to undergo conceptual change when warranted (Southerland & Sinatra, 2003; Stanovich, 1999).

Researchers have not yet systematically addressed the origins of various dispositions. Perhaps inherited temperamental differences (e.g., in stimulation seeking) are involved (Raine et al., 2002). Epistemological beliefs—for instance, the belief that knowledge is fixed and unchanging, on the one hand, or dynamic and continually evolving, on the other—may also play a role (King & Kitchener, 2002; Mason, 2003; also see Chapter 13). And quite possibly, teachers' actions in the classroom make a difference. In the following classroom interaction, a teacher actually seems to *discourage* any disposition to think analytically and critically about classroom material:

Teacher:	Write this on your paper . . . it's simply memorizing this pattern. We have meters, centimeters, and millimeters. Let's say . . . write millimeters, centimeters, and meters. We want to make sure that our metric measurement is the same. If I gave you this decimal, let's say .234 m (yes, write that). In order to come up with .234 m in centimeters, the only thing that is necessary is that you move the decimal. How do we move the decimal? You move it to the right two places. (Jason, sit up please.) If I move it to the right two places, what should .234 m look like, Daniel, in centimeters? What does it look like, Ashley?
Ashley:	23.4 cm.
Teacher:	Twenty-three point four. Simple stuff. In order to find meters, we're still moving that decimal to the right, but this time, boys and girls, we're only going to move it one place. So, if I move this decimal one place, what is my answer for millimeters? (dialogue from Turner, Meyer et al., 1998, p. 741)

Undoubtedly, this teacher means well: She wants her students to know how to convert from one unit of measurement to another. But notice the attitude she engenders: "Write this . . . it's simply memorizing this pattern."

Many of the dispositions that lead to effective learning and problem solving reflect considerable self-regulated learning. Truly effective learners regulate not only their approach to a learning task but also their motivation and affect. We now look at the interplay among motivation, affect, and self-regulation.

MOTIVATION, AFFECT, AND SELF-REGULATION

In Chapter 16, we discovered how motivation and affect are often interrelated. Motivation and affect also influence, and are influenced by, self-regulation. Furthermore, self-regulation may involve *internalizing* the motives, values, and goals of others. Let's explore each of these ideas in turn.

How Motivation and Affect Influence Self-Regulation

People are more likely to be self-regulated learners when they feel confident that they can be successful at a learning task and when they believe they can control the direction in which they are going. In other words, self-regulated learners have a sense of both competence (self-efficacy) and self-determination (Corno & Rohrkemper, 1985; McCombs, 1996; Paris & Turner, 1994; Schunk, 1995; Zimmerman, 1995; Zimmerman & Risemberg, 1997).

One aspect of self-regulated learning in which motivation and affect figure prominently is *help-seeking behavior.* Why do some students willingly seek others' assistance when they need it, whereas other struggling students consistently ignore opportunities and offers for assistance? Researchers have found that students are *less* likely to seek help (perhaps from teachers, perhaps from peers) when they

- Perceive requests for help as threatening their sense of competence and self-worth.
- Believe that asking for help will undermine their sense of autonomy and self-determination (in some instances, they may also think they can learn more if they persist on their own).[10]
- Have performance goals (rather than mastery goals) in combination with low ability.
- Are more concerned about making a good impression on others than in interacting with others, and worry that a request for help will make them look stupid.
- Worry that requests for help may be disparaged and rejected.
  (R. Ames, 1983; Butler, 1998b; Newman & Schwager, 1992; A. M. Ryan, Hicks, & Midgley, 1997; A. M. Ryan, Pintrich, & Midgley, 2001; Skaalvik & Valas, 2001; Turner, Husman, & Schallest, 2002)

How Self-Regulation Influences Motivation and Affect

Not only does motivation influence self-regulated learning, but self-regulated learners also *control* their motivation to some degree. They do so in a variety of ways:

- *Aligning assigned tasks with areas of interest.* When they have leeway in learning activities, they intentionally choose alternatives that interest them (Covington, 2000). For example, when thinking about research projects for an upcoming science fair, they might develop a project that relates to a current interest in lizards or a long-term goal of becoming a dentist.
- *Setting goals.* They set short-term as well as long-term goals for themselves (Locke & Latham, 2002; Zimmerman, 1998). For instance, they might tell themselves, "I need to finish reading this chapter on motivation before I go to lunch."
- *Minimizing distractions.* They create or find an environment in which they can concentrate as they study (Kuhl, 1987; Wolters, 2000; Wolters & Rosenthal, 2000). For instance, they might turn off the television while studying in the living room, or they might retreat to a quiet corner of the local library.
- *Reminding themselves of the importance of doing well.* They engage in self-talk that emphasizes reasons for completing a task or performing at high levels (Wolters, 2000; Wolters & Rosenthal, 2000). For instance, they might say, "I can help others in my

---

[10]Culture may also be a factor here. Many Western societies encourage students to be independent learners as much as possible and to minimize reliance on others (Karabenick & Sharma, 1994).

study group understand this only if I understand it myself" or "Getting an A on this test is important for my GPA."

- *Enhancing the appeal of a task.* They devise ways to make a boring task more interesting and enjoyable (Sansone, Weir, Harpster, & Morgan, 1992; Wolters, 2000; Wolters & Rosenthal, 2000). For example, they might try to make the task into a game of some sort, or they might embellish their written work with artful illustrations.
- *Self-imposing consequences.* They promise themselves, and then follow through on, rewards for doing well; they may also punish themselves in some way if they fail (Wolters, 2000; Wolters & Rosenthal, 2000; also see Chapter 7). For example, they might treat themselves to a night at the movies with friends if, but only if, they get at least a B on an assignment.

Although emotions are not as easy to control as motivation, self-regulated learners rein in unproductive ones as much as they can. For instance, they try to put worrisome thoughts out of their minds while they study (Zeidner, 1998). They try to think of upcoming exams as being challenges that they can overcome rather than as threatening events that foreshadow almost certain doom (Richards & Gross, 2000). And they bounce back quickly after a discouraging failure, renewing their efforts and finding reasons for optimism that they will be successful the next time (Corno, 1993; Turner et al., 2002).

Internalized Motivation

As I mentioned in Chapter 13, my son Alex and I once took an undergraduate course in art history. We were both taking the course primarily to gain a greater understanding of the many works of art we'd seen in museums over the years. Alex also had a second reason for taking the course: to earn credit toward his high school diploma. Alex, of course, had to get a passing grade in the course. As for me, it mattered little whether I got an A or an F. Yet I diligently studied for every test, often foregoing things I'd rather have been doing, such as reading a mystery novel or watching a television game show. Why did I do it? Although I enjoyed attending class, studying the material before a test was definitely *not* an intrinsically motivating activity for me; the textbook had lots of beautiful pictures, but its prose was about as interesting and engaging as the telephone book. There was no extrinsic motivation for me to study, either; the grade I got in the course would in no way affect my future physical, financial, or emotional well-being. The bottom line was that, in my many years as a student, I had acquired a desire to achieve good grades, more or less for their own sake.

In our discussion so far, we have thought of intrinsic versus extrinsic motivation as an either–or state of affairs. In fact, there is a third possibility. The concept of **internalized motivation** refers to situations in which, over time, people gradually adopt behaviors that other individuals value, without regard for the external consequences that such behaviors may or may not bring (Deci & Ryan, 1995; Deci, Vallerand, Pelletier, & Ryan, 1991; Harter, 1992; Ryan & Connell, 1989; Ryan, Connell, & Grolnick, 1992).

Deci and Ryan (1995; Deci et al., 1991; Ryan et al., 1992) have proposed that internalized motivation may evolve in the following sequence:

1. *External regulation.* The individual is motivated to behave, or else *not* to behave, in certain ways based primarily on the external consequences that will follow behaviors; in other words, the individual is extrinsically motivated. For instance, students may do schoolwork primarily to avoid being punished for poor grades, and they are likely to need a lot of prodding to complete assigned tasks.

2. *Introjection.* The individual behaves in particular ways to gain the approval of others; for example, a student may willingly complete an easy, boring assignment as a means of gaining a teacher's approval. At this point, we see some internal pressure to engage in desired behaviors; for instance, the individual may feel guilty if he or she violates certain standards or rules for behavior. However, the person does not fully understand the rationale behind such standards and rules. Instead, the primary motives appear to be avoiding a negative self-evaluation and protecting one's sense of self-worth.

3. *Identification.* The individual now sees certain behaviors as being personally important or valuable. For instance, a student is likely to value learning and academic success for their own sake, to perceive assigned classroom tasks as being essential for learning, and to need little prodding to get assigned work done.

4. *Integration.* The individual has fully accepted the desirability of certain behaviors and integrated them into an overall system of motives and values. For example, a student might have acquired a keen interest in science as a career goal; if so, we are likely to see that interest reflected in many things the student does on a regular basis.

Internalized motivation is an important aspect of self-regulated learning; it fosters a general work ethic in which the learner spontaneously engages in activities that, although not always fun or immediately gratifying, are essential for reaching long-term goals (Harter, 1992; McCombs, 1996; Ryan et al., 1992; Stipek, 1993).

Ryan and his colleagues (1992) have suggested that three conditions promote the development of internalized motivation:

- *The learner operates within the context of a warm, responsive, and supportive environment.* The learner feels a sense of relatedness to, and regard for, important other people (i.e., *significant others*) within his or her environment (also see Wentzel & Wigfield, 1998).
- *The learner is given some autonomy.* The significant others who are controlling the learner's behavior (e.g., parents, teachers) exert no more control than necessary, as a way of maximizing the extent to which the learner maintains a sense of self-determination. And, over time, they gradually relinquish that control to the learner.
- *The learner operates within a certain degree of structure.* The environment provides information about expected behaviors and why they are important. Response–consequence contingencies are clearly identified.

Fostering the development of internalized motivation, then, involves a delicate balancing act between giving the learner sufficient opportunities for experiencing self-determination and providing some guidance about how the learner should behave. In a sense, significant others scaffold desired behaviors at first, gradually reducing such scaffolding as the learner exhibits the behaviors more easily and frequently.

What other educational implications can we draw from what we have learned about cognitive factors in motivation? In the final section of the chapter we identify a number of strategies for fostering "motivating" cognitions in instructional settings.

ENCOURAGING COGNITIONS THAT MOTIVATE

We have considered several cognitive factors that influence motivation, including perceptions of competence and self-determination, expectancies, values, interests, goals, and dispositions. Following are some guidelines that we can derive from such factors:

- *Students must feel competent about classroom activities and have high expectations for academic success.* Throughout the book, we have encountered strategies for promoting students' academic success. For example, we have found that students learn classroom subject matter more successfully when teachers help them use effective cognitive processes—for instance, by providing advance organizers, visual aids, and mnemonics. We have also found that some learning and study strategies promote more effective learning and memory than others and that students can learn to use such strategies. And we have found that students often have more success on classroom tasks when they work with their peers rather than alone.

In addition to promoting success itself, teachers can use several other strategies to enhance students' sense of competence and expectations for academic success. They can communicate their own high expectations for student performance. They can help students develop a realistic perspective as to what success *is* (monthly improvement qualifies, consistent perfection does not). And they can cast students' errors in an appropriate light—as inevitable minor stumbling blocks on the road to success—and make sure that, despite such errors, students eventually do succeed with effort, persistence, and appropriate strategies.

- *Students should believe that they have some self-determination regarding classroom events.* For both pedagogical and logistical reasons, students often have little control over the things that happen in school. For example, society's needs and school district curricula often dictate the objectives that students must achieve. The use of the same facilities and resources by many different students requires adherence to certain schedules. To keep students' attention focused on school tasks, teachers must maintain some semblance of order in the classroom. And as we have seen, a certain amount of structure regarding expectations for students' behavior is an important condition for promoting internalized motivation.

Yet some degree of self-determination is essential for both intrinsic motivation and the development of internalized motivation. Teachers can do numerous little things to give students a sense of self-determination about classroom activities. For example, they can establish general routines and procedures that students should typically follow, thus minimizing the need to give explicit instructions for each and every assignment (Spaulding, 1992). They can inform students well ahead of time about upcoming deadlines, so that students can budget their time accordingly (Spaulding, 1992). They can ask for regular feedback about how classroom activities might be improved (Keller, 1987). They can structure classroom tasks sufficiently to facilitate successful performance but not so much that students feel unnecessarily constrained (deCharms, 1984; Reeve, Bolt, & Cai, 1999). They can provide opportunities for students to learn independently, perhaps through small-group work or computer-assisted instruction (Swan, Mitrani, Guerrero, Cheung, & Schoener, 1990). When the same objective can be accomplished in two or more different ways, they can give students a choice about how best to proceed (Hennessey & Amabile, 1987; Paris & Turner, 1994; Spaulding, 1992). When extrinsic reinforcers are used as a way of encouraging students to perform dull but necessary tasks, teachers can preserve students' sense of self-determination by giving them choices regarding the specific reinforcers they can earn by completing those tasks (Spaulding, 1992). And when evaluation is useful in promoting academic progress, teachers can provide mechanisms (e.g., checklists, feedback sheets) through which students can evaluate *themselves* (McCaslin & Good, 1996; Spaulding, 1992; Wlodkowski, 1978).

- *Feedback and other forms of extrinsic reinforcement should communicate information rather than decrease students' sense of control.* In an ideal world, all students would be intrinsically motivated to learn in the classroom and succeed at classroom activities. But in reality, external stimuli—feedback, praise, privileges, and so on—are sometimes necessary to keep students on task.

As we discovered earlier in the chapter, reinforcement may undermine students' intrinsic motivation, particularly if it conveys the idea that adults are trying to control students' behaviors. Yet feedback and other forms of reinforcement can be beneficial when they instead communicate information about students' current performances and offer suggestions for improvement (Bangert-Drowns et al., 1991; Clifford, 1990; Deci & Ryan, 1985, 1987; Harris & Rosenthal, 1985). Whenever possible, teachers should provide such information immediately so that students can store it in working memory simultaneously with their recollections of what they have just done; in this way, the two are easily integrated (J. R. Anderson, 1987).

- *Instruction should help students see value in learning school subject matter.* Some classroom activities will be naturally fun, interesting, or otherwise intrinsically motivating for students. But others—perhaps occasional drill and practice to promote automaticity of basic skills, or perhaps intensive study of dry but essential topics—may have little obvious appeal. Teachers can do many things to help students find value in school activities. For example, they can identify the specific knowledge and skills that students will acquire from an instructional unit (Keller, 1987). They can show how things learned in the classroom will help address students' present concerns and long-term goals (C. Ames, 1992; Brophy & Alleman, 1991; Ferrari & Elik, 2003). They can demonstrate how they themselves value academic activities—for example, by sharing their fascination with certain topics and describing how they use the things they've learned in school (Brophy, 1999; Brophy & Alleman, 1991). And they should refrain from asking students to engage in activities with little long-term benefit—memorizing trivial facts for no good reason, reading material that is clearly beyond students' comprehension levels, and so on (Brophy, 1987).

- *Students should find classroom material interesting as well as informative.* Almost all students learn more when a topic is interesting; students with little background knowledge in the topic are especially likely to benefit (Alexander, 1997; Garner et al., 1991). Yet students often report that they find little of interest in classroom subject matter, particularly as they reach the middle school and high school grades (Gentry, Gable, & Rizza, 2002; Larson, 2000).

Certainly teachers should capitalize on students' personal interests whenever possible (Alexander et al., 1994; Brophy, 1986, 1987; Wlodkowski, 1978). But situational interest factors can also be incorporated into classroom topics and activities. For example, students typically enjoy opportunities to respond actively during a learning activity—perhaps by manipulating and experimenting with physical objects, creating new products, discussing controversial issues, or teaching something they've learned to peers (Andre & Windschitl, 2003; Brophy, 1987; Hidi, Weiss, Berndorff, & Nolan, 1998; Zahorik, 1994). They enjoy subject matter to which they can relate on a personal level—for instance, math lessons that involve students' favorite foods, works of literature that feature characters with whom students can readily identify, or history textbooks that portray historical figures as real people with distinctly human qualities (Anand & Ross, 1987; Levstik, 1994). Students are often curious about things that are new and different and about events that are surprising and puzzling (Brophy, 1987; Lepper & Hodell, 1989; Sheveland, 1994; Stipek, 1993). They like to engage in fantasy and make-believe—for example, playing out the roles of key figures in historical events or imagining what it must be like to be weightless in space (Brophy, 1987; Lepper & Hodell, 1989). Keep in mind, however, that adding interesting but *irrelevant* information may sometimes be counterproductive, distracting students' attention from more important material (recall our earlier discussion of seductive details).

- *Teachers should encourage students to set goals for themselves.* When we talked about instructional objectives in Chapter 5, we were essentially talking about goals that teachers set for their students. But it is equally important that students set their *own* goals regarding what they want to accomplish at school (Wentzel, 1999). Self-chosen goals will help students make appropriate choices, direct students' efforts as they work in the classroom, and contribute to students' sense of self-determination.

Although teachers should certainly encourage students to develop long-term goals for themselves—perhaps to go to college or become an environmental scientist—such goals are often too general and abstract to guide students' immediate behaviors (Bandura, 1997; Husman & Freeman, 1999). Many students (younger ones especially) initially respond more favorably to fairly specific, concrete, short-term goals—perhaps learning a certain number of spelling words or solving a certain number of mathematics problems (Bandura & Schunk, 1981; Good & Brophy, 1994; Schunk & Rice, 1989).[11] By setting and working for a series of short-term goals, students get regular feedback about the progress they are making, develop a greater sense of self-efficacy that they can master school subject matter, and achieve at higher levels (Bandura, 1997; Kluger & DeNisi, 1998; Page-Voth & Graham, 1999; Schunk, 1996).

- *As much as possible, teachers should encourage students to focus on mastery goals rather than performance goals.* To some degree, performance goals (e.g., completing assigned tasks, earning high grades and test scores) are inevitable in today's schools and in society at large (Butler, 1989; Elliot & McGregor, 2000). Furthermore, children and adolescents will invariably look to their peers' performance as one means of evaluating their *own* performance, and many aspects of the adult world (gaining admission to college, seeking employment, working in private industry, playing professional sports, etc.) are inherently competitive in nature. But ultimately, mastery goals are the ones most likely to promote effective learning and performance over the long run. Mastery goals are especially motivating when they are specific ("I want to learn how to ride a bicycle"), challenging ("Writing a limerick looks difficult, but I'm sure I can do it"), and short-term ("I'm going to learn to count to 100 in French by the end of the month") (Alderman, 1990; Brophy, 1987; Good & Brophy, 1994).

Recently, some theorists (Schunk & Swartz, 1993; Schunk & Zimmerman, 1997; Zimmerman & Kitsantas, 1997) have proposed that different kinds of mastery goals may be more useful at different points in learning, especially when learners are trying to learn a skill of some sort (e.g., writing a good paragraph, playing basketball, throwing darts). Initially, learners may want to work toward a **process goal,** perfecting the form or procedure that the skill involves without regard to the final outcome. As the desired form or procedure becomes more automatized, they may then want to shift their attention to a **product goal,** striving for a certain standard of performance (e.g., getting a certain percentage of balls in the basket or a certain number of darts in the center of the target).

Through their own behaviors, teachers can demonstrate that improving and mastering knowledge and skills are the objectives most important for students to accomplish. For example, they can express their *own* belief that learning, understanding, and improving are ultimately more important than getting good grades, winning competitions, and so on (Roberts et al., 1997; Wentzel, 1999). They can present tasks that students find valuable in and of themselves (Ames, 1992; Dweck & Elliott, 1983; Pintrich et al., 1993). They can provide mechanisms and criteria through which students may easily record and assess academic progress (Good & Brophy, 1994;

---

[11]Some theorists use the terms *distal goals* and *proximal goals* when referring to long-term and short-term goals, respectively.

Spaulding, 1992). They can communicate the idea that mistakes are a normal part of learning and therefore to be expected (Ames, 1992; Clifford, 1990; Dweck & Elliott, 1983; Stipek, 1996). They can give specific feedback about how students can improve rather than simply reporting test scores or letter grades (Brophy, 1986; Butler, 1987; Graham & Weiner, 1996; Spaulding, 1992). And they should *not* repeatedly remind students that classwork will be evaluated and graded (Stipek, 1993; Thomas & Oldfather, 1997). Focusing learners' attention on mastery goals, especially when those goals relate to learners' own lives, may especially benefit students from diverse ethnic backgrounds and students at risk for academic failure (Alderman, 1990; Garcia, 1992; Wlodkowski & Ginsberg, 1995).

  • *Classroom activities are more effective when they enable students to meet several goals at once.* Students will be more productive when they can accomplish multiple goals simultaneously (M. E. Ford, 1992; Wentzel & Wigfield, 1998). For instance, students might work toward mastery goals by learning and practicing new skills within the context of group projects (thus meeting their social goals) and with evaluation criteria that allow for risk taking and mistakes (thus also meeting their performance goals). Students are *unlikely* to strive for mastery goals when assignments ask little of them (thereby not enhancing their self-efficacy), when they must compete with one another for resources or high test scores (so possibly thwarting attaining of social goals), and when any single failure has a significant impact on their final grades (impeding progress toward performance goals).

  • *Dispositions that involve actively and thoughtfully engaging with school subject matter should promote more effective cognitive processing and learning over the long run.* To date, researchers have focused more on how students differ in their dispositions than on how to *promote* certain dispositions. But we can reasonably assume that teachers who encourage and model productive dispositions—for example, by asking students to evaluate the quality of scientific evidence, insisting that students defend opinions about social issues with sound rationales, teaching strategies for constructing persuasive arguments, and consistently exhibiting their own open-mindedness about diverse perspectives—get students off to a good start (e.g., see Baron, 1987; Derry, Levin, Osana, & Jones, 1998; Halpern, 1998; Kuhn, 2001b).

Although we have identified numerous cognitive factors in motivation, we have largely ignored a very important one: the extent to which people make a *connection* between what they do and what happens to them. Certainly people are more eager to pursue an activity when they think their behaviors will lead to desired outcomes. But some individuals fail to recognize existing contingencies between the behaviors they exhibit and the consequences that result. To what sources do people attribute the events that occur in their lives? To what things do they give credit when they succeed? What things do they blame when they fail? We'll find out as we explore *attribution theory* in the next chapter.

SUMMARY

Many cognitive factors influence human motivation. Some motivation theorists believe that students are most likely to be intrinsically motivated when two conditions exist: (1) when they have a high sense of *competence* (high self-efficacy) regarding their ability to succeed at classroom tasks and (2) when they have a sense of *self-determination*—a sense that they have some control over the course that their lives will take.

From this perspective, possible strategies for promoting intrinsic motivation include giving competence-promoting feedback, presenting rules and evaluations in an informational rather than controlling fashion, minimizing reliance on extrinsic reinforcers, and occasionally allowing students to make choices and be involved in decision making.

Other theorists have proposed that motivation for performing a particular task depends on two subjective variables. First, people must have an *expectancy* that they will be successful; their expectations for success will depend not only on their own skill level but also on such outside factors as the quality of instruction and the availability of resources and support. Second, people must *value* the task: They must believe that there are direct or indirect benefits to performing it—perhaps achieving a desired goal, impressing others, or simply having fun. In classroom situations, students must believe that they will have the support they need to learn something successfully; they must also see how school subject matter has value for them personally.

An additional form of intrinsic motivation is *interest*, which can take either of two forms. *Situational interest* is temporary and evoked by something in the immediate environment. *Personal interest* is more stable and resides within the individual. Learners who are interested in the topic they are studying engage in more effective information processing and so remember the subject matter better over the long run. Teachers can often get students actively engaged in classroom subject matter both by capitalizing on individual personal interests and by provoking situational interest (e.g., through events that are new, different, or unexpected).

Learners have a wide variety of goals that may either contribute to or interfere with learning in instructional settings. Students who have *mastery goals* want to acquire additional knowledge or skills. Students who have *performance goals* either want to look competent in the eyes of others (a *performance-approach goal*) or else not to look incompetent (a *performance-avoidance goal*). The three kinds of goals are not necessarily mutually exclusive (a student might have two, or even all three), but generally speaking, students with mastery goals are more likely to recognize that competence comes only through effort and practice, to choose activities that maximize opportunities for learning, and to use errors constructively to improve future performance. Other common goals include *work-avoidance goals* (i.e., getting by with minimal effort), *social goals* (i.e., gaining and maintaining relationships with others), and *career goals*. Sometimes students are able to achieve two or more goals simultaneously; at other times, achieving one goal prevents them from satisfying others. Ideally, teachers should focus students' attention primarily on mastery goals, and they should encourage students to set some of their own goals, including short-term, concrete ones that will give them a sense of accomplishment and enable them to see the progress they are making.

Some learners have *dispositions*—general inclinations to approach learning and problem-solving situations in particular ways—that enhance their cognitive engagement and learning success. For example, they might frequently persevere at challenging tasks (learned industriousness), routinely consider multiple perspectives before coming to a conclusion (open-mindedness), and consistently evaluate information in terms of its probable accuracy and credibility (critical thinking).

Just as effective learners self-regulate their cognitive processes, so, too, do they intentionally try to bring productive motives and emotions to a learning situation, for instance by setting specific goals for a learning task, devising ways to make boring tasks more interesting, and trying to put worrisome thoughts out of mind. Self-regulation is also reflected in the phenomenon of *internalized motivation*: People gradually begin to value and adopt the behaviors that those around them value and encourage. Teachers and other adults can foster internalized motivation by creating a warm and supportive environment, giving learners some autonomy in what they do and learn, and providing sufficient structure to promote success.

CHAPTER 18

Attributions

You have undoubtedly gotten As on some of the classroom exams you have taken. On those occasions, why do you think you did so well? Did you study hard? Were the exams easy? Did you luck out and guess right on questions you knew little about? Or is it simply that you are an incredibly intelligent human being?

Now let's consider those exams on which you haven't done as well. To what did you attribute your failures? Did you spend too little time studying, or did you perhaps study the wrong things? Were the exams too difficult? Were the questions poorly worded, so that you misinterpreted many that you should have answered correctly? Were you too tired or ill to think clearly? Or do you just not have what it takes?

People's various explanations for success and failure—their beliefs about what causes what—are **attributions.** As we explore attribution theory in this chapter, we'll build on numerous ideas from earlier chapters. For instance, how people interpret the *reinforcement* and *punishment* they experience—whether they think an event is the result of something they themselves have done (and so might be able to control) or instead the result of something that has been done *to* them—influences the long-term effects that reinforcement and punishment are likely to have. In addition, attributions reflect *constructive processes* in long-term memory storage: People combine new information (in this case, a consequence they've just experienced) with their knowledge and beliefs about themselves and the world, and they then construct what is, to them, a reasonable interpretation of what has happened and why. As we examine the nature and effects of attributions, we'll also draw on many other concepts from our previous discussions of learning and motivation. For example, be on the lookout for references to *contingencies*, *self-efficacy*, *learning strategies*, *metacognition*, *self-regulated learning*, *self-worth*, *self-handicapping*, *relatedness*, *expectancies*, *values*, and *affect*.

We'll begin our exploration of attribution theory by considering three key dimensions that seem to underlie people's attributions. We'll then look separately at attributions for things that happen to *oneself* and attributions for things that happen to *other people*; as we shall see, self-attributions and attributions for others have somewhat different qualities and effects. Later, we'll revisit a phenomenon we first examined in Chapter 6, *learned helplessness*, reframing it within the context of attribution theory. Finally, we'll consider the effects of challenge and competition for attributions and other aspects of human motivation, and we'll identify strategies for fostering productive attributions in instructional settings.

DIMENSIONS UNDERLYING PEOPLE'S ATTRIBUTIONS

People are apt to explain events in a variety of ways. For example, school children may attribute their successes and failures in the classroom to such things as effort, ability, luck, task difficulty, health, mood, physical appearance, or teachers' or peers' behaviors (Schunk, 1990). Attributions are as much a function of *perception* as of reality; thus, they are often distorted in line with existing beliefs about oneself and about how the world operates (Dweck, 1978; Dweck & Elliott, 1983; Paris & Byrnes, 1989). For example, your poor performance on exams in years past may very well have been the result of ineffective study strategies; like many students, you may have tried to learn class material in a rote, meaningless fashion (you obviously hadn't read this book yet!). But because you thought of yourself as a smart person and believed that you *had* studied adequately, you perhaps instead attributed your low scores to the exceptional difficulty or "pickiness" of your tests or to arbitrary and irrational evaluations by your teachers.

People's attributions appear to vary in terms of three key dimensions: locus, stability, and controllability (Weiner, 1984, 1986, 2000).[1]

Locus ("Place"): Internal Versus External We sometimes attribute the causes of events to *internal* things—that is, to factors within ourselves. Thinking that a good grade is the result of your own hard work and believing that a poor grade is the result of your lack of ability are examples of internal attributions. At other times, we attribute events to *external* things—to factors outside of ourselves. Concluding that you received a scholarship because you were lucky and interpreting a classmate's scowl as being due to her bad mood (rather than to anything you might have done to deserve such a scowl) are examples of external attributions.

Some theorists have referred to the "locus" dimension as *locus of control*. However, Weiner (1986, 2000) has pointed out that *locus* and *control* are probably two distinctly different aspects of an attribution. For instance, one's singing ability may be internal but in many people's eyes it is not entirely controllable.

---

[1]In earlier writings, Weiner suggested two additional dimensions: *cross-situational generality* (global versus specific) and *intentionality* (intentional versus intentional). More recently, however, he has focused primarily on locus, stability, and controllability (Weiner, 2000).

Temporal Stability: Stable Versus Unstable Sometimes we think that events are a result of *stable* factors—things that probably won't change much in the near future. For example, if you believe that you do well in school because of inherited ability or that you have trouble making friends because you're too fat, then you are attributing events to stable, relatively unchangeable causes. But sometimes we instead believe that events are the result of *unstable* factors—things that can change from one time to the next. Thinking that winning a tennis game was simply a "fluke" and believing that you got a bad test grade because you were tired when you took the test are examples of attributions involving unstable factors.

Controllability: Controllable Versus Uncontrollable On some occasions we attribute events to *controllable* factors—to things we can influence and change. For example, if you believe that a classmate invited you to coffee because you always smile and say nice things to her, and if you think you probably failed a test simply because you didn't study the right things, then you are attributing these events to controllable factors. On other occasions, we attribute events to *uncontrollable* factors—to things over which we have no influence. For example, if you think that you were chosen for a title role in *Romeo and Juliet* because the director thinks you have the right face for the part, or that you played a lousy game of basketball because you had a mild case of the flu, then you are attributing these events to uncontrollable factors.

Attribution theory's notion of controllability overlaps with, yet is also somewhat different from, Deci and Ryan's concept of *self-determination* (Deci & Ryan, 1987). Attribution to controllable factors involves a belief that we can influence and alter environmental events and circumstances. In contrast, self-determination involves a belief that we can autonomously choose our behaviors and, ultimately, our fate. In other words, controllable attributions reflect control of one's *environment,* whereas self-determination reflects control of one's *behaviors*.

The controllability dimension possibly has two subcomponents (Weisz & Cameron, 1985). First, one must believe that there is a *contingency* between the behavior and the outcome—in other words, that a particular behavior can cause a certain event to occur. Second, one must have a sense of *competence* (i.e., self-efficacy) that one is actually capable of performing the necessary behavior. A person is apt to believe that an event is uncontrollable if either one of these components is missing. For example, a student may know that good grades will result from making correct responses in class but may not believe that he or she has the ability to make those responses; in this situation there is a sense of contingency but no sense of competence (Weisz, 1986). As another example, a person from a minority group may have high self-efficacy for achieving a particular goal yet feel that the racial prejudice and discrimination of others will, nevertheless, make success impossible; in this case there is a sense of competence but no sense of contingency (Pintrich & Schunk, 2002; Sue & Chin, 1983).

We can analyze virtually any attribution in terms of these three dimensions. For example, viewing success on a task as being the result of inherited ability is an internal, stable, and uncontrollable attribution. Believing failure on task was a case of bad luck is an external, unstable, and uncontrollable attribution. Table 18–1 analyzes eight common attributions in terms of the three dimensions.

As you look at Table 18–1, you might think to yourself that "ability can change with practice, so is unstable and controllable" or that "teachers' attitudes toward students often depend on how students behave in the classroom, so are really the result of internal, unstable, and controllable factors." Perhaps you are right, but keep in mind that people's *beliefs* about the locus, stability, and controllability of their attributions, not the reality of the situation, are what affect future behavior (Dweck & Leggett, 1988; Weiner, 1994).

Table 18–1
Analyzing various student attributions in terms of the three dimensions.

Success or Failure Attributed to	Locus	Stability	Controllability
Inherited "ability"	Internal	Stable	Uncontrollable
Personality	Internal	Stable	Uncontrollable
Effort	Internal	Unstable	Controllable
Health	Internal	Unstable	Uncontrollable
Energy level	Internal	Unstable	Uncontrollable
Task difficulty	External	Stable	Uncontrollable
Teachers' attitudes	External	Stable	Uncontrollable
Luck or chance	External	Unstable	Uncontrollable

What about *effort* (trying or not trying hard) and *luck* (either good or bad)? Are these temporary states of affairs, or are they more enduring qualities that tend to bless or haunt us time after time? People occasionally think of effort and luck as being relatively stable, enduring characteristics; for instance, they may believe that people are consistently lucky or unlucky (Weiner, 1986). To be consistent with much of the literature in attribution theory, however, in our discussions here we will treat both effort and luck as unstable, temporary factors.

And what about *intelligence*? Whether intelligence is actually a stable or unstable characteristic is a matter of considerable controversy among psychologists, and nonpsychologists—adults and children alike—are similarly divided on the matter. Some have an **entity view:** They believe that intelligence is a "thing" that is fairly permanent and unchangeable. Others have an **incremental view:** They believe that intelligence can and does improve with effort and practice (Dweck & Leggett, 1988; Weiner, 1994). Because I cannot give a definitive answer about the nature of intelligence, I have omitted it from Table 18–1; I have instead included "inherited" ability, which is presumably stable and uncontrollable.

ATTRIBUTIONS FOR ONESELF

We now zero in on the nature of people's attributions for the things that happen to *themselves*—that is, **intrapersonal attributions** (Weiner, 2000). We'll first look at the effects that such attributions are likely to have on people's behavior, cognition, motivation, and affective responses. We'll then identify several factors that seem to lead to different kinds of attributions.

Effects of Self-Attributions

Attributions appear to have a significant influence on many aspects of people's functioning, including their performance and achievement in classroom settings (Dweck, 1986; Graham, 1994; Weiner, 1984, 1986, 2000). They have fairly predictable effects on people's emotional reactions to success and failure, future expectations and self-efficacy, effort and persistence, learning strategies, responses to failure situations, and future choices. We'll consider each of these in turn.

Emotional Reactions to Success and Failure

People are, of course, happy when they succeed. But do they also feel *proud* of their accomplishments? When they believe that their successes are the result of the actions of another person or some other outside force, they are apt to feel grateful rather than proud.[2] Individuals feel pride and satisfaction about their successes only when they attribute those successes to internal causes—that is, to something that they themselves have done (Hareli & Weiner, 2002; Weiner, Russell, & Lerman, 1978, 1979).

Along a similar vein, people usually feel a certain amount of sadness after a failure. When they believe that failure is the result of external causes—to events and people outside of themselves—they are apt to feel angry and resentful. When they instead believe that the failure is caused by their own lack of ability or effort, they are apt to feel guilty or ashamed (Eccles & Wigfield, 1985; Hareli & Weiner, 2002; Neumann, 2000; Weiner et al., 1978, 1979). People who attribute failure to internal causes, and especially to their lack of ability, often have lower self-esteem as a result (Covington, Spratt, & Omelich, 1980).

Future Expectations and Self-Efficacy

When people attribute their successes and failures to stable factors, they will expect their future performance to be similar to their current performance. In this situation, success leads to an anticipation of future success, and failure breeds an expectation of more failure to come. In contrast, when people attribute their successes and failures to *unstable* factors—for example, to effort, strategies, or luck—then their current success rate will have less influence on their expectation for future success (Dweck, 1978; Fennema, 1987; Hong, Chiu, & Dweck, 1995; Weiner, 1986, 2000). The most optimistic individuals—those who have the highest expectancies for future success and, as a result, the highest self-efficacy—are the ones who attribute their successes to stable, dependable factors (such as high innate ability and a consistently supportive environment) and their failures to unstable yet controllable factors (such as lack of effort) (Eccles [Parsons], 1983; Murray & Jackson, 1982/1983; Pomerantz & Saxon, 2001; Weiner, 1984).

Effort and Persistence

When people believe that their failures are due to their own lack of effort—that they *do* have the ability to succeed if they try hard enough—they are likely to exert more effort in future situations and to persist in the face of difficulty. When they instead attribute failure to a lack of innate ability (they couldn't do it even if they tried), they give up easily and sometimes cannot even perform tasks they have previously accomplished successfully (Brophy, 1986; Dweck, 1978; Eccles [Parsons], 1983; Feather, 1982; Weiner, 1984). Students with a history of academic failure are especially likely to attribute their classroom difficulties to low ability, and they often stop trying as a result (Pressley, Borkowski, & Schneider, 1987).

---

[2]One recent study suggests that when college students believe that their teachers (rather than themselves) have control over the grades they receive, they feel *entitled* to good grades rather than grateful for them (Achacoso, Summers, & Schallert, 2002).

Learning Strategies

People's attributions and resulting expectations for future performance clearly affect the cognitive strategies they apply to learning tasks. Students who expect to succeed in the classroom and believe that academic success is a result of their own doing are more likely to apply effective study strategies, especially when trained in their use, and they are more likely to approach problem-solving tasks in a logical, systematic, and meaningful fashion (Palmer & Goetz, 1988; Pressley, Borkowski, & Schneider, 1987; Tyler, 1958). These students are also more likely to be self-regulated learners and to seek help when they need it (R. Ames, 1983; Zimmerman, 1998). In contrast, students who expect failure and believe that their academic performance is largely out of their hands often reject effective learning and problem-solving strategies in favor of rote-learning approaches.

Responses to Failure Situations

As we noted earlier, some people have an *entity* view of intelligence: They believe that intelligence is an uncontrollable, stable characteristic—a built-in, "natural" talent. These people also tend to believe that ability and effort are inversely related: Success with little effort reflects high ability, and success that comes only with a great deal of effort is a sign of low ability (Barker & Graham, 1987; Covington & Omelich, 1979; Dweck & Elliott, 1983; Eccles [Parsons], 1983; Graham, 1990). Such beliefs are especially prevalent when people have performance goals rather than learning goals (see Table 17–1 in the preceding chapter).

For such individuals, effort is probably a "double-edged sword" (Covington & Omelich, 1979; Covington et al., 1980; Eccles & Wigfield, 1985). Those who perceive themselves as having low ability are in a no-win situation. If they don't try hard, failure is inevitable. If they *do* try hard and fail anyway, they look "stupid," at least in their own eyes. Many of them therefore do not try very hard (one form of self-handicapping), perhaps as a way of saving face and hiding the low ability they believe they have (Covington, 1992; Covington & Beery, 1976; Covington et al., 1980; Dweck, 1986; Eccles & Wigfield, 1985; Jagacinski & Nicholls, 1990; Murray & Jackson, 1982/1983; Schunk, 1990). They may also decide that the activity isn't worth doing—in other words, they attach little value to it (Covington & Beery, 1976; Eccles & Wigfield, 1985).

Attribution theorists propose that people respond most favorably to failure situations when they attribute these failures to internal, unstable, and controllable variables such as effort and strategies (Clifford, 1984; Curtis & Graham, 1991; Pressley, Borkowski, & Schneider, 1987). Blaming lack of effort alone can backfire, however. Individuals who try hard and still fail are likely to reach the conclusion that they have low ability—that they simply don't have what it takes. Therefore, it is more beneficial to attribute failure to strategies as well—to believe that they could succeed if they did things *differently* (Curtis & Graham, 1991; Pressley, Borkowski, & Schneider, 1987). Such attributions often characterize good students who know that they need not only to work hard but also to work strategically (Brophy, 1987; Pressley, Borkowski, & Schneider, 1987; Weinstein et al., 1991).

Future Choices

As you might expect, individuals whose attributions lead them to expect success in a particular subject area are more likely to pursue that area—for instance, by enrolling in more courses in the same discipline (Dweck, 1986; Eccles [Parsons], 1984; Stipek & Gralinski, 1990; Weiner, 1986). Individuals who believe their chances for future success in an activity are slim will avoid that activity whenever they can. And when people don't continue to pursue an activity, they can't possibly get better at it.

Why do different people attribute the same events to different causes? For example, why does one individual believe that a failure is merely a temporary setback due to an inappropriate strategy, while another attributes the same failure to low ability, and still another believes it to be the result of someone else's capricious and unpredictable actions? We now look at variables affecting the development of different attributions.

Factors Influencing the Nature of Self-Attributions

Forming attributions is just one of the many ways in which people try to make better sense of their world (Tollefson, 2000; Weiner, 2000). In this case, they are trying to identify cause–effect relationships for events in their own lives. Researchers have identified numerous variables that influence the attributions that people construct. For now, we'll look at the effects of several variables: past history of success and failure, situational cues, degree to which successes and failures are followed by reinforcement or punishment, self-protective bias, age, gender, the necessity for image management, culture, and messages from others. Later in the chapter, we'll look at two additional ones: challenge and competition.

Past History of Success and Failure
The attributions that people develop result partly from their previous success and failure experiences (Klein, 1990; Paris & Byrnes, 1989; Pressley, Borkowski, & Schneider, 1987; Schunk, 1990; Stipek, 1993). Those who have tried and succeeded in the past are more likely to believe that success is the result of internal factors, such as effort or high ability. Those who have tried and failed, or who have had an inconsistent pattern of successes and failures, are likely to believe that success is due to something beyond their control—perhaps to an ability they don't possess or to such external factors as a tough break or poor instruction.

When we consider students in the classroom, metacognition plays a role here as well. In Chapter 13, we discovered that students often think they have learned something they actually have *not* learned; in other words, they have an *illusion of knowing.* When these students do poorly on an exam, they cannot attribute their performance to internal factors; after all, they studied hard and so "know" the material. Instead, they are likely to attribute poor performance to such external factors as bad luck, exam difficulty, or teacher capriciousness (Horgan, 1990).

Situational Cues
Characteristics specific to a particular situation may influence the attributions that people make. Features of the task being performed are one influential characteristic; for example, complex math problems (e.g., those that include more numbers) are perceived as being more difficult, and so failure to solve those problems can readily be attributed to task difficulty rather than to internal causes (Schunk, 1990). The performance of peers provides another cue; for example, a failure is apt to be attributed to task difficulty if everyone else is failing, whereas it is more likely to be attributed to an internal source (such as lack of ability) if others are succeeding (Schunk, 1990; Weiner, 1984).

Reinforcement and Punishment
Generally speaking, children are more likely to attribute events to internal, controllable causes when adults reinforce their successes but don't punish their failures. Conversely, children are more likely to make external attributions when adults punish failures and ignore successes

(Katkovsky, Crandall, & Good, 1967). It appears that people are more likely to accept responsibility for their failures if others don't made a big deal of them.

Self-Protective Bias

As a general rule, people tend to form attributions that maintain or enhance their sense of self-worth. For instance, we tend to attribute our successes to internal causes (e.g., high ability or hard work) and our failures to external causes (e.g., bad luck or the thoughtless behavior of others) (Igoe & Sullivan, 1991; Marsh, 1990; Weiner, 1992; Weisz & Cameron, 1985; Whitley & Frieze, 1985). By patting ourselves on the back for the things we do well and putting the blame elsewhere for poor performance, we are able to maintain positive self-perceptions (Katkovsky et al., 1967; Paris & Byrnes, 1989). This self-protective bias is not always in our best interest, however: If we inaccurately attribute our failures to factors outside of ourselves, we are unlikely to change our behavior in ways that will lead to greater success (Seligman, 1991).

Curiously, people may think they are in control even in situations where they are not, and this belief may enhance their optimism on future occasions (S. C. Thompson, 1999). For instance, we might believe that we have a better chance of winning the lottery if we pick the numbers ourselves rather than letting the computer pick them for us. In fact, only one behavior affects our chances of winning the lottery: actually buying a ticket. Every possible sequence of numbers has an equal chance of being the winning combination, regardless of how it was selected.

Age

As children get older, they become increasingly able to distinguish among various causes for events. Preschoolers don't have a clear understanding of the differences among the possible causes—effort, ability, luck, task difficulty, and so on—of their successes and failures (Eccles et al., 1998; Nicholls, 1990). At about age six, they begin to recognize that effort and ability are separate qualities but see them as positively correlated: People who try hardest have the greatest ability, and effort is the primary determiner of success (Nicholls, 1990). Thus, children in the early elementary grades tend to believe they have the ability to do well in school if they expend a reasonable amount of effort (Dweck & Elliott, 1983; Stipek & Gralinski, 1990).

Sometime around age nine, they begin to understand that effort and ability often compensate for one another and that people with less ability may have to exert greater effort to achieve the same outcome as their more able peers (Nicholls, 1990). By age 13 or so, they make a clear distinction between effort and ability: They realize that people differ both in their inherent ability to perform a task and in the amount of effort they exert on a task. At this point, they also know that ability and effort can compensate for each other but that a lack of ability sometimes precludes success no matter *how* much effort a person puts forth (Nicholls, 1990). With age, then, learners increasingly acquire an *entity* view of intelligence (Dweck, 1999). If they are usually successful at classroom tasks, they will have high self-efficacy about such tasks; if failures are frequent, their self-efficacy may plummet (Dweck, 1986; Eccles [Parsons], 1983; Schunk, 1990; E. A. Skinner, 1995).

This state of affairs may lead to a self-fulfilling prophecy. As we discovered in Chapter 7, people with low self-efficacy choose less challenging tasks and give up more easily than their more self-confident peers. As a result, they will have fewer opportunities to discover that success *can* come with effort. Further compounding the problem is the fact that some children with low self-efficacy may attribute the successes they do achieve to external factors and their failures to internal factors, thereby giving themselves little credit for the things they do well and blaming themselves for the things they do poorly (Ickes & Layden, 1978).

Gender

Gender differences sometimes, although not always, appear in research studies (Carr & Jessup, 1997; Deaux, 1984; Durkin, 1987; Dweck, 1978; Fennema, 1987; Huston, 1983; Stipek & Gralinski, 1990). In these instances, males are more likely to attribute their successes to ability and their failures to lack of effort, thus assuming the attitude that *I know I can do this because I have the ability.* Females show the reverse pattern: They attribute their successes to effort and their failures to lack of ability, believing that *I don't know if I can keep on doing it, because I'm not very good at this type of thing.* Such differences, which can appear even when boys' and girls' previous levels of achievement are equivalent, are more frequently observed in stereotypically male domains such as mathematics and sports (Eccles & Jacobs, 1986; Fennema, 1987; Stipek, 1984; Vermeer, Boekaerts, & Seegers, 2000).

Image Management

The attributions that individuals express do not always reflect their true beliefs about the sources of their successes and failures. As children get older, they discover that different kinds of attributions elicit different kinds of reactions from other people. To maintain positive interpersonal relationships (and thereby satisfy their need for relatedness), they begin to modify their attributions for the particular audience at hand. Juvonen (2000) calls this phenomenon *face-saving,* but I suggest using the broader term **image management.**

Teachers, parents, and other adults are often sympathetic and forgiving when students fail because of something beyond their control (illness, lack of ability, etc.) but frequently get angry when students fail simply because they didn't try very hard. By the time students reach fourth grade, most of them are aware of this fact and so may verbalize attributions that are likely to elicit favorable reactions (Juvonen, 1996, 2000; Weiner, 1995). To illustrate, a student who knows very well that she did poorly on an assignment because she didn't put forth her best effort may distort the truth, telling her teacher that she "can't seem to make sense of this stuff" or "wasn't feeling well."

Learners become equally adept at tailoring their attributions for the ears of their peers. Generally speaking, fourth graders believe that their peers value diligence and hard work, and so they are likely to tell their classmates that they did well on an assignment because they worked hard. By eighth grade, however, many students believe that their peers will disapprove of those who exert much effort on academic tasks, and so they often prefer to convey the impression that they *aren't* working very hard—for instance, that they "didn't study very much" for an important exam or "just lucked out" when they have performed at a high level (Howie, 2002; Juvonen, 1996, 2000).

Culture

People's cultural backgrounds influence their attributions as well. For instance, students from Asian backgrounds are more likely to attribute classroom success and failure to unstable factors—effort in the case of academic achievement, and temporary situational factors in the case of appropriate or inappropriate behaviors—than students brought up in mainstream Western culture (Hess, Chih-Mei, & McDevitt, 1987; Lillard, 1997; Steinberg, 1996). And some studies indicate a greater tendency for African American students to believe they have little control over whether they achieve academic success (Graham, 1989; Holliday, 1985). To some extent, racial prejudice may contribute to such an attribution: Some students may begin to believe that, because of the color of their skin, they have little chance of success no matter what they do (Sue & Chin, 1983; van Laar, 2000).

Messages From Others

Oftentimes attributions are derived in part from the explanations that others offer for a particular success or failure. In some instances, other people's messages are fairly straightforward ("Wow, you sure worked hard on this project!"). At other times, they are more subtle, perhaps taking the form of emotions (e.g., anger or pity) that indirectly suggest certain attributions. In the upcoming section, we look at the types of messages that others give to learners and at the various attributions that such messages may convey.

ATTRIBUTIONS FOR OTHERS

Just as we form attributions regarding the causes of our performance, those around us may form their own opinions regarding why we have succeeded or failed. We, in turn, have beliefs about why *they* have done well or poorly. In other words, people form **interpersonal attributions** as well as in*tra*personal ones.

I recall a conversation I had not too long ago with a well-educated man whose training was in mechanical engineering rather than psychology or education. We were discussing the fact that, on average, children in inner-city schools achieve at lower levels than children in suburban schools. Knowing that I was an educational psychologist, the man asked me why I thought there was such a difference in performance levels. I said that there were apt to be a number of reasons, probably including smaller school budgets, larger class sizes, more obligations and fewer resources at home, poor nutrition, fear for personal safety, a higher proportion of children with learning disabilities and other special needs, and so on. The man seemed quite surprised. "I always thought that the kids just weren't *motivated*," he said.

The three dimensions we identified earlier—locus, stability, and controllability—are as relevant to interpersonal attributions as they are to intrapersonal ones. Probably the most important one from an interpersonal standpoint is *controllability* (Weiner, 2000). The reasons I offered for the low achievement of many inner-city students—fewer resources, poor nutrition, a dangerous environment, and so on—all involved things beyond the students' control. In contrast, my conversational partner believed that the students performed poorly only because they didn't *want* to do well; in other words, high achievement was well within their grasp if they set their minds to it. (The man also had an overly simplistic idea of what motivation is. As should be clear by now, motivation involves many things—self-efficacy, self-determination, expectancies, values, and so on—and most of these cannot be voluntarily flicked on and off like a light switch.)

In this section, we will look at the ways in which people communicate their attributions for learners, the effects that such attributions are likely to have, and the various factors that may lead people to interpret learners' successes and failures in one way or another. We will then examine the nature and effects of attributions and expectations for students in the classroom.

How People Communicate Their Attributions

People communicate their attributions for a learner's performance both directly through the statements they make and indirectly through their evaluative and emotional reactions.

Statements

In some cases, people communicate their attributions verbally and explicitly. For example, consider the things a teacher might say about a student's success:

- "You did it! You're so smart!"
- "That's wonderful. Your hard work has really paid off, hasn't it?"
- "You've done very well. It's clear that you really know how to study."
- "Terrific! This is certainly your lucky day!"

Consider, also, the statements a teacher might make about a student's failure:

- "Hmmm, maybe this just isn't something you're good at. Perhaps we should try a different activity."
- "Why don't you practice a little more and then try again?"
- "Let's see whether we can come up with some study strategies that might work better for you."
- "Maybe you're just having a bad day."

All of these are well-intended comments, presumably designed to make someone feel good. But notice the different attributions they imply. In some cases success or failure is attributed to controllable (and therefore changeable) behaviors—that is, to hard work or lack of practice or to the use of effective or ineffective study strategies. But in other cases success or failure is attributed to uncontrollable ability—that is, to being smart or not "good at" something. And in still other cases an outcome is attributed to external, uncontrollable causes—that is, to a lucky break or a bad day.

Evaluative and Emotional Reactions

People also communicate their attributions—and indirectly, their beliefs about a learner's ability level—through the emotions they convey and the extent to which they praise or criticize performance (Graham, 1990, 1991, 1997; Hareli & Weiner, 2002; C. Reyna & Weiner, 2001; Weiner, 2000). Frequent praise is often a message that learners' successes are a result of their efforts; however, by praising a learner for *easy* tasks, people may simultaneously convey the message that success wasn't expected—in other words, that the learner has low ability. Here, then, we see a perspective very different from that of operant conditioning. Operant conditioning theorists propose that, as reinforcement, praise should increase the behavior it follows. From the standpoint of attribution theory, however, praise may be counterproductive for easy tasks. If it communicates low ability, learners may be unwilling to exert much effort on later tasks. Praise for effort is likely to be effective only when learners *have* exerted that effort.

Reactions to a learner's failures communicate attributions as well. When people criticize, express anger about, and perhaps punish a learner's poor performance, they convey the message that the learner has sufficient ability to master the task and simply isn't trying hard enough. But when people express pity or sympathy for the same performance, they communicate their belief that the learner's low ability is the reason for the failure.

Children readily draw inferences from other adults' evaluative and emotional reactions to their performance. As an illustration, Barker and Graham (1987) asked 4- to 12-year-old children to watch a videotape depicting two boys either solving single-digit math problems at the blackboard or throwing balls through a large hoop in the gymnasium; the two tasks appeared to be easy ones for the boys to accomplish. Some of the children saw a videotape in which both boys succeeded; the teacher praised one boy (e.g., "Great job!") but gave the other only neutral feedback (e.g., "Correct"). Other children saw a videotape in which the two boys failed at their task; one was criticized for this failure (e.g., "What's the matter with you? That's not the right answer!") and the other, again, given neutral feedback (e.g., "No, not quite"). The children were subsequently asked to rate the two boys for either intelligence (for the math problem videos) or throwing ability (for the ball throwing videos) on a 5-point scale. Younger children (4- and 5-year-olds) concluded that the boy praised for his success had higher ability than the other boy; in contrast, older children (11- and 12-year-olds) concluded that the praised boy had *lower* ability. At the same time, younger children deduced that the boy criticized for his failure had lower ability, while older children came to the opposite conclusion. Children who were 8 or 9 years old assigned similar ratings to both boys in both success and failure situations. Thus, we see a developmental change as children grow older: They become increasingly likely to interpret praise for an easy success as a sign of low ability and to interpret blame for failure on an easy task as an indication of high ability.

Effects of Interpersonal Attributions

Research indicates that children's attributions for their performance are often similar to the attributions that adults assign to that performance (Dweck, Davidson, Nelson, & Enna, 1978; Eccles et al., 1998; Lueptow, 1984; Parsons, Adler, & Kaczala, 1982; Schunk, 1982). Furthermore, when parents and teachers communicate their belief that children are incapable of mastering a task, children are likely to attribute their failures to low ability and may therefore conclude that there is little to be gained by trying harder (Butler, 1994; Weiner, 2000; Yee & Eccles, 1988).

When people don't know why they have succeeded or failed, they eagerly seek out information that can help them explain what has happened (Weiner, 2000). As an example, let's look at a recent study in a second-grade classroom (Gaskill, 2001). In a three-week unit on cursive writing, the teacher introduced a new cursive letter each day and showed her students how to write it correctly. After a short demonstration and discussion of the letter, she asked the students to practice it, first by "writing" it in the air using large arm movements and then by writing it numerous times on lined paper. As the children practiced, she gave different children different kinds of feedback. (She had randomly assigned the children to two groups and placed small stickers inconspicuously on each desk to remind her which children were in which group.) When children in the control (*praise*) group wrote a letter with good form, she gave them a "happy face" token, said "Great!" or "Perfect!" and either smiled at them or gave them a pat on the back. When children in the treatment (*attribution*) group wrote a letter with good form at least once, she gave them a happy face token and said something along the lines of "You sure are working hard," "You can write beautifully in cursive," or "You are a natural at this" (Gaskill, 2001, p. 8). If children in either group failed to meet her standards for good form, she gave them whatever corrective feedback they needed. Despite the seemingly minor differences in her behavior toward the two groups, the teacher observed significant differences in what the two groups said and did. During the unit, the children in the control group often seemed disappointed, sometimes even anxious, when they received their "positive" feedback. For instance, on one occasion, after overhearing the teacher say that a classmate was a natural at cursive writing, a particularly good writer in the control group (who was consistently getting feedback such as "Great!" or "Perfect!") asked, "Am *I* a natural at this?" After the unit was over, the children in the treatment group enjoyed cursive writing more, thought it was easier, and used it more frequently in their spelling tests, journal entries, and other writing tasks. Such findings remind us once again that learners are usually eager not only for information that tells them they are doing well but also for information that affirms their sense of self-worth more generally.

Factors Influencing Attributions for Others

Just as people base their self-attributions partly on past successes and failures and partly on cultural perspectives, so, too, are their attributions for others partially a function of prior performance and culture. In addition, a general bias toward stable attributions, conceptions of intelligence, stereotypes, and goals enter into the picture. Let's briefly look at each of these.

Past History of Success and Failure
One logical source of information for forming attributions is the pattern of performance that another has exhibited. Seeing consistent performance over time—whether it be consistently high or consistently low—should lead an observer to infer that stable factors, such as intelligence or some other general ability, are the cause of the performance. Seeing *inconsistent* performance from one time to the next should lead the observer to conclude that temporary factors (perhaps that switch-on–switch-off "motivation" my engineer friend had in mind) are the primary cause of performance.

Culture
Just as cultural beliefs influence people's self-attributions, so, too, do they affect people's attributions for others. For instance, compared to Chinese American and European American mothers, mothers in the People's Republic of China are much more likely to attribute their children's poor performance in math to low effort, rather than to more stable and less controllable factors such as ability (Hess et al., 1987).

General Bias Toward Stable Attributions
In forming their self-attributions, people often consider situational factors (how much help they're getting, whether irrelevant events are distracting their attention, etc.) that may be affecting their performance. In contrast, people tend to attribute *others'* behaviors to fairly stable personal characteristics, such as ability, disposition, or personality (Fiske & Taylor, 1991; Weiner, 1992). In part, this bias may be a result of the fact that an observer usually catches only an occasional snippet of a learner's performance and so does not have much opportunity to see variability across time and situations (Fiske & Taylor, 1991).

Conception of Intelligence
As noted earlier, people have differing views of intelligence, some believing it to be an *entity* that remains fairly stable and others believing that it can change *incrementally* over time. People who have an entity view of intelligence are more likely to attribute high and low performance to a stable ability, and so they will expect learners' future performance to be quite similar to current performance levels (Pintrich & Schunk, 2002).

Stereotypes

Gender stereotypes influence the attributions that adults form for boys and girls. For example, many parents have the impression that boys are "naturally" more mathematically talented than girls. Those who do are apt to attribute their sons' high math performance to ability and their daughters' high math performance to effort. Meanwhile, they attribute sons' low math performance to lack of effort and their daughters' low math performance to low ability. The reverse pattern is seen for English, which is stereotypically a "female" domain (Dunton, McDevitt, & Hess, 1988; Eccles et al., 1998; Jacobs & Eccles, 1992; Yee & Eccles, 1988).

Ethnic and racial stereotypes affect attributions as well (C. Reyna, 2000). For example, imagine that a student from a particular ethnic group fails an exam. A teacher who believes that people of that ethnic group are "lazy" is apt to attribute the poor performance to lack of effort, get angry, and refuse to help the student improve. In contrast, a teacher who believes that people of that ethnic group are the unfortunate victims of racial discrimination (as well as of the resulting poverty and poor living conditions that it brings about) is apt to attribute the poor performance to uncontrollable factors, be sympathetic, and work hard to help the student master the subject matter (C. Reyna, 2000).

Goals

Regardless of what observers actually believe about the causes of a learner's success and failure, the attributions they *communicate* may depend on their goals as they interact with the learner (Hareli & Weiner, 2002). For instance, imagine that John has just failed a classroom task. A teacher who wants to protect John's sense of self-worth may suggest that his poor performance was caused by something he can control (e.g., effort or study strategies) rather than low ability. If the teacher attributes the failure to low ability, however, more effort and a new approach may not work; an alternative way of protecting John's self-worth is to suggest that the task is a very difficult one—an external, uncontrollable attribution (Hareli & Weiner, 2002).

Attributions and Expectations in the Classroom

In the classroom, teachers' attributions affect the expectations they form for students' future behaviors. A teacher who thinks that a student's high performance is the result of something internal and stable (e.g., natural ability or a strong work ethic) will expect the student to do well in the future; a teacher who thinks the high performance is the result of temporary variables (e.g., an unusual burst of energy or a lucky break) won't be so sure. Similarly, a teacher who thinks that a student's poor performance is the result of internal, stable factors (e.g., low intelligence or chronic laziness) will expect poor performance on future occasions, but a teacher who attributes the performance to something temporary (e.g., a bad mood or the flu) will be more optimistic.

Yet teachers' expectations and prior beliefs influence their attributions as well. As we discovered in Chapter 10, expectations often affect encoding and storage of new information: To some degree, people see what they expect to see, and the new evidence they collect may very well confirm their initial attributions for someone else's performance (Weiner, 2000). Expectations are especially influential when stimuli are ambiguous, and other people's *behaviors* are prime examples of such ambiguity. For example, imagine that a student, Mary, fails to finish a classroom assignment on time. Her teacher, Mr. Jones, might possibly conclude that Mary (1) didn't try very hard, (2) wasn't capable of doing the task, or (3) used her time poorly.

Which conclusion Mr. Jones draws will depend to some extent on his prior beliefs about Mary—whether he thinks that she (1) is lazy and unmotivated, (2) has low ability, or (3) is both motivated and capable of doing the work.

To some extent, teachers' expectations are based on the performance students have previously demonstrated. Yet even when several students all have the same history of success and failure, teachers and other adults may hold different expectations for each of these students, and their expectations in turn lead to different student attributions and varying levels of performance (Brophy & Good, 1970; Eccles & Wigfield, 1985; Eccles [Parsons] et al., 1983; Harris & Rosenthal, 1985; Miller, Brickman, & Bolen, 1975; Murray & Jackson, 1982/1983; Palardy, 1969; Yee & Eccles, 1988).

Teachers typically draw conclusions about their students relatively early in the school year, forming opinions about each one's strengths, weaknesses, and potential for academic success. In many instances, teachers size up their students fairly accurately: They know which ones need help with reading skills, which ones have short attention spans, which ones have trouble working together in the same cooperative group, and so on, and they can adapt their instruction and assistance accordingly (Goldenberg, 1992; Good & Brophy, 1994; Good & Nichols, 2001). Yet even the best teachers inevitably make errors in their judgments. For example, teachers often underestimate the abilities of students who

- Are physically unattractive.
- Misbehave frequently in class.
- Speak in dialects other than Standard English.
- Are members of ethnic minority groups.
- Are recent immigrants.
- Come from low-income backgrounds.
  (Banks & Banks, 1995; Bennett et al., 1993; Knapp & Woolverton, 1995; McLoyd, 1998; Oakes & Guiton, 1995; Ritts et al., 1992)

All too often, teachers perceive students' ability levels to be relatively fixed and stable; in other words, they have an *entity* view of intelligence (Oakes & Guiton, 1995; C. Reyna, 2000). Their beliefs about these "stable" abilities affect their expectations for students' performance, which in turn lead them to behave differently toward different students. When teachers have high expectations for students, they create a warmer classroom climate, interact with students more frequently, provide more opportunities for students to respond, and give more positive and more specific feedback; they also present more course material and more challenging topics. In contrast, when teachers have low expectations for certain students, they offer fewer opportunities for speaking in class, ask easier questions, give less feedback about students' responses, present few if any challenging assignments, and overlook good performance when it occurs (Babad, 1993; Good & Brophy, 1994; Graham, 1990, 1991; Rosenthal, 1994). Minority students with a history of academic failure are especially likely to be the recipients of such low-ability signals (Graham, 1990).

Most children and adolescents are well aware of their teachers' differential treatment of individual students and use such treatment to draw logical inferences about their own and others' abilities (Butler, 1994; Good & Nichols, 2001; Weinstein, 1993). When their teachers repeatedly give them low-ability messages, they may begin to see themselves as their teachers see them. Furthermore, their behavior may mirror their self-perceptions; for instance, they may exert little effort on academic tasks, or they may frequently misbehave in class (Marachi, Friedel, & Midgley,

2001; Murdock, 1999). In some cases, then, teachers' expectations and attributions may lead to a **self-fulfilling prophecy:** What teachers expect students to achieve becomes what students actually *do* achieve.

With the effects of teacher expectations in mind, we should note that teacher assistance, though often a valuable source of scaffolding on difficult tasks, may be counterproductive if students don't really need it. When students struggle temporarily with a task, the unsolicited help of their teacher may communicate the message that they have low ability and little control regarding their own successes and failures. In contrast, allowing students to struggle on their own for a reasonable period of time conveys the belief that students do have the ability to succeed on their own (Graham, 1990, 1997; Graham & Barker, 1990; Stipek, 1996; Weiner, 1984).

Certainly teacher expectations don't always lead to self-fulfilling prophecies. In some cases, teachers follow up on low expectations by offering the kinds of instruction and assistance that students need to improve, and so students *do* improve (Goldenberg, 1992). In other cases, students may develop an "I'll show *you*" attitude that spurs them on to greater effort and achievement than a teacher anticipated (Good & Nichols, 2001). In still other cases, assertive parents may step in and offer evidence that their children are more capable than a teacher initially thought (Good & Nichols, 2001).

So how prevalent are self-fulfilling prophecies? In other words, to what extent do teacher expectations affect students' classroom performance and overall academic growth? Research on this topic yields mixed results (Eccles et al., 1998; Goldenberg, 1992; Rosenthal, 1994). Some research indicates that girls, students from low-income families, and students from ethnic minority groups are more susceptible to teacher expectations than boys from European American backgrounds (Graham, 1990; Jussim, Eccles, & Madon, 1996). Teacher expectations also appear to have a greater influence in the early elementary school years (first and second grades), in the first year of secondary school, and, more generally, within the first few weeks of school—in other words, at times when students are entering new and unfamiliar school environments (Jussim et al., 1996; Kuklinski & Weinstein, 2001; Raudenbush, 1984; Weinstein, Madison, & Kuklinski, 1995).

For a variety of reasons, then, different people may interpret the same events in very different ways. Over time, learners gradually develop predictable patterns of attributions and expectations for their future performance. Some remain optimistic, confident that they can master new tasks and succeed in a variety of endeavors. But others, either unsure of their own chances for success or else convinced that they *can't* succeed, display a growing sense of futility. Theorists have characterized this difference among people as being a difference in *explanatory style*.

EXPLANATORY STYLE: MASTERY ORIENTATION VERSUS LEARNED HELPLESSNESS

In Chapter 6, we encountered the phenomenon of learned helplessness: When organisms repeatedly encounter aversive stimuli that they cannot avoid, escape, or terminate, they eventually give up and passively accept those stimuli. Although much of the early research on learned helplessness was conducted with animals, this concept has been incorporated into attribution theory—which deals exclusively with human beings—and more specifically with cognitive theorists' notion of explanatory style.

A person's **explanatory style**[3] is the general way in which the individual interprets daily events and consequences. Some people typically attribute their accomplishments to their own abilities and efforts; they have an I-can-do-it attitude known as a **mastery orientation.** Others attribute successes to outside and uncontrollable factors and believe that their failures reflect a relatively permanent lack of ability; they have an I-can't-do-it attitude known as **learned helplessness** (Dweck, 1986; Eccles & Wigfield, 1985; Mikulincer, 1994; C. Peterson et al., 1993). You should think of this distinction as a continuum of individual differences rather than a complete dichotomy. You might also look at it as a difference between *optimists* and *pessimists* (C. Peterson, 1990; Seligman, 1991).

To illustrate, consider these two boys, keeping in mind that both boys have the same ability level:

- Jerry is an enthusiastic, energetic learner. He enjoys working hard at school activities and takes obvious pleasure in doing well. He is always looking for a challenge and especially likes to solve the brainteaser problems that his teacher assigns as extra-credit work each day. He can't always solve the problems, but he takes failure in stride and is eager for more problems the following day.
- Jason is an anxious, fidgety student. He doesn't seem to have much confidence in his ability to accomplish school tasks successfully. In fact, he is always underestimating what he can do; even when he has succeeded, he doubts that he can do it again. He seems to prefer filling out drill-and-practice worksheets that help him practice skills he's already mastered rather than attempting new tasks and problems. As for those daily brainteasers, he sometimes takes a stab at them, but he gives up quickly if the answer isn't readily apparent.

Jerry exhibits a mastery orientation: He clearly has his life (and his attributions) under control, and he is optimistic about his future performance. In contrast, Jason displays learned helplessness: He believes that challenging tasks are out of his reach and beyond his control, and he expects failure rather than success.

Researchers have identified a number of ways in which people with a mastery orientation differ from those with learned helplessness. In an academic context, those with a mastery orientation tend to perform better in the classroom than we would predict from their aptitude test scores and previous grade point averages (Seligman, 1991). In an athletic context, optimists bounce back from a lost game more readily, and overcome injuries more quickly, than do equally capable but more pessimistic athletes (C. Peterson, 1990). Table 18–2 lists additional differences between a mastery orientation and learned helplessness. As you can see from this table, people with a mastery orientation behave in ways that lead to higher achievement over the long run: They set high goals, seek challenging situations, and persist in the face of failure. People with learned helplessness behave very differently: Because they underestimate their own ability, they set goals they can easily accomplish, avoid situations likely to maximize their learning and growth, and respond to failure in counterproductive ways. They are also hampered by anxiety-related thoughts, which leave limited working memory capacity for concentrating on the task at hand (Mikulincer, 1994).

Even preschoolers can develop learned helplessness about a particular task if they consistently encounter failure when attempting it (Burhans & Dweck, 1995). By age 5 or 6, some children begin to show a consistent tendency either to persist at a task and express confidence that they can master

---

[3]You may also see the term *attributional style.*

Table 18–2
Characteristics of a mastery orientation versus learned helplessness.

People With a Mastery Orientation	People With Learned Helplessness
Have higher self-esteem and greater self-efficacy about their chances for success	Have low self-esteem and poor self-efficacy
Set high goals for themselves	Set low, easily accomplished goals for themselves
Prefer new and challenging tasks	Prefer easy tasks and tasks they have already completed successfully; avoid challenges
Strive for success	Try to avoid failure
Believe that prior successes are an indication of high ability and future success	Don't see prior successes as indicative of high ability and future success; *do* see prior failures as an indication of low ability and future failure
Accurately estimate their number of prior successes	Underestimate their prior successes; may even forget about them
View failure as a challenge to be met	Define themselves as "failures" when they fail
Persist when facing difficulty; try to determine the source of difficulty; seek assistance if needed	Become anxious and discouraged when facing difficulty; use ineffective strategies; may experience depression
Increase effort and concentration after failure	Decrease effort and concentration after failure; give up quickly
Take pride in their accomplishments	Don't take pride in their accomplishments because they don't believe they *caused* them; may take more responsibility for their failures than is warranted
Perform and achieve at higher levels	Perform and achieve at lower levels

Sources: Abramson, Seligman, & Teasdale, 1978; Diener & Dweck, 1978; Dweck, 1975, 1986; Dweck & Licht, 1980; Dweck & Reppucci, 1973; Meyer, Turner, & Spencer, 1994; Mikulincer, 1994; C. Peterson, 1990; Peterson & Barrett, 1987; Peterson, Colvin, & Lin, 1992; Peterson et al., 1993; Seligman, 1991; Wood, Schau, & Fiedler, 1990.

it, on the one hand, or to abandon a task quickly and say they don't have the ability to do it, on the other (Ziegert, Kistner, Castro, & Robertson, 2001). As a general rule, however, children younger than 8 rarely exhibit extreme forms of learned helplessness, perhaps because they still believe that success is largely the result of their own efforts (Eccles et al., 1998; Paris & Cunningham, 1996). By early adolescence, feelings of helplessness are more common: Some middle schoolers believe they cannot control the things that happen to them and are at a loss for strategies about how to avert future failures (Paris & Cunningham, 1996; C. Peterson et al., 1993).

As I indicated in Chapter 6, helplessness sometimes develops when people consistently find that they have little or no control over the things that happen to them. It may also develop when people observe *other* individuals having little control over their lives (Brown & Inouye, 1978; C. Peterson et al., 1993). In some cases, entire *groups* can begin to feel helpless when group members are asked to work together on tasks that, despite their best efforts, they cannot accomplish successfully (Simkin, Lederer, & Seligman, 1983). When people have a history of experiences in which they *have* had control of their successes and failures, however, they are less likely to succumb to learned helplessness in the face of temporarily uncontrollable events (C. Peterson et al., 1993).

Some theorists have suggested that learned helplessness may actually be a roundabout way in which people actually try to *maintain* a sense of control in chronically adverse conditions (Hall, Hladkyj, Ruthig, Pekrun, & Perry, 2002; Hall, Hladkyj, Taylor, & Perry, 2000; Rothbaum, Weisz, & Snyder, 1982). Because they are unable to change their environment, they instead accept their circumstances, recognize their limitations, acknowledge that factors beyond themselves (fate, God, etc.) are ultimately in charge, and try to find the silver lining in their unhappy situation.

Throughout the chapter, we have seen how numerous factors (past successes and failures, situational cues, others' messages and behaviors, etc.) influence people's self-attributions. I have saved two additional factors for last, because they have implications not only for attributions but for other key aspects of motivation as well. We turn now to the effects of these factors: challenge and competition.

EFFECTS OF CHALLENGE AND COMPETITION

In various places throughout the book I have alluded to the positive effects of challenging tasks. For example, as we discovered in Chapter 8, challenges promote cognitive development. From Piaget's perspective, accommodation occurs and new schemes emerge only when events cannot be readily assimilated into existing schemes. From Vygotsky's perspective, tasks within a child's zone of proximal development are optimal for long-term cognitive growth. Furthermore, as we learned in Chapter 13, students are most likely to develop maximally effective metacognitive strategies when the learning tasks they face are not easily accomplished using such simplistic strategies as repetition and rote memorization.

Competition and other forms of social comparison also play a role in learning. For example, when we examined the "good behavior game" in Chapter 5, we discovered that when two groups of students compete for privileges based on good behavior, students in both groups show marked improvements in classroom behavior. Furthermore, as we learned in Chapter 7, students develop high or low self-efficacy partially as a function of what they see their peers being able to do.

Challenge and competition have implications for human motivation as well as learning. Let's look at both of these within the context of the cognitive motivational factors we have explored in this and the preceding chapter.

Challenge

As I defined it in Chapter 16, a *challenge* is a situation in which individuals believe that, although they risk possible failure, they are likely to succeed if they exert sufficient effort. From a motivational standpoint, the advantages of challenges are threefold:

- *Success at challenging tasks promotes a greater sense of competence and self-efficacy* (Clifford, 1990; Deci & Ryan, 1992; Lan, Repman, Bradley, & Weller, 1994). Take a minute to do this little exercise:

Write the numbers 1 to 10 on a piece of paper. See if you can do it in less than 10 seconds.

Were you successful? If so, how good does your success make you feel? I just did the task in about four seconds' time, and I had little reason to feel particularly proud. After all, I'm 54 years old; if I can't write these numbers quickly and accurately by now, something must be terribly wrong.

Success on easy tasks, although virtually guaranteed, does little to enhance our sense of competence and self-efficacy. Sure, we can do it, but so can anyone else. However, challenges are not so easily accomplished: Perhaps we have failed to accomplish them in the past, or perhaps we know others who have failed. When we successfully meet a challenge, we must obviously be pretty competent folks. Success on a challenging task, then, gives us feelings of satisfaction that are not possible with an easier task. Furthermore, because it enhances our feelings of competency, success in a challenging situation also increases our intrinsic motivation (Clifford, 1990; Deci & Ryan, 1985; Stipek, 1996).

• *Challenges heighten interest and minimize boredom* (Csikszentmihalyi, 1990; Deci & Ryan, 1992; Malone & Lepper, 1987; Shernoff, Schneider, & Csikszentmihalyi, 2001; J. C. Turner et al., 1998). We typically become bored with easy tasks, yet we are frustrated by tasks at which we always seem to fail. Challenges provide a happy medium: They have those unexpected little twists and turns that maintain our interest, but we know that, with persistence, we can achieve success.

• *It is difficult to attribute success on challenging tasks to external factors, such as easiness of the task or luck* (Clifford, 1990; Eisenberger, 1992; Lan et al., 1994; C. Peterson, 1988, 1990). When we succeed at a very easy task—one on which we have exerted very little effort—we are likely to attribute our success to the fact that, hey, anybody can do it. When we succeed at an extremely difficult task—something we thought ourselves incapable of doing—we might attribute our success to good luck or somebody else's assistance. However, when we succeed on a challenging task—one that we know we can do if we try long and hard enough—we cannot dismiss it as being a result of task ease, and we have little reason to attribute our performance to luck or assistance. Our best alternative is to attribute our hard-won success to our own efforts and clever strategies.

When are learners most likely to take on new risks and challenges? Theorists suggest that conditions such as these are optimal:

• Standards for success are realistic for each individual.
• Scaffolding is sufficient to make success possible.
• There are few, if any, penalties for errors.
• The same rewards cannot be obtained by engaging in easier tasks, *or* rewards are greater for challenging tasks than they are for easy ones.
• Learners believe that success will probably be the result of their own knowledge, skills, efforts, and strategies (i.e., people have internal attributions).
• Learners have a sense of competence and a sense of self-determination.
  (Brophy & Alleman, 1992; Clifford, 1990; Corno & Rohrkemper, 1985; Deci & Ryan, 1985; Dweck & Elliott, 1983; Lan et al., 1994; Perry et al., 2002; Stipek, 1993)

A moment ago, I stated that success on challenging tasks promotes feelings of competence. But the last of the conditions I just listed indicates that the reverse is also true; that is, competence increases the challenges that people undertake. In other words, we have a happily "vicious" cycle here: Challenge promotes competence, and competence promotes a desire for more challenge.

Competition

In a competitive situation, success doesn't depend on absolute mastery of a task; instead, it results from outperforming others. Competition is a pervasive element in our society. In the business world, the people who have the best ideas, make the most money, or work the longest hours are (usually) the ones who get ahead. We often see competition in recreation, too—for instance, in the games we play and the athletic events we watch on television. And our democratic political system is based on competition in the most basic sense: Those who get the most votes are the ones who end up in office.

Competition is prevalent in our schools as well. We find school personnel comparing students in virtually every arena. For example, when teachers grade on the curve, their grades reflect how students stack up against one another, and only those at the top of the stack are identified as being successful. When students take college aptitude tests, their test scores reflect not what they know and can do but how their performance compares with that of their peers. Participation in sports is competitive, especially at the high school level: Even before students compete against other teams, they compete among themselves to make the team and achieve first-string status. And many of the concepts we use when we talk about students' abilities—intelligence, giftedness, learning disabilities, and so on—are defined by psychologists only in a normative sense.

What conditions promote a competitive atmosphere? One likely condition is uncertainty regarding others' expectations for our performance: In the absence of definitive criteria about what "good" performance is, we compare ourselves with our peers as a general indication of how well we are doing (C. Ames, 1984). A second condition, certainly, is a competitive reward structure, one that reinforces us for outperforming everyone else.

Many people are motivated by competition *if* they believe they have a reasonable chance of winning (Brophy, 1986; Deci & Ryan, 1992; Krampen, 1987; Stipek, 1996). But competition has several negative side effects, both motivational and behavioral, of which you should be aware:

- *Competition promotes performance goals rather than mastery goals* (C. Ames, 1984; Hagen, 1994; Nicholls, 1984; Spaulding, 1992; Stipek, 1996). When the key to success is doing better than everyone else, people inevitably focus their attention on how good they appear to others rather than on how much they are learning. And they define success as being better than everyone else rather than as improving their abilities and skills over time.

- *For the losers, competition promotes a low sense of competence and self-efficacy and diminishes self-worth* (C. Ames, 1984; C. Ames & Ames, 1981; Covington & Müeller, 2001). When people define success as mastery of a task or improvement in an activity over time, success is likely to come frequently and so will enhance self-efficacy. But when people instead define success as coming out on top, most will inevitably be losers. In the face of such "failure," they may understandably begin to believe themselves to be incompetent.

- *Competition promotes attributions to ability rather than to effort* (C. Ames, 1984; Nicholls, 1984; Stipek, 1993). Many people lose in competitive situations even when they exert a great deal of effort. They quite logically reach the conclusion that effort is not enough—that some sort of natural ability is the critical ingredient for success. Their failures, then, are due to their lack of that elusive ability, and they become pessimistic about their future chances for success.

- *Competition sometimes leads to undesirable or counterproductive behaviors* (C. Ames, 1984). In a competitive situation, people often behave in ways that interfere with their own learning and achievement or with the learning and achievement of others. For example, they may cheat if cheating puts them ahead of the pack. They may deny others access to the resources necessary for success. They may have little regard for equity and fairness. And because they are accustomed to working against one another, they may have a difficult time working cooperatively *with* one another.

- *Competition ultimately leads to lower achievement for most students.* When students' classroom success is judged on the basis of how well they perform relative to one another rather than on the basis of how much improvement they make, most students earn lower grades, show less creativity, and develop more negative attitudes toward school (Amabile & Hennessey, 1992; Covington, 1992; Graham & Golen, 1991; Krampen, 1987). Competitive classroom environments may be especially disadvantageous to female students (Eccles, 1989; Inglehart, Brown, & Vida, 1994).

As you can see, competition is not productive in situations in which we want and expect *all* learners to achieve at the highest possible levels. Thus, it is generally not a recommended strategy in school settings, where maximizing every student's achievement is the number one goal.

FOSTERING PRODUCTIVE ATTRIBUTIONS

Students of all ages are most likely to learn and achieve at high levels if they attribute successful learning and performance to things over which they have control (e.g., effort, persistence, and effective learning strategies). Yet *teachers'* attributions—not only for their students but also for themselves—are important as well. Teachers must believe that they themselves have some control over students' learning and achievement—that by using instructional methods that promote long-term memory storage, by scaffolding students' efforts at challenging tasks, and so on, they can genuinely help students master school subject matter. Following are additional principles to keep in mind:

- *Teachers should attribute students' successes to both stable and unstable internal factors but attribute their failures only to unstable and controllable internal factors.* To be most optimistic about their future performances, students should attribute their successes partly to stable internal factors, such as natural talent (thus, they will know that success wasn't a fluke), and partly to unstable but controllable factors, such as effort and strategies (thus, they will continue to work hard). At the same time, they should attribute their failures primarily to factors they can control and change.

Teachers can help promote such attributions in their students through the causes they themselves attribute to student performance (Alderman, 1990; Brophy, 1987; Schunk, 1990; Spaulding, 1992; Stipek, 1993). Consider these teacher statements as examples:

- "You've done very well. Obviously you're good at this, and you've been trying very hard to get better."
- "Your project shows a lot of talent and a lot of hard work."
- "The more you practice, the better you will get."
- "Perhaps you need to study a little more next time. And let me give you some suggestions on how you might study a little differently, too."

When students' failures are consistently attributed to ineffective learning strategies or a lack of effort, rather than to low ability or uncontrollable external factors, and when new strategies or increased effort *do* in fact produce success, then students work harder, persist longer in the face of failure, and seek help when they need it (Dweck & Elliott, 1983; Eccles & Wigfield, 1985; Graham, 1991; Paris & Paris, 2001).

Teachers should attribute student failures solely to a lack of effort only when students clearly haven't given classroom tasks their best shot. When students fail at a task at which they have expended a great deal of effort and are then told that they didn't try hard enough, they are likely to conclude that they simply don't have the ability to perform the task successfully (Alderman, 1990; Curtis & Graham, 1991; Schunk, 1990). In many cases, it may be more productive, and probably more accurate, to attribute failures to ineffective strategies and subsequently to help students acquire more effective ones (Clifford, 1984; Curtis & Graham, 1991; Pressley, Borkowski, & Schneider, 1987; Weinstein et al., 1991).

- *Attribution retraining can be helpful.* A number of studies have shown that, for school-age children at least, attributions can be altered, with more persistence in the face of failure being the result (Andrews & Debus, 1978; Chapin & Dyck, 1976; Dweck, 1975; Fowler & Peterson, 1981; Robertson, 2000). In these **attribution retraining** studies, children are asked to engage in a particular task (e.g., reading difficult sentences, solving arithmetic problems, or constructing geometric puzzles), with occasional failures interspersed among more frequent successes. Within this context, one viable approach for changing attributions is for an adult to interpret each success in terms of the effort a child has exerted and each failure in terms of insufficient effort (Chapin & Dyck, 1976; Dweck, 1975; Fowler & Peterson, 1981). Another effective approach is to reinforce children for attributing their *own* successes and failures to effort or a lack thereof (Andrews & Debus, 1978; Fowler & Peterson, 1981).

Early studies focused on effort attributions, but later studies indicated that effort attributions are not always the most beneficial attributions for children to acquire. For example, greater self-efficacy may result when an adult attributes a child's successes (but not failures) to ability rather than effort (e.g., "You're good at this") (Schunk, 1983a). And attributions to effective and ineffective learning strategies (for success and failure, respectively) are often more productive than effort attributions, particularly when such attribution retraining accompanies a study strategies training program (Pressley, Borkowski, & Schneider, 1987; Weinstein et al., 1991).

- *Efforts to change attributions must be an ongoing endeavor rather than a one-shot intervention.* Learners' views of themselves and their abilities are not likely to change dramatically overnight (Meece, 1994; Paris, 1990). In classroom contexts, teachers can do a variety of things to promote internal, controllable attributions and an overall mastery orientation. For instance, they can portray knowledge and skills as things that, with hard work and occasional inevitable errors, will undoubtedly increase over time (Good & Brophy, 1994). They can describe and model how they themselves learn—for example, by recalling situations in which they have mastered something only after they've exerted considerable effort or tried several different strategies (Good & Brophy, 1994). They can give students numerous opportunities to improve assignments and overall class grades (C. Ames, 1992). And they should certainly evaluate students on the basis of mastery of class material rather than on how students compare with one another (C. Ames, 1992; Good & Brophy, 1994).

- *Teachers should encourage students to take on challenges and risks.* Success on difficult and challenging tasks promotes feelings of competence and self-efficacy, as well as attributions to internal causes, in ways that easier tasks never can. Teachers should help students recognize that a hard-won success is far more significant than the "easy A." And they shouldn't penalize students for trying new approaches that don't pan out.

Yet the school day shouldn't necessarily be one challenge after another. Such a state of affairs would be absolutely exhausting, and probably quite discouraging as well. Instead, teachers should probably strike a balance between easy tasks—those that will boost students' self-confidence over the short run—and the challenging tasks so critical for a long-term sense of competence and self-efficacy (Keller, 1987; Spaulding, 1992; Stipek, 1993, 1996).

• *Most classroom activities should be noncompetitive in nature.* In any public situation, including the classroom, people will invariably compare themselves with one another. Yet teachers can take steps to minimize the extent to which comparison and competition among students occur. For example, they can keep students' performance on classroom tasks private and confidential, minimizing the degree to which students are even aware of classmates' performance levels (Schunk, 1990; Spaulding, 1992). At any one time, they can have different students doing different tasks (Stipek, 1996). They can assess students' performance independently of how well classmates are doing and encourage students to assess their own performance in a similar manner (Spaulding, 1992; Wlodkowski, 1978). When little competitions among students (e.g., debates, team math games) do seem appropriate, teachers can make sure that all students or teams have a reasonable (and, if possible, equal) chance of winning (Brophy, 1986, 1987) and make no big deal about whoever the ultimate winners are.

• *Teachers should have and communicate high expectations for students.* As we have seen, when teachers have high expectations for students' performance, they are more likely to *get* such performance. And when students consistently perform at high levels, teachers are more likely to recognize that their students do, in fact, have the potential for success and that they themselves are instrumental in making this success possible. In other words, high expectations lead to higher performance, which in turn leads to higher expectations and more optimistic attributions.

A study involving children's littering behavior (Miller et al., 1975) illustrates just how simply teachers might communicate their expectations and how powerful their expectations can be. One group of fifth graders was repeatedly labeled neat and clean; for example, a poster of a Peanuts character on the wall proclaimed that "We are Andersen's litter-conscious class," and, after noticing a piece of litter on the floor, the teacher stated that "Our class is clean and would not do that." For a second group of students, persuasion was used in various forms to alter littering behavior; for example, a poster of a Peanuts character advocated, "Don't be a litterbug," and the teacher explained why garbage should always be thrown away (e.g., it draws flies and endangers health). To test the relative effects of the two treatments, the experimenters provided opportunities for the students to litter (by distributing candy wrapped in cellophane and, two weeks later, by handing out toy puzzles in disposable plastic containers); they also scattered several candy wrappers and plastic puzzle containers on the floor while the students were at recess. A short time later, the experimenters counted the number of candy wrappers and plastic containers that remained on the floor. Students who had consistently been labeled neat and clean left significantly fewer pieces of litter than those who had specifically been persuaded not to litter.

But how do teachers acquire high expectations for students in the first place? First, teachers can *look for strengths in every student.* Sometimes students' weaknesses are all too evident. But it is essential that teachers also look for the many unique qualities and strengths that students inevitably bring to the classroom. For example, many African American students show considerable creativity when they converse; they joke, tease, and tell lively stories (Hale-Benson, 1986). Teachers can certainly take advantage of such playfulness in students' speech—perhaps by having students create songs, jokes, or short stories that relate to classroom subject matter.

Second, teachers should *learn more about students' backgrounds and home environments*. Teachers are most likely to have low expectations for students' performance when they have formed rigid stereotypes about students from certain ethnic or socioeconomic groups (McLoyd, 1998; Snow et al., 1996). And such stereotypes are often the result of ignorance about students' cultures and home environments (Alexander, Entwisle, & Thompson, 1987). When teachers have a clear picture of their students' activities, habits, values, and families, they are far more likely to think of their students as *individuals* than as stereotypical members of a particular group.

Third, teachers should *assume that ability can and often does improve with time, practice, and solid instructional practices.* In other words, teachers should take an incremental view, rather than an entity view, of students' intelligence and other abilities (Pintrich & Schunk, 2002).

Fourth, teachers should *assess students' progress regularly and objectively.* Because expectations for students' performance are likely to color any informal estimates of what students are actually accomplishing, teachers need to identify more objective ways of assessing learning and achievement. Furthermore, they should assess students' progress frequently so that students have ongoing and reasonably accurate information with which to make instructional decisions (Goldenberg, 1992).

Finally, teachers should *remember that they can definitely make a difference.* Teachers are more likely to have high expectations for students when they are confident in their *own* ability to promote learning and academic success (Ashton, 1985; Weinstein et al., 1995).

SUMMARY

Attributions are the cause–effect explanations that people construct for things that happen to themselves or to others. People may attribute events to causes that are (1) internal or external, (2) stable or unstable to oneself, and (3) controllable or uncontrollable.

People's attributions for themselves affect many aspects of behavior and cognition, including their reactions to success and failure, expectations for future success, expenditure of effort, learning strategies, and choice of activities. For instance, people are most likely to take pride in a success when they believe they themselves were responsible for it. And they are most likely to modify their behavior after a failure when they believe the failure was the result of internal factors they can control—factors such as effort and strategies.

People's self-attributions emerge from many sources. Their past history of success and failure certainly has an effect; for instance, if they consistently fail no matter what they do, they are apt to attribute such failure to something stable and uncontrollable, such as lack of natural talent. But other factors make a difference as well, including situational cues (e.g., the apparent difficulty of a task), self-protective biases (especially a need to protect self-worth), and age-related trends (e.g., a developing ability to distinguish between effort and ability).

The messages that other individuals convey are also an important source of information about cause–effect attributions. People tend to draw inferences not only about why things happen to themselves but also about why things happen to others, and they convey such interpersonal attributions through the things they say (e.g., "You certainly worked hard on this") and the ways they react (e.g., being angry rather than sympathetic when a student does poorly on an assigned task). As is true for self-attributions, people's attributions for others are sometimes accurate and sometimes not; they can be influenced not only by the observed pattern of previous successes and failures but also by cultural norms, a general bias toward stable rather than unstable attributions, beliefs about the nature of intelligence, and group stereotypes.

In the classroom, teachers attributions for students' successes and failures (e.g., whether they chalk up students' academic performance to intelligence, effort, or some other factor) influence their expectations for students' future performance. Premature and unwarranted expectations for students can be self-perpetuating; they influence teachers' behaviors toward students and so ultimately may also influence students' self-perceptions and academic achievement.

As children grow older, and especially as they reach adolescence or adulthood, many develop a general explanatory style, perhaps an I-can-do-it attitude (*mastery orientation*) that promotes effort, persistence, and preference for challenge, or perhaps an I-*can't*-do-it attitude (*learned helplessness*) that leads them to set easy goals for themselves and to give up quickly in the face of obstacles.

Challenging tasks have motivational benefits as well as cognitive ones; in particular, they enhance self-efficacy, heighten interest, and promote optimistic internal attributions. In contrast, competitive situations are usually detrimental to motivation: They encourage performance goals rather than mastery goals, and because most people inevitably come out losers rather than winners, they promote low self-efficacy and attributions to low ability.

Teachers should give students reasons for optimism about their future chances of success by attributing both successes and failures to factors students can control, including effort (if it has, in fact, influenced the outcome) and cognitive strategies. Teachers should also attribute students' successes (but not failures) partly to a fairly stable ability that will be a dependable resource time after time. Ultimately, to foster productive attributions in students, teachers must believe that students truly have the ability to achieve academic success and that they themselves have many effective techniques in their instructional toolboxes to help students learn.

References

Ablard, K. E., & Lipschultz, R. E. (1998). Self-regulated learning in high-achieving students: Relations to advanced reasoning, achievement goals, and gender. *Journal of Educational Psychology, 90,* 94–101.

Abrams, R. A. (1994). The forces that move the eyes. *Current Directions in Psychological Science, 3,* 65–67.

Abramson, L. Y., Seligman, M. E. P., & Teasdale, J. (1978). Learned helplessness in humans: Critique and reformulation. *Journal of Abnormal Psychology, 87,* 49–74.

Achacoso, M. V., Summers, J. J., & Schallert, D. L. (2002, April). *Entitlement as an attributional belief: A new venue for a model of academic motivation.* Paper presented at the annual meeting of the American Educational Research Association, New Orleans.

Achenbach, T. M. (1974). *Developmental psychopathology.* New York: Ronald Press.

Ackley, D. H., Hinton, G. E., & Sejnowski, T. J. (1985). A learning algorithm for Boltzmann machines. *Cognitive Science, 9,* 147–169.

Adolphs, R., & Damasion, A. R. (2001). The interaction of affect and cognition: A neurobiological perspective. In J. P. Forgas (Ed.), *Handbook of affect and social cognition* (pp. 27–49). Mahwah, NJ: Erlbaum.

Airasian, P. W. (1994). *Classroom assessment* (2nd ed.). New York: McGraw-Hill.

Alberto, P. A., & Troutman, A. C. (2003). *Applied behavior analysis for teachers* (6th ed.). Upper Saddle River, NJ: Merrill/Prentice Hall.

Alderman, K. (1990). Motivation for at-risk students. *Educational Leadership, 48*(1), 27–30.

Alegria, J. (1998). The origin and functions of phonological representations in deaf people. In C. Hulme & R. M. Joshi (Eds.), *Reading and spelling: Development and disorders.* Mahwah, NJ: Erlbaum.

Alexander, K., Entwisle, D., & Thompson, M. (1987). School performance, status relations, and the structure of sentiment: Bringing the teacher back in. *American Sociological Review, 52,* 665–682.

Alexander, L., Frankiewicz, R., & Williams, R. (1979). Facilitation of learning and retention of oral instruction using advance and post organizers. *Journal of Educational Psychology, 71,* 701–707.

Alexander, P. A. (1997). Mapping the multidimensional nature of domain learning: The interplay of cognitive, motivational, and strategic forces. In P. R. Pintrich & M. L. Maehr (Eds.), *Advances in motivation and achievement* (Vol. 10). Greenwich, CT: JAI Press.

Alexander, P. A. (1998). Positioning conceptual change within a model of domain literacy. In B. Guzzetti & C. Hynd (Eds.), *Perspectives on conceptual change: Multiple ways to understand knowing and learning in a complex world* (pp. 55–76). Mahwah, NJ: Erlbaum.

Alexander, P. A., Graham, S., & Harris, K. R. (1998). A perspective on strategy research: Progress and prospects. *Educational Psychology Review, 10,* 129–154.

Alexander, P. A., & Jetton, T. L. (1996). The role of importance and interest in the processing of text. *Educational Psychology Review, 8,* 89–121.

Alexander, P. A., & Judy, J. E. (1988). The interaction of domain-specific and strategic knowledge in academic performance. *Review of Educational Research, 58,* 375–404.

Alexander, P. A., Kulikowich, J. M., & Schulze, S. K. (1994). How subject-matter knowledge affects recall and interest. *American Educational Research Journal, 31,* 313–337.

Alexander, P. A., White, C. S., & Daugherty, M. (1997). Analogical reasoning and early mathematical learning. In L. D. English (Ed.), *Mathematical reasoning: Analogies, metaphors, and images* (pp. 117–147). Mahwah, NJ: Erlbaum.

Alfassi, M. (1998). Reading for meaning: The efficacy of reciprocal teaching in fostering reading comprehension in high school students in remedial reading classes. *American Educational Research Journal, 35,* 309–332.

Alford, G. S., & Rosenthal, T. L. (1973). Process and products of modeling in observational concept attainment. *Child Development, 44,* 714–720.

Alibali, M. W., Bassok, M., Solomon, K. O., Syc, S. E., & Goldin-Meadow, S. (1999). Illuminating mental representations through speech and gesture. *Psychological Science, 10,* 327–333.

Alleman, J., & Brophy, J. (1992). Analysis of the activities in a social studies curriculum. In J. Brophy (Ed.), *Advances in research on teaching: Vol. 3. Planning and managing learning tasks and activities.* Greenwich, CT: JAI Press.

Allen, K. D. (1998). The use of an enhanced simplified habit-reversal procedure to reduce disruptive outbursts during athletic performance. *Journal of Applied Behavior Analysis, 31,* 489–492.

Altmann, E. M., & Gray, W. D. (2002). Forgetting to remember: The functional relationship of decay and interference. *Psychological Science, 13,* 27–33.

Alvermann, D. E. (1981). The compensatory effect of graphic organizers on descriptive text. *Journal of Educational Research, 75,* 44–48.

Amabile, T. M., & Hennessey, B. A. (1992). The motivation for creativity in children. In A. K. Boggiano & T. S. Pittman (Eds.), *Achievement and motivation: A social-developmental perspective.* Cambridge, England: Cambridge University Press.

Ames, C. (1984). Competitive, cooperative, and individualistic goal structures: A cognitive-motivational analysis. In R. Ames & C. Ames (Eds.), *Research on motivation in education: Vol. 1. Student motivation.* Orlando: Academic Press.

Ames, C. (1992). Classrooms: Goals, structures, and student motivation. *Journal of Educational Psychology, 84,* 261–271.

Ames, C., & Ames, R. (1981). Competitive versus individualistic goal structures: The salience of past performance information for causal attributions and affect. *Journal of Educational Psychology, 73,* 411–418.

Ames, C., & Archer, J. (1988). Achievement goals in the classroom: Students' learning strategies and motivation processes. *Journal of Educational Psychology, 80,* 260–267.

Ames, R. (1983). Help-seeking and achievement orientation: Perspectives from attribution theory. In A. Nadler, J. Fisher, & B. DePaulo (Eds.), *New directions in helping* (Vol. 2). New York: Academic Press.

Amrein, A. L., & Berliner, D. C. (2002, March 28). High-stakes testing, uncertainty, and student learning. *Education Policy Analysis Archives, 10*(18). Retrieved April 9, 2002, from http://epaa.asu.edu/epaa/v10n18/.

Anand, P., & Ross, S. (1987). A computer-based strategy for personalizing verbal problems in teaching mathematics. *Educational Communication and Technology Journal, 35,* 151–162.

Anderman, E. M., Griesinger, T., & Westerfield, G. (1998). Motivation and cheating during early adolescence. *Journal of Educational Psychology, 90,* 84–93.

Anderman, E. M., & Maehr, M. L. (1994). Motivation and schooling in the middle grades. *Review of Educational Research, 64,* 287–309.

Anderman, L. H., & Anderman, E. M. (1999). Social predictors of changes in students' achievement goal orientation. *Contemporary Educational Psychology, 25,* 21–37.

Anderson, C. A., & Bushman, B. J. (2001). Effects of violent video games on aggressive behavior, aggressive cognition, aggressive affect, physiological arousal, and prosocial behavior: A meta-analytic review of the scientific literature. *Psychological Science, 12,* 353–359.

Anderson, C. W., Sheldon, T. H., & Dubay, J. (1990). The effects of instruction on college nonmajors' conceptions of respiration and photosynthesis. *Journal of Research in Science Teaching, 27,* 761–776.

Anderson, J. R. (1974). Retrieval of propositional information from long-term memory. *Cognitive Psychology, 6,* 451–474.

Anderson, J. R. (1976). *Language, memory, and thought.* Hillsdale, NJ: Erlbaum.

Anderson, J. R. (1983a). *The architecture of cognition.* Cambridge, MA: Harvard University Press.

Anderson, J. R. (1983b). A spreading activation theory of memory. *Journal of Verbal Learning and Verbal Behavior, 22,* 261–295.

Anderson, J. R. (1984). Spreading activation. In J. R. Anderson & S. M. Kosslyn (Eds.), *Tutorials in learning and memory.* San Francisco: W. H. Freeman.

Anderson, J. R. (1985). *Cognitive psychology and its implications* (2nd ed.). New York: W. H. Freeman.

Anderson, J. R. (1987). Skill acquisition: Compilation of weak-method problem solutions. *Psychological Review, 94,* 192–210.

Anderson, J. R. (1990). *Cognitive psychology and its implications* (3rd ed.). New York: W. H. Freeman.

Anderson, J. R. (1993). Problem solving and learning. *American Psychologist, 48,* 35–44.

Anderson, J. R. (1995). *Learning and memory: An integrated approach.* New York: Wiley.

Anderson, J. R., & Bower, G. H. (1973). *Human associative memory.* Washington, DC: Winston.

Anderson, J. R., Greeno, J. G., Reder, L. M., & Simon, H. A. (2000). Perspectives on learning, thinking, and activity. *Educational Researcher, 29*(4), 11–13.

Anderson, J. R., Reder, L. M., & Simon, H. A. (1996). Situated learning and education. *Educational Researcher, 25*(4), 5–11.

Anderson, J. R., Reder, L. M., & Simon, H. A. (1997). Situative versus cognitive perspectives: Form versus substance. *Educational Researcher, 26*(1), 18–21.

Anderson, J. R., & Schooler, L. J. (1991). Reflections of the environment in memory. *Psychological Science, 2,* 396–408.

Anderson, L. M. (1993). Auxiliary materials that accompany textbooks: Can they promote "higher-order" learning? In B. K. Britton, A. Woodward, & M. Binkley (Eds.), *Learning from textbooks: Theory and practice.* Hillsdale, NJ: Erlbaum.

Anderson, L. M. (1997, March). Taking students' entering knowledge and beliefs seriously when teaching about learning and teaching. In H. Borko (Chair), *Educational psychology and teacher education: Perennial issues.* Symposium conducted at the annual meeting of the American Educational Research Association, Chicago.

Anderson, L. W., Krathwohl, D. R., Airasian, P. W., Cruikshank, K. A., Mayer, R. E., Pintrich, P. R., Raths, J., & Wittrock, M. C. (Eds.) (2001). *A taxonomy for learning, teaching, and assessing: A revision of Bloom's taxonomy of educational objectives.* New York: Longman.

Anderson, R. C. (1984). Role of reader's schema in comprehension, learning, and memory. In R. C. Anderson, J. Osborn, & R. J. Tierney (Eds.), *Learning to read in American schools: Basal readers and content texts.* Hillsdale, NJ: Erlbaum.

Anderson, R. C., & Biddle, B. (1975). On asking people questions about what they are reading. In G. H. Bower (Ed.), *Psychology of learning and motivation* (Vol. 9). New York: Academic Press.

Anderson, R. C., Nguyen-Jahiel, K., McNurlen, B., Archodidou, A., Kim, S.-Y., Reznitskaya, A., Tillmanns, M., & Gilbert, L. (2001). The snowball phenomenon: Spread of ways of talking and ways of thinking across groups of children. *Cognition and Instruction, 19,* 1–46.

Anderson, R. C., & Pearson, P. D. (1984). A schema-theoretic view of basic processes in reading. In P. D. Pearson (Ed.), *Handbook of reading research.* New York: Longman.

Anderson, R. C., & Pichert, J. W. (1978). Recall of previously unrecallable information following a shift in perspective. *Journal of Verbal Learning and Verbal Behavior, 17,* 1–12.

Anderson, R. C., Reynolds, R. E., Schallert, D. L., & Goetz, E. T. (1977). Frameworks for comprehending discourse. *American Educational Research Journal, 14,* 367–381.

Anderson, V., & Hidi, S. (1988/1989). Teaching students to summarize. *Educational Leadership, 46*(4), 26–28.

Anderson-Inman, L., Walker, H. M., & Purcell, J. (1984). Promoting the transfer of skills across settings: Transenvironmental programming for handicapped students in the mainstream. In W. Heward, T. E. Heron, D. S. Hill, & J. Trap-Porter (Eds.), *Focus on behavior analysis in education.* Columbus, OH: Merrill.

Andre, T. (1979). Does answering higher-level questions while reading facilitate productive learning? *Review of Educational Research, 49,* 280–318.

Andre, T. (1986). Problem solving and education. In G. D. Phye & T. Andre (Eds.), *Cognitive classroom learning: Understanding, thinking, and problem solving.* Orlando: Academic Press.

Andre, T., & Windschitl, M. (2003). Interest, epistemological belief, and intentional conceptual change. In G. M. Sinatra & P. R. Pintrich (Eds.), *Intentional conceptual change* (pp. 173–197). Mahwah, NJ: Erlbaum.

Andrews, A. C. (1987). The analogy theme in geography. *Journal of Geography, 86,* 194–197.

Andrews, G. R., & Debus, R. L. (1978). Persistence and the causal perception of failure: Modifying cognitive attributions. *Journal of Educational Psychology, 70,* 154–166.

Anglin, J. M. (1977). *Word, object, and conceptual development.* New York: W. W. Norton.

Anker, A. L., & Crowley, T. J. (1982). Use of contingency contracts in specialty clinics for cocaine abuse. *National Institute on Drug Abuse: Research Monograph Series, 4,* 452–459.

Anzai, Y. (1991). Learning and use of representations for physics expertise. In K. A. Ericsson & J. Smith (Eds.), *Toward a general theory of expertise: Prospects and limits.* Cambridge, England: Cambridge University Press.

Appel, J. B., & Peterson, N. J. (1965). Punishment: Effects of shock intensity on response suppression. *Psychological Reports, 16,* 721–730.

Ariely, D. (2001). Seeing sets: Representation by statistical properties. *Psychological Science, 12,* 157–162.

Ariely, D., & Wertenbroch, K. (2002). Procrastination, deadlines, and performance: Self-control by precommitment. *Psychological Science, 13,* 219–224.

Arlin, M. (1984). Time, equality, and mastery learning. *Review of Educational Research, 54,* 65–86.

Armbruster, B. B. (1984). The problem of "inconsiderate text." In G. G. Duffy, L. R. Roehler, & J. Mason (Eds.), *Comprehension instruction: Perspectives and suggestions.* New York: Longman.

Armbruster, B. B., & Ostertag, J. (1993). Questions in elementary science and social studies textbooks. In B. K. Britton, A. Woodward, & M. Binkley (Eds.), *Learning from textbooks: Theory and practice.* Hillsdale, NJ: Erlbaum.

Armstrong, S. L., Gleitman, L. R., & Gleitman, H. G. (1983). What some concepts might not be. *Cognition, 13,* 263–308.

Aronfreed, J. (1968). Aversive control of socialization. In W. J. Arnold (Ed.), *Nebraska Symposium on Motivation.* Lincoln: University of Nebraska Press.

Aronfreed, J., & Reber, A. (1965). Internalized behavioral suppression and the timing of social punishment. *Journal of Personality and Social Psychology, 1*, 3–16.

Aronson, E. (1997). *The jigsaw classroom: Building cooperation in the classroom* (2nd ed.). New York: Longman.

Arrigo, J. M., & Pezdek, K. (1997). Lessons from the study of psychogenic amnesia. *Current Directions in Psychological Science, 6*, 148–152.

Ashton, P. (1985). Motivation and the teacher's sense of efficacy. In C. Ames & R. Ames (Eds.), *Research on motivation in education: Vol. 2. The classroom milieu.* San Diego: Academic Press.

Assor, A., & Connell, J. P. (1992). The validity of students' self-reports as measures of performance affecting self-appraisals. In D. H. Schunk & J. L. Meece (Eds.), *Student perceptions in the classroom.* Hillsdale, NJ: Erlbaum.

Astington, J. W., & Pelletier, J. (1996). The language of mind: Its role in teaching and learning. In D. R. Olson & N. Torrance (Eds.), *The handbook of education and human development: New models of learning, teaching, and schooling.* Cambridge, MA: Blackwell Publishers.

Atkinson, J. W. (1957). Motivational determinants of risk-taking behavior. *Psychological Review, 64*, 359–372.

Atkinson, J. W. (1958). *Motives in fantasy, action, and sobriety.* Princeton, NJ: Van Nostrand.

Atkinson, J. W. (1964). *Introduction to motivation.* Princeton, NJ: Van Nostrand.

Atkinson, J. W., & Birch, D. (1978). *Introduction to motivation* (2nd ed.). New York: Van Nostrand.

Atkinson, J. W., & Feather, N. T. (Eds.).(1966). *A theory of achievement motivation.* New York: Wiley.

Atkinson, J. W., & Litwin, G. H. (1960). Achievement motive and test anxiety conceived as motive to approach success and motive to avoid failure. *Journal of Abnormal and Social Psychology, 60*, 52–63.

Atkinson, J. W., & Raynor, J. O. (1978). *Personality, motivation, and achievement.* Washington, DC: Hemisphere.

Atkinson, R. C. (1975). Mnemotechnics in second-language learning. *American Psychologist, 30*, 821–828.

Atkinson, R. C., & Shiffrin, R. M. (1968). Human memory: A proposed system and its control processes. In K. W. Spence & J. T. Spence (Eds.), *The psychology of learning and motivation: Advances in research and theory* (Vol. 2). New York: Academic Press.

Atkinson, R. C., & Shiffrin, R. M. (1971). The control of short-term memory. *Scientific American, 225*(2), 82–90.

Atkinson, R. K., Derry, S. J., Renkl, A., & Wortham, D. (2000). Learning from examples: Instructional principles from the worked examples research. *Review of Educational Research, 70*, 181–214.

Atkinson, R. K., Levin, J. R., Kiewra, K. A., Meyers, T., Kim, S., Atkinson, L. A., Renandya, W. A., & Hwang, Y. (1999). Matrix and mnemonic text-processing adjuncts: Comparing and combining their components. *Journal of Educational Psychology, 91*, 342–357.

Attneave, A. (1957). Transfer of experience with a class schema to identification learning of patterns and shapes. *Journal of Experimental Psychology, 54*, 81–88.

Aulls, M. W. (1998). Contributions of classroom discourse to what content students learn during curriculum enactment. *Journal of Educational Psychology, 90*, 56–69.

Austin, J., Alvero, A. M., & Olson, R. (1998). Prompting patron safety belt use at a restaurant. *Journal of Applied Behavior Analysis, 31*, 655–657.

Ausubel, D. P. (1963). *The psychology of meaningful verbal learning.* New York: Grune & Stratton.

Ausubel, D. P. (1968). *Educational psychology: A cognitive view.* New York: Holt, Rinehart & Winston.

Ausubel, D. P., Novak, J. D., & Hanesian, H. (1978). *Educational psychology: A cognitive view* (2nd ed.). New York: Holt, Rinehart & Winston.

Ausubel, D. P., & Robinson, F. G. (1969). *School learning: An introduction to educational psychology.* New York: Holt, Rinehart & Winston.

Awh, E., Jonides, J., Smith, E. E., Schumacher, E. H., Koeppe, R. A., & Katz, S. (1996). Dissociation of storage and rehearsal in verbal working memory: Evidence from positron emission tomography. *Psychological Science, 7*, 25–31.

Ayllon, T., Layman, D., & Kandel, H. J. (1975). A behavioral–educational alternative to drug control of hyperactive children. *Journal of Applied Behavior Analysis, 8*, 137–146.

Azrin, N. H. (1960). Effects of punishment intensity during variable-interval reinforcement. *Journal of the Experimental Analysis of Behavior, 3*, 123–142.

Azrin, N. H. (1967, May). Pain and aggression. *Psychology Today, 1*, 27–33.

Azrin, N. H., & Holz, W. C. (1966). Punishment. In W. K. Honig (Ed.), *Operant behavior: Areas of research and application.* New York: Appleton-Century-Crofts.

Babad, E. (1993). Teachers' differential behavior. *Educational Psychology Review, 5*, 347–376.

Bachevalier, J., Malkova, L., & Beauregard, M. (1996). Multiple memory systems: A neuropsychological and developmental perspective. In G. R. Lyon & N. A. Krasnegor (Eds.), *Attention, memory, and executive function.* Baltimore: Paul H. Brookes.

Bach-y-Rita, P. (1981). Brain plasticity as a basis for therapeutic procedures. In P. Bach-y-Rita (Ed.), *Recovery of function: Theoretical considerations for brain injury rehabiliation.* Baltimore, MD: University Park Press.

Baddeley, A. D. (1978). The trouble with levels: A reexamination of Craik and Lockhart's framework for memory research. *Psychological Review, 85*, 139–152.

Baddeley, A. D. (1982). *Your memory: A user's guide.* New York: Macmillan.

Baddeley, A. D. (1986). *Working memory.* Oxford, England: Clarendon Press.

Baddeley, A. D. (1999). *Essentials of human memory.* Philadelphia: Psychology Press.

Baddeley, A. D. (2001). Is working memory still working? *American Psychologist, 56*, 851–864.

Baddeley, A. D., & Hitch, G. (1974). Working memory. In G. H. Bower (Ed.), *The psychology of learning and motivation* (Vol. 8). New York: Academic Press.

Baddeley, A. D., & Logie, R. (1992). Auditory imagery and working memory. In D. Reisberg (Ed.), *Auditory imagery.* Hillsdale, NJ: Erlbaum.

Bahrick, H. P. (1984). Semantic memory content in permastore: Fifty years of memory for Spanish learned in school. *Journal of Experimental Psychology: General, 113*, 1–29.

Bahrick, H. P., Bahrick, L. E., Bahrick, A. S., & Bahrick, P. E. (1993). Maintenance of foreign language vocabulary and the spacing effect. *Psychological Science, 4*, 316–321.

Baillargeon, R. (1994). How do infants learn about the physical world? *Current Directions in Psychological Science, 3*, 133–140.

Baker, L. (1989). Metacognition, comprehension monitoring, and the adult reader. *Educational Psychology Review, 1*, 3–38.

Baker, L., & Brown, A. L. (1984). Metacognitive skills of reading. In D. Pearson (Ed.), *Handbook of reading research.* New York: Longman.

Baker, L., Scher, D., & Mackler, K. (1997). Home and family influences on motivations for reading. *Educational Psychologist, 32*, 69–82.

Balch, W., Bowman, K., & Mohler, L. (1992). Music-dependent memory in immediate and delayed word recall. *Memory and Cognition, 20*, 21–28.

Ballard, D. H. (1986). Cortical connections and parallel processing. *Behavioural and Brain Sciences, 9*(1), 67–120.

Bandura, A. (1965a). Behavioral modification through modeling practices. In L. Krasner & L. Ullman (Eds.), *Research in behavior modification.* New York: Holt, Rinehart & Winston.

Bandura, A. (1965b). Influence of models' reinforcement contingencies on the acquisition of imitative responses. *Journal of Personality and Social Psychology, 1*, 589–595.

Bandura, A. (1969). *Principles of behavior modification.* New York: Holt, Rinehart & Winston.

Bandura, A. (1973). *Aggression: A social learning analysis.* Englewood Cliffs, NJ: Prentice Hall.

Bandura, A. (1977a). Self-efficacy: Toward a unifying theory of behavioral change. *Psychological Review*, 84, 191–215.

Bandura, A. (1977b). *Social learning theory.* Englewood Cliffs, NJ: Prentice Hall.

Bandura, A. (1982). Self-efficacy mechanism in human agency. *American Psychologist*, 37, 122–147.

Bandura, A. (1986). *Social foundations of thought and action: A social cognitive theory.* Englewood Cliffs, NJ: Prentice Hall.

Bandura, A. (1989). Human agency in social cognitive theory. *American Psychologist*, 44, 1175–1184.

Bandura, A. (1997). *Self-efficacy: The exercise of control.* New York: Freeman.

Bandura, A. (2000). Exercise of human agency through collective efficacy. *Current Directions in Psychological Science*, 9, 75–78.

Bandura, A., Barbaranelli, C., Caprara, G. V., & Pastorelli, C. (2001). Self-efficacy beliefs as shapers of children's aspirations and career trajectories. *Child Development*, 72, 187–206.

Bandura, A., Grusec, E., & Menlove, F. L. (1967). Vicarious extinction of avoidance behavior. *Journal of Personality and Social Psychology*, 5, 16–23.

Bandura, A., & Jeffery, R. W. (1973). Role of symbolic coding and rehearsal processes in observational learning. *Journal of Personality & Social Psychology*, 26, 122–130.

Bandura, A., Jeffery, R. W., & Bachicha, D. L. (1974). Analysis of memory codes and cumulative rehearsal in observational learning. *Journal of Research in Personality*, 7, 295–305.

Bandura, A., & Kupers, C. J. (1964). Transmission of patterns of self-reinforcement through modeling. *Journal of Abnormal and Social Psychology*, 69, 1–9.

Bandura, A., & McDonald, F. J. (1963). Influences of social reinforcement and the behavior of models in shaping children's moral judgments. *Journal of Abnormal and Social Psychology*, 67, 274–281.

Bandura, A., & Menlove, F. L. (1968). Factors determining vicarious extinction of avoidance behavior through symbolic modeling. *Journal of Personality and Social Psychology*, 5, 16–23.

Bandura, A., & Perloff, B. (1967). Relative efficacy of self-monitored and externally imposed reinforcement systems. *Journal of Personality and Social Psychology*, 7, 111–116.

Bandura, A., Ross, D., & Ross, S. A. (1961). Transmission of aggression through imitation of aggressive models. *Journal of Abnormal and Social Psychology*, 63, 575–582.

Bandura, A., Ross, D., & Ross, S. A. (1963). Imitation of film-mediated aggressive models. *Journal of Abnormal and Social Psychology*, 66, 3–11.

Bandura, A., & Schunk, D. (1981). Cultivating competence, self-efficacy, and intrinsic interest through proximal self-motivation. *Journal of Personality and Social Psychology*, 41, 586–598.

Bandura, A., & Walters, R. H. (1963). *Social learning and personality development.* New York: Holt, Rinehart & Winston.

Bandura, A., & Whalen, C. K. (1966). The influence of antecedent reinforcement and divergent modeling cues on patterns of self-reward. *Journal of Personality & Social Psychology*, 3, 373–382.

Bangert-Drowns, R. L., Kulik, C. C., Kulik, J. A., & Morgan, M. (1991). The instructional effect of feedback in test-like events. *Review of Educational Research*, 61, 213–238.

Banks, J. A. (1991). Multicultural literacy and curriculum reform. *Educational Horizons*, 69(3), 135–140.

Banks, J. A., & Banks, C. A. M. (Eds.). (1995). *Handbook of research on multicultural education.* New York: Macmillan.

Barbetta, P. M. (1990). GOALS: A group-oriented adapted levels system for children with behavior disorders. *Academic Therapy*, 25, 645–656.

Barbetta, P. M., Heward, W. L., Bradley, D. M., & Miller, A. D. (1994). Effects of immediate and delayed error correction on the acquisition and maintenance of sight words by students with developmental disabilities. *Journal of Applied Behavior Analysis*, 27, 177–178.

Barker, G. P., & Graham, S. (1987). Developmental study of praise and blame as attributional cues. *Journal of Educational Psychology*, 79, 62–66.

Barker, R. H., Dembo, T., & Lewin, K. (1941). Frustration and regression: An experiment with young children. *University of Iowa Studies in Child Welfare*, 18, 1–314.

Barkley, R. A. (1996a). Critical issues in research on attention. In G. R. Lyon & N. A. Krasnegor (Eds.), *Attention, memory, and executive function.* Baltimore: Paul H. Brookes.

Barkley, R. A. (1996b). Linkages between attention and executive functions. In G. R. Lyon & N. A. Krasnegor (Eds.), *Attention, memory, and executive function.* Baltimore: Paul H. Brookes.

Barnett, J. E. (1999, April). *Adaptive studying across disciplines: A think-aloud study.* Paper presented at the annual meeting of the American Educational Research Association, Montreal.

Barnett, J. E. (2001, April). *Study strategies and preparing for exams: A survey of middle and high school students.* Paper presented at the annual meeting of the American Educational Research Association, Seattle, WA.

Barnett, J. E., Di Vesta, F. J., & Rogozinski, J. T. (1981). What is learned in note taking? *Journal of Educational Psychology*, 73, 181–192.

Baron, A., Kaufman, A., & Stauber, K. A. (1969). Effects of instructions and reinforcement feedback on human operant behavior maintained by fixed-interval reinforcement. *Journal of the Experimental Analysis of Behavior*, 12, 701–712.

Baron, J. B. (1987). Evaluating thinking skills in the classroom. In J. B. Baron & R. J. Stern-berg (Eds.), *Teaching thinking skills: Theory and practice.* New York: W. H. Freeman.

Barrish, H. H., Saunders, M., & Wolf, M. M. (1969). Good behavior game: Effects of individual contingencies for group consequences on disruptive behavior in a classroom. *Journal of Applied Behavior Analysis*, 2, 119–124.

Barron, B. (2000). Problem solving in video-based microworlds: Collaborative and individual outcomes of high-achieving sixth-grade students. *Journal of Educational Psychology*, 92, 391–398.

Barth, R. (1979). Home-based reinforcement of school behavior: A review and analysis. *Review of Educational Research*, 49, 436–458.

Bartlett, F. C. (1932). *Remembering: A study in experimental and social psychology.* Cambridge, England: Cambridge University Press.

Bassok, M. (1997). Two types of reliance on correlations between content and structure in reasoning about word problems. In L. D. English (Ed.), *Mathematical reasoning: Analogies, metaphors, and images* (pp. 221–246). Mahwah, NJ: Erlbaum.

Bassok, M., & Holyoak, K. (1990, April). *Transfer of solution procedures between quantitative domains.* Paper presented at the annual meeting of the American Educational Research Association, Boston.

Bassok, M., & Holyoak, K. J. (1993). Pragmatic knowledge and conceptual structure: Determinants of transfer between quantitative domains. In D. K. Detterman & R. J. Sternberg (Eds.), *Transfer on trial: Intelligence, cognition, and instruction.* Norwood, NJ: Ablex.

Bates, J. A. (1979). Extrinsic reward and intrinsic motivation: A review with implications for the classroom. *Review of Educational Research*, 49, 557–576.

Bauer, P. J. (1995). Recalling past events: From infancy to early childhood. In R. Vasta (Ed.), *Annals of child development: A research annual* (Vol. 11, pp. 25–71). London: Jessica Kingsley.

Bauer, P. J. (2002). Long-term recall memory: Behavioral and neuro-developmental changes in the first 2 years of life. *Current Directions in Psychological Science*, 11, 137–141.

Baumrind, D. (1983). Rejoinder to Lewis's reinterpretation of parental firm control effects: Are authoritative families really harmonious? *Psychological Bulletin*, 94, 132–142.

Baumrind, D., Larzelere, R. E., & Cowan, P. A. (2002). Ordinary physical punishment: Is it harmful? Comment on Gershoff (2002). *Psychological Bulletin*, 128(4), 580–589.

Baxter Magolda, M. B. (2002). Epistemological reflection: The evolution of epistemological assumptions from age 18 to 30. In B. K. Hofer & P. R. Pintrich (Eds.), *Personal epistemology: The psychology of beliefs about knowledge and knowing* (pp. 89–102). Mahwah, NJ: Erlbaum.

Bay-Hinitz, A. K., Peterson, R. F., & Quilitch, H. R. (1994). Cooperative games: A way to modify aggressive and cooperative behaviors in young children. *Journal of Applied Behavior Analysis, 27*, 435–446.

Bean, T. W., & Steenwyk, F. L. (1984). The effect of three forms of summarization instruction on sixth graders' summary writing and comprehension. *Journal of Reading Behavior, 16*, 297–306.

Bechterev, V. M. (1913). *The psychologie objective*. Paris: Alcan.

Beck, I. L., & McKeown, M. G. (1988). Toward meaningful accounts in history texts for young learners. *Educational Researcher, 47*(6), 31–39.

Beck, I. L., & McKeown, M. G. (1994). Outcomes of history instruction: Paste-up accounts. In M. Carretero & J. F. Voss (Eds.), *Cognitive and instructional processes in history and the social sciences* (pp. 237–256). Mahwah, NJ: Erlbaum.

Becker, W. C. (1971). *Parents are teachers*. Champaign, IL: Research Press.

Becker, W. C., Madsen, C. H., Arnold, C. R., & Thomas, D. R. (1967). The contingent use of teacher attention and praise in reducing classroom behavior problems. *Journal of Special Education, 1*, 287–307.

Bédard, J., & Chi, M. T. H. (1992). Expertise. *Current Directions in Psychological Science, 1*, 135–139.

Beeman, M. J., & Chiarello, C. (1998). Complementary right- and left-hemisphere language comprehension. *Current Directions in Psychological Science, 7*, 2–8.

Begg, I., Anas, A., & Farinacci, S. (1992). Dissociation of processes in belief: Source recollection, statement familiarity, and the illusion of truth. *Journal of Experimental Psychology: General, 121*, 446–458.

Behl-Chadha, G. (1996). Basic-level and superordinate-like categorical representations in early infancy. *Cognition, 60*, 105–141.

Behr, M., & Harel, G. (1988, April). Cognitive conflict in procedure applications. In D. Tirosh (Chair), *The role of inconsistent ideas in learning mathematics*. Symposium conducted at the annual meeting of the American Educational Research Association, New Orleans.

Behrmann, M. (2000). The mind's eye mapped onto the brain's matter. *Current Directions in Psychological Science, 9*, 50–54.

Belenky, M., Clinchy, B., Goldberger, N. R., & Tarule, J. (1997). *Women's ways of knowing: The development of self, mind, and voice*. New York: Basic Books. (Originally published 1986)

Belfiore, P. J., & Hornyak, R. S. (1998). Operant theory and application to self-monitoring in adolescents. In D. H. Schunk and B. J. Zimmerman (Eds.), *Self-regulated learning: From teaching to self-reflective practice*. New York: Guilford Press.

Belfiore, P. J., Lee, D. L., Vargas, A. U., & Skinner, C. H. (1997). Effects of high-preference single-digit mathematics problem completion on multiple-digit mathematics problem performance. *Journal of Applied Behavior Analysis, 30*, 327–330.

Belfiore, P. J., Skinner, C. H., & Ferkis, M. A. (1995). Effects of response and trial repetition on sight-word training for students with learning disabilities. *Journal of Applied Behavior Analysis, 28*, 347–348.

Bell, P., & Linn, M. C. (2002). Beliefs about science: How does science instruction contribute? In B. K. Hofer & P. R. Pintrich (Eds.), *Personal epistemology: The psychology of beliefs about knowledge and knowing* (pp. 321–346). Mahwah, NJ: Erlbaum.

Bellezza, F. S. (1986). Mental cues and verbal reports in learning. In G. H. Bower (Ed.), *The psychology of learning and motivation: Advances in research and theory* (Vol. 20). Orlando: Academic Press.

Bell-Gredler, M. E. (1986). *Learning and instruction: Theory into practice*. New York: Macmillan.

Bendixen, L. (2002). A process model of epistemic belief change. In B. K. Hofer & P. R. Pintrich (Eds.), *Personal epistemology: The psychology of beliefs about knowledge and knowing* (pp. 191–208). Mahwah, NJ: Erlbaum.

Beneke, W. N., & Harris, M. B. (1972). Teaching self-control of study behavior. *Behaviour Research and Therapy, 10*, 35–41.

Bennett, R. E., Gottesman, R. L., Rock, D. A., & Cerullo, F. (1993). Influence of behavior perceptions and gender on teachers' judgments of students' academic skill. *Journal of Educational Psychology, 85*, 347–356.

Benton, S. L. (1997). Psychological foundations of elementary writing instruction. In G. D. Phye (Ed.), *Handbook of academic learning: Construction of knowledge*. San Diego: Academic Press.

Benton, S. L., Kiewra, K. A., Whitfill, J. M., & Dennison, R. (1993). Encoding and external-storage effects on writing processes. *Journal of Educational Psychology, 85*, 267–280.

Benware, C., & Deci, E. L. (1984). Quality of learning with an active versus passive motivational set. *American Educational Research Journal, 21*, 755–765.

Berardi-Coletta, B., Buyer, L. S., Dominowski, R. L., & Rellinger, E. A. (1995). Metacognition and problem solving: A process-oriented approach. *Journal of Experimental Psychology: Learning, Memory, and Cognition, 21*, 205–223.

Bereiter, C. (1994). Implications of postmodernism for science, or, science as progressive discourse. *Educational Psychologist, 29*(1), 3–12.

Bereiter, C. (1995). A dispositional view of transfer. In A. McKeough, J. Lupart, & A. Marini (Eds.), *Teaching for transfer: Fostering generalization in learning*. Mahwah, NJ: Erlbaum.

Bereiter, C. (1997). Situated cognition and how to overcome it. In D. Kirshner &

J. A. Whitson (Eds.), *Situated cognition: Social, semiotic, and psychological perspectives*. Mahwah, NJ: Erlbaum.

Bereiter, C., & Scardamalia, M. (1989). Intentional learning as a goal of instruction. In L. B. Resnick (Ed.), *Knowing, learning and instruction: Essays in honour of Robert Glaser* (pp. 361–392). Mahwah, NJ: Erlbaum.

Bereiter, C., & Scardamalia, M. (1996). Rethinking learning. In D. R. Olson & N. Torrance (Eds.), *The handbook of education and human development: New models of learning, teaching, and schooling*. Cambridge, MA: Blackwell.

Berg, C. A., & Calderone, K. S. (1994). The role of problem interpretations in understanding the development of everyday problem solving. In R. J. Sternberg & R. K. Wagner (Eds.), *Mind in context: Interactionist perspectives on human intelligence*. Cambridge, England: Cambridge University Press.

Berk, L. E. (1994). Why children talk to themselves. *Scientific American, 271*, 78–83.

Berkowitz, L., & LePage, A. (1967). Weapons as aggression-eliciting stimuli. *Journal of Personality and Social Psychology, 7*, 202–207.

Berliner, D. C. (1989). The place of process-product research in developing the agenda for research on teacher thinking. *Educational Psychologist, 24*, 325–344.

Berliner, D. C. (1997, March). Discussant's comments. In H. Borko (Chair), *Educational psychology and teacher education: Perennial issues*. Symposium conducted at the annual meeting of the American Educational Research Association, Chicago.

Berliner, D. C., & Biddle, B. J. (1995). *The manufactured crisis: Myths, fraud, and the attack on America's public schools*. Reading, MA: Addison-Wesley.

Berlyne, D. E. (1960). *Conflict, arousal, and curiosity*. New York: McGraw-Hill.

Berndt, T., & Perry, T. (1990). Distinctive features and effects of early adolescent friendships. In R. Montemayor, G. Adams, & T. Gullotta (Eds.), *From childhood to adolescence: A transitional period?* Newbury Park, CA: Sage.

Berndt, T. J., & Keefe, K. (1996). Friends' influence on school adjustment: A motivational analysis. In J. Juvonen & K. R. Wentzel (Eds.), *Social motivation: Understanding children's school adjustment* (pp. 248–278). Cambridge, England: Cambridge University Press.

Berninger, V. W., Fuller, F., & Whitaker, D. (1996). A process model of writing development across the life span. *Educational Psychology Review, 8*, 193–218.

Bersh, P. J. (1951). The influence of two variables upon the establishment of a secondary reinforcer for operant responses. *Journal of Experimental Psychology, 41*, 62–73.

Berti, A. E. (1994). Children's understanding of the concept of the state. In M. Carretero & J. F. Voss (Eds.), *Cognitive and instructional processes in history and the social sciences* (pp. 49–75). Mahwah, NJ: Erlbaum.

Bialystok, E. (1994a). Representation and ways of knowing: Three issues in second language acquisition. In N. C. Ellis (Ed.), *Implicit and explicit learning of languages.* London: Academic Press.

Bialystok, E. (1994b). Towards an explanation of second language acquisition. In G. Brown, K. Malmkjær, A. Pollitt, & J. Williams (Eds.), *Language and understanding.* Oxford, England: Oxford University Press.

Biemiller, A., Shany, M., Inglis, A., & Meichenbaum, D. (1998). Factors influencing children's acquisition and demonstration of self-regulation on academic tasks. In D. H. Schunk & B. J. Zimmerman (Eds.), *Self-regulated learning: From teaching to self-reflective practice* (pp. 203–224). New York: Guilford Press.

Bilodeau, I. M., & Schlosberg, H. (1951). Similarity in stimulating conditions as a variable in retroactive inhibition. *Journal of Experimental Psychology, 41,* 199–204.

Binder, L. M., Dixon, M. R., & Ghezzi, P. M. (2000). A procedure to teach self-control to children with attention deficit hyperactivity disorder. *Journal of Applied Behavior Analysis, 33,* 233–237.

Birch, H. G., & Rabinowitz, H. S. (1951). The negative effect of previous experience on productive thinking. *Journal of Experimental Psychology, 41,* 121–125.

Birnbaum, J. C. (1982). The reading and composing behaviors of selected fourth- and seventh-grade students. *Research in the Teaching of English, 16,* 241–260.

Bishop, B. A., & Anderson, C. W. (1990). Student conceptions of natural selection and its role in evolution. *Journal of Research in Science Teaching, 27,* 415–427.

Bivens, J. A., & Berk, L. E. (1990). A longitudinal study of the development of elementary school children's private speech. *Merrill-Palmer Quarterly, 36,* 443–463.

Bjork, R. A. (1972). Theoretical implications of directed forgetting. In A. W. Melton & E. Martin (Eds.), *Coding processes in human memory.* Washington, DC: V. H. Winston.

Bjorklund, D. F. (1987). How age changes in knowledge base contribute to the development of children's memory: An interpretive review. *Developmental Review, 7,* 93–130.

Bjorklund, D. F., & Coyle, T. R. (1995). Utilization deficiencies in the development of memory strategies. In F. E. Weinert & W. Schneider (Eds.), *Research on memory development: State of the art and future directions.* Hillsdale, NJ: Erlbaum.

Bjorklund, D. F., & Green, B. L. (1992). The adaptive nature of cognitive immaturity. *American Psychologist, 47,* 46–54.

Black, J. E., Isaacs, K. R., Anderson, B. J., Alcantara, A. A., & Greenough, W. T. (1990). Learning causes synaptogenesis, whereas motor activity causes angiogenesis, in cerebellar cortex of adult rats. *Proceedings of the National Academy of Sciences, 87,* 5568–5572.

Blanchard, F. A., Lilly, T., & Vaughn, L. A. (1991). Reducing the expression of racial prejudice. *Psychological Science, 2,* 101–105.

Block, J. H. (1980). Promoting excellence through mastery learning. *Theory into Practice, 19*(1), 66–74.

Block, J. H., & Burns, R. B. (1976). Mastery learning. In L. Shulman (Ed.), *Review of research in education* (Vol. 4). Itasca, IL: Peacock.

Blok, H., Oostdam, R., Otter, M. E., & Overmaat, M. (2002). Computer-assisted instruction in support of beginning reading instruction: A review. *Review of Educational Research, 72,* 101–103.

Bloom, B. S. (1968). Mastery learning. In *Evaluation comment* (Vol. 1, No. 2). Los Angeles: University of California at Los Angeles, Center for the Study of Evaluation of Instructional Programs.

Bloom, B. S. (1974). An introduction to mastery learning theory. In J. H. Block (Ed.), *Schools, society, and mastery learning.* New York: Holt, Rinehart & Winston.

Bloom, B. S. (1976). *Human characteristics and school learning.* New York: McGraw-Hill.

Bloom, B. S. (1981). *All our children learning.* New York: McGraw-Hill.

Bloom, B. S. (1984). The search for methods of group instruction as effective as one-to-one tutoring. *Educational Leadership, 41*(8), 4–17.

Bloom, B. S., & Broder, L. J. (1950). *Problem-solving processes of college students.* Chicago: University of Chicago Press.

Bloom, B. S., Englehart, M. B., Furst, E. J., Hill, W. H., & Krathwohl, D. R. (1956). *Taxonomy of educational objectives. The classification of educational goals. Handbook I: Cognitive domain.* New York: Longmans Green.

Bloom, L., & Tinker, E. (2001). The intentionality model and language acquisition. *Monographs of the Society for Research in Child Development, 66*(4, Serial No. 267).

Blumenfeld, P. C. (1992). The task and the teacher: Enhancing student thoughtfulness in science. In J. Brophy (Ed.), *Advances in research on teaching: Vol. 3. Planning and managing learning tasks and activities.* Greenwich, CT: JAI Press.

Blumenfeld, P. C., Hamilton, V. L., Bossert, S., Wessels, K., & Meece, C. (1983). Teacher talk and student thought: Socialization into the student role. In J. Levine & U. Wang (Eds.), *Teacher and student perceptions: Implications for learning.* Hillsdale, NJ: Erlbaum.

Blumenfeld, P. C., Marx, R. W., Soloway, E., & Krajcik, J. (1996). Learning with peers: From small group cooperation to collaborative communities. *Educational Researcher, 25*(8), 37–40.

Bobrow, S., & Bower, G. H. (1969). Comprehension and recall of sentences. *Journal of Experimental Psychology, 80,* 455–461.

Bochenhauer, M. H. (1990, April). *Connections: Geographic education and the National Geographic Society.* Paper presented at the annual meeting of the American Educational Research Association, Boston.

Boe, E. E., & Church, R. M. (1967). Permanent effects of punishment during extinction. *Journal of Comparative and Physiological Psychology, 63,* 486–492.

Boggiano, A. K., Main, D. S., & Katz, P. A. (1988). Children's preference for challenge: The role of perceived competence and control. *Journal of Personality and Social Psychology, 54,* 134–141.

Boggiano, A. K., & Pittman, T. S. (Eds.). (1992). *Achievement and motivation: A social-developmental perspective.* Cambridge, England: Cambridge University Press.

Bohannon, J. N., III, & Symons, V. L. (1992). Flashbulb memories: Confidence, consistency, and quantity. In E. Winograd & U. Neisser (Eds.), *Affect and accuracy in recall: Studies of "flashbulb" memories.* Cambridge, England: Cambridge University Press.

Bolles, R. C. (1975). *Theory of motivation* (2nd ed.). New York: Harper & Row.

Bolstad, O., & Johnson, S. (1972). Self-regulation in the modification of disruptive classroom behavior. *Journal of Applied Behavior Analysis, 5,* 443–454.

Bomba, P. C., & Siqueland, E. R. (1983). The nature and structure of infant form categories. *Journal of Experimental Child Psychology, 35,* 294–328.

Bong, M. (2001). Between- and within-domain relations of academic motivation among middle and high school students: Self-efficacy, task-value, and achievement goals. *Journal of Educational Psychology, 93,* 23–34.

Bong, M., & Clark, R. E. (1999). Comparison between self-concept and self-efficacy in academic motivation research. *Educational Psychologist, 34,* 139–153.

Borko, H., & Putnam, R. T. (1996). Learning to teach. In D. C. Berliner & R. C. Calfee (Eds.), *Handbook of educational psychology.* New York: Macmillan.

Born, D. G., & Davis, M. L. (1974). Amount and distribution of study in a personalized instruction course and in a lecture course. *Journal of Applied Behavior Analysis, 7,* 365–375.

Boschee, F., & Baron, M. A. (1993). *Outcome-based education: Developing programs through strategic planning.* Lancaster, PA: Technomic Publishing.

Bourbeau, P. E., Sowers, J., & Close, D. E. (1986). An experimental analysis of generalization of banking skills from classroom to bank settings in the community. *Education and Training of the Mentally Retarded, 21,* 98–107.

Bourne, L. E., Jr. (1967). Learning and utilization of conceptual rules. In B. Kleinmuntz (Ed.), *Concepts and the structure of memory.* New York: Wiley.

Bourne, L. E., Jr. (1982). Typicality effects in logically defined concepts. *Memory and Cognition, 10,* 3–9.

Bourne, L. E., Jr., Dominowski, R. L., Loftus, E. F., & Healy, A. F. (1986). *Cognitive processes* (2nd ed.). Englewood Cliffs, NJ: Prentice Hall.

Bourne, L. E., Jr., Ekstrand, D. R., & Dominowski, R. L. (1971). *The psychology of thinking.* Englewood Cliffs, NJ: Prentice Hall.

Bousfield, W. A. (1953). The occurrence of clustering in the recall of randomly arranged associates. *Journal of General Psychology, 49,* 229–240.

Bouton, M. E. (1994). Context, ambiguity, and classical conditioning. *Current Directions in Psychological Science, 3,* 49–53.

Bower, G. H. (1972). Mental imagery and associative learning. In L. W. Gregg (Ed.), *Cognition in learning and memory.* New York: Wiley.

Bower, G. H. (1994). Some relations between emotions and memory. In P. Ekman & R. J. Davidson (Eds.), *The nature of emotion: Fundamental questions.* New York: Oxford University Press.

Bower, G. H., Black, J. B., & Turner, T. J. (1979). Scripts in memory for text. *Cognitive Psychology, 11,* 177–220.

Bower, G. H., & Clark, M. C. (1969). Narrative stories as mediators for serial learning. *Psychonomic Science, 14,* 181–182.

Bower, G. H., Clark, M. C., Lesgold, A. M., & Winzenz, D. (1969). Hierarchical retrieval schemes in recall of categorized word lists. *Journal of Verbal Learning and Verbal Behavior, 8,* 323–343.

Bower, G. H., & Forgas, J. P. (2001). Mood and social memory. In J. P. Forgas (Ed.), *Handbook of affect and social cognition* (pp. 95–120). Mahwah, NJ: Erlbaum.

Bower, G. H., & Hilgard, E. R. (1981). *Theories of learning* (5th ed.). Englewood Cliffs, NJ: Prentice Hall.

Bower, G. H., & Holyoak, K. J. (1973). Encoding and recognition memory for naturalistic sounds. *Journal of Experimental Psychology, 101,* 360–366.

Bower, G. H., Karlin, M. B., & Dueck, A. (1975). Comprehension and memory for pictures. *Memory and Cognition, 3,* 216–220.

Bower, G. H., McLean, J., & Meachem, J. (1966). Value of knowing when reinforcement is due. *Journal of Comparative and Physiological Psychology, 62,* 184–192.

Bower, G. H., & Springston, F. (1970). Pauses as recoding points in letter series. *Journal of Experimental Psychology, 83,* 421–430.

Bowers, F. E., Woods, D. W., Carlyon, W. D., & Friman, P. C. (2000). Using positive peer reporting to improve the social interactions and acceptance of socially isolated adolescents in residential care: A systematic replication. *Journal of Applied Behavior Analysis, 33,* 239–242.

Bowman, L. G., Piazza, C. C., Fisher, W. W., Hagopian, L. P., & Kogan, J. S. (1997). Assessment of preference for varied versus constant reinforcers. *Journal of Applied Behavior Analysis, 30,* 451–458.

Boyatzis, R. E. (1973). Affiliation motivation. In D. C. McClelland & R. S. Steele (Eds.), *Human motivation: A book of readings.* Morristown, NJ: General Learning Press.

Boykin, A. W. (1994). Harvesting talent and culture: African-American children and educational reform. In R. J. Rossi (Ed.), *Schools and students at risk: Context and framework for positive change.* New York: Teachers College Press.

Braaksma, M. A. H., Rijlaarsdam, G., & van den Bergh, H. (2002). Observational learning and the effects of model–observer similarity. *Journal of Educational Psychology, 94,* 405–415.

Bragstad, B. J., & Stumpf, S. M. (1982). *A guidebook for teaching study skills and motivation.* Boston: Allyn & Bacon.

Brainerd, C. J., & Reyna, V. F. (1992). Explaining "memory free" reasoning. *Psychological Science, 3,* 332–339.

Brainerd, C. J., & Reyna, V. F. (1998). When things that were never experienced are easier to "remember" than things that were. *Psychological Science, 9,* 484–489.

Brainerd, C. J., Reyna, V. F., & Brandse, E. (1995). Are children's false memories more persistent than their true memories? *Psychological Science, 6,* 359–364.

Bramel, D., Taub, B., & Blum, B. (1968). An observer's reaction to the suffering of his enemy. *Journal of Personality and Social Psychology, 8,* 384–392.

Bransford, J. D., & Franks, J. J. (1971). The abstraction of linguistic ideas. *Cognitive Psychology, 2,* 331–350.

Bransford, J. D., Franks, J. J., Vye, N. J., & Sherwood, R. D. (1989). New approaches to instruction: Because wisdom can't be told. In S. Vosniadou & A. Ortony (Eds.), *Similarity and analogical reasoning* (pp. 470–497). Cambridge, England: Cambridge University Press.

Bransford, J. D., & Johnson, M. K. (1972). Contextual prerequisites for understanding: Some investigations of comprehension and recall. *Journal of Verbal Learning and Verbal Behavior, 11,* 717–726.

Braukmann, C. J., Ramp, K. K., & Wolf, M. M. (1981). Behavioral treatment of juvenile delinquency. In S. W. Bijou & R. Ruiz (Eds.), *Behavior modification: Contributions to education.* Hillsdale, NJ: Erlbaum.

Bredo, E. (1997). The social construction of learning. In G. D. Phye (Ed.), *Handbook of academic learning: Construction of knowledge.* San Diego: Academic Press.

Breitmeyer, B. B., & Ganz, L. (1976). Implications of sustained and transient channels for theories of visual pattern masking, saccadic suppression, and information processing. *Psychological Review, 83,* 1–36.

Bressler, S. L. (2002). Understanding cognition through large-scale cortical networks. *Current Directions in Psychological Science, 11,* 58–61.

Brewer, W. F. (1992). The theoretical and empirical status of the flashbulb memory hypothesis. In E. Winograd & U. Neisser (Eds.), *Affect and accuracy in recall: Studies of "flashbulb" memories.* Cambridge, England: Cambridge University Press.

Brewer, W. F., & Treyens, J. C. (1981). Role of schemata in memory for places. *Cognitive Psychology, 13,* 207–230.

Brickman, S., Miller, R. B., & Roedel, T. D. (1997, March). *Goal valuing and future consequences as predictors of cognitive engagement.* Paper presented at the annual meeting of the American Educational Research Association, Chicago.

Briggs, L. J., & Reed, H. B. (1943). The curve of retention for substance material. *Journal of Experimental Psychology, 32,* 513–517.

Britton, B. K., Stimson, M., Stennett, B., & Gülgöz, S. (1998). Learning from instructional text: Test of an individual differences model. *Journal of Educational Psychology, 90,* 476–491.

Broadbent, D. E. (1958). *Perception and communication.* London: Pergamon Press.

Broadhurst, P. L. (1959). The interaction of task difficulty and motivation: The Yerkes-Dodson law revived. *Acta Psychologia, 16,* 321–338.

Broekkamp, H., Van Hout-Wolters, B. H. A. M., Rijlaarsdam, G., & van den Bergh, H. (2002). Importance in instructional text: Teachers' and students' perceptions of task demands. *Journal of Educational Psychology, 94,* 260–271.

Bronfenbrenner, U. (1970). *Two worlds of childhood: U.S. and U.S.S.R.* New York: Russell Sage Foundation.

Bronfenbrenner, U. (1999). Is early intervention effective? Some studies of early education in familial and extra-familial settings. In A. Montagu (Ed.), *Race and IQ* (expanded ed., pp. 343–378). New York: Oxford University Press.

Bronson, M. B. (2000). *Self-regulation in early childhood: Nature and nurture.* New York: Guilford.

Brooke, R. R., & Ruthren, A. J. (1984). The effects of contingency contracting on student performance in a PSI class. *Teaching of Psychology, 11,* 87–89.

Brooks, L. R. (1978). Nonanalytic concept formation and memory for instances. In E. Rosch & B. B. Lloyd (Eds.), *Cognition and categorization.* Hillsdale, NJ: Erlbaum.

Brooks, L. W., & Dansereau, D. F. (1987). Transfer of information: An instructional perspective. In S. M. Cormier & J. D. Hagman (Eds.), *Transfer of learning: Contemporary research and applications.* San Diego: Academic Press.

Brophy, J. E. (1981). Teacher praise: A functional analysis. *Review of Educational Research, 51,* 5–32.

Brophy, J. E. (1986). *On motivating students*. Occasional Paper No. 101, Institute for Research on Teaching, Michigan State University, East Lansing.

Brophy, J. E. (1987). Synthesis of research on strategies for motivating students to learn. *Educational Leadership, 45*(2), 40–48.

Brophy, J. E. (1988). Research linking teacher behavior to student achievement: Potential implications for instruction of Chapter 1 students. *Educational Psychologist, 23*, 235–286.

Brophy, J. E. (1992a). Conclusions: Comments on an emerging field. In J. Brophy (Ed.), *Advances in research on teaching: Vol. 3. Planning and managing learning tasks and activities*. Greenwich, CT: JAI Press.

Brophy, J. E. (1992b). Probing the subtleties of subject-matter teaching. *Educational Leadership, 49*(7), 4–8.

Brophy, J. E. (1999). Toward a model of the value aspects of motivation in education: Developing appreciation for particular learning domains and activities. *Educational Psychologist, 34*, 75–85.

Brophy, J. E., & Alleman, J. (1991). Activities as instructional tools: A framework for analysis and evaluation. *Educational Researcher, 20*(4), 9–23.

Brophy, J. E. & Alleman, J. (1992). Planning and managing learning activities: Basic principles. In J. Brophy (Ed.), *Advances in research on teaching: Vol. 3. Planning and managing learning tasks and activities*. Greenwich, CT: JAI Press.

Brophy, J. E., & Good, T. L. (1970). Teachers' communication of differential expectations for children's classroom performance: Some behavioral data. *Journal of Educational Psychology, 61*, 365–374.

Brothers, K. J., Krantz, P. J., & McClannahan, L. E. (1994). Office paper recycling: A function of container proximity. *Journal of Applied Behavior Analysis, 27*, 153–160.

Brown, A. (1991). A review of the tip-of-the-tongue experience. *Psychological Bulletin, 109*, 204–223.

Brown, A. L. (1978). Knowing when, where, and how to remember: A problem of metacognition. In R. Glaser (Ed.), *Advances in instructional psychology*, Hillsdale, NJ: Erlbaum.

Brown, A. L., Ash, D., Rutherford, M., Nakagawa, K., Gordon, A., & Campione, J. C. (1993). Distributed expertise in the classroom. In G. Salomon (Ed.), *Distributed cognitions: Psychological and educational considerations*. Cambridge, England: Cambridge University Press.

Brown, A. L., Bransford, J. D., Ferrera, R. A., & Campione, J. C. (1983). Learning, remembering, and understanding. In J. Flavell & E. Mankman (Eds.), *Carmichael's manual of children psychology* (Vol. 1). New York: Wiley.

Brown, A. L., & Campione, J. C. (1972). Recognition memory for perceptually similar pictures in preschool children. *Journal of Experimental Psychology, 95*, 55–62.

Brown, A. L., & Campione, J. C. (1986). Psychological theory and the study of learning disabilities. *American Psychologist, 41*, 1059–1068.

Brown, A. L., & Campione, J. C. (1994). Guided discovery in a community of learners. In K. McGilly (Ed.), *Classroom lessons: Integrating cognitive theory and classroom practice*. Cambridge, MA: MIT Press/Bradford.

Brown, A. L., & Campione, J. C. (1996). Psychological theory and the design of innovative learning environments: On procedures, principles, and systems. In L. Schauble & R. Glaser (Eds.), *Innovations in learning: New environments for education*. Mahwah, NJ: Erlbaum.

Brown, A. L., Campione, J., & Day, J. (1981). Learning to learn: On training students to learn from texts. *Educational Researcher, 10*(2), 14–21.

Brown, A. L., & Day, J. D. (1983). Macrorules for summarizing texts: The development of expertise. *Journal of Verbal Learning and Verbal Behavior, 22*, 1–14.

Brown, A. L., Kane, M. J., & Echols, K. (1986). Young children's mental models determine analogical transfer across problems with a common goal structure. *Cognitive Development, 1*, 103–122.

Brown, A. L., & Palincsar, A. S. (1987). Reciprocal teaching of comprehension strategies: A natural history of one program for enhancing learning. In J. Borkowski & J. D. Day (Eds.), *Cognition in special education: Comparative approaches to retardation, learning disabilities, and giftedness*. Norwood, NJ: Ablex.

Brown, A. L., & Palincsar, A. S. (1989). Guided, cooperative learning and individual knowledge acquisition. In L. B. Resnick (Ed.), *Knowing, learning, and instruction: Essays in honor of Robert Glaser*. Hillsdale, NJ: Erlbaum.

Brown, A. L., Palincsar, A. S., & Armbruster, B. B. (1984). Instructing comprehension fostering activities in interactive learning situations. In H. Mandl, N. Stein, & T. Trabasso (Eds.), *Learning and comprehension of text*. Hillsdale, NJ: Erlbaum.

Brown, A. L., & Reeve, R. A. (1987). Bandwidths of competence: The role of supportive contexts in learning and development. In L. S. Liben (Ed.), *Development and learning: Conflict or congruence?* Hillsdale, NJ: Erlbaum.

Brown, A. L., & Scott, M. S. (1971). Recognition memory for pictures in preschool children. *Journal of Experimental Child Psychology, 11*, 401–412.

Brown, B. (1990). Peer groups. In S. Feldman & G. Elliott (Eds.), *At the threshold: The developing adolescent* (pp. 171–196). Cambridge, MA: Harvard University Press.

Brown, B. B., Eicher, S. A., & Petrie, S. (1986). The importance of peer group ("crowd") affiiation in adolescence. *Journal of Adolescence, 9*, 73–96.

Brown, D. E. (1992). Using examples and analogies to remediate misconceptions in physics: Factors influencing conceptual change. *Journal of Research in Science Teaching, 29*, 17–34.

Brown, I., & Inouye, D. K. (1978). Learned helplessness through modeling: The role of perceived similarity in competence. *Journal of Personality and Social Psychology, 36*, 900–908.

Brown, J. (1968). Reciprocal facilitation and impairment of free recall. *Psychonomic Science, 10*, 41–42.

Brown, J. S., Collins, A., & Duguid, P. (1989). Situated cognition and the culture of learning. *Educational Researcher, 18*(1), 32–42.

Brown, N. R., & Schopflocher, D. (1998). Event clusters: An organization of personal events in autobiographical memory. *Psychological Science, 9*, 470–475.

Brown, R., & Herrnstein, R. J. (1975). *Psychology*. Boston: Little, Brown.

Brown, R., & Kulik, J. (1977). Flashbulb memories. *Cognition, 5*, 73–99.

Brown, R., & McNeill, D. (1966). The "tip of the tongue" phenomenon. *Journal of Verbal Learning and Verbal Behavior, 5*, 325–337.

Brown, R. D., & Bjorklund, D. F. (1998). The biologizing of cognition, development, and education: Approach with cautious enthusiasm. *Educational Psychology Review, 10*, 355–373.

Brown, S. I., & Walter, M. I. (1990). *The art of problem posing* (2nd ed.). Hillsdale, NJ: Erlbaum.

Brown, W. H., Bryson-Brockmann, W., & Fox, J. J. (1986). The usefulness of J. R. Kantor's setting event concept for research on children's social behavior. *Child and Family Behavior Therapy, 8*(2), 15–25.

Brown, W. H., Fox, J. J., & Brady, M. P. (1987). Effects of spatial density on 3- and 4-year-old children's socially directed behavior during freeplay: An investigation of a setting factor. *Education and Treatment of Children, 10*, 247–258.

Brozo, W. G., Stahl, N. A., & Gordon, B. (1985). Training effects of summarizing, item writing, and knowledge of information sources on reading test performance. In J. A. Niles & R. V. Lalik (Eds.), *Issues in literacy*. Rochester, NY: National Reading Conference.

Bruck, M., Cavanagh, P., & Ceci, S. (1991). Fortysomething: Recognizing faces at one's 25th reunion. *Memory and Cognition, 19*, 221–228.

Bruck, M., & Ceci, S. J. (1997). The suggestibility of young children. *Current Directions in Psychological Science, 6*, 75–79.

Bruer, J. T. (1997). Education and the brain: A bridge too far. *Educational Researcher, 26*(8), 4–16.

Bruer, J. T. (1999). *The myth of the first three years: A new understanding of early brain development and lifelong learning*. New York: Free Press.

Bruner, J. S. (1957). On going beyond the information given. In *Contemporary approaches to cognition*. Cambridge, MA: Harvard University Press.

Bruner, J. S. (1961a). The act of discovery. *Harvard Educational Review, 31*, 21–32.

Bruner, J. S. (1961b). *The process of education*. Cambridge, MA: Harvard University Press.

Bruner, J. S. (1966). *Toward a theory of instruction*. New York: W. W. Norton.

Bruner, J. S., Goodnow, J., & Austin, G. (1956). *A study of thinking*. New York: Wiley.

Bruning, R. H., Schraw, G. J., & Ronning, R. R. (1995). *Cognitive psychology and instruction* (2nd ed.). Englewood Cliffs, NJ: Prentice Hall/Merrill.

Bryan, J. H. (1971). Model affect and children's imitative altruism. *Child Development, 42*, 2061–2065.

Bryan, J. H. (1975). Children's cooperation and helping behaviors. In E. M. Hetherington (Ed.), *Review of child development research* (Vol. 5). Chicago: University of Chicago Press.

Buckhout, R. (1974). Eyewitness testimony. *Scientific American, 231*(6), 23–31.

Buckland, P. R. (1968). The ordering of frames in a linear program. *Programmed Learning and Educational Technology, 5*, 197–205.

Buehl, M. M., & Alexander, P. A. (2001). Beliefs about academic knowledge. *Educational Psychology Review, 13*, 385–418.

Bufford, R. K. (1976). Evaluation of a reinforcement procedure for accelerating work rate in a self-paced course. *Journal of Applied Behavior Analysis, 9*, 208.

Bugelski, B. R. (1962). Presentation time, total time, and mediation in paired-associate learning. *Journal of Experimental Psychology, 63*, 409–412.

Bugelski, B. R., & Alampay, D. A. (1961). The role of frequency in developing perceptual sets. *Canadian Journal of Psychology, 15*, 205–211.

Bugelski, B. R., Kidd, E., & Segmen, J. (1968). Image as a mediator in one-trial paired-associate learning. *Journal of Experimental Psychology, 76*, 69–73.

Bulgren, J. A., Deshler, D. D., Schumaker, J. B., & Lenz, B. K. (2000). The use and effectiveness of analogical instruction in diverse secondary content classrooms. *Journal of Educational Psychology, 92*, 426–441.

Bulgren, J. A., Schumaker, J. B., & Deshler, D. D. (1994). The effects of a recall enhancement routine on the test performance of secondary students with and without learning disabilities. *Learning Disabilities Research and Practice, 9*, 2–11.

Burhans, K. K., & Dweck, C. S. (1995). Helplessness in early childhood: The role of contingent worth. *Child Development, 66*, 1719–1738.

Burnett, R. E., & Kastman, L. M. (1997). Teaching composition: Current theories and practices. In G. D. Phye (Ed.), *Handbook of academic learning: Construction of knowledge*. San Diego: Academic Press.

Burron, A., & Claybaugh, A. (1992). *Basic concepts in reading instruction: A programmed approach*. Longmont, CO: Sopris.

Buschke, H. (1977). Two-dimensional recall: Immediate identification of clusters in episodic and semantic memory. *Journal of Verbal Learning and Verbal Behavior, 16*, 201–215.

Bushell, D., Wrobel, P. A., & Michaelis, M. L. (1968). Applying "group" contingencies to the classroom study behavior of preschool children. *Journal of Applied Behavior Analysis, 1*, 55–61.

Butler, D. L., & Winne, P. H. (1995). Feedback and self-regulated learning: A theoretical synthesis. *Review of Educational Research, 65*, 245–281.

Butler, R. (1987). Task-involving and ego-involving properties of evaluation: Effects of different feedback conditions on motivational perceptions, interest, and performance. *Journal of Educational Psychology, 79*, 474–482.

Butler, R. (1988). Enhancing and undermining intrinsic motivation: The effects of task-involving and ego-involving evaluation on interest and performance. *British Journal of Educational Psychology, 58*, 1–14.

Butler, R. (1989). Mastery versus ability appraisal: A developmental study of children's observations of peers' work. *Child Development, 60*, 1350–1361.

Butler, R. (1994). Teacher communication and student interpretations: Effects of teacher responses to failing students on attributional inferences in two age groups. *British Journal of Educational Psychology, 64*, 277–294.

Butler, R. (1998a). Age trends in the use of social and temporal comparison for self-evaluation: Examination of a novel developmental hypothesis. *Child Development, 69*, 1054–1073.

Butler, R. (1998b). Determinants of help seeking: Relations between perceived reasons for classroom help-avoidance and help-seeking behaviors in an experimental context. *Journal of Educational Psychology, 90*, 630–644.

Butler, R., & Nisan, M. (1986). Effects of no feedback, task-related comments, and grades on intrinsic motivation and performance. *Journal of Educational Psychology, 78*, 210–216.

Butterworth, G. (1993). Context and cognition in models of cognitive growth. In P. Light & G. Butterworth (Eds.), *Context and cognition: Ways of learning and knowing*. Hillsdale, NJ: Erlbaum.

Byrnes, J. P. (1996). *Cognitive development and learning in instructional contexts*. Boston: Allyn & Bacon.

Byrnes, J. P. (2001). *Minds, brains, and learning: Understanding the psychological and educational relevance of neuroscientific research*. New York: Guilford Press.

Byrnes, J. P., & Fox, N. A. (1998). The educational relevance of research in cognitive neuroscience. *Educational Psychology Review, 10*, 297–342.

Cacioppo, J. T., Petty, R. E., Feinstein, J. A., & Jarvis, W. B. G. (1996). Dispositional differences in cognitive motivation: The life and times of individuals varying in need for cognition. *Psychological Bulletin, 119*, 197–253.

Cahill, L., Haier, R. J., Fallon, J., Alkire, M., Tang, C., Keator, D., Wu, J., & McGaugh, J. (1996). Amygdala activity at encoding correlated with long-term, free recall of emotional information. *Proceedings of the National Academy of Sciences, 93*, 8016–8321.

Cairns, H. S. (1996). *The acquisition of language* (2nd ed.). Austin, TX: Pro-Ed.

Calfee, R. (1981). Cognitive psychology and educational practice. In D. C. Berliner (Ed.), *Review of Research in Education* (Vol. 9). Washington, DC: American Educational Research Association.

Calfee, R., & Chambliss, M. J. (1988, April). *The structure of social studies textbooks: Where is the design?* Paper presented at the annual meeting of the American Educational Research Association, New Orleans.

Calfee, R., Dunlap, K., & Wat, A. (1994). Authentic discussion of texts in middle grade schooling: An analytic-narrative approach. *Journal of Reading, 37*, 546–556.

Cameron, J. (2001). Negative effects of reward on intrinsic motivation—A limited phenomenon: Comment on Deci, Koestner, and Ryan (2001). *Review of Educational Research, 71*, 29–42.

Campbell, F. A., & Ramey, C. T. (1995). Cognitive and school outcomes for high-risk African-American students at middle adolescence: Positive effects of early intervention. *American Educational Research Journal, 32*, 742–772.

Campione, J. C., Shapiro, A. M., & Brown, A. L. (1995). Forms of transfer in a community of learners: Flexible learning and understanding. In A. McKeough, J. Lupart, & A. Marini (Eds.), *Teaching for transfer: Fostering generalization in learning*. Mahwah, NJ: Erlbaum.

Cann, A., & Ross, D. (1989). Olfactory stimuli as context cues in human memory. *American Journal of Psychology, 102*, 91–102.

Cardelle-Elawar, M. (1992). Effects of teaching metacognitive skills to students with low mathematics ability. *Teaching and Teacher Education, 8*, 109–121.

Carey, R. G., & Bucher, B. D. (1986). Positive practice overcorrection: Effects of reinforcing correct performance. *Behavior Modification, 10*, 73–92.

Carey, S. (1985a). Are children fundamentally different kinds of thinkers and learners than adults? In S. F. Chipman, J. W. Segal, & R. Glaser (Eds.), *Learning and thinking skills: Vol. 2. Research and open questions*. Hillsdale, NJ: Erlbaum.

Carey, S. (1985b). *Conceptual change in childhood*. Cambridge, MA: MIT Press.

Carey, S. (1986). Cognitive science and science education. *American Psychologist, 41*, 1123–1130.

Carlson, B. E. (1984). The father's contribution to child care: Effects on children's perceptions of parental roles. *American Journal of Orthopsychiatry, 54*, 123–136.

Carlson, N. R. (1999). *Foundations of physiological psychology*. Boston: Allyn & Bacon.

Carlson, S. M., & Moses, L. J. (2001). Individual differences in inhibitory control and children's theory of mind. *Child Development, 72*, 1032–1053.

Carmichael, C. A., & Hayes, B. K. (2001). Prior knowledge and exemplar encoding in children's concept acquisition. *Child Development, 72*, 1071–1090.

Carmichael, L., Hogan, H. P., & Walters, A. A. (1932). An experimental study of the effect of language on the reproduction of visually perceived form. *Journal of Experimental Psychology, 15*, 73–86.

Carney, R. N., & Levin, J. R. (1994). Combining mnemonic strategies to remember who painted what when. *Contemporary Educational Psychology, 19*, 323–339.

Carney, R. N., & Levin, J. R. (2000). Mnemonic instruction, with a focus on transfer. *Journal of Educational Psychology, 92*, 783–790.

Carney, R. N., & Levin, J. R. (2002). Pictorial illustrations *still* improve students' learning from text. *Educational Psychology Review, 14*, 5–26.

Carney, R. N., Levin, J. R., & Stackhouse, T. L. (1997). The face-name mnemonic strategy from a different perspective. *Contemporary Educational Psychology, 22*, 399–412.

Carpenter, P. A., & Just, M. A. (1986). Cognitive processes in reading. In J. Orasanu (Ed.), *Reading comprehension: From research to practice*. Hillsdale, NJ: Erlbaum.

Carpenter, T. P. (1985). Learning to add and subtract: An exercise in problem solving. In E. A. Silver (Ed.), *Teaching and learning mathematical problem solving: Multiple research perspectives*. Hillsdale, NJ: Erlbaum.

Carr, M., & Biddlecomb, B. (1998). Metacognition in mathematics from a constructivist perspective. In D. J. Hacker, J. Dunlosky, & A. C. Graesser (Eds.), *Metacognition in educational theory and practice* (pp. 69–91). Mahwah, NJ: Erlbaum.

Carr, M., & Jessup, D. (1997). Gender differences in first grade mathematics strategy use: Social, metacognitive, and attributional differences. *Journal of Educational Psychology, 89*, 318–328.

Carr, M., & Schneider, W. (1991). Long-term maintenance of organizational strategies in kindergarten children. *Contemporary Educational Psychology, 16*, 61–75.

Carraher, T. N., Carraher, D. W., & Schliemann, A. D. (1985). Mathematics in the streets and in the schools. *British Journal of Developmental Psychology, 3*, 21–29.

Carroll, J. B. (1963). A model of school learning. *Teachers College Record, 64*, 723–733.

Carroll, J. B. (1989). The Carroll model: A 25-year retrospective and prospective view. *Educational Researcher, 18*(1), 26–31.

Carver, C. S., & Scheier, M. F. (1990). Origins and functions of positive and negative affect: A control-process view. *Psychological Review, 97*, 19–35.

Carver, R. P. (1971). *Sense and nonsense in speed reading*. Silver Springs, MD: Revrac.

Carver, R. P. (1990). *Reading rate: A review of research and theory*. San Diego: Academic Press.

Case, R. (1985). *Intellectual development: Birth to adulthood*. Orlando: Academic Press.

Case, R. (1996). Changing views of knowledge and their impact on educational research and practice. In D. R. Olson & N. Torrance (Eds.), *The handbook of education and human development: New models of learning, teaching, and schooling*. Cambridge, MA: Blackwell.

Cassady, J. C., & Johnson, R. E. (2002). Cognitive test anxiety and academic performance. *Contemporary Educational Psychology, 27*, 270–295.

Castro-Caldas, A., Miranda, P. C., Carmo, I., Reis, A., Leote, F., Ribeiro, C., & Ducla-Soares, E. (1999). Influence of learning to read and write on the morphology of the corpus callosum. *European Journal of Neurology, 6*, 23–28.

Catania, A. C. (1985). The two psychologies of learning: Blind alleys and nonsense syllables. In S. Koch & D. E. Leary (Eds.), *A century of psychology as science*. New York: McGraw-Hill.

Catania, A. C., & Reynolds, G. S. (1968). A quantitative analysis of the responding maintained by interval schedules of reinforcement. *Journal of the Experimental Analysis of Behavior, 11*, 327–383.

Ceci, S. J., & Roazzi, A. (1994). The effects of context on cognition: Postcards from Brazil. In R. J. Sternberg & R. K. Wagner (Eds.), *Mind in context: Interactionist perspectives on human intelligence*. Cambridge, England: Cambridge University Press.

Cermak, L. S. (1993). Automatic versus controlled processing and the implicit task performance of amnesic patients. In P. Graf & M. E. J. Masson (Eds.), *Implicit memory: New directions in cognition, development, and neuropsychology*. Hillsdale, NJ: Erlbaum.

Cermak, L. S., & Craik, F. I. M. (Eds.). (1979). *Levels of processing in human memory*. Hillsdale, NJ: Erlbaum.

Certo, J., Cauley, K. M., & Chafin, C. (2002, April). *Students' perspectives on their high school experience*. Paper presented at the annual meeting of the American Educational Research Association, New Orleans.

Chalmers, D. J. (1996). *The conscious mind: In search of a fundamental theory*. New York: Oxford University Press.

Chambers, D., & Reisberg, D. (1985). Can mental images be ambiguous? *Journal of Experimental Psychology: Human Perception and Performance, 11*, 317–328.

Chambliss, M. J. (1994). Why do readers fail to change their beliefs after reading persuasive text? In R. Garner & P. A. Alexander (Eds.), *Beliefs about text and instruction with text*. Hillsdale, NJ: Erlbaum.

Chambliss, M. J., Calfee, R. C., & Wong, I. (1990, April). *Structure and content in science textbooks: Where is the design?* Paper presented at the annual meeting of the American Educational Research Association, Boston.

Champagne, A. B., Klopfer, L. E., & Gunstone, R. F. (1982). Cognitive research and the design of science instruction. *Educational Psychologist, 17*, 31–53.

Chan, C., Burtis, J., & Bereiter, C. (1997). Knowledge building as a mediator of conflict in conceptual change. *Cognition and Instruction, 15*, 1–40.

Chan, C. K. K., Burtis, P. J., Scardamalia, M., & Bereiter, C. (1992). Constructive activity in learning from text. *American Educational Research Journal, 29*, 97–118.

Chapin, M., & Dyck, D. G. (1976). Persistence in children's reading behavior as a function of N length and attribution retraining. *Journal of Abnormal Psychology, 85*, 511–515.

Chase, W. G., & Chi, M. T. H. (1980). Cognitive skill: Implications for spatial skill in large-scale environments. In J. Harvey (Ed.), *Cognition, social behavior, and the environment*. Potomac, MD: Erlbaum.

Chase, W. G., & Simon, H. A. (1973). Perception in chess. *Cognitive Psychology, 4*, 55–81.

Chen, Z. (1999). Schema induction in children's analogical problem solving. *Journal of Educational Psychology, 91*, 703–715.

Cheng, P. W. (1985). Restructuring versus automaticity: Alternative accounts of skill acquisition. *Psychological Review, 92*, 414–423.

Cheng, P. W., Holyoak, K. J., Nisbett, R. E., & Oliver, L. M. (1986). Pragmatic versus syntactic approaches to training deductive reasoning. *Cognitive Psychology, 18*, 293–328.

Cherry, E. C. (1953). Some experiments on the recognition of speech, with one and with two ears. *Journal of the Acoustical Society of America, 25*, 975–979.

Cheyne, J. A., & Walters, R. H. (1970). Punishment and prohibition: Some origins of self-control. In T. M. Newcomb (Ed.), *New directions in psychology*. New York: Holt, Rinehart & Winston.

Chi, M. T. H. (1978). Knowledge structures and memory development. In R. S. Siegler (Ed.), *Children's thinking: What develops?* Hillsdale, NJ: Erlbaum.

Chi, M. T. H. (1981). Knowledge development and memory performance. In M. P. Friedman, J. P. Das, & N. O'Connor (Eds.), *Intelligence and learning*. New York: Plenum Press.

Chi, M. T. H., & Glaser, R. (1985). Problem-solving ability. In R. J. Sternberg (Ed.), *Human abilities: An information-processing approach*. New York: W. H. Freeman.

Chi, M. T. H., Glaser, R., & Farr, M. J. (Eds.). (1988). *The nature of expertise*. Hillsdale, NJ: Erlbaum.

Chi, M. T. H., Glaser, R., & Rees, E. (1982). Expertise in problem solving. In R. J. Sternberg (Ed.), *Advances in the psychology of human intelligence*. Hillsdale, NJ: Erlbaum.

Chiesi, H. L., Spilich, G. J., & Voss, J. F. (1979). Acquisition of domain-related information in relation to high and low domain knowledge. *Journal of Verbal Learning and Verbal Behavior, 18,* 257–273.

Chinn, C. A. (1998). A critique of social constructivist explanations of knowledge change. In B. Guzzetti & C. Hynd (Eds.), *Perspectives on conceptual change: Multiple ways to understand knowing and learning in a complex world* (pp. 77–115). Mahwah, NJ: Erlbaum.

Chinn, C. A., & Brewer, W. F. (1993). The role of anomalous data in knowledge acquisition: A theoretical framework and implications for science instruction. *Review of Educational Research, 63,* 1–49.

Chinn, C. A., & Malhotra, B. A. (2002). Children's responses to anomalous scientific data: How is conceptual change impeded? *Journal of Educational Psychology, 94,* 327–343.

Chipman, S. F., Krantz, D. H., & Silver, R. (1992). Mathematics anxiety and science careers among able college women. *Psychological Science, 3,* 292–295.

Chomsky, N. (1957). *Syntactic structures*. The Hague: Mouton.

Chomsky, N. (1959). Review of B. F. Skinner's *Verbal behavior, Language, 35,* 26–58.

Chomsky, N. (1972). *Language and mind* (Enl. ed.). San Diego: Harcourt Brace Jovanovich.

Christen, F., & Bjork, R. A. (1976). *On updating the loci in the method of loci*. Paper presented at the annual meeting of the Psychonomic Society, St. Louis.

Christie, J. F., & Johnsen, E. P. (1983). The role of play in social–intellectual development. *Review of Educational Research, 53,* 93–115.

Christmann, E., Badgett, J., & Lucking, R. (1997). Microcomputer-based computer-assisted instruction within differing subject areas: A statistical deduction. *Journal of Educational Computing Research, 16,* 281–296.

Church, M. A., Elliot, A. J., & Gable, S. L. (2001). Perceptions of classroom environment, achievement goals, and achievement outcomes. *Journal of Educational Psychology, 93,* 43–54.

Church, R. M. (1993). Human models of animal behavior. *Psychological Science, 4,* 170–173.

Clancey, W. J. (1997). *Situated cognition: On human knowledge and computer representations*. Cambridge, England: Cambridge University Press.

Clark, D. C. (1971). Teaching concepts in the classroom: A set of teaching prescriptions derived from experimental research. *Journal of Educational Psychology, 62,* 253–278.

Clark, H. H. (1969). Linguistic processes in deductive reasoning. *Psychological Review, 75,* 387–404.

Clark, J. M., & Paivio, A. (1991). Dual coding theory and education. *Educational Psychology Review, 3,* 149–210.

Clement, J. (1982). Students' preconceptions in elementary mechanics. *American Journal of Physics, 50,* 66–71.

Clement, J. (1987). Overcoming students' misconceptions in physics: The role of anchoring intuitions and analogical validity. In *Proceedings of the Second International Seminar on Misconceptions and Educational Strategies in Science and Mathematics* (Vol. 3). Ithaca, NY: Cornell University.

Clifford, M. M. (1984). Thoughts on a theory of constructive failure. *Educational Psychologist, 19,* 108–120.

Clifford, M. M. (1990). Students need challenge, not easy success. *Educational Leadership, 48*(1), 22–26.

Clore, G. L., Gasper, K., & Garvin, E. (2001). Affect as information. In J. P. Forgas (Ed.), *Handbook of affect and social cognition* (pp. 121–144). Mahwah, NJ: Erlbaum.

Coates, B., & Hartup, W. W. (1969). Age and verbalization in observational learning. *Developmental Psychology, 1,* 556–562.

Cobb, P., Wood, T., Yackel, E., Nicholls, J., Wheatley, G., Trigatti, B., & Perlwitz, M. (1991). Assessment of a problem centered second-grade mathematics project. *Journal for Research in Mathematics Education, 22,* 3–29.

Cobb, P., & Yackel, E. (1996). Constructivist, emergent, and sociocultural perspectives in the context of developmental research. *Educational Psychologist, 31,* 175–190.

Cobb, P., Yackel, E., & Wood, T. (1989). Young children's emotional acts while engaged in mathematical problem solving. In D. B. McLeod & V. M. Adams (Eds.), *Affect and mathematical problem solving: A new perspective*. New York: Springer-Verlag.

Cochran, K. F. (1988, April). *Cognitive structure representation in physics*. Paper presented at the annual meeting of the American Educational Research Association, New Orleans.

Cofer, C. (1971). Properties of verbal materials and verbal learning. In J. Kling & L. Riggs (Eds.), *Woodworth and Schlosberg's experimental psychology*. New York: Holt, Rinehart & Winston.

Cognition and Technology Group at Vanderbilt (1990). Anchored instruction and its relationship to situated cognition. *Educational Researcher, 19*(6), 2–10.

Cognition and Technology Group at Vanderbilt (1996). Looking at technology in con-text: A framework for understanding technology and education research. In D. C. Berliner & R. C. Calfee (Eds.), *Handbook of educational psychology* (pp. 807–840). New York: Macmillan.

Cohen, E. G. (1994). Restructuring the classroom: Conditions for productive small groups. *Review of Educational Research, 64,* 1–35.

Cohen, E. G., & Lotan, R. A. (1995). Producing equal-status interaction in the heterogeneous classroom. *American Educational Research Journal, 32,* 99–120.

Cohen, G. (1983). *The psychology of cognition* (2nd ed.). London: Academic Press.

Cohen, L. B., (1972). Attention-getting and attention-holding processes of infant visual preference. *Child Development, 43,* 869–879.

Cohen, R. L. (1989). Memory for action events: The power of enactment. *Educational Psychology Review, 1,* 57–80.

Cohn, S., Hult, R. E., & Engle, R. W. (1990, April). *Working memory, notetaking, and learning from a lecture*. Paper presented at the annual meeting of the American Educational Research Association, Boston.

Cole, N. S. (1990). Conceptions of educational achievement. *Educational Researcher, 19*(3), 2–7.

Coleman, C. L., & Holmes, P. A. (1998). The use of noncontingent escape to reduce disruptive behaviors in children with speech delays. *Journal of Applied Behavior Analysis, 31,* 687–690.

Collie, R., & Hayne, H. (1999). Deferred imitation by 6- and 9-month-old infants: More evidence for declarative memory. *Developmental Psychobiology, 35,* 83–90.

Collier, G., Hirsh, E., & Hamlin, P. H. (1972). The ecological determinants of reinforcement in the rat. *Physiology and Behavior, 9,* 705–716.

Collier, V. (1989). How long? A synthesis of research on academic achievement in a second language. *TESOL Quarterly, 23,* 509–523.

Collins, A., Brown, J. S., & Newman, S. E. (1989). Cognitive apprenticeship: Teaching the crafts of reading, writing, and mathematics. In L. B. Resnick (Ed.), *Knowing, learning, and instruction: Essays in honor of Robert Glaser*. Hillsdale, NJ: Erlbaum.

Collins, A. M., & Loftus, E. F. (1975). A spreading-activation theory of semantic processing. *Psychological Review, 82,* 407–428.

Collins, A. M., & Quillian, M. R. (1969). Retrieval time from semantic memory. *Journal of Verbal Learning and Verbal Behavior, 8,* 240–247.

Collins, A. M., & Quillian, M. R. (1972). How to make a language user. In E. Tulving & W. Donaldson (Eds.), *Organization of memory*. New York: Academic Press.

Coltheart, M., Lea, C. D., & Thompson, K. (1974). In defense of iconic memory. *Quarterly Journal of Experimental Psychology, 26,* 633–641.

Colwill, R. M. (1993). An associative analysis of instrumental learning. *Current Directions in Psychological Science, 2,* 111–116.

Colwill, R. M., & Rescorla, R. A. (1986). Associative structures in instrumental learning. In G. H. Bower (Ed.), *The psychology of learning and motivation* (Vol. 20). Orlando: Academic Press.

Combs, A. W., Richards, A. C., & Richards, F. (1976). *Perceptual psychology: A humanistic approach to the study of persons.* New York: Harper & Row.

Condry, J. (1977). Enemies of exploration: Self-initiated versus other-initiated learning. *Journal of Personality and Social Psychology, 35,* 459–477.

Conklin, H. M., & Iacono, W. G. (2002). Schizophrenia: A neurodevelopmental perspective. *Current Directions in Psychological Science, 11,* 33–37.

Connell, J. P. (1990). Context, self, and action: A motivational analysis of self-system processes across the life span. In D. Cicchetti & M. Beeghly (Eds.), *The self in transition: Infancy to childhood.* Chicago: University of Chicago Press.

Connell, J. P., & Wellborn, J. G. (1991). Competence, autonomy, and relatedness: A motivational analysis of self-system processes. In M. R. Gunnar & L. A. Sroufe (Eds.), *Self processes and development: The Minnesota Symposia on Child Psychology* (Vol. 23). Hillsdale, NJ: Erlbaum.

Connolly, F. W., & Eisenberg, T. E. (1990). The feedback classroom: Teaching's silent friend. *T.H.E. Journal, 17*(5), 75–77.

Conrad, R. (1962). An association between memory errors and errors due to acoustic masking of speech. *Nature, 193,* 1314–1315.

Conrad, R. (1964). Acoustic confusions in immediate memory. *British Journal of Psychology, 55,* 75–84.

Conrad, R. (1972). Short-term memory in the deaf: A test for speech coding. *British Journal of Psychology, 63,* 173–180.

Conrad, R., & Hull, A. J. (1964). Information, acoustic confusion, and memory span. *British Journal of Psychology, 55,* 429–432.

Conway, M. A., & Rubin, D. C. (1993). The structure of autobiographical memory. In A. F. Collins, S. E. Gathercole, M. A. Conway, & P. E. Morris (Eds.), *Theories of memory.* Hove, England: Erlbaum.

Cook, V., & Newson, M. (1996). *Chomsky's universal grammar: An introduction* (2nd ed.). Oxford, England: Blackwell.

Cooney, J. B. (1991). Reflections on the origin of mathematical intuition and some implications for instruction. *Learning and Individual Differences, 3,* 83–107.

Cooper, L. A., & Shepard, R. N. (1973). The time required to prepare for a rotated stimulus. *Memory and Cognition, 1,* 246–250.

Corbett, H. D., & Wilson, B. (1988). Raising the stakes in statewide mandatory minimum competency testing. *Politics of Education Association Yearbook,* 27–39.

Cordua, G. D., McGraw, K. O., & Drabman, R. S. (1979). Doctor or nurse: Children's perception of sex typed occupations. *Child Development, 50,* 590–593.

Corkill, A. J. (1992). Advance organizers: Facilitators of recall. *Educational Psychology Review, 4,* 33–67.

Corkill, A. J., Glover, J. A., & Bruning, R. H. (1988). Advance organizers: Concrete versus abstract. *Journal of Educational Research, 82,* 76–81.

Cormier, S. M. (1987). The structural processes underlying transfer of training. In S. M. Cormier & J. D. Hagman (Eds.), *Transfer of learning: Contemporary research and applications.* San Diego: Academic Press.

Cormier, S. M., & Hagman, J. D. (1987). Introduction. In S. M. Cormier & J. D. Hagman (Eds.), *Transfer of learning: Contemporary research and applications.* San Diego: Academic Press.

Corno, L. (1993). The best-laid plans: Modern conceptions of volition and educational research. *Educational Researcher, 22,* 14–22.

Corno, L., Cronbach, L. J., Kupermintz, H., Lohman, D. F., Mandinach, E. B., Porteus, A. W., & Talbert, J. E. (2002). *Remaking the concept of aptitude: Extending the legacy of Richard E. Snow.* Mahwah, NJ: Erlbaum.

Corno, L., & Rohrkemper, M. M. (1985). The intrinsic motivation to learn in classrooms. In C. Ames & R. Ames (Eds.), *Research on motivation in education: Vol. 2. The classroom milieu.* Orlando: Academic Press.

Corte, H. E., Wolf, M. M., & Locke, B. J. (1971). A comparison of procedures for eliminating self-injurious behavior of retarded adolescents. *Journal of Applied Behavior Analysis, 4,* 201–214.

Cothern, N. B., Konopak, B. C., & Willis, E. L. (1990). Using readers' imagery of literary characters to study text meaning construction. *Reading Research and Instruction, 30,* 15–29.

Covington, M. V. (1992). *Making the grade: A self-worth perspective on motivation and school reform.* Cambridge, England: Cambridge University Press.

Covington, M. V. (2000). Intrinsic versus extrinsic motivation in schools: A reconciliation. *Current Directions in Psychological Science, 9,* 22–25.

Covington, M. V., & Beery, R. M. (1976). *Self-worth and school learning.* New York: Holt, Rinehart & Winston.

Covington, M. V., & Müeller, K. J. (2001). Intrinsic versus extrinsic motivation: An approach/avoidance reformulation. *Educational Psychology Review, 13,* 157–176.

Covington, M. V., & Omelich, C. (1979). Effort: The double-edged sword in school achievement. *Journal of Educational Psychology, 71,* 169–182.

Covington, M. V., & Omelich, C. L. (1991). Need achievement revisited: Verification of Atkinson's original 2 × 2 model. In C. D. Spielberger, I. G. Sarason, Z. Kulc-

sar, & G. L. Van Heck (Eds.), *Stress and emotion* (Vol. 14). New York: Hemisphere.

Covington, M. V., Spratt, M., & Omelich, C. (1980). Is effort enough or does diligence count too? Student and teacher reactions to effort stability in failure. *Journal of Educational Psychology, 72,* 717–729.

Cowan, N. (1994). Mechanisms of verbal short-term memory. *Current Directions in Psychological Science, 3,* 185–189.

Cowan, N. (1995). *Attention and memory: An integrated framework.* New York: Oxford University Press.

Cowan, N., Wood, N. L., Nugent, L. D., & Treisman, M. (1997). There are two word-length effects in verbal short-term memory: Opposed effects of duration and complexity. *Psychological Science, 8,* 290–295.

Cox, B. D. (1997). The rediscovery of the active learner in adaptive contexts: A developmental–historical analysis of transfer of training. *Educational Psychologist, 32,* 41–55.

Craft, M. A., Alberg, S. R., & Heward, W. L. (1998). Teaching elementary students with developmental disabilities to recruit teacher attention in a general education classroom: Effects on teacher praise and academic productivity. *Journal of Applied Behavior Analysis, 31,* 399–415.

Craik, F. I. M., & Lockhart, R. S. (1972). Levels of processing: A framework for memory research. *Journal of Verbal Learning and Verbal Behavior, 11,* 671–684.

Craik, F. I. M., & Tulving, E. (1975). Depth of processing and the retention of words in episodic memory. *Journal of Experimental Psychology: General, 104,* 268–294.

Craik, F. I. M., & Watkins, M. J. (1973). The role of rehearsal in short-term memory. *Journal of Verbal Learning and Verbal Behavior, 12,* 598–607.

Crawley, A. M., Anderson, D. R., Wilder, A., Williams, M., & Santomero, A. (1999). Effects of repeated exposures to a single episode of the television program *Blue's Clues* on the viewing behaviors and comprehension of preschool children. *Journal of Educational Psychology 91,* 630–637.

Crespi, L. P. (1942). Quantitative variation of incentive and performance in the white rat. *American Journal of Psychology, 55,* 467–517.

Crill, W. E., & Raichle, M. E. (1982). Clinical evaluation of injury and recovery. In J. G. Nicholls (Ed.), *Repair and regeneration of the nervous system.* New York: Springer-Verlag.

Crisafi, M. A., & Brown, A. L. (1986). Analogical transfer in very young children: Combining two separately learned solutions to reach a goal. *Child Development, 57,* 953–968.

Critchfield, T. S., & Kollins, S. H. (2001). Temporal discounting: Basic research and the analysis of socially important behavior. *Journal of Applied Behavior Analysis, 34,* 101–122.

Cromer, R. F. (1993). Language growth with experience without feedback. In P. Bloom (Ed.), *Language acquisition: Core readings*. Cambridge, MA: MIT Press.

Crooks, T. J. (1988). The impact of classroom evaluation practices on students. *Review of Educational Research, 58*, 438–481.

Crosbie, J., & Kelly, G. (1994). Effects of imposed postfeedback delays in programmed instruction. *Journal of Applied Behavior Analysis, 27*, 483–491.

Cross, D. R., & Paris, S. G. (1988). Developmental and instructional analyses of children's metacognitive and reading comprehension. *Journal of Educational Psychology, 80*, 131–142.

Crowder, N. A., & Martin, G. (1961). *Trigonometry*. Garden City, NY: Doubleday.

Crowder, R. G. (1993). Short-term memory: Where do we stand? *Memory and Cognition, 21*, 142–145.

Crowder, R. G., & Wagner, R. K. (1992). *The psychology of reading: An introduction* (2nd ed.). New York: Oxford University Press.

Crowley, K., & Siegler, R. S. (1999). Explanation and generalization in young children's strategy learning. *Child Development, 70*, 304–316.

Crowley, T. J. (1984). Contingency contracting treatment of drug-abusing physicians, nurses, and dentists. *National Institute on Drug Abuse: Research Monograph Series, 46*, 68–83.

Crowne, D. P., & Marlowe, D. (1964). *The approval motive: Studies in evaluative dependence*. New York: Wiley.

Csikszentmihalyi, M. (1990). *Flow: The psychology of optimal experience*. New York: Harper & Row.

Csikszentmihalyi, M. (1996). *Creativity: Flow and the psychology of discovery and invention*. New York: HarperCollins.

Csikszentmihalyi, M., & Nakamura, J. (1989). The dynamics of intrinsic motivation: A study of adolescents. In C. Ames & R. Ames (Eds.), *Research on motivation in education: Vol. 3. Goals and cognitions*. Orlando: Academic Press.

Csikszentmihalyi, M., Rathunde, K., & Whalen, S. (1993). *Talented teenagers: A longitudinal study of their development*. New York: Cambridge University Press.

Curtis, K. A., & Graham, S. (1991, April). *Altering beliefs about the importance of strategy: An attributional intervention*. Paper presented at the annual meeting of the American Educational Research Association, Chicago.

Curtiss, S. (1977). *Genie: A psycholinguistic study of a modern-day "wild child."* New York: Academic Press.

Cushing, L. S., & Kennedy, C. H. (1997). Academic effects of providing peer support in general education classrooms on students without disabilities. *Journal of Applied Behavior Analysis, 30*, 139–151.

Cuvo, A. J. (1975). Developmental differences in rehearsal and free recall. *Journal of Experimental Child Psychology, 19*, 65–78.

Dai, D. Y. (2002, April). *Effects of need for cognition and reader beliefs on the comprehension of narrative text*. Paper presented at the annual meeting of the American Educational Research Association, New Orleans.

Dallett, K. M. (1964). Implicit mediators in paired-associate learning. *Journal of Verbal Learning and Verbal Behavior, 3*, 209–214.

D'Amato, M. R. (1955). Secondary reinforcement and magnitude of primary reinforcement. *Journal of Comparative and Physiological Psychology, 48*, 378–380.

D'Amato, M. R. (1970). *Experimental psychology: Methodology, psychophysics, and learning*. New York: McGraw-Hill.

Daneman, M. (1987). Reading and working memory. In J. R. Beech & A. M. Colley (Eds.), *Cognitive approaches to reading*. Chichester, England: Wiley.

Daneman, M., & Carpenter, P. A. (1980). Individual differences in working memory and reading. *Journal of Verbal Learning and Verbal Behavior, 19*, 450–466.

Danner, F. W., & Lonky, E. (1981). A cognitive-developmental approach to the effects of rewards on intrinsic motivation. *Child Development, 52*, 1043–1052.

Dansereau, D. F. (1978). The development of a learning strategies curriculum. In H. F. O'Neil, Jr. (Ed.), *Learning strategies*. New York: Academic Press.

Dansereau, D. F. (1988). Cooperative learning strategies. In C. E. Weinstein, E. T. Goetz, & P. A. Alexander (Eds.), *Learning and study strategies: Issues in assessment, instruction, and evaluation*. San Diego: Academic Press.

Dansereau, D. F. (1995). Derived structural schemas and the transfer of knowledge. In A. McKeough, J. Lupart, & A. Marini (Eds.), *Teaching for transfer: Fostering generalization in learning*. Mahwah, NJ: Erlbaum.

Darley, J. M., & Gross, P. H. (1983). A hypothesis-confirming bias in labeling effects. *Journal of Personality and Social Psychology, 44*, 20–33.

Darling-Hammond, L. (1991). The implications of testing policy for quality and equality. *Phi Delta Kappan, 73*, 220–225.

Darwin, C. J., Turvey, M. T., & Crowder, R. G. (1972). An auditory analogue of the Sperling partial report procedure: Evidence for brief auditory storage. *Cognitive Psychology, 3*, 255–267.

Davidson, J. E., & Sternberg, R. J. (1998). Smart problem solving: How metacognition helps. In D. J. Hacker, J. Dunlosky, & A. C. Graesser (Eds.), *Metacognition in educational theory and practice* (pp. 47–68). Mahwah, NJ: Erlbaum.

Davis, G. A. (1966). Current status of research and theory in human problem solving. *Psychological Bulletin, 66*, 36–54.

Davis, G. A., & Thomas, M. A. (1989). *Effective schools and effective teachers*. Boston: Allyn & Bacon.

Davis, P. J. (1987). Repression and the inaccessibility of affective memories. *Journal of Personality and Social Psychology, 53*, 585–593.

Davis, P. J., & Schwartz, G. E. (1987). Repression and the inaccessibility of affective memories. *Journal of Personality and Social Psychology, 52*, 155–162.

Deaux, K. (1984). From individual differences to social categories: Analysis of a decade's research on gender. *American Psychologist, 39*, 105–116.

DeCasper, A. J., & Spence, M. J. (1986). Prenatal maternal speech influences newborns' perception of speech sounds. *Infant Behavior and Development, 9*, 133–150.

deCharms, R. (1972). Personal causation training in the schools. *Journal of Applied Social Psychology, 2*, 95–113.

deCharms, R. (1984). Motivation enhancement in educational settings. In R. Ames & C. Ames (Eds.), *Research on motivation in education: Vol. 1. Student motivation*. Orlando: Academic Press.

Deci, E. L. (1971). Effects of externally mediated rewards on intrinsic motivation. *Journal of Personality and Social Psychology, 18*, 105–115.

Deci, E. L. (1992). The relation of interest to the motivation of behavior: A self-determination theory perspective. In K. A. Renninger, S. Hidi, & A. Krapp (Eds.), *The role of interest in learning and development*. Hillsdale, NJ: Erlbaum.

Deci, E. L., Koestner, R., & Ryan, R. M. (2001). Extrinsic rewards and intrinsic motivation in education: Reconsidered once again. *Review of Educational Research, 71*, 1–27.

Deci, E. L., & Ryan, R. M. (1985). *Intrinsic motivation and self-determination in human behavior*. New York: Plenum Press.

Deci, E. L., & Ryan, R. M. (1987). The support of autonomy and the control of behavior. *Journal of Personality and Social Psychology, 53*, 1024–1037.

Deci, E. L., & Ryan, R. M. (1992). The initiation and regulation of intrinsically motivated learning and achievement. In A. K. Boggiano & T. S. Pittman (Eds.), *Achievement and motivation: A social-developmental perspective*. Cambridge, England: Cambridge University Press.

Deci. E. L., & Ryan, R. M. (1995). Human autonomy: The basis for true self-esteem. In M. H. Kernis (Ed.), *Efficacy, agency, and self-esteem*. New York: Plenum Press.

Deci, E. L., Vallerand, R. J., Pelletier, L. G., & Ryan, R. M. (1991). Motivation and education: The self-determination perspective. *Educational Psychologist, 26*, 325–346.

De Corte, E., Greer, B., & Verschaffel, L. (1996). Mathematics teaching and learning. In D. C. Berliner & R. C. Calfee (Eds.), *Handbook of educational psychology*. New York: Macmillan.

De Corte, E., Op't Eynde, P., & Verschaffel, L. (2002). "Knowing what to believe": The relevance of students' mathematical beliefs for mathematics education. In B. K. Hofer & P. R. Pintrich (Eds.), *Personal epistemology: The psychology of beliefs about knowledge and knowing* (pp. 297–320). Mahwah, NJ: Erlbaum.

Dee-Lucas, D., & Larkin, J. H. (1991). Equations in scientific proofs: Effects on comprehension. *American Educational Research Journal, 28,* 661–682.

DeGrandpre, R. J. (2000). A science of meaning: Can behaviorism bring meaning to psychological science? *American Psychologist, 55,* pp. 721–739.

deGroot, A. D. (1965). *Thought and choice in chess.* The Hague: Mouton.

Delclos, V. R., & Harrington, C. (1991). Effects of strategy monitoring and proactive instruction on children's problem-solving performance. *Journal of Educational Psychology, 83,* 35–42.

deLeeuw, N., & Chi, M. T. H. (2003). Self-explanation: Enriching a situation model or repairing a domain model? In G. M. Sinatra & P. R. Pintrich (Eds.), *Intentional conceptual change* (pp. 55–78). Mahwah, NJ: Erlbaum.

De Lisi, R., & Golbeck, S. L. (1999). Implications of Piagetian theory for peer learning. In A. M. O'Donnell & A. King (Eds.), *Cognitive perspectives on peer learning* (pp. 3–37). Mahwah, NJ: Erlbaum.

DeLoache, J. S. (1995). Early understanding and use of symbols: The model model. *Current Directions in Psychological Science, 4,* 109–113.

Delval, J. (1994). Stages in the child's construction of social knowledge. In M. Carretero & J. F. Voss (Eds.), *Cognitive and instructional processes in history and the social sciences* (pp. 77–102). Mahwah, NJ: Erlbaum.

Demetriou, A., Christou, C., Spanoudis, G., & Platsidou, M. (2002). The development of mental processing: Efficiency, working memory, and thinking. *Monographs of the Society for Research in Child Development, 67*(1, Serial No. 268).

Dempster, F. N. (1991). Synthesis of research on reviews and tests. *Educational Leadership, 48*(7), 71–76.

Dempster, F. N. (1992). The rise and fall of the inhibitory mechanism: Toward a unified theory of cognitive development and aging. *Developmental Review, 12,* 45–75.

Dempster, F. N., & Corkill, A. J. (1999). Interference and inhibition in cognition and behavior: Unifying themes for educational psychology. *Educational Psychology Review, 11,* 1–88.

Dempster, F. N., & Rohwer, W. D. (1974). Component analysis of the elaborative encoding effect in paired-associate learning. *Journal of Experimental Psychology, 103,* 400–408.

Denny, M. R., & Weisman, R. G. (1964). Avoidance behavior as a function of the length of nonshock confinement. *Journal of Comparative and Physiological Psychology, 58,* 252–257.

Derry, S. J. (1996). Cognitive schema theory in the constructivist debate. *Educational Psychologist, 31,* 163–174.

Derry, S. J., DuRussel, L. A., & O'Donnell, A. M. (1998). Individual and distributed cognitions in interdisciplinary teamwork: A developing case study and emerging theory. *Educational Psychology Review, 10,* 25–56.

Derry, S. J., Levin, J. R., Osana, H. P., & Jones, M. S. (1998). Developing middle school students' statistical reasoning abilities through simulation gaming. In S. P. Lajoie (Ed.), *Reflections on statistics: Learning, teaching, and assessment in grades K–12* (pp. 175–195). Mahwah, NJ: Erlbaum.

Deutsch, M. (1993). Educating for a peaceful world. *American Psychologist, 48,* 510–517.

de Villiers, P. A. (1977). Choice in concurrent schedules and a quantitative formulation of the law of effect. In W. K. Honig & J. E. R. Staddon (Eds.), *Handbook of operant behavior.* Englewood Cliffs, NJ: Prentice Hall.

DeVries, R. (1969). Constancy of generic identity in the years three to six. *Monographs of the Society for Research in Child Development, 34* (Whole No. 127).

Dewhurst, S. A., & Conway, M. A. (1994). Pictures, images, and recollective experience. *Journal of Experimental Psychology: Learning, Memory, and Cognition, 20,* 1088–1098.

Diamond, M., & Hopson, J. (1998). *Magic trees of the mind.* New York: Dutton.

Diaz, R. M., Neal, C. J., & Amaya-Williams, M. (1990). The social origins of self-regulation. In L. C. Moll (Ed.), *Vygotsky and education: Instructional implications and applications of sociohistorical psychology.* Cambridge, England: Cambridge University Press.

Diener, C. I., & Dweck, C. S. (1978). An analysis of learned helplessness: Continuous changes in performance, strategy, and achievement cognitions following failure. *Journal of Personality and Social Psychology, 36,* 451–462.

Dinsmoor, J. A. (1954). Punishment: I. The avoidance hypothesis. *Psychological Review, 61,* 34–46.

Dinsmoor, J. A. (1955). Punishment: II. An interpretation of empirical findings. *Psychological Review, 62,* 96–105.

diSessa, A. A. (1982). Unlearning Aristotelian physics: A study of knowledge-based learning. *Cognitive Science, 6,* 37–75.

diSessa, A. A. (1996). What do "just plain folk" know about physics? In D. R. Olson & N. Torrance (Eds.), *The handbook of education and human development: New models of learning, teaching, and schooling.* Cambridge, MA: Blackwell.

diSessa, A. A., Elby, A., & Hammer, D. (2003). J's epistemological stance and strategies. In G. M. Sinatra & P. R. Pintrich (Eds.), *Intentional conceptual change* (pp. 237–290). Mahwah, NJ: Erlbaum.

Di Vesta, F. J., & Gray, S. G. (1972). Listening and notetaking. *Journal of Educational Psychology, 63,* 8–14.

Di Vesta, F. J., & Ingersoll, G. M. (1969). Influence of pronounceability, articulation, and test mode on paired-associate learning by the study-recall procedure. *Journal of Experimental Psychology, 79,* 104–108.

Di Vesta, F. J., & Peverly, S. T. (1984). The effects of encoding variability, processing activity and rule example sequences on the transfer of conceptual rules. *Journal of Educational Psychology, 76,* 108–119.

Dixon, M. R., & Cummings, A. (2001). Self-control in children with autism: Response allocation during delays to reinforcement. *Journal of Applied Behavior Analysis, 34,* 491–495.

Doctorow, M., Wittrock, M. C., & Marks, C. (1978). Generative processes in reading comprehension. *Journal of Educational Psychology, 70,* 109–118.

Dodd, D. H., & White, R. M. (1980). *Cognition: Mental structures and processes.* Boston: Allyn & Bacon.

Dodge, K. A., Asher, S. R., & Parkhurst, J. T. (1989). Social life as a goal-coordination task. In C. Ames & R. Ames (Eds.), *Research on motivation in education: Vol. 3. Goals and cognitions.* San Diego: Academic Press.

Dole, J. A., Duffy, G. G., Roehler, L. R., & Pearson, P. D. (1991). Moving from the old to the new: Research on reading comprehension instruction. *Review of Educational Research, 61,* 239–264.

Dollard, J. C., Doob, L., Miller, N., Mowrer, O., & Sears, R. (1939). *Frustration and aggression.* New Haven, CT: Yale University Press.

Dominowski, R. L. (1998). Verbalization and problem solving. In D. J. Hacker, J. Dunlosky, & A. C. Graesser (Eds.), *Metacognition in educational theory and practice* (pp. 25–45). Mahwah, NJ: Erlbaum.

Dominowski, R. L., & Jenrick, R. (1972). Effects of hints and interpolated activity on solution of an insight problem. *Psychonomic Science, 26,* 335–338.

Donaldson, M. (1978). *Children's minds.* New York: W. W. Norton.

Donnelly, C. M., & McDaniel, M. A. (1993). Use of analogy in learning scientific concepts. *Journal of Experimental Psychology: Learning, Memory, and Cognition, 19,* 975–987.

Dooling, D. J., & Christiaansen, R. E. (1977). Episodic and semantic aspects of memory for prose. *Journal of Experimental Psychology: Human Learning and Memory, 3,* 428–436.

Dorris, M. (1989). *The broken cord.* New York: Harper & Row.

Dowaliby, F. J., & Schumer, H. (1973). Teacher-centered versus student-centered mode of college classroom instruction as related to manifest anxiety. *Journal of Educational Psychology, 64,* 125–132.

Downing, P. E. (2000). Interactions between visual working memory and selective attention. *Psychological Science, 11,* 467–473.

Downs, R. M., & Stea, D. (1977). *Maps in minds*. New York: Harper & Row.

Dowson, M., & McInerney, D. M. (2001). Psychological parameters of students' social and work avoidance goals: A qualitative investigation. *Journal of Educational Psychology, 93*, 35–42.

Doyle, W. (1983). Academic work. *Review of Educational Research, 53*, 159–199.

Doyle, W. (1986a). Classroom organization and management. In M. C. Wittrock (Ed.), *Handbook of research on teaching* (3rd ed.). New York: Macmillan.

Doyle, W. (1986b). Content representation in teachers' definitions of academic work. *Journal of Curriculum Studies, 18*, 365–379.

Doyle, W. (1990). Classroom management techniques. In O. C. Moles (Ed.), *Student discipline strategies: Research and practice*. Albany: State University of New York Press.

Drabman, R. S. (1976). Behavior modification in the classroom. In W. E. Craighead & M. J. Mahoney (Eds.), *Behavior modification principles, issues, and applications*. Boston: Houghton Mifflin.

Dressel, P. L. (1977). The nature and role of objectives in instruction. *Educational Technology, 17*(5), 7–15.

Drevno, G. E., Kimball, J. W., Possi, M. K., Heward, W. L., Gardner, R., III, & Barbetta, P. M. (1994). Effects of active student responding during error correction on the acquisition, maintenance, and generalization of science vocabulary by elementary students: A systematic replication. *Journal of Applied Behavior Analysis, 27*, 179–180.

Driver, R., Asoko, H., Leach, J., Mortimer, E., & Scott, P. (1994). Constructing scientific knowledge in the classroom. *Educational Researcher, 23*(7), 5–12.

Dryden, M. A., & Jefferson, P. (1994, April). *Use of background knowledge and reading achievement among elementary school students*. Paper presented at the annual meeting of the American Educational Research Association, New Orleans.

DuBois, N. F., Kiewra, K. A., & Fraley, J. (1988, April). *Differential effects of a learning strategy course*. Paper presented at the annual meeting of the American Educational Research Association, New Orleans.

DuBois, N. F., Staley, R., Guzy, L., & DiNardo, P. (1995, April). *Durable effects of a study skills course on academic achievement*. Paper presented at the annual meeting of the American Educational Research Association, San Francisco.

Duell, O. K. (1994). Extended wait time and university student achievement. *American Educational Research Journal, 31*, 397–414.

Dufresne, A., & Kobasigawa, A. (1989). Children's spontaneous allocation of study time: Differential and sufficient aspects. *Journal of Experimental Child Psychology, 47*, 274–296.

Duit, R. (1990, April). *On the role of analogies, similes, and metaphors in learning science*. Paper presented at the annual meeting of

the American Educational Research Association, Boston.

Duit, R. (1991). Students' conceptual frameworks: Consequences for learning science. In S. M. Glynn, R. H. Yeany, & B. K. Britton (Eds.), *The psychology of learning science*. Hillsdale, NJ: Erlbaum.

DuNann, D. G., & Weber, S. J. (1976). Short- and long-term effects of contingency managed instruction on low, medium, and high GPA students. *Journal of Applied Behavior Analysis, 9*, 375–376.

Duncker, K. (1945). On problem solving. *Psychological Monographs, 58* (Whole No. 270).

Dunlap, G., dePerczel, M., Clarke, S., Wilson, D., Wright, S., White, R., & Gomez, A. (1994). Choice making to promote adaptive behavior for students with emotional and behavioral challenges. *Journal of Applied Behavior Analysis, 27*, 505–518.

Dunn, C. S. (1983). The influence of instructional methods on concept learning. *Science Education, 67*, 647–656.

Dunton, K. J., McDevitt, T. M., & Hess, R. D. (1988). Origins of mothers' attributions about their daughters' and sons' performance in mathematics in sixth grade. *Merrill-Palmer Quarterly, 34*, 47–70.

DuPaul, G. J., Ervin, R. A., Hook, C. L., & McGoey, K. E. (1998). Peer tutoring for children with attention deficit hyperactivity disorder: Effects on classroom behavior and academic performance. *Journal of Applied Behavior Analysis, 31*, 579–592.

Durkin, K. (1987). Social cognition and social context in the construction of sex differences. In M. A. Baker (Ed.), *Sex differences in human performance*. Chichester, England: Wiley.

Durkin, K. (1995). *Developmental social psychology: From infancy to old age*. Cambridge, MA: Blackwell.

Durst, R. K., & Newell, G. E. (1989). The uses of function: James Britton's category system and research on writing. *Review of Educational Research, 59*, 375–394.

Dusek, J. B. (1980). The development of test anxiety in children. In I. G. Sarason (Ed.), *Test anxiety: Theory, research, and applications*. Hillsdale, NJ: Erlbaum.

Dweck, C. S. (1975). The role of expectations and attributions in the alleviation of learned helplessness. *Journal of Personality and Social Psychology, 31*, 674–685.

Dweck, C. S. (1978). Achievement. In M. E. Lamb (Ed.), *Social and personality development*. New York: Holt, Rinehart & Winston.

Dweck, C. S. (1986). Motivational processes affecting learning. *American Psychologist, 41*, 1040–1048.

Dweck, C. S. (1999). *Self-theories: Their role in motivation, personality, and development*. Philadelphia: Taylor & Francis.

Dweck, C. S., Davidson, W., Nelson, S., & Enna, B. (1978). Sex differences in learned helplessness: II. The contingen-

cies of evaluative feedback in the classroom; III. An experimental analysis. *Developmental Psychology, 14*, 268–276.

Dweck, C. S., & Elliott, E. S. (1983). Achievement motivation. In E. M. Hetherington (Ed.), *Handbook of child psychology: Vol. 4. Socialization, personality, and social development* (4th ed.). New York: Wiley.

Dweck, C. S., Goetz, T. E., & Strauss, N. L. (1980). Sex differences in learned helplessness: IV. An experimental and naturalistic study of failure generalization and its mediators. *Journal of Personality and Social Psychology, 38*, 441–452.

Dweck, C. S., & Leggett, E. L. (1988). A social–cognitive approach to motivation and personality. *Psychological Review, 95*, 256–273.

Dweck, C. S., & Licht, B. (1980). Learned helplessness and intellectual achievement. In J. Garber & M. E. P. Seligman (Eds.), *Human helplessness: Theory and applications*. New York: Academic Press.

Dweck, C. S., & Reppucci, N. D. (1973). Learned helplessness and reinforcement responsibility in children. *Journal of Personality and Social Psychology, 25*, 109–116.

Dyer, H. S. (1967). The discovery and development of educational goals. *Proceedings of the 1966 Invitational Conference on Testing Problems*. Princeton, NJ: Educational Testing Service.

Eacott, M. J. (1999). Memory for the events of early childhood. *Current Directions in Psychological Science, 8*, 46–49.

Eagly, A. H., Kulesa, P., Chen, S., & Chaiken, S. (2001). Do attitudes affect memory? Tests of the congeniality hypothesis. *Current Directions in Psychological Science, 10*, 5–9.

Easterbrook, J. A. (1959). The effect of emotion on cue utilization and the organization of behavior. *Psychological Review, 66*, 183–201.

Eaton, J. F., Anderson, C. W., & Smith, E. L. (1984). Students' misconceptions interfere with science learning: Case studies of fifth-grade students. *Elementary School Journal, 84*, 365–379.

Ebbinghaus, H. (1913). *Memory: A contribution to experimental psychology* (H. A. Ruger & C. E. Bussenius, Trans.). New York: Teachers College. (Original work published 1885)

Eccles, J. S. (1989). Bringing young women to math and science. In M. Crawford & M. Gentry (Eds.), *Gender and thought: Psychological perspectives*. New York: Springer-Verlag.

Eccles, J. S., & Jacobs, J. E. (1986). Social forces shape math attitudes and performance. *Signs: Journal of Women in Culture and Society, 11*, 367–380.

Eccles, J. S., & Midgley, C. (1989). Stage-environment fit: Developmentally appropriate classrooms for young adolescents. In C. Ames & R. Ames (Eds.), *Research on motivation in education: Vol. 3. Goals and cognition*. New York: Academic Press.

Eccles, J. S., & Wigfield, A. (1985). Teacher expectations and student motivation. In J. B. Dusek (Ed.), *Teacher expectancies*. Hillsdale, NJ: Erlbaum.

Eccles, J. S., Wigfield, A., & Schiefele, U. (1998). Motivation to succeed. In W. Damon (Editor-in-Chief) and N. Eisenberg (Volume Editor), *Handbook of child psychology* (5th ed., Vol. 3). New York: Wiley.

Eccles (Parsons), J. (1983). Expectancies, values, and academic behaviors. In J. T. Spence (Ed.), *Achievement and achievement motivation*. San Francisco: W. H. Freeman.

Eccles (Parsons), J. (1984). Sex differences in mathematics participation. In M. Steinkamp & M. Maehr (Eds.), *Women in science*. Greenwich, CT: JAI Press.

Eccles (Parsons), J. S., Adler, T. F., Futterman, R., Goff, S. B., Kaczala, C. M., Meece, J. L., & Midgley, C. (1983). Expectations, values, and academic behaviors. In J. T. Spence (Ed.), *Achievement and achievement motivation*. San Francisco: W. H. Freeman.

Edens, K. M., & McCormick, C. B. (2000). How do adolescents process advertisements? The influence of ad characteristics, processing objective, and gender. *Contemporary Educational Psychology, 25*, 450–463.

Edens, K. M., & Potter, E. F. (2001). Promoting conceptual understanding through pictorial representation. *Studies in Art Education, 42*, 214–233.

Edwards, K., & Bryan, T. S. (1997). Judgmental biases produced by instructions to disregard: The (paradoxical) case of emotional information. *Personality and Social Psychology Bulletin, 23*, 849–864.

Eeds, M., & Wells, D. (1989). Grand conversations: An explanation of meaning construction in literature study groups. *Research in the Teaching of English, 23*, 4–29.

Eich, R. (1995). Searching for mood dependent memory. *Psychological Science, 6*, 67–75.

Eilam, B. (2001). Primary strategies for promoting homework performance. *American Educational Research Journal, 38*, 691–725.

Eimas, P. D., & Quinn, P. C. (1994). Studies on the formation of perceptually based basic-level categories in young infants. *Child Development, 65*, 903–917.

Eisenberg, N., Martin, C. L., & Fabes, R. A. (1996). Gender development and gender effects. In D. C. Berliner & R. C. Calfee (Eds.), *Handbook of educational psychology*. New York: Macmillan.

Eisenberger, R. (1992). Learned industriousness. *Psychological Review, 99*, 248–267.

Eisner, E. W. (1994). *Cognition and curriculum reconsidered*. New York: Teachers College Press.

Elbert, T., Pantev, C., & Taub, E. (1995). Increased cortical representation of the fingers of the left hand in string players. *Science, 270*, 305–307.

Elder, A. D. (2002). Characterizing fifth grade students' epistemological beliefs in science. In B. K. Hofer & P. R. Pintrich (Eds.), *Personal epistemology: The psychology of beliefs about knowledge and knowing* (pp. 347–363). Mahwah, NJ: Erlbaum.

Elkind, D. (1981). *Children and adolescents: Interpretive essays on Jean Piaget* (3rd ed.). New York: Oxford University Press.

Ellingson, S. A., Miltenberger, R. G., Stricker, J. M., Garlinghouse, M. A., Roberts, J., Galensky, T., L., & Rapp, J. T. (2000). Analysis and treatment of finger sucking. *Journal of Applied Behavior Analysis, 33*, 41–52.

Elliot, A. J. (1999). Approach and avoidance motivation and achievement goals. *Educational Psychologist, 34*, 169–189.

Elliot, A. J., & McGregor, H. A. (2000, April). Approach and avoidance goals and autonomous-controlled regulation: Empirical and conceptual relations. In A. Assor (Chair), *Self-determination theory and achievement goal theory: Convergences, divergences, and educational implications*. Symposium conducted at the annual meeting of the American Educational Research Association, New Orleans.

Elliot, A. J., & Thrash, T. M. (2001). Achievement goals and the hierarchical model of achievement motivation. *Educational Psychology Review, 13*, 139–156.

Elliott, D. J. (1995). *Music matters: A new philosophy of music education*. New York: Oxford University Press.

Elliott, R., & Vasta, R. (1970). The modeling of sharing: Effects associated with vicarious reinforcement, symbolization, age, and generalization. *Journal of Experimental Child Psychology, 10*, 8–15.

Elliott, S. N., & Busse, R. T. (1991). Social skills assessment and intervention with children and adolescents. *School Psychology International, 12*, 63–83.

Ellis, H. C., & Hunt, R. R. (1983). *Fundamentals of human memory and cognition* (3rd ed.). Dubuque, IA: Wm. C. Brown.

Ellis, J. O. (1975). *Cognitive processes in logical problem-solving: The three-term series problem*. Unpublished doctoral dissertation, The Pennsylvania State University, University Park.

Ellis, N. C. (Ed.) (1994). *Implicit and explicit learning of languages*. London: Academic Press.

Ellis, S., & Rogoff, B. (1986). Problem solving in children's management of instruction. In E. C. Mueller & C. R. Cooper (Eds.), *Process and outcome in peer relationships* (pp. 301–325). Orlando: Academic Press.

Emmer, E. T., & Evertson, C. M. (1981). Synthesis of research on classroom management. *Educational Leadership, 38*, 342–347.

Emmer, E. T., Evertson, C. M., Clements, B. S., & Worsham, M. E. (1994). *Classroom management for secondary teachers* (3rd ed.). Boston: Allyn & Bacon.

Emshoff, J. G., Redd, W. H., & Davidson, W. S. (1976). Generalization training and the transfer of treatment effects with delinquent adolescents. *Journal of Behavior Therapy and Experimental Psychiatry, 7*, 141–144.

Engerman, J. A., Austin, J., & Bailey, J. S. (1997). Prompting patron safety belt use at a supermarket. *Journal of Applied Behavior Analysis, 30*, 577–579.

Engle, R. W. (2002). Working memory capacity as executive attention. *Current Directions in Psychological Science, 11*, 19–23.

English, H. B., Welborn, E. L., & Killian, C. D. (1934). Studies in substance memorization. *Journal of General Psychology, 11*, 233–260.

English, L. D. (1997a). Analogies, metaphors, and images: Vehicles for mathematical reasoning. In L. D. English (Ed.), *Mathematical reasoning: Analogies, metaphors, and images* (pp. 3–18). Mahwah, NJ: Erlbaum.

English, L. D. (Ed.) (1997b). *Mathematical reasoning: Analogies, metaphors, and images*. Mahwah, NJ: Erlbaum.

Entwisle, N. J., & Ramsden, P. (1983). *Understanding student learning*. London: Croom Helm.

Epstein, H. (1978). Growth spurts during brain development: Implications for educational policy and practice. In J. Chall & A. Mirsky (Eds.), *Education and the brain: The 77th yearbook of the National Society for the Study of Education, Part II*. Chicago: University of Chicago Press.

Epstein, R. (1991). Skinner, creativity, and the problem of spontaneous behavior. *Psychological Science, 2*, 362–370.

Erdelyi, M. H. (1985). *Psychoanalysis: Freud's cognitive psychology*. New York: W. H. Freeman.

Erdelyi, M. H., & Goldberg, B. (1979). Let's not sweep repression under the rug: Toward a cognitive psychology of repression. In J. F. Kihlstrom & F. J. Evans (Eds.), *Functional disorders of memory*. Hillsdale, NJ: Erlbaum.

Ericsson, K. A. (1996). *The road to excellence: The acquisition of expert performance in the arts and science, sports, and games*. Mahwah, NJ: Erlbaum.

Ericsson, K. A., & Chalmers, N. (1994). Expert performance: Its structure and acquisition. *American Psychologist, 49*, 725–747.

Eriksen, C. W., & Kuethe, J. L. (1956). Avoidance conditioning of verbal behavior without awareness: A paradigm of repression. *Journal of Abnormal and Social Psychology, 53*, 203–209.

Estes, W. K. (1969a). New perspectives on some old issues in association theory. In N. J. Mackintosh & W. K. Honig (Eds.), *Fundamental issues in associative learning*. Halifax, Canada: Dalhousie University Press.

Estes, W. K. (1969b). Outline of a theory of punishment. In B. A. Campbell & R. M. Church (Eds.), *Punishment and aversive behavior*. New York: Appleton-Century-Crofts.

Evans, G. W., & Oswalt, G. L. (1968). Acceleration of academic progress through the manipulation of peer influence. *Behaviour Research and Therapy, 6,* 189–195.

Eysenck, M. W. (1979). Depth, elaboration, and distinctiveness. In L. S. Cermak & F. I. M. Craik (Eds.), *Levels of processing in human memory.* Hillsdale, NJ: Erlbaum.

Eysenck, M. W. (1992). *Anxiety: The cognitive perspective.* Hove, England: Erlbaum.

Eysenck, M. W., & Keane, M. T. (1990). *Cognitive psychology: A student's handbook.* Hove, England: Erlbaum.

Fabos, B., & Young, M. D. (1999). Telecommunication in the classroom: Rhetoric versus reality. *Review of Educational Research, 69,* 217–259.

Fagen, J. W., & Rovee, C. K. (1976). Effects of qualitative shifts in a visual reinforcer in the instrumental response of infants. *Journal of Experimental Child Psychology, 21,* 349–360.

Fantino, E. (1973). Aversive control. In J. A. Nevin & G. S. Reynolds (Eds.), *The study of behavior.* Glenview, IL: Scott Foresman.

Fantuzzo, J. W., King, J., & Heller, L. R. (1992). Effects of reciprocal peer tutoring on mathematics and school adjustment: A component analysis. *Journal of Educational Psychology, 84,* 331–339.

Farah, M. J., Hammond, K. M., Levine, D. N., & Calvanio, R. (1988). Visual and spatial mental imagery: Dissociable systems of representation. *Cognitive Psychology, 20,* 439–462.

Farnham-Diggory, S. (1972). The development of equivalence systems. In S. Farnham-Diggory (Ed.), *Information processing in children.* New York: Academic Press.

Farrar, M. J., & Goodman, G. S. (1992). Developmental changes in event memory. *Child Development, 63,* 173–187.

Farwell, L. A., & Smith, S. S. (2001). Using brain MERMER testing to detect knowledge despite efforts to conceal. *Journal of Forensic Sciences, 46*(1), 1–9.

Fashola, O. S., Drum, P. A., Mayer, R. E., & Kang, S. (1996). A cognitive theory of orthographic transitioning: Predictable errors in how Spanish-speaking children spell English words. *American Educational Research Journal, 33,* 825–843.

Faust, G. W., & Anderson, R. C. (1967). Effects of incidental material in a programmed Russian vocabulary lesson. *Journal of Educational Psychology, 58,* 3–10.

Feather, N. T. (1982). *Expectations and actions: Expectancy-value models in psychology.* Hillsdale, NJ: Erlbaum.

Feld, S., Ruhland, D., & Gold, M. (1979). Developmental changes in achievement motivation. *Merrill-Palmer Quarterly, 25,* 43–60.

Feltz, D. L., Chaase, M. A., Moritz, S. E., & Sullivan, P. J. (1999). A conceptual model of coaching efficacy: Preliminary investigation and instrument development. *Journal of Educational Psychology, 91,* 765–776.

Feltz, D. L., Landers, D. M., & Becker, B. J. (1988). A revised meta-analysis of the mental practice literature on motor skill performance. In D. Druckman & J. A. Swets (Eds.), *Enhancing human performance: Issues, theories, and techniques: Background papers.* Washington, DC: National Research Council.

Fennema, E. (1980). Sex-related differences in mathematics achievement: Where and why. In L. H. Fox, L. Brody, & D. Tobin (Eds.), *Women and the mathematical mystique.* Baltimore: Johns Hopkins University Press.

Fennema, E. (1987). Sex-related differences in education: Myths, realities, and interventions. In V. Richardson-Koehler (Ed.), *Educators' handbook: A research perspective.* New York: Longman.

Fennema, E., Carpenter, T. P., & Peterson, P. L. (1989). Learning mathematics with understanding: Cognitively guided instruction. In J. Brophy (Ed.), *Advances in research on teaching* (Vol. 1). Greenwich, CT: JAI Press.

Ferguson, E. L., & Hegarty, M. (1995). Learning with real machines or diagrams: Application of knowledge to real-world problems. *Cognition and Instruction, 13,* 129–160.

Ferrari, M., & Elik, N. (2003). Influences on intentional conceptual change. In G. M. Sinatra & P. R. Pintrich (Eds.), *Intentional conceptual change* (pp. 21–54). Mahwah, NJ: Erlbaum.

Ferster, C. B., & Skinner, B. F. (1957). *Schedules of reinforcement.* Englewood Cliffs, NJ: Prentice Hall.

Feuerstein, R. (1990). The theory of structural cognitive modifiability. In B. Z. Presseisen (Ed.), *Learning and thinking styles: Classroom interaction.* Washington, DC: National Education Association.

Feuerstein, R., Klein, P. R., & Tannenbaum, A. (Eds.). (1991). *Mediated learning experience: Theoretical, psychosocial, and learning implications.* London: Freund.

Field, D. (1987). A review of preschool conservation training: An analysis of analyses. *Developmental Review, 7,* 210–251.

Field, T. F., Woodson, R., Greenberg, R., & Cohen, D. (1982). Discrimination and imitation of facial expressions by neonates. *Science, 218*(8), 179–181.

Fischer, S. M., Iwata, B. A., & Mazaleski, J. L. (1997). Noncontingent delivery of arbitrary reinforcers as treatment for self-injurious behavior. *Journal of Applied Behavior Analysis, 30,* 239–249.

Fisher, W. W., & Mazur, J. E. (1997). Basic and applied research on choice responding. *Journal of Applied Behavior Analysis, 30,* 387–410.

Fiske, D. W., & Maddi, S. R. (1961). *Functions of varied experience.* Homewood, IL: Dorsey.

Fiske, S. T., & Taylor, S. (1991). *Social cognition.* New York: McGraw-Hill.

Flaherty, C. F. (1985). *Animal learning and cognition.* New York: Alfred Knopf.

Flaherty, C. F., Uzwiak, A. J., Levine, J., Smith, M., Hall, P., & Schuler, R. (1980). Apparent hypoglycemic conditioned responses with exogenous insulin as the unconditioned stimulus. *Animal Learning and Behavior, 8,* 382–386.

Flavell, J. H. (1963). *The developmental psychology of Jean Piaget.* New York: Van Nostrand Reinhold.

Flavell, J. H. (1979). Metacognition and cognitive monitoring: A new area of cognitive-developmental inquiry. *American Psychologist, 34,* 906–911.

Flavell, J. H. (1996). Piaget's legacy. *Psychological Science, 7,* 200–203.

Flavell, J. H. (2000). Development of children's knowledge about the mental world. *International Journal of Behavioral Development, 24*(1), 15–23.

Flavell, J. H., Friedrichs, A. G., & Hoyt, J. D. (1970). Developmental changes in memorization processes. *Cognitive Psychology, 1,* 324–340.

Flavell, J. H., Green, F. L., & Flavell, E. R. (2000). Development of children's awareness of their own thoughts. *Journal of Cognitive Development, 1,* 97–112.

Flavell, J. H., Miller, P. H., & Miller, S. A. (1993). *Cognitive development* (3rd ed.). Upper Saddle River, NJ: Prentice Hall.

Flege, J. E., Munro, M. J., & MacKay, I. R. A. (1995). Effects of age of second-language learning on the production of English consonants. *Speech Communication, 16*(1), 1–26.

Fletcher, K. L., & Bray, N. W. (1996). External memory strategy use in preschool children. *Merrill-Palmer Quarterly, 42,* 379–396.

Fletcher-Flinn, C. M., & Gravatt, B. (1995). The efficacy of computer-assisted instruction (CAI): A meta-analysis. *Journal of Educational Computing Research, 12,* 219–242.

Flink, C., Boggiano, A. K., Main, D. S., Barrett, M., & Katz, P. A. (1992). Children's achievement-related behaviors: The role of extrinsic and intrinsic motivational orientations. In A. K. Boggiano & T. S. Pittman (Eds.), *Achievement and motivation: A social–developmental perspective.* Cambridge, England: Cambridge University Press.

Flood, W. A., Wilder, D. A., Flood, A. L., & Masuda, A. (2002). Peer-mediated reinforcement plus prompting as treatment for off-task behavior in children with attention deficit hyperactivity disorder. *Journal of Applied Behavior Analysis, 35,* 199–204.

Flower, L. S., & Hayes, J. R. (1981). A cognitive process theory of writing. *College Composition and Communication, 32,* 365–387.

Fodor, J. A., & Pylyshyn, Z. W. (1988). Connectionism and cognitive architecture: A critical analysis. *Cognition, 28,* 3–71.

Foley, M. A., Harris, J., & Herman, S. (1994). Developmental comparisons of the ability to discriminate between memories for symbolic play enactments. *Developmental Psychology, 30*, 206–217.

Fong, G. T., Krantz, D. H., & Nisbett, R. E. (1986). The effects of statistical training on thinking about everyday problems. *Cognitive Psychology, 18*, 253–292.

Foos, P. W., & Fisher, R. P. (1988). Using tests as learning opportunities. *Journal of Educational Psychology, 80*, 179–183.

Ford, D. Y. (1996). *Reversing underachievement among gifted black students.* New York: Teachers College Press.

Ford, M. E. (1992). *Motivating humans: Goals, emotions, and personal agency beliefs.* Newbury Park, CA: Sage.

Ford, M. E. (1996). Motivational opportunities and obstacles associated with social responsibility and caring behavior in school contexts. In J. Juvonen & K. R. Wentzel (Eds.), *Social motivation: Understanding children's school adjustment* (pp. 126–153). Cambridge, England: Cambridge University Press.

Ford, M. E., & Nichols, C. W. (1991). Using goal assessments to identify motivational patterns and facilitate behavioral regulation and achievement. In M. Maehr & P. R. Pintrich (Eds.), *Advances in motivation and achievement: Vol. 7. Goals and self-regulatory processes.* Greenwich, CT: JAI Press.

Forgas, J. P. (2000). The role of affect in social cognition. In J. Forgas (Ed.), *Feeling and thinking: The role of affect in social cognition* (pp. 1–28). New York: Cambridge University Press.

Försterling, F., & Morgenstern, M. (2002). Accuracy of self-assessment and task performance: Does it pay to know the truth? *Journal of Educational Psychology, 94*, 576–585.

Forsyth, J. P., & Eifert, G. H. (1998). Phobic anxiety and panic: An integrative behavioral account of their origin and treatment. In J. J. Plaud & G. H. Eifert (Eds.), *From behavior theory to behavior therapy* (pp. 38–67). Needham Heights, MA: Allyn & Bacon.

Fosnot, C. T. (1996). Constructivism: A psychological theory of learning. In C. T. Fosnot (Ed.), *Constructivism: Theory, perspectives, and practice.* New York: Teachers College Press.

Foster-Johnson, L., Ferro, J., & Dunlap, G. (1994). Preferred curriculum activities and reduced problem behaviors in students with intellectual disabilities. *Journal of Applied Behavior Analysis, 27*, 493–504.

Fowler, J. W., & Peterson, P. L. (1981). Increasing reading persistence and altering attributional style of learned helpless children. *Journal of Educational Psychology, 73*, 251–260.

Fowler, S. A., & Baer, D. M. (1981). "Do I have to be good all day?" The timing of delayed reinforcement as a factor in generaliza-

tion. *Journal of Applied Behavior Analysis, 14*, 13–24.

Fox, P. W., & LeCount, J. (1991, April). *When more is less: Faculty misestimation of student learning.* Paper presented at the annual meeting of the American Educational Research Association, Chicago.

Foxx, R. M., & Azrin, N. H. (1973). The elimination of autistic self-stimulatory behavior by overcorrection. *Journal of Applied Behavior Analysis, 6*, 1–14.

Foxx, R. M., & Bechtel, D. R. (1983). Overcorrection: A review and analysis. In S. Axelrod & J. Apsche (Eds.), *The effects of punishment on human behavior.* New York: Academic Press.

Foxx, R. M., & Shapiro, S. T. (1978). The timeout ribbon: A nonexclusionary timeout procedure. *Journal of Applied Behavior Analysis, 11*, 125–136.

Frankel, F., & Simmons, J. Q. (1985). Behavioral treatment approaches to pathological unsocialized physical aggression in young children. *Journal of Child Psychiatry, 26*, 525–551.

Franks, J. J., & Bransford, J. D. (1971). Abstraction of visual patterns. *Journal of Experimental Psychology, 90*, 65–74.

Frase, L. T. (1975). Prose processing. In G. H. Bower (Ed.), *The psychology of learning and motivation* (Vol. 9). New York: Academic Press.

Frederiksen, J. R., & Collins, A. (1989). A systems approach to educational testing. *Educational Researcher, 18*(9), 27–32.

Frederiksen, N. (1984a). Implications of cognitive theory for instruction in problemsolving. *Review of Educational Research, 54*, 363–407.

Frederiksen, N. (1984b). The real test bias: Influences of testing on teaching and learning. *American Psychologist, 39*, 193–202.

Frederiksen, N., & Ward, W. C. (1978). Measures for the study of creativity in scientific problem solving. *Applied Psychological Measurement, 2*, 1–24.

Freeland, J. T., & Noell, G. H. (1999). Maintaining accurate math responses in elementary school students: The effects of delayed intermittent reinforcement and programming common stimuli. *Journal of Applied Behavior Analysis, 32*, 211–215.

Freiburgs, V., & Tulving, E. (1961). The effect of practice on utilization of information from positive and negative instances in concept identification. *Canadian Journal of Psychology, 15*, 101–106.

French, E. G. (1955). Some characteristics of achievement motivation. *Journal of Experimental Psychology, 50*, 232–236.

French, E. G. (1956). Motivation as a variable in work partner selection. *Journal of Abnormal and Social Psychology, 53*, 96–99.

Freud, S. (1922). *Beyond the pleasure principle.* London: International Psychoanalytic Press.

Freud, S. (1949). Instincts and their vicissitudes. In *Collected papers of Sigmund Freud*

(Vol. 4). (J. Riviere, Trans.). London: Hogarth. (Original work published 1915)

Freud, S. (1957). Repression. In J. Strachey (Ed.), *The standard edition of the complete psychological works of Sigmund Freud* (Vol. 14). London: Hogarth Press. (Original work published 1915)

Friedrich, L. K., & Stein, A. H. (1973). Aggressive and pro-social television programs and the natural behavior of preschool children. *Society for Research in Child Development Monographs, 38* (Whole No. 151).

Friman, P. C., & Poling, A. (1995). Making life easier with effort: Basic findings and applied research on response effort. *Journal of Applied Behavior Analysis, 28*, 583–590.

Frith, U. (1978). From print to meaning and from print to sound, or how to read without knowing how to spell. *Visible Language, 12*, 43–54.

Frith, U. (1980). Unexpected spelling problems. In U. Frith (Ed.), *Cognitive processes in spelling.* London: Academic Press.

Fuchs, D., Fuchs, L. S., Mathes, P. G., & Simmons, D. C. (1997). Peer-assisted learning strategies: Making classrooms more responsive to diversity. *American Educational Research Journal, 34*, 174–206.

Fuchs, L. S., Fuchs, D., Hamlett, C. L., & Karns, K. (1998). High-achieving students' interactions and performance on complex mathematical tasks as a function of homogeneous and heterogeneous pairings. *American Educational Research Journal, 35*, 227–267.

Fuchs, L. S., Fuchs, D., Karns, K., Hamlett, C. L., Dutka, S., & Katzaroff, M. (1996). The relation between student ability and the quality and effectiveness of explanations. *American Educational Research Journal, 33*, 631–664.

Fuchs, L. S., Fuchs, D., Karns, K., Hamlett, C. L., Katzaroff, M., & Dutka, S. (1997). Effects of task-focused goals on low-achieving students with and without learning disabilities. *American Educational Research Journal, 34*, 513–543.

Fueyo, V., & Bushell, D., Jr. (1998). Using number line procedures and peer tutoring to improve the mathematics computation of low-performing first graders. *Journal of Applied Behavior Analysis, 31*, 417–430.

Fukkink, R. G., & de Glopper, K. (1998). Effects of instruction in deriving word meanings from context: A meta-analysis. *Review of Educational Research, 68*, 450–469.

Fuller, M. L. (2001). Multicultural concerns and classroom management. In Grant, C. A., & Gomez, M. L., *Campus and classroom: Making schooling multicultural* (2nd ed., pp. 109–134). Upper Saddle River, NJ: Merrill/Prentice Hall.

Furedy, J. J., & Riley, D. M. (1987). Human Pavlovian autonomic conditioning and the cognitive paradigm. In G. Davey (Ed.), *Cognitive processes and Pavlovian conditioning in humans.* Chichester, England: Wiley.

Furst, E. J. (1981). Bloom's taxonomy of educational objectives for the cognitive domain: Philosophical and educational issues. *Review of Educational Research, 51,* 441–453.

Fuson, K. C., & Willis, G. B. (1989). Second graders' use of schematic drawings in solving addition and subtraction word problems. *Journal of Educational Psychology, 81,* 514–520.

Gabriele, A. J., & Boody, R. M. (2001, April). *The influence of achievement goals on the constructive activity of low achievers during collaborative problem solving.* Paper presented at the annual meeting of the American Educational Research Association, Seattle, WA.

Gabriele, A. J., & Montecinos, C. (2001). Collaborating with a skilled peer: The influence of achievement goals and perceptions of partner's competence on the participation and learning of low-achieving students. *Journal of Experimental Education, 69,* 152–178.

Gabrieli, J. D. E., Keane, M. M., Zarella, M. M., & Poldrack, R. A. (1997). Preservation of implicit memory for new associations in global amnesia. *Psychological Science, 8,* 326–329.

Gagné, E. D. (1985). *The cognitive psychology of school learning.* Boston: Little, Brown.

Gagné, R. M. (1983). Some issues in the psychology of mathematics instruction. *Journal of Research in Mathematics Education, 14*(1), 7–18.

Gagné, R. M. (1985). *The conditions of learning and theory of instruction* (4th ed.). New York: Holt, Rinehart & Winston.

Gagné, R. M., & Driscoll, M. P. (1988). *Essentials of learning for instruction* (2nd ed.). Englewood Cliffs, NJ: Prentice Hall.

Gallimore, R., & Tharp, R. (1990). Teaching mind in society: Teaching, schooling, and literate discourse. In L. C. Moll (Ed.), *Vygotsky and education: Instructional implications and applications of sociohistorical psychology.* Cambridge, England: Cambridge University Press.

Gallini, J. (2000, April). *An investigatin of self-regulation developments in early adolescence: A comparison between non at-risk and at-risk students.* Paper presented at the annual meeting of the American Educational Research Association, New Orleans.

Gallistel, C. R., & Gibbon, J. (2001). Computational versus associative models of simple conditioning. *Current Directions in Psychological Science, 10,* 146–150.

Gambrell, L. B., & Bales, R. J. (1986). Mental imagery and the comprehension-monitoring performance of fourth- and fifth-grade poor readers. *Reading Research Quarterly, 21,* 454–464.

Garb, J. L., & Stunkard, A. J. (1974). Taste aversions in man. *American Journal of Psychiatry, 131,* 1204–1207.

Garcia, E. E. (1992). "Hispanic" children: Theoretical, empirical, and related policy issues. *Educational Psychology Review, 4,* 69–93.

Garcia, E. E. (1994). *Understanding and meeting the challenge of student cultural diversity.* Boston: Houghton Mifflin.

Garcia, J., & Koelling, R. A. (1966). The relation of cue to consequence in avoidance learning. *Psychonomic Science, 4,* 123–124.

Gardner, H. (2000). *The disciplined mind: Beyond facts and standardized tests, the K–12 education that every child deserves.* New York: Penguin Books.

Gardner, H., Torff, B., & Hatch, T. (1996). The age of innocence reconsidered: Preserving the best of the progressive traditions in psychology and education. In D. R. Olson & N. Torrance (Eds.), *The handbook of education and human development: New models of learning, teaching, and schooling.* Cambridge, MA: Blackwell.

Gardner, M. (1978). *Aha! Insight.* New York: Scientific American.

Garner, R. (1998). Epilogue: Choosing to learn or not-learn in school. *Educational Psychology Review, 10,* 227–237.

Garner, R., Alexander, P. A., Gillingham, M. G., Kulikowich, J. M., & Brown, R. (1991). Interest and learning from text. *American Educational Research Journal, 28,* 643–659.

Garner, R., Brown, R., Sanders, S., & Menke, D. J. (1992). "Seductive details" and learning from text. In K. A. Renninger, S. Hidi, & A. Krapp (Eds.), *The role of interest in learning and development.* Hillsdale, NJ: Erlbaum.

Garner, R., Gillingham, M. G., & White, C. S. (1989). Effects of "seductive details" on macroprocessing and microprocessing in adults and children. *Cognition and Instruction, 6,* 41–57.

Garnier, H. E., Stein, J. A., & Jacobs, J. K. (1997). The process of dropping out of high school: A 19-year perspective. *American Educational Research Journal, 34,* 395–419.

Garry, M., & Polaschek, D. L. L. (2000). Imagination and memory. *Current Directions in Psychological Science, 9,* 6–10.

Gaskill, P. J. (2001, April). *Differential effects of reinforcement feedback and attributional feedback on second-graders' self-efficacy.* Paper presented at the annual meeting of the American Educational Research Association, Seattle, WA.

Gasper, K. L. (1980). The student perspective. *Teaching Political Science, 7,* 470–471.

Gathercole, S. E., & Hitch, G. J. (1993). Developmental changes in short-term memory: A revised working memory perspective. In A. F. Collins, S. E. Gathercole, M. A. Conway, & P. E. Morris (Eds.), *Theories of memory.* Hove, England: Erlbaum.

Gaudry, E., & Bradshaw, G. D. (1971). The differential effect of anxiety on performance in progressive and terminal school examinations. In E. Gaudry & C. D. Spielberger (Eds.), *Anxiety and educational achievement.* Sydney, Australia: Wiley.

Gaudry, E., & Spielberger, C. D. (Eds.) (1971). *Anxiety and educational achievement.* Sydney, Australia: Wiley.

Gauntt, H. L. (1991, April). *The roles of prior knowledge of text structure and prior knowledge of content in the comprehension and recall of expository text.* Paper presented at the annual meeting of the American Educational Research Association, Chicago.

Gauvain, M. (2001). *The social context of cognitive development.* New York: Guilford Press.

Gayford, C. (1992). Patterns of group behavior in open-ended problem solving in science classes of 15-year-old students in England. *Internal Journal of Science Education, 14,* 41–49.

Gaynor, J., & Millham, J. (1976). Student performance and evaluation under variant teaching and testing methods in a large college course. *Journal of Educational Psychology, 68,* 312–317.

Geary, D. C. (1994). *Children's mathematical development: Research and practical applications.* Washington, DC: American Psychological Association.

Geary, D. C. (1998). What is the function of mind and brain? *Educational Psychology Review, 10,* 377–387.

Geckeler, A. S., Libby, M. E., Graff, R. B., & Ahearn, W. H. (2000). Effects of reinforcer choice measured in single-operant and concurrent-schedule procedures. *Journal of Applied Behavior Analysis, 33,* 347–351.

Gentner, D., & Gentner, D. R. (1983). Flowing waters or teeming crowds: Mental models of electricity. In D. Gentner & A. L. Stevens (Eds.), *Mental models.* Hillsdale, NJ: Erlbaum.

Gentry, M., Gable, R. K., & Rizza, M. G. (2002). Students' perceptions of classroom activities: Are there grade-level and gender differences? *Journal of Educational Psychology, 94,* 539–544.

Gerst, M. S. (1971). Symbolic coding processes in observational learning. *Journal of Personality and Social Psychology, 19,* 7–17.

Giaconia, R. M. (1988). Teacher questioning and wait-time (Doctoral dissertation, Stanford University, 1988). *Dissertation Abstracts International, 49,* 462A.

Gibson, E., & Rader, N. (1979). Attention: The perceiver as performer. In G. A. Hale & M. Lewis (Eds.), *Attention and cognitive development.* New York: Plenum Press.

Gick, M. L. (1986). Problem-solving strategies. *Educational Psychologist, 21,* 99–120.

Gick, M. L., & Holyoak, K. J. (1980). Analogical problem solving. *Cognitive Psychology, 12,* 306–355.

Gick, M. L., & Holyoak, K. J. (1987). The cognitive basis of knowledge transfer. In S. M. Cormier & J. D. Hagman (Eds.), *Transfer of learning: Contemporary research and applications.* San Diego: Academic Press.

Giedd, J. N., Blumenthal, J., Jeffries, N. O., Rajapakse, J. C., Vaituzis, A. C., Liu, H., Berry, Y. C., Tobin, M., Nelson, J., &

Castellanos, F. X. (1999a). Development of the human corpus callosum during childhood and adolescence: A longitudinal MRI study. *Progress in Neuro-Psychopharmacology and Biological Psychiatry, 23,* 571–588.

Giedd, J. N., Jeffries, N. O., Blumenthal, J., Castellanos, F. X., Vaituzis, A. C., Fernandez, T., Hamburger, S. D., Liu, H., Nelson, J., Bedwell, J., Tran, L., Lenane, M., Nicolson, R., & Rapoport, J. L. (1999b). Childhood-onset schizophrenia: Progressive brain changes during adolescence. *Biological Psychiatry, 46,* 892–898.

Gillies, R. M., & Ashman, A. D. (1998). Behavior and interactions of children in cooperative groups in lower and middle elementary grades. *Journal of Educational Psychology, 90,* 746–757.

Ginsburg-Block, M. D., & Fantuzzo, J. W. (1998). An evaluation of the relative effectiveness of NCTM standards-based interventions for low-achieving urban elementary students. *Journal of Educational Psychology, 90,* 560–569.

Girotto, V., & Light, P. (1993). The pragmatic bases of children's reasoning. In P. Light & G. Butterworth (Eds.), *Context and cognition: Ways of learning and knowing.* Hillsdale, NJ: Erlbaum.

Glanzer, M., & Cunitz, A. R. (1966). Two storage mechanisms in free recall. *Journal of Verbal Learning and Verbal Behavior, 5,* 351–360.

Glaser, R. (1979). Trends and research questions in psychological research on learning and schooling. *Educational Researcher, 8,* 6–13.

Glaser, R. (1987). Thoughts on expertise. In C. Schooler & W. Schaie (Eds.), *Cognitive functioning and social structure over the life course.* Norwood, NJ: Ablex.

Glass, A. L., & Holyoak, K. J. (1975). Alternative conceptions of semantic memory. *Cognition, 3,* 313–339.

Glass, A. L., Holyoak, K. J., & O'Dell, C. (1974). Production frequency and the verification of quantified statements. *Journal of Verbal Learning and Verbal Behavior, 13,* 237–254.

Glass, A. L., Holyoak, K. J., & Santa, J. L. (1979). *Cognition.* Reading, MA: Addison-Wesley.

Gleitman, H. (1985). Some trends in the study of cognition. In S. Koch & D. E. Leary (Eds.), *A century of psychology as science.* New York: McGraw-Hill.

Glenberg, A. (1976). Monotonic and nonmonotonic lag effects in paired-associate and recognition memory paradigms. *Journal of Verbal Learning and Verbal Behavior, 15,* 1–16.

Glover, J., & Gary, A. L. (1976). Procedures to increase some aspects of creativity. *Journal of Applied Behavior Analysis, 9,* 79–84.

Glucksberg, S. (1962). The influence of strength of drive on functional fixedness and perceptual recognition. *Journal of Experimental Psychology, 63,* 36–41.

Glucksberg, S., & Weisberg, R. W. (1966). Verbal behavior and problem solving: Some effects of labeling in a functional fixedness problem. *Journal of Experimental Psychology, 71,* 659–664.

Glueck, S., & Glueck, E. (1950). *Unraveling juvenile delinquency.* Cambridge, MA: Harvard University Press.

Glynn, S. M. (1991). Explaining science concepts: A teaching-with-analogies model. In S. M. Glynn, R. H. Yeany, & B. K. Britton (Eds.), *The psychology of learning science.* Hillsdale, NJ: Erlbaum.

Glynn, S. M., & Di Vesta, F. J. (1977). Outline and hierarchical organization as aids for study and retrieval. *Journal of Educational Psychology, 69,* 89–95.

Glynn, S. M., Yeany, R. H., & Britton, B. K. (1991). A constructive view of learning science. In S. M. Glynn, R. H. Yeany, & B. K. Britton (Eds.), *The psychology of learning science.* Hillsdale, NJ: Erlbaum.

Goddard, R. D. (2001). Collective efficacy: A neglected construct in the study of schools and student achievement. *Journal of Educational Psychology, 93,* 467–476.

Godden, D. R., & Baddeley, A. D. (1975). Context-dependent memory in two natural environments: On land and underwater. *British Journal of Psychology, 66,* 325–332.

Goetz, E. T., Schallert, D. L., Reynolds, R. E., & Radin, D. I. (1983). Reading in perspective: What real cops and pretend burglars look for in a story. *Journal of Educational Psychology, 75,* 500–510.

Goldenberg, C. (1992). The limits of expectations: A case for case knowledge about teacher expectancy effects. *American Educational Research Journal, 29,* 517–544.

Goldin-Meadow, S. (1997). When gestures and words speak differently. *Current Directions in Psychological Science, 6,* 138–143.

Goldin-Meadow, S. (2001). Giving the mind a hand: The role of gesture in cognitive change. In J. L. McClelland & R. S. Siegler (Eds.), *Mechanisms of cognitive development: Behavioral and neural perspectives* (pp. 5–31). Mahwah, NJ: Erlbaum.

Goldman-Rakic, P. S. (1986). Setting the stage: Neural development before birth. In S. L. Friedman, K. A. Klivington, & R. W. Peterson (Eds.), *The brain, cognition, and education.* Orlando: Academic Press.

Goldman-Rakic, P. S. (1992). Working memory and the mind. *Scientific American, 90,* 111–117.

Goldstein, N. E., Arnold, D. H., Rosenberg, J. L., Stowe, R. M., & Ortiz, C. (2001). Contagion of aggression in day care classrooms as a function of peer and teacher responses. *Journal of Educational Psychology, 93,* 708–719.

Good, T. L., & Brophy, J. E. (1986). *Educational psychology: A realistic approach.* New York: Longman.

Good, T. L., & Brophy, J. E. (1994). *Looking in classrooms* (6th ed.). New York: HarperCollins.

Good, T. L., McCaslin, M. M., & Reys, B. J. (1992). Investigating work groups to promote problem solving in mathematics. In J. Brophy (Ed.), *Advances in research on teaching: Vol. 3. Planning and managing learning tasks and activities.* Greenwich, CT: JAI Press.

Good, T. L., & Nichols. S. L. (2001). Expectancy effects in the classroom: A special focus on improving the reading performance of minority students in first-grade classrooms. *Educational Psychologist, 36,* 113–126.

Goodenow, C. (1993). Classroom belonging among early adolescent students: Relationships to motivation and achievement. *Journal of Early Adolescence, 13*(1), 21–43.

Goodman, C. S., & Tessier-Lavigne, M. (1997). Molecular mechanisms of axon guidance and target recognition. In W. M. Cowan, T. M. Jessell, & S. L. Zipursky (Eds.), *Molecular and cellular approaches to neural development* (pp. 108–137). New York: Oxford University Press.

Gootman, M. E. (1998). Effective in-house suspension. *Educational Leadership, 56*(1), 39–41.

Gopnik, M. (Ed.) (1997). *The inheritance and innateness of grammars.* New York: Oxford University Press.

Gorman, A. M. (1961). Recognition memory for nouns as a function of abstractness and frequency. *Journal of Experimental Psychology, 61,* 23–29.

Gottfried, A. E. (1990). Academic intrinsic motivation in young elementary school children. *Journal of Educational Psychology, 82,* 525–538.

Gottfried, A. E., Fleming, J. S., & Gottfried, A. W. (2001). Continuity of academic intrinsic motivation from childhood through late adolescence: A longitudinal study. *Journal of Educational Psychology, 93,* 3–13.

Gould, E., Beylin, A., Tanapat, P., Reeves, A., & Shors, T. J. (1999). Learning enhances adult neurogenesis in the hippocampal formation. *Nature Neuroscience, 2,* 260–265.

Grabe, M. (1986). Attentional processes in education. In G. D. Phye & T. Andre (Eds.), *Cognitive classroom learning: Understanding, thinking, and problem solving.* Orlando: Academic Press.

Graesser, A. C., & Bower, G. H. (Eds.) (1990). *Inferences and text comprehension. The psychology of learning and motivation: Advances in research and theory* (Vol. 25). Orlando: Academic Press.

Graesser, A. C., & Person, N. K. (1994). Question asking during tutoring. *American Educational Research Journal, 31,* 104–137.

Graf, P., & Masson, M. E. J. (Eds.) (1993). *Implicit memory: New directions in cognition, development, and neuropsychology.* Hillsdale, NJ: Erlbaum.

Graham, S. (1989). Motivation in Afro-Americans. In G. L. Berry & J. K. Asamen (Eds.), *Black students: Psychosocial issues and academic achievement.* Newbury Park, CA: Sage.

Graham, S. (1990). Communicating low ability in the classroom: Bad things good teachers sometimes do. In S. Graham & V. S. Folkes (Eds.), *Attribution theory: Applications to achievement, mental health, and interpersonal conflict.* Hillsdale, NJ: Erlbaum.

Graham, S. (1991). A review of attribution theory in achievement contexts. *Educational Psychology Review, 3,* 5–39.

Graham, S. (1994). Classroom motivation from an attributional perspective. In H. F. O'Neil, Jr., & M. Drillings (Eds.), *Motivation: Theory and research.* Hillsdale, NJ: Erlbaum.

Graham, S. (1997). Using attribution theory to understand social and academic motivation in African American youth. *Educational Psychologist, 32,* 21–34.

Graham, S., & Barker, G. (1990). The downside of help: An attributional–developmental analysis of helping behavior as a low ability cue. *Journal of Educational Psychology, 82,* 7–14.

Graham, S., & Golen, S. (1991). Motivational influences on cognition: Task involvement, ego involvement, and depth of information processing. *Journal of Educational Psychology, 83,* 187–194.

Graham, S., & Weiner, B. (1996). Theories and principles of motivation. In D. C. Berliner & R. C. Calfee (Eds.), *Handbook of educational psychology.* New York: Macmillan.

Granger, R. H., Jr., & Schlimmer, J. C. (1986). The computation of contingency in classical conditioning. In G. H. Bower (Ed.), *The psychology of learning and motivation: Advances in research and theory* (Vol. 20). Orlando: Academic Press.

Gray, J. A., & Wedderburn, A. A. I. (1960). Grouping strategies with simultaneous stimuli. *Quarterly Journal of Experimental Psychology, 12,* 180–184.

Gray, W. D., & Orasanu, J. M. (1987). Transfer of cognitive skills. In S. M. Cormier & J. D. Hagman (Eds.), *Transfer of learning: Contemporary research and applications.* San Diego: Academic Press.

Green, L., Fry, A. F., & Myerson, J. (1994). Discounting of delayed rewards: A lifespan comparison. *Psychological Science, 5,* 33–36.

Green, L., & Rachlin, H. (1977). Pigeon's preferences for stimulus information: Effects of amount of information. *Journal of the Experimental Analysis of Behavior, 27,* 255–263.

Greene, B. A. (1994, April). *Instruction to enhance comprehension of unfamiliar text: Should it focus on domain-specific or strategy knowledge?* Paper presented at the annual meeting of the American Educational Research Association, New Orleans.

Greene, B. A., & Royer, J. M. (1994). A developmental review of response time data that support a cognitive components model of reading. *Educational Psychology Review, 6,* 141–172.

Greene, R. L. (1986). Sources of recency effects in free recall. *Psychological Bulletin, 99,* 221–228.

Greene, S., & Ackerman, J. M. (1995). Expanding the constructivist metaphor: A rhetorical perspective on literacy research and practice. *Review of Educational Research, 65,* 383–420.

Greeno, J. G. (1973). The structure of memory and the process of solving problems. In R. L. Solso (Ed.), *Contemporary issues in cognitive psychology: The Loyola Symposium.* Washington, DC: Winston.

Greeno, J. G. (1991). A view of mathematical problem solving in school. In M. U. Smith (Ed.), *Toward a unified theory of problem solving: Views from the content domains.* Hillsdale, NJ: Erlbaum.

Greeno, J. G., Collins, A. M., & Resnick, L. B. (1996). Cognition and learning. In D. C. Berliner & R. C. Calfee (Eds.), *Handbook of educational psychology.* New York: Macmillan.

Greeno, J. G., Moore, J. L., & Smith, D. R. (1993). Transfer of situated learning. In D. K. Detterman & R. J. Sternberg (Eds.), *Transfer on trial: Intelligence, cognition, and instruction.* Norwood, NJ: Ablex.

Greenough, W. T., Black, J. E., & Wallace, C. S. (1987). Experience and brain development. *Child Development, 58,* 539–559.

Greenough, W. T., Juraska, J. M., & Volkmar, F. R. (1979). Maze training effects on dendritic branching in occipital cortex of adult rats. *Behavioral and Neural Biology, 26,* 287–297.

Greenspoon, J., & Ranyard, R. (1957). Stimulus conditions and retroactive inhibition. *Journal of Experimental Psychology, 53,* 55–59.

Greenwood, C. R., Carta, J. J., & Hall, R. V. (1988). The use of peer tutoring strategies in classroom management and educational instruction. *School Psychology Review, 17,* 258–275.

Greer, R. D. (1983). Contingencies of the science and technology of teaching and prebehavioristic research practices in education. *Educational Researcher, 12*(1), 3–9.

Gregg, M., & Leinhardt, G. (1994a, April). *Constructing geography.* Paper presented at the annual meeting of the American Educational Research Association, New Orleans.

Gregg, M., & Leinhardt, G. (1994b). Mapping out geography: An example of epistemology and education. *Review of Educational Research, 64,* 311–361.

Greiner, J. M., & Karoly, P. (1976). Effects of self-control training on study activity and academic performance: An analysis of self-monitoring, self-reward, and systematic planning components. *Journal of Counseling Psychology, 23,* 495–502.

Griffin, M. M., & Griffin, B. W. (1994, April). *Some can get there from here: Situated learning, cognitive style, and map skills.* Paper presented at the annual meeting of the American Educational Research Association, New Orleans.

Griffore, R. J. (1981). *Child development: An educational perspective.* Springfield, IL: Charles C. Thomas.

Grimes, J. W., & Allinsmith, W. (1961). Compulsivity, anxiety, and school achievement. *Merrill-Palmer Quarterly, 7,* 247–271.

Grimes, J. W., & Allinsmith, W. (1970). Compulsivity, anxiety, and school achievement. In P. H. Mussen, J. J. Conger, & J. Kagan (Eds.), *Readings in child development and personality.* New York: Harper & Row.

Grolnick, W. S., & Ryan, R. M. (1987). Autonomy in children's learning: An experimental and individual difference investigation. *Journal of Personality and Social Psychology, 52,* 890–898.

Groninger, L. D. (1971). Mnemonic imagery and forgetting. *Psychonomic Science, 23,* 161–163.

Gronlund, N. E. (2000). *How to write and use instructional objectives* (6th ed.). Upper Saddle River, NJ: Merrill/Prentice Hall.

Gross, T. F., & Mastenbrook, M. (1980). Examination of the effects of state anxiety on problem-solving efficiency under high and low memory conditions. *Journal of Educational Psychology, 72,* 605–609.

Grossman, P. L. (1990). *The making of a teacher: Teacher knowledge and teacher education.* New York: Teachers College Press.

Guevremont, D. C., Osnes, P. G., & Stokes, T. F. (1988). The functional role of preschoolers' verbalization in the generalization of self-instructional training. *Journal of Applied Behavior Analysis, 21,* 45–55.

Gulya, M., Rovee-Collier, C., Galluccio, L., & Wilk, A. (1998). Memory processing of a serial list by young infants. *Psychological Science, 9,* 303–307.

Gunnoe, M. L., & Mariner, C. L. (1997). Toward a developmental–contextual model of the effects of parental spanking on children's aggression. *Archives of Pediatrics and Adolescent Medicine, 151,* 768–775.

Gunstone, R. F. (1994). The importance of specific science content in the enhancement of metacognition. In P. J. Fensham, R. F. Gunstone, & R. T. White (Eds.), *The content of science: A constructivist approach to its teaching and learning.* London: Falmer Press.

Guskey, T. R. (1985). *Implementing mastery learning.* Belmont, CA: Wadsworth.

Guskey, T. R. (1994, April). *Outcome-based education and mastery learning: Clarifying the differences.* Paper presented at the annual meeting of the American Educational Research Association, New Orleans.

Gustafsson, J., & Undheim, J. O. (1996). Individual differences in cognitive functions. In D. C. Berliner & R. C. Calfee (Eds.), *Handbook of educational psychology.* New York: Macmillan.

Guthrie, E. R. (1935). *The psychology of learning.* New York: Harper & Row.

Guthrie, E. R. (1942). Conditioning: A theory of learning in terms of stimulus, response, and association. In *The psychology of learning, 41st yearbook of the National Society for the Study of Education, Part II*. Chicago: University of Chicago Press.

Guttentag, R. E. (1984). The mental effort requirement of cumulative rehearsal: A developmental study. *Journal of Experimental Child Psychology, 37*, 92–106.

Guzzetti, B. J., Snyder, T. E., Glass, G. V., & Gamas, W. S. (1993). Promoting conceptual change in science: A comparative meta-analysis of instructional interventions from reading education and science education. *Reading Research Quarterly, 28*, 117–159.

Haberlandt, K. (1997). *Cognitive psychology* (2nd ed.). Needham Heights, MA: Allyn & Bacon.

Hacker, D. J. (1998a). Definitions and empirical foundations. In D. J. Hacker, J. Dunlosky, & A. C. Graesser (Eds.), *Metacognition in educational theory and practice* (pp. 1–23). Mahwah, NJ: Erlbaum.

Hacker, D. J. (1998b). Self-regulated comprehension during normal reading. In D. J. Hacker, J. Dunlosky, & A. C. Graesser (Eds.), *Metacognition in educational theory and practice* (pp. 165–191). Mahwah, NJ: Erlbaum.

Hacker, D. J., Bol, L., Horgan, D. D., & Rakow, E. A. (2000). Test prediction and performance in a classroom context. *Journal of Educational Psychology, 92*, 160–170.

Hacker, D. J., Dunlosky, J., & Graesser, A. C. (Eds.).(1998). *Metacognition in educational theory and practice* (pp. 145–164). Mahwah, NJ: Erlbaum.

Haden, C. A., Ornstein, P. A., Eckerman, C. O., & Didow, S. M. (2001). Mother–child conversational interactions as events unfold: Linkages to subsequent remembering. *Child Development, 72*, 1016–1031.

Haenan, J. (1996). Piotr Gal'perin's criticism and extension of Lev Vygotsky's work. *Journal of Russian and East European Psychology, 34*(2), 54–60.

Hagen, A. S. (1994, April). *Achievement motivation processes and the role of classroom context*. Paper presented at the annual meeting of the American Educational Research Association, New Orleans.

Hagopian, L. P., Crockett, J. L., van Stone, M., DeLeon, I. G., & Bowman, L. G. (2000). Effects of noncontingent reinforcement on problem behavior and stimulus engagement: The role of satiation, extinction, and alternative reinforcement. *Journal of Applied Behavior Analysis, 33*, 433–449.

Haier, R. J. (2001). PET studies of learning and individual differences. In J. L. McClelland & R. S. Siegler (Eds.), *Mechanisms of cognitive development: Behavioral and neural perspectives* (pp. 123–145). Mahwah, NJ: Erlbaum.

Hale, G. A. (1983). Students' predictions of prose forgetting and the effects of study strategies. *Journal of Educational Psychology, 75*, 708–715.

Hale-Benson, J. E. (1986). *Black children: Their roots, culture, and learning styles*. Baltimore: Johns Hopkins University Press.

Halford, G. S. (1993). *Children's understanding: The development of mental models*. Hillsdale, NJ: Erlbaum.

Hall, J. F. (1966). *The psychology of learning*. Philadelphia: J. B. Lippincott.

Hall, J. F. (1971). *Verbal learning and retention*. Philadelphia: J. B. Lippincott.

Hall, N. C., Hladkyj, S., Ruthig, J. C., Pekrun, R. H., & Perry, R. P. (2002, April). *The role of action control in moderating primary versus secondary control strategy use in college students*. Paper presented at the annual meeting of the American Educational Research Association, New Orleans.

Hall, N. C., Hladkyj, S., Taylor, J. R., & Perry, R. P. (2000, April). *Primary and secondary control: Empirical links to academic motivation, achievement, and failure*. Paper presented at the annual meeting of the American Educational Research Association, New Orleans.

Hall, R. V., Axelrod, S., Foundopoulos, M., Shellman, J., Campbell, R. A., & Cranston, S. S. (1971). The effective use of punishment to modify behavior in the classroom. *Educational Technology, 11*(4), 24–26. (Reprinted in *Classroom management: The successful use of behavior modification*, by K. D. O'Leary & S. O'Leary, Eds., 1972, New York: Pergamon.)

Hall, R. V., Cristler, C., Cranston, S. S., & Tucker, B. (1970). Teachers and parents as researchers using multiple baseline designs. *Journal of Applied Behavior Analysis, 3*, 247–255.

Hall, V. C., & Edmondson, B. (1992). Relative importance of aptitude and prior domain knowledge on immediate and delayed posttests. *Journal of Educational Psychology, 84*, 219–223.

Hall, W. S. (1989). Reading comprehension. *American Psychologist, 44*, 157–161.

Hallahan, D. P., Marshall, K. J., & Lloyd, J. W. (1981). Self-recording during group instruction: Effects of attention to task. *Learning Disabilities Quarterly, 4*, 407–413.

Halldén, O. (1994). On the paradox of understanding history in an educational setting. In G. Leinhardt, I. L. Beck, & C. Stainton (Eds.), *Teaching and learning in history*. Hillsdale, NJ: Erlbaum.

Haller, E. P., Child, D. A., & Walberg, H. J. (1988). Can comprehension be taught? A quantitative synthesis of "metacognitive" studies. *Educational Researcher, 17*(9), 5–8.

Halpern, D. F. (1985). The influence of sex-role stereotypes on prose recall. *Sex Roles, 12*, 363–375.

Halpern, D. F. (1997). *Critical thinking across the curriculum: A brief edition of thought and knowledge*. Mahwah, NJ: Erlbaum.

Halpern, D. F. (1998). Teaching critical thinking for transfer across domains: Dispositions, skills, structure, training, and metacognitive monitoring. *American Psychologist, 53*, 449–455.

Halpin, G., & Halpin, G. (1982). Experimental investigations of the effects of study and testing on student learning, retention, and ratings of instruction. *Journal of Educational Psychology, 74*, 32–38.

Hamman, D., Berthelot, J., Saia, J., & Crowley, E. (2000). Teachers' coaching of learning and its relation to students' strategic learning. *Journal of Educational Psychology, 92*, 342–348.

Hamman, D., Shell, D. F., Droesch, D., Husman, J., Handwerk, M., Park, Y., & Oppenheim, N. (1995, April). *Middle school readers' on-line cognitive processes: Influence of subject-matter knowledge and interest during reading*. Paper presented at the annual meeting of the American Educational Research Association, San Francisco.

Hammer, D. (1994). Epistemological beliefs in introductory physics. *Cognition and Instruction, 12*, 151–183.

Hammer, D., & Elby, A. (2002). On the form of a personal epistemology. In B. K. Hofer & P. R. Pintrich (Eds.), *Personal epistemology: The psychology of beliefs about knowledge and knowing* (pp. 169–190). Mahwah, NJ: Erlbaum.

Hampton, J. A. (1981). An investigation of the nature of abstract concepts. *Memory and Cognition, 9*, 149–156.

Hansen, J., & Pearson, P. D. (1983). An instructional study: Improving the inferential comprehension of good and poor fourth-grade readers. *Journal of Educational Psychology, 75*, 821–829.

Harackiewicz, J. M., Barron, K. E., Pintrich, P. R., Elliot, A. J., & Thrash, T. M. (2002). Revision of achievement goal theory: Necessary and illuminating. *Journal of Educational Psychology, 94*, 638–645.

Harari, H., & McDavid, J. W. (1973). Name stereotypes and teachers' expectations. *Journal of Educational Psychology, 65*, 222–225.

Hareli, S., & Weiner, B. (2002). Social emotions and personality inferences: A scaffold for a new direction in the study of achievement motivation. *Educational Psychologist, 37*, 183–193.

Haring, N. G., & Liberty, K. A. (1990). Matching strategies with performance in facilitating generalization. *Focus on Exceptional Children, 22*(8), 1–16.

Haring, T. G., Roger, B., Lee, M., Breen, C., & Gaylord-Ross, R. (1986). Teaching social language to moderately handicapped students. *Journal of Applied Behavior Analysis, 19*, 159–171.

Harlow, H. F. (1949). The formation of learning sets. *Psychological Review, 56*, 51–65.

Harlow, H. F. (1950). Analysis of discrimination learning by monkeys. *Journal of Experimental Psychology, 40*, 26–39.

Harlow, H. F. (1959). Learning set and error factor theory. In S. Koch (Ed.), *Psychology: A study of science.* New York: McGraw-Hill.

Harlow, H. F., & Zimmerman, R. R. (1959). Affectional responses in the infant monkey. *Science, 130,* 421–432.

Harmon-Jones, E. (2001). The role of affect in cognitive-dissonance processes. In J. P. Forgas (Ed.), *Handbook of affect and social cognition* (pp. 237–255). Mahwah, NJ: Erlbaum.

Harnishfeger, K. K. (1995). The development of cognitive inhibition: Theories, definitions, and research evidence. In F. N. Dempster & C. J. Brainerd (Eds.), *Interference and inhibition in cognition.* San Diego: Academic Press.

Harp, S. F., & Mayer, R. E. (1998). How seductive details do their damage: A theory of cognitive interest in science learning. *Journal of Educational Psychology, 90,* 414–434.

Harris, K. R. (1986). Self-monitoring of attentional behavior versus self-monitoring of productivity: Effects of on-task behavior and academic response rate among learning disabled children. *Journal of Applied Behavior Analysis, 19,* 417–423.

Harris, K. R., & Alexander, P. A. (1998). Integrated, constructivist education: Challenge and reality. *Educational Psychology Review, 10,* 115–127.

Harris, M. (1985). Visualization and spelling competence. *Journal of Developmental Education, 9*(2), 2–5, 31.

Harris, M. (1992). *Language experience and early language development: From input to uptake.* Hove, England: Erlbaum.

Harris, M. J., & Rosenthal, R. (1985). Mediation of interpersonal expectancy effects: 31 meta-analyses. *Psychological Bulletin, 97,* 363–386.

Harris, R. J. (1977). Comprehension of pragmatic implications in advertising. *Journal of Applied Psychology, 62,* 603–608.

Harris, V. W., & Sherman, J. A. (1973). Use and analysis of the "Good Behavior Game" to reduce disruptive classroom behavior. *Journal of Applied Behavior Analysis, 6,* 405–417.

Harrow, A. J. (1972). *A taxonomy of the psychomotor domain: A guide for developing behavioral objectives.* New York: David McKay.

Hart, E. R., & Speece, D. L. (1998). Reciprocal teaching goes to college: Effects for postsecondary students at risk for academic failure. *Journal of Educational Psychology, 90,* 670–681.

Harter, S. (1978). Pleasure derived from optimal challenge and the effects of extrinsic rewards on children's difficulty level choices. *Child Development, 49,* 788–799.

Harter, S. (1981a). A model of mastery motivation in children: Individual differences and developmental change. In W. A. Collins (Ed.), *The Minnesota symposia on child psychology: Vol. 14. Aspects of the development of competence.* Hillsdale, NJ: Erlbaum.

Harter, S. (1981b). A new self-report scale of intrinsic versus extrinsic orientation in the classroom: Motivational and informational components. *Developmental Psychology, 17,* 300–312.

Harter, S. (1983). Developmental perspectives on the self-system. In E. M. Hetherington (Ed.), *Handbook of child psychology: Vol. 4. Socialization, personality, and social development.* New York: Wiley.

Harter, S. (1988). The construction and conservation of the self: James and Cooley revisited. In D. K. Lapsley & F. C. Power (Eds.), *Self, ego, and identity: Integrative approaches* (pp. 43–69). New York: Springer-Verlag.

Harter, S. (1990). Causes, correlates, and the functional role of global self-worth: A life-span perspective. In R. J. Sternberg & J. Kolligian, Jr. (Eds.), *Competence considered.* New Haven, CT: Yale University Press.

Harter, S. (1992). The relationship between perceived competence, affect, and motivational orientation within the classroom: Processes and patterns of change. In A. K. Boggiano & T. S. Pittman (Eds.), *Achievement and motivation: A social-developmental perspective.* Cambridge, England: Cambridge University Press.

Harter, S., Whitesell, N. R., & Kowalski, P. (1992). Individual differences in the effects of educational transitions on young adolescents' perceptions of competence and motivational orientation. *American Educational Research Journal, 29,* 777–807.

Hartley, J., Bartlett, S., & Branthwaite, A. (1980). Underlining can make a difference—sometimes. *Journal of Educational Research, 73,* 218–224.

Hartley, J., & Trueman, M. (1982). The effects of summaries on the recall of information from prose: Five experimental studies. *Human Learning, 1,* 63–82.

Hartley, K., & Bendixen, L. D. (2001). Educational research in the Internet age: Examining the role of individual characteristics. *Educational Researcher, 30*(9), 22–26.

Hartmann, W. K., Miller, R., & Lee, P. (1984). *Out of the cradle: Exploring the frontiers beyond earth.* New York: Workman.

Hartup, W. W. (1983). Peer relations. In P. H. Mussen (Series Ed.) & E. M. Hetherington (Vol. Ed.), *Handbook of child psychology: Vol. 4. Socialization, personality, and social development* (pp. 103–196). New York: Wiley.

Haseman, A. L. (1999, April). *Cross talk: How students' epistemological beliefs impact the learning process in a constructivist course.* Paper presented at the annual meeting of the American Educational Research Association, Montreal.

Hasher, L., & Zacks, R. T. (1984). Automatic processing of fundamental information. *American Psychologist, 39,* 1372–1388.

Hastings, W. M. (1977). In praise of regurgitation. *Intellect, 105,* 349–350.

Hatano, G., & Inagaki, K. (1991). Sharing cognition through collective comprehension activity. In L. B. Resnick, J. M. Levine, & S. D. Teasley (Eds.), *Perspectives on socially shared cognition.* Washington, DC: American Psychological Association.

Hatano, G., & Inagaki, K. (1993). Desituating cognition through the construction of conceptual knowledge. In P. Light & G. Butterworth (Eds.), *Context and cognition: Ways of learning and knowing.* Hillsdale, NJ: Erlbaum.

Hatano, G., & Inagaki, K. (1996). Cognitive and cultural factors in the acquisition of intuitive biology. In D. R. Olson & N. Torrance (Eds.), *The handbook of education and human development: New models of learning, teaching, and schooling.* Cambridge, MA: Blackwell.

Hatano, G., & Inagaki, K. (2003). When is conceptual change intended? A cognitive–sociocultural view. In G. M. Sinatra & P. R. Pintrich (Eds.), *Intentional conceptual change* (pp. 407–427). Mahwah, NJ: Erlbaum.

Hativa, N., & Shorer, D. (1989). Socioeconomic status, aptitude, and gender differences in CAI gains of arithmetic. *Journal of Educational Research, 83*(1), 11–21.

Hattie, J., Biggs, J., & Purdie, N. (1996). Effects of learning skills interventions on student learning: A meta-analysis. *Review of Educational Research, 66,* 99–136.

Hawk, P. P. (1986). Using graphic organizers to increase achievement in middle school life science. *Science Education, 70,* 81–87.

Hay, I., Ashman, A. F., van Kraayenoord, C. E., & Stewart, A. L. (1999). Identification of self-verification in the formation of children's academic self-concept. *Journal of Educational Psychology, 91,* 225–229.

Hayes, D. A., & Henk, W. A. (1986). Understanding and remembering complex prose augmented by analogic and pictorial illustration. *Journal of Reading Behavior, 18,* 63–78.

Hayes, J. R., & Simon, H. A. (1974). Understanding written problem instructions. In L. W. Gregg (Ed.), *Knowledge and cognition.* Hillsdale, NJ: Erlbaum.

Hayes, K. J., & Hayes, C. (1952). Imitation in a home-raised chimpanzee. *Journal of Comparative and Physiological Psychology, 45,* 450–459.

Hayes, S. C., Rosenfarb, I., Wulfert, E., Munt, E. D., Korn, Z., & Zettle, R. D. (1985). Self-reinforcement effects: An artifact of social standard setting? *Journal of Applied Behavior Analysis, 18,* 201–214.

Hayes-Roth, B., & Thorndyke, P. W. (1979). Integration of knowledge from text. *Journal of Verbal Learning and Verbal Behavior, 18,* 91–108.

Haygood, R. C., & Bourne, L. E., Jr. (1965). Attribute- and rule-learning aspects of conceptual behavior. *Psychological Review, 72,* 175–195.

Hebb, D. O. (1955). Drives and the c. n. s. (conceptual nervous system). *Psychological Review, 62*, 243–254.

Heck, A., Collins, J., & Peterson, L. (2001). Decreasing children's risk taking on the playground. *Journal of Applied Behavior Analysis, 34*, 349–352.

Hegarty, M., & Kozhevnikov, M. (1999). Types of visual–spatial representations and mathematical problem solving. *Journal of Educational Psychology, 91*, 684–689.

Heil, M., Rösler, F., & Henninghausen, E. (1994). Dynamics of activation in long-term memory: The retrieval of verbal, pictorial, spatial, and color information. *Journal of Experimental Psychology: Learning, Memory, and Cognition, 20*, 169–184.

Heindel, P., & Kose, G. (1990). The effects of motoric action and organization on children's memory. *Journal of Experimental Child Psychology, 50*, 416–428.

Heins, E. D., Lloyd, J. W., & Hallahan, D. P. (1986). Cued and noncued self-recording of attention to task. *Behavior Modification, 10*, 235–254.

Heit, E. (1993). Modeling the effects of expectations on recognition memory. *Psychological Science, 4*, 244–251.

Heller, J. I., & Hungate, H. N. (1985). Implications for mathematics instruction of research on scientific problem solving. In E. A. Silver (Ed.), *Teaching and learning mathematical problem solving: Multiple research perspectives*. Hillsdale, NJ: Erlbaum.

Helmke, A. (1989). Affective student characteristics and cognitive development: Problems, pitfalls, perspectives. *International Journal of Educational Research, 13*, 915–932.

Hembree, R. (1988). Correlates, causes, effects, and treatment of test anxiety. *Review of Educational Research, 58*, 47–77.

Hemphill, L., & Snow, C. (1996). Language and literacy development: Discontinuities and differences. In D. R. Olson & N. Torrance (Eds.), *The handbook of education and human development: New models of learning, teaching, and schooling*. Cambridge, MA: Blackwell.

Henle, M. (1985). Rediscovering Gestalt psychology. In S. Koch & D. E. Leary (Eds.), *A century of psychology as science*. New York: McGraw-Hill.

Hennessey, B. A. (1995). Social, environmental, and developmental issues and creativity. *Educational Psychology Review, 7*, 163–183.

Hennessey, B. A., & Amabile, T. M. (1987). *Creativity and learning*. Washington, DC: National Education Association.

Hennessey, M. G. (2003). Metacognitive aspects of students' reflective discourse: Implications for intentional conceptual change teaching and learning. In G. M. Sinatra & P. R. Pintrich (Eds.), *Intentional conceptual change* (pp. 103–132). Mahwah, NJ: Erlbaum.

Herbert, J. J., & Harsh, C. M. (1944). Observational learning by cats. *Journal of Comparative Psychology, 37*, 81–95.

Heron, W. (1957). The pathology of boredom. *Scientific American, 196*(1), 52–56.

Herrenkohl, L. R., & Guerra, M. R. (1998). Participant structures, scientific discourse, and student engagement in fourth grade. *Cognition and Instruction, 16*, 431–473.

Herrnstein, R. J. (1969). Method and theory in the study of avoidance. *Psychological Review, 76*, 49–69.

Herrnstein, R. J. (1977). The evolution of behaviorism. *American Psychologist, 32*, 593–603.

Herrnstein, R. J. (1990). Behavior, reinforcement and utility. *Psychological Science, 1*, 217–223.

Herrnstein, R. J., Nickerson, R. S., de Sánchez, M., & Swets, J. A. (1986). Teaching thinking skills. *American Psychologist, 41*, 1279–1289.

Hertel, P. T. (1994). Depression and memory: Are impairments remediable through attentional control? *Current Directions in Psychological Science, 3*, 190–193.

Hess, R. D., Chih-Mei, C., & McDevitt, T. M. (1987). Cultural variations in family beliefs about children's performance in mathematics: Comparisons among People's Republic of China, Chinese-American, and Caucasian-American families. *Journal of Educational Psychology, 79*, 179–188.

Hess, R. D., & McDevitt, T. M. (1984). Some cognitive consequences of maternal intervention techniques: A longitudinal study. *Child Development, 55*, 2017–2030.

Hess, R. D., & McDevitt, T. M. (1989). Family. In E. Barnouw (Ed.), *International encyclopedia of communications*. New York: Oxford University Press.

Hettena, C. M., & Ballif, B. L. (1981). Effects of mood on learning. *Journal of Educational Psychology, 73*, 505–508.

Heuer, F., & Reisberg, D. (1990). Vivid memories of emotional events: The accuracy of remembered minutiae. *Memory and Cognition, 18*, 496–506.

Heuer, F., & Reisberg, D. (1992). Emotion, arousal, and memory for detail. In S. Christianson (Ed.), *Handbook of emotion and memory*. Hillsdale, NJ: Erlbaum.

Hewitt, J., & Scardamalia, M. (1996, April). *Design principles for the support of distributed processes*. Paper presented at the annual meeting of the American Educational Research Association, New York.

Hewitt, J., & Scardamalia, M. (1998). Design principles for distributed knowledge building processes. *Educational Psychology Review, 10*, 75–96.

Hickey, D. T. (1997). Motivation and contemporary socio-constructivist instructional perspectives. *Educational Psychologist, 32*, 175–193.

Hicks, L. (1997). Academic motivation and peer relationships—how do they mix in an adolescent world? *Middle School Journal, 28*, 18–22.

Hidi, S. (1990). Interest and its contribution as a mental resource for learning. *Review of Educational Research, 60*, 549–571.

Hidi, S., & Anderson, V. (1992). Situational interest and its impact on reading and expository writing. In K. A. Renninger, S. Hidi, & A. Krapp (Eds.), *The role of interest in learning and development*. Hillsdale, NJ: Erlbaum.

Hidi, S., & Harackiewicz, J. M. (2000). Motivating the academically unmotivated: A critical issue for the 21st century. *Review of Educational Research, 70*, 151–179.

Hidi, S., & McLaren, J. (1990). The effect of topic and theme interestingness on the production of school expositions. In H. Mandl, E. De Corte, N. Bennett, & H. F. Friedrich (Eds.), *Learning and instruction in an international context*. Oxford, England: Pergamon.

Hidi, S., Weiss, J., Berndorff, D., & Nolan, J. (1998). The role of gender, instruction, and a cooperative learning technique in science education across formal and informal settings. In L. Hoffman, A. Krapp, K. Renninger, & J. Baumert (Eds.), *Interest and learning: Proceedings of the Seeon Conference on interest and gender* (pp. 215–227). Kiel, Germany: IPN.

Hiebert, E. H., & Fisher, C. W. (1992). The tasks of school literacy: Trends and issues. In J. Brophy (Ed.), *Advances in research on teaching: Vol. 3. Planning and managing learning tasks and activities*. Greenwich, CT: JAI Press.

Hiebert, E. H., & Raphael, T. E. (1996). Psychological perspectives on literacy and extensions to educational practice. In D. C. Berliner & R. C. Calfee (Eds.), *Handbook of educational psychology*. New York: Macmillan.

Hiebert, J., Carpenter, T. P., Fennema, E., Fuson, K., Human, P., Murray, H., Olivier, A., & Wearne, D. (1996). Problem solving as a basis for reform in curriculum and instruction: The case of mathematics. *Educational Researcher, 25*(4), 12–21.

Hiebert, J., Carpenter, T. P., Fennema, E., Fuson, K. C., Wearne, D., Murray, H., Olivier, A., & Human, P. (1997). *Making sense: Teaching and learning mathematics with understanding*. Portsmouth, NH: Heinemann.

Hiebert, J., & Lefevre, P. (1986). Conceptual and procedural knowledge in mathematics: An introductory analysis. In J. Hiebert (Ed.), *Conceptual and procedural knowledge: The case of mathematics*. Hillsdale, NJ: Erlbaum.

Hiebert, J., & Wearne, D. (1992). Links between teaching and learning place value with understanding in first grade. *Journal for Research in Mathematics Education, 23*, 98–122.

Hiebert, J., & Wearne, D. (1993). Instructional tasks, classroom discourse, and students' learning in second-grade arithmetic. *American Educational Research Journal, 30*, 393–425.

Hiebert, J., & Wearne, D. (1996). Instruction, understanding, and skill in multidigit addition and subtraction. *Cognition and Instruction, 14*, 251–283.

Higbee, K. L. (1976). Can young children use mnemonics? *Psychological Reports, 38*, 18.

Hill, C. A. (1987). Affiliation motivation: People who need people . . . but in different ways. *Journal of Personality and Social Psychology, 52*, 1008–1018.

Hill, K. T. (1984). Debilitating motivation and testing: A major educational problem, possible solutions, and policy applications. In R. Ames & C. Ames (Eds.), *Research on motivation in education: Vol. 1. Student motivation*. New York: Academic Press.

Hill, K. T., & Wigfield, A. (1984). Test anxiety: A major educational problem and what can be done about it. *Elementary School Journal, 85*, 105–126.

Hinkley, J. W., McInerney, D. M., & Marsh, H. W. (2001, April). *The multifaceted structure of school achievement motivation: A case for social goals.* Paper presented at the annual meeting of the American Educational Research Association, Seattle, WA.

Hinsley, D., Hayes, J. R., & Simon, H. A. (1977). From words to equations. In P. Carpenter & M. Just (Eds.), *Cognitive processes in comprehension*. Hillsdale, NJ: Erlbaum.

Hinton, B. L. (1968). Environmental frustration and creative problem solving. *Journal of Applied Psychology, 52*, 211–217.

Hinton, G. E., & Anderson, J. A. (1981). *Parallel models of associative memory*. Hillsdale, NJ: Erlbaum.

Hinton, G. E., McClelland, J. L., & Rumelhart, D. E. (1986). Distributed representations. In D. E. Rumelhart, J. L. McClelland, & the PDP Research Group (Eds.), *Parallel distributed processing: Vol. 1. Foundations*. Cambridge, MA: MIT Press.

Hiroto, D. S. (1974). Locus of control and learned helplessness. *Journal of Experimental Psychology, 102*, 187–193.

Hiroto, D. S., & Seligman, M. E. P. (1975). Generality of learned helplessness in man. *Journal of Personality and Social Psychology, 31*, 311–327.

Hirsch, E. D., Jr. (1996). *The schools we need and why we don't have them*. New York: Doubleday.

Hirschfeld, L. A., & Gelman, S. A. (Eds.). (1994). *Mapping the mind: Domain specificity in cognition and culture*. Cambridge, England: Cambridge University Press.

Hirsh-Pasek, K., & Golinkoff, R. M. (1996). *The origins of grammar: Evidence from early language comprehension*. Cambridge, MA: MIT Press.

Hirst, W., Spelke, E., Reaves, C., Caharack, G., & Neisser, U. (1980). Dividing attention without alternation or automaticity. *Journal of Experimental Psychology: General, 109*, 98–117.

Ho, D. Y. F. (1994). Cognitive socialization in Confucian heritage cultures. In P. M. Greenfield & R. R. Cocking (Eds.), *Cross-cultural roots of minority child development*. Hillsdale, NJ: Erlbaum.

Hobbs, T. R., & Holt, M. M. (1976). The effects of token reinforcement on the behavior of delinquents in cottage settings. *Journal of Applied Behavior Analysis, 9*, 189–198.

Hoch, H., McComas, J. J., Johnson, L., Faranda, N., & Guenther, S. L. (2002). The effects of magnitude and quality of reinforcement on choice responding during play activities. *Journal of Applied Behavior Analysis, 35*, 171–181.

Hockman, C. H., & Lipsitt, L. P. (1961). Delay-of-reward gradients in discrimination learning with children for two levels of difficulty. *Journal of Comparative and Physiological Psychology, 54*, 24–27.

Hofer, B. K. (2000). Dimensionality and disciplinary differences in personal epistemology. *Contemporary Educational Psychology, 25*, 378–405.

Hofer, B. K. (2002). Personal epistemology as a psychological and educational construct: An introduction. In B. K. Hofer & P. R. Pintrich (Eds.), *Personal epistemology: The psychology of beliefs about knowledge and knowing* (pp. 3–14). Mahwah, NJ: Erlbaum.

Hofer, B. K., & Pintrich, P. R. (1997). The development of epistemological theories: Beliefs about knowledge and knowing and their relation to learning. *Review of Educational Research, 67*, 88–140.

Hofer, B. K., & Pintrich, P. R. (Eds.). (2002). *Personal epistemology: The psychology of beliefs about knowledge and knowing*. Mahwah, NJ: Erlbaum.

Hoffman, M. L. (1975). Altruistic behavior and the parent–child relationship. *Journal of Personality and Social Psychology, 31*, 937–943.

Hoffman, M. L. (1984). Interaction of affect and cognition in empathy. In C. E. Izard, J. Kagan, & R. B. Zajonc (Eds.), *Emotions, cognition, and behavior*. Cambridge, England: Cambridge University Press.

Hoffman, M. L. (1991). Empathy, social cognition, and moral action. In W. M. Kurtines & J. L. Gewirtz (Eds.), *Moral behavior and development: Vol. 1. Theory*. Hillsdale, NJ: Erlbaum.

Hogan, D. M., & Tudge, J. R. H. (1999). Implications of Vygotsky's theory for peer learning. In A. M. O'Donnell & A. King (Eds.), *Cognitive perspectives on peer learning* (pp. 39–65). Mahwah, NJ: Erlbaum.

Hogan, K. (1997, March). *Relating students' personal frameworks for science learning to their cognition in collaborative contexts.* Paper presented at the annual meeting of the American Educational Research Association, Chicago.

Hogan, K., Nastasi, B. K., & Pressley, M. (2000). Discourse patterns and collaborative scientific reasoning in peer and teacher-guided discussions. *Cognition and Instruction, 17*, 379–432.

Hokanson, J. E., & Burgess, M. (1962). The effects of three types of aggression on vascular processes. *Journal of Abnormal and Social Psychology, 64*, 446–449.

Holley, C. D., & Dansereau, D. F. (1984). *Spatial learning strategies: Techniques, applications, and related issues*. Orlando: Academic Press.

Holliday, B. G. (1985). Towards a model of teacher–child transactional processes affecting black children's academic achievement. In M. B. Spencer, G. K. Brookins, & W. R. Allen (Eds.), *Beginnings: The social and affective development of black children*. Hillsdale, NJ: Erlbaum.

Hollis, K. L. (1997). Contemporary research on Pavlovian conditioning: A "new" functional analysis. *American Psychologist, 52*, 956–965.

Hollon, R. E., Roth, K. J., & Anderson, C. W. (1991). Science teachers' conceptions of teaching and learning. In J. Brophy (Ed.), *Advances in research on teaching: Vol. 2. Teachers' knowledge of subject matter as it relates to their teaching practice*. Greenwich, CT: JAI Press.

Holmes, D. S. (1974). Investigation of repression: Differential recall of material experimentally or naturally associated with ego threat. *Psychological Bulletin, 81*, 632–653.

Holmes, D. S. (1990). The evidence for suppression: An examination of sixty years of research. In J. Singer (Ed.), *Repression and dissociation: Implications for personality theory, psychopathology, and health*. Chicago: University of Chicago Press.

Holt-Reynolds, D. (1992). Personal history-based beliefs as relevant prior knowledge in course work. *American Educational Research Journal, 29*, 325–349.

Holyoak, K. J. (1985). The pragmatics of analogical transfer. In G. H. Bower (Ed.), *The psychology of learning and motivation: Advances in research and theory* (Vol. 19). Orlando: Academic Press.

Holyoak, K. J. (1987). Review of parallel distributed processing. *Science, 236*, 992.

Holyoak, K. J., & Koh, K. (1987). Surface and structural similarity in analogical transfer. *Memory and Cognition, 15*, 332–340.

Holyoak, K. J., & Thagard, P. (1995). *Mental leaps*. Cambridge, MA: MIT Press.

Holz, W. C., & Azrin, N. H. (1962). Recovery during punishment by intense noise. *Psychological Reports, 11*, 655–657.

Hom, A., & Battistich, V. (1995, April). *Students' sense of school community as a factor in reducing drug use and delinquency.* Paper presented at the annual meeting of the American Educational Research Association, San Francisco.

Homme, L. E., Csanyi, A. P., Gonzales, M. A., & Rechs, J. R. (1970). *How to use contingency contracting in the classroom*. Champaign, IL: Research Press.

Homme, L. E., deBaca, P. C., Devine, J. V., Steinhorst, R., & Rickert, E. J. (1963). Use of the Premack principle in controlling the behavior of nursery school children. *Journal of the Experimental Analysis of Behavior, 6*, 544.

Hong, Y., Chiu, C., & Dweck, C. S. (1995). Implicit theories of intelligence: Reconsidering the role of confidence in achievement motivation. In M. H. Kernis (Ed.), *Efficacy, agency, and self-esteem*. New York: Plenum Press.

Hopkins, R. H., & Atkinson, R. C. (1968). Priming and the retrieval of names from long-term memory. *Psychonomic Science, 11*, 219–220.

Horgan, D. (1990, April). *Students' predictions of test grades: Calibration and metacognition*. Paper presented at the annual meeting of the American Educational Research Association, Boston.

Horstmann, G. (2002). Evidence for attentional capture by a surprising color singleton in visual search. *Psychological Science, 13*, 499–505.

Hovland, C. I., & Weiss, W. (1953). Transmission of information concerning concepts through positive and negative instances. *Journal of Experimental Psychology, 43*, 175–182.

Howard, D. V. (1983). *Cognitive psychology: Memory, language, and thought*. New York: Macmillan.

Howe, C., Tolmie, A., Greer, K., & Mackenzie, M. (1995). Peer collaboration and conceptual growth in physics: Task influences on children's understanding of heating and cooling. *Cognition and Instruction, 13*, 483–503.

Howe, M. J. A. (1970). Using students' notes to examine the role of the individual learner in acquiring meaningful subject matter. *Journal of Educational Research, 64*, 61–63.

Howe, M. L., & O'Sullivan, J. T. (1990). The development of strategic memory: Coordinating knowledge, metamemory, and resources. In D. F. Bjorklund (Ed.), *Children's strategies: Contemporary views of cognitive development*. Hillsdale, NJ: Erlbaum.

Howie, J. D. (2002, April). *Effects of audience, gender, and achievement level on adolescent students' communicated attributions and affect in response to academic success and failure*. Paper presented at the annual meeting of the American Educational Research Association, New Orleans.

Hubel, D. H., & Wiesel, T. N. (1970). The period of susceptibility to the physiological effects of unilateral eye closure in kittens. *Journal of Physiology, 206*, 419–436.

Hubel, D. H., Wiesel, T. N., & Levay, S. (1977). Plasticity of ocular dominance columns in monkey striate cortex, *Philosophical Transactions of the Royal Society of London, B 278*, 307–409.

Hudson, T. (1983). Correspondences and numerical differences between disjoint sets. *Child Development, 54*, 84–90.

Hudspeth, W. J. (1985). Developmental neuropsychology: Functional implications of quantitative EEG maturation [Abstract]. *Journal of Clinical and Experimental Neuropsychology, 7*, 606.

Huff, J. A. (1988). Personalized behavior modification: An in-school suspension

program that teaches students how to change. *School Counselor, 35*, 210–214.

Hughes, J. N. (1988). *Cognitive behavior therapy with children in schools*. New York: Pergamon.

Hull, C. L. (1920). Quantitative aspects of the evolution of concepts: An experimental study. *Psychological Monographs, 28* (Whole No. 123).

Hull, C. L. (1934). The concept of the habit-family hierarchy and maze learning. *Psychological Review, 41*, 33–54.

Hull, C. L. (1937). Mind, mechanism, and adaptive behavior. *Psychological Review, 44*, 1–32.

Hull, C. L. (1938). The goal-gradient hypothesis applied to some "field-force" problems in the behavior of young children. *Psychological Review, 45*, 271–299.

Hull, C. L. (1943). *Principles of behavior: An introduction to behavior theory*. New York: Appleton-Century-Crofts.

Hull, C. L. (1951). *Essentials of behavior*. New Haven, CT: Yale University Press.

Hull, C. L. (1952). *A behavior system: An introduction to behavior theory concerning the individual organism*. New Haven, CT: Yale University Press.

Hulse, S. H. (1993). The present status of animal cognition: An introduction. *Psychological Science, 4*, 154–155.

Humphreys, L. G. (1939). Acquisition and extinction of verbal expectations in a situation analogous to conditioning. *Journal of Experimental Psychology, 25*, 294–301.

Hundert, J. (1976). The effectiveness of reinforcement, response cost, and mixed programs on classroom behaviors. *Journal of Applied Behavior Analysis, 9*, 107.

Hunt, E. (1997). Nature vs. nurture: The feeling of *vujà dé*. In R. J. Sternberg & E. L. Grigorenko (Eds.), *Intelligence, heredity, and environment* (pp. 531–551). Cambridge, England: Cambridge University Press.

Hunter, M. (1982). *Mastery teaching*. El Segundo, CA: TIP Publications.

Husman, J., & Freeman, B. (1999, April). *The effect of perceptions of instrumentality on intrinsic motivation*. Paper presented at the annual meeting of the American Educational Research Association, Montreal.

Huston, A. C. (1983). Sex-typing. In E. M. Hetherington (Ed.), *Handbook of child psychology: Vol. 4. Socialization, personality, and social development* (4th ed.). New York: Wiley.

Huston, A. C., Watkins, B. A., & Kunkel, D. (1989). Public policy and children's television. *American Psychologist, 44*, 424–433.

Huttenlocher, J. (1968). Constructing spatial images: A strategy in reasoning. *Psychological Review, 75*, 550–560.

Huttenlocher, P. R. (1979). Synaptic density in human frontal cortex—developmental changes and effects of aging. *Brain Research, 163*, 195–205.

Huttenlocher, P. R. (1990). Morphometric study of human cerebral cortex development. *Neuropsychologia, 28*, 517–527.

Huttenlocher, P. R. (1993). Morphometric study of human cerebral cortex development. In M. H. Johnson (Ed.), *Brain development and cognition: A reader*. Cambridge, MA: Blackwell.

Huttenlocher, P. R., & Dabholkar, A. S. (1997). Regional differences in synaptogenesis in human cerebral cortex. *Journal of Comparative Neurology, 387*, 167–178.

Hyde, T. S., & Jenkins, J. J. (1969). Differential effects of incidental tasks on the organization of recall of a list of highly associated words. *Journal of Experimental Psychology, 82*, 472–481.

Hymel, S., Comfort, C., Schonert-Reichl, K., & McDougall, P. (1996). Academic failure and school dropout: The influence of peers. In J. Juvonen & K. R. Wentzel (Eds.), *Social motivation: Understanding children's school adjustment* (pp. 313–345). Cambridge, England: Cambridge University Press.

Hynd, C. (1998). Observing learning from different perspectives: What does it mean for Barry and his understanding of gravity?. In B. Guzzetti & C. Hynd (Eds.), *Perspectives on conceptual change: Multiple ways to understand knowing and learning in a complex world* (pp. 235–244). Mahwah, NJ: Erlbaum.

Hynd, C. (2003). Conceptual change in response to persuasive messages. In G. M. Sinatra & P. R. Pintrich (Eds.), *Intentional conceptual change* (pp. 291–315). Mahwah, NJ: Erlbaum.

Ickes, W. J., & Layden, M. A. (1978). Attributional styles. In J. Harvey, W. Ickes, & R. Kidd (Eds.), *New directions in attributional research* (Vol. 2). Hillsdale, NJ: Erlbaum.

Igoe, A. R., & Sullivan, H. (1991, April). *Gender and grade-level differences in student attributes related to school learning and motivation*. Paper presented at the annual meeting of the American Educational Research Association, Chicago.

Inglehart, M., Brown, D. R., & Vida, M. (1994). Competition, achievement, and gender: A stress theoretical analysis. In P. R. Pintrich, D. R. Brown, & C. E. Weinstein (Eds.), *Student motivation, cognition, and learning: Essays in honor of Wilbert J. McKeachie*. Hillsdale, NJ: Erlbaum.

Inglis, A., & Biemiller, A. (1997, March). *Fostering self-direction in mathematics: A cross-age tutoring program that enhances math problem solving*. Paper presented at the annual meeting of the American Educational Research Association, Chicago.

Inhelder, B., & Piaget, J. (1958). *The growth of logical thinking from childhood to adolescence* (A. Parsons & S. Milgram, Trans.). New York: Basic Books.

Intons-Peterson, M. J. (1992). Components of auditory imagery. In D. Reisberg (Ed.), *Auditory imagery*. Hillsdale, NJ: Erlbaum.

Intons-Peterson, M. J., Russell, W., & Dressel, S. (1992). The role of pitch in auditory imagery. *Journal of Experimental Psychology: Human Perception and Performance*, *18*, 233–240.

Irwin, D. E. (1996). Integrating information across saccadic eye movements. *Current Directions in Psychological Science*, *5*, 94–100.

Isaacson, R. L. (1964). Relation between achievement, test anxiety, and curricular choices. *Journal of Abnormal and Social Psychology*, *68*, 447–452.

Isen, A., Daubman, K. A., & Gorgoglione, J. M. (1987). The influence of positive affect on cognitive organization: Implications for education. In R. E. Snow & M. J. Farr (Eds.), *Aptitude, learning and instruction* (Vol. 3). Hillsdale, NJ: Erlbaum.

Ito, T. A., & Cacioppo, J. T. (2001). Affect and attitudes: A social neuroscience approach. In J. P. Forgas (Ed.), *Handbook of affect and social cognition* (pp. 50–74). Mahwah, NJ: Erlbaum.

Iwata, B. A. (1987). Negative reinforcement in applied behavior analysis: An emerging technology. *Journal of Applied Behavior Analysis*, *20*, 361–378.

Iwata, B. A., & Bailey, J. S. (1974). Reward versus cost token systems: An analysis of the effects on students and teacher. *Journal of Applied Behavior Analysis*, *7*, 567–576.

Iwata, B. A., Dorsey, M. F., Slifer, K. J., Bauman, K. E., & Richman, G. S. (1994). Toward a functional analysis of self-injury. *Journal of Applied Behavior Analysis*, *27*, 197–209. (Reprinted from *Analysis and Intervention in Developmental Disabilities*, *2*, 3–20, 1982)

Iwata, B. A., Pace, G. M., Cowdery, G. E., & Miltenberger, R. G. (1994). What makes extinction work: An analysis of procedural form and function. *Journal of Applied Behavior Analysis*, *27*, 131–144.

Jackson, D. L., Ormrod, J. E., & Salih, D. J. (1996, April). *The nature of students' metacognitive processes, as reflected in their self-generated questions and class notes.* Paper presented at the annual meeting of the American Educational Research Association, New York.

Jackson, D. L., Ormrod, J. E., & Salih, D. J. (1999, April). *Promoting students' achievement by teaching them to generate higher-order self-questions.* Paper presented at the annual meeting of the American Educational Research Association, Montreal.

Jacobs, J. E., & Eccles, J. S. (1992). The influence of parent stereotypes on parent and child ability beliefs in three domains. *Journal of Personality and Social Psychology*, *63*, 932–944.

Jacobsen, B., Lowery, B., & DuCette, J. (1986). Attributions of learning disabled children. *Journal of Educational Psychology*, *78*, 59–64.

Jacobsen, L. K., Giedd, J. N., Berquin, P. C., Krain, A. L., Hamburger, S. D., Kumra, S., & Rapoport, J. L. (1997a). Quantitative morphology of the cerebellum and fourth ventricle in childhood-onset schizophre-

nia. *American Journal of Psychiatry*, *154*, 1663–1669.

Jacobsen, L. K., Giedd, J. N., Castellanos, F. X., Vaituzis, A. C., Hamburger, S. D., Kumra, S., Lenane, M. C., & Rapoport, J. L. (1997b). Progressive reduction of temporal lobe structures in childhood-onset schizophrenia. *American Journal of Psychiatry*, *155*, 678–685.

Jagacinski, C. M., & Nicholls, J. (1984). Conceptions of ability and related affects in task involvement and ego involvement. *Journal of Educational Psychology*, *76*, 909–919.

Jagacinski, C. M., & Nicholls, J. (1987). Competence and affect in task involvement and ego involvement: The impact of social comparison information. *Journal of Educational Psychology*, *79*, 107–114.

Jagacinski, C. M., & Nicholls, J. G. (1990). Reducing effort to protect perceived ability: "They'd do it but I wouldn't." *Journal of Educational Psychology*, *82*, 15–21.

James, W. (1890). *Principles of psychology*. New York: Holt.

Jenkins, J. J., & Russell, W. A. (1952). Associative clustering during recall. *Journal of Abnormal and Social Psychology*, *47*, 818–821.

Jenlink, C. L. (1994, April). *Music: A lifeline for the self-esteem of at-risk students.* Paper presented at the annual meeting of the American Educational Research Association, New Orleans.

Johnson, D. W., & Johnson, R. T. (1985a). Classroom conflict: Controversy versus debate in learning groups. *American Educational Research Journal*, *22*, 237–256.

Johnson, D. W., & Johnson, R. T. (1985b). Motivational processes in cooperative, competitive, and individualistic learning situations. In C. Ames & R. Ames (Eds.), *Research on motivation in education: Vol. 2. The classroom milieu.* Orlando, FL: Academic Press.

Johnson, D. W., & Johnson, R. T. (1987). *Learning together and alone: Cooperative, competitive, and individualistic learning* (2nd ed.). Englewood Cliffs, NJ: Prentice Hall.

Johnson, D. W., & Johnson, R. T. (1991). *Learning together and alone: Cooperative, competitive, and individualistic learning* (3rd ed.). Upper Saddle River, NJ: Prentice Hall.

Johnson, J. S., & Newport, E. L. (1989). Critical period effects in second language learning. *Cognitive Psychology*, *21*, 60–99.

Johnson, M. H., & de Haan, M. (2001). Developing cortical specialization for visual-cognitive function: The case of face recognition. In J. L. McClelland & R. S. Siegler (Eds.), *Mechanisms of cognitive development: Behavioral and neural perspectives* (pp. 253–270). Mahwah, NJ: Erlbaum.

Johnson, M. K., Bransford, J. D., & Solomon, S. K. (1973). Memory for tacit implications of sentences. *Journal of Experimental Psychology*, *98*, 203–205.

Johnson, R. N. (1972). *Aggression in man and animals*. Philadelphia: Saunders.

Johnson-Laird, P. N., & Wason, P. C. (1977). Introduction to conceptual thinking. In P. N. Johnson-Laird & P. C. Wason (Eds.), *Thinking: Readings in cognitive science*. Cambridge, England: Cambridge University Press.

John-Steiner, V. (1997). *Notebooks of the mind: Explorations of thinking* (Rev. ed.). New York: Oxford University Press.

John-Steiner, V., & Mahn, H. (1996). Sociocultural approaches to learning and development: A Vygotskian framework. *Educational Psychologist*, *31*, 191–206.

Johnston, J. C., McCann, R. S., & Remington, R. W. (1995). Chronometric evidence for two types of attention. *Psychological Science*, *6*, 365–369.

Johnstone, A. H., & El-Banna, H. (1986). Capacities, demands, and processes—a predictive model for science education. *Education in Chemistry*, *23*, 80–84.

Jonassen, D. H., Hartley, J., & Trueman, M. (1986). The effects of learner-generated versus text-provided headings on immediate and delayed recall and comprehension: An exploratory study. *Human Learning*, *5*, 139–150.

Jones, B. F., & Hall, J. W. (1982). School applications of the mnemonic keyword method as a study strategy by eighth graders. *Journal of Educational Psychology*, *74*, 230–237.

Jones, B. F., Pierce, J., & Hunter, B. (1988/1989). Teaching students to construct graphic representations. *Educational Leadership*, *46*(4), 20–25.

Jones, B. P. (1993). Repression: The evolution of a psychoanalytic concept from the 1890's to the 1990's. *Journal of the American Psychoanalytic Association*, *41*(1), 63–93.

Jones, E. E., & Berglas, S. (1978). Control of attributions about the self through self-handicapping strategies: The appeal of alcohol and the role of underachievement. *Personality and Social Psychology Bulletin*, *4*, 200–206.

Jones, H. E., & English, H. B. (1926). Notional vs. rote memory. *American Journal of Psychology*, *37*, 602–603.

Jones, K. M., Drew, H. A., & Weber, N. L. (2000). Noncontingent peer attention as treatment for disruptive classroom behavior. *Journal of Applied Behavior Analysis*, *33*, 343–346.

Jones, M. C. (1924). The elimination of children's fears. *Journal of Experimental Psychology*, *7*, 382–390.

Jones, M. S., Levin, M. E., Levin, J. R., & Beitzel, B. D. (2000). Can vocabulary-learning strategies and pair-learning formats be profitably combined? *Journal of Educational Psychology*, *92*, 256–262.

Judd, C. H. (1932). Autobiography. In C. Murchison (Ed.), *History of psychology in autobiography* (Vol. 2). Worcester, MA: Clark University Press.

Jussim, L., Eccles, J., & Madon, S. (1996). Social perception, social stereotypes, and teacher expectations: Accuracy and the quest for the powerful self-fulfilling prophecy. In L. Berkowitz (Ed.), *Advances in experimental social psychology*. New York: Academic Press.

Just, M. A., Carpenter, P. A., Keller, T. A., Emery, L., Zajac, H., & Thulborn, K. R. (2001). Interdependence of nonoverlapping cortical systems in dual cognitive tasks. *NeuroImage, 14,* 417–426.

Juvonen, J. (1991, April). *The effect of attributions and interpersonal attitudes on social emotions and behavior.* Paper presented at the annual meeting of the American Educational Research Association, Chicago.

Juvonen, J. (1996). Self-presentation tactics promoting teacher and peer approval: The function of excuses and other clever explanations. In J. Juvonen & K. R. Wentzel (Eds.), *Social motivation: Understanding children's school adjustment* (pp. 43–65). Cambridge, England: Cambridge University Press.

Juvonen, J. (2000). The social functions of attributional face-saving tactics among early adolescents. *Educational Psychology Review, 12,* 15–32.

Juvonen, J., & Weiner, B. (1993). An attributional analysis of students' interactions: The social consequences of perceived responsibility. *Educational Psychology Review, 5,* 325–345.

Kahl, B., & Woloshyn, V. E. (1994). Using elaborative interrogation to facilitate acquisition of factual information in cooperative learning settings: One good strategy deserves another. *Applied Cognitive Psychology, 8,* 465–478.

Kahneman, D. (1973). *Attention and effort.* Englewood Cliffs, NJ: Prentice Hall.

Kahneman, D., & Tversky, A. (1972). Subjective probability: A judgment of representativeness. *Cognitive Psychology, 3,* 430–454.

Kahneman, D., & Tversky, A. (1973). On the psychology of prediction. *Psychological Review, 80,* 237–251.

Kail, R. (1990). *The development of memory in children* (3rd ed.). New York: W. H. Freeman.

Kaiser, D. H., Zentall, T. R., & Galef, B. G., Jr. (1997). Can imitation in pigeons by explained by local enhancement together with trial-and-error learning? *Psychological Science, 8,* 459–460.

Kaiser, M. K., McCloskey, M., & Proffitt, D. R. (1986). Development of intuitive theories of motion: Curvilinear motion in the absence of external forces. *Developmental Psychology, 22,* 67–71.

Kamin, L. J. (1956). The effects of termination of the CS and avoidance of the US on avoidance learning. *Journal of Comparative and Physiological Psychology, 49,* 420–424.

Kamin, L. J., Brimer, C. J., & Black, A. H. (1963). Conditioned suppression as a monitor of fear of the CS in the course of avoidance training. *Journal of Comparative and Physiological Psychology, 56,* 497–501.

Kantor, J. R. (1959). *Interbehavioral psychology.* Granville, OH: Principia Press.

Kaplan, A. (1998, April). *Task goal orientation and adaptive social interaction among students of diverse cultural backgrounds.* Paper presented at the annual meeting of the American Educational Research Association, San Diego.

Kaplan, A., & Midgley, C. (1997). The effect of achievement goals: Does level of perceived academic competence make a difference? *Contemporary Educational Psychology, 22,* 415–435.

Kaplan, A., & Midgley, C. (1999). The relationship between perceptions of the classroom goal structure and early adolescents' affect in school: The mediating role of coping strategies. *Learning and Individual Differences, 11,* 187–212.

Karabenick, S. A., & Sharma, R. (1994). Seeking academic assistance as a strategic learning resource. In P. R. Pintrich, D. R. Brown, & C. E. Weinstein (Eds.), *Student motivation, cognition, and learning: Essays in honor of Wilbert J. McKeachie.* Hillsdale, NJ: Erlbaum.

Karau, S. J., & Williams, K. D. (1995). Social loafing: Research findings, implications, and future directions. *Current Directions in Psychological Science, 4,* 134–140.

Kardash, C. A. M., & Amlund, J. T. (1991). Self-reported learning strategies and learning from expository text. *Contemporary Educational Psychology, 16,* 117–138.

Kardash, C. A. M., & Howell, K. L. (2000). Effects of epistemological beliefs and topic-specific beliefs on undergraduates' cognitive and strategic processing of dual-positional text. *Journal of Educational Psychology, 92,* 524–535.

Kardash, C. A. M., Royer, J. M., & Greene, B. A. (1988). Effects of schemata on both encoding and retrieval of information from prose. *Journal of Educational Psychology, 80,* 324–329.

Kardash, C. A. M., & Scholes, R. J. (1996). Effects of pre-existing beliefs, epistemological beliefs, and need for cognition on interpretation of controversial issues. *Journal of Educational Psychology, 88,* 260–271.

Karpov, Y. V., & Haywood, H. C. (1998). Two ways to elaborate Vygotsky's concept of mediation: Implications for instruction. *American Psychologist, 53,* 27–36.

Katayama, A. D., & Robinson, D. H. (2000). Getting students "partially" involved in note-taking using graphic organizers. *Journal of Experimental Education, 68,* 119–133.

Katkovsky, W., Crandall, V. C., & Good, S. (1967). Parental antecedents of children's beliefs in internal–external control of reinforcements in intellectual achievement situations. *Child Development, 38,* 765–776.

Kauffman, S. (1995). *At home in the universe: The search for laws of self-organization and complexity.* New York: Oxford University Press.

Kaufman, A., Baron, A., & Kopp, R. E. (1966). Some effects of instructions on human operant behavior. *Psychonomic Monograph Supplements, 1,* 243–250.

Kazdin, A. E. (1972). Response cost: The removal of conditional reinforcers for therapeutic change. *Behavior Therapy, 3,* 533–546.

Keele, S. W. (1973). *Attention and human performance.* Pacific Palisades, CA: Goodyear.

Keil, F. C. (1986). The acquisition of natural kind and artifact terms. In W. Demopolous & A. Marras (Eds.), *Language learning and concept acquisition.* Norwood, NJ: Ablex.

Keil, F. C. (1987). Conceptual development and category structure. In U. Neisser (Ed.), *Concepts and conceptual development: Ecological and intellectual factors in categorization.* Cambridge, England: Cambridge University Press.

Keil, F. C. (1989). *Concepts, kinds, and cognitive development.* Cambridge, MA: MIT Press.

Keil, F. C. (1991). Theories, concepts, and the acquisition of word meaning. In S. A. Gelman & J. P. Byrnes (Eds.), *Perspectives on language and thought: Interrelations in development.* Cambridge, England: Cambridge University Press.

Keil, F. C. (1994). The birth and nurturance of concepts by domains: The origins of concepts of living things. In L. A. Hirschfeld & S. A. Gelman (Eds.), *Mapping the mind: Domain specificity in cognition and culture.* Cambridge, England: Cambridge University Press.

Keil, F. C., & Silberstein, C. S. (1996). Schooling and the acquisition of theoretical knowledge. In D. R. Olson & N. Torrance (Eds.), *The handbook of education and human development: New models of learning, teaching, and schooling.* Cambridge, MA: Blackwell Publishers.

Kelemen, D. (1999). Why are rocks pointy? Children's preference for teleological explanations of the natural world. *Developmental Psychology, 35,* 1440–1452.

Keller, F. S. (1968). Goodbye teacher. *Journal of Applied Behavior Analysis, 1,* 79–89.

Keller, F. S. (1974). An international venture in behavior modification. In F. S. Keller & E. Ribes-Inesta (Eds.), *Behavior modification: Applications to education.* New York: Academic Press.

Keller, J. M. (1987). Development and use of the ARCS model of instructional design. *Journal of Instructional Development, 10*(3), 2–10.

Kelley, M. L., & Carper, L. B. (1988). Home-based reinforcement procedures. In J. C. Witt, S. N. Elliott, & F. M. Gresham (Eds.), *Handbook of behavior therapy in education.* New York: Plenum Press.

Kelly, S. W., Burton, A. M., Kato, T., & Akamatsu, S. (2001). Incidental learning of real-world regularities. *Psychological Science, 12,* 86–89.

Kemler Nelson, D. G. (1990). When experimental findings conflict with everyday observations: Reflections on children's category learning. *Child Development, 61,* 606–610.

Kendler, H. H. (1985). Behaviorism and psychology: An uneasy alliance. In S. Koch & D. E. Leary (Eds.), *A century of psychology as science.* New York: McGraw-Hill.

Kendler, H. H., & Kendler, T. S. (1961). Effect of verbalization on reversal shifts in children. *Science, 134,* 1619–1620.

Kendler, H. H., & Kendler, T. S. (1962). Vertical and horizontal processes in problem solving. *Psychological Review, 69,* 1–16.

Kendler, T. S., & Kendler, H. H. (1959). Reversal and nonreversal shifts in kindergarten children. *Journal of Experimental Psychology, 58,* 56–60.

Keppel, G., & Underwood, B. J. (1962). Proactive inhibition in short-term retention of single items. *Journal of Verbal Learning and Verbal Behavior, 1,* 153–161.

Kermani, H., & Moallem, M. (1997, March). *Cross-age tutoring: Exploring features and processes of peer-mediated learning.* Paper presented at the annual meeting of the American Educational Research Association, Chicago.

Kernaghan, K., & Woloshyn, V. E. (1994, April). *Explicit versus implicit multiple strategy instruction: Monitoring grade one students' spelling performances.* Paper presented at the annual meeting of the American Educational Research Association, New Orleans.

Kiewra, K. A. (1985). Investigating notetaking and review: A depth of processing alternative. *Educational Psychologist, 20,* 23–32.

Kiewra, K. A. (1989). A review of note-taking: The encoding-storage paradigm and beyond. *Educational Psychology Review, 1,* 147–172.

Kiewra, K. A., DuBois, N. F., Christian, D., McShane, A., Meyerhoffer, M., & Roskelly, D. (1988, April). *Theoretical and practical aspects of taking, reviewing, and borrowing conventional, skeletal, or matrix lecture notes.* Paper presented at the annual meeting of the American Educational Research Association, New Orleans.

Killeen, P. R. (1991). Behavior's time. In G. H. Bower (Ed.), *The psychology of learning and motivation: Advances in research and theory* (Vol. 27). San Diego: Academic Press.

Killeen, P. R. (2001). The four causes of behavior. *Current Directions in Psychological Science, 10,* 136–140.

Kilpatrick, J. (1985). A retrospective account of the past 25 years of research on teaching mathematical problem solving. In E. A. Silver (Ed.), *Teaching and learning mathematical problem solving: Multiple research perspectives.* Hillsdale, NJ: Erlbaum.

Kim, D., Solomon, D., & Roberts, W. (1995, April). *Classroom practices that enhance students' sense of community.* Paper presented at the annual meeting of the American Educational Research Association, San Francisco.

Kimberg, D. Y., D'Esposito, M., & Farah, M. J. (1997). Cognitive functions in the prefrontal cortex—working memory and executive control. *Current Directions in Psychological Science, 6,* 185–192.

Kimble, G. A. (2000). Behaviorism and unity in psychology. *Current Directions in Psychological Science, 9,* 208–212.

King, A. (1991). Effects of training in strategic questioning on children's problem-solving performance. *Journal of Educational Psychology, 83,* 307–317.

King, A. (1992). Comparison of self-questioning, summarizing, and notetaking—review as strategies for learning from lectures. *American Educational Research Journal, 29,* 303–323.

King, A. (1994). Guiding knowledge construction in the classroom: Effects of teaching children how to question and how to explain. *American Educational Research Journal, 31,* 338–368.

King, A. (1997). ASK to THINK–TEL WHY ®©: A model of transactive peer tutoring for scaffolding higher level complex learning. *Educational Psychologist, 32,* 221–235.

King, A. (1999). Discourse patterns for mediating peer learning. In A. M. O'Donnell & A. King (Eds.), *Cognitive perspectives on peer learning* (pp. 87–115). Mahwah, NJ: Erlbaum.

King, A., Staffieri, A., & Adelgais, A. (1998). Mutual peer tutoring: Effects of structuring tutorial interaction to scaffold peer learning. *Journal of Educational Psychology, 90,* 134–152.

King, N. J., & Ollendick, T. H. (1989). Children's anxiety and phobic disorders in school settings: Classification, assessment, and intervention issues. *Review of Educational Research, 59,* 431–470.

King, P. M., & Kitchener, K. S. (1994). *Developing reflective judgment: Understanding and promoting intellectual growth and critical thinking in adolescents and adults.* San Francisco: Jossey-Bass.

King, P. M., & Kitchener, K. S. (2002). The reflective judgment model: Twenty years of research on epistemic cognition. In B. K. Hofer & P. R. Pintrich (Eds.), *Personal epistemology: The psychology of beliefs about knowledge and knowing* (pp. 37–61). Mahwah, NJ: Erlbaum.

Kinnick, V. (1990). The effect of concept teaching in preparing nursing students for clinical practice. *Journal of Nursing Education, 29,* 362–366.

Kintsch, W. (1977). Reading comprehension as a function of text structure. In A. S. Reber & D. L. Scarborough (Eds.), *Toward a psychology of reading.* New York: Wiley.

Kintsch, W. (1980). Learning from text, levels of comprehension, or: Why anyone would read a story anyway. *Poetics, 9,* 87–98.

Kintsch, W. (1998). *Comprehension: A paradigm for cognition.* Cambridge, England: Cambridge University Press.

Kintsch, W., Mandel, T. S., & Kozminsky, E. (1977). Summarizing scrambled stories. *Memory and Cognition, 5,* 547–552.

Kintsch, W., & van Dijk, T. A. (1978). Toward a model of text comprehension and production. *Psychological Review, 85,* 363–394.

Kirkland, M. C. (1971). The effect of tests on students and schools. *Review of Educational Research, 41,* 303–350.

Kitsantas, A., Zimmerman, B. J., & Cleary, T. (2000). The role of observation and emulation in the development of athletic self-regulation. *Journal of Educational Psychology, 92,* 811–817.

Kladopoulos, C. N., & McComas, J. J. (2001). The effects of form training on foul-shooting performance in members of a women's college basketball team. *Journal of Applied Behavior Analysis, 34,* 329–332.

Klatzky, R. L. (1975). *Human memory.* San Francisco: W. H. Freeman.

Klausmeier, H. J. (1990). Conceptualizing. In B. F. Jones & L. Idol (Eds.), *Dimensions of thinking and cognitive instruction.* Hillsdale, NJ: Erlbaum.

Kleim, J. A., Swain, R. A., Armstrong, K. A., Napper, R. M. A., Jones, T. A., & Greenough, W. T. (1998). Selective synaptic plasticity within the cerebellar cortex following complex motor skill learning. *Neurobiology of Learning and Memory, 69,* 274–289.

Klein, J. D. (1990, April). *The effect of interest, task performance, and reward contingencies on self-efficacy.* Paper presented at the annual meeting of the American Educational Research Association, Boston.

Klein, P. S. (1975). Effects of open vs. structured teacher–student interaction on creativity of children with different levels of anxiety. *Psychology in the Schools, 12,* 286–288.

Klein, S. B. (1987). *Learning: Principles and applications.* New York: McGraw-Hill.

Kleinsmith, L. J., & Kaplan, S. (1963). Paired associate learning as a function of arousal and interpolated interval. *Journal of Experimental Psychology, 65,* 190–193.

Kletzien, S. B. (1988, April). *Achieving and non-achieving high school readers' use of comprehension strategies for reading expository text.* Paper presented at the annual meeting of the American Educational Research Association, New Orleans.

Kline, K., & Flowers, J. (1998, April). *A comparison of fourth graders' proportional reasoning in reform and traditional classrooms.* Paper presented at the annual meeting of the American Educational Research Association, San Diego.

Klinger, E. (1975). Consequences of commitment to and disengagement from incentives. *Psychological Review, 82,* 1–25.

Klinger, E. (1977). *Meaning and void: Inner experience and the incentives in people's lives.* Minneapolis: University of Minnesota Press.

Kluger, A. N., & DeNisi, A. (1998). Feedback interventions: Toward the understanding of a double-edged sword. *Current Directions in Psychological Science, 7*, 67–72.

Knapp, M. S., & Woolverton, S. (1995). Social class and schooling. In J. A. Banks & C. A. M. Banks (Eds.), *Handbook of research on multicultural education*. New York: Macmillan.

Koestner, R., Ryan, R. M., Bernieri, F., & Holt, K. (1984). Setting limits on children's behavior: The differential effects of controlling vs. informational styles on intrinsic motivation and creativity. *Journal of Personality, 52*, 233–248.

Koffka, K. (1935). *Principles of Gestalt psychology*. New York: Harcourt, Brace.

Köhler, W. (1925). *The mentality of apes*. London: Routledge & Kegan Paul.

Köhler, W. (1929). *Gestalt psychology*. New York: Liveright.

Köhler, W. (1938). *The place of value in a world of facts*. New York: Liveright.

Köhler, W. (1940). *Dynamics in psychology*. New York: Liveright.

Köhler, W. (1947). *Gestalt psychology: An introduction to new concepts in modern psychology*. New York: Liveright.

Köhler, W. (1959). Gestalt psychology today. *American Psychologist, 14*, 727–734.

Köhler, W. (1969). *The task of Gestalt psychology*. Princeton, NJ: Princeton University Press.

Kolb, B., & Whishaw, I. Q. (1990). *Fundamentals of human neuropsychology* (3rd ed.). New York: Freeman.

Kolers, P. A. (1975). Specificity of operations in sentence recognition. *Cognitive Psychology, 1*, 283–306.

Kolodner, J. (1985). Memory for experience. In G. H. Bower (Ed.), *The psychology of learning and motivation: Advances in research and theory* (Vol. 19). Orlando: Academic Press.

Konopak, B. C., Martin, S. H., & Martin, M. A. (1990). Using a writing strategy to enhance sixth-grade students' comprehension of content material. *Journal of Reading Behavior, 22*, 19–37.

Koschmann, T., & LeBaron, C. (2002). Learner articulation as interactional achievement: Studying the conversation of gesture. *Cognition and Instruction, 20*, 249–282.

Kosslyn, S. M. (1985). Mental imagery ability. In R. J. Sternberg (Ed.), *Human abilities: An information-processing approach*. New York: W. H. Freeman.

Kosslyn, S. M. (1994). *Image and brain: The resolution of the imagery debate*. Cambridge, MA: MIT Press.

Kotovsky, K., & Fallside, D. (1989). Representation and transfer in problem solving. In D. Klahr & K. Kotovsky (Eds.), *Complex information processing: The impact of Herbert A. Simon*. Hillsdale, NJ: Erlbaum.

Krajcik, J. S. (1991). Developing students' understanding of chemical concepts. In S. M. Glynn, R. H. Yeany, & B. K. Britton (Eds.), *The psychology of learning science*. Hillsdale, NJ: Erlbaum.

Krampen, G. (1987). Differential effects of teacher comments. *Journal of Educational Psychology, 79*, 137–146.

Krapp, A., Hidi, S., & Renninger, K. A. (1992). Interest, learning, and development. In K. A. Renninger, S. Hidi, & A. Krapp (Eds.), *The role of interest in learning and development*. Hillsdale, NJ: Erlbaum.

Krathwohl, D. R. (1994). Reflections on the taxonomy: Its past, present, and future. In L. W. Anderson & L. A. Sosniak (Eds.), *Bloom's taxonomy: A forty-year perspective. Ninety-third yearbook of the National Society for the Study of Education, Part II*. Chicago: National Society for the Study of Education.

Krathwohl, D. R., Bloom, B. S., & Masia, B. B. (1964). *Taxonomy of educational objectives. Handbook II: Affective domain*. New York: David McKay.

Krauss, R. M. (1998). Why do we gesture when we speak? *Current Directions in Psychological Science, 7*, 54–60.

Kritch, K. M., & Bostrow, D. E. (1998). Degree of constructed-response interaction in computer-based programmed instruction. *Journal of Applied Behavior Analysis, 31*, 387–398.

Krueger, W. C. F. (1929). The effect of overlearning on retention. *Journal of Experimental Psychology, 12*, 71–78.

Krumboltz, J. D., & Krumboltz, H. B. (1972). *Changing children's behavior*. Englewood Cliffs, NJ: Prentice Hall.

Kuhara-Kojima, K., & Hatano, G. (1991). Contribution of content knowledge and learning ability to the learning of facts. *Journal of Educational Psychology, 83*, 253–263.

Kuhl, J. (1985). Volitional mediators of cognition–behavior consistency: Self-regulatory processes and actions versus state orientation. In J. Kuhl & J. Beckmann (Eds.), *Action control: From cognition to behavior*. Berlin Germany: Springer-Verlag.

Kuhl, J. (1987). Action control: The maintenance of motivational states. In F. Halisch & J. Kuhl (Eds.), *Motivation, intention, and volition*. Berlin, Germany: Springer-Verlag.

Kuhl, P. K., Williams, K. A., & Lacerda, F. (1992). Linguistic experience alters phonetic perceptions in infants by 6 months of age. *Science, 255*, 606–608.

Kuhn, D. (1999). A developmental model of critical thinking. *Educational Researcher, 28*, 16–26.

Kuhn, D. (2000). Metacognitive development. *Current Directions in Psychological Science, 9*, 178–181.

Kuhn, D. (2001a). How do people know? *Psychological Science, 12*, 1–8.

Kuhn, D. (2001b). Why development does (and does not) occur: Evidence from the domain of inductive reasoning. In J. L. McClelland & R. S. Siegler (Eds.), *Mechanisms of cognitive development: Behavioral and neural perspectives* (pp. 221–249). Mahwah, NJ: Erlbaum.

Kuhn, D., Amsel, E., & O'Loughlin, M. (1988). *The development of scientific thinking skills*. San Diego: Academic Press.

Kuhn, D., Garcia-Mila, M., Zohar, A., & Andersen, C. (1995). Strategies of knowledge acquisition. *Monographs of the Society for Research in Child Development, 60*(245, Serial No. 4).

Kuhn, D., Shaw, V., & Felton, M. (1997). Effects of dyadic interaction on argumentative reasoning. *Cognition and Instruction, 15*, 287–315.

Kuhn, D., & Weinstock, M. (2002). What is epistemological thinking and why does it matter? In B. K. Hofer & P. R. Pintrich (Eds.), *Personal epistemology: The psychology of beliefs about knowledge and knowing* (pp. 121–144). Mahwah, NJ: Erlbaum.

Kuhn, T. (1970). *The structure of scientific revolutions* (2nd ed.). Chicago: University of Chicago Press.

Kuklinski, M. R., & Weinstein, R. S. (2001). Classroom and developmental differences in a path model of teacher expectancy effects. *Child Development, 72*, 1554–1578.

Kulhavy, R. W., Lee, J. B., & Caterino, L. C. (1985). Conjoint retention of maps and related discourse. *Contemporary Educational Psychology, 10*, 28–37.

Kulhavy, R. W., Peterson, S., & Schwartz, N. H. (1986). Working memory: The encoding process. In G. D. Phye & T. Andre (Eds.), *Cognitive classroom learning: Understanding, thinking, and problem solving*. Orlando: Academic Press.

Kulik, C. C., Kulik, J. A., & Bangert-Drowns, R. L. (1990). Effectiveness of mastery learning programs: A meta-analysis. *Review of Educational Research, 60*, 265–299.

Kulik, C. C., Kulik, J. A., & Shwalb, B. J. (1983). College programs for high-risk and disadvantaged students: A meta-analysis of findings. *Review of Educational Research, 53*, 397–414.

Kulik, C. C., Schwalb, B. J., & Kulik, J. A. (1982). Programmed instruction in secondary education: A meta-analysis of evaluation findings. *Journal of Educational Research, 75*(3), 133–138.

Kulik, J. A., Cohen, P. A., & Ebeling, B. J. (1980). Effectiveness of programmed instruction in higher education: A meta-analysis of findings. *Educational Evaluation and Policy Analysis, 2*(6), 51–64.

Kulik, J. A., & Kulik, C. C. (1988). Timing of feedback and verbal learning. *Review of Educational Research, 58*, 79–97.

Kulik, J. A., Kulik, C. C., & Cohen, P. A. (1979). A meta-analysis of outcome studies of Keller's Personalized System of Instruction. *American Psychologist, 34*, 307–318.

Kulik, J. A., Kulik, C. C., & Cohen, P. A. (1980). Effectiveness of computer-based college teaching: A meta-analysis of findings. *Review of Educational Research, 50*, 525–544.

Kupersmidt, J. B., Buchele, K. S., Voegler, M. E., & Sedikides, C. (1996). Social self-discrepancy: A theory relating peer relations problems and school maladjustment. In J. Juvonen & K. R. Wentzel (Eds.), *Social motivation: Understanding children's school adjustment* (pp. 66–97). Cambridge, England: Cambridge University Press.

Kyle, W. C., & Shymansky, J. A. (1989, April). Enhancing through conceptual change teaching. *NARST News, 31*, 7–8.

LaBerge, D., & Samuels, S. J. (1974). Toward a theory of automatic information processing in reading. *Cognitive Psychology, 6*, 293–323.

Labov, W. (1973). The boundaries of words and their meanings. In C.-J. N. Bailey & R. W. Shuy (Eds.), *New ways of analyzing variations in English*. Washington, DC: Georgetown University Press.

Lachter, J., & Bever, T. G. (1988). The relation between linguistic structure and associative theories of language learning—a critique of some connectionist learning models. *Cognition, 28*, 195–247.

Ladd, G. W. (1990). Having friends, keeping friends, making friends, and being liked by peers in the classroom: Predictors of children's early school adjustment? *Child Development, 61*, 1081–1100.

Lajoie, S. P., & Derry, S. J. (Eds.). (1993). *Computers as cognitive tools*. Hillsdale, NJ: Erlbaum.

Lakoff, G., & Núñez, R. E. (1997). The metaphorical structure of mathematics: Sketching out cognitive foundations for a mind-based mathematics. In L. D. English (Ed.), *Mathematical reasoning: Analogies, metaphors, and images* (pp. 21–89). Mahwah, NJ: Erlbaum.

Lambiotte, J. G., Dansereau, D. F., Cross, D. R., & Reynolds, S. B. (1989). Multirelational semantic maps. *Educational Psychology Review, 1*, 331–367.

Lamon, M., Chan, C., Scardamalia, M., Burtis, P. J., & Brett, C. (1993, April). *Beliefs about learning and constructive processes in reading: Effects of a computer supported intentional learning environment (CSILE)*. Paper presented at the annual meeting of the American Educational Research Association, Atlanta.

Lampert, M. (1990). When the problem is not the question and the solution is not the answer: Mathematical knowing and teaching. *American Educational Research Journal, 17*, 29–63.

Lampert, M., Rittenhouse, P., & Crumbaugh, C. (1996). Agreeing to disagree: Developing sociable mathematical discourse. In D. R. Olson & N. Torrance (Eds.), *The handbook of education and human development: New models of learning, teaching, and schooling*. Cambridge, MA: Blackwell.

Lan, W. Y., Repman, J., Bradley, L., & Weller, H. (1994, April). *Immediate and lasting effects of criterion and payoff on academic risk taking*. Paper presented at the annual meeting of the American Educational Research Association, New Orleans.

Landauer, T. K. (1962). Rate of implicit speech. *Perceptual and Motor Skills, 15*, 646.

Lange, G., & Pierce, S. H. (1992). Memory-strategy learning and maintenance in preschool children. *Developmental Psychology, 28*, 453–462.

Langer, E. J. (1997). *The power of mindful learning*. Reading, MA: Addison-Wesley.

Langer, E. J. (2000). Mindful learning. *Current Directions in Psychological Science, 9*, 220–223.

Larkin, J. H. (1983). The role of problem representation in physics. In D. Gentner & A. L. Stevens (Eds.), *Mental models*. Hillsdale, NJ: Erlbaum.

Larson, R. W. (2000). Toward a psychology of positive youth development. *American Psychologist, 55*, pp. 170–183.

Lashley, K. S. (1929). *Brain mechanisms and intelligence*. Chicago: University of Chicago Press.

Lave, J. (1988). *Cognition in practice: Mind, mathematics, and culture in everyday life*. Cambridge, England: Cambridge University Press.

Lave, J. (1991). Situating learning in communities of practice. In L. B. Resnick, J. M. Levine, & S. D. Teasley (Eds.), *Perspectives on socially shared cognition*. Washington, DC: American Psychological Association.

Lave, J. (1993). Word problems: A microcosm of theories of learning. In P. Light & G. Butterworth (Eds.), *Context and cognition: Ways of learning and knowing*. Hillsdale, NJ: Erlbaum.

Lave, J., & Wenger, E. (1991). *Situated learning: Legitimate peripheral participation*. Cambridge, England: Cambridge University Press.

Lawson, M. J., & Chinnappan, M. (1994). Generative activity during geometry problem solving: Comparison of the performance of high-achieving and low-achieving high school students. *Cognition and Instruction, 12*, 61–93.

Lazarus, R. S. (1991). *Emotion and adaptation*. New York: Oxford University Press.

Learning Technology Center at Vanderbilt. (1996). *Jasper in the Classroom* (Videodisc). Mahwah, NJ: Erlbaum.

LeDoux, J. (1998). *The emotional brain*. London: Weidenfeld and Nicholson.

Lee, J. F., Jr., & Pruitt, K. W. (1984). *Providing for individual differences in student learning: A mastery learning approach*. Springfield, IL: Charles C. Thomas.

Lee, O. (1991, April). *Motivation to learn subject matter content: The case of science*. Paper presented at the annual meeting of the American Educational Research Association, Chicago.

Lee, O., & Anderson, C. W. (1991, April). *Student motivation in middle school science classrooms*. Paper presented at the annual meeting of the American Educational Research Association, Chicago.

Lee, O., & Anderson, C. W. (1993). Task engagement and conceptual change in middle school science classrooms. *American Educational Research Journal, 30*, 585–610.

LeFevre, J., Bisanz, J., & Mrkonjic, J. (1988). Cognitive arithmetic: Evidence for obligatory activation of arithmetic facts. *Memory and Cognition, 16*, 45–53.

Leff, R. (1969). Effects of punishment intensity and consistency on the internalization of behavioral suppression in children. *Developmental Psychology, 1*, 345–356.

Leherissey, B. L., O'Neil, H. F., Jr., & Hansen, D. N. (1971). Effects of memory support on state anxiety and performance in computer-assisted learning. *Journal of Educational Psychology, 62*, 413–420.

Leichtman, M. D., & Ceci, S. J. (1995). The effects of stereotypes and suggestions on preschoolers' reports. *Developmental Psychology, 31*, 568–578.

Leinhardt, G. (1992). What research on learning tells us about teaching. *Educational Leadership, 49*(7), 20–25.

Leinhardt, G. (1994). History: A time to be mindful. In G. Leinhardt, I. L. Beck, & C. Stainton (Eds.), *Teaching and learning in history*. Hillsdale, NJ: Erlbaum.

Lejuez, C. W., Schaal, D. W., & O'Donnell, J. (1998). Behavioral pharmacology and the treatment of substance abuse. In J. J. Plaud & G. H. Eifert (Eds.), *From behavior theory to behavior therapy* (pp. 116–135). Needham Heights, MA: Allyn & Bacon.

Lenneberg, E. (1967). *Biological foundations of language*. New York: Wiley.

Lennon, R., Ormrod, J. E., Burger, S. F., & Warren, E. (1990, October). *Belief systems of teacher education majors and their possible influences on future classroom performance*. Paper presented at the annual meeting of the Northern Rocky Mountain Educational Research Association, Greeley, CO.

Lentz, F. E. (1988). Reductive procedures. In J. C. Witt, S. N. Elliott, & F. M. Gresham (Eds.), *Handbook of behavior therapy in education*. New York: Plenum Press.

Leon, J. A., & Pepe, H. J. (1983). Self-instructional training: Cognitive behavior modification for remediating arithmetic deficits. *Exceptional Children, 50*, 54–60.

Lepper, M. R. (1981). Intrinsic and extrinsic motivation in children: Detrimental effects of superfluous social controls. In W. A. Collins (Ed.), *Minnesota Symposia on Child Psychology* (Vol. 14). Hillsdale, NJ: Erlbaum.

Lepper, M. R., Aspinwall, L. G., Mumme, D. L., & Chabey, R. W. (1990). Self-perception and social-perception processes in tutoring: Subtle social control strategies of expert tutors. In J. M. Olson & M. P. Zanna (Eds.), *Self-inference processes: The Ontario Symposium*. Hillsdale, NJ: Erlbaum.

Lepper, M. R., Greene, D., & Nisbett, R. E. (1973). Understanding children's intrinsic interest with extrinsic reward: A test of the "overjustification" hypothesis. *Journal of Personality and Social Psychology, 28*, 129–137.

Lepper, M. R., & Gurtner, J. (1989). Children and computers: Approaching the twenty-first century. *American Psychologist, 44*, 170–178.

Lepper, M. R., & Hodell, M. (1989). Intrinsic motivation in the classroom. In C. Ames & R. Ames (Eds.), *Research on motivation in education: Vol. 3. Goals and cognitions.* San Diego: Academic Press.

Lerman, D. C., & Iwata, B. A. (1995). Prevalence of the extinction burst and its attenuation during treatment. *Journal of Applied Behavior Analysis, 28*, 93–94.

Lerman, D. C., Iwata, B. A., & Wallace, M. D. (1999). Side effects of extinction: Prevalence of bursting and aggression during the treatment of self-injurious behavior. *Journal of Applied Behavior Analysis, 32*, 1–8.

Lerman, D. C., Kelley, M. E., Vorndran, C. M., Kuhn, S. A. C., & LaRue, R. H., Jr. (2002). Reinforcement magnitude and responding during treatment with differential reinforcement. *Journal of Applied Behavior Analysis, 35*, 29–48.

Lesgold, A. M. (1983). A rationale for computer-based reading instruction. In A. C. Wilkinson (Ed.), *Classroom computers and cognitive science.* New York: Academic Press.

Lesgold, A. M., & Lajoie, S. (1991). Complex problem-solving in electronics. In R. J. Sternberg & P. A. Frensch (Eds.), *Complex problem solving: Principles and mechanisms.* Hillsdale, NJ: Erlbaum.

Lester, F. K., Jr. (1985). Methodological considerations in research on mathematical problem-solving instruction. In E. A. Silver (Ed.), *Teaching and learning mathematical problem solving: Multiple research perspectives.* Hillsdale, NJ: Erlbaum.

Lester, F. K., Jr., Lambdin, D. V., & Preston, R. V. (1997). A new vision of the nature and purposes of assessment in the mathematics classroom. In G. D. Phye (Ed.), *Handbook of classroom assessment: Learning, achievement, and adjustment.* San Diego: Academic Press.

Lett, B. T. (1973). Delayed reward learning: Disproof of the traditional theory. *Learning and Motivation, 4*, 237–246.

Lett, B. T. (1975). Long delay learning in the T-maze. *Learning and Motivation, 6*, 80–90.

Levay, S., Wiesel, T. N., & Hubel, D. H. (1980). The development of ocular dominance columns in normal and visually deprived monkeys, *Journal of Comparative Neurology, 19*, 11–51.

Levin, J. R. (1981). The mnemonic '80s: Keywords in the classroom. *Educational Psychologist, 16*, 65–82.

Levin, J. R., Anglin, G. J., & Carney, R. N. (1987). On empirically validating functions of pictures in prose. In D. M. Willows & H. A. Houghton (Eds.), *The psychology of illustration: I. Basic research.* New York: Springer-Verlag.

Levin, J. R., & Mayer, R. E. (1993). Understanding illustrations in text. In B. K. Britton, A. Woodward, & M. Binkley (Eds.), *Learning from textbooks: Theory and practice.* Hillsdale, NJ: Erlbaum.

Levin, J. R., McCormick, C. B., Miller, G. E., Berry, J. K., & Pressley, M. (1982). Mnemonic versus nonmnemonic vocabulary learning strategies for children. *American Educational Research Journal, 19*, 121–136.

Levine, M. (1966). Hypothesis behavior by humans during discrimination learning. *Journal of Experimental Psychology, 71*, 331–338.

Levstik, L. S. (1994). Building a sense of history in a first-grade classroom. In J. Brophy (Ed.), *Advances in research on teaching: Vol. 4. Case studies of teaching and learning in social studies.* Greenwich, CT: JAI Press.

Levy, I., Kaplan, A., & Patrick, H. (2000, April). *Early adolescents' achievement goals, intergroup processes, and attitudes towards collaboration.* Paper presented at the annual meeting of the American Educational Research Association, New Orleans.

Lewin, K., Lippitt, R., & White, R. (1939). Pattern of aggressive behavior in experimentally created "social climates." *Journal of Social Psychology, 10*, 271–299.

Lewis, D. J., & Maher, B. A. (1965). Neural consolidation and electroconvulsive shock. *Psychological Review, 72*, 225–239.

Lhyle, K. G., & Kulhavy, R. W. (1987). Feedback processing and error correction. *Journal of Educational Psychology, 79*, 320–322.

Liao, Y. K. (1992). Effects of computer-assisted instruction on cognitive outcomes: A meta-analysis. *Journal of Research on Computing in Education, 24*, 367–380.

Lickona, T. (1991). Moral development in the elementary school classroom. In W. M. Kurtines & J. L. Gewirtz (Eds.), *Moral behavior and development: Vol. 3. Application.* Hillsdale, NJ: Erlbaum.

Liebert, R. M., & Morris, L. W. (1967). Cognitive and emotional components of test anxiety: A distinction and some initial data. *Psychological Reports, 20*, 975–978.

Light, P., & Butterworth, G. (Eds.). (1993). *Context and cognition: Ways of learning and knowing.* Hillsdale, NJ: Erlbaum.

Lightfoot, D. (1999). *The development of language: Acquisition, change, and evolution.* Malden, MA: Blackwell.

Lillard, A. S. (1997). Other folks' theories of mind and behavior. *Psychological Science, 8*, 268–274.

Lillard, A. S. (1998). Ethnopsychologies: Cultural variations in theories of mind. *Psychological Bulletin, 123*, 3–33.

Lima, S. D. (1993). Word-initial letter sequences and reading. *Current Directions in Psychological Science, 2*, 139–142.

Lindberg, M. A. (1991). A taxonomy of suggestibility and eyewitness memory: Age, memory process, and focus of analysis. In J. L. Doris (Ed.), *The suggestibility of children's recollections.* Washington, DC: American Psychological Association.

Linderholm, T., Gustafson, M., van den Broek, P., & Lorch, R. F., Jr. (1997, March). *Effects of reading goals on inference generation.* Paper presented at the annual meeting of the American Educational Research Association, Chicago.

Lindsay, D. S. (1993). Eyewitness suggestibility. *Current Directions in Psychological Science, 2*, 86–89.

Lindsay, P. H., & Norman, D. A. (1977). *Human information processing.* New York: Academic Press.

Lindvall, C. M., Tamburino, J. L., & Robinson, L. (1982, March). *An exploratory investigation of the effect of teaching primary grade children to use specific problem-solving strategies in solving simple story problems.* Paper presented at the annual meeting of the American Educational Research Association, New York.

Linn, M. C., & Muilenburg, L. (1996). Creating lifelong science learners: What models form a firm foundation? *Educational Researcher, 25*(5), 18–24.

Linn, M. C., Songer, N. B., & Eylon, B. (1996). Shifts and convergences in science learning and instruction. In D. C. Berliner & R. C. Calfee (Eds.), *Handbook of educational psychology.* New York: Macmillan.

Linn, R. L. (2000). Assessments and accountability. *Educational Researcher, 29*(2), 4–16.

Linnenbrink, E. A., & Pintrich, P. R. (2002). Achievement goal theory and affect: An asymmetrical bidirectional model. *Educational Psychologist, 37*, 69–78.

Linnenbrink, E. A., & Pintrich, P. R. (2003). Achievement goals and intentional conceptual change. In G. M. Sinatra & P. R. Pintrich (Eds.), *Intentional conceptual change* (pp. 347–374). Mahwah, NJ: Erlbaum.

Linton, M. (1986). Ways of searching and the contents of memory. In D. C. Rubin (Ed.), *Autobiographical memory.* Cambridge, England: Cambridge University Press.

Lipsitt, L. P., & Kaye, H. (1964). Conditioned sucking in the human newborn. *Psychonomic Science, 1*, 29–30.

Lipsitt, L. P., & Kaye, H. (1965). Change in neonatal response to optimizing and non-optimizing sucking stimulation. *Psychonomic Science, 2*, 221–222.

Lipson, M. Y. (1982). Learning new information from text: The role of prior knowledge and reading ability. *Journal of Reading Behavior, 14*, 243–261.

Lipson, M. Y. (1983). The influence of religious affiliation on children's memory for text information. *Reading Research Quarterly, 18*, 448–457.

Littlewood, W. T. (1984). *Foreign and second language learning: Language-acquisition research and its implications for the classroom.* Cambridge, England: Cambridge University Press.

Liu, J., Golinkoff, R. M., & Sak, K. (2001). One cow does not an animal make: Young children can extend novel words at the superordinate level. *Child Development, 72,* 1674–1694.

Liu, L. G. (1990, April). *The use of causal questioning to promote narrative comprehension and memory.* Paper presented at the annual meeting of the American Educational Research Association, Boston.

Locke, E. A., & Latham, G. P. (2002). Building a practically useful theory of goal setting and task motivation: A 35-year odyssey. *American Psychologist, 57,* 705–717.

Locke, J. L. (1993). *The child's path to spoken language.* Cambridge, MA: Harvard University Press.

Loftus, E. F. (1991). Made in memory: Distortions in recollection after misleading information. In G. H. Bower (Ed.), *The psychology of learning and motivation: Advances in research and theory* (Vol. 27). San Diego: Academic Press.

Loftus, E. F. (1992). When a lie becomes memory's truth: Memory distortion after exposure to misinformation. *Current Directions in Psychological Science, 1,* 121–123.

Loftus, E. F. (1993). The reality of repressed memories. *American Psychologist, 48,* 518–537.

Loftus, E. F. (1997). Memory for a past that never was. *Current Directions in Psychological Science, 6,* 60–65.

Loftus, E. F., & Kaufman, L. (1992). Why do traumatic experiences sometimes produce good memory (flashbulbs) and sometimes no memory (repression)? In E. Winograd & U. Neisser (Eds.), *Affect and accuracy in recall: Studies of "flashbulb" memories.* Cambridge, England: Cambridge University Press.

Loftus, E. F., & Loftus, G. R. (1980). On the permanence of stored information in the human brain. *American Psychologist, 35,* 409–420.

Loftus, E. F., & Palmer, J. C. (1974). Reconstruction of automobile destruction: An example of the interaction between language and memory. *Journal of Verbal Learning and Verbal Behavior, 13,* 585–589.

Loftus, G. R., & Bell, S. M. (1975). Two types of information in picture memory. *Journal of Experimental Psychology: Human Learning and Perception, 104,* 103–113.

Loftus, G. R., & Loftus, E. F. (1976). *Human memory: The processing of information.* New York: Wiley.

Logue, A. W. (1979). Taste aversion and the generality of the laws of learning. *Psychological Bulletin, 86,* 276–296.

Loranger, A. L. (1994). The study strategies of successful and unsuccessful high school students. *Journal of Reading Behavior, 26,* 347–360.

Lorayne, H., & Lucas, J. (1974). *The memory book.* New York: Stein and Day.

Lorch, R. F., Jr., Lorch, E. P., & Inman, W. E. (1993). Effects of signaling topic structure on text recall. *Journal of Educational Psychology, 85,* 281–290.

Lou, Y., Abrami, P. C., & d'Apollonia, S. (2001). Small group and individual learning with technology: A meta-analysis. *Review of of Educational Research, 71,* 449–521.

Lou, Y., Abrami, P. C., Spence, J. C., Poulsen, C., Chambers, B., & d'Apollonia, S. (1996). Within-class grouping: A meta-analysis. *Review of Educational Research, 66,* 423–458.

Lovitt, T. C., Guppy, T. E., & Blattner, J. E. (1969). The use of free-time contingency with fourth graders to increase spelling accuracy. *Behaviour Research and Therapy, 7,* 151–156.

Luchins, A. S. (1942). Mechanization in problem solving: The effect of Einstellung. *Psychological Monographs, 54* (Whole No. 248).

Luchins, A. S., & Luchins, E. H. (1950). New experimental attempts at preventing mechanization in problem solving. *Journal of General Psychology, 42,* 279–297.

Ludwig, T. D., Gray, T. W., & Rowell, A. (1998). Increasing recycling in academic buildings: A systematic replication. *Journal of Applied Behavior Analysis, 31,* 683–686.

Lueptow, L. B. (1984). *Adolescent sex roles and social change.* New York: Columbia University Press.

Lundeberg, M. A., & Fox, P. W. (1991). Do laboratory findings on test expectancy generalize to classroom outcomes? *Review of Educational Research, 61,* 94–106.

Luque, M. L. (2003). The role of domain-specific knowledge in intentional conceptual change. In G. M. Sinatra & P. R. Pintrich (Eds.), *Intentional conceptual change* (pp. 133–170). Mahwah, NJ: Erlbaum.

Lynn, S. J., Lock, T. G., Myers, B., & Payne, D. G. (1997). Recalling the unrecallable: Should hypnosis be used to recover memories in psychotherapy? *Current Directions in Psychological Science, 6,* 79–83.

Lyon, T. D., & Flavell, J. H. (1994). Young children's understanding of "remember" and "forget." *Child Development, 65,* 1357–1371.

MacAndrew, D. K., Klatzky, R. L., Fiez, J. A., McClelland, J. L., & Becker, J. T. (2002). The phonological-similarity effect differentiates between two working memory tasks. *Psychological Science, 13,* 465–468.

Mace, F. C., Belfiore, P. J., & Shea, M. C. (1989). Operant theory and research on self-regulation. In B. J. Zimmerman & D. H. Schunk (Eds.), *Self-regulated learning and academic achievement: Theory, research, and practice.* New York: Springer-Verlag.

Mace, F. C., Hock, M. L., Lalli, J. S., West, B. J., Belfiore, P., Pinter, E., & Brown, D. K. (1988). Behavioral momentum in the treatment of noncompliance. *Journal of Applied Behavior Analysis, 21,* 123–141.

Mace, F. C., & Kratochwill, T. R. (1988). Self-monitoring. In J. C. Witt, S. N. Elliott, & F. M. Gresham (Eds.), *Handbook of behavior therapy in education.* New York: Plenum Press.

Mace, F. C., Page, T. J., Ivancic, M. T., & O'Brien, S. (1986). Effectiveness of brief time-out with and without contingent delay: A comparative analysis. *Journal of Applied Behavior Analysis, 19,* 79–86.

Macfarlane, A. (1978). What a baby knows. *Human Nature, 1,* 74–81.

Machiels-Bongaerts, M., Schmidt, H. G., & Boshuizen, H. P. A. (1991, April). *The effects of prior knowledge activation on free recall and study time allocation.* Paper presented at the annual meeting of the American Educational Research Association, Chicago.

MacIver, D., Stipek, D. J., & Daniels, D. (1991). Explaining within-semester changes in student effort in junior high school and senior high school courses. *Journal of Educational Psychology, 83,* 201–211.

MacPherson, E. M., Candee, B. L., & Hohman, R. J. (1974). A comparison of three methods for eliminating disruptive lunchroom behavior. *Journal of Applied Behavior Analysis, 7,* 287–297.

Madsen, C. H., Becker, W. C., & Thomas, D. R. (1968). Rules, praise, and ignoring: Elements of elementary classroom control. *Journal of Applied Behavior Analysis, 1,* 139–150.

Maehr, M. L. (1984). Meaning and motivation: Toward a theory of personal investment. In R. Ames & C. Ames (Eds.), *Research on motivation in education: Vol. 1. Student motivation.* Orlando: Academic Press.

Maehr, M. L., & Kaplan, A. (2000, April). It might be all about self: Self-consciousness as an organizing scheme for integrating understandings from self-determination theory and achievement goal theory. In A. Assor (Chair), *Self-determination theory and achievement goal theory: Convergences, divergences, and educational implications.* Symposium conducted at the annual meeting of the American Educational Research Association, New Orleans.

Maehr, M. L., & Meyer, H. A. (1997). Understanding motivation and schooling: Where we've been, where we are, and where we need to go. *Educational Psychology Review, 9,* 371–409.

Magee, S. K., & Ellis, J. (2000). Extinction effects during the assessment of multiple problem behaviors. *Journal of Applied Behavior Analysis, 33,* 313–316.

Mager, R. F. (1962). *Preparing instructional objectives.* Belmont, CA: Fearon.

Mager, R. F. (1972). *Goal analysis.* Belmont, CA: Fearon.

Mager, R. F. (1984). *Preparing instructional objectives* (2nd ed.). Belmont, CA: David S. Lake.

Mahoney, M. J., & Thoresen, C. E. (1974). *Self-control: Power to the person.* Monterey, CA: Brooks-Cole.

Maier, N. R. F. (1945). Reasoning in humans III: The mechanisms of equivalent stimuli and of reasoning. *Journal of Experimental Psychology, 35*, 349–360.

Maier, N. R. F., & Janzen, J. C. (1968). Functional values as aids and distractors in problem solving. *Psychological Reports, 22*, 1021–1034.

Maier, S. F., & Seligman, M. E. P. (1976). Learned helplessness: Theory and evidence. *Journal of Experimental Psychology: General, 105*, 3–46.

Maki, R. H. (1998). Test predictions over text material. In D. J. Hacker, J. Dunlosky, & A. C. Graesser (Eds.), *Metacognition in educational theory and practice* (pp. 117–144). Mahwah, NJ: Erlbaum.

Malone, T. W., & Lepper, M. R. (1987). Making learning fun: A taxonomy of intrinsic motivation for learning. In R. E. Snow & M. J. Farr (Eds.), *Aptitude, learning, and instruction: Vol. 3. Conative and affective process analyses.* Hillsdale, NJ: Erlbaum.

Mandler, J. M., & Johnson, N. S. (1976). Some of the thousand words a picture is worth. *Journal of Experimental Psychology: Human Learning and Memory, 2*, 529–540.

Mandler, J. M., & Parker, R. E. (1976). Memory for descriptive and spatial information in complex pictures. *Journal of Experimental Psychology: Human Learning and Memory, 2*, 38–48.

Mandler, J. M., & Ritchey, G. H. (1977). Long-term memory for pictures. *Journal of Experimental Psychology: Human Learning and Memory, 3*, 386–396.

Marachi, R., Friedel, J., & Midgley, C. (2001, April). *"I sometimes annoy my teacher during math": Relations between student perceptions of the teacher and disruptive behavior in the classroom.* Paper presented at the annual meeting of the American Educational Research Association, Seattle, WA.

Marcia, J. E. (1980). Identity in adolescence. In J. Adelson (Ed.), *Handbook of adolescent psychology.* New York: Wiley.

Markman, E. M. (1977). Realizing that you don't understand: A preliminary investigation. *Child Development, 48*, 986–992.

Marsh, H. W. (1990). A multidimensional, hierarchical model of self-concept: Theoretical and empirical justification. *Educational Psychology Review, 2*, 77–172.

Marsh, H. W., & Craven, R. (1997). Academic self-concept: Beyond the dustbowl. In G. D. Phye (Ed.), *Handbook of classroom assessment: Learning, achievement, and adjustment.* San Diego: Academic Press.

Marshall, H. H. (Ed.). (1992). *Redefining student learning: Roots of educational change.* Norwood, NJ: Ablex.

Marshall, J. (1987). The effects of writing on students' understanding of literary texts. *Research in the Teaching of English, 21*, 30–63.

Martin, A. J., Marsh, H. W., & Debus, R. L. (2001). A quadripolar need achievement representation of self-handicapping and defensive pessimism. *American Educational Research Journal, 38*, 583–610.

Martin, C. L., & Halverson, C. F. (1981). A schematic processing model of sex typing and stereotyping in children. *Child Development, 52*, 1119–1134.

Martin, I., & Levey, A. B. (1987). Learning what will happen next: Conditioning, evaluation, and cognitive processes. In G. Davey (Ed.), *Cognitive processes and Pavlovian conditioning in humans.* Chichester, England: Wiley.

Martin, S. S., Brady, M. P., & Williams, R. E. (1991). Effects of toys on the social behavior of preschool children in integrated and nonintegrated groups: Investigation of a setting event. *Journal of Early Intervention, 15*, 153–161.

Martin, V. L., & Pressley, M. (1991). Elaborative-interrogation effects depend on the nature of the question. *Journal of Educational Psychology, 83*, 113–119.

Marton, F., & Booth, S. (1997). *Learning and awareness.* Mahwah, NJ: Erlbaum.

Maslow, A. H. (1959). *New knowledge in human values.* New York: Harper & Row.

Maslow, A. H. (1973a). Self-actualizing people: A study of psychological health. In R. J. Lowry (Ed.), *Dominance, self-esteem, self-actualization: Germinal papers of A. H. Maslow.* Monterey, CA: Brooks-Cole.

Maslow, A. H. (1973b). Theory of human motivation. In R. J. Lowry (Ed.), *Dominance, self-esteem, self-actualization: Germinal papers of A. H. Maslow.* Monterey, CA: Brooks-Cole.

Maslow, A. H. (1987). *Motivation and personality* (3rd ed.). New York: Harper & Row.

Mason, L. (2003). Personal epistemologies and intentional conceptual change. In G. M. Sinatra & P. R. Pintrich (Eds.), *Intentional conceptual change* (pp. 199–236). Mahwah, NJ: Erlbaum.

Massey, C. M., & Gelman, R. (1988). Preschoolers' ability to decide whether a photographed unfamiliar object can move itself. *Developmental Psychology, 24*, 307–317.

Massialas, B. G., & Zevin, J. (1983). *Teaching creatively: Learning through discovery.* Malabar, FL: Robert E. Krieger.

Mastropieri, M. A., & Scruggs, T. E. (1989). Constructing more meaningful relationships: Mnemonic instruction for special populations. *Educational Psychology Review, 1*, 83–111.

Mastropieri, M. A., & Scruggs, T. E. (1992). Science for students with disabilities. *Review of Educational Research, 62*, 377–411.

Masur, E. F., McIntyre, C. W., & Flavell, J. H. (1973). Developmental changes in apportionment of study time among items in a multitrial free recall task. *Journal of Experimental Child Psychology, 15*, 237–246.

Mathes, P. G., Torgesen, J. K., & Allor, J. H. (2001). The effects of peer-assisted literacy strategies for first-grade readers with and without additional computer-assisted instruction. *American Educational Research Journal, 38*, 371–410.

Mathews, J. R., Friman, P. C., Barone, V. J., Ross, L. V., & Christophersen, E. R. (1987). Decreasing dangerous infant behaviors through parent instruction. *Journal of Applied Behavior Analysis, 20*, 165–169.

Maurer, A. (1974). Corporal punishment. *American Psychologist, 29*, 614–626.

Mayer, G. R., & Butterworth, T. N. (1979). A preventive approach to school violence and vandalism: An experimental study. *Personnel Guidance Journal, 57*, 436–441.

Mayer, R. E. (1974). Acquisition processes and resilience under varying testing conditions for structurally different problem solving procedures. *Journal of Educational Psychology, 66*, 644–656.

Mayer, R. E. (1975). Information processing variables in learning to solve problems. *Review of Educational Research, 45*, 525–541.

Mayer, R. E. (1977). *Thinking and problem solving: An introduction to human cognition and learning.* Glenview, IL: Scott Foresman.

Mayer, R. E. (1979a). Can advance organizers influence meaningful learning? *Review of Educational Research, 49*, 371–383.

Mayer, R. E. (1979b). Twenty years of research on advance organizers: Assimilation theory is still the best predictor of results. *Instructional Science, 8*, 133–167.

Mayer, R. E. (1982). Memory for algebra story problems. *Journal of Educational Psychology, 74*, 199–216.

Mayer, R. E. (1983). *Thinking, problem solving, and cognition.* New York: W. H. Freeman.

Mayer, R. E. (1984). Aids to text comprehension. *Educational Psychologist, 19*, 30–42.

Mayer, R. E. (1985). Implications of cognitive psychology for instruction in mathematical problem solving. In E. A. Silver (Ed.), *Teaching and learning mathematical problem solving: Multiple research perspectives.* Hillsdale, NJ: Erlbaum.

Mayer, R. E. (1986). Mathematics. In R. F. Dillon & R. J. Sternberg (Eds.), *Cognition and instruction.* San Diego: Academic Press.

Mayer, R. E. (1987). *Educational psychology: A cognitive approach.* Boston: Little, Brown.

Mayer, R. E. (1989a). Models for understanding. *Review of Educational Research, 59*, 43–64.

Mayer, R. E. (1989b). Teaching for thinking: Research on the teachability of thinking skills. In I. S. Cohen (Ed.), *The G. Stanley Hall Lecture Series* (Vol. 9). Washington, DC: American Psychological Association.

Mayer, R. E. (1992). *Thinking, problem solving, cognition* (2nd ed.). New York: W. H. Freeman.

Mayer, R. E. (1996a). Learners as information processors: Legacies and limitations of educational psychology's second metaphor. *Educational Psychologist, 31,* 151–161.

Mayer, R. E. (1996b). Learning strategies for making sense out of expository text: The SOI model for guiding three cognitive processes in knowledge construction. *Educational Psychology Review, 8,* 357–371.

Mayer, R. E. (1998). Does the brain have a place in educational psychology? *Educational Psychology Review, 10,* 389–396.

Mayer, R. E., & Bromage, B. (1980). Different recall protocols for technical texts due to advance organizers. *Journal of Educational Psychology, 72,* 209–225.

Mayer, R. E., & Greeno, J. G. (1972). Structural differences between learning outcomes produced by different instructional methods. *Journal of Educational Psychology, 63,* 165–173.

Mayer, R. E., & Moreno, R. (1998). A split-attention effect in multimedia learning: Evidence for dual processing systems in working memory. *Journal of Educational Psychology, 90,* 312–320.

Mayer, R. E., Moreno, R., Boire, M., & Vagge, S. (1999). Maximizing constructivist learning from multimedia communications by minimizing cognitive load. *Journal of Educational Psychology, 91,* 638–643.

Mayer, R. E., & Wittrock, M. C. (1996). Problem-solving transfer. In D. C. Berliner & R. C. Calfee (Eds.), *Handbook of educational psychology.* New York: Macmillan.

Mayfield, K. H., & Chase, P. N. (2002). The effects of cumulative practice on mathematics problem solving. *Journal of Applied Behavior Analysis, 35,* 105–123.

Mayzner, M. S., & Tresselt, M. E. (1958). Anagram solution times: A function of letter-order and word frequency. *Journal of Experimental Psychology, 56,* 350–376.

Mayzner, M. S., & Tresselt, M. E. (1966). Anagram solution times: A function of multiple-solution anagrams. *Journal of Experimental Psychology, 71,* 66–73.

Mazur, J. E. (1993). Predicting the strength of a conditioned reinforcer: Effects of delay and uncertainty. *Current Directions in Psychological Science, 2,* 70–74.

McAllister, W. R., & McAllister, D. E. (1965). Variables influencing the conditioning and the measurement of acquired fear. In W. F. Prokasy (Ed.), *Classical conditioning.* New York: Appleton-Century-Crofts.

McAndrew, D. A. (1983). Underlining and notetaking: Some suggestions from research. *Journal of Reading, 27,* 103–108.

McAshan, H. H. (1979). *Competency-based education and behavioral objectives.* Englewood Cliffs, NJ: Educational Technology.

McCallin, R. C., Ormrod, J. E., & Cochran, K. C. (1997, March). *Algorithmic and heuristic learning sets and their relationship to cognitive structure.* Paper presented at the annual meeting of the American Educational Research Association, Chicago.

McCaslin, M., & Good, T. L. (1996). The informal curriculum. In D. C. Berliner & R. C. Calfee (Eds.), *Handbook of educational psychology.* New York: Macmillan.

McCauley, R. N. (1987). The role of theories in a theory of concepts. In U. Neisser (Ed.), *Concepts and conceptual development: Ecological and intellectual factors in categorization.* Cambridge, England: Cambridge University Press.

McClelland, D. C. (1984). *Motives, personality, and society: Selected papers.* New York: Praeger.

McClelland, D. C., Atkinson, J. W., Clark, R. A., & Lowell, E. L. (1953). *The achievement motive.* New York: Appleton-Century-Crofts.

McClelland, J. L. (2001). Failures to learn and their remediation: A Hebbian account. In J. L. McClelland & R. S. Siegler (Eds.), *Mechanisms of cognitive development: Behavioral and neural perspectives* (pp. 97–121). Mahwah, NJ: Erlbaum.

McClelland, J. L., & Rumelhart, D. E. (1986). *Parallel distributed processing* (Vol. 2). Cambridge, MA: MIT Press.

McCloskey, M. E., & Glucksberg, S. (1978). Natural categories: Well-defined or fuzzy sets? *Memory and Cognition, 6,* 462–472.

McCombs, B. L. (1988). Motivational skills training: Combining metacognitive, cognitive, and affective learning strategies. In C. E. Weinstein, E. T. Goetz, & P. A. Alexander (Eds.), *Learning and study strategies: Issues in assessment, instruction, and evaluation.* San Diego: Harcourt Brace Jovanovich.

McCombs, B. L. (1996). Alternative perspectives for motivation. In L. Baker, P. Afflerbach, & D. Reinking (Eds.), *Developing engaged readers in school and home communities.* Hillsdale, NJ: Erlbaum.

McCord, W., McCord, J., & Zola, I. K. (1959). *Origins of crime: A new evaluation of the Cambridge–Somerville Youth Study.* New York: Columbia University Press.

McCoy, L. P. (1990, April). *Correlates of mathematics anxiety.* Paper presented at the annual meeting of the American Educational Research Association, Boston.

McCrary, J. W., & Hunter, W. S. (1953). Serial position curves in verbal learning. *Science, 117,* 131–134.

McCutchen, D. (1996). A capacity theory of writing: Working memory in composition. *Educational Psychology Review, 8,* 299–325.

McDaniel, M. A., & Einstein, G. O. (1989). Material-appropriate processing: A contextualist approach to reading and studying strategies. *Educational Psychology Review, 1,* 113–145.

McDaniel, M. A., Maier, S. F., & Einstein, G. O. (2002). "Brain-specific" nutrients: A memory cure? *Psychological Science in the Public Interest, 3*(1), 12–38.

McDaniel, M. A., & Masson, M. E. J. (1985). Altering memory representations through retrieval. *Journal of Experimental Psychology: Learning, Memory, and Cognition, 11,* 371–385.

McDaniel, M. A., & Schlager, M. S. (1990). Discovery learning and transfer of problem-solving skills. *Cognition and Instruction, 7,* 129–159.

McDaniel, M. A., Waddill, P. J., & Einstein, G. O. (1988). A contextual account of the generation effect: A three-factor theory. *Journal of Memory and Language, 27,* 521–536.

McDaniel, M. A., Waddill, P. J., Finstad, K., & Bourg, T. (2000). The effects of text-based interest on attention and recall. *Journal of Educational Psychology, 92,* 492–502.

McDevitt, T. M., Sheehan, E. P., Cooney, J. B., Smith, H. V., & Walker, I. (1994). Conceptions of listening, learning processes, and epistemologies held by American, Irish, and Australian university students. *Learning and Individual Differences, 6,* 231–256.

McDevitt, T. M., Spivey, N., Sheehan, E. P., Lennon, R., & Story, R. (1990). Children's beliefs about listening: Is it enough to be still and quiet? *Child Development, 55,* 810–820.

McGee, K. D., Knight, S. L., & Boudah, D. J. (2001, April). *Using reciprocal teaching in secondary inclusive English classroom instruction.* Paper presented at the annual meeting of the American Educational Research Association, Seattle, WA.

McGee, L. M. (1992). An exploration of meaning construction in first graders' grand conversations. In C. K. Kinzer & D. J. Leu (Eds.), *Literacy research, theory, and practice: Views from many perspectives.* Chicago: National Reading Conference.

McGeoch, J. A. (1942). *The psychology of human learning.* New York: David McKay.

McGill, P. (1999). Establishing operations: Implications for the assessment, treatment, and prevention of problem behavior. *Journal of Applied Behavior Analysis, 32,* 393–418.

McGregor, H. A., & Elliot, A. J. (2002). Achievement goals as predictors of achievement-relevant processes prior to task engagement. *Journal of Educational Psychology, 94,* 381–395.

McHale, M. A., Brooks, Z., & Wolach, A. H. (1982). Incentive shifts with different massed and spaced trial cues. *Psychological Record, 32,* 85–92.

McInerney, D. M., Roche, L. A., McInerney, V., & Marsh, H. W. (1997). Cultural perspectives on school motivation: The relevance and application of goal theory. *American Educational Research Journal, 34,* 207–236.

McKeachie, W. J. (1961). Motivation, teaching methods, and college learning. In M. R. Jones (Ed.), *Nebraska symposium on motivation.* Lincoln: University of Nebraska Press.

McKeachie, W. J., Lin, Y., Milholland, J., & Isaacson, R. (1966). Student affiliation motives, teacher warmth, and academic achievement. *Journal of Personality and Social Psychology, 4,* 457–461.

McKenzie, H. S., Clark, M., Wolf, M. M., Kothera, R., & Benson, C. (1968). Behavior modification of children with learning disabilities using grades as tokens and allowances as back up reinforcers. *Exceptional Children, 34,* 745–752.

McKeown, M. G., & Beck, I. L. (1990). The assessment and characterization of young learners' knowledge of a topic in history. *American Educational Research Journal, 27,* 688–726.

McLaughlin, T. F., & Malaby, J. (1972). Intrinsic reinforcers in a classroom token economy. *Journal of Applied Behavior Analysis, 5,* 263–270.

McLaughlin, T. F., & Williams, R. L. (1988). The token economy. In J. C. Witt, S. N. Elliott, & F. M. Gresham (Eds.), *Handbook of behavior therapy in education.* New York: Plenum Press.

McLeod, D. B., & Adams, V. M. (Eds.). (1989). *Affect and mathematical problem solving: A new perspective.* New York: Springer-Verlag.

McLoyd, V. C. (1998). Socioeconomic disadvantage and child development. *American Psychologist, 53,* 185–204.

McNamara, D. S., & Healy, A. F. (1995). A generation advantage for multiplication skill training and nonword vocabulary acquisition. In A. F. Healy & L. E. Bourne, Jr. (Eds.), *Learning and memory of knowledge and skills: Durability and specificity.* Thousand Oaks, CA: Sage.

McNamara, E. (1987). Behavioural approaches in the secondary school. In K. Wheldall (Ed.), *The behaviourist in the classroom.* London: Allen & Unwin.

McNeil, N. M., & Alibali, M. W. (2000). Learning mathematics from procedural instructin: Externally imposed goals influence what is learned. *Journal of Educational Psychology, 92,* 734–744.

Medin, D. L. (1989). Concepts and conceptual structure. *American Psychologist, 44,* 1469–1481.

Meece, J. L. (1994). The role of motivation in self-regulated learning. In D. H. Schunk & B. J. Zimmerman (Eds.), *Self-regulation of learning and performance: Issues and educational applications.* Hillsdale, NJ: Erlbaum.

Meece, J. L., & Holt, K. (1993). A pattern analysis of students' achievement goals. *Journal of Educational Psychology, 85,* 582–590.

Meece, J. L., Wigfield, A., & Eccles, J. S. (1990). Predictors of math anxiety and its influence on young adolescents' course enrollment intentions and performance in mathematics. *Journal of Educational Psychology, 82,* 60–70.

Meehl, P. E. (1950). On the circularity of the law of effect. *Psychological Bulletin, 47,* 52–75.

Mehan, H. (1979). *Social organization in the classroom.* Cambridge, MA: Harvard University Press.

Mehrens, W. A. (1992). Using performance assessment for accountability purposes. *Educational Measurement: Issues and Practices, 11*(1), 3–9.

Meichenbaum, D. (1977). *Cognitive-behavior modification: An integrative approach.* New York: Plenum Press.

Meichenbaum, D. (1985). Teaching thinking: A cognitive–behavioral perspective. In S. F. Chipman, J. W. Segal, & R. Glaser (Eds.), *Thinking and learning skills: Vol. 2. Research and open questions.* Hillsdale, NJ: Erlbaum.

Mellers, B. A., & McGraw, A. P. (2001). Anticipated emotions as guides to choice. *Current Directions in Psychological Science, 10,* 210–214.

Mellers, B. A., Schwartz, A., Ho, K., & Ritov, H. (1997). Decision affect theory: Emotional reactions to the outcomes of risky options. *Psychological Science, 8,* 423–429.

Meloth, M. S., & Deering, P. D. (1992). Effects of two cooperative conditions on peer-group discussions, reading comprehension, and metacognition. *Contemporary Educational Psychology, 17,* 175–193.

Meloth, M. S., & Deering, P. D. (1994). Task talk and task awareness under different cooperative learning conditions. *American Educational Research Journal, 31,* 138–165.

Meloth, M. S., & Deering, P. D. (1999). The role of the teacher in promoting cognitive processing during collaborative learning. In A. M. O'Donnell & A. King (Eds.), *Cognitive perspectives on peer learning* (pp. 235–255). Mahwah, NJ: Erlbaum.

Melton, A. W. (1963). Implications of short-term memory for a general theory of memory. *Journal of Verbal Learning and Verbal Behavior, 2,* 1–21.

Melton, A. W., & Irwin, J. M. (1940). The influence of degree of interpolated learning on retroactive inhibition and the overt transfer of specific responses. *American Journal of Psychology, 53,* 173–203.

Melton, R. F. (1978). Resolution of conflicting claims concerning the effect of behavioral objectives on student learning. *Review of Educational Research, 48,* 291–302.

Meltzoff, A. N. (1988a). Infant imitation after a 1-week delay: Long-term memory for novel acts and multiple stimuli. *Developmental Psychology, 24,* 470–476.

Meltzoff, A. N. (1988b). Infant imitation and memory: Ninth-month-old infants in immediate and deferred tests. *Child Development, 59,* 217–225.

Meltzoff, A. N., & Moore, M. K. (1977). Imitation of facial and manual gestures by human neonates. *Science, 198,* 75–78.

Merrill, M. D., & Tennyson, R. D. (1977). *Concept teaching: An instructional design guide.* Englewood Cliffs, NJ: Educational Technology.

Merrill, M. D., & Tennyson, R. D. (1978). Concept classification and classification errors as a function of relationships between examples and non-examples.

Improving Human Performance, 7, 351–364.

Merrill, P. F., Hammons, K., Vincent, B. R., Reynolds, P. L., Christensen, L., & Tolman, M. N. (1996). *Computers in education* (3rd ed.). Needham Heights, MA: Allyn & Bacon.

Mervis, C. B. (1987). Child-basic object categories and early lexical development. In U. Neisser (Ed.), *Concepts and conceptual development: Ecological and intellectual factors in categorization.* Cambridge, England: Cambridge University Press.

Merzenich, M. M. (2001). Cortical plasticity contributing to child development. In J. L. McClelland & R. S. Siegler (Eds.), *Mechanisms of cognitive development: Behavioral and neural perspectives* (pp. 67–95). Mahwah, NJ: Erlbaum.

Merzenich, M. M., Allard, T. T., & Jenkins, W. M. (1990). Neural ontogeny of higher brain function: Implications of some recent neurophysiological findings. In O. Franzen & P. Westman (Eds.), *Information processing in the somatosensory system* (pp. 293–311). London: Macmillan.

Metz, K. E. (1995). Reassessment of developmental constraints on children's science instruction. *Review of Educational Research, 65,* 93–127.

Meyer, B. J. F., Brandt, D. H., & Bluth, G. J. (1980). Use of top-level structure in text: Key for reading comprehension of ninth-grade students. *Reading Research Quarterly, 16,* 72–103.

Meyer, D. K., & Turner, J. C. (2002). Discovering emotion in classroom motivation research. *Educational Psychologist, 37,* 107–114.

Meyer, D. K., Turner, J. C., & Spencer, C. A. (1994, April). *Academic risk taking and motivation in an elementary mathematics classroom.* Paper presented at the annual meeting of the American Educational Research Association, New Orleans.

Meyer, K. A. (1999). Functional analysis and treatment of problem behavior exhibited by elementary school children. *Journal of Applied Behavior Analysis, 32,* 229–232.

Michael, J. (1993). Establishing operations. *The Behavior Analyst, 16,* 191–206.

Michael, J. (2000). Implications and refinements of the establishing operation concept. *Journal of Applied Behavior Analysis, 33,* 401–410.

Michael, J. L. (1974). The essential components of effective instruction and why most college teaching is not. In F. S. Keller & E. Ribes-Inesta (Eds.), *Behavior modification: Applications to education.* New York: Academic Press.

Middleton, M. J., & Midgley, C. (1997). Avoiding the demonstration of lack of ability: An under-explored aspect of goal theory. *Journal of Educational Psychology, 89,* 710–718.

Middleton, M. J., & Midgley, C. (2002). Beyond motivation: Middle school students' perceptions of press for understanding in math. *Contemporary Educational Psychology, 27,* 373–391.

Midgley, C. (1993). Motivation and middle level schools. In M. Maehr & P. R. Pintrich (Eds.), *Advances in motivation and achievement* (Vol. 8, pp. 217–274). Greenwich, CT: JAI Press.

Midgley, C., Kaplan, A., & Middleton, M. (2001). Performance-approach goals: Good for what, for whom, under what circumstances, and at what cost? *Journal of Educational Psychology, 93,* 77–86.

Midgley, C., Kaplan, A., Middleton, M., Maehr, M., Urdan, T., Anderman, L., Anderman, E., & Roeser, R. (1998). The development and validation of scales assessing students' achievement goal orientations. *Contemporary Educational Psychology, 23,* 113–131.

Mikulincer, M. (1994). *Human learned helplessness: A coping perspective.* New York: Plenum Press.

Miller, D. L., & Kelley, M. L. (1994). The use of goal setting and contingency contracting for improving children's homework performance. *Journal of Applied Behavior Analysis, 27,* 73–84.

Miller, G. A. (1956). The magical number seven, plus or minus two: Some limits on our capacity for processing information. *Psychological Review, 63,* 81–97.

Miller, G. A., Galanter, E., & Pribram, K. H. (1960). *Plans and the structure of behavior.* New York: Holt, Rinehart & Winston.

Miller, N. E. (1948). Studies of fear as an acquirable drive: I. Fear as motivation and fear-reduction as reinforcement in the learning of new responses. *Journal of Experimental Psychology, 38,* 89–101.

Miller, N. E., & Dollard, J. C. (1941). *Social learning and imitation.* New Haven, CT: Yale University Press.

Miller, R. L., Brickman, P., & Bolen, D. (1975). Attribution versus persuasion as a means for modifying behavior. *Journal of Personality and Social Psychology, 31,* 430–441.

Miller, R. R., & Barnet, R. C. (1993). The role of time in elementary associations. *Current Directions in Psychological Science, 2,* 106–111.

Millroy, W. L. (1991). An ethnographic study of the mathematical ideas of a group of carpenters. *Learning and Individual Differences, 3,* 1–25.

Minstrell, J., & Stimpson, V. (1996). A classroom environment for learning: Guiding students' reconstruction of understanding and reasoning. In L. Schauble & R. Glaser (Eds.), *Innovations in learning: New environments for education.* Mahwah, NJ: Erlbaum.

Mintzes, J. J., Trowbridge, J. E., Arnaudin, M. W., & Wandersee, J. H. (1991). Children's biology: Studies on conceptual development in the life sciences. In S. M. Glynn, R. H. Yeany, & B. K. Britton (Eds.), *The psychology of learning science.* Hillsdale, NJ: Erlbaum.

Mintzes, J. J., Wandersee, J. H., & Novak, J. D. (1997). Meaningful learning in science: The human constructivist perspective. In G. D. Phye (Ed.), *Handbook of academic learning: Construction of knowledge.* San Diego: Academic Press.

Mischel, W., & Grusec, J. E. (1966). Determinants of the rehearsal and transmission of neutral and aversive behaviors. *Journal of Personality and Social Psychology, 3,* 197–205.

Mitchell, J. B. (1989). Current theories on expert and novice thinking: A full faculty considers the implications for legal education. *Journal of Legal Education, 39,* 275–297.

Moely, B. E. (1977). Organizational factors in the development of memory. In R. V. Kail & J. W. Hagen (Eds.), *Perspectives on the development of memory and cognition.* Hillsdale, NJ: Erlbaum.

Mohatt, G., & Erickson, F. (1981). Cultural differences in teaching styles in an Odawa school: A sociolinguistic approach. In H. T. Trueba, G. P. Guthrie, & K. H. Au (Eds.), *Culture and the bilingual classroom: Studies in classroom ethnography.* Rowley, MA: Newbury House.

Moles, O. C. (Ed.) (1990). *Student discipline strategies: Research and practice.* Albany: State University of New York Press.

Moletzsky, B. (1974). Behavior recording as treatment: A brief note. *Behavior Therapy, 5,* 107–111.

Mooney, C. M. (1957). Age in the development of closure ability in children. *Canadian Journal of Psychology, 11,* 219–226.

Moray, N., Bates, A., & Barnett, R. (1965). Experiments on the four-eared man. *Journal of the Acoustical Society of America, 38,* 196–201.

Morgan, M. (1984). Reward-induced decrements and increments in intrinsic motivation. *Review of Educational Research, 54,* 5–30.

Morgan, M. (1985). Self-monitoring of attained subgoals in private study. *Journal of Educational Psychology, 77,* 623–630.

Morris, C. D., Bransford, J. D., & Franks, J. J. (1977). Levels of processing versus transfer appropriate processing. *Journal of Verbal Learning and Verbal Behavior, 16,* 519–533.

Morris, E. K. (1982). Some relationships between interbehavioral psychology and radical behaviorism. *Behaviorism, 10,* 187–216.

Morris, P. (1977). Practical strategies for human learning and remembering. In M. J. A. Howe (Ed.), *Adult learning: Psychological research and applications.* London: Wiley.

Morris, R. J. (1985). *Behavior modification with exceptional children: Principles and practices.* Glenview, IL: Scott Foresman.

Morris, R. J., Kratochwill, T. R., & Aldridge, K. (1988). Fears and phobias. In J. C. Witt, S. N. Elliott, & F. M. Gresham (Eds.), *Handbook of behavior therapy in education.* New York: Plenum Press.

Mowrer, O. H. (1938). Preparatory set (expectancy): A determinant in motivation and learning. *Psychological Review, 45,* 62–91.

Mowrer, O. H. (1939). A stimulus–response analysis and its role as a reinforcing agent. *Psychological Review, 46,* 553–565.

Mowrer, O. H. (1956). Two-factor learning theory reconsidered, with special reference to secondary reinforcement and the concept of habit. *Psychological Review, 63,* 114–128.

Mowrer, O. H. (1960). *Learning theory and behavior.* New York: Wiley.

Mowrer, O. H., & Lamoreaux, R. R. (1942). Avoidance conditioning and signal duration: A study of secondary motivation and reward. *Psychological Monographs, 54* (Whole No. 247).

Mueller, J. H. (1980). Test anxiety and the encoding and retrieval of information. In I. G. Sarason (Ed.), *Test anxiety: Theory, research, and applications.* Hillsdale, NJ: Erlbaum.

Mueller, M. M., Sterling-Turner, H. E., & Scattone, D. (2001). Functional assessment of hand flapping in a general education classroom. *Journal of Applied Behavior Analysis, 34,* 233–236.

Murdock, T. B. (1999). The social context of risk: Status and motivational predictors of alienation in middle school. *Journal of Educational Psychology, 91,* 62–75.

Murnane, R. J., & Raizen, S. A. (Eds.). (1988). *Improving indicators of the quality of science and mathematics education in grades K–12.* Washington, DC: National Academy Press.

Murphy, P. K. (2000). A motivated exploration of motivation terminology. *Contemporary Educational Psychology, 25,* 3–53.

Murphy, P. K., & Alexander, P. A. (2000). A motivated exploration of motivation terminology. *Contemporary Educational Psychology, 25,* 3–53.

Murray, C. B., & Jackson, J. S. (1982/1983). The conditioned failure model of black educational underachievement. *Humboldt Journal of Social Relations, 10,* 276–300.

Murray, F. B. (1978). Teaching strategies and conservation training. In A. M. Lesgold, J. W. Pellegrino, S. D. Fokkema, & R. Glaser (Eds.), *Cognitive psychology and instruction.* New York: Plenum Press.

Mwangi, W., & Sweller, J. (1998). Learning to solve compare word problems: The effect of example format and generating self-explanations. *Cognition and Instruction, 16,* 173–199.

Myers, J. L., & Duffy, S. A. (1990). Causal inferences and text memory. In A. C. Graessner & G. H. Bower (Eds.), *Inferences and text comprehension. The psychology of learning and motivation: Advances in research and theory* (Vol. 25). Orlando: Academic Press.

Nadel, L., & Jacobs, W. J. (1998). Traumatic memory is special. *Current Directions in Psychological Science, 7,* 154–157.

Natriello, G. (1987). The impact of evaluation processes on students. *Educational Psychologist, 22*, 155–175.

Natriello, G., & Dornbusch, S. M. (1984). *Teacher evaluative standards and student effort.* New York: Longman.

Naveh-Benjamin, M. (1991). A comparison of training programs intended for different types of text-anxious students: Further support for an information-processing model. *Journal of Educational Psychology, 83*, 134–139.

Neisser, U. (1967). *Cognitive psychology.* New York: Appleton-Century-Crofts.

Neisser, U. (1981). John Dean's memory: A case study. *Cognition, 9*, 1–22.

Neisser, U. (Ed.). (1987). *Concepts and conceptual development: Ecological and intellectual factors in categorization.* Cambridge, England: Cambridge University Press.

Neisser, U., & Harsch, N. (1992). Phantom flashbulbs: False recollections of hearing the news about *Challenger.* In E. Winograd & U. Neisser (Eds.), *Affect and accuracy in recall: Studies of "flashbulb" memories.* Cambridge, England: Cambridge University Press.

Neisser, U., & Weene, P. (1962). Hierarchies in concept formation. *Journal of Experimental Psychology, 64*, 644–645.

Nell, V. (2002). Why young men drive dangerously: Implications for injury prevention. *Current Directions in Psychological Science, 11*, 75–79.

Nelson, C. A. (1995). The ontogeny of human memory: A cognitive neuroscience perspective. *Developmental Psychology, 31*, 723–738.

Nelson, K. (1993a). Explaining the emergence of autobiographical memory in early childhood. In A. F. Collins, S. E. Gathercole, M. A. Conway, & P. E. Morris (Eds.), *Theories of memory.* Hove, England: Erlbaum.

Nelson, K. (1993b). The psychological and social origins of autobiographical memory. *Psychological Science, 4*, 7–14.

Nelson, K. (1996). Memory development from 4 to 7 years. In A. J. Sameroff & M. M. Haith (Eds.), *The 5 to 7 shift* (pp. 141–160). Chicago: University of Chicago Press.

Nelson, L. J., & Miller, D. T. (1995). The distinctiveness effect in social categorization: You are what makes you unusual. *Psychological Science, 6*, 246–249.

Nelson, T. O. (1971). Savings and forgetting from long-term memory. *Journal of Verbal Learning and Verbal Behavior, 10*, 568–576.

Nelson, T. O. (1977). Repetition and depth of processing. *Journal of Verbal Learning and Verbal Behavior, 16*, 151–171.

Nelson, T. O. (1978). Detecting small amounts of information in memory: Savings for nonrecognized items. *Journal of Experimental Psychology: Human Learning and Memory, 4*, 453–468.

Nelson, T. O., & Dunlosky, J. (1991). When people's judgments of learning (JOLs) are extremely accurate at predicting subsequent recall: The "delayed-JOL effect." *Psychological Science, 2*, 267–270.

Nelson, T. O., & Rothbart, R. (1972). Acoustic savings for items forgotten from long-term memory. *Journal of Experimental Psychology, 93*, 357–360.

Nenniger, P. (1992). Task motivation: An interaction between the cognitive and content-oriented dimensions in learning. In K. A. Renninger, S. Hidi, & A. Krapp (Eds.), *The role of interest in learning and development.* Hillsdale, NJ: Erlbaum.

Neumann, P. G. (1974). An attribute frequency model for the abstraction of prototypes. *Memory and Cognition, 2*, 241–248.

Neumann, P. G. (1977). Visual prototype formation with discontinuous representation of dimensions of variability. *Memory and Cognition, 5*, 187–197.

Neumann, R. (2000). The causal influences of attributions on emotions: A procedural priming approach. *Psychological Science, 11*, 179–182.

Nevin, J. A., Mandell, C., & Atak, J. R. (1983). The analysis of behavioral momentum. *Journal of the Experimental Analysis of Behavior, 39*, 49–59.

Newby, T. J., Ertmer, P. A., & Stepich, D. A. (1994, April). *Instructional analogies and the learning of concepts.* Paper presented at the annual meeting of the American Educational Research Association, New Orleans.

Newby, T. J., & Stepich, D. A. (1987). Learning about concepts: The use of analogies as a mediational strategy. *Journal of Instructional Development, 10*(2), 20–26.

Newcombe, N. S., Drummey, A. B., Fox, N. A., Lie, E., & Ottinger-Albergs, W. (2000). Remembering early childhood: How much, how, and why (or why not). *Current Directions in Psychological Science, 9*, 55–58.

Newcombe, N. S., & Fox, N. A. (1994). Infantile amnesia: Through a glass darkly. *Child Development, 65*, 31–40.

Newell, A., Shaw, J. C., & Simon, H. A. (1958). Elements of a theory of human problem solving. *Psychological Review, 65*, 151–166.

Newell, A., & Simon, H. A. (1972). *Human problem solving.* Englewood Cliffs, NJ: Prentice Hall.

Newman, R. S. (1998). Students' help seeking during problem solving: Influences of personal and contextual achievement goals. *Journal of Educational Psychology, 90*, 644–658.

Newman, R. S., & Schwager, M. T. (1992). Student perceptions and academic help seeking. In D. Schunk & J. Meece (Eds.), *Student perceptions in the classroom.* Hillsdale, NJ: Erlbaum.

Newman, R. S., & Schwager, M. T. (1995). Students' help seeking during problem solving: Effects of grade, goal, and prior achievement. *American Educational Research Journal, 32*, 352–376.

Newmann, F. M., & Wehlage, G. G. (1993). Five standards of authentic instruction. *Educational Leadership, 50*(7), 8–12.

Newport, E. L. (1990). Maturational constraints on language learning. *Cognitive Science, 14*, 11–28.

Nicholls, J. G. (1984). Conceptions of ability and achievement motivation. In R. Ames & C. Ames (Eds.), *Research on motivation in education: Vol. 1. Student motivation.* Orlando: Academic Press.

Nicholls, J. G. (1990). What is ability and why are we mindful of it? A developmental perspective. In R. J. Sternberg & J. Kolligian (Eds.), *Competence considered.* New Haven, CT: Yale University Press.

Nicholls, J. G. (1992). Students as educational theorists. In D. Schunk & J. L. Meece (Eds.), *Student perception in the classroom.* Hillsdale, NJ: Erlbaum.

Nicholls, J. G., Cobb, P., Yackel, E., Wood, T., & Wheatley, G. (1990). Students' theories of mathematics and their mathematical knowledge: Multiple dimensions of assessment. In G. Kulm (Ed.), *Assessing higher order thinking in mathematics.* Washington, DC: American Association for the Advancement of Science.

Nichols, J. D. (1996a). Cooperative learning: A motivational tool to enhance student persistence, self-regulation, and efforts to please teachers and parents. *Educational Research and Evaluation, 2*, 246–260.

Nichols, J. D. (1996b). The effects of cooperative learning on student achievement and motivation in a high school geometry class. *Contemporary Educational Psychology, 21*, 467–476.

Nichols, J. D., Ludwin, W. G., & Iadicola, P. (1999). A darker shade of gray: A year-end analysis of discipline and suspension data. *Equity and Excellence in Education, 32*(1), 43–55.

Nickerson, R. S. (1989). New directions in educational assessment. *Educational Researcher, 18*(9), 3–7.

Nisbett, R. E., & Bellows, N. (1977). Verbal reports about causal influences on social judgments: Private access versus public theories. *Journal of Personality and Social Psychology, 35*, 613–624.

Nisbett, R. E., & Wilson, T. D. (1977). Telling more than we can know: Verbal reports on mental processes. *Psychological Review, 84*, 231–259.

Nist, S. L., Simpson, M. L., Olejnik, S., & Mealey, D. L. (1991). The relation between self-selected study processes and test performance. *American Educational Research Journal, 28*, 849–874.

Noddings, N. (1985). Small groups as a setting for research on mathematical problem solving. In E. A. Silver (Ed.), *Teaching and learning mathematical problem solving: Multiple research perspectives.* Hillsdale, NJ: Erlbaum.

Nolen, S. B. (1996). Why study? How reasons for learning influence strategy selection. *Educational Psychology Review, 8*, 335–355.

Norman, D. A. (1969). *Memory and attention: An introduction to human information processing*. New York: Wiley.

Norman, D. A., & Bobrow, D. G. (1975). On data-limited and resource-limited processes. *Cognitive Psychology, 7*, 44–64.

Norman, D. A., & Rumelhart, D. E. (1975). *Explorations in cognition*. San Francisco: W. H. Freeman.

Northup, J. (2000). Further evaluation of the accuracy of reinforcer surveys: A systematic replication. *Journal of Applied Behavior Analysis, 33*, 335–338.

Northup, J., Broussard, C., Jones, K. George, T., Vollmer, T. R., & Herring, M. (1995). The differential effects of teachers and peer attention on the disruptive classroom behavior of three children with a diagnosis of attention deficit hyperactivity disorder. *Journal of Applied Behavior Analysis, 28*, 227–228.

Novak, J. D. (1998). *Learning, creating, and using knowledge: Concept maps as facilitative tools in schools and corporations*. Mahwah, NJ: Erlbaum.

Novak, J. D., & Gowin, D. B. (1984). *Learning how to learn*. Cambridge, England: Cambridge University Press.

Novak, J. D., & Musonda, D. (1991). A twelve-year longitudinal study of science concept learning. *American Educational Research Journal, 28*, 117–153.

Novick, L. R. (1988). Analogical transfer, problem similarity, and expertise. *Journal of Experimental Psychology: Learning, Memory, and Cognition, 14*, 510–520.

Nungester, R. J., & Duchastel, P. C. (1982). Testing versus review: Effects on retention. *Journal of Educational Psychology, 74*, 18–22.

Nussbaum, J. (1985). The earth as a cosmic body. In R. Driver (Ed.), *Children's ideas of science*. Philadelphia: Open University Press.

Nuthall, G. (2000). The anatomy of memory in the classroom: Understanding how students acquire memory processes from classroom activities in science and social studies units. *American Educational Research Journal, 37*, 247–304.

Oakes, J., & Guiton, G. (1995). Matchmaking: The dynamics of high school tracking decisions. *American Educational Research Journal, 32*, 3–33.

Oakhill, J. (1993). Children's difficulties in reading comprehension. *Educational Psychology Review, 5*, 223–237.

Oatley, K., & Nundy, S. (1996). Rethinking the role of emotions in education. In D. R. Olson & N. Torrance (Eds.), *The handbook of education and human development: New models of learning, teaching, and schooling*. Cambridge, MA: Blackwell.

Ochsner, K. N., & Lieberman, M. D. (2001). The emergence of social cognitive neuroscience. *American Psychologist, 56*, 717–734.

Oden, G. C. (1987). Concept, knowledge, and thought. *Annual Review of Psychology, 38*, 203–227.

O'Donnell, A. M. (1999). Structuring dyadic interaction through scripted cooperation. In A. M. O'Donnell & A. King (Eds.), *Cognitive perspectives on peer learning* (pp. 179–196). Mahwah, NJ: Erlbaum.

O'Donnell, A. M., Dansereau, D. F., & Hall, R. H. (2002). Knowledge maps as scaffolds for cognitive processing. *Educational Psychology Review, 14*, 71–86.

O'Donnell, A. M., & King, A. (Eds.). (1999). *Cognitive perspectives on peer learning*. Mahwah, NJ: Erlbaum.

O'Donnell, A. M., & O'Kelly, J. (1994). Learning from peers: Beyond the rhetoric of positive results. *Educational Psychology Review, 6*, 321–349.

Ohlsson, S. (1983). On natural and technical knowledge domains. *Scandinavian Journal of Psychology, 25*, 89–91.

Olds, J., & Milner, P. (1954). Positive reinforcement produced by electrical stimulation of septal area and other regions of rat brain. *Journal of Comparative and Physiological Psychology, 47*, 419–427.

O'Leary, K. D., & Becker, W. C. (1967). Behavior modification of an adjustment class: A token reinforcement program. *Exceptional Children, 33*, 637–642.

O'Leary, K. D., Kaufman, K. F., Kass, R. E., & Drabman, R. S. (1970). The effects of loud and soft reprimands on the behavior of disruptive students. *Exceptional Children, 37*, 145–155.

O'Leary, K. D., & O'Leary, S. G. (Eds.) (1972). *Classroom management: The successful use of behavior modification*. New York: Pergamon Press.

Olneck, M. R. (1995). Immigrants and education. In J. A. Banks & C. A. M. Banks (Eds.), *Handbook of research on multicultural education*. New York: Macmillan.

Olson, M. A., & Fazio, R. H. (2001). Implicit attitude formation through classical conditioning. *Psychological Science, 12*, 413–417.

Onosko, J. J. (1996). Exploring issues with students despite the barriers. *Social Education, 60*(1), 22–27.

Onosko, J. J., & Newmann, F. M. (1994). Creating more thoughtful learning environments. In J. N. Mangieri & C. C. Block (Eds.), *Creating powerful thinking in teachers and students: Diverse perspectives*. Fort Worth, TX: Harcourt Brace.

Ormrod, J. E. (1979). Cognitive processes in the solution of three-term series problems. *American Journal of Psychology, 92*, 235–255.

Ormrod, J. E. (1985). Proofreading *The Cat in the Hat*: Evidence for different reading styles of good and poor spellers. *Psychological Reports, 57*, 863–867.

Ormrod, J. E. (1986a). Differences between good and poor spellers in reading style and short-term memory. *Visible Language, 20*, 437–447.

Ormrod, J. E. (1986b). Learning to spell: Three studies at the university level. *Research in the Teaching of English, 20*, 160–173.

Ormrod, J. E. (1986c). Learning to spell while reading: A follow-up study. *Perceptual and Motor Skills, 63*, 652–654.

Ormrod, J. E., & Jenkins, L. (1988, April). *Study strategies for learning spelling: What works and what does not*. Paper presented at the annual meeting of the American Educational Research Association, New Orleans.

Ormrod, J. E., Ormrod, R. K., Wagner, E. D., & McCallin, R. C. (1988). Reconceptualizing map learning. *American Journal of Psychology, 101*, 425–433.

Ormrod, J. E., & Wagner, E. D. (1987, October). *Spelling conscience in undergraduate students: Ratings of spelling accuracy and dictionary use*. Paper presented at the annual meeting of the Northern Rocky Mountain Educational Research Association, Park City, UT.

Ornstein, P. A., & Haden, C. A. (2001). *Memory* development or the *development* of memory? *Current Directions in Psychological Science, 10*, 202–205.

Ornstein, R. (1972). *The psychology of consciousness*. San Francisco: W. H. Freeman.

Ornstein, R. (1997). *The right mind: Making sense of the hemispheres*. San Diego: Harcourt Brace.

Osborn, A. F. (1963). *Applied imagination* (3rd ed.). New York: Scribner.

Osborne, J. G. (1969). Free-time as a reinforcer in the management of classroom behavior. *Journal of Applied Behavior Analysis, 2*, 113–118.

Osborne, J. W., & Simmons, C. M. (2002, April). *Girls, math, stereotype threat, and anxiety: Physiological evidence*. Paper presented at the annual meeting of the American Educational Research Association, New Orleans.

Osgood, C. E. (1949). The similarity paradox in human learning: A resolution. *Psychological Review, 56*, 132–143.

Oskamp, S. (Ed.). (2000). *Reducing prejudice and discrimination*. Mahwah, NJ: Erlbaum.

Osterman, K. F. (2000). Students' need for belonging in the school community. *Review of Educational Research, 70*, 323–367.

O'Sullivan, J. T., & Joy, R. M. (1990, April). *Children's theories about reading difficulty: A developmental study*. Paper presented at the annual meeting of the American Educational Research Association, Boston.

Otero, J. (1998). Influence of knowledge activation and context on comprehension monitoring of science texts. In D. J. Hacker, J. Dunlosky, & A. C. Graesser (Eds.), *Metacognition in educational theory and practice* (pp. 145–164). Mahwah, NJ: Erlbaum.

Otero, J., & Kintsch, W. (1992). Failures to detect contradictions in a text: What readers believe versus what they read. *Psychological Science, 3*, 229–235.

Overmier, J. B., & Lawry, J. A. (1979). Pavlovian conditioning and the mediation of behavior. In G. H. Bower (Ed.), *The psychology of learning and motivation* (Vol. 13). New York: Academic Press.

Owens, J., Bower, G. H., & Black, J. B. (1979). The "soap opera" effect in story recall. *Memory and Cognition, 7,* 185–191.

Owens, R. E., Jr. (1996). *Language development* (4th ed.). Boston: Allyn & Bacon.

Packard, R. G. (1970). The control of "classroom attention": A group contingency for complex behavior. *Journal of Applied Behavior Analysis, 3,* 13–28.

Packer, M. J., & Goicoechea, J. (2000). Sociocultural and constructivist theories of learning: Ontology, not just epistemology. *Educational Psychologist, 35,* 227–241.

Page-Voth, V., & Graham, S. (1999). Effects of goal setting and strategy use on the writing performance and self-efficacy of students with writing and learning problems. *Journal of Educational Psychology, 91,* 230–240.

Paige, J. M., & Simon, H. A. (1966). Cognitive processes in solving algebra word problems. In B. Kleinmuntz (Ed.), *Problem solving.* New York: Wiley.

Paivio, A. (1963). Learning of adjective–noun paired associates as a function of adjective–noun word order and noun abstractness. *Canadian Journal of Psychology, 17,* 370–379.

Paivio, A. (1971). *Imagery and verbal processes.* New York: Holt, Rinehart & Winston.

Paivio, A. (1975). Coding distinctions and repetition effects in memory. In G. H. Bower (Ed.), *The psychology of learning and motivation* (Vol. 9). New York: Academic Press.

Paivio, A. (1986). *Mental representations: A dual-coding approach.* New York: Oxford University Press.

Pajares, F. (1996). Self-efficacy beliefs in academic settings. *Review of Educational Research, 66,* 543–578.

Palardy, J. M. (1969). What teachers believe—what children achieve. *Elementary School Journal, 69,* 370–374.

Palermo, D. S. (1973). More about less: A study of language comprehension. *Journal of Verbal Learning and Verbal Behavior, 12,* 211–221.

Palincsar, A. S. (1986, April). *Interactive cognition to promote listening comprehension.* Paper presented at the annual meeting of the American Educational Research Association, San Francisco.

Palincsar, A. S., Anderson, C., & David, Y. M. (1993). Pursuing scientific literacy in the middle grades through collaborative problem solving. *Elementary School Journal, 93,* 643–658.

Palincsar, A. S., & Brown, A. L. (1984). Reciprocal teaching of comprehension-fostering and comprehension-monitoring activities. *Cognition and Instruction, 1,* 117–175.

Palincsar, A. S., & Brown, A. L. (1989). Classroom dialogues to promote self-regulated comprehension. In J. Brophy (Ed.),

Advances in research on teaching (Vol. 1). Greenwich, CT: JAI Press.

Palincsar, A. S., & Herrenkohl, L. R. (1999). Designing collaborative contexts: Lessons from three research programs. In A. M. O'Donnell & A. King (Eds.), *Cognitive perspectives on peer learning* (pp. 151–177). Mahwah, NJ: Erlbaum.

Pallock, L., & Surber, J. R. (1997, March). *Effect of topic frequency and importance on recall of text.* Paper presented at the annual meeting of the American Educational Research Association, Chicago.

Palmer, D. J., & Goetz, E. T. (1988). Selection and use of study strategies: The role of the studier's beliefs about self and strategies. In C. E. Weinstein, E. T. Goetz, & P. A. Alexander (Eds.), *Learning and study strategies: Issues in assessment, instruction, and evaluation.* San Diego: Academic Press.

Papka, M., Ivry, R. B., & Woodruff-Pak, D. S. (1997). Eyeblink classical conditioning and awareness revisited. *Psychological Science, 8,* 404–408.

Paris, S. G. (1988). Models and metaphors of learning strategies. In C. E. Weinstein, E. T. Goetz, & P. A. Alexander (Eds.), *Learning and study strategies: Issues in assessment, instruction, and evaluation.* San Diego, CA: Academic Press.

Paris, S. G. (1990, April). Discussant's comments. In B. McCombs (Chair), *Theoretical perspectives on socialization and children's development of self-regulated learning.* Symposium presented at the annual meeting of the American Educational Research Association, Boston.

Paris, S. G., & Ayres, L. R. (1994). *Becoming reflective students and teachers with portfolios and authentic assessment.* Washington, DC: American Psychological Association.

Paris, S. G., & Byrnes, J. P. (1989). The constructivist approach to self-regulation and learning in the classroom. In B. J. Zimmerman & D. H. Schunk (Eds.), *Self-regulated learning and academic achievement: Theory, research, and practice.* New York: Springer-Verlag.

Paris, S. G., & Cunningham, A. E. (1996). Children becoming students. In D. C. Berliner & R. C. Calfee (Eds.), *Handbook of educational psychology.* New York: Macmillan.

Paris, S. G., Lawton, T. A., Turner, J. C., & Roth, J. L. (1991). A developmental perspective on standardized achievement testing. *Educational Researcher, 20*(5), 12–20, 40.

Paris, S. G., & Lindauer, B. K. (1976). The role of inference in children's comprehension and memory. *Cognitive Psychology, 8,* 217–227.

Paris, S. G., & Paris, A. H. (2001). Classroom applications of research on self-regulated learning. *Educational Psychologist, 36,* 89–101.

Paris, S. G., & Turner, J. C. (1994). Situated motivation. In P. R. Pintrich, D. R. Brown, & C. E. Weinstein (Eds.), *Student motiva-*

tion, cognition, and learning: Essays in honor of Wilbert J. McKeachie. Hillsdale, NJ: Erlbaum.

Paris, S. G., & Winograd, P. (1990). How metacognition can promote academic learning and instruction. In B. F. Jones & L. Idol (Eds.), *Dimensions of thinking and cognitive instruction.* Hillsdale, NJ: Erlbaum.

Park, O. (1984). Example comparison strategy versus attribute identification strategy in concept learning. *American Educational Research Journal, 21,* 145–162.

Parke, R. D. (1972). Some effects of punishment on children's behavior. In W. W. Hartup (Ed.), *The young child* (Vol. 2). Washington, DC: National Association for the Education of Young Children.

Parke, R. D. (1977). Some effects of punishment on children's behavior—revisited. In E. M. Hetherington & R. D. Parke (Eds.), *Contemporary readings in child psychology.* New York: McGraw-Hill.

Parke, R. D., & Deur, J. L. (1972). Schedule of punishment and inhibition of aggression in children. *Developmental Psychology, 7,* 266–269.

Parke, R. D., & Walters, R. H. (1967). Some factors determining the efficacy of punishment for inducing response inhibition. *Monograph for the Society for Research in Child Development, 32* (Whole No. 109).

Parker, J. (1995). Age differences in source monitoring of performed and imagined actions on immediate and delayed tests. *Journal of Experimental Child Psychology, 60,* 84–101.

Parrish, J. M., Cataldo, M. F., Kolko, D. J., Neef, N. A., & Egel, A. L. (1986). Experimental analysis of response covariations among compliant and inappropriate behaviors. *Journal of Applied Behavior Analysis, 19,* 241–254.

Parsons, J. E., Adler, T. F., & Kaczala, C. M. (1982). Socialization of achievement attitudes and beliefs: Parental influences. *Child Development, 53,* 310–321.

Parsons, J. E., Kaczala, C. M., & Meece, J. L. (1982). Socialization of achievement attitudes and beliefs: Classroom influences. *Child Development, 53,* 322–339.

Pascarella, E. T., & Terenzini, P. T. (1991). *How college affects students: Findings and insights from twenty years of research.* San Francisco: Jossey-Bass.

Pashler, H. (1992). Attentional limitations in doing two tasks at the same time. *Current Directions in Psychological Science, 1,* 44–48.

Patrick, H., & Middleton, M. J. (2002). Turning the kaleidoscope: What we see when self-regulated learning is viewed with a qualitative lens. *Educational Psychologist, 37,* 27–39.

Paus, T., Zijdenbos, A., Worsley, K., Collins, D. L., Blumenthal, J., Giedd, J. N., Rapoport, J. L., & Evans, A. C. (1999). Structural maturation of neural pathways in children and adolescents: In vivo study. *Science, 283,* 1908–1911.

Pavlov, I. P. (1927). *Conditioned reflexes* (G. V. Anrep, Trans.). London: Oxford University Press.

Pea, R. D. (1993). Practices of distributed intelligence and designs for education. In G. Salomon (Ed.), *Distributed cognitions: Psychological and educational considerations.* Cambridge, England: Cambridge University Press.

Pear, J. J., & Crone-Todd, D. E. (1999). Personalized system of instruction in cyberspace. *Journal of Applied Behavior Analysis, 32,* 205–209.

Pearson, P. D., Hansen, J., & Gordon, C. (1979). The effect of background knowledge on young children's comprehension of explicit and implicit information. *Journal of Reading Behavior, 11*(3), 201–209.

Pellegrini, A. D., & Bjorklund, D. F. (1997). The role of recess in children's cognitive performance. *Educational Psychologist, 32,* 35–40.

Pellegrini, A. D., Huberty, P. D., & Jones, I. (1995). The effects of recess timing on children's playground and classroom behaviors. *American Educational Research Journal, 32,* 845–864.

Penfield, W. (1958). Some mechanisms of consciousness discovered during electrical stimulation of the brain. *Proceedings of the National Academy of Sciences, 44,* 51–66.

Penfield, W. (1959). Consciousness, memory, and man's conditioned reflexes. In K. Pribram (Ed.), *On the biology of learning.* New York: Harcourt, Brace, & World.

Penfield, W., & Roberts, L. (1959). *Speech and brain-mechanisms.* Princeton, NJ: Princeton University Press.

Perfetti, C. A. (1983). Reading, vocabulary, and writing: Implications for computer-based instruction. In A. C. Wilkinson (Ed.), *Classroom computers and cognitive science.* New York: Academic Press.

Perfetti, C. A., Britt, M. A., Rouet, J.-F., Georgi, M. C., & Mason, R. A. (1994). How students use texts to learn and reason about historical uncertainty. In M. Carretero & J. F. Voss (Eds.), *Cognitive and instructional processes in history and the social sciences* (pp. 257–283). Mahwah, NJ: Erlbaum.

Perfetti, C. A., & Hogaboam, T. (1975). The relationship between single word coding and reading comprehension skill. *Journal of Educational Psychology, 67,* 461–469.

Perfetti, C. A., & Lesgold, A. M. (1979). Coding and comprehension in skilled reading and implications for reading instruction. In L. B. Resnick & P. Weaver (Eds.), *Theory and practice of early reading* (Vol. 1). Hillsdale, NJ: Erlbaum.

Perin, C. T. (1942). Behavior potentiality as a joint function of the amount of training and the degree of hunger at the time of extinction. *Journal of Experimental Psychology, 30,* 93–113.

Perin, C. T. (1943). A quantitative investigation of the delay-of-reinforcement gradi-ent. *Journal of Experimental Psychology, 32,* 37–51.

Perkins, D. (1992). *Smart schools: From training memories to educating minds.* New York: Free Press/Macmillan.

Perkins, D. (1995). *Outsmarting IQ: The emerging science of learnable intelligence.* New York: Free Press.

Perkins, D. N., & Salomon, G. (1987). Transfer and teaching thinking. In D. N. Perkins, J. Lochhead, & J. Bishop (Eds.), *Thinking: The second international conference.* Hillsdale, NJ: Erlbaum.

Perkins, D. N., & Salomon, G. (1989). Are cognitive skills context-bound? *Educational Researcher, 18*(1), 16–25.

Perkins, D. N., & Simmons, R. (1988). Patterns of misunderstanding: An integrative model for science, math, and programming. *Review of Educational Research, 58,* 303–326.

Perlmutter, M., & Lange, G. A. (1978). A developmental analysis of recall-recognition distinctions. In P. A. Ornstein (Ed.), *Memory development in children.* Hillsdale, NJ: Erlbaum.

Perone, M., & Baron, A. (1980). Reinforcement of human observing behavior by a stimulus correlated with extinction or increased effort. *Journal of the Experimental Analysis of Behavior, 34,* 239–261.

Perry, A. C., & Fisher, W. W. (2001). Behavioral economic influences on treatments designed to decrease destructive behavior. *Journal of Applied Behavior Analysis, 34,* 211–215.

Perry, D. G., & Perry, L. C. (1983). Social learning, causal attribution, and moral internalization. In J. Bisanz, G. L. Bisanz, & R. Kail (Eds.), *Learning in children: Progress in cognitive development research.* New York: Springer-Verlag.

Perry, M. (1991). Learning and transfer: Instructional conditions and conceptual change. *Cognitive Development, 6,* 449–468.

Perry, N. E. (1998). Young children's self-regulated learning and contexts that support it. *Journal of Educational Psychology, 90,* 715–729.

Perry, N. E., VandeKamp, K. O., Mercer, L. K., & Nordby, C. J. (2002). Investigating teacher-student interactions that foster self-regulated learning. *Educational Psychologist, 37,* 5–15.

Perry, R. P. (1985). Instructor expressivenss: Implications for improving teaching. In J. G. Donald & A. M. Sullivan (Eds.), *Using research to improve teaching* (pp. 35–49). San Francisco: Jossey-Bass.

Perry, W. G., Jr. (1968). *Forms of intellectual and ethical development in the college years.* Cambridge, MA: President and Fellows of Harvard College.

Peskin, J. (1998). Constructing meaning when reading poetry: An expert–novice study. *Cognition and Instruction, 16,* 235–263.

Peterson, C. (1988, August). *Explanatory style and academic performance.* Paper pre-sented at the annual meeting of the American Psychological Association, Atlanta.

Peterson, C. (1990). Explanatory style in the classroom and on the playing field. In S. Graham & V. S. Folkes (Eds.), *Attribution theory: Applications to achievement, mental health, and interpersonal conflict.* Hillsdale, NJ: Erlbaum.

Peterson, C., & Barrett, L. C. (1987). Explanatory style and academic performance among university freshmen. *Journal of Personality and Social Psychology, 53,* 603–607.

Peterson, C., Colvin, D., & Lin, E. H. (1992). Explanatory style and helplessness. *Social Behavior and Personality, 20*(1), 1–14.

Peterson, C., Maier, S. F., & Seligman, M. E. P. (1993). *Learned helplessness: A theory for the age of personal control.* New York: Oxford University Press.

Peterson, L. R., & Peterson, M. J. (1959). Short-term retention of individual items. *Journal of Experimental Psychology, 58,* 193–198.

Peterson, L. R., & Peterson, M. J. (1962). Minimal paired-associate learning. *Journal of Experimental Psychology, 63,* 521–527.

Peterson, M. A. (1994). Object recognition processes can and do operate before figure–ground organization. *Current Directions in Psychological Science, 3,* 105–111.

Peterson, M. A., & Gibson, B. S. (1994). Must figure–ground organization precede object recognition? An assumption in peril. *Psychological Science, 5,* 253–259.

Peterson, M. A., Kihlstrom, J. F., Rose, P. M., & Glisky, M. L. (1992). Mental images can be ambiguous: Reconstruals and reference-frame reversals. *Memory and Cognition, 20,* 107–123.

Peterson, S. E. (1993). The effects of prior achievement and group outcome on attributions and affect in cooperative tasks. *Contemporary Educational Psychology, 18,* 479–485.

Petri, H. L. (1991). *Motivation: Theory, research, and applications* (3rd ed.). Belmont, CA: Wadsworth.

Pezdek, K. (1977). Cross-modality semantic integration of sentence and picture memory. *Journal of Experimental Psychology: Human Learning and Memory, 3,* 515–524.

Pezdek, K., & Banks, W. P. (Eds.). (1996). *The recovered memory/false memory debate.* San Diego: Academic Press.

Pezdek, K., Finger, K., & Hodge, D. (1997). Planting false childhood memories: The role of event plausibility. *Psychological Science, 8,* 437–441.

Pfeiffer, K., Feinberg, G., & Gelber, S. (1987). Teaching productive problem solving attitudes. In D. Berger, K. Pezdek, & W. Banks (Eds.), *Applications in cognitive psychology: Problem solving education and computing.* Hillsdale, NJ: Erlbaum.

Pfiffner, L. J., & Barkley, R. A. (1998). t of ADHD in school settings. In R. A. Barkley, *Attention-deficit hyperactivy disorder: A handbook for diagnosis and treatment* (2nd ed., pp. 458–490). New York: Guilford Press.

Pfiffner, L. J., & O'Leary, S. G. (1987). The efficacy of all-positive management as a function of the prior use of negative consequences. *Journal of Applied Behavior Analysis, 20,* 265–271.

Pfiffner, L. J., & O'Leary, S. G. (1993). School-based psychological treatments. In J. L. Matson (Ed.), *Handbook of hyperactivity in children* (pp. 234–255). Boston: Allyn & Bacon.

Pfiffner, L. J., Rosén, L. A., & O'Leary, S. G. (1985). The efficacy of an all-positive approach to classroom management. *Journal of Applied Behavior Analysis, 18,* 257–261.

Phelan, P., Yu, H. C., & Davidson, A. L. (1994). Navigating the psychosocial pressures of adolescence: The voices and experiences of high school youth. *American Educational Research Journal, 31,* 415–447.

Phillips, B. N., Pitcher, G. D., Worsham, M. E., & Miller, S. C. (1980). Test anxiety and the school environment. In I. G. Sarason (Ed.), *Test anxiety: Theory, research, and applications.* Hillsdale, NJ: Erlbaum.

Phillips, D. A., & Zimmerman, M. (1990). The developmental course of perceived competence and incompetence among competent children. In R. J. Sternberg & J. Kolligian (Eds.), *Competence considered.* New Haven, CT: Yale University Press.

Phillips, E. L., Phillips, E. A., Fixsen, D. L., & Wolf, M. M. (1971). Achievement place: Modification of the behaviors of predelinquent boys within a token economy. *Journal of Applied Behavior Analysis, 4,* 45–59.

Phye, G. D. (1997). Learning and remembering: The basis for personal knowledge construction. In G. D. Phye (Ed.), *Handbook of academic learning: Construction of knowledge.* San Diego: Academic Press.

Phye, G. D. (2001). Problem-solving instruction and problem-solving transfer: The correspondence issue. *Journal of Educational Psychology, 93,* 571–578.

Piaget, J. (1928). *Judgment and reasoning in the child* (M. Warden, Trans.). New York: Harcourt, Brace.

Piaget, J. (1952). *The origins of intelligence in children* (M. Cook, Trans.). New York: W. W. Norton.

Piaget, J. (1959). *The language and thought of the child* (3rd ed.). (M. Gabain, Trans.). New York: Humanities Press.

Piaget, J. (1970). Piaget's theory. In P. H. Mussen (Ed.), *Carmichael's manual of psychology.* New York: Wiley.

Piaget, J. (1971). *Psychology and epistemology: Towards a theory of knowledge* (A. Rosin, Trans.). New York: Viking.

Piaget, J. (1972). *The principles of genetic epistemology* (W. Mays, Trans.). New York: Basic Books.

Piaget, J. (1980). *Adaptation and intelligence: Organic selection and phenocopy* (S. Eames, Trans.). Chicago: University of Chicago Press.

Piaget, J., & Inhelder, B. (1969). *The psychology of the child* (H. Weaver, Trans.). New York: Basic Books.

Pianko, S. (1979). A description of the composing processes of college freshmen writers. *Research in the Teaching of English, 13,* 5–22.

Piazza, C. C., Bowman, L. G., Contrucci, S. A., Delia, M. D., Adelinis, J. D., & Goh, H.-L. (1999). An evaluation of the properties of attention as reinforcement for destructive and appropriate behavior. *Journal of Applied Behavior Analysis, 32,* 437–449.

Pichert, J. W., & Anderson, R. C. (1977). Taking different perspectives on a story. *Journal of Educational Psychology, 69,* 309–315.

Piersel, W. C. (1987). Basic skills education. In C. A. Maher & S. G. Forman (Eds.), *A behavioral approach to education of children and youth.* Hillsdale, NJ: Erlbaum.

Pigott, H. E., Fantuzzo, J. W., & Clement, P. W. (1986). The effects of reciprocal peer tutoring and group contingencies on the academic performance of elementary school children. *Journal of Applied Behavior Analysis, 19,* 93–98.

Piliavin, I. M., Piliavin, J. A., & Rodin, J. (1975). Costs, diffusion, and the stigmatized victim. *Journal of Personality and Social Psychology, 32,* 429–438.

Piliavin, J. A., Dovidio, J. F., Gaertner, S. L., & Clark, R. D., III (1981). Responsive bystanders: The process of intervention. In J. Grzelak & V. Derlega (Eds.), *Living with other people: Theory and research on cooperation and helping.* New York: Academic Press.

Pillemer, D. B., & White, S. H. (1989). Childhood events recalled by children and adults. In H. W. Reese (Ed.), *Advances in child development and behavior* (Vol. 21). New York: Academic Press.

Pine, K. J., & Messer, D. J. (2000). The effect of explaining another's actions on children's implicit theories of balance. *Cognition and Instruction, 18,* 35–51.

Pinker, S. (1993). Rules of language. In P. Bloom (Ed.), *Language acquisition: Core readings.* Cambridge, MA: MIT Press.

Pinker, S., & Prince, A. (1988). On language and connectionism: Analysis of a parallel distributed processing model of language acquisition. *Cognition, 28,* 73–193.

Pinkston, E. M., Reese, N. M., LeBlanc, J. M., & Baer, D. M. (1973). Independent control of a preschool child's aggression and peer interaction by contingent teacher attention. *Journal of Applied Behavior Analysis, 6,* 223–224.

Pintrich, P. R. (2000). Multiple goals, multiple pathways: The role of goal orientation in learning and achievement. *Journal of Educational Psychology, 92,* 544–555.

Pintrich, P. R., & De Groot, E. V. (1990). Motivational and self-regulated learning components of classroom academic performance. *Journal of Educational Psychology, 82,* 33–40.

Pintrich, P. R., Marx, R. W., & Boyle, R. A. (1993). Beyond cold conceptual change: The role of motivational beliefs and classroom contextual factors in the process of conceptual change. *Review of Educational Research, 63,* 167–199.

Pintrich, P. R., & Schrauben, B. (1992). Students' motivational beliefs and their cognitive engagement in academic tasks. In D. Schunk & J. Meece (Eds.), *Students' perceptions in the classroom: Causes and consequences.* Hillsdale, NJ: Erlbaum.

Pintrich, P. R., & Schunk, D. H. (2002). *Motivation in education: Theory, research, and applications* (2nd ed.). Upper Saddle River, NJ: Merrill/Prentice Hall.

Piontkowski, D., & Calfee, R. (1979). Attention in the classroom. In G. A. Hale & M. Lewis (Eds.), *Attention and cognitive development.* New York: Plenum Press.

Plumert, J. M. (1994). Flexibility in children's use of spatial and categorical organizational strategies in recall. *Developmental Psychology, 30,* 738–747.

Plummer, S., Baer, D. M., & LeBlanc, J. M. (1977). Functional considerations in the use of procedural time out and an effective alternative. *Journal of Applied Behavior Analysis, 10,* 689–706.

Plunkett, K. (1996). *Connectionism and development: Neural networks and the study of change.* New York: Oxford University Press.

Poche, C., Yoder, P., & Miltenberger, R. (1988). Teaching self-protection to children using television techniques. *Journal of Applied Behavior Analysis, 21,* 253–261.

Polya, G. (1957). *How to solve it.* Garden City, NY: Doubleday.

Pomerantz, E. M., & Saxon, J. L. (2001). Conceptions of ability as stable and self-evaluative processes: A longitudinal examination. *Child Development, 72,* 152–173.

Pontecorvo, C. (1993). Social interaction in the acquisition of knowledge. *Educational Psychology Review, 5,* 293–310.

Poole, D. (1994). Routine testing practices and the linguistic construction of knowledge. *Cognition and Instruction, 12,* 125–150.

Popham, W. J. (1988). *Educational evaluation* (2nd ed.). Englewood Cliffs, NJ: Prentice Hall.

Popham, W. J. (1995). *Classroom assessment: What teachers need to know.* Boston: Allyn & Bacon.

Porter, A. (1989). A curriculum out of balance: The case of elementary school mathematics. *Educational Researcher, 18*(5), 9–15.

Posner, G. J., & Rudnitsky, A. N. (1986). *Course design: A guide to curriculum development for teachers* (3rd ed.). New York: Longman.

Posner, G. J., Strike, K. A., Hewson, P. W., & Gertzog, W. A. (1982). Accommodation of a scientific conception: Toward a theory of conceptual change. *Science Education, 66,* 211–227.

Posner, M. I., Goldsmith, R., & Welton, K. E., Jr. (1967). Perceived distance and the classification of distorted patterns. *Journal of Experimental Psychology, 73,* 28–38.

Posner, M. I., & Keele, S. W. (1968). On the genesis of abstract ideas. *Journal of Experimental Psychology*, 77, 353–363.

Posner, M. I., & Keele, S. W. (1970). Retention of abstract ideas. *Journal of Experimental Psychology*, 83, 304–308.

Postman, L. (1964). Short-term memory and incidental learning. In A. W. Melton (Ed.), *Categories of human learning*. New York: Academic Press.

Postman, L., & Phillips, L. (1965). Short-term temporal changes in free recall. *Quarterly Journal of Experimental Psychology*, 17, 132–138.

Postman, L., & Underwood, B. J. (1973). Critical issues in interference theory. *Memory and Cognition*, 1, 19–40.

Poulin-Dubois, D. (1999). Infants' distinction between animate and inanimate objects: The origins of naïve psychology. In P. Rochar (Ed.), *Early social cognition* (pp. 257–280). Mahwah, NJ: Erlbaum.

Powell, B. M. (1990, April). *Children's perceptions of classroom goal orientation: Relationship to learning strategies and intrinsic motivation*. Paper presented at the annual meeting of the American Educational Research Association, Boston.

Powell, S., & Nelson, B. (1997). Effects of choosing academic assignments on a study with attention deficit hyperactivity disorder. *Journal of Applied Behavior Analysis*, 30, 181–183.

Prawat, R. S. (1989). Promoting access to knowledge, strategy, and disposition in students: A research synthesis. *Review of Educational Research*, 59, 1–41.

Prawat, R. S. (1992). From individual differences to learning communities—our changing focus. *Educational Leadership*, 49(7), 9–13.

Prawat, R. S. (1993). The value of ideas: Problems versus possibilities in learning. *Educational Researcher*, 22(6), 5–16.

Prawat, R. S. (1996). Constructivisms, modern and postmodern. *Educational Psychologist*, 31, 215–225.

Premack, D. (1959). Toward empirical behavior laws: I. Positive reinforcement. *Psychological Review*, 66, 219–233.

Premack, D. (1963). Rate differential reinforcement in monkey manipulation. *Journal of Experimental Analysis of Behavior*, 6, 81–89.

Prentice, N. M. (1972). The influence of live and symbolic modeling on prompting moral judgments of adolescent delinquents. *Journal of Abnormal Psychology*, 80, 157–161.

Pressley, M. (1982). Elaboration and memory development. *Child Development*, 53, 296–309.

Pressley, M., Borkowski, J. G., & Schneider, W. (1987). Cognitive strategies: Good strategy users coordinate metacognition and knowledge. In R. Vasta & G. Whitehurst (Eds.), *Annals of child development* (Vol. 5). New York: JAI Press.

Pressley, M., El-Dinary, P. B., Marks, M. B., Brown, R., & Stein, S. (1992). Good strategy instruction is motivating and interesting. In K. A. Renninger, S. Hidi, & A. Krapp (Eds.), *The role of interest in learning and development*. Hillsdale, NJ: Erlbaum.

Pressley, M., Harris, K. R., & Marks, M. B. (1992). But good strategy instructors are constructivists! *Educational Psychology Review*, 4, 3–31.

Pressley, M., Johnson, C. J., Symons, S., McGoldrick, J., & Kurita, J. (1989). Strategies that improve children's memory and comprehension of what is read. *Elementary School Journal*, 90, 3–32.

Pressley, M., Levin, J. R., & Delaney, H. D. (1982). The mnemonic keyword method. *Review of Educational Research*, 52, 61–91.

Pressley, M., Levin, J. R., & Ghatala, E. S. (1984). Memory strategy monitoring in adults and children. *Journal of Verbal Learning and Verbal Behavior*, 23, 270–288.

Pressley, M., Levin, J. R., & Ghatala, E. S. (1988). Strategy-comparison opportunities promote long-term strategy use. *Contemporary Educational Psychology*, 13, 157–168.

Pressley, M. (with McCormick, C. B.). (1995). *Advanced educational psychology: For educators, researchers, and policymakers*. New York: HarperCollins.

Pressley, M., Ross, K. A., Levin, J. R., & Ghatala, E. S. (1984). The role of strategy utility knowledge in children's strategy decision making. *Journal of Experimental Child Psychology*, 38, 491–504.

Pressley, M., Snyder, B. L., & Cariglia-Bull, T. (1987). How can good strategy use be taught to children? Evaluation of six alternative approaches. In S. M. Cormier & J. D. Hagman (Eds.), *Transfer of learning: Contemporary research and applications*. San Diego: Academic Press.

Pressley, M., Wharton-McDonald, R., Rankin, J., El-Dinary, P. B., Brown, R., Afflerbach, P., Mistretta, J., & Yokoi, L. (1997). Elementary reading instruction. In G. D. Phye (Ed.), *Handbook of academic learning: Construction of knowledge*. San Diego: Academic Press.

Pressley, M., Woloshyn, V., Lysynchuk, L. M., Martin, V., Wood, E., & Willoughby, T. (1990). A primer of research on cognitive strategy instruction: The important issues and how to address them. *Educational Psychology Review*, 2, 1–58.

Pressley, M., Yokoi, L., Van Meter, P., Van Etten, S., & Freebern, G. (1997). Some of the reasons why preparing for exams is so hard: What can be done to make it easier? *Educational Psychology Review*, 9, 1–38.

Pribram, K. H. (1997). The work in working memory: Implications for development. In N. A. Krasnegor, G. R. Lyon, & P. S. Goldman-Rakic (Eds.), *Development of the prefrontal cortex: Evolution, neurobiology, and behavior* (pp. 359–378). Baltimore, MD: Brookes.

Proctor, R. W., & Dutta, A. (1995). *Skill acquisition and human performance*. Thousand Oaks, CA: Sage.

Pulos, S. (1980, August). *M capacity as a developmental constraint on structural learning*. Paper presented at the annual meeting of the American Psychological Association, Montreal.

Pulos, S., & Linn, M. C. (1981). Generality of the controlling variables scheme in early adolescence. *Journal of Early Adolescence*, 1, 26–37.

Purdie, N., & Hattie, J. (1996). Cultural differences in the use of strategies for self-regulated learning. *American Educational Research Journal*, 33, 845–871.

Purdie, N., Hattie, J., & Douglas, G. (1996). Student conceptions of learning and their use of self-regulated learning strategies: A cross-cultural comparison. *Journal of Educational Psychology*, 88, 87–100.

Pylyshyn, Z. W. (1973). What the mind's eye tells the mind's brain: A critique of mental imagery. *Psychological Bulletin*, 80, 1–24.

Pylyshyn, Z. W. (1979). Imagery theory: Not mysterious—just wrong. *Behavioural and Brain Sciences*, 2, 561–563.

Pylyshyn, Z. W. (1981). The imagery debate: Analogue media versus tacit knowledge. *Psychological Review*, 88, 16–45.

Pylyshyn, Z. W. (1984). *Computation and cognition*. Cambridge, MA: MIT Press.

Qian, G., & Alvermann, D. (1995). Role of epistemological beliefs and learned helplessness in secondary school students' learning science concepts from text. *Journal of Educational Psychology*, 87, 282–292.

Qian, G., & Pan, J. (2002). A comparison of epistemological beliefs and learning from science text between American and Chinese high school students. In B. K. Hofer & P. R. Pintrich (Eds.), *Personal epistemology: The psychology of beliefs about knowledge and knowing* (pp. 365–385). Mahwah, NJ: Erlbaum.

Qin, Z., Johnson, D. W., & Johnson, R. T. (1995). Cooperative versus competitive efforts and problem solving. *Review of Educational Research*, 65, 129–143.

Quartz, S. R., & Sejnowski, T. J. (1997). The neural basis of cognitive development: A constructivist manifesto. *Behavioral and Brain Sciences*, 20, 537–596.

Quinn, P. C. (2002). Category representation in young infants. *Current Directions in Psychological Science*, 11, 66–70.

Quinn, P. C. (2003). Concepts are not just for objects: Categorization of spatial relation information by young infants. In D. H. Rakison & L. M. Oakes (Eds.), *Early category and concept development: Making sense of the blooming, buzzing confusion*. Oxford, England: Oxford University Press.

Quinn, P. C., Bhatt, R. S., Brush, D., Grimes, A., & Sharpnack, H. (2002). Development of form similarity as a Gestalt grouping principles in infancy. *Psychological Science*, 13, 320–328.

Rabinowitz, M., & Glaser, R. (1985). Cognitive structure and process in highly competent performance. In F. D. Horowitz & M. O'Brien (Eds.), *The gifted and the talented: Developmental perspectives.* Washington, DC: American Psychological Association.

Rachlin, H. (1990). Why do people gamble and keep gambling despite heavy losses? *Psychological Science, 1,* 294–297.

Rachlin, H. (1991). *Introduction to modern behaviorism* (3rd ed.). New York: W. H. Freeman.

Rachlin, H. (1995) The value of temporal patterns in behavior. *Current Directions in Psychological Science, 4,* 188–192.

Rachlin, H., & Herrnstein, R. J. (1969). Hedonism revisited: On the negative law of effect. In B. A. Campbell & R. M. Church (Eds.), *Punishment and aversive behavior.* New York: Appleton-Century-Crofts.

Radebaugh, M. R. (1985). Children's perceptions of their spelling strategies. *The Reading Teacher, 38,* 532–536.

Radke-Yarrow, M., Zahn-Waxler, C., & Chapman, M. (1983). Children's prosocial dispositions and behavior. In E. M. Hetherington (Ed.), *Handbook of child psychology: Vol. 4. Socialization, personality, and social development.* New York: Wiley.

Radziszewska, B., & Rogoff, B. (1991). Children's guided participation in planning imaginary errands with skilled adult or peer partners. *Developmental Psychology, 27,* 381–389.

Raine, A., Reynolds, C., & Venables, P. H. (2002). Stimulation seeking and intelligence: A prospective longitudinal study. *Journal of Personality and Social Psychology, 82,* 663–674.

Rakow, S. J. (1984). What's happening in elementary science: A national assessment. *Science and children, 21*(4), 39–40.

Ramey, C. T. (1992). High-risk children and IQ: Altering intergenerational patterns. *Intelligence, 16,* 239–256.

Rapport, M. D., & Bostow, D. E. (1976). The effects of access to special activities on performance in four categories of academic tasks with third-grade students. *Journal of Applied Behavior Analysis, 9,* 372.

Rapport, M. D., Murphy, H. A., & Bailey, J. S. (1982). Ritalin vs. response cost in the control of hyperactive children: A within-subject comparison. *Journal of Applied Behavior Analysis, 15,* 205–216.

Ratcliff, R. (1990). Connectionist models of recognition memory: Constraints imposed by learning and forgetting functions. *Psychological Review, 97,* 285–308.

Ratcliff, R. A., & McKoon, G. (1981). Does activation really spread? *Psychological Review, 88,* 454–462.

Raudenbush, S. W. (1984). Magnitude of teacher expectancy effects on pupil IQ as a function of credibility induction: A synthesis of findings from 18 experiments. *Journal of Educational Psychology, 76,* 85–97.

Raudenbush, S. W., Rowan, B., & Cheong, Y. F. (1993). Higher order instructional goals in secondary schools: Class, teacher, and school influences. *American Educational Research Journal, 30,* 523–553.

Rawsthorne, L. J., & Elliot, A. J. (1999). Achievement goals and intrinsic motivation: A meta-analytic review. *Personality and Social Psychology Review, 3,* 326–344.

Rayner, K., Foorman, B. R., Perfetti, C. A., Pesetsky, D., & Seidenberg, M. S. (2001). How psychological science informs the teaching of reading. *Psychological Science in the Public Interest, 2,* 31–74.

Raynor, J. O. (1981). Future orientation and achievement motivation: Toward a theory of personality functioning and change. In G. Ydewalle & W. Lens (Eds.), *Cognition in human motivation and learning* (pp. 199–231). Hillsdale, NJ: Erlbaum.

Rayport, S. G. (1992). Cellular and molecular biology of the neuron. In S. C. Yudofsky & R. E. Hales (Eds.), *The American psychiatric press textbook of neuropsychiatry* (2nd ed., pp. 3–28). Washington, DC: American Psychiatric Press.

Reason, J., & Mycielska, K. (1982). *Absent-minded? The psychology of mental lapses and everyday errors.* Upper Saddle River, NJ: Prentice Hall.

Reber, A. S. (1993). *Implicit learning and tacit knowledge: An essay on the cognitive unconscious.* New York: Oxford University Press.

Reber, A. S., & Allen, R. (1978). Analogical and abstraction strategies in synthetic grammar learning: A functionalist interpretation. *Cognition, 6,* 189–221.

Reber, A. S., Kassin, S. M., Lewis, S., & Cantor, B. (1980). On the relationship between implicit and explicit modes in the learning of a complex rule structure. *Journal of Experimental Psychology: Human Learning and Memory, 6,* 492–502.

Redd, W. H., Morris, E. K., & Martin, J. A. (1975). Effects of positive and negative adult–child interactions on children's social preference. *Journal of Experimental Child Psychology, 19,* 153–164.

Reder, L. M. (1982). Plausibility judgment versus fact retrieval: Alternative strategies for sentence verification. *Psychological Review, 89,* 250–280.

Reder, L. M., & Ross, B. H. (1983). Integrated knowledge in different tasks: Positive and negative fan effects. *Journal of Experimental Psychology: Human Learning and Memory, 8,* 55–72.

Redfield, D. L., & Rousseau, E. W. (1981). A meta-analysis of experimental research on teacher questioning behavior. *Review of Educational Research, 51,* 237–245.

Reed, S. (1974). Structural descriptions and the limitations of visual images. *Memory and Cognition, 2,* 329–336.

Reed, S. K. (1993). A schema-based theory of transfer. In D. K. Detterman & R. J. Sternberg (Eds.), *Transfer on trial: Intelligence, cognition, and instruction.* Norwood, NJ: Ablex.

Reed, S. K., Ernst, G. W., & Banerji, R. (1974). The role of analogy in transfer between similar problem states. *Cognitive Psychology, 6,* 436–450.

Reese, H. W., & Lipsitt, L. P. (1970). *Experimental child psychology.* New York: Academic Press.

Reesink, C. J. (1984). Metric munchies. *Science and Children, 21*(7), 16–17.

Reeve, J., Bolt, E., & Cai, Y. (1999). Autonomy-supportive teachers: How they teach and motivate students. *Journal of Educational Psychology, 91,* 537–548.

Reif, F., & Heller, J. I. (1982). Knowledge structure and problem solving in physics. *Educational Psychologist, 17,* 102–127.

Reimann, P., & Schult, T. J. (1996). Turning examples into cases: Acquiring knowledge structures for analogical problem solving. *Educational Psychologist, 31,* 123–132.

Reiner, M., Slotta, J. D., Chi, M. T. H., & Resnick, L. B. (2000). Naïve physics reasoning: A commitment to substance-based conceptions. *Cognition and Instruction, 18,* 1–34.

Reisberg, D. (Ed.). (1992). *Auditory imagery.* Hillsdale, NJ: Erlbaum.

Reisberg, D. (1997). *Cognition: Exploring the science of the mind.* New York: W. W. Norton.

Reiser, R. A., & Sullivan, H. J. (1977). Effects of self-pacing and instructor-pacing in a PSI course. *Journal of Educational Research, 71,* 8–12.

Reissland, N. (1988). Neonatal imitation in the first hour of life: Observations in rural Nepal. *Developmental Psychology, 24,* 464–469.

Reiter, S. N. (1994). Teaching dialogically: Its relationship to critical thinking in college students. In P. R. Pintrich, D. R. Brown, & C. E. Weinstein (Eds.), *Student motivation, cognition, and learning: Essays in honor of Wilbert J. McKeachie.* Hillsdale, NJ: Erlbaum.

Reitman, J. S. (1974). Without surreptitious rehearsal, information in short-term memory decays. *Journal of Verbal Learning and Verbal Behavior, 13,* 365–377.

Reitman, W. R. (1964). Heuristic decision procedures, open constraints, and the structure of ill-defined problems. In M. W. Shelley & G. L. Bryan (Eds.), *Human judgments and optimality.* New York: Wiley.

Reitman, W. R. (1965). *Cognition and thought: An information processing approach.* New York: Wiley.

Renkl, A., Mandl, H., & Gruber, H. (1996). Inert knowledge: Analyses and remedies. *Educational Psychologist, 31,* 115–121.

Renninger, K. A. (1992). Individual interest and development: Implications for theory and practice. In K. A. Renninger, S. Hidi, & A. Krapp (Eds.).(1992). *The role of interest in learning and development.* Hillsdale, NJ: Erlbaum.

Renninger, K. A., Hidi, S., & Krapp, A. (Eds.). (1992). *The role of interest in learning and development.* Hillsdale, NJ: Erlbaum.

Repp, A. C., Barton, L., & Brulle, A. (1983). A comparison of two procedures for programming the differential reinforcement of other behavior. *Journal of Applied Behavior Analysis, 16,* 435–445.

Repp, A. C., & Deitz, S. M. (1974). Reducing aggressive and self-injurious behavior of institutionalized retarded children through reinforcement of other behaviors. *Journal of Applied Behavior Analysis, 7,* 313–325.

Rescorla, R. A. (1967). Pavlovian conditioning and its proper control procedures. *Psychological Review, 74,* 71–80.

Rescorla, R. A. (1987). A Pavlovian analysis of goal-directed behavior. *American Psychologist, 42,* 119–129.

Rescorla, R. A. (1988). Pavlovian conditioning: It's not what you think it is. *American Psychologist, 43,* 151–160.

Rescorla, R. A., & Wagner, A. R. (1972). A theory of Pavlovian conditioning: Variations in the effectiveness of reinforcement and non-reinforcement. In A. H. Black & W. F. Prokasy (Eds.), *The psychology of learning and motivation* (Vol. 4). New York: Academic Press.

Resnick, D. P., & Resnick, L. B. (1996). Performance assessment and the multiple functions of educational measurement. In M. B. Kane & R. Mitchell (Eds.), *Implementing performance assessment: Promises, problems, and challenges* (pp. 23–38). Mahwah, NJ: Erlbaum.

Resnick, L. B. (1976). Task analysis in instructional design: Some cases from mathematics. In D. Klahr (Ed.), *Cognition and instruction.* Hillsdale, NJ: Erlbaum.

Resnick, L. B. (1987). *Education and learning to think.* Washington, DC: National Academy Press.

Resnick, L. B. (1989). Developing mathematical knowledge. *American Psychologist, 44,* 162–169.

Resnick, L. B., Bill, V. L., Lesgold, S. B., & Leer, M. N. (1991). Thinking in arithmetic class. In B. Means, C. Chelemer, & M. S. Knapp (Eds.), *Teaching advanced skills to at-risk students.* San Francisco: Jossey-Bass.

Resnick, L. B., & Glaser, R. (1976). Problem solving and intelligence. In L. B. Resnick (Ed.), *The nature of intelligence.* Hillsdale, NJ: Erlbaum.

Resnick, L. B., & Johnson, A. (1988). Intelligent machines for intelligent people: Cognitive theory and the future of computer-assisted learning. In R. S. Nickerson & P. P. Zodhiates (Eds.), *Technology in education: Looking toward 2020.* Hillsdale, NJ: Erlbaum.

Restle, F., & Davis, J. H. (1962). Success and speed of problem solving by individuals and groups. *Psychological Review, 69,* 520–536.

Reyna, C. (2000). Lazy, dumb, or industrious: When stereotypes convey attribution information in the classroom. *Educational Psychology Review, 12,* 85–110.

Reyna, C., & Weiner, B. (2001). Justice and utility in the classroom: An attributional analysis of the goals of teachers' punishment and intervention strategies. *Journal of Educational Psychology, 93,* 309–319.

Reyna, V. F. (1995). Interference effects in memory and reasoning: A fuzzy-trace theory analysis. In F. N. Dempster & C. J. Brainerd (Eds.), *Interference and inhibition in cognition.* San Diego: Academic Press.

Reynolds, G. S. (1975). *A primer of operant conditioning* (Rev. ed.). Glenview, IL: Scott Foresman.

Reynolds, R. E., & Shirey, L. L. (1988). The role of attention in studying and learning. In C. E. Weinstein, E. T. Goetz, & P. A. Alexander (Eds.), *Learning and study strategies: Issues in assessment, instruction, and evaluation.* San Diego: Academic Press.

Reynolds, R. E., Sinatra, G. M., & Jetton, T. L. (1996). Views of knowledge acquisition and representation: A continuum from experience centered to mind centered. *Educational Psychologist, 31,* 93–104.

Reynolds, R. E., Taylor, M. A., Steffensen, M. S., Shirey, L. L., & Anderson, R. C. (1982). Cultural schemata and reading comprehension. *Reading Research Quarterly, 17,* 353–366.

Rice, M. S., Hauerwas, L. B., Ruggiero, J., & Carlisle, J. F. (1996, April). *Comprehension and recall of more and less imageable text by average and above average college readers.* Paper presented at the annual meeting of the American Educational Research Association, New York.

Richards, J. M., & Gross, J. J. (2000). Emotion regulation and memory: The cognitive costs of keeping one's cool. *Journal of Personality and Social Psychology, 79,* 410–424.

Riding, R. J., & Calvey, I. (1981). The assessment of verbal-imagery learning styles and their effect on the recall of concrete and abstract prose passages by 11-year-old children. *British Journal of Psychology, 72,* 59–64.

Riggs, J. M. (1992). Self-handicapping and achievement. In A. K. Boggiano & T. S. Pittman (Eds.), *Achievement and motivation: A social–developmental perspective.* Cambridge, England: Cambridge University Press.

Rimm, D. C., & Masters, J. C. (1974). *Behavior therapy: Techniques and empirical findings.* New York: Academic Press.

Rinehart, S. D., Stahl, S. A., & Erickson, L. G. (1986). Some effects of summarization training on reading and studying. *Reading Research Quarterly, 21,* 422–438.

Ringdahl, J. E., Vollmer, T. R., Borrero, J. C., & Connell, J. E. (2001). Fixed-time schedule effects as a function of baseline reinforcement rate. *Journal of Applied Behavior Analysis, 34,* 1–15.

Ringness, T. A. (1967). Identification patterns, motivation, and school achievement of bright junior high school boys. *Journal of Educational Psychology, 58,* 93–102.

Rips, L. J., Shoben, E. J., & Smith, E. E. (1973). Semantic distance and the verification of semantic relations. *Journal of Verbal Learning and Verbal Behavior, 12,* 1–20.

Rittle-Johnson, B., & Alibali, M. W. (1999). Conceptual and procedural knowledge of mathematics: Does one lead to the other? *Journal of Educational Psychology, 91,* 175–189.

Rittle-Johnson, B., Siegler, R. S., & Alibali, M. W. (2001). Developing conceptual understanding and procedural skill in mathematics: An iterative process. *Journal of Educational Psychology, 93,* 346–362.

Ritts, V., Patterson, M. L., & Tubbs, M. E. (1992). Expectations, impressions, and judgments of physically attractive students: A review. *Review of Educational Research, 62,* 413–426.

Roberts, G. C., Treasure, D. C., & Kavussanu, M. (1997). Motivation in physical activity contexts: An achievement goal perspective. *Advances in Motivation and Achievement, 10,* 413–447.

Roberts, K. T., & Ehri, L. C. (1983). Effects of two types of letter rehearsal on word memory in skilled and less skilled beginning readers. *Contemporary Educational Psychology, 8,* 375–390.

Roberts, T., & Kraft, R. (1987). Reading comprehension performance and laterality: Evidence for concurrent validity of dichotic, haptic, and EEG laterality measures. *Neuropsychologia, 25,* 817–828.

Robertson, J. S. (2000). Is attribution training a worthwhile classroom intervention for K–12 students with learning difficulties? *Educational Psychology Review, 12,* 111–134.

Robins, R. W., Gosling, S. D., & Craik, K. H. (1999). An empirical analysis of trends in psychology. *American Psychologist, 54,* pp. 117–128.

Robinson, F. P. (1961). *Effective study.* New York: Harper & Row.

Robinson, N. M., & Robinson, H. B. (1961). A method for the study of instrumental avoidance conditioning with children. *Journal of Comparative and Physiological Psychology, 54,* 20–23.

Robinson, T. R., Smith, S. W., Miller, M. D., & Brownell, M. T. (1999). Cognitive behavior modification of hyperactivity-impulsivity and aggression: A meta-analysis of school-based studies. *Journal of Educational Psychology, 91,* 195–203.

Roediger, H. L. (1980). Memory metaphors in cognitive psychology. *Memory and Cognition, 8,* 231–246.

Roediger, H. L., & Crowder, R. G. (1976). A serial position effect in recall of United States presidents. *Bulletin of the Psychonomic Society, 8,* 275–278.

Roediger, H. L., III. (1990). Implicit memory: Retention without remembering. *American Psychologist, 45,* 1043–1056.

Roediger, H. L., III, & McDermott, K. B. (2000). Tricks of memory. *Current Directions in Psychological Science, 9,* 123–127.

Rogers, C. R. (1951). *Client-centered therapy: Its current practice, implication, and theory*. Boston: Houghton Mifflin.

Rogers, C. R. (1961). *On becoming a person: A therapist's view of psychotherapy*. Boston: Houghton Mifflin.

Rogers, T. B., Kuiper, N. A., & Kirker, W. S. (1977). Self-reference and the encoding of personal information. *Journal of Personality and Social Psychology, 35*, 677–688.

Rogoff, B. (1990). *Apprenticeship in thinking: Cognitive development in social context*. New York: Oxford University Press.

Rogoff, B. (1991). Social interaction as apprenticeship in thinking: Guidance and participation in spatial planning. In L. B. Resnick, J. M. Levine, & S. D. Teasley (Eds.), *Perspectives on socially shared cognition*. Washington, DC: American Psychological Association.

Rogoff, B. (1994, April). *Developing understanding of the idea of communities of learners*. Paper presented at the annual meeting of the American Educational Research Association, New Orleans.

Rogoff, B. (1995). Observing sociocultural activity on three planes: Participatory appropriation, guided participation, and apprenticeship. In J. V. Wertsch, P. del Rio, & A. Alvarez (Eds.), *Sociocultural studies of mind*. Cambridge, England: Cambridge University Press.

Rogoff, B., Matusov, E., & White, C. (1996). Models of teaching and learning: Participation in a community of learners. In D. R. Olson & N. Torrance (Eds.), *The handbook of education and human development: New models of learning, teaching, and schooling*. Cambridge, MA: Blackwell.

Rortvedt, A. K., & Miltenberger, R. G. (1994). Analysis of a high-probability instructional sequence and time-out in the treatment of child noncompliance. *Journal of Applied Behavior Analysis, 27*, 327–330.

Rosales-Ruiz, J., & Baer, D. M. (1997). Behavioral cusps: A developmental and pragmatic concept for behavior analysis. *Journal of Applied Behavior Analysis, 30*, 533–544.

Rosch, E. H. (1973a). Natural categories. *Cognitive Psychology, 4*, 328–350.

Rosch, E. H. (1973b). On the internal structure of perceptual and semantic categories. In T. E. Moore (Ed.), *Cognitive development and the acquisition of language*. New York: Academic Press.

Rosch, E. H. (1977a). Classification of real-world objects: Origins and representations in cognition. In P. N. Johnson-Laird & P. C. Wason (Eds.), *Thinking: Readings in cognitive science*. Cambridge, MA: Cambridge University Press.

Rosch, E. H. (1977b). Human categorization. In N. Warren (Ed.), *Advances in cross-cultural psychology* (Vol. 1). London: Academic Press.

Rosch, E. H. (1978). Principles of categorization. In E. Rosch & B. Lloyd (Eds.), *Cognition and categorization*. Hillsdale, NJ: Erlbaum.

Rosch, E. H., & Mervis, C. B. (1975). Family resemblances: Studies in the internal structure of categories. *Cognitive Psychology, 7*, 573–605.

Rosch, E. H., Mervis, C. B., Gray, W. D., Johnson, D. M., & Boyes-Braem, P. (1976). Basic objects in natural categories. *Cognitive Psychology, 8*, 382–439.

Rosch, E. H., Simpson, C., & Miller, R. S. (1976). Structural bases of typicality effects. *Journal of Experimental Psychology: Human Perception and Performance, 2*, 491–502.

Rosenberg, E. L. (1998). Levels of analysis and the organization of affect. *Review of General Psychology, 2*, 247–270.

Rosenfield, I. (1988). *The invention of memory: A new view of the brain*. New York: Basic Books.

Rosenshine, B., & Meister, C. (1992). The use of scaffolds for teaching higher-level cognitive strategies. *Educational Leadership, 49*(7), 26–33.

Rosenshine, B., & Meister, C. (1994). Reciprocal teaching: A review of the research. *Review of Educational Research, 64*, 479–530.

Rosenshine, B., Meister, C., & Chapman, S. (1996). Teaching students to generate questions: A review of the intervention studies. *Review of Educational Research, 66*, 181–221.

Rosenshine, B., & Stevens, R. (1986). Teaching functions. In M. C. Wittrock (Ed.), *Handbook of research on teaching* (3rd ed.). New York: Macmillan.

Rosenthal, R. (1994). Interpersonal expectancy effects: A 30-year perspective. *Current Directions in Psychological Science, 3*, 176–179.

Rosenthal, T. L., Alford, G. S., & Rasp, L. M. (1972). Concept attainment, generalization, and retention through observation and verbal coding. *Journal of Experimental Child Psychology, 13*, 183–194.

Rosenthal, T. L., & Bandura, A. (1978). Psychological modeling: Theory and practice. In S. L. Garfield & A. E. Begia (Eds.), *Handbook of psychotherapy and behavior change: An empirical analysis* (2nd ed.). New York: Wiley.

Rosenthal, T. L., & Zimmerman, B. J. (1978). *Social learning and cognition*. New York: Academic Press.

Rosenzweig, M. R. (1986). Multiple models of memory. In S. L. Friedman, K. A. Klivington, & R. W. Peterson (Eds.), *The brain, cognition, and education*. Orlando: Academic Press.

Ross, B. H., & Spalding, T. L. (1994). Concepts and categories. In R. J. Sternberg (Ed.), *Handbook of perception and cognition* (Vol. 12). New York: Academic Press.

Rosser, R. (1994). *Cognitive development: Psychological and biological perspectives*. Boston: Allyn & Bacon.

Roth, K. (1990). Developing meaningful conceptual understanding in science. In B. F. Jones & L. Idol (Eds.), *Dimensions of thinking and cognitive instruction*. Hillsdale, NJ: Erlbaum.

Roth, K., & Anderson, C. (1988). Promoting conceptual change learning from science textbooks. In P. Ramsden (Ed.), *Improving learning: New perspectives*. London: Kogan Page.

Roth, W., & Bowen, G. M. (1995). Knowing and interacting: A study of culture, practices, and resources in a grade 8 open-inquiry science classroom guided by a cognitive apprenticeship metaphor. *Cognition and Instruction, 13*, 73–128.

Roth, W.-M. (2001). Gestures: Their role in teaching and learning. *Review of Educational Research, 71*, 365–392.

Rothbaum, F., Weisz, J. R., & Snyder, S. S. (1982). Changing the world and changing the self: A two-process model of perceived control. *Journal of Personality and Social Psychology, 42*, 5–37.

Rouet, J.-F., Favart, M., Britt, M. A., & Perfetti, C. A. (1997). Studying and using multiple documents in history: Effects of discipline expertise. *Cognition and Instruction, 15*, 85–106.

Rovee-Collier, C. (1993). The capacity for long-term memory in infancy. *Current Directions in Psychological Science, 2*, 130–135.

Rovee-Collier, C. (1999). The development of infant memory. *Current Directions in Psychological Science, 8*, 80–85.

Rowe, M. B. (1974). Wait-time and rewards as instructional variables, their influence on language, logic, and fate control: Part I. Wait time. *Journal of Research in Science Teaching, 11*, 81–94.

Rowe, M. B. (1987). Wait time: Slowing down may be a way of speeding up. *American Educator, 11*(1), 38–43, 47.

Royer, J. M., & Cable, G. W. (1976). Illustrations, analogies, and facilitation of transfer in prose learning. *Journal of Educational Psychology, 68*, 205–209.

Rubin, D. C. (1992). Constraints on memory. In E. Winograd & U. Neisser (Eds.), *Affect and accuracy in recall: Studies of "flashbulb" memories*. Cambridge, England: Cambridge University Press.

Ruble, D. N. (1980). A developmental perspective on theories of achievement motivation. In L. J. Fyans, Jr. (Ed.), *Achievement motivation: Recent trends in theory and research*. New York: Plenum Press.

Ruble, D. N., & Ruble, T. L. (1982). Sex stereotypes. In A. G. Miller (Ed.), *In the eye of the beholder*. New York: Praeger.

Rueda, R., & Moll, L. C. (1994). A sociocultural perspective on motivation. In H. F. O'Neil, Jr., & M. Drillings (Eds.), *Motivation: Theory and research*. Hillsdale, NJ: Erlbaum.

Ruef, M. B., Higgins, C., Glaeser, B., & Patnode, M. (1998). Positive behavioral support: Strategies for teachers. *Intervention in School and Clinic, 34*(1), 21–32.

Rueger, D. B., & Liberman, R. P. (1984). Behavioral family therapy for delinquent substance-abusing adolescents. *Journal of Drug Abuse, 14,* 403–418.

Rumberger, R. W. (1995). Dropping out of middle school: A multilevel analysis of students and schools. *American Educational Research Journal, 32,* 583–625.

Rumelhart, D. E. (1980). Schemata: The building blocks of cognition. In R. J. Spiro, B. C. Bruce, & W. F. Brewer (Eds.), *Theoretical issues in reading comprehension.* Hillsdale, NJ: Erlbaum.

Rumelhart, D. E., & McClelland, J. L. (1986). *Parallel distributed processing* (Vol. 1). Cambridge, MA: MIT Press.

Rumelhart, D. E., & Ortony, A. (1977). The representation of knowledge in memory. In R. C. Anderson, R. J. Spiro, & W. E. Montague (Eds.), *Schooling and the acquisition of knowledge.* Hillsdale, NJ: Erlbaum.

Rundus, D. (1971). Analysis of rehearsal processes in free recall. *Journal of Experimental Psychology, 89,* 63–77.

Rundus, D., & Atkinson, R. C. (1971). Rehearsal processes in free recall: A procedure for direct observation. *Journal of Verbal Learning and Verbal Behavior, 9,* 99–105.

Rusch, F., & Close, D. (1976). Overcorrection: A procedural evaluation. *AAESPH Review, 1,* 32–45.

Rushton, J. P. (1975). Generosity in children: Immediate and long-term effects of modeling, preaching, and moral judgment. *Journal of Personality and Social Psychology, 31,* 459–466.

Rushton, J. P. (1980). *Altruism, socialization, and society.* Englewood Cliffs, NJ: Prentice Hall.

Rushton, J. P. (1982). Social learning theory and the development of prosocial behavior. In N. Eisenberg (Ed.), *The development of prosocial behavior.* New York: Academic Press.

Russ, S. W. (1993). *Affect and creativity: The role of affect and play in the creative process.* Hillsdale, NJ: Erlbaum.

Ryan, A. M., Hicks, L., & Midgley, C. (1997). Social goals, academic goals, and avoiding seeking help in the classroom. *Journal of Early Adolescence, 17,* 152–171.

Ryan, A. M., & Patrick, H. (2001). The classroom social environment and changes in adolescents' motivation and engagement during middle school. *American Educational Research Journal, 38,* 437–460.

Ryan, A. M., Pintrich, P. R., & Midgley, C. (2001). Avoiding seeking help in the classroom: Who and why? *Educational Psychology Review, 13,* 93–114.

Ryan, R. M. (1982). Control and information in the intrapersonal sphere: An extension of cognitive evaluation theory. *Journal of Personality and Social Psychology, 43,* 450–461.

Ryan, R. M., & Connell, J. P. (1989). Perceived locus of causality and internalization: Examining reasons for acting in two domains. *Journal of Personality and Social Psychology, 57,* 749–761.

Ryan, R. M., Connell, J. P., & Grolnick, W. S. (1992). When achievement is *not* intrinsically motivated: A theory of internalization and self-regulation in school. In A. K. Boggiano & T. S. Pittman (Eds.), *Achievement and motivation: A social-developmental perspective.* Cambridge, England: Cambridge University Press.

Ryan, R.M., & Deci, E.L. (2000). Self-determination theory and the facilitation of intrinsic motivation, social development, and well-being. *American Psychologist, 55,* pp. 68–78.

Ryan, R. M., Mims, V., & Koestner, R. (1983). Relation of reward contingency and interpersonal context to intrinsic motivation: A review and test using cognitive evaluation theory. *Journal of Personality and Social Psychology, 45,* 736–750.

Sadoski, M., Goetz, E. T., & Fritz, J. B. (1993). Impact of concreteness on comprehensibility, interest, and memory for text: Implications for dual coding theory and text design. *Journal of Educational Psychology, 85,* 291–304.

Sadoski, M., & Paivio, A. (2001). *Imagery and text: A dual coding theory of reading and writing.* Mahwah, NJ: Erlbaum.

Sadoski, M., & Quast, Z. (1990). Reader response and long-term recall for journalistic text: The roles of imagery, affect, and importance. *Reading Research Quarterly, 25,* 256–272.

Safren, M. A. (1962). Associations, sets, and the solution of word problems. *Journal of Experimental Psychology, 64,* 40–45.

Saljo, R., & Wyndham, J. (1992). Solving everyday problems in the formal setting: An empirical study of the school as context for thought. In S. Chaiklin & J. Lave (Eds.), *Understanding practice.* New York: Cambridge University Press.

Salomon, G. (1993). No distribution without individuals' cognition: A dynamic interactional view. In G. Salomon (Ed.), *Distributed cognitions: Psychological and educational considerations* (pp. 111–138). Cambridge, England: Cambridge University Press.

Salomon, G. (1994). *Interaction of media, cognition, and learning.* Hillsdale, NJ: Erlbaum. (Original work published 1979)

Salthouse, T. A. (1991). Mediation of adult age differences in cognition by reductions in working memory and speed of processing. *Psychological Science, 2,* 179–183.

Saltz, E. (1971). *The cognitive bases of human learning.* Homewood, IL: Dorsey.

Samuel, A. L. (1963). Some studies in machine learning using the game of checkers. In E. A. Feigenbaum & J. Feldman (Eds.), *Computers and thought.* New York: McGraw-Hill.

Samuels, S. J. (1967). Attentional processes in reading: The effect of pictures in the acquisition of reading responses. *Journal of Educational Psychology, 58,* 337–342.

Samuels, S. J. (1970). Effects of pictures on learning to read, comprehension and attitudes. *Review of Educational Research, 40,* 397–407.

Samuels, S. J., & Turnure, J. E. (1974). Attention and reading achievement in first-grade boys and girls. *Journal of Educational Psychology, 66,* 29–32.

Sansone, C., Weir, C., Harpster, L., & Morgan, C. (1992). Once a boring task always a boring task? Interest as a self-regulatory mechanism. *Journal of Personality and Social Psychology, 63,* 379–390.

Sapolsky, R. M. (1999). Glucocorticoids, stress, and their adverse neurological effects: Relevance to aging. *Experimental Gerontology, 34,* 721–732.

Sarason, I. G. (1980). Introduction to the study of test anxiety. In I. G. Sarason (Ed.), *Test anxiety: Theory, research, and applications.* Hillsdale, NJ: Erlbaum.

Sarason, S. B. (1972). What research says about test anxiety in elementary school children. In A. R. Binter & S. H. Frey (Eds.), *The psychology of the elementary school child.* Chicago: Rand McNally.

Sasso, G. M., & Rude, H. A. (1987). Unprogrammed effects of training high-status peers to interact with severely handicapped children. *Journal of Applied Behavior Analysis, 20,* 35–44.

Sawyer, R. J., Graham, S., & Harris, K. R. (1992). Direct teaching, strategy instruction, and strategy instruction with explicit self-regulation: Effects on the composition skills and self-efficacy of students with learning disabilities. *Journal of Educational Psychology, 84,* 340–352.

Sax, G. (1989). *Principles of educational and psychological measurement and evaluation* (3rd ed.). Belmont, CA: Wadsworth.

Saxe, G. B. (1988). Candy selling and math learning. *Educational Researcher, 17*(6), 14–21.

Scandura, J. M. (1974). Role of higher order rules in problem solving. *Journal of Experimental Psychology, 102,* 984–991.

Scardamalia, M., & Bereiter, C. (1985). Fostering the development of self-regulation in children's knowledge processing. In S. F. Chipman, J. W. Segal, & R. Glaser (Eds.), *Thinking and learning skills: Vol. 2. Research and open questions.* Hillsdale, NJ: Erlbaum.

Scevak, J. J., Moore, P. J., & Kirby, J. R. (1993). Training students to use maps to increase text recall. *Contemporary Educational Psychology, 18,* 401–413.

Schab, F. (1990). Odors and the remembrance of things past. *Journal of Experimental Psychology: Learning, Memory, and Cognition, 16,* 648–655.

Schacter, D. L. (1989). Memory. In M. I. Posner (Ed.), *Foundations of cognitive science* (pp. 683–725). Cambridge, MA: MIT Press.

Schacter, D. L. (1993). Understanding implicit memory: A cognitive neuroscience approach. In A. F. Collins, S. E. Gathercole, M. A. Conway, & P. E. Morris (Eds.), *Theories of memory.* Hove, England: Erlbaum.

Schacter, D. L. (1999). The seven sins of memory: Insights from psychology and neuroscience. *American Psychologist, 54,* pp. 182–203.

Schacter, J. (2000). Does individual tutoring produce optimal learning? *American Educational Research Journal, 37,* 801–829.

Schank, R. C. (1975). *Conceptual information processing.* New York: Elsevier.

Schank, R. C. (1979). Interestingness: Controlling inferences. *Artificial Intelligence, 12,* 273–297.

Schank, R. C., & Abelson, R. P. (1977). *Scripts, plans, goals, and understanding: An inquiry into human knowledge structures.* Hillsdale, NJ: Erlbaum.

Schank, R. C., & Abelson, R. P. (1995). Knowledge and memory: The real story. In R. S. Wyer, Jr. (Ed.), *Advances in social cognition: Vol. 8. Knowledge and memory: The real story.* Hillsdale, NJ: Erlbaum.

Schauble, L. (1990). Belief revision in children: The role of prior knowledge and strategies for generating evidence. *Journal of Experimental Child Psychology, 49,* 31–57.

Schellings, G. L. M., Van Hout-Wolters, B., & Vermunt, J. D. (1996). Individual differences in adapting to three different tasks of selecting information from texts. *Contemporary Educational Psychology, 21,* 423–446.

Schiefele, U. (1991). Interest, learning, and motivation. *Educational Psychologist, 26,* 299–323.

Schiefele, U. (1992). Topic interest and levels of text comprehension. In K. A. Renninger, S. Hidi, & A. Krapp (Eds.), *The role of interest in learning and development.* Hillsdale, NJ: Erlbaum.

Schiefele, U. (1998). Individual interest and learning: What we know and what we don't know. In L. Hoffman, A. Krapp, K. Renninger, & J. Baumert (Eds.), *Interest and learning: Proceedings of the Seeon Conference on interest and gender* (pp. 91–104). Kiel, Germany: IPN.

Schiefele, U., Krapp, A., & Winteler, A. (1992). Interest as a predictor of academic achievement: A meta-analysis of research. In K. A. Renninger, S. Hidi, & A. Krapp (Eds.), *The role of interest in learning and development.* Hillsdale, NJ: Erlbaum.

Schiefele, U., & Wild, K. (1994, April). *Motivational predictors of strategy use and course grades.* Paper presented at the annual meeting of the American Educational Research Association, New Orleans.

Schimmoeller, M. A. (1998, April). *Influence of private speech on the writing behaviors of young children: Four case studies.* Paper presented at the annual meeting of the American Educational Research Association, San Diego.

Schliefer, M., & Douglas, V. I. (1973). Effects of training on the moral judgment of young children. *Journal of Personality and Social Psychology, 28,* 62–67.

Schliemann, A. D., & Carraher, D. W. (1993). Proportional reasoning in and out of school. In P. Light & G. Butterworth (Eds.), *Context and cognition: Ways of learning and knowing.* Hillsdale, NJ: Erlbaum.

Schloss, P. J., & Smith, M. A. (1994). *Applied behavior analysis in the classroom.* Boston: Allyn & Bacon.

Schmidt, R. A., & Bjork, R. A. (1992). New conceptualizations of practice: Common principles in three paradigms suggest new concepts for training. *Psychological Science, 3,* 207–217.

Schmidt, R. A., & Young, D. E. (1987). Transfer of movement control in motor skill learning. In S. M. Cormier & J. D. Hagman (Eds.), *Transfer of learning: Contemporary research and applications.* San Diego: Academic Press.

Schmolck, H., Buffalo, E. A., & Squire, L. R. (2000). Memory distortions develop over time: Recollections of the O. J. Simpson trial verdict after 15 and 32 months. *Psychological Science, 11,* 39–45.

Schneider, W. (1993). Domain-specific knowledge and memory performance in children. *Educational Psychology Review, 5,* 257–273.

Schneider, W., & Detweiler, M. (1987). A connectionist/control architecture for working memory. In G. H. Bower (Ed.), *The psychology of learning and motivation: Advances in research and theory* (Vol. 21). Orlando: Academic Press.

Schneider, W., Körkel, J., & Weinert, F. E. (1990). Expert knowledge, general abilities, and text processing. In W. Schneider & F. E. Weinert (Eds.), *Interactions among aptitudes, strategies, and knowledge in cognitive performance.* New York: Springer-Verlag.

Schneider, W., & Pressley, M. (1989). *Memory development between 2 and 20.* New York: Springer-Verlag.

Schneider, W., & Shiffrin, R. M. (1977). Controlled and automatic human information processing: I. Detection, search, and attention. *Psychological Review, 84,* 1–66.

Schoenfeld, A. H. (1979). Explicit heuristic training as a variable in problem solving performance. *Journal for Research in Mathematics Education, 10,* 173–187.

Schoenfeld, A. H. (1982). Measures of problem-solving performance and problem-solving instruction. *Journal for Research in Mathematics Education, 13,* 31–49.

Schoenfeld, A. H. (1985a). *Mathematical problem solving.* San Diego: Academic Press.

Schoenfeld, A. H. (1985b). Metacognitive and epistemological issues in mathematical understanding. In E. A. Silver (Ed.), *Teaching and learning mathematical problem solving: Multiple research perspectives.* Hillsdale, NJ: Erlbaum.

Schoenfeld, A. H. (1988). When good teaching leads to bad results: The disasters of "well-taught" mathematics courses. *Educational Psychologist, 23,* 145–166.

Schoenfeld, A. H. (1992). Learning to think mathematically: Problem solving, metacognition, and sense-making in mathematics. In D. A. Grouws (Ed.), *Handbook of research on mathematics teaching and learning.* New York: Macmillan.

Schoenfeld, A. H., & Herrmann, D. J. (1982). Problem perception and knowledge structure in expert and novice mathematical problem solvers. *Journal of Experimental Psychology: Learning, Memory, and Cognition, 8,* 484–494.

Schofield, J. W. (1995). Improving intergroup relations among students. In J. A. Banks & C. A. M. Banks (Eds.), *Handbook of research on multicultural education.* New York: Macmillan.

Schofield, N. J., & Kirby, J. R. (1994). Position location on topographical maps: Effects of task factors, training, and strategies. *Cognition and Instruction, 12,* 35–60.

Scholes, R. J., & Kardash, C. M. (1996, April). *The effect of topic interest on the relationship between text-based interest and importance in text comprehension.* Paper presented at the annual meeting of the American Educational Research Association, New York.

Schommer, M. (1990). Effects of beliefs about the nature of knowledge on comprehension. *Journal of Educational Psychology, 82,* 498–504.

Schommer, M. (1994a). An emerging conceptualization of epistemological beliefs and their role in learning. In R. Garner & P. A. Alexander (Eds.), *Beliefs about text and instruction with text.* Hillsdale, NJ: Erlbaum.

Schommer, M. (1994b). Synthesizing epistemological belief research: Tentative understandings and provocative confusions. *Educational Psychology Review, 6,* 293–319.

Schommer, M. (1997). The development of epistemological beliefs among secondary students: A longitudinal study. *Journal of Educational Psychology, 89,* 37–40.

Schommer-Aikins, M. (2002). An evolving theoretical framework for an epistemological belief system. In B. K. Hofer & P. R. Pintrich (Eds.), *Personal epistemology: The psychology of beliefs about knowledge and knowing* (pp. 103–118). Mahwah, NJ: Erlbaum.

Schraw, G. (1998). Processing and recall differences among seductive details. *Journal of Educational Psychology, 90,* 3–12.

Schraw, G. (2000). Reader beliefs and meaning construction in narrative text. *Journal of Educational Psychology, 92,* 96–106.

Schraw, G., Bendixen, L. D., & Dunkle, M. E. (2002). Development and validation of the Epistemic Belief Inventory (EBI). In B. K. Hofer & P. R. Pintrich (Eds.), *Personal epistemology: The psychology of beliefs about knowledge and knowing* (pp. 261–275). Mahwah, NJ: Erlbaum.

Schraw, G., & Bruning, R. (1995, April). *Reader beliefs and reading comprehension.* Paper presented at the annual meeting of the American Educational Research Association, San Francisco.

Schraw, G., Dunkle, M. E., & Bendixen, L. D. (1995). Cognitive processes in well-defined and ill-defined problem solving. *Applied Cognitive Psychology, 9*, 523–538.

Schraw, G., & Lehman, S. (2001). Situational interest: A review of the literature and directions for future research. *Educational Psychology Review, 13*, 23–52.

Schraw, G., & Moshman, D. (1995). Metacognitive theories. *Educational Psychology Review, 7*, 351–371.

Schraw, G., Potenza, M. T., & Nebelsick-Gullet, L. (1993). Constraints on the calibration of performance. *Contemporary Educational Psychology, 18*, 455–463.

Schroth, M. L. (1992). The effects of delay of feedback on a delayed concept formation transfer task. *Contemporary Educational Psychology, 17*, 78–82.

Schultz, K., & Lochhead, J. (1991). A view from physics. In M. U. Smith (Ed.), *Toward a unified theory of problem solving: Views from the content domains.* Hillsdale, NJ: Erlbaum.

Schunk, D. H. (1981). Modeling and attributional effects on children's achievement: A self-efficacy analysis. *Journal of Educational Psychology, 73*, 93–105.

Schunk, D. H. (1982). Effects of effort attributional feedback on children's perceived self-efficacy and achievement. *Journal of Educational Psychology, 74*, 548–556.

Schunk, D. H. (1983a). Ability versus effort attributional feedback: Differential effects on self-efficacy and achievement. *Journal of Educational Psychology, 75*, 848–856.

Schunk, D. H. (1983b). Developing children's self-efficacy and skills: The roles of social comparative information and goal setting. *Contemporary Educational Psychology, 8*, 76–86.

Schunk, D. H. (1985). Participation in goal setting: Effects on self-efficacy and skills of learning disabled children. *Journal of Special Education, 19*, 307–317.

Schunk, D. H. (1987). Peer models and children's behavioral change. *Review of Educational Research, 57*, 149–174.

Schunk, D. H. (1989a). Self-efficacy and achievement behaviors. *Educational Psychology Review, 1*, 173–208.

Schunk, D. H. (1989b). Self-efficacy and cognitive skill learning. In C. Ames & R. Ames (Eds.), *Research on motivation in education: Vol. 3. Goals and cognitions.* San Diego: Academic Press.

Schunk, D. H. (1989c). Social cognitive theory and self-regulated learning. In B. J. Zimmerman & D. H. Schunk (Eds.), *Self-regulated learning and academic achievement: Theory, research, and practice.* New York: Springer-Verlag.

Schunk, D. H. (1990, April). *Socialization and the development of self-regulated learning: The role of attributions.* Paper presented at the annual meeting of the American Educational Research Association, Boston.

Schunk, D. H. (1995). Inherent details of self-regulated learning include student perceptions. *Educational Psychologist, 30*, 213–216.

Schunk, D. H. (1996). Goal and self-evaluative influences during children's cognitive skill learning. *American Educational Research Journal, 33*, 359–382.

Schunk, D. H. (1998). Teaching elementary students to self-regulate practice of mathematical skills with modeling. In D. H. Schunk & B. J. Zimmerman (Eds.), *Self-regulated learning: From teaching to self-reflective practice* (pp. 137–159). New York: Guilford Press.

Schunk, D. H., & Hanson, A. R. (1985). Peer models: Influence on children's self-efficacy and achievement. *Journal of Educational Psychology, 77*, 313–322.

Schunk, D. H., Hanson, A. R., & Cox, P. D. (1987). Peer-model attributes and children's achievement behaviors. *Journal of Educational Psychology, 79*, 54–61.

Schunk, D. H., & Rice, J. (1989). Learning goals and children's reading comprehension. *Journal of Reading Behavior, 21*, 279–293.

Schunk, D. H., & Swartz, C. W. (1993). Goals and progress feedback: Effects on self-efficacy and writing achievement. *Contemporary Educational Psychology, 18*, 337–354.

Schunk, D. H., & Zimmerman, B. J. (Eds.). (1994). *Self-regulation of learning and performance: Issues and educational applications.* Hillsdale, NJ: Erlbaum.

Schunk, D. H., & Zimmerman, B. J. (1996). Modeling and self-efficacy influences on children's development of self-regulation. In J. Juvonen & K. R. Wentzel (Eds.), *Social motivation: Understanding children's school adjustment* (pp. 154–180). Cambridge, England: Cambridge University Press.

Schunk, D. H., & Zimmerman, B. J. (1997). Social origins of self-regulatory competence. *Educational Psychologist, 32*, 195–208.

Schutz, P. A. (1994). Goals as the transactive point between motivation and cognition. In P. R. Pintrich, D. R. Brown, & C. E. Weinstein (Eds.), *Student motivation, cognition, and learning: Essays in honor of Wilbert J. McKeachie.* Hillsdale, NJ: Erlbaum.

Schwartz, B., & Reisberg, D. (1991). *Learning and memory.* New York: W. W. Norton.

Schwartz, S. H. (1971). Modes of representation and problem solving: Well evolved is half solved. *Journal of Experimental Psychology, 91*, 347–350.

Schwarz, B. B., Neuman, Y., & Biezuner, S. (2000). Two wrongs may make a right . . . if they argue together! *Cognition and Instruction, 18*, 461–494.

Schwebel, A. I., & Cherlin, D. L. (1972). Physical and social distancing in teacher–pupil relationships. *Journal of Educational Psychology, 63*, 543–550.

Scoville, W. B., & Milner, B. (1957). Loss of recent memory after bilateral hippocampal lesions. *Journal of Neurology, Neurosurgery, and Psychiatry, 20*, 11–19.

Seamon, J. G., Luo, C. R., & Gallo, D. A. (1998). Creating false memories of words with or without recognition of list items: Evidence for nonconscious processes. *Psychological Science, 9*, 20–26.

Sears, R. R., Maccoby, E. E., & Levin, H. (1957). *Patterns of child rearing.* Evanston, IL: Row Peterson.

Seddon, G. M. (1978). The properties of Bloom's taxonomy of educational objectives for the cognitive domain. *Review of Educational Research, 48*, 303–323.

Seitz, V., Rosenbaum, L. K., & Apfel, N. H. (1985). Effects of family support intervention: A ten-year follow-up. *Child Development, 56*, 376–391.

Seligman, M. E. P. (1975). *Helplessness.* San Francisco: W. H. Freeman.

Seligman, M. E. P. (1991). *Learned optimism.* New York: Alfred Knopf.

Seligman, M. E. P., & Campbell, B. A. (1965). Effects of intensity and duration of punishment on extinction of an avoidance response. *Journal of Comparative and Physiological Psychology, 59*, 295–297.

Seligman, M. E. P., & Johnston, J. C. (1973). A cognitive theory of avoidance learning. In F. J. McGuigan & D. B. Lumsden (Eds.), *Contemporary approaches to conditioning and learning.* Washington, DC: V. H. Winston & Sons.

Seligman, M. E. P., & Maier, S. F. (1967). Failure to escape traumatic shock. *Journal of Experimental Psychology, 74*, 1–9.

Selkow, P. (1984). Effects of maternal employment on kindergarten and first-grade children's vocational aspirations. *Sex Roles, 11*, 677–690.

Semb, G. B., & Ellis, J. A. (1994). Knowledge taught in school: What is remembered? *Review of Educational Research, 64*, 253–286.

Semb, G. B., Ellis, J. A., & Araujo, J. (1993). Long-term memory for knowledge learned in school. *Journal of Educational Psychology, 85*, 305–316.

Sergeant, J. (1996). A theory of attention: An information processing perspective. In G. R. Lyon & N. A. Krasnegor (Eds.), *Attention, memory, and executive function.* Baltimore: Paul H. Brookes.

Sfard, A. (1997). Commentary: On metaphorical roots of conceptual growth. In L. D. English (Ed.), *Mathematical reasoning: Analogies, metaphors, and images* (pp. 339–371). Mahwah, NJ: Erlbaum.

Sfard, A. (1998). On two metaphors for learning and the dangers of choosing just one. *Educational Researcher, 27*(2), 4–13.

Shabani, D. B., Katz, R. C., Wilder, D. A., Beauchamp, K., Taylor, C. R., & Fischer, K. J. (2002). Increasing social initiations in children with autism: Effects of a tactile prompt. *Journal of Applied Behavior Analysis, 35*, 79–83.

Shachar, H., & Sharan, S. (1994). Talking, relating, and achieving: Effects of cooperative learning and whole-class instruction. *Cognition and Instruction, 12*, 313–353.

Shaffer, D. R. (1988). *Social and personality development* (2nd ed.). Pacific Grove, CA: Brooks-Cole.

Shafto, F., & Sulzbacher, S. (1977). Comparing treatment tactics with a hyperactive preschool child: Stimulant medication and programmed teacher intervention. *Journal of Applied Behavior Analysis, 10*, 13–20.

Shah, P., & Hoeffner, J. (2002). Review of graph comprehension research: Implications for instruction. *Educational Psychology Review, 14*, 47–69.

Shah, P., & Miyake, A. (1996). The separability of working memory resources for spatial thinking and language processing: An individual differences approach. *Journal of Experimental Psychology: General, 125*, 4–27.

Shapiro, K. L. (1994). The attentional blink: The brain's "eyeblink." *Current Directions in Psychological Science, 3*, 86–89.

Shapley, K. S. (1994, April). *Metacognition, motivation, and learning: A study of middle school students' use and development of self-regulated learning strategies.* Paper presented at the annual meeting of the American Educational Research Association, New Orleans.

Sheffield, F. D. (1966a). A drive-induction theory of reinforcement. In R. N. Haber (Ed.), *Current research in motivation.* New York: Holt, Rinehart & Winston.

Sheffield, F. D. (1966b). New evidence on the drive-induction theory of reinforcement. In R. N. Haber (Ed.), *Current research in motivation.* New York: Holt, Rinehart & Winston.

Sheffield, F. D., & Roby, T. B. (1950). Reward value of a non-nutritive sweet taste. *Journal of Comparative and Physiological Psychology, 43*, 471–481.

Sheffield, F. D., Roby, T. B., & Campbell, B. A. (1954). Drive reduction versus consummatory behavior as determinants of reinforcement. *Journal of Comparative and Physiological Psychology, 47*, 349–354.

Sheffield, F. D., Wulff, J. J., & Backer, R. (1951). Reward value of copulation without sex drive reduction. *Journal of Comparative and Physiological Psychology, 44*, 3–8.

Shepard, L. A. (2000). The role of assessment in a learning culture. *Educational Researcher, 29*(7), 4–14.

Shepard, R. N. (1967). Recognition memory for words, sentences, and pictures. *Journal of Verbal Learning and Verbal Behavior, 6*, 156–163.

Shepard, R. N., & Metzler, J. (1971). Mental rotation of three-dimensional objects. *Science, 171*, 701–703.

Shepperd, J. A., & McNulty, J. K. (2002). The affective consequences of expected and unexpected outcomes. *Psychological Science, 13*, 85–88.

Sherman, D. K., & Cohen, G. L. (2002). Accepting threatening information: Self-affirmation and the reduction of defensive biases. *Current Directions in Psychological Science, 11*, 119–123.

Sherman, J. W., & Bessenoff, G. R. (1999). Stereotypes as source-monitoring cues: On the interaction between episodic and semantic memory. *Psychological Science, 10*, 106–110.

Shernoff, D. J., & Hoogstra, L. A. (2001, April). *Exploring continuing interest: How engagement in high school classes relates to subsequent commitment.* Paper presented at the annual meeting of the American Educational Research Association, Seattle, WA.

Shernoff, D. J., Schneider, B., & Csikszentmihalyi, M. (2001, April). *An assessment of multiple influences on student engagement in high school classrooms.* Paper presented at the annual meeting of the American Educational Research Association, Seattle, WA.

Sheveland, D. E. (1994, April). *Motivational factors in the development of independent readers.* Paper presented at the annual meeting of the American Educational Research Association, New Orleans.

Shiffrin, R. M., & Cook, J. R. (1978). Short-term forgetting of item and order information. *Journal of Verbal Learning and Verbal Behavior, 17*, 189–218.

Shiffrin, R. M., & Schneider, W. (1977). Controlled and automatic human information processing: II. Perceptual learning, automatic attending, and a general theory. *Psychological Review, 84*, 127–190.

Shimmerlick, S. M., & Nolan, J. D. (1976). Reorganization and the recall of prose. *Journal of Educational Psychology, 68*, 779–786.

Shimoff, E., Catania, A. C., & Matthews, B. A. (1981). Uninstructed human responding: Sensitivity of low-rate performance to schedule contingencies. *Journal of the Experimental Analysis of Behavior, 36*, 207–220.

Shrager, L., & Mayer, R. E. (1989). Note-taking fosters generative learning strategies in novices. *Journal of Educational Psychology, 81*, 263–264.

Shuell, T. J. (1996). Teaching and learning in a classroom context. In D. C. Berliner & R. C. Calfee (Eds.), *Handbook of educational psychology.* New York: Macmillan.

Shulman, H. G. (1971). Similarity effects in short-term memory. *Psychological Bulletin, 75*, 399–415.

Shulman, H. G. (1972). Semantic confusion errors in short-term memory. *Journal of Verbal Learning and Verbal Behavior, 11*, 221–227.

Shymansky, J. A., Hedges, L. V., & Woodworth, G. (1990). A reassessment of the effects of inquiry-based science curricula of the 60's on student performance. *Journal of Research in Science Teaching, 27*, 127–144.

Sieber, J. E., Kameya, L. I., & Paulson, F. L. (1970). Effect of memory support on the problem-solving ability of test-anxious children. *Journal of Educational Psychology, 61*, 159–168.

Siegel, S. (1975). Evidence from rats that morphine tolerance is learned response. *Journal of Comparative and Physiological Psychology, 89*, 498–506.

Siegel, S. (1979). The role of conditioning in drug tolerance and addiction. In J. D. Keehn (Ed.), *Psychopathology in animals: Research and clinical implications.* New York: Academic Press.

Siegel, S., & Andrews, J. M. (1962). Magnitude of reinforcement and choice behavior in children. *Journal of Experimental Psychology, 63*, 337–341.

Siegel, S., Hinson, R. E., Krank, M. D., & McCully, J. (1982). Heroin "overdose" death: Contribution of drug-associated environmental cues. *Science, 216*, 436–437.

Siegler, R. S. (1978). The origins of scientific reasoning. In R. S. Siegler (Ed.), *Children's thinking: What develops?* Hillsdale, NJ: Erlbaum.

Siegler, R. S. (1998). *Children's thinking* (3rd ed.). Upper Saddle River, NJ: Prentice Hall.

Siegler, R. S. (2000). Unconscious insights. *Current Directions in Psychological Science, 9*, 79–83.

Siegler, R. S., & Ellis, S. (1996). Piaget on childhood. *Psychological Science, 7*, 211–215.

Siegler, R. S., & Jenkins, E. (1989). *How children discover new strategies.* Hillsdale, NJ: Erlbaum.

Sigman, M., & Whaley, S. E. (1998). The role of nutrition in the development of intelligence. In U. Neisser (Ed.), *The rising curve: Long-term gains in IQ and related measures* (pp. 155–182). Washington, DC: American Psychological Association.

Signorella, M. L., & Liben, L. S. (1984). Recall and reconstruction of gender-related pictures: Effects of attitude, task difficulty, and age. *Child Development, 55*, 393–405.

Silver, E. A. (1982). Knowledge organization and mathematical problem solving. In F. K. Lester & J. Garofalo (Eds.), *Mathematical problem solving: Issues in research.* Philadelphia: The Franklin Institute Press.

Silver, E. A., & Kenney, P. A. (1995). Sources of assessment information for instructional guidance in mathematics. In T. Romberg (Ed.), *Reform in school mathematics and authentic assessment.* Albany: State University of New York Press.

Silver, E. A., Shapiro, L. J., & Deutsch, A. (1993). Sense making and the solution of division problems involving remainders: An examination of middle school students' solution processes and their interpretations of solutions. *Journal of Research in Mathematics Education, 24*, 117–135.

Silverman, W. K., & Kearney, C. A. (1991). *Educational Psychology Review, 3*, 335–361.

Simcock, G., & Hayne, H. (2002). Breaking the barrier? Children fail to translate their preverbal memories into language. *Psychological Science, 13*, 225–231.

Simkin, D. K., Lederer, J. P., & Seligman, M. E. P. (1983). Learned helplessness in groups. *Behaviour Research and Therapy*, *21*, 613–622.

Simon, H. A. (1973). The structure of ill-structured problems. *Artificial Intelligence*, *4*, 181–201.

Simon, H. A. (1974). How big is a chunk? *Science*, *183*, 482–488.

Simon, H. A. (1978). Information-processing theory of human problem solving. In W. K. Estes (Ed.), *Handbook of learning and cognitive processes: Vol. 5. Human information processing*. Hillsdale, NJ: Erlbaum.

Simon, H. A. (1980). Problem solving and education. In D. T. Tuma & F. Reif (Eds.), *Problem-solving and education: Issues in teaching and research*. Hillsdale, NJ: Erlbaum.

Simons, P. R. J. (1984). Instructing with analogies. *Journal of Educational Psychology*, *76*, 513–527.

Sinatra, G. M., & Pintrich, P. R. (Eds.). (2003a). *Intentional conceptual change*. Mahwah, NJ: Erlbaum.

Sinatra, G. M., & Pintrich, P. R. (2003b). The role of intentions in conceptual change learning. In G. M. Sinatra & P. R. Pintrich (Eds.) *Intentional conceptual change* (pp. 1–18). Mahwah, NJ: Erlbaum.

Sinatra, G. M., Southerland, S. A., McConaughy, F., & Demastes, J. (in press). The role of intentions and beliefs in students' understanding and acceptance of biological evolution. *Journal of Research on Science Teaching*.

Sinclair, K. E. (1971). The influence of anxiety on several measures of classroom performance. In E. Gaudry & C. D. Spielberger (Eds.), *Anxiety and educational achievement*. Sydney, Australia: Wiley.

Singley, M. K., & Anderson, J. R. (1989). *The transfer of cognitive skill*. Cambridge, MA: Harvard University Press.

Sizer, T. R. (1992). *Horace's school: Redesigning the American high school*. Boston: Houghton Mifflin.

Skaalvik, E. M. (1997). Self-enhancing and self-defeating ego orientation: Relations with task avoidance orientation, achievement, self-perceptions, and anxiety. *Journal of Educational Psychology*, *89*, 71–81.

Skaalvik, E. M., & Valas, H. (2001, April). *Student help seeking: Relations with academic self-concept and goal-orientation*. Paper presented at the annual meeting of the American Educational Research Association, Seattle, WA.

Skiba, R., & Raison, J. (1990). Relationship between the use of timeout and academic achievement. *Exceptional Children*, *57*, 36–46.

Skinner, B. F. (1938). *The behavior of organisms: An experimental analysis*. Englewood Cliffs, NJ: Prentice Hall.

Skinner, B. F. (1948). Superstition in the pigeon. *Journal of Experimental Psychology*, *38*, 168–172.

Skinner, B. F. (1953). *Science and human behavior*. New York: Macmillan.

Skinner, B. F. (1954). The science of learning and the art of teaching. *Harvard Educational Review*, *24*, 86–97.

Skinner, B. F. (1958). Reinforcement today. *American Psychologist*, *13*, 94–99.

Skinner, B. F. (1966a). An operant analysis of problem solving. In B. Kleinmuntz (Ed.), *Problem solving: Research, method and theory*. New York: Wiley.

Skinner, B. F. (1966b). What is the experimental analysis of behavior? *Journal of the Experimental Analysis of Behavior*, *9*, 213–218.

Skinner, B. F. (1967). B. F. Skinner . . . An autobiography. In E. G. Boring & G. Lindzey (Eds.), *A history of psychology in autobiography* (Vol. 5). New York: Irvington.

Skinner, B. F. (1968). *The technology of teaching*. New York: Appleton-Century-Crofts.

Skinner, B. F. (1971). *Beyond freedom and dignity*. New York: Alfred Knopf.

Skinner, B. F. (1973). The free and happy student. *Phi Delta Kappan*, *55*, 13–16.

Skinner, B. F. (1989). The origins of cognitive thought. *American Psychologist*, *44*, 13–18.

Skinner, B. F., & Epstein, R. (1982). *Skinner for the classroom*. Champaign, IL: Research Press.

Skinner, E. A. (1995). *Perceived control, motivation, and coping*. Thousand Oaks, CA: Sage.

Slater, A., Mattock, A., & Brown, E. (1990). Size constancy at birth: Newborn infants' responses to retinal and real size. *Journal of Experimental Child Psychology*, *49*, 314–322.

Slavin, R. E. (1983a). *Cooperative learning*. New York: Longman.

Slavin, R. E. (1983b). When does cooperative learning increase student achievement? *Psychological Bulletin*, *94*, 429–445.

Slavin, R. E. (1987). Mastery learning reconsidered. *Review of Educational Research*, *57*, 175–213.

Slavin, R. E. (1990a). *Cooperative learning: Theory, research, and practice*. Upper Saddle River, NJ: Prentice Hall.

Slavin, R. E. (1990b). Mastery learning reconsidered. *Review of Educational Research*, *60*, 300–302.

Sloutsky, V. M., Lo, Y.-F., & Fisher, A. V. (2001). How much does a shared name make things similar? Linguistic labels, similarity, and the development of inductive inference. *Child Development*, *72*, 1695–1709.

Slusher, M. P., & Anderson, C. A. (1996). Using causal persuasive arguments to change beliefs and teach new information: The mediating role of explanation availability and evaluation bias in the acceptance of knowledge. *Journal of Educational Psychology*, *88*, 110–122.

Small, M. Y., Lovett, S. B., & Scher, M. S. (1993). Pictures facilitate children's recall of unillustrated expository prose. *Journal of Educational Psychology*, *85*, 520–528.

Small, S. L., Flores, D. K., & Noll, D. C. (1998). Different neural circuits subserve reading before and after therapy for acquired dyslexia. *Brain and Language*, *62*, 298–308.

Smith, B. L., & MacGregor, J. T. (1992). What is collaborative learning? In A. Goodsell, M. Maher, & V. Tinto (Eds.), *Collaborative learning: A sourcebook for higher education*. University Park, PA: National Center on Postsecondary Teaching, Learning, and Assessment, The Pennsylvania State University.

Smith, C. A., & Kirby, L. D. (2001). Affect and cognitive appraisal processes. In J. P. Forgas (Ed.), *Handbook of affect and social cognition* (pp. 75–92). Mahwah, NJ: Erlbaum.

Smith, C. L., Maclin, D., Grosslight, L., & Davis, H. (1997). Teaching for understanding: A study of students' preinstruction theories of matter and a comparison of the effectiveness of two approaches to teaching about matter and density. *Cognition and Instruction*, *15*, 317–393.

Smith, C. L., Maclin, D., Houghton, C., & Hennessey, M. G. (2000). Sixth-grade students' epistemologies of science: The impact of school science experiences on epistemological development. *Cognition and Instruction*, *18*, 349–422.

Smith, E. E. (1988). Concepts and thought. In R. J. Sternberg & E. E. Smith (Eds.), *The psychology of human thought*. New York: Cambridge University Press.

Smith, E. E. (2000). Neural bases of human working memory. *Current Directions in Psychological Science*, *9*, 45–49.

Smith, E. E., Shoben, E. J., & Rips, L. J. (1974). Structure and process in semantic memory: A feature model of semantic decisions. *Psychological Review*, *81*, 214–241.

Smith, K., Johnson, D. W., & Johnson, R. T. (1981). Can conflict be constructive? Controversy versus concurrence seeking in learning groups. *Journal of Educational Psychology*, *73*, 651–663.

Smith, P. K., & Dutton, S. (1979). Play and training on direct and innovative problem-solving. *Child Development*, *50*, 830–836.

Smith, R. E., & Smoll, F. L. (1997). Coaching the coaches: Youth sports as a scientific and applied behavioral setting. *Current Directions in Psychological Science*, *6*(1), 16–21.

Smith, S. M., Glenberg, A., & Bjork, R. A. (1978). Environmental context and human memory. *Memory and Cognition*, *6*, 342–353.

Smoke, K. L. (1932). An objective study of concept formation. *Psychological Monographs*, *42* (Whole No. 191).

Sneider, C., & Pulos, S. (1983). Children's cosmographies: Understanding the earth's shape and gravity. *Science Education*, *67*, 205–221.

Snow, R. E. (1989). Aptitude-treatment interaction as a framework for research on individual differences in learning. In P. L. Ackerman, R. J. Sternberg, & R. Glaser (Eds.), *Learning and individual differences: Advances in theory and research*. New York: W. H. Freeman.

Snow, R. E. (1994). Abilities in academic tasks. In R. J. Sternberg & R. K. Wagner (Eds.), *Mind in context: Interactionist perspectives on human intelligence.* Cambridge, England: Cambridge University Press.

Snow, R. E., Corno, L., & Jackson, D., III (1996). Individual differences in affective and conative functions. In D. C. Berliner & R. C. Calfee (Eds.), *Handbook of educational psychology.* New York: Macmillan.

Snowman, J. (1986). Learning tactics and strategies. In G. D. Phye & T. Andre (Eds.), *Cognitive classroom learning: Understanding, thinking, and problem solving.* Orlando: Academic Press.

Snyder, M., & Swann, W. B. (1978). Behavioral confirmation in social interaction: From social perception to social reality. *Journal of Experimental Social Psychology, 14,* 148–162.

Sokal, R. R. (1977). Classification: Purposes, principles, progress, prospects. In P. N. Johnson-Laird & P. C. Wason (Eds.), *Thinking: Readings in cognitive science.* Cambridge, England: Cambridge University Press.

Solnick, J. V., Rincover, A., & Peterson, C. R. (1977). Some determinants of the reinforcing and punishing effects of timeout. *Journal of Applied Behavior Analysis, 10,* 415–424.

Solomon, P., Kubzansky, P. E., Leiderman, P. H., Mendelson, J. H., Trumbull, R., & Wexler, D. (1961). *Sensory deprivation: A symposium held at Harvard Medical School.* Cambridge, MA: Harvard University Press.

Solomon, R. L., & Wynne, L. C. (1954). Traumatic avoidance learning: Acquisition in normal dogs. *Psychological Monographs, 67* (Whole No. 354).

Sosniak, L. A., & Stodolsky, S. S. (1994). Making connections: Social studies education in an urban fourth-grade classroom. In J. Brophy (Ed.), *Advances in research on teaching: Vol. 4. Case studies of teaching and learning in social studies.* Greenwich, CT: JAI Press.

Southerland, S. A., & Sinatra, G. M. (2003). Learning about biological evolution: A special case of intentional conceptual change. In G. M. Sinatra & P. R. Pintrich (Eds.), *Intentional conceptual change* (pp. 317–345). Mahwah, NJ: Erlbaum.

Sowell, E. R., & Jernigan, T. L. (1998). Further MRI evidence of late brain maturation: Limbic volume increases and changing asymmetries during childhood and adolescence. *Developmental Neuropsychology, 14,* 599–617.

Sowell, E. R., Thompson, P. M., Holmes, C. J., Jernigan, T. L., & Toga, A. W. (1999). *In vivo* evidence for post-adolescent brain maturation in frontal and striatal regions. *Nature Neuroscience, 2,* 859–861.

Spaulding, C. L. (1992). *Motivation in the classroom.* New York: McGraw-Hill.

Spelke, E. S. (1994). Initial knowledge: Six suggestions. *Cognition, 50,* 431–445.

Spelke, E. S. (2000). Core knowledge. *American Psychologist, 55,* 1233–1243.

Spelke, E. S., Breinlinger, K., Macomber, J., & Jacobson, K. (1992). Origins of knowledge. *Psychological Review, 99,* 605–632.

Spelke, E.S., Hirst, W., & Neisser, U. (1976). The skills of divided attention. *Cognition, 4,* 215–230.

Spence, K. W. (1956). *Behavior theory and conditioning.* New Haven, CT: Yale University Press.

Sperling, G. (1960). The information available in brief visual presentations. *Psychological Monographs, 74* (Whole No. 498).

Sperling, G. (1967). Successive approximations to a model for short-term memory. *Acta Psychologia, 27,* 285–292.

Spielberger, C. D. (1966). The effects of anxiety on complex learning in academic achievement. In C. D. Spielberger (Ed.), *Anxiety and behavior.* New York: Academic Press.

Spielberger, C. D., & DeNike, L. D. (1966). Descriptive behaviorism versus cognitive theory in verbal operant conditioning. *Psychological Review, 73,* 306–326.

Spilich, G. J., Vesonder, G. T., Chiesi, H. L., & Voss, J. F. (1979). Text processing of domain-related information for individuals with high and low domain knowledge. *Journal of Verbal Learning and Verbal Behavior, 18,* 275–290.

Spires, H. A. (1990, April). *Learning from a lecture: Effects of comprehension monitoring.* Paper presented at the annual meeting of the American Educational Research Association, Boston.

Spires, H. A., & Donley, J. (1998). Prior knowledge activation: Inducing engagement with informational texts. *Journal of Educational Psychology, 90,* 249–260.

Spires, H. A., Donley, J., & Penrose, A. M. (1990, April). *Prior knowledge activation: Inducing text engagement in reading to learn.* Paper presented at the annual meeting of the American Educational Research Association, Boston.

Spiro, R. J. (1977). Remembering information from text: The "state of schema" approach. In R. C. Anderson, R. J. Spiro, & W. E. Montague (Eds.), *Schooling and the acquisition of knowledge.* Hillsdale, NJ: Erlbaum.

Spiro, R. J. (1980a). Accommodative reconstruction in prose recall. *Journal of Verbal Learning and Verbal Behavior, 19,* 84–95.

Spiro, R. J. (1980b). Constructive processes in prose comprehension and recall. In R. J. Spiro, B. C. Bruce, & W. F. Brewer (Eds.), *Theoretical issues in reading comprehension.* Hillsdale, NJ: Erlbaum.

Spivey, N. N. (1997). *The constructivist metaphor: Reading, writing, and the making of meaning.* San Diego: Academic Press.

Sporer, S. (1991). Deep-deeper-deepest? Encoding strategies and the recognition of human faces. *Journal of Experimental Psychology: Learning, Memory, and Cognition, 17,* 323–333.

Squire, L. R., & Alvarez, P. (1998). Retrograde amnesia and memory consolidation: A neurobiological perspective. In L. R. Squire & S. M. Kosslyn (Eds.), *Findings and current opinion in cognitive neuroscience* (pp. 75–84). Cambridge, MA: MIT Press.

Stacey, K. (1992). Mathematical problem solving in groups: Are two heads better than one? *Journal of Mathematical Behavior, 11,* 261–275.

Staddon, J. E. R., & Higa, J. J. (1991). Temporal learning. In G. H. Bower (Ed.), *The psychology of learning and motivation: Advances in research and theory* (Vol. 27). San Diego: Academic Press.

Standing, L. (1973). Learning 10,000 pictures. *Quarterly Journal of Experimental Psychology, 25,* 207–222.

Stanovich, K. E. (1998). Cognitive neuroscience and educational psychology: What season is it? *Educational Psychology Review, 10,* 419–426.

Stanovich, K. E. (1999). *Who is rational? Studies of individual differences in reasoning.* Mahwah, NJ: Erlbaum.

Starr, E. J., & Lovett, S. B. (2000). The ability to distinguish between comprehension and memory: Failing to succeed. *Journal of Educational Psychology, 92,* 761–771.

Stazyk, E. H., Ashcraft, M. H., & Hamann, M. S. (1982). A network approach to mental multiplication. *Journal of Experimental Psychology: Learning, Memory, and Cognition, 8,* 320–335.

Steele, B. G., & Pollack, C. B. (1968). A psychiatric study of parents who abuse infants and small children. In R. E. Helfer & C. H. Kempe (Eds.), *The battered child.* Chicago: University of Chicago Press.

Steele, C. (1997). A threat in the air: How stereotypes shape intellectual identify and performance. *American Psychologist, 52,* 613–629.

Steffensen, M. S., Joag-Dev, C., & Anderson, R. C. (1979). A cross-cultural perspective on reading comprehension. *Reading Research Quarterly, 15,* 10–29.

Stein, B. S. (1978). Depth of processing reexamined: The effects of the precision of encoding and test appropriateness. *Journal of Verbal Learning and Verbal Behavior, 17,* 165–174.

Stein, B. S. (1989). Memory and creativity. In J. A. Glover, R. R. Ronning, & C. R. Reynolds (Eds.), *Handbook of creativity.* New York: Plenum Press.

Stein, B. S., & Bransford, J. D. (1979). Constraints on effective elaboration: Effects of precision and subject generation. *Journal of Verbal Learning and Verbal Behavior, 18,* 769–777.

Stein, B. S., Bransford, J. D., Franks, J. J., Owings, R. A., Vye, N. J., & McGraw, W. (1982). Differences in the precision of self-generated elaborations. *Journal of Experimental Psychology: General, 111,* 399–405.

Steinberg, L. (1996). *Beyond the classroom: Why school reform has failed and what parents need to do.* New York: Touchstone.

Steinmetz, S. K. (1977). *The cycle of violence.* New York: Praeger.

Stensvold, M. S., & Wilson, J. T. (1990). The interaction of verbal ability with concept mapping in learning from a chemistry laboratory activity. *Science Education, 74,* 473–480.

Stepans, J. (1991). Developmental patterns in students' understanding of physics concepts. In S. M. Glynn, R. H. Yeany, & B. K. Britton (Eds.), *The psychology of learning science.* Hillsdale, NJ: Erlbaum.

Stephan, W. G., & Stephan, C. W. (2000). An integrated threat theory of prejudice. In S. Oskamp (Ed.), *Reducing prejudice and discrimination* (pp. 23–45). Mahwah, NJ: Erlbaum.

Stephens, C. E., Pear, J. J., Wray, L. D., & Jackson, G. C. (1975). Some effects of reinforcement schedules in teaching picture names to retarded children. *Journal of Applied Behavior Analysis, 8,* 435–447.

Stepich, D. A., & Newby, T. J. (1988). Analogical instruction within the information processing paradigm: Effective means to facilitate learning. *Instructional Science, 17,* 129–144.

Sternberg, R. J. (1985). *Beyond IQ: A triarchic theory of human intelligence.* Cambridge, England: Cambridge University Press.

Sternberg, R. J. (1996). *Cognitive psychology.* Fort Worth, TX: Harcourt Brace.

Sternberg, R. J., & Davidson, J. E. (1982). Componential analysis and componential theory. *Behavioural and Brain Sciences, 53,* 352–353.

Sternberg, R. J., & Davidson, J. E. (1983). Insight in the gifted. *Educational Psychologist, 18,* 51–57.

Sternberg, R. J., Forsythe, G. B., Hedlund, J., Horvath, J. A., Wagner, R. K., Williams, W. M., Snook, S. A., & Grigorenko. E. L. (2000). *Practical intelligence in everyday life.* Cambridge, England: Cambridge University Press.

Sternberg, R. J., & Frensch, P. A. (1993). Mechanisms of transfer. In D. K. Detterman & R. J. Sternberg (Eds.), *Transfer on trial: Intelligence, cognition, and instruction.* Norwood, NJ: Ablex.

Sternberg, R. J., & Wagner, R. K. (Eds.) (1994). *Mind in context: Interactionist perspectives on human intelligence.* Cambridge, England: Cambridge University Press.

Sternberg, S. (1966). High-speed scanning in human memory. *Science, 153,* 652–654.

Steuer, F. B., Applefield, J. M., & Smith, R. (1971). Televised aggression and the interpersonal aggression of preschool children. *Journal of Experimental Child Psychology, 11,* 442–447.

Stevens, R. J., & Slavin, R. E. (1995). The cooperative elementary school: Effects of students' achievement, attitudes, and social relations. *American Educational Research Journal, 32,* 321–351.

Stevenson, H. C., & Fantuzzo, J. W. (1986). The generality and social validity of a competency-based self-control training intervention for underachieving students. *Journal of Applied Behavior Analysis, 19,* 269–276.

Stevenson, H. W., Chen, C., & Uttal, D. H. (1990). Beliefs and achievement: A study of black, white, and Hispanic children. *Child Development, 61,* 508–523.

Stiggins, R. J. (2001). *Student-involved classroom assessment* (3rd ed.). Upper Saddle River, NJ: Merrill/Prentice Hall.

Stiles, J., & Thal, D. (1993). Linguistic and spatial cognitive development following early focal brain injury: Patterns of deficit and recovery. In M. Johnson (Ed.), *Brain development and cognition.* Oxford, England: Blackwell.

Stipek, D. J. (1984). Sex differences in children's attributions for success and failure on math and spelling tests. *Sex Roles, 11,* 969–981.

Stipek, D. J. (1993). *Motivation to learn: From theory to practice* (2nd ed.). Boston: Allyn & Bacon.

Stipek, D. J. (1996). Motivation and instruction. In D. C. Berliner & R. C. Calfee (Eds.), *Handbook of educational psychology.* New York: Macmillan.

Stipek, D. J., & Gralinski, H. (1990, April). *Gender differences in children's achievement-related beliefs and emotional responses to success and failure in math.* Paper presented at the annual meeting of the American Educational Research Association, Boston.

Stipek, D. J., & Kowalski, P. S. (1989). Learned helplessness in task-orienting versus performance-orienting testing conditions. *Journal of Educational Psychology, 81,* 384–391.

Stodolsky, S. S., Salk, S., & Glaessner, B. (1991). Student views about learning math and social studies. *American Educational Research Journal, 28,* 89–116.

Stokes, T. F., & Baer, D. M. (1977). An implicit technology of generalization. *Journal of Applied Behavior Analysis, 10,* 349–367.

Stone, N. J. (2000). Exploring the relationship between calibration and self-regulated learning. *Educational Psychology Review, 12,* 437–475.

Strage, A., Christopoulos, J., Rohwer, W. D., Thomas, J. W., Delucchi, J. J., & Curley, R. G. (1988, April). *Grade-level differences in study activities as a function of perceived and observed course characteristics.* Paper presented at the American Educational Research Association, New Orleans.

Straus, M. A. (2000a). The benefits of never spanking: New and more definitive evidence. In M. A. Straus, *Beating the devil out of them: Corporal punishment by American families and its effects on children.* New Brunswick, NJ: Transaction.

Straus, M. A. (2000b). Corporal punishment by parents: The cradle of violence in the family and society. *The Virginia Journal of Social Policy & the Law, 8(1),* 7–60.

Straus, M. A., Gelles, R. J., & Steinmetz, S. K. (1980). *Behind closed doors: Violence in the American family.* Garden City, NY: Doubleday.

Strayer, D. L., & Johnston, W. A. (2001). Driven to distraction: Dual-task studies of simulated driving and conversing on a cellular telephone. *Psychological Science, 12,* 462–466.

Stright, A. D., Neitzel, C., Sears, K. G., & Hoke-Sinex, L. (2001). Instruction begins in the home: Relations between parental instruction and children's self-regulation in the classroom. *Journal of Educational Psychology, 93,* 456–466.

Strike, K. A., & Posner, G. J. (1992). A revisionist theory of conceptual change. In R. A. Duschl & R. J. Hamilton (Eds.), *Philosophy of science, cognitive psychology, and educational theory and practice.* Albany: State University of New York Press.

Strozer, J. R. (1994). *Language acquisition after puberty.* Washington, DC: Georgetown University Press.

Sue, S., & Chin, R. (1983). The mental health of Chinese-American children: Stressors and resources. In G. J. Powell (Ed.), *The psychosocial development of minority children.* New York: Brunner/Mazel.

Suina, J. H., & Smolkin, L. B. (1994). From natal culture to school culture to dominant society culture: Supporting transitions for Pueblo Indian students. In P. M. Greenfield & R. R. Cocking (Eds.), *Cross-cultural roots of minority child development.* Hillsdale, NJ: Erlbaum.

Sulin, R. A., & Dooling, D. J. (1974). Intrusions of a thematic idea in retention of prose. *Journal of Experimental Psychology, 103,* 255–262.

Sullivan, J. S. (1989). Planning, implementing, and maintaining an effective in-school suspension program. *Clearing House, 62,* 409–410.

Sullivan, R. C. (1994). Autism: Definitions past and present. *Journal of Vocational Rehabilitation, 4,* 4–9.

Surber, J. R. (2001). Effect of topic label repetition and importance on reading time and recall of text. *Journal of Educational Psychology, 93,* 279–287.

Sussman, D. M. (1981). PSI: Variations on a theme. In S. W. Bijou & R. Ruiz (Eds.), *Behavior modification: Contributions to education.* Hillsdale, NJ: Erlbaum.

Swan, K., Mitrani, M., Guerrero, F., Cheung, M., & Schoener, J. (1990, April). *Perceived locus of control and computer-based instruction.* Paper presented at the annual meeting of the American Educational Research Association, Boston.

Swanson, H. L. (1987). Information processing theory and learning disabilities: An overview. *Journal of Learning Disabilities, 20,* 3–7.

Swanson, H. L., O'Connor, J. E., & Cooney, J. B. (1990). An information processing analysis of expert and novice teachers' problem solving. *American Educational Research Journal, 27,* 533–556.

Sweller, J., & Levine, M. (1982). Effects of goal specificity on means–end analysis and learning. *Journal of Experimental Psychology: Learning, Memory, and Cognition, 8,* 463–474.

Swenson, L. C. (1980). *Theories of learning: Traditional perspectives/contemporary developments.* Belmont, CA: Wadsworth.

Sylva, K., Bruner, J. S., & Genova, P. (1976). The role of play in the problem solving of children 3 to 5 years old. In J. Bruner, A. Jolly, & K. Sylva (Eds.), *Play: Its role in development and evolution.* New York: Basic Books.

Tang, J.-C., Kennedy, C. H., Koppekin, A., & Caruso, M. (2002). Functional analysis of sterotypical ear covering in a child with autism. *Journal of Applied Behavior Analysis, 35,* 95–98.

Tanner, B. A., & Zeiler, M. (1975). Punishment of self-injurious behavior using aromatic ammonia as the aversive stimulus. *Journal of Applied Behavior Analysis, 8,* 53–57.

Tarver, S. G. (1992). Direct Instruction. In W. Stainback & S. Stainback (Eds.), *Controversial issues confronting special education.* Boston: Allyn & Bacon.

Taylor, B. A., & Levin, L. (1998). Teaching a student with autism to make verbal initiations: Effects of a tactile prompt. *Journal of Applied Behavior Analysis, 31,* 651–654.

Taylor, B. M. (1982). Text structure and children's comprehension and memory for expository material. *Journal of Educational Psychology, 74,* 323–340.

Taylor, J. C., & Romanczyk, R. G. (1994). Generating hypotheses about the function of student problem behavior by observing teacher behavior. *Journal of Applied Behavior Analysis, 27,* 251–265.

Taylor, M., Esbensen, B. M., & Bennett, R. T. (1994). Children's understanding of knowledge acquisition: The tendency for children to report they have always known what they have just learned. *Child Development, 65,* 1581–1604.

Taylor, M. J., & Kratochwill, T. R. (1978). Modification of preschool children's bathroom behaviors by contingent teacher attention. *Journal of School Psychology, 16,* 64–71.

Taylor, S. M. (1994, April). *Staying in school against the odds: Voices of minority adolescent girls.* Paper presented at the annual meeting of the American Educational Research Association, New Orleans.

Teasley, S. D., & Roschelle, J. (1993). Constructing a joint problem space: The computer as a tool for sharing information. In S. P. Lajoie & S. J. Derry (Eds.), *Computers as cognitive tools* (pp. 229–258). Hillsdale, NJ: Erlbaum.

Tennyson, C. L., Tennyson, R. D., & Rothen, W. (1980). Content structure and instructional control strategies as design variables in concept acquisition. *Journal of Educational Psychology, 72,* 499–505.

Tennyson, R. D., & Cocchiarella, M. J. (1986). An empirically based instructional design theory for teaching concepts. *Review of Educational Research, 56,* 40–71.

Tennyson, R. D., & Park, O. (1980). The teaching of concepts: A review of instructional design literature. *Review of Educational Research, 50,* 55–70.

Tennyson, R. D., & Tennyson, C. L. (1975). Rule acquisition design strategy variables: Degree of instance divergence, sequence, and instance analysis. *Journal of Educational Psychology, 67,* 852–859.

Tennyson, R. D., Youngers, J., & Suebsonthi, P. (1983). Concept learning by children using instructional presentation forms for prototype formation and classification-skill development. *Journal of Educational Psychology, 75,* 280–291.

Terrell, G., & Ware, R. (1961). Role of delay of reward in speed of size and form discrimination learning in childhood. *Child Development, 32,* 409–415.

Tessler, M., & Nelson, K. (1994). Making memories: The influence of joint encoding on later recall by young children. *Consciousness and Cognition, 3,* 307–326.

Thapar, A., & Greene, R. (1993). Evidence against a short-term store account of long-term recency effects. *Memory and Cognition, 21,* 329–337.

Tharp, R. G. (1989). Psychocultural variables and constants: Effects on teaching and learning in schools. *American Psychologist, 44,* 349–359.

Théberge, C. L. (1994, April). *Small-group vs. whole-class discussion: Gaining the floor in science lessons.* Paper presented at the annual meeting of the American Educational Research Association, New Orleans.

Thelen, D. (1989). Memory and American history. *Journal of American History, 75,* 1117–1129.

Thelen, E., & Smith, L. B. (1998). Dynamic systems theories. In W. Damon (Ed.-in-chief) and R. M. Lerner (Vol. Ed.), *Handbook of child psychology: Vol. 1. Theoretical models of human development.* New York: Wiley.

Thiagarajan, S. (1989). Interactive lectures: Seven more strategies. *Performance and Instruction, 28*(2), 35–37.

Thomas, E. L., & Robinson, H. A. (1972). *Improving reading in every class: A sourcebook for teachers.* Boston: Allyn & Bacon.

Thomas, J. W. (1993). Expectations and effort: Course demands, students' study practices, and academic achievement. In T. M. Tomlinson (Ed.), *Motivating students to learn: Overcoming barriers to high achievement.* Berkeley, CA: McCutchan.

Thomas, S., & Oldfather, P. (1997). Intrinsic motivations, literacy, and assessment practices: "That's my grade. That's me." *Educational Psychologist, 32,* 107–123.

Thompson, A. G., & Thompson, P. W. (1989). Affect and problem solving in an elementary school mathematics classroom. In D. B. McLeod & V. M. Adams (Eds.), *Affect and mathematical problem solving: A new perspective.* New York: Springer-Verlag.

Thompson, R., & McConnell, J. (1955). Classical conditioning in the planarian, *Dugesia dorotocephala. Journal of Comparative and Physiological Psychology, 48,* 65–68.

Thompson, R. A., & Nelson, C. A. (2001). Developmental science and the media: Early brain development. *American Psychologist, 56,* 5–15.

Thompson, R. F. (1985). *The brain: An introduction to neuroscience.* New York: W. H. Freeman.

Thompson, S. C. (1999). Illusions of control: How we overestimate our personal influence. *Current Directions in Psychological Science, 8,* 187–190.

Thorndike, E. L. (1898). Animal intelligence: An experimental study of the associative processes in animals. *Psychological Review Monograph Supplement, 2*(8).

Thorndike, E. L. (1903). *Educational psychology.* New York: Lemcke & Buechner.

Thorndike, E. L. (1911). *Animal intelligence.* New York: Macmillan.

Thorndike, E. L. (1913). *Educational psychology: The psychology of learning* (Vol. 2). New York: Teachers College Press.

Thorndike, E. L. (1924). Mental discipline in high school studies. *Journal of Educational Psychology, 15,* 1–22, 83–98.

Thorndike, E. L. (1932a). *The fundamentals of learning.* New York: Teachers College Press.

Thorndike, E. L. (1932b). Reward and punishment in animal learning. *Comparative Psychology Monograph, 8*(39).

Thorndike, E. L. (1935). *The psychology of wants, interests, and attitudes.* New York: Appleton-Century-Crofts.

Thorndike, E. L., & Woodworth, R. S. (1901). The influence of improvement in one mental function upon the efficiency of other functions. *Psychological Review, 8,* 247–261, 384–395, 553–564.

Thrailkill, N. J., & Ormrod, J. E. (1994, April). *Facilitating lecture recall: Effects of embedded imagery-evoking phrases on memory for proximal and non-proximal material.* Paper presented at the annual meeting of the American Educational Research Association, New Orleans.

Thyne, J. M. (1963). *The psychology of learning and techniques of teaching.* London: University of London Press.

Tiffany, S. T., & Baker, T. B. (1981). Morphine tolerance in rats: Congruence with a Pavlovian paradigm. *Journal of Comparative and Physiological Psychology, 95,* 747–762.

Timberlake, W., & Allison, J. (1974). Response deprivation: An empirical approach to instrumental performance. *Psychological Review, 81,* 146–164.

Timberlake, W., & Lucas, G. A. (1989). Behavior systems and learning: From misbehavior to general principles. In S. B. Klein & R. R. Mowrer (Eds.), *Contemporary learning theories: Instrumental conditioning theory and the impact of biological constraints on learning.* Mahwah, NJ: Erlbaum.

Tirosh, D., & Graeber, A. O. (1990). Evoking cognitive conflict to explore preservice teachers' thinking about division. *Journal for Research in Mathematics Education, 21,* 98–108.

Titcomb, A. L., & Reyna, V. F. (1995). Memory interference and misinformation effects. In F. N. Dempster & C. J. Brainerd (Eds.), *Interference and inhibition in cognition.* San Diego: Academic Press.

Tobias, S. (1980). Anxiety and instruction. In I. G. Sarason (Ed.), *Test anxiety: Theory, research, and applications.* Hillsdale, NJ: Erlbaum.

Tobias, S. (1985). Test anxiety: Interference, defective skills, and cognitive capacity. *Educational Psychologist, 20,* 135–142.

Tobias, S. (1994). Interest, prior knowledge, and learning. *Review of Educational Research, 64,* 37–54.

Tobin, K. (1986). Student task involvement and achievement in process-oriented science activities. *Science Education, 70*(1), 61–72.

Tobin, K. (1987). The role of wait time in higher cognitive level learning. *Review of Educational Research, 57,* 69–95.

Tobin, K., & Tippins, D. (1993). Constructivism as a reference for teaching and learning. In K. Tobin (Ed.), *The practice of constructivism in science education.* Washington, DC: American Association for the Advancement of Science.

Toglia, M. P. (1996). Recovered memories: Lost and found? In K. Pezdek & W. P. Banks (Eds.), *The recovered memory/false memory debate.* San Diego: Academic Press.

Tollefson, N. (2000). Classroom applications of cognitive theories of motivation. *Educational Psychology Review, 12,* 63–83.

Tolman, E. C. (1932). *Purposive behavior in animals and men.* New York: Century.

Tolman, E. C. (1938). The determiners of behavior at a choice point. *Psychological Review, 45,* 1–41.

Tolman, E. C. (1942). *Drives toward war.* New York: Appleton-Century Crofts.

Tolman, E. C. (1959). Principles of purposive behavior. In S. Koch (Ed.), *Psychology: A study of a science* (Vol. 2). New York: McGraw-Hill.

Tolman, E. C., & Honzik, C. H. (1930). Introduction and removal of reward, and maze performance in rats. *University of California Publications in Psychology, 4,* 257–275.

Tolman, E. C., Ritchie, B. F., & Kalish, D. (1946). Studies in spatial learning: I. Orientation and the short-cut. *Journal of Experimental Psychology, 36,* 13–24.

Toplak, M. E., & Stanovich, K. E. (2002). The domain specificity and generality of disjunctive searching for a generalizable critical thinking skill. *Journal of Educational Psychology, 94,* 197–209.

Torney-Purta, J. (1994). Dimensions of adolescents' reasoning about political and historical issues: Ontological switches, developmental processes, and situated learning. In M. Carretero & J. F. Voss (Eds.), *Cognitive and instructional processes in history and the social sciences* (pp. 103–122). Mahwah, NJ: Erlbaum.

Torrance, E. P., & Myers, R. E. (1970). *Creative learning and teaching.* New York: Dodd, Mead & Company.

Tourniaire, F., & Pulos, S. (1985). Proportional reasoning: A review of the literature. *Educational Studies in Mathematics, 16,* 181–204.

Trachtenberg, D. (1974). Student tasks in text material. What cognitive skills do they tap? *Peabody Journal of Education, 52,* 54–57.

Trawick-Smith, J. (2000). *Early childhood development: A multicultural perspective* (2nd ed.). Upper Saddle River, NJ: Merrill/Prentice Hall.

Treisman, A. M. (1964). Verbal cues, language and meaning in selective attention. *American Journal of Psychology, 77,* 215–216.

Trenholme, I. A., & Baron, A. (1975). Intermediate and delayed punishment of human behavior by loss of reinforcement. *Learning and Motivation, 6,* 62–79.

Trowbridge, M. H., & Cason, H. (1932). An experimental study of Thorndike's theory of learning. *Journal of General Psychology, 7,* 245–252.

Tryon, G. S. (1980). The measurement and treatment of test anxiety. *Review of Educational Research, 50,* 343–372.

Tschannen-Moran, M., Woolfolk Hoy, A., & Hoy, W. K. (1998). Teacher efficacy: Its meaning and measure. *Review of Educational Research, 68,* 202–248.

Tudge, J. (1990). Vygotsky, the zone of proximal development, and peer collaboration: Implications for classroom practice. In L. C. Moll (Ed.), *Vygotsky and education: Instructional implications and applications of sociohistorical psychology.* Cambridge, England: Cambridge University Press.

Tudor, R. M. (1995). Isolating the effects of active responding in computer-based instruction. *Journal of Applied Behavior Analysis, 28,* 343–344.

Tulving, E. (1962). Subjective organization in free recall of "unrelated" words. *Psychological Review, 69,* 344–354.

Tulving, E. (1968). Theoretical issues in free recall. In T. R. Dixon & D. L. Horton (Eds.), *Verbal behavior and general behavior theory.* Englewood Cliffs, NJ: Prentice Hall.

Tulving, E. (1975). Ecphoric processes in recall and recognition. In J. Brown (Ed.), *Recall and recognition.* London: Wiley.

Tulving, E. (1983). *Elements of episodic memory.* Oxford, England: Oxford University Press.

Tulving, E. (1991). Concepts of human memory. In L. R. Squire, N. M. Weinberger, G. Lynch, & J. L. McGaugh (Eds.), *Organization and locus of change.* New York: Oxford University Press.

Tulving, E. (1993). What is episodic memory? *Current Directions in Psychological Science, 2,* 67–70.

Tulving, E., & Psotka, J. (1971). Retroactive inhibition in free recall: Inaccessibility of information available in the memory store. *Journal of Experimental Psychology, 87,* 1–8.

Tulving, E., & Thomson, D. M. (1971). Retrieval processes in recognition memory: Effects of associative context. *Journal of Experimental Psychology, 87,* 116–124.

Turnbull, C. M. (1961). *The forest people.* New York: Simon & Schuster.

Turner, J. C. (1995). The influence of classroom contexts on young children's motivation for literacy. *Reading Research Quarterly, 30,* 410–441.

Turner, J. C., Meyer, D. K., Cox, K. E., Logan, C., DiCintio, M., & Thomas, C. T. (1998). Creating contexts for involvement in mathematics. *Journal of Educational Psychology, 90,* 730–745.

Turner, J. C., Thorpe, P. K., & Meyer, D. K. (1998). Students' reports of motivation and negative affect: A theoretical and empirical analysis. *Journal of Educational Psychology, 90,* 758–771.

Turner, J. E., Husman, J., & Schallert, D. L. (2002). The importance of students' goals in their emotional experience of academic failure: Investigating the precursors and consequences of shame. *Educational Psychologist, 37,* 79–89.

Turnure, J., Buium, N., & Thurlow, M. (1976). The effectiveness of interrogatives for promoting verbal elaboration productivity in young children. *Child Development, 47,* 851–855.

Turvey, M. T., & Kravetz, S. (1970). Retrieval from iconic memory with shape as the selection criterion. *Perception and Psychophysics, 8,* 171–172.

Tversky, A., & Kahneman, D. (1973). Availability: A heuristic for judging frequency and probability. *Cognitive Psychology, 5,* 207–232.

Tversky, A., & Kahneman, D. (1974). Judgment under uncertainty: Heuristics and biases. *Science, 185,* 1124–1131.

Tversky, B. (1981). Distortions in memory for maps. *Cognitive Psychology, 13,* 407–433.

Tweed, R. G., & Lehman, D. R. (2002). Learning considered within a cultural context. *American Psychologist, 57,* 89–99.

Tyler, B. (1958). Expectancy for eventual success as a factor in problem solving behavior. *Journal of Educational Psychology, 49,* 166–172.

Uhl, C. N. (1973). Eliminating behavior with omission and extinction after varying amounts of training. *Animal Learning and Behavior, 1,* 237–240.

Uhl, C. N., & Garcia, E. E. (1969). Comparison of omission with extinction in response elimination in rats. *Journal of Comparative and Physiological Psychology, 69,* 554–562.

Underwood, B. J. (1948). "Spontaneous recovery" of verbal associations. *Journal of Experimental Psychology, 38,* 429–439.

Underwood, B. J. (1954). Studies of distributed practice: XII. Retention following varying degrees of original learning. *Journal of Experimental Psychology, 47,* 294–300.

Underwood, B. J. (1957). Interference and forgetting. *Psychological Review, 64,* 49–60.

Underwood, B. J. (1961). Ten years of massed practice on distributed practice. *Psychological Review, 68,* 229–247.

Underwood, B. J. (1983). *Attributes of memory.* Glenview, IL: Scott Foresman.

Underwood, B. J., & Erlebacher, A. H. (1965). Studies of coding in verbal behavior. *Psychological Monographs, 79* (Whole No. 606).

Underwood, B. J., Kapelak, S., & Malmi, R. (1976). The spacing effect: Additions to the theoretical and empirical puzzles. *Memory and Cognition, 4,* 391–400.

Underwood, B. J., & Schulz, R. W. (1960). *Meaningfulness and verbal learning.* Philadelphia: J. B. Lippincott.

Urdan, T. C. (1997). Achievement goal theory: Past results, future directions. In M. L. Maehr & P. R. Pintrich (Eds.), *Advances in motivation and achievement* (Vol. 10, pp. 99–141). Greenwich, CT: JAI Press.

Urdan, T. C. (2000, April). The intersection of self-determination and achievement goal theories: Do we need to have goals? In A. Assor (Chair), *Self-determination theory and achievement goal theory: Convergences, divergences, and educational implications.* Symposium conducted at the annual meeting of the American Educational Research Association, New Orleans.

Urdan, T. C., & Maehr, M. L. (1995). Beyond a two-goal theory of motivation and achievement: A case for social goals. *Review of Educational Research, 65,* 213–243.

Urdan, T. C., & Midgley, C. (2001). Academic self-handicapping: What we know, what more there is to learn. *Educational Psychology Review, 13,* 115–138.

Urdan, T. C., Midgley, C., & Anderman, E. M. (1998). The role of classroom goal structure in students' use of self-handicapping strategies. *American Educational Research Journal, 35,* 101–122.

Van Camp, C. M., Lerman, D. C., Kelley, M. E., Roane, H. S., Contrucci, S. A., & Vorndran, C. M. (2000). Further analysis of idiosyncratic antecedent influences during the assessment and treatment of problem behavior. *Journal of Applied Behavior Analysis, 33,* 207–221.

van der Broek, P. (1990). Causal inferences and the comprehension of narrative text. In A. C. Graessner & G. H. Bower (Eds.), *Inferences and text comprehension. The*

psychology of learning and motivation: Advances in research and theory (Vol. 25). Orlando: Academic Press.

van Dijk, T. A., & Kintsch, W. (1983). *Strategies of discourse comprehension.* New York: Academic Press.

Van Houten, R., Nau, P., MacKenzie-Keating, S., Sameoto, D., & Colavecchia, B. (1982). An analysis of some variables influencing the effectiveness of reprimands. *Journal of Applied Behavior Analysis, 15,* 65–83.

van Kraayenoord, C. E., & Paris, S. G. (1997). Children's self-appraisal of their worksamples and academic progress. *Elementary School Journal, 97,* 523–5537.

van Laar, C. (2000). The paradox of low academic achievement but high self-esteem in African American students: An attributional account. *Educational Psychology Review, 12,* 33–61.

Van Meter, P. (2001). Drawing construction as a strategy for learning from text. *Journal of Educational Psychology, 93,* 129–140.

Van Meter, P., Yokoi, L., & Pressley, M. (1994). College students' theory of notetaking derived from their perceptions of notetaking. *Journal of Educational Psychology, 86,* 323–338.

Van Patten, J. R., Chao, C. I., & Reigeluth, C. M. (1986). A review of strategies for sequencing and synthesizing information. *Review of Educational Research, 56,* 437–472.

Van Rossum, E. J., & Schenk, S. M. (1984). The relationship between learning conception, study strategy and learning outcome. *British Journal of Educational Psychology, 54,* 73–83.

VanSledright, B., & Brophy, J. (1992). Storytelling, imagination, and fanciful elaboration in children's historical reconstructions. *American Educational Research Journal, 29,* 837–859.

Vaughan, W. (1988). Formation of equivalence sets in pigeons. *Journal of Experimental Psychology: Animal Behavior Processes, 14,* 36–42.

Vaughn, B. J., & Horner, R. H. (1997). Identifying instructional tasks that occasion problem behaviors and assessing the effects of teacher versus teacher choice among these tasks. *Journal of Applied Behavior Analysis, 30,* 299–312.

Vecera, S. P., Vogel, E. K., & Woodman, G. F. (2002). Lower region: A new cue for figure–ground assignment. *Journal of Experimental Psychology: General, 131,* 194–205.

Vekiri, I. (2002). What is the value of graphical displays in learning? *Educational Psychology Review, 14,* 261–312.

Verdi, M. P., & Kulhavy, R. W. (2002). Learning with maps and texts: An overview. *Educational Psychology Review, 14,* 27–46.

Verdi, M. P., Kulhavy, R. W., Stock, W. A., Rittschof, K. A., & Johnson, J. T. (1996). Text learning using scientific diagrams: Implications for classroom use.

Contemporary Educational Psychology, 21, 487–499.

Vermeer, H. J., Boekaerts, M., & Seegers, G. (2000). Motivational and gender differences: Sixth-grade students' mathematical problem-solving behavior. *Journal of Educational Psychology, 92,* 308–315.

Vernon, M. D. (1969). *Human motivation.* Cambridge, England: Cambridge University Press.

Veroff, J., McClelland, L., & Ruhland, D. (1975). Varieties of achievement motivation. In M. T. S. Mednick, S. S. Tangri, & L. W. Hoffman (Eds.), *Women and achievement: Social and motivational analyses.* New York: Halsted.

Viken, R. J., & McFall, R. M. (1994). Paradox lost: Implications of contemporary reinforcement theory for behavior therapy. *Current Directions in Psychological Science, 3,* 121–125.

Vollmer, T. R., & Hackenberg, T. D. (2001). Reinforcement contingencies and social reinforcement: Some reciprocal relations between basic and applied research. *Journal of Applied Behavior Analysis, 34,* 241–253.

Vollmer, T. R., Roane, H. S., Ringdahl, J. E., & Marcus, B. A. (1999). Evaluating treatment challenges with differential reinforcement of alternative behavior. *Journal of Applied Behavior Analysis, 32,* 9–23.

von Glasersfeld, E. (1995). A constructivist approach to teaching. In L. P. Steffe & J. Gale (Eds.), *Constructivism in education* (pp. 3–15). Mahwah, NJ: Erlbaum.

Vosniadou, S. (1991). Conceptual development in astronomy. In S. M. Glynn, R. H. Yeany, & B. K. Britton (Eds.), *The psychology of learning science.* Hillsdale, NJ: Erlbaum.

Vosniadou, S. (1994). Universal and culture-specific properties of children's mental models of the earth. In L. A. Hirschfeld & S. A. Gelman (Eds.), *Mapping the mind: Domain specificity in cognition and culture.* Cambridge, England: Cambridge University Press.

Vosniadou, S., & Brewer, W. F. (1987). Theories of knowledge restructuring in development. *Review of Educational Research, 57,* 51–67.

Voss, J. F. (1987). Learning and transfer in subject-matter learning: A problem-solving model. *International Journal of Educational Research, 11,* 607–622.

Voss, J. F., Greene, T. R., Post, T. A., & Penner, B. D. (1983). Problem-solving skill in the social sciences. In G. H. Bower (Ed.), *The psychology of learning and motivation* (Vol. 17). New York: Academic Press.

Voss, J. F., & Schauble, L. (1992). Is interest educationally interesting? An interest-related model of learning. In K. A. Renninger, S. Hidi, & A. Krapp (Eds.), *The role of interest in learning and development.* Hillsdale, NJ: Erlbaum.

Voss, J. F., Tyler, S. W., & Yengo, L. A. (1983). Individual differences in the solving of social science problems. In R. F. Dillon & R. R. Schmeck (Eds.), *Individual differences in cognition*. New York: Academic Press.

Voss, J. F., Wolfe, C. R., Lawrence, J. A., & Engle, R. A. (1991). From representation to decision: An analysis of problem solving in international relations. In R. J. Sternberg & P. A. Frensch (Eds.), *Complex problem solving: Principles and mechanisms*. Hillsdale, NJ: Erlbaum.

Vurpillot, E., & Ball, W. A. (1979). The concept of identity and children's selective attention. In G. A. Hale & M. Lewis (Eds.), *Attention and cognitive development*. New York: Plenum Press.

Vye, N. J., Schwartz, D. L., Bransford, J. D., Barron, B. J., Zech, L., & The Cognition and Technology Group at Vanderbilt (1998). SMART environments that support monitoring, reflection, and revision. In D. J. Hacker, J. Dunlosky, & A. C. Graesser (Eds.), *Metacognition in educational theory and practice* (pp. 305–346). Mahwah, NJ: Erlbaum.

Vygotsky, L. S. (1962). *Thought and language* (E. Haufmann & G. Vakar, Eds. and Trans.). Cambridge, MA: MIT Press.

Vygotsky, L. S. (1978). *Mind in society: The development of higher psychological processes*. Cambridge, MA: Harvard University Press.

Vygotsky, L. S. (1987). *The collected works of L. S. Vygotsky* (R. W. Rieber & A. S. Carton, Eds.). New York: Plenum Press.

Vygotsky, L. S. (1997). *Educational psychology*. Boca Raton, FL: St. Lucie Press.

Waddill, P. J., McDaniel, M. A., & Einstein, G. O. (1988). Illustrations as adjuncts to prose: A text-appropriate processing approach. *Journal of Educational Psychology, 80*, 457–464.

Wade, S. E. (1983). A synthesis of the research for improving reading in the social studies. *Review of Educational Research, 53*, 461–497.

Wade, S. E. (1992). How interest affects learning from text. In K. A. Renninger, S. Hidi, & A. Krapp (Eds.), *The role of interest in learning and development*. Hillsdale, NJ: Erlbaum.

Wadsworth, B. J. (1996). *Piaget's theory of cognitive and affective development* (5th ed.). New York: Addison-Wesley-Longman.

Wagner, A. R. (1981). SOP: A model of automatic memory processing in animal behavior. In N. E. Spear & R. R. Miller (Eds.), *Information processing in animals: Memory mechanisms*. Hillsdale, NJ: Erlbaum.

Wagner, A. R., & Rescorla, R. A. (1972). Inhibition in Pavlovian conditioning: Applications of a theory. In R. A. Boakes & M. S. Halliday (Eds.), *Inhibition and learning*. New York: Academic Press.

Wahler, R. G., & Fox, J. J. (1981). Setting events in applied behavior analysis: Toward a conceptual and methodological expansion. *Journal of Applied Behavior Analysis, 14*, 327–338.

Walker, E. F. (2002). Adolescent neurodevelopment and psychopathology. *Current Directions in Psychological Science, 11*, 24–28.

Walker, H. M., Mattsen, R. H., & Buckley, N. K. (1971). The functional analysis of behavior within an experimental class setting. In W. C. Becker (Ed.), *An empirical basis for change in education*. Chicago: Science Research Associates.

Walker, J. E., & Shea, T. M. (1995). *Behavior management: A practical approach for educators* (6th ed.). Englewood Cliffs, NJ: Merrill/Prentice Hall.

Wallas, G. (1926). *The art of thought*. New York: Harcourt Brace Jovanovich.

Walters, G. C., & Grusec, J. E. (1977). *Punishment*. San Francisco: W. H. Freeman.

Walters, R. H. (1964). Delay of reinforcement gradients in children's learning. *Psychonomic Science, 1*, 307–308.

Walters, R. H., & Parke, R. D. (1964). Influence of response consequences to a social model on resistance to deviation. *Journal of Experimental Child Psychology, 1*, 269–280.

Walters, R. H., Parke, R. D., & Cane, V. A. (1965). Timing of punishment and the observation of consequences to others as determinants of response inhibition. *Journal of Experimental Child Psychology, 2*, 10–30.

Walters, R. H., & Thomas, E. L. (1963). Enhancement of punitiveness by visual and audiovisual displays. *Canadian Journal of Psychology, 17*, 244–255.

Walters, R. H., Thomas, E. L., & Acker, W. (1962). Enhancement of punitive behavior by audio-visual displays. *Science, 136*, 872–873.

Walton, G. E., & Bower, T. G. R. (1993). Newborns form "prototypes" in less than 1 minute. *Psychological Science, 4*, 203–205.

Wang, M. C., & Stiles, B. (1976). An investigation of children's concept of self-responsibility for their school learning. *American Educational Research Journal, 13*, 159–179.

Want, S. C., & Harris, P. L. (2001). Learning from other people's mistakes: Causal understanding in learning to use a tool. *Child Development, 72*, 431–443.

Ward, S. L., & Overton, W. F. (1990). Semantic familiarity, relevance, and the development of deductive reasoning. *Developmental Psychology, 26*, 488–493.

Ward, T. B., Vela, E., & Haas, S. D. (1990). Children and adults learn family-resemblance categories analytically. *Child Development, 61*, 593–605.

Ward, T. J., Jr. (1991, April). The effects of field articulation and interestingness on text processing. In G. Schraw (Chair), *Cognitive processing and text comprehension in specific knowledge domains*. Symposium presented at the annual meeting of the American Educational Research Association, Chicago.

Wasserman, E. A. (1993). Comparative cognition: Toward a general understanding of cognition in behavior. *Psychological Science, 4*, 156–161.

Wasserman, E. A., DeVolder, C. L., & Coppage, D. J. (1992). Non-similarity–based conceptualization in pigeons via secondary or mediated generalization. *Psychological Science, 3*, 374–379.

Waters, H. S. (1982). Memory development in adolescence: Relationships between metamemory, strategy use, and performance. *Journal of Experimental Child Psychology, 33*, 183–195.

Watkins, M. J., & Watkins, O. C. (1974). Processing of recency items for free-recall. *Journal of Experimental Psychology, 102*, 488–493.

Watson, J. B. (1913). Psychology as the behaviorist views it. *Psychological Review, 20*, 158–177.

Watson, J. B. (1914). *Behavior: An introduction to comparative psychology*. New York: Holt, Rinehart & Winston.

Watson, J. B. (1916). The place of a conditioned reflex in psychology. *Psychological Review, 23*, 89–116.

Watson, J. B. (1919). *Psychology from the standpoint of a behaviorist*. Philadelphia: J. B. Lippincott.

Watson, J. B. (1925). *Behaviorism*. New York: W. W. Norton.

Watson, J. B., & Rayner, R. (1920). Conditioned emotional reactions. *Journal of Experimental Psychology, 3*, 1–14.

Watts, G. H., & Anderson, R. C. (1971). Effects of three types of inserted questions on learning from prose. *Journal of Educational Psychology, 62*, 387–394.

Weaver, C. A., III, & Kelemen, W. L. (1997). Judgments of learning at delays: Shifts in response patterns or increased metamemory accuracy? *Psychological Science, 8*, 318–321.

Weaver, C. A., III, & Kintsch, W. (1991). Expository text. In R. Barr, M. L. Kamil, P. B. Mosenthal, & P. D. Pearson (Eds.), *Handbook of reading research* (Vol. 2). New York: Longman.

Webb, N. M. (1989). Peer interaction and learning in small groups. *International Journal of Educational Research, 13*, 21–39.

Webb, N. M., & Farivar, S. (1994). Promoting helping behavior in cooperative small groups in middle school mathematics. *American Educational Research Journal, 31*, 369–395.

Webb, N. M., & Farivar, S. (1999). Developing productive group interaction in middle school mathematics. In A. M. O'Donnell & A. King (Eds.), *Cognitive perspectives on peer learning* (pp. 117–149). Mahwah, NJ: Erlbaum.

Webb, N. M., Nemer, K. M., Chizhik, A. W., & Sugrue, B. (1998). Equity issues in collaborative group assessment: Group composition and performance. *American Educational Research Journal, 35*, 607–651.

Webb, N. M., & Palincsar, A. S. (1996). Group processes in the classroom. In D. C. Berliner & R. C. Calfee (Eds.), *Handbook of educational psychology*. New York: Macmillan.

Webber, J., Scheuermann, B., McCall, C., & Coleman, M. (1993). Research on self-monitoring as a behavior management technique in special education classrooms: A descriptive review. *Remedial and Special Education, 14*(2), 38–56.

Wegman, C. (1985). *Psychoanalysis and cognitive psychology*. London: Academic Press.

Weiner, B. (1984). Principles for a theory of student motivation and their application within an attributional framework. In R. Ames & C. Ames (Eds.), *Research on motivation in education: Vol. 1. Student motivation*. Orlando: Academic Press.

Weiner, B. (1986). *An attributional theory of motivation and emotion*. New York: Springer-Verlag.

Weiner, B. (1992). *Human motivation: Metaphors, theories, and research*. Newbury Park, CA: Sage.

Weiner, B. (1994). Ability versus effort revisited: The moral determinants of achievement evaluation and achievement as a moral system. *Educational Psychologist, 29*, 163–172.

Weiner, B. (1995). *Judgments of responsibility: Foundations for a theory of social conduct*. New York: Guilford Press.

Weiner, B. (2000). Intrapersonal and interpersonal theories of motivation from an attributional perspective. *Educational Psychology Review, 12*, 1–14.

Weiner, B., Russell, D., & Lerman, D. (1978). Affective consequences of causal ascriptions. In J. Harvey, W. Ickes, & R. Kidd (Eds.), *New directions in attribution research* (Vol. 2). Hillsdale, NJ: Erlbaum.

Weiner, B., Russell, D., & Lerman, D. (1979). The cognition–emotion process in achievement-related contexts. *Journal of Personality and Social Psychology, 37*, 1211–1220.

Weinert, F. E., & Helmke, A. (1995). Learning from wise Mother Nature or Big Brother Instructor: The wrong choice as seen from an educational perspective. *Educational Psychologist, 30*, 135–142.

Weinraub, M., Clemens, L. P., Sockloff, A., Ethridge, T., Gracely, E., & Myers, B. (1984). The development of sex role stereotypes in the third year: Relationships to gender labeling, gender identity, sex-typed toy preference, and family characteristics. *Child Development, 55*, 1493–1503.

Weinstein, C. E. (1978). Elaboration skills as a learning strategy. In H. F. O'Neil, Jr. (Ed.), *Learning strategies*. New York: Academic Press.

Weinstein, C. E., Goetz, E. T., & Alexander, P. A. (Eds.) (1988). *Learning and study strategies: Issues in assessment, instruction, and evaluation*. San Diego: Academic Press.

Weinstein, C. E., Hagen, A. S., & Meyer, D. K. (1991, April). Work smart. . . not hard: The effects of combining instruction in using strategies, goal using, and executive control on attributions and academic performance. Paper presented at the annual meeting of the American Educational Research Association, Chicago.

Weinstein, C. E., & Mayer, R. E. (1986). The teaching of learning strategies. In M. C. Wittrock (Ed.), *Handbook of research on teaching* (3rd ed.). New York: Macmillan.

Weinstein, R. S. (1993). Children's knowledge of differential treatment in school: Implications for motivation. In T. M. Tomlinson (Ed.), *Motivating students to learn: Overcoming barriers to high achievement*. Berkeley, CA: McCutchan.

Weinstein, R. S., Madison, S. M., & Kuklinski, M. R. (1995). Raising expectations in schooling: Obstacles and opportunities for change. *American Educational Research Journal, 32*, 121–159.

Weisberg, R. W., DiCamillo, M., & Phillips, D. (1979). Transferring old associations to new situations: A nonautomatic process. *Journal of Verbal Learning and Verbal Behavior, 17*, 219–228.

Weiss, M. R., & Klint, K. A. (1987). "Show and tell" in the gymnasium: An investigation of developmental differences in modeling and verbal rehearsal of motor skills. *Research Quarterly for Exercise and Sport, 58*, 234–241.

Weisz, J. R. (1986). Understanding the developing understanding of control. In M. Perlmutter (Ed.), *Cognitive perspectives on children's social and behavioral development. Minnesota Symposia on Child Psychology* (Vol. 18). Hillsdale, NJ: Erlbaum.

Weisz, J. R., & Cameron, A. M. (1985). Individual differences in the student's sense of control. In C. Ames & R. Ames (Eds.), *Research on motivation in education: Vol. 2. The classroom milieu*. Orlando: Academic Press.

Welch, G. J. (1985). Contingency contracting with a delinquent and his family. *Journal of Behavior Therapy and Experimental Psychiatry, 16*, 253–259.

Welder, A. N., & Graham, S. A. (2001). The influence of shape similarity and shared labels on infants' inductive inferences about nonobvious object properties. *Child Development, 72*, 1653–1673.

Welford, A. T. (1977). Serial reaction-times, continuity of task, single-channel effects and age. In S. Dornic (Ed.), *Attention and performance* (Vol. 6). Hillsdale, NJ: Erlbaum.

Wellman, H. M. (1990). *The child's theory of mind*. Cambridge, MA: MIT Press.

Wellman, H. M., & Gelman, S. A. (1992). Cognitive development: Foundational theories of core domains. In M. R. Rosenzweig & L. W. Porter (Eds.), *Annual review of psychology* (Vol. 43). Palo Alto, CA: Annual Reviews.

Wellman, H. M., & Gelman, S. A. (1998). Knowledge acquisition in functional domains. In W. Damon (Series Ed.), D. Kuhn & R. S. Siegler (Vol. Eds.), *Handbook of child psychology: Vol. 2. Cognition, perception, and language* (5th ed., pp. 523–573). New York: Wiley.

Wellman, H. M., & Hickling, A. K. (1994). The mind's "I": Children's conception of the mind as an active agent. *Child Development, 65*, 1564–1580.

Wells, G. L., & Bradfield, A. L. (1999). Distortions in eyewitnesses' recollections: Can the postidentification-feedback effect be moderated? *Psychological Science, 10*, 138–144.

Wentzel, K. R. (1989). Adolescent classroom grades, standards for performance, and academic achievement: An interactionist perspective. *Journal of Educational Psychology, 81*, 131–142.

Wentzel, K. R. (1999). Social-motivational processes and interpersonal relationships: Implications for understanding motivation at school. *Journal of Educational Psychology, 91*, 76–97.

Wentzel, K. R., & Wigfield, A. (1998). Academic and social motivational influences on students' academic performance. *Educational Psychology Review, 10*, 155–175.

Wertheimer, M. (1912). Experimentelle Studien über das Sehen von Bewegung. *Zeitschrift für Psychologie, 61*, 161–265.

Wertheimer, M. (1945). *Productive thinking*. New York: Harper.

Wertheimer, M. (1959). *Productive thinking* (Enl. ed., M. Wertheimer, Ed.). New York: Harper.

Wertsch, J. V. (1984). The zone of proximal development: Some conceptual issues. *Children's learning in the zone of proximal development: New directions for child development* (No. 23). San Francisco: Jossey-Bass.

West, R. F., & Stanovich, K. E. (1991). The incidental acquisition of information from reading. *Psychological Science, 2*, 325–329.

Wheatley, G. H. (1997). Reasoning with images in mathematical activity. In L. D. English (Ed.), *Mathematical reasoning: Analogies, metaphors, and images* (pp. 281–297). Mahwah, NJ: Erlbaum.

Whimbey, A., & Lochhead, J. (1986). *Problem solving and comprehension* (4th ed.). Hillsdale, NJ: Erlbaum.

White, J. J., & Rumsey, S. (1994). Teaching for understanding in a third-grade geography lesson. In J. Brophy (Ed.), *Advances in research on teaching: Vol. 4. Case studies of teaching and learning in social studies*. Greenwich, CT: JAI Press.

White, R. (1959). Motivation reconsidered: The concept of competence. *Psychological Review, 66*, 297–333.

Whitehead, A. N. (1929). *The aims of education and other essays*. New York: Macmillan.

Whiting, B. B., & Edwards, C. P. (1988). *Children of different worlds*. Cambridge, MA: Harvard University Press.

Whitley, B. E., Jr., & Frieze, I. H. (1985). Children's causal attributions for success and failure in achievement settings: A meta-analysis. *Journal of Educational Psychology, 77*, 608–616.

Whitlock, C. (1966). Note on reading acquisition: An extension of laboratory principles. *Journal of Experimental Child Psychology, 3,* 83–85.

Wickelgren, W. A. (1973). The long and the short of memory. *Psychological Bulletin, 80,* 425–438.

Wickelgren, W. A. (1974). *How to solve problems: Elements of a theory of problems and problem solving.* San Francisco: W. H. Freeman.

Wielkiewicz, R. M. (1986). *Behavior management in the schools: Principles and procedures.* New York: Pergamon Press.

Wigfield, A. (1994). Expectancy-value theory of achievement motivation: A developmental perspective. *Educational Psychology Review, 6,* 49–78.

Wigfield, A. (1997). Reading motivation: A domain-specific approach to motivation. *Educational Psychologist, 32,* 59–68.

Wigfield, A., & Eccles, J. (1992). The development of achievement task values: A theoretical analysis. *Developmental Review, 12,* 265–310.

Wigfield, A., & Eccles, J. (2000). Expectancy-value theory of achievement motivation. *Contemporary Educational Psychology, 25,* 68–81.

Wigfield, A., Eccles, J. S., Mac Iver, D., Reuman, D., & Midgley, C. (1991). Transitions at early adolescence: Changes in children's domain-specific self-perceptions and general self-esteem across the transition to junior high school. *Developmental Psychology, 27,* 552–565.

Wigfield, A., Eccles, J. S., & Pintrich, P. R. (1996). Development between the ages of 11 and 25. In D. C. Berliner & R. C. Calfee (Eds.), *Handbook of educational psychology.* New York: Macmillan.

Wigfield, A., & Meece, J. L. (1988). Math anxiety in elementary and secondary school students. *Journal of Educational Psychology, 80,* 210–216.

Wiley, J., & Voss, J. F. (1999). Constructing arguments from multiple sources: Tasks that promote understanding and not just memory for text. *Journal of Educational Psychology, 91,* 301–311.

Wilkins, A. T. (1971). Conjoint frequency, category size, and categorization time. *Journal of Verbal Learning and Verbal Behavior, 10,* 382–385.

Willatts, P. (1990). Development of problem solving strategies in infancy. In D. F. Bjorklund (Ed.), *Children's strategies.* Hillsdale, NJ: Erlbaum.

Williams, D. (1996). *Autism: An inside-out approach.* London: Jessica Kingsley Publishers.

Williams, S. B. (1938). Resistance to extinction as a function of the number of reinforcements. Journal of Experimental Psychology, 23, 506–522.

Willingham, D. B. (1999). The neural basis of motor-skill learning. *Current Directions in Psychological Science, 8,* 178–182.

Willingham, D. B., & Goedert-Eschmann, K. (1999). The relation between implicit and explicit learning: Evidence for parallel development. *Psychological Science, 10,* 531–534.

Wilson, J. E. (1988). Implications of learning strategy research and training: What it has to say to the practitioner. In Weinstein, C. E., Goetz, E. T., & Alexander, P. A. (Eds.), *Learning and study strategies: Issues in assessment, instruction, and evaluation.* San Diego: Academic Press.

Wilson, P. S. (1988, April). The relationship of students' definitions and example choices in geometry. In D. Tirosh (Chair), *The role of inconsistent ideas in learning mathematics.* Symposium conducted at the annual meeting of the American Educational Research Association, New Orleans.

Wilson, P. T., & Anderson, R. C. (1986). What they don't know will hurt them: The role of prior knowledge in comprehension. In J. Orasanu (Ed.), *Reading comprehension: From research to practice.* Hillsdale, NJ: Erlbaum.

Wine, J. D. (1980). Cognitive-attentional theory of test anxiety. In I. G. Sarason (Ed.), *Test anxiety: Theory, research, and applications.* Hillsdale, NJ: Erlbaum.

Winer, G. A., & Cottrell, J. E. (1996). Does anything leave the eye when we see? Extramission beliefs of children and adults. *Current Directions in Psychological Science, 5,* 137–142.

Winer, G. A., Cottrell, J. E., Gregg, V., Fournier, J. S., & Bica, L. A. (2002). Fundamentally misunderstanding visual perception: Adults' belief in visual emissions. *American Psychologist, 57,* 417–424.

Wingfield, A., & Byrnes, D. L. (1981). *The psychology of human memory.* New York: Academic Press.

Winik, M. (1994). *Telling.* New York: Random House.

Winn, W. (1991). Learning from maps and diagrams. *Educational Psychology Review, 3,* 211–247.

Winn, W. (2002). Current trends in educational technology research: The study of learning environments. *Educational Psychology Review, 14,* 331–351.

Winne, P. H. (1995a). Inherent details in self-regulated learning. *Educational Psychologist, 30,* 173–187.

Winne, P. H. (1995b). Self-regulation is ubiquitous but its forms vary with knowledge. *Educational Psychologist, 30,* 223–228.

Winne, P. H., & Hadwin, A. F. (1998). Studying as self-regulated learning. In D. J. Hacker, J. Dunlosky, & A. C. Graesser (Eds.), *Metacognition in educational theory and practice* (pp. 277–304). Mahwah, NJ: Erlbaum.

Winne, P. H., & Jamieson-Noel, D. (2001, April). *How self perceptions of prior knowledge and self-regulated learning interact to affect learning.* Paper presented at the annual meeting of the American Educational Research Association, Seattle, WA.

Winne, P. H., & Marx, R. W. (1989). A cognitive-processing analysis of motivation within classroom tasks. In C. Ames & R. Ames (Eds.), *Research on motivation in education: Vol. 3. Goals and cognitions.* San Diego: Academic Press.

Winne, P. H., & Stockley, D. B. (1998). Computing technologies as sites for developing self-regulated learning. In D. H. Schunk & B. J. Zimmerman (Eds.), *Self-regulated learning: From teaching to self-reflective practice* (pp. 106–136). New York: Guilford press.

Winograd, E., & Neisser, U. (1992). *Affect and accuracy in recall: Studies of "flashbulb" memories.* Cambridge, England: Cambridge University Press.

Winston, P. (1973). Learning to identify toy block structures. In R. L. Solso (Ed.), *Contemporary issues in cognitive psychology: The Loyola Symposium.* Washington, DC: V. H. Winston.

Witt, J. C., Elliott, S. N., & Gresham, F. M. (Eds.). (1988). *Handbook of behavior therapy in education.* New York: Plenum Press.

Wittenbaum, G. M., & Park, E. S. (2001). The collective preference for shared information. *Current Directions in Psychological Science, 10,* 70–73.

Wittgenstein, L. (1958). *Philosophical investigations* (2nd ed.). Oxford, England: Blackwell.

Wittrock, M. C., & Alesandrini, K. (1990). Generation of summaries and analogies and analytic and holistic abilities. *American Educational Research Journal, 27,* 489–502.

Wixson, K. K. (1984). Level of importance of post-questions and children's learning from text. *American Educational Research Journal, 21,* 419–433.

Wixted, J. T., & Ebbesen, E. B. (1991). On the form of forgetting. *Psychological Science, 2,* 409–415.

Wlodkowski, R. J. (1978). *Motivation and teaching: A practical guide.* Washington, DC: National Education Association.

Wlodkowski, R. J., & Ginsberg, M. B. (1995). *Diversity and motivation: Culturally responsive teaching.* San Francisco: Jossey-Bass.

Wolf, M. M., Braukmann, C. J., & Ramp, K. A. (1987). Serious delinquent behavior as part of a significantly handicapping condition: Cures and supportive environments. *Journal of Applied Behavior Analysis, 20,* 347–359.

Wolf, T. M., & Cheyne, J. A. (1972). Persistence of effects of live behavioral, televised behavioral, and live verbal models on resistance to temptation. *Child Development, 43,* 1429–1436.

Wolfe, J. B. (1936). Effectiveness of token-rewards for chimps. *Comparative Psychology Monographs, 12* (60).

Woloshyn, V. E., Pressley, M., & Schneider, W. (1992). Elaborative-interrogation and prior-knowledge effects on learning of facts. *Journal of Educational Psychology, 84,* 115–124.

Wolpe, J. (1958). *Psychotherapy by reciprocal inhibition*. Stanford CA: Stanford University Press.

Wolpe, J. (1969). *The practice of behavior therapy*. Oxford, England: Pergamon.

Wolpe, J., & Plaud, J. J. (1997). Pavlov's contributions to behavior therapy: The obvious and the not so obvious. *American Psychologist, 52,* 966–972.

Wolters, C. A. (1998). Self-regulated learning and college students' regulation of motivation. *Journal of Educational Psychology, 90,* 224–235.

Wolters, C. A. (2000). The relation between high school students' motivational regulation and their use of learning strategies, effort, and classroom performance. *Learning and Individual Differences, 3,* 281–299.

Wolters, C. A., & Rosenthal, H. (2000). The relation between students' motivational beliefs and their use of motivational regulation strategies. *International Journal of Educational Research, 33,* 801–820.

Wong, B. Y. L. (1985). Self-questioning instructional research: A review. *Review of Educational Research, 55,* 227–268.

Wood, C. J., Schau, C., & Fiedler, M. L. (1990, April). *Attribution, motivation, and self-perception: A comparative study—elementary, middle, and high school students.* Paper presented at the annual meeting of the American Educational Research Association, Boston.

Wood, D., Bruner, J. S., & Ross, G. (1976). The role of tutoring in problem-solving. *Journal of Child Psychology and Psychiatry, 17,* 89–100.

Wood, D., Wood, H., Ainsworth, S., & O'Malley, C. (1995). On becoming a tutor: Toward an ontogenetic model. *Cognition and Instruction, 13,* 565–581.

Wood, E., Motz, M., & Willoughby, T. (1997, April). *Examining students' retrospective memories of strategy development.* Paper presented at the annual meeting of the American Educational Research Association, Chicago.

Wood, P., & Kardash, C. A. M. (2002). Critical elements in the design and analysis of studies of epistemology. In B. K. Hofer & P. R. Pintrich (Eds.), *Personal epistemology: The psychology of beliefs about knowledge and knowing* (pp. 231–260). Mahwah, NJ: Erlbaum.

Woodman, G. F., Vogel, E. K., & Luck, S. J. (2001). Visual search remains efficient when visual working memory is full. *Psychological Science, 12,* 219–224.

Woods, D. W., & Miltenberger, R. G. (1995). Habit reversal: A review of applications and variations. *Journal of Behavior Therapy and Experimental Psychiatry, 26,* 123–131.

Woodworth, R. S. (1918). *Dynamic psychology.* New York: Columbia University Press.

Wright, R. (1994). *The moral animal: The new science of evolutionary psychology.* New York: Pantheon Books.

Wulbert, M., & Dries, R. (1977). The relative efficacy of methylphenidate (Ritalin) and behavior-modification techniques in the treatment of a hyperacive child. *Journal of Applied Behavior Analysis, 10,* 21–31.

Wynn, K., & Chiang, W. (1998). Limits to infants' knowledge of objects: The case of magical appearance. *Psychological Science, 9,* 448–455.

Yager, S., Johnson, D. W., & Johnson, R. T. (1985). Oral discussion, group to individual transfer, and achievement in cooperative learning groups. *Journal of Educational Psychology, 77,* 60–66.

Yarmey, A. D. (1973). I recognize your face but I can't remember your name: Further evidence on the tip-of-the-tongue phenomenon. *Memory and Cognition, 1,* 287–290.

Yee, D. K., & Eccles, J. S. (1988). Parent perceptions and attributions for children's math achievement. *Sex Roles, 19,* 317–333.

Yell, M. L., Robinson, T. R., & Drasgow, E. (2001). Cognitive behavior modification. In T. J. Zirpoli & K. J. Melloy, *Behavior management: Applications for teachers* (3rd ed., pp. 200–246). Upper Saddle River, NJ: Merrill/Prentice Hall.

Yerkes, R. M., & Dodson, J. D. (1908). The relation of strength of stimulus to rapidity of habit-formation. *Journal of Comparative Neurology and Psychology, 18,* 459–482.

Yokoi, L. (1997, March). *The developmental context of notetaking: A qualitative examination of notetaking at the secondary level.* Paper presented at the annual meeting of the American Educational Research Association, Chicago.

Zacks, R. T., Hasher, L., & Hock, H. S. (1986). Inevitability and automaticity: A response to Fisk. *American Psychologist, 41,* 216–218.

Zahorik, J. A. (1994, April). *Making things interesting.* Paper presented at the annual meeting of the American Educational Research Association, New Orleans.

Zajonc, R. B. (1980). Feeling and thinking: Preferences need no inferences. *American Psychologist, 35,* 151–175.

Zajonc, R. B. (2000). Feeling and thinking: Closing the debate on the primacy of affect. In J. P Forgas (Ed.), *Feeling and thinking: The role of affect in social cognition* (pp. 31–58). New York: Cambridge University Press.

Zajonc, R. B. (2001). Mere exposure: A gateway to the subliminal. *Current Directions in Psychological Science, 10,* 224–228.

Zaragoza, M. S., & Mitchell, K. J. (1996). Repeated exposure to suggestion and the creation of false memories. *Psychological Science, 7,* 294–300.

Zaragoza, M. S., Payment, K. E., Ackil, J. K., Drivdahl, S. B., & Beck, M. (2001). Interviewing witnesses: Forced confabulation and confirmatory feedback increase false memories. *Psychological Science, 12,* 473–477.

Zazdeh, L. A., Fu, K. S., Tanak, K., & Shimura, M. (Eds.). (1975). *Fuzzy sets and their applications to cognitive and decision processes.* New York: Academic Press.

Zechmeister, E. B., & Nyberg, S. E. (1982). *Human memory: An introduction to research and theory.* Monterey, CA: Brooks-Cole.

Zeidner, M. (1998). *Test anxiety: The state of the art.* New York: Plenum Press.

Zeiler, M. D. (1971). Eliminating behavior with reinforcement. *Journal of the Experimental Analysis of Behavior, 16,* 401–405.

Zeitz, C. M. (1994). Expert–novice differences in memory, abstraction, and reasoning in the domain of literature. *Cognition and Instruction, 12,* 277–312.

Zeller, A. F. (1950). An experimental analogue of repression: II. The effect of individual failure and success on memory measured by relearning. *Journal of Experimental Psychology, 40,* 411–422.

Zentall, T. R., Sutton, J. E., & Sherburne, L. M. (1996). True imitative learning in pigeons. *Psychological Science, 7,* 343–346.

Zhu, X., & Simon, H. A. (1987). Learning mathematics from examples and by doing. *Cognition and Instruction, 4,* 137–166.

Ziegert, D. I., Kistner, J. A., Castro, R., & Robertson, B. (2001). Longitudinal study of young children's responses to challenging achievement situations. *Child Development, 72,* 609–624.

Ziegler, S. G. (1987). Effects of stimulus cueing on the acquisition of groundstrokes by beginning tennis players. *Journal of Applied Behavior Analysis, 20,* 405–411.

Zigler, E., & Hodapp, R. M. (1986). *Understanding mental retardation.* Cambridge, England: Cambridge University Press.

Zigler, E. F., & Finn-Stevenson, M. (1987). *Children: Development and social issues.* Lexington, MA: Heath.

Zimmerman, B. J. (1981). Social learning theory and cognitive constructivism. In I. E. Sigel, D. M. Brodzinsky, & R. M. Golinkoff (Eds.), *New directions in Piagetian theory and practice.* Hillsdale, NJ: Erlbaum.

Zimmerman, B. J. (1989). Models of self-regulated learning and academic achievement. In B. J. Zimmerman & D. H. Schunk (Eds.), *Self-regulated learning and academic achievement: Theory, research, and practice.* New York: Springer-Verlag.

Zimmerman, B. J. (1994, April). *From modeling to self-efficacy: A social cognitive view of students' development of motivation to self-regulate.* Paper presented at the annual meeting of the American Educational Research Association, New Orleans.

Zimmerman, B. J. (1995). Self-regulation involves more than metacognition: A social cognitive perspective. *Educational Psychologist, 30,* 217–221.

Zimmerman, B. J. (1998). Developing self-fulfilling cycles of academic regulation: An analysis of exemplary instructional models. In D. H. Schunk & B. J. Zimmerman (Eds.), *Self-regulated learning: From teaching to self-reflective practice* (pp. 1–19). New York: Guilford Press.

Zimmerman, B. J., & Bandura, A. (1994). Impact of self-regulatory influences on writing course attainment. *American Educational Research Journal, 31*, 845–862.

Zimmerman, B. J., Bandura, A., & Martinez-Pons, M. (1992). Self-motivation for academic attainment: The role of self-efficacy beliefs and personal goal setting. *American Educational Research Journal, 29*, 663–676.

Zimmerman, B. J., & Kitsantas, A. (1997). Developmental phases in self-regulation: Shifting from process to outcome goals. *Journal of Educational Psychology, 89*, 29–36.

Zimmerman, B. J., & Kitsantas, A. (1999). Acquiring writing revision skill: Shifting from process to outcome self-regulatory goals. *Journal of Educational Psychology, 91*, 241–250.

Zimmerman, B. J., & Risemberg, R. (1997). Self-regulatory dimensions of academic learning and motivation. In G. D. Phye (Ed.), *Handbook of academic learning: Construction of knowledge.* San Diego: Academic Press.

Zirin, G. (1974). How to make a boring thing more boring. *Child Development, 45*, 232–236.

Zirpoli, T. J., & Melloy, K. J. (2001). *Behavior management: Applications for teachers.* Upper Saddle River, NJ: Merrill/Prentice Hall.

Zola-Morgan, S. M., & Squire, L. R. (1990). The primate hippocampal formation: Evidence for a time-limited role in memory storage. *Science, 250*, 288–290.

Zook, K. B. (1991). Effects of analogical processes on learning and misrepresentation. *Educational Psychology Review, 3*, 41–72.

Zook, K. B., & Di Vesta, F. J. (1991). Instructional analogies and conceptual misrepresentations. *Journal of Educational Psychology, 83*, 246–252.

Zuckerman, G. (1994). A pilot study of a 10-day course in cooperative learning for beginning Russian first graders. *Elementary School Journal, 94*, 405–420.

Zuriff, G. E. (1985). *Behaviorism: A conceptual reconstruction.* New York: Columbia University Press.

Author Index

Subject Index